The Complete Guide to
MARKETING and the LAW

Robert J. Posch, Jr.

PRENTICE HALL
Englewood Cliffs, New Jersey 07632

Prentice Hall International, Inc., *London*
Prentice Hall of Australia, Pty. Ltd., *Sydney*
Prentice Hall Canada, Inc., *Toronto*
Prentice Hall of India Private Ltd., *New Delhi*
Prentice Hall of Japan, Inc., *Tokyo*
Prentice Hall of Southeast Asia Pte. Ltd., *Singapore*
Editora Prentice Hall do Brasil Ltda., *Rio de Janeiro*
Prentice Hall Hispanoamericana, S.A., *Mexico*

This publication is designed to provide accurate and authoritative information in regard to the subject matter covered. It is sold with the understanding that the publisher is not engaged in rendering legal, accounting, or other professional service. If legal advice or other expert assistance is required, the services of a competent professional person should be sought. . . . *From the Declaration of Principles jointly adopted by a Committee of the American Bar Association and a Committee of Publishers and Associations.*

Library of Congress Cataloging-in-Publication Data

Posch, Robert J., Jr.
  The Complete Guide to Marketing and the Law
  Includes index.

ISBN 0-13-160904-1

Printed in the United States of America

DEDICATION

GERARD H. TONER

"A wise man will make more opportunities than he initially finds."

ABOUT THE AUTHOR

Robert J. Posch, Jr. brings to the reader a unique perspective on marketing and the law. As an attorney with J.D. and M.B.A. degrees from Hofstra University, he is Counsel for the Book Clubs Group at Doubleday & Company. He has authored two successful books on marketing law, as well as hundreds of articles for publications such as *Direct Marketing.*

ACKNOWLEDGEMENTS

This book bears the imprint of many persons. The Acknowledgement is the fun part of any book because I have the chance to thank people in the permanence of print. Although it goes without saying that it is impossible to list acknowledgements to all those who influenced this book, I'm going to try. I'd like to note special thanks to those individuals who, since I left Hofstra Law School, contributed decisively to my integration of law and marketing.

At Doubleday over the past twelve years I've received much hands-on knowledge from a host of individuals who have assisted me in integrating law and business. If you, the manager, find this book lucid yet cogent, you can thank the following (I've listed them in alphabetical order): Jean Anderson, Andy Danek, Bruce De Palma, Bob Di Pietro, Maureen Egen, Rick Engle, Bob Galway, Bill Gatti, Dr. Walter Gerstgrasser, Marjorie Goldstein, Tom Kraemer, George Larie, Ed Leonard, Mike McCormack, Jon Mulford, Pete Muller, Marty Pendergast, Peter von Puttkamer, Lou Re, Georg Richter, Betsy Sherer, Diane Silverman, Ilene Skeen, Howard Weill, Markus Wilhelm, and the late James T. McGrath.

Other professionals who've had a direct impact include Dick Barton, John Beach, Courtland Bovee, Jackie Chasey, Leonard Charney, Anne Darr, Ron Docksai, Harriette Dorsen, Joe Fletcher, Heather Florence, Jonah Gitlitz, Chris Goff, Sarah Goodman, Craig Havemeyer, Dan Hoffman, Rand Hoffman, Henry Hoke, Henry Kaufman, Dr. Manfred Kuehn, Harry Johnson, Heather Kilpatrick, Dr. Juergen Kraemer, Ted Krebsbach, Jim Larocca, Robert Levering, Sen. Norman Levy, Dick Malina, Jack Mandell, Terry McGoldrick, Ed Nash, Bill Newton, Clarence O'Connor, Mitch Pally, J. Gardiner Pieper (who operates New York State's best bar review course), Howard Phillips, Mike Pollack, Ray Roel, Claus Rossin, William Sabin, Ray Schuler, Sandra Stiles, Dan Walsh, Edward Walsh, Howard Weber, Leo Yochim, and four outstanding professors in the Hofstra MBA programs, Dr. Dorothy Cohen, Dr. Joel Evans, Dr. Saul Sands, and Dr. Herman Berliner.

Specific editorial input came from many sources. Of particular note: Robert Callagy provided a fine legal review. Then there were the incisive editorial comments by Eileen DeMilt, who was particularly helpful in offering insights into Section VIII, one area of her current expertise. I extend deep gratitude to Lisa Capone and Lorri Rabell for their diligence and expertise in word processing and work beyond the call of duty.

I also want to extend my warmest appreciation to the dedicated professionals at Prentice Hall: Joe Coniglio, Frances Jeffery, Jon Koschei, Arthur Rosenberg, Bette Schwartzberg, and to those who are usually unsung but make any project work.

My overriding debt is to my wife, Mary Lou, who has been a star to steer by in helping to shape the contents (and index) of this book. The tone is hers as well as mine, and I hope that the reader will appreciate that the relative absence of legalese results from her efforts. Her patience and that of my children, Judi and Robert III, were greatly appreciated. To extol the merits of Mary Lou is to say the same about her parents, Vernon and Mary Collins. Finally, I thank my parents, Robert and Maryrose Posch, and my sister Eileen, who always encouraged me to write; now that I'm prolific, I trust they feel vindicated.

Robert J. Posch, Jr.

TABLE OF CONTENTS

xi

PREFACE

A good manager "manages" to overcome obstacles—"muddling through" is not the way to manage. Having as much information as you can get avoids much needless risk. This book significantly reduces your risk while relating in conversational style both how to get things done within the framework of government regulations and how to keep government regulations from impinging on your management discretion.

A business person in the 1980s who is not at least familiar with spotting legal issues is guilty of gross professional negligence. As all *effective* managers are aware, government legislation and government agencies create and destroy marketing objectives or opportunities at a rate not even considered a decade ago. For example, permitting comparative advertising creates opportunities, and banning cigarette advertising on television destroys them.

As knowledge increases, so will government intrusion in the form of laws, taxes, mandated copy, and the like. Today's manager who wants to be tomorrow's manager must know the current law and trends and how he or she can anticipate (and possibly influence) the government *before* it jeopardizes a market, a trademark, or a pricing or distribution policy. Failure to anticipate and interact with government and other political environments can lead your firm down the path of the nuclear power industry or the automakers in the 1960s. It will also justify your outplacement.

This book will assist today's broad-visioned, multidimensional manager to include government in the "marketing concept." Traditionally, the marketing concept is the philosophy of focusing all the activities of the organization on satisfying customer needs through the use of integrated marketing to achieve maximum profits through customer satisfaction. However, all the positive publicity campaigns in the world won't overcome a government press release picked up by a wire service that alleges (but your buying public reads "states" or "confirms") that you've cheated customers or sold them television sets with excess radiation. You and your firm must be aware of the government at every stage of your management decision-making process—from obtaining a trademark for a new product idea through post-sale warranty service.

This book will provide timely insights into your markets and the law. "The law" represents changes made in public forums with a weather eye on re-election. The voters who are clamoring for laws in a given area are your customers. The trend of the law is your customers' voting their wishes into action. Your advertising and market strategy must reflect current public sentiment.

The relatively low cost of this book may be tax deductible. It may help you interact with your counsel to avoid millions of dollars in fines, which are *not* deductible. This book is written for *all* committed management professionals (because everyone in private enterprise is in marketing or assists marketing) who do not want to see the government feasting on their firms' profits or otherwise interfering in their business operations.

The writing has been kept simple, so you'll find no gratuitous legalese. Further, you'll find many checklists for easy review and overview—a feature that does not exist in current literature in the field. Finally you have to read the book—you can't plan on just catching the movie.

A primary goal of this book is to help managers to spot issues or situations that may become legal issues. As we'll discuss, you're not just being a team player assisting your business to avoid fines or bad publicity. There are criminal sanctions now, too, even at your level! Any professional knows that in our complex world it's hard to fight all the fires. When you see a legal issue or anticipate that one may develop, review the matter with your counsel. Prompt consultation with your counsel in these circumstances could be the best career move you ever made.

ROBERT J. POSCH, JR.

HOW TO READ THIS BOOK

The chapters in this book are not arranged in order of "importance" but rather are designed to follow one form of traditional decision analysis. Obviously, managers do not make their marketing decisions in "chapter-by-chapter" isolation, but some sequence was needed. This is a reference book to skim from time to time and read *before* you invest a lot of time in planning in a given area. For example, if you're considering franchising your business (or buying one), read the chapter before you devote any expenditure in time to consultants, "finders," and the like.

Today's manager must interact with the organization's total marketing program, goals, and political environment. It's all covered somewhere inside; so if what you're interested in doesn't jump out of the table of contents, check the detailed index.

The chapter on profit preservation centers is written primarily for the small concern that can't afford to retain ongoing in-house counsel, since the monitoring function can be done by any manager who wants to avoid adverse visibility to government. More importantly, this monitoring is fun—it's "newspaper law" or current events. Staying atop these areas will assist your professional career as well as make you a better citizen.

Management at all levels of responsibility must plan for government change the same way it does for technological changes, tax changes, or competitive changes. The failure to do so will hurt your firm's future as well as your career advancement.

After you've reviewed this section, pick out the section you're most involved with professionally, that is, product development, channel design, pricing, or promotional policy. If you encounter "legalese," it will usually be explained in plain English. The Glossary is a handy reference tool when you need a quick definition of a term. Also, give the references a chance; they have a lot of information useful to you without further follow-up.

After you've read a section, use the index to locate related information that may be of interest. While each section is built around a "core theme," all are integrated. For example, contracts have their own section, but special contract issues are targeted in-depth in most other sections, too.

Finally, no book can replace decent gut reaction to a questionable practice. Posch's Rule of Regulatory Compliance is simple: If you would not like to be treated this way (unfair pricing, deceptive advertising, bait and switch, etc.), then someone else wouldn't either, and one of those "someone elses" probably has a law or regulation on point.

If you encounter a questionable area of importance, never rely on a book such as this as your sole source of information. *You must consult your attorney.* If you don't have an attorney who specializes in your field, contact your local bar association for a referral. Or, in today's climate of competitive advertising, even your yellow pages can be a place to begin by topic.

I hope you have resolved to stay abreast of legal areas of concern to you and your firm. One way to do this is to follow trade association newsletters, and most business magazines allude to legal areas. Three periodicals that will keep you abreast of current marketing law are *Advertising Age, Journal of Marketing*'s "Legal Briefs" (each issue), and *Direct Marketing* (my own column, "Legal Outlook").

Finally, take your lawyer to lunch, even when nothing in particular is on the horizon. Your counsel can discuss with you the topical areas you've read about as well as marketing ideas you're thinking of. This type of personal contact builds mutual trust and friendship for when you need each other in more serious matters.

I'd appreciate any comments and opinions you have as to any topic covered. Write to me at 242 Elsie Avenue, Merrick, N.Y. 11566, or call me at (516) 868-9849 (evenings) or (516) 873-4628 (days). All correspondence and calls will be answered. I look forward to hearing from you.

I hope you enjoy reading and using this book.

SECTION I

WHAT YOU SHOULD KNOW ABOUT THE LAW AFFECTING PRODUCT DECISIONS

In the truly marketing-oriented firm, the "customer is king." A good manager therefore develops products that appeal to the general public or to a previously defined target market.

Before your product-development program is put into effect, your company will decide its strategy and policy regarding product ideas. Traditionally, you answer various product-marketing questions such as the identity of the product's primary user and whether such primary user is the primary purchaser. You want to know where the product is purchased and whether this place of purchase is the optimum site. You'll consider whether you have the necessary distribution channels or the ability to develop them. These and many other routine questions affect the legal environment. If you approach your product-marketing decisions in a legal vacuum, you may find your firm encountering legal problems you hadn't anticipated.

This section will assist you in understanding the legal issues so that you'll be more likely to spot a potential problem. *This* is the time to consult your counsel, *before* you make significant investments of your time and budget into market research and other initial preproduction investments. *Prior* involvement with counsel is imperative, whether it is to evaluate your product wording for trademark or patent purposes, or whether your warning label or warranty language is well written *and* directed to its targeted audience. Then, obviously, there are a lot of contractual issues to be thought through. The section also includes a few pointers on potential issues involving both the production phase and the contractual phase.

Chapter 1 addresses your product-liability exposure and how it can vary depending on the target market, communications mix, or distribution-channel strategy you use. The chapter briefs you on useful areas to

1

document and provides some tips on how to build in and emphasize safety as a form of sales strategy. Products liability is a broad area that is actually made up of several different legal theories. A product manufacturer can be liable to an injured user based upon a theory of breach of contract (e.g., breach of an express or implied warranty), negligence, or strict liability. We'll cover each of these, as well as the recent cases that would impose product-liability costs on manufacturers *without* proof that their product caused the injury or damage. We'll also briefly explore some issues relevant to your potential criminal liability. Finally, we'll review the mission, composition, and current activities of the Consumer Product Safety Commission.

As a marketer you are a seller, and selling is the transfer of enthusiasm for your product downstream to your customer. Chapter 1 encourages you to see the benefits of transferring enthusiasm for product safety upstream to your design and manufacturing people.

Chapter 2 reviews another essential in your sales strategy—your product's packaging. Does it look attractive on the shelf? Does it catch the eye? Can you mail it safely? A lot of marketing input goes into packaging, and your customers are increasingly relying on label information in their purchase decisions. The growth of self-service accelerates this trend. Visualize yourself as a consumer, and you'll find useful information. You should have an idea of the complexity of the regulations affecting packaging and labeling. Chapter 2 touches on these areas with a review of the Fair Packaging and Labeling Act.

Chapter 3 explains warranties; it covers both the Magnuson-Moss requirements (for consumers only) and those of the Uniform Commercial Code (UCC). You know from recent automobile ads that a warranty is a valuable marketing vehicle. Your competitors are offering them, and your customer wants them—good ones. Knowing your obligations here is essential to the success of any warranty promotion. Just as important, don't forget that once you leave your office you are "one of them"— you're a consumer. *The law you learn here (as well as in other sections) will help you protect your own rights in the marketplace.*

Chapter 4 takes a look at what a patent is and how you might use patent protection. We'll explain the steps in getting one as well as a few legal strategies you should use to exploit the patent at each stage of the registration process, *not* just after formal ownership. Finally, we'll discuss protection options.

Chapter 5 covers trademarks. In a more traditional book, you'd find this topic under advertising. But the reality nowadays is "image," and your brand name and image can be as much a part of your strategy as any other factor. This chapter gives managers a thorough grasp of traditional trademark law, the Lanham Act, and prepares them to use legal strategies to enhance their competitive position in the world of product image built around such a mark.

So read on and enjoy, and consult the fairly extensive references as often as possible. Although many provide follow-up for the specialist, often you'll find general, useful facts pertinent to your needs.

The Birth of Modern Products Liability

In 1916 the U.S. was in transition from an agricultural to an urban society. Its goods were being produced by faceless manufacturers and often distributed via faceless catalogs and impersonal stores in larger populated areas. The self-sufficient individual no longer understood many available items, so the purchaser was relying on adequate inspection by one who did.

While products proliferated, American products liability law remained largely rooted in the concept of privity. This specified that the manufacturer of a negligently manufactured product was liable only to a consumer who bought the product directly from the manufacturer. If the manufacturer used retailers, wholesalers, and the like as a buffer, the manufacturer was immune from liability for its negligence. Although privity helped a locally based industrial economy, it was obsolete to carry the U.S. through the 20th century of mass production.

Gradually, inroads were made toward aligning rules for the liability of manufacturers with those applicable to other negligent defendants. The most significant of these steps was the rule that manufacturers who produced goods that were imminently dangerous to consumers would be liable to those consumers because of their negligence. The list of imminently dangerous products fluctuated and was broadening slowly when Judge Cardozo decided the following famous case.[1]

The End of Privity for Personal Injuries

The defendant was an auto manufacturer. It sold a car to a retail dealer. The retail dealer sold to the plaintiff. While the plaintiff was in the moving car, it suddenly collapsed.[2] He was thrown out and injured. One of the wheels was made of defective wood (this was 1914) and its spokes crumbled into fragments. The wheel was not made by the defendant; it was bought from another manufacturer. There was evidence, however, that its defects could have been discovered by reasonable inspection, and that no inspection was made. There was no claim that the defendant knew of the defect and willfully concealed it. The charge was negligence, not fraud. The question to be determined was whether the defendant owed a duty of care and vigilance to anyone but the immediate purchaser.[3]

The court's holding would protect a retail purchaser by imposing liability against a manufacturer who delivered a car with a defective wheel to an independent distributor, even though the wheel itself had been manufactured by another. As the court stated in adopting another opinion:

> Whenever one person supplies goods, or machinery, or the like, for the purpose of their being used by another person under such circumstances that every one of ordinary sense would, if he thought, recognize at once that unless he used ordinary care and skill with regard to the condition of the thing supplied or the mode of supplying it, there will be danger of injury to the person or property of him for whose use the thing is supplied, and who is to use it, a duty arises to use ordinary care and skill as to the condition or manner of supplying such thing. He then points out that for a neglect of such ordinary care or skill whereby injury happens, the appropriate remedy is an action for negligence. The right to enforce this liability is not to be confined to the immediate buyer. The right, he says, extends to the persons or class of persons for whose use the thing is supplied. It is enough that the goods "would in all probability be used at once before a reasonable opportunity for discovering any defect which might exist," and that the thing supplied is of such a nature that neglect of ordinary care or skill as to its condition or the manner of supplying it would probably cause danger to the person or property of the person for whose use it was supplied, and who was about to use it.[4]

The court then expanded this principle beyond its earlier limitations to poisons, explosives, and other things that in their normal operation are implements of destruction.

> Other products must be included from this decision, because there thus emerges a definition of the duty of a manufacturer which enables us to measure this defendant's liability. Beyond all question, the nature of an automobile gives warning of probable danger if its construction is defective. This automobile was designed to go 50 miles an hour. Unless its wheels were sound and strong, injury was almost certain. It was as much a thing of danger as a defective engine for a railroad. The defendant knew the danger. It knew also that the car would be used by persons other than the buyer, because there were seats for three persons.[5]

The court dismissed the argument that the supplier was primarily responsible.

> The law does not lead us to so inconsequent a conclusion. Precedents drawn from the days of travel by stage coach do not fit the conditions of travel today. The principle that the danger must be imminent does not change, but the things subject to the principle do change. They are whatever the needs of life in a developing civilization require them to be.[6]

The court went on:

> There is nothing anomalous in a rule which imposes upon A, who has contracted with B, a duty to C and D and others according as he knows or does not know that the subject matter of the contract is intended for their use. We may find an analogy in the law which measures the liability of

landlords. If A leases to B a tumble-down house, he is not liable, in the absence of fraud, to B's guests who enter it and are injured. This is because B is then under the duty to repair it; the lessor has the right to suppose that he will fulfill that duty, and, if he omits to do so, his guests must look to him. [Citation omitted.] But if A leases a building to be used by the lessee at once as a place of public entertainment, the rule is different. The injury to persons other than the lessee is to be foreseen, and foresight of the consequences involves the creation of a duty.

In this view of the defendant's liability there is nothing inconsistent with the theory of liability on which the case was tried. It is true that the court told the jury that "an automobile is not an inherently dangerous vehicle." The meaning, however, is made plain by the context. The meaning is that danger is not to be expected when the vehicle is well constructed. The court left it to the jury to say whether the defendant ought to have foreseen that the car, if negligently constructed, would become "imminently dangerous." Subtle distinctions are drawn by the defendant between things imminently dangerous, but the case does not turn upon these verbal niceties. If danger was to be expected as reasonably certain, there was a duty of vigilance, and this whether you call the danger inherent or imminent. In varying forms that thought was put before the jury. We do not say that the court would not have been justified in ruling as a matter of law that the car was a dangerous thing. If there was any error, it was none of which the defendant can complain.

We think the defendant was not absolved from a duty of inspection because it bought the wheels from a reputable manufacturer. It was not merely a dealer in automobiles. It was a manufacturer of automobiles. It was responsible for the finished product. It was not at liberty to put the finished product on the market without subjecting the component parts to ordinary and simple tests. Under the charge of the trial judge nothing more was required of it. *The obligation to inspect must vary with the nature of the thing to be inspected. The more probable the danger, the greater the need of caution. . . .* [7]

Conclusion

This was a landmark case in abolishing privity. Once privity was gone, the scope of a plaintiff's targets was (and is) open to judicial creativity. The balance of this chapter focuses on such creativity.

It also focuses on the issue of duty. When we know a customer will use a product without an inspection, (or have it inspected by someone who is not a professional), then the manufacturer must inspect, and prove that it inspected the product as to defects. The manufacturer has a duty not only to turn out a working product, but one that is carefully constructed.

MacPherson took the buyer beyond liability for obvious implements of destruction to include the full gamut of the consumer market; this ushered in the birth of the modern consumer movement of the mass-produced goods era.

Finally, the case points out, the courts are looking for ways to compensate injured plaintiffs. The manufacturer cannot isolate itself behind a component part maker any more than a retailer. The manufacturer, not the buyer, is in the best position to protect itself with indemnification from any party involved in producing its product. The courts also believed the manufacturer was in the best position to obtain insurance—though this ability no longer exists for many manufacturers.

We'll take a look at the various theories of recovery. Such theories of recovery have so broadened that the once radical, precedent-setting *MacPherson* case is now one of "simple negligence."

ENDNOTES

(1) *MacPherson v. Buick Motor Company*, 217 NY 382 (1916).

(2) *Id.*, p. 384.

(3) *Id.*, p. 385.

(4) *Id.*, p. 388-389.

(5) *Id.*, p. 390-391.

(6) *Id.*, p. 391.

(7) *Id.*, p. 393-395 (emphasis added).

CHAPTER 1

YOUR PRODUCT
LIABILITY EXPOSURE

Why product liability? Isn't this an area of safety design for manufacturing? Although primary responsibility for a safe product rests in the product design and testing areas of your firm, your firm's communications mix, distribution system, labeling, and written instructions are all important factors in legal exposure. You can reduce your firm's risk of legal exposure to product liability as well as broaden your overall business knowledge by familiarizing yourself with the points raised in this chapter.

We'll review three traditional aspects of product liability and then discuss some evolving areas, including criminal exposure. We'll also briefly discuss the role of the Consumer Product Safety Commission, since this relates directly to product liability. However, first it is important to stress that your firm must have a comprehensive in-house product liability program with your in-house counsel playing a leading role.

This program (depending on product) should consist of a routine legal review of all warranties you offer, specifications and handling information, purchase and sales forms, your insurance coverage, adequacy of packaging, new and revised labels and instructions books, adequacy of warnings, document retention programs, and other relevant areas. Then your counsel should review with you basic issues as to your product's design, assembly, and manufacture, as well as the selection of components and materials. Then you'll tie all this in with the strategy of your advertising and promotional efforts. Finally you'll review your product liability program as to its flexibility and overall ability to react to a possible duty to issue post-sale warnings or recalls. Such a program needs the absolute and honest cooperation of all concerned parties. One way you can assist this program is to be aware of areas of exposure so that you can quickly contact your counsel if you see any problems develop.

When people are injured because of some defect in a product, they may have a claim for traditional negligence, strict product liability, or breach of warranty. Each of these three areas will be examined.

As we review the issues you'll note that product liability law grew out of a public policy that people needed more protection from dangerous products than was afforded by the law of contract warranty.[1] Under contract law the disgruntled consumer had to plea that the manufacturer was bound by a warranty (implied or expressed) that the product was reasonably fit to do what it was supposed to do without injury to the user. In the absence of a direct contract between the manufacturer and the consumer (privity), the courts would hold that the plaintiff had no case against the producer but had to sue the retailer.

The courts began to expand tort law in the area of consumer product safety.[2] The manufacturer was to be liable whether or not it was negligent because "public policy demands that responsibility be fixed wherever it will most effectively reduce the hazards to life and health inherent in defective products that reach the market."[3]

For similar reasons of safety, the manufacturer's duty of care was broadened to include protection against property damage.[4] Such damage is considered so akin to personal injury that the two are treated alike.[5]

The lines were drawn and an area of tension was created at consumer[6] vs. commercial[7] property/product damages. The courts did not wish to see tort law encompassing purely arm's-length agreements resulting only in monetary loss, or contracts would drown in a sea of tort and unrealistic damages.[8] In short, the courts attempted to differentiate between "the disappointed users . . . and the endangered ones."[9] The determination of who is in the latter class turns on the nature of the defect, the type of risk, and the manner in which the injury arose. This tension of how to determine such standards is evident in each of the following topics we'll review.

All of the various theories of products liability are interpreted and applied largely by state and local courts. As a result, products liability law is far from uniform.

Further, a new element is likely to enter into the law shortly due to the tort liability insurance crunch. For years, courts have quaintly and naively sought to legislate no-fault transfers of wealth from business to individuals, whether or not the former could have prevented injury to the latter. This transfer was always under the guise of who could best obtain insurance against "the risk."

Today, insurance is often not obtainable, and when it is, the social and financial hurdles are often prohibitive. In the future, the state and federal legislatures will have to enact tort reform. In the interim, we'll look at the law as it is today—beginning with the "oldest"—negligence.

Negligence

In early transactions, the rule was *caveat emptor* (let the buyer beware). The buyer had to make his or her own inspection, rely on his or her own judgment, and assume the risk of any defect in the goods purchased. This wasn't as harsh as it sounded because the buyer and seller knew each other. As this personal relationship changed, so did the law of negligence. Gradually, this approach changed. Today, a seller of goods is under a duty to exercise the care of a reasonable person to see that the goods do not harm a buyer.

The definition of negligence in products liability, and the standard of care required, is the same as in other cases based on negligence. Negligence is the failure to use the amount of care you should reasonably have exercised under the circumstances, thereby resulting in injury to a person or property. As with much of the law, there is an emphasis on reasonableness, that is, the common sense maturity the public has a right to expect from one in your position in a given set of circumstances. The specific elements a plaintiff must allege and prove in a products-liability lawsuit are as follows:[10]

- There was a defect in the product (usually latent in nature, not known or apparent to him/her, though this standard is weakening in many jurisdictions).[11]
- The defect arose out of the lack of reasonable care by the defendant (objective standard of the reasonable person).
- The defendant foresaw or should have foreseen a danger to the plaintiff as one foreseeably affected thereby, when the product is used for its intended purpose.[12]
- The plaintiff was damaged or otherwise injured in an accident or other mishap.
- And finally, there is a proximate relationship between the defect and the plaintiff's damage or injury. The causal connection need not be proved with absolute certainty or to the exclusion of every possible cause. It is a fact to be established, like any other, by a preponderance of the evidence, including circumstantial evidence.

If a manufacturer fails to exercise its duty of care, it will be liable for the physical harm caused by the product. Negligence looks to the defendant's conduct as to any foreseeable plaintiff. There is no duty that plaintiff and defendant be in privity of contract.[13]

The duty to exercise reasonable care extends to all phases of the design, production, and distribution process. In general, this duty rests on the manufacturer, particularly if the wholesaler or retailer merely passes along sealed packages manufactured by reputable firms. The standard is that of an ordinary, reasonably prudent manufacturer in like circumstances.[14] If you don't manufacture the product, you cannot be held liable (under negligence) for injuries sustained from the contents of a sealed product, even though a test might have disclosed a potential danger not known to you at the time of sale. You may be held liable for failure to exercise reasonable care in designing, manufacturing, assembling, packaging, or labeling the product.[15]

You are under a duty to discover any defects that a *reasonable* inspection would disclose. You are negligent if you fail to test or to inspect, *or* if a careless test or inspection results in your failure to discover a defect. Likewise, you can be liable for negligence in the actual design of a product which exposed users to an unreasonable risk of injury.[16]

Industry standards can be relevant and useful, but are not a defense in a negligent design defect case.[17] Disclaimers in contracts generally won't shield a manufacturer (or seller) against his or her liability for negligence.[18]

Further, a manufacturer that relies on its channels to inspect the product or perform other services can be held negligent if such channel members are lax in their duties or if the manufacturer fails to instruct them accordingly. A manufacturer has a duty to all whom it should expect to use its product and to exercise reasonable care in the adoption of a safe plan or design. The manufacturer's duty as to intervening agents and markets broadens with the channels it selects. For example, the instruction booklet furnished to a supplier with a heater stated:

> IMPORTANT! To obtain the maximum efficiency and economy of operation from any baseboard heating system, it is important that there be free circulation of air through the units. *Do not block the air inlet (bottom) or air outlet (top) with draperies, rugs, furniture or other materials that will prevent or restrict the free flow of air.* [Underscored in original.]

The supplier installed the heater behind drapes, resulting in a fire. The Court held the manufacturer was liable for negligent instruction since the above warning pertained to the operating efficiency of the heater but did not provide knowledge or warning of a potential fire hazard. The manufacturer could demonstrate no knowledge or notice was ever given to the supplier as to the potentially dangerous situation created by its products about which it should be reasonably aware. As such, it—not the supplier—was liable.[19] A designer and/or manufacturer has a duty to warn its chain of distribution of all potential harm to users resulting from the nature of its finished product. It has no duty to warn of a risk that at the time of the design decision was unknown, and not reasonably foreseen[20] (except as cited below in a "post-sale duty to warn" situation). Further, a manufacturer is not liable for miscarriages in the communication process that are not attributable to its failure to give adequate warning.[21]

Then there is the issue of whether you should repair a product after an accident. Generally, the fact that you repaired a product after it injured someone is not relevant to show the product was defective at the time of the injury. The social policy is to encourage repair, and the defense is that it was repaired to make it even safer.

However, you're not off the hook. There are a number of ways you can expose yourself to liability in the postmanufacturing process. If you distribute the product of another as your own, the burden of liability shifts to you as well as the manufacturer. If you assume responsibility for assembling the product or otherwise preparing it for sale, you are charged with the responsibility for proper assemblage as well as for discovering and correcting obvious defects or other apparent problems.

For example, a firm designed a saw using all reasonable care at the time of design. However, after placing the saw into the marketplace, new safety improvements were introduced. A worker was injured and recovered $250,000. The court held that with little inconvenience or expense the firm could have instructed its dealers not to sell the saw without the latest safety attachment.[22] In another situation a firm was put on notice of its defective product (shattered glasses) by its rate of returns in such condition. Its failure to act and warn users was negligent.[23]

We'll discuss this issue in greater detail in "strict products liability," but you should be alert to the fact that the duty of post-sale warnings due to new technology, design, etc. is expanding. Such post-sale vigilance must be a part of your in-house product liability contingency planning program.

A retailer may risk exposure by selling an otherwise safe product to the wrong consumer; for example, selling firearms, fireworks, or flammables such as kerosene or automotive flares to minors.[24] Here the test is the predictability of harm as well as the duty of care owed the particular buyer.

Products for children are especially important. It is estimated that there are as many as 750,000 injuries as a result of toy-related incidents each year.[25] You may be liable for an unintentional injury through faulty assembly, failure to warn, or selling to a child obviously not mature enough to handle such a toy.

Both a wholesaler and a retailer have a duty to warn when they know about a product's dangerous condition and the next recipient in the channel probably will not discover the danger. You should be aware that the negligent acts or omissions of one distribution-channel member may result in other channel members being liable if they should have anticipated the negligent act.

Obviously, if the distribution of a potentially dangerous product is strictly controlled and if there's no chance it will fall into the hands of outsiders unfamiliar with its specific hazards, your need to warn is greatly reduced. However, if there is even a remote chance that your product will find its way into the open market, you must post conspicuous warnings or give explicit explanations concerning safe and correct handling.

Labeling is important. Whenever you have a duty to warn (and you have such duty whenever you know or should anticipate that an inexperienced purchaser might use the item in a dangerous manner or might not comprehend the danger of such use), it is advisable to have a carefully worded, descriptive label on your product. The label must be worded in language the intended audience can grasp, which means basic English (or in the language of your particular target group). When adequate warnings are given, the seller may reasonably assume that they will be read and followed. Here is where manufacturing, legal, and marketing sections must work together. Manufacturing must carefully explain the product's uses and dangers to counsel. You must work with your counsel to draft a well-worded label or instruction booklet. To make such a booklet and/or label readable to your audience, you must take into account who your audience is when reviewing the comprehensibility of the booklet or label. You might also suggest that a Flesch readability test (see Glossary of terms) be run.[26]

Fortunately, the courts recognize common sense realities in the areas of what is inherently a dangerous product versus what is a dangerous product if handled with a lack of basic common sense. For example, a seller of firearms is obligated to exercise ordinary care in the sale of firearms. This satisfies the seller's duty. A subsequent act of murder with such gun is an independent intervening act which superseded the act of sale.[27] You will not be held negligently liable for an employee's mental state which is sudden and unrelated to his or her employment.[28] Further, you as a manufacturer are not liable *in a negligence* action for accidents resulting from a product to which you've surrendered control unless the plaintiff can *prove* that a defect attributable to you caused the injury.[29] Finally, in any suit the plaintiff must be able to prove the product injured him or her while being subjected to its "normal use." Likewise, there is no liability when the product is harmless to normal persons and the plaintiff's injury from the use of the product is attributable to his or her hypersensitivity or allergy, unless defendant manufacturer had actual knowledge of the plaintiff's condition. If such knowledge exists, then there is a duty to warn the user.

A final issue in negligence is the doctrine of res ipsa loquitor. This doctrine requires proof

- that the product which caused the injury was under the control and management of the defendant; and
- that the occurrence was such as, in the ordinary course of things, would not happen if those who had its control and management used proper care.

If both of these are present, this is evidence that the injury was caused by the defendant's lack of care. Such proof permits an inference that the defendant was guilty of negligence. Of course, the application of this doctrine does not relieve the plaintiff of the further necessity of showing that the product was actually defective and was the proximate cause of his or her injury.

The above areas of negligence concern themselves with tangibles. An area to look for in the future is product liability for the negligent dissemination of intangibles, i.e., ideas. One publisher[30] lost a jury verdict for the negligent failure to test experiments in its textbooks and for the publisher's failure to adequately warn students and teachers about the dangerous qualities of the experiments. Most publishers will now require an author to warrant that his or her book contains no "injurious formulas, recipes, or instructions." To date, free expression of ideas has controlled most decisions. Others still hold there is no duty of a publisher to verify the material it publishes. This field bears watching in our "information economy."[31]

Fraud, Deceit, Misrepresentation

A manufacturer or seller may be liable for injury or damage caused by a defective product on the ground of fraud or deceit, independent of other major grounds on which products liability is based (negligence, breach of warranty, and strict liability in tort). One who sells an article and represents it to be safe for the purposes or uses which it is designed to serve, knowing it to be dangerous because of concealed defects, commits a wrong, independent of his or her contract. The seller may be liable to a third person using the article, without knowledge of its defective character, for any injury sustained by reason of the seller's deceit and concealment which may be reasonably contemplated as likely to result and which does in fact result regardless of lack of privity of contract between the seller and such third person. Fraudulent representations are frequently in the form of advertisements, labels, radio or television commercials, or pamphlets. The liability of the manufacturer or seller is more obvious when he or she takes active steps to conceal dangerous defects in the article sold. To recover on the ground of fraud, the consumer must establish that the manufacturer or seller knew that its representations were false.

Even if the positive elements of fraud and deceit are lacking, a manufacturer or seller may be liable for injury caused by a defective product, on the ground of misrepresentation or even "innocent misrepresentation." A seller who, by advertising, labels, or otherwise makes a public misrepresentation of a material fact concerning the character or quality of a thing sold is subject to liability for physical harm to a consumer caused by justifiable reliance on the misrepresentation, even though it is not made fraudulently or negligently, and even though the consumer had no contractual relation with the defendant.

Strict Liability

Strict liability law is a rapidly emerging area; it represents the greatest potential hazard to you and your firm. The standards you are held to are much greater under strict liability than under negligence law. For example, in negligence the exercise of due care will exonerate you from liability. In strict liability law, the exercise of due care is little defense. Manufacturers of defective products may be strictly liable for injury caused by their products, regardless of privity, foreseeability, or due care.

Fault or negligence is *not* an essential element of liability (and no contractual relationship need be established). The plaintiff need only show that the defendant was connected with the product, that the product was defective and "unreasonably dangerous" when sold, and that it caused injury. As one court stated: "a manufacturer is strictly liable in tort when an article he places on the market, knowing that it will be used without inspection, proves to have a defect that causes injury to a human being."[32] Imposition of this onerous liability rests largely on considerations of public policy. Given the increased complexity of modern products and modern production methods, most often only the manufacturer can fairly be said to know and to understand when an article is suitably designed and safely made for its intended purpose. By the same token, the manufacturer most often alone has the practical opportunity, as well as a considerable incentive, to turn out useful, attractive, but safe products.

Policy considerations have also been advanced for the imposition of strict liability on certain sellers, such as retailers and distributors of allegedly defective products. When products are sold in the normal course of business, sellers, by reason of their continuing relationships with manufacturers, are most often in a position to exert pressure for the improved safety of products and can recover increased costs within their commercial dealings, or through contribution or indemnification in litigation. Additionally, by marketing the products as a regular part of their business, such sellers may be said to have assumed a special responsibility to the public which has come to expect them to stand behind their goods.

When strict liability is imposed, sellers (and everyone also in the seller's distributive chain)[33] are made, in effect, the virtual insurers of their products. Even when an injured plaintiff *knows* of a danger inherent in using a product, that will not defeat his or her claim if the manufacturer could reasonably have guarded against the danger in designing the product.[34]

The essential aspects of strict liability are expressed in Section 402A of the *Restatement of Torts (Second),* which reads as follows:

Section 402A. Special Liability of Seller of Product for Physical Harm to User or Consumer.

1. One who sells any product in a defective condition unreasonably dangerous to the user or consumer or to his property, is subject to liability for physical harm thereby caused to the ultimate user or consumer, or to his property, if (a) the seller is engaged in the business of selling such a product, and (b) it is expected to and does reach the consumer or user without substantial change in the condition in which it is sold.

2. The rule stated in subsection (1) applies although (a) the seller has exercised all possible care in the preparation and sale of his product, and (b) the user or consumer had not bought the product from or entered into any contractual relation with the seller.

The issue is the quality of the product. The product—not the defendant—is on trial. In strict product liability law, a defective product may involve:

- A mistake in manufacturing, i.e., a flaw;
- A design defect (a product may be meticulously made but if it presents an unreasonable risk of harm it is defectively designed);[35]
- An inadequate or nonexistent warning in connection with the use of the product, or a failure to correctly instruct the end user.

If one of the above arguments is available, the plaintiff must prove a proximate connection between the product's defect and the harm suffered. Further, he or she must also prove that such defect existed, even if not manifested, when the product left the hands of the manufacturer/defendant. A product manufactured with structural weaknesses which injures the user in the process of normal usage will impose liability on the seller, even if the defect did not become evident until after leaving such seller's control. Finally, the plaintiff must prove the product injured him or her while being subjected to "normal use."

To determine whether the product was reasonably dangerous to the user, the court will consider the following factors:

- usefulness and desirability of the product;
- availability of other and safer products which can meet the same need;
- obviousness of the danger or lack of same (the analysis by the court will reflect on targeted market, advertising, etc.);
- likelihood of injury *vis a vis* the common expectation that the product is or can be dangerous; and
- the ability to eliminate the danger without seriously impairing the usefulness of the product or making it unduly expensive to the consumer.

Let's review the above in the context of the court decisions.

Mistake in Manufacturing

A mistake in manufacturing is fairly straightforward: you have produced a "lemon." A traditional comment in this area is that "a manufacturer is strictly liable in tort when an article he places on the market, knowing that it presents a safety risk if defectively made or designed and that it is to be used without inspection for defects, proves to have a defect that causes injury to a human being."[36] In one case strict liability was imposed "to insure that the costs of injuries resulting from defective products are borne by the manufacturers that put such products on the market rather than by the injured persons who are powerless to protect themselves."[37] As one court elaborated (emphasis my own):

. . . The justification for imposing liability is that: "[T]he seller, by marketing his product for use and consumption, has undertaken and assumed a special responsibility toward any member of the consuming public who may be injured by it; that the public has the right to and does expect, in the case of products which it needs and for which it is forced to rely upon the seller, that reputable sellers will stand behind their goods; that public policy demands that the burden of accidental injuries caused by products intended for consumption be placed upon those who market them, and be treated as a cost of production *against which liability insurance can be obtained;* and that the consumer of such products is entitled to the maximum of protection at the hands of someone, and the proper persons to afford it are those who market the products . . ."[38]

Other justifications by the Court in *Mead* included that the retailer may

- seek contribution from the manufacturer as a joint tortfeasor; or
- provide for contractual indemnity; or
- seek indemnity from the manufacturer itself based upon strict liability.[39]

The fact that all of the above may not be realistic options has yet to seriously penetrate the courts' cloister. Insurance may not be available to even mid-size businesses and the contractual comments do not reflect the realities of a small business at any level of the distribution chain.

The social policy involved is based both on consumer reliance on the manufacturer's expertise for protection when consumers are induced to purchase and on the manufacturer's superior ability to spread out the cost of injury through insurance. Also involved is the basic element of deterrence, whereby the ease of making out a strict product liability claim, along with the potential of losing large judgments, is thought to induce a manufacturer to impose greater control over product development and manufacture. However, such strict standards are not generally applied to *commercial* purchases between two companies of relatively equal bargaining power. Here the commercial firm is presumed to have the personnel and expertise necessary to adequately inspect and protect its own interest. In short, " . . . the doctrine of products liability does not apply as between parties who: (1) deal in a commercial setting; (2) from positions of relatively equal economic strength; (3) bargain the specifications of the product; and (4) negotiate concerning the risk of loss from defects in it."[40]

As you can see, this is an area of primary concern to manufacturers. However, those in the marketing distribution channels can involve themselves in product defect situations.[41] One example occurred in a classic case on point, that of the "burning TV." As the court stated, "we can say that a television set properly manufactured and properly serviced by the seller does not, in normal operation, combust."[42] As a result, a retailer was held strictly liable. The court noted that some accidents do not ordinarily occur in the absence of a defect and that in those situations a defect may be inferred from the circumstances as long as no alterations were made to the product. The court further commented that the retailer should have known about this danger because of the retailer's size, merchandising skills, and power to control the quality of its products.

Further, you can become liable for a product defect if you service the product. The doctrine of strict liability does not require a new product, but it does require that the product be in substantially the same condition after being serviced as when it was initially delivered to the purchaser.[43] Therefore, if "the seller takes possession of the product, whether it is done on the seller's premises or on the premises of the purchaser, the effect is a re-delivery of the product with the same assurances and with the same obligations as the original sale."[44]

Although this discussion concerns your exposure to your customer, it does not mean that you have no right of recovery. Your attorney should have included an indemnification clause in your contract with the manufacturer. The social policy for allowing a recovery by the consumer here is that you are distributing the goods and have an obligation of accountability. Even more important, you are the visible party a consumer will turn to for redress.

Design Defect

When a design defect is involved, there is a balance between the likelihood of harm and the burden of taking precautions against the harm. A manufacturer is under a duty to design a product with reasonable care. He or she is held to the standard of an ordinary, reasonably prudent designer in like circumstances. A product, even if meticulously made, is defective if the danger posed by the product is unreasonable in light of the product's utility. The test is whether a reasonable manufacturer, knowing of the hazards associated with the design, would have marketed the product in the same way as the defendant.[45] Stated another way:

> In a strict products liability action based upon design defect, whether the product as marketed was reasonably safe for its intended use is determined by whether a reasonable person with knowledge of the potential for injury of the product and of the available alternatives, balancing the product's risks against its utility and costs and against the risks, utility and cost of the alternatives, would have concluded that it should not have been marketed in the condition that it was.[46]

Courts do not defer to the design decisions reached by corporate management.[47] Courts do wish to see documentation that management "anticipate the environment in which its product will be used, and . . . design against the reasonably foreseeable risks attending the product's use in that setting."[48] The responsibility of a manufacturer is gauged as of the time the product left the manufacturer. This legal trade-off is important.

Once the injured party alleges that there is something about the design of your product which caused the injury, you must demonstrate that the design was safe, that a safer design was not known to you or reasonably in use in the industry, or that there was a substantial modification by the purchaser which subsequently altered the product. The latter involves testing the defective product to demonstrate that it was modified by the owner. Your duty is to produce items free of defects, not to produce products impossible to abuse (within reasonable predictability) or to incorporate safety features into your products so as to reasonably be assured that no harm will result from reasonable use, no matter how careless or even reckless.[49] The test here is whether the product has reached the user or consumer without substantial changes in the condition in which it is sold.[50]

When the issues of a safe product or safest practical product are involved, you must document, document, and then document. Here the "big three" (manufacturer, manager, and counsel) must work together carefully. Some topics your documents should show include:

- Safety of the design of the product.
- All procedures, research, and testing that went into the design of the product.
- Documents detailing prior accidents or complaints (or lack of same) and how you responded.
- Records of parts and materials, quality control documents, and sales and marketing records to show what warranties were made.
- Proof that all government standards were met or, preferably, exceeded.

Don't expect to rely on your buyer's compliance with Occupational Safety and Health Administration (OSHA) regulations. If you have the duty to install safety features (or your sales personnel must follow up on this during the installation of machinery), assume that the employer and/or buyer *won't.*[51]

One final note: Where possible, don't offer safety equipment as optional if it can be designed into the product. Although safety equipment offered as an option to reduce initial cost resistance or as a "sweetener" might seem preferable, in general it greatly increases your potential liability. It is not necessary that the likelihood of an accident be high for a court to find you should have added the safety features rather than making them optional.

No product can be absolutely safe. In design-defect cases the injured party must show that a safer design would have been practical.[52] For example:

[T]here is a case for the jury if the plaintiff can show an available design modification which would reduce the risk without undue cost or interference with the performance of the machinery." . . . In evaluating the adequacy of a product's design, the jury must weigh "the gravity of the danger posed by the challenged design, the likelihood that such danger would occur, the mechanical feasibility of a safer alternative design, the financial cost of an improved design, and the adverse consequences to the product and to the consumer that would result from an alternative design.[53]

Again, be able to document. The following precautions are advised:

☐ Be able to document that any later design improvements were new to the state of the art and not a result of the inadequacy of your product's original design. In some states, postaccident design changes can be used as evidence against a manufacturer in product liability cases. Be alert to this issue and consult your counsel.

☐ Prepare your documentation to show that you are committed to safety but that you must be able to price the product within the limits of your customer's ability to pay. Never phrase any cost-benefit analyses as a safety trade-off.

☐ When in doubt, phrase the documents in technical terms; don't draw conclusions. Never use words such as "defective."

☐ Whenever possible, document that the design in question was in accordance with or mandated by the buyer's specifications and/or that the buyer refused to purchase safety devices offered by you, the absence of which caused the design defect. Complying with the buyer's specifications is usually a good defense unless the designs supplied contain defects so extraordinarily dangerous that a prudent manufacturer would decline to produce them.[54]

☐ Document all efforts to keep abreast of scientific, technological, and other developments in your ongoing product design and improvement efforts. Make sure you are prepared to warn purchasers of any material data that comes to light as a result of such updates.

☐ A manufacturer or retailer may, however, incur liability for failing to warn concerning dangers in the use of a product which come to his attention after manufacture or sale, through advancements in the state of the art, with which he is expected to stay abreast, or through being made aware of later accidents involving dangers in the product of which warning should be given to users . . .

. . . The nature of the warning to be given and to whom it should be given likewise turn upon a number of factors, including the harm that may result from use of the product without notice, the reliability and any possible adverse interest of the person, if other than the user, to whom notice is given, the burden on the manufacturer or vendor involved in locating the persons to whom notice is required to be given, the attention which it can be expected a notice in the form given will receive from the recipient, the kind of product involved and the number manufactured or sold and the steps taken, other than the giving of notice, to correct the problem . . .

. . . Germane also will be any governmental regulation dealing with notice, whose function will be to assess the reasonableness of the steps taken by the manufacturer or vendor in light of the evidence concerning the factors listed above presented in the particular case, as well as any expert testimony adduced on the question. The manufacturer and the vendor do not necessarily have the same obligation to warn concerning dangers learned of after delivery of the product.[55]

Stress to your people that they should keep all documentation in writing, assuming that it will someday be used as evidence in litigation.

Without adequate documentation, defending yourself in an action alleging design defect will be difficult. With adequate documentation you should be able to establish the inherent safety of your product and that your testing revealed that there was no safer *state-of-the-art design* technology at the time of production. The documents must show that you tested the product for use as intended as well as for all unintended yet reasonably foreseeable uses. Further, they must show that there was no available design modification that would reduce the risk of harm without *undue* cost to the consumer or interference with the performance of the product. This documentation enables you to establish the balancing test of the likelihood of your product's causing harm against the burdens of taking realistic precautions against that harm.[56]

Finally, it will establish you were not negligent. Even though we're dealing with strict liability, many courts require evidence of negligence in design and warning cases.[57] Such lack of negligence has to improve your halo effect with a jury.

Duty to Warn

Duty to warn is the area of greatest legal exposure for those in the distribution chain, although here, as elsewhere, the primary burdens fall on the manufacturer. The content and meaning of all labels, warnings, assembly instructions, sales brochures (and sales force presentations) and instruction booklets are evaluated as to size of print, location, and effectiveness.

In some situations, products not defective by design and manufacture can be rendered defective due to inadequate warning labels. One of the most important things you can do to prevent a products liability suit is to provide with your products proper warnings that adequately convey the degree of danger associated with the normal (or foreseeable) use of the product. Warnings, no matter how adequate, however, cannot absolve the manufacturer or designer of all responsibility for product safety. A warning alone is never a satisfactory replacement for a safety device.[58] Further, and this is all-important, the *ultimate user* must receive the warning if it is to have any value at all to you (or the user). In many cases this will mean you must warn the actual product users (e.g., employees) not just the purchaser (employer or corporate purchasing staff). Such warning must involve not only a statement that a danger exists, but a precise description of the extent of such danger.[59] Your goal must be to warn any member of the consuming public who might use the product.

There is no duty to warn of a product-connected danger that is apparent on its face or actually known to the person who claims to be entitled to the warning. "Awareness" is a defense when the consumer is aware of a possible defect and its potential danger but proceeds *unreasonably* to use the product.[60] While failure to warn can make a product unreasonably dangerous, there is no duty to warn where the product is not defectively designed or manufactured and where the possibility of injury results from a common propensity of the product which is open and obvious.[61] Further, if a warning has been communicated, a manufacturer is entitled to assume that the user will read and follow the furnished instructions.

Place in your contracts a paragraph that your purchaser will read all instruction books and/or warning labels you provide and pass them along to the ultimate consumer. If the purchaser's employees will use the product, then the purchaser should agree to pass along all warnings to employees.

Write your instruction booklets as if you were preparing for a lawsuit. All warnings on the product should be included in the booklet. Work with your lawyer so that neither legalese nor needlessly complicated jargon is included in the book. If necessary, design and enclose a couple of instruction booklets addressed to varied individuals to whom your instructions are applicable.

On your product labels include a warning that the user must read the instruction booklet before using the product. All product labels should be screened by your attorney as well as by experts who can determine the adequacy and audience "understandability" of your text. Understandability might include technical or complex wording analysis, convenience of the placement of the label to the reader, and the size of the print. Finally, remember that the label decal must stay affixed to the product for the life of the product.

Be alert to the frequency and duration of your advertising campaign for a product—especially one directed at consumers. Advertisements may increase consumers' expectations regarding product performance.[62] One court stated:

> The commercial advertising of a product will be the guiding force upon the expectations of consumers with regard to the safety of a product, and is highly relevant to the formulation of what those expectations might be. The particular manner in which a product is advertised as being used is also relevant to a determination of the intended and reasonably foreseeable uses of the product. Therefore, it was not error to admit the commercial advertising in evidence to establish consumer expectation of safety and intended use.[63]

Your marketing communications can result in liability due to the *innocent omission* of facts. Retailers can be held liable for the goods they sell if they do not make the user aware of certain dangers. In one case the court held that the responsibility of a retailer was the same as that of a manufacturer, because the retailer held the product out as its own and because its size, volume, and merchandising practices brought it within the class of "professional vendors," who are presumed to know of defects in their wares. This relationship permits the retailer to exert pressure on the manufacturer to control its quality.[64] This case concerned a chipped hammer. It is well known in the tool industry that once a hammer is chipped it is dangerous and should be discarded. However, the court felt that the entire buying public should be made aware of this fact and went so far as to suggest a warning label stating "if this hammer chips, return to seller."[65]

If you did not actively design a warning label, or the product itself, but merely printed a label, be able to document this. The mere printing of the label is strictly ministerial and tangential, and will not "rise to a level sufficient to bring you within the class of those who may be responsible in strict liability."[66]

Finally, as in all areas of products liability, if you become aware of defects or dangers associated with a product which has already been distributed into the marketplace, you must take reasonable steps to provide an appropriate warning to the product users. This is the manufacturer's "post–sale" or "post–manufacture" duty to warn. Whether there is a "post–sale" duty to warn may depend on such factors as the degree of danger involved, the probable response that a warning would generate, the number of products involved, and the ease in locating the purchasers. Regrettably, such warnings sent out after an accident are admissible to rebut testimony that your product was not dangerous.[67]

The courts are interpreting defective labels, instruction books, and packaging as defective products. They have created the presumption in favor of warnings. When a product has no warning, the court will presume that the consumer would have read and heeded a proper warning.[68] These are not product decisions strictly for the manufacturing and legal departments. Managers must get involved in these areas.

There is no one formula that will tell you whether or not your product warnings are adequate. Therefore, you need to use the strongest warning possible given your product, your targeted and foreseeable market's perceptions about your product, the nature of the potential harm, whether you are using "individual" (e. g. pharmaceuticals) or mass-distribution marketing,[69] and any laws governing disclosures. However, the law as to strict products liability recovery continues to become more "creative"[70] and you must try to stay ahead of it to design equally creative defenses.

One hopes that the courts will one day cease their overkill and adopt in black letter law the following (emphasis my own):

> . . . *Warnings, in order to be effective, must be selective. They must call the consumer's attention to a danger that has a real probability of occurring and whose impact will be significant. One must warn with discrimination since*

the consumer is being asked to discriminate and react accordingly. The story of the boy who cried wolf is an analogy worth contemplating when considering the imposition of a warning in a case of rather marginal risk . . . Those who argue for warning as *the* judicial solution to latent defect cases labor under a naive belief that one can warn against all significant risks. The truth is that such a marketing scheme is not feasible. The warning process, in order to have impact, will have to select carefully the items which are to become part of the consumer's mental apparatus while using the product. Making the consumer account mentally for trivia or guard against risks that are not likely to occur imposes a very real societal cost . . .

In short, when calculating the burden of precaution which is part of the risk-utility calculus, *it will be necessary to focus on costs other than the cost of label printing. The efficacy of warning is a societal cost of substantial importance.* [71]

Finally it should be noted that not every seller is subject to strict liability. The policy considerations that have been advanced to justify the imposition of strict liability on manufacturers and sellers in the normal course of business obviously lack applicability in the case of a party who is not engaged in the sale of the product in issue as a regular part of its business. Specifically, "[t]his Section is also not intended to apply to sales of the stock of merchants out of the usual course of business, such as execution sales, bankruptcy sales, bulk sales, and the like."[72] The casual or occasional seller of a product does not undertake the special responsibility for public safety assumed by those in the business of regularly supplying those products, nor is there the corollary element of forced reliance on that undertaking by purchasers of such goods. As a practical matter, the occasional seller has neither the opportunity, nor the incentive, nor the protection of the manufacturer or seller who puts that product into the stream of commerce as a normal part of its business, and the public consumer does not have the same expectation when it buys from such a seller.

To conclude on a note of "optimism," it appears (to date) that a provider of professional services is not subject to suit on grounds of strict products liability—only negligence.[73]

Breach of Warranty

A warranty is a representation by the seller about the product's qualities or characteristics. Warranties are discussed in more depth elsewhere in this Section, but for now you should distinguish breach of warranty from the areas of negligence and strict products liability. The cause of action for breach of warranty is a contractual relationship, and only the parties to the contract may assert it. However, warranty protection is extended to a subpurchaser who bought the product under warranty and who justifiably relied on representations made by the seller to the public through advertisements or labels attached to the goods.

The distinction between tort and warranty are ingrained in the substance of law. When a product "injures only itself" and aggravates the economic situation of its buyer, the reasons for imposing a tort duty are weak and those for leaving the party to its contractual remedies are strong.

> The distinction that the law has drawn between tort recovery for physical injuries and warranty recovery for economic loss is not arbitrary and does not rest on the 'luck' of one plaintiff in having an accident causing physical injury. The distinction rests, rather, on an understanding of the nature of the responsibility a manufacturer must undertake in distributing his products.[74]

The tort concern with safety is reduced when an injury is only to the product itself. When a person is injured, the "cost of an injury and the loss of time or health may be an overwhelming misfortune," and one the person is not prepared to meet.[75] In contrast, when a product injures itself, the commercial user stands to lose the value of the product, risks the displeasure of its customers who find that the product does not meet their needs, or experiences increased costs in performing a service. Losses like these can be insured. The small cost to the public that would result from holding a manufacturer liable in tort for purely economic loss is not justified and even the courts have yet to "reach" for it (though it is "broadening"). The Supreme Court went on record that "permitting recovery for all foreseeable claims for purely economic loss could make a manufacturer liable for vast sums. It would be difficult for a manufacturer to take into account the expectations of persons downstream who may encounter its product."[76]

Damage to a product itself is most naturally understood as a warranty claim. Such damage means simply that the product has not met the customer's expectations, or, in other words, that the customer has received "insufficient product value."[77] The maintenance of product value and quality is precisely the purpose of express and implied warranties. In the contractual value of warranties, a manufacturer can restrict its liability within contractually defined limits (based on foreseeability and privity) by disclaiming or limiting the remedies available to the purchaser. In exchange for this risk, the purchaser should pay less for the goods.

An initial question in the warranty area is the degree of reliance the buyer placed on the salesperson's "pitch." A certain amount of puffery is permitted. However, any affirmation of fact which relates to the goods and becomes a part of the basis of the bargain will create an express warranty. An express warranty may be created in one of three ways:

- by a promise made by the seller to the buyer that relates to the goods (e.g., how it would function or perform);
- by a specific description of the goods made by the seller; or

• by the seller's sample or model.[78]

In general, catalog statements and other written advertisements for a product are express warranties.[79]

Other warranties may be created by law. One such type of warranty is the implied warranty of merchantability. Only a merchant seller creates such a warranty. The foremost question in deciding whether goods are merchantable or not is whether the goods are fit for the ordinary purposes for which such goods are used.[80]

Another warranty created by law is the implied warranty of fitness for a particular purpose. If at the time of contracting the seller has reason to know any particular purpose for which the goods are required and that the buyer is relying on the seller's skill or judgment to select or furnish suitable goods, there is an implied warranty that the goods shall be fit for such purpose.[81]

The contractual issues are discussed in other sections. There is a suit for personal injuries available under warranty law.

Breach of Warranty as a Basis for a Products Liability Suit

If a plaintiff demonstrates that a seller extended an express warranty or an implied warranty exists, and the seller breached this warranty (article not as warranted), a person *injured* as a result of the breach of warranty may bring suit to recover for his or her injuries if the plaintiff also establishes the express or implied warranty was part of the basis of the bargain between the parties. Any attempt by a seller to limit consequential damages for injury caused to a person by consumer goods is unconscionable, though limitation of damages where the loss is commercial is not.[82] Under various state "dangerous instrumentality" laws, disclaimers cannot hold up if a product causes an accident.

The law of warranty is congruent in many, if not all, respects with the principles of strict liability expressed in the Restatement (Second) of Torts section 402(A).[83] In deciding the issue of warranty liability:

> . . . the jury must weigh competing factors much as they would in determining the fault of the defendant in a negligence case. The inquiry focuses on product characteristics rather than on the defendant's conduct, but the nature of the decision is essentially the same. In evaluating the adequacy of a product's design, the jury should consider, among other factors, the gravity of the danger posed by the challenged design, the likelihood that such danger would occur, the mechanical feasibility of a safer alternative design, the financial cost of an improved design, and the adverse consequences to the product and to the consumer that would result from an alternative design.[84]

In another case the court stated:

[T]he plaintiff in a warranty action . . . may not recover if it is found that, after discovering the product's defect and being made aware of its danger, he nevertheless proceeded unreasonably to make use of the product and was injured by it.[85]

In a franchising situation where a franchisor consents to the distribution of a defective product bearing its name, the obligation of the franchisor to compensate the injured consumer for *breach of implied warranty,* arises from several factors in combination:

- the risk created by approving for distribution of an unsafe product likely to cause injury,
- the franchisor's ability and opportunity to eliminate the unsafe character of the product and prevent the loss,
- the consumer's lack of knowledge of the danger, and
- the consumer's reliance on the trade name which gives the intended impression that the franchisor is responsible for and stands behind the product.

Liability is based on the franchisor's control and the public's assumption, induced by the franchisor conduct, that it does in fact control and vouch for the product.[86] Even without the trademark on the product, franchisors have been held to express warranties based on their advertising claims.[87]

Because of the outright state bans on disclaimers, varied laws and their court interpretations in each state due to our federal system, and for other reasons, the whole issue of warranties will have to be re-reviewed by management. There is no escaping product injury, but creative approaches to economic exposure are being argued in the trade press. One idea is expanded, up-front consumer redress or liquidated damages in a commercial setting.[88]

You can't escape the above exposure with disclaimers, franchising, etc. In many cases if you sell your firm outright, the product liability issues travel to your successor. When and if this happens in a given situation is our next discussion.

Successor Corporations

The general rule of successor liability provides for nonliability on the part of a successor corporation. The rule states that when one company sells or otherwise transfers all its assets to another company the latter is not liable for the debts and liabilities of the transferor, *except when*

- the purchaser expressly or impliedly agrees to assume such debts;
- the transaction amounts to a consolidation or merger of the seller and purchaser;
- the purchasing corporation is merely a continuation of the selling corporation;

- the transaction is entered into fraudulently in order to escape liability for such debts; or
- the court reviews the assetless condition of the original manufacturer and the availability of resources to the successor corporation and the fairness of the successor in taking the benefit with the burden—the "product line" concept.

The traditional rule of nonliability of successor corporations (and its exceptions) were developed prior to the adoption of strict products liability law. Recognizing this reality, many states have moved all over the map to find (justify) recovery for injured persons who suddenly find the seller defunct. In pursuing the successor liability concept, the debate has centered on two schools of thought—"product line" and "continuation of the enterprise."

Product Line Theory

This originated in California[89] and was adopted elsewhere.[90] Generally, California does not impose liability on a successor corporation that purchases the assets of a predecessor in an arm's length transaction.[91] However, in *Ray,* the California Supreme Court created an exception to that rule. In holding a successor corporation liable for the defective product of the predecessor corporation, the *Ray* court concluded:

> . . . that a party which acquires a manufacturing business and continues the output of its line of products under the circumstances here presented assumes strict tort liability for defects in units of the same product line previously manufactured and distributed by the entity from which the business was acquired.[92]

The circumstances presented in *Ray* were as follows:[93]

1. The successor corporation (Alad II) purchased the entire assets of the predecessor corporation (Alad I) which previously had manufactured the defective ladder;

2. Pursuant to a written sales contract, Alad I agreed "to dissolve its corporate existence as soon as practical and [to] assist and cooperate with [Alad II] in the organization of a new corporation to be formed by [Alad II] under the name ALAD CORPORATION";

3. After the acquisition of Alad I, Alad II continued to manufacture the same line of ladders under the Alad name, using the same manufacturing equipment and designs and the same personnel;

4. Alad II continued to solicit Alad I's customers through the same sales representatives;

5. There was no outward indication of a change in the ownership of the business;

6. There was no express or implied agreement to assume liability for injury from defective products previously manufactured by Alad I;

7. The record did not disclose whether Alad II had liability insurance to cover the plaintiff's claims;

8. The plaintiff's practical ability to recover from Alad I as manufacturer of the defective product was vitiated by the purchase of Alad I's tangible assets, trade name and good will, and the dissolution of Alad I within two months thereafter.

The California Supreme Court imposed strict tort liability on Alad II for the defective ladder manufactured by Alad I. The court reasoned:

> Justification for imposing strict liability upon a *successor* to a manufacturer under the circumstances here presented rests upon (1) the virtual destruction of the plaintiff's remedies against the original manufacturer caused by the successor's acquisition of the business, (2) the successor's ability to assume the original manufacturer's risk-spreading role, and (3) the fairness of requiring the successor to assume a responsibility for defective products that was a burden necessarily attached to the original manufacturer's good will being enjoyed by the successor in the continued operation of the business.[93]

The court relied upon the facts that the new Alad Company continued to make the same line of ladders, and that it exploited its purchase of the original Alad's trade name, good will, and customer lists in order to hold itself out as the same enterprise. The court emphasized throughout the opinion that it applied the exception "under the narrow circumstances here presented . . . "

Subsequently, a California decision clarified this by holding that for the *Ray* exception to apply, the asset sale to the successor corporation must have contributed to the curtailing or destruction of the plaintiff's remedies.[94] The required causation was present in *Ray*. There, the successor purchased the predecessor's assets pursuant to a written sales contract that required the dissolution of the predecessor. The purchase of all assets and the required dissolution eliminated the possibility of recovery from the predecessor.[95]

New Jersey adopted this theory, as has Pennsylvania[96] and Washington.[97] It has been rejected in Colorado,[98] Illinois,[99] Kansas,[100] Alabama,[101] Florida,[102] Nebraska,[103] New York,[104] Vermont,[105] Wisconsin,[106] Missouri,[107] and Louisiana.[108] In rejecting "product line," many state courts argue that *Ray* looks "primarily to the availability of a remedy and implicitly to the location of a 'deep pocket' to furnish that remedy."[109] Another court commented on basic equity, i.e., "if the product line exception is utilized, liability will be imposed on a successor corporation not for something it has done, but rather because it may be able to afford liability."[110] Finally, some courts acknowledge:

> There is little justification for generally holding a successor accountable for its predecessor's product defects. And it is no justification for such a conclusion to reason that a small business successor may protect itself from liability by purchasing products liability insurance. Insurance is no

longer the apparent panacea which it may have been at one time: where insurance is available at all, its high cost may make it prohibitively expensive for the average business to purchase. . . .

. . . Where insurance is an unaffordable or unavailable alternative for protection from successor liability, businesses will have an increasingly difficult time selling or transferring corporate assets.[111]

Most courts will echo Colorado's:

It is clear the weight of authority approves the traditional notions of successor corporation nonliability. We elect to follow the majority trend of nonliability of successor corporations . . .

. . . We recognize the result reached in this matter is harsh; however, we believe it is consistent with the current status of Colorado law. For us to come to any other conclusion would be an unwarranted exercise in decision making. We decline to apply the product line theory or the continuity of enterprise theory as urged by the Plaintiff.[112]

Other courts elect to follow all or part of the enterprise theory referred to by the Colorado court.

Continuation-of-Enterprise Liability

The leading case here was *Turner v. Bituminous Casualty Co.* [113] The machine at issue had been manufactured by a company which was taken over lock, stock, and barrel by a new company which continued to make the same products in the same plant with the same people under the same name. As the court there observed, "continuity is the purpose, continuity is the watch word, continuity is the fact." The court relied upon this continuity, in which the successor corporation held itself out as continuing the original enterprise, as the basis for imposing liability. The court noted that it would be unjust to allow the successor to hold itself out in this manner for the purpose of sales, while allowing it to deny continuity in order to defeat products liability claims.

The court adopted three criteria to test for the existence of continuity: whether there was a continuation of the enterprise of the original entity (including retention of key personnel, assets, name, etc.); whether the original entity ceased its ordinary business operations and dissolved promptly after the transaction; and whether the purchasing entity assumed those liabilities and obligations of the seller normally required for an uninterrupted continuation of the sellers' operation (and holding itself out to the world as the effective continuation of the seller corporation).

These criteria were adopted from cases which set forth a concept of "de facto merger." The court took pains to point out that the form of transaction was of secondary importance, so long as the necessary continuity was found.[114] A New York court preferred *Turner,* stating:

The *Turner* approach has the virtue that it based its imposition of liability upon the successor corporation's own acts, in holding itself out to be an unbroken continuation of the original enterprise. This approach is grounded in traditional tort principles.[115]

In contrast, a New Jersey Court found "product line" preferable to the "continuation of enterprise" theory set forth in *Turner*, since it believed that the primary focus should be on a continuation of the actual manufacturing operation rather than on the continuation of ownership and management. The court considered the unavailability of a remedy against the original manufacturer, the ability of the successor to spread the risk, and the justice of imposing liability on the successor as a burden necessarily attached to its enjoyment of the original company's name and trade.[116]

The debate will go on. The social policy articulated in some theories is that "solvent corporations, going concerns, should not be permitted to discharge their liabilities to injured persons simply by shuffling paper and manipulating corporate entities.[117] Again, courts are seeking to impose liability based on the public policy of spreading loss across society rather than on an individual. This burden is imposed on the firm, even though the successor corporation has not put the defective article into commerce, as strict product liability mandates.[118] The majority position remains that no one should be liable for torts they did not create.

For your planning and insurance purposes, it is important to review with counsel your state legal exposure when you seek to acquire the assets of another firm or to sell your firm. Further, awareness of your exposure here will enable you to include this potential liability when negotiating for your acquisition. You should then either purchase adequate product liability insurance or enter into an agreement under which your predecessor will indemnify you for any liability occasioned by the predecessor's product defects.

Now we'll move on to another creative way of funding deep pocket defendants when an aggrieved client searches for someone to sue.

Enterprise, Market-Share, and Concerted-Action Liability

In the 1930s a generic drug, diethystilbestrol (DES), was developed from a coal derivative in England. It was two and a half times more potent than natural estrogen. It was never patented and a number of firms marketed it for the treatment of certain pregnancy complications. This chemical, more than any other factor, has spurred the legal debate concerning industry-wide liability.

There are roughly five theories advanced to support industry-wide liability:

- civil conspiracy;
- concerted action;

- alternate liability;
- enterprise liability; and
- market share liability.

Civil Conspiracy

Generally, a cause of action here requires that two or more persons combine or enter an agreement to commit an unlawful act or to do an otherwise lawful act by unlawful means. Proof of malice must be shown. Three recent DES cases are representative of the lack of success of civil conspiracy to date.

In one case, the U.S. District Court[119] held that in order to state and prove a cause of action for civil conspiracy, the plaintiffs were required to allege and prove that the defendant had entered into an unlawful agreement for the express purpose of committing either a criminal act or an intentional tort. Negligence, the court held, was insufficient. After reviewing the elements of civil conspiracy under South Carolina law, the court concluded that the plaintiff, as a matter of law, could not make out a cause of action for civil conspiracy:

> Plaintiff has shown no meetings, no conferences, no telephone calls, no joint filings, no cooperation, no consolidation, no licensing—nothing that any two companies did together. Each company had its own distinct FDA filings, package literature, warnings, indications, manufacturing processes, trade names, and marketing practices . . . No evidence supports plaintiff's allegations of common efforts or concerted, conspiratorial action. In fact, all of the evidence proves that no defendant entered into any agreement or even cooperated with any other drug company in the licensing, manufacturing, marketing, or promotion of Stilbestrol [DES] for the use that plaintiff claims produced her injuries.[120]

Finally, a Pennsylvania court held that:

> Like the DES daughters in *Ryan* and *Collins*, the plaintiffs in the instant case have failed to allege the manner in which a conspiratorial scheme was devised and carried out. The complaint contains no averments of meetings, conferences, telephone calls, joint filings, cooperation, consolidation, or joint licensing. The plaintiffs have alleged no more than a contemporaneous and negligent failure to act. This was insufficient to state either a conspiratorial agreement or the requisite intent to cause injury. Similarly, the completed discovery fails to demonstrate facts necessary to a cause of action for conspiracy. The trial court correctly held, therefore, that the appellees were not liable to the plaintiffs on a theory of civil conspiracy.[121]

Concerted Action

The theory of concerted action is to be found in Section 876 of the Restatement (Second) of Torts. That Section provides that for harm resulting to a third person from the tortious conduct of another, one is subject to liability if he

(a) does a tortious act in concert with the other or pursuant to a common design with him,

(b) knows that the other's conduct constitutes a breach of duty and gives substantial assistance or encouragement to the other to so conduct himself, or

(c) gives substantial assistance to the other in accomplishing a tortious result and his own conduct, separately considered, constitutes a breach of duty to the third person.

The theory represents an expansion of product liability law, since it does not require that the defendant be guilty of any particular injurious conduct. The major cases on point arose from other DES litigation.[121] The injured party can proceed against any of the manufacturers, and they in turn may recover against manufacturers not brought into the action by the injured party.

Most courts have not supported this theory in DES actions due to the concern that a manufacturer would become liable for defects in its competitor's products.[122] As stated in one court:

The gravamen of the charge of concert is that defendants failed to adequately test the drug or to give sufficient warning of its dangers and that they relied upon the tests performed by one another and took advantage of each other's promotional and marketing techniques. These allegations do not amount to a charge that there was a tacit understanding or a common plan among defendants to fail to conduct adequate tests or give sufficient warnings, and that they substantially aided and encouraged one another in these omissions . . .

What the complaint appears to charge is defendants' parallel or imitative conduct in that they relied upon each other's testing and promotion methods. But such conduct describes a common practice in industry: a producer avails himself of the experiences and methods of others making the same or similar products. Application of the concept of concert of action to the situation would expand the doctrine far beyond its intended scope and *would render virtually any manufacturer liable for the defective products of an entire industry, even if it could be demonstrated that the product which caused the injury was not made by the defendant.*[123]

A minority of courts reflect the following view:

The specific problems presented by the widespread use of generic drugs, which render identification almost impossible to the user, let alone the ultimately harmed person, plus the absence of any uniform requirement for pharmacies to keep and maintain records over extended periods, cannot be permitted to prevent valid recoveries nor to allow some manufacturers to escape their liability altogether by means of this shroud of anonymity. We of this court, too, adhere to the view of Dean Pound that "[t]he Law must be stable but must not stand still."

It does not strain one's sense of fairness to allow a limited expansion of the doctrine of concerted action to cover the type of circumstances faced in a DES case where the traditional evidentiary requirements of tort law may be insurmountable.[124]

In this case the court found ample evidence from which a jury could determine the defendant was engaged in concerted action.

The original cooperation by the twelve manufacturers and pooling of information, the agreement on the same basic chemical formula, and the adoption of Lilly's literature as a model for package inserts for joint submission to the FDA in 1941, can rationally be construed as an express agreement for purposes of finding concerted action, even if such cooperation was first invited by the FDA. And Lilly, it will be remembered, was the leader of the voluntarily formed Small Committee, which organized and expedited the effort for the twelve. By this activity, these manufacturers were acting on behalf of all later manufacturers of DES inasmuch as they set the pattern for acceptance by the FDA.[125]

The court also invoked a unique comparison to conscious parallelism in antitrust. The court found it worthy of note that in antitrust cases, evidence of conscious parallel behavior without express agreement of conspiracy has long been accepted by the Supreme Court as a basis for finding of conspiracy.

The court believed that there was evidence in abundance of conscious parallel activity thereafter of the drug companies which later sought FDA approval of DES for use in treating risks of pregnancy—evidence from which may be inferred a tacit understanding. In fact, by terms of the FDA supplemental application form, applicants for this new usage of DES could, and did, rely on the data contained in the original application for DES usage concerning which no change was proposed.

Getting carried away with its desire to invent a right of recovery, the court eventually concluded that it "can easily be seen, the evidence implicating Lilly in this concerted action was overwhelming."[126] Eventually certain courts will simply announce an injury and then use a dart board to determine who will pay for the courts' "beneficence." Another dart board recovery theory discussed in the courts is "alternative liability."

Alternative Liability

Again, we'll be presented with a case where someone is injured, so it is presumed the wrongful conduct of one or more defendants in a defined class caused the injury. Rather than have a plaintiff demonstrate that the manufacture of the product by a specified defendant was the proximate cause of the injury, the court would reverse the burden and have the defendants determine which one of them caused the injury.

The American Law Institute succinctly states the theory in section 433B(3) of the Restatement (Second) of Torts (1965): "Where the conduct of two or more actors is tortious, and it is proved that harm has been caused to the plaintiff by only one of them, but there is uncertainty as to which one has caused it, the burden is upon each such actor to prove that he has not caused the harm."

The basis for this exception is said to be the injustice of permitting proved wrongdoers, who among them have inflicted an injury upon the entirely innocent plaintiff, to escape liability merely because the nature of their conduct and the resulting harm has made it difficult or impossible to prove which of them has caused the harm.

The classic case which inspired the Restatement (and clearly has no application to a mass defendant grouping tort such as the DES cases) is summarized as follows. Three men went bird hunting. When a bird was flushed, both defendants fired at it even though plaintiff Summers was directly in the line of fire and clearly visible. Summers was hit once in the eye and once in the lip. It was determined that both defendant hunters were negligent in firing their guns in the direction of plaintiff and that plaintiff could not identify which of the negligent defendants' shots hit him. The court shifted the burden of proof as to whose shot actually hit plaintiff to the two admittedly negligent hunters, the only possible tortfeasors.[127]

Only a few courts (and one is divided) agree that alternative liability is not clearly distinguishable in a mass tortfeasor case where the defendants are neither few, present, nor acting simultaneously.[128] The principle is criticized as imposing liability without fault on a class of manufacturers. It would result in the taking of the property of all the named defendants in order to pay for harm which may have been caused by only one of the defendants, or even by one who is not a party to the lawsuit, who is unknown to the defendants, over whom they have no control or even any meaningful contact.

Another theory that works better with a small group of easily defined tortfeasors, rather than an ill-defined class, is enterprise liability. Here again some courts have attempted to adapt what worked well as a clearly-distinguished fact scenario to another fact pattern where there is no commonality. Alternative and enterprise liability are vaguely similar in principle to group defamation. Where defamatory language refers to all members of a small, easily personified group, each member of such group may establish that the defamatory statement could be understood by the community to be of and concerning him or her.[129] If, however, the group grows too large, it is no longer possible to state precisely that the defamatory language could be understood to be "of or concerning the plaintiff."

Enterprise or Industry-Wide Liability[130]

This theory was first advanced in Judge Weinstein's 1972 opinion.[131] In that case, 13 children sued six blasting cap manufacturers alleging that they had been injured in explosions of the caps. Although the six defendants were not the only possible sources of blasting caps, they did comprise virtually the entire blasting cap industry in this country. Plaintiffs based their claim on the practices of that industry in failing to take reasonable safety precautions and make reasonable warnings. They alleged that members of the industry had adhered to industry-wide safety standards and had delegated substantial safety investigation and design functions to their trade association.

The court focused on the joint conduct of the defendants, finding that their joint control of the risk presented by their industry warranted the imposition of joint liability. Judge Weinstein limited his holding by warning against its application to a "decentralized" industry with many individual members.[132]

Enterprise liability, where it has found any favor, has had to establish at a minimum the following criteria:[133]

- The injury-causing product was manufactured by one of a small number of defendants in an industry.
- The defendants had joint knowledge of the risks inherent in the product and possessed a joint capacity to reduce those risks; and
- Each of them failed to take steps to reduce the risk but, rather, delegated this responsibility to a trade association.

When it has come to the fore in DES and similar tort cases, the courts have all appeared to quote the original *Hall* qualifications: "[w]hat would be fair and feasible with regard to an industry of five or ten producers might be manifestly unreasonable if applied to a decentralized industry composed of thousands of small producers."[134]

In the DES cases:

- There were a large number of defendants. Such numbers mitigate against group conduct requiring the imposition of liability on all for the acts of the unidentified wrongdoer.
- The DES manufacturers did not control their conduct by jointly imposed safety standards.
- The DES firms did not delegate control or responsibility for safety functions to a trade association.

A final theory in this area is that of market share liability.

Market-Share Liability

Market-share liability is based on a similar social principle, that is, that these costs are foreseeable and should be borne by those financially able to spread the risk rather than by an individual.

Market-share liability was announced in California in 1980.[135] A 22-year-old woman developed cervical cancer. Her mother had taken DES when she was pregnant with her daughter. The court held that she could sue all the drug makers collectively because she could not prove which one produced the particular DES her mother had taken. The reasoning was that all the makers of this drug should be jointly and severally liable for the young woman's cancer and that, provided that she joined enough manufacturers in her suit to account for a broad market share (here about 85 percent of the entire market was joined), there would be enough likelihood that the defendant would be "caught." Each defendant was held liable for the percentage of its share of the market sales unless it could show that it could not have manufactured the pills.

A major problem with this line of reasoning is the lack of a clear market. In this case national market shares were used, but equity would have seemed to dictate that the state where the injured party's mother resided or even the local market would have been a more realistic basis of market share.

In order to state a cause of action for market share liability,[136] a DES plaintiff must prove the following elements:

- that the plaintiff's mother took DES;
- that DES caused the plaintiff's subsequent injuries;
- that the defendant produced or marketed the type of DES taken by the plaintiff's mother; and
- that the defendant's conduct in producing or marketing the DES constituted a breach of a legally recognized duty to the plaintiff.

The court explained the plaintiff's burden of proof as follows:

[T]he plaintiff need not prove that a defendant produced or marketed the precise DES taken by the plaintiff's mother. Rather, the plaintiff need only establish by a preponderance of the evidence that a defendant produced or marketed the type (e.g., dosage, color, shape, markings, size or other identifiable characteristics) of DES taken by the plaintiff's mother; the plaintiff need not allege or prove any facts related to the time or geographic distribution of the subject DES.

After the plaintiff has made out a prima facie case, the burden will then shift to the defendants to establish their freedom from liability:

Individual defendants are entitled to exculpate themselves from liability by establishing, by a preponderance of the evidence, that they did not produce or market the particular type [of] DES taken by the plaintiff's mother; that they did not market the DES in the geographic area of the plaintiff mother's obtaining the drug; or that it did not distribute DES in the time period of plaintiff mother's ingestion of the drug.[137]

While California, Michigan, South Dakota, Washington, and Wisconsin have dropped the causation requirement at least as to DES, other courts are proving more responsive to the larger social picture as well as the proper function of the judiciary. In correctly rejecting this theory, the Iowa Supreme Court stated as follows:

> We reject the market share liability theory on a broad policy basis. We acknowledge that plaintiff in a DES case with an unidentified product manufacturer presents an appealing claim for relief. Endeavoring to provide relief, courts have developed theories which in one way or another provided plaintiff's recovery of loss by a kind of court-constructed insurance plan. The result is that manufacturers are required to pay or contribute to payment for injuries which their product may not have caused.
>
> This may or may not be a desireable result. We believe, however, that awarding damages to an admitted innocent party by means of a court-constructed device that places liability on manufacturers who were not proved to have caused the injury *involves social engineering more appropriate within the legislative domain.* In order to reach such a determination, three broad policy questions must be answered. *One is whether the burden of damages for these injuries should be transferred in a constitutional manner to the industry irrespective of an individual manufacturer's connection with the particular injury.* If so, the second question relates to the principles and procedures by which the burden would be transferred. Finally, how do we ascertain the extent of damages to be assessed against each manufacturer? As to the latter, we note a wide divergency of solutions advanced by courts in fashioning relief without the benefit of legislation.
>
> Our General Assembly has not entered this field, and we in the judicial branch adhere to our established principles of legal cause.
>
> . . . Plaintiffs request that we make a substantial departure from our fundamental negligence requirement of proving causation, without previous warning or guidelines. The imposition of liability upon a manufacturer for harm that it may not have caused is the very legal legerdemain, at least by our long held traditional standards, that we believe the courts should avoid unless prior warnings remain unheeded. It is an act more closely identified as a function assigned to the legislature under its power to enact.
>
> . . . We hold correspondingly that under Iowa common law a plaintiff in a products liability case must prove that the injury-causing product was a product manufactured or supplied by the defendant.

The Iowa court correctly did not allow itself to jettison its proper role for the emotional satisfaction of attempting to invent a remedy for isolated victims. The logic of a policy of dart-board recoveries where industries can face catastrophic losses at the whim of a judge who is prepared to ignore the common law precedents as well as his/her proper role *vis-a-vis* the legislators is short-sighted at best.

Judicial transfers of wealth have already made liability insurance impossible for many small firms and adequate insurance beyond the reach of many others. If insurance carriers believe they will be hostage to open-ended commitments of judicial social engineering, then insurance will become a luxury for the firms who have the mission of finding cures for cancer, AIDS, etc. The imposition of all "share the liability" remedies on firms who were not proved to have caused an injury is a legislative role. Courts carrying out erratic free-lance legislative agendas will chill research and development in the pharmaceutical and other risk industries by making them de facto insurers of their customers. In a balance of equities, society must move forward in a predictable manner. It can't if enterprise liabilities flourish.

Criminal Liability

The Ford Pinto case was a controversial criminal case in the product liability field. In 1980, Ford Motor Company was acquitted on reckless homicide charges stemming from the 1979 accident. The company and executives justifiably came out acquitted, but the firm lost the valuable Pinto as a viable sales product. Although there is little precedential value in the case, do not disregard it.

In general, reckless homicide (and similar charges) may result from a reckless failure to perform an act which one was under a duty to perform. Managers should assist the corporation in developing a product safety attitude. In light of the discussions throughout this chapter, such an attitude is clearly more than just good business.

For example, when involved in a product decision, be alert as to how much of the product's obvious (and occasionally fatal) defects you are aware of or someone could accuse you of being aware of. Failure to ask questions (if you have some) and to disassociate yourself from a potential injury-producing product could be as fatal to your career as it is to the product's user. Further, a criminal conviction not only can involve incarceration, but it also allows victims or their families to press forward with civil liability suits.

You should also be sensitive to your criminal liability exposure in the plant where you conduct your business. Products liability safety should begin at the design phase and carry through the proper assembly to the customer's hands. One such stage is a safe work environment.

A Polish immigrant who overstayed his visa died of cyanide poisoning while employed by Film Recovery Systems, Inc. After he died, his superiors reportedly ordered fellow workers, most of them illegal aliens like him, to dump the body outside, where it lay in subfreezing weather until an ambulance arrived. Three employees—the president, plant manager and foreman—were found guilty of murder and sentenced to 25-year prison terms.

As a business executive, you are familiar with your corporate criminal liability exposure in areas such as antitrust, securities, governmental contracting, or even the knowing transport of hazardous waste to a facility that does not have a permit.[138] A sensitivity here as well as a knowledge of the black letter law can save your firm the loss of goodwill and you, yourself, can avoid a trip to a federal/state facility.

Now we'll wind up this chapter by taking a look at one agency which is doing a lot of good for the consumer without being a negative factor for responsible firms.

The Consumer Product Safety Commission

The Consumer Product Safety Commission (CPSC) is an independent regulatory agency which was formed on May 14, 1973, under the provisions of the Consumer Product Safety Act (CPSA). The Commission has five members—three constitute a quorum for the transaction of business. The purpose of the Commission under the CPSA is

- to protect the public against *unreasonable* risks of injury associated with consumer products;
- to assist consumers in evaluating the comparative safety of consumer products;
- to develop uniform safety standards for consumer products (usually voluntary regulations as opposed to mandatory rules) and to minimize conflicting State and local regulations (such standards cover the design, construction, contents, performance and labeling of more than 15,000 consumer products); and
- to promote research and investigation into the causes and prevention of product-related deaths, illnesses, and injuries.

The Commission is composed of five members appointed by the President, by and with the advice and consent of the Senate, for terms of seven years.[139] It administers five safety acts:

- The Consumer Product Safety Act[140]
- The Flammable Fabrics Act[141]
- The Federal Hazardous Substances Act[142]
- The Poison Prevention Packaging Act of 1970;[143] and
- The Refrigerator Safety Act of 1956.[144]

The term "consumer product"

means any article, or component part thereof, produced or distributed (i) for sales to a consumer for use in or around a permanent or temporary household or residence, a school, in recreation, or otherwise, or (ii) for the personal use, consumption or enjoyment of a consumer in or around a permanent or temporary household or residence, a school, in recreation, or otherwise; but such term does not include: (A) any article which is not customarily produced or distributed for sale to, or use or consumption by, or enjoyment of, a consumer.

This statutory definition requires that the product be "customarily" (not just occasionally) produced or distributed for the use of consumers.[145]

Any interested person may petition the Commission to issue, amend, or revoke a rule or regulation by submitting a written request to the Secretary, Consumer Product Safety Commission, Washington, D.C. 20207.[146]

Consumer product safety standards come in two forms—standards and outright bans of a product. Throughout this standard-setting process the CPSC must confront subjective questions such as how safe is safe? How much risk should consumers be expected to assume in relation to how much cost they must incur? If it proceeds to develop any standard, the CPSC will publish a notice in the *Federal Register* and will afford a reasonable opportunity for interested persons to present relevant testimony and data.[147]

A product safety standard consists of one or more of the following: (1) requirements as to performance, composition, contents, design, construction, finish, or packaging of a consumer product; (2) requirements that a consumer product be marked with or accompanied by clear and adequate warnings or instructions, or requirements respecting the form of warnings or instructions. Any standard must be reasonably necessary to prevent or reduce any *unreasonable* risk of injury associated with such products.

The CPSA directs that a safety standard's provisions "shall, whenever feasible, be expressed in terms of performance requirements." The statutory preference for performance requirements is rooted in the belief that this mode of regulation stimulates product innovation, promotes the search for cost-effective means of compliance, and fosters competition by offering consumers a range of choices in the market place. In contrast, design-restrictive rules tend to freeze technology, stifle research aimed at better and cheaper compliance measures and deprive consumers of the opportunity to choose among competing designs.[148]

The CPSC has the power to ban products. The commission must establish that the product presents an unreasonable risk of injury to the public, which could not be eliminated through the issuance of a consumer product safety standard. It lacks the power to ban a product that through an improved design, or by the use of warnings and instructions, might be sold without an unreasonable risk of harm to the public.[149]

The commission may investigate a product within its jurisdiction. If it presents an "unreasonable risk of injury," it may develop rules to reduce the product's risk or, if no safety standard can protect the consumer, it may (although it rarely does) ban the product in question.[150]

Under the act, a proceeding to declare a product unsafe may also be initiated by any interested person (such as your disgruntled customer) or organization.[151] The commission must respond to this petition within 120 days. If it determines a need for such action, the commission follows the same procedure it would follow if the commission had started the proceeding. If the petition is denied or there is no action within 120 days, the petitioner may go to a United States district court to compel the commission to initiate the proceedings. If the petitioner convinces the court that a product presents an unreasonable risk of injury, the court may order the commission to initiate the action requested. The commission may then elect to investigate further. The CPSA provides for an informal rule making.[152]

Naturally you'll bring in your counsel immediately. From a marketing point of view, you must ensure that your counsel knows exactly what information provided by your firm is confidential and/or a trade secret. The commission has a duty not to disclose data that may injure a company. One decision[153] stated your rights well. The court noted that Congress specified that some information would be completely exempt from disclosure:

> All information reported to or otherwise obtained by the Commission or its representative under this Act which information contains or relates to a trade secret or other matter . . . shall be considered confidential and shall not be disclosed. . . .

> It is wholly improper, and forbidden by this section, for the Commission to disclose information provided by a company if, taking a realistic view of the environment in which that company operates, such disclosure would result in any significant competitive harm to the company. While no conclusive formula can be devised, factors such as these are to be taken into account in determining whether a document comes within the prohibition: whether the information is considered confidential by the submittor and given appropriate protection; whether the information would reveal to competitors operational strengths and weaknesses or other valuable information to which the submittor does not have access about these competitors; whether the information is readily available from other sources.[154]

What the Commission Will Look At

Congress expects the commission to weigh economic impact of their standards against the cost of their absence.[155] In view of this, each product is then reviewed as to:

> (A) the degree and nature of the risk of injury the rule is designed to eliminate or reduce;

> (B) the approximate number of consumer products, or types or classes thereof, subject to such rule;

> (C) the need of the public for the consumer products subject to such rule, and the probable effect of such rule upon the utility, cost, or availability of such products to meet such need; and

(D) any means of achieving the objective of the order while minimizing adverse effects on competition or disruption or dislocation of manufacturing and other commercial practices consistent with the public health and safety.[156]

Then the Commission must also find:

(A) that the rule (including its effective date) is reasonably necessary to eliminate or reduce an unreasonable risk of injury associated with such product;

(B) that the promulgation of the rule is in the public interest; . . .[157]

For example, a court held on review that requirements to reduce the hazard of accidentally ignited matches were "reasonably necessary" under the act, since there was substantial evidence that a sizable number of persons are injured annually by matchbooks which accidentally ignite and since the cost of reducing such hazard to the industry was relatively small.[158]

This balancing test illustrates the need for the written documentation concerning the testing of your product as to safety that we discussed earlier in this chapter. Such documentation may be a critical element in establishing that the risk of any harm inherent in your product is balanced by other compelling factors. Can you demonstrate through your market research that a safety improvement will greatly increase the cost of your product beyond the reach of your customer's ability to purchase it? Consumers in lower-income brackets may willingly accept greater risks to save money. If you can document the utility of your product to them, you may be able to convince the commission (or a court) that denying the product to them is not worth a slight improvement in safety.

The commission has authority (see below) to order the manufacturer or any distributor or retailer of the product to give public notice of any product that fails to comply with an applicable consumer product safety rule or has a defect that creates a substantial risk or injury to the public. The commission may order the manufacturer, distributor, or retailer of the product either to repair or replace the product, or to refund the purchase price of such product. Finally, the commission can correct the problem by issuing labeling and/or packaging standards.

The CPSA makes violations of the act subject to a civil fine of up to $2,000 for each violation of the act. The maximum civil penalty is $500,000 for any related series of violations. The act also makes a knowing and willful violation of the act subject to a fine of not more than $5,000, or imprisonment for not more than one year, or both. A failure to properly report a product defect (see below) can also result in a private cause of action against you under the act.

Your Firm's Obligations If You Discover a Hazard

Manufacturers, distributors, and retailers have a responsibility to report to the CPSC any product they suspect could cause a substantial hazard to consumers, even if such hazard is not immediately confirmed. The CPSA requires every manufacturer (including an importer), distributor or retailer of a consumer product who obtains information which reasonably supports the conclusion that such a product either fails to comply with an applicable consumer product safety rule, or contains a *defect,* which *could* (when in doubt—contact the CPSC) create a substantial product hazard, to *immediately* (within 24 hours after you obtain the information, even if not all the details are available) inform the commission, unless the firm has actual knowledge that the commission has been adequately informed. A defect not only includes patent defects, but latent ones also. If your assembly instructions omit an important assembly feature, an otherwise safe product may have a dangerous defect.

The act defines substantial product hazard to include "a product defect which (because of the pattern of defect, the number of defective products distributed in commerce, the severity of the risk, or otherwise) creates a substantial risk of injury to the public." The definition is not precise, and requires a balancing of the relevant factors to determine whether a product presents a substantial risk of injury. A product that could cause death may be a substantial product hazard even though very few of them have been sold; conversely, a product that presents a risk of minor injury could be a substantial product hazard if a great many have been sold.

The first report to the CPSC must include:

- the nature of the hazard described with the best information you have available;
- an estimate of the number of your products involved;
- information, if any, about any injuries and/or complaints; and
- your plans for corrective action and the corrective action taken to date, if any.

Subsequent reports must fill in the details as listed in the CPSC regulations,[159] including

- estimates of the number, nature and severity of injuries;
- whether your product is still being manufactured; and
- copies of relevant consumer complaints.

A retailer or distributor of a possibly defective product, who is neither a manufacturer nor an importer of the product, can satisfy its reporting obligations by either

First—telephoning or writing the Product Defect Correction Division of the CPSC;

Second—sending a letter describing the defective product to the manufacturer of the product with a copy of the letter to the Product Defect Correction Division; or

Third—forwarding to the Product Defect Correction Division reportable information received from another firm.

These simplified reporting procedures are helpful in complying with the Act, and recognize that the retailer is frequently in a poor position to evaluate the potential hazards associated with a product.[160]

The CPSC will then determine whether the hazards are serious enough to warrant a recall or some lesser drastic form of corrective relief (you would be advised to order the CPSC's "Hazard Priority and Corrective Action Guidelines"). The CPSC Compliance Officer will negotiate the wording of the press release with the manufacturer. Then, if a recall is required, your basic responsibilities include getting the recalled products off the shelves or back from consumers; informing consumers of the recall; and, arranging for replacement or repair of the product or refund of the customer's money.

Your Target Audience

As a manager you know your market, and your target market may greatly increase your exposure to the commission's scrutiny. The commission has been criticized for relying on the National Electronic Injury Surveillance System (NEISS—the acronym is pronounced "nice") injury data to the exclusion of almost all else. NEISS (at least initially) only reported product-related accidents which caused problems because certain products may relate to accidents without causing them. Also, the NEISS data counted only actual injuries, ignoring exposures.

If the old, the infirm, and children are your market, you may have increased exposure to the commission. For example, children under 10 years of age receive added weight. Accidents affecting this group are counted twice in the compilation of data as a result of the age-adjusted frequency severity index.

Products not remotely affecting children may come before the commission. Such an innocuous product as an extension cord warranted a specific safety standard to protect children, who had a high frequency of injuries resulting from such cord.

Sample Internal Policies/Controls to Enhance Product Safety

You should regard the standards of the CPSC as a minimum. Exceeding their standards is helpful in other ways for the mere compliance with the CPSC's standards is *not* a defense in a products liability suit. The following checklist should be considered in avoiding a products liability action and/or exposure to the CPSC and, on a positive note, in preserving your goodwill.

Before We Begin

☐ Do I have adequate information systems? Careful record keeping from design through marketing is a good management tool. It can assist you to spot defects as they arise, assist in recalling defective products, and act to mitigate your adverse exposure in a lawsuit. The downside is that such records may be subpoenaed and used against you. However, the failure to produce such records may be equally damaging in court.

☐ Do we have an internal safety review committee supported by top management?

Design Phase

☐ Are we careful to document all steps of our design, testing results and manufacturing efforts?

☐ Did we document all changes in design?

☐ Did we selectively and routinely test (internally as well as with independent groups and/or labs) for allergies, toxicity, etc.? (For example, videotape a child playing with a toy to see if the "child's approach" might turn up something—even remote—your adult design people didn't consider.) Did we test our products for safety as to their market and use by children where it is reasonable to anticipate that a child might come into contact with your product?

☐ Did we test again in the United States a product we tested/manufactured overseas? What special considerations are given to a product which will be self-installed or assembled by an amateur?

☐ Did we utilize an independent laboratory to test materials, components, prototypes and final products for safety and performance? Can we verify that such standards satisfy both voluntary and mandatory standards?

☐ Have we identified all select hazard sources in our product such as chemicals, subjectivity to temperatures, etc.? Have all hazards been identified in the product, such as electrical exposure?

Prepare for Production

☐ Do we develop sources of raw materials and suppliers who are safety conscious?

☐ Have we developed purchasing specifications and contracts to protect ourselves as to raw materials and supplies?

☐ Are all workers properly trained for the production to be done as well as inculcated in the need for safety consciousness?

☐ Are we consistent by showing the same regard for our workers' safety while they construct our safe product? Are we sensitive to noise levels, deficient or aging machines, unsafe storage of chemicals, slippery floors, missing machine guides, etc.?

☐ Do we periodically test the product?

☐ Are all our instructions and procedures in writing?

Product Distribution

☐ *Advertising/Use Instruction.* Is our advertising directed to the proper audience? If it is complicated, you might wish to set up safety demonstrations in departments of your or your retailers' stores.

☐ *Packaging.* Has the package been tested to assure that it (as well as the product inside) can withstand its expected mode of transportation (truck, mail, etc.)?

☐ *Labels/Warnings.* Are these affixed outside the package when necessary as well as on our product? Have we anticipated any special language needs of our recipients? Have we attempted to anticipate misuse? (Have your counsel review such tests and documents plus your labels, catalogs, and other promotional material as to wording and suitability to your target audience. If you are investigated, identify for your counsel all documents which must be kept confidential.)

☐ *Retailers.* Are they safety conscious? They can provide you with valuable feedback. You should actively solicit this feedback from them.

☐ *Merchandise Displays.* Are we sure our stores are designed in such a way that no merchandise is hazardously displayed (clear risks, no sharp, protruding edges, etc.)?

☐ *Instruction.* Are all our instructions clearly worded for our targeted audience? Have we included any instructions for repairs/maintenance our customers can make? Do we exaggerate our safety features, possibly giving the user a false sense of security?

☐ *Warranties.* Are all warranties displayed and/or provided for, in compliance with the Magnuson Moss Act (see following chapter)?

Customer Contact

☐ Is correspondence audited and followed up on?

☐ Do we provide a toll-free number to facilitate prompt resolution as well as a rapid source of customer feedback concerning any product problem?

☐ Do we follow up immediately upon complaints/injuries which might reasonably indicate we have a defective product?

☐ Have we established by contract with distributors and retailers any recall obligations?

☐ Have we provided for returning such products to service centers and for distributing replacement parts?

☐ Have we conducted a dry run to make sure our CPSC contacts and recall procedures would work under the exigencies of stress/time?

Management Support

☐ Do we have written procedures and a clear chain of command so all personnel know what action is required and who is in charge (press, regulatory agencies contact, managing product recall campaigns, et al) if a product safety incident occurs?

☐ Is our senior management actively and visibly committed to our product safety campaign? This commitment will influence management down the vertical chain.

☐ Finally, have we discussed with our counsel in advance any unique characteristics of our product which might remove it from the statutory jurisdiction of the Consumer Products Safety Commission?

Conclusion

This chapter has covered many diverse areas. You must be alert to product design, safety features, the target audience variable, and many other areas of liability. This information will help you avoid risk—a goal dear to all business executives.

In view of the variety of court decisions and the varied state and federal legislative and regulatory activity on point, it is difficult to predict the future of industry liability (and your own). You must work closely with your counsel, particularly in drafting contracts with firms with whom you deal and for whom you distribute and in dealing with your advertising agency regarding their promotional proposals. You should also work with your counsel in establishing your own internal procedures for product selection and testing and control of product promotions that will reach the public (and come to the attention of federal and state government agencies). Your attorney's skilled input will see that you have proper indemnification and insurance protection.

ENDNOTES

(1) *Seely v. White Motor Co.,* 63 Cal 2d 9, 15, 403 P2d 149 (1965). For an excellent overview of the tort/contract issues see "The Role of the Judge In Tort Law," (three articles by Messrs. Fischer, Henderson, and Twerski), *Hofstra Law Review,* Vol. II, No. 3, Spring 1983, p. 845–996.

(2) *MacPherson v. Buick Motor Company,* 217 NY 382, 111 NE (1916).

(3) *Escola v. Coca Cola Bottling Co.,* 24 Cal 2d 462, 150 P2d 141 (1944) (concurring opinion).

(4) *Marsh Wood Products Co. v. Babcock & Wilcox Co.,* 207 Wis 209, 226, 240 NW 392, 399 (1932); *Genesee County Patrons Fire Relief Ass'n v. L. Sonneborn Sons, Inc.,* 263 NY 463, 469–473, 189 NE 551, 553–555 (1934).

(5) See Note 1, 63 Cal 2d 9, 19 and 403 P2d 149, 152 (1965).

(6) *Santor v. A and M Karagheusian, Inc.,* 44 NJ 52, 66-67, 207 A2d 305, 312–313 (1965).

(7) *In Spring Motors Distributors, Inc. v. Ford Motor Co.,* 98 NJ 579, 489 A2d 672 (N.J. Court rejected holding of *Santor;* see Note 6 in a commercial context). See also

Jones & Laughlin Steel Corp. v. Johns-Manville Sales Corp., 626 F2d 280, 287 and n.13 (CA3 1980).

(8) *Northern Power & Engineering Corp. v. Caterpillar Tractor Co.*, 623 P2d 324, 330 (Alaska 1981).

(9) *Russell v. Ford Motor Co.*, 281 Ore 587, 595, 575 P2d 1383, 1387 (1978). See also *East River S.S. v. Transamerica Delaval*, 90 LEd 2d 865, 54 L.W. 4649 (1986) (unanimous decision).

(10) See note 2 and *Campo v. Scofield*, 301 NY 468, 95 NE2d 802 (1950) (for a succinct statement of the latent-patent rule), though see its demise in *Micallef v. Miehle Co.*, 39 NY2d 376, 385-86, 348 NE2d 571, 577-78, 384 NYS2d 115, 120-21 (1976). See also *Meyer v. Gehl Co.*, 42 AD2d 461, 36 NY2d 760 (1975).

(11) *Holm v. Sponco Mfg., Inc.*, 324 NW2d 207 (Minn. 1982). See also *Davis v. Fox River Tractor Co.*, 518 F2d 481 (10th Cir. 1975) (applying Oklahoma law); *Beloit Corp. v. Harrell*, 339 S2d 992 (Ala. 1976); *Byrns v. Riddle, Inc.*, 113 Ariz 264, 550 P2d 1065 (1976); *Pike v. Frank G. Hough Co.*, 2 Cal 3d 465, 467 P2d 229, 85 Cal Rptr 629 (1970); *Auburn Machine Works Co. v. Jones*, 366 S2d 1167 (Fla. 1979); *Brown v. Clark Equipment Co.*, 62 Haw 530, 618 P2d 267 (1980); *Uloth v. City Tank Corp.*, 376 Mass 874, 384 NE2d 1188 (1978); *Stenberg v. Beatrice Foods Co.*, 176 Mont 123, 576 P2d 725 (1978); *Casey v. Gifford Wood Co.*, 61 Mich App 208, 232 NW 2d 360 (1975); *Thibault v. Sears, Roebuck, & Co.*, 118 NH 802, 395 A2d 843 (1978); *Ferrigno v. Eli Lilly and Co.*, 175 NJ Super 551, 420 A2d 1305 (1980); *Micallef v. Miehle Co.*, 39 NY2d 376, 385-86, 348 NE2d 571, 577-78, 384 NYS2d 115, 120-21 (1976) (overruling Campo in note 10); *Olson v. A.W. Chesterton Co.*, 256 NW2d 530 (N.D. 1977); *Palmer v. Massey-Ferguson, Inc.*, 3 Wash App. 508, 476 P2d 713 (1970). But see *Vineyard v. Empire Machine Co.*, 119 Ariz 502, 504–05, 581 P2d, 1152, 1154-55 (1978).

(12) *Smith v. General Paving Co.*, 58 Ill App 3d 336, 16 Ill Dec 359, 374 NE 2d 1134 (1978); *Clinton v. Commonwealth Edison Co.*, 36 Ill App 3d 1064, 344 NE 2d 509 (1976).

(13) *McLaughlin v. Mine Safety Appliance Co.*, 11 NY 2d 62 (1967).

(14) *Bach v. Wiches Corp.*, 375 Mass 633, 643, 378 NE 2d 964 (1978) Brownstone v. Times Square Stage Lighting, 39 AD2d 892, 333 NYS2d 781 (1972).

(15) *Alfieri v. Cabot Corp.*, 13 NY2d 1027 (1963). See also *Pigone v. Sarita Anita Mfg. Corp.*, 457 NE2d 642 (Mass. App. 1983) and *Kalivas v. A.J. Feliz Co.*, 446 NE 2d 726 (1983).

(16) *Richard v. American Mfg. Co., Inc.*, 489 NE 2d 214 (Mass. App. 1986). See *Smith v. Ariens*, 375 Mass 620, 625, 377 NE2d 954 (1978). See also *Uloth v. City Tank Corp.*, 376 Mass 874, 881, 384 NE2d 1188 (1978); *Fahey v. Rockwell Graphic Systems, Inc.*, 20 Mass App Ct 642, 649, 482 NE 2d 519 (1985).

(17) *Pigone v. Santa Anita Mfg. Corp.*, 457 NE2d 642 (Mass. App. 1983). See also *Torre v. Harris-Seybold Co.*, 9 Mass App 660, 671-673, 677, 404 NE2d 96 (1980).

(18) *Larsen v. General Motors Corp.*, 391 F2d 495 (8th Cir. 1968).

(19) *Schmidt v. Plains Electrics, Inc.*, 281 NW2d 794 (1979). As to pre-purchase "trials," see *Thorpe v. Robert Bullock, Inc.*, 348 S.E.2d 55 (1986).

(20) *Alm v. Aluminum Co. of America*, 717 SW2d 588 (Tex. 1986).

(21) Id. p. 598 (here bottler had control of labeling and so the bottler, not manufacturer, is the one possessing the adequate means to pass warnings on to consumers). See also *Magro v. Ragsdale Brothers, Inc.*, 721 S.W. 2d 832 (Tex. 1986).

(22) *Perkins v. Emerson Elec. Co.*, 482 FSupp 1347 (1980).

(23) *Filler v. Royex Corp.*, 435 F2d 336 (7th Cir. 1970).

(24) *Lake Washington School Dist. No. 414 v. Schuch's Auto Supply, Inc.*, 613 P2d 561 (1980).

(25) Edward M. Swartz, "Toys-R-Dangerous," *Trial*, February 1982, p. 29.

(26) See Rudolph Flesch, *How to Test Readability,* Harper & Brothers, New York, 1951.

(27) *Hulsman v. Hemmeter Development Corp.,* 647 P2d 713 (Hawaii, 1982).

(28) *Hill v. Acme Markets, Inc.,* 504 A2d 324, 325-26 (Pa Super 1986).

(29) *Corsetti v. Stone Co.,* 483 NE2d 793, 805-806 (Mass 1985).

(30) *Carter v. Rand McNally & Co.,* No. 76-1864-F (D. Mass 9/4/80); *contra Alm v. Van Nostrand Reinhold Co., Inc.,* 480 NE2d 1263 (Ill App. 1 Dist. 1985) (adverse effect of such liability upon public's free access to ideas would be too high a price to pay). See also *Columbia Broadcasting System, Inc. v. Democratic National Committee,* 412 US 94, 93 SCt 2080, 36 LEd 2d 772 (1973). See also Alan J. Hoetnick, "Responsibility for Poison in Recipe: 1st Amendment or Products Liability?", *New York Law Journal,* Dec. 1986, p. 5; Donald Wallis, "Negligent Publishing: Implications for University Publishers," *Journal of College and University Law,* Vol. 9 No 2, p. 209–227 (1982-83) and Kathleen McDermott, "Liability for Negligent Dissemination of Product Information: A Proposal for Assuring a More Responsible Writership," *The Forum,* p. 557–576 (1983).

(31) *Dun & Bradstreet, Inc. v. Greenmoss Builders, Inc.,* 105 SCt 2939 (1985).

(32) *Greenman v. Yuba Power Products, Inc.,* 59 Cal 2d 57, 377 P2d 897, 900, 27 Cal Rptr 697, 700 (1963). The doctrine of strict liability in tort applies to *both* physical harm to the ultimate purchaser and harm to his/her property. See *Mendleson v. General Motors,* 432 NYS2D 132, *aff'd* 441 NYS2d (AD 4/10/81).

(33) See *Cover v. Cohen,* 61 NY2d 261, 473 NYS2d 378, 461 NE2d 864 (1984); *Mead v. Warner Pruyn Division, Finch Pruyn Sales, Inc.,* 57 AD2d 340, 394 NYS2d 483 (3d Dept. 1977); *Queensbury Union Free School District v. Jim Walter Corporation,* 91 Misc 2d 804, 398 NYS2d 832 (Sup. Ct. Warren Co. 1977).

(34) *Micallef v. Miehle Co.,* 39 NY2d 376, 348 NE2d 571, 384 NYS2d 115 (1976).

(35) *Robinson v. Reed-Prentice Division,* 49 NY2d 471, 479, 403 NE2d 440, 446-7 (1980).

(36) See note 32. Also of interest is the landmark case *MacPherson v. Buick Motor Co.,* 217 NY 382, 11 NE 1050 (1916).

(37) See note 32.

(38) *Mead v. Warner-Pruyn Division, Finch Pruyn Sales, Inc.,* 57 AD2d 340, 394 NYS2d 483 (3d Dept. 1977) (A retailer was held liable to the last purchaser for his death nearly two years after the purchase by the decedent. Save your receipts—forever.). See also *Vandermark v. Ford Motor Co.,* 61 Cal 2d 256, 37 Cal Rptr 896, 391 P2d 168 (1964).

(39) *Infante v. Montgomery Ward & Co.,* 49 AD2d 72, 75, 371 NY2d 500 (1975).

(40) *Scandinavian Airlines Sys. v. United Aircraft Corp.,* 601 F2d 425 (9th Cir. 1979).

(41) *Kirby v. Rouselle Corp.,* 437 NYS2d 512 (1981).

(42) *Winters v. Sears, Roebuck & Co.,* 554 SW2d 565, 571 (1977).

(43) Id. at 570.

(44) Id. at 572.

(45) *Phillips v. Kinwood Mach. Co.,* 269 Or 485, 492, 525 P2d 1033, 1036 (1974).

(46) *Cover v. Cohen,* 92 AD2d 928, 61 NY2d 261, 461 NE2d 864, 866 (1984).

(47) *T.J. Hooper,* 60 F2d 737 (2d Cir.), *cert. denied,* 387 US 662 (1932).

(48) *Fahey v. Rockwell Graphic Systems, Inc.,* 482 NE2d 519, 523 (Mass App 1985). See also *Rhoads v. Service Mach. Co.,* 329 FSupp 367 (E.D. Ark 1971); *Pike v. Frank G. Hough Co.,* 2 Cal 3d 465, 467 P2d 229, 85 Cal Rptr 629 (1970).

(49) See note 35.

(50) *Hatcher v. American Motors Corp.,* 241 S2d 147 (1970). After purchase, an independent auto mechanic improperly installed overload springs in a car. This subsequent modification, and not a design defect, resulted in the injury. For a more recent decision, see *Daberko v. Heil Co.,* 661 F2d 445 (1982). Again, the fact that a manufacturer might have designed a safer product doesn't necessarily mean that the current one is unreasonably dangerous.

(51) *Jasper v. Skyhood Corp.,* 547 P2d 1140 (1976).

(52) *Wilson v. Piper Aircraft Corp.,* 579 P2d 1287 (1978). But contra see *Azzarello v. Black Brothers Co.,* 480 P 547, 391 A2d 1020 (1978).

(53) See note 48.

(54) *McCabe Powers Body Co. v. Sharp,* 594 SW2d 592, 595 (1980).

(55) See note 47, 461 NE2d 864, 871-72 (1984). See also *Schumacher v. Richards Shear Co.,* 59 NY2d 239, 247, 464 NYS2d 437, 451 NE2d 195 (198?).

(56) See note 34. Such documentation can also come back to haunt you; an injured party was permitted to show that about 4 years after the accident the manufacturer modified its design and cured the alleged defect by modification known 8 years *before* the accident. See *Capara v. Chrysler Corp.,* 52 NY2d 114, 417 NE2d 545 (1981).

(57) *Melia v. Ford Motor Co.,* 534 F2d 795 (8th Cir. 1976) (Nebraska law); *Karjala v. Johns-Manville Prods. Corp.,* 523 F2d 155 (8th Cir. 1975) (Minnesota law); *Borel v. Fibreboard Paper Products Corp.,* 493 F2d 1076 (5th Cir. 1973), *cert. denied,* 419 US 869 (1974).

(58) *Uloth v. City Tank Corp.,* 384 NE2d 1188, 1192 (1978).

(59) *Holm v. Sponco Mfg., Inc.,* 324 NW2d 207 (Minn 1982); *Schmidt* v. *Plains Electric, Inc.,* 281 NW2d 794 (ND 1979).

(60) *Hunt v. Harley-Davidson Motor Co.,* 248 SE2d 15 (1978). See also *LeBoeuf v. Goodyear Tire & Rubber Co.,* 623 F2d 985, 988 (5th Cir. 1980) and *Moran v. Fabrege, Inc.,* 273 Md. 538, 332 A2d 11 (1975).

(61) *Taylor v. Gerry's Ridgewood, Inc.,* 90 NE2d 987, 991 (Ill App. 3d Dist. 1986). In other situations make sure you demand the history of your product's servicing and maintenance record (or lack of same). See *Glass v. Allis-Chalmers Corp.,* 618 FSupp 314 (D.C. Mo. 1985).

(62) *Curry v. Louis Allis Co.,* 100 Ill App 3d 910, 56 Ill Dec 174, 427 NE2d 254 (1981).

(63) *Leichtomer v. American Motors Corp.,* 67 Ohio St 2d 456, 469, 424 NE2d 568, 578 (1981). See also *McCann v. Atlas Supply Co.,* 325 FSupp 701 (1971).

(64) *Chappins v. Sears, Roebuck & Co.,* 358 S2d 926 (1978).

(65) Id. at 930.

(66) *Blackburn v. Johnson Chemical Co., Inc.,* 490 NYS2d 452, 455 (Sup 1985).

(67) *Howard v. Fabrege, Inc.,* 679 SW2d 644 (Tex App. 1 Dist. 1984). See also *Kenny v. Southeastern Transport,* 581 F2d 351 (3d Cir. 1978) (evidence of increased lighting after accident admitted).

(68) Id., p. 650.

(69) *Reyes v. Wyeth Labs,* 498 F2d 1264, 1277 (5th Cir. 1974), *cert. denied,* 419 US 1096 (1974). (Since the manufacturer had reason to know that the vaccine was "dispensed without the sort of individualized medical balancing of the risks to the vaccinee that is contemplated by the prescription drug exception," it was under a duty to warn the plaintiff of the dangers inherent in its vaccine.) See also *Petty v. U.S.,* 740 F2d 1428 (8th Cir. 1984) and *Unthank v. U.S.,* 732 F2d 1517 (10th Cir 1984). As to what constitutes reasonable steps to bring warnings to the attention of the medical profession, see *Baker v. St. Agnes Hospital,* 421 NYS2d 81 (1979) and *Wolfgumber v. Upjohn Co.,* 52 NY2d 768 (1981).

(70) *The Trustees of Columbia University v. Exposaic Industries, Inc.,* AD2d (1st Dep't, Aug. 28, 1986).

(71) *Dunn v. Lederle Laboratories,* 121 Mich App 73, 81-82, 328 NW2d 576, 581 (1982).

(72) Restatement of Torts (Second), section 402A, comment (f). See also *Gobhai v. KLM Royal Dutch Airlines,* 57 NY2d 839, *affd.* 85 AD2d 566 (where distribution of an allegedly defective product is incidental to defendant's regular business the principles of strict product liability have no relevance).

(73) *Hall v. State,* 106 Misc 2d 860, 435 NYS2d 663 (1981).

(74) *Seely v. White Motor Co.,* 63 Cal 2d 18, 403 P2d 151 (1965).

(75) *Escola v. Coca Cola Bottling Co.,* 24 Cal 2d 462, 150 P2d 441 (1944) (concurring opinion).

(76) *East River S.S. v. Transamerica Delaval,* 90 LEd 2d 865, 879, 54 CW 4649 (1986).

(77) See J. White and R. Summers, Uniform Commercial Code 406 (2d ed. 1980).

(78) UCC sec. 2-313 1(a).

(79) *Klages v. General Ordnance Equipment Corp.,* 367 A2d 304, 310 (Pa. Super. 1976) and *Filler* v. *Rayex Corp.,* 435 F2d 336 (7th Cir. 1970).

(80) UCC sec. 2-314. For an excellent review of the traditional areas of liability, see Fred W. Morgan, "Marketing and Product Liability: A Review and Update," *Journal of Marketing,* vol. 46, no. 3, Summer 1982, pp. 69–78. Table 2 is particularly useful in highlighting reference cases according to your marketing function (e.g., selling, advertising, wholesaling). If you're serving food you should review 656 F. Supp 445, (D. Md. 1987).

(81) USS sec. 2-315. Efforts to exclude or modify implied warranties of merchantability or fitness for consumers are usually unenforceable, e.g., see Section 75-2-315.1, *Mississippi Code* (1972).

(82) UCC sec. 2-719(3) and UCC sec. 2-316 (approximately 10 states prohibit *all* warranty disclaimers). Further, the UCC drastically curtails the requirement of privity between the persons injured by a defective product and the manufacturer and/or seller in actions based on breach of warranty. See UCC sec. 2-318 and Comment 2.

(83) See Notes 48 and 79 and *Swartz v. General Motors Corp.,* 375 Mass 628, 630, 378 NE2d 61 (1978); *Correia v. Firestone Tire & Rubber Co.,* 388 Mass 342, 353, 446 NE2d 1033 (1983).

(84) *Barker v. Lull Engr. Co.,* 20 Cal 3d 431, 143 Cal Rptr 225, 573 P2d 443 (1978).

(85) *Richard v. American Mfg. Co., Inc.,* 489 NE 214 (Mass. App. 1986).

(86) *Kosters v. Seven-Up Co.,* 595 F2d 347 (6th Cir. 1979). See also Note, *Trademark—Strict Tort Liability in Warranty of a Franchisor-Consumer Reliance on Trade Names, Kosters v. Seven-Up Co.,* 7 N Ky Law Rev 113, 116 (1980).

(87) *Gizzi v. Texaco, Inc.,* 437 F2d 308 (3d Cir. 1971). See in general, Stephen E. Carr, "Liability of Franchisors and Franchisees for the Sale of Defective Products—Placing the Burden with the Blame, " *Franchise Law Journal,* Vol. 4, No. 3, Winter 1985.

(88) Ben-Aaron, Diana, "User Lawsuit Puts Lotus on the Defensive," *Information Week,* 8/25/86, p. 14-16.

(89) *Ray v. Alad Corp.,* 19 Cal 3d 22, 560 P2d 3, 136 Cal Rptr 574 (1977). See also *Corsetti v. Stone Co.,* 483 NE2d 793, 805 (Mass 1985).

(90) *Ramirez v. Amstel Ind., Inc.,* 86 NJ 332, 431 A2d 811 (1981).

(91) *Kline v. Johns-Manville,* 745 F2d 1217, 1219 (9th Cir. 1984).

(92) Note 89, 19 Cal 3d 34, 560 P2d 11, 136 Cal Rptr 582.

(93) Note 88, 19 Cal 3d 3, 560 P2d 8, 9, 136 Cal Rptr 579-80.

(94) *Nelson v. Tiffany Industries, Inc.,* 778 F2d 533, 535-36 (9th Cir. 1985). The most widely followed rules of successor corporation liability were noted by the United States Supreme Court in *Golden State Bottling Co. v. NLRB,* 414 US 169, 94 SCt 414, 38 LEd 2d 388 (1973).

(95) Note 90, p. 1219-20.

(96) *Darvejko v. Jorgensen Steel Co.,* 290 Pa Super Ct 15, 434 A2d 106, 109 (1981).

(97) *Hall v. Armstrong,* 103 Wash 2d 258, 692 P2d 787 (1984). See also *Martin v. Abbott Laboratories,* 102 Wash 2d 581, 689 P2d 368 (1984).

(98) *Florum v. Elliot Mfg. Co.,* 629 FSupp 1145 (D. Colo. 1986).

(99) *Gonzalez v. Rock Wool Eng. and Equipment Co.,* 117 Ill App 3d 435, 72 Ill Dec 917, 453 NE2d 792 (1983); *Freeman v. White Way Sign & Maintenance Co.,* 82 Ill App 3d 884, 38 Ill Dec 264, 403 NE2d 495 (1980).

(100) *Stratton v. Garvey Intern., Inc.,* 9 Kan App 2d 254, 676 P2d 1290 (1984).

(101) *Andrews v. John E. Smith's Sons Co.,* 369 S2d 781 (Ala 1979).

(102) *Bernard v. Kee Manuf. Co., Inc.,* 409 S2d 1047 (1982).

(103) *Jones v. Johnson Machine & Press,* 211 Neb 724, 320 NW2d 481 (1982).

(104) *Salvati v. Blaw-Knox Food & Chemical Equipment,* 497 NYS 2d 242 (Sup. 1985).

(105) *Ostrowski Hydra-Tool Corp.,* 144 Vt 305, 479 A2d 126, 127 (1984).

(106) *Fish* v. *Amsted Industries, Inc.* 376 NW2d 820 (Wis. 1985).

(107) *Young* v. *Fulton Iron Works Co.,* 709 SW2d 927 (Mo App. 1986).

(108) *Bourque v. Lehmann Lathe, Inc., 476 S2d 1125 (La App. 3 Cir. 1985).*

(109) Note 103, p. 247.

(110) Note 106, p. 827.

(111) Note 105, p. 830 (concurrence—emphasis my own.).

(112) Note 97, p. 1149 citing *MacMillan Bloedel Ltd. v. Flinkote Co.,* 760 F2d 580 (5th Cir. 1985); *Bud Antle, Inc. v.Eastern Foods, Inc.,* 758 F2d 1451 (11th Cir. 1985); *Mozingo v. Correct Manufacturing Corp.,* 752 F2d 168 (5th Cir. 1985); *Dayton v. Peck, Stow and Wilcox Co.,* 739 F2d 690 (1st Cir. 1984); *Weaver v. Nash International, Inc.,* 730 F2d 547 (8th cir. 1984); *Travis v. Harris Corp.,* 565 F2d 443 (7th cir. 1977); see also to the same effect: *Products Liability—Successor Corporations—Liability for Defects in Predecessor's Products, Stratton* v. *Gravey International, Inc.,* 33 U. Kan. L. Rev. 791 (1985); *Annot,* 66 *A.L.R.* 3D 824, 827 (1975).

(113) Mich 406, 244 NW2d (1976.)

(114) Id., 397 Mich 406, 420, 430, 244 NW2d 873, 879, 883. See also Note 105, p. 829.

(115) Note 104, p. 244.

(116) Id., p. 247.

(117) *Shannon v. Samuel Langston Co.,* 379 FSupp 797, 803 (W.D. Mich 1979). For a similar articulation of social policy, see *Dawejho v. Jorgensen Steel Co.,* 434 A2d 106, 109 (1981).

(118) *Tucker v. Paxson Mach. Co.,* 645 F2d 620 (8th Cir. 1981). See also *Bernard v. Kee Mfg. Co.,* 394 S2d 552 (Fla Dist. Ct. App. 1981). But see *Armour Dial, Inc.* v. *Albar Eng'r Corp.,* 469 FSupp 1198 (1979).

(119) *Ryan v. Eli Lilly & Co.,* 514 FSupp 1004 (D.S.C. 1981).

(120) Id., p. 1014.

(121) *Burnside v. Abbott Laboratories,* 505 A2d 973, 982 (Pa Super. 1985).

(122) Id., p. 982 and *Bichler v. Eli Lilly & Co.,* 436 NYS2d 625, 79 AD2d 317 (1981).

(123) Note 119 and *Payton v. Abbott Laboratories,* 512 FSupp 1031 (1981); *Conley v. Boyle Drug Co.,* 477 S2d 600 (Fla Dist. Ct. App. 1985); *Ferrigno v. Eli Lilly & Co.,* 175 NJ Super 551, 420 A2d 1305 (1980). Contra: *Abel v. Eli Lilly & Co.,* 418 Mich 311, 343 NW2d 164 (1984), *cert. denied sub nom.,* E.R. Squibb & Sons, Inc. v. Abel, __ US __ 105 SCt 123, 83 LEd 2d 65 (1984).

(124) *Sindell v. Abbott Laboratories,* 26 Cal 3d 588, 605, 607 P2d 924, 932-33, 163 Cal Rptr 132, 141, *cert. denied,* 449 US 912, 101 SCt 285, 66 LEd 2d 140 (1980).

(125) *Bichler v. Eli Lilly & Co.,* 436 NYS2d 625, 632 (1981).

(126) Id., p. 633. For a criticism of the "conscious parallelism" reaching see *Surdell v. Abbott Laboratories,* 26 Cal 3d 588, 597, 163 Cal Rptr 132, 141, 607 P2d 924, 933 (1980).

(127) *Summers v. Tice,* 33 Cal 2d 80, 199 P2d 1 (1948). See also *Mulcahy* v. *Eli Lilly & Co.,* 386 NW 67, 73 (Iowa 1986) and *Namm* v. *Charles E. Frosst & Co.,* 178 NJ Super 19, 32, 427 A2d 1121, 1127-28 (App. Div. 1981).

(128) *Abel v. Eli Lilly & Co.,* 418 Mich 311, 343 NW2d 164 (1984). See also *Ferrigno v. Eli Lilly & Co.,* 175 NJSuper 551, 420 A2d 1305 (Law Div. 1980) (agrees). *Namm* (see note 127) expressly disagrees with *Ferrigno. Namm,* 178 NJSuper 32, 427 A2d 1127 n. 3.

(129) *Bornmann v. Star Co.,* 174 NY 213 (1903).

(130) See *Starling v. Seaboard Coast Line Railroad,* 533 FSupp 183, 187 (S.D. Ga 1982); *Zafft v. Eli Lilly & Co.,* 676 SW2d 241, 245 (Mo 1984).

(131) *Hall v. E.I. DuPont DeNemours & Co.,* 345 FSupp 353 (E.D.N.Y. 1972). See also *Morton v. Abbott Laboratories,* 538 FSupp 593, 598 (M.D. Fla 1982).

(132) *Hall v. E.I. DuPont DeNemours & Co.,* 345 FSupp 353, 371.

(133) Note 123.

(134) Note 132, p. 378.

(135) Note 123.

(136) Note 97, 102 Wash 2d 604, 689 P2d 382. See also Note, Market Share Liability: An Answer to the DES Causation Problem, 94 *Harvard L. Rev.* 668, 670-672 (1981).

(137) *Mulcahy v. Eli Lilly & Co.,* 386 NW2d 67, 75-76 (Iowa).

(138) *U.S. v. Hayes International Corporation,* 786 F2d 1499 (11th Cir. 1986).

(139) 16 CFR 1001.1 (1986) (emphasis my own).

(140) 15 USC 2051 et seq.

(141) 15 USC 1191 et seq.

(142) 15 USC 1261 et seq.

(143) 15 USC 1471 et seq.

(144) 15 USC 1211 et seq.

(145) 15 USC 2052. See also 43 ALR Fed 827.

(146) 16 CFR 1000.5.

(147) 16 CFR 1000.8 (c and d).

(148) *Southland Mower Co.* v. *Consumer Product Safety Commission,* 619 F2d 499 (5th Cir. 1980).

(149) 15 USC 2503-508. It is advisable to get on their mailing list. You might also wish to order a copy of the Commission's "Report of the Recall Effectiveness Task Force of the Consumer Product Safety Commission." To do so, write to the Office of the Secretary, Consumer Product Safety Commission, Washington, D.C., 20207. The Commission operates a toll-free telephone Hotline by which the public can communicate with the Commission. The number for use in all 50 states, Puerto Rico, and the U.S. Virgin Islands is 1-800-638-CPSC (800-638-2772).

(150) 15 USC 2058(c)(2)(c).

(151) See Note 149 and 15 USC 2059(a).

(152) *Gulf South Insul v. U.S. CPSC,* 701 F2d 1137, 1148 (1983). Review is in accordance with the Administrative Procedure Act, 5 USC sec. 701 et seq.

(153) *Fountainhead Group v. Consumer Product Safety Commission,* 527 FSupp 294 (1981).

(154) Id., p. 298-99.

(155) 15 USC 2058(c)(1)(c).

(156) 15 USC 2058(c)(1).

(157) 15 USC 2058(c)(2).

(158) *D.D. Bean & Sons Co. v. Consumer Product Safety Commission,* 574 F2d 643 (1978).

(159) 16 CFR 1115.13(b).

(160) All concerned should be alert to the imputed seller negligence, *Philips v. Kinwood Machine Co.,* 269 Or 485, 525 P2d 1033 (1974).

CHAPTER 2

PACKAGING/LABELING LAW, PROMOTIONAL STRATEGY, AND COMPLIANCE

Once most marketing was based on the personal advice and guidance of someone you knew in the local general store. The growth of the suburbs, resulting in large, impersonal shopping centers, as well as the growth of direct marketing has brought many innovations.

One such innovation has been self-service, which puts a premium on packaging. The package helps sell the product. The color and shape of the package calls attention to the product and describes it.

The shape may even give you a competitive advantage you'd like to patent or trademark. A label may discuss warranty information specifically or inadvertently.

The world of high-volume marketing has resulted in both the marketing and legal professions paying greater attention to the area of packaging and labeling.

Why is this area important to you? Well, you may not sell through "self-service," but your sales must employ labels, containers, boxes, etc.

Your product enclosures must conform to packaging and labeling laws. It's also helpful for you to be aware of your legal protections when you're shopping on your own. So, this law is essential to your firm and you personally.

There is a lot of law covering this area. However, we'll lead off and focus on the federal Fair Packaging and Labeling Act.

There is state regulation in this area, but the primary basis of compliance you should be aware of is the Fair Packaging and Labeling Act.[1]

The basic purpose of the act is to enable your consumers to obtain accurate information which will facilitate value comparison between products. Ideally the purchaser will use this information in his or her purchase decision and not be swayed or misled by extraneous considerations.

We'll now briefly review the general principles of the act as well as the FTC's very lucid interpretations.[2] For your general enforcement overview, the act is enforced primarily by two federal agencies, the Food and Drug Administration and the Federal Trade Commission. The FDA's jurisdiction applies "to any consumer commodity that is a food, drug, device or cosmetic" as defined by the Food, Drug and Cosmetic Act. The Federal Trade Commission's jurisdiction applies to any other consumer commodity.[3]

Definitions You Should Know

It is always good to review law with a clear idea of what the salient terms mean. There are four definitions in the act with which you should be familiar: "consumer commodity," "package," "label," and "principal display panel."

Consumer commodity means: any food, drug, device or cosmetic (as those terms are defined by the Federal Food, Drug, and Cosmetic Act 21 USC § 301 et seq.), and any other article, product, or commodity of any kind or class which is customarily produced or distributed for sale through retail sales agencies or instrumentalities for consumption by individuals, or use by individuals for purposes of personal care or in the performance of services ordinarily rendered within the household, and which usually is consumed or expended in the course of such consumption or use.[4]

Package means: "any container or wrapping in which any consumer commodity is enclosed for use in the delivery or display of that commodity to retail purchasers."[5]

There are specific containers and wrappings which are not included. This is fairly technical, and your specific circumstances and promotional product needs should be reviewed with your counsel.

Label is any written, printed or graphic matter affixed to or appearing upon any consumer commodity or affixed to or appearing upon a package containing any consumer commodity; except that: (1) an inspector's tag or other non-promotional matter affixed to or appearing upon a consumer commodity shall not be deemed to be a label requiring the repetition of the label information required by this part; and (2) for the purposes of the regulations in this part the term "label" does not include written, printed, or graphic matter affixed to or appearing upon containers or wrappers for commodities sold or distributed to industrial or institutional user.[6]

Principal display panel means: "that part of a label that is most likely to be displayed, presented, shown, or examined under normal and customary conditions of display for retail sale. The principal display panel must be large enough to accommodate all the mandatory label information required to be placed thereon by this part without obscuring designs, vignettes, or crowding. The definition does not preclude utilization of alternate principal display panels on the label of a package, but alternate principal display panels must duplicate the information required to be placed on the principal display panel by this part."[7]

Labels

The primary purpose of a label is to identify merchandise and give directions for its use. The principal display panel of a consumer commodity must identify the original marketer of the commodity in a type size and location which will be understandable to the consumer.[8]

This requires that the name (including corporate name) and address of the manufacturer, packer, or distributor be on the label.

When the consumer commodity is not manufactured by the person whose name appears on the label, the name should be qualified by a phrase that reveals the connection such person has with the commodity, such as "Manufactured for. . .," "Distributed by. . .," or any other wording that clearly expresses the facts of your situation.[9]

The net quantity must appear in the front in a fixed location as a distinct item on the principal display panel. It must be separated from other printed label information appearing above or below the declaration by at least a space equal to the height of the lettering used in the declaration.

The net quantity statement must not include any term qualifying a unit of weight, measure, or count such as "jumbo quart", "full gallon," "when packed," "minimum," or words of similar import. This prevents consumer confusion in comparison shopping where the consumer could be confronted by one company's referring to its size as "jumbo" while its competitor referred to the same size as "large."

The declaration of net quantity must be separated from the other printed label information appearing to the left or right of the declaration by at least a space equal to twice the width of the letter "N" of the style of type used in the net quantity statement.[10]

The quantity must be stated in standard measurements known to your purchasers so as to give accurate information regarding the net quantity of the contents to facilitate comparison shopping.

The act states specific measurements as to weight and measure,[11] units of fluid measure,[12] length and width,[13] area,[14] cubic measure and dry measure,[15] units of count,[16] measurement of container type,[17] and how to set forth fractional amounts[18] of any of the previous measurements.

The act requires ingredient disclosure on labels unless a given substance is a trade secret.[19]

As you can see, the above label information (and how to word and present it) is specified by law quite precisely. All such required information must appear in conspicuous and easily readable boldface type or print in distinct contrast (by layout, color, etc.) to the other matter on your package.[20]

The type size must be uniform for all labels and packages of substantially the same size. An "official" listing of definitions is also set forth.[21]

Variations from the stated weight or measure are permitted when caused by ordinary factors that are "conditions which normally occur in good distribution practices and which unavoidably result in a change of weight or measure."[22]

An example of this was in a California case where the state's labeling laws did not permit variations caused by moisture. A firm was in trouble because the average net weight of its flour was less than the net weight stated on the packages.

The Supreme Court, relying on the principle of the utility of the national marketplace for goods, held that varied state laws affecting weight measurements would defeat the Act's purpose of facilitating value comparisons by consumers of similar products. The goal of the act is to facilitate value comparisons among similar products and such goal cannot be accomplished unless packages that bear the same indicated weight in fact contain the same quantity of the product for which the consumer is paying.[23]

The federal act permitted weight variations in flour packages caused by humidity. Unless allowance was made for moisture loss, consumers throughout the country would be misled by attempting to compare the value of identically labeled packages that did not contain identical amounts of flour solids. The Court struck down the state law because the federal act superseded any state law that requires information "different from" the act.[24] Such superseding power is not all encompassing. For example, such superseding governs "net contents" and not the state's power to regulate product names.[25]

If you see a potential issue as to temperature, humidity, etc., affecting the weight of your product, consult your counsel as to your potential adverse legal exposure (or lack of same). Copies of published product standards are available.[26]

The act presents a variety of regulations as to multi-unit packages, [27] variety of packages,[28] and combination packages.[29] Then there are certain exemptions affecting certain varied products such as camera film,[30] Christmas tree ornaments,[31] and pillowcases.[32]

As usual, you must review your particular circumstances with your counsel, who can advise you as to your specific needs and compliance.

Specific Regulations

Perhaps of most interest to direct marketers is the section establishing requirements for the labeling and characterization of certain retail sale price representations. As a result, we'll relate these areas in greater detail.

Cents-Off. Any offer of a certain amount off the regular price is a powerful incentive to buy. You may not place a "cents-off" statement on your package label unless:

(1) "The commodity has been sold by the packager or labeler at an ordinary and customary price in the most recent and regular course of business in the trade area in which the 'cents-off' promotion is made."[33]

(2) It is sold "at a reduction from the ordinary and customary price, which reduction is at least equal to the amount of the 'cents-off' representation imprinted on the commodity package or label."[34]

(3) "Each 'cents-off' representation imprinted on the package or label is limited to a phrase which reflects that the price marked by the retailer represents the savings in the amount of the 'cents-off' the retailer's price, e.g., 'Price Marked is $ __ Off the Regular Price' 'Price Marked is __ Cents Off the Regular Price of This Package .'"[35]

Further, you may not initiate more than three "cents-off" promotions of any single size commodity in the same trade area within a 12-month period.[36] You must allow at least 30 days to lapse between "cents-off" promotions of any particular size packaged or labeled commodity in a specific trade area.[37]

Finally, there are common sense requirements that state that you must not allow a "cents-off" promotion to be used in a deceptive manner and that you must retain invoices and/or other records for one year after the "cents-off" promotion occurs to verify your compliance with the above requirements.

Introductory Offers. The principles are similar to those for "cents-off." To place this term on your package or label, you must use the exact words "Introductory Offer."

The product must be new (or new to your trade area) or changed in a functionally significant and substantial respect.[38] Your introductory offer may not be made for longer than six months.[39]

The requirements as to avoiding deception and the one-year period for recordkeeping are the same as those for "cents-off."

Economy Size. Size characterization is important to comparison shopping because it affects the comparison of the same product by different manufacturers and/or distributors. To use this wording on your package or label, the following are required.

(1) You must have at least one other size of the same brand available when you have an "economy size."

(2) You must sell the commodity labeled with an "economy size" representation at a price per unit of weight, volume, measure, or count which is substantially reduced (i.e., at least 5% from the actual price of all other packaged or labeled units of the same brand of that commodity offered simultaneously.[40]

Final Thoughts on the Act

Compliance with this act is important to you because a federal (i.e., national) standard avoids the chaos that state-by-state regulation would bring and because your consumer wants benchmark standards to facilitate comparison shopping.

In the context of a national economy, uniform standards are a prerequisite to assuring the free flow of goods throughout the country. Such uniformity is of particular utility to a direct marketer operating in some, if not all 50 states.

Without this act, your customer would lack a national and rational value comparison for products as to their size, weight, etc. If you have a good product that stands up to your competitors' in objective comparisons, then you'll appreciate the uniformity of standards imposed by this act. Your best approach is to forward the format for your proposed market research as well as suggested packaging, wording, labeling, etc., to your counsel before formal research/testing is begun.

This early review will save both time and money, especially if the initial claims are not legally supportable as designed. If your package/label plans are approved, you should also conduct a legal review of the finished materials.

Your counsel should then retain in his or her file a complete set of supporting documents for all claims, statements, and similar items included in all your packaging and labeling material.

Another reason you'll want a legal review is to determine whether your warranty is worded correctly, or possibly whether your promotional wording is setting forth a warranty you don't want to offer.

Warranty Issues

A short discussion concerning this topic is in order here (though, see more in-depth review elsewhere in this section) as it is a common practice to stress safety or other affirmations of objective selling criteria on labels or on your package.

Often these statements will create one or more warranties for which you are liable—warranties that are usually separate and apart from any offered (possibly in greater detail) inside your package.

It is important for you to review any declarative statement of merit with your counsel. If your statement is clearly a subjective opinion about the merits of your product it might pass as "puffing."

However, a factual description of an important characteristic of your product will probably expose you to a warranty action or an action for misrepresentation or negligence.

A good example was where a 13-year-old boy bought a "Golfing Gizmo."[41] The label on the shipping carton urged players to "drive the ball with full power" and further stated that the "completely safe ball will not hit player." The boy used it as instructed and was severely injured in the head by the golf ball.

The court found that the safety statement went to the basis of the bargain as "anyone learning to play golf searches for a product that will enable him to learn safely."

The court held this constituted an express warranty. "It is not necessary to the creation of an express warranty that the seller use formal words such as 'warranty' or 'guarantee' or that he have a specific intention to make a warranty."[42]

In fact, the court noted that:

(1) Any affirmation of fact or promise made by the seller to the buyer which relates to the goods and becomes part of the basis of the bargain creates an express warranty that the goods shall conform to the affirmation or promise.

(2) Any description of the goods which is made part of the basis of the bargain creates an express warranty that the goods shall conform to the description.[43]

An implied warranty of merchantability was created by operation of law unless specifically excluded or modified. Specifically, as to packaging or labeling, goods must:

(1) Be fit for the ordinary purposes for which such goods are used.

(2) Be adequately contained, packaged and labeled as the agreement may require.

(3) Conform to the promises or affirmations of fact made on the container or label.[44]

Finally, the label sets forth a warranty of fitness for a particular purpose. Where the seller has reason to know the particular purpose for which its product is required and knows (or should know) that the buyer is relying on the seller's skill in furnishing such goods, there is (unless excluded) an implied warranty that the goods shall be fit for such purpose.[45]

Here the risk of harm was found to be greatest when the "Gizmo" was being used by its intended user, a player of limited ability.

This latter point is very important in considering your package/label warning. The target audience is a key to any warranty analysis. If you are offering any product to a child, a "beginner," or a sophisticated product to anyone, it is "seller beware."

This is true for warranty or misrepresentation claims, and you will not have a defense by alleging such statement was not fraudulent or negligent.

Further, you should assume the worst as to your targeted recipient. A seven-year-old child may not be your targeted audience for sparklers, but you had better warn of all dangers on the box in language clear even to a child.[46]

Even where your language is clearly understandable to a child, if you place an illustration on your box that encourages a child to a course of action resulting in injury, you will lose.[47]

If your marketing department is setting forth promotional wording on your packages or labels without a legal review, you are recklessly exposing your firm to fines, lawsuits, significant adverse media publicity, and possibly recalls of or injunctions against your product. This is not a business judgment, but conduct bordering on professional malfeasance.

Can I Register My Container?

You may believe the package or container you've designed is distinctive and merits a trademark (see discussion below in this section).

Traditionally, U.S. trademark law has held that the configuration is dictated by functional considerations, i.e., those considerations that add to the usefulness of the product. Public policy requires that a primarily functional designation be available to all competitors.

However, this area is subject to various interpretations and such exceptions appear to be broadening.[48] If your container is distinctive, either inherently or through "secondary meaning" (i.e., your customers identify the configuration of the container as yours) and you've adopted and promoted its design with the intent that it function as a source identifying mark, then you should review with your counsel whether your package is qualified for registration.

An example of a container configuration which was demonstrated to identify the source of its goods (and, therefore, was registrable) was the traditional Coca-Cola bottle.

Conclusion

Packaging and labeling practices are an area of significant if unglamorous exposure and you'd be well-advised to review your current and future promotional wording on your package and labels as your customer would. The expansion of product liability and warranty law as well as compliance with this act mandates such wording be proper and precise. Don't feel insulated by disclaimers inside the box.

ENDNOTES

(1) 15 U.S.C. 1451-61.

(2) 16 C.F.R. 500 Subchapter E—Rules, Regulations, Statement of General Policy or Interpretation and Exemptions Under the Fair Packaging and Labeling Act.

(3) 15 U.S.C. 1454(a).

(4) 15 U.S.C. 1459(a).

(5) 16 C.F.R. 502.2(d).

(6) 16 C.F.R. 502.2(e).

(7) 16 C.F.R. 502.2(h).

(8) 16 C.F.R. 500.4.

(9) 16 C.F.R. 500.5(a).

(10) 16 C.F.R. 500.6(b).

(11) 16 C.F.R. 500.8 and 500.9.

(12) 16 C.F.R. 500.10.

(13) 16 C.F.R. 500.11 and 500.12.

(14) 16 C.F.R. 500.13.

(15) 16 C.F.R. 500.14.

(16) 16 C.F.R. 500.15.

(17) 16 C.F.R. 500.15(a).

(18) 16 C.F.R. 500.16.

(19) 15 U.S.C. 1454. See also *Zotos International, Inc. v. Kennedy,* 460 F. Supp. 268, 277 (1978).

(20) 16 C.F.R. 500.17.

(21) 16 C.F.R. 500.19.

(22) 16 C.F.R. 500.22(b).

(23) *Jones v. Rath Packing Co.,* 430 U.S. 519, 51 L.Ed.2d 604, 96 S.Ct. 1305 (1977).

(24) 15 U.S.C. 1461.

(25) *Atlantic Ocean Products, Inc. v. Leth,* 292 F.Supp. 615, 618 (1968).

(26) Write to the National Bureau of Standards, Department of Commerce, Washington, D.C.

(27) 16 C.F.R. 500.24.

(28) 16 C.F.R. 500.25.

(29) 16 C.F.R. 500.26.

(30) 16 C.F.R. 501.1.

(31) 16 C.F.R. 501.2.

(32) 16 C.F.R. 501.5. See C.F.R. 500.1-501.8.

(33) 16 C.F.R. 502.100(b)(1).

(34) 16 C.F.R. 502.100(b)(2).

(35) 16 C.F.R. 502.100(b)(3).

(36) 16 C.F.R. 502.100(b)(5)(i).

(37) 16 C.F.R. 502.100(b)(5)(ii).

(38) 16 C.F.R. 502.101(b)(2). Obviously mere new packaging is not enough. Being able to qualify for a patent would be enough to comply with this section.

(39) 16 C.F.R. 502.101(b)(3).

(40) 16 C.F.R. 502.102(b)(3).

(41) *Hauter v. Zogarts,* 14 Cal.3d.104 (1975). See also *Filler v. Royex Corp.,* 435 F.2d 336 (1970).

(42) UCC Sec. 2-313(2).

(43) UCC Sec. 2-313(1)(a), (b).

(44) UCC Sec. 2-314(2)(c), 2-314(2)(e), 2-314(2)(f).

(45) UCC Sec. 2-315.

(46) *Henry v. Cook,* 195 N.Y.S. 642 (1922).

(47) *Tirino v. Kenner Products Company,* 72 Misc.2d. 1094; 341 N.Y.S.2d 61 (1973).

(48) *In Re Morton-Norwich Products, Inc.,* 671 F.2d 1332 (CCPA 1982). See also *Oxford Pendaflex Corp. v. Rolodex Corp.,* 204 U.S.P.Q. 249 (TTAB 1979) and *In re Ovation Instruments, Inc.,* 201 U.S.P.Q. 116 (TTAB 1978).

CHAPTER 3
WARRANTY COMPLIANCE

A warranty is the assumption of responsibility by the seller for the quality, character, or suitability of the goods he or she has put into the stream of commerce. Sellers are more accountable today because of a variety of factors including societal changes and perceived costs to the consumer.

We once made most of our goods, and much of the rest were purchased in face-to-face negotiations from people we knew. As society became more fragmented and the source of goods more remote, we retained the fiction a buyer could appraise the quality of the goods and the seller's veracity. The standard was: "buyer beware." Over the last generation, society's concept of who can best bear the responsibility for the quality of goods and the accuracy of their presentation to the public has changed significantly.

As your products cost more, or seem to, any failure to live up to advertised expectations becomes increasingly irksome to the consumer. A relatively no-growth economy also produces a customer who wants a long-life product. A pleasurable or unsatisfactory purchase experience will determine whether you retain your customer. A key determinant here is how well you honor your warranty or that of your supplier. As discussed later, as a retailer or distributor you may not be liable for a manufacturer's warranty. However, your customer will look to you for information and assistance, and ignorance of the pertinent law may jeopardize a repeat purchase.

There is a lot of warranty activity in the news; the court calendars are filling up with varied claims. Certain states have enacted laws to give new car buyers the right to receive a new car or refund if their automobile cannot be repaired within four tries for the same problem or if the car is out of service for more than 30 days due to one or more defects.

Many states require that a written warranty be delivered to the consumer at or before the time the sales contract is signed.[1] These laws generally provide that the warranty and notice may be set forth on one sheet or on separate sheets and may be separate from, attached to, or a part of the contract. If incorporated in the contract, the warranty and notice must be headed by a conspicuous title. Increasingly, consumers want useful warranties, and they know how to enforce them. Your competitive position may be significantly affected by how well you satisfy the public demand for this benefit.

In developing your warranty policy, consider the following: performance data obtained from company research and development and product performance testing, consumer expectations and experience based on market testing and complaint data, and the differences between full and limited warranties. Weigh the costs to the company against the costs to consumers of any limitations or conditions on warranty coverage. Then consider the federal and state laws and regulations governing warranties.[2]

Finally, it is important to reflect on how warranties arise so that you can maximize the likelihood that your business will get them on the purchasing side and control them on the selling side. Warranties arise by contract and by operation of law.

Contract. "A warranty, express or implied, is contractual in nature. Whether considered collateral thereto or an integral part thereof, a warranty is an element of a contract of sale."[3]

You want a signed contract that pays careful attention to contingencies that might arise in your business. For example, you'll wish to specifically exclude certain forms of misuse of your product. You may wish to extend the warranty to the future performance of the goods. If you're selling, you want to avoid a haphazard "battle of the forms." Unless you clearly pin the buyer down, the court may impose general provisions of the Uniform Commercial Code that inevitably favor the buyer. Obviously, you'll want an effective integration clause.

Operation of Law. We'll shortly review a number of statutory warranty principles for commercial and consumer marketing and how they are triggered. One important principle in the commercial or consumer marketing warranty area is that if you want to enforce legal or contractual rights against someone, you must enforce them against the person with whom you have a contract. For example, there is an action for breach of warranty when the action is based on an express or implied contract. If liability is imposed on a retailer for breach of warranty, he or she must proceed against the supplier. The supplier in turn is entitled to indemnity on the warranty payout from the distributor with whom the former is in privity.[4]

This can put you at a disadvantage if you are buying from a distributor or are involved in third-party leasing. Here, there is no privity of contract between a user and the manufacturer. You must contractually require the intermediary distributor or lessor to give you such warranties as it has. In drafting the agreement you usually insert the requirement in the section where they waive any warranty flowing to you from such lessor or distributor, but you want them to pass along the manufacturer's warranties regarding the equipment to be leased. For example:

> Lessor represents that it has purchased the leased equipment from the manufacturer thereof, under an agreement between Lessor and ABC Company, dated _____ , a copy of which is annexed hereto as Exhibit A. Lessor hereby assigns to Lessee all of Lessor's right, title and interest in and to said purchase agreement and hereby appoints Lessee its attorney-in-fact, irrevocable during the term of this lease, and coupled with an interest to exercise and enforce all of the rights granted to Lessor under said purchase agreement, in Lessor's name.

> The failure to insert this can leave you holding the bag as to enforcing any rights if a dispute occurs.[5]

Remember we are discussing commercial and consumer damages. As we reviewed in the introduction to this section, there is today no privity of contract requirement in personal injury cases. The cause of action for breach of warranty is contractual and at common-law only those persons who were parties to the bargain, sue for a breach of it. However, the courts today permit an injured purchaser to recover directly from the manufacturer.

The Uniform Commercial Code (UCC) drastically curtails the requirement of privity between the person injured by a defective product and the manufacturer or seller thereof, in actions based on breach of warranty. It provides[6] three alternative provisions; the choice is left to each adopting state. As Comment 2 states, "the purpose of this section is to give certain beneficiaries the benefit of the same warranty which the buyer received in the contract of sale, thereby freeing any such beneficiaries from any technical rules to 'privity'."

According to the UCC first alternative, a seller's warranty, express or implied, extends to any natural person who is in the family or household of the buyer or who is a guest in his home, if it is reasonable to expect that such person may use, consume, or be affected by the goods, and who is injured in person by breach of the warranty; and a seller may not exclude or limit the operation of this provision. Under the second alternative, a seller's warranty, express or implied, extends to any natural person who may reasonably be expected to use, consume, or be affected by the goods and who is injured in person by breach of the warranty; and this alternative also provides that a seller may not exclude or limit its operation. The third alternative extends the warranty to any person who may reasonably be expected to use, consume, or be affected by the goods and who is injured by breach of the warranty; and it provides that the seller may not exclude or limit its operation with respect to injury to the person.

A seller cannot exclude or limit the operation of this recovery. Additionally, the warranty protection is extended to a sub-purchaser that justifiably relied upon representations made by the manufacturer to the public through advertisements or labels tagged to the goods.[7]

With the above background in mind we'll look at the salient laws on point. The following discussion of federal and state laws first reviews the scope and coverage of the Magnuson-Moss law for marketing compliance, which requires that your customer receive a complete and understandable explanation of written product warranties *before* a purchase is made (this emphasis on disclosure is increasingly found in all FTC related remedies). Warranties under the UCC, including traditional title, express, and implied warranties are reviewed later in this chapter.

Warranties Under the Magnuson-Moss Warranty Act

A warranty is an expression of your firm's willingness to stand behind its product *after* the purchase is complete. The social policy behind the Magnuson-Moss Act is that your warranty is part of the product you sell and should be as readily available for examination prior to the sale as is the product itself.

The act applies only to *written* warranties[8] on tangible consumer property that is normally used for personal, family, or household purposes (not products sold for resale or services).[9] The controlling consideration in each sale is how *this* purchaser will use this product. The percentage of sales or the use to which a product is put by any individual buyer is not determinative. For example, products such as automobiles and typewriters that are used for both personal and commercial purposes come within the definition of consumer product. When it is unclear whether a particular product is covered under the definition of consumer product, any ambiguity will be resolved in favor of coverage.[10]

Another area of "ambiguity" is how you emphasize your warranty in advertising. You have the privilege of selecting one or more points in your warranty to feature in advertising. If you do, you have the responsibility to point out that warranties differ in many respects, and that other features not cited may be of importance to the purchaser in advertising.

Certain representations, such as energy efficiency ratings for electrical appliances, care labeling of wearing apparel, and other product information disclosures may be express warranties under the UCC. However, these disclosures alone are not written warranties under this Act unless there is a written reaffirmance of this related to a specific period of time.[11]

This written warranty must be part of the "basis of the bargain." Thus it must be given at the time of sale, and the purchaser must not give any additional payment exceeding the purchase price of the product to benefit from the warranty. Again, the product must *not* be purchased by the consumer for resale purposes.

Generally, the threshold figure for warranty compliance is where the *actual* cost to the consumer exceeds $10 (excluding taxes or shipping and handling charges). The $10 minimum will be interpreted to include multiple-packaged items which may individually sell for less than $10, but which have been packaged in a manner that does not permit breaking the package to purchase an item or items at a price less than $10. Thus, a written warranty on a dozen items packaged and priced for sale at $12 must be designated, even though identical items may be offered in smaller quantities at under $10.[12]

The warranty must cover a specified period of time to be considered a written warranty.[13] Taken alone, terms of sale such as "free examination period" or any other promotional wording allowing the consumer an unconditional right to revoke acceptance of your goods within a certain number of days after delivery are not sufficient for compliance under the act. Congress's purpose in enacting the Magnuson-Moss Act was threefold.

First were the information purposes:

(1) A warranty is part of the basic contract of sale of a product. You, as business people, know how important it is to know the terms on which you are going to buy a product before you buy it. The easier you make it for your customers to know what they are offered, the more likely it is that they will be satisfied with what the warranty really provides.

(2) Your customers need to understand the limitations in warranties, and differences among them, so that they can shop wisely for the best "deal." A warranty is part of the product you sell and customers need a chance to examine the whole package before they buy.

(3) Congress wanted to make sure that as customers started to look at differences in warranties they would let business know—in all the various ways that businesses know what customers want—just what kind of warranty protection is really wanted on each product, and at what price.

Second, Congress sought to provide minimum warranty protection for consumers by providing not only disclosure rights but useful remedies including federal court jurisdiction of a dispute and counsel fees to the subsequent plaintiff. The FTC Regulations further provide less formal overuse of settlement.[14] The consumer action may only be against the person actually making a written warranty making them liable for purposes of FTC and private enforcement of the act. A supplier who does no more than distribute or sell a consumer product covered by a written warranty offered by another person or business and which identifies that person or business as the warrantor is not liable for failure of the written warranty to comply with the act or rules thereunder. However, other actions as well as written and oral representations of such a supplier in connection with the offer or sale of a warranted product may obligate that supplier under the act. If under state law the supplier is deemed to have "adopted" the written affirmation of fact, promise, or undertaking, the supplier is also obligated under the Act. Suppliers are advised to consult state law to determine those actions and representations which may make them co-warrantors, and therefore obligated under the warranty of the other person or business.[15]

Third, Congress sought to encourage greater product reliability by making it easier for consumers to choose among products on the basis of their probable reliability.

Full or Limited Warranty

What is a written warranty? As set forth by the FTC,[16] a written warranty means:

(1) Any written affirmation of fact or written promise made in connection with the sale of a consumer product by a supplier to a buyer which relates to the nature of the material or workmanship and affirms or promises that such material or workmanship is defect free or will meet a specified level of performance over a specified period of time, or

(2) Any undertaking in writing in connection with the sale by a supplier of a consumer product to refund, repair, replace, or take other remedial action with respect to such product in the event that such product fails to meet the specifications set forth in the undertaking, which written affirmation, promise or undertaking becomes part of the basis of the bargain between a supplier and a buyer for purposes other than resale of such product.[17]

"On the face of the warranty" means:

(1) Where the warranty is a single sheet with printing on both sides of the sheet or where the warranty is comprised of more than one sheet, the page on which the warranty text begins;

(2) Where the warranty is included as part of a larger document, such as a use and care manual, the page in such document on which the warranty text begins.[18]

Keep in mind that you are not obligated to offer any warranties at all on your product. The act *does not require* any product or service to carry a *written* warranty regardless of product category or price of the item. However, once you elect to offer a *written* warranty on a product costing the consumer more than $10 (again, excluding sales tax and other charges), it must be designated as either a "full" or a "limited" warranty. Such designations should appear conspicuously as a caption or prominent title, *clearly separated* from the text of your warranty. This creates a headline that your customers will be able to recognize easily.

A full warranty promises the customer the following:

► A defective product will be fixed (or replaced) free, including removal and reinstallation, if necessary.

► A defective product will be fixed within a reasonable time after the first complaint.

► Your customer will not have to do anything unreasonable to get warranty service. Any duties imposed on your customer must be conspicuously disclosed in advance.

► The warranty is good for anyone who owns the product during the warranty period unless it is materially altered. However, you may limit this in *clear and conspicuous* language by stating that the duration of the warranty expires automatically if the consumer transfers the item.[19] For example, an automobile battery or muffler warranty may be designated as "full warranty for as long as you own your car."[20]

► If the product cannot be fixed (or hasn't been after a reasonable number of tries), the customer is entitled to the choice of a new product or his or her money back.[21] The warrantor can't elect to initiate a refund unless:

• The warrantor is unable to provide replacement and repair is not commercially practicable or cannot be timely made, or

• The consumer is willing to accept such refund.[22]

► Warranty coverage is not contingent on returning a registration card (either expressly or even implicitly).[23] This does not prohibit the use of such cards as a proof of the date of purchase. You might encourage the return of these cards (useful for market research) by stating that you may need to use them to notify your customer of a defect or recall. However, you must include a notice that the failure to return the card will not affect rights or service under the warranty, so long as the customer can show in a reasonable manner the date the product was purchased.[24] Therefore, it may be useful for you to encourage your customers to save their sales slip with their warranty. Together they document the date of purchase, your coverage, and the fact of first ownership, if that is a limitation of the warranty.

► Implied warranties may not be disclaimed or limited during the duration of the full warranty. There is one important thing that the word "full" doesn't promise—a full warranty doesn't have to cover the whole product. It may cover only part of the product, like the picture tube of a television. Or it may leave out some parts, like tires on a car. If your warranty covers only the picture tube and the sound goes bad, the customer pays.[25]

Again, it must be stressed that if you do nothing to limit your warranty, the FTC will assume it is a full warranty. If you clearly and conspicuously label a warranty as limited, you can avoid some of the above burdens.

A limited warranty gives anything less than what a full warranty offers. A product may have both limited and full warranties for different parts or aspects of performance. A limited warranty might cover parts only, and your customer would have to pay labor or vice versa. You may require the return of a registration card for a limited warranty only if you do not provide service on products for which the card has not been returned.

You may charge for shipping and handling, as well as require the return of a warranty.

Unless you are selling a product "as is" (see below) you must give at least an implied warranty that your product is merchantable. This means the seller promises that the product will do what it is supposed to do (i.e., purchased to do); for example, that a toaster will toast. Implied warranties can not be disclaimed but implied warranties can be limited to the duration of the written warranty if the duration isn't so short that it's unconscionable. (A one-year limited warranty can state that both express and implied warranties last for one year.)

Both forms of warranty prohibit any tying arrangement that *conditions* warranty coverage on the consumer's use of an article or service identified by brand, trade, or corporate name unless that article or service is provided free of charge to the consumer.[26] Likewise, no warranty may condition its continued validity on the use of only authorized repair service and/or authorized replacement parts for nonwarranty service and maintenance. For example, a provision such as "this warranty is void if service is performed by anyone other than an authorized ABC dealer and all replacement parts must be genuine ABC parts" is prohibited when the service and parts are not covered by the warranty.[27]

Neither form of warranty need be honored if the warrantor demonstrates that the defect, malfunction, or failure of the product resulted from consumer misuse.

Disclosure of Warranty Terms

Besides the protections just mentioned, the warranty must disclose clearly and conspicuously in a single document in readily understood language, the following information:

☐ The identity of the party or parties to whom the written warranty is extended (if the enforceability of the written warranty is limited to the original consumer purchaser or is otherwise limited to persons other than every consumer owner during the term of the warranty);

☐ A clear description and identification of products, parts, characteristics, components, properties covered by, and, where necessary for clarification, excluded from the warranty;

☐ A statement of what the warrantor will do in the event of a defect, malfunction or failure to conform with the written warranty, including the items or services the warrantor will pay for or provide, and, where necessary for clarification, those which the warrantor will not pay for or provide;

☐ The point in time or event on which the warranty term commences, if different from the purchase date, and the time period or other measurement of warranty duration;

☐ A step-by-step explanation of the procedure which the consumer should follow in order to obtain performance of any warranty obligation, including the persons or class of persons authorized to perform warranty obligations. This includes the name(s) of the warrantor(s), together with: The mailing address(es) of the warrantor, and/or the name or title and the address of any employee or department of the warrantor responsible for the performance of warranty obligations, and/or a telephone number which consumers may use without charge to obtain information on warranty performance;

☐ Information concerning the availability of any informal dispute settlement mechanism elected by the warrantor.

☐ Any limitations on the duration of implied warranties, disclosed on the face of the warranty as provided in Section 108 of the act, accompanied by the following statement:

"Some States do not allow limitations on how long an implied warranty lasts, so the above limitation may not apply to you."

☐ Any exclusions of or limitations on relief such as incidental or consequential damages, accompanied by the following statement, which may be combined with the statement above:

"Some states do not allow the exclusion or limitation of incidental or consequential damages, so the above limitation or exclusion may not apply to you."

☐ A statement in the following language:

"This warranty gives you specific legal rights, and you may also have other rights, which vary from State to State."[28]

These disclosures must be written "with such clarity and prominence as will be noticed and understood by prospective purchasers."[29] The use of easy to understand examples can help a customer through a difficult point.[30] However, you are not responsible for your customer's ability or inability to digest information, although you should consider printing instructions and other terms in languages other than English when justified by your market. The inability to understand the warranty remains a major impediment to the usefulness of warranty protection.

If you are the party extending the warranty, you should establish standardized forms for warranty repairs and all warranty procedures. These forms should be consistent with or identical to your warranty disclosure material and should spell out to your service agent what is included and excluded from warranty coverage. One way to facilitate understanding and goodwill by your customers is to use subheadings:

- WHAT IS COVERED
- FOR HOW LONG
- WHAT WE WILL AND WILL NOT DO
- WHAT THE CUSTOMER MUST DO
- OTHER CONDITIONS
- STATE LAW RIGHTS

Now, let's look at exactly when and how these warranties must be presented to would-be buyers.

Presale Availability

When products cost more than $15, retail sellers must display the text of any written warranty (assuming one exists) in close conjunction with each warranted product or retain a binder with copies of all written warranties, displaying the binder or placing signs in prominent locations in the store "in a manner calculated to elicit the prospective buyer's attention."[31] A major problem for the consumer is clutter and the lack of systematic organization. Written warranties are often organized differently for different brands, inhibiting comparison price shopping.

The Magnuson-Moss Act offers the retailer four methods of making warranties available to consumers. You may elect one or more of the following:

▶ Clearly and conspicuously display the text of your written warranty in close conjunction to each warranted product.

▶ Maintain binders that contain copies of your warranties for the products sold in each department in which any consumer product with a written warranty is offered for sale. Such binders should be maintained in each department or in a location that provides the prospective buyer with ready access to such binders; they should be clearly identified as the binders containing the warranties. You may display the binders in such a way as to catch the prospective buyer's attention. Or, you may make the binders available to prospective buyers on request. If you choose the latter, you must post signs that will catch prospective buyer's attention in the store or department. These signs must advise them of the availability of the binders and must include instructions for obtaining access to them.

▶ Display the package of any consumer product on which the text of the written warranty is disclosed in a manner such that the warranty is clearly visible to your prospective buyers at the point of sale.

▶ Place a notice that discloses the text of the written warranty in close proximity to the warranted product in a manner which clearly identifies to your prospective buyers the product to which the notice applies.[32]

▶ In television advertising, the advertisement should make the necessary disclosure simultaneously with or immediately following the warranty claim and the disclosure is made in the audio portion, or, if in the video portion, if it remains on the screen for at least five seconds.[33] You should be aware of whatever warranties are offered by the manufacturers of merchandise you sell. The nature of such warranties (if available) should be spelled out in all contracts you sign with your vendors. You might discuss with counsel whether to insert a clause in your merchandise contract requiring your vendor to explicitly state what warranties, if any, are expressed or implied.[34]

What if you are involved in direct marketing? Do you have to disclose the presale availability of any warranties, and, if so, how? The act specifically addresses two forms of direct-marketing categories—mail and door-to-door sales.

Direct Mail.   First, what constitutes a catalog or mail-order sale? "Catalog or Mail Order Sale means *any offer for sale or any solicitation* for an order for a consumer product with a written warranty, which includes instructions for ordering the product which do not require a personal visit to the seller's establishment."[35]

If you sell via catalog or mail order, you must include in your catalog or solicitation either the full text of the written warranty or the fact that the warranty can be obtained from you free on specific written request. The address to which such requests may be sent must be included, and if this option is elected you must *promptly* provide requested copies to the consumer. If the buyer doesn't request the warranty and reading it would have saved the buyer from difficulty, the buyer will not be able to benefit against you for his or her failure to exercise common diligence.[36] The text of your warranty or the statement that your warranty will be provided on request must appear close to the description of your warranted product or must be clearly referenced to an information section of the catalog or solicitation, including a page number. "Close" here means on the same page as the description of the product or on the facing page.

Be careful as to your own promotional copy. If your catalog describes the product in specific terms, the description may very likely be considered a warranty. Be careful as to any embellishment of the manufacturer's description or you may find yourself between a rock and a hard place.

Don't adopt as your own the manufacturer's literature. If you mark the literature with your name, you may be sued (at least initially) for any defects.

Finally, when a retailer takes full responsibility for part of the warranty service, this constitutes a separate retailer's warranty. Furthermore, promotional representations in connection with making a sale may make the retailer a "co-warrantor" and therefore obligated under the warranty. Advertising and verbal representation such as "We stand behind our products" may bind the retailer as well.

Assuming you avoid the pitfalls described above, and even if you did not mention the warranty your vendor has provided for the product you're selling, your vendor alone is liable for any defect in the warranty or in performance under it.[37] You should also make sure that your vendor is required by contract to inform you of the existence of any warranties offered on a product—even if you are not actually promoting them.

Door-to-Door Sales.   Anyone involved in door-to-door sales should be aware of the following warranty provisions directly impacting their operations:

> Any seller who offers for sale to consumers consumer products with written warranties by means of door-to-door sales shall, prior to the consummation of the sale, disclose the fact that the sales representative has copies of the warranties for the warranted products being offered for sale which may be inspected by the prospective buyer at any time during the

sales presentation. Such disclosure shall be made orally and shall be included in any written materials shown to the prospective buyers.[38]

A further wild card here is that the courts are looking less favorably upon sales puffery today, especially where less knowledgeable consumers are the targeted market. When your salesperson makes claims or promises of an *objective* or *factual* nature regarding your product's inherent capabilities, you may have a warranty. Such a warranty is more likely to be found where the salesperson was understood to know the capabilities of your product and the purchaser relied on the "pitch" to his or her detriment (see the discussion of "puffing" later in this chapter).

Broadcast Media and Telephone Sales

In broadcast media, your customers have a limited time to absorb information. Your customer cannot control the sequence and the rate of the information presentation, and the continuous pace does not permit careful study.

The broad definition of "mail order," that is, "any solicitation for an order which does not require a personal visit to the seller's establishment," appears to include radio, television, telephone, and cable sales. Interactive cable (and related technologies such as videotext) have the capabilities to provide instant access to a central data base and thereby obtain the warranty information through the media itself. This instantaneous retrieval could offer a significant competitive advantage over all other media both per product and in overall comparison shopping. Review your media communications mix disclosure strategy with your counsel.

Informal Dispute Settlement Procedures

Voluntary procedures to settle a dispute informally should be carefully reviewed with counsel.[39] The trade-off is often the burden of setting them up and disclosing them versus the possibility of saving a costly litigation fee.[40] This saving may result from your ability to require the consumer to resort to the informal procedures (specifically arbitration) before taking you to court.

An informal settlement procedure is called a "mechanism."[41] Your mechanism must comply with the standards of the FTC's dispute settlement rule,[42] which governs the disclosure of the mechanism in written warranties as well as the mechanism's organization, operation, and recordkeeping. An example of a qualifying mechanism is a panel established by a trade association, a local better business bureau, an accounting firm, or other sponsor insulated from your influence and in no way a party to the dispute.

The warrantor shall disclose clearly and conspicuously at least the following information *on the face of the written warranty:*

1. A statement of the availability of the informal dispute settlement mechanism;

2. The name and address of the mechanism, or the name and a telephone number of the mechanism which consumers may use without charge;

3. A statement of any requirement that the consumer resort to the mechanism before exercising rights or seeking remedies created by Title I of the act; together with the disclosure that if a consumer chooses to seek redress by pursuing rights and remedies not created by Title I of the act, resort to the mechanism would not be required by any provision of the act; and

4. A statement, if applicable, indicating where further information on the mechanism can be found in materials accompanying the product, as provided *in this section.*

(c) The warrantor shall include in the written warranty or in a separate section of materials accompanying the product, the following information:

1. Either (i) a form addressed to the mechanism containing spaces requesting the information which the mechanism may require for prompt resolution of warranty disputes; or (ii) a telephone number of the mechanism which consumers may use without charge;

2. The name and address of the mechanism;

3. A brief description of mechanism procedures;

4. The time limits adhered to by the mechanism; and

5. The types of information which the mechanism may require for prompt resolution of warranty disputes.[43]

With one narrow exception, you may require consumers to resort to a qualifying mechanism before suing (including small claims court).[44] However, your customers are free at any time to pursue alternative state or federal remedies. Warrantors with mechanisms may also encourage, but may not require, consumers to seek redress from the warrantor directly without raising a complaint to the level of a dispute.[45] The decisions are not binding on the parties but are admissible in evidence in any related civil action.[46] The nonbinding feature of the procedure may, of course, significantly diminish the procedure's utility to both warrantors and consumers.

Meetings are open to observers, and either party has access to all records of the hearings, including the right to copy the records. Records must be retained for four years after the final disposition of the dispute.

It is good customer relations to treat these informal hearings as customer service rather than as adversarial proceedings. You should use the consumer experience and complaints as a means for improving quality, discovering latent defects, and designing products for simplified serviceability.

Before moving on to the UCC warranties, we'll briefly review two concepts related to this act—"as is" and "service contracts."

"As Is"

If you're doing your buying from private individuals, street peddlers in NYC, or Anytown, U.S.A.'s "flea markets," you are buying your goods "as is."

In more formal sales, the words "as is" disclaim implied warranties but not express warranties (in a dozen states and D.C., no consumer product may be sold "as is").

If you use "as is," you need take no further responsibility. The customer is alerted by the "as is" language and presumably accepts any shortcomings because the sales price is also reduced.

If you want to sell a product "as is," you must communicate to the customer that if the product is defective, breaks down, or is faulty for any reason, you will not be responsible for it. You must state this in writing, as a conspicuous part of the sales contract. You must refer to "merchantability" specifically as something you don't warrant, or else use the phrase "as is" or "with all faults." For example, you can state in large, prominent letters: "Product sold as is," or "No warranty of merchantability or otherwise given as to the condition of the product," or the like. You would be well advised also to make this clear orally to the customer before he or she decides on the purchase. Under no circumstances should you promise something when you're selling the product and then use a contract form disclaiming all warranties.

So, in about 35 states you can sell "as is." However, with the growth of consumerism, small claims courts, etc., the hurdles and lost goodwill may not be worth the reduced paperwork in compliance.

Service Contracts

Although often called "extended warranties," service contracts are not warranties. Warranties are included in the price of the product. Service contracts are separate from the product and are extended at extra cost. Further, the disclosures are not as detailed as the warranty rules.

To decide whether you, as a consumer, need a service contract, you should consider several factors: whether the warranty already covers the repairs that you would get under the service contract; whether the product is likely to need repairs and their potential costs; how long the service contract is in effect; and the reputation of the dealer offering the service contract. The key issue is whether the service contract will offer real value after deductible amounts and other loopholes.

If you wish to offer real value and provide service contracts, then you must be careful as to the following:

▶ A service contract must not seem to be a warranty so you are not permitted to call it an "extended warranty" or "limited service contract."

► Your customers must be able to read and understand all material terms, such as

- what they're getting,
- for how long.
- the name and address of the company that takes legal responsibility for the contract as well as where and how to get service.
- the price of the service contract, clearly disclosed. (A blank space for the current price to be inserted is fine.)
- full disclosure by name of what the contract covers and does not cover and what the servicer will or will not do.
- what must happen before the customer may make a claim under the contract.
- what must be done to keep the agreement valid (e.g., a customer may have to perform maintenance to keep the contract in effect).
- whether the customer can cancel or transfer the contract or get a refund. Any cancellation fees, transfer fees, or method of calculating a refund should be disclosed.

Conclusions on the Magnuson-Moss Warranty Act

Magnuson-Moss is a truth-in-warranty law. It mandates that all warranties be written so as to be understandable to your average lay customer. If you can't understand it, chances are your customer also can't and may not buy your product as a result. Therefore, review your warranty as to who is protected, what parts of the product are covered, whether it is full or limited, and what are the effective date and total life of the warranty. Also, does the warrantor attempt to disclaim any implied warranty? This is illegal. Finally, review the steps your buyer must take if the product is defective. Is notification of the seller (you) involved? If so, review with counsel whether to establish informal procedure mechanisms to deal with such contingencies. Consumer goodwill and your company's reputation may depend on how well you exercise this option.[47]

Product Warranties Under the UCC

The UCC (Uniform Commercial Code) warranties are in many ways similar to the Magnuson-Moss warranties. The scope of the UCC (adopted in all states except Louisiana) covers many commercial transactions concerning "goods." You must take both the UCC and Magnuson-Moss consumer warranty provisions into account, depending on the parties to the contractual relationship into which you are entering.

In this section will be reviewed four UCC warranties: warranties of title, express warranties, implied warranties of merchantability, and implied warranties of fitness for a particular purpose. Warranties are important because of their effect on your firm's goodwill. Further, approximately 25% of all UCC litigation involves warranty disputes; clearly, we are discussing a very significant area of commercial law. You may best enjoy this section if you first refer to the chapter on sales law in Section 3. Remember that UCC warranties are limited to the sale of goods only; they do not affect services.

Since the warranty field is technical, I strongly suggest that you have your counsel review all your warranties in light of your marketing objectives. Failure to use the UCC-prescribed language creates some additional warranty exposure, and your counsel can describe the amount of that exposure so that you can evaluate your risks.

Warranties of Title

The warranty of title is the most common warranty.[48] The seller need not be a merchant dealing in goods of the kind involved.[49] *Any* sales contract warrants as to the goods that the title conveyed is good, its transfer rightful, and that the goods are free from all encumbrances and liens of which the *seller* at the time of contracting has *no* knowledge[50] (though seller's lack of knowledge is no defense). Comment 1 states that a buyer is entitled to "receive a good, clean title transferred to him also in a rightful manner so that he will not be exposed to a lawsuit in order to protect it."

The implied warranty of title differs from other warranties in that it protects the buyer in ownership of the goods bought. In contrast, the other warranties discussed in this chapter relate to the quality of the goods sold.

Problems in this area ordinarily will not arise when new goods are sold to consumers from inventory held by a person regularly involved in selling these goods. But when the goods are used, such as traded-in goods, then it is possible that the goods may be subject to an outstanding security interest, and this will not be cut off upon sale, or that the goods may have been stolen. Since, in every case of a sale of goods there is an implied warranty of title (unless excluded or modified), it is incumbent on counsel to anticipate problems in at least the obvious areas of exposure.

The title warranty can be disclaimed or modified only by specific language in your contract or by circumstances which give your buyer notice that you do not claim title or that you are purporting to sell only such right or titles as you may have.[51]

The disclaimer should specifically mention the word "title." For example, we're discussing that the words "as is" exclude the implied warranty of merchantability and fitness for a particular purpose. However, "as is" standing alone does not exclude the warranty of title.

Finally, there is the warranty against infringement. Here, unless otherwise agreed, a seller who is a merchant regularly dealing in goods of the kind warrants that the goods shall be delivered free of the rightful claim of any third person by way of infringement or the like, but a buyer who furnishes specifications to the seller must hold the seller harmless against any such claim which arises out of compliance with the specifications.[52]

Express Warranties

Any affirmation of fact or promise made by a seller to a buyer can result in an express warranty if such statement is part of the basis of the bargain. For example, a promise of service for one year, being a part of the basis of a bargain, gives rise to an express warranty of service for one year.[53]

As one court phrased it, "the purpose of the law of warranty is to determine what it is that the seller has in essence agreed to sell."[54] Nowhere is this more true than in the area of express warranties where there are many declarative statements.

A statement becomes part of the basis of a bargain when your buyer *could* (not did) have relied on it when she or he entered into the contract or agreement of sale. A seller need not use the words "warrant" or "guarantee."[55]

Express affirmations of fact can be created by *objective* promises or descriptions such as those found on a label or in a brochure or catalog. *Subjective* statements relating merely to the value of the goods or a statement purporting to be only the seller's opinion or commendation of the goods does not create an express warranty. A statement that an article is "excellent," "well made," "unbeatable," or "the best machine made" is rarely a warranty. Rather, it is usually considered puffery. "Puffery" is "an affirmation merely of the value of the goods or a statement purporting to be merely the seller's opinion of commendation of the goods and does not create a warranty."[56]

Examples always seem to include used car dealers making rosy statements about their cars such as "Ford (or Chrysler or General Motors) cars are better." However, this is an audience sophistication issue. If you are selling to sophisticated businesspersons in your field, you have greater latitude in making claims than if you were selling to the "average" consumer. Even with sophisticated buyers, if you move from subjective conjecture, opinions, guessing, or predictions into the realm of a commitment (such as, "we'll meet your deadline"), you create an express warranty.[57]

For example, Redmac (a family corporation) sought to purchase a computer system. It relied on a salesperson's verbal assurances that the computer system would be "free of defects" on delivery or be repaired during the manufacturer's warranty period and would "work for a reasonable period of time"—statements that cannot be readily classified as mere sales puffery. The Court held that taken together these statements constituted an affirmation of fact that the equipment would be installed so that it would operate properly and, in the event that it did not, the seller promised to render it operational for a reasonable period of time.[58]

As discussed throughout this book, the old standby is fast fading. Once courts could blithely state that "the decisive test for whether a given representation is a warranty or merely an expression of the seller's opinion is whether the seller asserts a fact of which the buyer is ignorant or merely states an opinion or judgment on a matter of which the seller has no special knowledge and on which the buyer may be expected also to have an opinion and to exercise his judgment."[59]

However, why should an agent's fabrications in sophisticated situations be dismissed as mere puffing? No one is likely to buy a home computer or a computer system because a salesperson says it's "really nifty." Cars today cost what houses did a generation ago, so no prudent buyer would rely solely on the assurance that "it'll give you no problems." The lie should not be able to insulate a buyer from obtaining what he seeks to purchase in the first place.

Firms know this. Their salesforce is pushed on quota systems. They hope they don't get caught. As a precaution, many firms highlight bold disclaimers in purchase documents warning customers that "no employee, agent, or representative of the company has the authority to bind the company to any oral representation or warranty concerning the system," and that "any written representation or warranty made prior to execution of the contract and not expressly contained therein shall not be enforceable by the customer." You should do this, too, if only to mitigate damages.

However, while you can structure your documents to negate any salesperson's oral or written warranties by virtue of this "integration clause," you cannot completely guard against the situation where the salesperson's statements to the buyer are so misleading as to amount to "fraud in the inducement." If the court finds that situation, it will simply disregard all of the contractual documents—including the disclaimers—and use the general principles of law found in the Uniform Commercial Code. As discussed, the UCC warranty provisions are so broad that the buyer will almost always win when they are applied.

Besides disclaimers in your agreement as related above, you should do the following:

- Educate your salesforce to avoid statements of fact; where the cost/benefit warrants it, provide scripts.
- Offer a phone number prominently displayed on the contract and state that a "buyer has a duty to look beyond the assertions of a salesperson and investigate the product(s) on his or her own." The phone number will provide another channel.
- Review your own (or a manufacturer's) promotional pieces to make sure their recitation won't hang you.[60]

- Keep current with all design changes and revise your manuals and scripts accordingly.

- If *Consumer Reports* or another source gives you a good write-up, display these articles and provide hand-outs.

- In lieu of the second suggestion above, have your people trained to state that if they don't know the answer to a customer's question, they shouldn't ad lib. They should tell the customer they don't know the answer but will get back promptly with the information. It is always safest to stick to the facts.

In addition to puffing and the above-described ways to create an express warranty, there are numerous other ways such a warranty may be created. *Remember:* an express warranty is any affirmation of fact made to induce the buyer to buy, and relied on by the buyer; the affirmation of fact becomes part of the basis of the bargain in the actual purchase decision.

Any description of the goods on which your buyer relies creates an express warranty that your goods will conform to that description. The FTC and state regulatory agencies are increasingly active in protecting consumers in this area, and thus your catalog wording must be submitted to your counsel as well as to your promotional personnel or advertising agency.

When dealing in commercial transactions, remember that your catalog is provided to induce the purchase of your product and, thus, such statements form the basis of the bargain. Technical specifications in a contract do not supersede catalog statements unless they expressly state that they do. For example, a court ordered a company to pay damages when the television transmitting tower it built for a customer collapsed in heavy winds. In the company's catalog (although not in the contractual wording), performance specifications stated that the tower could withstand maximum wind velocities. The courts stated that the catalog's "broad affirmations were not superseded or corrected by the technical specifications in the contract."[61]

Illustrations as well as words in a catalog or brochure are descriptions of goods and, as such, are express warranties if they become part of the basis of the bargain. In one instance the court noted that such promotional vehicles "are thrust upon the public as invitation to purchase" and are replacements for the traveling salesperson.[62] In another case, the use of an illustrated booklet constituted a description and the goods must, therefore, conform to such description.[63] If you have any questions, consult your counsel as to the advisability of placing in your catalog any indication that the items are not as illustrated. This may relieve you of express warranty responsibility for your illustrations.

In addition to the express warranty of description, there is a warranty created by sample. When you offer the buyer the right to inspect samples and your buyer relies on the samples in the purchase decision, then such samples become part of the basis of the bargain.

Thereafter your buyer has the right to assume that *all* goods covered by the order will take the form of the sample you showed.[64]

Managers must know when a distributor or dealer has *adopted* a manufacturer's express warranty. A seller is liable for the breach of an express warranty only when through conduct or communication the seller creates or adopts a warranty and the buyer relies on it as the basis of the bargain.[65] If a dealer only passes on a manufacturer's warranty and does not adopt it, the dealer is not bound by the warranty.[66] A dealer adopts the manufacturer's warranty when it attempts to carry out the repair obligations under the warranty.[67] Note that if you as a purchaser want the warranty period tolled during downtime for repairs, such provision must be stated in your express warranty.[68]

Then there is the situation as to post-sale actions and statements by the seller. For example, when the seller has made additional promises to the buyer after the sale is concluded, perhaps to induce the buyer not to reject the goods or revoke acceptance, these promises may become part of the basis of the bargain, although the buyer could not possibly have relied on them at the time of the sale; that is, the "bargain" is in a sense a continuing relationship. Promises or warranties made after the sale can be treated as modifications of the contract requiring no consideration to be binding.[69]

In certain cases, post-sale action by the seller waived its warranty disclaimers.[70] However, the seller can also improve things. In one case, post-sale warnings which were received and ignored were adequate to defeat subsequent express and implied warranty claims.[71]

Finally, you should be aware of the disclaimer issues for express warranties. Between merchants there is little second-guessing if your documents follow UCC provisions correctly once both parties sign on. You can disclaim warranties and limit your liability in a commercial setting without too much fear of a court's imposing liability on the grounds of public policy or fairness. You need not have the disclaimer on the front of the form or in different color ink. All you need do is follow the UCC's wording. The precise language of the UCC is that "words or conduct relevant to the creation of an express warranty and words or conduct tending to negate or limit such warranty shall be construed wherever reasonable as consistent with each other."[72] The negation of such warranties is inoperative to the extent that such construction is unreasonable.

For example, if a sales contract which includes an express warranty also includes a clause excluding "all warranties, express or implied," that clause would be inoperative since it would be inconsistent with the express warranty. The inconsistency between the two clauses renders the disclaimer inoperative.

Any disclaimer must be conspicuous. As stated by a New Jersey court: "an exclusion or limitation of express warranties is strongly disfavored in the UCC." A court will not uphold a warranty disclaimer which is a linguistic maze.[73] As in all such cases, a disclaimer cannot be favored vis-a-vis fraud in the inducement.[74]

State after state is reducing, if not eliminating, your right to disclaim warranties in consumer sales without at least extensive warnings.[75]

One idea is to have separate paragraphs where you state your warranty and then disclaim it! Never use the back of your documents to disclaim a warranty unless you call attention to your disclaimer language on the front page. Then the disclaimers, too, become part of the basis of the bargain. Equally important is to have a well-drafted integration or merger clause. This will indicate that this writing was meant as a final and exclusive expression of your agreement and prevent parol evidence or consistent, additional terms from getting in.[76]

Only your counsel should create disclaimer wording and decide on its location. When dealing with two commercial enterprises on a relatively equal footing, your counsel can usually disclaim express warranties.[77] However, the situation is much more complicated when dealing with a consumer, because of the requirements of Magnuson-Moss as well as the general UCC provisions as to unconscionability.[78]

As to "remedies" such as "cover, damages,"[79] and the like," please refer to the chapter on sales in Section II.

Implied Warranties of Merchantability

Since people began trading with one another, it became obvious to all concerned that in each transaction, however simple or silent, a variety of understandings were assumed, some even subconsciously. Since these assumptions reflected elementary societal mores and were necessary to facilitate commerce, the courts and legislatures sought to give them formal legal status. As merits became complex, such inclusions into codified law became an absolute necessity.

Today, a buyer has little or no opportunity to *meaningfully* examine goods before making a decision to purchase them. In addition, because of the complexity and nature of many goods, buyers are often not in a position to test them adequately to determine their quality prior to buying them. To try to rectify this imbalance, the law "implies" or imposes by law certain warranties.

The implied warranty of merchantability can be made *only* by a *merchant* who deals in goods of the kind sold (see the discussion relating to merchants in Section II). In every sale by a merchant who deals in goods of the kind sold, there is an implied warranty that the goods are merchantable. The buyer need not rely on the seller for this warranty. One example is the serving of food or drink on the premises. This would be a sale of goods subject to the warranty of merchantability. The full text of the seven elements of this warranty is as follows:[80]

To be merchantable, goods must be at least such as (a) pass without objection in the trade under the contract description; (b) in the case of tangible goods, are of fair average quality within that description; (c) are fit for the ordinary purposes for which such goods are used; (d) run of even kind, quality and quantity within each unit; (e) are adequately packaged and labelled as the agreement may require;[81] (f) conform to promises and affirmations made in the contract or label, if any; (g) unless excused or modified, other implied warranties may arise from course of dealing or usage of trade.[82]

These elements are fairly straightforward though it should be noted that not all of them apply to a given sales contract. One area not readily apparent but included is the sale of used or second-hand goods. The UCC does not distinguish between new and used goods, and so the sale of used goods gives rise to implied warranties. If you sell used goods, you are warranting that they are fit for the purpose for which they are sold.[83]

One final point you will note in subsection (f) is that the UCC makes conformity to the affirmation on a container or label into an implied warranty. Thus, you need only show that the statement was there, not that it was part of the "basis of the bargain" (i.e., an express warranty).

To exclude or modify any part of the implied warranty of merchantability, you must use language that mentions merchantability in the exclusion. The exclusion does not have to be in writing, but if the warranty is in writing the disclaimer must be conspicuous.[84] A term or clause is conspicuous when it is so written that a reasonable person against whom it is to operate ought to notice it. A printed heading in capitals is conspicuous. Language in the body of a form is conspicuous if it is in larger type or in a contrasting color.[85] Indenting and underlining the language will also assist in distinguishing and setting apart your disclaimer language from the text of the other contractual provisions.[86] Other ways to exclude this warranty include:

▶ The use of expressions such as "as is" or "with all faults" are generally understood to call to your buyer's attention the fact that you are offering no implied warranties. They are equivalent to the phrase "there are no warranties which extend beyond the description on the face hereof."[87]

▶ When you have demanded that your buyer inspect the goods and the buyer has refused, then there is no warranty as to patent defects that a reasonable examination would have revealed. Still, you remain liable under the warranty for any latent defect.[88]

▶ Under certain circumstances implied warranties may be disclaimed by the course of dealing, course of performance, sequence of conduct, or usage of trade.[89]

▶ Have the buyer separately initial the disclaimer clause.

Finally, review the suggestions made in the prior discussion of express warranties, concerning where to locate your disclaimers, how to set them apart, etc.[90] You must have counsel draft your warranty provisions and any modifications and disclaimers in your commercial dealings. In general, you won't be able to disclaim a written warranty given to a consumer.[91] The UCC also provides that express warranties displace inconsistent implied warranties other than an implied warranty of fitness for a particular purpose.[92] In addition to the law, there is the issue of your goodwill, since the buyer may think that any small-print disclaimers are in bad faith, and you may lose a repeat purchase. However, you should consult with counsel as to the as-is sale and other options available to you in consumer warranty limitations.

Implied Warranties of Fitness for a Particular Purpose

The implied warranty of fitness for a particular purpose basically means that the buyer is relying on your specific skill and expertise and that you know the buyer is so relying.[93] For this warranty you need not be a merchant. You are held to a higher standard of care here than for the warranty of merchantability (i.e., for fitness for the ordinary purposes for which such goods are used). As the comment to the UCC says: "A particular purpose differs from an ordinary purpose for which goods are used in that it envisages a specific use by the buyer which is peculiar to the nature of his business whereas the ordinary purposes for which goods are used are those envisaged in the concept of merchantability."[94]

Specifically, a warranty of fitness for a particular purpose requires the following:

- The seller must have reason to know the buyer's particular purpose.
- The seller must have reason to know that the buyer is relying on the seller's skill or judgment to furnish appropriate goods.
- The buyer must, in fact, rely upon the seller's skill or judgment.[95]

Two of the comments to this UCC provision are worth reviewing in depth.[96]

1. Whether or not this warranty arises in any individual case is basically a question of fact to be determined by the circumstances of the contracting. Under this section the buyer need not bring home to the seller actual knowledge of the particular purpose for which the goods are intended or of his reliance on the seller's skill and judgment, if the circumstances are such that the seller has reason to realize the purpose intended or that the reliance exists. The buyer, of course, must actually be relying on the seller.

2. A "particular purpose" differs from the ordinary purpose for which the goods are used in that it envisages a specific use by the buyer which is peculiar to the nature of his business whereas the ordinary purposes for which goods are used are those envisaged in the concept of merchantability and go to uses which are customarily made of the goods in question.

Many goods that are perfectly merchantable will not meet the implied warranty of fitness for a particular purpose.

This warranty is intended to protect the buyer of goods from bearing the burden of loss when goods, although not violating express warranties, do not meet the buyer's particular purpose. Such expertise can vary from your expertise in electronic circuitry design[97] to your knowledge of the age and dependability of a punch press.[98]

Another area of increasing importance to managers is compliance with various flammability acts. If your buyer requests clothing fit for the particular purpose of compliance with these flammability acts, and you agree to provide such clothing, the clothing you provide must be fit for your buyer's purposes.[99]

However, common sense tells you that a buyer receives no warranty of fitness for a particular purpose if you manufacture or supply goods on the basis of specifications provided by the buyer (and on the buyer's advice as to a particular brand or design).[100] In one case a buyer ordered carts, supplying the exact specifications, and then inspected them. The buyer then claimed that the goods breached the warranty of fitness. The court actually moved the carts about in front of the courthouse and found them fit for the purpose intended! Since the buyer designed them and they were found fit, the buyer received no further warranty protection.[101] As a general rule, the warranty will not be found to exist when the buyer selected goods under their trade name, or if a buyer asks for a particular brand of goods. In that case, the buyer probably knows as much about whether they can be assumed to fill the buyer's needs as the seller knows. The buyer is simply not relying on the seller's skill of judgment.[102]

To disclaim these warranties, refer to the general disclaimers previously discussed (as is, inspection or refusal to inspect, course of dealing, conspicuous language, and so on). Wording such as "There are no warranties which extend beyond the description of the face hereof" is sufficient to exclude a warranty of fitness for a particular purpose.[103]

Disclaimer language properly drafted by your counsel will invariably accomplish its purposes with parties who have equal bargaining power and expertise. However, when dealing with consumers, a court may hold your disclaimer unconscionable even though it is in literal compliance with the formal requirements we've discussed. The court may find that your customer's lack of bargaining position, lack of choice, lack of expertise concerning your goods, failure to understand the language, or other matters are more important issues than the mere fact that your disclaimer wording was correct. Consult with counsel as to your specific exposure with your specific market.

Cumulation and Conflict of Warranties Express or Implied

Finally, the "priority" of warranties when there is a problem of ambiguity is a UCC issue. The UCC reads concisely here:

All warranties, express or implied, are to be construed as consistent and cumulative, but if this is unreasonable, the parties' intention determines which warranty is dominant. To get that result, certain rules are followed:

► Exact or technical specifications displace an inconsistent sample or model or general descriptive language.

► A sample from an existing bulk displaces general inconsistent language of description.

► Express warranties displace inconsistent implied warranties, other than an implied warranty of fitness for a particular purpose. Thus, though the seller delivers an item as described in the contract, it would not bar an action for breach of warranty of fitness for the purpose intended, if it was not suited for the work intended as known by the seller and upon whose judgment the buyer relied.[104]

Conclusion

Your warranty is the expression of your willingness to stand behind your products. There is much goodwill at stake. Sears' simple "we service what we sell" has been an excellent warranty used in conjunction with its promotional campaigns. Anyone offering a warranty must be acquainted with the laws on point. This knowledge will help you become a better manager and well-rounded business executive; it also informs you of your own rights and protection as a consumer.

ENDNOTES

(1) E.g., NYS General Business Law §198(b).

(2) Note that law of a given state in which you do business may be narrower than construed by federal agencies or the courts. For example, Sections 1793.1 and 1975.6 of the California Civil Code require that all orders or repair invoices contain a statement, in 10-point boldface type, informing consumers of their rights. These sections also extend the warranty period by the number of days a product is out of a customer's hands because of repairs. Review the particular statutes and the various deceptive trade practices acts with counsel. You might also contact your trade association to see if they compile and distribute information as to consumer rights and remedies applicable in the various states. See also Robert J. Posch, Jr., "Warranty Disclosure for Direct Marketers," *Direct Marketing,* November 1982, pp. 110-112.

(3) *Harris v. Tractor Co.,* 202 Va. 958, 961-62, 121 S.E. 2d 471, 473 (1961).

(4) *Guyot v. Al Charyn, Inc.,* 417 N.Y.S.2d 941 (1979). See also *Cedars of Lebanon Hospital Corp. v. European X-Ray Distributors of America, Inc.,* 444 So.2d 1068, (Fla. 1984).

(5) *Loews Corp. v. Sperry Corp.,* 86 AD.2d 221, 449 N.Y.S. 2d 715 (1982).

(6) UCC 2-318. See also *Henningsen v. Bloomfield Motors, Inc.,* 161 A.2d 69 (Sup. Ct. N.J.) (1960).

(7) *Knitwear v. American Cyanamid Co.* 11 N.Y.2d 946 (1962); *Maure v. Fordham Motor Sales,* 414 N.Y.S.2d 882 (1979).

(8) For the purposes of this act, there is no legal difference between the words "warranty" and "guarantee." For you, they both mean you promise to stand behind your products.

(9) 16 C.F.R. 700.1(a). and 700.1(h) (1986) "Subchapter G, Rules, Regulations, Statements and Interpretations Under the Magnuson-Moss Warranty Act." If an oral express warranty is at issue, your customer may have protection under the UCC Sec. 2-213 or under the states' "little FTC acts." For this reason, it is particularly important to familiarize your sales staff with the proper presentation of warranty information.

(10) 16 C.F.R. 700.1(a).

(11) 16 C.F.R. 700.3.

(12) 16 C.F.R. 700.1(a) and 15 U.S.C. 2301 Sec. 103. The act covers consumer products that cost more than $10 but the regulations adopted by the Federal Trade Commission to implement the act cover only products that cost more than $15.

(13) 16 C.F.R. 700.3.

(14) 16 C.F.R. 703.3-8 (1986).

(15) 16 C.F.R. 700.4.

(16) See note 12 above—FTC Reg. 701.2 regulates beginning at $15.00, not $10.00.

(17) 16 C.F.R. 701.1(c).

(18) 16 C.F.R. 701.1(i).

(19) The act does not define "conspicuous," but UCC language [Sec. 1-201(10)] may be useful as a guide. It defines "conspicuous" as a term or clause that is "so written that a reasonable person against whom it is to operate ought to have noticed it. . .Language in the body of a form is conspicuous if it is in larger or other contrasting type or color. But in a telegram any stated term is conspicuous."

(20) See Federal Trade Commission, "Warranties: There Ought to Be a Law. . .," FTC informational pamphlet.

(21) 16 C.F.R. 700.6(b).

(22) 16 C.F.R. 701(e)(3).

(23) 16 C.F.R. 700.7(b).

(24) 16 C.F.R. 700.7(c). The information you request should be limited to that necessary to fulfill your warranty program. Before you request additional information (such as retail prices), you should consult your counsel.

(25) See note 9.

(26) 16 C.F.R. 700.10(a). See also Robert J. Posch, Jr., "How to Avoid Getting Tied Up with Tie-Ins," *Direct Marketing,* August 1982, pp. 104-106.

(27) 16 C.F.R. 700.10(c).

(28) 16 C.F.R. 701.3.

(29) 16 C.F.R. 239.2, "Guides for the Advertising of Warranties and Guarantees."

(30) See 16 C.F.R. 239 for a variety of suggested examples.

(31) 16 C.F.R. 702.3.

(32) "Reasonably calculated to elicit the prospective buyer's attention" must be read, in context with the three nonbinder options, to require that notice of the availability of warranty information in the form of binders or signs be in sufficient proximity to the point of sale so that buyers are likely to see such notice before making their purchases.

(33) 16 C.F.R. 239.2(a) of note 1.

(34) 16 C.F.R. 702.3(a).

(35) 16 C.F.R. 702.3(c)(i) (emphasis added).

(36) *A-Larms, Inc. v. Alarms Devil Manufacturing Co.,* 300 S.E. 2d 311 (1983).

(37) 16 C.F.R. 700.4. Again, it is important to review your purchase agreements with counsel. If you are merely a supplier of a product, you should make sure you know if the manufacturer is offering a warranty with the product as delivered.

(38) 16 C.F.R. 702.3(d)(2).

(39) 16 C.F.R. 703.

(40) 16 C.F.R. 703.2.

(41) 16 C.F.R. 703.2(a).

(42) Specifically, 16 C.F.R. 703.3-703.8 (1986).

(43) 16 C.F.R. 703.2 (b) and (c).

(44) 16 C.F.R. 703.2(b)(3).

(45) 16 C.F.R. 703.2(d).

(46) 16 C.F.R. 703.5(j).

(47) Related to the issue of warranties is the disclosure of unassembled merchandise (with the logical exception of toy hobby kits). Review this area with your counsel. Although there are no specific formal guidelines as to the exact language needed in the promotion piece, failure to include some form of clear, up-front (not buried in copy text) language indicating that the product requires assembly or special tools could result in a charge of deceptive advertising based on FTC case history and also certain state laws (e.g., New York).

Finally, you may wish to review a few FTC decisions discussing the extent of disclosure and manner of performance for the warranty under the act:

a. *Redman Indus., Inc.,* 85 FTC 309 (1975).

b. *Fleetwood Enters. Inc.,* 85 FTC 414 (1975).

c. *Skyline Corp.,* 85 FTC 444 (1975).

d. *Soxomy Pools,* 86 FTC 349 (1975).

e. *North American Pools, Inc.,* 86 FTC 615 (1975).

f. *Lifetime Filter Equip. Corp.,* 86 FTC 608 (1975).

g. *Mutual Const. Co.,* 87 FTC 608 (1975).

h. *Levitz Furniture Corp.,* 88 FTC 263 (1976).

i. *Korvette's, Inc.,* 94 FTC 318 (1979).

j. *Montgomery Ward & Co.,* 97 FTC 363 (1979).

k. *George's Radio and Television Co.,* 94 FTC 1135 (1979).

(48) UCC Sec. 2-312. Although we'll be citing federal statutes, all types of warranties are governed by state law. Further, different states have modified their own UCC's in different ways, and their courts have rendered varying interpretations. Complying with the federal law on point may not be enough, so review with your counsel the laws of the states in which you're doing business.

(49) UCC Sec. 2-104. A "merchant" is "a person who deals in goods of the kind or otherwise by his occupation holds himself out as having knowledge or skill peculiar to the practices or goods involved in the transaction or to whom such knowledge or skill may be attributed by his employment of an agent or broker or other intermediary who by his occupation holds himself out as having such knowledge or skill." As to the warranty against infringement's application only to merchants, see UCC Sec. 2-312(5) and Comment 3.

(50) U.S.C. 2-312(1). See also *Pineau v. White,* 101 N.H. 119, 135 A.2d 716 (1957).

(51) UCC Sec. 2-312(2), and see Comment (5). Unlike the warranties in Sections 2-314 and 2-315, this warranty of title is not governed by the disclaimer provision of Sec. 2-316.

(52) UCC Sec. 2-312(3) and see Comment (5).

(53) UCC 2-313.

(54) *Keith v. Buchanan,* 220 Cal. Rptr. 392, 395, 42 U.C.C. Rep. Serv. 386, 390 (1985) citing *A.A. Boxter Corp. v. Cold Industries, Inc.,* 88 Cal. Rptr. 842 (1970).

(55) UCC Sec. 2-312(2).

(56) Id.

(57) *Vance Pearson, Inc., v. Alexander,* 408 N.E.2d 782 (1980). *Royal Business Machines v. Lorraine Corp.,* 633 F.2d 34 (7th Cir. 1986). See also *Investors Premium Corp. v. Burroughs Corp.,* 389 F. Supp. 39 (D.S.C. 1974), and *O'Hara v. Derschug,* 241 A.D. 513, 5B 272 NYS (A.D.) 189 (1934).

(58) *Redmac, Inc. v. Computerland of Peoria,* 489 N.E.2d 380, 383 (III App. 3 Dist. 1986).

(59) 633 F.2d 34 (7th Cir. 1986).

(60) It has long been established that an advertisement can be part of the basis of the bargain. *Harris v. Dalton,* 258 Cal. App. 2d 595; 65 Cal. Rptr. 808 (1968).

(61) UCC Sec. 2-313(1)(b). *Community Television Servs., Inc. v. Dresser Industries, Inc.,* 586 F.2d 637, 640 (1978). See also *M-A-S-H, Inc. v. Fiat-Allis Constr. Mach. Inc.,* 461 F. Supp.79 (1978).

(62) *Arlis, Inc. v. Gojer, Inc.,* 75 Misc.2d 962, 349; N.Y.S.2d 948 (Civ. Ct. Queens Co., 1973).

(63) *Antonucci v. Stevens Dodge,* 73 Misc. 2d 173 (1973). See also *Mahasco, Inc. v. Anderson Halverson Corp.,* 90 Nev. 114, 520 P.2d 234 (1974) (customized carpet).

(64) *Indus-Ri-Chem Par Laboratory, Inc. v. Pak Co.,* 602 S.W.2d 282 (1980).

(65) Id. at 296. However, consistent with the UCC's overall policy of commercial reasons, you should be aware of the comment in Sec. 2-313 with regard to express warranties: "Of course, all descriptions by merchants must be read against the applicable trade usages with the general rules as to merchantability resolving any doubts." Thus, express warranties running to your buyer and the buyer's objections must be read in terms of their significance in the trade and relative to what would normally pass in the trade without objection under the catalog description.

(66) *Courtesy Motor Sales, Inc. v. Farrior,* 298 So. 2d 26 (1974).

(67) *Matthews v. Ford Motor Co.,* 479 F.2d 399 (1973).

(68) *Mountain Fuel Supply Co., v. Central En'g and Equip. Co.,* 611 P.2d 863 (1980).

(69) UCC Sec. 2-313, Comment 7. See also *Downie v. Apex Corp.,* (Ca 10 Utah), 741 F.2d 1235.

(70) *Oregon Bank v. Nautilus Crane and Equipment Corp.,* 68 Or. App. 131; 683 P.2d 95 (1984).

(71) *Temple v. Velcro USA, Inc.,* 148 Cal. App. 3d 1090; 196 Cal. Reptr. 531 (1983).

(72) UCC Sec. 2-316(1). You should be alert to UCC Sec. 2-202 (see discussion in Section II), since consistent additional oral express warranties may be proven unless the written contract is stated to be complete or unless the writing negates any other warranties. This leaves open modification under UCC Sec. 2-209(1).

(73) *Henningsen v. Bloomfield Motors, Inc.,* 32 N.J. 358, 373; 161 A.2d 69 (1960). See also *Gladden v. Cadillac Motor Car Div.,* 416 A.2d 394, 399, 401 (1980); or bordering on unconscionable, see *McCarthy v. E.J. Korvette, Inc.,* 347 A.2d 253 (Md. 1975).

(74) *Tinker v. De Maria Porsche Audi, Inc.,* 459 So.2d 487 (Fla. Dist. Ct. App. 1984).

(75) Examples include: Conn. Gen. State. 42a-2-316 (must be specifically marked as such); N.H. Rev. Stat. Ann. 38-A:2-316(4) (a consumer must sign a waiver and be given same); Kan. Stat. Ann. 50-639 (no limitation of implied warranty of merchantability). See also *Dale v. King Lincoln-Mercury, Inc.,* 234 Kan. 840; 676 P.2d 744.

(76) UCC Sec. 2-316(1).

(77) See *Filures, Inc. v. Proctor & Schwartz, Inc.,* 509 F.2d 1043 (1979).

(78) UCC Sec. 2-714(2).

(79) UCC Sec. 2-711(1)(a), 2-712(1).

(80) UCC Sec. 2-314(1) and *Stark v. Chock Full O' Nuts,* 356 NYS 2d 403 (1974).

(81) UCC Sec. 2-301.

(82) See the discussion of the Fair Labeling and Packaging Act in this section.

(83) UCC Sec. 2-314(2). *Bly v. Otis Elevator Co.,* 713 F.2d 1040 (4th Cir. 1983) and *Harris v. Aluminum Co. of America,* 550 F.Supp. 1024 (W.D. Va. 1982).

(84) *Perry v. Lawson Ford Tractor Co.,* 613 P.2d 458 (1980). See also *Weisz v. Parke–Bernet Galleries, Inc.,* 325 N.Y.S.2d 576 (1971).

(85) UCC Sec. 2-316.

(86) UCC Sec. 2-201(10). See also *Transcontinental Refrigeration Co. v. Figgins,* 585 P.2d 1301 (1978).

(87) *R.D. Lowrance, Inc. v. Peterson,* 178 N.W.2d 277 (1970).

(88) UCC Sec. 2-316(2).

(89) *Country Clubs, Inc. v. Allis-Chalmers Mfg. Co.,* 430 F.2d 1394 (1970). As to "usage of trade" see UCC Sec. 1-205(2).

(90) See *Hunt v. Perkings Mach. Co.,* 226 N.E.2d 228 (1967). See also *DeKalb Agresearch, Inc. v. Abbott,* 391 F.Supp. 152 (1974).

(91) 15 U.S.C. Sec. 2308. However, see 15 U.S.C. Sec. 2308(b) and 15 U.S.C. Sec. 2304(a)(3). Obviously, you and your counsel must discuss the applicable state laws governing your warranty.

(92) UCC Sec. 2-317.

(93) UCC Sec. 2-315. *Addis v. Bernadin, Inc.,* 597 P.2d 250 (Kan. 1979).

(94) UCC Sec. 2-315, Comment 2. See also *Coisson Corp. v. Ingersoll-Rand Co.,* 622 F.2d 672 (1980).

(95) UCC Sec. 2-315.

(96) *Controltek, Inc. v. Kwikee Enters, Inc.,* 585 P.2d 670 (1978).

(97) UCC Sec. 2-315, Comments 1 and 2.

(98) *Miller v. Hubbard-Wrory Co.,* 630 P.2d 880 (1981).

(99) *Trinkle v. Schumacher Co.,* 301 N.W. 2d 255 (1980). See Flammable Fabrics Act, 15 U.S.C. Secs. 1191-1204.

(100) *Sam's v. Admar Bar,* 425 N.Y.S. 2d 743 (1980).

(101) *Sam's Marine Park Enters, Inc. v. Admar Bar & Kitchen Equip. Corp.,* 103 Misc.2d 276; 425 N.Y.S.2d 743 (1980).

(102) *United States Leasing Corp. v. Comerald Assocs., Inc. v. Pitney Bowes, Inc.,* 101 Misc. 2d 773; 421 N.Y.S.2d 1003 (1979); but see *Ewers v. Eisenzopf,* 88 Wis.2d 482; 276 N.W.2d 802 (1979).

(103) UCC Sec. 2-316(2).

(104) UCC Sec. 2-317.

CHAPTER 4

PATENT PROTECTION

This area of intellectual property, when contrasted to copyrights, trademarks, and trade secrets, is not as important to the business manager. However, it can be useful to consider patent protection in your overall product development and promotion strategies. Generally, there are two ways to go with a product invention. One, patent it and use the patent to beat back all competition. The second is to forget about patent laws and use the invention to build a production and marketing organization that always stays one step ahead of the competition. Where it can be employed, patent protection can be decisive in giving you almost absolute market preemption.

In this chapter we'll review what a patent is, why you should get one, how to go about applying for one, and how patent law relates to other legal areas.

What Is a Patentable Invention?

The initial law you must take a look at is Title 35 of the U.S. Code[1] and the Manual of Patent Office Procedures. The source of federal authority to grant patents is the United States Constitution, which authorizes Congress "to promote the Progress of Science and useful Arts, by securing for limited Times to Authors and Inventors the exclusive Right to their respective Writings and Discoveries."[2]

As with copyrights, the common law gives to an inventor the right to introduce his or her creation to the public. Similarly, federal statutory law provides protection after the first introduction. In contrast to trademark law (but similar to copyrights), there is no requirement for the patented product to be in interstate commerce. The states have no authority whatsoever as to the issuing of a patent, as the subject matter is one of national, not local, commerce. The statutory law is purely federal. The patent is a federal statutorily granted monopoly to make, use, or sell a machine, a manufacture, a composition of matter, or a process. Because of its monopoly potential as a restriction on information and the development of information, the right to a patent has traditionally been severely limited.

The patent statute[3] enumerates in Section 101 the categories into which your invention must fall to qualify for patent protection. "Whoever invents or discovers any new and useful process, machine, manufacture, or composition of matter, or any new and useful improvement thereof, may obtain a patent therefor. . ."

An invention not falling within one of these four classes is deemed nonstatutory subject matter and is not eligible for patent protection. In addition to meeting the Section 101 requirements, an invention must also be:

☐ *NOVEL.* That which already is anticipated or generally known (e.g. described in a trade journal), or is a law of nature (e.g., mathematical laws), cannot be patented. A combination of "generally known" elements or components may be patentable if their combination results in a new and beneficial use to society.[4]

☐ *NONOBVIOUS.* Even though an invention is novel, it cannot be patented if it is merely a trivial advance that would have been obvious to one "ordinarily skilled in the art."

☐ *USEFUL.* The invention must actually work (not be frivolous or immoral) or otherwise be useful, though it need not be better than what is available. Utility is seldom a problem, except in the area of chemical process patents.

Patents are classified in three general groupings:

▶ *Utility or Functional Patent*—Obtained for processes (chemical, mechanical, or electrical procedures), machines, articles of manufacture, and compositions of matter. These patents are addressed to the workings of the articles themselves, protecting their functional, rather than aesthetic, qualities.[5]

▶ *Design Patent*—Obtained for inventing a new, original and ornamental design for an article of manufacture. Its stress is on the beautification in manufactured articles so as to increase their desirability and satisfy the aesthetic sense of the purchaser.[6] Design patent protection does not extend to the functional aspects of the item; only to its appearance.[7]

▶ *Plant Patent*—Obtained for a new variety of a cultivated asexually reproduced plant.

Who May Obtain a Patent?

A patent application must be filed only in the name of the individual inventor or group of inventors who actually invented the patentable invention. Joint applicants are not required to delineate their contributions to the invention, only to authenticate their cooperation.

Conversely, no one may obtain a patent on anything unless he or she in fact invented it.

Then, there is the gray area of employees who create patentable inventions.[7a] Does the employer own it? Yes, if either of the following exists:

- the employer can demonstrate the employee was recruited specifically to develop, produce, or invent the patentable invention; or
- the employer can demonstrate that the employee used the employer's knowledge and material in developing an invention.

What happens if two similar or identical patentable products arrive at the U.S. Patent Office? An interference may be declared between an application and an issued patent if the application is filed within one year of the issue date of the patent. If it is unclear about who was the first to invent it, then you must be able to prove you were the first to conceive it. Conception requires you to demonstrate you had an idea of a useful result together with a specific means for achieving that result.

It is important to plan for this eventuality from day one by keeping thorough records. To do this:

- keep a notebook, diary, or log in which you update your thoughts and procedures in a regular or systematic manner;
- date all your sketches and drawings;
- have a notary authenticate the above from time to time by signing and dating entries when made;
- routinely file all bills for materials, subcontractors, labor, progress reports, and other third party contacts, which establish a "flow" for your invention's development; and
- use confidentiality agreements when approaching any third party as to significant input, license, or sale (see Section IX).

These steps will demonstrate your progress and that you and others were systematically acknowledging that certain progress benchmarks were being made. All such data will be useful if you must file a sealed statement with exhibits, should an "interference" proceeding be necessary.

OK, you are the inventor who is satisfied he or she can proceed to apply for a patent registration. What must you do now?

Find a Patent Attorney.   Your general practitioner probably can't assist you in the complicated patent area. For example, the patent lawyer must have a specific educational foundation in scientific areas and must take an exam over and above the state bar exam. Your attorney or in-house counsel will know of an effective practitioner. Otherwise, the *Martindale Hubbel Legal Directory,* or your local bar association can direct you to specialists in this field.

The patent attorney is necessary to advise you whether your invention will justify going further. If so, he would proceed to order and review the search, frame the application, and file any appeals. He or she will also be able to advise you on the mundane but necessary areas of compiling all the records of your invention, the cost of the process (varies as to routine, complexity, and even whether it's chemical or mechanical) and the time frame you're looking at. This can be very important advice to you.

Your attorney will advise you as to your legal exposure during the patent's filing. He or she might review whether other protections would be more timely or cost effective. For example, if you are marketing a product with a short technological life, your counsel will alert you as to the fact the approval may take 2–3 years, during which time your product may become obsolete or at least less marketable, owing to technological changes. During the period of time between your application and the approval, you will have no enforceable rights under the patent laws (though he or she will review other interim strategies), thereby rendering your potential protection meaningless during the time when you might consider it most valuable. Furthermore, the information that is the background or basis of the patent is publicly revealed on the grant of your patent, and there can be no secrecy about patented inventions nor restrictions on their use. Your counsel will review with you whether trade secret protection might be a better approach.

On the plus side, your attorney may suggest creative ways for you to trade off risks (and gains) and hit the ground running faster.

Your counsel may suggest you license your invention to others while the application process drags on. The licensee will look on this as an opportunity to pick up a useful invention at bargain basement rates because he or she has you over the barrel. The licensee can capitalize on your uncertainty regarding the eventual patent approval.

This is a two-way street, of course; that's why your counsel suggested it. If you lack the resources (including counsel fees) to develop your invention further or sustain the outflow of the registration process, your licensee's royalties will enter the picture with a fresh cash flow and carry you forward. Your licensee will also contribute to a more rapid commercialization of your invention. Yet, when potential competitors get wind of your royalty remuneration, they may have no incentive to enter your market.

So for the trade-off of speculative future royalties on the patent's grant to you, you have in hand a cash flow, promotional assistance and possible preemption of the market for a longer period of time. A final advantage is that the licensor will not have to offer patent indemnity to the licensee. Normally (see below and Section VII) a licensor/seller must agree to hold the licensee/buyer harmless against any infringement of patents that the use of the invention may cause, and that the licensor/seller will defend the licensee/buyer in any actions arising therefrom.

Your counsel will also assist you in developing both an in-house confidentiality policy as well as a confidentiality agreement to be signed by would-be licensees before divulging any material data to them about your invention. Since *a patent application filing* is not a public record until the patent is actually issued, such application will not destroy any existing trade secret rights. Your counsel will coordinate these respective protections if you elect to go forward with the application.

Your counsel will prepare a short document preserving your protection while not "turning off" potential licensees. He or she will include the following items:

☐ Description of parties

☐ Definitions, if technical

☐ A statement of principle as to why you're getting together, for example:

"In order to proceed with our discussions concerning the potential opportunities pertaining to _____ , it is advisable for us to establish a basis upon which each of us can communicate and exchange information about the (invention). Accordingly, in consideration of the execution of this Agreement and the covenants contained herein, the following conditions will govern our relationship:

"Whereas, Irving Inventor (hereafter "Inventor") is the possessor of a certain valuable and confidential invention and the unauthorized disclosure of which will be injurious to it.

"Whereas, Lorraine Licensee (hereafter "Licensee") will have access to and use of the aforesaid information and invention in order to pursue our discussions further."

☐ Confidentiality provisions set forth such as:

"**(a)** Now, therefore, it is agreed between Inventor and Licensee that any and all information and data about the invention (regardless of the manner in which it is embodied) supplied by Inventor or otherwise obtained by Licensee during the course of the above-mentioned discussion shall be treated as confidential by Licensee, safeguarded by it and not revealed, divulged by it, or made known to any other person, firm, or corporation or otherwise used directly or indirectly by it (except for the specific purposes of this Agreement) without the express written permission of Inventor, and returned to Inventor at the end of the period of our discussions or at any time upon the request of Inventor."

"**(b)** Licensee agrees to hold all identified and accepted confidential information about said invention in connection with this business opportunity in confidence for a period of five (5) years from the date hereof, to use such information only for the purpose of this Agreement, and to use the same degree of care which it uses for its own information of like importance about a similar invention to prevent dissemination of the same. However, Licensee shall have no obligation with respect to any such information which is known to it prior to the disclosure, which is or becomes publicly known through no wrongful act by it, which is received by it from a third party without restriction and without breach of this Agreement, which is approved for use or release by written authorization by either of us to the other, which is independently developed by Licensee, which is or may be derived from examination of publicly available information or was ascertained without use of the disclosed information about Inventor's Invention."

☐ For discussion purposes only:

"(a) While each of us is willing to undertake the time and effort necessary to determine its degree of interest in the contemplated transaction of developing the Invention; there is, of course, no certainty of the final outcome of the matter. With this in mind, Inventor will not forgo any other opportunity with regards to this opportunity and is free to explore the same without any obligation whatsoever to Licensee except as provided by the terms hereof, while awaiting the outcome of this matter."

"(b) However, unless Inventor expressly advises Licensee to the contrary, Inventor does hereby covenant and warrant that it has not at any time prior to the making of this agreement in any manner made known, divulged or communicated the said opportunity to any person, firm, or corporation, and such therewith is known only to Inventor."

☐ Irreparable harm—Whenever you deal with intellectual property you must convey to the other party that such party's divulgence will cause you irreparable harm. For example:

"It is understood that this document is of the essence to any future agreement and that any breach thereof will cause Inventor irreparable harm."

Then there are the "traditional boilerplate" paragraphs (see Section VII), e.g.,

☐ No joint venture

☐ Governing law

☐ Term/Termination (if any)

☐ Integration or merger clause—Once you've decided on licensing your rights, you've obviously elected to proceed to registration. Let's briefly take a look at what this entails.

Obtaining the Registration

A preliminary patentability search is indispensable to find out if your invention is novel. Regardless of the results, your attorney will prepare a written opinion as to whether you should go forward in light of the search. If you do, the search information also assists your attorney in drafting the application. With this knowledge of the market, your attorney will merge into your patent petition the object of your invention, its structure (by a detailed drawing) and all known and potential benefits for the examiner's review and consideration (the wording on a design application may be a bit different from an application for a utility patent).

You will then mail your patent application enclosing the prescribed governmental filing fees. On acceptance of the application, you will be assigned an official serial number. All correspondence henceforth must reference such number.

Your attorney will then advise you to use the legend "patent pending" or similar words on your patented articles or processes and in all advertisements, correspondence, or other public affirmations of your invention.

Within a year, the Patent Office will

- accept the application,
- reject it for specific cause, or
- request further information or a re-draft of your drawings.

Your time to respond will be set forth in the official notice. The amendment and appeal process in your circumstances is best reviewed with your counsel. For our purposes we'll assume you were accepted.

Patent Protections Designation

After your patent has been issued, the following patent notice may be used: the word "patent" or "pat." and the number of the patent. This notice is not mandatory but may be necessary to get damages from an infringer. On the other hand, use of an improper patent notice is punishable by a fine. Obviously, you should review all such indications of ownership terminology with your counsel.

Length of Protection.   A design patent will be issued for a period of 3½, 7, or 14 years as selected by the applicant and approved by the Patent Office. The various time periods require different fees.

A utility patent or plant patent can last three years longer or 17 years from the date of issuance of the patent. It can expire earlier if specified maintenance fees are not paid 3½ years, 7½ years, and 11½ years after grant (plus a six-month grace period). A patent cannot be renewed, and since it is publicly disclosed when issued, anyone can make, use, or sell in the U.S. devices embodying the formerly patented invention after the patent has expired or has been declared invalid.

Patent Infringement.   In general, using or selling a patented invention (or the active inducement of another to do so) without the authority of the patent owner is an infringement. Whether the allegedly infringing device is the same is determined by whether it accomplishes essentially the same result by essentially the same means as that stated in the patent claims. Copying is not a requisite element of patent infringement under the patent statute.

Exclusive jurisdiction to enforce your remedies is vested in the federal courts and the governing law is exclusively federal law.

If you establish infringement and wish to recover damages, you must be prepared to prove either the infringer had actual notice of the infringement (i.e., you wrote asking him or her to cease and desist), or your patented invention bore the proper patent notice conspicuous to a reasonable person or conspicuous in the circumstances of your trade.

You can receive compensatory damages, punitive damages, or a preliminary and permanent injunction against future infringement.[8] You may also be entitled to attorney's fees and interest for any losses suffered from the infringement, including a "reasonable royalty." However, you must be prepared to defend a counterclaim contesting the underlying validity of your patent.

In any event, you will probably be forced to assert your claim *against* infringement by contract with any buyer or licensee you might have contracted with.

If you are sued for infringement, you will probably be obligated to defend the user against any such infringement claim and to hold such user harmless. First, you will give a warranty of title that there are no threats of infringement and/or actions pending. Then you'll provide a "hold harmless" warranty. The typical (similar for copyright, trademark, and other proprietary rights protection) "hold harmless clause" will read as follows:

> Inventor warrants that the invention is original to the Inventor and that neither the invention nor any of its elements nor the use thereof does or will violate or infringe upon any patent of any other person.

> The inventor will defend and hold the user harmless from any loss, cost, or liability finally awarded arising out of any breach of this warranty.

This will be conditioned on:

(a) a specified period which constitutes "prompt notice,"

(b) Inventor will have sole control over any defense and all negotiations as to settlement,

(c) you didn't alter the Inventor's product specifications operating procedures, etc. in any way or add on "improvements" or other ancillary features without the contractual right to do so and/or prior approval in writing.

Depending on Leverage:

Strong Inventor—may require you to accept a "comparable" replacement or force you to accept a credit for the balance of the useful life of the machine (buyer) or limited if any liquidated damages (licensee).

Strong Licensee/Buyer—The Inventor might be required to furnish an indemnification bond. More commonly the licensee/buyer will retain the right (by contract) to withhold payment of any royalty or other sums required to be paid during the pendency of the action. The contract might provide for an escrow account in this contingency. Any licensee should require that he or she be able to withhold royalties for any downtime due to injunctions and the like. The licensee will also retain a contractual right to terminate the agreement in the event of a final judicial determination of infringement (or adverse settlement acknowledging same).

The buyer loses some leverage but, as discussed in Section VII, well-drafted benchmarks and maintenance agreements will preserve some continuity of an ongoing relationship.

Antitrust

There is a lot of built-in tension here. The patent laws are predicated on the assumption that progress in the sciences and in the useful arts is best promoted by granting to the inventor a legal monopoly of his or her discovery. Thus, in a sense, the patent laws may be viewed as exceptions to our antitrust policy of preserving competition. In another sense, however, the patent laws appear as instruments designed to accelerate technological progress by granting short-term monopoly privileges as offsets to the risks involved in introducing a new product or process; i.e., they may stimulate competition in the long run. See also the Section II discussion of tie-ins. However, licensing is essential to patent exploitation, so we'll briefly review a few issues here.

First, the good news. The Antitrust Division no longer has a list of nine illegal per se restrictions, and the courts are shifting on the issue of patent licensing.[9]

Nevertheless, the courts generally still look harshly at the potential of tying a natural monopoly such as a patent to nonpatented goods. This is especially true if there is no close substitute for the patented items (otherwise the patentee probably will not have the requisite economic power in the tied product). There is much authority, however, that presumes economic power in a tying product when a patent is involved. This situation can arise if the licensor seeks to tie a supply contract to its patent.[10] This is no problem as long as there is no compulsion.

Another issue the courts will look at is whether this is a simple cross-licensee agreement or a patent interchange agreement. In the latter case, the *enhanced* power to exclude (due to the combined patent holdings) is the reason these interchanges are usually viewed adversely by the courts.[11] The courts have long held that what a single patent could do is not necessarily permissible conduct for two or more patentees acting through cross-licensing agreements.[12] However, cross-license agreements which do not enhance the patent position of either party for licensing or litigation purposes possess minimum antitrust risk.

Another area of patent licensing exposure is the exclusive "grant back." This is a contractual provision whereby the Licensee must grant back (by assignment or exclusive license) to the Licensor any patent which was issued to the Licensee after the license agreement was finalized.

This is odious to competition because it tends to reduce the incentive for a licensee so bound to invest in innovation for its own sale and for its potential competition to the licensor's monopoly position.

Overall, as discussed in Section III, the patent licensor has probably the greatest hurdles of negative presumptions left in antitrust law today. Such factor is an obvious consideration to review with your attorney whenever you are considering the exploitation of this property right.

Patent Exploitation in the Future

We shouldn't leave on a "down" antitrust theme. There is a growing rule-of-reason lobby here in the literature, Justice Department, and some courts. Elsewhere patent rights are expanding.

First, the Patent Office has succeeded somewhat and is trying to do more to facilitate its reviews.

Second, patent rights are being expanded by the courts into the various "high-tech" areas. For example, as stated earlier:

> The most common example of what can't be patented is mathematical formula.[13] If it does not involve such a formula, you have a good chance to obtain a patent (assuming all the above-quoted statutory requirements are met).

If your software involves a mathematical formula (algorithm), then you must show that your claim does not attempt to wholly preclude other people from using it, but is using it only as one specific application of the mathematical formula.[14] For example, you can show that while the mathematical formula you're using is well known, you've used it in a new and very efficient way.[15] In this case, the Court allowed computer programs to be patented when they were part of a longer process or apparatus which is patentable (software cannot be patented by itself).[16]

Checklist for Basic Patent Consideration

☐ Do I have a novel, nonobvious, useful invention or design that will pass the initial statutory review? If so,

☐ Am I the lawful inventor?

☐ If I am, can I prove it?

☐ This is the first question if you're only starting to tinker with a potentially patentable idea—have I:

- organized a diary to record my step-by-step progress from idea to embodiment?

- authenticated such diary's dates and insertions with a neutral third party?

- organized all other business transactions to support my contention of ownership?

☐ Have I retained a *patent* attorney who says I may have a patent?

☐ Have we reviewed alternatives to patents (factoring time to obtain, costs and comparative protections against practical dangers)?[17]

☐ Is my registration application proper in form?

☐ Have we reviewed pre-acceptance as well as post acceptance exploitation?

☐ Am I proceeding only with adequate paperwork (confidentiality agreements, licensee agreements, narrowly worded indemnification, etc.)?

☐ Are all drafted with antitrust sensitivity?

☐ Now that I have the registration, am I labeling my identification of ownership correctly?

☐ Am I paying the renewal fees at the proper intervals?

☐ Have I reviewed with counsel steps to take to protect my property after the expiration of the patent protected term?

A review with your own patent counsel will best serve your interest. Unlike other areas of intellectual property, patents are more product-specific and don't lend themselves to broad-brush reviews.

Conclusion

As the U.S. comes to realize it is in global competition and that most antitrust laws were a luxury of a bygone era, it will continue to release undue restrictions on competition. Then the antitrust area will begin to open up just as other patent utility strategies are becoming more available to today's marketing manager's short- and long-term strategies.

Patent protection (because of time and costs) is not a routine option. However, if you have a valuable invention worth a long-term investment to you or offering a significant competitive advantage in marketing, sales, or other bottom-line impact, then it is an option you must review with your counsel.

ENDNOTES

(1) 35 U.S.C. 100 et seq.

(2) Article I, Section 8 of the U.S. Constitution. See also *U.S. v. Univis Lens Co.,* 316 U.S. 241, 250 (1982). See also *Graham v. John Deere Co.,* 383 U.S. 1,5 (1966).

(3) See note 1 above.

(4) Often referred to as an "algorithm," which the Supreme Court in *Gottschalk v. Benson,* 409 U.S. 63, 65 (1972), defined as a "procedure for solving a given type of mathematical problem." See also *Smith v. Acme General Corp.,* 614 F.2d 1086, 1088 n. 6 (6th Cir. 1980) as to "anticipation."

(5) See *Ropat Corp. v. McGraw-Edison Co.,* 535 F.2d 378, 381 (7th Cir. 1976); *Trimble Prods. Inc. v. W.T. Grant Co.,* 283 F.Supp. 707, 716 (S.D.N.Y.), aff'd; 404 F.2d 344 (2d Cir. 1968).

(6) *Rains v. Cascade Indus,* 269 F.Supp. 688, 693 (D.N.J. 1967) (citation omitted), rev'd on other grounds; 402 F.2d 241 (3rd Cir. 1968).

(7) See *Barofsky v. General Elec. Corp.,* 396 F.2d 340, 344 (9th Cir. 1968), cert. denied; 393 U.S. 1031 (1969); and *Gorham Co. v. White,* 81 U.S. (14 Wall.) 511, 525 (1871).

(7a) *Mainland Ind. v. Timberland Mach.,* 649 P.2d 613 (1982). A key question is always whether the invention was related to the company's products.

(8) *KSM Fastening Systems v. H.A. Jones Co.,* 776 F.2d 1522 (1985) de minimus claims are not favored, see *Condenser Corp. of America v. Micanold Radio Corp.,* 145 F.2d 878 (1944), and the courts will be loath to grant a preliminary injunction unless the validity of the patent is clear and beyond question, *Bercy Industries, Inc. v. Mechanical Minor Works, Inc.,* 274 F.Supp. 157 (1967).

(9) *U.S. v. Westinghouse Corp.,* 648 F.2d 642 (9th Cir. 1981).

(10) *International Salt Co., Inc. v. U.S.,* 332 U.S. 392 (1947) (required lessers to purchase from appellant all unpatented salt and salt tablets consumed in the lease machinery). But see also *U.S. v. General Electric,* 272 U.S. 476 (1920) (per se legality stamp on price-restrictive licensing).

(11) *U.S. v. Line Material Co.,* 333 U.S. 287 (1948); *U.S. v. Singer Mfg. Co.,* 374 U.S. 174 (1963).

(12) *Hartford Empire Co. v. U.S.,* 323 U.S. 386 (1945).

(13) See note 9 above.

(14) *In re Freeman,* 573 F.2d 1237 (C.C.P.A. 1978).

(15) *Diamond v. Diehr,* 450 U.S. 175, 182-84 (1981).

(16) See note 9 above and *Parker v. Flooh,* 437 U.S. 584 (1978). See also *In re Walter,* 618 F.2d 758. (1980); *In re Taner,* 681 F.2d 787 (1981); *In re Pardo,* 684 F.2d 912 (1982); and *In re Meyer,* 688 F.2d 789 (1982).

(17) *Mager v. Stein,* 347 U.S. 201, 217 (1954) (Election of one form of protection over another is not required.) *In re Yardley,* 493 F.2d 1389 (1974).

CHAPTER 5

YOUR TRADEMARK AS
PART OF YOUR PACKAGE

Today many marketers are increasingly emphasizing a product or service name rather than stressing price or quality. These marketers are using "image" to sell their merchandise. They carefully select their market segments and then protect their specific and well-differentiated audience by hooking them on an image.

This is not the advent of a new historical epoch in marketing. Since the birth of modern free enterprise, merchants and guildsmen distinguished their products or services with unique and personal marks and signs (the red-and-white striped barber's pole being one of the more enduring). These signs were necessary to communicate immediate benefits to an illiterate society. Buyers learned to recognize these symbols and to use them as a basis for purchasing.

What has changed today is the shift in emphasis of symbolism or image from being merely one factor in selling to being the leading factor. A number of social and economic reasons have produced this stress on "image":

- Increasing labor costs have forced cutbacks on servicing in many firms.
- Location is less of an advantage because of the proliferation of competitive outlets an easy drive away.
- Product proliferation and wide distribution (compounded by the demise of fair trade laws) have robbed many firms of merchandise exclusivity.
- The gospel of "work hard, save, and buy goods with a significant utility" is giving way to social hedonism. This factor is most clearly manifest in modern catalog marketing. In an increasingly impersonal nation, your buyers are showing a growing need for individuality in their style and products.
- Finally, what worked in merchandising before doesn't work as well now. People's habits and tastes have changed and they've begun to make and spend more money. Shopping has become not a begrudged chore (contrary

to the unfounded arguments of some direct marketers), but a fun thing to do, a weekend sport, a way to be entertained. The shopping mall itself as well as direct marketers' catalogs are presented with ambience and layouts to please the eye and often to simply be "fun."

Strong brand identification is the most important factor in a product's success. But, if you are going to spend a lot of money on name selection, packaging, generation of publicity, consumer testing and promotion, you had better have a brand you can obtain a monopoly on. A brand with a legal monopoly is a trademark.[1]

As used in this book, the words "trademark," "mark," and "brand" are synonymous. You will want to work closely with your counsel in developing your mark. In fact, your involvement here may be the most practical interaction you can have with your lawyer to ensure your product's success. Since marketers are the primary users of trademarks, they should accept the responsibility for creating an effective corporate strategy for implementing this tool. Familiarize yourself with this entire section and reread it before beginning any significant product development plans. This is not a time to make business decisions in isolation from legal realities.

What Is a Trademark?

The purpose of a trademark is to identify a product and its origin. Secondarily, it serves to guarantee the quality of the goods bearing the mark. In a sense it is a handy, abbreviated form for identifying something. A good trademark requires no additional attribution. The trademark is its own attribution.

The term trademark "includes any word, name, symbol or device or any combination thereof adopted and used by a manufacturer or merchant to identify his or her goods and distinguish them from those manufactured or sold by others."[2] Making a name into an asset is usually quite expensive so it's natural to want to protect its value and restrict its use. You'll be glad to know the law is very protective of your rights here. For example, Supreme Court Justice Frankfurter once commented on the importance of trademarks to the marketer in our economic system:

> The protection of trademarks is the law's recognition of the psychological function of symbols. If it is true that we live by symbols, it is no less true that we purchase goods by them. A trademark is a merchandising shortcut which induces a purchaser to select what he wants, or what he has been led to believe he wants. The owner of a mark exploits this human propensity by making every effort to impregnate the atmosphere of the market with the drawing power of a congenial symbol. Whatever the means employed, the aim is the same—to convey through the mark, in the midst of potential customers, the desirability of the commodity upon which it appears. Once this is attained, the trademark owner has something of value. If another

poaches upon the commercial magnetism the symbol has created, the owner can obtain legal redress.[3]

In a society with a high literacy rate, words are the most common and most favored form of trademark. You can use any type of symbol or design for your mark provided that it functions as a trademark. Essentially a trademark is used for three reasons:

- To distinguish and identify your goods.
- To serve as a guarantee of consistent quality.
- To advertise and sell your products.

A product packaged in an unmistakable color and stamped with a famous logo in a stylish script typeface can serve all of the above three functions. Your goal is to get across the message that "this product is mine and no one else's."

In addition to trademarks, there are service marks. The trademark identifies a "thing" whereas a service mark is a "mark" used in the sale or advertising of services to identify the services of one person and distinguish them from the services of others.[4] For example, the titles, character names, and other distinctive features of a television program are registrable as service marks.

You are allowed to amortize certain trademark (and trade name) expenditures over a period of not less than 60 months. The amortizable expenditures include those directly connected with the acquisition, protection, expansion, and defense of your trademarks (and trade names), if such expenditures are chargeable to your capital account. They do *not* include any amounts paid for the purchase of a trademark (or trade name) *already* in existence. The amounts paid for an existing trademark (or trade name) are regarded as in essence paid-for goodwill, an asset having an indefinite useful life, and consequently no amortization is allowed.

Choosing Your Trademark

The trademarks and service marks of your business are among your most important assets. You'll want brand-name wording that best communicates to your target audience your product's novel and important benefits, as well as one that's able to accommodate future innovation. You might also wish to study a distinctive package shape to complement your product. You may wish to bring it in line with your other house marks or you may wish to adopt Procter & Gamble's theory of brand management, which is that any brand stands as an independent, self-sustaining competitive unit. A drawback here is that customers satisfied with the house mark are unfamiliar with your new mark. A plus is that, to the extent that any brand becomes the victim of adverse publicity, the damage will be limited to that brand and will not spill over to the company's other brands.[5]

In general, a strong trademark is one that

- is brief and easy to remember, read, and pronounce;
- is readily adaptable to all media; and
- has no unpleasant connotations (including in foreign languages if the products are to be exported).

Once you've developed what you consider to be a good mark, see your counsel. It is not cost-effective to see your lawyer after a lot of money is spent developing and advertising the product. Your counsel will review with you your wording and the thrust of your marketing plans, and may be able to tell you immediately whether your wording is generic, descriptive, or distinctive. If it is the latter, your counsel will make sure you have a present intent to market the goods. You'll also want to verify that the mark will not be offensive. An acceptable mark in one geographical area might not be equally acceptable in another region or to another "ethnic" group. With this in mind, consider not just your target markets but the sensitivities of the overall market so as to avoid a bad press or worse.

Trademark protection in the U.S. comes from use—this will differ for international registration[6]—not mere adoption. Shipment of goods in interstate commerce to which your mark is attached will suffice for registration. If you intend to use your mark shortly, your counsel will then undertake a search to see if the mark is already in use. If it is in use, your counsel may be able to recommend certain strategies to save your mark. Let's briefly review the different types of marks—in their ascending order of value to you.

Types of Marks

Not all marks are created equal. We'll review three areas as to their scope of protection.

Generic.   To be valid, a trademark must serve a source-denoting function. The basic reason a generic term cannot be utilized as a trademark is that it does not identify goods and distinguish them from those manufactured or sold by others,[7] i.e., a generic term denotes a product and not the specific producer of a product. Its status no longer identifies and distinguishes the goods of *one* owner as the *sole* source.

The generic doctrine is directly related to the communicative function of your language. Exclusive trademark rights cannot be claimed to be the name of an article either in the English language or its equivalent in any foreign language.[8] This doctrine applies even to phonetic foreign equivalents.[9]

A term may become generic. Your own advertising may be the culprit. Trademark cases are very fact-intensive. The Court will look at your advertising as well as other corporate materials in considering "genericide." If you allow your arbitrary mark to become changed in the minds of the public so that they become "ordinary words," you're well on your way to losing your mark. At one time aspirin, escalator, cellophane, and thermos were all privately owned.[10] Now their firms have lost them forever because once a term becomes generic, it remains so. These are now part of the common or universal terms whose words are the property of all who wish to use them. No one can later claim them as their own.

A good tactic here is to review your advertising copy and make sure your trademarks are used only as *adjectives* (use as a noun can result in its loss).[11] A trademark identifies a particular brand of some product. If it becomes a noun (name of the product itself), you're well on your way to losing it. When you're using your mark as an adjective, the noun it will modify is the generic name of the product. As long as your policing follows this grammatical guideline, you're probably effectively using your mark.

Finally, don't expect to get away with a slight modification of a generic name. "Lite" was held not to be a valid trademark for a low-calorie beer due to its similarity to the generic term "light,"[12] and "Alo" is not a valid trademark for a skin creme due to its likeness to the generic "aloe." A generic term cannot be appropriated through the device of misspelling it (e.g., "Lite" for "light").

Descriptive.   An error frequently made by business is the selection of a mark that clearly describes or identifies a product or service. A descriptive mark is one that describes the product as to its quality, function or place of origination. In general, a descriptive term, one which characterizes your product—its uses, functions, or characteristics—is available to "all the world" in a descriptive sense. This is because the basic principle of trademark law is its source-denoting function. A descriptive term will not unambiguously advise the public of a product's source because of the high probability other firms will also use the term descriptively.

For example, one firm put out a mark "Trim," which the court felt was a weak mark at best because it was descriptive of the product's function.[13] However, unlike a generic term, a descriptive term can acquire trademark rights by taking on a "secondary meaning." This may occur when a mark has been so extensively advertised or promoted that your purchasers have come to associate the mark with your firm as the source or origin of the product.[14]

Therefore, if there are compelling reasons for you to employ a descriptive mark, your counsel will conduct a search on the mark. If there is danger of infringement, your counsel will work with you to develop a descriptive mark into a distinctive mark. Your counsel may suggest alternate registration.

Supplemental Registration is the appropriate procedure for registering marks that are not inherently distinctive but that are capable of acquiring trademark significance in the future through exclusive use by the registrant. The Supplemental Register is also the only proper place for registering marks that are not truly in the nature of marks but that are more like slogans (like "You deserve a break today").

Once you are actively using the mark, your counsel may argue that it has developed a secondary meaning because you can show your purchasing public has come to associate your mark as the producer of the product through the extent of its use, sales volume, the extent of your steady advertising, distribution, market share, and publicity of your mark which indicated source or origin of the product, along with write-ups in the media that identify your products on which your mark has been used and acknowledged as yours. Secondary meaning is achieved by an association between a name and a source. Does the mark denote to your consumer a single thing coming from a single source?[15]

Finally, proof of exact copying, without any opposing proof, can be sufficient to establish secondary meaning. "There is no logical reason for the precise copying save an attempt to realize upon a secondary meaning[16] that is in existence."

Distinctive.   A distinctive mark is one that uses words that are arbitrary, "fanciful," or "meaningless" (a strong mark is not a dictionary word) or suggestive without being descriptive. A "meaningless" word mark is not meaningless to you, as this kind is the most protectable. Any arbitrary wording that connotes nothing about a product or its use can be a strong trademark.

Examples of these include purely fanciful coined words such as EXXON, common words such as SHELL for gasoline, or a character or picture mark such as the famous Green Giant. A suggestive word hints at, but does not describe characteristics or properties of a product. A classic here is Ivory soap. The word evokes an image of purity and luxury. Finally, consider using ordinary words in an unusual way. For example, look at the wholly nondescriptive mark "apple," which the public recognizes as a computer company, not a fruit stand.

You might consider the shape of your product or its container. Will it be primarily functional? If so, then it probably won't be entitled to registration. Since your package often helps to sell itself in a catalog, you might consider designing it less for utility features and more for selling features, possibly entitling it to protection.

Finally, there are times when registering a joint mark of the design and name together will strengthen your mark. Explore this with your counsel.

The Search

OK, you have a good mark or a good mark plus design. Now your counsel will conduct a search in the U.S. Patent and Trademark Office and elsewhere (e.g., trade directories, telephone directories, and a variety of other data bases) to determine whether your contemplated mark might infringe on an existing mark. Obviously this is an important step for you as you don't want to pursue this further in dollars and time only to find out you can't use the product of your efforts, or worse, to subsequently have to change your packaging or advertising.

You should be aware that an exhaustive search is never possible since no one can guarantee you that your proposed mark is not in use in some obscure area by a company that never registered its mark. Though there is no guarantee that a search eliminates all risks, a good one should insulate you from adverse legal exposure as well as possibly providing you with some useful marketing information. Many search reports are rich in such information.

You should use your mark as soon as possible after completing the search process. If not, then you should obtain an updated search before using it to confirm availability. You should review your search report as to your mark's potential to infringe. The test for infringement is whether the use of the word in question is likely to cause confusion, to cause a mistake as to origin, to result in division of goods, or to deceive the public.[17] There is no need to show actual deception or confusion—merely that such deception or confusion would be a natural and probable result.[18] The weaker your mark, the more the likelihood of confusion, and therefore the more limited the protection available to you.[19] The following are areas to consider when you read the search report (and also when you are evaluating whether someone is infringing on your mark):

► The degree of resemblance between the designation and the other's trade name, trademark, or certification mark in the following:
  • Appearance (shape of package, artwork, and lettering),
  • Pronunciation of the words involved,
  • Translation of the words involved,
  • Verbal translation of the pictures or designs involved,
  • Suggestiveness, connotation, or meaning of the actor's designation and trade name, trademark, or certification mark involved,
  • Identity of retail outlets and other retail channels and purchasers, and
  • Identity and similarity of advertising media used.
► The intent of the user in adopting and using the designation.
► The similarity of circumstances and conditions surrounding the purchase of the goods or services involved.
► The degree of care likely to be exercised by purchasers of the goods or services involved.[20] (Who is your buying audience, e.g. are they mature adults, children, etc.).
► Examination of prior litigation history of the user (the claimant):
  • The public record may demonstrate whether the mark is weak or strong.
  • An examination of prior litigation may also reveal the degree to which a competitor is willing to litigate to protect its marks. If a company has been aggressive in policing its rights against third parties, your counsel

may advise you to refrain from using a potentially conflicting mark unless you are willing to expend substantial sums in litigation defending it.

► Abandonment of the mark. Two years of nonuse constitutes abandonment.[21]

► Finally, no trademark can be registered if it

- Consists of or comprises immoral, deceptive, or scandalous matter or matter that may disparage or falsely suggest a connection with persons, living or dead, institutions, beliefs, or national symbols, or bring them into contempt or disrepute.

- Consists of or comprises the flag or coat or arms or other insignia of the United States, or of any state or municipality, or of any foreign nation, or any simulation thereof.

- Consists of or comprises a name, portrait, or signature identifying a particular living individual except by his or her written consent, of the name, signature, or portrait of a deceased President of the United States during the life of his widow, if any, except by the written consent of the widow.

- Consists of or comprises a mark which so resembles a mark registered in the Patent and Trademark Office or a mark or trade name previously used in the United States by another and not abandoned, as to be likely, when applied to the goods of another person, to cause confusion, or to cause mistake, or to deceive.

- Constitutes a generic term.

Assuming your mark survives the above analysis, your next step is to register your mark, a confusing issue for a variety of reasons. One is historical. Although the Constitution explicitly gives the federal government patent and copyright jurisdiction, trademark jurisdiction was originally left to the states, resulting in an inconsistent evolution nationwide. Only in the last century has federal trademark law emerged from Congress. This historical scenario aside, it's a good idea to register your mark. Let's talk about why.

Why Registration?

The question always comes up as to whether this process is cost effective. You'll have a minimum of up-front legal costs and then possibly further costs if you must appeal the Examiner's initial decision. You have first use—isn't this enough?

Use protects you in the geographical area in which you're using it and for as long as you use your mark. The more use, the greater the protection afforded your mark. The quality as well as quantity of mark use may be more important

- when your product comes from only one source (possibly due to patent protection); or
- when your product category is new and, therefore, has no well-established generic term to hang your hat on.

Priority of use alone is the basic criterion (your rights arise through the use of the mark, not the registration), but use is rarely preferable to registration. Prior registration of your mark with the U.S. Patent and Trademark Office will enable you to obtain the following advantages.

Other firms receive constructive notice of your right to use the mark. With registration, notice to the world is presumed in your favor. It creates valuable legal presumptions as to ownership and the exclusive right to use it as an indication of the origin of the source of ownership. The constructive notice in effect means that the use of a name or mark that is the same or confusingly similar cannot be justified by any claim of innocence, good faith, or lack of knowledge.[22]

This notice is superior to the rights conveyed by "use" for other reasons. For example, while trademark rights of use are created only in the area where actual use takes place, federal registration achieves nationwide protection regardless of the area of actual utilization.

As another example, if you're a mailer testing a product in New York and New Jersey prior to a full rollout, "use" only protects your mark in New York and New Jersey. You wouldn't be protected in the other 48 states. In theory, two organizations in the same business could use the identical mark if they did business in geographically separate areas. The geographic division is enough to distinguish the different products. However, you avoid these problems if you register your mark. REGISTRATION PROTECTS YOUR MARK IN ALL 50 STATES EVEN BEFORE IT'S USED IN THEM.

Registration gives you the right to sue in a federal rather than state court (getting your case into a federal court otherwise presents you with a variety of hurdles). Federal courts tend to be more sophisticated in these matters and may also be more inclined to stop the infringement than state courts, which might favor a local interest.

The notice discourages a good faith firm from "accidentally" infringing. Even when there is no intention to infringe, it still costs money and time to alert and stop the infringer. Further, you've lost exclusive use of your mark even if only for a short period of time.

It may be used as a basis for obtaining registration in foreign countries that are parties to an international agreement commonly known as the Paris Convention. Many nations require your trademark to be registered in your own country before it can be registered in theirs. It also gives you the right to have the Bureau of Customs exclude imports of goods bearing an infringing mark.

Aside from an infringement situation, registration asserts and increases distinctiveness. A trademark, otherwise protectable, could conceivably lose its distinctiveness if the owner is not careful in asserting it (see the discussion earlier concerning "generic marks").

Registration permits certain of your rights to become "incontestable" after five years of continuous use (this requires a special affidavit with the U.S. Patent and Trademark Office).[23]

What is incontestability? For a layperson's purposes, it is a status acquired after an affidavit is filed by your counsel stating that your mark has been in continuous use in commerce for a period of five years after registration, and is still in use in commerce (specify the nature of such commerce); there has been no final decision adverse to your claim of ownership for such mark for such goods or services, or to your right to register the same or to keep the same on the register; there is no proceeding involving said rights pending in the Patent and Trademark Office or in a court and not finally disposed of.

Incontestable status makes it nearly impossible for anyone to challenge your rights to your mark on any grounds. Your mark is now nondescriptive and/or has acquired secondary meaning (if either is an issue). Once you obtain this status all you need to do to keep your protection (except for a few areas specified by statute, such as fraud or a failure to disclose relevant information to the Patent and Trademark Office) is to properly renew.

Finally, consider state registration, which is relatively inexpensive. State trademark law differs little, if at all, from state to state and departs only insignificantly from federal law in its basic premises. The cost/benefit trade-offs here should be reviewed with your counsel, especially if federal registration is unavailable. Further, state registration offers some backup protection if your federal registration is cancelled.

Renewal. Trademark rights continue indefinitely as long as you properly use your mark and don't abandon it (i.e., not use it for two consecutive years). Your registration remains in force for 20 years from the date of your registration and may be renewed for periods of 20 years from the expiring period unless you've previously cancelled or surrendered it.

Your registration may be renewed provided the mark is in use in commerce at the time the application for renewal is filed. (However, if the mark is not in use in commerce, the registration will be eligible for renewal provided the nonuse is due to special circumstances that excuse the nonuse and not due to any intention to abandon the mark.)

Renewal requires a verified application setting forth certain specific requirements as to your use of your mark, current specimens, a fee, etc. Your application must be executed not more than six months before the expiration of your registration or three months after.

Supplemental Register

We briefly discussed this option earlier in our review of "descriptive" marks. However, it may be important to your overall trademark strategy so we'll review it more thoroughly here. The Trademark Act of 1946 provided for the establishment of two registers, designated as the Principal Register and the Supplemental Register. Coined, arbitrary, fanciful, or suggestive marks, generally referred to as "technical marks," may, if otherwise qualified, be registered on the Principal Register. Marks not qualified for registration on the principal register but which, nevertheless, are capable of distinguishing the applicant's goods and have been in lawful use in commerce for at least one year, may be registered on the Supplemental Register.

Registrable Marks—Principal Register.   A trademark, if otherwise eligible, may be registered on the Principal Register unless it consists of a mark which,

- when applied to the goods/services of the applicant is merely descriptive or deceptively misdescriptive of them,
- when applied to the goods/services of the applicant is primarily geographically descriptive or deceptively misdescriptive of them, except as indications of regional origin, or
- is primarily merely a surname.

Such marks, however, may be registered on the Principal Register, provided they have become distinctive as applied to the applicant's goods in commerce. The proof of substantially exclusive and continuous use thereof as a mark by the applicant in commerce for the five years preceding the date of filing of the application for registration is required.

All marks capable of distinguishing an applicant's goods and not registrable on the Principal Register, which have been in lawful use in commerce for the year preceding the filing of the registration application, may be registered on the Supplemental Register. For the purpose of registration on the Supplemental Register, a mark may consist of any trademark, symbol, label, package, configuration of goods, name, word, slogan, phrase, surname, geographical name, numeral, or device, or any combination of these.

If an application for registration on the Supplemental Register is based on prior use, the application must indicate that the mark has been in continuous use in commerce by the applicant for the preceding year. The nature of the commerce must be specified in the application.

Registration on the Supplemental Register does not constitute constructive notice of prima facie evidence and does not give the right to prevent importation of goods bearing an infringing mark, but does give the right to sue in the United States courts.

The Supplemental Register is as it appears—a second-class citizen when it comes to protection. However, it enables you to get your foot in the door as well as provides other options a creative counsel can review with you when he or she is apprised of your own particular situation. Eventually your mark may acquire distinction and be accepted for the Principal Register.

Applying for Registration

You should solicit the advice of an attorney experienced in this field as the procedure is formalistic and, if not presented in the precise manner required, can result in a lengthy appeal process. The U.S. Patent and Trademark Office reviews all applications very thoroughly, and barely 10% of applications are accepted on the first attempt. A registration is usually secured only after extended responses are made to the Examiner's questions and objections. The following is a brief checklist generic to all applications:

Your typewritten application (in English on one side of legal size paper) must state the following:

- ☐ The name of the applicant;
- ☐ The citizenship of the applicant; if the applicant is a partnership, the names and citizenship of the general partners or, if the applicant is a corporation or association, the state or nation under the laws of which organized;
- ☐ The domicile and post office address of the applicant;
- ☐ That the applicant has adopted and is using the mark shown in the accompanying drawing. The drawing must be a substantially exact representation of the mark as actually used in connection with the goods or services. The drawing of a service mark may be dispensed with if the mark is not capable of representation by a drawing, but in such case the written application must contain an adequate description of the mark.
- ☐ Date of such first use of the mark on or in connection with the goods specified in the application;
- ☐ Mode or manner in which the mark is used with the goods; and
- ☐ What classification you are seeking to come under.

Before mailing the application, make sure that it is signed, that the proper fee is enclosed, and that five specimens demonstrating the manner of use are also enclosed. As in any important legal correspondence, you should use only certified or registered mail, return receipt requested.

Once your application has arrived in the Patent and Trademark Office the following takes place:

- ▶ Your application will be docketed and examined in the order in which it is received. In the event it is found that the mark is not entitled to registration for any reason, you will be notified and advised of the reasons therefor and of any formal requirements or objections.
- ▶ You have six months from the date of mailing of any action by the Patent and Trademark Office to respond to it. Your failure to respond within this period will result in abandonment of the application. Response may be made with or without amendment and must include such proper action by the applicant as the nature of the action and the condition of the case may require.
- ▶ After your response, your application will be reexamined or reconsidered. If on further examination or consideration, registration is refused, you may appeal to the Trademark Trial and Appeal Board.

► If, on examination or reexamination of an application for registration on the Principal Register, it appears that the applicant is entitled to have his or her mark registered, it will be published in the *Official Gazette* and will be subject to opposition. Any person who believes he or she would be damaged by the registration of a mark on the Principal Register may oppose it within 30 days after publication. Oppositions are transmitted to the Trademark Trial and Appeal Board and are governed by the rules applicable to adversary proceedings.

► If you survive all of the above hurdles, you'll probably receive your mark after a reasonable interval.

Displaying Your Mark

What is formal identification? The usual, but not required, procedure is to use the symbol TM (or SM for a service mark) on all material where the mark is used (such as stationery, business forms, and in advertising) while the registration procedure is pending. Once the product or service mark is registered, the mark is followed by the letter "R" enclosed within a circle (®),[24] which shouts to all the world that you have a legal trademark.

This notice should appear with all uses or references to the trademark and be used at least once in every piece of printed matter—preferably in conjunction with the first time (or most prominent place) the trademark appears (certainly, more frequent use is helpful). As to size, you need not spoil the aesthetic appearance of your promotion (legibility is the only standard in regard to your mark's size). It is important to remember that these notices can be used only when the trademark already has been registered in the United States Patent and Trademark Office. If you make deliberate use of a false registration notice and the Patent and Trademark Office finds out about it, they will refuse to register your trademark and the mark also may be unenforceable in court against an infringer as a kind of penalty for using the false notice.[25]

Once you're registered, don't let your company's trademark cross the line from a unique product designation to a common descriptive term for all products of that type. You'll lose your exclusive protection. The following checklist will help you protect such exclusivity and distinctiveness by taking these precautions (this checklist is not meant to be exclusive but a starting point to your review with your own counsel):

☐ Where there is a risk of generic adaptation, use your mark in conjunction with the generic name for the product. One method is to insert the word "brand" between the trademark and the generic term, e.g., "Scotch brand tape" (see below).

☐ Always spell your trademark in exactly the same manner and spell it correctly (changes in form detract from its status). Neither abbreviate your mark nor delete or insert hyphens.

☐ Always use a beginning capital letter when referring to the trademark in advertisements and general correspondence. *Never* capitalize the generic product name. In ruling that cellophane had become generic, the court indicated that the trademark owner's use in correspondence of the work "cellophane" with a small "c" showed that the trademark owner considered the mark to be generic.[26]

☐ Always use the trademark in a distinctive way so that its wording will be distinguished from the text around it.

☐ Have the trademark appear in the type of printing in which it is registered whenever possible.

☐ Use the symbol ® after registration is secured. Consistency of use builds consumer awareness and recognition. Utilization of this symbol increases the likelihood that the public will understand the mark to be a trademark.

☐ Tell your customers it is a brand name—for example, you'll often see "Sanka brand coffee" in the ads. The word "brand" will reduce the possibility that your mark will be thought of as a generic name for your product, or line of products. The appearance of the word "brand" between your mark and the generic term makes it unmistakably clear that your trademark is a trademark. When used, "brand" *must* always appear in small print.

☐ Grammatically, always use your mark as a proper adjective only (not as a common descriptive adjective), never as a verb, noun,[27] or possessive word. As an adjective it should be followed whenever possible by the common descriptive name (noun) of the product.

☐ Since a trademark is *not* a noun, it should never be used in the plural form.

☐ Your grammatical usage can be checked by a simple test. Would a grammatically correct sentence (i.e., a complete thought) be expressed if my trademark was omitted from the sentence?

☐ Be concerned with how your mark is used on products. If an unauthorized use occurs, there may be no confusion or deception per se, but the use may reflect adversely on your image. Under state as well as federal laws, you may have an action for "dilution" of your mark.

☐ Also be careful how you display your mark with another (even your own). When more than one mark is displayed, the careful placement of statutory notice is absolutely necessary so as to clarify which mark is registered, *or* that both are.

☐ Be careful if you cease use—even temporarily. While a short period of nonuse may be permissible, nonuse for two years or more may result in the presumption of abandonment.

☐ Finally, be prepared to fight infringement immediately. The test is whether the other mark would confuse or deceive the normal purchaser in your market.

Policing Your Mark

If you begin to receive misdelivered mail, or experience mix-ups in equipment deliveries and/or telephone calls or orders intended for a competitor,[28] contact your counsel immediately. A competitor may be employing a mark similar to your own which is *"likely* to cause confusion or to cause mistake or to deceive" the public as to the source of the product. Note the emphasis on *"likely."* Evidence of actual confusion is not necessary to prove likelihood of confusion, but if you can establish it, then it is entitled to great weight by the court.[29] For example, courts rely heavily on auditory, visual and reasoning reactions in ascertaining whether the public would be likely to be confused by the use of a trademark. The courts attempt to place themselves in the position of the consumer exposed to the infringing mark under actual market conditions.[30]

The problem may be a competitor's use of your geographic area's name. While you are not entitled to the exclusive use of geographic terms, you do have the right to prevent others from misleading the public as to geographic origin. "Black Hills jewelry" must come from the Black Hills.[31]

Then there is the obvious situation where a competitor is employing a similar trade dress on its product. Such similarities tend to obscure whatever differences exist between the marks themselves and may contribute significantly to the likelihood of confusion in the minds of your purchasers. Ask yourself whether your customers are likely to purchase another product in the mistaken belief that it is yours. For example, a court felt that a firm was copying the unique trade dress of certain Johnson & Johnson products. Their clear plastic baby oil bottle was identical, and their baby powder was packaged in a straight, rectangular-shaped white plastic container that was also identical to Johnson & Johnson's.

Then again, there may be no confusion you can demonstrate. Your company can't have trademark protection for obvious configurations or where the marks are not so similar that the average viewer could not readily detect the differences.[32] The sophistication of your customers is as relevant to the likelihood that confusion will occur as is their degree of care and attention devoted to the decision to purchase your product.[33] However, the persons to be considered in determining whether confusion is likely to be caused are "not only the intelligent, the experienced, and the astute, but also the ignorant, the inexperienced, and the gullible."[34]

Your counsel will review your particular situation by asking the following questions, which you can use as a checklist:

☐ Who has superior rights (use, registrations, assignment)? If you haven't registered, then your counsel will have to analyze whether your competitor might also have superior rights in a limited geographic area based on innocent adoption and use.

☐ Is there a likelihood of confusion[35] as to (same analysis as you earlier conducted after your "Search"—see above):

• Similarity of marks (appearance, sound, similar shape of packaging, artwork, lettering).[36]

• Similarity of goods or services (and the nature of the goods).[37]

• Similarity of distribution channels.

- Similarity of communications mix employed.
- Similarity of trade dress.
- Strength of respective marks.
- Purchase audience.

☐ Was there wrongful or innocent intent in the appropriation of the mark? This issue of "good faith" goes to mitigation of damages but is not a defense to liability for infringement.

☐ What defenses might another user have to defeat our claim of infringement?

☐ What is the quality of notoriety of your mark? If you have a fine one, this is good news for you. Famous trademarks, especially those that embody an aura of preeminent excellence and quality, are generally given broad protection, even though the products do not compete. It is considered that the public is likely, on encountering a mark that is virtually synonymous with quality, to assume that even entirely different products are at least sponsored by the trademark owner. Rolls Royce, for automobile and airplanes, has been enforced against Rolls Royce for radio tubes[38] and Tiffany for a theater, a restaurant, and ornamental tile.[39]

☐ Is the reference by another to your mark truthful?[40]

Remember the social policy behind trademarks—protection of its selling power. This is intertwined with the impression made on your public. The ability to impact a favorable impression is dependent on the uniqueness of your mark. The use of a similar mark vitiates this uniqueness by associating your mark with different products or producers. Your goal is to prevent this. The better the quality of your mark, the greater your exposure to those who'll want to tie their product to yours, as the above discussion made clear.

If you fail to clamp down on infringers, the legal situation will be the equivalent of acquiescence in the unauthorized use. This can be considered a type of abandonment by acts of omission. Therefore, once you are aware of an infringement, ignoring it is not an option for you to entertain.

In most cases you will want to enforce your mark by a cease and desist letter from your counsel, followed by litigation, if things can't be worked out amicably.

Finally, don't overlook obvious aids to policing your mark. Telephone directories, competitors' catalogs, and major trade journals will disclose advertisements for potential infringers. You should have a media monitoring program ready to contact any editor, publisher, broadcaster, public figure, or other individual who has misused your mark.

If you see a potential infringement, move quickly to avoid an argument by a competitor that you sat too long on your rights (laches).

Counterfeiting

An effective program of policing should be three-tiered. It should include efforts to prevent your trademark from becoming generic, instituting suits for infringement, as well as an attempt to use civil and the new federal/state remedies to reduce trademark counterfeiting.

For years the trademark laws were essentially toothless and counterfeiters could write off any losses as the risk of doing business. There are no international treaties agreements to which the U.S. is a party that affect counterfeiting. Domestically, the only U.S. law was the Lanham Act, which is a civil law that only bans a company from using another's mark and, in certain situations, awards damages. Firms damaged by counterfeiting had to track down the violators, build a case against them, and then win the case in court.

The statistics were appalling. U.S. business lost $18 billion in 1984, up from $3 billion in 1978. Congress had to act. In 1984 Congress passed a tough law as part of the Continuing Appropriations Comprehensive Crime Control Act.[41] The law provides for up to five years imprisonment and a $250,000 fine for first-time traffickers of counterfeit goods with registered trademarks. Corporate offenders may be fined up to $1 million for the first offense, and federal courts are authorized to issue orders without notice to seize bogus goods with counterfeit marks.

You should review with your counsel a variety of tough new state laws that have been recently enacted.

The law here is traditional but hardly static. There are a number of currents developing.

Counterfeiting penalties are being increased at the state level. Louisiana,[42] a short while back, prohibited the sale or transfer of any item with a counterfeit trademark (without the owner's consent) and backed the law up with stiff penalties. Violators of the law are subject to a maximum fine of $10,000 or five years of imprisonment, or both. Violators may also be required to pay a fine of up to three times the gross value gained or three times the gross loss, whichever is greater.

California[43] subjects anyone who uses a registered mark or a confusingly similar mark on products, in order to enhance their commercial value or to sell or solicit sales, to an injunction against the use.

Wisconsin[44] has defined the crime of "trafficking in counterfeit marks" and increased the civil damages that a court may award in cases of counterfeiting trademarks from reasonable damages (including defendant's profits) to actual damages or three times the defendant's profits (whichever is greater) plus the costs of investigation and litigation.

Finally, if counterfeiting is a problem for you or your firm, you should join The International Anticounterfeiting Coalition, Inc.[45]

Licensing Your Mark

An increasingly lucrative form of income, especially in these days of brand image and entertainment spinoffs, is fees from licensing subsidiary rights to your property. Once trademarks were primarily used to indicate sources. Now it is recognized that marks also have a function as a symbol of the quality of a product.

Traditionally, some of the most successful types of merchandise were low-priced, impulse products. However, this is changing to higher markup items. These properties can also be valuable to your competitors. A trademark license must be carefully drawn. If you aren't sure whether you're taking adequate precautions to protect your competitive advantage, your existing or projected licensing program, then read on.

A trademark license is the key to most franchise agreements under which the franchisor grants the franchisee the use of its mark.[46] This requires the owner of the mark to exercise strict control over the nature and quality of its product supplied by its licensees. When done in this manner, the mark continues to identify the single ultimate source of the good despite the "licensee middleman."

You may begin to license your mark once it is registered on either the Principal Register or the Supplemental Register. Besides franchises, you have a whole host of options to consider. This is another area of teamwork between the marketing and legal departments. One emerging area is merchandising properties as "status" properties, "personification" properties, "popularity" properties, and "character" properties. Let's take a brief look at what these are.

Status properties.   These involve status symbols used on merchandise, such as JORDACHE. These are bought for quality, but more importantly as "ego merchandise." The other properties discussed below are more likely associated with low-priced "impulse" products.

Personification properties.   These marks create demand by association. For example, "Be a Pepper, Drink Dr. Pepper." For some reason people aspire to associate with certain commercial efforts—for example, the "Pepsi generation." These marks on almost any product are not of a symbol of quality but a mere "lifestyle statement." A classic "lifestyle statement" firm is Playboy, which has always capitalized on its sex/fantasy mystique to successfully license and market products bearing the Playboy emblem.[47]

Popularity properties.   These marks result from mass-media hype given movies such as *Annie* or *E.T.,* sports events, etc.

Character properties.   With these marks you have both service and/or trademarks so the terms can be used interchangeably.[48] If you wore a Beatles wig, a coonskin cap, or mouse-ears at one time in your life, you have an idea what these are. A possible problem down the road is that these "marks" have jettisoned traditional trademark concepts. These are both functional and not representative to the public of a uniform source of quality of a particular product or products. However, in these areas the public doesn't seem to care and functionality has been broadly defined.[49]

Ownership rights will vary. If you own one of these properties, review with your counsel whether you should approach these as distinctive, or immediately develop a strategy for developing evidence of a secondary meaning. This secondary meaning can result from licensing efforts and the extent of the popularity of the particular property.[50] You will also have to be alert to others developing confusingly similar properties, such as when Columbia Pictures successfully opposed the registration of the mark "Clothes Encounters" of clothing, based on its movie *Close Encounters of the Third Kind* and its own merchandising program.[51]

It is important to review your merchandising program early on, both for the obvious product line potential as well as spinoffs into the ancillary properties discussed above and to be sure that the legal requirements of trademark licensing agreements are adequately carried out. Your in-house trademark program is a key in developing all these properties. For example, your failure to police your mark will alienate licensees as they will be paying for a "non-privilege" as competitors undersell them.

Preparing Your Agreement

You are the owner of a merchandising property who has both developed it and taken the steps to protect it. You now wish to exploit it by licensing. Consider the following checklist.

☐ Get a mental handle on the different natures of properties that may be licensed (some of which were discussed earlier) so as to be able to mold the license terms and related royalty and obligation of confidence terms into patterns that are compatible with each other, the law, the tax environment, and other realities of your marketplace (including distribution and servicing).

☐ Consider whether such licensing may give away your know-how and eventually set up your future competitor.

☐ What are you licensing? There may be many separate rights available to license. There's the right to make, use, lease, sell, etc. Each such right must be considered separately in your planning.

☐ Do your overall homework. A license agreement is only as good for you as the firm standing behind it. Investigate your licensee's financial strength, sales capacity, geography of their market structure, and their familiarity with the subject matter to be licensed.

☐ Remember to integrate the other topics. If you are aloof from the licensee's operations, they may risk abandonment of their mark. If you supervise too closely, you increase the likelihood of being held jointly liable for injuries arising from their activities or even directly liable. In recent years the Courts have moved toward the position that a licensor of a trademark can be held strictly liable for injuries even if the product is manufactured and/or distributed by another distributor (see Section on

Products Liability). Another dilemma is antitrust, particularly as to tie-ins (see Section on Antitrust, particularly as to intellectual property).

☐ To minimize potential licensing problems, have your counsel draft language addressing these issues. Such language should include specifications for minimum quality standards, a description of sanctions for the failure to meet those standards and a requirement that your license carry comprehensive liability insurance to cover you as well as the licensee.

If you've satisfied yourself as to your review of the above issues, you should consult a lawyer with a good understanding of contracts. The following points will constitute a checklist of 20 points for you to review with your lawyer (and if any of the checklist points are omitted, ask your lawyer why). You should include the following terms, at a minimum.

1. *Preamble* —or "Whereas Clause,"—This is a standard beginning. To avoid antitrust exposure and to preempt any future disputes, it is essential to recite specifically here why the license is being granted and to whom.

2. *License Grant*—Here you should be clear as to what your grant of a license does or does not include. Then, one of the basic questions to be answered in a licensing agreement is whether the rights to be transferred are exclusive or nonexclusive.

The word "exclusive" raises the spectre of antitrust since you're licensing an intellectual monopoly property with unique economic power. Under an exclusive license, the licensee has been given the exclusive right to use, exclusive even as to the licensor unless expressly provided for otherwise.

A nonexclusive right is not without problems. For example (as discussed below), a trademark owner must maintain quality control. A situation could arise where one licensee demands you take legal action against another.

Territorial Limits of License—This must be carefully reviewed with counsel as to the rational and objectively verifiable business reasons for such restriction.

3. *Assignment*—You want to have some veto power over the licensee's ability to sublicense the agreement without your advance approval. If the license is silent on the right of assignment or reserves an unrestricted right of assignment, then you may have little recourse to prevent this.

More subtly, but just as ominously, you might find the agreement assigned to a bank in your credit line (this could restrict your future borrowing) or a competitor's parent or subsidiary (implication obvious). Finally you'll review with your counsel any of the technical provisions against the assignment or licensing of marks "in gross."

4. *Strict Quality Control Procedures*—This is a must for certain licenses, especially trademarks. It is fundamental that a trademark license contain quality control provisions. Control is the key to uniformity and it enhances goodwill and maintains quality. However, not only must the provision be written into the agreement, it must be enforced.

This relates back to the very basis on which trademarks are permitted to be licensed. Since trademarks represent source of origin, which to the public means goods of consistent quality, the licensor must control the nature and quality of the goods to prevent public deception.

The licensor must insist that (to make sure there are no misrepresentations as well as random sampling of the products) license agreements include a provision requiring its approval of all advertising and labeling.

In addition, the licensor must vigorously follow up on this for the duration of the license at adequate intervals including visits to the licensee's plants and warehouses. Direct mailers should also set up a few test accounts.

All of the above controls must be reviewed with an attorney sensitive to your antitrust exposure in areas of pricing, territorial controls, tying, etc., as well as the fact that you must assure your trademarked goods are of standard quality and character.

The failure to enforce the latter could result in your mark becoming lost, owing to its becoming descriptive of its goods.

5. *Indemnification*—You should obtain indemnification from your licensee for a variety of negligence as well as for product liability and have such survive the term of the license.

You should also require the licensee to name you, as licensor, co-insured in the licensee's liability insurance policy and to require the insurance company to notify you in the event the premiums are not paid or the policy is being revised, modified, or canceled. This will then allow you to pay the premiums or somehow otherwise insure yourself to avoid losing the benefits of insurance.

Failure to maintain such payments could also be grounds for termination of the license at your sole option.

Note: As licensor, you will probably be asked to warrant that your proprietary right does not infringe on or violate the right of any third party. You should require the licensee to promptly notify you if action is commenced and to cooperate (at your expense) in the defense.

You should include language that if the licensee on its own initiative settles any claims, demands, or actions without your prior written consent, then you are released from this indemnity in this instance.

6. *Terms of Agreement*—This will usually commence on the date of execution and run for a certain amount of time as per mutual agreement. If both parties are amenable, you should consider language setting forth automatic extensions.

7. *Confidential Property*—You'll want to specify that the licensee must use the same care in guarding your specified confidential property as the licensee would for its own proprietary information of like importance. The disclosure by the licensee of any such property will cause you irreparable harm. Depending on the sensitivity of your needs, this is an important paragraph to review with your counsel.

8. *Compliance with Laws*—A provision should be included that both parties will comply with all current laws as well as monitor legislation so as to comply with future laws arising during the term of the license.

9. *Registration*—The licensee will not seek any copyright or trademark registration for the property without your prior written consent; will cooperate fully with reasonable requests by you in connection with any applications you may choose to file for such registrations; will execute any documents reasonably requested by you to confirm your rights; and will appoint you its authorized attorney-in-fact to execute and deliver such documents in the licensee's name, should the licensee fail or refuse to do so.

10. *Royalties*—To be negotiated, as per your needs as to the type to be used, and whether you'll receive a guaranteed minimum in royalty as well as sales (to insure that the market is being adequately exploited).

11. *Advertising*—At a minimum, you'll want language specifying that the licensee will in good faith use its best efforts to promote your product. You may also require the licensee to spend a certain stated minimum in advertising in a given market. You might also set forth a cooperative advertising plan (see Section IV).

12. *Force Majeure*—This paragraph was once titled "Act of God" and still retains a religious amount of tolerance. What much of it means is that your business is to be placed at risk, because the drafter failed to anticipate a reasonable business eventuality. Have your counsel draft a provision for recovery for catastrophic failure for the "Acts of God" that can be reasonably anticipated and planned for. Scheduled strikes, etc., are not Acts of God.

13. *Governing Law*—This paragraph defines the law of the state under which the contract will be governed. You should be aware that if you commence a tort action, your original choice of law may go by the boards since contracting parties can't choose the law applicable to a tort claim arising from the relationship.

14. *Joint Venture*—You'll want specific language stating that your license in no way implies an agency relationship or joint venture between the parties.

15. *Trademark/Copyright Notices*—You will specifically set forth the licensee's requirement to cause each item to bear an appropriate trademark, copyright, or other notice. You might specifically state that trademarks are "under license granted by you." For copyrights, you must make it clear that any copyrightable contributions licensee may make in any reproduction of your property will be deemed a work made for hire for you, or if it does not so qualify, all rights, title, and interest in it shall be deemed automatically transferred to you, subject to the rights granted the licensee under this agreement.

16. *Reserved Rights*—All rights not expressly granted in the agreement are reserved by you, including without limitation . . . (set forth your rights in detail if you wish).

17. *Termination*—This should spell out that upon the completion of a specified amount of time or a specified event, all rights granted will automatically revert back to you as licensor. The licensee will immediately cease using your property. Some provision should also be made for disposing of the licensed products at termination.

18. *Waiver*—The waiver of any breach of any condition or part of the license by either party is not to be viewed as a waiver of any subsequent breach.

19. *Severability*—You might include language such as: "If any provision of this license shall be adjudged by a court to be void or unenforceable, the same shall in no way affect any other provision, or the validity or enforceability of this license."

This language, while reasonable on its face, is not always in your best interest, so review its utility with your counsel.

20. *Notices*—Notices should be in writing, mailed (registered or certified mail), telegraphed, or hand-delivered to the party concerned, effective on the date so sent, at the address specified in the opening paragraph of this license or at such other addresses as may be subsequently designated in writing by such party (you should specify a title rather than a person to receive these).

21. *Merger or Integration Clause*—Here you'll get language such as: "This contract constitutes the entire agreement between the parties with respect to the subject matter; all prior agreements, representations, statements, negotiations, and undertakings are superseded hereby."

This means that all letters, brochures, demonstrations, and other prior representations you relied on are inoperative as to the contract obligations.

22. *Signature Line*—It goes without saying that all agreements should be signed by all parties to be bound.

The above discussion is not intended to cover all clauses that should be included in a license agreement, but it does cover many of the more important clauses. Each license situation involves unique considerations, and care must be exercised accordingly.

Conclusion

Trademarks communicate information about your product by providing consumers with a handy reference point that summarizes their past experience and information obtained about brands using the same mark. It acquires meaning over a period of time by associations formed in the minds of the public about the quality standards identified with the mark. Repeat purchases eventually build up a positive reputation for your brand as consumers come to associate it with satisfaction of their needs.

Without a favorable reputation, no promised benefits of yours will sell well. Therefore, before any important marketing campaign, it is important to see to it that your firm gets good publicity. Such publicity reflects on your key communications headliner, the trademark. If your firm enjoys a good reputation and your product's name is associated with high quality, by all means use that name. As the old saying goes, if you've got it, flaunt it. But, as the new saying goes, *if you've got it, protect it!* A trademark can be an incredibly useful device, so long as you're vigilant and don't allow your competitor to abscond with it while your guard is down.

All marketers who are considering developing future properties for licensing or who are about to embark on licensing existing properties should protect themselves as follows:

▶ Before a lot of money is spent on the creation and exploitation of a potential merchandising property or character, you should review your proposals with an attorney skilled in licensing.

► A merchandising program should be considered for each of your qualifying properties and products.

► The properties should be analyzed with your counsel to identify what types of protection are available to you, i.e., patent, trademark, copyright, etc., with appropriate steps taken as legally recommended.

► Your enforcement program should be agreed upon and established prior to any infringement by a competitor.

► As a licensee, the agreement should be created or accepted only after a careful review with your counsel reflecting upon the above points reviewed.

► Finally, always be alert to new opportunities opening up to you in trademark exploitation. An example of such new opportunity is broadcasting. At one time broadcasters could trademark only their logos, not their call letters. The Patent and Trademark Office always took the position that call letters were owned by the FCC. This changed in early 1985 when the Appeals Board of the Patent and Trademark Office[52] permitted a station to register its call letters, stating that while the FCC has the duty to regulate broadcasting, the FCC has no "ownership" interest in the call signs of a radio station. There is no requirement that the call letters be used in a distinctive style to be registrable. The protection of such registration will also guarantee the exclusive use of a call sign even against nonbroadcasters. For example, a broadcaster in your area who registers the call letters WXYZ could very well preclude an electrician from calling his or her business "WXYZ Electricians."

GOOD LUCK![53]

ENDNOTES

(1) A "trade name" refers to the name of a business. There is a well-recognized distinction between the term "trade name" and the terms "trademark" or "brand," which refer to the product sold by the business. *Philip Morris v. Imperial Tobacco Co.,* 282 F. Supp. 931 (1967). For a good, enduring article on image marketing, see Cohen, A.I. and A. Jones, "Brand Marketing in the New Retail Environment," *Harvard Business Review,* September-October, 1978, p. 141.

(2) 15 U.S.C. Sec. 1127. A trade name need not be affixed to your product. It is a name that has been used long and intensely enough so that the public associates it with your product. A trade name, like a trademark, can be a valuable asset in your communications strategy. However, trade names are not subject to registration unless actually used as trademarks.

(3) *Mishawaka Rubber and Woolen Mfg. Co. v. S.S. Kresge Co.,* 316 U.S. 203, 205; 62 S.Ct. 1022, 1024; 86 L.Ed. 381 (1942).

(4) 15 U.S.C. Sec. 1127.

(5) *Procter & Gamble Co. v. Johnson & Johnson Inc.,* 485 F.Supp. 1185 (1979).

(6) International registration—as a general rule, your trademark may be protected through registration without *prior* use. See your attorney about the particular country you're considering.

(7) *Anti-Monopoly, Inc. v. General Mills Fun Group, Inc.,* 515 F. Supp. 448 (1981) ("Monopoly" has become a generic word describing a kind of board game—the name primarily denotes the product, not the producer). See also the following representative cases: *Kellogg Co. v. National Biscuit Co.* 305 U.S. 111, 116 (1938) ("shredded wheat" is a

generic term). *Abercrombie and Fitch Co. v. Hunting World, Inc.,* 537 F.2d 4 (1976); *Raizk v. Southland Corp.,* 591 P.2d 985 (1978) (why a "hoagie" is a generic name for a sandwich); *King-Seely Thermos Co. v. Aladdin Industries, Inc.* 321 F.2d 577 (1963); *Centaur Co. v. Heinsfurter,* 84 F.2d 955 (1898) ("castoria" generic for a medicine).

(8) *Nestlé's Milk Products, Inc. v. Baker Importing Co.,* 182 F.2d 193 (1950).

(9) *Weiss Noodle Co. v. Golden Trachnel and Specialty Co.* 298 F.2d 845 (1961).

(10) *American Thermos Products Co. v. Aladdin Industries, Inc.,* 207 F.Supp. 9 (1962), aff'd; 321 F.2d 577 (1963), remanded; 418 F.2d 31 (1966), mod.; 320 F.Supp. 1156 (1970), policing order; 169 U.S.P.Q. 85 (1970) ("thermos" generic for vacuum bottles). *Haughton Elevator Co. v. Seeberger,* 85 U.S.P.Q. 80 (1950) ("escalator" generic for moving stairway). *DuPont Cellophane Co. v. Waxed Prods. Co.,* 85 F.2d 75 (2d Cir.), cert. den.; 299 U.S. 601 (1936); *Bayer Co. v. United Drug Co.,* 272 F. 505 (S.D.N.Y. 1921). You will note most generic words came about through private litigation.

"High-tech" isn't immune; see *Intel Corp. v. Radiation Inc.,* 184 U.S.P.Q. 54 (1974) (loss of "PROM").

For a successful defense as to an argument of generic status see *Selchow & Righter Co. v. McGraw Hill Book Co.* 439 F.Supp. 243 (1977).

(11) See *Intel* case supra, note 10.

(12) *Miller Brewing Co. v. Jas-Schlitz Brewing Co.* 605 F.2d 990 cert. den.; 444 U.S. 1102 (1979); and *Miller Brewing Co. v. G. Heilman Brewing Co.* 561 F.2d 75 cert. den.; 434 U.S. 1025 (1977). A generic term "light" could not be appropriated through the device of misspelling it "lite." Neither the word nor its phonetic equivalent could be appropriated for beer. See also *Finkler v. Schussel,* 469 F.Supp. 674 (1979).

(13) *Sheraton Corp. of America v. Sheffield Watch, Inc.,* 103 F.2d 917 (C.C.P.A. 1939); *Lever Brothers Co. v. Nobio Prods. Inc.,* 103 F.2d 917 (C.C.P.A. 1939). *Note:* While the use of a trademark in advertising ordinarily provides no protectable trademark rights, the use of a service mark in advertising constitutes valid service mark use and creates a protectable interest. See 15 U.S.C. Sec. 1127 and 15 U.S.C. Sec. 1052(e).

(14) *W.E. Basset Co. v. Revlon, Inc.* 435 F.2d 656 (1972).

(15) *American Scientific Chemical, Inc. v. American Hospital Supply Corp.* 690 F.2d 791 (9th Cir. 1982); *Glovatorium, Inc. v. NCR Corp.,* 684 F.2d 658 (9th Cir. 1982); *Transgo, Inc. v. Ajac Transmissions Parts Corp.,* 768 F.2d 1001 (1985); *American Footwear Corp. v. General Goodware Co. and Universal Studios, Inc.,* 609 F.2d 655, 663 (1979). See also *Procter & Gamble Co. v. Johnson & Johnson, Inc.,* 485 F.Supp. 1185, 1197 (1979) and *Ball v. United Artists,* 214 N.Y.S.2d 219 (1939); and *Kellogg Co. v. National Biscuit Co.,* U.S. 111; 59 S.Ct. 109; 83 L.Ed. 73 (1938).

(16) *Audio Fidelity, Inc. v. High Fidelity Recordings, Inc.,* 283 F.2d 551, 557-8 (9th Cir. 1960).

(17) 15 U.S.C. Sec. 1114(1)(a). See also *St. Charles Mfg. Co. v. St. Charles Furniture Corp.,* 482 F.Supp. 397 (1979) (mistake as to origin); *Clairol Inc. v. Budget Discount, Inc.,* 168 U.S.P.Q. 315 (1970); and *Smith v. Chanel, Inc.,* 402 F.2d 562 (1968), aff'd, 528 F.2d 284 (1976).

(18) *Household Fin. Corp. of Del. v. Household Fin. Corp. of W.Va.,* 11 F.Supp. 3 (1935). See also *Roto-Rooter Corp. v. O'Neal,* 513 F.2d 44 (1975) and *Puritan Furniture Co. v. Comerc. Inc.,* 519 F.Supp 56 (1981). See also *NFE International, Ltd. v. General Resource Corp.,* 558 F.Supp. 1137 (1983) where two products though not identical had similar pronunciations and spelling.

(19) 15 U.S.C.A. Sec. 1125(a)

(20) *Reddy Communications v. Envtl. Action,* 477 F.Supp. 936, 947 (1979) (a case holding that the use of a caricature was incidental to the sale and did not result in confusion).

(21) 15 U.S.C. Sec. 1127. See also 15 U.S.C. Sec. 1115(b)(2). *Dawn Donut Co. v. Hart's Food Stores, Inc.,* 267 F.2d 358 (1959). See also *Interstate Brands Corp. v. Way Baking*

Co., 403 Mich. 479, 270 N.W.2d 103 (1978) (intermittent periods of nonuse and reduced use do not constitute "abandonment" of a trademark).

(22) See 15 U.S.C. Sec. 1072 and 15 U.S.C. Sec. 1111. See also *St. Charles Mfg. Co. v. St. Charles Furniture Corp.,* 482 F.Supp. 397, 402 (1979).

(23) 15 U.S.C. Sec. 1065 and 15 U.S.C. Sec. 1115(b)

(24) Other notices are "Registered in U.S. Patent and Trademark Office" or "Reg. U.S. Pat. & Tm. Off.", which can be rather obtrusive in ad copy. If you use these notices, they can be footnoted, which may be helpful in the aesthetic sense.

(25) *Fox-Stanley Photo Products, Inc. v. Otaguro,* 339 F.Supp. 1293 (1972) and *Four Roses Products Co. v. Small Grain Distilling & Drug Co.,* 29 F.2d 959 (1928).

(26) *DuPont Cellophane Co. v. Waxed Products Co.* 85 F.2d 75, cert. den. 299 U.S. 601 (1936).

(27) *Intel Corp. v. Radiation Inc.,* 184 U.S.P.Q. 54, 59 (1974).

(28) *Taylor v. Quebedeaux,* 617 P. 2d 23 (1980).

(29) *Union Carbide Corp. v. Ever-Ready, Inc.* 531 F.2d 366, 383 (1976). However, the party alleging infringement has the burden of proving the likelihood of confusion. See *Lindy Pen Co. v. Bic Pen Corp.,* 725 F.2d 1240, 1243 (9th Cir. 1984) cert. den. 469 U.S. 1188 (1985).

(30) *G.D. Searle & Co. v. Chas. Pfizer & Co.,* 265 F.2d 385, cert. den. 361 U.S. 819 (1959). See also *San Francisco Arts & Athletics, Inc. v. U.S. Olympic Comm.,* 107 S.Ct. 2971 (1987). ("Confusion occurs when consumers make an incorrect mental association between the involved commercial products or their producers"). See also Restatement of Torts Sec. 729 (1938).

(31) *Black Hills Jewelery Mfg. Co. v. LaBelle's,* 489 F.Supp. 754 (1980).

(32) *United Artists Corp. v. Ford Motor Co.,* 483 F.Supp. 89 (1980). See also *Volkswagenwerk Aktiengesellschaft v. Rosevear Enterprise, Inc.,* 592 F.2d 1180 (1979), and *Burger Chef Systems, Inc. v. Sandwich Chef, Inc.,* 608 F.2d 875 (1979).

(33) *Procter & Gamble Co. v. Johnson & Johnson, Inc.,* 485 F.Supp. 1185 (1979).

(34) *Tisch Hotels, Inc. v. Americana Inn.* 350 F.2d 609 (1965).

(35) 15 U.S.C. Sec. 1114(1). See also *Monte Carlo Shirt, Inc. v. Daewoo International Corp.,* 707 F.2d 1054 (1983).

(36) *NFE International, Ltd. v. General Resource Corp.,* 558 F.Supp. 1137 (1983). See also *Grotrain, Helfferick, Schultz, Noch v. Steinway & Sons,* 523 F.2d 1331, 1340 (1975); *L.L. Bean, Inc. v. Drake Publishing, Inc.,* 625 F.Supp. 1531 (D. Me. 1986); *Beer Nuts, Inc. v. Clover Club Foods Co.,* 805 F.2d 920, 925 (1986) (similarities between marks are to be given more wieght than differences).

(37) Here issues as to audience sophistication are taken into account, but if the goods can have a dangerous effect (e.g., medical products), the courts will exercise greater vigilance. See *Morgenstern Chemical Co. v. G.D. Searle & Co.,* 253 F.2d 390 (1958). For a related case of interest see *Aircraft Novelties Corp. v. Baxter Lane Co. of Amarillo,* 685 F.2d 988 (1982).

(38) *Wall v. Rolls Royce of America, Inc.,* 4 F.2d 333 (1925).

(39) *Tiffany & Co. v. Tiffany Productions, Inc.,* 147 Misc. 679; 264 N.Y. 459 aff'd per curiam, 262 N.Y. 482 188 NE.30 (1933).

(40) *G.D. Searle & Co. v. Hudson Pharmaceutical Corp.,* 715 F.2d 837 (1983).

(41) Trademarks Counterfeiting Act of 1984, 15 U.S.C. Sec. 1126 and 18 U.S.C. Sec. 2320, which authorizes the ex parte seizure of infringing goods. See also *General Motors Corp. v. Gibson Chemical & Oil,* 786 F.2d 105 (2d Cir. 1986).

(42) *Louisiana Revised Statutes* 14:228.1 (1986).

(43) Section 14330 of the *Business and Professions Code of California* (1986).

(44) *Wisconsin Statutes* (1986) 132.001 et seq.

(45) They're at 101 California Street, San Francisco, CA 94111-5874; (415)986-2380. Get involved and make your voice heard.

(46) Posch, Robert J., Jr., "Legally Protect Your Product with Merchandising License," *Direct Marketing,* January 1985, pp. 118-121, and "Avoiding Antitrust Exposure in Intellectual Property Licensing," *Direct Marketing,* May 1985, pp. 128-131.

For a story concerning how problems can develop in these areas, see Machalaba, Daniel, "The Christmas Tale Pits Toy Railroads Against Little Kitten," *Wall Street Journal,* 12/20/83, p. 1. For one on growth, see Forhan, James, "Toy Makers Play to Strength of Licensing," *Advertising Age,* March 14, 1983, p. 32.

(47) Finally, for solid overview of the overall area of these properties see Monterosso, Ronald, "Companies Find Trademarks Valuable Source for Direct Profits Due to Changes in Law," *New York Law Journal,* 8/1/86. See Tully, Shawn, "Playboy Makes the Boss's Daughter Boss," *Fortune,* August 23 1982, pp. 105-118. I'd venture a guess that Christie Hefner will not be a success once her father leaves. Playboy is basically an autobiographical sketch of the father that stimulates male fantasies. Since Ms. Hefner cannot replace the fantasy, she'll be a victim of reverse image marketing.

(48) *Boston Prof. Hockey Assoc., Inc. v. Dallas Corp. & Emblem Mfg., Inc.,* 510 F.2d 1004, 1009 (5th Cir.), cert. den., 423 U.S. 868, reh den., 423 U.S. 991 (1975).

(49) *Pagliero v. Wallace China Co.,* 198 F.2d 339 (9th Cir. 1952).

(50) See *American Footwear Corp. v. General Goodware Co. and Universal Studios, Inc.,* 609 F.2d 655, 663 (1979). See also Agnew, Joe, "Brand Licensers Become Increasingly Clothes-Minded" *Marketing News* 8/31/87 p.1.

(51) *Columbia Pictures Indus., Inc. v. Miller,* 211 U.S.P.Q. 816 (1981).

(52) In re: *WSM, Inc.,* 225 U.S.P.Q. 883 (TTAB 1983).

(53) *More Information:* If you are considering major efforts in this area, have your counsel become active in the United States Trademark Association, 6 East 45th Street, New York, NY 10017; (212)986-5880 as well as in his or her local, state, and federal bars—all of which have active intellectual property groups. As an individual starting out, or wishing other primers, contact the U.S. Department of Commerce, Patent and Trademark Office, Washington, D.C. 20402. They usually have a variety of general information, booklets, etc., for the asking. Ask.

SECTION II

CHANNEL POLICY: IT'S EASIER TO TERMINATE YOUR DISTRIBUTOR TODAY

One rule of thumb is that your greatest inadvertent legal exposure today is the involuntary termination of your distributor. The *Monsanto* [1] decision has eliminated the inadvertent aspect. To lose now you are, at best, careless; more likely, you acted either capriciously or worse.

The *Monsanto* case is an excellent overview of the political and the legal debate, as well as of the undercurrents concerning distributor terminations, rule of reason, and the whole topic of vertical territorial arrangements. Let's take a look first at what was not said.

Background

Any professional who cares enough about the legal issues of his or her business to be reading a book like this knows there has been a strong clash of cultures over antitrust enforcement during the Reagan administration. It was elected to "get government off the backs of business" and during the 1980 to 1984 elections managed to carry all states except Minnesota. Just as interesting, you had politicians actually seek to keep their promises. As 1986 FTC Chairman Daniel Oliver was quoted, "his plan is to do no harm to the marketplace." [2]

As in the case of Robinson Patman (with small business), the curtailment of enforcement against resale price maintenance raised a constituency. People really want these laws! The then-head of the Antitrust Division publicly voiced his criticism of the established doctrine that resale price maintenance is per se illegal. He did not believe it advanced consumer welfare. He wrote a friend of the court brief concerning *Monsanto,* urging the Court to replace the per se rule with a rule-of-reason analysis. Such analysis had already been sanctioned for

133

non-price restrictions when there had been no evidence of communications among competing distributors.

As we shall see, the Supreme Court declined to reach this issue because neither party had raised it.[3] Congress was in an uproar, and took the unusual step of attaching a rider to the appropriations bill forbidding the Justice Department from spending any funds for overturning the established law on vertical price fixing. Simultaneously, 46 state attorneys general joined as friends of the court to urge the continuation of the per se rule against price fixing, joined by the National Mass Retailing Institute and the Small Business Legal Defense Committee, among others.

At the same time, a number of Circuits are on record that not all vertical arrangements affecting price constitute resale price maintenance agreements.[4] Congress appears to want a case-by-case review whereas the Justice Department appears to wish to interject greater flexibility so that the marketplace can more readily anticipate court challenges before it designs its distribution strategy.

The long and the short of it is we'll have to wait for another case to overturn precedent. However, *Monsanto* clarified a few things. Let's review the case that caused all the fuss.

Monsanto's Relationship With Spray-Rite

Monsanto is a large chemicals producer with a specialty in agricultural chemicals. Spray-Rite was a family business engaged in the wholesale distribution of agricultural chemicals. It bought in large quantities and sold at a low margin. For 10 uneventful years it was an authorized distributor of Monsanto herbicides.

In the fall of 1967, Monsanto announced that it would appoint distributors for one-year terms, and that it would renew distributorships according to several new criteria. Among the criteria were:

- whether the distributor's primary activity was soliciting sales to retail dealers;
- whether the distributor employed trained salesmen capable of educating its customers on the technical aspects of Monsanto's herbicides; and
- whether the distributor could be expected "to exploit fully" the market in its geographical area of primary responsibility.

Shortly thereafter, Monsanto also introduced a number of incentive programs, such as making cash payments to distributors that sent salesmen to training classes, and providing free deliveries of products to customers within a distributor's area of primary responsibility. Such areas of primary responsibility were not exclusive territorial restrictions. Approximately 10 to 20 distributors were assigned to each area, and distributors were permitted to sell outside their assigned area.[5]

In October 1968, Monsanto declined to renew Spray-Rite's distributorship. At that time, Spray-Rite was the tenth largest out of approximately 100 distributors of Monsanto's primary corn herbicide. Ninety percent of Spray-Rite's sales volume was devoted to herbicide sales, and 16% of its sales were of Monsanto products. The action severely hurt its business, which continued until 1972.

The Lower Court's Holdings

Spray-Rite sued under Section 1 of the Sherman Act. It alleged that Monsanto and some of its distributors conspired to fix the resale prices of Monsanto herbicides. Its complaint further alleged that Monsanto terminated Spray-Rite's distributorship, adopted compensation programs and shipping policies, and encouraged distributors to boycott Spray-Rite in furtherance of this conspiracy. Monsanto denied the allegations of conspiracy, and asserted that Spray-Rite's distributorship had been terminated because of its failure to hire trained salesmen and adequately promote sales to dealers.[6]

The jury found for Spray-Rite and awarded a judgment of $10,500,000! Monsanto appealed on the question of proof. The Court of Appeals affirmed,[7] stating that there was sufficient evidence to satisfy the burden of proving a conspiracy to set prices. The court stated that "proof of termination following competitor complaints is sufficient to support an inference of concerted action."[8]

The Supreme Court granted certiorari to resolve differences among the circuits as to what evidence was needed to sustain a verdict for a terminated dealer in these circumstances. The difference among the circuits related to the importance to be attached to complaints from other dealers that the terminated dealer was price-cutting. The Seventh Circuit had stated that if there was evidence of such complaints followed by a termination, it was permissible for the jury to infer the existence of a conspiracy.[9] Other circuits required evidence that the termination was actually in response to the complaints.[10] The resulting holding of the Court is important to all marketers in their relationship with their distributors.

Supreme Court Holding

The Supreme Court set forth the two important distinctions in any distributor-termination case, including the importance of distinguishing concerted action to set prices and concerted action on nonprice restrictions.[11]

First, there is the basic distinction between concerted and independent action—a distinction not always clearly drawn by parties and courts. Section 1 of the Sherman Act requires that there be a "contract, combination. . .or conspiracy" between the manufacturer and other distributors in order to establish a violation. Independent action is not proscribed. A manufacturer, of course, generally has a right to deal, or refuse to deal, with whomever it likes, as long as it does so independently.[12] Under this approach, the manufacturer can announce its resale prices in advance and refuse to deal with those who fail to comply. And a distributor is free to acquiesce in the manufacturer's demand in order to avoid termination.

Second, there is the important distinction between concerted action to set prices and concerted action on nonprice restrictions. The former have been per se illegal since the early years of national antitrust enforcement.[13] The latter are judged under the rule of reason, which requires a weighing of the relevant circumstances of a case to decide whether a restrictive practice constitutes an unreasonable restraint on competition.[14]

The Court reviewed the relevant circumstances and gave great latitude to the exchange and market information in these settings:

". . .the fact that a manufacturer and its distributors are in constant communication about prices and marketing strategy does not alone show that the distributors are not making independent pricing decisions. A manufacturer and its distributors have legitimate reasons to exchange information about the prices and the reception of their products in the market. Moreover, it is precisely in cases in which the manufacturer attempts to further a particular marketing strategy by means of agreements on often costly nonprice restrictions that it will have the most interest in the distributors' resale prices. The manufacturer often will want to ensure that its distributors earn sufficient profit to pay for programs such as hiring and training additional salesmen or demonstrating the technical features of the product, and will want to see that "free-riders" do not interfere."[15]

What then, is evidence of price-fixing agreements as distinguished from this ongoing exchange of price information? The Court wants more than ambiguous inferences so as to retain the integrity of the *Colgate* and *Sylvania* doctrines.[16] The Court held that you can't build a case on self-serving complaints by other distributors. Something more is needed. There must be evidence that tends to exclude the possibility that the manufacturer and nonterminated distributors were acting independently. A plaintiff should present direct or circumstantial evidence that reasonably tends to prove that the manufacturer and others had a conscious commitment (meeting of the minds) to a common scheme designed to achieve an unlawful objective.[17]

Applying its evidentiary requirement to the facts before it, the Supreme Court found sufficient evidence to enable the jury to conclude that Monsanto and some of its distributors were parties to an agreement to maintain resale prices and terminate price-cutters. The Court cited evidence of an agreement between Monsanto and another distributor to charge Monsanto's suggested price despite the distributor's initial objection. It also referred to a distributor newsletter which it said could be reasonably interpreted to indicate such an understanding. As evidence that Plaintiff's termination was pursuant to the understanding, it relied on evidence that Monsanto had informed the plaintiff of other distributors' requests that prices be maintained and had later explicitly threatened to terminate the distributor unless it raised prices.[18]

Beyond Monsanto's striking out in all three courts, what does the Supreme Court's holding leave us with? (One thing it didn't leave Monsanto with was $10,500,000—the original judgment was left intact. These issues are costly.)

Terminating a Distributor Today

The Supreme Court continued to endorse the *Colgate* Doctrine, which permits you to unilaterally terminate a distributor—even a price-cutting distributor. The Court unanimously recognized the value of restricted dealing.

The Court also recognized the normal give-and-take market realities. The intrabrand dealers talking to each other, or their participation in informing the manufacturer/supplier regarding market conditions *including prices* is not an automatic horizontal agreement, but may be procompetitive by assisting the manufacturer/supplier to compete in the interbrand market more effectively, and to increase its market share.

If you are sued, the court will want the plaintiff to actually prove that there was an unlawful agreement between the supplier and competing distributors. It is not enough for a jury to infer this from complaints alone or even that dealers and manufacturers are in constant communication about price. There must be evidence predicated by conduct that will tend to exclude the possibility that the manufacturer and the non-terminated dealers were acting independently.[19] Such evidence must show a "conscious commitment to common scheme designed to achieve an unlawful objective."[20] This gets away from the traditional reliance on agreement motions (e.g., complaints, letters, etc.) and moves us more to an analysis of precisely what concrete conduct took place.

What the Court was not clear on is exactly what additional evidence it does require. Does the Court want a plaintiff to meet the standards necessary to demonstrate a criminal conspiracy, or some other lesser standard of "additional evidence"?[21]

We shall await the decisions of future courts. As stated earlier, in the interim it is clear from the conduct emphasis that it will be hard for you to "inadvertently" become involved in an illegal termination. It will be almost impossible if you handle your distributor termination situations in a thoughtful, thorough, and cautious manner.[22]

For ways to avoid such inference (especially the creation of documentary records at each and every state of your relationship), see the latter part of the next chapter for suggestions on point. First, we'll look at the overall map of vertical territorial restraints, both price and nonprice.

ENDNOTES

(1) *Monsanto Co. v. Spray-Rite Service Corporation,* 104 S.Ct. 1464 (1984).

(2) Seller, David, "To Regulate a Regulatory Agency," *Insight* , 12/8/86, p. 45-46 (a good review of FTC and Justice Dept. enforcement or lack of same in the current administration).

(3) Note 1, p. 1469, n. 7 and Justice Brennan's concurrence, p. 1473.

(4) *Lewis Service Center, Inc. v. Mack Trucks, Inc.,* 714 F.2d 842 (8th Cir.), *cert. den.,* 104 S.Ct. 2678 (1984) (manufacturer's system of discounts to enable dealers to meet retail price competition evaluated under the rule of reason); *AAA Liquors, Inc. v. Joseph F. Seagram & Son,* 705 F.2d 1203, 1205 (9th Cir.), *cert. den.,* 461 US 919 (1983) (liquor distiller's system of price supports to wholesaler, which in turn offered discounts to large volume dealers not resale price maintenance); *Eastern Scientific Co. v. Wild Heerburg Instruments, Inc.,* 572 F.2d 883 (1st Cir.), *cert. den.* , 439 US 833 (1978) (use of both nonprice and price restrictions analyzed under the rule of reason); *Butera v. Sun Oil Co.,* 496 F.2d 434 (1st Cir. 1974) (gasoline supplier's discount system, whereby supplier credited dealers for discount amount, was not resale price maintenance); *Sun Oil Co. v. Vickers Refining Co.,* 414 F.2d 383 (8th Cir. 1969) (allowing a contract formula between two gasoline suppliers in which first supplier sold to a second supplier and guaranteed a minimum profit to second supplier based on the price actually received by second supplier from its jobbers).

(5) Note 1, p. 1467 n.1.

(6) Note 1, p. 1467.

(7) 684 F.2d 1226 (7th Cir. 1982).

(8) Note 1, p. 1468.

(9) Note 7, p. 1228.

(10) Note 1, p. 1468, n.5.

(11) Note 1, p. 1469.

(12) *U.S. v. Colgate & Co.,* 250 US 300, 307, 39 S.Ct. 465, 468; 63 L.Ed. 992 (1919); cf., *U.S. v. Parke, Davis & Co.,* 362 US 29; 80 S.Ct. 503; 4 L.Ed.2d 505 (1960).

(13) See *Dr. Miles Medical Co. v. John D. Park & Sons Co.,* 220 US 373, 404-409, 31 S.Ct. 376, 383-385; 55 L.Ed. 502 (1911).

(14) See *Continental TV, Inc. v. GTE Sylvania, Inc.,* 433 U.S. 36; 97 S.Ct. 2549, 53 L.Ed.2d 568 (1977).

(15) Note 1, p. 1470.

(16) Id.

(17) Note 1, p. 1473.

(18) Note 1, p. 1471-72.

(19) Note 1, p. 1471, n.8 and possibly n.9 as to "clues."

(20) Note 1, p. 1473.

(21) Note 1, p. 1471.

(22) Stoll, Neal A. and Goldfein, Shepard "Breaking Up Is Easier to Do." *NY Law Journal* 7/21/87 p.1.

CHAPTER 6

ANTITRUST ISSUES IN CHANNEL DISTRIBUTION

In this chapter, we'll take a look at restrictive distribution systems employing vertical restraints, an area that has been the subject of much antitrust literature. Then we'll discuss the often thorny legal ramifications of terminating your distributor. You *can* do it without causing antitrust problems, provided that you understand the rules. Along the way we'll discuss boycotts and horizontal restrictions. We'll wrap up the chapter with a comprehensive question-and-answer review of the legal highlights in this area.

Remember that your understanding of these antitrust issues is essential to the entire marketing process. Although this is not the most thrilling subject, shelling out a large sum of money (from your personal or your corporate piggybank) as a fine is a lot *less* thrilling! Even *less* enticing is the thought of designing all your wonderful marketing strategies from your own exclusive prison cell!

Distribution Plans With Vertical Strings Attached

You, like every manager, want to get your product from the warehouse to the customers' hands. You'll do this either as a direct marketer (see the next chapter) or by distribution. The *difference* between wholesale and retail price is the cost of distribution. Some of these *differences* will result from a variety of locational or service restrictions you might contractually negotiate. These restrictions may include limits that a supplier may impose on its distributions or retailers as to pricing, product, quality control, and the geographic market in which they may sell.

Any proposed restrictions must be reviewed by counsel, lest your firm leave itself open to unnecessary litigation. This doesn't mean that

139

you can't consider any kind of restrictions in your distribution plan, but you should have a working notion of what is legally feasible. Knowledge of the present state of the law and of the direction in which it is heading will enable you to blueprint distribution plans that will get a green light from your own counsel, thereby saving time, energy, and costs for all concerned.

We'll first address the two theories of analysis upon which all decisions in this area chart their initial point of reference.

Per Se Approach vs. Rule of Reason

The key antitrust legal question always is this: At what point do the actions of free marketplace choices become unreasonable restrictions on free commerce? The courts have addressed this dilemma through two approaches: by adopting "per se" rules of illegality and by using a "rule of reason" approach that analyzes each case on its merits. Understanding the distinction between these approaches is important, since these terms appear throughout your antitrust reading in all texts and trade journals.

Violations of the antitrust laws traditionally have been classified into two specific categories and subjected to different treatment by the courts. Certain business agreements, conduct, or other interaction (such as price fixing, boycotts, agreements to retard technological development, horizontal territorial restrictions, and some tie-ins) are considered by the courts to be so inherently anticompetitive as to be considered illegal per se (in and of themselves) without any inquiry into the reasonableness of the activity involved or their actual effect on competition. The definitive statement on point is from Justice Black:[1]

> The Sherman Act was designed to be a comprehensive charter of economic liberty aimed at preserving free and unfettered competition as the rule of trade. It rests on the premise that the unrestrained interaction of competitive forces will yield the best allocation of our economic resources, the lowest prices, the highest quality and the greatest material progress, while at the same time providing an environment conducive to the preservation of our democratic political and social institutions. But even were that premise open to question, the policy unequivocally laid down by the Act is competition. And to this end it prohibits "Every Contract, combination . . . or conspiracy, in restraint of trade or commerce among the several States." Although this prohibition is literally all-encompassing, the courts have construed it as precluding only those contracts or combinations which "unreasonably" restrain competition. . .
>
> However, there are certain agreements or practices which because of their pernicious effect on competition and lack of any redeeming virtue are conclusively presumed to be unreasonable and therefore illegal without elaborate inquiry as to the precise harm they have caused or the business excuse for their use. This principal of *per se* unreasonableness not only

makes the type of restraints which are proscribed by the Sherman Act more certain to the benefit of everyone concerned, but it also avoids the necessity for an incredibly complicated and prolonged economic investigation into the entire history of the industry involved, as well as related industries, in an effort to determine at large whether a particular restraint has been unreasonable—an inquiry so often wholly fruitless when undertaken. Among the practices which the courts have heretofore deemed to be unlawful in and of themselves are price fixing, *United States v. Socony-Vacuum Oil Co.* [2]. . . .; division of markets, *United States v. Addyston Pipe & Steel Co.* [3]. . . .; group boycotts, *Fashion Originator's Guild of America, Inc. v. Federal Trade Commission* [4]. . . .; and tying arrangements, *International Salt Co. v. United States.* [5]

Violations of this nature are usually proven by circumstantial evidence, one example of which is a meeting between competitors followed by actions leading to restraint of trade. Any facts that show communications between direct competitors and that indicate some restraining effect are admissible as evidence. Courts are influenced by patterns of contact among competitors, so you must be alert in your conversations and contacts with your competitors, even at informal lunches and trade association meetings. When in doubt, don't talk— talk to your lawyer first.

Although the courts use the per se approach when the conduct fits into one of its categories, the more common and increasingly preferred standard is the rule of reason. The rule of reason inquiry focuses on the competitive significance of a particular restraint. Using the rule of reason, a court inquires into the purpose of the activity, its socially redeeming virtues (for example, if the practice actually promotes interbrand competition by allowing a new competitor to enter or a failing competitor to remain solvent), and the existence of practical but less restrictive alternatives. The court proceeds to weigh each fact presented to determine its overall reasonability and therefore its legality. The definitive statement on the rule of reason test is set forth by Justice Brandeis:[6]

> [T]he legality of an agreement or regulation cannot be determined by so simple a test, as whether it restrains competition. Every agreement concerning trade, every regulation of trade, restrains. To bind, to restrain, is of their very essence. The true test of legality is whether the restraint imposed is such as merely regulates and perhaps thereby promotes competition to whether it is such as may suppress or even destroy competition. To determine that question the court must ordinarily consider the facts peculiar to the business to which the restraint is applied; its condition before and after the restraint was imposed; the nature of the restraint and its effect, actual or probable. The history of the restraint, the evil believed to exist, the reason for adopting the particular remedy, the purpose or end sought to be attained, are all relevant facts. This is not because a good intention will save an otherwise objectionable regulation or

the reverse; but because knowledge of intent may help the court to interpret facts and predict consequences.

The case that effectively enshrined the rule of reason approach was *Continental TV, Inc. v. GTE Sylvania, Inc.* [7] *Sylvania* represented a growing awareness by the Supreme Court that the marketplace is a dynamic forum and not a closed zone to be refereed by a few judges. It preserved the competitive spirit of the Sherman Act while reflecting on the particular activities of the industry involved. The crucial factors to analyze are the following:

- The market power or dominance of the company imposing the restraints in its relevant market;
- The extent to which the restraints impede intrabrand competition;
- The justifications asserted for the restraints in terms of promoting interbrand competition.

The drawback most often cited by critics when referring to the rule of reason is the ensuing increase in litigation. This, however, can be minimized by a working knowledge of the checklist set forth in the conclusion of this chapter. But first, we'll briefly review some sticky issues involved in distinguishing horizontal and vertical distribution arrangements.

Horizontal v. Vertical Territorial Allocations

Until the last decade the distinction between horizontal and vertical distribution systems was academic. All were considered per se illegal whether or not price was a factor. You will still have a per se issue as to price, but nonprice vertical restraints are governed by the rule of reason. [8]

Horizontal agreements are those that are made between firms operating at the same level of market structure, e.g., agreements between competing distributors as well as competing manufacturers. [9] Such firms need not be in direct competition with each other, but it is necessary that the parties be at least potential competitors. [10]

Vertical agreements, in contrast, are restraints on dealers or distributors imposed by a firm higher up in the distribution hierarchy, acting in pursuit *of its own market strategy,* e.g., bona fide licensing restrictions imposed by a manufacturer on its distributors. [11]

Horizontal price agreements are always illegal per se as a violation of Section 1 of the Sherman Act. [12] There is some debate whether vertical (resale price maintenance) agreements were also to remain per se illegal. The historical reason these agreements were per se illegal since 1911 is that they hindered, if not prevented, effective competition between retailers.

As discussed in the introductory case [13] Congress expressly refused the Justice Department permission to spend any funds for overturning the established law with respect to the illegality of vertical price fixing. Congress was merely holding up a long tradition in this area.

The Supreme Court has long held that *vertical price fixing* is a *per se* violation of Section 1 of the Sherman Act.[14] In an early resale price maintenance case,[15] the Supreme Court ruled that when a manufacturer parts with title to his property, he may not require the person or company with whom he dealt to resell the product at a particular price. In that case, a manufacturer of patent medicines entered into an agreement with its dealers on the minimum price at which the patent medicine could be resold. The Court acknowledged that such a price-fixing scheme helped increase the profits of dealers handling this patent medicine, and seemed to imply there may also be some advantage to Dr. Miles as well. Without determining what that advantage might be, the Court held that a manufacturer may not enter into an agreement with its dealers, that restrains trade in this fashion. A resale-price-maintenance scheme of this nature is illegal per se.

The practice is unlawful because it restricts the freedom of traders who are at lower levels of the product or service distribution system to set their own prices. Establishing a *per se* violation of the Sherman Act in a private action brought under a vertical price fixing theory requires proof of four elements.

First, the defendant must have intended to fix prices charged by traders at lower levels in the distribution system.[16] *Second* , the defendant must have coerced the plaintiff into charging higher or lower prices.[17] Coercion in the vertical price fixing context is actual or threatened affirmative action, beyond suggestion or persuasion, taken by a defendant in order to induce the plaintiff (i.e., the distributor) to follow its price.[18] For example, threatening to terminate a franchisee in order to induce compliance with suggested retail prices is coercion.[19] Similarly, while *Colgate* [20] permits you to refuse to deal with discounters and others, you may not condition their reinstatement of terminated dealers on their assurance of future compliance.[21] *Third,* the defendant's conduct must have caused antitrust injury.[22] Finally, a plaintiff must show entitlement to relief.

One court examined leading Supreme Court decisions concerning both vertical price fixing and lawful unilateral refusals to deal, and summed up the salient rules as follows: first, that the "required combination" for a finding of illegal resale price fixing must be demonstrated by proof of "(1) an express or implied agreement, or (2) the securing of actual adherence to prices by means beyond mere refusal to deal;" and second, that the use of "coercion that achieves actual price-fixing is illegal."[23]

What can you do? You can suggest retail prices so long as you allow departure from them.[24] You can also act as a cheerleader and "exhort your dealers to adhere" so long as you take no further action.[25] You can even preticket so long as this is only a suggestion and your retailer is free to set his/her own price.[26] You can try to argue your premium image is to everyone's benefit or the value to you of financially sound distributors (i.e., keep the distributor focused on profits—not on price). Finally, it is not a per se violation for a supplier to withdraw preferential pricing from a favored dealer.[27]

Neither the Courts nor Congress will look with indulgence on any effort to be creative in skirting the rules as to either a horizontal or vertical pricing scheme. Horizontal territorial allocation will not receive any better treatment.[28]

Finally, don't become involved in any distribution scheme which could appear as a concerted refusal to deal or a boycott without the clearance of counsel.[29] As the Supreme Court held recently:

> . . .and frequently the boycotting firms possess a dominant position in the relevant market. . . . In addition, the practices [are] generally not justified by plausible arguments that they were intended to enhance overall efficiency and make markets more competitive. Under such circumstances the likelihood of anticompetitive effects is clear and the possibility of countervailing procompetitive effects is remote.[30]

However, it should be noted that the above case first required thorough analysis of market power in the defined product and geographic market before applying a presumption of anticompetitive power. The Court, therefore, approved a rule-of-reason analysis for the conduct of the cooperative's expulsion procedure.

What happened in the *Northwest Wholesalers* case is that a regional group of wholesale stationery distributors acted jointly to expel from membership a wholesale distributor who also sold at retail, enabling them to earn extra profits while selling at discounted retail prices. In the absence of a "dominant" position in the product and geographic market or "unique access to a business element necessary for effective competition," the Court held there was insufficient "market power" to warrant *per se* evaluation.

The Court has a precedent that horizontal trade association activity is to be judged under a rule of reason regardless of its impact on prices. Traditionally, the courts have given great leeway to trade association lobbying under Noerr-Pennington, or as to a cooperative group's right to expel a member (see below). It remains to be seen if this holding is an isolated one or a watershed in the general category of concerted activity.

A mere substitution of dealers will be considered a non-price restraint governed by the rule of reason.[31] A cooperative group may expel a member in the pursuit of valid self-regulation.[32] Generally there are three points that must be established for self-regulation:

(1) There is a legislative mandate for self-regulation;[33]

(2) The collective action (a) is intended to accomplish an end consistent with the policy justifying self-regulation, (b) is reasonably related to that goal, and (c) is no more extensive than necessary;[34]

(3) The association provides procedural safeguards that assure that the restraints are not arbitrary and that furnish a basis for judicial review.[35]

If these points are established, the group activity will come under a rule-of-reason analysis. These matters are often in a gray, close-call area, as a recent case clearly demonstrates. Let's take a look at the Indiana dentists.[36] In an effort to contain costs, Indiana group health care insurers devised a dental insurance plan that required dentists to submit to the insurer copies of a patient's dental X-rays along with the insurance claim form. The form and X-rays were reviewed by lay personnel employed by the insurance company. If any procedure was questioned, the X-rays and the form were turned over to a dentist hired by the insurer. Based solely on the information on the form and the X-rays, the dentist decided what would be the least expensive type of treatment that would provide good dental care.

For the above and other reasons, a number of dentists opposed the plan. They formed the Indiana Federation of Dentists (IFD) to refuse collectively to provide the insurers with the requested X-rays.[37] The FTC brought suit against the IFD alleging that the IFD's collective refusal to submit X-rays constituted a conspiracy in restraint of trade in violation of Section 1 of the Sherman Act, and hence of Section 5 of the FTC Act. The FTC held this boycott constituted a per se unlawful restraint of trade.[38]

The Court of Appeals ruled against the FTC on both the per-se-illegality and the rule-of-reason analyses and found no anticompetitive effect on the relevant market.[39] The Supreme Court, on the other hand, applying a rule-of-reason analysis,[40] concluded that the IFD's actions constituted an unreasonable restraint of trade and an unfair method of competition.[41] The X-ray policy took the form of a horizontal agreement among the IFD members to withhold from their customers a particular service they desired. Under the rule of reason, such an agreement cannot be sustained unless a countervailing procompetitive purpose can be demonstrated.

With boycotts, you should see if there is concerted commercial activity in which the parties agree not to deal with a company or companies or demand that others not deal with a company or companies. This will be treated as a classic boycott when the purpose of the conspirators is to deprive a competitor of a needed resource and make it harder for the competitor to compete. Such concerted commercial activity constitutes a per se violation of the Sherman Act. The courts regard such activity as inherently harmful to competition.[42]

If there is not a commercial purpose to the agreement but rather an attempt at industry self-regulation, any group boycott charge will almost inevitably be subject to a rule-of-reason analysis.[43]

We've saved discussing the most flexible option for last. Now is the time to review it.

The Nonprice Vertical Territorial Option

When the production processes are completed, your product is ready for distribution to the consuming public. The type of good determines whether you desire an intensive or selective distribution.

The distribution systems available range from dealing with independent distributors to the supplier's development of a complete, vertically integrated system for merchandising the product. Trade-offs involved include the costs and benefits of the available delivery mechanisms and the degree of control the manufacturer needs or wants to retain over the product. In general, costs to the manufacturer increase in proportion to the degree of control exercised. Therefore, suppliers have sometimes sought the advantages of vertical integration without the disadvantages of the required capital investment and ensuing operational costs by arranging contractually a variety of vertical restrictions.

Vertical restrictions on distributors are limits that a channel member at one level of the distribution system (usually the supplier) imposes on a channel member at a different level of the distribution system (such as a wholesaler or retailer). The five most common examples of such contractually arranged restrictions are:

► *Location agreements,* which limit the distributor's resale operations to a specified physical site (have been upheld uniformly by the courts).[44]

► *Territorial sales restrictions,* which limit a distributor to sales within a defined territory and which often include an agreement by the supplier to prohibit other distributors from selling within that area.

► *Areas of primary responsibility,* which give a particular distributor primary responsibility for selling in an assigned territory. As long as the distributor represents you in his or her area of primary responsibility, he or she is free to sell anywhere else.[45]

► *Profit preservation clause,* which gives your distributor the right to sell anywhere, *but* if the distributor "sells into" someone else's territory, the distributor must reimburse that other distributor for the sales and marketing he or she has done in the territory.[46] That latter reimbursement is equitable to compensate the nonselling distributor for the goodwill it generated, laying the seed through advertising expenditure.

► *Customer restrictions,* which limit a distributor's choice of customers, such as when the supplier rather than the distributor sells to and services a large national customer.

Basically, there are three types of vertical distribution relationships:

• exclusive-dealing relationships,
• independent sales contracts (franchising, or any contracted long-term distribution arrangement), and
• full vertical integration.

The most efficient distribution relationship is generally defined by the marketplace. However, regrettable abuses have occurred that have resulted in the enactment of legislation primarily designed to guide rather than to define marketplace conduct. The inherent tension between the manager's desire to maximize efficiency and profit in distribution and society's attempts to maintain the antiquated nineteenth-century concept of atomistic "free" competition has acted as a major constraint on short- and long-term distribution strategies.

Congress began seeking to resolve the tension of varied competing interests almost a century ago. Recognizing the increasingly dynamic economic environment of the day, it sought a legal posture that would evolve with the marketplace without constraining it. Since we are only a few years from the centennial of the famous Sherman Act, it is obvious that these laws usually work well.

With competitive markets, the consumer benefits from lower prices and a greater selection of goods accomplished by mass economies of scale as well as by efficient and economical distribution. History has demonstrated that marketplace competition thrives when efficient firms are permitted to enjoy the fruits of their superior planning, organizational, and capital investment skills. The need to maximize efficiency often encourages a firm to control its distribution through vertical territorial restrictions for both economic and social reasons.

Economically, the modern firm requires specialist expertise, a large capital investment, increasingly sophisticated technological resources, and marketing know-how to stay competitive. Years of research, development, and planning may be invested before an item is ready to be produced. To reduce risk, the firm seeks some advantage over its competition, such as a more desirable product, more appropriate positioning, the right degree of segmentation, loyal customers and wholesalers, and so on.

One way of gaining this advantage lies in controlling the firm's distribution system so that the firm can reduce *intrabrand* competition in the interest of succeeding against *interbrand* competition. Interbrand competition is competition among producers of a generic product, for example, competition among producers of washing machines. Intrabrand competition is competition among retailers to sell a specific brand of washing machine. The costs the firm incurs in production will be constant regardless of which distribution system is employed. Therefore, the distribution system will generally be a key variable. Its proper selection and creative structure can significantly affect your bottom line.

By imposing nonprice territorial restrictions (that is, restrictions that do not result in price restraints) on where and how a distributor can sell its product, the supplier maintains a degree of control over the distribution without assuming the distribution function. The supplier enjoys the expertise of the distributor and its client contact while avoiding the cost burden of establishing its own distribution system through vertical integration. In addition, by choosing territorial restrictions instead of vertical integration, a manager may retain a necessary local flavor by taking advantage of the knowledge of the distributor's sales personnel concerning local demands, desires, and needs. The imposition of vertical territorial restrictions on the distributor can be especially beneficial to the supplier when the supplier is entering new markets, in inducing higher levels of distributor service and in encouraging distributors to provide a full product line to a full range of customers. Nevertheless such nonprice territorial restrictions may still be a violation if the restraint is an unreasonable one.

The courts are not about to make per se lawful practices which were per se unlawful. For example, the value of intrabrand competition should not be dismissed lightly. Plaintiffs do win some cases in the vertical nonprice restraint area:

> The argument, pressed by Itek at length here, that the reduction or elimination of intrabrand competition is, by itself, never sufficient to show that a trade restraint is anticompetitive must rest, at bottom, on the view that intrabrand competition—regardless of the circumstances—is never a significant source of consumer welfare. This view is simply not supported by economic analysis, or by the cases. A seller with considerable market power in the interbrand market—whether stemming from its dominant position in the market structure or from the successful differentiation of its products—will necessarily have some power over price. In that situation, intrabrand competition will be a significant source of consumer welfare because it alone can exert downward pressure on the retail price at which the good is sold. Dealers, by competing against each other and bidding the retail price down, will in turn exert downward pressure on the seller's wholesale price in order to maintain their profit margins. Thus, in situations of manufacturer market power, intrabrand restrictions on distributor competition can have a substantial adverse effect on consumer welfare by eliminating an important source of competitive pressure on price. Rather than promoting nonprice competition, vertical restraints in this context may enable a manufacturer to retain monopoly profits arising from an interbrand competitive advantage[47]. . .

> We note that the Sixth and Third Circuits, respectively,[48] agree with the Second Circuit that intrabrand competition alone can be a significant concern of antitrust law, notwithstanding the *Sylvania* Court's observation that interbrand competition is "the primary concern of antitrust law."[49]

Itek lost because, among other reasons, Graphic Products demonstrated clear adverse impact on competition by evidence that Itek's products were sufficiently differentiated so that the only competitive balance was provided by intrabrand competition.

In any rule of reason analysis we look at the market power (i.e., the ability to raise prices significantly above the competitive level without losing so many sales that the increase is unprofitable) of the defendant in a well-defined, relevant market.[50] Such market will consist of a relevant product and geographic market in which both the manufacturer, supplier and distributor operate. Market definition turns on discovering patterns of trade that are followed in practice (such as demand substitutes and supply substitutes). The key element is that the market(s) must correspond to commercial realities; theoretical arguments of interchangeability of products always fail.

Specific, "non-theoretical" questions to ask yourself about your product market include:

- Is your product so clearly differentiated from your competition that there is little impact on interbrand distribution as a result of your controls?
- What does your own internal analysis say about the physical characteristics or end use of your competitors' products in comparison to your own concerning whether interchangeability is feasible?
- How does the trade literature, industry experts, et al. classify the competition among products in your market?
- Is your product clearly differentiated by an ancillary service or trained staff which dominates customer preference?
- What is the cross-elasticity of demand resulting from your pricing strategy analysis?

Specific, "nontheoretical" questions to ask yourself about your geographic market include:

- Does overall effective competition at the national market disguise large regional market segments in which your products are clearly dominant?
- What alternative sources of supply of your product are available in the national or regional market segments?
- What is your overall market share?
- What is the nature of the restraint imposed in light of the above? Such inquiry of your restraint's possible anticompetitive impact must examine both the short-term as well as the long-term impact at both the manufacturer/supplier and distributor levels. You should be able to argue why interbrand competition is enhanced. If intrabrand competition is hurt, show the procompetitive overall trade-off.

If the plaintiff can cross the threshold by demonstrating the anticompetitive effect of the nonprice, vertical restraint, the defendant must then counter that it has a legitimate, procompetitive benefit or justification when the purpose and effect of the restraint is viewed as a whole. In determining its effect on competition in totality *both* interbrand and intrabrand effects must be considered. If the nonprice territorial restriction is air-tight and completely eliminates intrabrand competition *and* intrabrand competition is shown to be important to consumer welfare you'll have a problem sustaining your argument that your restrictions are indeed pro-competitive.

The Courts remain in flux in this area and the U.S. as well as state Attorneys General are issuing various "guidelines." These are merely opinions on their view of the law. They are not law. Considering their reaction vis a vis Congress, the U.S. Justice Department Guidelines are at best likely to surface in a few ominous opinions—if their finding isn't blatantly cut off. Unless something more definitive comes along, the courts have provided the only direction.

You can help yourself by avoiding problems before they arise. The best problem-avoidance strategy when dealing with nonprice vertical issues is to be as careful as possible in terminating your distributors. We'll take a look at this issue right now.

Terminating Your Distributor

Your right to unilaterally conduct your business in a manner you see fit and to choose customers with whom you wish to deal is acknowledged.[51] However, once you've freely elected to do business with a distributor, terminating that distributor can be a bit risky—unless you've done your homework. And "homework" in law means *documentation.*

First consider whether to enter into a formal contractual relationship (though contracts are no longer sacrosanct as they once were in these areas).[52] The following lists some questions you'll want to ask yourself in determining the terms beyond the basics which you'll want to include in your contract (see Section VIII on the Generic Contract):

☐ What is the term (be sure to clearly define)? Is it automatically renewable and, if so, by which (or both) parties?

☐ Exactly what services will the distributor provide? (e.g., how often will he/she call on customers, will warranties be serviced, etc.) Will you utilize a "best efforts" or "reasonable efforts" standard?[53] What type of reports (and their frequency) do you want?

☐ What products will the distributor handle and not handle, and to which customers?

☐ What territory will this include, and are there other restrictions such as location, profit-passover and other clauses?

☐ Will there be quotas?

☐ Will you dabble in the dangerous area of recommended price?

☐ Are you going to try to set up any non-compete agreements (see Section VIII on point)?

☐ If you are franchising or assigning a trademark, have you drawn up the proper quality control agreement? Are any other rights assignable?

☐ Do you have a clearly spelled-out insolvency clause?

☐ Has your termination provision been negotiated and put into the contract? This will head off later bad feelings better than any boilerplate language. You can cite the "spirit" of your prior negotiations. Also, it is a good idea to spell out which level of management can terminate the agreement *and* that no member of the sales force has authority to terminate it.

☐ Do you have an arbitration clause? Arbitration will act as a buffer between you and the courts. You can avoid discovery and have time for the terminated distributor to cool off and get involved in other things.

☐ Finally, do you have a proper waiver clause?

Second, document all complaints as they arise and try to head off a problem at its inception. Make sure your sales force knows the distinction between inquiry and complaint, and segregates the contact accordingly. When in doubt, *don't* label the communication as a complaint.

If competing distributors complain to you, tell them you don't want their input in these matters. Don't use distributors as a *source of pricing* concerning their competing distributors.

If a distributor is terminated as a result of this form of complaint, it may be used as evidence that "tends to exclude the possibility that the manufacturer and non-terminated distributors were acting independently" and "that reasonably tends to prove that the manufacturer and others had a conscious commitment to a common scheme to achieve an unlawful objective."[54]

If you do take any action at this time, make sure you document

- the time interval between complaint and action;
- the credibility (and why) of the complaining party;
- whether this is the usual way you handle this form of complaint or whether this distributor was singled out;
- whether your action was a significant one (e.g., cutting a credit line[55]) or merely a contact one (e.g., letter or call); and
- whether all of your actions were clearly within your economic interest (at all times in any pre- or post-termination activity, be able to show you didn't act against your own interest).

Remember, you *can* act upon complaints from other distributors to secure compliance with legitimate corporate policy if you can document your motivation was self-interest of a clear corporate purpose, and not dictated by or to the benefit of such complaining distributors.

Third, document the termination situation thoroughly. Remember that termination is (and is viewed as) a threat the manufacturer or supplier can use to force compliance with an illegal resale price maintenance scheme. To properly document, you must show a legitimate business reason for the dissatisfaction, such as the distributor's lack of cooperation with your marketing plans or poor payment record or your own internal reorganization. Many states (check franchise laws here too, as many are broadly drafted and will pull you in) now require a showing of "just cause" and a period of advance written notice — specific areas you must review with your counsel. Make sure you can't be accused of terminating a non-complying distributor who opposed your attempts to use distribution restrictions to raise the barriers to entry by competitors.

With all of the above caveats stated, if you have a poor distributor, don't be intimated — see your counsel. The trend is that fewer and fewer terminated distributors are satisfying this burden of proof (that's legalese for they're losing most of the time). Since the distributor must prove that the termination had an anticompetitive effect, how do you deprive the distributor of possible proof?

Document all your business reasons for termination and the procedures you employed. Check your files, letters, and contracts, and review any significant conversations. Then examine your own motives. Is the termination based on sound business judgment?[56] You may terminate for the following reasons:

1. To reduce the number of your dealers, especially if an alternate supply of your product is available to the terminated distributor.[57]

2. To end a relationship that has grown uneconomic. This might mean that even though the distributor's sales have not fallen off, its failure to enthusiastically adopt your new or current marketing strategy might be enough to terminate.[58] In addition to the distributor's policy of late payments "plus more" may be sufficient grounds for just cause to terminate. Likewise, disloyalty in promoting the line of a competitor is just cause[59] as is terminating a distributor who violated your longstanding policy in a material way. Here you'll document your policy as well as the extent of the violation.

You will help yourself with a jury by showing you tried to let the distributor "down easy", with respect and dignity. It is a good idea for the termination letter to be a personal one from a senior executive (reviewed by counsel) and for it to set forth precisely the reasons for termination and/or the contractual provision letting you escape (similarly, make sure you have a policy that low-level management *cannot* terminate a distributor). The considered decision of top corporate management will create a better halo effect to a fact finder.

If the termination is not for cause, thank the distributor for his/her period of service. Don't imply you won't recommend him or her elsewhere and if you feel up to it offer yourself as a reference in the trade (again only for contractual, end-of-term terminations—*not* terminations for cause).

Finally, your case is greatly improved if your terminated distributor cannot show that the termination lessened competition or created an "unreasonable restraint of trade" in the affected industry.[60] You want to show it improved interbrand competition.[61] The fact that the distributor alone is injured does not convert your decision into a violation of the antitrust laws.[62]

If conscious parallelism (a number of competitors raise prices together with no explicit agreement to do so) is alleged, the plaintiff who claims price-fixing must show one of several "plus factors" beyond the "coincidence" to demonstrate a real agreement. One such factor is that the parallel conduct is individually irrational in the absence of cooperation from the other participants but becomes rational with their cooperation. Naturally, if you can document that you had different interests from your alleged "co-conspirators" and, therefore, would not have benefitted from the alleged conspiracy, you are pretty much home free from the allegation as well as other "plus" factors.[63]

In general, courts won't compel a manufacturer to renew a dealership if there is no public harm even if the distributor is hurt. This rule will hold even when the court recognizes that subjective hostility might be involved, for example, when former employees compete with you.[64]

Again, a thorough interview with your counsel is essential before termination—particularly if pricing motives are even partly involved in your termination decision.

To Wrap Up the Distribution Area

The following checklist will enable the manager employing or considering a restrictive distribution system to review it in light of the current judicial climate. You must review with your counsel the relevant court cases for any of the points which are applicable to your company and/or your distribution plan. Although the rule of reason enhances flexibility in designing channel strategy by leaving open areas of interpretation, it presents the possibility of adverse interpretation. As usual, a text or checklist is a general planning aid but is no substitute for a counsel who knows your unique needs.

☐ *Can I create or participate in a horizontal territorial allocation of the market under any circumstances?* No—not even if you can show it will bring "stability." Market sharing limits aggressive well-run firms and protects less efficient ones.

☐ *Could a complainant objectively demonstrate in a challenge that a portion of the relevant market is being effectively eliminated by the distribution plan?* Vertical territorial distribution restrictions may be valid even if they make distributor sales outside of assigned territories economically unattractive, provided that they do not totally bar such sales and can be shown to be reasonable to the maintenance of an efficient distribution system. Note that the exclusion of a portion of the relevant market may also be justified in the wake of *Sylvania* if necessary to safeguard unique quality standards. Again, before you pursue any of your ideas, it is important to review the specifics of your restrictions with your counsel.

☐ *Could a complainant objectively demonstrate in a challenge that the distribution plan has substantially lessened interbrand competition or has tended to create a monopoly?* The reviewing court will judge harshly any plan which tends to make a monopolistic effect and to stifle competition. An important issue here will be whether you have sufficient market power in the relevant market.[65]

☐ *Could a complainant objectively demonstrate in a challenge that prices are becoming artificially high as a result of a decline in intrabrand competition?* This area is fraught with peril and any such plan should certainly be reviewed by counsel.

☐ *Can we demonstrate that the success of a challenge to our plan would result in incentives to vertically integrate our industry fully, thereby diminishing intrabrand competition?* We should be able to demonstrate without complex economic analysis that the restraint in question will promote interbrand competition in the relevant market while minimizing a decline in intrabrand competition. In the wake of *Sylvania,* such an argument would be judged by the rule of reason; the vertical restrictions inherent in the plan would be considered preferable to full vertical integration which increases marketplace concentration.[66]

☐ *Do we possess monopoly power?* The necessary ingredients for monopoly power are the percentage of market share controlled by the firm, the number and strength of firms already established in the market, and the ease of entry into the market by potential competitors. In general, the more monopoly or market power (i.e., the ability to raise and sustain prices above the prevailing competitive market price) a firm has, the more likely that its vertical territorial distribution plan will be challenged.[67]

☐ *Is our monopoly power the result of purpose or intent to exercise that power through anticompetitive conduct?* To prove unlawful practices, the firm must have both the power to control prices and the *intent* to exclude competition in the relevant market.[68] If the firm's actions show that it means to keep and does keep a complete and exclusive hold on the market, it is monopolizing the market, no matter how innocently it may otherwise proceed.

☐ *Is our monopoly power the result of a superior product, business acumen, or historic accident?* These would be considered mitigating factors in determining the question of unlawful practices, providing that the firm did not deliberately retain exclusive control of the market subsequently. A firm will not be penalized for growth or development as a consequence of a superior product, business acumen, or historic accident.[69]

☐ *To what extent do we actually enforce any written restrictions?* Written restrictions which are firmly and resolutely enforced and which result in securing compliance with "suggested" prices are illegal.[70]

☐ *Are we a new entrant into a highly competitive market?* If so, the use of vertical restrictions to gain a foothold in the marketplace might survive a rule of reason test, because any decrease in intrabrand competition would be more than compensated for by an increase in interbrand competition.[71]

☐ *Are we an established seller struggling to survive?* The arguments in favor of vertical restrictions for a failing firm are the same as those for a new entrant into a competitive market.[72]

☐ *Is our market share declining or increasing?* If the firm's market share is declining, the arguments for vertical restrictions are improved insofar as those restrictions will enable the firm to survive in the marketplace and will increase intrabrand competition.[73] If, however, the firm's market share is increasing, it must be able to prove an increase in interbrand competition as a result of such restrictions.

☐ *How does our absolute size compare to the size of the distributor on whom we're imposing our restrictions?* The smaller the firm's absolute size is in relation to the size of the distributor's, the less likely the firm's ability and intent to monopolize. Conversely, the larger the firm is compared with the distributor, the greater the burden of proof. Each case will be judged accordingly under the rule of reason.[74]

☐ *Is there any presence of a direct or indirect relationship which could be conclusively presumed unreasonable and therefore constitute a per se violation (i.e., a naked restraint of trade with no purpose except stifling of competition) such as:*

a. *Price-fixing?* Managers should be wary of instituting illegal practices in regard to price-fixing. This area is reviewed in depth in Chapter 12. Price-fixing is generally a naked restraint of trade, and as such a per se violation of the Sherman Act. However, there are certain limited exceptions you should review with your counsel.[75] For example, an importer of scientific equipment had assigned areas of primary responsibility to its dealers (the entire State of Rhode Island was the territory), coupled with resale price restrictions. The dealers were free to set any price they wished when selling within their respective assigned areas. When selling outside those areas, however, they were prohibited from selling at less than the list price recommended by the defendant. The court concluded that the price restrictions at issue were "not the kind that require per se treatment."[76] The court reasoned that the "effect" of the restraints involved in the case was, if anything, less "anti-competitive" than a pure policy of exclusive territories, since dealers remained free to compete in price with other dealers charging greater than list price.[77]

b. *Group boycotts?* These generally (some exceptions noted above) involve concentrated efforts to avoid competitors and would be considered per se illegal.[78]

c. *Horizontal division of markets?* Agreements between competitors producing the same generic product to price fix or to impose horizontal territorial restrictions (i.e., to divide up the market geographically) are per se illegal. The effect is to stifle interbrand competition, and no such plan would be upheld in court.[79]

d. *Allocation of business by collusive bidding?* Again, there are no reasonableness factors to consider, and such practices are per se illegal.

e. *Tying arrangements?* The lower courts (and the current Justice Department) increasingly review many of these devices by a rule of reason analysis. The crucial test involves whether the tie-in represents the firm's attempt to extend its monopoly power from one area into another. Any such arrangement should be reviewed carefully by your counsel.[80]

☐ *Must we retain distributors as long as they return a profit?* You must consult with your counsel as to whether the particular state involved has passed a law requiring that good faith and just cause be shown before a distribution agreement may be terminated. However, the refusal of a distributor to go along with a reasonable marketing plan not involving price-fixing or other anticompetitive requirements is sufficient grounds to terminate.[81] As stated earlier, you need solid documentation of your reasons. Then do the following:

- Give the proper notice required by your contract; if length of notice is not specified in the contract, give the longest reasonable notice.

- Consider whether to give objective reasons for the termination to document your just cause or to give no reason, relying on your contract provisions.

- Allow the distributor to complete all short-term agreements on which it acted in reliance. Show you're attempting to minimize any financial losses for the distributor.

☐ *Is our product inherently dangerous?* The uniqueness of a product may justify vertical restraints. Restrictions on resale of potentially dangerous products may be justified to protect the public from harm and to protect the firm from potential product liability (discussed in Section I). For any exposure in this area you must consult your counsel.

☐ *Is the product essentially safe with certain safeguards we must control?* Where health and safety concerns (as well as adverse publicity and legal exposure) can be clearly shown by the manufacturer, distributors and sellers may be required to carefully abide by the firm's specifications as to resale restrictions.[82]

☐ *Is the product highly perishable?* Under a rule of reason analysis, vertical restrictions employed to protect the quality of a product (and therefore the commercial reputation of its producer), such as one which is highly perishable, would in the absence of anticompetitive intent most likely be upheld.

☐ *Is the product protected by patent or trademark?* If so, the restriction reasonably necessary to protect the integrity of the patent and/or trademark may be justifiable, as distinguished from collateral restrictions relating to price or other competitive factors.[83]

☐ *Are there specific legal requirements as to the method of distribution?* Specific legal requirements as to the method of distribution (for example, under the Magnuson-Moss Consumer Products Warranties Act or as required by the Consumer Product Safety Commission) are compelling arguments for the particular distribution plan chosen. In general, this is applicable only in specialized situations involving licensed dealers, such as those who sell prescription drugs or alcoholic beverages.

☐ *Are there any other relevant factors in the nature of our market?* Carefully analyze with your counsel your distribution plan in light of any particularly unique characteristics of the product and/or firm which would further justify the use of a distribution system employing vertical territorial restrictions. The need to ensure prompt and skillful after-sale service for machinery might be strong grounds to demonstrate that the restrictions had sufficient potential to improve interbrand competition.[84]

☐ *Could we establish a consignment, agency, or franchise relationship to justify distributor restrictions nominally questionable in arm's-length transactions?* These arrangements, if challenged, must still be defensible under the rule of reason. Examine the various alternatives to determine which will best suit the needs of your firm and will survive a legal challenge.

☐ *Have we detailed any necessary investment in capital or labor required by the retailer to market the product efficiently and safely, therefore necessitating our territorial restrictions?* Although not yet a recognized defense, it might be helpful to argue that in order for your firm to protect its investment, it was necessary to create a distribution system employing vertical territorial restrictions. Keep detailed and accurate records of all such investments as well as the marketing strategy necessitating the restrictions in anticipation of any litigious challenges.

☐ *What is our exposure if we operate a dual-distribution plan?* In a dual distribution system, the manufacturer is both a supplier and a competitor. It sees it can create some distribution more cheaply than other dealers but at the same time sees potential retail costs as a constraint in other areas of distribution. So a dual system is created. An issue of characterization is presented as there is both a vertical relationship[85] and a horizontal one (manufacturer is in direct or potential competition with its distributors).[86]

A landmark case (though no longer in favor) involved Holiday Inns'[87] method of franchising. Holiday Inns operated approximately 300 motels internally and franchised another 1,100 motels under the Holiday Inn service mark. To protect its own company-owned motel operations, it refused to franchise independents in areas where company-owned units already existed.[88] It also sent a letter to the three nearest existing franchisees and solicited comments on proposed franchisees. In addition, its franchise agreements expressly prohibited its franchisees from operating non-Holiday Inn motels without prior permission.[89] An objection by one or more carried near-veto power.

The court held that the combination of these practices constituted a horizontal conspiracy between Holiday Inn, "operating on the retail level as a motel-operator," and its motel franchisees.[90] The "horizontal" label was summarily attached to the restrictions on the ground that Holiday Inn, "in one of its capacities" was "dealing on the same market level as its franchisees."[91]

The clear trend since has been to adopt a more flexible approach which stresses a rule of reason unless the horizontal aspect is the controlling one as to *both* design *and* purpose.[92] As with all restraints, be prepared to demonstrate its competitive value to interbrand competition while minimizing its impact on intrabrand competition.

☐ *Will the U.S. Department of Justice's Antitrust Guidelines radically alter the trends in this area in the future?* All 50 State Attorney Generals have unanimously refused to follow these Guidelines! This may actually lead to a less uniform pattern of holdings in the future.

Conclusion

The foregoing checklist is not meant to be a comprehensive study of the legal implications of vertical territorial restrictions. Rather, it provides food for thought and a brief overview of the major factors examined when a distribution program employing such restrictions is tested using the rule of reason. You should design the program to be cost-effective as well as efficient. Likewise you should attempt to "litigation-proof" your exposure to distributors by emphasis on proper documentation. Be able to demonstrate that:

- any distributional change or decision to impose vertical restrictions was made by your firm acting alone (unilaterally); and
- there is no intent to impose any restriction on resale prices.

The good news is that since *Sylvania* almost every challenge to a *non*-price vertical restraint was upheld. If you avoid a price restraint or dealer cartel your restriction should also be upheld. However, since this area historically is fluid and subject to differences of persuasion, any distribution program incorporating territorial restrictions should be reviewed by your counsel, preferably annually and certainly when modifications are undertaken.[93]

ENDNOTES

(1) *Northern Pacific Railway Co. v. United States,* 356 US 1, 5 (1958).

(2) 310 US 150 (1940).

(3) 85 F.271, *aff'd,* 175 US 211 (1899).

(4) 312 US 457 (1941).

(5) 322 US 392 (1947). One should also consider the comment by Justice Stevens that once the Court establishes a per se rule, only Congress may alter the rule. See *Arizona v. Maricopa County Medical Society,* 457 US 332, 454-55 (1982) (Court condemned a horizontal arrangement even on the assumption it saved consumers millions of dollars).

(6) *Board of Trade of the City of Chicago v. United States,* 246 US 231, 238 (1918). See also *National Society of Professional Engineers v. United States,* 435 US 679, 688 (1978) (purpose of the rule of reason analysis is to form a judgment about the competitive significance of the restraint) and *U.S. v. Penn-Olin Chemical Co.,* 378 US 158, 176-77 (1964).

(7) 433 US 36, 53 (1977).

(8) Id.

(9) *Timken Roller Bearing Co. v. United States,* 341 US 593 (1951). See also *Abadir & Co. v. First Mississippi Corp.,* 651 F.2d 422, 427, n.5 (5th Cir. 1981) (market-distributing agreements which are initiated by distributors are horizontal even if the supplier is nominally a party to the contract); *P. Stone, Inc. v. Koppers Corp.,* 631 F.2d 241 (1980) and *U.S. v. Topco Assoc., Inc.,* 405 US 596 (1972).

(10) Id. and *United States v. Sealy, Inc.,* 388 US 352 (1967). See also *Jayco Systems v. Savin Business Machines Corp.,* 777 F.2d 306 (5th Cir. 1985); but contrast to *Broadcast Music, Inc. v. CBS, Inc.,* 441 US 1 (1979) (a combination of horizontal competitors in the creation and licensing of musical compositions was examined under the rule of reason where defendants presented substantial evidence that the challenged combination was absolutely necessary to the creation and marketing of its products).

(11) *Continental TV, Inc. v. GTE Sylvania, Inc.,* 433 US 36 (1977). See also *Zidill Explorations, Inc. v. Conval Intern. Ltd.,* 719 F.2d 1465, 1470 (1983).

(12) See note 9 — *Timken* .

(13) *Monsanto Co. v. Spray-Rite Service Corp.,* 104 S.Ct. 1464, 79 L.Ed.2d 775 (1984) (see discussion in introduction to this section). See also *Helicopter Support Systems, Inc. v. Hughes Helicopter, Inc.,* 818 F.2d 1530 (11th Cir. 1987) and *Beach v. Viking Sewing Machine Co.,* 784 F.2d 746 (6th Cir.).

(14) Id. See also *Albrecht v. Herald Co.,* 390 US 145, 151-53, 88 S.Ct. 869, 872-73, 19 L.Ed.2d 998 (1968); *United States v. Parke, Davis & Co.,* 362 US 29, 47, 80 S.Ct. 503, 513, 4 L.Ed.2d 505 (1960); *Kiefer-Stewart Co. v. Joseph E. Seagram & Sons, Inc.,* 340 US 211, 213, 71 S.Ct. 259, 260, 95 L.Ed. 219 (1951).

(15) *Dr. Miles Medical Co. v. John D. Park & Sons Co.,* 220 US 373, 31 S.Ct. 376, 55 L.Ed.502 (1911).

(16) See note 13 plus *Edward J. Sweeney & Sons, Inc. v. Texaco, Inc.,* 637 F.2d 105, 111 (3d Cir. 1980), *aff'd.,* 478 F.Supp 243, 259 (E.D.Pa. 1979); *Mowery v. Standard Oil Company of Ohio,* 463 F.Supp. 762, 767 (N.D.Ohio 1976), *aff'd.,* 590 F.2d 335 (6th Cir. 1978).

(17) *Carlson Machine Tools, Inc. v. American Tool, Inc.* 678 F.2d 1253, 1261 (5th Cir. 1982); *Yentsch v. Texaco, Inc.,* 630 F.2d 46, 52-54 (2d Cir. 1980); *Santa Clara Valley Distributing Co., Inc. v. Pabst Brewing Co.,* 556 F.2d 942, 945 (9th Cir. 1977); *Hanson v. Shell Oil Co.,* 541 F.2d 1352, 1356 (9th Cir. 1976), *cert. den.,* 429 US 1074, 97 S.Ct. 813, 50 L. Ed. 2d 792 (1977).

(18) *Binder v. Southland Corp.,* 749 F.2d 1205, 1213 (1984); *Newberry v. Washington Post Co.,* 438 F.Supp. 470, 479 (D.D.C. 1977). See also *Skokie Gold Standard Liquors, Inc. v. Joseph Seagram & Sons* , 692 F.2d 759 (7th Cir. 1982).

(19) *In re Coordinated Pretrial Proceedings in Petroleum Products Antitrust Litigation,* 691 F.2d 1335, 1343 (9th Cir. 1982).

(20) *U.S. v. Colgate & Co.,* 250 US 300 (1919). See also *U.S. v. General Electric Co.* (resale price maintenance not illegal as to consignment sales).

(21) *FTC v. Beech-Nut Packing Co.,* 257 US 441 (1922).

(22) *General Cinema Corp. v. Buena Vista Distribution Co., Inc.* , 681 F.2d 594, 596 (9th Cir. 1982); *Belk-Avery, Inc. v. Henry I. Siegel Co. Inc.,* 457 F.Supp. 1330, 1336 (M.D. Ala. 1978).

(23) *Yentsch v. Texaco, Inc.,* 630 F.2d 46, 51-52 (2d Cir. 1980).

(24) *Susser v. Carvel Corp.,* 332 F.2d 505 (2d Cir 1964), *cert. den.,* 381 US 125 (1965).

(25) *Sargent-Welch Scientific Co. v. Ventron Corp.,* 567 F.2d 701, 707 (7th Cir. 1977), *cert. den.,* 439 US 822 (1978).

(26) *In re Nissan Antitrust Litigation,* 577 F.2d 910 (5th Cir. 1978), *cert. denied,* 439 US 1072 (1979).

(27) *Westinghouse Electronics Corp. v. CS Processing Laboratories,* 523 F.2d 668, 675-76 (9th Cir. 1975).

(28) See note 3 above.

(29) See, e.g., *Northwest Stationers v. Pacific Stationery,* 472 US, 105 S.Ct. 2613, 2620, 86 L.Ed.2d 202 (1985) (requires a showing of dominance in both the defined product and geographic markets). See also *Silver v. N.Y. Stock Exchange,* 373 US 341 (1963).

(30) Id., 105 S.Ct. at 2619-20, 861 L.Ed. 2d at 211 (1985).

(31) *Carlson Machine Tools, Inc. v. American Tool, Inc.,* 678 F.2d 1253, 1259 (1982).

(32) See note 29.

(33) *Gordon v. N. Y. Stock Exchange,* 422 US 659 (1975). See also *National Society of Professional Engineers v. U.S.,* 435 US 679 (1978) (per se standard should be applied sparingly to rules adopted by professional associations).

(34) *Denver Rockets v. All-Pro Management, Inc.,* 325 F.Supp. 1049, 1064 (C.D. Cal. 1971).

(35) *McCreery Angus Farms v. American Angus Ass'n.,* 379 F.Supp. 1008, 1018 (S.D. Ill. 1974), aff'd, 506 F.2d 1404 (7th Cir); *Villani v. N.Y. Stock Exchange,* 348 F.Supp. 1185 (S.D.N.Y. 1972).

(36) *FTC v. Indiana Federation of Dentists,* 54 USLW 4531 (1986).

(37) *In re Indiana Federation of Dentists,* 101 FTC 57 (1983).

(38) Id., p. 124.

(39) *Indiana Federation of Dentists v. FTC,* 745 F.2d 1124, 1144 (1984).

(40) see note 36, p. 4534.

(41) Id.

(42) See note 4. See also *Olsen v. Progressive Music Supply, Inc.,* 703 F.2d 432 (10th Cir. 1983), cert. den. 464 US 866, 104 S.Ct. 197, 78 L.Ed.2d 172 (1984) and *Gould v. Control Laser Corp.,* 462 F.Supp. 685 (M.D. Fla, 1978), aff'd, 650 F.2d 617 (5th Cir. 1981).

(43) See notes 33 and 36. See also *Reazin v. Blue Cross & Blue Shield of Kansas, Inc.,* 635 F.Supp. 1287, 1322-28 (D.Kan. 1986) and *U.S. v. Insurance Board of Cleveland,* 144 F.Supp. 684 (N.D. Ohio 1956).

(44) *Jack Kahn Music Co. v. Baldwin Piano & Organ Co.,* 604 F.2d 755 (2d Cir. 1979); *Gate Acceptance Corp. v. General Motors Corp.,* 597 F.2d 676 (9th Cir. 1979); *Salco Corp. v. General Motors Corp.,* 517 F.2d 567 (10th Cir. 1975); *Kaiser v. General Motors Corp.,* 396 F.Supp. 33 (E.D. Pa. 1975), aff'd per curiam, 530 F.2d 964 (3d Cir. 1976).

(45) *Kestenbaum v. Falstaff Brewing Corp.,* 575 F.2d 564, 572-73 (5th Cir. 1978), cert. den. 440 US 909 (1979); *Santa Clara Valley Distrib. Co. v. Pabst Brewing Co.,* 556 F.2d 942 (9th Cir. 1977); *Knutson v. Daily Review, Inc.,* 548 F.2d 795, 807-810 (9th Cir. 1976), cert. den., 433 US 910 (1977); *Colorado Pump & Supply Co. v. Febco, Inc.,* 472 F.2d 637 (10th Cir.), cert. den., 411 US 987 (1973).

(46) *Ohio-Sealy Mattress Mfg. Co. v. Sealy, Inc.,* 585 F.2d 821 (7th Cir. 1978), cert. den., 440 US 930 (1979).

(47) *Graphic Products Distributors v. Itek Corp.,* 717 F.2d 1560, 1572 (1983).

(48) See *Com-Tel, Inc. v. DuKane Corp.,* 669 F.2d 404, 412 (6th Cir. 1982); *Cernuto, Inc. v. United Cabinet Corp.,* 595 F.2d 164, 166 n. 11 (3d Cir. 1979). See also *Business Electronics Corp. v. Sharp Electronics Corp.,* 780 F.2d 1212 (5th Cir. 1986), cert. granted, 55 U.S.L.W. 3815 (1987).

(49) *Eiberger v. Sony Corp.,* 622 F.2d 1068, 1076 (2d Cir. 1920).

(50) See *U.S. v. Waste Management, Inc.,* 743 F.2d 976, 984 (1984) (large share may not reflect future market power, while 70% - 75% market share during relevant period plus strong product differentiation will sustain threshold requirements); see also Landes and Posner, "Market Power in Antitrust Cases," 94 *Harvard Law Review* 937 (1981).

(51) *U.S. v. Colgate & Co.,* 250 US 300, 307 (1919).

(52) Lappen, Alyssa A., "Revolt of the Reps," *Forbes,* Sept. 1, 1985, p. 51.

(53) *Bloor v. Flastaff Brewing Corp.,* 601 F.2d 609 (2d Cir. 1979).

(54) See note 13, p. 1471.

(55) *World of Sleep v. La-Z-Boy Chair Co.,* 765 F.2d 1467 (10th Cir. 1985).

(56) *R.E. Spriggs Co. v. Adolph Coors Co.,* 156 Cal. Rptr. 738, 94 Cal. 3d 419 (1979).

(57) *Excello Wine Co. v. Monsieur Henri Wines,,* 474 F.Supp. 203, 210 (1979). See also *Hood v. Tenneco Texas Life Insurance Co.* , 739 F.2d 1012 (1984).

(58) *Muenster Butone, Inc. v. Stewart Co.,* 651 F.2d 292 (5th Cir. 1981). See also *Valley Liquors, Inc. v. Renfield Importers, Ltd.,* 678 F.2d 742 (7th Cir. 1982).

(59) *Pierce v. Ramsey Winch Co.,* 753 F.2d 416 (5th Cir. 1985) or *Landmark Development Corp. v. Chambers Corp.,* 752 F.2d 369 (9th Cir. 1985).

(60) *Oreck Co. v. Whirlpool Corp.,* 579 F.2d 126 (2d Cir. 1978), cert. den., 439 US 946, 99 S.Ct. 340 (1979). See also *Valley Liquors, Inc. v. Renfield Importers, Ltd.,* 822 F.2d 656 (7th Cir. 1987). *Gregoris Motors v. Nissan Motor Corp. in USA,* 630 F.Supp. 902 (E.D.N.Y. 1986); *Daniels v. All Steel Equipment, Inc.,* 590 F.2d 111 (1979) and *Gilchrist Machinery Co., Inc. v. Komatsu America Corp.,* 601 F.Supp. 1192, 1201, (S.D. Miss. 1984).

(61) See note 31.

(62) *Nifty Foods Corp. v. A & P,* 614 F.2d 832, 842 (1980).

(63) *First National Bank v. Cities Service Co.,* 391 US 253 (1968).

(64) *Blair Foods, Inc. v. Ronchers Cotton Oil,* 610 F.2d 665 (1980).

(65) *Donald B. Rice Tire v. Michelin Tire Corp.,* 483 F.Supp. 750 (D. Md. 1980), *aff'd,* 638 F.2d 15 (4th Cir.), *cert. denied* , 102 S.Ct. 324 (1981). See also *Eiberger v. Sony Corp. of America* , 622 F.2d 1068, 1080, n. 23 (2d Cir. 1980).

(66) See note 11, p. 53.

(67) *U.S. v. Aluminum Co. of America,* 148 F.2d 416 (1945).

(68) *Greyhound Computer Corp. v. IBM,* 559 F.2d 488, 492 (9th Cir. 1977).

(69) *United States v. Grinnell Corp.,* 384 US 563 (1966).

(70) *Adolph Coors Co. v. FTC,* 497 F.2d 1178 (10th Cir. 1974), cert. den., 419 US 1105 (1975).

(71) But see *Munsters Corp. v. Burgess Industries Inc.,* 450 F.Supp. 1196 (S.D.N.Y. 1978) (rejection of market penetration rationale).

(72) See note 11.

(73) Id.

(74) *United States v. O.M. Scott & Sons Co.,* 303 F.Supp. 141 (D.D.C. 1969).

(75) *Eastern Scientific Co. v. Wild Heerburgg Instruments, Inc.* , 572 F.2d 833 (1st Cir. 1978) (CA-119781), cert. den., 439 US 833 (1978).

(76) Id., p. 885.

(77) Id., pp. 885-86.

(78) *Klor's Inc. v. Broadway-Hal Stores,* 359 US 207 (1959). See also *United States v. General Motors,* 384 US 127 (1966) and *Montague & Co. v. Lowry,* 193 US 38 (1904).

(79) See note 9.

(80) *United States v. American Can Co.,* 87 F.Supp. 18 (N.D. Cal. 1949). See also note 1.

(81) See notes 5 and 6.

(82) *Clairol, Inc. v. Boston Discount Center of Berkeley,* 608 F.2d 1114 (1979) (cosmetics).

(83) *United States v. General Electric Co.,* 358 F.Supp. 141 (D.D.C. 1969). See also note 69.

(84) *Copy-Data Sys., Inc. v. Toshiba America, Inc.,* 663 F.2d 405, 408-09 (2d Cir. 1981).

(85) See note 65, *Rice Tire* . See also *Reed Diamond Supply, Inc. v. Liquid Carbonic Corp.,* 637 F.2d 1001, 1004-07 (5th Cir.), *cert. den.,* 102 SCt 119 (1981) and *Abadir & Co. v. First Mississippi Corp.,* 651 F.2d 422, 427 (5th Cir. 1981) and *FTC v. Coca-Cola Co.,* 91 FTC 517 (1978), rev'd on other grounds, 642 F.2d 1387 (D.C. Cir. 1981).

(86) *Fortuna Aviation, Inc. v. Beech Aircraft Corp.,* 432 F.2d 1080 (7th Cir. 1970).

(87) *America Motor Inns, Inc. v. Holiday Inns, Inc.,* 521 F.2d 1230 (3d Cir. 1975). See also *In re Amway Corp.,* 93 FTC 618 (1979); *Pitchford v. PEPI, Inc.,* 531 F.2d 92, 104 (3d Cir. 1975), cert. den., 96 S.Ct. 2649 (1975); *Interphoto Corp. v. Minolta Corp.* , 417 F.2d 621 (2d Cir. 1969).

(88) Id., p.1239.

(89) Id., p.1238.

(90) Id., p. 1253.

(91) Id., p. 1254.

(92) *Dart Indus., Inc. v. Plunkett Co.,* 704 F.2d 496, 498-99 (10th Cir. 1983); *Davis-Watkins Co. v. Service Merchandise,* 686 F.2d 1190, 1201-02 (6th Cir. 1982), *cert. den. sub nom., Service Merchandise Co. v. Amana Refrigeration, Inc.,* 104 S.Ct. 1718 (1984). See also *Krehl v. Baskin-Robbins Ice Cream Co.,* 664 F.2d 1348 (9th Cir. 1982); *Barnosky Oils, Inc. v. Union Oil of California,* 665 F.2d 74, 80, n. 10 (6th Cir. 1981); *H & B Equipment Co. v. International Harvester Co.,* 577 F.2d 239 (5th Cir. 1978). See also Section 2.2 and 2.3 of the Justice Department's Vertical Guidelines.

(93) For an article on point, see Robert J. Posch, Jr. and Dr. Saul Sands, "Legal Ramifications of Vertical Territorial Restrictive Distribution Plans for the 1980s," *Journal of Marketing,* Summer 1982, pp. 38-43.

CHAPTER 7

WHAT YOU NEED TO KNOW ABOUT PHYSICAL HANDLING RELATIONSHIPS

One unglamorous area of marketing involves the various physical handling relationships which make up your unique distribution process. You should be concerned about the safe storage and warehousing of your goods during the distribution process. This chapter will take a broad look at bailments, so that you can spot legal issues and discuss them with your counsel before they spell trouble and before you have to be bailed out of a tight spot!

What Kind of Transfer Is Your Transaction?

You've heard the term "bailment." Is a bailment a contract? Yes. Is it a sale? No. Bailments are important in the warehousing and storage of your goods at every stage of the distribution process. For your purposes, a bailment is the relationship created by the transfer of *possession* (not title) of an item of *personal* property[1] by one, the bailor, to another, the bailee, for the accomplishment of a particular purpose. Whenever you transfer, lend, or store personal property to or for another, think bailment.

Your best clue as to whether a bailment relationship exists is whether the identical article is to be returned in the same or in an agreed-on altered form. If another thing of equal value is to be returned, the transaction is a sale. Examples of bailments include your product's being stored in a warehouse pending sale or a dairy farmer's transferring milk to receive back milk or cheese.

Legal Elements of the Generic Bailment .   Any kind of *personal* property may be the subject of a bailment. A bailment is the delivery of personal property by one person (the bailor) to another person (the bailee) who accepts it and is under an express or implied agreement to return it to the bailor or to someone designated by the bailor. The essential elements are:

- the bailor has title to or the right to possess the item of property;
- possession and temporary control of the property must be given to the bailee; and
- the bailee must owe a duty to return the property as directed by the bailor or when the purpose of the bailment is complete depending on the terms of the creation of the bailment.

Creation of Relation. As a general rule, a bailment is created by an express or implied contract. Whether or not a bailment exists must be determined from all the facts and circumstances of the particular situation. Generally there are three classifications of bailments:

- bailments for the sole benefit of the bailor,
- bailments for the sole benefit of the bailee, and
- mutual benefit bailments.

The type of bailment may be important in determining the liability of the bailee for loss of or damages to the property. A broader classification frequently observed in terminology describes a bailment as a gratuitous bailment or one for compensation or hire. Bailments sometimes arise without any agreement between the parties, as when a person holds possession of personal property under such circumstances that the law imposes on him the obligation to deliver it to another. This is called a constructive bailment. We'll briefly take a look at their definitions and distinguishments.

Bailment for Sole Benefit of Bailor. A bailment for the sole benefit of the bailor is one in which the bailee renders some service but does not receive a benefit in return. For example, you allow a neighbor to park her car in your garage while she is on vacation and she does not pay you anything. The neighbor (bailor) has received a benefit from you (bailee), but you have not received a benefit from them in return. In such gratuitous bailments, the bailee is liable only for gross negligence — which would be an intentional failure to carry out a manifest duty in reckless disregard of the consequences.[2] Only in the event of an emergency is such bailee required to take steps of ordinary prudence for the preservation of the property as the emergency may require. The bailee is obligated to explain a failure to return the property as such failure establishes a prima facie case of gross negligence.

Bailment for Sole Benefit of Bailee. Here the owner of the goods allows someone else to use them free of charge, e.g., you lend a ladder to your neighbor. The bailor owes only the duty of giving warning of any defects of which he or she has knowledge and which in reasonable probability would imperil the user.[3] You can hold your neighbor to a high standard of care and (in an ideal neighborhood) can receive compensation for damage to your ladder resulting from even slight negligence. If, however, the property is stolen or damaged by another, the bailee is usually not liable if he or she can be proven to have exercised the standard of care required.

Mutual Benefit Bailments.   This is the most common situation. If both the bailee and the bailor receive benefits from the bailment, it is a mutual benefit bailment. Consider bringing your car to the service station for repairs. In return for payment by you (bailor) the bailee is obligated to exercise that degree of care which you, yourself (as owner) would exercise under the same circumstances.

He is under a legal obligation to redeliver the article (car) exactly as received with the improvements, if any, contracted for. Failure to so deliver may result in the legal action of conversion. In general, for all mutual bailments, the standard of care for the bailee is that which a reasonable owner of the goods would exercise under the same circumstances for the protection and preservation of the product and its special characteristics, if any (e.g., perishability).

Finally, there is the ambiguous status of the *"constructive bailment."* A person who, in the absence of a mutual contract of bailment, lawfully acquires the possession of another's personal property is generally considered to be a constructive bailee. A constructive bailee is a person who acquires possession of another's property by mistake, accident, or through force of circumstances under which the law imposes on him the duties of a bailee. Such bailment is ordinarily considered gratuitous, if there is no reasonable basis for implying an intent of mutual benefit. A finder of lost property is a typical case of gratuitous bailee.[4]

For all bailments, a bailee has a right of possession of the article committed to his charge and may institute a suit to recover against everybody but the owner, and can deliver it only to the owner or someone authorized by him to take it.

Action for Conversion.   You'll see this tort discussed a lot in the bailment area. Conversion is a tort consisting of a *distinct act* of dominion wrongfully exerted over another's *tangible, personal property* in denial of or inconsistent with his title or rights therein, or in derogation, exclusion, or defiance of such title or rights. There is a conversion when a person does such acts in reference to the personal property of another as amount to the appropriation of the property to himself and a denial or violation of the plaintiff's dominion over or rights in the property. Some affirmative act on the part of the defendant is usually regarded as necessary to constitute a conversion. Neither a mere intention to do a particular act nor a wrongful assertion of ownership is ordinarily enough to support an action for conversion.

The motive with which the defendant acts is generally immaterial. Liability in such an action does not depend on the defendant's knowledge or intent, and it is generally immaterial that he or she acted without malice and in good faith or in ignorance of the plaintiff's interest in the property.

Now let's see how this all affects your daily, personal life.

Bailments in Your Personal Life

Do bailments sound complicated? You probably engage in these transactions daily in your personal life. You are a bailor and your bank a bailee each time you place an item in your safe deposit box. The last time you left your watch for repair at the jeweler's or your suit at the cleaners, you entered a bailment relationship. As such, those businesses are responsible for the property (e.g., the contents of the box, the watch, or the suit). The bailee is obligated to use due care and to come forward and explain loss or damages to the property entrusted to it. Conversely, a *lien* is created for rental or work (e.g., the watch) until payment is tendered. However, persons engaged in some of these occupations may be held liable in contract for acts of their employees even if those employees act outside the scope of their duties.[5]

Perhaps the last time you went to the city it was impossible to find a parking spot. Finally, you found a parking lot, and were grateful to just dump the auto with the attendant. What took place? If you parked your car in the parking lot, you may be merely renting parking space or you may be a bailor! Did you retain your keys? If so, you are probably renting space. If the attendant (bailee) retained your keys, then you have a bailment. The bailee is expected to exercise the degree of care over your car which a reasonable owner of such automobile would exercise under the same circumstances for its protection. Further, there is a similar obligation of care as to all items reasonably expected to be in your car (such as a spare tire or jack) but not as to items not expected to be in a car (such as a coat). While the garage is liable for damage, it may not be liable for auto theft since such theft is outside the scope of employment.[6]

What if the small print on the back of your ticket exempts the garage or lot from negligence? In many states this will fail if the parking facility has the capacity to park four or more vehicles.[7] However, if you tell the Court you make it a practice never to inform the garage of your contents you'll walk away empty-handed.[8]

If you stopped at a hotel and the hotel's service people park your car with the actual authority of the hotel and took your keys, the vehicle *and* its contents were accepted by the hotel. The hotel could reasonably anticipate that people in transit would leave luggage, apparel and other personal belongings in the car not necessary for a night's lodging.[9] This may not hold true for a week's stay at a resort.

What if you skipped the lot and the hotel and just went to a nice restaurant featuring valet parking? You pull up to your restaurant and give the keys to the attendant, so you have a bailment. You enter the restaurant, sit down, and hang your coat on a hook in close proximity to your seat. There was no bailment as to the coat, since you could take the coat at any time and the restaurant owner exercised no control over it.

This is true even if your waiter helped you remove it and hung it up for you.[10] But, if the owner operated a checkroom to which you delivered your coat and received a receipt, a bailment was created, although liability might be limited by statute.[11] This protection may be less for an owner who allows a private concessionaire to operate the checkroom.[12]

Say you have mink coats and fine drapes, which you store in a warehouse, and for which you get a receipt. Here you have to watch out for hidden exculpatory language. By law, "[d]amages may be limited by a term in the warehouse receipt or storage agreement limiting the amount of liability in case of loss or damage, and setting forth a specific liability per article or item, or value per unit of weight, beyond which the warehouseman shall not be liable."[13] The bailee can't contract away his or her duty of care, but he or she can limit it. If it's not conspicuous, your mink's loss can't be limited to $100 or some other paltry sum.[14] This case applied the standard contract formation analysis to determine whether the limitation is part of the contract. Another court took it further and spelled out what facts are relevant to determine the reasonableness of a bailee's belief that a fur storage (or similar property) agreement limited the bailee's liability. The Court set up seven criteria:

- Whether bailee notified bailor of the limitation;
- The conspicuousness of the limitation;
- The intelligibility of the language of the limitation provision to a lay person;
- Whether bailor signed the storage receipt;
- Whether bailor assented to the limitation of valuation;
- The status of the bailor as business person or lay person; and
- The purpose of the limitation.[15]

Putting all of the above elements together, the Court held for the bailor as follows:

> In this case, bailee did not discuss the valuation with bailor, nor did he notify her of the limitation. He did not ask her to read or sign the receipt, and she did neither. The limitation is inconspicuously placed in the midst of a lengthy paragraph printed in small type. A lay person may not readily understand the import of the limitation provision, which is couched in legalese and which by its terms refers to bailor's representations as to the value of the article stored. Bailor is a lay person, not a business person chargeable with the general knowledge that bailment contracts often contain liability limitations. Bailee arbitrarily limited a known risk, as opposed to sheltering himself from an undisclosed, extraordinary risk. Although the $100 valuation clearly appears on the face of the receipt, this at most created a jury question as to whether bailor's failure to object to, or inquire about, the valuation was so unreasonable as to justify the reasonable belief that bailor thereby agreed to the limitation. . .

> . . .We conclude that under all the circumstances of this case, bailor's conduct did not manifest or assent to the terms and conditions of the

receipt. The limitation of bailee's liability for negligent care of the mink, therefore, is unenforceable.[16]

Similarly, if someone inspects your drapes, states he can clean them and proceeds to do so, any damage to the drapes in the bailee's custody is his fault even if he asserts it was due to their age or wear and tear:[17]

Having satisfied himself the fabric had sufficient strength to withstand cleaning, Pringle accepted the drapes. His unqualified acceptance was an implied assurance to the plaintiff-customer that the drapes could withstand the cleaning process to which they would be subjected. It created the relationship of a bailment for hire between the parties, thereby imposing upon the defendant the duty of diligent care of a prudent administrator as exacted.[18]

Bailments in Your Business Life

Now that you know what a bailment is and how it operates in your personal life, let's review some common bailment relationships your product may pass through between your firm and your customer.

Warehouse

Warehousing is a business engaged in storing goods for hire.[19] As you will note throughout this book, society grants greater legal protection to an individual consumer, and seeks to protect those with unequal bargaining power.[20] In a commercial warehousing relationship, the law will presume parity of arm's-length bargaining. Therefore, your warehouse representative may try to limit its duty of care. Without such a limit, the warehouser must exercise such care as a reasonable person would under such circumstances but, *unless otherwise agreed,* "is not liable for damages which would not have been avoided by the exercise of such care."[21] Your warehouse may also limit its liability for other damages in writing in the receipt or storage agreement. However, you have the right to request in writing that the warehouse increase its liability on all or part of your goods. The warehouse must honor this written request although it has the right to increase its rates based on the increased valuations.[22]

Therefore, it is incumbent on you not to treat the receipt or storage agreement as a nonnegotiable "boilerplate" agreement. Carefully review the small print with your counsel. Discuss the minimum protection you need (consider your current insurance protection), and have your attorney draft an agreement accordingly. The added psychological value, plus stressing the goods' value and your desire to protect them, might in and of itself encourage greater vigilance at the warehouse.

What other contractual issues should you be on the lookout for? (See "Generic Contract" in Section VIII as well as the Glossary of Terms for some "shorthand" below.) The following checklist will help.

☐ Generally, you want to make sure the warehouse is an independent contractor and not in any way your agent.

☐ You want to specify all the merchandise (with estimated value of all items) you are warehousing and that you will retain title.

☐ The merchandise will not be transferred or delivered to anyone without your prior written consent.

☐ No assignment by the warehouse is permitted without your prior written permission and __ days notice.

☐ No merchandise will be removed from the address specified without your prior written consent even if there is no assignment — just an internal move.

☐ You will have the right to inspect the warehouse and your goods, including a physical count of your goods.

☐ Your goods will be stored in an area specifically designated for the purpose and will not be mixed with any other inventory.

☐ You will receive a warranty that the warehouse will use its best efforts to prevent and indemnify you against unexplained shortages, theft or other destruction from any and all causes.

☐ Because an indemnification doesn't help you as to lost goodwill, failure to comply with the Thirty Day Rule (see chapter on Direct Marketing) or a host of other eventualities you may consider a liquidated damages provision here as well as indemnification.

☐ You'll want to examine their fire and other applicable insurance policies, make it an express part of the agreement, and have the insurer agree to give you 30 days notice prior to cancellation or lapse (or whatever your reasonable termination period is).

☐ A termination period which will allow you to transfer your goods with a minimum of dislocation.

☐ The usual boilerplate as to governing law, integration clause, etc. (Again, see "Generic Contract" in Section VIII.)

☐ All warranties, representations and indemnities (where applicable) should survive termination of the agreement.

Prior to making any important warehousing arrangement or other similar agreement, check the firm out with a Dun & Bradstreet or similar report. The quality of the firm you're doing business with is at least as important as the quality of your contract.

A warehouse is a professional bailee.[23] Warehouses make it their living or principle business to act as a bailee and deal with the public on a uniform (and not individual) basis. Such "professional" bailees impose predetermined conditions on bailors whose bargaining power lacks parity with such bailees. Depending on your size and expertise, the courts may treat you favorably in a dispute vis a vis a professional bailee and a limitation of liability clause.[24] One clause such bailees frequently impose is a limitation on the time you may recover for a loss. These are legal so long as they are printed or placed in the contract, where they can be seen (by a nonprofessional) or negotiated in somewhere with a firm at arm's length.[25]

If you end up with a warehouse full of merchandise, financing costs alone may doom you! However, don't expect any indulgences from your warehouse owner since he or she faces the same interest rate problems.

Before the goods have been stored, be prepared to pay in advance (unless otherwise agreed to in writing) to have your goods released to you or placed on a carrier. Again, the agreement controls. The warehouse owner has a legal right or lien to retain your goods until storage, transportation, insurance, labor, or other agreed-on charges in relation to the goods are paid for.[26] The warehouse will be loath to release the goods to you because the lien is lost on voluntary delivery to you.[27] You probably wouldn't even consider going to the dry cleaner's to pick up your suit if you didn't have the necessary cash to pay for it! In addition to this lien, the warehouse has all other legal remedies afforded to a creditor against a debtor.[28]

As to damages, the UCC states:

> Damages may be limited by a term in the warehouse receipt or storage agreement limiting the amount of liability in case of loss or damage, and setting forth a specific liability per article or item, or value per unit of weight, beyond which the warehouseman shall not be liable; provided, however, that such liability may be on written request of the bailor at the time of signing such storage agreement or within a reasonable time after receipt of the warehouse receipt be increased. . .in which event increased rates may be charged based on such increased valuation. . .No such limitation is effective with respect to the warehouseman's liability for conversion to his own use.[29]

How do you establish conversion by the warehouse? Here you must establish proof of delivery to the warehouseman and his failure to return your property on proper demand. The warehouseman must then come forward with evidence sufficient to prove that the failure to return the goods was not the result of conversion.

If the warehouseman has no evidence or loses on the merits, you can recover two forms of damages: direct damages in the form of loss or injury to your goods themselves; you may also be able to recover consequential damages, such as lost profits. The latter is particularly important to, among others, seasonal sellers.[30]

Common Carriers

A common carrier[31] takes goods from anyone in return for payment[32] up to the capacity of its facilities with certain exceptions, such as lack of correct packaging,[33] the goods are not of the character and description ordinarily carried by them, or other circumstances. Common carriers are often licensed by government agencies. They are usually permitted to limit their liability to a stated value unless the bailor declares a higher value for the property and pays an additional fee. They also have a lien on the goods themselves for freight and for advances made to other carriers and may hold them until this is paid.

The common carrier is distinguishable from a private carrier (also a bailee), which may be more selective as to users. The liability of a private carrier is limited to negligence. The common carrier, however, is an *absolute insurer* of your goods (but not of the safety of their passengers) on their receipt, with certain exceptions.[34] It is liable for a missing shipment of your goods irrespective of any exculpatory language in the bill of lading or its exercise of reasonable care. Further, it can't exempt itself if another connecting carrier causes a loss or damage to your goods. The carrier is held to the degree of care a reasonable person would exercise in like circumstances both as to carriage and to the delivery date.

An important document in this relationship is the bill of lading. The bill of lading serves a threefold purpose:

- receipt of goods,
- contract for their carriage and delivery, and
- document of title.[35]

Here the carrier will set forth any exemption from responsibility which the carrier can or does claim. Known usage and custom will be read into all such contracts unless they clearly stipulate the contrary.

You want to be sure you receive a "clean bill of lading" from your carrier. This signifies that the goods as delivered were in good order and condition. This clean bill of health puts you in a strong recovery position in the event of damage to the goods while in transit *and* until your buyer assumes control.[36] For example, under the Uniform Straight Bill of Lading Act, as a condition precedent to recovery, a written claim must be filed with the receiving or delivering carrier, or carrier on whose line the damage occurred, or who then had possession, within nine months after delivery of the property or, if not delivered, within nine months after a reasonable time for delivery had elapsed. A suit must be commenced within two years and a day from the time written notice is given by the carrier that there has been disallowance of the claim.[37]

If there is no dispute, the bill of lading is negotiated by endorsing it to a specified person or firm.[38] A holder to whom a negotiable document has been duly negotiated acquires title to the document and to the goods. If there was a transfer rather than a negotiation of the negotiable or nonnegotiable document, the transferee acquires the title and rights of the transferor.

In the case of a nonnegotiable document, *until* the bailee receives notice of the transfer, the rights of the transferee may be defeated by creditors of the transferor who could treat the sale as void under UCC section 2-402 or by a buyer from the transferor in the ordinary course of business who had received delivery or been notified of his rights or as against the bailee by good faith dealings of the bailee with the transferor.[39]

The carrier can become a bailee in a number of ways. Two important instances are when it holds the goods pending orders to ship[40] or when, after timely notice of arrival is given, the goods are not picked up by the buyer or consignee.[41] As with the warehouse operator, a carrier (common or private) has a lien on the goods covered by the bill of lading for charges subsequent to the date of its receipt of the goods for storage or transportation and for expenses necessary for the preservation of the goods incident to their sale pursuant to law.[42] As with the warehouse lien, the carrier lien is lost on any goods voluntarily delivered.[43]

Generally a carrier is liable in conversion (irrespective of negligence or the exercise of due care) when it delivers the goods to anyone except the person designated by the shipper as the recipient. Contracts or notices which purport to exempt a common carrier entirely from liability for its negligence are void as they are against public policy. A carrier may limit its liability for damages caused even by its own negligence, if the carrier's rates are dependent upon value and the consignor is afforded an opportunity to declare the higher true value or the value allowed in the tariff, and obtain complete coverage. However, no limitation is effective with respect to the carrier's liability for conversion to its own use.[44] Likewise a carrier can contract to exempt itself from liability to passengers in return for a lower rate, provided the passenger has the option to pay the full fare without giving any exemptions. This rule may be different if you're traveling on a "free pass."

Finally, the telegraph and telephone companies are carriers whose efficient service can be vital to you. If you are injured in your business dealings as a result of their foul-ups, you may not have to simply swallow it. Consult with your counsel. A telegraph company may be liable for miswording your message; their outright failure to deliver improves your chances for recovery. The telephone company is liable for gross negligence or willful misconduct. A public utility is limited to damages arising from its willful misconduct or gross negligence. The latter has been termed as a failure to exercise even slight care.[45] State law will vary, so see your attorney if you believe you've been injured.

Conclusion

When you surrender custody and control of personal property to another but you do not sell it, think bailment. Then ask yourself:

- Did an actual or constructive delivery by the bailor to the bailee take place?
- Did the bailee take possession with *intent* to possess it (think of who controls the car keys in the parking example)?
- Was custody and control — but not title — transferred? If so, you have a bailment. If not, think contract.
- If you have a bailment, determine what type and proceed accordingly.

ENDNOTES

(1) Personal property is defined in the Glossary.

(2) *Belofsky v. State Insurance Fund* 260 N.Y.S.2d 855 (1965) and *Voorhis v. Consolidated Rail Co.,* 60 N.Y.S.2d 828.

(3) *Hood v. State,* 264 N.Y.S.2d 134 (1942), aff'd 283 N.Y.S.2d (AD) 695 (1967).

(4) *Hertz Corp. v. Paloni,* 619 P.2d 1256 (1980).

(5) *O'Malley v. Putnam Safe Deposit Vaults,* 458 E.2d 752 (Mass. App. 1983) (missing coins in safe deposit box).

(6) *Garlock v. Multiple Parking Services,* 427 N.Y.S.2d 670 (1980). For a good discussion of possession and sale of stolen goods see *State v. Serrino,* 509 A.2d 1039 (1986).

(7) See, e.g., N.Y. Gen.Oblig. Law Sec. 5-325 (Consol. 1986).

(8) *Ampco Auto Parks, Inc. v. Williams,* 517 S.W.2d 401, 405 (1974).

(9) *Hallman v. Federal Parking Services,* 134 A.2d 382 (Ct. App. D.C. 1957).

(10) *Wieler v. Silver Standard Ins.,* 263 AD 521, 33 N.Y.S.2d 617 (App. Div. 1942).

(11) See, e.g., N.Y. Gen. Oblig. Law Sec. 201(1) (Consol. 1986). See also the law's ancient roots in *Buttman v. Dennett,* 9 Misc. 462, 30 NY 247, (N.Y. Ct. C.P. 1894, per curiam). Also note the growing emphasis on public accommodations liability in other areas, e.g., the duty to police guests' liquor consumption: *Kane v. Fields Corner Grille, Inc.,* 341 Mass. 640, 171 N.E.2d 287 (1961); *Adamian v. Three Sons, Inc.,* 353 Mass. 498; 233 N.E.2d 18 (1968); and *Irwin v. Town of Ware,* 467 N.E.2d 1292 (1984) (municipal liability).

(12) *Aldrich v. Waldorf-Astoria,* 343 N.Y.S.2d 2830 (1973).

(13) UCC Sec. 7-204.

(14) *Carter v. Reichlin Furriers,* 34 Conn. Sup. 661, 386 A.2d 648 (1977).

(15) *Lerner v. Brettshneider,* 598 P.2d 515, 518-19 (Ariz. App. 1979).

(16) Id., p. 519.

(17) *Axelrod v. Wardrobe Cleaners, Inc.,* 289 So.2d 847 (Ct. App. La. 1974). For a related case as to damages see *Devine v. Buckley,* 603 S.2d 558 (1979).

(18) Id., p. 849

(19) UCC Sec. 7-102(h).

(20) For example, UCC Sec. 2-302 (unconscionable contracts or clauses), discussed in greater detail infra.

(21) UCC Sec. 7-204(1).

(22) UCC Sec. 7-204(2).

(23) *Miller's Mutual Fire Insurance Association v. Parker,* 234 NC 20, 65 S.E.2d 341 (1951).

(24) *Griffin v. Nationwide Moving and Storage Co.,* 187 Conn 405, 446 A 799 (1982).

(25) *Refrigeration Sales Co. v. Mitchell-Jackson, Inc.,* 770 F.2d 98 (1985).

(26) UCC Sec. 7-209(1).

(27) UCC Sec. 7-209(4). See also *James Talcott v. Stagz,* 252 N.Y.S.2d 628 (1964).

(28) UCC Sec. 7-210(7), 7-210(2). See also *Hughes v. Accredited Movers, Inc., 461 A.2d 1203* (N.J. Super. Ct. App. Div. 1983).

(29) UCC Sec. 7-204(2).

(30) The UCC isn't particularly clear here, though creative arguments by your counsel should be effective when 7-204(1) is read with 1-103 and 1-106 of the UCC.

(31) These relationships are not always bailments. However, they often result in this form of relationship. Either way they can be an important factor in your channel decision (e.g., whether to send by private carrier or the U.S. Postal Service). The duties of a carrier will be specified in the bill of lading. If the transaction is intrastate, Article 7 of the UCC governs. If it is interstate, the Federal Bill of Lading Act (U.S.C. Title 49) governs.

(32) A common carrier takes goods *or* persons. However, there are distinctions made between the two.

(33) *Sprague v. Louis Picciano, Inc.,* 474 N.Y.S.2d (AD) 591 (1984) (a carrier must warn of or correct obvious defects in packaging). See also *Paquet v. Dart,* 343 N.Y.S.2d 446 (1982).

(34) Act of God, act of state, act of public enemy, act or order of the government or public authority (e.g., goods are removed by valid legal process), or negligence of shipper (e.g., bailor who improperly packs the goods or damages them due to the inherent nature of the goods themselves). *Frosty Land Foods Int'l Inc. v. Refrigerated Transp. Co.,* 613 F.2d 1344 (1980).

(35) UCC Sec. 7-104. The document lists the goods received by the carrier and states the agreed destination for the goods and the terms on which the carrier undertakes to deliver them.

(36) *Instrument Systems v. Association Rig,* 416 N.Y.S.2d (AD) 5 (1979).

(37) *Cooper-Janett v. Melody Stationery Co.,* 385 N.Y.S.2d (AD) 394 (1986).

(38) UCC Sec. 7-501 (3, 5).

(39) UCC Sec. 7-504 (1, 2).

(40) Liability is the same as that of a warehouser.

(41) This is a traditional bailment relationship.

(42) UCC Sec. 7-307(1).

(43) UCC Sec. 7-307(3).

(44) Interstate Commerce Act, Sec. 201, UCC Sec. 7-309.

(45) For an interesting (pre-deregulation) case on being omitted from the Yellow Pages, see *Wille v. Southwestern Bell Telephone Co.,* 549 P.2d 903 (Sup. Ct. Kan. 1976).

CHAPTER 8
SALIENT ISSUES IN SALES LAW

If you have a product to sell, you should familiarize yourself with the law of sales. In designing your channel strategy, this overview will give you a working knowledge of certain commercial practices that our society expects from a sophisticated manager. Reading this chapter is not intended to substitute for specific legal advice from your company's lawyer. However, it should alert you to the salient issues, so that you'll be aware of a legal issue in advance.

To have a thorough grasp of this area, your attorney must know some sophisticated distinctions and construction language, but this chapter will not place a premium on vocabulary; rather, it will get you through this area with a minimum of pain, a maximum of depth, and with some practical examples.

Selling You on the UCC

Article 2 of the UCC (Uniform Commercial Code) applies to all *commercial* (not *consumer*) "transactions in goods."[1] Any other transaction (personal services, real estate, etc.) is governed by traditional contract law. For example, you wish to paint your office. The paint is a *good*—covered by the UCC. The painter provides a *service*—covered by contract law. A car wash is a service, your car is a good. Most examples are fairly clear-cut. When you have a "mixed transaction," its main thrust will determine whether it is covered by the UCC or by contract law.

This chapter will highlight areas of the UCC's flexibility and its occasional more-restrictive sections vis-a-vis common-law contract law.

While it is fair to say that the UCC contractual provisions are more flexible than traditional, common-law contractual principles, even freedom of contract must be limited if the formation of a contract is to remain a meaningful and viable concept. The UCC does *restrict* your freedom of contract in a number of ways. For example, you may not disclaim your obligations of good faith and fair dealing, reasonableness, diligence, and care, and you may not contract around the statute of frauds.[2] You are also restricted in a few instances from choosing the law to govern your contract.[3]

Once you've determined that you are covered by the UCC, you'll want to consider four questions:

- What does this agreement consist of?
- Is it enforceable?
- If it is enforceable, what is the extent of the performance I can expect to receive (or have to provide)?
- If I fail to receive performance (or fail to perform), what are my remedies? (Or what penalties will I be subject to?)

The answers to these issues are found in the UCC. They will be discussed here, along with some representative cases. You will find that you can apply your understanding of the UCC to your daily business transactions.

General Principles of the UCC

The UCC is the "constitution" of the commercial world.[4] The writers of our U.S. Constitution intended it to be dynamic and to grow and mature with our nation. Likewise, the UCC provides "its own machinery for expansion of commercial practices. It is intended to make it possible for the law embodied in this Act to be developed by the courts in the light of unforeseen and new circumstances and practices."[5] Further, it was intended to coordinate commercial dealings in interstate commerce to produce one national marketplace with a set of common rules that all participants could understand. A number of key themes run throughout the UCC; read the following twice to get a good grasp of the underlying principles of sales law:

Executed Sale.   An executed sale is one that is final and complete in all contractual terms.

Executory Sale.   An executory sale is one in which all terms and conditions were definitely agreed upon but which has not yet been carried into full effect in respect to some of its terms or details (such as price, quantity, or delivery).

Good Faith.   By reading books such as this, you are making a good-faith effort to stay on top of all areas of your business or profession. The UCC expects all your competitors and associates to live up to similar standards. Good faith is simple honesty in fact. For merchants this means observance of commercial reasonableness and fair dealing in their trade. *Every* contract (can't be waived) or duty under Article 2 of the

UCC imposes an obligation of good faith in its performance and enforcement. Even if all parties agree at arm's length, they may not waive or disclaim the obligation of good faith.[6]

Goods.   In general, goods are all things except real property and personal services (including specially manufactured goods) that are movable at the time of identification to the contract for sale. "Identifying" goods means designating them as the ones to be delivered under your contract. For example, "we designate 500 widgets to be shipped as per the contract."[7]

Material Term.   A material term is one that, when included in the contract, would make a difference as to whether the parties would agree to the contract. (Deciding whether a term is material is similar to applying the principles in consumer law analysis, i.e., simply consider whether it makes a difference.)

Merchants.   Merchants are held to higher standards of skill concerning the goods involved as well as business practices in their particular fields. Who is a merchant? As defined by the UCC, merchants are those who deal in goods of the kind or otherwise hold themselves out as having knowledge peculiar to the practices or goods involved in the transaction.[8] Merchants *impliedly warrant* their goods as merchantable. This implied warranty means that the merchant's goods must at least pass without objection in the trade. As a business professional, you're probably being held to the merchant standards.

Payment.   Payment can be rendered in any manner current in the usual course of the business. If the seller demands payment in legal tender, the seller must grant a reasonable extension of time to enable the buyer to procure it. No credit terms are ever assumed—such terms must be specified.

Reasonableness.   This word or a variation is a dominant theme of the article. No specific definition is given, so it can be used with flexibility in varied transactions. (On the other hand, negative limit exists in the determination of what is "unconscionability," which is discussed below.) On the whole, it may be said that if you're acting in good faith, you're acting reasonably.

Sale.   A sale is a contract under which title passes from the seller to the buyer for consideration. Note that bailment is not a sale; it transfers possession only, not title. A gift transfers title without consideration.

Unconscionability.[9]   To be deemed unconscionable, an agreement must be found to be unconscionable when made. It can arise from *unequal bargaining* position (adhesion contracts), *misrepresentations, oppressive terms,* and the like. The parties will be allowed to introduce evidence that such terms are reasonable or customary in their business. If an agreement is found to be unconscionable, the court may void the contract, or give effect to the contract without the provision found unconscionable, or it may limit the application of the unconscionable clause so as to avoid any unconscionable result.

No damages are mandated by law. Unconscionability is a defense for nonfulfillment of a contract obligation and does not give rise to an affirmative cause of action. As yet no court has held that a party is obligated to act "conscionably," though that condition would seem to be implied by the term "in good faith."

In a nutshell: If you're a responsible business person and you buy or sell goods in good faith, the UCC is on your side.[10] If your competitor did likewise and yet you both made a few errors or omissions in evidencing the agreement (which shouldn't happen if you properly consult your attorney from the beginning!), the UCC will help you. Let's see how.

What Does Your Agreement Consist Of?

A written agreement between two commercial enterprises dealing on an equal basis, which states that it is the exclusive statement of the terms of the agreement, will have priority over the UCC-supplied terms.

The courts will not use the UCC to create a result contrary to the clearly understood intentions of the parties. The parties are generally free to agree to terms not encouraged by the specific UCC provisions. However, few contracts are this clear-cut.

The UCC provisions are designed to assist two parties to achieve the benefit of the arm's-length bargain they sought. Under the UCC, the agreement for the sale of goods may be made in any manner sufficient to show agreement, including conduct by both parties that recognizes the existence of a contract. Such conduct is sufficient to establish a contract for sale even though the parties' writings don't. The contract will not fail on the basis of indefiniteness if the UCC can provide the "missing links."[11]

The courts will accept testimony as to custom and usage in your trade, and they will examine whether there was a pattern of prior dealings between the parties.[12]

Let's look at the specifics of what it takes for your agreement to pass muster.

Is Your Agreement Enforceable?

The most important idea underlying the discussion of UCC Article 2 is that the code will work to assist all parties in realizing their good faith commercial expectations. This is in contrast to the common law, whose formalism (that is, its emphasis on form over substance) has defeated valid contractual expectations in two ways.

Terms of Your Offer

An offer is effective when communicated and accepted. In many states the offer is effective when accepted in an *authorized* manner. In general this means that, absent any indication to the contrary, the acceptance must be communicated in the same manner as the offer. Thus, if you received the offer by mail, your acceptance must likewise be by mail to be considered made in an authorized manner. If the acceptance is by mail, it is effective when *sent.* However, if you used a telegram or other vehicle, the acceptance is effective only when *received* by the offeror. This is often referred to as the "minor acceptance" rule and is interpreted literally. This law clings to a mystique of a world before the communications evolution.

Nowhere is the UCC's greater flexibility more evident. Under the UCC, the assumption is made that offerors in buying and selling goods are not exacting about the methods of acceptance.[13] If the parties think they have a contract, they probably do.

The UCC permits acceptance in any manner and by any medium reasonable under the circumstances, unless the offeror unambiguously indicates how acceptance is to be made.[14] Communication of acceptance can also be accomplished by conduct that recognizes the contract's existence. For example, if your buyer orders 200 widgets, you can indicate acceptance by immediately shipping goods conforming to the order.[15]

Another common-law exception applies to *merchants.* Contract law requires that firm offers "be sustained by some valid consideration to bind the offeror." Again, the UCC is flexible in light of commercial realities. An offer by a *merchant* to buy or sell in a signed agreement that gives assurance that it will be held open needs no consideration to be irrevocable for a stated time. If no time period is stated, then the period of irrevocability may extend to 90 days.[16]

Offers at Auction

"What am I bid for this antique lamp?" is generally not an offer but an invitation to offer bids.

The UCC[17] states that in auctions of goods conducted *without reserve,* the auctioneer is the offeror and is bound by the offeree's bid; that is, he has not reserved his right to remove the goods from the auction if they do not receive an equitable bid. An auction with reserve actually reserves for the auctioneer the right to remove from auction an item that has not received a fair bid.

The Offer Results in Conflicting Writings ("Battle of the Forms")

Conflicting writings constitute a common problem in your everyday ordering. Your business transactions are often conducted by phone, followed by a standardized form. After your phone conversation you receive a form from the buyer, but things don't exactly jell; some terms are open, and others are at variance.

Traditionally, the parties were limited to acceptance or rejection, or acceptance of the offer with treatment of all additional terms as "counteroffers." There also was the strong influence of the "mirror acceptance" rule, which stated that a purported "acceptance" that is not identical to the offer (in terms or as discussed earlier in the manner of its transmission to the offeror) does not operate as an acceptance but as a repetition and a counter-offer. What about situations where both parties proceed to perform? In these cases, the common law creates a contract whose terms are those of the offeree's! This resulted in an unfair burden on commercial expectations—a burden the UCC attempted to address.

Under the UCC you have a contract provided you have a specified *quantity term.* This is the one essential. Your contract is not enforceable beyond the quantity term. If there is none present, there is no contract.[18] Otherwise, the courts can assist you in forming one and will help fill in the gaps. The courts will proceed under the overall spirit of the UCC as well as the general formation section, which states that "even though one or more terms are left open, a contract for sale does not fail for indefiniteness if the parties have intended to make a contract and there is a reasonably certain basis for giving an appropriate remedy."[19]

However, merchants have special privileges to facilitate the contract formation process. The UCC recognizes that the realities of business life make it impossible for every routine sales transaction to be accompanied by proposals that agree on all terms. Therefore, a written confirmation sent to your buyer within a reasonable time operates as an acceptance, even if it states terms different from or additional to those offered originally. Between merchants, such terms become part of the contract unless[20]

- the offer *expressly* limits acceptance to the terms of the offer, or conditions any acceptance to any additional terms upon a written consent which was not given;
- the offeror objects to the extra terms within a reasonable time; or
- the additional terms *materially* alter the contract. Depending on the circumstances, trade practice, etc.,[21] the contract is materially altered if the additional terms do any of the following:

  (a) limit tort liability arising out of the good's use; (Note: Although written agreements shortening the statute of limitations are authorized, such a shortened period cannot be less than one year generally—in some states it is longer.)[22]

  (b) shorten the time to make complaints concerning the goods;

  (c) add an arbitration clause;[23]

(d) alter the risk of loss on the goods; or

(e) negate the standard warranties (of merchantability, fitness for a particular purpose, etc.).

The "choice of law" your attorney places in your contract is usually not a material term, though this is not true as to form selection.[24] Cases can turn on *minor* matters. For example, a seller shipped goods on receiving the buyer's purchase order, but sent an invoice containing different terms. The battle of forms began as to what exactly was accepted. The buyer's purchase was FOB destination, while the seller's invoice contained the term "Our liability ceases upon delivery of the merchandise to the carrier." If the shipment occurred before the seller dispatched the invoice (and there is some indication of this), at best the invoice was a request for modification not accepted by the buyer. If the dispatch of the invoice occurred before the shipment, it could constitute a counteroffer. If it was construed as, or contained "a definite and reasonable expression of acceptance," the UCC would come in. The court concluded that even if it were part of the contract, "the term in the invoice. . . does not clearly negate the provision that. . .defendant bore the responsibility for delivery of the goods [to buyer]. . ."[25] and therefore the risk of loss until destination.

To avoid these issues you should review all additional proposals with your counsel—both those you send and those you receive. As to the former, you may not wish to offer your buyer an "out" without knowing all legal consequences. If you are the recipient, your counsel will explain your legal exposure if you fulfill the agreement as is. Whether the additional term is material is a matter for your counsel. If you want out, you should immediately direct your counsel to draft a letter that complies with the "*prompt* notification of objection" exception.

Finally, even if you don't believe your writings are a contract, conduct by both you and your buyer that recognizes the existence of a contract will establish a contract: "In such case the terms of the particular contract consist of those terms on which the parties agree, together with any supplementary terms incorporated under any other provisions of this Act."[26] The latter may include custom or evidence of course of performance. These will be considered and weighed on a priority basis. Express contractual terms control over all else. Course of performance controls over evidence of both course of dealings and usage of trade.[27]

Insufficient Writing—The Oral Contract

We've reviewed how the UCC attempts to sort out too many writings. What about too few writings? Take the case of the classic order over the telephone: You receive a bid from XYZ supplier over the phone for the $8,000 worth of merchandise necessary for your fulfillment of a lucrative contract. You accept the bid, hang up the phone, and calculate your total cost after considering XYZ's bid, your costs, and a reasonable profit. You then call your buyer, B, who accepts immediately. You're elated. Three days later a memo arrives from B, confirming the conversation and stating the agreed-on quantity ordered. Three weeks later you call XYZ, and they can't honor the bid. Can you sue XYZ? Can you opt out of your agreement with B?

You can't sue XYZ. With some exceptions, discussed below, a contract for the sale of goods for the price of $500 or more is voidable unless made in writing and signed by the party to be charged for its fulfillment.[28] The contract is *voidable* rather than *void* because your supplier still has the option to fulfill its moral obligation on the oral agreement. Still, your supplier is not *legally* bound to fulfill without a written confirmation.[29] The social policy of the writing requirement in the Statute of Frauds is to prevent fraud or perjury on claims of substance.

You won't be able to void your contract with B—even if your lawyer found it missing a material term such as the price, or even if it wasn't signed by you or B (unless you can prove that availability of your supplies from XYZ is a material term). A contract for the sale of goods need not contain all material terms (just the quantity term), and the material terms need not be precisely stated. The only requirement is that the writing afford a basis for believing that there is a real transaction resulting from the oral evidence—the phone calls plus the memo from B.[30] What's more, the memo need not have been signed! A memo containing B's letterhead, quantity designation, and other identifying criteria is a sufficient writing confirming the contract.[31]

Again, there is a special section for merchants. You didn't have to sign an acceptance to B's memo. If you, the party to be charged, are a merchant and you receive a written confirmation of your oral sales contract, this confirmation binds you *unless you object within 10 days*.[32] If you had seen your attorney concerning this matter, you'd have been told to follow up your conversation with XYZ; if XYZ didn't object within 10 days, you could hold it to the agreement just as B is holding you.

These are other exceptions to the statute of frauds:

1. Partial acceptance or partial payment for the goods. The goods that are paid for are not covered by the statute, but the balance of the unpaid goods is.[33] However, the acceptance of part of any commercial unit is an acceptance of the entire unit. A commercial unit is a unit which by commercial usage is a single whole for the purpose of a sale, depending on the relevant market.[34]

2. An admission by the party against whom enforcement of the contract is sought, but only to the extent of the quantity of goods admitted.[35]

3. A substantial beginning in manufacturing or procurement of special goods for the buyer before you receive a notice of repudiation from the buyer. In this case, the contract is enforceable despite the lack of a writing.[36]

To best protect yourself as a buyer, you should never rely on an exception. Once you've placed your order by phone, you should send a confirmatory letter by certified mail. Depending on your total exposure, you might require the seller to sign such a letter.[37] One way or the other, a mailing addressed to a large corporation may be considered "received" because this type of document is "not spurious" and will be passed along to those who have reason to know of its contents.[38] The moral: make sure your mailroom red-flags this type of correspondence.

What about a long-term relationship? Here, course of performance will argue for a contract. In one relationship, the parties gave each other oral assurances as to termination. After sales and purchases over 30 years' duration, the buyer terminated the agreement without the agreed-upon notice. The seller brought suit and lost in the lower court because there was no enforceable agreement under the Statute of Frauds.

The appeals court reversed the decision, however. Its rationale was that the UCC Statute of Frauds, on which the lower court relied, did not apply to the transaction because the deal extended beyond the mere sale of goods. The 30-year relationship and the substantial dealings between the parties placed them somewhere between a "distributorship" and the normal UCC "sale."[39]

Here's a recap of a few Code-approved methods of acceptance:

1. You may accept an offer either by a promise or an act (i.e., a prompt shipment of the goods or the notice of your intent to ship them).

2. Identical cross-offers are a contract as are (usually) conflicting forms (see above). A strong course of prior dealing will certainly assist your argument for contract formation.

3. Any reasonable form of acceptance is permissible *unless* the offer expressly calls for a particular method *and* the violation of same will result in a counteroffer.[40]

In short, acceptance of the contract may be made in any manner sufficient to show agreement, including conduct by both parties that recognizes the existence of such a contract.

Note: Acceptance of the contract is not acceptance of the goods.

Now let's move on to a few other factors that enable us to form or define an otherwise ambiguous or less than satisfactory agreement.

Parol Evidence Rule

In your contracts you've often seen the familiar "integration clause," which generally states that "this instrument contains the entire agreement between the seller and buyer and no statement, promise, or inducements made by either party or agent of either party that is not contained in this written agreement shall be valid or binding; this agreement may not be enlarged, modified, or altered except in writing signed by both the seller and the buyer and endorsed hereon."[41]

This clause may or may not work to your advantage. If it is included, then your written agreement is the complete, final, and exclusive statement of the terms of the agreement. If the integration clause is not in the agreement, then the agreement is not to be taken as including all matters agreed upon. Later you may be able to get in evidence of prior written or oral agreements or consistent additional terms and you may have the opportunity to explain or interpret by oral evidence your current terms by demonstrating usage of trade, course of dealings, or course of performance.[42] This is because the UCC's Parol Evidence Rule permits you to bring in trade usage, not to contradict, but to explain terms; it also allows additional terms *unless* the court finds the parties intended your writing as the complete and exclusive statement of your contract.

Discuss this subject carefully with your attorney. If you need a narrow contract, your attorney will carefully negate the permissible introduction of anything but that within the contract. If you need greater flexibility now or anticipate that you might as your marketing effort develops, advise your attorney accordingly.

Finally, while you may sign an agreement that excludes oral modification or recision, except by a signed writing, in the following exception parol evidence can be used in any contractual dispute:

- mutual mistake;
- fraud;
- duress, illegality, overreaching or lack of sufficient capacity to enter into this particular agreement;
- invalidity (e.g., when a liquidated damages provision is put into a contract, parol evidence can be used to show that it was intended to be a penalty and thus invalid);[43] or
- a showing by a non-merchant that a merchant imposed this clause in a sales slip or receipt and that the non-merchant never agreed to this restriction.

The exceptions are best summed up by a classic English case:[44]

"The distinction. . .is that evidence to vary the terms of an agreement in writing is not admissible, but evidence to show that there is not an agreement at all is admissible."

Finally, it almost goes without saying that a single transaction can never be a prior course of dealing "because it cannot explain nor supplement an agreement."[45]

Unconscionability

Another way of challenging the validity of a contractual clause or perhaps even the entire contract is to demonstrate, in cases of "extreme overreaching," that the matter in question is unconscionable. The basic test is whether, in the light of the general commercial climate then existing and within the framework of a particular transaction, the clauses involved are so one-sided that they are unconscionable as of the *time of making the contract*.[46]

> This time qualification is important because the UCC is not intended to prop up poor negotiators or someone who simply blew a deal. For example, making a too-low bid on the basis of a miscalculation isn't enough—the court won't rescue you from a negligent mistake that may not have been initially apparent but that becomes obvious as the transaction proceeds.[47]

A court wants to see real pain suffered in a situation of disparate bargaining posture. This setting can defeat the necessary mutuality of agreement and obligation. A good working definition of a rule of thumb is contained in the court's decision in a case involving a consumer who couldn't speak English, much less read and understand the fine-print terms: "the doctrine of unconscionability is used by the court to protect those who are unable to protect themselves and to prevent injustice. . .Unequal bargaining powers and the absence of meaningful choice on the part of one of the parties, together with contract terms which unreasonably favor the other party *may* spell out unconscionability."[48]

When you wish to preserve the general contract, but have reservations about any clause, discuss with your counsel adding a paragraph such as this: "The doctrine of severability shall be applied to this agreement. In the event that any term of this agreement is declared illegal, void, or unenforceable, such declaration shall not affect or impair the other terms." A court may second-guess you on a particular clause; if the clause is severable, you may be able to save the rest of the contract. The downside is, of course, that if you don't want the contract without that paragraph, then you don't want the severability option included.

Some Contractual Gap Fillers

We've emphasized the UCC's flexibility as well as its desire to uphold the intent of the parties. As you know from experience, it is a rare sales contract that satisfies every term that might come back to haunt you. The following are a few more ways the UCC will help once it has been established that all parties have an "agreement to agree." However, you should note that these gap-fillers tend to favor the buyer over the seller. For example, the implied warranty of merchantability is automatically "gap filled in" unless properly disclaimed, whenever the seller is a merchant with respect to goods of that kind.

Open Price. When your contract is silent as to price, it is assumed that both parties intended a reasonable price at the time of delivery.[49] If the price is to be fixed by the seller or buyer, then such price must be set in good faith.[50]

Open Duration of Contractual Relationship. The Code provides that such a contract is valid for a reasonable time,[51] though terminable by either party at any time subject to reasonable notice.[52] This requires good faith, and the notice period must reflect the amount of time necessary for the other party to protect itself. For example, how much time will it take to secure a new source of supply?[53] In all these situations "reasonable notice" is when one has actual knowledge or has received notice (duly delivered to his or her place of business) or has, under all the facts and circumstances, reason to know.[54]

Open Quantity Terms. Again, a contract must specify the quantity you're selling or purchasing to satisfy the Statute of Frauds. However, the quantity need not be specified in numerical figures. An agreement that your buyer will purchase all requirements from you for a defined period is a "valid requirements contract."[55] Likewise, your buyer may agree to take all goods produced by you from a specific production unit during a given period of time. This is a "valid output contract."[56]

Single Lots. If the parties are silent in their agreement, the UCC requires them to make (and take) delivery in a single-lot shipment. *Note:* A commercial unit is a single whole for purposes of a sale. For example, the seller ships a commercial unit of 10 watches; the buyer returns 4. The seller need not accept the returned watches because if the buyer has accepted any item in a commercial unit, the buyer has accepted all the items in the unit.[57]

Place of Delivery. If the parties are silent and delivery by carrier is not an issue,[58] the place of delivery is the seller's place of business or, if none exists, the seller's residence.[59]

Time of Delivery. If the parties are silent, then a reasonable time for delivery is implied. Such reasonable time must be determined by the good-faith commercial standards of your industry.[60]

Time of Payment or Credit. If the parties are silent, payment and delivery are concurrent conditions. Payment is due at the time and place at which the buyer is to receive the goods, that is, where and when the buyer takes physical possession of the goods.[61] If the delivery is authorized and made by documents (e.g., a bill of lading or warehouse receipt),[62] then payment is due at the time and place that the buyer receives the documents.[63] The credit period begins to run from the date of shipment, subject to verifiable delays.[64]

Open Shipping Arrangements. If the parties are silent, the duty to make shipping arrangements falls on the seller.[65] Generally, the courts will narrowly interpret your force majeure (acts of God) clause and expect you to get the delivery through.[66] If you are specific, they are more lenient. For example, in one case a firm agreed to deliver by rail *unless otherwise agreed* by both parties. When the rains came and the rails went, the seller was excused, even though other carriers were getting through.[67]

Although the courts will read these significant gap-fillers into an agreement when it appears that the parties intended an enforceable contract, sloppy work on your part or your failure to review your agreement with counsel is not encouraged. The more gaps you permit, the more difficult establishing a bona fide contractual intent will be. The gap-fillers are helpful, but nothing is preferable to having your own counsel draft an agreement customized to your needs.

Commercial Delivery Obligations

Your invoices may contain myriad shipment terms. For nonmaritime contracts, the leading shorthand term you'll see is FOB (free on board).[68] There are varied uses for the term, but the most common are the following:

FOB point of shipment. If this is specified in the contract, the seller must bear the risk and expense only of bringing the goods into the possession of the carrier.[69] The seller does not bear the expense of loading.[70] As a seller, this is the wording you want.

FOB carrier. This wording means that the seller is obligated to bear the expense and risk of having the goods loaded on board.[71]

FOB destination. This wording obligates the seller to bear the expense and risk of having the goods brought to the point of destination. This is the language the buyer wants.[72]

F.A.S. The term F.A.S. means "free alongside" and, when followed by the name of a port, means that the seller at his or her own expense and risk must deliver the goods alongside the vessel in that port or on a dock designated and provided by the buyer; the seller must also get and tender a receipt for the goods, in exchange for which the carrier has a duty to issue a bill of lading.

When a shipment is FOB place of shipment, or FOB vessel or vehicle, or F.A.S. vessel, the buyer must give delivery instructions. Failure to give needed instructions may be treated by the seller as a failure to cooperate because of which the seller is excused for any resulting delay and may proceed to perform in any reasonable manner or to treat the failure to cooperate as a breach similar to failing to accept the goods.[73]

C.I.F. The letters C.I.F. stand for "cost, insurance, and freight." A C.I.F. sale means that the agreed price includes the cost of the goods plus insurance and freight to the named destination. The terms "C & F" and "C.F." mean that the price includes cost and freight to the named destination.

Unless otherwise agreed, these terms require the seller at his or her expense and risk to do the following:

• deliver to the carrier and obtain a negotiable bill of lading covering the transportation to the named destination;

- load the goods and obtain a receipt (which may be included in the bill of lading) showing that payment of freight has been made;
- obtain insurance covering the goods in favor of the buyer or for the account of whom it may concern;
- prepare an invoice and documents required in order to ship and comply with the contract;
- forward and tender with commercial promptness all documents in such form as necessary to protect the buyer.

Unless otherwise agreed, the buyer must pay against tender of the required documents. The seller may not tender nor the buyer demand the goods in substitution of the documents.[74]

If the agreement is silent, the UCC will read in a point-of-shipment contract. If you don't want this, make sure you specify what you want in your contract. Remember that at all times the parties are free to prescribe terms and conditions of delivery that are controlling. As a seller, one final protection you might like to have your counsel draft into your contract is a "no arrival, no sale" clause, which means that you promise to ship conforming goods but assume no obligation for the actual arrival of the goods, unless you are responsible for their nonarrival.[75]

"Sale on Approval" and "Sale or Return"

In a sale on approval, you deliver your goods to a potential purchaser for examination. This is a bailment relationship; the bailee (recipient of the goods) has the option to purchase. This will not usually occur unless the purchaser sells it. In effect, the seller is acting as an agent for the owner of the goods. The owner is called the "consignor," the salesperson is the "consignee," and the merchandise itself is called the "consignment." When it's sold, the salesperson takes a percentage commission of the sales price under prior agreement with the consignor, even though the salesperson has made no investment in the goods. Title to the goods does not pass until the option is exercised by an indicated approval or until the expiration of a reasonable time, when a time limit for approval has not been agreed upon.[76] At this time the goods are not subject to any claims by the consignor's creditors either.

This presupposes both an actual receipt by your buyer as well as a reasonable opportunity to inspect the goods. This is a tricky area. For instance, a coin dealer sent samples to a customer by registered mail. A so-called unknown person signed the receipt. The coin dealer argued that the buyer received them and that registered mail was adequate protection. Not so, said the court—a buyer must actually take delivery *and* accept.[77]

In a purchase subject to return, the goods belong to the buyer until she or he actually returns them. Any loss or damage to the goods while in the buyer's possession falls on the buyer. If the buyer elects to return the goods, they must be returned in their original condition with the buyer bearing risk and expense.[78]

Seller's Performance Obligations

The UCC embodies the pre-Code rule of "perfect tender" (although this rule is weakened by the seller's right to cure).[79] The doctrine of substantial performance does not apply to a contract for the sale of goods[80] except when specifically modified.[81] If the goods or tender of delivery fail in any respect to conform to the contract, "the buyer may reject the whole, accept the whole, or accept part and reject part."[82]

To satisfy proper delivery, the seller must put and hold goods conforming to the contract at its buyer's disposition as well as give the buyer any notification reasonably necessary to enable the buyer to take delivery.[83] If the seller's original tender of the goods is rejected as nonconforming and the time for performance has not yet expired, the seller may promptly notify the buyer of an intention to "cure" and then, within the contract time for performance, make a conforming delivery.[84] This option is available even when the seller has taken back the nonconforming goods and refunded the purchase price.

You also have the right to cure after expiration because of a "surprise rejection," when the seller's tender was nonconforming but the seller had good reason to believe it would be accepted. The reasonable grounds might be prior course of dealings or trade usage. Also, there is good-faith common sense, such as where a buyer orders an older model hearing aid, but the seller sends the new model, believing the buyer would want it. Upon rejection, the seller may cure even after the expiration date.[85] Make sure that you retain your insurance coverage for the goods during the cure effort.[86]

The buyer has a right to inspect the goods before payment or acceptance unless the goods are sent COD (cash on delivery) or the buyer pays against an order bill of lading or unless otherwise specified in the contract. Inspection expenses are borne by the buyer but are recoverable from you (the seller) if the goods don't conform and are rejected.[87]

Fraudulent Transfers.   As part of the obligation of good faith and fair dealing, the seller is obligated to pass along to the buyer good title. Title may pass from the seller to the buyer in any manner and on any conditions explicitly agreed to by the parties.[88] Unless agreed otherwise, the title will pass when the seller completes its performance with reference to the physical delivery of the goods.[89] If the transfer is made to a bona fide purchaser for value, such purchaser is protected despite the intentions of the *transferor* (who may not be the same person as a seller who can transfer valid title).[90]

If you receive title of stolen property from a thief, you lose and the true owner may recover. Then there is the "voidable-title" situation where there is a consentual transfer of title but in circumstances to rescind and revest title in itself. Where a legal title is thereafter passed by the transferee to a bona fide purchaser, the purchaser prevails over the equity of rescission. In the third case, a true owner has parted with less than full title. This is the "entrusting" situation.[91] The recipients of the transfer, who have the power but not the right to divest the true owner's title, are a more limited class as they must be "dealers in goods of that kind." Equally, the purchasers are a more limited kind, namely buyers in the ordinary course of business.[92]

These situations are unlikely to arise if you do a credit screening on a seller before doing business, inspect its insurance, and draft a solid indemnification clause.

Closely related to the issue of fraudulent transfers is the protection offered creditors as to bulk transfers.

Bulk Transfers. Article 6 of the UCC, which deals with bulk transfers, was enacted to prevent fraud on creditors. The bulk transfer laws are intended to prevent the commercial fraud in which a merchant, owing debts, sells out his or her stock in trade for cash, pockets the proceeds, and then disappears, leaving creditors unpaid. This law covers a transfer in bulk and not in the ordinary course of the transferor's business. The transferor is selling a substantial portion of its inventory, materials, supplies, or equipment.[93] Except where they are narrowly exempted or in the ordinary course of the transferor's business,[94] notice of such transfer must be given to the transferor's creditors.[95]

The purpose of the statute is to avoid having a debtor-merchant leave creditors high and dry. A transfer that is not in compliance is ineffective in protecting transferor's creditors. The creditor may move to set aside the transfer or sell such equitable remedies as are warranted by the circumstances.[96] The businesses subject to the bulk transfer law are those whose principal business is the sale of merchandise from stock, including retailers, wholesalers, and manufacturers.

The notice to the creditors must be given by certified mail in a timely and descriptive manner as set forth in the UCC.[97] You need not give such notice for an executory contract or one for a sale far into the future. Until sold, the inventory or equipment remains subject to the creditors. A sale for the benefit of the creditors would also be exempt.[98]

As to who the creditors are, they are those holding claims based on transactions occurring prior to the bulk transfer. Those who become creditors after proper notice to the creditors is given, are not entitled to notice.[99] One whose claim is not liquidated is not a creditor.[100]

To balance the interests of the innocent purchaser as well as the defrauded creditors, there is a short statute of limitations. No action under the Bulk Transfer Article can be brought to assert a right on a levy made more than six months after the transferee took possession of the goods unless the transfer had been concealed (e.g., by improper notice or failure of notice by *either* the transferor or the purchaser). If it was concealed, the action may be brought or levy made within six months after its discovery.[101]

The purchaser is also protected by the seller being required to give the purchasers a sworn schedule of the property to be transferred and a sworn list of the seller's creditors. The purchaser is required to give the creditors on the list, and any other known creditors, notice of the pending transfer at least ten days before he or she takes possession of the goods. The purchaser must make sure that the requirements of the bulk transfer law are met or be deemed to hold the goods in trust for the creditors of the seller. The purchaser should not only send notice of the impending transfer to all listed creditors and to all other creditors known to hold or assert claims against the seller but should also place notices in the relevant trade papers and magazines as is deemed prudent. Having taken these precautions, a creditor cannot state the buyer has not complied, and the transfer will be effective against any creditor omitted unless the creditor can prove the buyer had actual notice of the claim. Otherwise the buyer must pursue the transferor.[102]

To touch all bases properly, make sure you check with your local tax office if you are the purchaser. For example, New York State requires that the purchaser give the state tax commission a minimum of 10 days' notice of a bulk sale. Failure to do so gives the commission a priority right or lien on the consideration for any sales tax due.[103] Finally, be aware that failure to comply will result in fines in many states plus criminal sanctions.

Now that we've reviewed all that the seller "owes" prior to and on delivery, let's look at the buyer's remedies.

Buyer's Remedies Upon Breach

We've discussed the buyer's rights upon improper delivery, but there are other rights you should be aware of.

When the seller breaches the actual or implied sales contract (usually by failing to deliver, or where the seller's tender is nonconforming to time or quantity), then the buyer may seek to do one of the following:

- exercise its right of rejection;
- revoke its prior acceptance upon discovering a defect;
- exercise its right to cover;
- seek specific performance for unique goods;
- sue on warranty; or
- sue for incidental or consequential damages.

Let's look at each of these remedies in detail.

Exercising the Right of Rejection

If the goods or tender of delivery fail in any way to conform to the contract the buyer may:[104]

- reject the whole;
- accept the whole; or
- accept any reasonable commercial unit.

The seller must be notified of rejection within a reasonable time after delivery of tender.[105] An exercise of ownership by the buyer is wrongful and destroys the effect of the rejection should the seller decide to treat it as an acceptance. If rightfully rejected, the buyer's duty to pay never arises, the goods remain the seller's property, and risk of loss also remains with the seller.

When rejecting the goods, the buyer needs to particularize the defect[106] and give notice to the seller[107] to allow him or her to solve the problem.[108] The buyer actually has to tell the seller that the buyer considered the seller in breach of contract. It is not enough for the seller to be aware that the buyer was having difficulty with the goods or that they were defective.

The buyer is required to hold the goods with reasonable care at the seller's disposition for a time sufficient to enable the seller to remove them (the buyer becomes a bailee for the seller).[109] If the seller fails to provide reasonable instructions to the buyer, the buyer may store the goods on the seller's account, reship them, or resell the goods for the seller's account. At all times the buyer has a security interest in the goods to the extent of the down payment. However, the buyer must maintain records in case the seller demands an accounting.[110]

Revoking Prior Acceptance

Acceptance occurs when:

- After reasonable opportunity, the buyer signifies to the seller that the goods are conforming or that he or she will take them despite their nonconformity; or
- The buyer fails to reject within a reasonable time after delivery; or
- The buyer commits any act inconsistent with the owner's ownership.[111]

Acceptance of goods by the buyer precludes *rejection* of the goods accepted and, if the acceptance was made with knowledge of a nonconformity, it cannot be *revoked* because of the nonconformity unless the acceptance was made on the reasonable assumption that the nonconformity would be cured by the seller.[112]

When revoking *prior* acceptance, the original acceptance might have been on documents. On inspection the buyer notices a latent, substantial, or material defect not observable sooner. The buyer must immediately notify the seller, and the notification should identify the particular goods revoked, detailing the nonconformity in detail.[113] A buyer who so revokes has the same rights and duties with regard to the goods as if they were rejected outright. Here the risk of loss is on the seller only to the extent of any insurance deficiency of the buyer.

If, after rejecting goods or revoking acceptance, the erstwhile buyer maintains possession, he or she must hold them for a reasonable time and in a reasonable manner and care; the "buyer" is now a bailee. If the bailee is a merchant and not in the seller's geographic area, then he or she has a duty to follow any reasonable instructions received from the seller. Instructions are not reasonable if expenses for undertaking those instructions are not absorbed by the seller.

If the nonconforming goods are perishable or rapidly depreciable and the non-accepting buyer-*merchant* has received no instructions, then he or she *must* make a reasonable effort to sell them for the seller.

Exercising the Right to Cover

In conformity with the UCC's emphasis on reducing damages in situations of breach, the buyer must in good faith and without reasonable delay make a reasonable purchase or contract for purchase of goods in substitution of those due from the seller.[114] This is known as "cover."

If the buyer is unable, after due diligence, to effect cover he or she may be able to replevy the identified goods from the seller.[115] A reasonable attempt to cover is a condition precedent to the buyer's recovering consequential damages from the seller.

The buyer can also recover any incidental damages sustained but must give the seller credit for any expenses saved. The buyer is not *required* to cover, however. If the buyer does not cover, the other remedies under the Code are still available.

The buyer may receive as damages the difference between the cost of cover and the contract price together with incidental and consequential damages.[116] The seller is liable for cost of cover even if the buyer makes a substitute purchase that is not identical to the goods originally ordered.[117]

Seeking Specific Performance

This is an equitable remedy whereby the court compels the seller to specifically perform in whole or in part as promised in the agreement. This remedy is available when the property contracted for is unique and there is difficulty and uncertainty in accurately estimating dollar damages. When the seller repudiates or fails to deliver, or when the goods are unique, the buyer may obtain specific performance or replevy the goods designated as the ones to be delivered under the contract of sale.[118]

Suing for Warranty Based on Breach of Contract

This option is available after the goods have been accepted and the time for revocation of acceptance has elapsed. The buyer may recover for the difference of the value of the goods accepted and the value they would have had if they were as warranted.[119]

Pursuing Damages[120]

The buyer can seek incidental damages for the expense of storage, transportation, insurance, custody, and care of the seller's goods incurred because of seller's breach. In a situation where the seller is more aggrieved than the buyer, he or she can pursue consequential damages. These are damages that do not flow directly from the breach sued upon but from the consequences resulting from the breach and arising from the general or particular needs or requirements of the buyer. This can even include interest on money borrowed to make repairs due to seller's breach.[121]

To be recoverable, the particular needs of the buyer must generally be made known to the seller, while the *general* needs (the buyer had "reason to know") do not need to be made known to the seller. Sellers argue that such damages are only recoverable if specifically contemplated at the time of contracting, but they consistently lose on this argument.[122]

Note: The Code does not favor noncompensatory damages:

"The remedies provided by this Act shall be administered to the end that the aggrieved party may be put in as good a position as if the other party had fully performed but neither consequential or special or penal damages may be had except as specifically provided in this Act or by other rule of law.

". . . to make it clear that compensatory damages are limited to compensation. They do not include consequential or special damages, or penal damages; and the Act elsewhere makes it clear that damages must be minimized [Cf. Sections 1-203, 2-706(1), and 2-712(2)]. The third purpose of subsection (1) is to reject any doctrine that damages must be calculable with mathematical accuracy. Compensatory damages are often at best approximate: they have to be proved with whatever definiteness and accuracy the facts permit, but no more."[123]

Despite any of the above remedies or lack of same, acceptance of an improper delivery or payment does not prejudice the aggrieved party's right to demand adequate assurance of future performance. And when there are reasonable grounds for feeling insecure about performance (and this applies to both parties), determined according to commercial standards, a written demand may be made for adequate assurance. If this is not forthcoming within 30 days after receipt of a justified demand, it is a repudiation of the contract. When a buyer is behind in payments to the seller, even on other unrelated transactions, this may justify the seller's feeling of insecurity. And if a seller is failing to deliver under a contract to others, the same feeling on the part of the buyer may be justified.[124]

Seller's Remedies Upon Breach

A buyer may breach a contract in a variety of ways:

- by wrongfully refusing to accept goods,
- by wrongfully returning goods,
- by failing to pay for goods when payment is due, and
- by indicating an unwillingness to go ahead with the contract.

The following are significant remedies available to the seller upon a full or partial breach by buyer (or expectations of same by seller):

- cancel the contract;
- withhold delivery or further delivery;
- reclaim the goods;
- resell the goods and seek damages; or
- sue on the price.

Cancellation. Upon the buyer's breach, the seller has the right to cancel the contract and to cease performance agreed to in the contract. The seller may then set aside any goods that were intended to fill the seller's obligations under the contract.[125]

If the seller is in the process of manufacturing the goods, the seller has two choices: complete manufacture of the goods, or stop manufacturing and sell the uncompleted goods for their scrap or salvage value. In choosing between these alternatives, the seller should select the alternative that will minimize the loss.[126] A seller would be justified in completing the manufacture of goods that could be resold readily at the contract price. However, a seller would not be justified in completing specially manufactured goods that could not be sold to anyone other than the buyer who ordered them. The purpose of this rule is to permit the seller to follow a reasonable course of action to minimize the damages.

Withhold Delivery of Goods. If the buyer wrongfully rejects or revokes, then the seller may withhold any of the undelivered goods at its place of business or stop them in transit.[127] Where a buyer is *insolvent* the seller can stop any amount in transit no matter how small. The seller is liable for the costs incurred by the carrier.

An effective way for the seller to control goods in transit is to ship them under a negotiable bill of lading, as the carrier will not surrender the goods with the bill outstanding. The buyer must pay to receive the endorsement.

Reclamation. Where the seller discovers that the buyer has received goods on credit while insolvent, the seller may reclaim the goods upon demand made within 10 days after receipt. But if a misrepresentation of solvency has been made to this particular seller in writing within three months prior to delivery, the 10-day limitation does not apply. This right to reclaim is subject to the rights of any buyer in the ordinary course of business.[128] Successful reclamation excludes all other remedies with respect to the goods because the right to reclaim is really a preferential treatment over the insolvent buyer's other creditors.[129]

Resell and Recover Damages. Resale is to be done in good faith in a commercially accepted, reasonable manner. The seller may recover the difference between the resale price and contract price plus incidental damages *less* expenses saved because of the buyer's breach.[130]

Such incidental damages include any commercially reasonable charges, expenses, commissions incurred in shipping, delivery, transportation, care, and custody after breach and in connection with the resale. They do not include attorneys' fees in the absence of a contract specifying them.[131]

If the goods were of the inventory type (cars or other goods of an "unlimited inventory"), the seller may be entitled to lost profits. If you regularly deal in goods of any kind (assuming you aren't selling a one-of-a-kind Picasso), discuss with your counsel whether you can recover the profits you would have made if the contract had been completed.[132]

Sue on the Price. The seller may sue on the price only when

- goods were delivered to a buyer who accepted them, or
- the conforming goods were destroyed after risk of loss passed to the buyer but while the goods were still in the hands of the carrier.

The seller may be permitted to recover expected profit, including reasonable overload.

Except as stated above, the seller must choose another remedy.[133]

Rights Inherent in Both Parties

Whether you are the buyer or seller in a transaction, the following may apply to you.

Right to Adequate Assurance of Performance. With bankruptcy courts doing a booming business, you don't want to be left holding the bag as a general creditor. The UCC also does not want the commercial world to slow down in anticipation of insolvency by their counterparts in sales transactions.

When reasonable grounds for financial or credit insecurity arise with respect to your buyer or seller, you may demand adequate assurance of due performance. Until you receive such assurance, you may suspend further performance. If you don't receive a response within 30 days, you may treat this as an automatic repudiation of the contract. Any acceptance of an improper delivery or payment does not prejudice your right to demand adequate assurances of future performances. As between merchants, the courts will look to what assurances are customary in the trade.[134]

If the seller first learns of the buyer's insolvency while the goods are in transit (including those in the possession of any bailee), the seller may stop the transfer of such goods and also reclaim the goods upon demand within 10 days (or possibly 90 days, if the buyer had misrepresented solvency in writing) after their receipt by the buyer. Henceforth the seller may refuse to send all deliveries except for those made for cash.[135]

Anticipatory Repudiation. An unconditional repudiation by either party as to its future performance is a breach of the contract. The aggrieved party has three options:

- Await performance by the repudiating party for a commercially reasonable period of time.[136]
- Resort to any legal remedy even while awaiting the repudiating party's retraction.
- In either case, to suspend performance. If the aggrieved seller is in the process of manufacturing to the buyer's order, the seller may complete the manufacturing process and identify the goods for the contract or cease manufacture and resell for salvage value.[137]

The buyer and seller may provide their own remedies to be applied in the event that one of the parties fails to perform.

Contractual Limitation of Remedies. A contract can expressly modify or limit the UCC remedies, e.g., to just allowing the buyer to return the goods in exchange for the purchase price or to just replacing the goods or having them repaired.[138] Compensatory damages may be limited unless this would be deemed to be unconscionable. The Code states that the parties agree on the amount of damages that is known as "liquidated damages." An agreement for liquidated damages is enforced if the amount is reasonable and if actual damages would be difficult to prove in the event of a breach of the contract. The amount is considered reasonable if it is not so large as to be a penalty or so small as to be unconscionable.[139] "Unconscionability" will also be found if an attempt is made to limit consequential damages for injuries caused to a person by consumer goods.[140]

For all remedies for either party there is a presumption that they are cumulative rather than exclusive.[141]

Conclusion

This chapter has provided a brief look at the dynamics that affect various commercial arrangements entered into on a regular basis, and the references provide valuable follow-up. The law will definitely influence a manager's strategic channel decisions. An informed professional understands the need to consult with experts in particular fields. These transactions require a counsel who is familiar with your firm, its trade, and the law. No guidebook can do you a better service than to urge you to consult with counsel as you enter into these transactions to avoid the various problems that can arise. If problems result despite your precautions, you have an expert familiar with the transaction since its inception.

ENDNOTES

(1) UCC Sec. 2-102. (Hereafter all references to the UCC, unless otherwise specified, refer to UCC Article 2–"Sales as defined in 2-101.") The sale itself consists in the passing

of title from the seller to the buyer for a price, UCC Secs. 2-103(1)(a), 2-103(1)(d), 2-106(1). See also *Bonebaker v. Cox,* 499 F.2d 951 (1974).

(2) UCC Sec. 1-102 (3) and the official Comment 2 to UCC Sec. 1-102.

(3) UCC Sec. 1-105.

(4) The UCC has been adopted by 49 of the 50 states (Louisiana is the partial exception).

(5) UCC Sec. 1-102 Comment 1.

(6) UCC Sec. 1-203, should be read with 1-203(3) and 1-106(2).

(7) UCC Sec. 2-105, which should be read with Sec. 2-107. See UCC Sec. 2-105(1) (when "identification occurs" if you don't have an "explicit agreement" between the parties evidencing same).

(8) UCC Sec. 2-104(1).

(9) UCC Sec. 2-302. For a good analysis of the expanding influence of unconscionability, see Robert J. Posch, Jr., "New Laws Deemed Necessary for a Competitive Environment," *Direct Marketing* , March 1985, pp. 184-188.

(10) In general, this discussion assumes that you're marketing or selling, so it adopts the seller's perspective.

(11) UCC Secs. 2-204, 2-207(3), 2-311(1).

(12) A proper reading of a sales contract requires a full review of the general trade background (UCC Secs. 1-205, 2-208). These realities, not merely a written contract, will structure the agreement. See also UCC Secs. 1-201(1) and 1-201(3).

(13) *McGregor v. Dimon* , 422 N.Y.S.2d 806 (1979).

(14) UCC Sec. 2-206(1)(a). See also *South Hampton Co. v. Stimmes Corp.* 733 F.2d 1108 mc—reverse case (5th Cir. 1984).

(15) UCC Sec. 2-206(1)(b). See also *American Bronze Corp. v. Streamway Products,* 8 Ohio App. 223; 456 N.E.2d 1295 (1982).

(16) UCC Sec. 2-205. See also *City University of New York v. Finalco, Inc.,* 461 N.Y.S.2d 830 (N.Y. App. Div. 1983).

(17) UCC Sec. 2-328(3).

(18) UCC Sec. 2-201; see also *Dandoli v. Asiatic Petroleum Co.,* 395 N.Y.S.2d (A.D.) 15 (1977).

(19) UCC Sec. 2-204(3).

(20) UCC Sec. 2-207(2). See also *Trust Co. Bank v. Barrett Distribs., Inc.* , 459 F.Supp. 959 (1978). As a practical matter, be aware that many of your buyers have "magic language" in their purchase forms that *automatically* objects to additional or different terms.

(21) *Coastal Indus., Inc. v. Automatic Steam Prods. Corp.,* 654 F.2d 375, 378 (1981). *Note:* Where both parties are merchants, nonmaterial terms are accepted by silence. However, if the terms are material, silence is not an acceptance.

(22) *Snyder v. Gallagher Truck Center* 453 N.Y.S.2d(AD) 826 (1982).

(23) Note 21. Id. at 379. See also *Fairfield-Noble Corp. v. Pressman-Gutman Co.,* 475 F.Supp. 899 (1979). (Arbitration is determined on a state by state basis.)

(24) *Product Components, Inc. v. Regency Door & Hardware, Inc.,* 568 F. Supp.651 (S.D. Ind. 1983).

(25) *In re Isis Foods, Inc.* 38 UCC Rep. Serv. 1134, 1137/1983). See also *Howard Construction Co. v. Jeff-Cole Quarries, Inc.,* 669 S.W. 2d 221 (1983).

(26) UCC Sec. 2-207(3). Again, the clear pattern and intent of Article 2 is to recognize and uphold a contract where there is evidence of intent to contract. See also *Diamond Fruit Growers, Inc. v. Krack Corp.* 794 F.2d 1440 (9th Cir., 1986) also *Clifford-Jacobs Forging Co. v. Capital Eng'g & Mfg. Co.,* 437 N.E.2d 22 (1982).

(27) UCC Secs. 1-205, 2-208(2).

(28) UCC Sec. 2-201(1). Note the emphasis on the tangible price. The UCC does not look to the more intangible "value."

(29) *C.G. Campbell & Son, Inc. v. COMDEQ Corp.* , 586 S.W. 2d 40 (1979). Note: The social policy for the statute of frauds is to prevent fraud or perjury on claims of substance.

(30) UCC Sec. 2-201. See also *Iandoli v. Asiatic Petro Co.* , 57 A.D. 2d 815, 395 NYS.2d 15 (1977). *Allen M. Campbell Co. v. Virginia Metal Industries* 708 F.2d 930 (1983).
*Note that all references to the UCC are to the official text. In drafting your agreements, your counsel will also consult applicable state law that contains local variations of these sections.

(31) *Alarm Device Mfg. Co. v. Arnold Indus., Inc.,* 417 N.E.2d 1284 (1979). See also *Barber & Ross, Co. v. Lifetime Doors. Inc.,* 810 F.2d 1276, 1280 (4th Cir. 1987) (a trademark affixed to a brochure can be a signature!).

(32) UCC Secs. 2-104(1), 2-104(3), 2-210(2). See also *Great Western Sugar Co. v. Long Star Donut Co.* 567 F. Supp. 340, aff'd., 721 F.2d 510 (5th Cir. 1983).

(33) UCC Sec. 2-201(3)(c). See *Starr v. Freeport Dodge,* 54 Misc. 2d 271, 282 N.Y.S.2d 58 (1967). Partial payment for an automobile constitutes payment for the entire automobile.

(34) UCC Secs. 2-105(6), 2-201, 2-606.

(35) UCC Sec. 2-201(3)(b)., but see *Slocomb Industries, Inc. v. Chelsea Industries* , 36 UCC Ref. 1543 (1983).

(36) UCC Sec. 2-201(3)(a).

(37) UCC Sec. 2-206.

(38) UCC Sec. 2-204.

(39) *Bethlehem Steel Corp., v. Litton Industries, Inc.* , 468 A.2d 748, (Pa. Super. Ct. 1983).

(40) UCC Sec. 2-206.

(41) UCC Sec. 2-209(2).

(42) UCC Sec. 2-202. A writing intended as the final expression of the parties' agreement cannot be contradicted but may be explained or supplemented by consistent additional terms, course of dealings, usage of trade or business, or prior course of performance. See also *Stender v. Twin City Foods, Inc.,* 510 P.2d 221 (1973).

(43) *U.S. v. Bethlehem Steel Co.* , 205 U.S. 105.

(44) *Pym v. Campbell,* Queens Bench (Eng.) 6 Ellis & Black baru 370 (1856).

(45) *Kern Oil and Refining Co. v. Tenneco Oil Co.* 792 F.2d 1380, 1385 (9th Cir. 1986).

(46) UCC Sec. 2-302. See also *Industralease v. R.M.E. Enter.,* 58 A.D. 2d 482, 396 N.Y.S. 2d 427 (1977).

(47) *Tierney, Inc. v. T. Wellington Carpets, Inc.* , 392 N.E. 2d 1066 (1979). For a decision on how to get out of a mistake, see *Confrancesco Const. Co. v. Superior Components, Inc.* 371 S.W. 2d 821 (1963). At a minimum you'll have to demonstrate a nonnegligent unilateral mistake accompanied by other facts, such as a typographical error or price that is both out of line and obvious to the other party and that the other party is not injured by the cancellation.

(48) *Brooklyn Union Gas Co. v. Jiminez* , 82 Misc. 2d 948, 951, 371 N.Y.S. 2d. 289, 292 (1975) (emphasis added).

(49) UCC Sec. 2-305(1). See *Bethlehem Steel Corp. v. Litton Industries, Inc.* 468 A.2d 748, 755-758 (Pa. Super 1983) (escalation clauses too complex to be "filled in as a gap").

(50) UCC Sec. 2-305(2). A proper reading of a sales contract always requires a full review of the general trade background (UCC Sec. 1-205) and the particular trade dealings between buyer and seller (UCC Sec. 1-205, 2-208). See also *Applied Disposal v. Bob's Home Service,* 595 S.W. 2d 417 (Ct. App. Mo. 1980).

(51) UCC Sec. 2-309 (2).

(52) UCC Sec. 2-309 (3).

(53) *Lidell Explorations, Inc. v. Conval International, Inc.,* 719 F.2d 1465.

(54) UCC Sec. 1-201 (25 & 26).

(55) UCC Sec. 2-306(1).

(56) UCC Sec. 2-306(1). See *Barber & Ross Co. v. Lifetime Doors, Inc.,* 810 F.2d 1276, 1277, (continuous production availability . . . insured purchasers could order . . . desired number).

(57) UCC Sec. 2-307.

(58) See UCC Sec. 2-504, which controls, not 2-308.

(59) UCC Sec. 2-308.

(60) UCC Secs. 1-203, 1-204, 2-103, 2-309. See also *Capital Steel Co. v. Foster and Creighton Co.,* 574 S.W. 2d 256 (1981).

(61) UCC Sec. 2-310(a).

(62) UCC Sec. 2-103(1)(c).

(63) UCC Sec. 2-103(c).

(64) UCC Sec. 2-310(d).

(65) UCC Sec. 2-311(2).

(66) 247 N.W. 2d 744 (Sup. Ct.-Iowa, 1976).

(67) *Jon-T Chemicals, Inc. v. Freeport Chemical Co.*, 704 F.2d 1412, 1416(1983).

(68) For "F.A.S.," "C.I.F.," or "C & F," see UCC Secs. 2-319(2), 2-320.

(69) Carrier obligations were discussed earlier in this chapter.

(70) UCC Sec. 2-319(1)(a).

(71) UCC Sec. 2-319(c).

(72) UCC Sec. 2-319(1)(b).

(73) UCC Sec. 2-319(3).

(74) UCC Sec. 2-320.

(75) UCC Secs. 2-324, 2-613.

(76) *Fulater v. Palmer's Gronite* , 456 N.Y.S.2d 289.

(77) UCC Secs. 2-326(1)(a), 2-327(1)(a), 2-327(1)(c) and *First Coin Investors v. Coppola* , 88 Misc.2d 495, 388 N.Y.S.2d 833 (1976) as discussed. Sale on approval has similarities to consignment sales. As to consignments, see Glossary.

(78) UCC Secs. 2-326(1)(b), 2-327(2)(a), 2-327(2)(b).

(79) UCC Sec. 2-508. See also *Monte Carlo Shirt, Inc. v. Daewoo International Corp.* 707 F.2d 1054 (9th Cir. 1983) and *T.W. Oil Inc., v. Consolidated Edison Co.* 443 N.E. 2d, 932 (N.Y. Ct. App. 1982).

(80) "Substantial performance" requires a buyer, under certain circumstances, to accept something less than perfectly conforming tender. See *Moulton Cavity & Mould, Inc. v. Lyn-Flex Indus. Inc.,* 396 A.2d 1024 (1979).

(81) UCC Sec. 2-612 (substantial performance permitted in installment sales contracts).

(82) UCC Sec. 2-601.

(83) UCC Sec. 2-503(1).

(84) UCC Sec. 2-508(1).

(85) UCC Sec. 2-508(2). See also *Gappelberg v. Candrun* , 666 S.W. 2d 88 (Tex. 1984); *Zabriskie Chevrolet, Inc. v. Smith* , 99 N.J. Super. 441, 240 A2d 195(1968); and *Bartus v. Riccardi* , 55 Misc. 2d, 3, 284 N.Y.S. 2d 222 (1967).

(86) UCC Sec. 2-509(3); *Ramos v. Wheel Sports Center* , 96 Misc. 2d 646, 409 N.Y.S. 2d 505 (1978).

(87) UCC Sec. 2-513(1)(b).

(88) UCC Sec. 2-401(1).

(89) UCC Sec. 2-401(2).

(90) UCC Sec. 2-403.

(91) UCC Sec. 2-403(2) and 2-403(3).

(92) UCC Sec. 2-201(a), defining "buyer in ordinary course of business," requires that the buyer buy "in ordinary course from a person in the business of selling goods of that kind. . . ." Buying "does not include a transfer in bulk or as security for or in total or partial satisfaction of a money debt."

(93) UCC Sec. 6-102.

(94) UCC Sec. 6-103. See *Allsbrook v. Azalea Radiator Service, Inc.* , 316 S.E. 2d 743 (VA. 1984).

(95) UCC Sec. 6-105.

(96) *Gracii v. Denaro* , 413 N.Y.S. 2d 607 (1979).

(97) UCC Sec. 6-107, *Columbia Rope Co. v. Rinek Cordage Company* , 461 A.2d 312 (Pa. Super. Ct. 1983).

(98) *Ouachita Electric Co-Op v. Evans St. Clair* , 672 S.W. 2d 660 (1984).

(99) UCC Sec. 6-109.

(100) *Friedman v. Baron* , 295 N.Y.S. 2d(AD) 874(1968).

(101) UCC Sec. 6-111.

(102) *FICO, Inc. v. Ghingher* , 28 UCC Rep. 498 (Ct. App. MD 1980).

(103) NYS Tax Law 1141c (McKinneys); *Arthur Treacher v. N.Y.S. Tax Commission* , 419 N.Y.S. 2d(AD) 768 (1979).

(104) UCC Sec. 2-601. See also *V. Zeppola v. Pyramid Co.* , 439 N.Y.D. 2d (AD) 765 (1981).

(105) *Roth Steel Products v. Sharon Steel Corp.* 705 F.2d 134, 1435 (6th Cir. 1983).

(106) UCC Sec. 2-605.

(107) UCC Sec. 2-602.

(108) UCC Sec. 2-508. See also *Running Springs Associates v. Masonite Corp.* 680 F.2d 469 (1982) and *K and M Joint Ventures v. Smith International* 669 F2d 106 (1982).

(109) UCC Secs. 2-510(1), 2-602. Again, you must be careful as to your position in these areas, since the UCC prefers to uphold contracts. Carefully review any rejection agreements with your counsel before acting to your possible prejudice. If the buyer has taken reasonable steps to safeguard the Seller's goods, the Seller is liable for goods stolen from Buyer's premises. *Lykins Oil Co. v. Fekkos,* 507 N.E.2d 795 (1986).

(110) *Kleiderfabrik v. Peters Sportwear Co.*, 483 F. Supp. 1228 (1980). UCC Secs. 2-602-604-706(6).

(111) UCC Sec. 2-607. See also *Columbia Can Co. of New Jersey v. Africa–Middle East Marketing, Inc.* , 455 A.2d 1143 (N.J. Super. Ct. App. Div. 1983).

(112) *Lenkay Products v. Benitey* , 362 N.Y.S. 2d (AD) 572 (1975). See also *Summer v. Fel-Air, Inc.* 680 P.2d. 1109 (Alaska 1984).

(113) UCC Sec. 2-106(2), 2-606(1)(b), 2-607, 2-608. See *Eastern Airlines v. McDonnell Douglas Corp.* 532 F.2d 957. See also *Lynx, Inc. v. Ordnance Prods. Inc.* , 327 A.2d 502 (1974). Note: If the use of the goods is necessary to allow proper evaluation of them, such use does not constitute acceptance (UCC Secs. 2-606, 2-608. See also *United Airlines, Inc. v. Conductron Corp.* 387 N.E. 1272 (1979).

(114) UCC Sec. 2-712. See also *Fertico Belgium, S.A. v. Phosphate Chemicals Export Assoc., Inc.,* 70 N.Y.2d 76 (1987).

(115) UCC Sec. 2-617.

(116) UCC Sec. 2-715; *Lowes Glove Co. v. Acme Fast Freight Co.* , 54 Misc. 2d 429, 282 N.Y.S. 2d 869 (1967). See also UCC Secs. 2-712(1), 2-712(3); *American Carpet Mills v. Grinny Corp.* , 649 F.2d 1056 (1981).

(117) UCC Secs. 2-711, 2-725; *Thorstenson v. Mobridge Iron Works* , 208 N.W. 2d 715 (1973).

(118) UCC Sec. 2-716. See also Sec. 2-502.

(119) UCC Sec. 2-714.

(120) UCC Sec. 2-715.

(121) *Metropolitan Transfer Station, Inc. v. Design Structures, Inc.* 328 N.W. 2d 532 (Iowa Ct. App. 1982).

(122) *Elar Invs., Inc. v. Southwest Culvert Co.* , 139 Ariz. 25, 676 P.2d 659 (1983).

(123) UCC Sec. 2-106 and Comment 1.

(124) UCC Sec. 2-609. See also *Clem Perrin Marine Towing, Inc. v. Panama Canal Co.,* 730 F.2d 186 (5th Cir. 1986).

(125) UCC Sec. 2-704.

(126) UCC Sec. 2-704(2).

(127) UCC Sec. 2-609, 2-610, 2-703(a), 2-705.

(128) UCC Sec. 2-403.

(129) UCC Sec. 2-702, 705.

(130) UCC 2-708(1) and (2). See *Union Carbide Corp. v. Consumers Power Co.,* 636 F.Supp. 1498 (E.D. Mich. 1986); *Trans World Metals, Inc. v. Southwire Co.,* 769 F.2d 902 (2nd Cir. 1985); and *Nobs Chemical, U.S.A., Inc. v. Koppers Co.,* 606 F.2d 212 (5th Cir. 1980).

(131) UCC Sec. 2-710; *Brownie's Army & Navy Store v. Burke* , 424 N.Y.S. 2d (AD) 800 (1980).

(132) UCC Sec. 2-706.

(133) UCC Sec. 2-708 and Comment 2 to 2-708.

(134) UCC Sec. 2-609 (defines insolvency).

(135) UCC Sec. 2-702(1)(b).

(136) Such party can retract its anticipatory repudiation, subject to UCC Sec. 2-611.

(137) UCC Sec. 2-610(a), 2-610(c), 2-704(2).

(138) UCC Sec. 2-719.

(139) UCC Sec. 2-718(1). See also *Speedi Lubrication Centers, Inc. v. Atlas Match Corp.,* 595 S.W. 2d 912 (Tex. 1980). For a good case on UCC2-718(2) see *Maxton Builders, Inc. v. Gallo,* 68 N.Y. 2d, 373, 377 (1987).

(140) UCC Sec. 2-719 (3).

(141) UCC Sec. 2-719(1)(b).

CHAPTER 9

YOUR GUIDE TO DIRECT-MARKETING LEGAL COMPLIANCE

Retailing has moved off Main Street into the malls. It now includes door-to-door, party selling, video catalogs, direct mail, direct telephone, home shopping networks, and the like. All of this new marketing is loosely grouped under the umbrella of direct or database marketing.

What is direct marketing? Who is a direct marketer? Henry R. Hoke, Jr., who runs a leading think tank in the field sets forth a flowchart in each of his magazines.[1] Specifically, "direct marketing is an interactive system of marketing that uses one or more advertising media to effect a measurable response and/or transaction at any location." Hoke has defined a direct marketer as "one who owns and maintains a mailing list, used to support any and all methods of selling. The list is the cornerstone."[2]

Detractors often dismiss this channel as "junk mail" or "junk calls." Invariably, you will find that such detractors are from newspapers and other media that are losing revenue to database marketing. This hypocrisy is rarely commented upon since it would require self-criticism in their own media. If home shopping keeps growing, maybe you'll soon be hearing about "junk TV channels", or "junk videotext."

More important, however, is the ability of the direct marketing channel to enable entrepreneurs with a little capital to rapidly enter national markets. One graphic way to demonstrate the power of direct mail is to look at its influence in politics. The conservative movement's unique mastery of the art of political communication through direct mail enabled it to dominate politics during 1977 to 1980. As a leading creative genius in the field, Richard Viguerie, stated:

> Direct mail has been our basic form of communication. The liberals have had control not only of all three branches of government, but of the major universities, the three major networks, the biggest newspapers, the news

weeklies, and Hollywood. . . .Fortunately, or rather providentially, a whole new technology has become available just in time—direct mail, backed by computer science, has allowed us to bypass all the media controlled by our adversaries.[3]

A great boost to direct marketing has come from the number of industry-input rules affecting this channel. These rules, rather than being counterproductive, have led to the great increase in public acceptance of direct marketing.

I find it amusing when I read other "reasons" given for the channel's recent success, e.g., the alleged energy shortages, poor retail service, women working outside the home, etc. None of these arguments has any serious basis in fact or marketing experience. Targeted marketing sells targeted products not available or perceived as not available in a nearby mall. It will do well or not depending on the crime rate of an area and public confidence.

The fundamental basis of the increased acceptance of ordering over the phone or through the mail has been an increase in customer satisfaction and trust in this marketing channel. A good deal of this is simply due to the fact that quality firms are earning and retaining this satisfaction. An equally valid fact is that government regulations have enhanced customer acceptance of this channel.

The Cooling-Off Period Rule increases customer trust in this form of direct selling. People are entering more sweepstakes today (see Section IV) because there is greater trust. No one likes a game with undue hassles. The Federal Trade Commission's promulgation and enforcement of fair marketplace rules is as necessary as an umpire. Take him away and who would be the neutral arbiter?

I doubt that any reader could point to any FTC rules which, since their inception, have had a negative impact on sales in the objective sense. Further, the subjective benefits of customer trust in the channel and knowledge of its rules of operation simply encourage the consumer to enter the "game" and buy.

The rule of greatest potential benefit to all mailers is the Trade Regulation Rule Concerning Mail Order Merchandise.[4] This rule was written with much industry input and should be preserved as is. However, there is a growing perception that it is not working. Mail order complaints remain at or near the top of most Better Business Bureau lists as well as the FTC's own.[5]

This public perception has led some states[6] to attempt to change the 30-Day Rule's requirement from *ship* within 30 days to *deliver* within 30 days. These bills were amended to delete the burden of "deliver" due to one of the trade's legislative lobbying groups, DeHart and Darr Associates, with input from its members. Other states, such as Wisconsin, acted more directly by legally pursuing firms that act improperly. In one year, lawsuits against mail order companies not complying with the state mail order law resulted in combined civil forfeitures of $203,840.[7]

The FTC has also been active. For example, one consent decree in 1984 resulted in, among other things, a mail order firm's paying $200,000 in settlement. (See footnote 9 for a variety of other firms cited.) As reported in DMA's *Washington Report,* [8] JS&A Group and Me-Books Publishing Company will pay $115,000 and $20,000, respectively, in civil penalties.

You will also note in many of these cases the firm not only had to pay fines and consumer restitution but that the individuals who ran the firms were often personally cited and became personally responsible. At least one officer was banned for life from the direct marketing channel![9]

This stepped-up enforcement is to be applauded. Violations of this rule, or even the appearance of same, generate publicity that is not in the best interest of direct mail marketers. Each unresolved complaint may represent someone who will return to the stores and ignore his or her mailbox. Besides lost orders, a continued volume of complaints may encourage not only overkill enforcement, but a rewording of the rule to require delivery rather than mere shipment within 30 days.[10]

This channel's potential is unlimited, but you must know the rules. We'll review here a few rules of the most interest which form a vital core to managers using this channel. For a more in-depth study, see my first book, *The Direct Marketer's Legal Adviser.* [11] After you read it, place it into the hands of your associates who need to know the basics of legal compliance. So read on for a brief review of what you need to know to keep your firm in compliance. In the long run this will contribute to customer satisfaction with your firm and with direct marketing in general.

The Mailstream of Commerce

Direct marketers have less difficulty than most in determining the length of the product-marketing channel needed to reach their markets. No matter how rapidly your customer registers the desire to purchase your product or even pays (e.g., instantaneous electronic fund transfer), you must contend with the delivery constraints of the U.S. Postal Service or a private carrier.[12] Intermediaries are few, although drop shippers may be used. Once the direct marketer was mainly concerned with postal regulations and costs and with physical distribution management. Recently, however, four major areas of compliance have arisen: The 30-day rules, the unordered-merchandise statutes, merchandise substitution, and telephone marketing.

With increases in costs for almost all aspects of mail-order selling (e.g., postage, printing, and the goods themselves), most firms have cut back on inventories. As a result, they can't always fill incoming orders promptly. Further, some marginal companies caught in the vise of inflation have sought interest-free, or "dry," loans, that is, holding their cash flow vis-a-vis fulfillment for as long as possible.

The FTC and many states have enacted 30-day rules or laws.[13] These state laws must be consulted, especially the laws of the state in which your corporation is located. Note 5 of the FTC rule specifically states that the FTC does not wish to preempt consistent but narrower state laws on point. Therefore, you may find that your firm must comply with a narrower state law. For our purposes, we'll focus on the FTC rules.[14]

The Thirty-Day Rule

The Mail Order Rule was based on proceedings begun in 1971. It was finally adopted in 1976. It will be enforced literally and penalties up to $10,000 may be issued for each violation. Since it is only three and a half pages long, it is worth your time to review it. It was written for laymen and avoids legalese. It all boils down to four areas:

(1) Initial solicitation requirements;

(2) First and subsequent delay notification;

(3) Internal Procedures;

(4) State laws on point which may be more narrowly drawn.

Initial Solicitation

It is an unfair or deceptive act to solicit any order through the mails unless you have a reasonable basis (arrived at in good faith, with objective substantiation) to believe you can fulfill the order within the time you specify or, if no time is specified, then 30 days after the receipt of a *properly completed order* from your buyer. This means that the mail order company must have received the cash, check, or money order, or charged a credit account, and that it has all the information needed to process and ship the order. For example, if you fail to specify the size or color of an ordered item, the order is not complete.

The FTC has indicated in a consent agreement that it wants you to state clearly and conspicuously, on each order form for premium merchandise, all the requirements for a properly completed order. To avoid the float situation (and to protect ethical sellers) it wants you to notify the sender within 15 days of the receipt of an improperly completed order. The notice should tell the sender why it is incomplete and how to complete it.

What is a reasonable basis to solicit the initial order is reflected by the variables of your industry and market—a factual issue affected by the interplay of many considerations. We all know the value of a dollar in hand and the retention of same. The FTC understands the "float" value of money too, and doesn't want your customers providing you with interest free loans. Your best protection as to your good faith and reasonable expectations at the time of solicitation is to maintain internal records which will objectively validate your expectations.

However, remember *you elect* to become involved with the 30-day aspect of this rule. You can insulate yourself from problems here if you state at the outset a date you can live with clearly and conspicuously on your promotion piece. You might state "60 days from receipt" of order. Then there is no first delay problem (see below) until 60 days have elapsed, not 30. The trade-off here might be a loss of "spontaneity," since customers might be discouraged by a long wait. However, the choice is yours.

You also elect to come within the provisions of this rule by accepting cash orders. Bill only by outside credit cards (may help your bad debt, too) or by a system of internal credit adjustments or even C.O.D. In none of these cases will you bill before delivery and, therefore, in none of these cases will you be affected by the "30-Day Rule."

Finally, there are methods to decrease potential legal problems as well as customer dissatisfaction. Remember a customer complaint to the FTC, a State Attorney General Office, or Better Business Bureau is not helpful even if totally unjustified. Such complaints attract unwanted attention to your firm and may accumulate with valid ones to reach a threshold number whereby adverse reaction is triggered. Examine the following as possible ways to lessen complaints:

▶ Don't wait until checks clear. The 30-day meter is running. Test whether this delay is resulting in 30-day shipment problems. If so, does the trade–off vis–a–vis your bad debt picture justify this practice?

▶ Test different post offices or even the time of day you ship (if this option is available to you.) Yes, it is true that your legal requirement is to ship—not deliver—within 30 days. Legally, your customer must then contend with the inherent delays in the U.S. Postal Service or some other similar system of distribution you employ. However, your customer knows only that he or she is waiting. Maximizing your deliveries by finding the best post office (and they vary) will enhance goodwill and possibly avoid complaints to the regulatory agencies.

▶ The 30-day meter begins to run only after you receive in-house a properly completed order. If you write back to your customer, make sure you keep a record of this. He or she may forget the initial delay was not prompted by you but by him or her. When he or she complains to you or an agency, it will satisfy both the individual and the agency if you can demonstrate that once a properly completed order was returned you fulfilled it and shipped it within the required time.

The reality of any marketplace is that unanticipated delays occur; for example, a welcome deluge of orders or a simple delay by your supplier. When you are unable to ship the merchandise within the applicable time (for instance, the specific time you stated in your promotion or 30 days if no time is specified), you have the option to cancel the agreement, and so inform your buyer, or attempt to preserve the sale.

"First Delay" Situations

To exercise this option, you must send a postage-paid return notice to the buyer clearly and conspicuously offering the buyer the choice to either cancel the order and receive a full and prompt refund or extend the time for shipment to a specified revised shipping date. Tactically, you have an advantage here as inertia is in your favor. If the buyer does not answer at all, you get the delay. Silence is construed as acceptance.

Don't attempt to improve on the prepaid reply device (postcard or letter). You may feel a toll–free 800 number is more spontaneous and actually a greater benefit in facilitating the customer's response. The FTC won't. Just use a prepaid response letter.

"Multiple Delay" Situations

You're unhappy you are not able to ship. The buyer is unhappy he or she has no product. The initial time to ship and now the "first delay" grace period has eclipsed. You might still be able to save the order.

You must notify the buyer of the additional delay. You may request the buyer's permission to ship at a future date or even a vague, indefinite date. At this time you must also notify the buyer that if he or she consents to the delay, he or she may still cancel at any subsequent time by notifying the seller prior to the actual shipment. The buyer may then cancel or affirmatively agree to extend the time for delivery.

The situation is most distinguishable from the "first delay" insofar as silence by the buyer cannot be construed as acceptance. If the buyer remains "silent" (for example, fails to return the postage-paid card), then you must treat the order as cancelled and return a refund promptly to the buyer.

What is a prompt refund? This depends on the payment option elected. If the buyer sent cash or a check, he or she is entitled to have mailed first-class a refund in full within seven business days. If a credit card or other form of credit adjustment is required, then you have a full billing cycle from the date on which the buyer's right to a refund begins. Under no circumstances are credit vouchers or scrip permitted.

The Mail Order Rule stresses the need for adequate systems and procedures to create a presumption of a good faith effort present to satisfy customer inquiries and or complaints. These systems and procedures should also be adequate to establish your good faith basis upon which to solicit the initial order or request a delay(s).

The rule does not apply to negative option forms of selling or to magazine sales (except for the initial shipment) as well as to C.O.D. orders, orders for seeds and growing plants, and credit orders where the buyer's account is not charged before you ship the merchandise.[15]

Narrower State Laws

As usual, you cannot be a 50-state marketer without following the legislatures of the 50 states.[16] The rule states that there is no preemption of consistent state laws offering equal or greater protection. You might find some state laws do, and if more narrowly drawn as to consumer protection, the FTC will defer to these where applicable. Direct marketers do not enjoy a uniform system of compliance. In certain states companies must maintain *two separate* systems for fulfilling a customer order, one to comply with the state and another to comply with the FTC *or* choose the more restrictive for a single fulfillment system.

For example, New York's law allows a *maximum* of 65 days. There is no "multiple-delay" or "extended-delay" provision available to a seller. The entire order *must* be shipped or the full payment refunded within a maximum of 65 days. Also, the exclusion found as to negative option, C.O.D., and so forth, discussed above under "Internal Procedures" are not found in the New York Law.[17]

Finally, certain states such as New York have extended the provisions of their Mail Order Rule to *include* telephone order merchandise though it did not change the fact that in New York State there are different delivery requirements for a credit card order mailed to the seller and a credit card order placed by telephone to the seller.

In signing the bill on August 8, 1984, the governor stated, "this measure will protect the growing number of persons, particularly elderly and disabled persons, who regularly rely on mail and telephone orders for their shopping needs." It is essential you learn, keep up with, and follow the laws of each state you do business in. You owe it to the goodwill of your firm and the direct marketing channel in general to avoid undue visibility to public regulatory scrutiny. Vigilant compliance with the Mail Order Rule should be a long step in this direction. Now let's move on to the Unordered Merchandise Rule.

Avoiding the Pitfalls of Unordered Merchandise

In an effort to maximize season ordering, many marketers are tempted to "substitute" orders. Others may accidentally mail to an incorrect address. On the other hand, many customers who order too quickly or without thinking receive what they ordered but didn't really want. As a result, certain items may not be paid for. You wish to dun.

Dunning for unordered merchandise can be the trigger for unwanted involvement with the Federal Trade Commission, a state attorney general, or simply bad customer relations. Dunning accomplishes this in two ways:

(1) The billing or dunning for unordered merchandise is, itself, an unfair practice; and

(2) Many customers do not complain to a regulatory body until dunning begins, because they were not aware of the problem or violation.

What is the rule concerning the mailing of unordered merchandise, and how can you avoid problems with it? We shall review it paragraph by paragraph and then discuss its exceptions.

Mailing of Unordered Merchandise

(a) Except for (1) free samples clearly and conspicuously marked as such, and (2) merchandise mailed by a charitable organization soliciting contributions, the mailing of unordered merchandise or of communications prohibited by subsection (c) of this section constitutes an unfair method of competition and an unfair trade practice in violation of section 45(a)(1) of Title 15 (15 USCS) Sec. 45(a)(1).[18]

This paragraph quite clearly makes it a per se violation of the unfair trade laws to ship unordered merchandise which is defined as "merchandise mailed without the prior expressed request or consent of the recipient."[19] The only ambiguity here was the reference to "mailed."

Because the original pronouncement referred to the Postal Reorganization Act, some thought enforcement would be limited to those marketers utilizing the United States Postal Service. The FTC clarified its position in 1978 in stating that *all* unordered merchandise was included whether shipped by mail, United Parcel, other private alternate delivery or any other carrier.

(b) Any merchandise mailed in violation of subsection (a) of this section, or within the exceptions contained therein, may be treated as a gift by the recipient, who shall have the right to retain, use, discard, or dispose of it in any manner he sees fit without any obligation whatsoever to the sender. All such merchandise shall have attached to it a clear and conspicuous statement informing the recipient that he may treat the merchandise as a gift to him and has the right to retain, use, discard, or dispose of it in any manner he sees fit without any obligation to the sender.

It should be noted that it is a *separate* violation (apart from the initial sending itself) for anyone to mail unordered merchandise without attaching a clear and conspicuous statement informing the recipient that he/she may treat it as a gift.

(c) No mailer of any merchandise mailed in violation of subsection (a) of this section, or within the exceptions contained therein, shall mail to any recipient of such merchandise a bill for such merchandise or any dunning communications.

It is a third violation of this statute for any sender of unordered merchandise (including correctly marked free samples and merchandise sent by charitable organizations) to send the recipient any bill or dunning communication (or suggestion of same) in connection with such unordered merchandise.

In fact, your best strategy may well be *"when in doubt, don't dun."* A customer complaint to a regulatory body or his/her own private action (discussed below) will rarely occur unless an effort is made to compel payment. Now we've reviewed the law. A number of questions arise.

What Are the Penalties? The penalties for both firms and individuals are up to $10,000 *per violation.* State laws may carry varied penalties and also may be more narrowly drawn. You should review the law for each state in which you're doing business as well as routinely monitor legislation/regulations in such state.

Must the Consumer Obtain His/Her Remedy by Complaint to an Agency? No. It was Congress' intent to permit the consumer to protect him or herself under the terms of the Unordered Merchandise Statute. This was clearly established in a 1977 case.[20] This case hits many issues of interest to you in this area and will be related in detail.

Academy Life mailed Mr. Kipperman and others unsolicited promotional material concerning the term notice "Student Protection Policy" with a face value of $2,000. Each recipient's name and address were printed by computer on the face of the "policy." At the bottom of such "policy" was a tear-off application form indicating a Premium Amount Now Due of $9.00.

The form itself and an enclosed brochure indicated coverage could be effected only on the return of the completed application and payment of the first premium (there was no "simulation" or "free" issue involved).

Kipperman brought a class action which sought, among other things, to have this term insurance policy declared "merchandise" within the meaning of the statute which allows the recipient of unsolicited merchandise to treat it as a gift, and therefore fully in effect without any payment of a premium.

In rejecting the contention that this unaccepted offer to insure was "merchandise" resulting in free insurance coverage, the 9th Circuit Court of Appeals stated:

> It is no more merchandise than is an unsolicited offer to sell kitchen appliances. The receipt of such an offer does not permit the recipient under Section 3009 to obtain a judicial determination that he is the owner of such appliances. No insurance coverage could arise until the recipient completed the application and forwarded it with the premium amount.[21]

While establishing that the consumer has the right to sue a firm in federal court, the decision also held that such consumer cannot obtain injunctive relief. This right to sue may become more important in the future as budget cutbacks and Reagan-appointed personnel at the FTC may lessen the FTC's ability or interest in following up on this area with the same consumerist zeal as they exhibited formerly.

What if the Customer Denies the Existence of an Agreement?

You are in a strong posture if you have a signed order, and such order unequivocally states the contractual relationship to which the individual is subscribing. If the signature was a forgery and/or contested by the recipient in good faith, you would be on firm ground to request the customer return such item at your expense (postage).

Prior course of dealings, such as a call with follow-up shipment, is not a valid argument when dealing with a consumer on a one-shot basis. Under the Uniform Commercial Code (UCC), two merchants can develop such prior course of dealings. However, the UCC is not applicable to consumers. The fact that you have shipped before and the customer has paid for similar items by check or otherwise really proves nothing in this particular instance of shipment.

If you dun, expect problems if the recipient complains to a public body. Your common law implied contract would probably not be compelling to the FTC or a state regulatory body—though by all means argue it, as it might establish good faith.

The weakest position of all is the telephone marketer making a "cold call order"[22] whereby without a prior business relationship, the seller ships upon order with no confirming documents. There is little possibility of enforcing such a call against a complaint filed under the Unordered Merchandise Statute. You have no acceptable proof at all of an order. Some ways you might consider to protect yourself include:

- Send all orders C.O.D. so that unordered merchandise might be rejected up front;
- Send a postage paid envelope with the order so that those recipients who receive unordered merchandise may be encouraged to return such goods immediately, at no cost to themselves, thereby saving the merchandise, itself;
- Comply with the cooling off provisions as worded or provide your customer with a follow-up written confirmation which could be responded to in a positive or negative option manner (the former response would probably negate any problems as to cold calls); and/or
- Follow up all orders with a subsequent phone call confirming the original order. This is still weaker protection than the above options because it is oral, but a procedure which, if routine, may move an agency to believe that you employ bona fide methods to avoid unordered merchandise problems.

No matter what the safeguards you employ, an oral order is not a provable order and this must be considered at all stages—especially before you dun.

We'll leave this topic on a note of optimism. Telephone marketing will prosper as long as you can hail a taxi outside your office. The cabbie is in a business similar to yours. He/she must depend on people's intrinsic honesty. If more than a few customers bolt, then there is no more profit in driving a cab. So people are basically honest—and so long as you can get a taxi you can sell "safely" by cold calling.

How Does This Statute Affect Negative Option Plans?   During the commitment period and at all subsequent times, there is an ongoing business relationship subject to the FTC's rule on point.[23] However, a contract-complete member may wish to cancel. For example, midway through a cycle, the seller receives from such contract-complete member a written notice of cancellation. But it is too late to stop the current product shipment. Is this unordered merchandise?

No. The trade regulation rule on point permits the sending of this last product if your cancellation (correct in form) was not received in time to be stopped in the routine course of business. Further, the rule[24] permits the sender to ask for its return (but not bill) this one time. Any subsequent shipments after this one constitute unordered merchandise.

What About a Continuity Plan?   Your rights are less clear as there is no rule on point. You could use a similar approach as to the one isolated shipment after cancellation, but I wouldn't dun.

What About Substituted Merchandise?   The entire area is fraught with peril, even if the substitution is of equivalent or superior quality. Artistic property by its very nature is too unique to ever substitute. If a seasonal surge or other unanticipated ordering deluge is overwhelming your inventory reserve, get expressed consent in writing before you substitute.

This will save your sale as well as satisfy a customer who prefers the substitution to nothing as he/she needs a gift by a given date. Substitution without the prior expressed consent or request of the recipient falls within the literal terms of the statute and will be considered an unfair trade practice.

Conclusion

The above is a review (by no means exhaustive) of the Federal Unordered Merchandise Statute. The law is short and is written in uncomplicated language and is entirely reproduced herein. Most states have similar laws on their books, some of them more narrowly drawn.

Whenever possible, coupons or order forms authorizing the shipment of merchandise to a consumer should be signed and clearly laid out in separate and distinct paragraphs. All wording should be in layman's English, and the merchandise or purchase plan should be described in detail. When a serious doubt arises as to the validity of your efforts to recover payment—don't dun.

Now let's take a look at some other telephone marketing legal issues.

Telephone Marketing—Personnel Training

The social benefits of telephone marketing are legion. Telephone marketing is utilized (with a greater potential to directly and indirectly achieve affirmative action goals). It is an excellent means of employment for handicapped and functionally older citizens. Further, the 24-hour-a-day 800 numbers will encourage you to hire for irregular shifts, thus opening the doors of employment opportunity to those at home with children during "normal" hours (such 24-hour service also lets you avoid "blue laws" where they still exist). The social utility of this marketing medium is apparent even before the financial benefit accumulates!

The utility of the telephone in various aspects of direct marketing is only now coming into its own. Telephone marketing is the fastest growing medium in marketing goods and services and is now #1 in direct marketing sales generation. Society is familiar with the traditional cold calls from various salespersons. It is only beginning to realize that commercial television, cable, and radio are no longer passive media but interactive, once the toll-free 800 number flashes across the screen.

Beyond marketing, telephone dunning is demonstrating a better cost/benefit ratio each time the postal rates go up. More and more modern customer service departments are encouraging telephone feedback as to service and product problems. The customer enjoys talking to someone besides a computer and the firm receives valuable market data. Yet, all phone contact depends on one key ingredient - the person representing your firm.

This person has to be articulate and employ proper diction. He/she must be motivated and be naturally adept at sustained human interaction. Your representative must know your product and possibly be a problem solver. Then, there is a rapid fatigue rate possibly compounded by irregular hours (the 800 number is often a 24-hour-a-day operation). Finally, this person must have the intestinal fortitude to withstand rejection and possibly verbal abuse (e.g., the debt collector).

One note of optimism is that just as telephone technology is understood and accepted by the receiver of the call, your staff callers arrive with some experience in operating and talking on the phone. However, all new personnel must be acclimated to the firm and trained in their specific area of operations. A training program without the ability to monitor "live" calls is a training program severely handicapped at its inception. But, in these days of post-Watergate consciousness, will the law allow a firm to monitor live calls to an outside party? Federal law says you can, and most states[25] have modeled their laws accordingly.

Federal Law

In 1968, Congress passed a comprehensive electronic surveillance law in Title III of the Omnibus Crime Control and Safe Streets Act of

1968.[26] This Act was intended to deal with increasing threats to privacy resulting from the growing use of sophisticated electronic monitoring devices which threatened an average citizen's reasonable expectation of privacy.

Unlike many pieces of legislative overkill, this Act was worded so as to strike a fair balance between privacy rights and legitimate business practices. For your business needs, an understanding of certain definitions in 18 USC 2510 is important. We'll review them here.

To violate the Act, you must intercept an oral or wire communication. A telephone conversation is a wire communication. However, an interception does not occur unless an "electronic, mechanical, or other device" is employed. The definition of these devices specifically excludes a telephone used in the regular course of the subscriber's business. Specifically, 18 USC 2510 (5) (a) (1) grants an exception to:

(a) any telephone or telegraph instrument, equipment or facility or any component thereof,

(i) furnished to the subscriber or user by a communication common carrier in the ordinary course of its business and being used by the subscriber or user in the ordinary course of its business;. . .

The means of intercepting the communication, as long as the device is attached to an extension phone outlet is irrelevant insofar as it relates to whether the interception is in the ordinary course of business.[27] If you request the telephone company to install a monitoring device which will permit you to listen in on telephone conversations between employees and customers only in the "ordinary course of business," there will be no interception. This is predicated on the fact that "ordinary course of business" duties include only lawful and proper activities.

Lawful and Proper Activities

The courts that have reviewed the issue do not want to see evidence of surreptitious monitoring or monitoring for personal gain or gossip. At all times you should be able to demonstrate that the monitoring was undertaken for the sole interest of the company's business operations. At no time do you wish to appear to have monitored a strictly "private" call. Some examples follow.

The Bell system installed monitoring equipment on telephones in a newspaper organization's departments that have direct contact with the public. The business purpose of this monitoring was to assist the employee training program as well as to serve as protection for employees from abusive calls. The monitoring was not surreptitious. On the contrary, it was performed with the prior knowledge of management and all affected employees (who were informed in writing). The Court held that there was no interception since the equipment was used in the ordinary course of the employer's business.[28]

Then there is the situation where monitoring is performed over a simple extension phone. One sobering case[29] was where a supervisor was invited to listen to a call. The employee had been visibly upset by a previous call from this person and this aroused the curiosity of the supervisor. The caller issued a death threat to the employee, a threat he proved only too capable of following through on. The trial court convicted the murderer, based in part, on the supervisor's testimony.

This decision was reversed by the Appellate Court. The Florida Supreme Court upheld the trial court's conclusion that there was no interception despite the issue of the supervisor's "curiosity." The supervisor was acting in her official capacity, concerned with the employee's emotional state affecting her job. The employee gave prior consent. The business purpose performed during business hours satisfied the "ordinary course of business" test establishing no interception.

Is monitoring permitted without employee's prior consent or at least being placed on notice? Yes—in limited circumstances. A manager had justifiable suspicion to believe an employee was acting in concert with an agent of a competitor to the possible detriment of the manager's corporation. The manager warned the employee not to disclose confidential information to this outside party. The manager continued to believe something was not right.

When the manager subsequently was informed by his secretary that the parties were on the phone with each other, he decided to validate his suspicions. He listened to and recorded a part of a telephone conversation by means of an extension phone without the prior knowledge of the employee or the third party.

The act of listening in was limited in purpose and time—just enough time to confirm his suspicions. The U.S. District Court[30] held no interception, because the manager was acting in what he legitimately believed was the company's best interest. While in no way condoning the manager's actions, the Court held that his use of the telephone satisfied the "ordinary course of a business test" due to the close business relationship between the content of the call and the reason behind the manager's monitoring.

In distinguishable circumstances, another court held that in the context of a business office, "a personal call may not be intercepted in the ordinary course of business . . . except to the extent necessary to guard against unauthorized use of the telephone or to determine whether a call is personal or not."[31]

Finally, it should be noted that the use of an extension telephone to intercept a phone call by someone who is not authorized to use the telephone (e.g., non-management employee if phones are restricted to management) under any circumstances cannot be considered conduct "in the ordinary course of business."[32]

Protecting Your Monitoring

If, after reviewing the above discussion, you can demonstrate that your employee telephone monitoring procedures are used in a manner which is lawful and proper and in the ordinary course of business, you are in fairly good shape. However, your worries are not over, and the following precautions are in order.

☐ State and local legislative and regulatory activity should be routinely audited. The law in place should be reviewed with counsel. The Federal Law we have discussed permits more stringent state standards, and some states do have more stringent laws on point. Others are trying to get some new laws on the books. Such burdens include requiring marked telephones, beep tones, or consent of one or more individuals in advance. The increased legislative activity here follows an increased attention to direct response advertising (36 states and Congress introduced one or more bills adversely affecting such advertising in 1985 and 1986). The ability to monitor live calls is an area telephone marketers would be wise to stay alert to.[33]

☐ Neither the surreptitious use of a telephone extension to record a private telephone conversation nor a general practice of surreptitious monitoring would qualify as a legal exception. You should never tape a call as "evidence" that a customer agreed to do something. The DMA Suggested Guidelines for Marketing by Telephone also discuss taping telephone conversations. For a copy of these industry self-regulation guidelines, call the New York DMA Office at (212) 689-4977.

☐ Do not attempt to monitor personal calls to "prove" a violation of a legitimate business policy against such calls without extending prior warnings to an individual concerning such violation of a no-personal-call policy.

☐ To meet the ordinary course of business test:

(a) state this purpose when you procure the equipment from the common carrier;

(b) give advance written notice to all managers and employees involved, stating the business purpose of the monitoring; and

(c) obtain a written release from each employee involved, stating that they are aware of the fact that their supervisor will listen in unannounced and that they agree to this policy.

☐ With the increased growth of international business in general and marketing in particular, one final comment is useful. The provisions of the Wire Interception and Interception of Oral Communications Act apply only within the territorial jurisdiction of the United States. The law of the nation where the monitoring takes place (situs) governs the validity of such monitoring.

This is true even though a United States citizen is involved and/or the intercepted telephone conversation traveled in part over the U.S. communications system. Therefore, a U.S.–based firm physically located in the U.S. may monitor calls to Canadian customers subject to U.S. law. Likewise, a Canadian–based firm monitoring calls to U.S. customers is bound by Canadian law on this point.

☐ Finally, in your personnel practices don't overlook the stress issues imposed on employees. There is a variety of software in use for monitoring the performance of telephone salespeople by computer. The sales manager can tell how many calls, closings and sales are made per hour and the dollar volume for each salesperson. This can be an important new tool for making personnel decisions. . .and for judging the effectiveness of various selling approaches—if done humanely. The failure to be alert to human needs may result in a union-organizing campaign at your office.

Conclusion

The direct marketer, in monitoring any aspect of employee calls, must be careful that he/she does not monitor in a manner which would "intercept" calls. There is no interception under federal law (and most state laws) if the acquisition of the contents of the communication is accomplished through telephone equipment used in the ordinary course of business. The main legal issues remain speculative and are based on the chimera of "privacy." Let's take a look now at the privacy non-issue.

Telephone Marketing—Overview of Regulatory Issues

Less than a decade ago there was a near hysterical chorus to overregulate and/or ban out of existence one of the major marketing devices of the present and future. In 1978, H.R. 9505 was introduced to effectively ban commercial speech by phone. In 23 states, 54 similar bills (and 50 other forms) were modeled after H.R. 9505. Then nothing significant happened! Why?

Essentially there were two reasons. First, the detractors had no "social" case in the terms of representing even a large segment of public opinion. Second, they had no legal case.

For the "cause people" to raise an issue successfully they need the media to hype interest which must in turn be translated into people willing to be counted. Initially, as you might remember, the media was vocal. However, the newspapers lost their concern with "junk calls" when they realized how many of their subscriptions were generated by phone. Broadcast media followed the print media and stopped hitting the issue.

Without the hype, an issue must really have substance in the public psyche. The FCC began a formal investigation of rulemaking citing "widespread public concern."[34] The FCC eventually dropped all efforts to regulate this form of speech.[35] The FTC ended its inquiry two months earlier.

Certain states acted. The main thrust was to ban automatic dialing devices.[36] Other states incorporated telephone sales into their Home Solicitation Sales Laws.[37] Each year a general potpourri of bills is introduced in the state legislatures. Even less compelling than the lack of public demand for these laws is the lack of legal basis.

There are four areas that were argued by those who do not wish telephone marketers well.

- Telephone solicitations are not "protected" speech.
- Telephone solicitations invade the listener's privacy.
- The tactics employed are "high-pressure."
- There are less intrusive alternatives.

We'll briefly review each of these areas both in reflection and because the issue may arise again, examining the lack of sufficient legal grounds in each case.

Commercial Speech

The Supreme Court first encountered the issue of determining the first amendment status of commercial speech in 1942.[38] The court considered commercial speech to be outside the zone of First Amendment protection, though the court failed to address a constitutional distinguishment between commercial and private speech or, for that matter, even define "commercial speech." This opinion was later characterized by Justice Douglas as "casual, almost offhand."[39]

Commercial speech protection began to emerge in *New York Times Co. v. Sullivan,*[40] where the court distinguished between commercial speech and editorial advertising. The content of the advertising was found to convey more than a commercial purpose. Because the advertisement contained information of the "highest public interest and concern," it was constitutionally protected.[41]

Twelve years later came a decision which was squarely based on the principle that the free flow of information in the commercial sector is as much a part of First Amendment values as the robust and open debate of political issues.[42] In fact, the court went so far as to state the "particular consumer's interest in the free flow of commercial information. . .may be as keen if not keener by far, than his interest in the day's most urgent political debate."[43] This statement, while criticized by some, is patently obvious. A lot more people may remember a Lite Beer commercial than a news brief or even the name of their local assemblyman. More obvious (and seasonal), a lot more people actively shopped in the December Christmas season than voted in the November election.

However, the strongest endorsement from the court came in the following quote (emphasis my own):

> Advertising, however tasteless and excessive it sometimes may seem, is nonetheless dissemination of information as to who is producing and selling what product, for what reason, and at what price. So long as we preserve a predominantly free enterprise economy, the allocation of our resources in large measure will be made through numerous private

economic decisions. *It is a matter of public interest that those decisions, in the aggregate, be intelligent and well-informed. To this end, the free flow of commercial information is indispensable.* . . And if it is indispensable to the proper allocation of resources in a free enterprise system, it is also indispensable to the formation of intelligent opinions as to how that system ought to be regulated or altered.

This last point is important as to the content issue. If commercial information were outside the protection of the First Amendment, the "consumer advocate" as well as the commercial speaker would be left unprotected. Ralph Nader and *Consumer Reports* magazine are two speakers whose message deserves (and receives) constitutional protection.

True, there are differences in the state's ability to regulate private and commercial speech. This is because the latter is more than mere content, but content leading to a sale. The states retain the right to protect their citizens as to content which would mislead an individual into a contract. Most cases will turn on whether a regulation on commercial speech is based on the information function or the contractual function of the message.

The test most useful was articulated by the Supreme Court in *U.S. v. O'Brien,* a case involving a private citizen's burning his draft card. Here was a case in which speech and non-speech elements were combined in the same course of conduct. O'Brien lost. The test employed by the court was as follows:

(a) government regulation is sufficiently justified if it. . .furthers an important or substantial government interest; if the government interest is unrelated to the suppression of free expression; and if the incidental restriction on alleged First Amendment freedoms is no greater than is essential to the furtherance of that interest.[44]

As part of "contractual regulation" government may regulate false or deceptive advertising. This is not a regulation of an advertiser's message content but of the fact the advertiser did not make do on the contract as promised *subsequent* to the content dissemination. Likewise, the state may compel affirmative disclosure where a deception might arise from incomplete disclosure. Finally, corrective advertising might be ordered not as a regulation of content but as a remedy for inducing a contract by deceptive means. Yes, there is such a thing as a wrong product claim. As the court noted:

There is no First Amendment Rule. . .requiring a state to allow deceptive or misleading commercial speech whenever the publication of additional information can clarify or offset the effects of spurious communication.[45]

However, the existence of varied forms of truth-in-advertising regulation should be considered to result in commercial speech as a "secondary" speech. Commercial speech claims are more verifiable and add to a contractual relationship. They are more than mere "opinion." When it goes beyond mere opinion, private speech is not without its own standards. As stated in *Gertz,* false statements of fact do not enjoy constitutional protection for their own sake. There is no constitutional value in false "statements of fact,"[46] many "fighting words," or yelling "Fire!" in a crowded theatre.

When any regulation goes beyond the contractual aspects of the commercial speech it will be analyzed under general First Amendment principles. This is important to all direct marketers in defending overbroad regulations on lists in the legislatures and inevitably in the courts.

The Privacy Chimera

Privacy is being argued on emotional terms in the legislatures. Privacy is a statutory right—not a constitutional one — and as such is entitled to less protection than First Amendment rights such as commercial free speech.

The Supreme Court did invent a form of constitutional "right of privacy" in an access to contraceptives case[47] without a majority agreeing on the constitutional text on which to base this new right. A plurality discovered "that specific guarantees in the Bill of Rights have penumbras, formed by emanations from those guarantees that help give them life and substance." Others found such "right" in the Ninth Amendment and others in the Fourteenth Amendment's "due process clause" (even though the text and history make it plain that only procedural not substantive rights were intended by this clause). Mr. Justice Stewart asked in dissent (and went unanswered): "What provision of the Constitution, then, does make this state law invalid?"

In a hierarchy of constitutional values the court invented right of privacy is not sufficiently grounded in the Constitution to survive a head-on test with commercial free speech in a constitution adjudication. The court will find that calls are content, and as such may be proscribed only if the speech actually infringes on another, is illegal, is untruthful or leads to uninformed acquiescence.[48] Telephone calls do none of the above and even if they did, there are less restrictive alternatives to further an individual's interest. "Infringement" or "uninformed acquiescence" are already protected by narrow regulations such as cooling-off periods. Illegality and untruthfulness are content issues, so they can be dealt with through in-place truth-in-advertising regulations.

The Constitution guarantees only the right to speak—not the right to force others to listen. The opponents of telephone marketing argued that they were forced to listen and such forced listening invaded the individual's right to be left alone.

If the telephone was such an intrusion, 99.9% of Americans wouldn't have them (many have two, three, or four). They are not there for outgoing calls only. The telephone seller's medium is the telephone wire. He calls you with the honest intent to make a sale. No firm is investing in his salary, support staff and, yes, phone bill with the intent to try to sell you a product you don't want at 3 a.m. after 11 rings of the phone.

Each call is costly. The calling firm has probably screened you carefully as a potential sale. The calling firm does not want to antagonize you so they probably have in-house guidelines similar to the Direct Marketing Association's "Suggested Guidelines for Marketing by Telephone." Calling late or early with too many rings will not produce a receptive buyer. The lack of business acumen of the critics is apparent here. Few sellers are making blind, cold calls to harass. If even one firm is, the market realities are that it will soon be out of business.

Sure, the phone ringing is a "disturbance," but such a "disturbance" disappears when the caller is providing me with a service I want. Move to a house and within days you have the option of various oil contracts—comparison of price, service contracts, and the like. It saves time and money. The cable company calls offering a discount which isn't available if you call them, etc., etc. Only a showing that a substantial privacy interest was being invaded in an intolerable manner would qualify as a substantial state interest justifying protection through regulation.[49] None exists to regulate legitimate telephone marketing channels.

The mask comes off the "privacy people" when they exclude in their legislation the charities, politicians, etc. Such distinctions are an attempt to distinguish the good guys from the bad. The latter are usually profitable enterprises.

If there really is a privacy issue in the phone's ringing, then treat all equally. But as was apparent, this regulatory effort was in essence a political issue—*not* a privacy issue. "Privacy" is now raised against all in the direct marketing technologies. There is a consistent bias against science, marketing, and, of course, profit, by opponents of lists, interactive cable, telephone, etc.

High-Pressure Tactics

High-pressure tactics can be an issue in the door-to door salesperson "confrontation" (and a growing one in telephone—see below). They're polished at their craft. Almost all are honest, but as good salespeople they believe in and are enthusiastic about their product. Their infectious enthusiasm can be catching. Further, you are a bit intimidated and after their presentation is complete, you don't want to appear "rude" by asking him or her to physically leave your premises. We have a cooling-off period for this form of sale.[50] This is a rational response to a "problem" of certain sensibilities.

The telephone is impersonal. You don't see the other person. There is no physical "presence." You are not a captive audience that cannot avoid the alleged "objectional" speech. Because you don't know the stranger on the other end of the phone, the added anonymity makes it easier to end the conversation without the guilt feelings one might otherwise have after asking a physically present salesperson to leave.

A click of the receiver and the person is gone. If a state wishes to entertain adopting a cooling-off period for its people, it has the option.[51] However, this exercise of a state's police power presupposes a rational need compelling such action. Overregulating or imposing unjustifiable burdens on commercial free speech to placate a vocal few with inordinate sensibilities is not a rational exercise of power.

Less Intrusive Alternatives

The ability to frame the question is often the ability to frame the answer. You'll often see the above "intrusion" argument. You are then caught defending an "intrusion" rather than talking up your service or convenience.

This argument again evidences an anti-business bias and lack of comprehension of marketing. As you know, your customers aren't interchangeable by media. Telephone may reach certain people better than mail or vice versa. Both mail and telephone may be better than TV.

Further, the uninformed "business is rich" attitude again surfaces. Most firms *don't* have a realistic access to TV. Telephone technology is decreasing in cost while other forms of access are increasing. Therefore, the marketing reality is that

- many customers whom you wouldn't otherwise have access to respond to the telephone, and
- telephone marketing may be the most financially feasible targeted marketing for the small firm or individual entrepreneur.

Conclusion

Government should have two priorities with regard to commercial speech: (1) to prohibit deceptive messages to consumers and (2) to do what it can to facilitate the maximum flow of truthful speech to consumers so that they can make realistic choices as to their needs.

The mere speculation of harm (the best that can be said of the critics' position) is not a compelling governmental interest justifying regulation. Telephone marketing assists society in achieving the second objective listed above. If a few dishonest or poorly managed firms enter the field, they'll be made short work of by the fine and desired firms. Your consistent customer purchasing volume is the purest form of democratic choice. And the consumer knows he or she can simply hang up the phone.

Telephone Marketing—Further Regulatory Issues

We've looked at commercial free speech—an essential platform for all marketers — database and traditional. However, telephone is a bit more intrusive in the public's mind than other forms of marketing. It has survived[52] but many compliance hurdles were enacted. Let's take a look at a few by state.

Cooling Off Telephone Marketing's Spontaneity

The home solicitation laws (see Section IV) were designed to head off the salesperson at your door. They were "Dagwood Bumstead" laws—designed to protect the unwary from high pressure sales. Rather than reenact Dagwood's brawls at the door, stairs, or in his tub, all you have to do is hang up the phone. These laws pertaining to telephone marketing make little sense when viewed in light of the original legislative intent. The laws were enacted to prevent overbearing salespersons from being able to successfully accomplish their stereotyped sales by intimidation.

The reasoning was that customers succumbed to sales persuasion because of intimidation or a lack of desire to hurt the feelings of another human being they just encountered in their living room and spent time with.

All such reasoning would fail if the nature of telephone marketing was understood. Intimidation ends with the click of the phone. An impersonal voice is much more easily dismissed than an individual you've met in person, albeit briefly.

Then there are "twists" in many laws. For example, Arkansas requires compliance for more than $25, while Oregon requires it for $25 or more—a penny variable for planning!

Louisiana incorporates telephone sales but it excludes catalog credit sales. Then there are local and municipal ordinances on point. Finally, the FTC has begun selective incorporation as to abusive telephone marketers on a case by case basis.

An interesting "hybrid" law related to this area is Maine's Transient Seller Law.[53] (Be aware that since 1977 this regulation applies to mail as well, and if you are doing business in Maine you might review it with your counsel.) The definition of transient seller includes companies that sell by telephone if the company does not maintain any permanent place of business in Maine. The law further requires "transient sellers" to file for a consumer merchandise license, and to make a security deposit or a bond to the state of $10,000 or the anticipated annual gross revenue in Maine, whichever is less. There are, however, exceptions, which include:

- If you swear you have engaged in consumer sales in Maine for a period of at least three years;
- You swear that none of your employees has been convicted of theft or deceptive business practice in any United States jurisdiction (a possible civil liberties issue);
- The attorney general in the state where the applicant seller does maintain principal place of business states in a letter that the applicant does not have complaints on file; or
- The applicant seller produces a letter of recommendation from an appropriate trade association which promotes sound and ethical business practices stating the applicant is a member in good standing.

The Department of Business Regulation shall respond to any application for waiver within 15 days. If issued, a waiver can be revoked if a seller is convicted of fraudulent business practices or fails to negotiate consumer complaints filed with the attorney general.

A variety of other states have sought these incorporations and you should stay alert to them for future compliance changes. Ten representative states are presented below for contrast:

1. Arizona (no threshold amount).[54]

2. Arkansas (threshold more than $25 in sales.)[55]

3. Indiana (applies to consumer *credit* sales in any amount).[56]

4. Louisiana (similar to the above although it excludes catalog credit sales).[57]

5. Michigan (threshold figure is sales of *more* than $25).[58]

6. North Dakota (all telephone sales).[59]

7. Oregon (affects sales of $25 or more with certain qualifications).[60]

8. Utah (affects sales over $25).[61]

9. Virginia (telephone and other "electronic means" of $25 and above—non-compliance results in the goods' being a gift to the recipient).[62]

10. Wyoming (sales of $25 or more).[63]

Then there are a variety of local ordinances, cease and desist orders, and voluntary guidelines you should be aware of (see endnotes for representative locations).[64] Finally, expect the courts to interpret all rules/laws narrowly to favor inclusion and consumer protection. For example, the law of Ohio was as follows (emphasis my own):

"Home solicitation sale" is defined in R.C. 1345.21 in pertinent part, as follows:

As used in sections 1345.21 to 1345.28 of the Revised Code:

"(A) 'Home solicitation sale' means a sale of consumer goods or services in which the seller or a person acting for him engages in a personal solicitation of the sale at a residence of the buyer, and the buyer's agreement or offer to purchase is there given to the seller or a person acting for him, or in which the buyer's agreement or offer to purchase is made at a place other than the seller's place of business. It does not include a transaction or transactions which: . . .(2) The transaction was conducted and consummated entirely by mail *or by telephone if initiated by the buyer* and without any other contact between the seller or his representative prior to the delivery of goods or performances of the service;"[65]

The court criticized the lower court for holding that "the statute was meant to cover sales actually made in the home of the buyer and in the physical presence of the salesperson."[66] Hanging its hat on the language "if initiated by the buyer" the court held that the law intended to include within the meaning of "home solicitation sale" those sales which are accomplished solely by telephone solicitation initiated by the *seller.* [67] If you call into Ohio, make sure your paperwork conforms to the state and federal cooling-off requirements.

Recorded Advertisements

President Reagan "cold-called" thousands of people with a taped message prior to the 1986 election. He lost eight Senate seats. If he had to conform to the state laws on point (political messages usually, if not always, are exempt as "content" or "ideas" under the First Amendment), he would have saved the dollars and maybe a few seats.

Automated selection/dialing is the most diversely regulated area, judging by state enactments. A state which recently expanded its legal coverage in this area was Florida (see endnote 68). The new law would amend an existing law which already bans the use of an automated system that selects and dials telephone numbers and now prohibits the use of automated systems that select and/or dial telephone numbers. Again, this is a new law, not a bill.

At least a dozen states have laws which would ban or significantly regulate various segments of automated calls. Other states try each year. Just as ominous to all marketers is the attempt to regulate message content. Formerly the only message requirement was the benign requirement that the recipient be able to hang up and thereby disconnect the call immediately.

In a recent session of the Massachusetts legislature, a bill was introduced requiring a prerecorded message to begin with a statement clearly setting forth that it is a recorded call. The statement must then be repeated every minute during the course of the message. Responses by the person you call may not be recorded unless such person gives his or her express consent. Finally, your message may not be personalized so as to suggest that it is directed to an individual.

Eventually telephone marketers may be forced to abandon the technology or sue and win on the grounds of commercial free speech. Obviously, a message content regulation presents a potential target of opportunity. So if you want to tape messages, there are a large variety of restrictions as to hours to call, automatic hang-ups upon recipient's disconnect, whether a live voice must introduce it, a caller's registration with agencies prior to doing business, whether a taped message is permissible at all, etc. Please refer to the endnotes[68] for representative samples of over a dozen states and their laws impacting your promotional wording, technology, etc.

Finally, you should be alert for the increasing trend to incorporate telephone selling into the states' 30-day rules or mail order merchandise statutes.[69]

Now we'll briefly take a look at another channel—satellite marketing and some of its legal overtones.

Direct Broadcast Satellites

The use of satellites for television transmission and other multipoint applications has been growing rapidly since the introduction of a domestic satellite communications system in 1974. The potential of direct broadcast satellites is enormous, because the costs of such satellites are distance insensitive, and they have the potential to reach anyone who wants them to.

Satellites differ from existing video programming distribution media, which depend on elaborate interconnection systems, and are hampered by terrestrial limitations on microwave transmissions (at present most terrestrial communications over long distances are handled through microwave systems). Such microwaves travel in a straight line and can be obstructed by any solid objects in the transmission path, including the curvature of the earth. This mandates a series of individual microwave stations be placed at specified intervals along a route to relay signals. Further, this system (at present) is not feasible for transmitting microwaves across oceans. The satellite transmitting from space will not have the problem of signal blockage by terrain.[70] The "direct" enters the picture when the consumer's dish is included in the equation. A number of manufacturers have developed receiving dishes which would allow the consumer to receive these programs directly into his or her home. The dish is about four feet in diameter and can be purchased for approximately $600.

The initial DBS systems are expected to provide three or more channels of programming transmitted via medium or high-powered satellites (the success of the former will relate directly to the evolution of the ground station technology). The programming will be sent from a transmit station to the satellite which will retransmit it to individual home receiver "dishes."

The primary market for DBS will be those households without access to mixed and other multichannel services. This will *not* be solely a rural market. The rural market is obvious, since the cable alternative is often not feasible because of the costs of wiring isolated towns and homes. DBS systems have potential as a statewide service to states such as Alaska.

Another area of opportunity is zoned subscribers where the minimum acreage often makes wiring each home economically unattractive to cable operators. Further, as the costs of satellite operations come down and the costs of cable wiring go up in urban areas, another potential market is large urban apartment and condominium complexes. This is no longer theoretical. One need only witness the success satellite master antenna television has begun to have.

DBS potentially promises several significant advantages over existing television technology including the following:

► Its higher-powered satellites can operate to increasingly smaller terminals and provide service to rural or remote areas where household density is too sparse to attract cable operators or where conventional broadcasting is inefficient.

► Service to urban centers not yet wired for cable or suburban zoned tracts where the minimum acreage often makes wiring each home economically unattractive to cable operators. Further, while the costs of wiring are escalating, DBS costs are declining significantly. For example:

• NASA's Space Shuttle has been launching satellites into orbit for substantially less than the expendable rockets used in the 1950s.

• Each satellite has a dramatically greater payload insofar as the dramatic reduction of communication capability vis-a-vis the overall mass volume of the satellite staff. These changes make possible greater efficiencies in the use of radio frequency communication capacity and overall cost efficiency.

• Significant reductions in the cost of earth stations have been and will continue to be achieved.

► Narrowcasting of programs to specialized audiences through its ability to aggregate small, widely dispersed audiences especially as the newer, advanced antenna structures increase their ability to concentrate beams more directly at specific earth stations;

► Offering pay-per-view events that non-addressable cable systems can't;

► Development of higher quality visual and audio signals through the use of high-definition television signals; and

► Information and the way it will be used is the key strategic variable for most commercial and non-profit businesses.

DBS's market for the transmission of non-entertainment programming for corporate, medical or educational use (aided by expanded use of shared earth stations) should exceed its entertainment market within this decade. Already many businesses are utilizing this technology for videoconferencing and other related purposes. We can also see tremendous potential growth through private satellite networks, operating from a corporate main office to small receiving antennas at field offices. This form of communication is only one-way (like DBS entertainment) but the telephone provides an easy response.

In short, the technology is in place. It is distance insensitive, and costs are declining, so the potential to reach anyone is there. The final equation of government noninterference was present under the Reagan Justice Department and the FCC. However, the courts are another matter and, as is often the case, present a hostile forum to technological growth. Let's review signs of regulatory encouragement.

Privacy and Piracy

Whenever targeted marketing is at issue, privacy laws are at issue, because targeting requires a trade-off between acquiring information needed to personally serve an individual and what such individual wants you to have. For a dated but related report on this topic, obtain the 1982 report by The National Telecommunications and Information Administration submitted to the Organization for Economic Cooperation and Development.[71]

Then there is the issue of piracy. The home interception of satellite-relayed signals by non-subscribers could become a very costly drain on DBS operations. However, these initial problems are largely being overcome with the new, sophisticated encoding/decoding capabilities, which no longer interfere with picture quality. Of greater initial concern in this overall area is the issue of copyright.

Finally, there might be an issue as to broadcast localism. This whole area is in flux, and it is probably impractical for a DBS applicant to demonstrate a familiarity with the community they seek to serve. These rules, however, are being eased.

Copyright

If DBS were a common carrier, then there would be no violation if it transmitted material for which no copyright royalty was paid, since a common carrier merely provides the public a means of transmitting the subscriber's communications.

The issue in regard to DBS was as clouded as cable until 1976. Prior to the new copyright law, the Supreme Court held that cable retransmission of a television broadcast did not constitute copyright infringement[72] even if it involved the importation of signals from a distant location from which reception would not be possible using conventional receiving equipment.[73]

Under 1976 amendments to the Copyright Act, cable operators must pay copyright owners royalties for retransmission of television broadcast signals. The copyright revision gives cable systems a "compulsory license" (i.e., users are entitled to make limited use of a copyrighted work upon payment of a set fee) to import distant television stations without the consent of the station or program owners.[74] The royalty payments[75] are then distributed to copyright owners by the Copyright Royalty Tribunal system. However, it may already be dated (see the following). Cable companies are highly leveraged and each potential loss of market share delays the payback investment because the company's capital costs aren't reduced with the reduction in market share. Further, the whole issue of cable companies, customer relations is coming under increasing scrutiny, particularly their failure to follow up and personalize their customer service base during service and when such customer threatens to depart.[76] There is tremendous market opportunity for a customer-first philosophy among the competition.

At present the pay subscriber route is probably the way to go. The size of the DBS receiver market may be too small and too low in subscriber density for some national advertising campaigns. However, generic products (household, supplies, parpared foods, etc.) would be suitable and targeted marketing to local or regional audiences could present excellent opportunities.

FCC and DBS

Very important to the equation is the fact that the Federal Communications Commission generally has adopted a policy of encouragement to the new communications. The FCC Advisory Committee on the 1983 Regional Administrative Radio Conference recommended that the United States obtain four eclipse-protected orbital slots corresponding approximately to the United States time zones.

A further example of this policy of encouragement was the flexibility demonstrated by the FCC in selecting its regulatory options for DBS operations. Rather than adopt either the conventional broadcasting regulation option or the common carrier regulatory alternative model, the FCC chose a flexible approach. The DBS operator will be regulated as to how it characterizes itself. The FCC has reserved the right to give priority in the sale of transponders to common carrier applicants. Eventually as the character of the services is defined, the regulatory pattern will likewise follow. However, for the present, this flexible approach permits ample room for DBS operators to chart their course governed more by technological and market restraints than by the twilight zone of governmental regulation.

The FCC then consolidated its media bureaus into one—the "Mass Media Bureau." It consists of four divisions: Audio Services, Enforcement, Policy and Rules, and Video Services. The latter will assume the responsibilities of the former Cable Bureau and oversee among its various duties, DBS systems.

There was also a change in the number of commissioners. As of June 30, 1983, the FCC was reduced from seven to five commissioners (their term remains seven years). A majority of the five are expected to support the philosophy of deregulation of communications.

As long as the requirements of Section 111 are met, resale carriers are able to pick up the programming of a broadcast station and send that programming to a satellite, which in turn can relay it directly to each subscriber.

It is always a good idea for you to obtain copyright indemnification in your contracts with program suppliers, when such programs are supplied under contract.

Antitrust and Economic Injury

The avowed goal of the antitrust laws is to prohibit conduct that directly or indirectly forecloses entry into and competition within any type of economic product and geographic market.

An unresolved legal issue for the future is what is the product market for the communications media? Should it be divided, e.g., advertiser-supported vs. subscriber based? Are videodiscs and cassettes a separate product category, because they offer their viewers complete control of scheduling?

The geographic market is the area in which a firm sells in active competition with other firms. The DBS geographic market is partly defined by the product market. For example, the DBS geographic market might be only other DBS competitors in the same time zone or it might be all video media competitors. Under Reagan, the Antitrust Division of the U.S. Justice Department also helped out.[77] The Direct Broadcast Satellite Association Standards Committee sought to formulate voluntary technical standards for all aspects of its service. The association argued[78] that such technical standards are needed in order to promote compatibility among components of competing systems and between direct broadcast satellite equipment manufacturers and operators. Such standards would relate to the areas of the location of satellites and bandwidth channels, the compatibility of satellites with various components of home receiving equipment and formats for direct broadcast satellite signals.

While the above areas remain nebulous, some traditional antitrust issues should be considered. Obvious violations such as price fixing, division of markets or boycott of available DBS channels from a new entrant would probably *not* arise, since the industry has a high visibility to government due to the already in-place regulations.

Less obviously, competitors might attempt to impose uniform technical standards for equipment. This might foreclose the wholesale or retail market for some equipment suppliers. It might discourage potential new entrants, who might not be able to capitalize on the dramatic fall in capital prices (e.g., space shuttles will carry into space improved and larger satellites at less than a quarter of the cost of launching today's smaller satellites).

Finally, some of the vertically integrated firms might attempt to transfer their market power in one area to control a market in another area. This use of market power is the classic tying arrangement whereby the seller refuses to sell a tying product or service unless the buyer also agrees to purchase an unwanted "tied product or service." Such market power is particularly apparent if the firm possesses a patent in the field.

The issue as to "economic injury" is less apparent than that of antitrust problems. However, as DBS becomes more common in small communities (its natural initial market), the economic injury argument is bound to be alleged by some of the local stations which have sought to serve local needs for years.

A competitor may allege and prove that the entry of a DBS operation into a given market would create definite and irreplaceable loss of programming in the given area. Such complainant must demonstrate:

(1) The revenue potential of the market will cause the petitioner to lose a significant amount of income.

(2) The loss will force the petitioner to eliminate some or all of its public service programming.

(3) The loss of programming cannot be offset by increased non-network programming proposed by the DBS applicant.[79]

This test imposes on the FCC the duty to consider the effects of competition on a station's ability to provide programming in the public interest.[80] It is in keeping with the philosophy of the First Amendment that diversity of viewpoints is instrumental to the survival of a democratic society. The loss of diversity of ideas and *not* economic injury must be proven by the complainant to have any hope of succeeding on the merits of a claim.

The FCC has attempted to be flexible on these developing issues. However, it is an open question whether the courts will be. Let's take a look at a few decisions.

The Courts vs. the FCC

In two recent cases[81] the D.C. Circuit Court endorsed most of the FCC regulatory approach to DBS. The court recognized that the FCC must re-evaluate its regulations over time and alter them in light of developments in the evolving communications industry. The court agreed with the FCC's not impeding new technologies and its general approach to the subject of spectrum management and letting the market forces determine price, range of service, and quality of service to customers.

However, the Court disagreed with the FCC's conclusions in one very important respect: The Court believes DBS is broadcasting, and for the FCC to determine otherwise would be "forbidden statutory experimentation." This means DBS operators are subject to the traditional broadcast regulatory burdens, such as the fairness and equal opportunity obligations. In vacating the exemption for customer programmers of DBS from the statutory requirements imposed on broadcasters, the court argued as follows:

> "Section 3(o) of the Communications Act defines 'broadcasting' as 'the dissemination of radio communications intended to be received by the public, directly or by the intermediary of relay stations.[82] We have previously held that the test for whether a particular activity constitutes broadcasting is whether there is 'an intent for public distribution' and whether the programming is 'of interest to the general . . . audience.'"

When DBS systems transmit signals directly to homes with the intent that those signals be received by the public, such transmissions rather clearly fit the definition of broadcasting; radio communications are being disseminated with the intent that they be received by the public. The Court went on to state that:

> "We also do not suggest that all uses of DBS constitute broadcasting; activity that would provide non-general interest, point-to-point service, where the format is of interest to only a narrow class of subscribers and does not implicate the broadcasting objectives of the Act, need not be regulated as broadcasting."

The long and the short of it is that DBS operators will be subjected to the full scope of broadcast regulation imposed under Title III of the Communications Act. It unsettles much of the FCC's efforts to devise a reasonable, flexible regulatory framework for DBS and, by analogy, other new technologies, such as multipoint distribution service (MDS) or teletext.

Title III requires of broadcasters (to cite three examples):

- The now-familiar fairness doctrine (specifically cited as a need in the *National Association of Broadcasters*). [83] Under this requirement, a federal candidate who wants access to a DBS system will gain access.
- The requirement to identify program sponsors; and
- A license necessary for any Title II common carrier spectrum use.

If these decisions go unchallenged, Title III will now regulate every line of communication used to disseminate messages to a general audience. This will hinder the development of existing technologies as well as dictate an inflexible regulatory framework which may discourage potential entrants in the future. Finally, the FCC's trend towards creativity will be, at best, dampened.

Concluding Thoughts on DBS

For the rest of this century, space telecommunications (as well as terrestrial systems) should experience dramatic growth while enjoying a significant drop in costs.

However, recent decisions by the D.C. Circuit Court put a cloud over all communications development. This bodes ill for communications development in the United States, and for the United States' envied position as a technological leader in this field. Finally, one can't dismiss an all-out assault on this industry from the self-anointed "environmentalist" lobby. A landscape dotted with millions of metal dishes may give rise to an effort similar to that of the 1960's billboard debate. Already, certain towns such as Harpers Ferry, West Virginia, have adopted ordinances effectively banning the dishes. Whether this trend will grow and survive court challenge by individuals denied access bears watching.[84]

Now we'll take a look at some of the issues confronting direct marketers utilizing in-home video, i.e., cable.

Cable TV's Cloudy Promotional and Legal Outlook

There is no doubt that cable TV has great potential. Interactive cable TV has the potential to give the audio-visual direct marketer more precise audience-demographic data. It could make much of network TV (mass audience) obsolete, similar to the way the segmented audience magazines adversely affected the generalist ones. It will also affect our culture and strengthen the conservative trend politically.

This latter area is subtle and not often discussed. The three major networks have often been accused of reflecting the liberal bias of the Eastern Seaboard. These arbiters of opinion are having their audience increasingly diluted by the switch to more varied and alternate news programming. As a campaign tool, cable will be seized upon as was direct mail for issue advocacy and fund raising.

Yes, cable TV will be the most revolutionary cultural medium since the birth of commercial television, and politically, it has the potential to be every bit as useful as targeted direct mail. There are great opportunities for marketers who understand where the nation is going. Companies which don't adapt to the new technology may not be in business in ten to fifteen years.

However, the pioneers of the new technological frontiers should not make the mistake which has been made by other major industries in the last decade and a half. The mistake is to underestimate the power of government to destroy the best laid plans of the marketers. Marketers enamored of the possibilities of cable TV should not lose sight of the fact that government has already artificially restrained its growth.

Cable was developed in the late 1940s for use in communities unable to receive broadcast television signals because of terrain or distance factors. Over the years, it developed a non-broadcast entertainment package promotional aspect as well as the clear transmission. However, its growth was severely hindered by the Federal Trade Commission, which issued rules that discouraged the entry of cable systems into the top 100 urban markets which at that time represented 85% of the population of the United States! The Federal Communications Commission only began to relax such entry barriers in 1973.

Subsequently, this highly capital intensive industry had to chart a course through some of the least predictable years of the fluctuating credit markets as well as myriad franchising laws and fees. Then the industry had to go to court[85] to overturn FCC rules which specified that most films could be cablecast on premium channels only if they had been in general release for less than three years or more than ten years.

Finally, effective January 1, 1978, the new Copyright Act[86] mandated compulsory license fees for all cable systems. Out of the woods yet? Not by a long shot. The *other opportunity* is for the industry professionals to identify the future legal issues before they occur. This will give them time to develop position papers and legislative education programs before the eleventh hour. Anyone who believes cable is a historical inevitability in the 1980s should look to two former historical inevitabilities of the 1970s—autos and nuclear power.

As to the former, I could recommend no better book than *Going For Broke.* [87] It is the best book on Detroit in general and Chrysler in particular, which have been driven to the wall and possible extinction by haphazard governmental regulation.

As to the latter, few people realize that during the 1960s the leading proponents of nuclear power were the environmentalists! These groups began their activities by focusing on the scenic damage being done by hydroelectric plants and on the growing urban air pollution problems. The Sierra Club (to cite one example), in various lawsuits, cited atomic energy as a reasonable alternative to dirty coal or new dams.

Things change. Yet, these industries simply did not adequately interact with the political environment in a systematic way until they were on the ropes.

I believe cable marketers have a high degree of potential governmental and consumerist visibility in three legally defined areas: privacy, obscenity, and the potential blurring of information/advertising in the infomercial. If you are a market leader or care enough about the legal environment to read books such as this, you may be in a position to anticipate and head off potential problems here.

Privacy

The issue is lifestyle profile, and it will be more visible than the list issue (see below). Interactive cable presents the most fertile field for audience segmentation and legal problems. It all sounds simple . . . from your little box at home you can order a product or answer an opinion poll. Each such action—your order, type of product, time of day or night you ordered it, etc. form a very descriptive profile of your life—that is why it is so valuable to marketers.

Then in certain other systems, the computer "knows" if you are watching a paid channel. If you are watching a particular movie, it will bill you for that movie. Your viewing selections—"cultural," "popular," "pornographic," etc., become part of your profile. To date the profile issue has been muted as certain firms have made laudable efforts to head off problems here. Certain contracts state up-front that customer records will be kept confidential. However, the capacity for such a profile to exist may, in itself, disturb certain people.

Further, the world of electronics is being tied together with electronic funds transfer and other banking records. A cashless society means more records. If you believe the coming debate will be initiated by the "left," then read the critics. Conservatives such as Howard Ruff[88] argued against various non-cash purchases precisely to avoid this type of private information's winding up in the hands of various government agencies, e.g., the IRS. The IRS may be very interested in your spending habits and other lifestyle information that is available concerning non-cash transactions.

The question for the future is whether consumers will be willing to sacrifice (if they perceive it as such) privacy for the convenience of direct electronic ordering. Will they accept centralized recording and storing of information concerning their individual tastes, finances, purchasing behavior, viewing habits and answers to opinion polls? If so, will they add on other devices (such as certain fire and burglar alarm systems) which will record when they come and go?

Responsible professionals in this field know these fears are exaggerated but so were they in lists, and that area continues to fester.

Obscenity

This is not the time to debate what it is. The viewer will know. Already certain groups who don't believe the commercial TV industry can clean its house are threatening a boycott. The obscenity laws generally observe the "contemporary community" standard. Cable by its very nature is more local intensive, and what plays in Manhattan may not find favor in Charleston, West Virginia. The airing of "blue" movies on Escapade or Midnight Blue could prompt laws restricting such programming (legislation to bar or restrict such programming has been introduced in Florida, Massachusetts, and New York).

To give praise where praise is due, Home Box Office has adopted certain programming policies as to the time of day certain movies will be shown. The solution may be a locked box. It is hoped that the industry and not government will decide the outcome.

'Infomercials'

The FTC has been studying a "blurring" of the lines resulting in the electronic media's longer and more informative commercials, often dubbed infomercials. Can the consumer differentiate what is matter-of-fact product information from creative advertising? Longer messages may contain more errors or even contribute to an "information overload." On the positive side, such infomercials, where properly designed and worded, will greatly enhance comparison shopping.

The cable advertiser should simply stress the truth and follow the law on the books when it comes to demonstrations. For example:

(1) The demonstration must actually prove something relating to the quality of the product. Truthful demonstrations which are not relevant to the major attribute of your product will present problems.

(2) The demonstration must accurately reflect the honest experience a user would have.

(3) The consumer is entitled to see what he/she is told is being shown. As to this point, if you read one case in this field, read *FTC v. Colgate-Palmolive Company.* [89]

Note: All prior rules/regulations you've learned about copy must still be disclosed on cable. For example, an endorsement must follow the FTC Guides Concerning Use of Endorsements and Testimonials in Advertising.[90] The law is cumulative.

Who Is the Audience?

To narrowcast, it must be demonstrated that different audience segments will watch different commercials rather than a mass audience watching a general spot. Cable programmers are having a hard time verifying their audience, while the audience (where it exists) may be having an even harder time finding its desired program or even becoming aware of the opportunity to view a program of special interest.

No state of the art quantitative measurement standard is in place and no criteria yet exist that will measure the qualitative nature of the selective viewers. So, advertisers are not sure how many people are watching a given channel, though they may be able to vaguely hypothesize who the viewers are. This lack of viewer data will doom any major influx of advertisers into the cable market.

Then there is the audience problem. Did you ever try to find a consistently accurate cable program guide for the varied channels? Sure *TV Guide,* the daily newspapers, and your monthly channel guide can fill you in as to HBO and a few other programs. After that, you must skim, especially for exact times. Cable viewers are skimmers for this reason and others. They have less viewer loyalty to most channels/programs than do commercial viewers. The lack of adequate program listings and the viewer tendency to skim can have interesting results. Nickelodeon research showed that initially 90% of its young viewers came upon it accidentally through skimming.

Besides the lack of audience measurement criteria, adequate program guides and a skimming viewer body, you have a sociological problem as to when and where your audience is available. Cable will not change the availability of people who watch. Will people watch weekday sports? If so, who are these people, what sports do they like and are they the decision-makers for the purchase decision concerning your product?

Has flexitime produced a significant male weekday audience? If so, might there be a renewed market for day baseball games again? Is it valid to assume women are a significant daytime audience in your specific locale for a given program? Can the later afternoons still be considered childrens' hours or do they now dominate 6 p.m. to 8 p.m. viewing? Do the movies that attract the 17- to 25-year-olds really have a market on a home set?

In other words, is it the movies themselves or the physical requirement of *going* to the movie theatre that has caused the older segment to see fewer movies? Direct marketers can't have it both ways. They can't gloat over changing social norms encouraging shop at home and not see the trade-off in programming problems for determining cable audience demographics.

Cable has two futures. It can follow the arguments that programmers must seek the largest possible broad-based audience to support themselves or it can narrowcast as a local medium serving local advertisers. Either option will usher new legal regulation which will establish adverse precedents for all direct marketers.

The Regulatory Forces Have Begun to Stir

As you are aware, unlike broadcast television stations which are licensed by the FCC,[91] cable television systems receive franchises from local governments. Most FCC regulations were overturned by the Supreme Court[92] and what remains are the signal registration[93] and other areas of less regulatory impact on operators. While this lack of regulation may change if the FCC eliminates its 12-year-old ban on network ownership of cable TV systems, the fact is that no rules are not always good rules as the vacuum invites regulatory mischief.

For example, the FCC has not placed any significant obligations on cable systems as to commercial content with the exception of the sponsor identification requirement.[94] Industry self-regulatory codes may not help too much at least until the NAB Code shakes out.

The legal arena might be complicated by unduly restrictive laws resulting from small, nonprofessional operations entering the local area advertising. Just as there were the legislative battles between 1977 and 1980 concerning telephone marketing and prior to that there was the "junk mail" controversy, the new entries may generate legislative activity through errors of omission.

Already the privacy debate has ended its somnolent state. A number of states now have laws on the books or are considering same which establish the worst direct marketing precedents to date. In one editorial, Henry Hoke Jr. stated that:

> We feel comfortable in the idea that a direct marketer is one who owns and maintains a mailing list, used to support any and all methods of selling. The list is the cornerstone. It is the vehicle through which advertising effectiveness can be measured, the database which houses information as to where the sale was consummated, by whom, what was purchased, the vehicle which reveals the next logical steps in the process of generating new sales.[95]

Few would argue with him. Yet *commercial* list restrictions or bans are passing with 1984 overtones. Wisconsin banned the release of cable subscriber lists in 1982.[96] Illinois almost did, but I'm less sanguine on this law than some recent commentary. As I read the law, it would severely restrict the utility of Illinois cable subscriber lists for narrowcasting purposes. True, it may be permissible to rent names of subscribers in isolation if subscribers are notified in advance and permitted to withdraw their name.

However, advertisers or direct marketers rarely want a mere name. They want to know specifics on which to target their sales promotion. OK, the individual is a subscriber to a cable TV system. That's all you get. Does he watch boating shows? Does she watch the stock report? You'll never know—it's banned. Section 3 is of interest and is quoted below (emphasis added):

> (a) It shall be unlawful for a communications company to: (1) *install and use any equipment which would allow a communications company to visually observe or listen to what is occurring in an individual subscriber's household* without the knowledge or permission of the subscriber; (2) provide any person or public or private organization with a list containing the name of a subscriber, unless the communications company gives notice thereof to the subscriber; (3) disclose the television viewing habits of any individual subscriber without the subscriber's consent; or (4) install or maintain a home-protection scanning device in a dwelling as part of a communication service without the express written consent of the occupant.[97]

Paragraph (a)(1) deals with electronic surveillance and the visual observance reminiscent of Big Brother in *1984*! Then, with barely a breath, lists are thrown in the category. Subscriber identification sales are effectively banned. Paragraph (a)(4) then neatly tidies up the package.

Minnesota's Cable Communications Board Code of Agency Rules contains the following language (emphasis my own):

No information or data obtained by monitoring transmission of a signal from a subscriber terminal, *including but not limited to lists of the names and addresses of such subscribers or any lists* that identify the viewing habits of subscribers shall be sold or otherwise made available to any party other than to the company and its employees for internal business use, and also to the subscriber subject of that information, *unless the company has received specific written authorization from the subscriber to make such data available.*[98]

The attorney general of New York State enthusiastically introduced an effective ban on cable list sales. Other states are considering similar legislation. So did Congress.

Legislation is more than a legal exercise. It is a reflection of public comment, concern and sentiment. If just the four states quoted above are expressing concern for list data then there is strong sentiment the industry must address. In quantitative terms, these four states alone represented one-third of all electoral votes needed to elect a president in 1984.

So, commercial lists are under fire on privacy grounds again. This is not surprising as legislation curbing access to state governmental lists is on the rise. Further, the victories of the late 1970s only bought time. Lists are not sold for their names and addresses. They are sold as capsules of personalities, interests, professions, etc. You often *want* to know a potential customer's age, sex, buying habits, marital status, etc. If you want names and addresses in isolation the telephone book is full of them.

Direct marketing will always have privacy trade-offs because of its more *direct* (i.e., personal and private), targeted nature. The next legal round should find the industry prepared not to argue on its opponents' terms (privacy) but on its own terms (commercial free speech). Unlike the more speculative aspect of future cable laws, this list survival task is already upon us and, regrettably, not doing well.

VCRs and Direct Marketing

Today any marketer who wishes to communicate by television may do so by making a promotional tape and distributing it to stores or individual owners of VCRs (video cassette recorders). No publicly controlled interconnection or transmission system is involved.

While the marketing potential is almost limitless, a few legal landmarks will also fall by the wayside. The proliferation and diversity of communications media today has made the "fairness" doctrine obsolete, and the FTC has acted accordingly. There is little weight left to an argument predicated upon the scarcity of broadcast facilities.[99] In fact, it may actually chill free expression.[100]

The opening up of the marketplace of ideas and commerce through the VCR will usher in the era of the video entrepreneur! The 1988 political campaign has witnessed candidates using videos. The catalog houses already are there.

Conclusion

Cable systems will survive because localities will desire them as a tax-cow. Whether they will prosper and in what form will be known within this decade. Such prosperity remains likely, though no longer the foregone event it once was. Direct satellite to backyard (or apartment rooftop) TV transmission and other technologies may replace it. Perhaps the disk antenna and not the cable will be the historical inevitability.

Legally, laws and regulations will flow as the public and its representatives get a feel for what systems will prosper and in what formats. The laws will evolve in the future. Where the governmental bodies have familiarity (e.g., lists) they are becoming more active. The list ban activity will affect not only cable operators but set precedents for all commercial list users. For list users, the legal future is now. Let's take a look at lists.

Will Quality Lists Be Available in 1990?

Independent or public mailings are the lifeline of database marketing. Without the list, that lifeline would cease to exist as there would be no market. The quality of the list determines the success of your promotion; the more refined the list, the better the response. With increasing costs such as postage, paper, and labor, the direct marketer cannot afford a shotgun approach. The tendency, therefore, has been to seek more efficient methods of targeting one's markets via lists, relying more heavily on sophisticated compiled lists of individuals in order to effect more positive results from the mailings.

What happens in the courtrooms and legislatures throughout the country in the next decade could spell either disaster or continued success for direct marketing. If direct marketers are organized and prepared to be involved in some tough legal battles over the privacy issue, chances of a favorable outcome will be greatly increased.

As discussed in the prior chapter, there were a lot of cable lists lost. Motor vehicle lists are ending and library lists are largely banned. So you don't rent library lists. In fact, you don't rent any compiled lists. Well, chances are you do, albeit indirectly. Do you rent a list from *any source* using public sources? If such lists are eliminated, there will be fewer private sector lists available from your source.

Every list ban, no matter how innocuous to your immediate marketing effort, dries up the universe of names available. So, in the past

18 months, 27 states have sought to dry up private lists by eliminating access to compiled sources. Any legislative watcher can tell you that it's easier to amend an existing law than to enact a new one. Compiled lists bans on the statute books are potentially amendable to become more restrictive, and even if never amended, they establish laws in place for adverse court precedents.

Worst-Case Scenario

Two cases on point have compiled list triggers which, though not controlling, could carry enough weight to ban commercial lists in a worst-case scenario. For example, in *Shibley v. Times,*[101] Norman W. Shibley sought to maintain a class action, representing those aggrieved by publishers and credit card companies, which would prohibit such firms from selling or renting the lists of their subscribers. The claim was a dubious one, but some language of the Court is relevant to the issue of compiled list bans. I've quoted it at length, emphasizing areas of particular interest to the direct marketer involved in lists (i.e., *all* direct marketers):

> 1. As defendants have pointed out, plaintiff and intervenor should look for relief to the legislative branch. The General Assembly has acted in the area of sales of names and addresses to direct mail advertisers in two instances. One concerns the sale by the state of Ohio of names and addresses of registrants of motor vehicles. . .

> . . .Ohio R.C. 4503.26 authorizes the sale of lists of names and addresses of registrants of motor vehicles. In authorizing such sales the Legislature impliedly indicates that sales of lists of names and addresses is not an invasion of the right of privacy. . .

> 2. As we pointed out in the New York case, *Lamont v. Commissioner of Motor Vehicles,* such a statute is not subject to attack as being unconstitutional. . .

> 3. Ohio House Bill No. 1056 introduced by Mr. P. Sweeney in January of this year to repeal R.C. 4503.26 only affirms defendants' contention that the legislative branch should make decisions in this area. . .

> 4. Ours is a nation of laws and not of men. This court happens to sympathize with the position of the plaintiffs, but just as each citizen must obey the law as it exists, whether or not he agrees with it, so must the court follow the law as it is and not as the court would wish it to be. Therefore, since the law as it now exists prevents the plaintiff from succeeding, for the reasons stated above the court must find that as of now the plaintiff has failed to state a claim on which relief can be granted.

To recap:

The Court clearly favored the plaintiff's position, reflecting an overt bias on the part of that particular Court against the free exchange of governmental lists. It was restrained from deciding in favor of the plaintiff, however, because of statutes previously enacted by the Ohio legislature. The message of the decision was clear: had the Ohio legislature not previously authorized the sale of state lists (as the defendant, Time, Inc., astutely pointed out), the Court's decision might well have been different. Similarly, the Ohio Appellate Court in its opinion agreed with the lower court, again giving weight to legislative intent.

The Court further pointed out that a bill was introduced to the Ohio General Assembly to repeal the existing statute which, although not passed, only serves as a warning that such laws *can* be overturned (other bills of similar import have been introduced subsequently). Certainly as times change, laws can and sometimes do change - often by means of the opposition's "whittling away" at an issue. . . a case here, an amendment there. . . until the legislature reflects such changes and overturns its previous decision.

Finally, the Court cited *Lamont* as precedent. Here a non-compelling privacy claim was made in the days of long ago (1967) when privacy was not an issue on the front burner. The sale of motor vehicle records was at issue. In its decision, the court (as in *Shibley*) gave some weight to the state legislature. It also reviewed the law of the 50 states:

> . . .reports its findings of provisions in every State except Kentucky making public records of vehicle registration information. The substantially uniform state practice is not decisive, but it is another item of some weight against plaintiff's constitutional theory.[102]

The "item of some weight" is shifting. Other states have joined Kentucky (e.g., Hawaii and Nevada) and many others are trying. If the government list bans are successful (and gradually they are being enacted):

(1) Won't legislative intent (a weathervane of public opinion) be given great weight where a legislature overrules prior practice and bans governmental lists? Perhaps.

(2) As more and more states ban the rental of various governmental lists, won't the courts give the quantitative trend "some weight" in their decision to ban? Perhaps. Five states banned library lists alone (to name one type) in 1985![103]

It does not require a great leap of faith to realize that if intellectual property direct marketers abdicate their educational role, their lists can easily be banned down the road by an analysis similar to *Shibley v. Time, Inc.* [104] The bottom line is that direct marketers agreed by their silence that a list of what one reads, or listens to, or otherwise represents "private" thoughts, is private!

The distinguishment between a library list ban and a commercial book or record club or continuity series list ban clearly indicates that these direct marketers' databases contain more information about a reader's habits than a library could ever hope to. The direct marketer also merges in credit history, age, marital status, data from other lists—all constituting greater "privacy" intrusions. Further, the act of associating with a *public* library as opposed to a *private* club is at least on the par in the public forum.

The precedent value to private list users is ominous but unrecognized by direct marketers including those dealing primarily in books or other intellectual property. This abdication of involvement in the legislative debate will haunt these sellers as soon as their opponents consolidate their precedents. Approximately half the states will have banned these by 1988.

Only one firm I'm aware of has raised any concern over the steady erosion of library lists during the last three or four years. While these lists may seem esoteric to the uninformed, it is a shame so few firms in the intellectual property field spoke out. A few years from now they'll have their own intellectual property glut and dearth of names (similar to "catalog glut"). This trend will nickel and dime to death commercial lists as commercial list sources are dried up. The trend will set up laws subject to broader ban amendments. Finally, this trend if allowed to go unchecked will potentially set up court challenges overturning favorable precedents on the books. At present, the loss of names is disguised as "catalog glut." In the future there may be no catalogs as there will be few names available to make the mailings worthwhile.

To Summarize

(1) You can't market successfully in direct marketing—*in any medium*—without a quality list.

(2) Public list sources affect your list whether you rent them directly or you rent from one who has already homogenized public source names into his or her own list.

(3) The increasing attempts to ban public lists at the state level might result in a precedent foundation leading to a ban of many, if not all, lists by various courts.

(4) If lists are banned, *you're out of business.*

What Can You Do?

You basically have three choices. You can

- act on your own,
- do nothing, or

• join a concerted group effort.

Few firms can afford the time, talent and general expense involved in choosing the first option beyond a narrow, selected area. As a practical matter, this isn't an option.

Sadly, too many have elected the second option. You wait for the other person to carry his/her load as well as your own. This "let the other guy do it" attitude is a sad commentary on a marketing channel heavily endowed with the entrepreneurial spirit.

However, maybe you just don't know where to go to get involved or feel your gross profits too small to make an effective contribution. Well, I'll tell you two organizations to go to. If you don't, you may have no gross profit left in a few years (I stress gross profit because a contribution to either group is a deductible expense).

(1) Call the Direct Marketing Association at (202)347-1222. Ask for information on Freedom to Mail groups interested in education of state legislators before a problem arises, and defeating bills which would create adverse impact on the direct marketing channel.

The Direct Marketing Association (DMA) became a truly effective trade group as a result of a change in leadership during the past few years and the support of an activist chairman cognizant of the legislative threats. The true purpose of any association is to provide for the common defense. Social gatherings are at best of secondary value. The new leadership raised the money to do the necessary: They retained DeHart & Darr Associates, a legislative intelligence/lobbying group that had represented (and continues to do so) an activist group of members who pioneered effective interaction with public bodies for direct marketers.

Each year DMA has increased funding toward preserving free access to lists, a national mail order merchandise rule and more. Not coincidentally, each increase in funding has witnessed a decrease in the passage of adverse legislation—and during a period where introduction had actually increased.

A successful defense budget is often taken for granted. The uninformed don't see a crisis and assume it's overhead. Actually, a crisis atmosphere in any organization usually indicates a substandard management performance. Saviors are often the ones whose neglect or apathy caused the problems in the first place. Without an adequate in-place political intelligence and lobby effort, all other budgets can become academic. An organized legislative program is like any insurance program; it is purchased for protection against the risks of the unknown, the unexpected.

(2) Contact DeHart and Darr directly.[105] This group works with DMA in defeating list bans. They have particular expertise in selecting counsel in a given state to protect the free distribution of lists. If you are already a DMA member, it may be in your interest to investigate this group. Now is a good time to get involved. The long-term effect of doing nothing will be a lot more costly than the incidental business cost of

getting involved. Remember, it's your business future we're talking about.

Now we'll move on to four miscellaneous specialized areas of direct marketing law: shipping and handling, negative option, sales tax, and a few comments on postal areas and minor nuisance issues.

MISCELLANEOUS LEGAL ISSUES

Shipping and Handling Charges

Four questions concerning shipping and handling charges frequently arise:

- Are shipping and handling charges a material term?
- Must sales tax be charged on them?
- What can shipping and handling bills actually comprise?
- Can I make a profit on these charges?

Let's take a look at each of these questions.

▶ Are shipping and handling charges a material term? Yes. And your failure to disclose same will result in a violation of the free rule, negative option rule, deceptive pricing or whatever general rule governs your specific promotion.

▶ What about sales tax? Many if not all states impose a sales or use tax on postage charges within a shipping and handling expense when these aren't separately stated. However, if the charge for postage is separately shown, your customers shouldn't be taxed on it. Check with your tax manager as to the requirements for each state you do business in.

▶ What may it comprise? A variety of factors can come into play. You're looking at actual postage charges plus carton/envelope expense, labels, packing material(filler, tape, etc.), labor costs to process the order, and other incidental but related costs.

▶ Can I make a profit? The answer is NO, despite some misleading headlines to the contrary.[106] Let's take a look at the case history should you have any doubts. Below are a few of the landmark rulings.

In the Matter of Alter & Co.[107]

The defendant dealt with so-called certificates of guarantee purporting to replace a defective article at a nominal charge which was to cover solely the postage, packing and shipping of the new article. It was found that such charges actually afforded Alter a profit equal to a full sale (e.g. actual postage and handling was 3¢; they charged 25¢-35¢). The defendant was ordered to cease and desist:

"From representing that the postage charges or the charges for postage, packing and shipping of rings or other articles of jewelry or merchandise sold or offered for sale by respondent *are a sum or sums of money more than said charges actually are at the time of the sale* of jewelry in interstate commerce."

In the Matter of Barnes[108]

Similar to *Alter & Co.* above, the purchaser received a five-year "certificate of guarantee" when he purchased a ring. Such certificate would be redeemed upon its submission with a 25¢ postage and handling fee. The defendant was ordered to cease and desist:

> "From representing that he will give free a new ring in exchange for any ring manufactured and sold by him which becomes defective or in which the setting becomes loose within five years from the date of purchase upon the payment of 25 cents for packing and shipping charges, unless and until a new ring is actually given free under such circumstances, *the purchaser paying only the amount required for packing and shipping* of the new ring."

In the Matter of Falcon Camera Company[109]

Defendants were distributing and selling cameras. Twenty-five trade tickets plus 30¢ purported to cover only the cost of packing and shipping and one trial roll of film. A camera was allegedly included "free." The court held that:

> "The sum of 30 cents which is remitted by each person sending in trade tickets for redemption *does not cover solely the cost of packing and shipping the camera* but actually covers the entire cost to the respondents of said camera."

Bronzed Baby Shoe Co.[110]

Again, a corporation was charging specified shipping and handling charges which exceeded the actual cost of such shipping and handling. The corporation was ordered to cease and desist:

> "From representing directly or by implication that the cost of the postage covering the shipment of the aforesaid products to individual customers amounts to only a few cents *or that such cost is other than that which has been established as a matter of fact.*"

U.S. v. Bill Crouch Foreign, Inc.[111]

Customers paid "freight" charges that exceeded the actual cost of transporting the cars to the dealer's showroom. The FTC held (in line with prior policy) that no amount may be paid "for freight or a charge of similar import in excess of actual outlays to *third parties* to transport" such goods. A "good faith estimate" is not valid if it exceeds actual outlays. Specifically:

> . . ."eligible class member" means those persons who purchased any new Honda Accord automobile at the respondent's showrooms between July

15, 1976 and the date of service of this order, and who paid any amount for "freight," or charge of similar import, in excess of respondent's actual outlays to third parties to transport the automobile from the port-of-entry to respondent's showrooms, if such actual outlays are known, or, if unknown, in excess of respondent's outlays as computed pursuant to subparagraph 10(b) below.

. . ."If at the time of sale the charge made by the respondent for "freight" to a person who purchased a new Honda Accord automobile between July 15, 1976 and the date of service of this order was a "good faith estimate" of the respondent's actual freight outlays to third parties, such person shall not be an "eligible class member" within the meaning of this Consent Order. Any charge for freight made by the respondent shall be deemed a "good faith estimate" by the respondent if such charge cannot be shown to have exceeded the respondent's subsequent actual outlays, or, if unknown, its estimated outlays, as determined under subparagraph 10(b) below, to third parties for transportation of the automobile from the port-of-entry to the respondent's showrooms by more than thirty dollars ($30.00)."

The above five decisions should provide ample examples to support the position that shipping and handling charges may not include an element of profit to the seller. This is not "gravy." To treat it as such will not only expose you to fines, penalties, and loss of goodwill, but it is an open invitation to the IRS if you treat it as unreported income. If you report it, you see the Catch 22.

Negative Option Rule[112]

This is the much maligned tool of the book, record, and other clubs as well as the governing law (in principle) of continuity and related programs. It's not permitted in Hawaii, and the Swedish Consumer Protection Agency has declared it illegal. Even the FTC considered abolishing it in 1971. Negative option has never lost in a state where business has sought to defend it. The reason that there has been no erosion since the early 1970s is because a number of enlightened firms hired a lobbying firm to defeat these proposals, and they did year after year—every year.[113]

The case for negative option is that it permits volume manufacturing and distribution. The major costs of books (and related costs for other products) is in the initial typesetting and plate-etching. The unit cost drops significantly with long single runs if there is no major scrappage later of unsold copies. The underlying economic requirement of a book club is accurately predictable high volume. To keep members, some of the savings are passed along to the member. Other savings enhance the First Amendment as it permits the clubs to publish authors/books/ideas that otherwise never would have had a shot. Book clubs bring literature to all 39,500-odd zip codes.

The average citizen understands economies of scale. He or she knows he or she can subscribe to a magazine, commit to receive every copy, and pay a lower price per copy, or buy it at a newsstand and pay a premium. This system is approaching its 70th birthday and public acceptance is at an all-time high. The ultimate consumer democracy is the freedom for the consumer to choose how he or she will spend discretionary income.

Literal compliance with the rule's wording is mandated, as a few firms discovered to their detriment in 1978.[114] A direct marketer employing negative option plans would do well to commit to memory the mandatory disclosures and practices or, better yet, devise a compliance checklist against which all copy is reviewed in advance. The checklist would include all mandatory disclosures. They are as follows.

All promotional material must clearly and conspicuously state the material terms of the plan, including the following:

☐ That a negative option plan is being used.

☐ The full obligation to purchase a minimum amount of merchandise.

☐ That the member may cancel his or her membership any time after completion of the agreement to purchase the minimum amount of merchandise specified.

☐ Whether billing charges include postage and handling. It should be noted that the FTC negative option proceeding considered the advance disclosure of the specific amount of the member's shipping and handling charges. However, the FTC decided not to require specific charges—you may merely indicate up front that such charges exist. However, you must be aware that the FTC has stated on record that shipping and handling charges may not include an element of profit to the seller (see the discussion supra).

☐ That the member will be given 10 days to notify the seller that the selected merchandise is not desired or that he or she wishes to order alternative merchandise being offered. If the member receives less than 10 days, the account will be credited for returned merchandise. The seller must give full credit and pay the return postage for merchandise sent to members who have not been sent a proper form or who have not been given the required time to respond.

☐ The frequency with which the advance announcement or merchandise will be sent to the member (i.e., the maximum received in a 12-month period).

☐ A statement to the effect that introductory, bonus, and/or premium merchandise must be shipped within four weeks of the order, unless otherwise disclosed.

☐ A form contained in or accompanying the announcement clearly and conspicuously disclosing the procedure required to reject the selection.

With regard to book clubs, you have no doubt often seen the phrase "Book Club Edition" on book jackets; this is not required by the FTC. It is a matter of negotiation between the book club and the licensing publisher.

The Rule should be followed verbatim. No discretion is permissible even if you don't think it is applicable to your particular plan or product. Any direct marketer utilizing or planning on utilizing negative option would be wise to review the various "how to complain" publications to keep abreast of and to anticipate the growth of consumer awareness and activism in this area. It always helps to know what the opposition's strategy is!

Finally (while not implicitly required by the Rule), a statement up front that sales tax will be charged enhances full disclosure of all pertinent charges. Since a mail-order house will not have physical presence or situs in most states, a statement to the effect that "sales tax will be added where applicable" is sufficient.

As long as we're talking sales tax, let's move on and discuss where we are in the current sales tax debate. We'll look at the prior legal history and what compliance will look like for the balance of this decade.

Who Pays the Sales Tax?

"Our decisions are not always clear as to the grounds on which a tax is supported, especially where more than one exists; nor are all of our pronouncements during the experimental period of this type of taxation consistent or reconcilable. A few have been specifically overruled, while others no longer fully represent the present state of the law. But the course of decisions does reflect at least consistent adherence to one time-honored concept: that due process requires some definite link, some minimum connection, between a state and the person, property or transaction it seeks to tax."[115]

The above candidly worded statement from the Supreme Court more than 30 years ago summarizes the problems of the entire sales/use tax debate that has now arrived for direct mailers. There is no clear court or congressional standard of precisely where the states can draw the line. However, the line is being drawn for direct mailers, even closer to interstate seller compliance for four primary reasons:

- Direct mail is growing in visibility and deep pockets;
- The increases in sales/use taxes result in a self-fulfilling momentum; as the rates increase, the amount not collected increases, resulting in a greater target;
- Such a target incites the aggressiveness of state tax authorities and the trend of many state legislatures and courts to support the revenue needs of their state; and
- Despite its own self-proclaimed shortcomings in the tax area, the Supreme Court decisions concerning state taxation of interstate business do demonstrate a readily identifiable trend toward the progressive removal of constitutional barriers to such taxation.[116]

Sales and Use Taxes—What Are They?

Sales taxes are convenient to finance socialism. As government programs grow, they need indirect forms of taxation to recapture constituent "benefits payments" they cannot pay for directly (politically unpopular) or ever cut (politically unpopular). As raids on the treasury grow, so grow the tax rates and the states' desires to *effectively* increase the net of payors.

Sales taxes are popular because they require the retailer, not the state, to collect and remit the tax. It is no accident that such state taxes were relatively unknown prior to the New Deal.[117] Sales and use taxes have become the most significant source of state revenue.

As a general rule, a sales tax is imposed upon the transfer of title or possession of tangible personal property at either the retail or wholesale level and on certain services within the state. The sales tax had one obvious drawback as a levy on the sales transaction itself: it could only reach sales within the state. Further, it was perceived that a sales tax placed an in-state or intrastate seller at a competitive disadvantage with the out-of-state seller who is selling the same product but is not subject to the sales tax.

To remedy this perceived loss of revenue due to out-of-state purchases, the state passed the use tax. Use taxes are imposed upon the use, storage or consumption of tangible personal property not subject to state sales taxes. It is complementary *in rate* to the sales tax. Its purpose is to discourage residents of the taxing state from purchasing goods in another state where the sales tax is lower or non-existent.

While complementary in rate, sales and use taxes often differ with respect to exemptions, time of payment and application of constitutional provisions. The latter is quite significant for interstate mailers who are not collecting the use tax from their customers.

A state's right to collect a sales tax through in-state sellers is an obvious constitutional right. However, before a state can constitutionally require an out-of-state seller to collect its use tax, the seller must be subject to the state's jurisdiction, which is determined by the due process clause of the Fourteenth Amendment. Specifically, due process requires that there be "some definite link, some minimum connection, between a state and the person, property or transaction it seeks to tax."[118] This link is the much debated nexus. Let's take a look at where the courts have gone on this.

The Courts Narrow the Nexus

"Congress shall have the power to regulate commerce among the several states."[119] We'll briefly review the leading cases that have impact on our debate. Such cases lead us toward what we can expect in the future as to "minimum contact." In determining whether this minimum contact requirement has been satisfied, two constitutional issues must be decided:

(1) Whether the due process requirements have been met so as to create state jurisdiction over the out-of-state vendor, and

(2) Whether collection of the tax constitutes an undue burden on interstate commerce.

Since 1973[120] the use tax has been held clearly constitutional when the tax was imposed not on interstate commerce but when the use after commerce was not burdened. The same result was reached where a mail order seller not only sold through interstate channels but maintained local retail stores in the taxing state.

In *Nelson v. Sears, Roebuck & Co.,* [121] the court shifted its focus to the benefits that the taxing state provided to the seller by holding that a state could justifiably exact a price for those benefits. Sears resisted Iowa's attempts to impose use tax obligations on its mail order sales within the state by arguing that those sales had no connection with its retail stores in Iowa.

The Court, however, reasoned that a seller's collection obligations should be established on the basis of benefits received by the entire economic unit without regard to departmentalization. It concluded that the crux of the due process inquiry was whether the state gave anything for which it could ask return.

Three years later[122] the Court held that the mere solicitation by in-state traveling salesmen with order acceptance and shipment by common carrier out of state was sufficient to provide jurisdiction to impose the use tax on the seller. However, the onward march of the trend to greater inclusion was slowed a bit 10 years later.

In *Miller Brothers Co. v. Maryland,* [123] a Delaware furniture seller who was neither qualified to do business nor employed salesmen or agents in Maryland was required to collect taxes on retail purchases for delivery in that state. The firm did not accept mail or telephone orders and advertised only in Delaware media which indirectly reached some Maryland residents.

On these facts, the court was unable to find a nexus sufficient to meet the due process requirement that there exist "some definite link, some minimum connection, between a state and the person, property or transaction it seeks to tax."[124] The court found that:

> "There is a wide gulf between this type of active and aggressive operation within a taxing state and the occasional delivery of goods sold at an out-of-state store with no solicitation other than the incidental effects of general advertising. There was no invasion or exploitation of the consumer market in Maryland."[125]

Six years later[126] the court held that jurisdiction existed where the out-of-state seller used local independent contractors to solicit orders for out-of-state acceptance. In finding seller collection jurisdiction, the court noted that simply by using independent contractors rather than its own employees, the vendor's sales practices did not differ significantly from General Trading's. *Miller Brothers* was distinguished by contrasting the seller's lack of solicitation or marketing exploitation in that case with the active search for customers in the taxing jurisdiction in this situation.

Subsequent to this decision, two cases were rendered by the Supreme Court and one by a state court clearly stating that soliciting by mail/telephone followed by a mailing using a common carrier provides no nexus on which a state can compel an interstate seller to collect the use tax. The test for seller collection jurisdiction, as begun in 1967, was whether or not the seller engaged in solicitation and market exploitation.

The court in *National Bellas Hess v. Department of Revenue* [127] shifted emphasis from solicitation and market exploitation to whether or not there was a use of state facilities. The ability to frame the question is the ability to frame the answer. As direct marketers look to defend the status quo, they must debate within this decision's framework, not on grounds raised by their opponents.

Favorable Cases

National Bellas Hess, a Missouri mail order house, solicited sales from and shipped goods to consumers in Illinois. It had neither retail outlets nor sales representatives in Illinois. All solicitations were conducted through the mail and all shipments were delivered by mail or common carrier.

The Illinois Department of Revenue, pursuant to the Illinois Use Tax Act, assessed use tax collection liability against the mail order house for all sales to Illinois purchasers from July 17, 1961, to October 30, 1962. In an action to determine the propriety of this assessment, the Illinois trial court ruled for the state. This decision was affirmed by the Supreme Court of Illinois but was reversed by the U.S. Supreme Court.

In holding for the mail order seller, the court specifically addressed three points at issue in the current debate:

(1) State taxation falling on interstate commerce can only be justified as designed to make such commerce bear a fair share of the cost of the local government whose protection it enjoys. The "simple and controlling question is whether the state has given anything for which it can ask for in return."[128] A firm whose only contacts with a state are via the U.S. Postal Service or common carrier clearly does not enjoy such protection.

(2) The court indirectly acknowledged the fiction that the firm is not being taxed but the customer is. The firm is made liable for payment of the tax whether collected or not, so the practical reality is that the firm is the payee.

(3) This is precisely the interstate burden on the firm: it must pay the tax. It is a massive and unreasonable burden on an interstate carrier when viewed in context—it won't stop at the state level. As the court stated:

"If the power of Illinois to impose use tax burdens upon National were upheld, the resulting impediments upon the free conduct of its interstate business would be neither imaginary nor remote. For if Illinois can impose such burdens, so can every other State, and so, indeed, can every municipality, every school district, and every other political subdivision throughout the Nation with power to impose sales and use taxes. The many variations in rates of tax, in allowable exemptions, and in administrative and record-keeping requirements could entangle National's interstate business in a virtual welter of complicated obligations to local jurisdictions with no legitimate claim to impose 'a fair share of the cost of local government.'"

"The very purpose of the Commerce Clause was to ensure a national economy free from such unjustifiable local entanglements. Under the Constitution, this is a domain where Congress alone has the power of regulation and control."[129]

In footnote 14, the court stated further:

"The prevailing system requires (the seller) to administer rules which differ from one State to another and whose application—especially for the industrial retailer—turns on facts which are often too remote and uncertain for the level of accuracy demanded by the prescribed system. . .

"Given the broad spread of sales of even small and moderate sized companies, it is clear that if just the localities which now impose the tax were to realize anything like their potential of out-of-state registrants the recordkeeping tasks of multistate sellers would be clearly intolerable."[130]

The same year as *Bellas Hess,* another court[131] clearly understood the need to distinguish the states' revenue needs and the demands of a truly national economy.

"MacFadden-Bartell Corp. was not licensed or qualified to do business in the State of Alabama and had no designated agent for service of process in Alabama. It did not own, lease, operate or maintain any office or place of business in Alabama. It has never had any telephone listing or bank account in the state. No employee of MacFadden-Bartell came into the State of Alabama for the purpose of soliciting, promoting or encouraging the sale of subscriptions, and there was no employee of MacFadden-Bartell who resided in Alabama."

"During the assessment period subscriptions were sold to residents of Alabama in two different ways. Approximately one-half were sold by EBSCO, an Alabama corporation. The other half was sold by what was termed 'direct mail subscriptions.' EBSCO is a corporation engaged in many business enterprises, one of which is the sale of magazine subscriptions. It sells subscriptions to publications of many different publishers. MacFadden-Bartell is one of the publishers whose magazines it sells and MacFadden-Bartell has no financial interest in EBSCO, exercises no control over it and furnishes no sales or promotional material to it in connection with its magazines. . ."[132]

"The orders for subscriptions and payment therefore were sent directly to the appellee in New York by the Alabama subscriber. These subscriptions were the result of circulars sent by mail by appellee over the United States, including Alabama, advertising a particular magazine. The magazines were delivered to the Alabama subscriber by U.S. mail."

"EBSCO was registered with the Department of Revenue as a dealer and collected the Alabama sales tax on each subscription it sold and remitted to the State the sales tax collected."

"From these facts the State contends that it is apparent that EBSCO is an agent of MacFadden-Bartell so as to bring MacFadden-Bartell within the purview of the foregoing sections, requiring it to collect the use tax both on the sales made by EBSCO and on those made directly. The Court held that the evidence fails to sustain the State's contention."[133]

Distinguishing *Scripto,* the court held that:

(1) EBSCO was not an "agent," "representative," or "independent contractor" for MacFadden-Bartell.

(2) The seller had not established any distinct connection with the State of Alabama.

Finally, the third favorable decision was *National Geographic Society v. The California Board of Equalization,*[134] which was decided with 10 years' reflection on *Bellas Hess.* This is often remembered as a defeat for direct marketers because the Society's challenge to California's use tax imposition failed. However, the Society had a continuous presence in California in two offices, so its failure was to be anticipated.

What is important constitutionally is that the Supreme Court chose to review the case at all. It did so to strike down California's holding that the "slightest presence" of a seller in California established a nexus. The U.S. Supreme Court, in rejecting the "slightest presence" test, held that there must be some "definite link" or "minimum connection" before a state can impose the responsibility of its use tax collection on the seller.

This rejection is being clearly overlooked by many states and the Advisory Commission on Intergovernmental Relations (ACIR) study as they seek to eliminate even a "slightest presence" standard.

Confronting the Challenge

The DMA has been active in an effective state effort to block a number of adverse bills at the state and federal level. There are a number of legal arguments which should be stressed. Beyond the reasons stated above, it might be useful to explore the antitrust laws because the tax compliance costs and company characteristics clearly correlate. Such costs are higher for smaller companies since the cost per transaction varies inversely with the number of transactions.

Economic Burdens. To state as the Advisory Commission on Intergovernmental Relations (ACIR) has that this is fair to local retailers and of no greater burden is simply intellectual dishonesty.

- A national seller must keep track of the laws of all states (localities?) while the local seller need only keep track of one. It is obvious a local cash system will be less burdensome than a national data processing oriented firm. Score one for the local seller.

- The ability to determine whether a particular sale is subject to a use tax is more complicated than just rate percentages. The national marketer must constantly check all jurisdictions' rates and exemptions. Such check is more than mere legislative monitoring. It must reference state court decisions and announcements by state tax administrators. This reference to red tape is an impossibility for small firms. It is difficult for a small firm to seriously keep abreast of the relevant law in those states where it must ship, bill, collect, account, report the tax due and subject its business records to the various auditing procedures.

- As a consequence, most small firms can't/won't comply. The states' limited enforcement powers will arbitrarily come down on a few but compliance by the other sellers will place them at a disadvantage vis–a–vis their non-complying competitors. Score another for the local in-state seller.

- The ACIR's answer to this is a bureaucrat's solution but a real world nightmare. They'd milk the 6,000 or so local jurisdictions into one tax rate for each state. A complying firm faces a goodwill nightmare as it attempts to collect the "common denominator tax" in a jurisdiction where it is significantly higher. Score another for the local retailers.

- Another inequity for the interstate seller is that any collection costs incurred by sellers are likely to remain uncompensated since less than half the states imposing sales and use taxes allow the vendor to retain a portion of the taxes collected to help defray the collection expenses. Again, the larger companies apparently can discharge their collection obligations at a lower cost per unit of output than a small or medium-sized company. If equity was seriously being considered, the ACIR would mandate sellers discounts for collections and timely payments. The DMA should also push this.

- As part of a comprehensive program of equity, there should be a mandated provision that the tax is imposed only on actual sales and that all bad debt is nontaxable. This is not the case in at least 11 states as of 1987.

- Finally, it should be stressed that the inclusion is merely part of a political agenda. For example, the first bill to authorize states to tax without regard to nexus was introduced by Sen. Mondale in 1973. His tax crusade ended in 1984 but the effort to tax the free market at all costs (regardless of constitutional constraints) has to be kept in mind.

Social Value. It's not a legal argument, but a fact that targeted marketing:

- Brings literature and other products into the homes of those in areas inaccessible to retail outlets. Such areas are numerous; they are traditionally rural areas cut off from the stores or inner cities where people are afraid to go out and prefer door-to-door purchasing over being mugged downtown. The elderly or the handicapped can live anywhere and depend on their mail or telephone for purchasing. These people are constituents of representatives who are voting to hinder their access to such purchases. All concerned should be informed.

- Direct mailers, like the postal system, service America. Congress has seen the need to keep a number of post offices open to service rural and other constituents. If this has a valid social purpose so does the product that arrives at the post office. Such post offices have other nationalist purposes such as a national organization to handle.

- Finally, direct mailers, unlike retailers, subsidize through higher postal rates these unprofitable post offices.

While not "law," the fact is the use tax, red tape and financial cost implementation will cut back on or eliminate the varied literature, and merchandise that many people would otherwise have access to. If society sees the need to subsidize a national post office, it can leave the Constitution as it is and indirectly "subsidize" the national supermarket accessible through the mail.

The States Are Moving

For the long term, we should look to a uniform use tax as a possible compromise or to be prepared to fight an endless legislative battle of attrition in the states. In the average session at least half the states will draft legislation on point. To date, none have had impact due to constitutional contraints. This is another issue that's not going to go away. It, like the decrease in subsidies to the postal system, is putting increased pressure on the profit margins. Now let's briefly scan a few postal issues.[135]

A Few Issues to Be Aware Of in the Postal Area

Throughout this book, shipping and handling and other postal-related issues have been discussed. The *Domestic Mail Manual* should be reviewed by your in-house specialist as to your particular promotions (e.g., mail classification, inserts, etc.). However, we'll touch on a few generic areas all marketers should be up on. We'll begin with an overview of the Board of Governors.

The Board of Governors

The Board of Governors of the Postal Service is the organization's governing body, comparable to the board of directors of a private corporation. The Board has 11 members. Nine of them are appointed by the President, subject to confirmation by the Senate. No more than five of the nine can be members of the same political party.

The first nine appointments were for staggered terms lasting from one to nine years. Subsequent appointments have been for full nine-year terms or the remainder of unexpired terms. The nine Presidentially appointed governors choose a Postmaster General, who also serves as a member of the Board. These 10, in turn, choose a Deputy Postmaster General, who becomes the 11th member of the Board. The Postmaster General and the Deputy Postmaster General serve at the pleasure of the governors.

The Postal Reorganization Act provides that the Board shall direct the exercise of the powers of the Postal Service, direct and control its expenditures, and review its practices and policies. The Board generally meets once a month. The governors receive $10,000 annually plus $300 per day for not more than 30 days of meetings per year.

History of the Postal Service and Its Key Monopoly

Everyone knows changes are coming.[136] The USPS is the oldest communications infrastructure in the United States. Is it now "that overworked, malfunctioning, classically Second Wave Institution"[137] as described by Alvin Toffler? Or, more positively, does the USPS owe its longevity to its own dynamism in growing with our nation through its various commercial epochs? This section will

- take a look at the law on point;
- review why it's there;
- take a look at the criminal and civil mail fraud statutes;
- examine whether it should stay there; and
- comment on the future of the USPS in general.

The Law

First, the text of 18 USCS Section 1696 is as follows:

1696. PRIVATE EXPRESS FOR LETTERS AND PACKETS.

(a) Whoever establishes any private express for the conveyance of letters or packets, or in any manner causes or provides for the conveyance of the same by regular trips or at stated periods over any post route which is or may be established by law, or from any city, town or place to any other city, town, or place, between which the mail is regularly carried, shall be fined not more than $500 or imprisoned not more than six months, or both.

This section shall not prohibit any person from receiving and delivering to the nearest post office, postal car, or other authorized depository for mail matter any mail matter properly stamped.

(b) Whoever transmits by private express or other unlawful means, or delivers to any agent thereof, or deposits at any appointed place, for the purpose of being so transmitted any letter or packet, shall be fined not more than $50.

(c) This chapter (sections 1691 to 1734) shall not prohibit the conveyance or transmission of letters or packets by private hands without compensation, or by special messenger employed for the particular occasion only. Whenever more than twenty-five such letters or packets are conveyed or transmitted by such special messenger, the requirements of section 500 of Title 39, shall be observed as to each piece.

Origins of the Law

In 1692, far removed from our electronic age (Ben Franklin hadn't even flown his kite yet), a Mr. Thomas Neale was granted a 21-year royal patent to operate the colonial postal service. Mr. Neale began one tradition immediately - he lost money! In 1707, the British postmaster general purchased the colonial operation for $1,664.

After years of lackluster management, Benjamin Franklin was appointed Postmaster General in 1753. Within eight years, he was showing a profit! However, his success was short-lived and eventually lost in the Stamp Act controversy (1765). Then a war was fought resulting in new management for the post office.

By 1782, Yorktown was won and the Continental Congress adopted a postal monopoly, specifically (emphasis added):

> The Postmaster General of these United States for the time being, and his deputy and deputies, thereunto by him sufficiently authorised (sic), and his and their agents, post-riders, expresses and messengers respectively, and *no other person whatsoever,* shall have the receiving taking up, ordering, despatching (sic), sending post or speed, carrying and delivering of any letters, packets or other despatches (sic) from any place within these United States for hire, reward, or other profit or advantage. . ."[138]

This monopoly principle was written into the Constitution in Article I, Section 8 which provides, among other things, that Congress shall have the power to establish post offices and post roads and to make all laws necessary for carrying into execution that order. There is no doubt the language of Section 8 is vague. However, it should be noted that despite such vague language, the framers and populace of the time (otherwise jealous of powers granted the national government) acquiesced to this clause with no acrimony whatsoever—in fact, with virtually no debate at all!

The current USCS section 1696 was "born" in 1845. Senator William Merrick of Maryland feared for the financial health of the post office, which was gradually being eroded by various private expresses. The 1845 act marked the first time in U.S. postal evolution that Congress employed the term "private express" in describing the activities of private companies which were carrying such items for compensation.

Under the 1845 statute, the monopoly covered "letters, packets *or packages of letters, or other matter properly transmittable in the U.S. mail,* except newspapers, pamphlets, magazines and periodicals."[139] This language might well be construed as encompassing all commercial information.

To date this monopoly has survived various Congressional attempts at Congressional repeal as well as court challenges.[140] For the record, such monopoly has been shown to encompass advertising circulars addressed to particular persons or locations but not merchandise.

Dubious Independence

In an effort to eliminate political influence over the postal service, Congress abolished the post office as a cabinet-level department in 1970 and replaced it with a quasi-independent corporation, the current USPS. At that time, Congress ordered the Governors of the USPS to undertake a thorough reevaluation of the monopoly. By 1973, this study was completed—though regulations were changed in 1979 to allow private delivery of "extremely urgent" mail.

The 11 years that followed showed laudatory improvements. This labor-intensive service (approximately 85% of operating costs) reduced its payroll by 75,000 while increasing its overall volume of business. The USPS was forced to raise significant amounts of capital for modernization—modernization long neglected by the former Post Office Department.

This made its overall expenditure volume compare unfavorably to its mail volume, particularly in the short run. Then there was OPEC, which forced dramatic increases in the fuel budget on the USPS, one of the nation's largest users of fuel.

The whole operation was shrouded with the myth of "independence." No independent firm is forced to retain unprofitable branches in remote areas, incur mandated minimum days to be open or set uniform rates. An example of the whole political domination is the ZIP + 4 issue. A private corporation would be allowed to risk innovation. The USPS has Congress on its back at every step of the process.

Other examples of dubious artificial market conditions sought to be placed on the USPS for solely political reasons (which no private firm would be hampered with) include—since just 1978:

(a) Carter's "Citizen's Rate" for first-class mail. As Henry Hoke stated at the time,[141] "Certainly the proposed 13 cents Citizen's Rate for first-class mail that Mr. Carter shoved down Mr. Bailor's throat was not a business decision. It was a political sop."

(b) Then there were other forms of bills proposed, which included (but were *not* limited to) bills to

- authorize "free" unrestricted citizen mailing of all letter mail to the President, Vice President and *all* members of Congress;
- force USPS to use Amtrak;
- mandate door delivery of mail to the physically handicapped regardless of delivery system in place (i.e., rural pickup, cluster boxes, etc.)
- prohibit the USPS from using its own funds to implement or even advertise ZIP + 4.
- permit non-profit health clinics receiving federal financial assistance to mail "free" of charge.

Fortunately, none of the above legislation has passed to date. No one would expect Emery Air Freight or Federal Express to be forced to "compete" under similar rules (and threats of others) that the USPS routinely must handle and, yes, amazingly master!

The USPS has two competitive advantages at present: significant advantages as state/federal level and the private express statutes. Eliminating one of these advantages without also granting the post office free-market discretion as to the five-days-a-week delivery, closing some rural post offices, etc., is simply another nail in the coffin of an indispensable system of national commerce and unity.

Recognizing this, society retains the private express statutes despite lawsuits to the contrary.[142] In opposing the First Amendment challenges, the Court went clearly on record that "there is neither historical nor constitutional support for the characterization of a letter box as a public forum.[143]

Now we'll move from the general to the criminal and civil enforcement aspects of the Postal Service. When you consider recent postal issues nowadays you think of rates, electronic mail, or nine-digit zip codes. Yet, there is another significant issue—that of the postal service's enforcement powers. We'll take a look at the Postal Service's current powers to combat mail fraud—both civil and criminal. After reviewing such powers we'll examine the constitutional debate.

Criminal Mail Fraud Statute

18 USC section 1341 is the criminal mail fraud statute under which the Postal Service may seek criminal prosecution for mail fraud

violations. Here the accused is entitled to normal due process safeguards, specifically, that the intent to defraud must be proven by the government. The statute reads, in pertinent part, as follows:

> Whoever, having devised or intending to devise any scheme or artifice to defraud, or for obtaining money or property by means of false or fraudulent pretenses, representations, or promises. . .for the purpose of executing such scheme or artifice or attempting to do so, places in any post office or authorized depository for mail matter, any matter or thing whatever to be sent or delivered by the Postal Service, or takes or receives therefrom, any such matter or thing, or knowingly causes to be delivered by mail according to the direction thereon. . .any such matter or thing, shall be fined not more than $1,000 or imprisoned not more than five years, or both.

The traditional elements of fraud are whereby the actor:

- Devises a deceptive scheme.
- The deceptive scheme is such that, if successful, it will probably injure another.
- He intends to defraud.

For purposes of the mail fraud statute, the necessary elements to look for are the scheme to defraud *and* the mailing of a letter (or "otherwise knowingly cause mail to be delivered") for the purpose of executing the scheme.[144] Such defendant is deemed to have "caused" a mailing if he could reasonably have foreseen it.

The original federal mail fraud statute was enacted in 1872. Five years later a unanimous Supreme Court upheld its constitutionality.

> The power possessed by Congress embraces the regulation of the entire postal system of the country. The right to designate what shall be carried necessarily involves the right to determine what shall be excluded.[145] From that premise, it followed that Congress was entirely free "to prescribe regulations as to what shall constitute mail matter" and that the sole limitation on such regulations would derive "from the necessity of enforcing them consistently with rights reserved to the People."[146]

The Court only mentioned two such rights: the Fourth Amendment right against unwarranted searches and seizures and the First Amendment freedom of the press. Freedom of speech was not specified until 1965.[147]

It is clear that Congress has established adequate criminal procedures to (hopefully) discourage, and where necessary prosecute, individuals engaged in mail fraud. We also see that the courts are wary of Congress's granting exclusionary powers over mail which involved constitutional issues. This tension remains in the current legislative debate concerning expanding the civil enforcement powers of the Postal Service.

Civil Statutes

There are two *civil* statutes which give the Postal Service authority to combat mail fraud. One statute is 39 USC 3005. This statute is employed to combat "false representations" delivered in the mail. This statute might be used, for example, to prohibit the advertising in the mail of a deceptive lottery scheme, or even the advertisement of books and other publications that contain false or questionable theories (e.g., the *Magnolia Lab* case discussed below).

Under current Section 3005, the Postal Service may, after an administrative hearing, issue a "stop order" which returns to sender the mail of an individual suspected of sending false representations through the mail. *The intent to defraud need not be proven* by the Postal Service. Following the administrative proceeding, the respondent may appeal the decision to the District Court.

Under Section 3007, the Postal Service may seek a temporary restraining order or preliminary injunction to detain the respondent's incoming mail before a "stop order" has been issued. The District Court may also allow the Postal Service to *open* and review this incoming mail. Finally, Section 3007 provides that the court *shall* issue such an injunction upon the showing that probable cause exists that the respondent is guilty of violating Section 3005.

Case Example

It is an established constitutional principle that there is no such thing as a wrong idea. However, any idea can be falsely advertised in the commercial free speech arena. The distinction the Postal Service must make between attacking a false idea in an advertisement and false ideas in a book or other material expressing ideas is often difficult to maintain. For example, there was the much celebrated and debated *Magnolia Lab* case.[148]

Prior to *Magnolia Lab,* the Postal Service had been criticized for "suppressing" books on martial arts, natural healing, nutrition and oriental philosophy. The Postal Service argues that it is not suppressing books, just the "false" advertisements promoting such books. However, what this amounts to is that it will suppress a truthful ad which accurately portrays a "false" idea contained in a book.

Critics charge that this is wrong in itself, since many such false ideas merely represent opinions which run counter to established thought such as that of the American Medical Association. Further, any such suppression can act to chill the mailing of a book. Finally (hypothetically), what of a truthful advertisement suppressed because the idea of a political candidate or "unacceptable" religious leader written in a book was "judged" to be "false" by the Postal Service?

The problem with the critics' argument is that it states that anyone has the license to state anything. A product sold through the mail is a commercial product. As such, its commercial advertising must be truthful on its face, and the claims in the book which relate to the claims in the advertisement must be true.

In *Magnolia Lab,* Robert Ford mailed out his booklet *Stale Food vs. Fresh Food* with an advertisement stating that "ARTERIES CAN CLEANSE THEMSELVES WITHOUT SURGERY BY DIET ALONE." It goes on to state:

> A startling new discovery shows how arteries can cleanse themselves without surgery. Just as your skin can cast out thorns, your arteries can cast out lumps when you stop forming them with the wrong foods. . . Now by my discovery you can now enjoy many of the rich and tasty foods denied you by the old humbug cholesterol diets, while your own natural blood flow washes your arteries clean. . .[149]

The claims encouraged self-medication. Further, the administrative law judge found that these representations (and others) were materially false representations in violation of 39 USC 3005. Finally, this was not a "suppressed minority opinion." The methods used to test this "diet" were not performed by the acceptable methods employed in the scientific and medical fields for proving a thesis. As was neatly summarized in another postal decision:

> Even though an advertisement correctly describes a booklet, if the results represented in the booklet cannot be achieved by following the procedures outlined in the booklet, the advertiser is in violation of 39 USC 3005.[150]

This decision does not attempt to or convey the threat of the suppression of ideas. Section 39 USC 3005 cannot be used to censor or edit *The Conservative Manifesto* or *Mother Jones.* It does not in any way restrict the *content* or ideas conveyed in a product sold through the mail. It is simply in line with traditional restrictions on commercial free speech, i.e., that the commercial advertisement/content not be false or deceptive either overtly or where deception might arise from incomplete disclosure. There is (constitutionally) such a thing as a wrong product claim. The enforcement of truth in advertising in the commercial area will enhance, not chill commercial free speech. It will have no impact whatsoever on the free dissemination of ideas through the mail.

The postal system impacts us in a variety of ways. Let's take a look at how large it is and a few suggestions for improvement.

It's a Real Business—And Can Be Improved

If compared to a Fortune 500 company, the Postal Service would be (approximately):

- Number 1 in total domestic employees (since AT&T's breakup), i.e., 725,000;
- Second largest retail chain (40,000 locations); and
- The *largest* transportation company in the U.S. (already)!

The postal system needs hands-off dealing from the Congress. It needs the ability to close unneeded post offices or a subsidy to keep them open if forced to. It should be able to set its own hours. Three suggestions:

(1) It should be encouraged to be a bit more innovative. For example, air transportation costs have jumped 23% (30% of mail travels by air). Deregulation meant the Civil Aeronautics Bureau (CAB) no longer exists to set uniform airmail rates. The USPS must now negotiate individually with each airline about costs and volume. Deregulation has led airlines to abandon unprofitable routes, increasing cost and time to deliver to many areas. The USPS has to contract with overnight freight carriers to replace these abandoned schedules.

The Postal Service should buy aircraft or buy into an airline. Their competitors in overnight delivery have their own fleets. The USPS's operations justify it. Surplus aircraft exist.

(2) Another area to cut costs would be to allow domestic corporations and U.S. citizens to promote their messages on stamps. The stamp would be sold through a competitive bidding process and then *resold* to the public. (USPS would continue to print, sell and distribute the stamps). Other advertising areas include:

- Postal vehicles (similar to public transit);
- The unmarked sides of stamp booklets;
- The backside of stamps (emulating other countries); and
- Specially designated areas of the Post Office.

(3) All Government funded housing as well as all new multi-dwelling units should have cluster boxes mandated by Congress and a multi-tier charge could be imposed for direct door convenience. A USPS study showed delivery costs per person to be:

- $105 for door service (even more in rural areas);
- $83 for curbline; and
- $53 for cluster boxes, or a 50% savings.

This carrier cost factor is essential to rates and you should reflect on it (no one else there has). The Postal Service operation can be divided into three parts: delivery, mail processing and all other. Postal Service costs are divided almost equally among these three segments. In fact, a recent Postal Service report estimated delivery costs to be 39% of total costs. THE CARRIER OPERATION, IN PARTICULAR CARRIER DELIVERY OR OUT-OF-OFFICE TIME, IS THE LEAST RESPONSIVE TO PRODUCTIVITY IMPROVEMENT.

Automation in mail processing has the potential to improve carrier productivity in his or her "in-office" casing operation by sorting the mail in walk sequence. Saturation mail can be and often is sorted in walk sequence by the mailer, thus improving the carriers' productivity. It is the carriers' street time that presents the challenge. A modest effort to improve carrier productivity is the use of cluster boxes in new developments.

Carrier street costs must increase with volume. As volume increases, overtime is required. If volume continues to increase, more carriers must be added. Volume could conceivably push this 39% of total costs even higher if productivity improvements continue to be made to the mail-processing third and to the all-other third. Ironically, carrier street costs in the past have been treated mostly as a volume variable, and therefore the costs are institutional. Institutional costs are spread over all classes of mail.

Considering its great impact on service, profit margins, etc., the direct marketing trade groups and firms have been extremely uncreative. Their lack of creativity in pushing for postal rejuvenation could haunt their cost-effective distribution channel in the future.

Now let's wind up with a few other legal areas of immediate and potential impact to this channel. Fortunately they are at present in the "legislative stage" and you can defeat them there.

Nuisance Issues of the 1980s

While none of these issues are going to severely affect your business, they do complicate it, and the cumulative effect of a lot of these will affect your bottom line.

Ten-Point Type.   These bills usually mandate that your contractual wording be printed in at least ten-point type, have a high Flesch scale readability score and be organized by descriptive captions with each paragraph in easily understood language.

None of this assists your marketing program. You're going to make sure your promotional copy is readable, anyway. The ten-point type problem is bad for you, because it impedes creative copy design. Your space to market is contracted by the type size. This is further amplified by the fact that many of you already have to include mandated legal copy. The larger legal copy takes up even more space while your reduced area for creative copy must contend with larger print size.

Cash Discounts.   These bills have abounded over the last few years. They might as well be entitled the "direct marketer's automatic discount act" where they require cash discounts to be available to all buyers including mail/phone whether or not such buyers have a card in the first place.

Almost everyone is going to take the discount unless it is a very large order. This presents you with a number of problems, including the fact that one reason for offering the credit card is for their "insurance protection." In exchange for their fee, the card issuer is insulating you from bad debt. Many of these bills require the discount to reflect the *largest* credit card fee you offer: If two cards are 5% and the third is 7% discount, you must offer a 7% discount. Dropping the latter card may be painless, or it may result in a fall-off of orders or even a loss of prestige.

Mail Order Licensing.   This topic has begun to surface. For example, a recent bill would have established a Mail Order Licensing Board and required all mail order businesses to be *licensed annually* and bonded. The board would have had broad authority to receive and mediate complaints, hold hearings into alleged violations, award compensation to customers and determine which companies should be refused a license to do business.

You would have had to print the fact that you were licensed on *all* contracts, invoices and receipts (a copy clutter burden which dwarfs ten point type).

VDTs.   A hot topic—as evidenced by the volume of legislative activity—is legislation regulating the use of video display terminals (VDTs). At least 20 states will have introduced legislation on this topic in the 1987–88 sessions alone.

Legislators who introduce these bills represent constituencies. Some of their constituents may be your employees. This legislative area promises to grow as concern will be fed by unions who see the safety issue as an excellent organizing tool and the media which has begun to sense a story.

If the restrictive lobby is correct in certain assumptions, the costs to business would make the asbestos problem appear minor. Unlike other employee safety legislation, such as nonsmokers' rights in the workplace, a VDT is essential to direct marketers. Thus, they should be active in this area. Many firms are blind to the implications of this topic. What have your legislators and other government people done to alert you? What has your trade press written? If you don't think your opponents are active, contact 9 to 5,[151] and ask them what they're doing.

New Mexico already has established guidelines for state employees and Rhode Island has directed its Department of Labor to create an informational brochure for all employees. The private sector had better move to keep this at the public employee and information stage.

Amendment Alert.   Another need for vigilance legislatively is that no bill ever dies. There are the bills that start out innocuously. If they look remotely applicable, you must track these because amendments can be tacked on which are adverse to you. You must be prepared to react swiftly or accept the consequences to your bottom line.

More ominous are the laws you worked on and now believe are safely on the books. Any bill you permit to be enacted which can affect you *will* affect you. For example, in the early 1970s, most states enacted

Home Solicitation Laws. There was little industry input, as many felt that because they didn't sell door-to-door the law didn't affect them.

Then suddenly in the late 1970s states rushed to incorporate telephone marketing in the "cooling off" and other provisions of the statutes. Almost 20 states now have these. Arguably (though not by me), telephone is a "high pressure" intrusive sales effort from which a consumer might need to cool off. However, states have recently sought fit to include mail order sellers despite the fact that mail by its very nature is "cool," passive, and low-key.

The same principle applies to lists. Laws are put on the books which become more inclusive through amendment. You need not be too future–oriented to see this inevitability.

Conclusion

With the velocity of legislation increasing greatly through computerization and the general growth of government itself, the trade group classed as direct or database marketers remains exposed to the government's altering of its way of doing business.

Paying a small percentage of trade association dues to retard or eliminate such threats is both cost-effective and necessary. However, merely forking over money does not buy defense. Each member has to be active in regard to his or her own personal interests. At times he or she must unite with smaller groups or go it alone.

Euphemisms will not provide the bottom line. Catalog glut won't rationalize the loss of lists. Being subjected to an assortment of state use taxes won't facilitate fulfillment of the bottom line. Government-mandated copy wording size will provide impact upon creativity. Changing the mail order merchandise law's requirement from *ship* in 30 days to *deliver* in 30 days could devastate inventory planning and fulfillment. These and other issues are being decided in the state legislatures each year. Make sure you are present and that your presence is felt.

ENDNOTES

(1) See under "Departments" the "Direct Marketing Flow Chart/Explanation" in each issue of *Direct Marketing Magazine*.

(2) Henry R. Hoke, Jr., "Editorial," *Direct Marketing,* July 1982, p. 238.

(3) Richard Viguerie, "Ends and Means," *The New Right Papers,* Robert W. Whitaker (ed.), St. Martin's, New York, 1982, p. 31.

(4) 16 CFR 435.

(5) See any quarter's *Digest of Consumer Complaints Correspondence.* Mail Order Merchandise will rank either first or second in the Violation Categories.

(6) E.g., Alabama and Utah.

(7) Assistant Attorney General Mark E. Smith press release September 10, 1982.

(8) *Washington Report,* April 30, 1985, p. 8.

(9) *FTC v. Hosiery Corporation of America, Inc.,* (E.D. Pa. 8/14/86). See Kent, Felix "Mail Order Advertising and Sales" *NY Law Journal* 11/28/86 p.1. Other recent penalties handed down by the FTC of interest to the direct marketer include:

   a. *U.S. v. Star Crest Product of California, Inc.,* No. CV-82-2404 (Kn) (C.D. Col. 5/24/82) ($50,000).

   b. *U.S. v. J.S. & A. Group, Inc. et al,* 547 F Supp 20 (N.D. Ill. 1982), aff'd, 716 F.2d 451 (7th Cir. 1983) (president personally liable for $115,000 fine).

   c. *U.S. v. Klein,* (C.D. Cal. 3/21/85) (officers of company must notify FTC of any employment or business they obtain in the next 10 years).

   d. *U.S. v. Encore House, Inc.,* (S.D.N.Y. 9/25/85) ($350,000 total payments plus one officer of the company was enjoined from engaging in the mail order business for the remainder of his natural life.)

   e. *U.S. v. Del Monte Corp.,* (N.D. Cal. 11/18/85) ($100,000 fine).

   f. *U.S. v. Raffoler, Ltd., No. CV-86-3519 (E.D.N.Y. 10/17/86)* ($150,000 fine).

(10) Both the Alabama and Utah legislatures seriously examined this wording recently.

(11) Robert J. Posch, Jr., *The Direct Marketer's Legal Adviser,* McGraw-Hill, New York, 1983.

(12) Robert J. Posch, Jr., "The U.S. Postal Service: Dinosaur or Dynamic Carrier?," *Direct Marketing,* March 1982, pp. 128-131 (reprinted in *Postal Bulletin*) and Posch, "New Postal Legislation: More Power to the Postal Service," *Direct Marketing,* June 1983, pp. 114-116.

(13) For example, review N.Y. Gen. Bus. Law sec. 396(m).

(14) See note 9 above.

(15) 16 C.F.R. 435 notes 1-4.

(16) NYS General Business Law 196(m).

(17) See note 11 above. Note: If following most or all of the state laws is a problem for you—it needn't be. See Section VII, Establishing Your Profit Preservation Center.

(18) 39 U.S.C.S. 3009.

(19) 39 U.S.C.S. 3009(d).

(20) *Kipperman v. Academy Life Insurance Company,* (CA9 Cal.), 599 F.2d 377, (1977).

(21) Id., pp. 380-1.

(22) Such marketer should note that more than 10 states have incorporated such calls into their respective Home Solicitation Laws requiring a three-day cooling-off period (see below). The FTC also has acted here on a situation by situation basis, e.g., see *In Re Commercial Lighting Products, Inc.,* File No. 792 3053 (1980).

(23) 16 C.F.R. 425.

(24) 16 C.F.R. 425.1(b)(1)(iii).

(25) Though not all: for example, see Georgia Codes Annotated, Article 26-3001 to 3010. Also, to make the calls it might be helpful to have a "neutral voice," i.e., Carlson, Eugene, "Neutral Accents Help Attract Telemarketers to the Midwest," *Wall Street Journal,* April 8, 1986, p. 33.

(26) 18 U.S.C. 2510 through 2520 (1970).

(27) *Abel v. Bonfanti,* 625 F.Supp. 263, 270 (S.D.N.Y. 1985).

(28) *James v. Newspaper Agency Corporation,* 591 F.2d 579 (10th Cir. 1979).

(29) *State of Florida v. Nova,* 261 S.2d 411 (1978).

(30) *Briggs v. American Air Filter Company, Inc.* 630 F.2d 414 (5th Cir. 1980).

(31) *Watkins v. C. M. Berry & Co.,* 704 F.2d 577, 583 (11th Cir. 1983).

(32) *United States v. Harpel,* 493 F.2d 346 (10th Cir. 1974). See also *United States v. Jones,* 542 F.2d 661 (6th Cir. 1976), and *United States v. Schrimsher,* 493 F.2d 848 (5th Cir. 1974).

(33) One must also watch future court interpretations of related statutes enacted in this area. For example, in 1986 Louisiana enacted R.S. 14:323 as to illegal possession and importation of eavesdropping devices. As to legislation, see the Annual Direct Marketing Supplement on Direct Marketing—it always has a legislative overview. For example, see Rupp, John, "Sorry, Wrong Number," *Advertising Age,* May 24, 1982, p. M-8

(34) FCC Report No. 13862, 3/16/78. Eventually a highly publicized effort to solicit complaints resulted in 4,500 informal comments.

(35) FCC Docket No. 78-100; RM 2955; p. 37740 Fed. Reg. 45, 109 (1980).

(36) Arkansas prohibited the use of automatic dialing systems with recorded messages to make telephone solicitation calls, except when initiated by the receiver. Other representative state samples include: Alaska, California, Colorado, Florida, Maryland, Michigan, Nebraska, North Carolina, Virginia, and Wisconsin.

(37) A number of states have mandated or voluntary compliance here. These include: Arizona, Arkansas, Indiana, Louisiana, Michigan, North Dakota, Ohio, Oregon, Utah, Virginia, Wisconsin, and Wyoming.

(38) *Valentine v. Chrestensen,* 316 US 52 (1942). See also *Beard v. Alexandria,* 341 US 622 (1951).

(39) *Commrano v. U.S.,* 358 US 498, 514 (1959).

(40) 376 US 254 (1954).

(41) Id. at 266.

(42) *Virginia State Board of Pharmacy v. Virginia Citizens Consumer Council,* 425 US 748 (1976).

(43) Id. at 763.

(44) 391 US 367, 377 (1968) (emphasis added). The crucial element to lowering the First Amendment shield is the *imminence* of a threatened evil. See *Herceg v. Hustler Magazine, Inc.,* 814 F.2d 1017, 1022 (1987). See also *Norwood v. Soldier of Fortune Magazine, Inc.,* 651 F.Supp 1397 (W.D. Ark. 1987).

(45) *Friedman v. Rogers,* 440 US 1, 8 (1979). See also *Posadas de Puerto Rico Assoc. v. Tourisma Co. of Puerto Rico,* 106 S.Ct. 2968 (1986).

(46) *Gertz v. Robert Welch, Inc.,* 418 US 323, 340 (1974).

(47) *Griswold v. Connecticut,* 381 US 479 (1965).

(48) See note 41 above and *Lindmark Assoc., Inc. v. Willingboro,* 431 US 85 (1977).

(49) *Central Hudson Gas & Electric Corp. v. Public Service Commission,* 100 S.Ct.2343, 2350 (1980). Two other decisions of not advancing corporate free speech (political) are: *First National Bank v. Belotti,* 435 US 765 (1978) and *Consolidated Edison Company v. Public Service Commission,* 100 S.Ct. 2326 (1980). Calls aren't a nuisance either see *Sefka v. Thal* 662 S.W.2d 502 (mo. banc 1983).

(50) Cooling-off period for door-to-door sales, 16 C.F.R. 233.

(51) See note 29. Also see *Brown v. Martinelli,* 419 N.E.2d 1081 (1981), where the Ohio Supreme Court ruled that telephone solicitation sales must have written contracts and a three-day cooling-off period for all sales over $25 initiated by the seller. If you wish to read a blistering attack on telephone marketing, see Nedelman, Alec G., "Smile and Dial: Regulating Telephone Sales," 32 *Federal Communications Law Journal* 371 (1980).

(52) Robert J. Posch, Jr., "Telephone Marketing—It Survived and Prospered!" *Direct Marketing,* September 1982, pp. 106–109. and "How The Laws of Privacy Impact Your Business" *Direct Marketing,* October, 1987, p. 74–102.

(53) *Maine Revised Statutes Annotated* Section 4681, Sub. 7, 32 MRSA section 4682-A et seq., Maine also requires "transient sellers" (includes telemarketers) to be licensed in the cities and town in which they do business. See Section 1 *Maine Revised Statutes Annotated* Section 2151, Sub. 35, Subchapter XI, Section 3231(4).

(54) *Ariz. Rev. Stat.* Chap. 80, amending Sec. 44-5004, 5992.

(55) *Ark. Stat.* Sec. 70-914 et seq. Arkansas is active in this field and you should get on their gem of a newsletter, "Consumer Alert" published by the Office of the Attorney General, Consumer Protection Division, Little Rock, Arkansas, 72201; or call (501) 371-2341 or their hotline 1-800-482-8982.

(56) *Ind. Code* Sec. 501 1C 24 4.5 2-501.

(57) *La. Rev. Stat.* Louisiana Consumer Credit Law, Tit. 9, Sec. 3516, para. 17.

(58) *Mich. Comp. Laws* Sec. 445.111.

(59) *N.D. Cent. Code* Secs. 51-18-01-51-18-07.

(60) *Or. Rev. Stat.* Sec. 83.710, 646.608.

(61) *Utah Code Ann.* Sec. 1, Section 13-11-4(1).

(62) *Virginia Code* Sec. 59-1-21-2.

(63) *Wyo. Stat.* Sec. 40194-251.

(64) There are local ordinances, for example:

a. Sheffield, Ala., Code Sec. 18-51.1 (1965).

b. Carlsbad, New Mexico, Ordinance 727 (1972).

c. Bedford, Ohio, Ordinance 4788-78, Sec. 719.01(b)(1)(c) (1978).

d. Bedford Heights, Ohio, Ordinance 76-45, Sec. 1 para. 733.02 (1976).

e. *Alabama Law Enforcement Officers, Inc. v. City of Anniston,* 131 S 897 (1961) [declaring that a municipality (Anniston, Alabama) may declare "unwanted" telephone calls a nuisance].

There are a few select FTC consent orders requiring cooling-off periods for specific firms including the following representative samples:

a. *United States v. Neighborhood Periodical Club, Inc.,* Civ. C-2246 (S.D. Ohio 1980) (for various reasons, the defendant was, among other things, fined $150,000).

b. *In re Commercial Lighting Prods., Inc.,* 95 FTC 750 (1980).

c. *In re Perfect Film & Chem Corp., Perfect Subscription Co. and Keystone Readers' Serv. Inc.,* 78 FTC 990 (1980).

Finally, at least one state has voluntary guidelines on point: For a booklet detailing same, contact the Virginia Telephone Solicitation Ethics Council, P.O. Box 10011, Richmond, Virginia, 23240. See also Va. Code Sec. 40.1-112 (regulating the solicitation of book and magazine contracts).

(65) *Brown v. Martinelli,* 419 N.E.2d 1081, 1082 (Ohio 1981).

(66) Id., p. 1083.

(67) Id., p. 1084. See *Celebreeze v. Hughes,* 18 Ohio St. 3d 71; 479 N.E.2d 886 (1985) (consumer statutes will be interpreted broadly).

(68) a. Alaska Stat., secs. 45.50.472(a), (b), and (c) (banning a "telephone call made for the purpose of advertising through the use of a recorded advertisement").

b. Arizona Revised Statutes, Title 13, Chapter 29, Section 13-2918 (1986) (prohibits automated system that selects and dials telephone numbers and plays a recorded message to solicit for the purchase of goods and services).

c. Arkansas Act 947 of 1981 prohibited the use of automatic dialing systems with recorded messages to make telephone solicitation calls except when initiated by the receiver.

d. Cal. Pub. Util. Code, Ch. 10, Arts. 2871-2875 (certain qualifications placed on "automatic dialing-announcing devices"). Cal. Chapt. 1 Part 3 of Div. 7 of the *Business and Professions Code,* Sec. 17511 Art. 1.4 (requires a "telephone seller" to register with the Department of Justice at least 10 days before doing business).

e. Colo. Rev. Stat. Title 18, Art. 9, pt. 3 (generally bans "cold calls" employing the use of automated dialing systems with prerecorded messages soliciting a purchase of goods or services.).

f. Fl. Stat. Ann. Sec. 365.165 (bans the "use of an automated system for the selection or dialing of telephone numbers and the playing of a recorded message when a connection is completed to the called number").

g. Md. Ann. Code Art. 78, Sec. 55c, (banning the use of automated dialing).

h. Mich. Comp. Laws Ann. Art. 445.111(a) (bans cold calls using recorded messages).

i. Neb. Rev. Stat. Sec. 87-302 (requires a permit to make these calls).

j. N.C. Gen Stat. Sec. 75-30, Ch. 75, Sec. 1, Art. 1 (regulates but does not ban commercial calls).

k. Vernon's Texas Civ. Stat., Art. 1446(c), Sec. 87B(b)(2) (regulates hours and days of the calls and automatic dialing) and PUC Rules 052.02.05.051(h).

l. Virginia Code Art. 6, Sec. 18-2-425.1 (as of 1986 *bans all* cold calls and requires any permissible recorded call to terminate as soon as the receiver hangs up).

m. Washington Revised Codes, Chapter 80.36.1-2 (bans automatic dialing devices and requires other callers to identify company for which the call is being made).

n. Regulation of Trade, Wis. Stat. Ann. Sec. 134.72 (requiring prior consent for prerecorded messages).
For a representative article on what is prompting this legislation, see Tharpe, G., *Helpline* ((404) 688-4147) "Computer Phone Calls Invade Man's Privacy," *The Atlantic Constitution,* May 5, 1986, p. 8-B. This was followed two days later by an editorial ("Why Wait for 'Daddy' to Limit Calls?") in the same paper, May 7, 1986, p. 18-A, demanding the Public Service Commission and Assembly to act. This is the conservative "pro-business" Sunbelt.

(69) For example, as to the "top two" see California (effective 1/1/87) *Business and Professions Code* Sections 17538 and 17538.3 or New York State *General Business Law* 396-m (effective 1/85).

(70) *National Association of Broadcasters v. FCC,* 740 F2d 1190, 1195 (1984). See also Cooney, John, "Lowering Skies for the Satellite Business," *Fortune,* December 13, 1982, pp. 148-161. Because DBS satellites aren't much more powerful overall than conventional ones, but each signal is, the power is allocated over fewer channels per satellite.

(71) For a related article, see Guillo, Jean B., "Detouring Disconnects," *CableVision,* September 27, 1982, p. 20.

(72) "Privacy Protection Law In the United States" ($12) from the National Technical Information Service, 5285 Port Royal Road, Springfield, Va. 22161.

(73) *Fortnightly Corp. v. United Artists Television, Inc.,* 392 US 390 (1968).

(74) *Teleprompter Corp. v. Columbia Broadcasting System, Inc.,* 415 US 394 (1974).

(75) 17 U.S.C. 111(c) and 111(d)(2)(b).

(76) 17 U.S.C. 111(d)(4) and (5).

(77) *WLVA, Inc., Lynchburg, Virginia v. FTC,* 459 F.2d 1286, 1297 (1972).

(78) Id., 1298.

(79) See also Department of Justice press release issued October 15, 1984.

(80) Under the Department's business review procedure, an organization may submit a proposed action to the Antitrust Division and receive a statement as to whether the Division would challenge that action under the antitrust laws.

(81) *United States Satellite Broadcasting, Inc. v. FCC,* 740 F.2d 1177 (1984) and *National Association of Broadcasters v. FCC,* 740 F.2d 1190, 1195 (1984).

(82) 47 U.S.C. 153(o).

(83) *National Association of Broadcasters v. FCC,* 740 F.2d 1190, 1201 (1984).

(84) For an excellent review of the motives of the "environmentalists" see William Tucker, *Progress and Privilege,* Anchor Press/Doubleday, 1982.

(85) *Home Box Office, Inc. v. FCC,* 567 F.2d 9 (1977); cert. den. 434 US 829 (1977).

(86) U.S.C. Section III (1976).

(87) Moritz, Michael and Barrett Seaman, *Going for Broke,* Doubleday and Company, Inc., 1981.

(88) Ruff, Howard, *How to Prosper During the Coming Bad Years,* Time Books (1979). Certain pages of interest are 91-2 and 115.

(89) 380 US 374 (1964).

(90) FTC 16 C.F.R. Part 255.

(91) 47 USC 307 (1976).

(92) *FCC v. Midwest Video Corp.,* 440 US 689 (1979).

(93) 47 C.F.R. 76.12 (1980).

(94) 47 C.F.R. 76.221 (1980).

(95) Hoke, Henry R Jr., "Editorial," *Direct Marketing,* 9/82.

(96) Wisconsin Laws of 1981, Chapter 271.

(97) The Illinois Communications Consumer Privacy Act, Public Act 82-526 (former House Bill 893).

(98) Section 4.202(w)(1).

(99) *Red Lion Broadcasting Co., Inc. v. FCC,* 395 US 367 (1969).

(100) *FCC v. League of Women Voters of California,* 104 S.Ct. 3106 (1984).

(101) 45 Ohio App. 2d 69 (1975), 341 NE 2d 337, 40 Ohio Misc. 51 (1974), 321 N.E.2d 791, 795.

(102) *Lamont v. Commissioner of Motor Vehicles,* 269 F.Supp. 880 (D.C. S.D.N.Y. 1967), aff, 2 Cn. 386 F.2d 449 (1968).

(103) Alaska, Arizona, Montana, Oklahoma and South Carolina.

(104) See note 101 above.

(105) DeHart and Darr Associates, Inc., 1360 Beverly Rd., Suite 201, McLean, Va. 22101; (703)448-1000.

(106) "Shipping & Handling Gravy," *Direct Marketing,* July 1985., pp. 4-6.

(107) 14 FTC 232, 244 (1930).

(108) 15 FTC 398, 401 (1931).

(109) 22 FTC 668, 673 (1936).

(110) 49 FTC 1647, 1651 (1953).

(111) Docket 5 No. C-3030 (1979).

(112) 16 C.F.R. 425 ("Use of Negative Option Plans by Sellers in Commerce"). The FTC Rule is the model for the trade, but the state laws must be consulted. Kentucky and many other states have adopted the FTC Rule, while Hawaii at present is the only state to effectively *ban* the use of negative option plans).

(113) See note 105 above.

(114) Verlon Industries, Inc., was fined $25,000 (concerning lack of disclosures by its Camera Arts Book Club) and had to comply with various notification requirements. Book-of-the-Month Club, Inc., (78 Civ. 4093) in its consent judgment was fined $85,000, and it incurred mailing costs and a potential loss of membership by agreeing to notify members who joined in response to the challenged ads that it would cancel the minimum purchase obligations.

Conservative Book Club went through a similar ordeal. Its violations included (1) no notice of the 10-day right to cancel, (2) no indication of the advance announcement or how often it was sent, and (3) no indication that there would be an additional charge for shipping and handling.

(115) *Miller Brothers Co. v. Maryland,* 347 US 340, 344-45 (1954).

(116) Consider *Robbins v. Shelby County Taxing District,* 120 US 489, 497 (1887)—"Interstate commerce cannot be taxed at all. . ." to today's narrow interpretation of what interstate activity can escape. See also Posch, Robert J. Jr., "Is The Collection of the Use Tax An Historical Inevitability?" *Direct Marketing,* August 1987, p. 138—141.

(117) In 1930 two states levied sales taxes; in 1933 15 states levied sales taxes; in 1985 44 states levied sales taxes.

(118) See note 113 above.

(119) U.S. Constitution Article 1, 8, Clause 3.

(120) *Henneford v. Sclas Mason Co.,* 300 US 577 (1937). "When the account is made up, the stranger from afar is subject to no greater burdens as a consequence of ownership than the dweller within the gates."

(121) 312 US 359 (1941). See also *Nelson v. Montgomery Ward and Co.,* 312 US 377 (1941) and the earlier *Wisconsin v. J. C. Penney Co.,* 311 US 435 (1940).

(122) *General Trading Co. v. State Tax Commission,* 322 US 335 (1944).

(123) 347 US 340 (1954).

(124) See note 113.

(125) 347 US 340, 347 (1954).

(126) *Scripto, Inc. v. Carson,* 362 US 207 (1960).

(127) 386 US 753 (1967).

(128) Id., p. 756.

(129) Id., p. 759-760.

(130) Id.

(131) *State v. MacFadden-Bartell Corp.,* 194 S2d 543 (1967).

(132) Id., p. 545.

(133) Id., p. 546.

(134) 430 US 551 (1977).

(135) If interested, one should contact Robert J. Levering, Director of Government Affairs/Legislative Counsel at the DMA D.C. Office or call (202)347-1222 and ask for his studies/arguments/updates on the State Taxation of Interstate Mail Order Sales. You might also ask who you can contact immediately as to the federal matter and (if applicable) state matters.

(136) Posch, Robert J. Jr., "The U.S. Postal Service: Dinosaur or Dynamic Carrier?", *Postal Bulletin,* 1982, pp. 18-20.

(137) Toffler, Alvin, *The Third Wave.* New York: William Morrow and Co., Inc. 1980, p. 177, see also p. 161.

(138) Act of 10/18/1782, 23 J.C.C. 670, 672-73. Black's Law Dictionary defines "Post Roads" as "The roads or highways, *by land or sea,* designated by law as the avenues over which the mails shall be transported. . . a 'post route' on the other hand, is the appointed course or prescribed line of transportation of the mail. . .." (Emphasis added.)

(139) Act of 3/3/1845, Ch. 4359, Stat. 732.

(140) E.G., *U.S.A. v. Black and Alternate Systems, Inc.,* 569 F2d 1111 (CA 10), 1978.

(141) Hoke, Henry, "Editorial," *Direct Marketing,* 2/23/78, p. 134.

(142) *United States Postal Service v. Council of Greenburgh Civic Associations* et al, 453 U.S. 114 (1981).

(143) Id., p. 14.

(144) *Pereira v. United States,* 347 US 1, 8 (1954).

(145) *Ex Parte Jackson,* 96 US 727 (1877).

(146) 96 US at 732 (emphasis added).

(147) Id.

(148) *Lamont v. Postmaster General,* 381 US 301 (1965).

(149) *Magnolia Lab and Magnolia Laboratory,* P. S. Docket No. 10/123, G.C.-40-81-F (2/11/82).

(150) Id.

(151) 9 to 5, 614 Superior Ave., N.W., Room 852, Cleveland, Ohio 44113, (216) 566-9308. See also Posch, Robert J. Jr., "The Debate Won't Go Away," *Direct Marketing,* September, 1987 p. 104—105.

CHAPTER 10

PRIMER IN FRANCHISING LEGAL COMPLIANCE

This chapter incorporates all areas discussed elsewhere in this book. As such, it is a good "review course." Topics of particular importance include advertising, antitrust, intellectual property and licensing, UCC, contracts, covenants not to compete, and product liability.

Franchising is a contractual agreement to sell products built around a strong, visible trademark. The franchise relationship is a form of vertical distribution. It is a revenue stream rather than an aggregation of physical assets. Like direct marketing, franchising is often thought to be a form of generic business or industry. As discussed in our sojourn through direct marketing, it can be database marketing in any business. As one court noted:

> The franchise, therefore, is the agreement between the parties, and not the business operated by the franchisee. The franchise might exist quite independently of the franchisee's business, as for example where the franchise agreement is concluded before any business operations commence. It follows, therefore, that cessation of the franchisee's business operations does not necessarily constitute termination of the franchise.[1]

Franchising thus involves some risks to the franchisor: it must be careful to avoid dilution of its trademark or loss of goodwill. However, if franchising is managed effectively, the benefits outweigh the risks. For example, as we shall see, the franchisor will be able to effectuate vertical distribution control and reduce the costs of expansion because the franchisee provides the capital through up-front license fees and then ongoing percentages, advertising pool contributions and the like. In essence the relationship is analogous to that of a tenant and landlord. The former's rent pays the carrying charges while the landlord builds equity. In addition, a regional managerial flavor is possible by judicious recruitment. Finally, your franchisees will be motivated by the most

275

effective free-market tool ever designed—each franchisee has invested a sizable amount upfront. The incentive to succeed is self-evident.

Besides the thrill of substituting for and assuming most of the franchisor's vertical integration costs, what does a franchisee gain?

If the franchisee has done his or her legwork, then a relationship was created whereby an individual has signed on to receive expert managerial assistance from a central source in every aspect of management, advertising, and financing. Without such assistance, the prospective franchisee would not be able to enter or compete successfully in the long run. The franchisor reduces the risks of entrepreneurship.

After the start-up, there is ongoing assistance through marketing analysis, field supervisors, centralized purchasing, and national and local advertising. The franchisee gets access not only to the company's products or trademarks, but also to its business plans and corporate support services.

This business franchise format is the fastest-growing form today. Despite criticism to the contrary, franchising has been elected by the public as something they want. The true test of economic democracy is the allocation of the citizen's freely disposable wealth. Since World War II, franchising has been the fastest-growing method of distribution. People have joined and operated and wish to continue their franchises.

The areas of primary importance to anyone involved in this field are the up-front disclosures required by law and the termination provisions. Then there is the drafting of the contract. The acquisition process sets the tone for all that follows. These themes will be covered here in depth, along with a review of a number of ancillary areas such as products liability exposure, unconscionability, antitrust and fiduciaries (or lack of same).

We'll start with the disclosure requirements because these must be complied with and, it is hoped, digested by a prospective franchisee prior to sitting down to contract.

The Scope of Franchise Compliance Regulation

As stated at the outset, franchising is not an industry. As a result it is not amenable to broad-brush legislation. The legislative preference has been for disclosure or restrictions on termination and other substantive aspects of the agreement.

Disclosure is favored in an attempt to neutralize the disparity of bargaining power. With full disclosure, a franchisee can make a reasoned evaluation of the guaranteed and potential costs, overall risks and, of course, the benefits of franchising. Nineteen states[2] now have some form of full disclosure law, including the 15 states that use a registration and prospectus format administered by a state agency.

The motivation for passage of franchise laws is much the same as that behind the securities laws.[3] They have become fairly uniform in part by the universal adoption of the Uniform Franchise Offering Circular (UFOC) rules and guidelines, recommended by the North American Securities Administrators Association. While the multistate form can be easier than a state-by-state effort, certain states require modifications and the instructions on putting together a UFOC are over 200 pages long. Nevertheless, they have achieved a measure of uniformity in the application and processing of state disclosure regulations.

The protection afforded is often even broader. In effect, the franchisee is viewed as an investor entitled to certain information and safeguards. Violation of these statutes is usually considered criminal and gives rise to civil liability to injured franchisees. On December 21, 1978, after almost eight years of study, the FTC promulgated its Rule,[4] with a Statement of Basis and Purpose.[5] The Rule became effective on October 21, 1979, and has remained in full force and effect ever since.

The Rule will be reviewed in detail because of its national impact and because its definitions of the relationships covered are similar to many of the state franchise and business opportunity laws. One non-requirement is that there is no requirement to register the franchise.

The FTC Rule

The Rule was designed to centralize in one federal agency effective and complete franchise regulation. Its goal of "completeness" as a federal pre-sale disclosure standard was diluted by its failure to provide for private enforcement and lack of preemptiveness. This enforcement is subject to the political winds blowing through the FTC as well as a variety of competing priorities.

What Is a Franchise?

The first requirement in reviewing any rule is to see whether it applies to you and your prospective relationship. The FTC has defined the term broadly to mean any *continuing commercial relationship* whereby:

. . .a person (hereinafter "franchisee") offers, sells, or distributes to any person other than a "franchisor" (as hereinafter defined), goods, commodities, or services which are:

(1) Identified by a trademark, service mark, trade name, advertising or other commercial symbol designating another person (hereinafter "franchisor"), or

(2) Indirectly or directly required or advised to meet the quality standards prescribed by another person (hereinafter "franchisor") where the franchi-

see operates under a name using the trademark, service mark, trade name, advertising or other commercial symbol designating the franchisor; and

(B)(1) The franchisor exerts or has authority to exert a significant degree of control over the franchisee's method of operation, including but not limited to, the franchisee's business organization, promotional activities, management, marketing plan or business affairs; or

(2) The franchisor gives significant assistance to the franchisee in the latter's method of operation, including, but not limited to, the franchisee's business organization, management, marketing plan, promotional activities, or business affairs; *Provided, however,* that assistance in the franchisee's promotional activities shall not, in the absence of assistance in other areas of the franchisee's method of operation, constitute significant assistance; or

(ii)(A) A person (hereinafter "franchisee") offers, sells, or distributes to any person other than a "franchisor" (as hereinafter defined), goods, commodities, or services which are:

(1) Supplied by another person (hereinafter "franchisor"), or

(2) Supplied by a third person (e.g., a supplier) with whom the franchisee is directly or indirectly required to do business by another person (hereinafter "franchisor"); or

(3) Supplied by a third person (e.g., a supplier) with whom the franchisee is directly or indirectly required to do business by another person (hereinafter "franchisor") where such third person is affiliated with the franchisor; and

(B) The franchisor:

(1) Secures for the franchisee retail outlets or accounts for said goods, commodities, or services; or

(2) Secures for the franchisee locations or sites for vending machines, rack displays, or any other product sales display used by the franchisee in the offering, sale, or distribution of said goods, commodities, or services; or

(3) Provides to the franchisee the services of a person able to secure the retail outlets, accounts, sites or locations referred to in paragraphs (a)(1)(ii)(B)(1) and (2) of this section; and

The franchisee is required as a condition of obtaining or commencing the franchise operation to make a payment or a commitment to pay to the franchisor, or to a person affiliated with the franchisor.[6]

Two types of franchises are included—package and product franchises—plus business opportunity ventures.

A *package franchise* permits the franchisee to do business under a prepackaged business format. The franchisor sets the rules of operation in strict boilerplate and protects its trademark with a strict quality control agreement (see discussion below of both). This is service-oriented.

In a *product franchise* the franchisee distributes a good produced by or under the control of the franchisor. In this arrangement is found the twin pillars of business management controls and a strong identification with the franchisor's trademark.

Finally, there is the hybrid "conversion franchising." This probably was first popularized by Century 21 Real Estate Corp. and followed by other services. The idea is to convince independent businesses to become franchisees. Recently some manufacturers have joined the trend to build their distribution channels around existing channels. The franchisor has a more highly committed sales force without giving up control, and the franchisees have the traditional security of the advertising pool, trademark, staff services, and other franchise benefits.

Each franchise also has the element of an up-front franchise fee. Such fee can include rent, advertising pool contributions, exclusive territorial fees, or other companion contracts. The payment to the franchisor or its affiliate must be $500 or more. Payments made to the franchisor for reasonable amounts of inventory purchased at bona fide wholesale prices for resale are not included in the fee. A "reasonable amount" is an amount that a businessperson would normally spend to start an inventory or to maintain a going inventory.

Business opportunity ventures are covered by the Rule if

- the buyer of the opportunity sells goods or services supplied by the seller or its affiliates[7] or suppliers with whom the buyer is *required* to do business;
- the seller secures or assists in securing outlets or accounts for the goods or services or sites of vending machines or displays or provides the services of a person to do either; and
- the buyer is required to pay the seller at least $500 prior to the seventh month after the buyer begins operations.

Then there are important exceptions from the definition of franchise contained in the Rule (again, many state laws are similar). Many would-be franchisors might consider attempting to structure a viable relationship which can fall between the cracks. Then they can avoid the disclosure burdens we'll review shortly.

The exceptions and exclusions are as follows:

- "fractional franchises"—where *less* than 20% of a franchisee's dollar volume comes from the franchisor's product;[8]
- leased departments;[9]
- when there is *no* writing which evidences any *material* term or aspect of the relationship or arrangement (oral agreements)—this is strictly construed as checks, letters, etc.—may be construed to be a written agreement.[10] Further the Rule provides that ". . .any relationship which is represented either orally or in writing to be a franchise (as defined in the paragraphs (a)(1) and (2) of this section) is subject to the requirements of this part";[11]

- employment relationships;[12]
- minimal investments such as franchises where the total payments required to be made by the franchise within 6 months after commencing the operation of the franchise is less than $500;[13]
- membership in bona fide cooperative associations;[14] and
- "single trademark licensing," an arrangement in which only a single licensee is granted the exclusive right to use the trademark (such exclusive right must be clearly spelled out in unambiguous language in your agreement).

However, it should be noted that merely because a licensor is not excluded, this does not necessarily mean he or she is included as a franchisor. The test will be how much control is enjoyed by the licensor.

Further, there are three other forms of licenses which remain excluded despite a "control" factor:

- One-on-one trademark license, which is an arrangement where the owner licenses the trademark to a single licensee who manufacturers the trademarked goods to the licensor's specifications.
- Collateral product licensing, which covers use of a trademark for clearly "collateral" or non-related goods.
- Infringement settlement arrangements, where the infringer avoided an affidavit of destination. The alleged infringer agrees to continue his infringement and is "licensed" for a limited period of time to dispose of the alleged infringing stock on hand.

The Disclosure Statement

If you have a franchise or the arrangement is initially represented as a franchise (as the term is defined) you have to make a variety of detailed, up-front disclosures. The heart of the Rule is the disclosure statement, which must be given to a "prospective franchisee" at the *earlier* of the "time for making of disclosures" or the first "personal meeting."[15] In any event, it must be given prior to a franchisee's committing any consideration or legally committing him/herself to a purchase. The term "personal meeting" appears to exclude communications by mail or telephone.[16]

The FTC affords franchisors the option of using either the 20-item format of disclosure prescribed in the Rule ("FTC Format") or the 23-item format commonly known as the Uniform Franchise Offering Circular ("UFOC"). Either way the FTC requires you have the following mandated disclosure in hand ten days prior to the execution of the franchise agreement. Its required disclosures fall generally into three groups:

- information relating to the franchisor,
- obligations upon the franchisee, and
- important terms contained within the franchise agreement.

Information Related to the Franchisor

It is important to examine the background of the people at the franchise organization because they also become your partners. Before you proceed you have the right to know

- the official name, address and principal place of business of the franchisor, and of the parent firm or holding company of the franchisor, if any;
- the name under which the franchisor is doing or intends to do business; and
- the trademarks, trade names, service marks, advertising or other commercial symbols which identify the goods, commodities, or services to be offered, sold, or distributed by the prospective franchisee, or under which the prospective franchisee will be operating.[17]

Beyond the mundane, the disclosures require a thorough relation of the franchisor's business experience as well as criminal and bankruptcy history. You might look at other clues - are all the key players from the same family, a husband/wife or other relationship which might warrant a further investigation as to the depth of the capitalizations or bona fide talent you'll be offered in the short and long term?

Relevant business disclosures include:

. . .The business experience during the past 5 years, stated individually, of each of the franchisor's current directors and executive officers. . . With regard to each person listed, those person's principal occupations and employers must be included.

. . .The business experience of the franchisor and the franchisor's parent firm (if any), including the length of time each: (i) Has conducted a business of the type to be operated by the franchisee; (ii) has offered or sold a franchise for such business; (iii) has conducted a business or offered or sold a franchise for a business (A) operating under a name using any mark set forth under paragraph (a)(1)(iii) of this section, or (B) involving the sale, offering, or distribution of goods, commodities, or services which are identified by any mark set forth under paragraph (a)(1)(iii) of this section; and (iv) has offered for sale or sold franchises in other lines of business, together with a description of such other lines of business.[18]

Then you have a right to a statement as to the above-named individuals:

- any felony conviction or nolo contendere pleadings (felony charges) during the last year if relevant, e.g., crimes of fraud (obvious one such as violation of a franchise law), embezzlement, restraint of trade and related crimes;[19]
- civil results over the past 7-year period for similar/related offenses such as fraud;[20]
- any pending matters concerning these areas.

The statement is a sophisticated rap sheet on the individuals, which must include the identity and location of the court or agency; the date of conviction, judgment, or decision; the penalty imposed; the damages assessed; the terms of settlement or the terms of the order; and the date, nature, and issuer of each such order or ruling. A franchisor may include a summary opinion of counsel as to any pending litigation, but only if counsel's consent to the use of such opinion is included in the disclosure statement.[21]

Then there is the bankruptcy history of the individuals identified as officers, directors, and others. Such information must include, over the prior seven-year period, the individuals who have:

- Filed in bankruptcy;
- Been adjudged bankrupt;
- Been reorganized due to insolvency; or
- Been a principal, director, executive officer, or partner of any other person that has so filed or was so adjudged or reorganized, during or within 1 year after the period that such person held such position in such other person. If so, the name and location of the person having so filed, or having been so adjudged or reorganized, the date thereof, and any other material facts relating thereto, shall be set forth.[22]

Finally, the franchisor must provide a factual description of the franchise being offered.[23]

Obligations of the Franchisee

The material burdens which must be set forth in detail include

- the total funds needed for franchisee fees, prepaid rent, equipment, etc.;[24]
- the recurring funds needed such as training, advertising pool and related on-going charges;[25]
- related firms, landlords, et al. which the franchisee will be expected to deal with.[26]

Material Terms Contained in the Agreement

These will include (a) financing;[27] (b) limitations of goods/services the franchisee may offer;[28] (c) territorial or customer restrictions or protections;[29] (d) personal, hands-on management requirements by the franchisee;[30] and (e) term renewals, extensions, terminations, assignment rights, and other contractual boilerplate.[31]

Then there are disclosures that invite or compel a prospective franchisee to act in his or her self interest. The franchisor must provide a statement disclosing, with respect to the franchisor and as to the particular named business being offered:

- The total number of franchises operating at the end of the preceding fiscal year;
- The total number of company-owned outlets operating at the end of the preceding fiscal year;

- The names, addresses, and telephone numbers of (a) the 10 franchised outlets of the named franchise business nearest the prospective franchisee's intended location; or (b) all franchisees of the franchisor, or (c) all franchisees of the franchisor in the state in which the prospective franchisee lives or where the proposed franchise is to be located, *provided however,* that there are more than 10 such franchisees. . .

- The number of franchises voluntarily terminated or not renewed by franchisees within, or at the conclusion of, the term of the franchise agreement, during the preceding fiscal year;

- The number of franchises reacquired by purchase by the franchisor during the term of the franchise agreement, and upon the conclusion of the term of the franchise agreement, during the preceding fiscal year;

- The number of franchises otherwise reacquired by the franchisor during the term of the franchisor during the term of the franchise agreement, and upon the conclusion of the term of the franchise agreement, during the preceding fiscal year;

- The number of franchises for which the franchisor refused renewal of the franchise agreement or other agreements relating to the franchise during the preceding fiscal year; and

- The number of franchises that were canceled or terminated by the franchisor during the term of the franchise agreement, and upon conclusion of the term.[32]

This gives you a window on your future. You should seize the opportunity and talk to current owners. If anything develops that you'd like to rely on, send a follow-up letter confirming your conversation—by certified mail, of course. Remember, nothing left orally exists in law as to your future reliance. At a minimum, you should ask about site selection assistance/intervals,[33] earnings claims in *their* experience/area, follow-up support by franchisor,[34] and the like.

The disclosure statement also covers public figure endorsements [35] and the balance sheets for the past three years.[36] It goes without saying you should obtain professional assistance (tax deductible) as to the law, accuracy and reliability of the accounting methods/data, and of what value the past data as to future market, product, and service performance is.

All of the above disclosure information:

. . .shall be contained in a single disclosure statement or prospectus, which shall not contain any materials or information other than that required by this part or by State law not preempted by this part. This does not preclude franchisors or franchise brokers from giving other nondeceptive information orally, visually, or in separate literature so long as such information is not contradictory to the information in the disclosure's statement required by paragraph (a) of this section. This disclosure statement shall carry a cover sheet distinctively and conspicuously showing the name of the franchisor, the date of issuance of the disclosure statement, and the following notice imprinted thereon in upper and lower case bold-face type of not less than 12 point size:

Information for Prospective Franchisees
Required by Federal Trade Commission

To protect you, we've required your franchisor to give you this information. *We haven't checked it, and don't know if it's correct.* It should help you make up your mind. Study it carefully. While it includes some information about your contract, don't rely on it alone to understand your contract. Read all of your contract carefully. Buying a franchise is a complicated investment. Take your time to decide. If possible, show your contract and this information to an advisor, like a lawyer or an accountant. If you find anything important that's been left out, you should let us know about it. It may be against the law.

There may also be laws on franchising in your state. Ask your state agencies about them.

FEDERAL TRADE COMMISSION

Washington, D.C.[37]

. . .All information contained in the disclosure statement shall be current as of the close of the franchisor's most recent fiscal year. After the close of each fiscal year, the franchisor shall be given a period not exceeding 90 days to prepare a revised disclosure statement and, following such 90 days, may distribute only the revised prospectus and no other. The franchisor shall, within a reasonable time after the close of each quarter of the fiscal year, prepare revisions to be attached to the disclosure statement to reflect any material change in the franchisor or relating to the franchise business of the franchisor, about which the franchisor or franchise broker, or any agent, representative, or employee thereof, knows or should know.[38]

The above "cover page" language is necessary if you are utilizing the UFOC, too. If a UFOC is utilized to comply with the Rule, its use in a state in which the franchisor has a currently effective franchise registration must still include the addition required by the FTC as set forth above as well as the date of the issuance of the prospectus.

The above gives you more than a flavor of the Rule. The franchisee clearly benefits, though there is an accuracy that defeats itself by an overemphasis on detail. Whether there really is a cost benefit to individual franchisees may be debatable. The information assembling exercise by the franchisor undoubtedly contributes to the confidence the public has in the franchise field.

As noted earlier, this Rule's enforcement has to date been fairly toothless. Private parties can't utilize it and the FTC often lacks the ideological motivation to do so. Further, their interpretations are further diluted by the weaker standard of what constitutes misrepresentation. At present, the misrepresentation must be likely to deceive a *reasonable* consumer acting reasonably under the circumstances and where it is likely to cause injury to a reasonably relying consumer.[39] The FTC's arsenal is strong with potential remedies ranging from damages and refunds to the equitable remedies of recision, injunction and accounting.

As stated earlier, the FTC isn't the final or sole rule on point. A number of federal and state laws are on the books. Before moving on to contracts, we'll take a look at a few of the targeted laws on point as to other issues besides disclosure—especially those whose language or enforcement history makes them of interest.

Automobile Dealer's Franchise Act[40]

In 1956 Congress enacted legislation which imposed liability on automobile manufacturers if they exercised coercion against a dealer to such dealer's detriment. Again, the issue is bargaining power. When the time for renewal comes around, the dealer, particularly one who has been operating the dealership for several years and has built up its business and clientele cannot afford to risk a confrontation. He or she just signs on the dotted line.[41]

The term "franchise" is defined to include "the written agreement or contract between any automobile manufacturer engaged in commerce and any automobile dealer which purports to fix the legal rights and liabilities of the parties to such agreement or contract."[42]

The basic theme is to prevent arbitrary and capricious nonrenewal by the manufacturer. The duty of good faith[43] is required during the entire ongoing relationship, though it does not regulate the initial negotiations of the franchise agreement itself.

Nonrenewal requires a legitimate business purpose—a broad standard. The failure to meet sales goals is a valid reason to deny renewal[44] as are failures to uphold the quality standards and goodwill of the manufacturer's mark.[45]

Petroleum Marketing Practices Act[46]

A more recent federal law (1979) provides 90 days' notice prior to termination[47] (except in certain extreme circumstances such as the franchisee's fraud, mental incapacity, condemnation, failure to uphold the reasonable quality safeguards of the mark and conviction of a felony).

"Good faith" is left undefined. As with most laws on point, it resulted from a perception by Congress that the individual dealer's disparity in bargaining power was too great to be socially desirable.

State Legislation

Over half the states have acted in the area of franchisee termination protections[48] as well as disclosure laws and laws targeted at certain specific industries including farm equipment, alcoholic beverages, petro-leum products, and automobiles (the latter two are similar to the federal laws discussed above).

Some states such as Mississippi require only a minimum notice period for termination, while others impose restrictions varying in severity. Most require a defined "good cause" standard. Unlike the federal laws noted above, the failure to meet sales quotas or other economic criteria alone[49] without additional reasons may not constitute good cause. However, failure to meet sales quotas clearly set forth and specifically quantifiable in a contractual agreement (see discussion below) will usually constitute good cause for termination.

Bankruptcy or insolvency alone may not pass muster under the new federal bankruptcy law. You'll need to fall back on precise default language in your agreement. Such agreement may set forth definable standards such as the franchisee's inability to pay bills or maintain specified servicing levels therefore diluting the franchisor's goodwill and overall trademark value to itself and other franchisees. It will bolster the franchisor's position if it can demonstrate that it is acting to protect the legitimate expectations of its franchisees in maintaining a strong trademark.

Finally, the franchisor must be sure its agreement adequately addresses the potential problem of a franchisee's leaving the territory of its own initiative. This is not a "runaway franchisee" situation (see below) but an exit from an unprofitable territory or departure for other legitimate reasons. Unless adequately protected by contract, a franchisor may be in a weak position in the event of such franchisee departure.[50] Even when the termination proceeds smoothly, many of the states cited in the footnotes require the franchisor to repurchase its inventory.[51]

Other Theories Concerning Termination

The debate concerning termination continues with arguments concerning unconscionability and fiduciary duty. The doctrine on unconscionability requires some showing of an absence of meaningful choice on the part of one of the parties together with contract terms which are unreasonably favorable to the other party. A franchisee will generally not prevail here because the standard of review is at the time of contract formation (see Chapter 8, on Sales). As discussed in Chapter 26 (as to shrink wrap licenses and other issues of unique bargaining power), this doctrine needs to be updated. A franchisee should avoid any argument here under the UCC because, at the time of signing he or she wasn't a merchant dealing in goods of that kind. The UCC is addressed to bona fide arm's-length commercial transactions.[52] The franchise relationship does not even resemble such a situation. Once signed on, franchisees lose almost all leverage and are not free to change franchisors or the latter's trademark, products, etc. Franchisees are under contractual restraints as to activities, location, supply, and other matters. The franchisor knows that they are not free to leave its system. The "commercially reasonable" standard is inadequate for the unique system of franchising.

Trade custom and usage arguments may compound the problem. The franchisee should resort to common law tort remedies such as fraud or lack of good faith, i.e., "dishonesty in fact."[53]

As to the argument of fiduciary duty, historically the courts have rejected the concept of fiduciary obligations in franchise relationships.[54] The general position of the courts is that a "franchise relationship is inherently a business relationship, not a fiduciary relationship. While Holiday Inns had a duty to deal fairly with Picture Lake, it did not have the duty of a fiduciary with all of the obligations and responsibilities pertaining thereto."[55]

Both as to the fiduciary duty and the idea of unconscionability the courts appear to be in a suspension-of-belief mode. The imbalance of power is real here. The disclosure statements, UFOCs, etc. are legalese and incomprehensible to the average layperson. While most franchise relationships are mutually rewarding, the traditional remedies should be available to protect the obviously weaker party.

Our courts have long held to a broad standard of fiduciary relationships. Such relationship is not restricted to "such confined relations as trustee and beneficiary, partners, principal and agent, guardian and ward, managing directors and corporation, etc. It applies to all persons who occupy a position out of which the duty of good faith ought in equity and good conscience to arise."[56] As one court noted: "One commentator noted that an inherent aspect of franchise relationships was the economic disparity of the parties: 'Were it not for this disparity, why would the franchisee have sought out the assistance of such a franchisor'?"[57]

Obviously, the courts would consider the franchisor's handling of its franchisees' funds in the advertising pool or elsewhere to be under a fiduciary duty of care. It works both ways. The franchisor would want this relationship in situations where it offers confidential materials such as manuals, software, marketing information, processes, etc.[58]

This debate will continue. On one hand you have the compelling situation of a truly aggrieved franchisee who might be a "victim." On the other hand you not only have a contract and related remedies but the franchise system needs a fair degree of latitude in the termination decision. This latitude enables the franchisor to police the system for the general good—not only of itself, but of all other present (and future) franchisees. Often the threat or actual act of termination is the only serious card the franchisor can play in policing its various agreements.

Speaking of policing, we'll briefly review trademark licensing and a few other issues prior to reviewing the overall contractual provisions.

Trademark Licensing Issues

A fundamental concept in franchising is that the franchisee operates its business according to a marketing and operations plan substantially prescribed by the franchisor, and thereby participates in a uniform distribution system identified by the franchisor's trademark. The franchisor's trademark is valuable because it identifies for consumers the nature and quality of the goods sold or services rendered by all franchisees operating under that trademark. The trademark, the source of the "licensed know-how," is at the core of all franchising.

The Lanham Act[59] and its various state counterparts requires the franchisor to exercise quality control. The failure to exercise such control (i.e., "naked licensing") may result in the trademark's being abandoned. Such lack of control might also permit franchisees to individually deviate from the general standards, thereby injuring all other franchisees. A franchisor may also seek income from such licensing to offset the slow development of its revenue stream from the product or service being licensed.

There is a fine line between trademark licensing and package franchising. If the degree of control is "significant," then it becomes a franchise; otherwise, it remains a trademark license. It may turn on whether the licensor's mark is included in the franchisee's business name.[60]

You'll hire a specialist in either if it is of importance to your career. The Trademark Chapter and the Licensing Chapter are both useful reading for someone contemplating franchising.

Antitrust Exposure

A franchise is a vertical relationship. As such, any restrictions are judged by a rule of reason test. Suppression of intrabrand competition generally is lawful if interbrand competition acts as a check on the exploitation of the intrabrand market power.[61]

The leading source of litigation has been the *tying issue.* In many of these cases, the plaintiff franchisees sought class action status. The cases were often prompted by the franchisees' obligation to contribute to a national advertising fund administered by the franchisor. Generally, the plaintiffs have argued that a franchisor is selling two or more distinct products, which may include franchise, trademark, and lease—to name the big three. For the most part, plaintiffs are losing on tying.

The courts are holding that:

> . . .the modern franchisee pays not only for the right to use a trademark but for the right to become a part of a system whose business methods virtually guarantee his success. It is most unrealistic to view a franchise agreement as little more than a trademark license.

Given the realities of modern franchising, we think the proper inquiry is not whether the allegedly tied products are associated in the public mind with the franchisor's trademark, but whether they are integral components of the business method being franchised. Where the challenged aggregation is an essential ingredient of the franchised system's formula for success, there is but a single product and no tie-in exists as a matter of law.[62]

As to *vertical territorial restraints,* in general you must analyze your product market and your geographic market, and look at other overall indications of market power you (as the "imposer") might possess, e.g.:

- whether your product is readily interchangeable;
- whether a patent/copyright/trade secret and possibly a trademark provides built-in monopoly power in your marketplace;
- whether your product requires unique servicing;
- what the overall cross-elasticity of demand is; and
- whether the size of the franchise fee may be so large as to be evidence of your market power.

Finally, review with your counsel the advertising pool expenditures and their impact on both intrabrand and interbrand competition.

In terms of *Robinson-Patman,* your exposure is greatest as to the pooled advertising contributions and any spin-off aid from the franchisor which might be applied in a manner not to help small franchisees or not assist the common group at all. Any cooperative advertising program administered in an uneven manner so that competing franchisees are not treated on proportionally equal terms presents the possibility of antitrust exposure.

Then, as to the *Sherman Act,* you have to watch enforced resale price maintenance by the franchisor as well as a possible impact of favoritism towards franchisees who "go along" with "passive" suggestions of resale prices. Similarly, a franchisor can't enforce discounting, either.[63]

Finally, you must be alert to agreements among competing franchisees to advertise or not, restrain entry, assign markets, etc. And you must be alert to the expanding influence of state antitrust laws (and aggressive state attorneys general), both as to exposure and the dilution of a national marketplace due to inconsistent interpretations. You also have to be alert to private consumer actions[64] as well as those of your franchisees.

Personnel Issues

Is a franchisor vicariously liable for the actions (authorized or otherwise) of its franchisee? Apparent authority may arise out of the uniform appearance of franchisee- and franchisor-operated outlets and the absence of any notice to the public that the outlet is operated by anyone other than the company whose trademark is prominently displayed there. Actual authority is found when the franchisor has imposed sufficient restrictions on or reserved sufficient controls over the operation of the franchisee's business as to be deemed to control day-to-day operations.[65] Franchisors are carrying (where available) insurance for this and contractually compelling franchisees to do the same.

Another problem in recent years (particularly where the franchisor doesn't lease the franchisee's premises) is the drop-out or break-away franchisee. This break-away can be accomplished by failing to pay royalties, contribute to the advertising pool, violating a covenant not to compete, or otherwise, "leaving the system's" obligations while continuing to enjoy its benefits while remaining under a contract. Franchisors are countering with expanded rights of entry, retaining lease control, utilizing options to buy and devising more flexible covenants not to compete.

Another employee issue is that under the exception to the FTC's Rule (and many state laws) where the relationship is that of an employer/employee.[66] To determine this you will consider whether the franchisor set the hours of operation, number of employees, placement of advertising signs and equipment loans. In addition, it is relevant to the issue of the franchisor's control whether the franchisor hired the employees, provided the management training, established the sales quotas, or offered financial support.

If you can document this exception, then you can avoid a lot of disclosure burdens. If you can't, then you'll proceed to review whether the operation of the business was substantially associated with the alleged franchisor's trade name.

All of these issues may well turn on a thorough review of your contract. Let's take a look at what goes into the contractual negotiation, the boilerplate and the reasoning behind it.

What to Look for in a Standard Franchise Agreement

You have done the preliminaries. . .

You've searched the seller's title and the seller's trademarks.

You've reviewed the data the seller gave you pursuant to an UFOC or the FTC's Rule with your attorney and accountant as to the following:

- Is the system growing?
- What is the leverage?
- What is the turnover?
- How are they insured?
- What is the quality of top management (your prospective partners)?
- How steady is the current revenue stream?

While your professional people reviewed the disclosures you were contacting the references provided, the Better Business Bureau, and State

Consumer Affairs and performed a Dun & Bradstreet check or similar commercial credit analysis.

During the sales presentation you looked for signs of pressure tactics such as promised price increases in ten days; offer not available in another ten days; operations are "easy"; or little things like whether the representative you spoke with signed in his/her official capacity and not as an individual.

Hopefully you have reached the point of pre-drafting acceptance and are entering this agreement because you believe no greater benefit can be derived by expending elsewhere the resources you are now committing. You've now retained an attorney experienced in this field. If you are a franchisee, this is particularly important because you are the discretion-granting party. You get the franchisor's boilerplate. Within the boilerplate the franchisor has retained a variety of exclusive powers and at least equal power as to every other issue.

Your Disclosure Package and Contract[67]

You have in hand a valid disclosure information package which complies with the FTC Rule[68] and state law (in our example, New York State's[69]). The following may be a handy checklist for a first glance at your contract. First you'll find the FTC letter, followed by NYS Compliance Disclosures (including initial franchise fee, effective date of offering, address of Franchisor's agent for service of process, etc.). Following these are the Operating History and the Table of Contents, in which are listed the 20–23 required disclosure topics in order. At their completion you'll find at least two exhibits: (1) franchise agreement and (2) financial statement.

At this time the prospective franchisee may enter a preliminary agreement such as a letter of intent. The franchisee's going forward may be conditioned on obtaining financing as well as an investigation of the franchisor. The franchisor may make available certain records such as its royalty revenues on which it may be basing its price or the status of its dependency on outside lenders, but only with confidentiality agreements exchanged for separate consideration. Once satisfied as to the value of going forward, the prospective franchisee and its attorney are ready to negotiate an agreement.

Let's review the salient paragraphs of a hypothetical franchise agreement one by one. Such paragraph-by-paragraph review is the best form of "checklist" in this area. (Your franchisor will have a table of contents to facilitate your review.)

I. *Parties.*

Here will be the blank part for the date of the agreement and the next lucky franchisee (you?). The legal name and address of the franchisor's principal office will be typed in.

II. *Whereas Clauses.*

Here the franchisor will set forth a statement of principles and business policy, introduce its ownership of trademarks, copyrights, patents, logotypes, and other assets as well as a business system whose development was the result of much time, skill, and investment.

The investment in its intellectual property and business operations is ongoing. You'll want to include by reference and incorporate as an exhibit the description of the business and other material provided in the disclosure document.

Finally, if there isn't a specific section of defined terms, have your counsel set forth agreed-upon definitions up front so there is no second guessing later on.

III. *Grant of Franchise and License.*

Will it be exclusive or nonexclusive? For how many sites, and will your rights vary by site? Are the currently outstanding franchise agreements legal and not under challenge?

IV. *Territory.*

You'll receive a map or written description (or both) of what you should expect to be an exclusive territory of some relevant size to your *target* population. Such exclusion must apply to the franchisor as well as the other franchisees.

The franchisor will reserve the right at its sole discretion to grant other franchises outside your designated territory and will probably prohibit you from offering or selling your services or products outside your territory without prior written consent. If interested, you might negotiate a pass-along agreement so as to be able to pick off some sales or goodwill from boundary areas.

V. *Term.*

You'll negotiate an initial term to which the franchisor will attach conditions (see below).

VI. *Renewal.*

The renewal will address the following:

a. Form and procedure of renewal, i.e., automatic, conditional, how much prior notice, fees upon renewal (make sure you are not obligated to pay any new Initial Franchise fee and try to negotiate out any renewal fee).

b. Renewal terms. Try for same period, automatically, if you have complied faithfully with all the material terms of the agreement and again, make sure both parties are clear as to the precise notice of expiration and any other conditions precedent to the renewal.

VII. *Payments to Franchisor.*

Here you'll encounter a great variety of methods including, but not limited to:

a. The *Initial Franchise Fee* usually payable upon execution. This is usually not refundable in whole or in part. If you have reservations, make sure they're expressed in writing. Verbal understandings or "gentlemen's agreements" are worthless.

b. The *Continuing Royalty.* This will be a percentage of monthly/quarterly gross revenues. Gross revenues will be defined (generally) to include the amount of all monies received by the franchisee from, through, by, or on account of the operation by his/her franchised business, whether received in cash, in services, in kind or on credit (and if on credit, whether or not payment is received therefor). There shall be deducted from gross revenues for purposes of said computation (but only to the extent they have been included) the amount of all sales tax receipts or similar tax receipts which, by law, are chargeable to customers, if such taxes are separately stated when the customer is charged and paid to the appropriate taxing authority, and the amount of any documented refunds, credits, and allowances given to customers by the franchisee in good faith.

Often these royalties will be on a sliding scale (i.e., the percentage increases after you've had a decent interval to settle in). You've reviewed the financial statements already. If expenses run high, you should aim for a percentage of the *net* revenue you receive. The gross may put too intolerable a burden upon you vis-a-vis mandated expenses.

Try to avoid any such boost. Tell the franchisor you intend to be successful. As an incentive, include certain benchmarks at which the royalty eventually drops back to the initial rate. Both you and the franchisor will benefit from this incentive. Your franchisor can't get a royalty on nonsales.

c. *Advertising Fee.* This will also be a percentage of your gross. You want to know if suppliers and the franchisor are contributing. If not, why not? It goes without saying all the franchisees are contributing their pro rata share but you want this in writing, anyway.

Do you have any guarantees about a minimum regional support? Coupons in the paper are worth more sometimes than national TV.

d. *Reporting.* You'll receive a schedule of dates as well as model forms approved by the franchisor on which to report all gross revenues. The franchisor will want its royalties concurrent with the submission of the report. You'll wish to reserve the right to withhold any matters reasonably in dispute, by including a clause such as this: "Franchisee shall not be subject to any interest or penalty charge for failure to make the above royalty payment when such payment or part of same is subject to a reasonable dispute by franchisee. Franchisee shall communicate such dispute to franchisor within ten (10) days of its occurrence or the discovery of same, whichever is longer."

e. *Commencement Date.* Will usually begin the day you commence operations (make sure it isn't from the date of the agreement in I above).

f. *Training Fees.* You and one or two of your employees should get initial courses "free" (though you will cover your own lodging, food, travel, and incidental expenses). The courses are in the franchisor's interest to assist its quality control program.

VIII. *Option for Additional Locations.*

If you work out well (i.e., to the franchisor's subjective as well as objective satisfaction), the franchisor may, at its sole and exclusive direction, give you the option to purchase one or more additional franchises. Often there is a discount extended as an incentive to invest further.

You'll want the specified option agreement attached as an exhibit and expressly incorporated therein. This will prevent later "surprises."

IX. *Proprietary Marks, Manuals and Confidential Information.*

A. *Proprietary Marks*

Proprietary marks comprise the essence of what it's all about and so we'll go into this topic in depth. You want a piece of the goodwill created by these marks. You'll be presented with quality control boilerplate similar in theme if not wording to the following:

Franchisee agrees that it will use trademark, or trade name, _____ , (herein called "Franchisor's mark") only in connection with the conduct and operation of the Franchise under this Agreement. Franchisee expressly recognizes and acknowledges that the use of the Franchisor's marks shall not confer upon Franchisee any proprietary rights to Franchisor's mark. Upon expiration or upon termination of Franchisee's rights to use Franchisor's mark for any cause, the Franchisee shall immediately cease all use of Franchisor's mark and will not use any such Franchisor's mark thereafter. Franchisee agrees not to question, contest or challenge the ownership by Franchisor of Franchisor's mark, except the right to use the same pursuant to the terms and conditions of this Agreement, and will not seek to register the Franchisor's mark. Franchisee agrees that upon expiration or termination of rights to use Franchisor's mark pursuant to this Agreement for any cause or without cause, it will execute all necessary or appropriate documents to confirm Franchisor's said ownership or to transfer any rights it may have acquired from Franchisor.

Franchisee recognizes that Franchisor's mark possesses a special, unique and extraordinary character which makes it difficult to assess the monetary damage which Franchisor would sustain in the event of unauthorized use. Franchisee expressly recognizes and agrees that irreparable injury would be caused to Franchisor by such unauthorized use and agrees that preliminary or permanent injunctive relief would be appropriate in the event of breach of this Paragraph by Franchisee provided that such remedy shall not be exclusive of other legal remedies otherwise available.

Franchisee agrees that if it receives knowledge of any manufacture or sale by anyone else of the products or services offered under the Franchise as would be confusingly similar in the minds of the public and which bear or are promoted in association with any of Franchisor's mark, or any names, symbols, emblems, designs or colors which would be confusingly similar in the minds of the public, Franchisee will promptly notify Franchisor.

Franchisor shall have the sole right, at its sole expense, to take such action with respect thereto as it determines, in its sole discretion, is appropriate. Franchisee undertakes to reasonably cooperate and assist in such protest or legal action at Franchisor's expense. Franchisee shall not undertake such protest or legal action on its own without first securing Franchisor's written permission to do so. In the event Franchisor shall permit Franchisee to undertake such protest or legal action, it is clearly understood that such protest or legal action shall be at Franchisee's expense. For the purposes of the foregoing, expenses shall include reasonable attorneys' fees. All recovery in the form of legal damages or settlement shall belong to the party bearing the expense of such protest or legal action. It is expressly understood upon expiration or termination of Franchisee rights to use Franchisor's mark pursuant to this Agreement for any cause, that nothing in this Agreement shall be construed to bar Franchisor from protecting its right to the exclusive use of its trademarks, service marks or trade names against infringement thereof by any party or parties, including Franchisee.

STANDARDS

Franchisor shall provide Franchisee with copies of its written procedures/policies establishing minimum standards of quality and/or performance for this Franchise. Franchisor shall immediately advise Franchisee of any changes in said standards. Franchisor agrees to observe no less than said minimum standards of quality and/or performance. Franchisor agrees that Franchisee has the right to visit Franchisor's offices, work sites and/or other places of business at any reasonable time and upon ten (10) days prior notice for the purpose of verifying Franchisor's compliance with said standards of quality and/or performance.

Related trademark issues will include non-ownership of trademarks and warranty/indemnification clauses. As to *Non-Ownership of Trademarks,* the Franchisor will clearly state that:

Nothing herein shall give Franchisee any right, title or interest in or to any of the Proprietary Marks except as a mere privilege and non-exclusive license during the term hereof to display and use the same according to the limitations set forth herein, and upon the termination or expiration of this Franchise Agreement for any reason, Franchisee shall forthwith deliver and surrender to Franchisor each and all of the Proprietary Marks, and any physical objects bearing or containing any of the Proprietary Marks, or alternatively, at Franchisee's election, shall obliterate or destroy any such Proprietary Marks in his/her possession.

There may be redundant language found herein that the franchisee won't dispute the franchisor's right to its marks. Finally, there will be specific language setting forth exactly how and where to display the franchisor's trademarks and how to proceed if the franchisor elects to change its proprietary marks. The franchisor will also include language obligating the franchisee at termination or for whatever reason to pull its association from all on going advertisements, including the Yellow Pages or similar registries.

As to *Warranty and Indemnification,* the franchisee must receive a warranty from the Franchisor that its title to its trademarks is clear and unencumbered. As to indemnification, the franchisee will be obligated to notify the franchisor if it receives notice or learns that any third party is using the franchisor's mark without authorization. The franchisor will offer you boilerplate protection. You want at *least* the following:

> The Franchisor shall promptly take such action as may be necessary to protect and defend Franchisee against any such claim by any third party and shall indemnify Franchisee against any loss, cost or expense incurred in connection therewith. Franchisee shall not settle or compromise any such claim by a third party without the prior written consent of Franchisor. Franchisor shall have the right to defend, compromise or settle any such claim at Franchisor's sole cost and expense, using attorneys of its own choosing, and Franchisee agrees to cooperate fully with Franchisor in connection with the defense of any such claim. Franchisor is hereby irrevocably granted authority and power of attorney of Franchisee to defend or settle all of such claims, demands or suits. Franchisee may participate at his own expense in such defense or settlement, but Franchisor's decisions with regard thereto shall be final. Notwithstanding anything herein contained to the contrary, Franchisor shall have no obligation to defend or indemnify Franchisee pursuant to this section if the claim, suit or demand against Franchisee arises out of or relates to Franchisee's use of the marks in violation of the terms of this agreement.

You will add "the provisions of this paragraph shall survive the termination, abandonment or other cancellation of this Agreement."

B. *Manuals*

> There may be a separate paragraph depending on its overall value to the parties. The manual may address issues such as testing material; instructional materials; business forms; educational forms; furniture and fixtures; product and service order forms; cash controls; bookkeeping procedures; general operations; personnel; revenue reports; customer lists; payroll procedures; training and accounting; display of signs and notices; authorized and required equipment; appliances and appurtenances, including specifications thereof; proprietary mark usage; insurance requirements; license requirements; standards for management and personnel; hours of operation; Yellow Page and other local advertising formats; standards of maintenance and appearance; report submissions; meeting and conference requirements; training requirements; site selection specifications; training specifications for directors, assistant directors, and teachers; telephone procedures; initial conference procedures; and all other components, specifications, and standards.

C. *Confidential Information*

As to Restrictions on Use, the Franchisor will set forth a variety of specifics and then a general wrap-up. The franchisee will "agree" that such disclosure will cause the franchisor irreparable harm. The franchisee's counsel will draft exceptions such as:

    a. information already known;

    b. information in the public domain; or

    c. information independently acquired by a third party.

X. *Advertising*

This will vary in complexity depending on the franchise. Many controls on presentation, wording, media, etc., will have been set forth in the earlier sections, the Manual, etc.

As to *Royalty for and Administration of the Advertising Pool,* the issues addressed here include:

    a. fee and its gradations;

    b. the franchisor shall have sole discretion over the allocation of funds, media selection, national and regional strategies, etc;

    c. procedures to be utilized if rebates or individual franchisee aid is offered;

    d. whether franchisor, suppliers, et al will participate;

    e. any requirement that franchisee must place local ads. If so, the franchisor may require:

        i. a minimum amount of media space per promotion or per annum or both;

        ii. that a primary medium must be used for at least half such promotion (such primary medium could be the newspaper with the largest circulation in the franchisee's territory according to the Audit Bureau of Circulation);

        iii. that a certain size ad may be mandated in the Yellow Pages; and

        iv. prior clearance by franchisor of all promotional wording, strategies and the like.

    f. any requirements as to signs that must be erected on the premises. The franchisee must make sure that the franchisor warrants there are no IRS or other challenges to the advertising fund.

XI. *Duties of the Franchisor*

Here, in narrowly drafted language, will be set forth what the franchisor must provide, such as:

    a. training and supervision (initially and on-going);

    b. field support and other advisory assistance;

    c. assistance in obtaining your premises, including:

        i. site selection;

        ii. market strategy;

        iii. relocation;

        iv. whether you need Franchisor's prior written approval;

    d. bookkeeping, tax, comparative statistical information, insurance packages (very important today due to the difficulty in obtaining commercial liability insurance) and related services, if any;

    e. start-up promotional material and ads;

f. what must be purchased from Franchisor to assure uniformity of concept and quality for example: "these products are unique and are not available from any other source";

g. what may be purchased elsewhere and the approval steps for same, for example:

i. Franchisee must submit a written request to Franchisor for approval of the suppliers;

ii. The supplier must demonstrate to Franchisor's reasonable satisfaction that it is able to supply a product or service to Franchisee meeting Franchisor's specifications for such commodities; and

iii. The supplier must demonstrate to Franchisor's reasonable satisfaction that the supplier is in good standing in the business community with respect to its financial soundness and reliability of its product or service.

h. suggested pricing strategies and consultation on same with the Franchisee with two reservations:

i. such suggested prices are not a guarantee that the Franchisee will optimize profits; and

ii. language indicating that such prices are only suggestions and . . . (whatever is needed to avoid the appearance that this particular program is seeking to effectuate resale price maintenance);

i. audits—if there are audit discrepancies there may be a percentage penalty for understatements below a certain specified amount;

j. possible business referrals;

k. on-going research and development (where applicable);

l. franchisor-sponsored warranty programs;

The franchisor should offer something along the following lines as indemnification for any claims by third parties against the franchisee for proprietary information violations:

Franchisor warrants that the Franchisor's proprietary products licensed hereby do not infringe upon or violate any patent, copyright, trade secret or other proprietary right of any third parties; in the event of any claim by any third party against the Franchisee, Franchisee shall promptly notify Franchisor and Franchisor shall defend such claim, in the Franchisee's name, at Franchisor's expense and shall indemnify Franchisee against any money judgment by a court of competent jurisdiction. If such claim is rendered successful Franchisor shall, at its option, modify or replace such product with a non-infringing product of equivalent performance or secure for the Franchisee the right to continue such infringing product.

The Franchisor will also reserve to itself the final determination as to any matters of potential interpretation, e.g., "the Franchisor's determination in this regard shall be final." Finally, the franchisor must at all times remain in compliance with all franchise registration, disclosure and other federal/state/local laws on point.

XII. *General Duties of Franchisee*

The franchisee invariably must perform the following obligations:

a. Pay royalties as per the schedule;

b. Pay all taxes required to be collected by the Franchisor on all goods and services it furnished to the Franchisee;

c. Inform and update itself so that it can comply with all applicable laws/regulations at the federal/state/local level;

d. Permit on-premises supervision and actual physical presence as required by the Franchise Agreement;

e. Comply with the agreed-upon manner of operation and hours of operation;

f. Conduct advertising campaigns either alone or in cooperation with Franchisor;

g. Provide necessary maintenance and repairs (if Franchisor *requires* you to purchase certain equipment, make sure it will furnish all maintenance, service and parts to you to keep it working);

h. Obtain prior written approval of any lease/site;

i. Avail itself of on-going training required by Franchisor;

j. Uphold its agreement on quality control;

k. Permit non-intrusive inspection by Franchisor during normal business hours;

l. Submit all required reports prepared in the form required by the Franchisor.

m. Agree to indemnify the Franchisor. (As stressed throughout this book, an indemnity is only as good as the indemnitor.) At a minimum, you'll see the following:

Franchisee hereby agrees to protect, defend and indemnify Franchisor, its subsidiaries, affiliates, and designees, and hold them harmless from and against any and all costs, expenses (including attorneys' fees), court costs, losses, liabilities, damages, claims, and demand of every kind or nature, arising in any way out of franchisee's operation of the franchised business, including (without limitation) the occupation of the franchised business location, the use or operation of any fixtures or equipment located therein, or the sale or rendition of services, materials, goods or products used or sold in, at or from the franchised business location and any satellite location thereof.

The provisions of this paragraph shall survive the termination, abandonment or other cancellation of this agreement.

n. Purchase insurance as prescribed by the contract, manual, or otherwise specifically set forth. All insurance purchased by Franchisee shall name Franchisor as an additional insured, and shall provide that Franchisor shall be given at least ten (10) days' prior written notice of any termination, amendment, cancellation, or modification thereof. Franchisee shall promptly provide Franchisor with Certificates of Insurance evidencing such coverage no later than ten (10) days prior to the date the franchised business will be open for business to the public.

o. Comply with Non-Compete Clause(s). The Franchisee will agree that during the term of this Agreement it will not, either directly or indirectly, engage in any business giving, offering or selling products/services in direct competition with Franchisor. Such restriction will be reasonable in time, geographic area and in specified businesses. This covenant will run following the expiration or termination of the Agreement *for any reason whatsoever.*

Because these covenants have fallen into disfavor (even banned in a few states[70]), the Franchisor will probably also include a clause authorizing judicial reduction in the geographic or time scope of the covenant.

> p. Agree to No Encumbrances—i.e., that Franchisee can't permit liens without the Franchisor's prior approval.

> XIII. *Assignment*

The franchisor will reserve a broad right to assign the agreement. You want a guarantee of quiet enjoyment as follows:

> The Franchisee shall be entitled during the term of this Franchise and any extension thereof to enjoy all its rights as hereunder set forth in this Agreement without disturbance, subject only to its obligations to make the required payments hereunder. Franchisor represents that this Agreement is not subject or subordinate to any right of Franchisor's creditors, or if such subordination exists, that the Agreement creating same provides for non-disturbance of the user so long as it shall not be in default hereunder.

You also need to reserve the right to terminate the agreement upon _____ days prior notice. Your "new partner" may not be someone you wish to be associated with.

Your rights to assign aren't as freely granted. You'll see language such as:

> This Franchise Agreement is personal, being entered into in reliance upon and in consideration of the singular personal skill and qualifications of the Franchisee and the trust and confidence reposed in Franchisee by Franchisor or, in the case of a corporate franchisee, the principal shareholders and officers thereof. Therefore, neither Franchisee's interest in this Franchise Agreement nor any of his rights or privileges hereunder, nor the franchised business or any interest therein, may be assigned, transferred, shared or divided, voluntarily or involuntarily, directly or indirectly, by operation of law or otherwise, in any manner, without the prior written consent of the Franchisor. Such consent shall not be unreasonably withheld.

The franchisor will then itemize a number of specific instances of when it will be unreasonable, with a general catchall at the end. The Franchisor will probably impose an assignment fee which will be a percentage of the initial franchise fee paid to acquire the franchise.

> XIV. *Miscellaneous*

A. *Right of First Refusal*

Franchisor will reserve this as to any assignment, transfer or sale of Franchisee's interest by such Franchisee.

B. *Relationship of the Parties*

Franchisee is an independent contractor - not an agent of Franchisor and the Franchisor has no intention of entering into a joint venture.

C. *Waiver*

No waiver or delay in the enforcement of any breach of any material term of the Agreement will be construed as a waiver of any preceding or succeeding breach or delay in enforcement.

D. *Merger*

Here you'll see wording such as:

> Franchisee acknowledges that he is entering into this Franchise Agreement as a result of his own independent investigation of the business and not as a result of any representations about the Franchisor by its agents, officers or employees that are contrary to the terms herein set forth or that are contrary to the terms of any offering, circular, prospectus, disclosure document or other similar document required or permitted to be given to Franchisee pursuant to applicable law.

> This Franchise Agreement may not be amended orally, but may be amended only by a written instrument signed by the parties hereto. Franchisee expressly acknowledges that no oral promises or declarations were made to it and that the obligations of the Franchisor are confined exclusively to the terms herein. Franchisee understands and assumes the business risks inherent in this enterprise.

E. *Governing Law.*

More than routine as courts will not always give effect to the parties' choice of law as expressed in the Franchise Agreement, particularly as to covenants not to compete.[71]

F. *Notices.*

Title as well as individual to whom any notices specified in the Agreement are to be sent.

G. *Termination.*

This will include specified time; default by a party/cure; insolvency; what obligations are placed upon the parties at the time of termination or expiration.

H. *Arbitration,*[72] *Severability, Signature Lines.*

See discussion on the contractual clauses in Chapter 9.

Conclusion

The public no longer confuses franchises and pyramid schemes. The best incentive to cleaning up certain earlier abuses is the high entry franchise fee. The prudent investor has learned to retain professional advice prior to immediately signing to "get in on the ground floor." Such advice will focus on two salient legal issues—disclosure and then a contractual review.

The franchisee must be wary in choosing legal and financial advice. Its attorney must know the nuances of franchise law and the structuring of such agreements. Both franchisee and franchisor must carefully screen any professional consultants or "arrangers." The consultants in this field are not licensed, held to a professional standard of excellence, or monitored by governmental agencies (beyond the obvious unfair and deceptive trade practice laws).

Franchising is a popular growth strategy for firms looking to obtain "outside" franchising and an efficient distribution network based on a workforce of business owners who have a built-in incentive to succeed. The franchisor must carefully analyze its capitalization and attitude as to whether he/she is prepared to treat franchisees as partners.

This field is far from shaken out. As contractual paragraphs are argued in court and/or the fiduciary principles develop, they will be updated in subsequent supplements to this book.

ENDNOTES

(1) *Coast to Coast v. Gruschus,* 667 P.2d 619 (Wash. 1983).

(2) California Corp. Code Sec. 31000-31516 (specific definition of "franchise" at 31005(a), and 31300, private rights against officers, directors and employers in their individual capacities). See also California Civil Code 1812.201 (regulation of business opportunities);

Connecticut Gen. Statutes Sec. 42-133(e) to 42-133(h) (Connecticut Franchise Act);

Florida Statues Sec. 559.801 (business opportunity statute);

Hawaii Rev. Stat. Sec. 482E to 482E-12;

Illinois Ann. Stat. Ch. 121 ½, Sec. 701-740;

Indiana Code Ann. Sec. 23-2-2.5-1 to .5-50 and Sec. 23-2-2.7 to .7-7;

Maryland Ann. Code Art. 56, Sec. 345-365;

Michigan Comp. Laws Sec. 445.1501 to .1545;

Minnesota Stat. Ann. Sec. 80C.01-.22;

North Dakota Cent. Code Sec. 51-19-01 to 51-19-17;

Oregon Rev. Stat. Sec. 650.005-.086;

Rhode Island Gen. Laws Sec. 19-28-1 to 19-28-15;

South Dakota Codified Laws Ann. Sec. 37-5A-1 to 37-5A-85;

Virginia Code Sec. 13.1-557 to.1-574;

Washington Rev. Code Ann. Sec. 19.100.010 to .19.100.940;

Wisconsin Stat. Ann. Sec. 553.01-.78. See also Florida Stat. Sec. 817.416 and Mississippi Code Ann. Sec. 75-24-55. See also *Bailey Employment Systems, Inc. v. Hahn,* 655 F2d 473 (2d Cir. 1981) and *Ger-Ro-Mar, Inc. v. FTC,* 518 F.2d 33 (2d Cir. 1975).

(3) See *SEC v. W. J. Horvey Co.,* 328 US 293 (1946).

(4) 16 C.F.R. 436.

(5) 43 Fed. Reg. 59,614.

(6) 16 C.F.R. 436.2(a).

(7) 16 C.F.R. 436.2(i) as to who is an "affiliated person."

(8) 16 C.F.R. 436.2(3)(i). See also definition of same in 436.2(h).

(9) 16 C.F.R. 436.2 (3)(ii).

(10) 16 C.F.R. 436.2(3)(iv) (emphasis added). For the definition of *material,* see 16 C.F.R. 436.2(n).

(11) 16 C.F.R. 436.2(5).

(12) 16 C.F.R. 436.2(4)(i).

(13) 16 C.F.R. 436.2(3)(iii).

(14) 16 C.F.R. 436.2(4)(ii). For the definition of cooperative association, see 436.2(1) and 43 Fed. Reg. 59,710 fn. 108 (1978).

(15) 16 C.F.R. 436.2(4)(iv).

(16) 16 C.F.R. 436.2 (o). Some relief may be available from the Racketeer Influenced and Corrupt Organizations Act (RICO), 18 U.S.C. 1861 et seq. The federal statute and state complements have been designed for relief from deceptive schemes using the U.S. mail or interstate wire. Then there is the ever present 15 U.S.C. 45 (a) of the FTC Act. E.g., see *FTC v. Engage-A-Car Services, Inc.,* Civ. Action No. 86-3758 (9/24/86).

(17) 16 C.F.R. 436.1(a)1(i-iii).

(18) 16 C.F.R. 436(a)(2-3).

(19) 16 C.F.R. 436(a)(4)(i).

(20) 16 C.F.R. 436(a)(4)(ii).

(21) 16 C.F.R. 436(a)(4)(iii).

(22) 16 C.F.R. 436(a)(5).

(23) 16 C.F.R. 436(a)(6).

(24) 16 C.F.R. 436.1(a)(7).

(25) 16 C.F.R. 436.1(a)(8).

(26) 16 C.F.R. 436.1(a)(10).

(27) 16 C.F.R. 436.1(a)(11 and 12).

(28) 16 C.F.R. 436.1(a)(13)(i).

(29) 16 C.F.R. 436.1(a)(13)(iii and iv).

(30) 16 C.F.R. 436.1(a)(14).

(31) 16 C.F.R. 436.1(a)(15).

(32) 16 C.F.R. 436.1(a)(16). You might consult an accountant or a statistician here.

(33) 16 C.F.R. 436.1(a)(17).

(34) 16 C.F.R. 436.1(a)(18).

(35) 16 C.F.R. 436.1(a)(19). See also Section V(A) on Endorsements and Testimonials.

(36) 16 C.F.R. 436.1(a)(20).

(37) 16 C.F.R. 436.1(a)(21).

(38) 16 C.F.R. 436.1(a)(22).

(39) *Amrep Corp. v. FTC,* 768 F.2d 1171, 1179 (10th Cir. 1985). The FTC does recommend you purchase the following: *The Franchise Opportunities Handbook,* published annually by the U.S. Department of Commerce. For a copy, send check or money order ($10 as of 1987) to: Superintendent of Documents, U.S. Government Printing Office, Washington D.C. 20402. You should also contact: International Franchise Association, 1025 Connecticut Ave. NW, Suite 1005, Washington, D.C. 20036; (202)659-0790.

(40) 15 USC Sec. 1221-25.

(41) *Compare Shell Oil Co. v. Marinello,* 307 A.2d 598 (Sup. Ct. N.J. 1973).

(42) 15 USC Sec. 1221(b).

(43) 15 USC Sec. 1222.

(44) *Russ Thompson Motors, Inc. v. Chrysler Corp.,* 425 F.Supp. 1218 (D.N.H. 1977).

(45) *Woodward v. General Motors Corp.,* 298 F2d 121 (5th Cir. 1962).

(46) 15 U.S.C. Sec. 2801-06.

(47) 15 U.S.C. Sec. 2804.

(48) a. Arkansas Stat. Ann. Sec. 70-808-70-816;

b. California Bus. & Prof. Code Sec. 20000-20043;

c. Connecticut Gen. Statutes Sec. 42-133(e) - 42-133(h);

d. Delaware Code Ann. Sec. 2551-56;

e. Hawaii Rev. Stat. Sec. 482E;

f. Illinois Ann. Stat. Ch. 121-112, Sec. 704.3 et seq.;

g. Indiana Code Ann. Title 23, Art. 2.2-2.7-1 et seq.;

h. Michigan Stat. Ann. Sec. 19,854;

i. Minnesota Stat. Ann. Sec. 80C; (80C.14(b) sets forth a variety of definitions of good cause);

j. Mississippi Code Ann. Sec 75-24-53 et seq. (Mississippi does not regulate grounds for termination or nonrenewal requiring only 90 days advance written notice);

k. Missouri Ann. Stat. Sec. 407.400 et seq.;

l. Nebraska Rev. Stat. Sec. 87-402 et seq.;

m. New Jersey Rev. Stat. Sec. 56:10-1-56:10-12;

n. Virginia Code Sec. 13.1-564 et seq.;

o. Washington Rev. Code Sec. 19.100.180;

p. Wisconsin Stat. Ann. Sec. 135.01-135.07.

(49) *Westfield Centre Service, Inc. v. Cities Service Oil Co.* , 158 NJ Super 455, 386 A.2d 448 (1978) (termination based on new marketing strategy shifting from full service to "straight gas"—an otherwise productive and contractually complying dealer should not be terminated). See also *Larese v. Creamland Dairies, Inc.,* 767 F.2d 716 (10th Cir. 1985) and *Seamen's Direct Buying Service, Inc. v. Standard Oil Co. of California,* 36 Cal. 3d 752, 206 Cal. Rptr. 362, 686 P.2d 1166 (1984).

(50) *Kealy Pharmacy & Home Care Services, Inc. v. Walgreen Co.* , 539 F.Supp. 1357 (W.D. Wis. 1982), aff'd 761 F.2d 345 (7th Cir. 1985). (In discussing the applicability of the Wisconsin Fair Dealership Law particularly as to Section 135.03, the Court stated: "The burden of proving good cause is on the grantor with respect to the termination of every dealership." p. 350).

(51) See note 47. Three specific examples include Ark. 70-815, Cal. 20035 and Hawaii 482E-6(3).

(52) UCC Sec. 2-302. See also *W.L. May Co. v. Philco-Ford Corp.,* 273 Or. 701, 543 P.2d 283 (1975) and *Williamson v. Walker-Thomas Furniture Co.,* 350 F.2d 445449.

(53) *Larese v. Creamland Dairies, Inc.,* 767 F.2d 716 (10th Cir. 1985). See also Spandorf, Gurmich & Fern, "Implications of the Covenant of Good Faith: Its Extension to Franchising," 5 *Franchising Law Journal* 3 (1985).

(54) *Arnott v. American Oil Co.,* 609 F.2d 873 (8th Cir. 1979). cert den. 446 US 918 (1980); but see *Bellmore v. Mobile Oil Corp.,* 524 F.Supp. 850, F.2d (2d Cir. 1986); See also *Phillips v. Chevron,* 792 F.2d 521 (5th Cir. 1986); *Dunkin' Donuts of America, Inc. v. Middletown Donut Corp.,* 495 A.2d 66 (N.J. Sup. Ct. 1985); *Domed Stadium Hotel, Inc. v. Holiday Inns, Inc.,* 732 F.2d 480 (5th Cir. 1984); *Bain et al v. Champlin Petroleum Co.,* 692 F.2d 43 (8th cir. 1982); *John Deere Industrial Equipment Co.,* 681 F.2d 386 (5th Cir. 1982); *Picture Lake Campground v. Holiday Inns, Inc.,* 497 F.Supp. 858, 869 (E.D. Va. 1980); *Atlantic Richfield Co. v. Razumic,* 480 Pa 366; 390 A.2d 736 (1978).

(55) *Picture Lake Campground v. Holiday Inns, Inc.,* 497 F.Supp. 858, 869 (Ed-Va 1980).

(56) *Parker v. Lewis Grocery Co.,* 246 Miss 873, 153 S.2d 261 (1963), relying in turn on substantial precedent in *Risk v. Risher* , 197 Miss 155, 19 S.2d 484 (1944). See *DeTenorio v. McGorwan,* 510 F.2d 92 (5th Cir. 1975). See also Brown, Harold, "Franchising: A Fiduciary Relationship," 49 *Texas Law Review,* 650 (1971) (Mr. Brown has a regular column on Franchising in the *New York Law Journal* as well as *Franchising* (ABA's Magazine), in which he regularly updates lawyers on the fiduciary debate).

(57) *Grand Light & Supply Co., Inc. v. Honeywell, Inc.,* 771 F.2d 672, 677 (1985).

(58) *Stranp v. Times Herald Co.,* 423 A. 2d 713 (Pa. Sup. Ct. App. 1980) (customer lists); *Auburn News Co., Inc. v. Providence Journal Co.,* 504 F.Supp. 292 (D.R.I. 1980), rev'd on other grounds, 659 F.2d 273 (1st Cir. 1981), cert. den. 102 US 1277 (1982).

(59) 15 U.S.C. Sec. 1055, 1064 (e), and 1127 (1986).

(60) *Finlay & Associates, Inc. v. Borg-Warner Corp.,* 146 NJ Super 210, 369 A.2d 541 (1976).

(61) *Aladdin Oil Co. v. Texaco, Inc.,* 603 F.2d 1107, 1116 (5th Cir. 1979). See also *Hydro Air of Connecticut, Inc. v. Versa Technologies,* 599 F.Supp. 1119 (1984).

(62) *Principe v. McDonald's Corp.,* 631 F.2d 303 (4th Cir. 1980). See also *Bender v. Southland Corp.,* 749 F.2d 1205, 1215 (1984).

(63) See 16 C.F.R. 240 (1986).

(64) For some latitude, see *U.S. v. Colgate & Co.,* 250 US 300 (1919).

(65) *Reiter v. Sonotone Corp.,* 442 US 330 (1979).

(66) *Jordan v. Robert Half Personnel Agencies of Kansas City, Inc.,* 615 S.W.2d 574 (1981). But see *O'Boyle v. Avis Rent-A-Car System, Inc.,* 435 N.Y.S. 2d 296, 78 AD2d 431 (N.Y. App. Div. 1981).

(67) The franchisee has one consolation. Any ambiguity will be strictly construed against the drafting franchisor, especially where there are two alternative applications from which to choose. See *TGI Friday's, Inc. v. International Restaurant, Inc.,* 569 F.2d 895 (5th Cir. 1978). Other States have certain conduct and contractual restrictions by franchisors, e.g., Indiana Code, Sec. 2.7.1-1.

(68) 16 C.F.R. 436.2(a)(4)(i).

(69) NYS General Business Law Art. 33.

(70) Michigan (Mich. Stat. Ann. sec. 28.61) prohibits post-term franchise covenants against competition, while Indiana (Ind. Code Ann. Sec. 23-2-2.7-1(9)) has limited their duration. Florida (Fla. Stat. Ann. Sec. 542.33(2)(b)), on the other hand, has expressly approved by statute such covenants in the franchising context.

(71) *Blacock v. Perfect Subscription Co.,* 458 F.Supp. 123, 127 (S.D. Ala. 1978).

(72) Carefully review these clauses with your counsel. The U.S. Supreme Court states the Federal Arbitration Act (9 USC 2) preempts state law. Arbitration may be proposed at the Franchisor's Home Office. See *Burger King Corp. v. Rudzewicz,* 471 U.S. 62 (1985) and *Southland Corp. v. Keating,* 465 U.S. 1 (1984).

CHAPTER 11

HOW TO AVOID GETTING TIED UP WITH TIE-INS

When you were young, your parents may have told you that you could to go the movies only if you took your pesty little brother. Since this was your only alternative if you were to see the film, you decided to go—brother and all. Your parents were using a tie-in when they insisted that you take your brother (the "tied" product) if you wanted to go to the movies (the "tying" product)! Was their request reasonable? Did they have per se market power over your allowance? In this chapter we'll examine the legal issues that may arise when you use a tie-in.

A tying arrangement may be defined as an agreement by a party to sell one product (the "tying" product) only on the condition that the buyer also purchase a different (or "tied") product, or at least not purchase that product from any other supplier. It is analogous to vertical integration because you are deciding how much of your products will be put in one bundle and how much will be sold separately.

The selling of two products together is not automatically a restraint on competition. The antitrust problem with tying is that it leverages a company's market position from one product to another without regard to the competitive advantages of the second product. Meanwhile, buyers are forced to surrender their independent judgment as to whether to purchase the tied product. This does not further the goal of antitrust policy, which is the efficient allocation of economic resources through free competition.

Tying agreements are outlawed by Section 3 of the Clayton Act, which states:

> It shall be unlawful for any person engaged in commerce, in the course of such commerce, to lease or make a sale or contract for sale of goods, wares, merchandise, machinery, supplies, or other commodities, whether patented or unpatented, for use, consumption, or resale within the

U.S. . . .on the condition, agreement, or understanding that the lessee or purchaser thereof shall not use or deal in the goods. . .of a competitor or competitors of the . . .seller, where the effect of such lease, sale, or contract for sale or such condition, agreement, or understanding may be to substantially lessen competition or tend to create a monopoly in any line of commerce.[1]

It should be noted that tying agreements may also violate Section 1 of the Sherman Act. Section 3 of the Clayton Act applies only to the sale or lease of a commodity (e.g. credit is not a commodity under Section 3)[2] on the condition that the lessee or purchaser not use or deal in commodities of the seller's or lessor's competitors. If a tying arrangement deals with the sale of services, suit must be brought on the basis of Section 1 of the Sherman Act.

When do you have an illegal tying arrangement? If you had read this book five years ago, this chapter would have been a lot shorter. Then, tie-ins were generally presumed to be per se illegal. Now a per se illegal tying arrangement will be found only where there is a substantial volume of commerce foreclosed and anticompetitive forcing is apparent or likely. There are five elements of tying violations:

- there must be a tying arrangement between two distinct products or services,
- the defendant must have sufficient economic power in the tying product market to impose significant restrictions in the tied product market,
- the amount of commerce in the tied product market must not be insubstantial,
- the seller of the tying product must have interest in the tied product, *and*
- there must be a strong element of coercion shown,[3] (i.e., existence of forcing is probable).

When all five factors are not present, an antitrust violation can be found only through rule-of-reason analysis, i.e., that there was an unreasonable restraint on competition. The whole is always more complex than the sum of its parts. Therefore, we shall address each of the elements individually.

The Tying Arrangement

You can have a formal tie-in by an express contract, or such agreement can be inferred from the conduct of the parties. Any formal or informal arrangement which will involve two or more products or services in a "package" or a desired product with a less desired product should be reviewed with your counsel for tie-in exposure.

The issue, with regard to separate and distinct products, can be subtle. Marketplace realities, not the intent of the parties, is what controls. A left shoe and a right shoe are individual items but are sold as one product—a pair of shoes. Likewise, shirts for buttons or tires for cars are less expensive when put in one package. Obviously the lack of two separate markets will tend to show a single product.

The existence of dual markets is one way to determine the separateness of products. Another way to view the separate product issue is to examine whether the item is normally purchased as a distinct whole (e.g., an automobile manufacturer requiring its own engine to be installed) or whether the products are accessory and capable of being purchased as distinct products from other suppliers. For example, can they be returned separately for credit?

Here a common-sense test can be applied. Often the tying product is simply less desirable. One example here is the former practice of block booking movie licenses. To get certain desired pictures, theaters were forced to also license less desirable ones. These arrangements were found legal. Most artistic or literary property is a unique product, and compelling the purchase of one property with another *may* constitute a separate product for tie-in purposes.

A defense to the above can be the new entrant in a new field.

You may or may not be aware of the town of Lansford, Pennsylvania. Nestled in Carbon County, this town once was unable to receive television signals through conventional equipment because of its location. An entrepreneur, Milton Shapp, set up a CATV system on a nearby hilltop and a new direct marketing channel was born.

Mr. Shapp, as president of Jerrold Electronics Corporation, saw a great promise in CATV. An obvious reason was that many communities, because of distance or other topographical features, were unable to obtain television reception.

Jerrold Electronics sold its CATV systems on the condition that the purchaser accept its installation and maintenance services. Such conditions were elaborately detailed in its contracts. Due to this and other related contractual requirements, the Justice Department filed a complaint charging that these provisions constituted illegal tie-in sales.

The lower court recognized that the tie-ins were utilized "in the launching of a new business with a highly uncertain future."[4] The Supreme Court had generally stated (at that time) that "tying arrangements serve hardly any purpose beyond the suppression of competition."[5] However, here the Supreme Court did approve the restraint of an engineering service contract for highly complex equipment, during the *early stages* of a business when technology was advanced but not yet proven.

The court was also impressed by the fact that a large capital expenditure was involved. Jerrold, unlike its limited competition, lacked the resources of a diversified business. Therefore, an initial tie-in requirement actually enhanced competition.

The long and the short of it is that a tying arrangement, which may otherwise be illegal under the federal antitrust law, may sometimes be justified in limited circumstances during the development period of a new industry.

Note : It is important to remember this was a new entrant at an early stage. Recovery of investment costs is not permissible generally from the narrowly construed exceptions to the per se rule (when applicable against tie-ins).[6]

Sufficient Economic Power

"The hallmark of a tie-in is that it denies competitors free access to the tied product market, not because the party imposing the arrangement has a superior product in that market, but because of the power or leverage exerted by the tying product. . .Rules governing tying arrangements are designed to strike, not at the mere coupling of physically separable objects, but rather at the use of dominant desired product to compel the purchase of second, distinct commodity. . .In effect, the forced purchase of the second, tied product is a price exacted for the purchase of the dominant, tying product. By shutting competitors out of the tied product market, tying arrangements serve hardly any purpose other than the suppression of competition."[7]

The purpose of the rule against certain tying arrangements is to stop the extension of market power from one product (tying product) to another (tied product).[8]

The idea is that a firm with a monopoly of one product may refuse to deal except on terms that will lead to a monopoly of another. It also may be possible to use tying arrangements to extract a higher profit through price discrimination. Both the extension of power and the practice of price discrimination are impossible unless the seller has substantial market power. This means power over price—the ability to induce buyers to pay more money by cutting back the supply of goods available for purchase.[9]

The best way to show power over price is to establish directly that the price of the tied package is higher than the price of components sold in competitive markets and that significant barriers to entry exist.

Market Power Isn't Enough

Both the Courts and the U.S. Justice Department are holding that a market share of 30% or less is presumptively lawful.[10] If a supplier's market share exceeds the 30% threshold, the Guidelines indicate, the Department will determine whether the supplier possesses "dominant" market power. If so, the tie-in will be deemed per se unlawful. If dominant market power cannot be established, the Justice Department will employ the rule of reason analysis.

Note: The guidelines are referenced occasionally in the text but are not set forth as an alternative to case law. They are subject to change and do not have the force of law. They merely set out the Antitrust Division's current analysis of vertical practices. They apply only to vertical nonprice restraints (such as tie-ins). The guidelines specifically do not apply to vertical price restraints including price maintenance (concedes per se) restrictions related to the licensing of intellectual property rights (favor a very liberal rule of reason analysis) or restraints imposed upon regulated industries.[11]

Uniqueness Isn't Enough

Uniqueness does not require that the defendant have a monopoly or even a dominant position throughout the market for a tying product. It does, however, focus attention on the question whether the seller has the power within the market for the tying product, to raise prices or to require purchasers to accept burdensome terms that could not be exacted in a completely competitive market. The question is whether the seller has some advantages not shared by his competitors in the market for the tying product.

This can only be done by an assessment of "market power" in the tying product within a realistically defined relevant market. Then you must calculate an economic analysis and the consideration of possible economic justification.[12]

In other words, the plaintiff must show a barrier to entry that prevents competition. If rivals *may* design and offer a similar package for a similar cost, there is no barrier, and without a barrier there is no market power.[13] The term *may* is important. The uniqueness means the *inability* of a seller's rivals to offer a similar product, not simply the fact that no rival has chosen to do so.[14]

The *Will*[15] Court criticized the holding in *Digidyne*[16] because it required an exact reproduction as a barrier to entry. It then set forth what it defines as a true barrier to entry:

> "Sellers may strive to differentiate their products from others in order to compete for the custom of patrons with slightly different needs or tastes. It would be perverse to turn this ordinary attribute of the competitive struggle into a source of illegality. No one may copy Comprehensive's trademark or its copyrighted materials precisely, but rivals may create similar items for similar costs. Only when there is a barrier to entry–when rivals' cost of creating similar items is higher than the full costs of the original creator–may differences in the decision of the package be treated as proof of market power. . ."[17]

This court's emphasis on barriers might be extreme to the extent that it is practically closing the door to any argument short of patents. The opinion in *Hyde*[18] it is fond of citing actually makes it clear that the requisite power over the tying product exists where the product is patented, where the market share is high or where the tying product is "unique."

Thus, the law draws a distinction between the exploitation of market power by merely enhancing the price of the tying product, on the one hand, and by attempting to impose restraints on competition in the market for a tied product, on the other. When the seller's power is just used to maximize its return in the tying product market, where presumably its product enjoys some justifiable advantage over its competitors, the competitive ideal of the Sherman Act is not necessarily compromised, but can be seen to be fading fast. The latter is significantly different (by traditional antitrust interpretation) from patents and copyrights in terms of economic or market power:

> "The trademark gives the owner the right to prevent use of the mark by others when that use is likely to cause confusion, mistake or to deceive. . .but, where a patentee or copyright owner may prevent others from copying the product upon which he holds a patent or copyright, the holder of a trademark, merely by virtue of the trademark, may not prevent others from copying his product and selling the product under a different mark. . .Such monopolistic power is obtainable only with a patent or copyright . . ."

The "exclusive right" of a trademark owner to prevent the unauthorized use of his mark may present a legal barrier to the use of the mark, but does not present a barrier to competition in the sale of the same product under different marks. In other words, the mere exclusive ownership of a trademark does not monopolize or foreclose competition in the market for the product.[19]

In fact, in the case of a trademark, your competitor remains free to produce even an *identical* product, provided they do not employ a mark on such product which is likely to confuse or deceive consumers as to the product's source.

Courts are looking very closely to see if the trademark is actually a "tying product" to the product with which it is associated or whether the items are separate. The courts are looking at whether the items are normally sold or used as a unit, rather than separately; whether the defendant itself offers the items separately; whether other firms offer comparable items separately or only together; whether the purchaser is charged individually for each item; and whether the items are viewed as essential components of a larger product or service package.

With the growth of franchising (see elsewhere in this Section), the courts have been forced to consistently retreat from *Chicken Delight.* [20] In that case the court concluded that the trademark was a separable item from the packaging mixes and equipment because it reflected the goodwill and quality standards of the enterprise it identified and did not attach to the multitude of separate articles used in the operation of the franchise. Further, it was not essential that the items be purchased from the franchisor. Finally the court felt that the economic power inherent in a franchisor was the fact that a franchisee either accepts the tie-in restrictions or is foreclosed from using the name.

The franchisor kept on fighting. They won on ice cream where the trademark served to identify the ice cream, and thus the trademark and ice cream were not separate products so the tying rules were inapplicable. The ice cream was a "distinctive" article "made in accordance with secret formulae and processes" developed by Baskin-Robbins and, therefore, available only from it or its licensed manufacturers. The court concluded that the trademark and the product it represented were so "inextricably interrelated in the mind of the consumer" as to "preclude any finding that the trademark [was] a separate item for tie-in purposes."[21]

The steak houses won.[22] Here the franchisees argued that they were assigned a contractor to build their restaurant. Was the trademark the tying product and the building the tied? No, said the court. You can't have your steak and eat it, too! You are buying a franchise—the franchisor wants quality standards in the construction. More importantly, the franchisor had no financial interest in the contractor and received no income at all from the sales or the rental of the building. This issue arose in a similar context with McDonald's. The court held that this was a franchise package.

> Given the realities of modern franchising, we think the proper inquiry is not whether the allegedly tied products are associated in the public mind with the franchisor's trademark, but whether they are integral components of the business method being franchised. Where the challenged aggregation is an essential ingredient of the franchised system's formula for success, there is but a single product and no tie-in exists as a matter of law.

In short, the modern franchisee pays not only for the right to use a trademark but the right to become a part of a system whose business methods virtually guarantee his success. It is often unrealistic to view a franchise agreement as little more than a trademark license.[23] The court also found the franchisor's policy of owning all of its franchised stores justifiable because it furthered its legitimate interests in maintaining the continuity and quality control of its business.

Similarly the issue of whether or not it should be considered a separate product and/or quality control of same was controlling as to gas station owners.[24]

The pattern continues in franchise cases; the courts are generally holding that the trademark is not separately licensed but is attached to each product as an emblem of their origin.[25] Economic or market power is being given short shrift. As one court said after distinguishing *Chicken Delight:*

> "To infer economic power from the mere existence of a trademark which identifies the origin of the product would render the requirement that the seller have economic power in the relevant market virtually meaningless. The great majority of consumer products are sold under trademarks. The mere use of a trademark does not give a manufacturer an advantage not shared by his competitors whose products are also sold under trademarks,

and does not give the economic power in the tying market necessary to have an impact on competition.[26]

Also you won't get uniqueness or economic power from most trademarks. You still will from most patents and copyrights under attack by the Justice Department.[27]

However, the case for monopoly power in copyright and patents is clear.[28] As to the former, a court said recently:[29]

The copyright confers upon defendant "some advantages not shared by his competitors in the market for the tying product."[30] "The copyright monopolies represented tying products that the Court regarded as sufficiently unique to give rise to a presumption of economic power." [429 U.S. at 619, 97 S.Ct. at 867]. "[P]er se prohibition is appropriate if anticompetitive forcing is likely. For example, if the government has granted the seller a patent or similar monopoly over a product, it is fair to presume that the inability to buy the product elsewhere gives the seller market power."

This copyright power (as would a "patent power") enabled the owner to lock in its customers. This leverage was shown to result in a 93% repeat business by those locked in.[31] Such a lock-in created the presumption of economic power sufficient to render the tying arrangement illegal per se.

The prerequisites of per se illegality are:

- separate products, the purchase of one (tying product) being conditioned on purchase of the other (tied product);
- sufficient economic power with respect to the tying product to restrain competition appreciably in the tied product; and
- an effect upon a substantial amount of commerce in the tied product. If these prerequisites are satisfied, a court need not determine whether competition was in fact unreasonably restrained.

The court related other precedents:[32]

Market dominance–some power to control price and to exclude competition–is by no means the only test of whether the seller has the requisite economic power. Even absent a showing of market dominance, the crucial economic power may be inferred from the tying product's desirability to consumers or from uniqueness in its attributes.

Since the requisite economic power may be found on the basis of either uniqueness or consumer appeal, and since market dominance in the present context does not necessitate a demonstration of market power in the sense of Section 2 of the Sherman Act, it should seldom be necessary in a tie-in sale case to embark upon a full-scale factual inquiry into the scope of the relevant market for the tying product and into the corollary problem of the seller's percentage share in that market. This is even more obviously true when the tying product is patented or copyrighted, in which case, as appears in greater detail below, sufficiency of economic power is presumed.

This position was reaffirmed in the *Fortner* cases. In *Fortner I* :

"The standard of 'sufficient economic power' does not, as the District Court held, require that the defendant have a monopoly or even a dominant position throughout the market for the tying product. Our tie-in cases have made unmistakably clear that the economic power over the tying product can be sufficient even though the power falls far short of dominance and even though the power exists only with respect to some of the buyers in the market. . . .

. . .[T]he presence of any appreciable restraint on competition provides a sufficient reason for invalidating the tie. Such appreciable restraint results whenever the seller can exert some power over some of the buyers in the market, even if his power is not complete over them and over all other buyers in the market. . .[D]espite the freedom of some or many buyers from the seller's power, other buyers—whether few or many, whether scattered throughout the market or part of some group within the market—can be forced to accept the higher price because of their stronger preferences for the product, and the seller could therefore choose instead to force them to accept a tying arrangement that would prevent free competition for their patronage in the market for the tied product. Accordingly, the proper focus of concern is whether the seller has the power to raise prices, to impose other burdensome terms such as a tie-in, with respect to any appreciable number of buyers within the market. . . ."[394 U.S. at 502-04, 89 S.Ct. at 1258-59](emphasis added).

The court spoke of this final (though debated) indicator of sufficient economic power, that of leverage. In recent decisions, the Supreme Court again made it clear that a tying arrangement is illegal per se if the seller of the tying product has the capacity to force some buyers to purchase a tied product they do not want or would have preferred to purchase elsewhere. When such forcing occurs "competition on the merits in the market for the tied item is restrained."[33] The Court went on: "Thus, what is required in a per se case is not power over the whole market for the tying product, but only, as the Court said, a *"type of market power [that] has sometimes been referred* to as leverage. . .defined here as a supplier's ability to induce his customers for one product to buy a second product from him that would not be purchased solely on the merit of that second product."'. . ."[We] have condemned tying arrangements," the Court said, "when the seller has some special ability—usually called 'market power'—to force a purchaser to do something that he would not do in a competitive market."[34]

Effect on Commerce

Here, again, a principal problem the courts have with tie-ins is that they deny competitors free access to the market for the tied product, not because the tying product is of better quality or at a lower price but simply because of leverage in another (and possibly unrelated) market.

Interstate commerce consists of sales across state lines. A "substantial" amount is a subjective issue. A key point here is that the market in question and not merely gross sales will be the controlling factor. In one case,[35] an amount of $60,800 was found to be a substantial amount of dollar volume affecting the market involved (Note: This figure is over 25 years old!).

Seller Must Have an Interest in The Tied Product

This issue can arise when the seller of the tied product requires (tying product) the buyer to do business with a specific firm to effectuate the contract. For example, as we discussed above, a franchisor may require a restaurant to be built by a particular contractor. The franchisee may claim that this was an illegal tying arrangement.

The franchisor will win if it can satisfy the standards set out in *Kenner*[36] and *Principle,*[37] i.e., that it has no financial or other interest with the contractor (including rentals). The franchisor believed this contractor would erect a better building than its competitors.

However, as we discussed above as to credit financing requirements—be careful whenever you require an additional, separate and distinct purchase to do business.

Showing of Coercion

A buyer must be able to prove that he/she was *coerced* and not merely persuaded to buy an allegedly tied product. If you have an express provision in your contract, no coercion need be proven as coercion is implied.

If you are attempting to demonstrate coercion by implication—look for the following: have other buyers accepted similar burdensome terms? Some concrete inference is important because a seller may have the economic power in your market, but unless it actually employed its economic power in a *coercive* manner to force the purchase of the tied product, you may not be able to prove a tie-in.

Seller's Defenses

None of the following are "guaranteed," but all could be helpful (the usual caveat—consult your counsel in *advance* as to the specific details of a possible tie-in arrangement).

- Demonstrate the alleged tie-in is a single product.[38]

- Demonstrate you are a new entrant, infant industry or a firm trying to introduce a new type of product or service to the marketplace.[39]

- If goodwill and/or quality control is essential, this may be a defense to an alleged tie-in.[40]

- The tie-ins contribution to economic efficiency outweighs its anticompetitive effect.[41]

The Supreme Court, however, has said that the last justifications fail in the usual situation, because specifications of the type and quality of the products to be used in connection with the tying product is protection enough. On the other hand, this view is becoming dated in light of the direction the courts are setting. Increasingly courts and commentators view these arrangements as vertical and judge them according to a true rule of reason analysis. There will be a realistic assessment of market power and a rule of reason analysis as to whether there really is any interbrand competitive effect of the tying arrangement. Short of a patent, license, or copyright, your counsel should be able to devise a method by which you can tie your two products. Such strategy will attract a careful review of your two products, the relevant market and the economic impact of the tie.

To sum up the current state of per se analysis, the Supreme Court is on record as follows:

Per se condemnation—condemnation without inquiry into actual conditions—is only appropriate if the existence of forcing is probable. Thus, application of the per se rule focuses on the probability of anticompetitive consequences. Of course, as a threshold matter there must be a substantial potential for impact on competition in order to justify per se condemnation. If only a single purchaser was "forced" with respect to the purchase of a tied item, the resultant impact on competition would not be sufficient to warrant the concern of antitrust law. It is for this reason that we have refused to condemn tying arrangements unless a substantial volume of commerce is foreclosed thereby. Similarly, when a purchaser is "forced" to buy a product he would not have otherwise bought even from another seller in the tied product market, there can be no adverse impact on competition because no portion of the market which would otherwise have been available to other sellers has been foreclosed.

Once this threshold is surmounted, per se prohibition is appropriate if anticompetitive forcing is likely. For example, if the government has granted the seller a patent or similar monopoly over a product, it is fair to presume that the inability to buy the product elsewhere gives the seller market power. Any effort to enlarge the scope of the patent monopoly by using the market power it confers to restrain competition in the market for a second product will undermine competition on the merits in that second market. Thus, the sale or lease of a patented item on condition that the buyer make all his purchases of a separate tied product from the patentee is unlawful.

The same strict rule is appropriate in other situations in which the existence of market power is probable. When the seller's share of the market is high, or when the seller offers a unique product that competitors are not able to offer, the Court has held that the likelihood that market power exists and is being used to restrain competition in a separate market is sufficient to make per se condemnation appropriate. . .When, however, the seller does not have either the degree or the kind of market power that enables him to force customers to purchase a second, unwanted product in order to obtain the tying product, an antitrust violation can be established only by evidence of an unreasonable restraint on competition in the relevant market.

In sum, any inquiry into the validity of a tying arrangement must focus on the market or markets in which the two products are sold, for that is where the anticompetitive forcing has its impact. Thus, in this case our analysis of the tying issue must focus on the hospital's sale of services to its patients, rather than its contractual arrangements with the providers of anesthesiological services. In making that analysis, we must consider whether petitioners are selling two separate products that may be tied together, and, if so, whether they have used their market power to force their patients to accept the tying arrangement.[42]

Exclusive-Dealing Arrangements

Exclusive dealing arrangements (a form of short-term vertical integration) normally take the form of an agreement whereby a purchaser agrees to buy exclusively for a significant period of time from one supplier. The antitrust implication is that the agreement forecloses the supplier's competitors from the market (often substantial) represented by the purchaser for the period of time involved. The arrangement may also take the form of an agreement forbidding the purchaser to buy from the seller's competitors, or it may take the form of a requirements contract. Exclusive dealing arrangements have traditionally been treated somewhat more leniently than tying arrangements because of the recognition that exclusive dealing arrangements, unlike nearly all tying arrangements, may have a procompetitive effect, especially when employed by new entrants or nondominant firms. As such they were always evaluated under the rule of reason and rarely if ever under the per se rule.

In particular, such an analysis must consider whether the competition eliminated by the restraint is "significant" within the context of the "total competition extant in the industry." The court will consider several relevant market factors, including the number and size of competing firms in the industry and possible business justifications for the practices. The plaintiff must demonstrate not only that an exclusive dealing arrangement exists but the performance of such an arrangement will foreclose competition in a substantial share of the relevant product and geographic markets.[43]

In its landmark decision on point, the Supreme Court[44] set forth the precise economic analysis it would conduct.

> In practical application, even though a contract is found to be an exclusive-dealing arrangement, it does not violate the section unless the court believes it probable that performance of the contract will foreclose competition in a substantial share of the line of commerce affected. Following the guidelines of earlier decisions, certain considerations must be taken. First, the line of commerce, i.e., the type of goods, wares, or merchandise, etc., involved must be determined, where it is in controversy, on the basis of the facts peculiar to the case. Second, the area of effective competition in the known line of commerce must be charted by careful selection of the market area in which the seller operates, and to which the purchaser can practically turn for supplies. In short, the threatened foreclosure of competition must be substantial in relation to the market affected.[45]

To determine substantiality in a given case, it is necessary to weigh the probable effect of the contract on the relevant area of effective competition, taking into account the relative strength of the parties, the proportionate volume of commerce involved in relation to the total volume of commerce in the relevant market area, and the possible immediate and future effects which preemption of that share of the market might have on effective competition therein. It follows that a mere showing that the contract itself involves a substantial number of dollars is ordinarily of little consequence.[46]

Statistical evidence of market foreclosure, relative strength of the parties and economic justifications all are reviewed by the courts.[47]

The statutory provision generally employed has been Clayton Act 3 (this also governs tying arrangements), which makes it unlawful to sell or lease a commodity on the condition that the buyer will not deal in the commodities of the seller's competitors, where the effect may be to substantially lessen competition or tend to create a monopoly.[48] Three significant limitations are inherent in the statute, i.e. the transaction must involve a commodity, involve a sale, lease or "contract of sale" (no consignments)[49] and must restrict the purchaser as opposed to the seller itself. Therefore, plaintiffs have also utilized Sherman Sections 1 and 2 and Section 5 of the FTC Act to challenge the arrangements.

Finally, there is the related reciprocal dealing arrangement. Here large firms typically buy large quantities of goods from suppliers. In many cases these supplying companies need goods manufactured by the companies they supply. Under these circumstances, a large firm may find it advantageous to use its buying power as a means of "encouraging" its suppliers to purchase all or most of their requirements for such goods from it. This use of purchasing power to promote sales, called "reciprocity," may involve antitrust consequences. The analysis is similar to that utilized for tying and exclusive dealing arrangements.

All these arrangements involve the attachment of terms and conditions to the purchase of a given product. However, the courts will generally favor exclusive dealing agreements which were freely entered into by both parties to serve a legitimate economic need and not to foreclose competition. For example, if a new business uses this agreement to gain a foothold in the market, thereby improving competition, the agreement will in all likelihood be upheld.

Conclusion

The crucial test in a tying agreement is whether the tie-in involves a product or services in which your firm enjoys significant economic power. Ask yourself whether reasonable appearances would indicate that you are attempting to exert leverage so that your monopoly power in one area (the tied product) may be extended into another (the tying area).

While this topic is increasingly being governed by the rule of reason analysis, you have per se hurdles in certain unique areas as well as concerns about copyrights and patents.

ENDNOTES

(1) 15 U.S.C.A. 14.

(2) *Stepp v. Ford Motor Credit Company,* 623 F.Supp. 583, 593 (D.C. Wisc., 1985). See also *Bouldis v. U.S. Suzuki Motor Corp.,* 711 F.2d 1319 (6th Cir. 1983).

(3) *Krehl v. Baskin-Robbins Ice Cream Co.,* 664 F.2d 1348 (9th Cir. 1982). See also *Jefferson Parish Hospital District No. 2 v. Hyde,* 466 U.S. 2, 104 S.Ct. 1551, 80 L.Ed.2d 2 (1984) and *Times Picayune Publishing Co. v. United States,* 345 U.S. 594 (1953).

(4) *U. S. v. Jerrold Electronics Corp.,* 187 F.Supp. 545 (E.D. Pa. 1960) aff'd per curiam, 365 U.S. 567 (1961).

(5) *Standard Oil Company of California v. U.S.,* 337 U.S. 293 (1949).

(6) *Data General Corp. v. Digidyne Corp.,* 734 F.2d 1336, 1344 (9th Cir. 1984) cert. den., 105 S.Ct. 898 (1985) (Court declined to review manufacturer's refusal to license its copyrighted computer operating system to anyone that did not purchase its CPU) (contrasting its situation to *Jerrold*).

(7) *Siegel v. Chicken Delight,* 448 F.2d 43, (9th Cir. 1971) cert. den., 405 U.S. 955 (1972).

(8) *Jefferson Parish Hospital District No. 2 v. Hyde,* 466 U.S. 2, 104 S.Ct. 1551, 1558-60, n.20; 80 L.Ed.2d (1984). See also *Northern Pacific Ry. v. United States,* 365 U.S. 1; 78 S.Ct. 514; 2 L.Ed.2d 545 (1958); *International Salt Co. v. United States,* 332 U.S. 392; 68 S.Ct. 12; 92 L.Ed. 20 (1947); *Carl Sandburg Village Condominium Ass'n No. 1 v. First Condominium Development Company,* 758 F.2d 203 (7th Cir. 1985).

(9) *Broadcast Music, Inc. v. Columbia Broadcasting System, Inc.,* 441 U.S. 1, 9-10, 22, n.40; 99 S.Ct. 1551, 1556-57, 1562-63, 1564, n. 40; 60L.Ed.2d 1 (1979); *National Collegiate Athletic Ass'n v. Board of Regents,* 468 U.S. 85; 104 S.Ct. 2948, 2961-63, 2967-68; 82 L.Ed. 70 (1984); and *Yentsch v. Texaco, Inc.* 630 F.2d 46 (2d Cir. 1980).

(10) See *Hyde* case (note 8), *Vertical Restraint Guidelines* Section 5.3 (1985), and statement of Charles F. Rale before the Committee on the Judiciary, U.S. Senate 7/16/85, p. 18. See also *United States v. Waste Management, Inc.,* 743 F.2d 976 (2d Cir.

1984) (market share exceeding 50% does not establish power over price when entry is easy).

(11) See Vertical Restraint Guidelines Sections 23, 24, and 3.3 (1985).

(12) *United States Steel Corp. v. Fortner Enterprises, Inc.* (a unique form of credit arrangement, but the firm supplied less than 1% of the nation's credit so there was no market power), 429 U.S. 610; 97 S.Ct. 861; 51 L.Ed.2d 80. See also *General Business Systems v. North American Philips Corp.*, 699 F.2d 965, 977 (1983).

(13) Id., p. 429; U.S. at 622; 97 S.Ct. at 868.

(14) *Spartan Grain & Mill Co. v. Ayers*, 735 F.2d 1284 (11th Cir. 1984), cert. den., 105 S.Ct. 785, 83 L.Ed.2d 779 (1985).

(15) *Will v. Comprehensive Accounting Corp.*, 776 F.2d 665, 673, (1985). (uniqueness not enough without proof such uniqueness conferred market power).

(16) See note 6 above.

(17) Id., p. 673.

(18) See note 8 above.

(19) *Golden West Insulation, Inc. v. Stardust Investment Corp.*, 615 P.2d 1048, 1054 (Ore. Ct. App. 1980).

(20) See note 7. See also *Photovest Corp. v. Fotomat Corp.*, 606 F.2d 704 (7th Cir. 1979), cert. den., 445 U.S. 917 (1980).

(21) See note 3 above, p. 1354.

(22) *Kenner v. Sizzler Family Steak Houses*, 597 F.2d 453 (CA 5 1979).

(23) *Principe v. McDonald's Corp.*, 631 F.2d 303, 309 (CA 4 1980), cert. den. (1981) and *Kentucky Fried Chicken Corp. v. Diversified Packaging Corp.*, 549 F.2d 368 (5th Cir. 1977). See also Linger, Elliott R.: "The McDonald's Antitrust Litigation: Real Estate Tying Agreements in Trademark Franchising," 13 *John Marshall Law Review* 603 (1980).

(24) *Redd v. Shell Oil Co.*, 524 F.2d 1054 (CA 10 1975); *Edward J. Sweeney & Sons Inc. v. Texaco, Inc.* 478 F.Supp. 243.

(25) *JRL Enterprises, Inc. v. Jhirmack Enterprises, Inc.* 509 F.Supp. 357, 377 (ND Cal. 1981).

(26) Id. at 378.

(27) U.S. Dept. of Justice Vertical Restraints (January 23, 1985), Section 5 at p.12.

(28) *U.S. v. Loew's Inc.*, 371 U.S. 38, 45, (1962) (the requisite economic power is presumed when the tying product is patented or copyrighted).

(29) *Digidyne Corp. v. Data General Corp.*, 734 F.2d 1336, 1341-42 (1984).

(30) See note 12 above.

(31) Note 28, p. 1343.

(32) Id., p. 1340.

(33) See *Hyde* case, note 8, p. 1558.

(34) Id., p. 1559. See also *Aspen Skiing Company v. Aspen Skiing Corp.*, 105 S.Ct. 2847 (1985) (affirmed a monopolization judgment that was in part based upon a tying or leveraging theory).

(35) *Anderson v. Home Style Stores, Inc.*, (D.C. PA) 58 F.R.D. 125 (E.D. Pa 1972).

(36) See note 21.

(37) See note 22.

(38) *Dehydrating Process Co. v. A.O. Smith Corp.*, 292 F.2d 653 (1st Cir.) cert. den., 368 U.S. 931 (1961).

(39) See *Jerrold Electronics* discussion below as well as note 7 and *Carpa, Inc. v. Ward Foods, Inc.,* 536 F.2d 39, 47 (5th Cir. 1976).

(40) *FTC v. Sinclair Refining Co.,* 261 U.S. 463 (1923). See also *Bender v. Southland Corp.,* 749 F.2d 1205, 1215 (1984) and *Fortner Enterprises, Inc., v. U.S. Steel Corp.,* 394 U.S. 495, 507; 89 S.Ct. 1252, 1260; 22 L.Ed.2d. 495 (1969).

(41) See note 8 above.

(42) Id. See also *Arizona v. Maricopa County Medical Soc.,* 457 U.S. 322, 444; 102 S.Ct. 2466, 2473, n.15; 73 L.Ed.2d 48 (1982); *Wilk v. AMA,* 719 F.2d 207 (7th Cir. 1983), cert. den. 467 U.S. 1210; 104 S.Ct. 2398; 81 L.Ed.2d. 355 (1984); see also *Reazin v. Blue Cross & Blue Shield of Kansas, Inc.,* 635 F. Supp. 1287, 1322 (D. Kansas, 1986).

(43) *D & A Distributing Co., Inc. v. Chambers Corp.,* 608 F.Supp. 1290 (D.C. Cal. 1984).

(44) *Tampa Electric Co. v. Nashville Coal Co.,* 365 U.S. 320 (1961).

(45) Id., p. 327.

(46) Id., p. 328.

(47) *American Motor Inns, Inc. v. Holiday Inns,* 521 F.2d 1230, 1252-53 (3d Cir. 1973).

(48) See note 40 above and *Mangus Petroleum Co. v. Skelly Oil Company,* 599 F. 2d 196 (7th Cir.), cert. den., 444 U.S. 916 (1979).

(49) *Simpson v. Union Oil Company of California,* 377 U.S. 13, 18 (1964).

SECTION III

HOW THE LAW AFFECTS PRICING POLICY

Economic activity is at its root cooperative, but the antitrust rules are written so that business transactions don't get too cozy. You are expected to set prices and make deals at "arm's length." When you meet with friends from other firms or attend trade association meetings, you must always remember that the law goes with you. Penalties for price agreements include fines and jail sentences. People *do* go to jail, and fines are not tax deductible as business expenses. Even a suspended sentence can kill a career of otherwise admirable achievement.

In this section we'll examine price-fixing. Then we'll join a hypothetical trade association meeting and see how unwary participants can become involved in antitrust activity through their words, actions, and *lack of actions.* From there we'll proceed through the myriad areas of the Robinson-Patman Act to learn how the law will look at your discriminatory pricing policies.

The "Summary Judgment Rule" Replaces Per Se Rules

Much ballyhoo has been made in the legal press that the U.S. Supreme Court has evolved from the "rigid" per se formula to a rule-of-reason "analysis." This is all very good if the Court rules reasonably.

Sadly, what may be taking place is the Court's using one shorthand (summary judgment) to make up for the loss of another (per se). The latter made some economic sense based on experience with certain economic relationships. Summary judgment makes all antitrust law more arbitrary, as the rule-of-reason analysis is merely distorted to justify a summary judgment. There were three tragic examples of this disposition recently.[1] We'll focus on one of these, *Matsushita,*[2] as it once again confirms the disadvantage U.S. firms are under in international competition. Our neutral umpire plays by "economic rules" that force U.S. firms into hopeless situations.

Japan Wins Another One

It is not a unique observation that the Japanese firms often are organized defensively at home so as to offensively maximize overseas markets that continue to be governed by the rules of fair trade. American manufacturers of television sets brought suit against Japanese manufacturers alleging that the Japanese manufacturers had illegally conspired to drive the American manufacturers from the American market by engaging in a scheme to (1) fix and maintain artificially high prices for television sets sold by the Japanese manufacturers in Japan and (2) fix and maintain low prices for the sets exported to and sold in the United States. The cases dragged on for over a decade. The United States District Court for the Eastern District of Pennsylvania granted summary judgment in favor of the Japanese manufacturers. The Third Circuit Court of Appeals affirmed in part and reversed in part.

The Japanese market for consumer electronic products (CEPs) was characterized by oligopolistic behavior, with a small number of producers meeting regularly and exchanging information on price and other matters. This created the opportunity for a stable combination to raise both prices and profits in Japan. American firms could not attack such a combination because the Japanese government imposed significant barriers to entry.[3]

In other words, Japanese firms can meet and operate at an unfair advantage because U.S. firms employing similar strategies would risk Sherman Act felony exposure. Japanese firms could then raise prices (plus receive export tax incentives) in Japan so as to lower prices artificially in the United States.

As stated earlier, per se rules lent predictability. The new "rule of reason" by summary judgment leaves the United States business executive at risk to whims of arbitrariness where precedent, economic argument, and economic realities are all ignored. Let's take a look at the views of the DePodwin Report, which the U.S. Court of Appeals and the Supreme Court minority thought quite persuading:

"When we consider the injuries inflicted on United States producers, we must again look at the Japanese television manufacturers' export agreement as part of a generally collusive scheme embracing the Japanese domestic market as well. This scheme increased the supply of television receivers to the United States market while restricting supply in the Japanese market. If the Japanese manufacturers had competed in both domestic and export markets, they would have sold more in the domestic market and less in the United States. A greater proportion of Japanese production capacity would have been devoted to domestic sales. Domestic prices would have been lower and export markets would have diminished practically to the vanishing point. Consequently, competition among Japanese producers in both markets would have resulted in reducing exports to the United States and Unites States prices would have risen. In addition, investment by the United States industry would have increased. As it was, however, the influx of sets at depressed prices cut the rates of return on television receiver production facilities in the United States to so low a level as to make such investment uneconomic.

"We can therefore conclude that the American manufacturers of television receivers would have made larger sales at higher prices in the absence of the Japanese cartel agreements. Thus, the collusive behavior of Japanese television manufacturers resulted in a very severe injury to those American television manufacturers, particularly to National Union Electric Corporation, which produced a preponderance of television sets with screen sizes of nineteen inches and lower, especially those in the lower range of prices." [5 App. to Brief for Appellants in No. 81-2331 (CA3), pp. 1629a-1630a.]

"The impact of Japanese anti-competitive practices on United States manufacturers is evident when one considers the nature of competition. When a market is fully competitive, firms pit their resources against one another in an attempt to secure the business of individual customers. However, when firms collude, they violate a basic tenet of competitive behavior, i.e., that they act independently. United States firms were confronted with Japanese competitors who collusively were seeking to destroy their established customer relationships. Each Japanese company had targeted customers which it could service with reasonable assurance that its fellow Japanese cartel members would not become involved. But just as importantly, each Japanese firm would be assured that what was already a low price level for Japanese television receivers in the United States market would not be further depressed by the actions of its Japanese associates.

"The result was a phenomenal growth in exports, particularly to the United States. Concurrently, Japanese manufacturers, and the defendants in particular, made large investments in new plant and equipment and expanded production capacity. It is obvious, therefore, that the effect of the investment on Japanese television industry was greater than otherwise would have been the case. This added capacity both enabled and encouraged the Japanese to penetrate the United States market more deeply than they would have had they competed lawfully." [5 App. to Brief for Appellant in No. 81-2331 (CA3), pp. 1628a-1629a.][4]

As the minority stated:

"The DePodwin Report, on which the Court of Appeals relied along with other material, indicates that respondents were harmed in two ways that are independent of whether petitioners priced their products below 'the level necessary to sell their products or . . . some appropriate measure of cost' [*Ibid.*]. First, the Report explains that the price-raising scheme in Japan resulted in lower consumption of petitioners' goods in that country and the exporting of more of petitioners' goods to this country than would have occurred had prices in Japan been at the competitive level. Increasing exports to this country resulted in depressed prices here, which harmed respondents. Second, the DePodwin Report indicates that petitioners exchanged confidential proprietary information and entered into agreements such as the five company rule with the goal of avoiding intragroup competition in the United States market. The Report explains that petitioners' restrictions on the intragroup competition caused respondents to lose business that they would not have lost had petitioners competed with one another."[5]

Here, we are not arguing the merits or who is right. We are arguing the U.S. firms' rights to go to the factfinder (i.e., jury) to rule on these issues. In summarily dismissing the United States firms' arguments:

▶ The majority held that U.S. antitrust laws do not regulate the competitive conditions of other nations' economics.[6] Yet the Court went on to acknowledge that the Sherman Act does reach conduct that has an *effect* on American commerce.[7]

▶ The Court placed great weight on an apparent lack of incentive to engage in predatory pricing. The Court dwelt at length on the fact that predatory pricing incurs upfront losses that must be recouped by raising prices once a monopoly has been achieved. It completely ignored the issue of market share as an incentive.

▶ The court imposed a heavier burden of proof on U.S. firms, which, in addition to showing a conspiracy in violation of the antitrust laws, must also show injury to them resulting from the illegal conduct.[8]

As already noted, the Court intended to ignore that U.S. firms' depressed selling prices hurt their R & D expenses. Even more bizarre, the Court ignored the fact that the "Japan, Inc." firms' collective market share rose from "one-fifth or less of the relevant markets to close to 50%!"[9] The Court attempted to obfuscate what should have been the most telling statistics by stating:

Two decades after their conspiracy is alleged to have commenced, petitioners appear to be far from achieving this goal: the two largest shares of the retail market in television sets are held by RCA and respondent Zenith, not by any of the petitioners. . . .Moreover, those shares, which together approximate 40% of sales, did not decline appreciably during the 1970's.[10]

The U.S. firms have "not declined appreciably"? The Japanese cartel has *captured* 50% of the entire market. Yet nothing is amiss by this Court's analysis. The Court disguised the 50% market share by isolating the percentages captured by numerous foreign firms. This was the issue for the jury: Was the cartel of Japanese firms as a unit engaging in predatory pricing? The Court is attempting to view the Japanese cartel as similar to OPEC. Yet the homogenity of the Japanese firms is completely distinguishable.

▶ The Court's only telling point (if isolated from all facts and economic data) is that "courts should not permit factfinders to infer conspiracies when such inferences are implausible, because the effect of such practices is often to deter pro-competitive conduct."[11] The Court was reiterating its policy that it doesn't want a firm to prosper by utilizing the chilling effect of expensive antitrust lawsuits to deter competition. In this case the survival of the United States consumer electronic products industry is at stake, so the lawsuit is hardly spurious.

▶ Finally, the majority somehow came to the conclusion that the cartel sought to raise prices (in the U.S.) rather than lower them.

"The 'direct evidence' on which the [Appeals] court relied was evidence of *other* combinations, not of a predatory pricing conspiracy. Evidence that petitioners conspired to raise prices in Japan provides little, if any, support for respondents' claims: a conspiracy to increase profits in one market does not tend to show a conspiracy to sustain losses in another. Evidence that petitioners agreed to fix *minimum* prices (through the "check price" agreements) for the American market actually works in petitioners' favor because it suggests that petitioners were seeking to place a floor under prices rather than to lower them. . . .

. . ."Here, the conduct in question consists largely of (i) pricing at levels that succeeded in taking business away from respondents, and (ii) arrangements that may have limited petitioners' ability to compete with each other (and thus kept prices from going even lower). This conduct suggests either that petitioners behaved competitively, or that petitioners conspired to *raise* prices. Neither possibility is consistent with an agreement among 21 companies to price below market levels. Moreover, the predatory pricing scheme that this conduct is said to provide is one that makes no practical sense: it calls for petitioners to destroy companies larger and better established than themselves, a goal that remains far distant more than two decades after the conspiracy's birth."[12]

Again, a nice legal argument in isolation. However, it ignores the economic realities of international competition as well as the text of the record before it:

• The cartel was to raise prices at home so it could (and did) lower them in the United States market; and

• The Court's emphasis on "two decades" again completely ignores that in such period the cartel went from a negligible presence in the American market to a 50% market share. Conceivably the cartel could capture over 90% of the market share and the U.S. firms would still be "larger" in isolated percentage terms.

Conclusion

This case deals with a number of issues that have been touched on throughout the text and in this introduction (rule of reason, predatory pricing, monopolies, etc.). It graphically demonstrates the hurdles U.S.

management must overcome when the Court refuses even to attempt to create a level playing field, for example, by

- ignoring an overseas cartel's impact on the stream of domestic commerce;
- ignoring market share as a marketing goal;
- acknowledging and then ignoring the fact that the United States has no free access to the Japanese market; and
- maintaining the misguided notion that U.S. firms can compete against foreign firms organized so as to penetrate our markets.

The legal literature generally hailed the departure from per se rule "rigidity" to rule-of-reason "analysis." What they hadn't anticipated was that per se rules were adopted for very real reasons such as the Court's docket overload. Therefore, a substitute must be found. It could be the new and surprising liberal attitude toward summary judgment for case resolution—even in complicated areas. If this is true, then a new era of arbitrariness will result in case precedent much to the detriment of U.S. firms, which must attempt to anticipate such "rules of reason."

ENDNOTES

(1) Two were: *Anderson v. Liberty Lobby, Inc.,* 106 S.Ct. 2505 (1986) and *Argus, Inc. v. Eastman Kodak Co.,* 612 F.Supp. 904 (S.D.N.Y. 1985), *aff'd* 801 F.2d 38 (2d Cir. 1986), cert. den. 107 S.Ct. 1295 (1987).

(2) *Matsushita Electric Industrial Co. v. Zenith Radio Corp.,* 106 S.Ct. 1348 (1986).

(3) Id., p. 1353.

(4) Id., p. 1365-66.

(5) Id., p. 1365.

(6) Id., p. 1354.

(7) Id., and see *Continental Ore Co. v. Union Carbide & Carbon Corp.,* 370 U.S. 690, 704; 82 S.Ct. 1404, 1413; 8 L.Ed.2d 277 (1962).

(8) Id., p. 1356.

(9) Id., p. 1358.

(10) Id.

(11) Id., p. 1360 citing *Monsanto v. Spray-Rite Corp.,* 465 U.S. 762-764; 104 S.Ct. 1470 (1984).

(12) Id., p. 1361.

CHAPTER 12

ANTITRUST ISSUES AFFECTING PRICE-FIXING

This chapter addresses issues you will undoubtedly encounter in your career, if you haven't already. Your best guide to everyday legal compliance is to remember the underlying social policy. Antitrust policy remains rooted in the assumption that free competition will promote optimal economic performance. Therefore, whenever you spot a potential antitrust issue, ask yourself whether the activity you are undertaking will add to or diminish market concentration; if the latter result appears likely, ask yourself: Is it reasonable in light of the following?

Price-Fixing

Section 1 of the Sherman Act states that "Every contract, combination in the form of trust or otherwise, or conspiracy, in restraint of trade or commerce among the several states, or with foreign nations is declared to be illegal."[1] The "contract" is the agreement to restrain competition. A "combination" occurs when two or more persons join together for the purpose of carrying out united action. A "conspiracy" is a continuing partnership in restraint of trade. At least two persons are required under all of these forms of joint activity.

When confronted with a Section 1 case, the Court first asks if the parties entered into an agreement. Price-fixing is an *agreement* among two or more parties on the prices they will charge for their product or service.[2] The traditional definition is any combination formed for the purpose of and with the effect of raising, depressing, fixing, pegging, or stabilizing prices.

It is not necessary to find an express agreement, either oral or written, in order to find a conspiracy, but it is sufficient that a concert of action be contemplated and that defendants conform to the arrangement.

Mutual consent need not be based on express agreement, for any conformance to an agreed or contemplated pattern of conduct will warrant an inference of conspiracy. Thus not only action, but even a lack of action, may be enough from which to infer a combination or conspiracy. "Agreement" as used in antitrust laws means no more than adherence to or participation in a common scheme. A "knowing wink" can mean more than words.[3]

Any mutual understanding of this nature, written or oral, explicit or tacit, is illegal. This can include "gentlemen's agreements" and off-the-record conversations as well. Moreover, it is not essential in establishing a violation that the parties actually perform the agreement.

Proof of collusion or agreement can be based on seemingly isolated facts that, when viewed together, present a chain of circumstantial evidence from which an agreement or conspiracy may be inferred. Any decision or agreement that would dilute traditional arm's-length bargaining should alert you to possible price-fixing situations. One question to ask is whether price uniformity is developing among competitors, customers, or suppliers. Be aware, also, that not just prices, but any factor influencing prices, such as warranties, division of markets or customers, and shipping terms, may not lawfully be the subject of an agreement among competitors.

The following are some questions that frequently confront managers.

1. *What is horizontal price-fixing?* This is a price-fixing agreement or other agreement limiting price competition among competitors on the same (horizontal) level of competition. For example, a horizontal price-fixing conspiracy may be aimed at eliminating discounters and raising prices at which consumers purchase goods.

2. *What is vertical price-fixing?* This is a price-fixing agreement or other agreement limiting price competition with a firm in your distribution channel (for example, a supplier or a wholesaler). For instance, here the conspirators might agree with intermediaries to set resale prices to be charged to third parties.

3. *Will the law treat violators differently?* Generally, no. Whether you engage in vertical or horizontal price-fixing, the penalties will be the same. (Though there might be some latitude evolving as to vertical price-fixing.)

4. *What are the penalties?* Section 1 of the Sherman Act is straightforward: Every person who shall make any contract or engage in any combination or conspiracy hereby declared to be illegal *shall be deemed guilty of a felony and, on conviction thereof, shall be punished by fine not exceeding one million dollars if a corporation, or, if any other person, one hundred thousand dollars, or be imprisoned not exceeding three years, or by both said punishments,* in the discretion of the court. [Emphasis added.]

5. *What if I intentionally engage in price-fixing to benefit the consumer?* *Any* agreement to fix prices or reduce price competition is illegal. This includes agreements that fix prices at lower than market levels, even if the agreement would mean lower prices for the consumer!

6. *What about agreements concerning credit terms among competitors?* It is unlawful for competitors not only to set maximum or minimum prices but to enter into any agreement affecting or relating to credit terms.

As the Supreme Court stated, it is virtually self-evident that extending interest-free credit for a period of time is equivalent to giving a discount equal to the value of the use of the purchase price for that period of time. Thus, credit terms must be characterized as an inseparable part of the price. An agreement to terminate the practice of giving credit is tantamount to an agreement to eliminate discounts, and thus falls squarely within the traditional *per se* rule against price-fixing. While eliminating a practice of giving variable discounts may ultimately lead (in a competitive market) to corresponding decreases in the invoice price, that is not necessarily to be anticipated. It is more realistic to view an agreement to eliminate credit sales as extinguishing one form of competition among the sellers.

In any event, when a particular concerted activity entails an obvious risk of anticompetitive impact with no apparent potentially redeeming value, the fact that a practice may turn out to be harmless in a particular set of circumstances will not prevent its being declared unlawful *per se.*

An agreement among competing wholesalers to refuse to sell unless the retailer makes payment in cash, either in advance or upon delivery, is "plainly anticompetitive." Since it is merely one form of price-fixing, and since price-fixing agreements have been adjudged to lack any "redeeming virtue," it is conclusively presumed illegal without further examination under the rule of reason.[4]

Again, the key here is "agreement." Exchanges of credit information with competitors are permissible, provided there is no agreement to adopt common credit policies or to refuse to extend credit to any customer.

7. *What if I don't deal directly with competitors?* Your exposure is now minimal. Until recently the Supreme Court has held that "the fact that there is common ownership or control of the contracting corporations does not liberate them from the impact of the antitrust laws.[5] The courts had held that since you've availed yourself of the privilege of doing business through separate corporations, common ownership (generally) could not save you from any of the obligations that the law imposes on separate entities. There was an exception if all corporations involved were owned and controlled by one person who made all decisions for them. A conspiracy involves two or more people. One person acting alone cannot have the requisite "meeting of two or more minds."[6] This exception was commonly referred to as the "sole decision maker rule."

In keeping with its new emphasis on realistic business analysis in its decisions, in 1984 the Court recognized the political realities of corporate life and held that a parent corporation and its *wholly owned* subsidiary were not legally capable of conspiring with each other under Section 1 of the Sherman Act.[7] (Purely *unilateral* conduct is illegal only under

Section 2— *never* under Section 1.) Philosophically, the Court summed up the law in this area:

> The reason Congress treated concerted behavior more strictly than unilateral behavior is readily appreciated. Concerted activity inherently is fraught with anticompetitive risk. It deprives the marketplace of the independent centers of decisionmaking that competition assumes and demands. In any conspiracy, two or more entities that previously pursued their own interests separately are combining to act as one for their common benefit. This not only reduces the diverse directions in which economic power is aimed but suddenly increases the economic power moving in one particular direction. Of course, such mergings of resources may well lead to efficiencies that benefit consumers, but their anti-competitive potential is sufficient to warrant scrutiny even in the absence of inherent monopoly.
>
> . . . The distinction between unilateral and concerted conduct is necessary for proper understanding of the terms "contract, combination . . . or conspiracy" in Section 1. Nothing in the literal meaning of those terms excludes coordinated conduct among officers or employees of the *same* company. But it is perfectly plain that an internal "agreement" to implement a single, unitary firm's policies does not raise the antitrust dangers that Section 1 was designed to police. The officers of a single firm are not separate economic actors pursuing separate economic interests, so agreements among them do not suddenly bring together economic power that was previously pursuing divergent goals. Coordination within a firm is as likely to result from an effort to compete as from an effort to stifle competition. In the marketplace, such coordination may be necessary if a business enterprise is to compete effectively. For these reasons, officers or employees of the same firm do not provide the plurality of actors imperative for a Section 1 conspiracy.[8]

The "sole decision maker rule" is no longer an exception but the rule. The Court will now hold that the ultimate interests of the wholly owned subsidiary and parent are identical, so that the parent and wholly owned subsidiary must be viewed as a single economic unit.

Whether or not a *non*-wholly owned subsidiary is governed by the traditional analysis of "intra-enterprise conspiracy" remains to be seen. A corporation may, however, conspire with its agents if the agents are *aware* of the anticompetitive purpose for which they are being used.[9] For the present, any wholly owned or largely controlled subsidiary will be treated under the *Copperweld* analysis, both as to alleged conspiracy between such entities and as to alleged conspiracy with its own officers or employees.

Another area of risk not involving *your* competitors could be multiple customer or franchise arrangements in which the courts will deem a horizontal constraint to exist by reason of the acquiescence of the intermediaries for which you are the source of a common pricing or other distribution policy.

8. *What if we use divisions?* No problem—now, or even prior to *Copperweld*. Divisions are *not* separate legal entities capable of conspiracy.

9. *What if I engage in price-fixing to avoid ruinous competition?* The Court has held that any combination that tampers with price structures is engaged in an unlawful activity regardless of motive.[10]

10. *Who enforces these laws?* The primary responsibility for enforcing the federal antitrust laws lies with the Antitrust Division of the Department of Justice and the FTC. There is state action under state antitrust laws and some enforcement authority under the federal laws. In addition, private rights of action in injunctions or treble damages are provided, and criminal fines and penalties are covered.

11. *Can consumers sue?* Yes, a private consumer can sue under the antitrust laws. The law states that the illegal conduct must inflict injury directly on the consumer's business or property. If a consumer can demonstrate that he or she paid higher prices because of violations of antitrust laws, then that consumer suffered injury to property (i.e., money) and may have grounds to sue. The plaintiff must prove: (1) that the causal connection between an antitrust violation and an injury is sufficient to establish the violation as a substantial factor in the occurrence of the damage; and (2) that the illegal act was linked to activities of the plaintiff that the antitrust laws were intended to protect.

12. *What about conscious parallelism?* Similar practices by competitors alone will rarely support the inference of an agreement. Only when the pattern of action undertaken is consistent with the self-interest of the individual actors, were they acting alone, may an agreement be inferred solely from such parallel action. Otherwise, you must demonstrate through additional facts that the conscious parallel actions of the alleged conspirators were concerted and interdependent.

13. *What about fair trade laws?* The courts have ruled consistently that resale price maintenance illegally restrains trade. Such arrangements are designed to maintain prices and to prevent competition among those who trade on competing goods. For many years, however, the Miller-Tydings Act of 1937 permitted the states to authorize resale price maintenance. The goal of that statute was to allow the states to protect small retail establishments that Congress thought might otherwise be driven from the marketplace by large-volume discounters. But in 1975 that congressional permission was rescinded. The Consumer Goods Pricing Act of 1975 repealed the Miller-Tydings Act and related legislation. Consequently, the Sherman Act's ban on resale price maintenance now applies to fair trade contracts unless an industry or program enjoys a special antitrust immunity.

Conspiracies and Monopolies

A conspiracy isn't something that just takes place in a novel, nor does a monopoly mean controlling Boardwalk and Park Place. A look at the Sherman Act in a little more detail explains what constitutes conspiracy and monopolization violations.

A conspiracy has always had an odious connotation in the law, because it establishes that the offense has moved beyond the random act of an individual to an organized group of calculating individuals or institutions. This ability to magnify a violation through a larger body of participants demands that the law act swiftly and punitively. If a price conspiracy is agreed on among competitors, nothing further (such as harmful effects) need be proven to establish a violation of the Sherman Act.

To establish a *conspiracy* in violation of Section 1 of the Sherman Act, your accuser must establish that you and at least one other party got together to impose unreasonable restraints on interstate commerce. To prove a conspiracy, it must be demonstrated that you and one or more other parties combined to accomplish some unlawful purpose or to accomplish a lawful purpose by unlawful means. The kind of agreement or understanding that existed as to each defendant must also be established. To prove that the parties were involved in a conspiracy in unreasonable restraint of trade, your accuser must show either that any conspiracy that is proved falls within one of the categories of per se offenses,[11] such as price-fixing, group boycotts[12] (traditional, but fast eroding), or division of markets or customers, or that any such conspiracy is unreasonable when tested by the rule of reason.

If the court analyzes a case under the rule of reason, it looks for harmful effects. It then examines the legitimate beneficial effects of the agreement, that is, those that are procompetitive. In determining the effects, courts often look at the *purposes* of the defendants as a guide to interpreting effects. (The court does not examine broader social policy arguments other than the furtherance of competition and efficiency.) Finally, the court examines whether *less restrictive alternatives* exist for achieving the goals the defendants wish to achieve. If they are able to achieve the same results in another way, which does not injure competition, the court likely will rule against the defendants.

The law does not look with favor on overwhelming monopoly power that is *consciously* acquired, as opposed to monopoly power that is thrust on a firm or is a rational response to underlying economic forces such as scaled economies. *Unlike conspiracy,* monopoly power can be acquired by one firm with an intent to monopolize. No evidence of a conspiracy with other firms is necessary. Monopoly power enables a firm to fix prices on its own initiative without the "need" to depend on or seek out others to achieve this goal through a conspiracy. Overwhelming monopoly power, consciously acquired, necessarily runs afoul of the Sherman Act.

As noted above, the Sherman Act outlaws monopolies and attempts to monopolize. Section 2 of the Act reads as follows:

> "Every person who shall monopolize, or attempt to monopolize, or combine or conspire with any other person or persons, to monopolize any part of the trade or commerce among the several states, or with foreign

nations, shall be deemed guilty of a felony, and, on conviction thereof, shall be punished by fine not exceeding one million dollars if a corporation, or, if any other person, one hundred thousand dollars, or by imprisonment not exceeding three years or by both said punishments, in the discretion of the court."[13]

Most challenges of monopolistic behavior are brought under Section 2 of the Sherman Act. To establish a *monopolization* violation of Section 2 of the Sherman Act, your accuser must establish (1) that a relevant product and geographic market exists and (2) that you and one or more other parties possessed monopoly power within that relevant market and that you willfully acquired or maintained this power with the intent to monopolize.

To establish an *attempt* to monopolize the accuser must establish the following:

- intent to control prices or destroy competition with respect to a part of commerce;
- predatory or anticompetitive conduct directed at accomplishing the unlawful purpose; and
- a dangerous probability of success.[14]

We'll take a look at each of these three criteria in detail.

Intent

Unlike per se violations of Section 1, establishing per se violations of Section 2 is a highly complex area of law requiring considerable economic, marketing, and accounting data and analysis. The initial problem in analyzing an antitrust claim is in defining the correct market. Such analysis will encompass reliable measures of supply and demand elasticities and what barriers to entry surround this market.

A court first determines the *geographic* market in which a business operates (usually fairly obvious). Then it takes a look at the *product market* and submarket(s). The relevant product market is composed of products that are reasonably interchangeable for the purposes of cross-elasticity of demand, i.e.:

The controlling concept for market definition in this case is that of cross-elasticity or reasonable substitutability. Where different products may be substituted easily for each other, they are part of the same product market. Cross-elasticity varies according to many factors, including: uses, barriers to entry by new firms, physical characteristics, public or economic recognition of submarkets, distinct customers or specialized vendors . . . . . . Cross-elasticity differs, depending upon the buyer's or seller's point of view. A product may have a great amount of cross-elasticity for a seller who regards the producers of slightly different products as competitors, but little cross-elasticity for certain buyers who, regardless of price, must continue to use a specific product. The exact measure of cross-elasticity is determined by the number of buyers who, at a specified price, will shift and buy a different product. The greater the number of reasonable substitutes, the higher the measure of cross-elasticity.[15]

As to relevant submarkets, the courts will delineate them by *quality* coupled with differences. However, the threshold to delineate your submarkets may be difficult to determine. In the *Brown Shoe* case,[16] the government challenged a proposed merger between Brown Shoe and another shoe company on the grounds that it would create a risk of monopolization and would adversely affect competition. Brown Shoe contended that the two companies competed in different product markets: medium-priced shoes and low-priced shoes. The Court rejected this argument, holding that the district court had properly found that the division of product lines based on "price/quality" was "unrealistic."[17]

You won't have any better luck trying to argue a relevant submarket in waffles that are distinguishable by label and price but not quality;[18] or cosmetic quality differences such as "premium" vs. "economy" dog food[19] or beer.[20]

Conduct

After examining the defendant's intent to control prices to destroy competition, the court will determine the *anticompetitive effects* of the firm's activities. For example, is it engaged in predatory pricing? This is the dominant firm's deliberate sacrifice of current revenues through lower prices for the purpose of driving rivals out of the market. Once it has vanquished its rivals, the dominant firm can more than recoup its short-term losses through higher profits earned in the absence of competition.[21]

The effect of the firm's conduct will be determined by evaluating a variety of cost analysis factors. Two cost-based tests are the average variable cost test, which focuses on short-term cost, and the long-run incremental cost test, which measures the long-term incremental cost caused by the production of the product.[22] The general consensus is that the essential element of a predatory pricing case is proof that the defendant's prices were below average variable or long-range incremental costs. In quoting the MCI decision[23] a recent decision has again endorsed this criterion:

> . . . The ultimate danger of monopoly power is that prices will be too high, not too low. A rule of predation based on the failure to maximize profits would rob consumers of the benefits of any price reductions by dominant firms facing new competition. Such a rule would tend to freeze the prices of dominant firms at the monopoly levels and would prevent many pro-competitive price cuts beneficial to consumers in other purchases . . . . It is in the interests of competition to permit dominant firms to engage in vigorous competition, including price competition. We

therefore reject MCI's "profit maximization" theory and reaffirm this circuit's holding that liability for predatory pricing must be based upon proof of pricing below cost.[24]

Not addressed is the situation where a dominant firm uses extensive and expensive advertising aimed at product differentiation to eliminate new entrants. The firm then passes along to consumers the cost of such advertising by raising its price after it has defeated the new entrant. Is such advertising another form of predatory pricing?

In all of the above the Court is seeking to balance the interest of a competitive marketplace free of abuse without damaging the countervailing interest. So long as the dominant or monopolist's conduct is not predatory or exclusionary, the firm may compete vigorously to maintain or build its market share. This is the general trend of the cases, though it is a bit clouded by the Court's recent language in *Aspen Skiing,*[25] where the Court put undue weight on a firm's ability to offer an efficiency justification for its conduct.[26]

Probability of Success

Finally, the Court will look at the defendant's "dangerous probability of success." A firm may violate Section 2 of the Sherman Act not only by achieving a monopoly, but also by *attempting* to monopolize a market. As stated earlier, a monopolist possesses the power to control prices or exclude competition in some part of the trade or commerce. Thus, a firm embarking on a course of willful acquisition or maintenance of monopoly power in a relevant market is trying to achieve a position in a market whereby it may control prices or exclude competition,[27] and such conduct makes sense only because it eliminates competition.[28]

In an attempt-to-monopolize case, courts require evidence that the defendant possesses a significant market share. (Intent alone is not enough.) A firm that intends to monopolize a market and engages in conduct designed to achieve this goal is *not* guilty of a violation of Section 2 *until* it achieves a significant market share. The firm must have enough of the market in question to pose a dangerous probability of succeeding in achieving a monopoly.

As a matter of law, a successful monopolization claim requires a large market share of the relevant market. (Generally, a 75%-80% share of the market would justify a successful monopolization finding under Section 2.[29] Most courts and commentators agree that when a company's absolute market share is small, it may not be liable for attempts to monopolize because there is no dangerous probability that it will succeed.[30]

However, unlike geographic and product markets and anticompetitive conduct, the courts permit more subjectivity as to a "dangerous probability of success." In establishing the presence of these elements, the

Court will permit a dangerous probability of success to be inferred from proof of specific intent, which in turn can be inferred from conduct that forms the basis of a substantial claim of restraint of trade, or conduct that is exclusionary or threatening to competition.[31]

We've reviewed three illegal strategies: price-fixings, monopolization, and attempting to monopolize. Now we'll briefly review a narrow way in which, under certain circumstances, companies can legally enforce retail prices.

The Colgate Doctrine

Because it requires that there be a "contract, combination . . . or conspiracy," Sherman Act Section 1 does not proscribe independent action by a manufacturer; a manufacturer generally has a right to deal, or refuse to deal, with whomever it chooses, as long as it does so independently.[32]

The *Colgate* doctrine is often argued by those involved in price-fixing. The *Colgate* case attempted to reconcile the prohibition on agreements between manufacturers and distributors to fix prices with the freedom of a manufacturer to sell to whom it chooses. The Supreme Court observed that a manufacturer may freely exercise its own independent discretion as to the parties with which it will deal and may announce in advance the circumstances under which it will refuse to sell to customers that fail to abide by its prices. A manufacturer may also terminate business dealings with dealers who sell its products above the stated price, or who don't follow its distribution requirements as to resale.[33]

However, cases setting forth what does violate the Sherman Act indicate that, as a practical matter, price-fixing will rarely be sustainable under *Colgate*. The firm's right to exercise independent judgment as to whom it will deal with is limited to cases where the absence of any purpose to create or maintain a monopoly is found.[34] The manufacturer may not enter into agreements with its customer obliging them to sell at fixed prices or use any other form of coercion, including termination and possibly even the threat of termination.

One example was the *Coors* case. Coors argued the *Colgate* doctrine in defense of the termination of its distributor. The distributor argued that the "suggested prices" were enforced. The court noted that:

> Coors' ideas about proper prices at the wholesale and retail level may only have been couched in terms of suggestions, but having in mind Coors' relative economic clout, particularly its power to cancel valuable distributor franchises almost at will, it seems clear that there is evidence that Coors engaged in price maintenance through suggestions which the distributors could not refuse.[35]

In a related case[36] the Court held that Colgate applies only to the manufacturer/retailer relationship and that a manufacturer may not threaten to cut off wholesalers that sell below the specified price. If you fix prices or enforce suggested prices, you are exposing yourself to Sherman Act enforcement. One suggestion to help you protect yourself is to print "suggested price" immediately adjacent to the preprinted price— and don't do any arm-twisting to enforce your suggested price.

Reciprocal Dealing Agreements

Although collusion between competitors constitutes the most obvious and most dangerous violation of the antitrust laws, violations may be found in restrictive arrangements with customers and suppliers. Unlike price-fixing, which is per se illegal (i.e., absolutely illegal without regard to the reasonableness of the activity involved), the legality of a reciprocal agreement is judged by the rule of reason. Often reciprocal agreements (see Section II on tie-ins—a related legal issue) are a naked abuse of market power and will be viewed as such. You must review all such agreements or arrangements in advance with your counsel.

Reciprocity occurs when you use your large purchasing power with a supplier to achieve a coercive or voluntary agreement that "I will buy from you if you will buy from me." Reciprocity is generally considered an anticompetitive practice, because it denies competitors an equal opportunity to sell on the basis of price, quality, service. Such dealings are always unlawful when your company is using its strong market position and purchasing power to promote sales—that is, you buy products from a supplier only on the condition that such supplier buys from you.

These agreements are to be distinguished from "mutual patronage" reciprocity, where both parties are on an equal footing. As one court stated:

> [T]he actual or potential implementation of coercive reciprocity, which presupposes the existence of leverage (i.e., large purchases from, and currently small sales to, the prospect), is inimical to a competitive economic society. "Mutual patronage" reciprocity, on the other hand, occurs when both parties stand on equal footing with reference to purchasing power inter se, yet agree to purchase from one another. While the former practice certainly is the more offensive, the latter arrangements are equally disruptive of the competitive processes.[37]

As with price-fixing, an agreement or understanding to deal reciprocally may be proved by circumstantial evidence. To avoid even the appearance of this situation, document that each purchasing decision by your company is made independently of any consideration of whether the supplier is purchasing other products from your company. Demonstrate that profit maximization is your overriding goal. One way to decrease your exposure here is to prohibit marketing and purchasing personnel from dealing jointly with customers or suppliers. Likewise, do not keep statistical records that combine the sales and purchase activity of various suppliers or customers.

Conclusion

The exchange of price information among competitors has a chilling effect on the vigor of price competition. Regardless of whether they improve competition or even lower prices, actual price-fixing agreements among competitors are illegal.

Don't forget that areas such as warranties and credit terms are essential, bargained-for competitive assets that must not be fixed any more than price. Watch "suggested price," and don't enforce resale prices after you've sold an item. If you want better pricing control, explore with your counsel a consignment relationship. Here, you will retain title as well as risk of loss until the item is purchased by the ultimate buyer.

Finally, watch your intracompany statements and memoranda. Such communications may one day be analyzed by government investigators or private litigants as possible evidence in antitrust litigation. Will an outsider misconstrue certain statements? For example, if you are preparing an analysis of market data, including pricing or other competitive elements, specify your information source and internal research purpose to prevent the misapprehension that you resorted to illicit communication with your competitors.

Stay alert—your career is on the line! When in doubt, consult your attorney at once. It will almost always be a false alarm, but here your attorney can give you a few "but fors" on how close you might have come to adverse exposure.

ENDNOTES

(1) 15 USCA Sec. 1.

(2) For purposes of this discussion, assume that all transactions are in interstate commerce. See *Brillhart v. Mutual Medical Ins., Inc.,* 768 F.2d 196 (7th Cir. 1985).

(3) *Esco Corp. v. United States,* 340 F.2d 1000 (9th Cir. 1965).

(4) *Catalino, Inc. et al, v. Target Sales, Inc. et al.,* 446 US 643 (1980).

(5) *Timken Roller Bearing Co. v. United States,* 341 US 593, 598 (1951). See also *United States v. Yellow Cab,* 322 US 218 (1947); *Kiefer-Steward Co. v. Joseph E. Seagram and Sons, Inc.,* 340 US 211 (1951); *Perma Life Mufflers, Inc. v. International Parts Corp.,* 392 US 134 (1968); and *Minnesota Bearing Co. v. White Motor Corp.,* 470 F.2d 1323 (8th Cir. 1973).

(6) *Harvey v. Fearless Ferris Wholesale, Inc.,* 589 F.2d 451, 457 (9th Cir. 1979).

(7) *Copperweld Corp. v. Independence Tube Corp.,* 104 S.Ct. 2731 (1984).

(8) Id., p. 2740. See also *Schwimmer v. Sony Corp. of America,* 677 F.2d 946, 953 (CA2), cert. den., 459 US 1007, 103 S.Ct. 362, 74 L.Ed.2d 398 (1982); *Tose v. First Pennsylvania Bank, N.A.,* 648 F.2d 879, 893-894 (CA3), cert. den., 454 US 893, 102 S.Ct. 390, 70 L.Ed.2d 208 (1981). For a look at Section 1 and the professions, see *Smith v. Northern Michigan Hospitals, Inc.,* 703 F.2d 942 (1983).

(9) *Albrecht v. Herald Co.,* 390 US 145, 88 S.Ct. 869, 19 L.Ed.2d 998 (1968).

(10) *United States v. Socony Vacuum Oil Co.,* 310 US 150 (1940).

(11) *Broadcast Music, Inc. v. CBS,* 441 US 1 (1979).

(12) *Pacific Stationery and Printing Co. v. Northwest Wholesale Stationers, Inc.,* 715 F.2d 1393 (9th Cir. 1983), rev'd, 105 S.Ct. 2613 (1985). See also *Goss v. Memorial Hospital System* 789 F.2d 353 (5th Cir. 1986); *FTC v. Indiana Federation of Dentists,* 54 U.S.L.W. 4531 (1986); *Rothery Storage and Van Co., et al. v. Atlas Van Lines, Inc.,* 792 F.2d 210 (1986) cert. den. 107 S.Ct. 880 (1987); *Silver v. N.Y. Stock Exchange,* 373 US 341 (1963); *Fashion Originators Guild of America, Inc. v. FTC,* 312 US 457 (1941).

(13) 15 USCA Sec. 2.

(14) *Chillicothe Sand & Gravel Co. v. Martin Marietta Corp.,* 615 F.2d 427, 430 (7th Cir. 1980). See also *Eliason Corp. v. National Sanitation Foundation,* 485 F.Supp. 1062, 1075 (1977).

(15) *Stepp v. Ford Motor Credit Co.,* 673 F.Supp. 583 (D.C. Wisc. 1985). See also *U.S. v. E. I. DuPont de Nemours,* 351 US 377, 404, 76 S.Ct. 994, 100 L.Ed. 1264 (1956) (product market determined to be not only cellophane, but all flexible packaging materials) and *American Key Corp. v. Cole Nat. Corp.,* 762 F.2d 1569 (1985).

(16) *Brown Shoe Co. v. United States,* 370 US 294, 325, 82 S.Ct. 1502, 1523, 8 L.Ed.2d 510 (1962); see, e.g., *M.A.P. v. Texaco, Inc.,* 691 F.2d 1303, 1307-08 (9th Cir. 1982).

(17) Id. at 326, 82 S.Ct. at 1524.

(18) *Nifty Foods Corp. v. Great Atlantic & Pacific Tea Co.,* 614 F.2d 832, 840 (1980).

(19) *Liggett & Myers, Inc. v. FTC,* 567 F.2d 1273 (4th Cir. 1977). See also *Gregoris Motors v. Nissan Motor Corp. in USA,* 630 F.Supp. 902 (E.D.N.Y. 1986) (Nissan v. "all car" market).

(20) *United States v. Jos. Schlitz Brewing Co.,* 253 F.Supp. 129 (N.D. Cal.), *aff'd per curiam,* 385 US 37, 87 S.Ct. 240, 17 L.Ed. 2d 35, reh. den., 385 US 1021, 87 S.Ct. 702, 17 L.Ed.2d 560 (1966).

(21) *MCI Communications Corp. v. American Telephone & Telegraph Co.,* 708 F.2d 1081, 1112 (7th Cir.), cert. den., 104 S.Ct. 234, 78 L.Ed.2d 226 (1983). See also *Janich Bros., Inc. v. American Distilling Co.,* 570 F.2d 848, 856 (9th Cir. 1977), cert. den., 439 US 829, 99 S.Ct. 103, 58 L.Ed.2d 122 (1978).

(22) For a good in-depth analysis comparison of a variety of these tests see *Jays Foods, Inc. v. Frito-Lay, Inc.,* 614 F.Supp. 1073 (D.C. Ill. 1985).

(23) See note 21, 708 F.2d at 1114.

(24) See note 22, p. 1082.

(25) *Aspen Skiing Co. v. Aspen Highlands Skiing Corp.,* 105 S.Ct. 2847 (1985). See also *Shoppin' Bag of Pueblo, Inc. v. Dillon Companies, Inc.* 783 F.2d 159 (10th Cir. 1986).

(26) Id., p. 2860. For more "traditional" case law see *Transamerica Computer Co. v. IBM,* 698 F.2d 1377 (9th Cir.), cert. den., 104 S.Ct. 370 (1983); see, e.g., *Foremost Pro Color, Inc. v. Eastman Kodak Co.,* 703 F.2d 534 (9th Cir. 1983), cert. den., 104 S.Ct. 1315 (1948); *Berkey Photo, Inc. v. Eastman Kodak Co.,* 603 F.2d 263 (2d Cir. 1979), cert. den., 444 US 1093 (1980) and *Telex Corp. v. IBM,* 510 F.2d 894 (10th Cir.), cert. den., 423 US 802 (1975).

(27) *United States v. Grinnell Corp.,* 384 US 563, 570-71, 86 S.Ct. 1698, 1703-04, 16 L.Ed.2d 778 (1966); *Greyhound Computer Corp. v. IBM,* 559 F.2d 488, 492 (9th Cir. 1977), cert. den., 434 US 1040, 98 S.Ct. 782, 54 L.Ed. 2d 790 (1978), and the existence of actual injury to competition in that market. See *Betaseed,* 681 F.2d at 1231-32 (1982); *California Computer Products v. IBM,* 613 F.2d 727, 735 (9th Cir. 1979) and *United States v. Aluminum Co. of America,* 148 F.2d 416 (2d Cir. 1945).

(28) *Trace X Chemical, Inc. v. Canadian Industries, Inc.,* 738 F.2d 261 (8th Cir. 1984), cert. den., 105 S.Ct. 911, 83 L.Ed.2d 925 (1985). See also *Conoco, Inc, v. Inman Oil Co., Inc.,* 774 F.2d 895 (1985) and *Times-Picayune Publishing Co. v. U.S.,* 345 US 594 (1953).

(29) *United States v. Aluminum Co. of America,* 148 F.2d 416 (2d Cir. 1945). See also *Hiland Dairy, Inc. v. Kroger Co.,* 402 F.2d 968, 623 F.Supp. 583 (1985), 974 (8th Cir. 1968), cert. den., 395 US 961 (1969).

(30) *Domed Stadium Hotel, Inc. v. Holiday Inns, Inc.,* 732 F.2d 480, 490-491 (5th Cir. 1984).

(31) *William Inglis & Sons Baking Co. v. ITT Continental Baking Co.,* 668 F.2d 1014, 1027, 1029 (9th Cir. 1981), cert. den., 103 S.Ct. 57, 74 L.Ed.2d 61 (1982). See also *General Business Systems v. North American Philips Corp.,* 699 F.2d 965 (1983).

(32) *Monsanto Co. v. Spray-Rite Service Corp.,* 465 US 752, 104 S.Ct. 1464, 1469, 79 L.Ed. 2d 775 (1984); *United States v. Colgate & Co.,* 250 US 300, 307, 39 S.Ct. 465, 468 (1919).

(33) *Pants 'N' Stuff Shed House v. Levi Strauss,* 619 F.Supp.945 (D.C.N.Y. 1985).

(34) Id. note 32, *Colgate,* p. 307, 39 S.Ct. 475.

(35) *R. E. Spriggs Co. v. Adolph Coors Co.,* 156 Cal Rptr 738, 741, 94 Cal.3d 419, cert. den., 444 US 1076 (1979).

(36) *U.S. v. Parke-Davis and Co.,* 362 U.S. 29 (1960).

(37) *U.S. v. General Dynamics,* 258 F.Supp. 36, 59 (S.D.N.Y. 1966).

CHAPTER 13

TRADE ASSOCIATION MEMBERS— COMPETITORS OR CO-CONSPIRATORS?

You've most likely attended one or more trade association meetings; at almost all such meetings or similar meetings, you rub elbows with your competitors. These affairs can be socially useful, provide information, and assist an industry in self-policing. These affairs can also result in fines and prison terms for unwary participants.

Trade associations have always been fraught with potential antitrust problems, because they constitute ready-made combinations of competitors. In this chapter, we discuss how a trade association can create problems as well as avoid them. If you have doubts as to any activity you might be involved in, consult with your firm's counsel immediately. Your firm's antitrust compliance committee (discussed later in this chapter) should be made aware of all participation in trade association activities.

Certain agreements, such as those concerned with the dissemination of general, relevant information, are lawful so long as there is no indication of a purpose to inhibit an individual firm's competitive decision making. Other agreements that directly (and often, indirectly) involve price-fixing (depression, pegging, stabilizing, etc.), boycotts, standard industry contracts, product specifications, or allocation of customers or territories will (if discovered) probably involve you with the Antitrust Division of the U.S. Department of Justice (at least for an initial screening as to the reasonableness of your agreements).

Their subsequent action against you may well result in severe, non-tax-deductible fines or an undesired sojourn in a federal facility. You may also have some Section 5 (FTC Act) exposure. This is broader than the antitrust laws. Section 5's prohibition against unfair methods of competition applies to "incipient" restraint of trade. This consists of acts and practices that are only potential violations of the Sherman Act (and thus not prohibited by the Sherman Act) but, if allowed to continue, would result in unreasonable restraint of trade.

343

The Federal Trade Commission Act has been interpreted to give the Commission the authority to cut short such acts and practices. Thus, the Federal Trade Commission has the power to intervene where a potential violation is seen, and there is a reasonable probability the violation will actually occur. Remember that the downside risk of a Section 5 FTC violation is not terribly large an injunction. Section 5 is not an "antitrust law" within the meaning of the Clayton Act, which would allow private plaintiffs to sue.

Any agreement among competitors that limits their competition in some significant respect will prompt close scrutiny; such agreements include gentlemen's agreements and those that "improve" competition. This chapter takes a look at antitrust issues related to trade associations (and also at "sham litigation") and, finally, discusses the heavy costs of Sherman Act violations.

You And Your Trade Association

The following scenario takes you through some of the "gray area" issues that could arise at a hypothetical trade association gathering. As you read this, you might consider which resolutions you would endorse, which you might oppose, and the point at which you would formally and physically withdraw from the meeting.

At the Meeting

In April, a number of firms send representatives to attend a specially convened meeting of the Widget Trade Association. Attendance is large, because the industry has seen increased price competition in the face of declining demand. Some firms are threatened with bankruptcy, while newer firms are entering the marketplace, further jeopardizing the others.

This disturbs all involved, since over the years the members have developed a pleasant rapport. All realize that those let go from the failing firms will enter a market that is not hiring. Individual careers will be destroyed, and no one's bottom line is being enhanced by the price wars. The general consensus is to reach some form of accommodation.

The meeting is called to order. Mary, a financial analyst representing a New York City widget firm, proposes that the association obtain and publish for members average price data so that the membership may have an idea of what is going on in the industry. The motion is carried, and the association designates one of its statisticians to set up a procedure immediately. However, Joe, an attorney for a Dallas firm, leaves the meeting, protesting that this is price-fixing. To allay Joe's fears, a new motion is entertained and approved to retain an independent outside accounting firm to gather and disseminate the data in question. Informed of this action, Joe still refuses to accept this policy.

Then George, a buyer of widgets for the eastern region, argues that all the price data in the world is useless, because the association would be comparing apples with oranges. Without a uniform warranty for quality, different types of widgets could be sold. He cites numerous instances of widgets that vary from firm to firm and demands that the trade association certify one standard widget to "protect" the consumer.

The association agrees to promulgate a set of standards and a certification procedure that would identify widgets that meet a definable quality standard. A number of members argue that this is policing of the industry. Counsel for the association states that the standards would not be enforced by a boycott of noncertified products.

John, a legislative administrator for the association, then states that the group is spinning its wheels. He proposes that the association voluntarily raise a war chest to lobby Congress to bar new firms from entering the market. Judith, also a legislative expert for the association, protests that this could take years. John then proposes that the association organize an initiative in California, the most visible state and also the base of the larger widget employers, to get this issue before the voters. The vote in seven months would receive national attention similar to that given Proposition 13; Congress would be moved to act accordingly.

Judith counters that any measure to bar competitors might be unconstitutional. Further, the high visibility the association would attain in attempting to eliminate competition would invariably bring indictments before a vote could be taken. Judith argues that the members' money would be better spent in an intimidation campaign of publicity against various key legislators. Judith's motion is defeated; before John's motion is voted on, Judith asks that the minutes show she left before the vote. She leaves and John's motion carries.

The members leave the meeting generally pleased that they finally are doing something constructive. Later that night, Mary, George, and John meet at John's home. They are a bit uneasy. Judith had phoned each one earlier, stating that she was glad she formally left and that they would wish they had done likewise. She has accused them and the association of involving themselves in price-fixing, controlling prices, establishing a constructive boycott, and blatantly and unethically attempting to manipulate government bodies to legislate illegal laws. Was Judith correct?

Price-Fixing Issue

Price-fixing has been defined as "any combination formed for the purpose of and with the effect of raising, depressing, fixing, pegging or stabilizing the price of a commodity in interstate commerce."[1] Did the Widget Trade Association create an inference of in price-fixing?

Probably not—the motion itself as carried was not price-fixing. However, the surrounding atmosphere could invite scrutiny, since the meeting was called to try to stabilize a chaotic price market. Keep in mind that the existence of the unlawful agreement may be inferred from a course of conduct or business behavior.[2] In fact, conspiracies are usually proved on the basis of circumstantial evidence. Considered separately, the circumstances may be entirely innocent. But viewed as a whole, they may be sufficient to permit an inference of a conspiracy to fix prices. On close examination, the association's motion as carried appears to be an effort to circulate information pertaining to general, *past* industry pricing which would *not* identify specific parties or transactions. Further, and more importantly, we are not dealing with a concentrated market that might tend to stabilize prices based on this information.

In this case, the trade association is fulfilling one of its primary and necessary functions—providing general information to assist members in more efficient competition. However, any exchange of information, whatever its nature or purpose, may be presumed to have an anticompetitive effect if prices *stabilize*. The association should note this in each information paper disseminated to its members. It should also specify that there is no association commitment to comply with these prices and that in fact the association expressly discourages any such conformity. Finally, the association should (as it did here) retain an *independent third party* to collect and disseminate the data. Doing this internally invites investigations and other problems.

Taking these steps is about as far as you should go, even in a highly competitive industry lacking oligopolistic tendencies. If the association had agreed to disseminate data relating to current prices or current production or relating to specific members, then a serious anticompetitive situation would have existed.[3] Obviously, had the association published suggested prices or required members to adhere to such prices, this would present a price-fixing situation.

In conclusion, the circulation of price information can give rise to an agreement to fix prices. However, general, average, dated, and unidentifiable industry price data collected and disseminated by an independent accounting firm should not present an anticompetitive problem, unless there is a tendency toward price stabilization or evidence that such exchanges were undertaken for the purpose of regulating prices.

Certification of Standards

There are two issues here—uniform warranties and the formal adoption of standards. The former should be avoided. Generalized guidelines are probably lawful, but they tend to promote uniformity.

Uniform warranties by competitors are prohibited. The warranty can be an essential, bargained-for, competitive asset every bit as significant as a bargained-for price.

As to the proposed standard of minimum quality, this can present problems even though designed with the best of motives, that is, consumer protection and preserving the reputation of the industry from inferior product entrants. When in doubt, you should discuss with your counsel whether an advisory opinion rather than a set of standards would be preferable. Good intent, in and of itself, is no defense if it results in an unlawful restraint of trade. A trade association will not be treated differently from a business competitor, especially when it is the association's standing and influence that makes the conspiracy effective and possible.[4] However, our hypothetical widget association's set of standards and certification procedure would probably survive because

- there is a statement expressly providing that no boycott or other restriction will be imposed on members or others,
- no sanctions will be imposed on members for a departure from the recommended standards, and
- not stated, but necessary, is that the association will not attempt to restrict the activities of members in any way relating to prices or conditions of sale.

If any of the three points are omitted, the standards and certification procedure would probably be proscribed. An example of the certification issue concerns a trade group's setting standards for refrigerators in the food service industry. A manufacturer that failed to qualify argued that the certification was an illegal restraint of trade. The court disagreed, stating that there was no direct or indirect boycott or evidence of price-fixing, division of markets, or division of customers. The court held the certification to be pro-competitive:

> [T]he record demonstrates that the primary purpose behind the NSF standards program has been pro-competitive in attempting to promote uniform standards among public health jurisdictions, thereby minimizing the number of differing, even conflicting, requirements, reducing costs for all manufacturers, and increasing the number of manufacturers able to compete in each jurisdiction.[5]

In conclusion, an association should not adopt uniform warranties. An association may adopt a reasonable product standard and certification program, provided it does not effect a boycott, fix prices, exclude members or other competitors, or control production.

Legislative Campaign

There is no doubt that the legislative campaign would seek official sanction for anticompetitive practices. Ironically, this strategy is most likely legal! Attempts by an association to lobby a government body are absolutely immune from antitrust liability, according to the Supreme Court.[6] This was a triumph of the First Amendment over the Sherman Act.

The legality of these activities turns on the applicability of the *Noerr-Pennington* doctrine. That doctrine allows individuals or businesses to petition the government, free of the threat of antitrust liability, for action that may have anticompetitive consequences. *Noerr-Pennington* protection is guaranteed by the First Amendment and extends to petitions for selfish, even anticompetitive ends. As the Court explained:

> . . . construction of the Sherman Act that would disqualify people from taking a public position on matters in which they were financially interested would thus deprive the government of a valuable source of information and, at the same time, deprive the people of their right to petition in the very instances in which that right may be of the most importance to them.[7]

In short, the association's purpose in seeking the political action is irrelevant. Further, Judith's question on the constitutionality of measures to bar competition is not controlling—an association is constitutionally protected in any activity that is a genuine effort to influence legislation. Once the genuine effort is established, the association is not obligated or expected to predict the results of a constitutional challenge in the courts. A subsequent declaration by the court of unconstitutionality will not expose the association or its members to antitrust penalties, regardless of their anticompetitive purpose.

These same principles govern attempts to influence the full gamut of political life: legislative, executive, administrative, and judicial bodies, as well as attempts to legislate through the initiative process.[8] Ironically, Judith's suggested publicity campaign (ostensibly at less cost and exposure) would probably come under the "sham" exception, that is, "[t]here may be situations in which a publicity campaign, ostensibly directed toward influencing governmental action, is a mere sham to cover what is actually nothing more than an attempt to interfere directly with the business relationships of a competitor and the application of the Sherman Act would be justified."[9]

The sham exception comes into play when the participant is not seeking official action by a governmental body. Over the years, as competitors have attempted, with greater frequency, to succeed in the courts rather than by competition on the merits in the marketplace, the courts have struggled to define precisely what constitutes unprotected sham litigation and how it must be proved. A publicity campaign aimed at intimidation rather than concerted government action probably would result in the courts' imposing sanctions for an unlawful violation of the antitrust laws. The sham exception would encompass lobbying or litigation efforts that are solely directed toward either interfering with another's business interests or seeking to bar another from meaningful access to adjudicatory tribunals.[10]

One suit *generally* is not enough to create a sham. As the Court stated:

> One claim, which a court or agency may think baseless, may go unnoticed; but a pattern of baseless, repetitive claims may emerge which leads the factfinder to conclude that the administrative and judicial processes have been abused.[11]

However, if a lawsuit is filed solely to interfere with another's business relationships or to deny another access to a tribunal, it should not be necessary that a second, third, fourth, or fifth lawsuit be filed before this conduct is considered a sham.[12] The Court quoted another figurative opinion:

> I am not convinced that the court intended to give every dog one free bite, thus making it an irrebuttable presumption that the first lawsuit was not a sham regardless of overwhelming evidence indicating otherwise. . . .Although the frequency of litigation is a probative factor in a putatively sham litigation situation, it is not by any means determinative.[13]

Your best defense if accused of a sham is simply to *win*. The fact that you obtained the relief you are seeking from the legislature indicates your efforts were not a sham. As held by one court:

> It should also be noted the Defendants were successful in their lobbying efforts. They went to the legislature with a proposal and the legislature adopted this proposal. This is a classic case of a group of persons petitioning their government for relief and receiving the relief they request. Such activity is protected by the Sherman Act.[14]

In addition to these so-called sham exceptions, some courts have also declined to apply *Noerr-Pennington* protection in situations where the government acted as a buyer or seller in the marketplace and was made a victim of anticompetitive conduct.[15]

In conclusion, the First Amendment offers an association and its membership free and unlimited access to petition its government regardless of intent or purpose so long as its efforts are "genuine." A publicity campaign undertaken for purposes other than influencing government action would probably not be protected and, therefore, could result in antitrust sanctions on the association and its members.[16] This whole discussion should encourage you to vigorously pursue the profit preservation center/governmental interaction suggestions set forth in Chapter 24.

Non-Price Predation

Non-price predation is strategic behavior designed to raise a competitor's costs through litigation, administrative action, and the like.

A competitor might be delayed or even barred from market entry because of legal costs and inability to attract capital.

The anticompetitive strategy may be hard for your opponent to define to a court. It might be easier if you are seeking to wrap him or her up in a week of bureaucratic red tape. As for the sham, the court looks to infer improper intent, primarily from objective factors—in particular, the likelihood that the relief ostensibly sought could not repay the costs of invoking governmental processes. This approach does not require baselessness but rather an evaluation of the petitioner's economic incentives, costs, and potential rewards in petitioning a court or government agency. As one court noted:

> If all nonmalicious litigation were immunized from government regulation by the First Amendment, the tort of abuse of process would be unconstitutional—something that, so far as we know, no one believes. . . . If abuse of process is not constitutionally protected, no more should litigation that has an improper anticompetitive purpose be protected, even though the plaintiff has a colorable claim.
>
> . . . [I]t has long been thought that litigation could be used for improper purposes even where there is probable cause for litigation; and if the improper purpose is to use litigation as a tool for suppressing competition in its antitrust sense, it becomes a matter of antitrust concern.[17]

Failing all of the above appeals, you might utilize Section 5 of the FTC Act. The FTC's remedial rights may be more effective in these ambiguous areas.

To Sum Up

Distinguishing between trade association activities that serve to enhance competition by improving a member's knowledge and those whose purpose is to eliminate competition is difficult.[18]

As a general rule, any activity (such as price stabilization, production, or allocation of territory or customers) that substitutes handshake cooperation for arm's-length competition is suspect. Obviously, as an informed business person, you are aware of your duty to anticipate activities or involvement that might place you in a compromising situation for both yourself and your firm. As a general rule, avoid even being present at discussions of an improper nature. If nothing else, it reflects on your professional judgment.

If, however, you are unwittingly placed in a situation where you might be linked to the questionable acts of an association or its individual members, make every effort to demonstrate that *you* did not condone such acts. Once you are aware of even the inference of questionable conversation/or proposals, immediately and formally disassociate yourself from the group and the meeting. If minutes are kept, have this disassociation reflected in them. Then immediately speak to your firm's counsel. Relate exactly what was said and ratified, exactly what steps you were involved in, and when you disassociated yourself (if at all) from the meeting. The conversation is confidential, and the advice will be specific and personally geared to your individual situation.[19]

This chapter reviewed at length trade association exposure because the obvious accessibility of competitors in a congenial manner is fertile ground for subtle understandings that may result in a felony conviction. However, an unwary individual can be just as vulnerable at a lunch meeting, or even when talking on the phone. *Prompt consultation with counsel in these circumstances could be the best career move you ever make.*

Are There Other Exceptions?

As discussed above, you are permitted to join with others to lobby for government action, even if the desired intent is to act with an anticompetitive purpose. Other exemptions include

- organized labor (except where collusion with industry members is involved).[20]
- agricultural and fishing cooperatives.
- certain contracts necessary to the national defense.
- the insurance industry. (Congress has delegated to the states the power to regulate and tax this industry.[21])
- state action which, if done by private parties, would be illegal.[22]

The so-called sovereign compulsion doctrine[23] has been narrowed.[24] For example, cities are not necessarily states for the purpose of the state action doctrine.[25] To come within the parameters of the state action doctrine it probably remains law that you must show a clear articulation of state policy, and active supervision of such policy should be in evidence.

A Word About Memberships

You and those working under you should not hold membership in any trade association in which you don't actively participate. A "paper membership" may look good on your resume, but it won't help you learn what's really going on. Without active participation you are not in a position to quickly disassociate yourself from a questionable course of conduct.

Your attendance is also necessary to make sure a responsible and accountable officer of the association itself is in attendance. Finally, active participation includes a review of the agenda prior to the meeting. You should make it clear that you will not support any "informal" ad hoc groups or any meeting where an agenda has not been prepared in advance.

The High Cost Of Sherman Act Violations

With the Reagan administration's emphasis on economic growth and deemphasis on overkill regulations during the last several years, a tendency to deemphasize legal compliance can crop up. That would be a mistake for you personally and for your business. This "New Opportunity" society has not lessened the enforcement of the Sherman Act.

Price Violations Hurt

As you are aware, the role of the IRS auditor is to collect more taxes. Few individuals or businesses consider an encounter with the IRS pleasant. It is something we prefer to avoid and so we adjust our affairs accordingly.

By the same token, the prime objective of the Antitrust Division attorney is to put people in jail. It is a mark of professional success if the attorney can obtain a long jail sentence. Fines and other deterrents are widely perceived as mere slaps on the wrist—not adequate punishment for white collar crime.

You may already be familiar with the *Paper Labels* [26] case. The defendants were members of the industry that manufactures paper labels that are affixed to the containers of a variety of canned and bottled products. The industry had a diffuse structure with low barriers to entry for an undifferentiated product. The possibility that purchasers would ship to another, more competitive supplier forced companies in the industry to keep their costs and prices as low as possible.

These businesses were under constant pressure to maintain their market position. Manufacturers of paper labels began to exchange (primarily at trade association meetings) increasingly explicit information concerning pricing decisions and policies, and eventually divided the market through pricing agreements.

The indictment that followed charged nine corporate and eight individual defendants with Sherman Act violations. All eight of the individual defendants and eight of the nine corporate defendants ultimately pleaded nolo contendere. (There is a difference between a nolo contendere plea and a plea of guilty as far as your legal exposure is concerned; the extent of jail sentences as well as fines may be affected.)

In *Paper Labels,* the corporate defendants were fined from $10,000 to $50,000 each. Three individual defendants were fined from $4,000 to $15,000 and received suspended jail sentences ranging from three to six months. They were placed on one year's probation conditioned on the making of 12 speeches to business or civic groups about the acts for which they were convicted.

These alternatives were met with much criticism as to leniency and because of First Amendment considerations. They also fueled the ongoing crime/punishment debate. One school of thought holds that antitrust crimes generally are not committed for personal gain, and that most defendants have no prior criminal record and are typically perceived as respected members of the community. The contrary view is that these are not crimes of passion but of calculation, and only vigorous and punitive sentencing will deter others.

In the *Alton Box* [27] case, most of the large corporations in the paper folding carton industry were charged with conspiring to fix prices. Price accommodation was accomplished by suppliers offering exceptionally high bids for short-term contracts so a competitor would receive the contract.

This conduct was reciprocated by the other members of the paper folding carton industry. Through these cover bids, the container suppliers could maintain their contracts and prices. This practice virtually eliminated competition within the industry.

Forty-seven defendants pleaded nolo contendere. Initially all of the individual defendants were imprisoned for terms of between 24 hours and 15 days. Subsequently 15 of them (including CEOs) were sentenced to brief prison terms and were personally fined as much as $35,000. Seventeen others were fined between $500 and $30,000 and placed on probation. The remaining 15 were fined between $100 and $2,500.

While not the slaughter seen in the famed electrical contracts conspiracy, these executives' careers were certainly not helped by the criminal convictions. Nevertheless, the Antitrust Division sought greater penalties. When the presiding judge indicated he was considering alternatives to imprisonment, Assistant Attorney General Donald I. Baker appeared before the judge to criticize sentences imposed in previous price-fixing cases and to ask the court to permit the division to submit sentencing recommendations for the individuals involved.

During the course of that appearance, Baker argued strongly for substantial prison sentences to deter others from committing antitrust violations. The judge eventually allowed the division to submit its recommendations and entered tentative sentences for the individuals ranging up to 60 days imprisonment, with alternative community service for a few added on.

While not achieving all its goals in the courts, the Antitrust Division's message reached Congress. The penal provisions of Section 1 were raised to felony status to allow a $1 million maximum fine for corporate defendants and a $100,000 maximum fine with a three-year jail sentence for individual defendants. This felony exposure and increase in fines eliminates much of the earlier attractiveness of a nolo contendere plea. [28]

Commenting on this new law and refuting the argument that such defendants are not "socially dangerous" and deserving of incarceration, the attorney general at that time stated:

"Antitrust violations are not casual crimes. Business tycoons are not seized by a fit of passion that compels them to rig bids. Corporate executives do not gather in the board room to fix prices because they are in the throes of a joint, irresistible impulse.

They violate the antitrust laws deliberately—because they want to and because they feel it's good for business.

Well, it's not good for the public's business. It's not good for the free enterprise system. And we are determined that this kind of lawbreaking will be uncovered and prosecuted as vigorously as any other.

Those in the business community who would break the laws had better face one hard fact of life: The day of the easy gouge, the fast ripoff is over. The Department of Justice will not look the other way when business imposes upon the public what are nothing more than totalitarian practices and totalitarian disdain for our democratic way of life.

Imprisonment has been increasingly accepted as the sanction which fits the antitrust offender. During the past five years, over 30 individuals have been sentenced to jail upon conviction in at least a dozen separate cases. Prior to 1970, individual defendants who participated in the massive Electrical Equipment and Plumbing Fixtures price fixing conspiracies, cases which in their enormity approach this conspiracy, were sentenced to imprisonment. The appropriateness of incarceration for price fixing has been recently emphasized by Congress in adopting legislation which raised the maximum jail term which may be imposed upon price fixers to three years."[29]

Are fines and prison all there are? No—fines and prison are compounded by the expensive legal fees—personal and corporate (and these astronomical costs are borne whether you win or lose), poor morale, damaged public image, and civil suits. Even more catastrophic to a firm (especially a small one) is the availability of treble damages.

Treble damages not only are an incentive to the government but are even more so to a private individual who wants to challenge your corporation. Can a private individual sue you under the antitrust laws? Yes. The law states that the illegal conduct must be shown to have inflicted injury directly on the individual's business or property. If a consumer can demonstrate that he or she paid higher prices because of violations of antitrust laws, then that consumer suffered injury (i.e., loss of money) and may have grounds to sue.

How do treble damages work? Under the antitrust laws if the plaintiff obtains a judgment and the jury sets the damages at, let's say, $10 million, that's automatically trebled to $30 million. The jury (one that may think you have insurance anyway) is not told that it's going to be trebled, so its members don't know precisely what devastation they're visiting on a company when they return a damage verdict. But it's automatic. It's not left to the discretion of the jury. It's not left to the discretion of the judge. The damages are simply trebled. And that's done to deter antitrust violations. And, of course, a class action multiplies the number of potential plaintiffs who might collect damages. It is easy to calculate your potential ruin.

What You Can Do About It

Your company and its managers must commit themselves to developing a comprehensive antitrust compliance program. The purpose of such a program is not to make employees into mini-lawyers, but to make each employee antitrust-sensitive. Do you have such a program? If you don't know whether you do, you don't—whether it exists on paper somewhere or not.

An antitrust program educates the managers on the firing line and can be a significant defense as to the issue of criminal intent. A criminal violation of the Sherman Act requires proof of criminal intent. An effectively communicated antitrust compliance program carries weight here. It will keep you out of prison and can save your firm millions. Antitrust compliance programs no longer serve only the function of helping to prevent government antitrust prosecutions of corporations, but also may be used to defend any such prosecutions the government might bring.

It is also possible that once such evidence is admitted, the district court will allow an expert in antitrust compliance programs to testify as to the strength and bona fides of the defendant corporation's program (i.e., the exculpatory value of the program).

In the corrugated box cases the following final instruction was given to the jury concerning two defendants:

> . . . One of the factors you may consider in determining the intent of each corporation, among other evidence, is whether or not that corporation had an antitrust compliance policy. In this regard, you are instructed that the mere existence of an antitrust compliance policy does not automatically mean that a corporation did not have the necessary intent. If, however, you find that a corporation acted diligently in the promulgation, dissemination, and enforcement of an antitrust compliance program in an active good faith effort to ensure that the employees would abide by the law, you may take this fact into account in determining whether or not the corporation had the required intent . . .[30]

The instruction has been criticized, but the jury came down on the side of the defendants and acquitted them. You, too, want an antitrust program and record of antitrust compliance you could take to a jury to save your career. Make sure you have it, and that it's effective for your specific business needs.

Summing Up Your Trade Association Exposure

Price-fixing exposure is bad news and it's getting worse. A defendant faces enormous penalties here—perhaps more than under any other public law that must be complied with. There is potential for enormous treble damages as a result of class actions, criminal penalties, legal expenses, adverse publicity, all of the disclosure problems, and perhaps even direct liability under certain circumstances.

If you think you're immune, consider that more individuals have antitrust exposure (and resulting criminal sanctions imposed) through trade associations than from any other business contacts. Is your trade association sensitive to this fact, or does it merely serve a social function, with no effort to lessen such exposure?

It's your career. If you plan to go beyond number crunching and paper shuffling to becoming a manager who makes bottom-line decisions, then you'll have to face the issues of antitrust exposure.

You should educate yourself accordingly. The most dangerous kind of ignorance is not knowing you don't know something. You are vulnerable—and you have to protect yourself.

ENDNOTES

(1) *United States v. Socony Vacuum Oil Co.*, 310 US 150, 221 (1940).

(2) See note 1 and *United States v. Container Corp. of America*, 393 US 333 (1969).

(3) *Eastern State Retail Lumber Dealers Association v. U.S.*, 234 US 600, 612 (1914).

(4) *Hydrolevel Corp. v. American Society of Mechanical Engineers, Inc.*, 635 F.2d 118 (1980).

(5) *Eliason Corp. v. National Sanitation Foundation*, 485 F. Supp. 1076 (1977). See also *Radiant Burners, Inc. v. Peoples Gas Light & Coke Co.*, 273 F.2d 196 (7th Cir.), *rev'd per curiam*, 364 US 656 (1961).

(6) *Eastern R. R. Presidents Conference v. Noerr Motor Freight, Inc.*, 365 US 127, 81 S.Ct. 523, 5 L.Ed.2d 464 (1961) and *United Mine Workers v. Burlington*, 318 US 657 (1965).

(7) Id., p. 139, 81 S.Ct. 530-31. See also *Greenwood Utilities v. Mississippi Power Co.*, 751 F.2d 1484 (1985).

(8) *California Motor Transport Co. v. Trucking Unlimited*, 404 US 508, 92 S.Ct. 609, 30 L.Ed.2d 642 (1972). See also *Razorback Ready Mix Concrete Co. v. Weaver*, 761 F.2d 484 (8th Cir. 1985); *Subscription TV v. Southern Cal. Theatre Owners*, 576 F.2d 230 (1978).

(9) *Eastern R. R. Presidents Conference v. Noerr Motor Freight, Inc.*, 365 US 127, 144, 81 S.Ct. 523, 5 L.Ed.2d 464 (1961).

(10) *First American Title Co., Etc. v. S. D. Land, Etc.*, 541 F.Supp. 1147 (1982).

(11) See note 8, *Cal. Motor et al,* p. 513, 92 S.Ct. at 613. But see *Richards v. Corneal Eye Registration Foundation,* 783 F.2d 1329 (9th Cir. 1986).

(12) A different opinion was expressed in *First National Bank of Omaha v. Marquette National Bank of Minneapolis,* 482 F.Supp. 514 (D. Minn. 1979).

(13) See note 10, p. 1159.

(14) *Colorado Petroleum Marketers Association v. Southland Corp.,* 476 F.Supp. 373, 378-79 (D. Colo. 1979).

(15) *Hecht v. Pro-Football, Inc.,* 444 F.2d 931, 940-42 (D.C. Cir. 1971), *cert. den.,* 404 US 1047, 92 S.Ct. 701, 30 L.Ed.2d 736 (1972). But see *In re Airport Car Rental Antitrust Litigation,* 693 F.2d 84, 87-88 (9th Cir. 1982), *cert. den.,* 103 S.Ct. 3114, 77 L.Ed.2d 1368 (1983) (holding that there is no "commercial exception" to the *Noerr-Pennington* doctrine).

(16) *Grip Pak, Inc. v. Illinois Tool Works, Inc.,* 694 F.2d 466 (7th Cir. 1982), *cert. den.,* 103 S.Ct. 2430 (1983) (sham exception applies even to a meritorious claim if it was brought solely to suppress competition). See also *Friedman, Inc. v. Kroger Co.,* 581 F.2d 1068 (3d Cir. 1978), *Franchise Realty Interstate Corp. v. San Francisco Local Joint Executive Board of Culinary Workers,* 542 F.2d 1076 (9th Cir. 1976); but see contra *Westmac, Inc. v. Smith* AFTR Vol. 51 No. 1277 at 213 (6th Cir. 1986).

(17) *Grip Pak,* pp. 470-472.

(18) *FTC v. Sperry & Hutchinson Co.,* 405 US 233 (1972).

(19) The exception to this is if you actually engaged in criminal activity. If you did, the attorney will interrupt you immediately if it appears you are confessing to criminal wrongdoing. The attorney represents the company; and he or she will inform you that you should refer to a list of competent specialists in antitrust defense.

(20) 29 USC at 52 et seq.

(21) 15 USC 1011-15.

(22) *Parker v. Brown,* 317 US 341 (1943).

(23) *Goldfarb v. Virginia State Bar,* 421 US 773 (1975).

(24) *California Retail Liquor Dealers Assoc. v. Medical Aluminum, Inc.,* 445 US 97 (1980).

(25) *Community Communications Co. v. City of Boulder,* 445 US 40 (1982); *City of Lafayette v. Louisiana Power & Light Co.,* 435 US 389 (1978).

(26) No. CR-74-182 CBR (N.D. Cal. 1974).

(27) For a solid in-depth view of this area and specific cases, see J. Sonnefeld and P. Lawrence, "Why Do Companies Succumb to Price Fixing?" *Harvard Business Review,* July-August 1978, p. 145.

(28) From the defendant's point of view, a nolo contendere plea offers two advantages. First, it avoids the expense of litigating the case. Second, the judgment entered by the court on such a plea cannot be used against the defendant in subsequent litigation, especially private treble damage actions.

(29) See note 26.

(30) *In Re Corrugated Antitrust Litigation,* Multidistrict Litigation No. 301 (S.D. Tex. 1979). For a good article on setting up your company's in-house antitrust program see Andre R. Jaglom, "How to Develop a Corporate Antitrust Compliance Program," *The Practical Lawyer* (Vol. 31, No. 5), July 15, 1985, pp. 75-86.

Note: All managers/attorneys concerned with these issues should obtain the movie "The Price." Call or write for a catalog: Commonwealth Films, Inc.
(Thomas McCann & Associates), 223 Commonwealth Avenue, Boston, MA 02116; phone (617) 262-5634.

CHAPTER 14

PRICE DISCRIMINATION AND THE ROBINSON-PATMAN ACT

The Robinson-Patman Act was passed when the American economic community was on the threshold of a revolutionary marketing change at the retail level. In the 1920s, chain stores, especially grocery stores, gradually entered the retailing field in competition with small, locally owned businesses. The chain store maximized economies of scale by eliminating many middlemen and dealing directly on a volume basis with the manufacturers.

Manufacturers wished to obtain the business of these chain stores, as they purchased much larger quantities of a product than an independent retailer could. The chains demanded larger discounts from the manufacturers because they purchased huge quantities. The chains then were able to sell the goods at a lower retail price than other competing retailers. Here, the courts refer to the injury as a *secondary-line* injury: damage occurs not to sellers, but to *buyers*. If the large chain stores obtain substantial discounts, these discounts put the chains in a more favorable position than the independent retailer which, because it used the traditional brokerage route, failed to obtain a volume discount.

The Robinson-Patman Act originated in a period when price uniformity was widely considered a positive value. During this same period legally supported resale price maintenance ("fair trade") began to take hold in various states.[1] An antitrust exemption for such statutes was enacted the following year, in 1937, and was to last until it was repealed in 1975 (see Chapter 12 on antitrust issues affecting price fixing).

The act is aimed at preventing price and other forms of discrimination, but not conspiracy. Its intent is to prohibit preferential pricing, allowances, or services that place the seller's customers or competitors at a significant economic disadvantage. Many critics have argued that Robinson-Patman encourages price uniformity.

Still, the act may become an anachronism simply through decreased enforcement. It has been almost 25 years since the Justice Department instituted a Robinson-Patman suit.[2] Aggressive FTC enforcement is minimal at present, and the Department of Justice has actually urged the act's repeal.[3] Increasingly, the FTC and others are asserting that Robinson-Patman is designed to protect competitors, not competition.[4]

Then the *Payne* decision was handed down in 1981.[5] Before *Payne,* a company proving price discrimination was held by some courts to be entitled to "automatic damages," (damages automatically allowed in an amount equal to the dollar value of the illegal discrimination experienced). The Supreme Court rejected automatic damages, thus raising a private litigant's burden of proof (and lessening the chances of monetary recovery). Now a plaintiff must prove specific injury—such as lost sales because favored competitors had reduced their prices, or lost profits because it had to reduce prices to meet those of competitors. Proof of a violation establishes only that injury *may* result (and may justify injunctive relief).

However, small businesses want and need to ensure hard competition in a free enterprise system. Their lobbies are staunch advocates and will keep the act on the books, and they may eventually obtain greater enforcement.

We'll look at each section of the act and explore in detail the sections that deal with discounts and allowances—Sections 2(d) and 2(e)—because, as far as today's manager is concerned, they are the real meat of the act.

The Statutory Prerequisites

A number of statutory elements are written right into Section 2(a) of the Robinson-Patman Act, and if the plaintiff cannot prove *any one* of these elements, or if the defendant can disprove just one, then the statute will not apply. First let's take a look at the text of the law, then break it down element by element.

Sec. 13. Discrimination in price, services, or facilities

(a) Price; cost justification; quantity limits; selection of customers; changing market conditions. It shall be unlawful for any person engaged in commerce, in the course of such commerce, either directly or indirectly, to discriminate in price between different purchasers of commodities of like grade and quality, where either or any of the purchases involved in such discrimination are in commerce, where such commodities are sold for use, consumption, or resale within the United States or any Territory thereof or the District of Columbia or any insular possession or other place under the jurisdiction of the United States, and where the effect of such discrimination may be substantially to lessen competition or tend to create a monopoly in any line of commerce, or to injure, destroy, or prevent competition with any person who either grants or knowingly receives the benefit of such discrimination, or with customers of either of them: Provided, That nothing herein contained shall prevent differentials which make only due allowance for differences in the cost of manufacture, sale, or delivery resulting from the differing methods or quantities in which such commodities are to such purchaser sold or delivered: Provided, however, That the Federal Trade Commission may, after due investigation and hearing to all interested parties, fix and establish quantity limits, and revise the same as it finds necessary, as to particular commodities or classes of commodities, where it finds that available purchasers in greater quantities are so few as to render differentials on account thereof unjustly discriminatory or promotive of monopoly in any line of commerce; and the foregoing shall then not be construed to permit differentials based on differences in quantities greater than those so fixed and established: And provided further, That nothing herein contained shall prevent persons engaged in selling goods, wares, or merchandise in commerce from selecting their own customers in bona fide transactions and not in restraint of trade: And, provided further, That nothing herein contained shall prevent price changes from time to time where in response to changing conditions affecting the market for or the marketability of the goods concerned, such as but not limited to actual or imminent deterioration of perishable goods, obsolescence of seasonal goods, distress sales under court process, or sales in good faith in discontinuance of business in the goods concerned.[6]

Seven distinct elements are discussed above; let's look at each individually.

(1) *Two Sales.* Under Robinson-Patman, the alleged discrimination must involve at least two actual, *contemporaneous, consummated* sales by the *same* seller. An offer to sell[7] is not a sale, though an executory contract is a sale. A license is not a sale. (A refusal to deal does not violate the Act.[8]) The two actual, consummated sales must be at *different* prices. Likewise, a sale to one buyer and a consignment to another cannot normally be reached under Section 2(a). Transfers from a parent corporation to its wholly owned subsidiary can never be considered a separate sale.[9] If a nonsale transaction is involved, you have avoided coverage by the act. Finally, the two sales must be at *different prices.*

(2) *Interstate Commerce.* At least one of the two sales must cross state lines. Whereas the Sherman Act covers transactions merely "affecting" commerce, Robinson-Patman is inapplicable unless the transactions complained of are actually in interstate commerce.[10] For example, if a local seller in Illinois unlawfully discriminates between its two Chicago buyers, the act wouldn't apply.

The courts have interpreted the commerce requirement differently in primary-line competition (between sellers) and secondary-line competition (at the buyer level) Section 2(a) cases. In primary-line cases it is sufficient to establish that the seller made sales at different prices in two or more states, even though the areas in which the discriminatory sales were made are not part of the same geographic market.

The commerce requirement for secondary-line cases is more restrictive. In determining whether "either or any" discriminatory gain is in commerce, only the purchases of the allegedly injured party and its competitors can be considered.[11]

Note: All sales covered by the act must be for use, consumption, or resale within the United States or any of its territories. *Export sales are exempted.* Thus, a U.S. seller *can* discriminate "unlawfully" between foreign buyers. However, this language does not exempt discriminatory sales for import into the United States. Furthermore, the same limitation does not appear in Sections 2(c), 2(d), and 2(e) of the act. Thus, the brokerage provisions of 2(c) have been applied to export sales in which a discriminatory rebate to the buyer was involved.

Finally, there is the *de minimis* principle, under which relatively small or insignificant amounts of interstate transactions have been held not to result in Section 2(a) coverage. If only a small sale is involved, the court will refuse to conclude that this relatively insignificant, isolated transaction served "to make a federal case out of what basically constitutes a local problem." What is considered "de minimis" will vary by industry, product, and other specifics of the case and should be reviewed with your counsel.

(3) *Discrimination in Price.* A price discrimination is merely a price difference.[12] This alone is not enough to bring Robinson-Patman into play. Such price discrimination must pose potential harm to competition. The plaintiff must prove that the price discrimination produced a requisite effect on competition.[13] The Supreme Court has defined this effect as "a reasonable possibility that a price difference may harm competition."[14] Price concession made to one competing purchaser and not another, such as free merchandise, preferred credit terms, and similar competitive benefits, may be found to discriminate if there is the possibility of injury to competition. For a hauling allowance to be considered a violation of the act, for example, injury to competition must be shown.[15]

In a recent case the court found a rebate program resulted in retailers receiving products at lower prices than wholesalers. The court stated that the wholesaler had established price discrimination (a "mere difference in price") but had failed to make a prima facie case of a reasonable possibility of resulting injury to competition. The court noted that the retailer was only one of many sellers in a market that was highly competitive before and after the rebate program.[16]

In a number of cases involving consumers and coupons the courts are clear that the purpose of a coupon is to promote a product, not offer a retailer a hidden price concession.[17] You will note that a lower threshold for competitive harm is set under Robinson-Patman than under the Sherman Act. Both are similar as to proof of anticompetitive conduct and intent from below-cost pricing, but they part company when it comes to proof of injury to competition. The offense of attempted monopolization requires proof of a dangerous probability of success, while Section 2(a) of the Robinson-Patman Act requires only a showing that a price discrimination "may" substantially lessen competition.

(4) *Different Purchasers.* The sales must be contemporaneous to at least two different purchasers at different prices. "The term purchaser. . . does not mean one who seeks to purchase. . . [I]t does not mean a prospective purchaser, or one who wishes to purchase. . ."[18]

What about the indirect purchaser situation? The indirect purchaser doctrine provides that, although the actual sale takes place through an intermediary, if a manufacturer in fact deals directly with a purchaser of its products by controlling the terms on which the purchaser buys, then that purchaser will be within the terms of the act.[19] The indirect purchaser doctrine requires, however, that the plaintiff prove in some way that the intermediary is in fact controlled by the manufacturer.[20]

(5) *Commodities.* The sale must be of a commodity (tangible goods such as wares or merchandise) *only.* (Advertising, real estate, and similar services are not covered.)[21] In a sale of services and goods, the court will look to the "dominant nature" of the transaction.[22] There is no price discrimination under Section 2(a) when intangible factors constitute a dominant portion of the contract price. However, as stressed throughout, Section 5 may overlap areas not covered by antitrust laws. Service discriminations may also be illegal, as "unfair methods of competition," so review them carefully with your counsel.

(6) *Like Grade and Quality.* The interpretation of "like grade and quality" goes further than a requirement that the goods be absolutely identical. If a difference is not significant so that there is true interchangeability and substitutability with the same performance results for the proposed use, goods may be found to be of like grade and quality.

Different prices cannot be justified merely because the label or packaging of the products differ. It has been held that private labeling of such goods as food products and appliances does not make them different from the same goods carrying the seller's house brand. If a seller can establish that there is an actual physical difference in grade or quality between two products, such as substantial differences affecting consumer use, preference, or marketability, then any price differential can be justified. Otherwise, the seller will meet a fate as did Borden, in the leading case in this area.[23]

The extent to which a product is of like grade and quality as another product depends on the characteristics of the products themselves. In *Borden* the court held that evaporated milk produced and sold under the Borden name was of like grade and quality as that which Borden produced for sale at lower prices under other brand names. The physical and chemical identity of the two products, rather than brand names and consumer preferences, are conclusive of the like grade and quality in question.[24]

Judicial refusal to recognize brand names and trademark differences in considering like grade and quality is not completely consistent with marketing realities. Marketing executives well appreciate that two identical products standing side by side on a shelf will not sell alike where only one is a widely advertised, national brand. The courts haven't caught up with image marketing yet.

One way a firm may circumvent the "like grade and quality" provision is to use its superior buying power to obtain exclusive merchandise not offered others. This reality flies against the intent of the drafters of the act but is perfectly legal.[25]

(7) *Injury to Competition.* Section 2(a) applies only to discrimination that has the reasonable probability of lessening competition. You must be able to demonstrate significant, *actual competitive injury.* To demonstrate competitive injury you must be able to show injury to competition, not just to yourself or your business. The effect of the price discrimination must be shown to substantially lessen competition or tend to create a monopoly in your market. You must be able to demonstrate this for cases involving primary-line competition and for cases involving secondary-line competition. Again, primary-line competition is between the competitors of the company alleged to have granted the discriminatory low price. Secondary-line competition pertains to the customers who receive the discriminatory low price versus those who do not.

When you are examining whether there is injury at the primary line, the traditional approach is to ask whether there has been "predatory pricing" (usually sales below marginal cost).[26] As to injury at the secondary line, any difference in price that is substantial or sufficient to influence the resale prices will be presumed to affect competition. A customer has a cause of action only if the alleged discrimination involved a competitor. The term competitor refers to *both* functional and geographic competition.[27] If the functional levels are different (e.g., retailer and wholesaler) there is probably no injury to competition.[28] Likewise, the competitors must compete in the same geographic markets.[29]

The Supreme Court has indicated that substantial price differentials between competing purchasers over time are sufficient to give rise to an inference of injury to competition.[30] It has also recognized that the difference in wholesale prices may be accounted for by the existence of a consumer preference for an advertised label product, and that preference "should receive due legal recognition" in determining whether an injury to competition has occurred.[31]

Exemptions and Defenses to Robinson-Patman Violations

If the plaintiff can overcome all seven statutory hurdles described above, he or she has established a prima facie price discrimination case and the defendant must set forth an exemption or defense. Exemptions let you off the hook. They include:

- cooperative distributions of earnings;
- sales to schools, colleges, libraries, churches, hospitals, and other charitable institutions *not* operated for a profit (their purchase from you must be designated for their use only and not for resale);[32] and
- sales directly to the federal government and its agencies, though the plain language of the act strongly suggests that there is no exemption for purchases used to compete with private enterprise.[33]

Let's take a look at the defenses. An absolute defense of changing market conditions is written into the act. Here are the obvious: perishable goods (e.g., reducing the price of Christmas trees as the number of days to Christmas decreases), discontinued items, seasonal goods, "going out of business" sales (honest ones, that is), and distress sales under court order. These areas are interpreted broadly. For example, cars may be considered seasonal goods, and wide latitude may be permitted in the normal change in a car model year.[34] Another example is remaindering—here books no longer in great demand (not this one, it is hoped) are sold for a nominal price and then discounted to the customer, often on large table sales you've seen in bookstores. Check with your counsel for practices in areas such as clothing, tools, and leisure goods.

Then there are the two better-known and more common defenses of cost justification and meeting competition.

Cost justification. This defense is predicated on services performed and the purchasing practices of the customer. You are permitted price differentials if you can demonstrate legitimate cost justification for differences in the costs of manufacture, sale, or delivery resulting from different methods or quantities in which the commodities are sold or delivered.[35] Here, if the selling, shipping, or other arrangements with a buyer result in a substantial savings to you (the seller), the saving may be passed on to the buyer in the form of a discount.

For example, one buyer may purchase the seller's product in reusable containers that may be handled by forklift and in carload lots at the seller's own warehouse, while another buyer may require store door delivery of a few units at a time in small cartons. Obviously, the cost to the seller will be lower in the first case, and the seller may pass on such savings to the first buyer through a lower price. Quantity discounts based on the annual volume of purchases can seldom be justified on a cost-saving basis.

However, no more than the *exact* cost savings attributable to the discount may be passed on. Finally, quantity discounts are generally lawful if the discounts are available to all competing customers and if all customers can realistically buy in quantities required to obtain the largest discounts. However, quantity discounts must be distinguished from volume discounts (discounts based on cumulative purchases during a stated period) and from rebates not based on cost savings (price concessions reserved for large and powerful buyers).

You should review and establish your cost-justification study *before* passing on savings to a favored customer. The study will determine whether (and at what level) the discounts may be granted. However, studies created after the sale will still be upheld so long as they comply with the statute and are not a mere afterthought.[36]

Meeting competition. We now move on to Section 13(b).[37] The statute reads as follows:

> **(b) Burden of rebutting prima-facie case of discrimination; good faith meeting competition.** Upon proof being made, at any hearing on a complaint under this section, that there has been discrimination in price or services or facilities furnished, the burden of rebutting the prima-facie case thus made by showing justification shall be upon the person charged with a violation of this section, and unless justification shall be affirmatively shown, the Commission is authorized to issue an order terminating the discrimination: Provided, however, *That nothing herein contained shall prevent a seller rebutting the prima-facie case thus made by showing that his lower price or the furnishing of services or facilities to any purchaser or purchasers was made in good faith to meet an equally low price of a competitor, or the services or facilities furnished by a competitor.*

Selling Beer in Indiana

The leading case as to the interpretation of this defense is *Falls City.*[38] Here the Court dealt with the question of whether a business may lower its price to meet a competitor's lower price to gain new customers, and whether a seller may lower a price in an entire territory rather than for specific customers.

Vanco is a beer distributor in Evansville, Indiana, near the Kentucky border. Falls City, a brewer, sold beer to wholesalers in Indiana, Kentucky, and other states. In Evansville, Vanco was Falls City's sole distributor. Because state law provisions required beer wholesalers to sell only to in-state retailers, Vanco did not compete directly with Falls City's Kentucky wholesalers, and Falls City sold its beer to Kentucky wholesalers at prices lower than those charged to Vanco and other Indiana wholesalers. In so doing, Falls City had structured its pricing practices like the larger brewers that sold beer in Kentucky and Indiana.

Vanco sued Falls City to recover for injuries resulting from the brewer's allegedly discriminatory pricing of beer in violation of the Robinson-Patman Act. Vanco claimed that the difference in wholesale prices injured it, since it affected retail prices and ultimately caused Vanco to sell less Falls City beer through Indiana retailers. Falls City did not deny that its Indiana and Kentucky prices differed, but it defended its pricing practices on the basis that the lower Kentucky prices were designed to meet competition and that Vanco had failed to establish the requisite competitive injury.

Plaintiff Vanco won in the district court and at the appeals level. It was granted certiorari. The Supreme Court reversed, however, and established or reestablished the criteria for the defense of "in good faith to meet an equally low price of your *own* competitor": You are not *required* to meet competition. It is an option you elect. However, to justify this defense, you must demonstrate the following.

▶ A good-faith belief (rather than an objective certainty) that your competitor is offering a certain lower price. The courts have viewed it as the "existence of facts leading a reasonable and prudent person to believe that the granting of a lower price would meet the equally low price of a competitor."[39] This is a flexible and pragmatic concept, not technical or doctrinaire.

▶ Evidence of the competitor's price that you are seeking to meet. This evidence may not result from direct verification through the competitor; you may obtain it from the customer in writing or from published sources. However, note that the Supreme Court has held that what would otherwise be an unlawful exchange of price information between competitors is *not* excusable or defensible on the grounds that the supposed purpose of the exchange was to verify a buyer's claim of a lower competing offer and thereby establish a "meeting competition defense to price discrimination under the Robinson-Patman Act."[40]

The Court has recognized that casual reliance on unverified reports of buyers or sales representatives may be insufficient to establish that you acted in good faith in proving that your competitors were offering the same product for a lower price. The Court concluded that where you have "only vague, generalized doubts about the reliability" of a buyer's information, you are permitted to offer a competitive price to make the sale.[41] It further recognized that where a customer's veracity or the accuracy of reports received by the seller may seriously be in doubt, this defense is likely to be unavailable should you grant a discriminatory price.[42]

The Court does not want direct verification as a defense to a Sherman Act price-fixing charge, because "the most likely consequence of any agreement to exchange price information would be the stabilization of industry prices."[43]

▶ The reduction was made to meet an individual competitive situation. The decision to meet a competitor's price should be made on a case-by-case basis (whether it covers all products in a line or just one segment), and it should never be automatic, pursuant to an established policy or practice. However, it is not always necessary to meet a competitive offer customer by customer. If you reasonably believe you are facing a territorial price reduction by a competitor you can lower your price accordingly in the territory without verifying that the lower price was in fact offered to each customer in the territory.[44]

▶ Only a lawful price may be met (though not undercut). Further, the seller cannot use the defense to meet a competitor's price for goods of a lower quality or in a larger quantity than those involved in the seller's quotation. This is common sense, since you can't have a "good-faith" argument of meeting competition if you have knowledge or reason to believe that the price being met is an unlawful one. The plaintiff has the burden to prove this, however.[45]

► A meeting-competition reduction may be granted and kept in place only as long as the competitive prices that prompted it persist.[46] Consequently, you must periodically review price reductions with your customer(s) to determine whether they are still justified by the realities of your marketplace. If you learn that the competitive offer no longer exists, you must likewise discontinue your price reduction.

At all times you should document your actions. Such documentation will include:

☐ Did you request a copy of the competitive invoice or price list? If so, what did it document? (Attach it to your meeting-competition form.) If not, why not?

☐ What is your previous record of dealings with the company (if any) as to its honesty and as to whether the customer will take his or her business elsewhere if the price is not met?

☐ Who had the authority to modify prices to meet competition? Have all responsible persons signed off properly?

☐ Has counsel signed off as to the modification?

☐ General information such as quantity, shipping and handling, and any non-cash factors.

If you do not meet competition, and intend to lower your price, you might notify your customer as follows:

Dear Customer:

After reviewing your recent letter (supporting discounts), the conversations of our respective staffs, and information available from trade sources, we have determined to our satisfaction that our discount to you is not currently competitive with that offered by certain of our major competitors. Since we realize that meeting competitive discounts is essential to our securing an appropriate share of your business, we are prepared to increase the discount available to you on your purchase of our products to xx percent, effective _____ . This new discount will apply until further notice and is predicated on the continuing substantiated availability of comparable discounts from our competitors.

Yours truly,

Brokerage Payments and Allowances—Section 2(c)

This section was enacted to eliminate discriminatory rebates granted large sellers under the guise of "brokerage fees" that were never actually earned, i.e., "under the table" price concessions that eventually fall into the hands of the buyer. This occurs when seller's brokers yield to the economic pressures of large buying organizations to grant preferences related to size rather than to cost efficiency. As Congress stated in its legislative history:

> . . .it prohibits the direct or indirect payment of brokerage fees except for . . . services (actually) rendered. It prohibits its allowance by the buyer direct to the seller, or by the seller direct to the buyer; and it prohibits its payment by either to an agent or intermediary acting in fact for or in behalf, or subject to the direct or indirect control of the other.[47]

Section 2(c), being self-contained, does not permit a defense of meeting competition or cost justification. Also, unlike Section 2(a), only one transaction—one payment by a seller to a buyer's broker—comprises a Section 2(c) violation, and a specific effect on competition need not be shown. For these reasons it is a far simpler task to prove a Section 2(c) violation than a Section 2(a) violation.

Here's the actual test:

> **(c) Payment or acceptance of commission, brokerage, or other compensation.** It shall be unlawful for any person engaged in commerce, in the course of such commerce, to pay or grant, or to receive or accept, anything of value as a commission, brokerage, or other compensation, or any allowance or discount in lieu thereof, except for services rendered in connection with the sale or purchase of goods, wares, or merchandise, either to the other party to such transaction or to an agent, representative, or other intermediary therein where such intermediary is acting in fact for or in behalf, or is subject to the direct or indirect control of any party to such transaction other than the person by whom such compensation is so granted or paid.[48]

As one court stated recently: "The law on the interpretation and application of section 2(c) of the Robinson-Patman Act is sparse and not particularly settled. Briefly, Section 2(c), 15 USC Section 13(c), forbids commercial bribery in connection with the sale or purchase of goods or services."[49]

No effect on competition need be shown to prove the violation. Such requirement would be unduly restrictive and is not part of the plain language of the statute.[50] Although the Robinson-Patman Act is directed mainly at price discrimination, Section 2(c) does not specifically mention price discrimination as the forbidden goal of the bribery. Increasingly, the case law supports the conclusion that a violation of Section 2(c) can be based on indirect price discrimination. In fact, business practices other than price discrimination can give rise to a Section 2(c) action.[51]

In particular, "indirect price discrimination," whereby the bribes or kickbacks can be calculated as a cost to a company is recognized as an injury giving rise to a Section 2(c) violation. Finally, nonprice injuries, including harm to a fiduciary relationship and preferential treatment, are recognized bases for a Section 2(c) cause of action. Even when a buyer's broker renders a service such as warehousing or breaking bulk, payment for such service has been held to be a violation. Therefore, any commission or allowance to a person directly or indirectly controlled by the buyer is prohibited, whether or not any of the payment ever reaches the buyer.

You will run afoul of this section if you reduce the brokerage fee received by the agent for *tangible* goods and pass the reduction on to the buyer in some form.[52]

Whenever both the buyer and seller are in a brokerage relationship, or there is a third party performing services for either, you must carefully review your brokerage payment schedules with counsel to ensure that large buyers are not gaining discriminatory preferences over smaller ones solely by virtue of their greater purchasing power.[53] If you are employing brokerage commissions in this manner you are engaged in price discrimination regardless of your lack of intent or motive to discriminate or cause injury to competition.

Payment for or Furnishing of Services or Facilities: Sections 2(d) and 2(e)

Sections 2(d) and 2(e) are the heart of the act for most readers, and we'll review these sections in detail as well as refer to the applicable FTC guides on point.

With the increasing costs of all forms of customer communication, many managers are expanding their involvement in cooperative promotions. Many hail the practice as increasing the flow of prime selection information to the consumer. Others, including Marcus Stanley, one of cooperative promotion's originators, have deemed it a "pernicious influence" in advertising that "restricts the customer's freedom of choice, encourages greater standardization, and makes it less likely that the best can get a chance to reach the marketplace."[54] One reason for strong reservations about cooperative advertising is the economic reality that firms that are better endowed financially have a big advantage in providing subsidies. This economic leverage could crowd out smaller firms that might have high-quality merchandise to offer but no cooperative advertising money to support a public awareness campaign.[55]

If you are involved or may be involved in cooperative promotions, you should know your rights and responsibilities in this area.

Sections 2(d) and 2(e) of the Robinson-Patman Act prohibit a seller from granting advertising and promotional allowances or services to customers unless they are available to all competing customers on proportionally equal terms. In Section 2(d) the buyer supplies the services or facilities and the seller pays all or an agreed-on portion of the bill; in Section 2(e) the seller supplies the services and facilities for the use of the buyer in facilitating resales. (For brevity's sake, the FTC guides on point have stated that the terms "services" and "facilities" have the same meaning.)[56]

For your cooperative promotional program to comply with sections 2(d) and 2(e) as well as the FTC guides, you must overcome three small hurdles.[57]

- What must you do to make your promotion "available" and on "proportionally equal terms"?
- To whom must you make your promotion available: that is, who are your actual competing customers?
- How does this affect issues such as credit granting, and what defenses are available?

In the following review of these questions, keep in mind that the purpose of the law and the guides is to eliminate direct or indirect devices by which large buyers obtain discriminatory preferences under the guise of promotional allowances. First we'll set forth the precise statutory language.

(d) Payment for services or facilities. It shall be unlawful for any person engaged in commerce to pay or contract for the payment of anything of value to or for the benefit of a customer of such person in the course of such commerce as compensation or in consideration for any services or facilities furnished by or through such customer in connection with the processing, handling, sale, or offering for sale, of any products or commodities manufactured, sold, or offered for sale by such person, unless such payment or consideration is available on proportionally equal terms to all other customers competing in the distribution of such products or commodities."[58]

(e) Furnishing services or facilities. It shall be unlawful for any person to discriminate in favor of one purchaser against another purchaser or purchasers of a commodity bought for resale, with or without processing, by contracting to furnish or furnishing, or by contributing to the furnishing of, any services or facilities connected with the processing, handling, sale, or offering for sale of such commodity so purchased upon terms not accorded to all purchasers on proportionally equal terms."[59]

Availability of Your Promotional Plan

Section 2(d) requires the seller to make a promotional payment available to competing customers on proportionally equal terms. Section 2(e) requires the seller to offer a promotional arrangement on terms accorded to all buyers. The seller who intends to institute a promotional arrangement, therefore, must solve the problem of how to make that program proportionally available to competing customers. There is no requirement that your customers accept your offer—just that they receive notice of a proportionally equal offer that is usable to them specifically.

The seller's obligation to make promotional arrangements available imposes the obligation to (1) inform all competing buyers that promotional programs are available to them and (2) offer a promotional plan that contains meaningful alternatives for all competing buyers.

The main goal of the Robinson-Patman Act is to strengthen the prohibition of unfair price discrimination contained in Section 2(a) by prohibiting "secret" discrimination, such as sellers providing promotional services or advertising allowances to their favorite customers.[60]

How to inform is clearly spelled out in the relevant FTC guide, which provides that the seller should take some action to inform *all* its customers competing with any participating customer of the availability of its plan.[61] You might elect to use letters or mailgrams, or you may choose to publish notice of the availability and essential features of the promotional plan in a publication of general distribution in the trade. Preferably the seller should use the *same media* to announce the availability of a particular form of merchandising assistance to *all* competing customers.

For example, placing such a notice of the terms of cooperative advertising or other promotional allowances in a specific trade magazine should satisfy the seller's duty to inform.[62] Further, you might use the direct mail channel "advising customers from accurate and reasonably complete mailing lists."[63]

Word-of-mouth publicity through your sales force is also a possibility, but receipt and retention of such notice isn't always provable.[64] The best way to be able to prove you actually informed *all* your customers is to follow the specific advice of the FTC:

> The seller can make the required notification by any means he chooses, but if he wants to be able to show later that he gave notice to a certain customer, he is in a better position to do so if it was given in writing.[65]

To summarize, detailed written notification to all your customers communicated in ample time for them to use the available promotional services will almost always satisfy your requirements to notify and inform.

After your customers are informed and understand the essential features of your plan comes the hard part: How can you tailor your plan to make it meaningfully available to all your customers? Again, the FTC is fairly emphatic that more than a minimal effort to proportionalize in good faith must be made:

> *The plan should be such that all types of competing customers may participate. It should not be tailored to favor or discriminate against a particular customer or class of customers but should, in its terms, be usable in a practical business sense by all competing customers.* This may require offering all such customers more than one way to participate in the plan or offering alternative terms and conditions to customers for whom the basic plan is not usable and suitable. *The seller should not either expressly, or by the way the plan operates, eliminate some competing customers, although he may offer alternative plans designed for different customer classes. If he*

offers alternative plans, all of the plans offered should provide the same proportionate equality, and the seller should inform competing customers of the various alternative plans. (Emphasis added.)[66]

In one situation it was found that in lieu of a cooperative newspaper advertising program that precluded reaching many smaller customers,[67] the firm in question could offer in-store promotional aids of display racks or handbills to satisfy the proportionally equal test.[68]

In the celebrated *A&P* case, a wholly owned subsidiary corporation published *Woman's Day* magazine solely for the competitive advantage of A&P retail stores.[69] The magazine was available only in A&P stores, *not* at newsstands or by subscription (except in Colorado, where A&P had no retail stores). The state wholesale grocers (none of which owned a magazine) sued, claiming that the advertising dollars spent in *Woman's Day* were not available to all grocers on proportionally equal terms. The court of appeals held that grocery suppliers (here specifically General Foods Corporation, Morton Salt Corporation, and Hunt Foods, Inc.) that placed ads in *Woman's Day* violated Section 2(d) unless they made similar payments available on proportionally equal terms to other grocery companies in competition with A&P.

Who Are the Relevant Competing Customers?

A seller who decides to make promotions available to a particular buyer must determine whether that buyer sells to other purchasers who compete with the buyer, since any promotional plan developed must cover *all* customers who compete with any customer participating in the plan.[70] This is the *Fred Meyer* doctrine, which holds that when the allowance is made to a direct-purchasing retailer a proportional offer must be made to competitors of that retailer who obtain the supplier's merchandise from distributors. Determining which buyers are subject to the act's protections involves problems in these areas:

(1) Sales involving retailers buying directly and retailers buying through wholesalers.

(2) The geographic area of competition, that is, any area in which two competitive buyers are competing for a customer.[71] The seller that makes payments for customers' merchandising services has, according to the FTC, a duty to ensure that the payments are actually used for that purpose. You might obtain a certificate from the recipient that the promotional funds are used only within the geographical area in which your promotion is being offered (an issue with chain stores).[72]

Essentially, the seller should treat all purchasers that buy from wholesalers as though they were buying directly from the seller with regard to all promotional arrangements.[73] Also, the FTC warns that the "seller should be careful here not to discriminate against customers located on the fringes but outside the area selected for the special promotion, since they may be actually competing with those participating."

Miscellaneous Provisions

In addition to promotional allowances, Sections 2(d) and 2(e) have been used to curb most other schemes by which large buyers are favored over smaller ones. These include discriminatory impact in warehousing and storage compensation and allowing credit for returns of merchandise.[74] However, the extension of credit itself in *not* within the purview of Section 2(d) or 2(e). Credit is too subjective a question because of differences in the borrower's financial strength, business expertise, and simple seat-of-the-pants judgment often needed in these decisions.

Finally, you may be displeased to know that one of the traditional defenses—cost justification, discussed earlier—is not available to you in a Section 2(d) or 2(e) claim.[75] The guide on point states that "It is no defense to a charge of unlawful discrimination in the payment of an allowance or the furnishing of the service for a seller to show that such payment, service or facility could be justified through savings in the course of manufacture, sale (e.g., returnable v. nonreturnable allowances), or delivery.[76] As to delivery of allowances, one court said:

> Section 2(e) should *not* be confined to the conventional type of promotional services such as window displays, demonstrators, exhibits and prizes, for Section 2(d), and therefore its companion Section 2(e), was "made intentionally broader than this one sphere [payments for advertising and promotional services] in order to prevent evasion in resort to others [nonadvertising and nonpromotional services] by which the same purpose might be accomplished. . . 2(e) was meant to cover "advertising, sales, and other facilities. . ."[77]

Thus, a seller may not discriminate as to delivery times, effectiveness, convenience, etc. To avoid the applicability of Section 2(e) to preferential differences in delivery times, sellers can formulate and announce delivery plans that will satisfy the "proportionally equal terms" requirement of the statute.[78]

This is in keeping with the long history of decisions holding that:

> Congress. . .imposed stricter standards of legality respecting promotional discriminations than price discrimination. Price discrimination is lawful if it can be justified under several exculpatory provisos or has no effect on competition. In contrast, promotional discrimination is illegal per se, irrespective of competitive impact and without resort to statutory justification. . .
>
> [Plaintiff's] argument would have us collapse the distinction in schemes and standards and would have us find that the two sections are mere surplusage. This we decline to do. In view of the strict standards of

sections 2(d) and 2(e), which focus on resale, it appears quite clear that Congress carefully considered the deficiency in the original law proscribing price discrimination in the supplier-customer sale and drafted sections 2(d) and 2(e) to apply exclusively to promotional discrimination like those alleged in this case.[79]

However, this restriction like many others in antitrust law (especially Robinson-Patman) appears to be on its way to becoming eased if not eliminated. While citing *Centex-Winston* (see note 77) and other traditional cases, another court has concluded:

> The weight of authority appears to conclude, however, that section 2(e) was aimed at advertising, merchandising, and other promotional services, and not intended to pertain to delivery. . . A review of the legislative history of section 2(e) (services such as deliveries were never mentioned) as well as these precedents and commentary, convinces the court that the scope of section 2(e) does not reach discrimination in the delivery of products.[80]

Likewise, the "test exception" (there is none) also appears to be dying a slow death. This meant that proposed advertising and promotional plans offered as a "test" to select or favored customers were banned. This is because, unlike Section 2(a), under Sections 2(d) and 2(e) there is no need to prove any injury to competition, only that you discriminated among competing customers. This ban may have changed in the absence of FTC or Justice Department enforcement. A private plaintiff must show *actual competitive injury* to obtain treble damages in a suit instituted under Section 2(d) or 2(e) as well as in a price discrimination suit.[81]

Recent decisions have shown that this is an extremely difficult burden of proof when a discriminatory advertising or promotional program has been offered for a limited period, or when the amount involved in the discrimination has been so small that the plaintiff is unable to prove that it actually lost sales or had to reduce prices as a result.[82] Here one firm received comparative advertising support for one product. A retailer selling a product with, at most, cosmetic differences sued. No one argued there was a violation. The defendant argued that it was error for this issue to have gone to the jury because the plaintiff had failed to put forward evidence that it suffered "actual injury." Unfortunately for the plaintiff, he failed to show that he was adversely affected by this disadvantage in advertising allowance. The Court of Appeals found that, without evidence to establish injury in fact, the award of damages would have to be reversed.

Similarly, an introductory discount offered to new, but not to current, customers does not constitute illegal price discrimination so long as it is offered to any new customer on an equal basis. Such discount promotions effectively encourage new customers for your product, resulting in both interbrand and intrabrand competition as your new customers compete with your current ones.[83] Again, no one is arguing these introductory discounts or coupons are not price discrimination. Rather, they are not illegal price discrimination because they promote competition, not impede it.

Today if you are running a limited test, it should not be sufficiently injurious to nonparticipating customers to attract the attention of the FTC (which has been inactive in this area for the past few years) or the nonparticipating customers who probably can't show real or compelling injury to justify the cost of a lawsuit.

Once the program has been designed, your staff should prepare a brief memo to your counsel that sets forth the terms and conditions of the program and of the test itself. Specifically, the memo should include the date the test will expire, the objectives of the test, and your probable reaction if the test is favorable or unfavorable. The goal of the memo will be to show that this is a true test, not a subterfuge for illegal and persistent price discrimination.

Another possible way to end-run the whole area is a copayment allowance policy. Here you will pay a certain amount of money for advertising allowances *only* if the distributor, or your customer, matches that amount. You will inform all your customers of the availability of this and make it available to them. You do not, however, have to sell it with equal vigor to all customers. The goal is to discourage small accounts that don't want to contribute any up-front money. You can then go around to your big accounts, where you feel it will be helpful, to sell the program with vigor. Make sure you review copayment tactics with your counsel.

Meeting competition remains a defense in this form of action.[84] Also, in today's world of leasing, remember Sections 2(d) and 2(e) violations apply only to sales. However, as we stated earlier, the FTC has broad powers to declare trade practices unfair under Section 5 of the FTC Act when the practice conflicts with the basic policies of the Sherman and Clayton Acts.

Buyer's Inducing or Receiving a Discriminatory Price— Section 2(f)

Like Section 2(a), Section 2(f) relates solely to price discrimination. Its text is short:

(f) Knowingly inducing or receiving discriminatory price. It shall be unlawful for any person engaged in commerce, in the course of such commerce, knowingly to induce or receive a discrimination in price which is prohibited by this section.[85]

Sometimes it's natural to assume that antitrust problems are strictly the seller's realm. Remember again the congressional concern over the purchasing power wielded by large buyers to exact price discrimination; Section 2(f) covers all bases by prohibiting such a buyer from *knowingly* inducing or receiving a discriminatory price unlawful under Section 2(a) of the act.[86] Section 2(f) does not apply to promotional payments or services prohibited by Sections 2(d) and 2(e).[87] Your only remedy is to try Section 5 of the FTC Act.[88] The knowledge requirement can be satisfied by showing that the buyer possessed "trade experience" in the industry. The legal question posed is to what extent can a buyer bargain, and to what extent can the uncertain seller reduce a price, before there is Robinson-Patman exposure?

Short of outright fraud or the "lying buyer situation," a buyer is not liable under this section if the lower prices induced are within one of the seller's defenses (for example, meeting competition) or if the buyer does not know that the lower prices are not within one of these defenses.[89] The court has held that a precondition of finding an inducement or receipt of an illegal price was the granting of a discriminatory price by the seller. This interpretation was tested again in 1979, and the Court again held that there is no inducement of price discrimination by a buyer if the seller has a valid defense of meeting competition. The clear language of Section 2(f) states that a buyer can be liable only if he receives a price discrimination "prohibited by this section." Buyer liability under Section 2(f) is dependent on seller liability under Section 2(a). If a seller has a valid meeting competition defense, there is simply no prohibited price discrimination. The Court left unresolved the question of a price induced by the buyer's fraud.[90]

The "lying buyer" has been argued by the FTC in a number of cases.[91] The Supreme Court shot down the theory in *A&P* because the meeting competition defense was available to Borden and so the complaint had to be dismissed against A&P regardless of what it knew.[92]

Conclusion

If you're a seller and you don't offer discriminatory preferences—including price discounts, favorable credit terms, cooperative advertising promotions, and the like—you should have no trouble avoiding adverse action under the Robinson-Patman Act. Nor should you encounter problems under this act if you're a buyer and you don't deceive your seller into granting you a discriminatory price not justifiable under one or more of the act's defenses.

But a word of warning: although enforcement of this act may be diminished at present, legal climates *do* change (witness the abrupt U.S. Senate turnaround in November 1986 with a more "activist" Judiciary Committee Chairman). So violations of any of the sections discussed above could come back to haunt you.

ENDNOTES

(1) For background see *Schwegmann Bros. v. Calvert Distillers Corp.,* 341 US 384 (1951).

(2) *U.S. v. National Dairy Products Corp.,* 372 US 29 (1963).

(3) U.S. Department of Justice, Report on the *Robinson-Patman Act,* 1977.

(4) *Brunswick Corp. v. Pueblo Bowl-O-Mat, Inc.,* 429 US 477, 487 (1977).

(5) *J. Truett Payne Co. v. Chrysler Motors Corp.,* 451 US 557, 101 S.Ct. 1923, 68 L.Ed. 2d 412 (1981); *Chrysler Credit Corp. v. J. Truett Payne Co.,* 670 F.2d 575 (5th Cir. 1982), *cert. den.,* 459 US 908 (1982) (directed verdict for defendant on remand). See also *D & R Distributing Co., Inc. v. Chambers Corp.,* 608 F.Supp. 1290 (D.C. Cal. 1984) and *Crowl Distrib. Corp. v. Singer Corp.,* 543 F.Supp. 1033, 1035 (1982) (no automatic damages, but you must show actual injury to yourself attributable to something the antitrust laws were designed to prevent).

(6) 15 USC 13(a).

(7) *Foremost Pro Color, Inc. v. Eastman Kodak Co.,* 703 F.2d 534, 547 (9th Cir. 1983), *cert. den.,* 465 US 1038 (1984).

(8) *L & L Oil Co. v. Murphy Oil Corp.,* 674 F.2d 1113 (5th Cir. 1982). See also *Mullis v. Arco Petroleum Corp.,* 502 F.2d 290, 294 (7th Cir. 1974).

(9) See note 5 above and *Security Tire & Rubber Co. v. Gates Rubber Co.,* 598 F.2d 962, 965-67 (5th Cir. 1979), *cert. den.,* 444 US 942 (1979).

(10) *Standard Oil Co. v. FTC,* 340 US 231 (1951).

(11) *Mayer Paving & Asphalt Co. v. General Dynamics Corp.,* 486 F.2d 763, 770 (7th Cir. 1973). See also *International Telephone & Telegraph Corp. et al.,* 104 FTC 280 (1984).

(12) *FTC v. Anheuser-Busch, Inc.,* 363 US 536, 549 (1960).

(13) *William Inglis & Sons Baking Co. v. ITT Continental Baking Co.,* 668 F.2d 1014, 1040 (9th Cir., 1981), *cert. den.,* 103 S.Ct. 58 (1982).

(14) *Falls City Industries, Inc. v. Vanco Beverage, Inc.,* 103 S.Ct. 1282, 1288 (1983). See also *FTC v. Morton Salt Co.,* 334 US 37, 43-47 (1948).

(15) *Edward J. Sweeney & Sons, Inc. v. Texaco, Inc.,* 478 F.Supp. 243 (1979).

(16) *Short Oil Co. v. Texaco, Inc.,* 799 F.2d 415 (8th Cir, 1986).

(17) *Indian Coffee Corp. v. Procter & Gamble Co.,* 482 F.Supp. 1104 (W.D. Pa. 1980).

(18) *Chicago Seating Co. v. S. Karpen & Bros.,* 177 F.2d 863, 867 (7th Cir. 1949), quoting *Shaw, Inc. v. Wilson-Jones, Co.,* 105 F.2d 331 (3d Cir. 1939). See also *Wales Home Remodeling Co., Inc. v. Alside Aluminum,* 443 F.Supp. 908, 911-12 (1978).

(19) *Checker Motors Corporation v. Chrysler Corporation* (S.D.N.Y. 1968), 283 F.Supp. 876, 887, *aff'd,* 405 F.2d 319 (1969), *cert. den.,* 394 US 999, 89 S.Ct. 1595, 22 L.Ed. 2d 777 (1969).

(20) *Purolator Products, Inc. v. FTC,* 352 F.2d 874 (7th Cir. 1965).

(21) *Baum v. Investors Diversified Services, Inc.,* 409 F.2d 872, 874 (7th Cir. 1969).

(22) *May Department Store v. Graphic Process Co.,* 637 F.2d 1211 (9th Cir. 1980).

(23) *FTC v. Borden Co.,* 383 US 637, 641, 86 S.Ct. 1092. See also note 19. (The courts will look to several factors to determine if goods are of like grade or quality, including whether one type of product will satisfy the demand for another, whether one product may be used in another's place, and whether the products physically resemble one another.)

(24) Id., p. 639-640, 86 S.Ct. at 1094-1095. See also *Jays Foods, Inc. v. Frito-Lay, Inc.,* 614 F.Supp. 1073, 1085 (C.D. Ill. 1985), and *Quaker Oats Co.,* 66 FTC 1131 (1964).

(25) See note 19. (Elements to consider here are whether the physical and chemical properties of the products are the same: cross-elasticity of demand, substitutability, physical appearance, and identity of performance.)

(26) The "substantial lessening of competition" component of a Section 2(a) offense may be somewhat easier to satisfy than the "dangerous probability of successful monopolization" requirement for proving attempted monopolization under the Sherman Act. *William Inglis & Sons Baking Co. v. ITT Continental Baking Co.,* 668 F.2d 1014, 1040 (9th Cir., 1981). However, when *no* showing of predatory conduct can be made it is highly unlikely that the Section 2(a) meeting competition requirement can be satisfied by direct evidence, which is often ambiguous and misleading or, as the Court stated herein (p. 1028, n. 6):

> ". . .direct evidence of intent alone can be ambiguous and misleading. . .Especially misleading here is the inveterate tendency of sales executives to brag to their superiors about their competitive prowess, often using metaphors of coercion that are compelling evidence of predatory intent to the naive. Any doctrine that relies upon proof of intent is going to be applied erratically at best."

See also *O. Hommel Co. v. Ferro Corp.,* 659 F.2d 340 (3d Cir. 1981), *cert. den.,* 455 US 1017 (1982).

(27) *National Distiller & Chem. Corp. v. Brad's Machine Products, Inc.,* 666 F.2d 492 (11th Cir. 1982).

(28) *Doubleday & Co., Inc.,* 152 FTC 169, 207-08 (1955). See also *O'Byrne v. Checker Oil Co.,* 530 F.Supp. 70 (N.D. Ill. 1981), *aff'd* 727 F.2d 159 (7th Cir. 1984).

(29) *Lupia v. Stella D'Oro Biscuit Co.,* 586 F.2d 1163 (7th Cir. 1978), *cert. den.,* 440 US 982 (1979).

(30) *FTC v. Morton Salt Co.,* 334 US 37, 43-47 (1948). See also *Foremost Pro Color, Inc. v. Eastman Kodak Co.,* 703 F.2d 534, 547 (9th Cir. 1983), *cert. den.,* 465 US 1038 (1984) and *Foremost Dairies, Inc. v. FTC,* 348 F.2d 674 (5th Cir.), *cert. den.,* 382 US 959 (1965) and *Beatrice Foods Co.,* 76 FTC 719, 801 (1969).

(31) *FTC v. The Borden Co.,* 383 US 637, 646 (1966); *accord, Borden Co. v. FTC,* 381 F.2d 175, 180-81 (5th Cir. 1967).

(32) *Abbott Laboratories v. Portland Retail Druggists Association,* 425 US 1 (1976). But see also *Jefferson County Pharmaceuticals Association v. Abbott Laboratories,* 460 US 150 (1983).

(33) *Champaign-Urbana News Agency v. J. L. Cummins News Co.,* 632 F.2d 680 (7th Cir. 1980) (sales to military PX are exempt).

(34) *Valley Plymouth v. Studebaker-Packard Corp.,* 219 F.Supp. 608 (S.D. Cal. 1963).

(35) 15 USC Sec. 2(a).

(36) *Reid v. Harper & Brothers,* 235 F.2d 420 (2d Cir. 1956).

(37) 15 USC Sec. 2(b) (emphasis added).

(38) *Falls City Industries, Inc. v. Vanco Beverage, Inc.,* 460 US 428 (1983).

(39) Id., p. 441, 449. See also *Covey Oil Co. v. Continental Oil Co.,* 340 F.2d 993, *cert. den.,* 380 US 964 (1965) and *Sunshine Biscuits, Inc. v. FTC,* 306 F.2d 48 (7th Cir. 1962).

(40) *United States v. United States Gypsum Co.,* 438 US 422 (1978).

(41) Id. at 454, n. 29.

(42) Id. at 455-6.

(43) Id. at 457.

(44) See note 38, p. 451. See also notes 13 and 17.

(45) See note 38, p. 439-41.

(46) See note 38, p. 451.

(47) H. R. 2287, 74th Congress 2d Sess. 15 (1936).

(48) 15 USC Sec. 2(e).

(49) *Gregoris Motors v. Nissan Motor Corp. in USA,* 630 F.Supp. 902 (E.D.N.Y. 1986).

(50) *Id.,* p. 910. See also *Seaboard Supply Co. v. Congoleum Corp.,* 770 F.2d 367 (3d Cir. 1985); *Metrix Warehouse Inc. v. Daimler-Benz Aktiengesellschaft,* 716 F.2d 245 (4th Cir. 1983); *Municipality of Anchorage v. Hitachi Cable Ltd.,* 547 F.Supp. 633 (D. Alaska 1982).

(51) *Wales Home Remodeling Co., Inc. v. Alside Aluminum,* 443 F.Supp. 908 (1978). See also *FTC v. Simplicity Pattern Co.,* 360 US 55, 65, 79 S.Ct. 1005, 1011 (1959) and *Computer Statistics, Inc. v. Blair,* 418 F.Supp. 1339 (S.D. Tex. 1976).

(52) *Grace v. E. J. Kozin Co.,* 538 F.2d 170 (7th Cir. 1976).

(53) See note 51.

(54) Marcus, Stanley, *Quest for the Best.* New York: Viking, 1979, p. 136. See Chapter 8, "The Seduction of the Buyer," in the same work.

(55) *Id.,* p. 133.

(56) Guides for Advertising Allowances and Other Merchandise Payments and Services, 16 CFR 240.5 (see "Note") (1986).

(57) Advertising is a service, but if it is involved with *commodities* (as we discussed earlier) the advertiser is covered by the laws on point.

(58) 15 USCA 13(d) (emphasis added). See also *Reid v. Doubleday & Co., Inc.,* 109 F.Supp. 354, 356 (1952).

(59) 15 USCA 13(e).

(60) *Cecil Corley Motor Co. v. GMC,* 380 F.Supp. 819, 848 (M.D. Tenn. 1974).

(61) 16 CFR 240.8(a)(3).

(62) 16 CFR 240.8. However, this is sufficient notice only if your customers ordinarily read this magazine. See *Exquisite Form Brassiere, Inc. v. FTC,* 301 F.2d 499 (1961), *cert. den.,* 382 US 888 (1962).

(63) 16 CFR 240.8(b)(3)(C).

(64) *Vanity Fair Paper Mills, Inc. v. FTC,* 311 F.2d 480 (2d Cir. 1968).

(65) 16 CFR 240.8(a) (1986).

(66) 16 CFR 240.9(a) (1986).

(67) *Surprise Brassiere Co. v. FTC,* 406 F.2d 711 (5th Cir. 1969).

(68) For a discussion of the flexibility as to display racks, see *Allen Pen Co. v. Springfield Photo Morent Co.,* 653 F.2d 17 (1981).

(69) *State Wholesale Grocers v. Great Atlantic and Pacific Tea Co.,* 258 F.2d 831 (7th Cir. 1958), *cert. den.,* 358 US 947 (1959).

(70) *FTC v. Fred Meyer, Inc.,* 390 US 341 (1968). See also *FLM Collision Parts, Inc. v. Ford Motor Co.,* 543 F.2d 1019 (2d Cir. 1976), *cert. den.,* 429 US 1097 (1977) (Doctrine not applicable to Section 2(a)).

(71) *FTC v. Simplicity Pattern Co.,* 360 US 55 (1959).

(72) *Abbott Laboratories v. Portland Retail Druggists Association,* 425 US 1 (1976).

(73) 16 CFR 240.12.

(74) There are FTC advisory opinions indicating that there is a limited exemption from Robinson-Patman under the Motor Carriers Act of 1980. This exemption is limited to "products sold primarily in grocery stores." If you deal in these products discuss this with your counsel. See *In re Procter & Gamble Co.,* 98 FTC 909, July 19, 1981, and *Nifty Foods Corp. v. Great Atlantic and Pacific Tea Co.,* 614 F.2d 832 (2d Cir. 1981).

(75) *Covey Oil Co. v. Continental Oil Co.,* 340 F.2d 993, *cert. den.,* 380 US 964 (1965).

(76) 16 CFR 240.17 (1986).

(77) *Centex-Winston Corp. v. Edward Hines Lumber Co.,* 447 F.2d 585, 587 (1971).

(78) Id., p. 589.

(79) In *Kirby v. P.R. Mallory & Co.,* 489 F.2d 904, 910-11 (7th Cir. 1973), *cert. den.,* 417 US 911 (1974).

(80) *John Peterson Motors, Inc. v. General Motors Corp.,* 613 F.Supp. 887, 898-99 (D. Minn. 1985).

(81) See note 5.

(82) *World of Sleep v. La-Z-Boy Chair Company,* 765 F.2d 1467 (10th Cir. 1985).

(83) *Interstate Cigar Co. v. Sterling Drug, Inc.,* 655 F.2d 29 (2d Cir. 1981).

(84) *Rabiner & Jontow v. FTC,* 386 F.2d 667 (2d Cir. 1967), *cert. den.,* 390 US 1004 (1968).

(85) 15 USC 13(f).

(86) 16 CFR 240.16 (1986).

(87) *Sofa Gallery v. Mohasco Upholstered Furniture Corp.,* 1986-2 Trade Cas. Par. 67,286 (D. Minn.).

(88) *General Beverage Sales Co.—Oshkosh v. East Side Winery,* 396 F.Supp. 590 (E.D. Wis. 1975), *rev'd on other grounds,* 568 F.2d 1147 (7th Cir. 1978). *Rickles, Inc. v. Francis Denney Corp.,* 508 F.Supp. 4 (1981).

(89) *Automatic Canteen Co. v. FTC,* 346 US 61 (1953).

(90) *Great Atlantic & Pacific Tea Co. v. FTC,* 440 US 69 (1979).

(91) *Beatrice Foods,* 76 FTC 719 (1969) and again in note 89 above.

(92) See note 89, p. 82-85.

Note: There are related state and federal laws and rules on point governing particular industries. For example, there is the FTC's "Guides for the Greeting Card Industry Relating to Discriminatory Practices," 16 CFR 244. This addresses specific industry wide guides for price discrimination generally and promotional assistance specifically. Consult your counsel as to any specific guides or rules for your industry.

SECTION IV

PROMOTIONAL POLICIES

A successful promotion must communicate in a persuasive manner, blending creativity and time with thorough product analysis. However, the promotion manager must realize that advertising is the most regulated form of communications and that all compliance procedures must be monitored and updated regularly. Legal compliance issues affect all the traditional product promotion questions.

Before undertaking any promotional campaign, you must conduct a thorough product analysis. Your product—whatever is to be marketed—must be understood as to its use and performance. Is it seasonal? What conditions surround its manufacture? What is the competitive environment? To best understand the product, analysis—and re-analysis—is necessary. The product must be examined, tested, critiqued, evaluated, and put to the various uses for which it was designed.

This analysis must be done regularly, since the product most likely will change as demand changes, and each such change will require reexamining your legal compliance requirements. A major aim of research is to know demand intimately, to adapt accordingly, to show the targeted audience that it needs the product (through benefits offered), and to create a preference for this product over others in its class.

This section addresses the three major areas of promotional policy: traditional advertising, personal selling, and nonpersonal sales promotion. Traditional advertising, which includes visual demonstrations, endorsements and testimonials, copyrighting of promotional material, and comparative and corrective advertising, is reviewed in detail in Chapter 15.

Personal selling is the process of assisting and persuading a prospect to buy a product or to act on an idea through the use of person-to-person communication. Chapter 16 addresses the issues of door-to-door sales, customer referrals, and telephone sales, and arms you with the knowledge you need to avoid "bait and switch" tactics.

Nonpersonal sales promotions include marketing activities (other than personal selling, advertising, and publicity) that stimulate consumer purchasing and dealer effectiveness. Chapter 17 looks at promotions using displays, shows and exhibitions, demonstrations, and various nonrecurrent nonroutine selling efforts (e.g., a sweepstakes promotion).

The easiest way to stay in compliance is to draft, with your counsel, a compliance checklist for promotion policy that is up to date based on all relevant legal and regulatory information affecting your particular promotional strategy. Consult this checklist routinely, and again each time you embark on a new promotion.

The following topical areas include questions you should consider when drafting such a checklist. These questions are broad, and you should consult your counsel as to the particulars of your own promotional strategy. It's counterproductive to spend valuable time and dollars convincing people to buy your product or service only to have a big chunk of your profits drained off by fines, legal fees, and damages paid, not to mention lost staff time.

The following case exemplifies many of the issues you will have to be concerned with.

Listerine Loses One

Advertising is a vast field, and it's difficult to find the one case that symbolizes the difficulties a firm can encounter when it doesn't substantiate its promotional campaign. However, the Listerine case is of interest because it illustrates a wide variety of problems you wish to avoid—administrative and court costs, substantial direct or indirect financial penalties, and the resulting bad publicity.

Listerine has been on the market since 1879. Its formula had never changed. Ever since its introduction it had been represented as being beneficial in fighting colds, cold symptoms, and sore throats. Direct advertising to the consumer, including the cold claims, began in 1921 and presented no problem for 50 years.

Then in 1972 the FTC issued a complaint charging Warner-Lambert Co., the manufacturer, with violations of Section 59(a)(1) of the FTC Act by misrepresenting the efficacy of Listerine against the common cold.[1] An administrative marathon ensued, producing a record 4,800 pages and the testimony of 46 witnesses. Warner-Lambert lost the case and, in effect, approximately $10,000,000, which it had to use for "corrective advertising."

Here's the scenario: After a number of administrative hearings they went to court.[2] The court began by endorsing its precedent-imposed marching orders that the FTC's findings (as any agency's) must be sustained if supported by substantial evidence or the record viewed as a whole. "The Commission is the expert body to determine what remedy is necessary to eliminate the unfair or deceptive trade practices which have been disclosed. It has wide latitude for judgment and the courts will not interfere except where the remedy selected has no reasonable relation to the unlawful practices found to exist."[3]

Then the court went into an exhaustive review of the controlling record. The following is representative of the type of substantiation your firm must be prepared to make.[4]

Both the administrative law judge (ALJ) and the Commission carefully analyzed the evidence. They gave full consideration to the studies submitted by the petitioner. The ultimate conclusion that Listerine is not an effective cold remedy was based on six specific findings of fact.

First, the Commission found that the ingredients of Listerine are not present in sufficient quantities to have any therapeutic effect. This was concluded by way of testimony of two leading pharmacologists called by Commission counsel. The Commission was justified in concluding that the testimony of Listerine's experts was not sufficiently persuasive to counter this testimony.

Second, the Commission found that gargling doesn't allow the mouthwash to reach the critical areas of the body in medically significant concentration. The liquid is confined to the mouth chamber. The Commission charged that any vapors that might reach the nasal passages would not be in therapeutic concentration, and Warner-Lambert did not offer evidence to the contrary.

Third, the Commission found that even if significant quantities of the active ingredients of Listerine were to reach the critical sites where cold viruses enter and infect the body, they could not interfere with the activities of the virus because they could not penetrate the tissue cells.

Fourth, the Commission discounted the results of a clinical study that Warner-Lambert conducted and relied on heavily. Warner-Lambert claimed that, in a four-year study, schoolchildren who gargled with Listerine had fewer colds and cold symptoms than those who did not gargle with Listerine. The Commission found that the design and execution of the "St. Barnabas study" made its results unreliable. For the first two years of the four-year test no placebo was given to the control group. For the last two years the placebo was inadequate: The control group was given colored water that did not resemble Listerine in smell or taste. There was also evidence that the physician who examined the test subjects was not blinded from knowing which children were using Listerine and which were not, that his evaluation of the cold symptoms of each child each day may have been imprecise, and that he necessarily relied on the child's subjective reporting. Both the ALJ and the Commission analyzed the study and the expert testimony about it in depth, and were justified in concluding that its results were unreliable.

Fifth, the Commission found that the ability of Listerine to kill germs by millions on contact is of no medical significance in the treatment of colds or sore throats. Expert testimony showed that bacteria in the oral cavity, the "germs" that Listerine purportedly kills, do not cause colds and play no role in cold symptoms. Colds are caused by viruses. Further, it found, "while Listerine kills millions of bacteria in the mouth, it also leaves millions. It is impossible to sterilize any area of the mouth, let alone the entire mouth."

Sixth, the Commission found that Listerine has no significant beneficial effect on the symptoms of sore throat. The Commission recognized that gargling with Listerine could provide temporary relief from a sore throat by removing accumulated debris irritating the throat. But this type of relief can also be obtained by gargling with salt water or even plain warm water. The Commission found that this is not the significant relief promised by advertisements. It was reasonable to conclude that "such temporary relief does not 'lessen the severity' of sore throat any more than expectorating or blowing one's nose 'lessens the severity' of a cold."

Warner-Lambert countered with the following arguments:

(1) There was a disparity between FTC and FDA analyses.

(2) The order exceeded the FTC's authority (this was also argued in the dissent to this case).

(3) The order interfered with its First Amendment rights.

(4) The duration of the corrective advertising required by the order was excessive.

The court paid short shrift to the first argument. As to the second, the court held the FTC has the power to shape remedies beyond the simple cease and desist order. As to the commercial free speech argument, the court felt that an order such as this triggers a special responsibility on the part of the FTC to order a remedy infringing its "commercial speech," only if the restriction inherent in its order is no greater than necessary to serve the interest involved. The court expressly noted that the First Amendment presents no obstacle to government regulation of false or misleading advertising.

Finally, in terms of the duration of the corrective advertising order, the court argued that Listerine had built up a widespread reputation over a period of many years. When it was ascertained that this reputation no longer applied to the product, it was necessary to take action to correct it. It is the accumulated effect of past advertising that necessitates disclosure in future advertising. To allow consumers to continue to buy the product on the strength of the impression built by prior advertising—an impression that is now known to be false—would be unfair and false. In a bit of irony the court held that "it is more than a little peculiar to hear petitioner assert that its commercials really have no effect on consumer belief."[5]

The specific sum to be spent was the advertising budget for Listerine from April 1962 to March 1972, approximately $10,000,000![6] The court felt this was a fair trade-off for 100 years of false cold-combatting (not noting the real-dollar cost was much less with inflation calculated into the equation).

The Listerine Case and Advertising Law

What are some themes of advertising law running through this case?

- This case gives us a good idea of the FTC's influence on advertising regulatory enforcement, its broad powers to adopt a remedy, and the courts' general deference to the agency's expertise (as well as that of other agencies acting within their own areas of authority).
- It is a good example of how the enforcement authority of government agencies such as the FTC and FDA can overlap.
- Commercial free speech, unheard of 20 years ago, is now almost as protected as individual free speech. The only real difference is that while there is no such thing as an individual's having a wrong idea in public discourse, a firm can make a false or deceptive statement about an objective fact.
- The reviewing bodies want to see objective substantiation (tests, surveys) to back up product claims. Such substantiation must be conducted professionally and scientifically, and not haphazardly.
- Losing an advertising regulatory dispute can be costly; some of the cost is in the loss of goodwill.
- This case directly focuses on corrective advertising.
- Finally, the case indirectly raises the questions of comparative advertising, whether an advertising agency can be a codefendant in this promotion, and what advertising deception is.

The Administrative Agency

Administrative agencies exist at all levels of government. They are creations of the state and federal legislative branch. Like political parties and other aspects of government that we take for granted, there is no mention in our Constitution of their role or utility. Administrative agencies are practical legal responses to complex problems that neither the legislature nor the courts have the resources to handle.

Sometimes a problem confronting the legislature requires a great deal of study and expertise before a proper response can be crafted. The legislators have neither the time nor the expertise to deal with issues that arise in such a situation. So the legislature will draft an enabling act, which briefly outlines the desired policy goals of the legislature, to be carried out by the administrative agency established for that purpose.

The agency has three broad forms of power, all of which were demonstrated in the Listerine case.

(1) They can legislate—make rules, draft regulations, and draft guidelines.

(2) They have executive powers of investigation.

(3) They have judiciary power to decide cases in the area of their expertise.

The courts may review whether agency decisions were made within the bounds of the agency's authority, whether the hearings met the due process standards, and whether the agency acted reasonably or arbitrarily and capriciously in its decision making.

Judicial review is limited. For example, in reviewing an agency adjudication (as in the Listerine case), the courts are loath to involve themselves in the facts of a given case. The courts have long held[7] that the agencies have acquired unique expertise by dealing continually with related themes, while "courts generally lack the expertise of the FTC (and other agencies) when it comes to evaluating advertising practices."[8] They will not substitute their judgment for that of an agency. They will review the record to ensure that the decision adequately considered all relevant factors and that it was not arbitrary, capricious, an abuse of discretion, or otherwise not in accordance with the law.

In reviewing a rule or regulation the courts will review the record to determine that there was a rational relationship between the rule-making and the agency's role as defined by the enabling act, and that proper due process safeguards were met. This includes the public's right to advance notice and right to comment.

> At the federal level the Administrative Procedure Act requires that the administrative agency give notice to the public of its proposed rule-making activity. Notice is given through publication in the *Federal Register* —the official public notice organ of the federal agencies. Thereafter, interested persons are given the opportunity to participate in the process. Once the rule has been promulgated, it must be made public, also through publication in the *Federal Register,* at least 30 days before it is to become effective. This gives those who are affected by the rule the opportunity to learn of it and conform to its provisions.

In the final step of the process, the courts will determine whether the rule is reasonable and not arbitrary.

A number of agencies at the local level involve themselves in advertising regulation. Many counties have consumer fraud divisions. Your state attorney general's office can enforce a variety of laws on the books. How broadly this is done often reflects the personality and political views of the incumbent's appointees.

At the federal level a variety of agencies are involved in regulating advertisements, including the Federal Communications Commission (FCC), Federal Drug Administration (FDA, whose interest is labels and labeling of foods, drugs, and cosmetics),[9] the Environmental Protection Agency (EPA)[10] and the United States Postal Service (USPS). The latter two are often overlooked, yet they possess fairly broad powers as to fraud, deceptive advertising, lotteries, and other matters. We'll review them here, starting with the Postal Service.

Criminal Mail Fraud Statute

There is a criminal mail fraud statute (18 USC Sec. 1341) under which the Postal Service may seek criminal prosecution for mail fraud violations through the office of the U.S. Attorney General. Here the accused is entitled to normal due process safeguards, specifically that the government must prove that the intent to defraud was willful and deliberate. The statute reads, in pertinent part, as follows:

> Whoever, having devised or intending to devise any scheme or artifice to defraud, or for obtaining money or property by means of false or fraudulent pretenses, representations, or promises. . .for the purpose of executing such scheme or artifice or attempting to do so, places in any post office or authorized depository for mail matter, any matter of thing whatever to be sent or delivered by the Postal Service, or takes or receives therefrom, any such matter or thing, or knowingly causes to be delivered by mail according to the direction thereon. . .any such matter or thing, shall be fined not more than $1,000 or imprisoned not more than five years, or both.

> Fraud traditionally includes the following elements:

- One or more persons devise a deceptive scheme;
- The deceptive scheme, if successful, will probably injure another;
- The person(s) *intend* to defraud.

Under the mail fraud statute, the key elements are the scheme to defraud *and* the mailing of a letter (or "otherwise knowingly cause mail to be delivered") for the purpose of executing the scheme.[11] A defendant is deemed to have "caused" a mailing if he or she could reasonably have foreseen it.

Civil Statutes

A number of statutes govern nonmailable matter such as mail bearing a fictitious name or address (39 USC Sec. 3003) or the solicitation in the form of a bill or invoice without specified disclaimers (39 USC Sec. 3001). Two *civil* statutes give the Postal Service authority to combat mail fraud. One is 39 USC Sec. 3005.

This statute is employed to combat "false representations" delivered in the mail. This statute might be used, for example, to prohibit the advertising by mail of a deceptive lottery scheme, or even the advertisement of books and other publications that contain false or questionable theories (e.g., see the *Magnolia* case discussed below).

Under current Section 3005, the Postal Service may, after an administrative hearing, issue a "stop order," which returns to sender the mail of an individual suspected of sending false or misleading representations through the mail. *The intent to defraud need not be proven* by the Postal Service. Following the administrative proceeding, the respondent may appeal the decision to the district court.

Then there is 39 USC Sec. 3007. Under this statute the Postal Service may seek a temporary restraining order or preliminary injunction to detain the respondent's incoming mail before a "stop order" has been issued. The district court may also allow the Postal Service to *open* and review this incoming mail. Finally, Section 3007 provides that the court *shall* issue such an injunction upon the showing of probable cause that the respondent is guilty of violating Section 3005.

The Statutes as Applied

The Postal Service cannot prohibit the mailing of any advertisement for a book or publication that is "not materially false or misleading in its description of the publication," or that accurately discloses the source of any statements derived or quoted from the publication and any opinions expressed about the publication—book reviews, for example.

It is an established constitutional principle that there is no such thing as a false idea. However, an idea can be falsely advertised in the commercial free speech arena. The distinction the Postal Service must make between attacking a false idea in an advertisement and false ideas in a book or other material expressing ideas is often difficult to justify. For example, there was the much celebrated and much debated *Magnolia Lab* case.[12] In *Magnolia Lab,* Robert Ford mailed out his booklet *Stale Food vs. Fresh Food* with an advertisement stating that "Arteries Can Cleanse Themselves Without Surgery by Diet Alone." It goes on to state:

> A startling new discovery shows how arteries can cleanse themselves without surgery. Just as your skin can cast out thorns, your arteries can cast out lumps when you stop forming them with the wrong food . . . Now by my discovery you can now enjoy many of the rich and tasty foods denied you by the old humbug cholesterol diets, while your own natural blood flow washes your arteries clean . . .

The claims encouraged self-medication. Further, the administrative law judge found that these representations (and others) were materially false representations in violation of 39 USC Sec. 3005. Finally, this was not a "suppressed minority opinion." The methods used to test this "diet" were not performed by the acceptable procedures employed in the scientific and medical fields for proving a thesis. As was neatly summarized in another postal decision:

Even though an advertisement correctly describes a booklet, if the results cannot be achieved by following the procedures outlined in the booklet, the advertiser is in violation of 39 USC Sec. 3005.[13]

This decision does not attempt to suppress, nor does it convey the threat to suppress ideas; 39 USC Sec. 3005 cannot be used to censor or edit *The Conservative Manifesto* or *Mother Jones.* It does not in any way restrict the *content* or ideas conveyed in a product sold through the mail. It is simply in line with traditional restrictions on commercial free speech—that the content of commercial advertisement not be false or deceptive either overtly or as a result of incomplete disclosure. There is (constitutionally) such a thing as a wrong product claim. The enforcement of truth in advertising in the commercial area will enhance, not chill commercial free speech. It will not affect the free dissemination of ideas through the mail.

As to criminal enforcement, one will be sobered by *U.S. v. Townley*[14] where the *omission* of material facts in a mailed advertisement was found to render the communication misleading, and resulted in a five-year prison sentence for an individual involved.

Label or Advertisement?

Any firm controlled by the Food and Drug Administration (FDA) or covered by a broad interpretation of its authority (e.g., a firm marketing any form of diet aid, even if all the ingredients are 100% "natural")[15] must consult counsel as to the FDA's and the FTC's separate (and sometimes overlapping) jurisdiction.

The FDA is charged with regulating the safety, effectiveness, and labeling of food, drugs, cosmetics, and medical devices to protect the public against potential health hazards. It is also charged with enforcing advertising claims appearing on the label or package of food, drug, and cosmetic items. (For prescription drugs the FDA controls *all* advertised claims, and can grant or deny *premarketing* approval of such claims.) It may even seize shipments of goods on receipt of evidence that its regulations have been violated. Labeling or packaging includes written, printed, or graphic material accompanying the article, as well as certain point-of-purchase materials.[16]

The FDA tests the product efficacy in the areas of its mission. The results of these experiments may then be used by the FTC as it enforces its mission to ban misrepresentation or fraud from marketplace advertising.

At first glance the jurisdiction of the FTC and of the FDA appears to overlap significantly. However, there is a functional difference between advertising and labeling. The former affects all product or service promotions the consumer will see in the mass media. However, once consumers purchase a product within the jurisdiction of the FDA, they are concerned with the instructions on the label.

Often labeling instructions are more narrowly drawn by the FDA than they are by the broader mission of the FTC. For example, a drug is considered misbranded unless its labeling bears adequate directions for use *and* adequate warnings against unsafe use.[17] Further, while the FDA is concerned with evaluating the absolute safety and efficacy of a product, it is not concerned with questions of comparative safety in areas once labeled "safe", such as over-the-counter drug advertising, which often utilizes comparative advertising tactics.

The FDA's influence is increasing in the marketplace because the food, drug, and cosmetic industries are among the largest purchasers of advertising time and space. Further, misfortunes such as the events surrounding the cyanide poisoning of Tylenol, Excedrin, and Anacin have prompted greater consumer demand for accountability. If you are at all in doubt about FDA compliance, FTC compliance, and general product liability and warranty principles, consult your counsel. (For more about product liability, see PH *Product Liability: Cases and Trends,* with monthly updates on leading cases.)

The Federal Communications Commission (FCC)

The Federal Communications Commission (FCC) was established as a result of the Communications Act of 1934. It has jurisdiction over the radio, television, telephone, and telegraph industries. Through its authority to license broadcasting stations and to remove a license or deny license renewal, the FCC has indirect control over broadcast advertising. This authority derives from the right of public domain over the airwaves and the mandate of broadcasting stations to operate in the public interest.

The FCC stringently controls the airing of obscenity and profanity. It has restricted both advertising content and the type of products that may be advertised on radio and television. Stations that do not comply with FCC policies may risk losing their licenses.

Under the impetus of deregulation, the FCC has dropped many of its rules and regulations for both radio and television stations, deciding marketplace forces can adequately police them. For example, the FCC no longer limits the amount of time that can be devoted to commercials. It has dropped minimum requirements for local programs and news and public affairs programs. And stations no longer have to maintain detailed program and commercial logs.

The FTC—Generic Standards for All Advertisers

The agencies discussed above are just the "appetizers." The main course is the Federal Trade Commission (FTC)—the agency charged with overseeing most advertising compliance. The Federal Trade Commission Act was passed in 1914 because its proponents believed that the Sherman Act had not sufficiently curtailed certain monopolistic practices and tendencies in the economy. In addition, the FTC jurisdiction was to police false advertising and other deceptive practices for which it is now better known.

The FTC has a broad mandate to root out "unfair methods of competition in or affecting commerce, and unfair or deceptive acts or practices in or affecting commerce."[18] It may act against materially deceptive speech ("material" is something that may influence the consumer's purchasing decision) when the injury is either to the consumer or to the advertiser's competitor, and such action would be in the public interest.[19] This deception need not deal with substantive qualities of a product or service; *any* intrinsic fact that may influence the purchasing decision may be material.[20]

Generally an act will be considered deceptive if the claim or omission is likely to mislead consumers, the consumer has acted reasonably under the circumstances, and the infraction is to the consumer's detriment.[21] To ascertain the meaning of an advertisement and its possible deception, the following checklist, while not all-inclusive, may be useful.

☐ Who is your audience? The nature of the audience will be a factor in determining whether an advertisement is deceptive. Advertisements directed at vulnerable groups such as children receive closer scrutiny than others.[22] However, in reviewing misleading advertising, the FTC does not always adopt law school's traditional "reasonable person" standard. Rather, they can be concerned with the public, "that vast multitude which includes the ignorant, the unthinking and the credulous, who, in making purchases, do not stop to analyze, but are governed by appearances and general impressions."[23] In summary, the appearances and general impressions you convey to the lowest common denominator—the audience segment that is more likely to be influenced by an impression gleaned from a first glance and not tempered by mature reflection or judgment—may be controlling.

☐ The FTC will view an advertisement in its entirety; total net impression governs.[24] A headline will outweigh any subsequent disclaimers or clarifying material.[25]

☐ Literal truth will not save your advertisement if it is misleading when read in the context of the entire advertisement. Here you must avoid deception by half-truth or the failure to disclose material facts.[26] The advertisement usually does not have to state all the facts, but must contain a reasonably complete statement.

☐ An advertisement may be found false and deceptive if either of two possible meanings is false.[27]

☐ Expressions of subjective opinion (puffery) are not actionable unless they convey the impression of factual representations or relate to material terms. Opinion of the superiority or the merits of a product seems to be generally acceptable until the phrase becomes a fact. "We believe (an opinion) that our razor blades will never cut your face (fact)." The claim of fact may cross the line from puffery to deception. Likewise, exaggerating the qualities of a product is usually permissible, but assigning qualities that do not exist reaches too far. Stating that you're the "number one" seller requires substantiation with supporting evidence and documentation.

☐ If you are employing a mock-up that is not an accurate representation of a consumer experience, it must not pertain to the product you are specifically selling.

☐ All research quoted must be significant and must have been professionally obtained through state-of-the-art research techniques.[28]

☐ You have a *continuing* obligation to make sure all your material claims are substantiated, including test results, price claims, and endorsements.

Throughout its history, the FTC has tried to follow the ideal that its regulation would serve two objectives—to provide useful and truthful data and to maintain effective competition. One way to accomplish this is to enforce minimal standards of marketplace compliance such as the examples above. Another way is to affirmatively encourage broader consumer information.

Marketplace Compliance Enforcement—FTC Procedures

Most FTC investigations arise from the commission's monitoring efforts, from public complaints (usually based on a noticeable volume), or from other governmental agencies. This information is referred to a staff attorney in the Bureau of Consumer Protection. If a scientific study is necessary, it might be referred to the Commission's Division of Scientific Operations.

Your first indication of any FTC scrutiny will generally come from an official-looking but informal request for information. High visibility is important so as to establish good faith. Your failure to cooperate could result in a formal investigation even if the actual situation as you know it (but have failed to clarify) doesn't merit this.

The FTC has broad data-gathering powers. It can subpoena witnesses and documents, inspect books, require substantiation, or visit your premises all on "mere suspicion."[29] After the investigation the attorney in charge will recommend that:

• your file be closed;
• informal enforcement measures be taken; or
• a complaint be issued. (This occurs rarely.)

If informal enforcement procedures are to be taken you will want to actively negotiate a consent agreement. Retain an attorney with specific expertise in this area.

FTC rules allow companies to "shop" among the five commissioners to get favorable rulings. All matters are not presented to the full commission; a single commissioner will be authorized to limit agency investigations or to quash subpoenas entirely. By watching who has that duty and in which months, a company can present its case to the commissioner most amenable to curbing the investigation. The petition can be tailored to the arguments that will convince that individual, rather than having to appeal to five people with different sets of values. Once entered, the consent order is in all respects effective in the same manner as an order of the FTC entered after adjudication.

If the violation is serious or a complaint is issued, you will have a hearing before an administrative law judge. Adjudication of a dispute by the FTC is similar to the adjudication function of a court. You must be given notice and will have the right to counsel. Witnesses are heard, discovery rules parallel the Federal Rules of Civil Procedure, evidence is submitted, cross examination is utilized, the law and policy are applied to the facts at hand, and a decision is reached. The materials on judicial decision-making would be applicable also to decision-making by an administrative law judge or hearing examiner.

However, there are some major differences between hearings conducted by the judicial system and by the FTC (and other agencies). Agency hearings are *never* heard by a jury. The decisions are made solely by a hearing examiner. As a result, the evidentiary rules designed to insulate juries from unreliable evidence are not applied as stringently in an administrative hearing.

As to appeal, the ruling becomes final after 30 days if neither party appeals to the commission. If the commission takes (and accepts) an appeal, the case is heard before the full commission. If the party charged is found to be in violation of the law and no settlement (consent order) is reached, a cease and desist order is issued. The order becomes final unless it is appealed to the courts within 60 days.

If a cease and desist order is issued against you (depending on appeal strategies), you'll have 60 days to submit a compliance report. In tailoring such an order, the FTC may take into account your or your firm's history of compliance.[30]

You should keep up on these orders whether or not you or your firm is directly involved. Under Section 5(m) of the FTC Act, you and your firm are bound by any cease and desist order (and possibly consent orders), regardless of your firm's lack of involvement, if you or your firm had actual knowledge that the act or practice was unfair or deceptive and unlawful under Section 5(a)(1). Specifically, the FTC can commence a civil action in federal district court against any person, partner, or corporation that engages in an act or practice the commission has determined in a cease and desist proceeding to be unfair or deceptive and prohibited by the FTC's decision. A violation of any such order may result in a civil penalty of up to $10,000 as well as in monitoring by the FTC, which will have access to internal records in matters pertaining to the order. The practical effect is that cease and desist orders are elevated to the level of trade regulation rules once you have actual knowledge. To establish such actual knowledge, the FTC will send copies of the order to industry members that may be engaging in the prohibited practice, or possibly as general information.

This may not afford you or your firm sufficient time to change policy. A more efficient way to do this is to routinely monitor all orders through an internal profit preservation center (see Chapter 24). This will keep you up to date as to compliance and will help you plan for future trends. At a minimum, get on the FTC's mailing list. Request that your name be added by writing to the Federal Trade Commission's Press Office, Washington, D.C., 20580.

While the cease and desist is the most common order, the FTC may utilize other forms of disclosure. Some examples:

(1) affirmative disclosures, such as those that appear on all cigarette advertising;[31]

(2) corrective advertising;

(3) restitution orders; or

(4) prior substantiation after assertions are made.[32]

Whenever the FTC fashions a remedy it may (under the "fencing-in" doctrine) frame one that extends beyond the precise illegal conduct found.[33]

FTC Improvement Act

Before 1980, for a variety of reasons, the FTC was perceived as an unelected body out of control. This perception crystallized with the Kid-Vid hearings and the unpopular actions of certain members. To curb these abuses, Congress enacted the FTC Improvement Act[34] in 1980.

The act strengthened the protection given to confidential business documents submitted to the agency. Now the FTC may refuse to disclose not only trade secrets and customer names but also "privileged" and "confidential" material. Documents submitted in the course of FTC enforcement procedures are assigned to a custodian and cannot be released to the public without 10 days' advance notice to the business providing the documents (with certain exceptions for specified government officials).

The FTC's investigative powers with regard to unfair or deceptive practices were curtailed. In addition, procedural changes were made that are designed to provide more protection for the rights of those charged with violations of the laws under the FTC's jurisdiction.

Do You Want an Advisory Opinion?

As you can see, there are many regulatory hurdles involved with regulatory agencies, particularly the FTC. Why not clear your promotion in advance with the FTC concerning the legality of anything within the scope of the laws under its jurisdiction? Obviously, you'll have to review the trade-offs with counsel. One drawback may be that you don't wish to heighten your general exposure to the FTC. However, if you do want an opinion from the FTC, you should review the following current requirements.

In 1979 the FTC substantially changed its advisory opinion procedures. The FTC will issue formal opinions at its election on written application by specified parties (unnamed parties may not receive a response) in the following areas:

(1) where the matter involves a substantial or novel question of law and there is no clear precedent;

(2) where a proposed merger or acquisition is involved;

(3) where the subject matter is of significant public interest.

Requests for advice and the FTC's response are placed on the public record immediately after the requesting party has received the advisory opinion. Any advice you receive does not preclude the FTC's right to reconsider, rescind, or revoke. There is an important reason in the public interest that an agency may not be considered legally bound by advice given by its employees. If such advice could bind the agency, there would be a danger that the agency could begin to assume powers that the legislature didn't wish it to have solely because of its inability to disavow any acts by its employees. However, the original requesting party will be notified in advance.

The FTC will not proceed against you if you rely in good faith on its advice, provided that you gave the commission all relevant facts, completely and accurately, and that your promotion is promptly discontinued if you're notified that the FTC has rescinded its approval. If you are concerned whether an advisory opinion is still valid, call the FTC at (202)523-3598.

To Sum Up

You can't plan an organized game of baseball without the umpire. The administrative agencies perform a similar role. For marketers the key agency is the FTC. Over the years the Federal Trade Commission has issued numerous trade regulation rules, guidelines for specific industries, consent orders, and opinions. The trade regulation rules and guidelines are usually issued after problems have arisen and have been heard by the commission, and they reflect the commission's findings and opinions. The trade regulation rules and guidelines are fundamental for anyone responsible for preparing any advertisement.

ENDNOTES

(1) *In the Matter of Warner-Lambert Co.,* 86 FTC 1398 (1975).

(2) *Warner-Lambert Co. v. FTC,* 562 F.2d 749 (D.C. Cir. 1977), *cert den.,* 435 US 950 (1978).

(3) Id., p. 735 and 762; see also *Universal Camera Corp v. NLRB,* 340 US 474, 71 S.Ct. 456; 95 L.Ed.456 (1951); *Jacob Siegel Co. v. FTC,* 327 US 608, 612-613, 66 S.Ct. 758, 760, 90 L.Ed. 888 (1946); *Carter Products, Inc. v. FTC,* 268 F.2d 461, 498 (9th Cir) *cert den.,* 361 US 884, 80 S.Ct. 155, 4 L.Ed.2d 120 (1959).

(4) Id., p. 753 and 754 (footnotes excluded.)

(5) Id., p. 762.

(6) Id., p. 763–764.

(7) See note 3 above.

(8) *American Home Products Corp. v. Johnson & Johnson,* 577 F.2d 160, 172 n.27 (2d Cir. 1978). See also *FTC v. Colgate-Palmolive Co.,* 380 US 374 (1964); *Fedders Corp. v. FTC,* 529 F.2d 1938 (2d Cir. 1976); and *FTC v. Mandel Bros., Inc.,* 359 US 385, 79 S.Ct. 818, 3 L.Ed.2d 893 (1959).

(9) 21 USC 301-392.

(10) See *Union Carbide Corp.,* 84 FTC 591 (1974), *mod.* 94 FTC 315 (1979); *Hercules, Inc.,* 84 FTC 605 (1974), *mod.* 94 FTC 315 (1979); and *Farnam Companies, Inc.,* 96 FTC 826 (1980).

(11) *Pereira v. U.S.,* 347 US 1, 8 (1954). See also Robert J. Posch, Jr., "New Postal Legislation: More Power to the Postal Service?," *Direct Marketing,* June, 1983, pp. 114-116.

(12) *Magnolia Lab and Magnolia Laboratory,* P.S. Docket No. 10/123, G.C.-40-81-F (2/11/82).

(13) *Health Purifiers, Inc.,* P.S. Docket 6/78 (P.S.D. March 22, 1979), p. 7.

(14) 665 F.2d 579 (5th Cir. 1982).

(15) For a good example of marketplace confusion and debate that can occur see Nancy Giges, "Diet Aids Face FDA Block", *Advertising Age,* June 21, 1982, p. 3. The FDA serves a useful role in enhancing consumer confidence. For example, if you buy peanut butter, you know that you're getting 92% or more peanuts. Without a national standard here and elsewhere, consumers would be more reluctant to purchase.

(16) FDA Act Sec. 201(m).

(17) FDA Act Sec. 502(f)(1).

(18) 15 USC 45(a)(1)(1986). See also *FTC v. Sperry & Hutchinson,* 405 US 233 (1972). The FTC also has jurisdiction over a host of other acts including Wool Products Labeling Act, Fur Products Labeling Act, Flammable Fabric Act, Lanham Trade-Mark Act, the Fair Packaging and Labeling Act, and others, including consumer credit acts.

(19) *In re Pfizer,* 81 FTC 23 (1972).

(20) *FTC v. Colgate Palmolive Co.,* 380 US 344, 386 (1965).

(21) *Cliffdale Associates, Inc.* et al, 104 FTC 110 (1984), *Thompson Medical Co., Inc.,* TRR par.22,045 (11/23/84) and *International Harvester Co.,* 104 FTC 949 (1984). These indicate little change in results since the "new" standard.

(22) *ITT Continental Baking Co. v. FTC,* 532 F.2d 207 (2d Cir. 1976). See also *Stupell Originals, Inc.,* 67 FTC 173 (1965); *Topper,* 79 FTC 667 (1971), *mod.,* TRR par. 22,202 (9/24/84); and *Hudson Pharmaceutical Corp.* ("Spiderman" vitamins), 89 FTC 82 (1977).

(23) *FTC v. Standard Education Society,* 302 US 113 (1937); *Charles of the Ritz v. FTC,* 143 F.2d 676 (2d Cir. 1944).

(24) *Charles of the Ritz Distributors Corp. v. FTC,* 143 F.2d 676 (2d Cir. 1944); *FTC v. Sterling Drug,* 317 F.2d 669 (2d Cir., 1963). See also *Kimberly Jewels, Inc.* (1981), P.S. Docket No. 9/65.

(25) *Thompson Medical Co., Inc.,* 104 FTC 648 (1984).

(26) *Kalwastys v. FTC,* 237 F.2d 654 (1956).

(27) *Murray Space Shoe Corp. v. FTC,* 304 F.2d 270 (2d Cir. 1962).

(28) *American Home Products Corp. v. Abbott Labs,* 522 F.Supp. 1035 (S.D.N.Y. 1981); *Vidal Sassoon, Inc. v. Bristol-Myers Co.,* 661 F.2d 272 (2d Cir. 1981).

(29) *U.S. v. Morton Salt Co.,* 338 US 632 (1950).

(30) *Motion Picture Studio Mechanics, Local 52 v. NLRB,* 593 F.2d 197, 200-201 (2d Cir. 1979).

(31) *In the Matter of Lorillard et al.,* 80 FTC 455 (1972) (consent order requiring six cigarette manufacturers and distributors to include the Surgeon General's warning label).

(32) *Jay Norris, Inc. v. FTC,* 598 F.2d 1244 (2d Cir. 1979), *cert den.,* 444 US 980, 100 S.Ct. 481, 62 L.Ed. 2d 406 (1979).

(33) *Bristol Myers Co. v. FTC,* 738 F.2d 554 (1984); *Sears, Roebuck & Co. v. FTC,* 676 F.2d 385 (9th Cir. 1982); *FTC v. Colgate-Palmolive Co.,* 380 US 374, 85 S.Ct. 1035, 13 L.Ed.2d 904 (1965).

(34) 15 USC §45 et seq. (1980).

CHAPTER 15

TRADITIONAL ADVERTISING

Marketing and advertising. . .can you conceive of one without the other? Indeed, advertising is such an integral part of the marketing process that it warrants our most lengthy review. Advertising is the communications tool most singled out for review by state and federal governmental agencies. Government can create advertising opportunities (e.g., by fostering comparative advertising) or hinder them (e.g., by banning broadcast of cigarette advertisement).

This chapter examines the most prominent form of advertising—traditional advertising, consisting of promotions such as visual demonstrations, endorsements and testimonials, copy headliners, and comparative advertising. It also looks at issues that may affect your promotion, including an advertising agency's liability for promotional claims, and at finding an alternate solution to some of your potential legal problems through the National Advertising Division of the Council of Better Business Bureaus. One area that you may have overlooked is copyright protection. Yet, this has broad and useful applicability to advertisers in general.

EFFECTIVE USE OF COPYRIGHT PROTECTION IN PROMOTIONAL STRATEGY

Copyright confers exclusive ownership of limited scope and duration on the author of a work, who is permitted to control the exploitation of his or her creation. We're all familiar with this area when it comes to novels, plays, and other products of the mind. Your catalogs and other promotional pieces are copyrightable, too. Creative works are no less artistic or literary simply because they are used for commercial purposes. Titles to books and other works are *not* subject to copyright protection but rather to "secondary meaning" trademark protection.

There are many ways a copyright can be utilized as part of an overall strategic advertising program. This chapter reviews the law and then shows how to protect, through copyright, your catalogs, lists, photos, and work made for hire.

The Constitution[1] granted Congress the power "To promote the Progress of Science and useful Arts, by securing for limited Times to Authors and Inventors the exclusive right to their respective writings and discoveries." Pursuant to the constitutional mandate "To promote the Progress of Science and useful Arts," the federal copyright act provides that "any person entitled thereto, upon complying with the provisions of this title, shall have the exclusive right to print, reprint, publish, copy, and vend the copyrighted work. . ."

The act is designed to encourage and protect many forms of intellectual effort by giving the author the exclusive right to reproduce and sell the author's creative idea. This may sound solemn and onerous, but the fact is that your catalogs and other promotional pieces do not have to involve creative genius to be copyrighted. Your advertisements must be created by your own efforts (original) in a fixed form (your advertisement). Copyright will then protect the expression of your ideas, though not the ideas themselves. Copyright won't protect record books, blank forms, information that comprises common property, pen names, slogans, lists of ingredients, and several other categories that your counsel will fill you in on.

Since copyright law is designed to promote creativity and encourage the development of the arts, one of the primary requirements for copyright protection is originality of expression. For *originality,* only a minimal amount of creativity is necessary to support a copyright. In fact, the 1976 Copyright Act deliberately avoids any definition of what constitutes "originality." This is simply a response to commercial reality as well as a deference to established judiciary precedent in the area.

You may have the best idea in the world—the theme for a great promotion—but until you set it down in tangible form so that it can be perceived, reproduced, or otherwise communicated, it's not protectable under the Copyright Act.

For *fixation,* it is no longer necessary that a work be formally communicated or published (as under former copyright law). Copyright occurs when your work is fixed in a tangible medium. Since the medium does not determine copyrightability, you can copyright your video catalog or film promotion as easily as works in print.

Once you have an original analysis, arrangement, mode of expression, or other novel form of presentation that is of utility to your marketing program and that doesn't fall into a category that cannot be copyrighted, you should obtain an application for Copyright Registration for a Nondramatic Literary Work (Form TX),[2] to register your claim to a copyright. Class TX includes reference works, catalogs, advertising copy, and compilations of information. The form is free for the asking. Once you complete the application form, simply return it with a $10 check payable to the Register of Copyrights. Deposit one complete copy of the material to be copyrighted with your application for unpublished works (copy, catalogs, etc.), or two complete of the best editions for published works. These rules may vary for works in machine-readable form, such as computer programs and data bases.

If you want to do it right, consult with counsel, particularly if you're copyrighting important proprietary information or getting involved in what exactly is an "identifying portion" of a computer program or data base.

Another area you might need expert opinion on is the Manufacturing Requirements of Form TX. Don't rely solely on the instructions provided with the form for matters of importance to you or your firm.

After copyright protection has been obtained, make sure you identify your copyrightable materials accordingly. Inclusion of copyright notice is important. If you omit the notice, make sure you make a reasonable effort to notify recipients of your copies. Such notice must entail something beyond normal business communications to the recipient. We'll discuss copyright notices in greater detail a little later.

Should You Register?

The instant your work becomes fixed, copyrightability exists *automatically* whether you want it or not![3] With the initial automatic vesting of copyright, the issue of whether you should pursue elective registration presents itself. Generally you should, for the following reasons:

Registration is a precondition to your being able to sue on your copyright.[4] This is the controlling reason.

To collect statutory damages (ranging from $250 to $50,000 per infringement) and attorneys fees, your registration must have occurred before the infringement of the unpublished work and, for a published work, within three months after first publication.[5]

The registration certificate is prima facie evidence of the validity of the copyright and of the facts stated if registration occurs within five years of the first publication.[6]

In addition to the above, there are numerous other factors[7] you should review with your counsel in light of your individual circumstances.

What is Fair Use?

The doctrine of fair use creates a "privilege in others other than the owner of the copyright to use the copyrighted material in a reasonable manner without consent, notwithstanding the monopoly granted to the owner."[8] This issue can arise in promotional wording, an excerpt you use, a parody, etc. It can be an important legal concept for any advertising professional. The doctrine is meant to balance the exclusive rights of the copyright holder against the public interest in the dissemination of information. It is justified to avoid the rigid application of the copyright statute when on occasion it would stifle the very creativity the law was designed to foster.[9] In the Copyright Act of 1976, Congress first codified the fair use doctrine. The statute is short and reads as follows:

> Notwithstanding the provisions of section 106, the fair use of a copyrighted work, including such use by reproduction in copies or phonorecords or by any other means specified by that section, for purposes such as criticism, comment, news reporting, teaching (including multiple copies for classroom use), scholarship, or research, is not an infringement of copyright. In determining whether the use made of a work in any particular case is a fair use the factors to be considered shall include:
>
> (1) the purpose and character of the use, including whether such use is of a commercial nature or is for nonprofit educational purposes;
>
> (2) the nature of the copyrighted work;
>
> (3) the amount and substantiality of the portion used in relation to the copyrighted work as a whole; and
>
> (4) the effect of the use upon the potential market for or value of the copyrighted work.[10]

The statute restates but does not change the pre–1976 law. The same four criteria must be reviewed, though the statute does not *require* a court to consider all four factors or to give greater weight to one than to another.

Purpose and Character of Use. Nonprofit educational users will find judicial preference. Commercial users will not find a similar warm reception, though the courts will look closely at the character of the use. If a commercial also conveys useful and factual information to the viewer, it will much more likely find favor in a fair use analysis.[11]

Nature of the Work. "The scope of fair use is greater when informational-type works (such as scientific material or articles, as opposed to more creative products) are involved."[12]

Amount and Substantiality of the Portion Used. For advertising (but not always for computer areas) the quantitative test generally applies. While 100 words taken from an encyclopedia *may* be fair use, 100 words taken from a short story may not be, because in the latter, that quantity represents a substantial part of the work (though it will be considered with other factors set forth in the statute).

Likewise, quotations from letters and newspaper columns (for example, a favorable write-up of your product) warrant careful scrutiny.

Because these are such brief works to begin with, even a very short quotation may constitute a "substantial portion" of the work. Finally, while it is always correct to give credit to the author of the copyrighted material, this alone will not shield you from liability for the use.

Market Effect.   This is traditionally the most important evaluative criterion or at least the one best understood by the public. A use that supplants any part of your normal market for a copyrighted work will ordinarily be considered an infringement.[13]

A final test is that "fair use presupposes good faith and fair dealing."[14] For advertising this criterior is applied most often to people particularly in the area of off-color humor. For parody you must show critical commentary on the copyrighted material,[15] and the parody must not reduce the demand for the copyrighted work.[16]

The courts are clear that "the first amendment is not a license to trammel on legally recognized rights in intellectual property."[17] If you design a calendar similar to another your parody defense may fail.[18] Likewise, case law bars using Walt Disney characters as members of a "promiscuous, drug-ingesting counterculture."[19] You must show your use was fair and reasonable, stimulated artistic creativity under the circumstances, and was a new idea, not merely the unauthorized copying of the expression of someone else's idea.

Distinguishments of Promotion Piece Classes

It may be useful to review certain legal rights you have in each type of promotion piece you might consider copyrighting.

Advertisements.   Any advertisement that you have created by your own skill, labor, and judgment may be copyrighted so long as it is not misleading and deceptive (another good compliance reason to have counsel scrutinize your ad copy) and is not so *descriptive* of a product that it doesn't comply even with the slight requirement of originality.[20]

A direct mail piece stands apart, and you'll protect it accordingly. What if you advertise in a newspaper or magazine? The registration of a claim of copyright by the publisher of the media vehicle you are currently utilizing does not protect individual advertisements featured. You must separately register your ad. This is different from an article that appears in the same media—the author and the periodical itself are protected. *Note:* The newspaper or magazine has no proprietary right to your ad. In the absence of an *express* agreement to the contrary, you, as the advertiser who prepared the ad, retain copyright and merely grant a license to print it.

The social policy behind this, as enunciated by the court, is that persons who submit their advertisements intend to advertise in as many publications as their resources permit. They have little knowledge of copyright law and, if they did, wouldn't elect to assign away their ads.[21]

The publisher can get ownership, but only through an express written agreement which might involve a work-made-for-hire relationship (see the discussion in this chapter).

Finally, remember you are copyrighting an expression of an idea, not an idea itself. Other persons are permitted to describe the same item so long as the portrayal is drawn from the product itself and not from your copyrighted advertisement.[22]

Catalogs. As discussed, the essence of copyright protection is a modicum of originality, not a great work of art. You can create originality through layout, background, spacing, color, and other means of individual expression. After you've put your time, money, and original thought into creating, in a tangible form, your "silent salesman,"[23] you're ready to copyright the catalog.

A copyright of your catalog as a whole protects all copyrightable contents, including each illustration.[24] This is an important protection for you. Otherwise, if only the whole catalog were protected, and not each of its parts, then your competitors could select just a few items from your copyrighted catalog and selectively pirate them. Therefore, protection of your catalog extends to both the description of each item or component part *and* the total arrangement of the catalog.[25] Your protection does not give you a monopoly on the articles described in the catalogs but only in the manner you portray and describe them.[26] Portrayal is held to a standard of reasonableness. Merely cutting out a competitor's illustrations and decreasing them in size is not an original contribution but a blatant copyright infringement.[27]

Photographs. You may use these in a variety of promotions. Again, you can get a copyright here if you make an original contribution to the posed subject. This contribution can be in arrangement, lighting, angle, or other form of unique expression you portray. Again, any other individual may photograph the same subject and copyright the result so long as it is not merely a copy of your photograph. Copyright protection for your photographs is discussed in greater detail below.

Lists. Compiling public domain information in an original way through independent research will entitle such list or directory information to copyright protection. This applies to telephone directories[28] and the mailing lists[29] essential to your marketing. The copyright is not in names and addresses but in the compilation you do. If you're interested in copyrighting your list, you'll be able to further utilize your seed names. Errors in the spelling of names and addresses that are faithfully copied by your malfeasant competitor create a prima facie case of copying for your copyright infringement action.

Copyright Protection for Your Photographs

As stated earlier, our Constitution sought "to promote the Progress of Science and useful Arts" so as to encourage and protect intellectual expression. At one time there was some question as to the validity of a copyright in photographs due to a lack of a "writing" and a mechanical process.

The Supreme Court ended this dispute by holding that a photograph of a person, in the production of which the photographer poses the subject, selects and arranges the costume, draperies, and other accessories, adjusts the lights and shades, and suggests and evokes the expression, must be deemed work of art and its maker an author, inventor, or designer of it, within the meaning and protection of the copyright statute.[30] The photographer was a creator of fine art.

A later court stated, "no photograph, however simple, can be unaffected by the personal influence of the author, and no two will be absolutely alike."[31] The latter was a bit of hyperhole, but it is well established that one can copyright an *original* photo. Originality is important, though it is often a difficult question if the alleged infringement of copyright is committed not by copying directly from the photograph but by knowingly posing the same subject in exactly the same manner, with identical light and shade, angle, and position.

A less difficult issue is where the author merely copies a preexisting work without exerting any intellectual effort. A recent decision[32] is instructive. A plaintiff's catalog contained photographic reproductions of its merchandise. The defendant's catalogs used line drawing. To prove a copyright violation, the plaintiff has to show more than similarity; it has to show actual copying. If it can do so, then the copyright law protects against unauthorized copy not only in the original medium in which the work was produced but also in any other medium.

The court reveiwed both catalogs and found that the merchandise was identically featured, positioned, and set at identical angles to the viewer. Identical props were used also. The court found actual copying of copyrighted material and that the plaintiff's copyright in catalog photos precluded unauthorized copying by drawing or in any other form.

We've reviewed your right to copyright and the need to obtain a warranty of originality. Another important issue to you is who will own the photo. The independent photographers you retain own their work from the instant they create them, unless they agree to waive that ownership right by means of a "work made for hire" (discussed below).

A commissioned work is not a work made for hire unless the parties expressly agree *in writing* that the work is to be considered made for hire. Specifically, a photograph would be a work made for hire if:

(1) It is prepared by an employee within the scope of his or her employment (as an employer you are considered the author of a photo produced by your employees who perform such duties); *or*

(2) It is specifically ordered or commissioned for use as a contribution to a collective work, as part of a motion picture or other audio-visual work, as a translation, as a supplementary work, as a compilation, as an instructional text, as a test, as answer material for a test, or as an atlas, *if*

all parties expressly agree in a written instrument signed by them that the work shall be considered a work made for hire.

You should review with counsel whether it is in your interest to seek a work made for hire or whether one-time use is sufficient. The precise wording of your agreement is important if you seek a work made for hire. If it is not a work made for hire, you will have to renegotiate with the photographer for further specific rights. Many agencies and their clients are looking for full buyouts, a trend that has sparked debate in the trade press.[33]

You might also review with your counsel the extent to which your photo(s) will be exposed to the "fair use" doctrine (again, the privilege others have to use copyrighted material in a reasonable manner without your consent).

Finally, you should be aware that if the photographer sells you all rights to a photo (instead of signing a work-made-for-hire agreement) he or she *still retains* authorship and the right to terminate the agreement in 35 years.

Alleging Infringement

As you'll see on Form TX, the required form of notice consists of three elements:

- The symbol "C" or the word "Copyright", or the abbreviation "Copr.";
- The year of first publication;
- The name of the owner of the copyright.

This will put your rights on public notice. However, not all your competitors are honest, and someone may violate your exclusive rights. If this happens, what do you do?

If you are the legal or beneficial owner (check with counsel) of any exclusive right under copyright, you can bring a civil action within three years after your claim accrues. Your counsel will confer with you as to whether you've recorded the pertinent instrument(s) in the Copyright Office.[34] There are narrow exceptions here, and if necessary you'll discuss them. Then, you will have to prove that the other party (defendant) has copied your protected work. To do this, you must prove both access and substantial similarity as to "material and substantial" part of the reproduction.

To establish *access,* you can show that the defendant had actually read or seen your copyrighted work or had a "reasonable opportunity to view your work."[35] Evidence that a third party with whom you and the defendant were both dealing had possession of your work is sufficient to establish access.

Assuming you can prove defendants had access, you must also demonstrate (depending on the circumstances a presumption of access will exist if you establish substantial similarity) that there is *substantial similarity* between the copyrighted work and allegedly infringing work in both ideas and the expression of those ideas. Here you'll have an "extrinsic" and an "intrinsic" test.[36] The extrinsic test focuses on a visual comparison of the two works as to specific criteria which can be listed and analyzed. Do they look substantially similar (as to appearance or text) to the average lay observer? For example, you will review overall page format, drawings, and their scale, shading and detail, and the like. Expert testimony may be introduced.

The intrinsic test focuses on a substantial similarity between the forms of expression presented in each work. This is a reasonable-person standard and can be demonstrated by a lay person's evaluation or indirectly, through orders mistakenly placed as a result of the substantial similarity of the promotion pieces or catalogs.

Finally, if you license another party to use your copyrighted material, the licensee must use the material in accordance with the terms of the license. In an action for infringement, the defendant bears the burden of proving that their use of the infringing material was authorized by the copyright owner.[37]

Besides statutory damages, a copyright proprietor is entitled to "all the profits which the infringer shall have made from the infringement."[38] Such profits (so long as they are not remote or speculative[39]) may be indirect as well as direct profits.[40]

WORK MADE FOR HIRE

Employment Relationship

There is an exception to the concept of copyright ownership initially vesting in the creator. This occurs when an employee created a work for an employer within the scope of the employment relationship. Unless the parties expressly agree otherwise in a written instrument signed by them, the employer owns all of the rights comprised in the copyright.[41] The key is the employer's control over the employee and the exercise of such control. Factors bearing on whether a work is one made for hire include:

(1) Was the author paid for the work?

(2) Was the work created at the employer's own volition?

(3) Was there an express contract for hire (especially one restricting the author's freedom to engage in other related creative activities)?

(4) Did the author maintain regular working hours, controlled and directed by the employer?

(5) Did the employer withhold income tax?

(6) Was the work created at the employer's place of business?[42]

If you can answer yes to all of the above questions, you probably have an employee employed by the employer for the purposes of the copyright law. In this case, the employer owns the creation. If factors 4 and 6 were questionable, you'll still probably have a happy employer. Creativity cannot be regulated, and the insights or artwork may come at any time, not necessarily during office hours. Such productivity will be part of the terms of your employment if the subject matter is reasonably within the scope of your employment.

There is a stong social utility to this doctrine. First, where the employer conceives a project and bears the financial risks, the employer should be entitled to the authorship of the work. Second, many creative efforts we take for granted could not be accomplished any other way. A company that creates a daily newspaper simply could not afford the ongoing financial and time cost of daily negotiations. A dictionary requires a blending of many creative efforts, a feat that could not be accomplished if each employee-contributor could arbitrarily pull out his or her individual work product.

A motion picture studio creates an animated film. Hundreds of animators, directors, writers, and others are involved in the final product. It would be an undue burden to obtain a copyright assignment from each contributor and to risk cancellation of such assignments after the 35-year statutory period expires.

None of this precludes your obtaining the employee's written assignment of his or her rights in "your" work to you. If it's important, ask, negotiate, or beg as the case may warrant.

Statutory Works Made for Hire

If you do not have an employer-employee relationship, there is another way you can enter a work-for-hire relationship in certain specified instances—you can specifically order or commission an independent contractor to prepare a certain type of work. This limitation is in significant contrast to the general contractual rule that parties are free to put whatever provisions they want in their contracts so long as these are legal and not contrary to public policy. It is also in contrast to the former law on copyright.

Until January 1, 1978, almost any commissioned work, even one made on a one-time commission, could be considered a work made for hire, and the copyright belonged to the purchaser instead of the creator of the work.[43] Under the new law, only certain types of commissioned works can be treated as works made for hire, and then only if the creator and the person or entity commissioning the work expressly agree that this is to be the case. Such express agreement must be in writing signed by both parties.

Prior to January 1, 1978, the "intent" of the parties had to be ascertained. Now, a writing controls only that there is no permissible issue of extraneous intent. Outside of these situations, the initial copyright in a commissioned work will belong to the creator regardless of whatever agreement may be made. The copyright law clearly defines what specific categories of works will be deemed works made for hire:[44]

(1) A contribution to a collective work. A "collective work" is defined as a work, such as a periodical issue, anthology, or encyclopedia, in which a number of contributions, constituting separate and idependent works in themselves, are assembled into a collective whole. A contribution to a collective work could be a photograph for a book of photographs or a painting for a multimedia work. Copyright ownership in each separate contribution is distinct from copyright ownership in the collective work as a whole.[45]

(2) Part of a motion picture or other audiovisual work.

(3) A translation.

(4) A supplementary work. "Supplementary work" is defined as a work prepared for publication as a secondary adjunct to a work by another author for the purpose of introducing, concluding, illustrating, explaining, revising, commenting upon or assisting in the use of the other work, such as forewords, afterwards, pictorial illustrations, maps, charts, tables, editorial notes, musical arrangements, answer material for tests, bibliographies, appendixes, and indexes. An illustration for a book jacket could possibly be a "supplementary work."

(5) A compilation. A "compilation" is defined as a work formed by the collection and assembly of preexisting materials or of data that are selected, coordinated, or arranged in such a way that the resulting work as a whole constitutes an original work of authorship. The copyright in a compilation covers the arrangement and selection of the material.

(6) An instructional text. An "instructional text" is defined as a literary, pictorial, or graphic work prepared for publication and with the purpose of use in systematic instructional activities.

(7) A test.

(8) Answer material for a test.

(9) An atlas.

To recap, then, your agreement must be *express* (incorporating specific unambiguous language). The phrase "work made for hire" is a legal term and should be specifically used wherever that is your intent. You should make it clear that you shall be the sole proprietor of all rights in such work including (but not limited to) all copyrights and renewals. You should also clearly set forth your right (at your sole discretion) to alter, expand on, adapt, advertise and so forth, said work as you see fit. For example, your agreement may be worded along the following lines:

(1) The said work (or "works") and all other works produced and supplied by the artist pursuant to this agreement shall be considered a work made for hire. This work has been specially ordered or commissioned by (you/your firm) within the meaning provided by the definition of such terms set forth in section 101 of the Copyright Revision Act. (You/your firm) shall be the sole proprietor of all rights in such work including, but not limited to, all copyrights and renewals thereof. Further, it is specifically understood that (you/your firm) has the right to alter, expand,

adapt and make any arrangements of said work, and (you/your firm) shall have the sole right to decide whether and in what manner said work shall be published, advertised, publicized, performed, or exploited by (you/your firm), its successors and assigns.

(2) (You/your firm) agrees to pay to the artist, and artist agrees to accept in full consideration for all services and materials provided by artist pursuant to the Agreement, the sum of $ _____ .

(3) Artist represents and warrants to (you/your firm) that:

(a) The work created by him/her is original.

(b) It does not and will not infringe upon or violate the copyrights or any other rights whatsoever of any person or entity.

(c) No adverse claim exists with respect to it.

(d) It has not heretofore been published or exploited in any form anywhere in the world.

(e) He/she has the full and exclusive right and authority to enter into this agreement.

(4) The artist will indemnify and save harmless (you/your firm) as well as any other person, firm or corporation making use of such work from and against all loss, damage or expense including reasonable attorney's fees, resulting from or by reason of the breach of any representation or warranty herein made by the artist.

These agreements can be used to clarify the "scope of employment" and to make appropriate provisions for works arguably outside that scope. They can also be used to address related trade secret ownership issues (review with counsel any such issues you believe should be integrated into the agreement).

On the other hand, the independent contractor will be attempting to reserve certain rights, such as the right to reproduce the work in another medium or to reproduce it after the commissioning party has had a specified period of time in which to exploit the work.

In addition to being express, your agreement must be *in writing* (verbal understandings are no good) and *signed by each party*. The work itself must be *"specially ordered or commissioned"* (to be commissioned, a work must be prepared at the request of the person for whom it is done). The agreement *applies only to special categories of work prepared for certain specified purposes.* The particular types of works are listed above, and that list is not merely illustrative, it is exhaustive—if a work doesn't fall within any of these categories, then it cannot be a work made for hire, even if it has been prepared by one person upon the special order or commission of another.

Thus, for example, the ordinary trade book (or novel), even though specially ordered or commissioned by a publisher, cannot be converted into a work made for hire simply by including in the contract a clause such as the one above because the ordinary trade book is not within any of the categories in the statutory definition. But it would appear that most textbook material (whether or not in book form or prepared in the form of text matter) would be classified as an "instructional text," one of the specific categories of commissioned works that can be considered a work made for hire (the definition of "instructional text" appears in the statute).

Note: No work of the United States Government can be covered by the work-made-for-hire relationship when such work is prepared by an officer or employee of the U.S. Government as part of that person's official duties. This provision applies to any covered work, whether published or unpublished. Such works are in the public domain.

Finally, while copyright law generally follows the "life plus 50" rule (copyright protection extends for the life of the author plus 50 years), work for hire is an exception. Here, the copyright protection endures for 75 years from the first publication or 100 years from the year of creation, whichever expires first.

Legislative Changes Coming and Those Already Here

Politics is the present tense of history. As such, it is always important to view every law not just in the textbook but in the context of the dynamic legal marketplace (the state and federal legislatures and agencies and the courts). These can be as important to market planning as census tracts. Over the past few years there have been a number of proposed state and federal changes to the work-for-hire relationship. Some would remove certain categories from among the types of assignments that can be done as work-for-hire. At the state level, legislation has passed affecting the relationship as to compensation.

California enacted S.B. 1755 to amend its Labor and Unemployment Code[46] to include within the definition of employee "any person while engaged by contract for the creation of a specially ordered or commissioned work of authorship in which the parties expressly agree in a written instrument signed by them that the work shall be considered a work made for hire," as defined in the 1976 act, where the ordering or commissioning party obtains ownership of all the rights comprised in the copyright in the work.

The California law also added a section to its Unemployment Insurance Code, defining an employer as "any person contracting for the creation of " a specially ordered or commissioned work or authorship as defined in the Labor Code. Similar legislation has been introduced in other states. If this area is important to you, ask your counsel to monitor state activity, or do it through your own profit preservation center (see Chapter 24).

Recently, groups representing graphic artists and other creators of works that are generally produced on a work-for-hire basis have sought to limit the doctrine or to ensure that their members receive certain benefits accorded employees. Such persons want it both ways. They want an independent lifestyle with employee benefits and the right to promote their artistry with the commissioning party assuming all risk. Finally, the result of their legislative agenda would be to nullify Congress's intent to create opportunities outside the workplace environment which will foster the maximum cost/benefit in creating/exploiting original expression.

A Final Word on Copyrights

Every person who creates, publishes, or owns a copyrightable work (or wishes to acquire one) has a vested interest in knowing how to protect the varied subsidiary rights in his or her property. These topics are essential to modern advertising.

This chapter should be read in conjunction with other chapters relating to intellectual property rights, such as trademarks (see Chapter 5), patents (Chapter 4), or product/character licensing (Chapter 28).

PHOTOS AS A MARKETING TOOL

If it's even half true that one picture is worth a thousand words, then photographs can save a lot of copy space. Photographs know no literary restrictions. Often they are essential to a successful catalog. As with anything of such marketing utility, you should be familiar with some core law impacting this area. We'll review the (somewhat) dry but necessary areas of law you will find useful and must consider before you proceed further.

Before You Shoot

As with any business commitment, you'll proceed to draft a binding agreement with your photographer. A photographer's bid for your work often suffices in lieu of a contract, but this is not a safe way for you to do business. Get all the details you can in writing. These written agreements may be form agreements, invoice forms, purchase orders, or some other operative writing probably designed by an agency. Your form of agreement should include (at a minimum) the following points:

- Name, address, and designation of each party.
- Licenses if needed (including applicable fees and taxes).
- Statement of agreement specifically detailing the nature and requirement of the job to be done, for example:
  (1) Black-and-white or color.
  (2) How the photo will be used.
  (3) Single-page or double-page.

(4) Whether you will receive one selected photo or all the photos taken during the photo session.

(5) What type of shooting is required (fashion or product).

(6) How many shots the photographer can do per day, etc.

- The terms of the agreement as well as any factor that may limit or expand such term. Make sure the photographer and any assistants, as well as the models you need, all will adhere to your agreed-on schedule (include specific "weather-permitting" days if needed).

- Place of performance (whether you'll need a studio or location setting).

- Copyright interests, including a warranty that such photo is original, does not invade an individual's privacy, etc. (see discussion below).

- Compensation, including which expenses (e.g., labor, film, special equipment, specialist assistance and transportation) are reimbursable.

- Effect of termination (whether a fee will be paid and how far in advance a cancellation may be made without penalty) or of noncompletion of the project. Spell out the variety of reasons that could prompt a postponement or a re-shoot.

- Indemnification provisions, such as the usual negligence protections as well as who is responsible for loss of or damage to film (see below), photo, etc., and who is responsible for which releases (see below). Finally, make sure the photographer has insurance for himself or herself and for employees.

- Arbitration of disputes.

- Assignability.

- Governing law.

- Date of contract and signatures of parties to be bound.

At this time it is important to define the copyright interests and reach an accord as to the releases. Both matters are essential to your adequate protection. Copyright protection has been reviewed in depth, releases are covered below.

Releases

Once you have finalized your agreement and copyright rights, you should obtain releases of all subjects prior to the shooting. For all photos (or TV and movies) you should obtain an affidavit setting forth the time and place of taking the photograph. This is preferable to merely dating the photo. Then you'll want to consider a variety of releases depending on location, subject, age, etc. A release is no cure-all, but it may protect you from a lawsuit for invasion of privacy or libel. (Be sure to get adequate errors-and-omissions insurance against these risks in addition to receiving a release.)

What may seem like a poignant moment or a photographic scoop may also result in exposure similar to the use of retained talent. Any photo that would or could place an individual in an embarrassing situation, be it an unreasonable intrusion upon a person's seclusion or an appropriation of a person's likeness (or name) for commercial purposes, should be reviewed with your counsel.

The following checklist is a minimum review for your photo release. (Many of these issues should be considered in *any* release you draft for any situation in advertising or similar creative ventures).

- Consider the location. A building has no right of privacy, and generally naming or depicting buildings in your promotions is not a problem. However, certain states such as New York[47] give protection to those buildings of nonprofit, religious, benevolent, educational, fraternal, and similar organizations. Review with your counsel whether you'll need a written property release to use any building if you have any doubt whatsoever. You may also need releases from neighboring premises or permits from local governments to work in the adjoining streets and sidewalks.

- If your subject is an adult, you'll want to include (at a minimum) the following points in your release:

  (1) The specific purpose of the release, such as "grant of right to use photographs for advertising purposes." As the buyer you'll wish to include here the photographer, advertising agency, and similar professionals involved in creating and disseminating the photo.

  (2) The names and addresses of the parties to be bound and protected.

  (3) The consideration bargained for and exchanged.

  (4) A waiver of any liability due to blurring, distortion, alteration, optical illusion, use in composite form, color, or otherwise, even though it might hold the subject up to "ridicule, scandal, reproach, scorn, or indignity."

  (5) The location of where photos will be shot.

  (6) Whether the subject's name will be used with the photo (or whether a fictitious name will be given to it).

  (7) A statement that you will retain all rights and interest in the negatives as well as in finished prints and reproductions. Such rights should specify copyright, publication for any lawful purpose whatsoever in any medium in color or black and white. Another such right is not to use the photo at all.

  (8) The right of the subject to inspect or approve the final product or copy in which he or she will be featured *or* a specific waiver of this right.

  (9) A statement that the subject is of full age and has read and understood the release and is fully familiar with its contents and effect. Finally, that such release endures to the benefit of the subject's legal representatives, successors, heirs, licensees, and assigns.

- If you're using a professional model, you'll have to consider all of the above issues as well as indicate a minimum amount of different poses (and times or dates, if more than one) as well as the right of the model to receive copies of each pose at no cost as well as the option to purchase others at a specified price.

- If you're photographing a minor (check laws of each state as to what constitutes a "minor"), you'll need a parent or guardian to sign the release. Such individual will specifically warrant that she or he is of full age and has every right to contract for the minor in this regard. Sometimes there is resistance to a carte blanche release, and you might have to obtain a release after the original photographs have been inspected.

- Keep track of any alternate models you use or have had referred from an agency. An alternate is not bound by the release of an earlier photo subject. In case of illness, accident, etc., forcing you to select an alternate, make sure the release is duly executed individually with that person.

- If you are dealing with nude models make sure the picture itself isn't obscene for your targeted market. "Community standards" usually define your exposure, and attitudes vary. Obscenity charges are backed by penal sanctions, so you should review any questionable photos and markets with your counsel.

- If using an animal, get the consent of the owner of the animal.

- If you shoot random crowd shots in public places you're generally safe, except as noted above. However, any use of a photo that would imply endorsement (or that outright endorses) of your product or service will require a release.

Taking the Photo

You've got contracts, insurance, and releases protecting you. However, you should remain alert as to your legal exposure regarding "candid" shots of individuals you have not contracted with. The mere taking of someone's photograph without his or her consent has not ordinarily been considered by the courts as an invasion of privacy. Most people do not object to having their picture taken. It is not until the picture is published — usually for some purpose that is offensive to them, or for some commercial purpose—that they ordinarily become offended. Then a key issue is one of location.

Generally, when the picture is taken on the public streets, or in a public place such as a courtroom or a sporting event, the courts have refused to consider the photo-taking as an invasion of privacy even if the individual was disturbed by it. An invasion of privacy usually requires the following:[48]

(1) An intrusion into an area or activity the subject had a right to believe would be private.

(2) Such intrusion must be one that would cause emotional distress (shame, humiliation, outrage, or the like) to a person of ordinary sensibilities. Without such evidence of emotional distress a court is unlikely to find the photographer pecuniarily liable.

It is wise to get consent for any photographic shooting that might result in an intrusion. The consent should be documented in writing and must exist at the time the alleged intrusion takes effect. A noncontemporaneous consent will probably fail as a defense.

Liability for Lost Film

After the photography has been accomplished, all efforts can go down the drain if the film is lost or stolen while in the hands of an independent developer. What can you salvage from such loss? This is the classic bailment situation reviewed in Chapter 7. A bailment is the relationship created by the transfer of possession (but not title) of an item of personal property by one, the bailer, to another, the bailee, for the accomplishment of a particular purpose. The failure to return the film on demand by the bailee is an indication of the failure to exercise ordinary care under the circumstances.

Ordinarily, actual value is held to be a proper measure of damages. Sometimes intrinsic (though not mere fanciful or sentimental) value will be awarded. This is because the film may have a peculiar value to its owner that is not measurable in terms of market value.

At a minimum, you can usually recover the cost of film and an amount sufficient to cover the costs of retaking the pictures *if* you've planned properly. However, you should be able to demonstrate that you clearly informed the developer as to the particular or peculiar value of the film to you.

Finally, watch out for disclaimers. If the film is important to you, you should negotiate around these. Failing that, you might be able to argue that the disclaimer was unconscionable—depending on the adequacy of disclosure, bargaining power of the parties, etc. However, if you merely accept a disclaimer, you may later find that "the limitation remedy was adapted to the general commercial background and commercial needs of the film industry."

This is not meant to be an all-inclusive explanation of the legal issues surrounding the photographs you're utilizing. The fact that you are aware of the legal exposure and are acting accordingly does not mean you're totally insulated. If you have encountered any ideas you haven't considered previously, follow up on them as soon as possible with your own counsel.

Privacy Rights—Expansion or Explosion?

The area of privacy rights is among the fastest expanding in law today. Models, employees, licensees, and others are broadening the traditional four tort privacy areas of one's "right to be let alone": intrusion, public disclosure of private facts, false light, and appropriation of name or likeness. This discussion is included here because of the potentially significant impact on your use of photographs in your promotions. The general privacy principles apply to any aspect of your promotional policy.

The appropriation of names or likenesses is of particular concern to someone whose career involves advertising. New York is the advertising and media capital of the world, and so it is useful to reflect on its state law on point. In New York the right to be let alone is purely statutory and can be interpreted quite literally. Its Civil Rights Law[49] sets forth five elements to be actionable:

(1) the misappropriation to one's own use or benefit,

(2) of a *living person's* (not a business associations),

(3) name, likeness, photo or any other sufficiently clear representation of such person,

(4) without *written* consent, *and*

(5) for purposes of not incidental commercial gain.

If you merely *suggest* certain characteristics of a person, without literally using his or her name, portrait, or picture, there is no cause of action.[50]

The diversity of decisions arising in our nation's media and advertising capital include cases of look-alikes.

In one case, a look-alike model was used to represent Jacqueline Onassis.[51] The illusion was created that Mrs. Onassis actually appeared in the advertisement. This decision, favoring Mrs. Onassis, should be limited to its narrow holding in a commercial context.

Note: An actor's face has sales value, and the substitution of a look-alike dilutes that value, especially when no disclaimer accompanies the ad.[52] Physical differences (such as a wider face, larger eyebrows, and different glasses) may be a defense, so you should consider planning accordingly.[53] It then "requires the court to answer the almost metaphysical question of when one person's face, presented in a certain context, becomes, as a matter of law, the face of another."[54]

One argument on which you will prevail is that the use of a look-alike's photograph in the advertisement created a likelihood of consumer confusion over the celebrity's endorsement or involvement, thus violating Section 43(a) of the Lanham Act (see discussion later in this chapter on Comparative Advertising).

A photo of a nude parent and child showing their bodies from behind may constitute an invasion of privacy if they are sufficiently identifiable and the photo is used commercially, even if such photo was taken in a public place.[55]

Rules of privacy and release requirements may apply to employees. In *Caeser v. Chemical Bank*,[56] the New York State Court of Appeals (this is the *highest* state court—not its Supreme Court) held against Chemical Bank for the commercial use of a photo of its own employees because there was *no written consent from such employees.* A class action suit had been instigated by employees of Chemical Bank when it displayed a photograph of them at a trade show. The defendant argued that all of the employees knew the purpose for which the photograph was taken and orally or impliedly consented to the display of the photograph in connection with the Bank's business. The appeals court held that "oral and implied consent are available as partial defense in mitigation of damages." They do not provide any defense to liability.

In New York State at least, whenever you use the names of employee(s) in advertising, such as who customers should contact, the employer should obtain written consent to the use of the employees' names. Such consent probably may be reflected simply by having the employee OK and initial a copy for the advertisement, but in the absence of written consent there will always be the possibility of a claim by the employee. The only way to safely use a person's photograph or name in advertising is to obtain a written release that covers the specific use. This includes the publicity announcements corporate PR departments send to the trade press.[57]

What about your voice? A number of promotions utilize a "sound-alike." To date most cases follow the reasoning of the California courts in the Nancy Sinatra case.[58] Here, the singer sued a tire company for using the music and revised lyrics from "These Boots Are Made for Walking," a song she was (and is) closely identified with. However, she had no copyright ownership of the song itself. Imitation alone did not give rise to an action for unfair competition.

Defenses

In any action for these forms of appropriation your counsel will review with you whether:

(a) the likeness is published concerning a newsworthy event or matter of public interest;[59] and

(b) such news stories and articles of public interest can be those of consumer interest such as merchandise, fashion, and the like.[60] The manner of use, not your motive, determines whether it is a newsworthy item or primarily one for trade usage.[61] All of these intricacies point up the necessity for you to review with your counsel both marketing strategies and then particular promotions.[62]

Rights of Estates and Heirs

A final factor to consider is the rights one's estate and heirs have to one's likeness. Obviously, this applies to celebrities and others in the limelight. A number of states have enacted laws in this area, including the following two representative samples:

Kentucky[63] extended an individual's right to protection from unauthorized commercial use of his or her name and likeness for 50 years after the person's death.

Oklahoma[64] made a deceased personality's right to the use of his or her name, voice, signature, photograph, or likeness a property right, which is transferable or which passes to the personality's spouse, children or parents for 100 years after the personality's death. Anyone who uses a deceased personality's name, voice, signature, photograph, or likeness in any manner, for commercial purposes without prior consent is liable for damages. Any profits from the unauthorized use will be taken into account in computing the actual damages. Punitive damages also may be awarded. Uses of a name, voice, signature, etc., that do not require consent include any use in connection with a news, public affairs or sports broadcast, or a political campaign; use in a play, book, magazine, newspaper, musical composition, etc., other than an advertisement or commercial; use in a single and original work of fine art. Anyone who knowingly uses another person's name, voice, signature, photograph, or likeness for commercial purposes without prior consent is also liable for any damages. Any profits from the unauthorized use shall be taken into account when actual damages are computed.

While this is the trend, the courts remain in flux.[65]

Copy Headliner Compliance

All promotional wording must be true (within the bounds of "puffing") and must be able to be substantiated when necessary. You know that certain words catch your targeted customer's eye and make the customer want to read on, or otherwise stay tuned. Using such words effectively is often essential in getting an individual to stay on the phone, open your envelope, or get past your front window.

However, in any offer you employ, you must be cognizant of the words you use in your advertisement for the premium (or any other promotion) and the direct or indirect price comparisons you convey to your recipient. A few years ago my wife and I received a circular from a local store addressed to its "preferred" customers. The circular aroused our interest for the four "magic word" reasons. I'm sure they figured it would. First, it advertised the store's semi-annual *sale.* Second, it offered a 20% *discount* to its preferred customers during the two-day promotion. Third, it stated that all items were *new.* Finally, it promised a *free* bottle of wine just for responding to the ad. Judging by the thriving business they did the evening we dropped by, their promotion was obviously successful (at least for pulling in people). Yours will be, too. We'll look at the law behind those particular words that always capture your viewer's eye and interest immediately.

Your Choice of Headliners

The FTC and your attorney general, and probably your local authorities, have a broad mandate to root out "unfair methods of competition in or affecting commerce, and unfair or deceptive acts or practices in or affecting commerce."[66] They will act against materially deceptive speech (speech that may influence your customer's purchasing decision) when your customer is injured, and such action would be in the public interest.[67] This deception need not deal with substantive qualities of your advertisement copy; any intrinsic fact that may influence your customer's purchasing decision may be material.[68]

Sale

The term "sale" will always catch your customer's eye. The FTC knows this and has enacted guides.[69] Most states, the District of Columbia, Guam, Puerto Rico, and the U.S. Virgin Islands have enacted so-called little FTC acts to prevent deceptive and unfair trade practices. Your customers are familiar with the general terms, and you should be, too. Long-term goodwill as well as legal compliance are at stake.

What Is a Sale?[70]

One of the most frequently used forms of bargain advertising is an offer of a reduction from the advertiser's former price for an article. If the former price was the actual, bona fide price at which the article was offered and *sold* to the public on a regular basis for a substantial period, it provides a *legitimate* basis of price comparison. I emphasize "sold" since this criterion must be demonstrated with objective evidence.

A former price is not necessarily fictitious merely because no sales were made. However, you must be able to objectively prove that the item was openly and actively offered for sale at the unreduced price, for a reasonable period, in the recent, regular course of your business, honestly, and in good faith.

In any sale, you must confirm that the amount of your reduction is not so insignificant as to be meaningless. Because it is a material term (one that influences the buyer's decision of whether to purchase the item), it must be objectively truthful and avoid the tendency or capacity to mislead the consumer. It is particularly important that you consider the nature of your audience. A sale of computer equipment to professionals will receive much less scrutiny than a sale directed to a particularly vulnerable group such as children. A nominal reduction of your price (for example, less than 5%) may be such an omission. Depending on your targeted audience, ticket price, and trade practices, a 10% or greater reduction from the most recent actual going price would be a safe *starting* point, although this may vary in certain state laws or municipal codes. Review these with your counsel.

In general, the product sold at a sale price must not be on sale for more than six months of the year. Further, you must be careful that the sale price doesn't become the "regular" price. The threshold is when more than 50% of your sales are at your sale price. Certainly, words of similar import such as "discount" are governed accordingly.

Must Every Item in a Sale Promotion Be Reduced?

Segregate your catalog pages. If only certain items are on sale, only those items may be so identified. If you call your catalog a "sale catalog" or a similar name, then *every* item advertised in the "sale catalog," or every item included in the "annual sale," "Fall sale," or other such term must represent a reduction from a recent former price that was openly and actively offered for sale for a reasonable period of time in the regular course of business. Also, if you state "at our lowest price ever," *all* merchandise included in this description must actually be at its lowest price ever.

The manufacturer, distributor, or retailer must in *every* case act honestly and in good faith when advertising in any local or trade area (a trade area is one where you do business). Likewise, retailers should not advertise a retail price as a wholesale price. They should not represent that they are selling at "factory" prices when they are not selling at prices paid by those purchasing directly from the manufacturer. When it comes to price reductions, objective verification is the rule, and puffery is not permitted.

Use the following checklist to monitor your sale to ensure that you don't "donate" your profits from the sale to some local, state, or federal agency.

- If quantities are in some way limited, you must disclose any limitation up front. Otherwise you might encounter time requirements. For example, at least one state requires that if your ad does not state a specific time during which your merchandise will be available, you must maintain a sufficient quantity to meet reasonably anticipated demand during three consecutive business days beginning with the effective date of the ad. This does not apply to exclusively in-store ads.
- Your sale price must be a reasonable and honest statement of a valid and recent actual former market price that is now temporarily reduced. Sales that are permanent or continue for a long time are always suspect.
- All items advertised as being on sale in a sales promotion should represent a bona fide reduction from your previous benchmark price.
- Be prepared to substantiate your claim that every item in a sale was *sold* previously in the relevant marketplace (and was not merely offered).
- The duration of the sale offer and items not on sale in a sales promotion must be distinctly identified and distinguished.

What Is a New Item?

This rule is in keeping with common sense: You can't describe a product as new unless it is in fact new in a way significant to your customer. "New" is used to promote a product that either has not yet been introduced into the marketplace or has been "improved" (in which case the marketer may advertise the item as "new and improved").

Also, a new product should constitute the latest model in a particular product line that has not been offered for more than six months.[71] However, in a bona fide test marketing of a new product that does not cover more than 16% of the U.S. population and does not exceed six months in duration from your initial general marketing, the six-months rule does not apply until the test period has ended. For example, say you test marketed a product in Colorado for six months and rolled it out nationally three months ago. It is acceptable to refer to the product as new.

Common sense and basic honesty dictate that your product may not be offered as "new" if it has been used, refurbished, rebuilt, or reconditioned or if *parts* of the item have been so remanufactured. This means returned merchandise may not be cleaned or "improved" in any way and then returned to inventory.

It is a deceptive practice to offer seconds, imperfect or irregular merchandise, at a reduced price without disclosing this fact. Unless stated otherwise, merchandise offered as new may not have been used during a trial period or otherwise (see the discussion of trial versus examination in this chapter under the discussion of the "Free" Rule.) This means that your customer is not obligated to inquire as to whether articles for sale are new, used, or refurbished. There is an implied warranty in all your promotions to the customer that the article is new (that is, not previously sold or used) unless you specifically and clearly disclose otherwise.[72]

Certain states[73] have very exact disclosure requirements and, therefore, you must make sure your counsel reviews all state law affecting your current and contemplated operations and routinely monitors their legislatures.

Finally, be aware that there are a variety of specific guidelines pertaining to different types of merchants and product lines. For example, as to certain book supplementations:

> §256.5 Representations, express or implied, describing a work as "new," "current" or "up-to-date."

> No direct-mail promotional materials or oral representations soliciting the sale of specific industry products should:

> (a) Expressly or impliedly represent that the industry product is new when said industry product was first distributed more than 18 months prior to the time of the offer or dissemination of the advertisement (some examples, but not all inclusive, of terms suggesting new publications are: "Announcing," "Newly revised," "New 8th Edition," "Up-to-date," "New");

> (b) Represent an industry product as current or up-to-date unless the work itself, or the supplementation thereto, is current or up-to-date, considering

the amount and nature of legal activity in the particular area of law covered on the date of issuance of the advertisement; but in no event should any representation be made that the industry product is current or up-to-date when either the copyright date for supplementation of such industry product is more than 18 months from the date of issuance of the advertisement.

Note: Some areas of the law require that some works be supplemented monthly to be considered current, while others may be kept sufficiently current by annual or, in exceptional cases, even less frequent supplementation. In some exceptional cases, for example, where legislatures meet on a biannual basis only, supplementation based thereon may be designated as current and up-to-date.[74]

"Free" Rule

The cardinal rule of any promotion is that your ad must immediately hold your customer's attention. One way to do this is to open with your highest card, namely, whatever is of most significant benefit to the customer, especially if that benefit appeals to the self-interest of your reader or listener. Many people would like to receive something for nothing; the beauty of the simple word "free," therefore, is that it inspires self-interest.

However, it is often subject to abuse by certain firms. For example, if you have ever followed up on a "free checking" sign only to find a host of strings attached—minimum balances, a limit on the number of checks, the required purchase of other services—you are doubtless aware of how costly "free" can be. The lack of clear and conspicuous disclosure of the costs and conditions of services is no defense in promotions (although the consumer of services is free to complain). Your test is that use of the word "free" in an advertisement is prohibited by the FTC unless the item is truly without cost or undisclosed obligation.

What Is a Free Item?

Consumers understand that, except in the case of introductory offers in connection with the sale of a product or service, an offer of free merchandise or service is contingent on a purchase at regular cost of another merchandise or service. The word "free" indicates that they are paying nothing for one article and no more than the regular price for the other and, where applicable, that the regular quality of the goods or services is not being reduced. Thus, a purchaser has a right to believe that the merchant will not directly or immediately recover, in whole or in part, the cost of the free merchandise or service by marking up the price of the article that must be purchased, by substituting inferior merchandise or services, or otherwise.[75]

If you are a direct marketer, such immediate recovery includes shipping and handling charges. Shipping and handling charges cannot be built into or added to a free item (nor can you make a profit on them). For example, if a package is sent to a customer for a "free 15-day examination," the cost of returning the article must not be borne by the customer. A prepaid mailing label must be provided *or* some other device must be used to guarantee no postage costs, such as refunding the cost of the postage or crediting the customer's account for the expense incurred. The use of an item during a trial or examination period is not considered free if recipients must pay the cost of returning the item, should they so desire. This area is often overlooked but is enforced, so review your copy clearly to make sure shipping and handling charges are included in a free order.

Disclosure of Conditions

When making free or similar offers, you must clearly and conspicuously set forth at the outset of the offer all the terms, conditions, and obligations on which receipt and retention of the free item are contingent (including credit limitations and prepayments)[76] to leave no reasonable probability that the offer might be misunderstood. This information should appear in close conjunction with the offer of free merchandise or service. For example, disclosing the terms of the offer in a footnote to which reference is made in the advertisement by an asterisk or other symbol placed next to the offer is not regarded as disclosure at the outset. However, mere notice of the existence of a free offer on the main display panel of a label or package is not precluded, provided that:

☐ The notice does not constitute an offer or identify the item being offered as free.

☐ The notice informs the customer of the location, elsewhere on the package or label, of the disclosures required by this section.

☐ No purchase or other such material affirmative act is required to discover the terms and conditions of the offer.

☐ The notice and the offer are not otherwise deceptive.

Continuous or repeated "free" offers are deceptive acts or practices since the supplier's regular price for goods or services to be purchased by consumers to avail themselves of the "free" offer will, in time, become the regular price for the "free" item plus the contingency purchase. Under such circumstances, therefore, an offer of "free" goods or services is merely illusory and deceptive. As always, review with your counsel any narrower state laws and regulations. For example, in Oregon it is an unlawful trade practice to offer something free conditioned on the purchase of another item (e.g., a car) that is usually sold on the basis of *negotiated* rather than fixed prices.[77]

The following checklist summarizes the Free Rule.

- Any and all terms, conditions, and obligations you are imposing should appear in close conjunction with (physically adjacent to) your offer of "free" merchandise, so that the elements are naturally read together without undue difficulty. If you don't set forth your limitations, the item is free to all, even to those individuals who you know have a definite history of credit delinquency.

- The type size must be at least half as large as the largest type size of the word "free" in the introductory offer copy, exclusive of numerals. This is the rule in New York City and may be the rule in your state as well.[78]

- The qualification terms must be stated together in the same location of your ad, not separated by copy or graphics.

- Disclosure of the terms of the offer set forth in a footnote of an advertisement to which reference is made by an asterisk or similar symbol does *not* constitute disclosure at the outset and will result in noncompliance.

- You may not substitute inferior quality merchandise or services to offset your cost of offering an item as free.

- Be aware that any wording having the practical effect of a free offer is governed by the Free Rule. Words of similar expectation such as "gift," "no cost or obligation," "given without charge," "bonus," or the like "which tend to convey the impression to the consuming public that an article of merchandise is Free" are governed by the Free Rule.[79]

- It is always a good idea to expressly contract with your wholesalers and distributors to pass along promotions as advertised. If a free offer you are promoting is not being passed on by a reseller or is otherwise being used by a reseller as an instrument of deception, it may be improper for you to continue to offer the product as promoted to such reseller. You should consult your counsel and take appropriate steps to bring an end to such deception, including the withdrawal of the offer from your customers. This policing of your resellers is good business as well as good legal compliance.

- Finally, as to timing your free promotion, you should know that:
  (a) A single size of a product should not be advertised with a "free" offer for more than six months in any 12-month period, and at least 30 days should elapse before another such offer is promoted.
  (b) No more than three such offers should be made in any 12 month period.
  (c) During this period, your sale of the product in the size promoted should not exceed 50% of the total volume of your sales of the product, in the same size.

Trial Versus Examination

The distinction between "trial" and "examination" is an important subtlety of regulatory law. If you review various advertisements you see each day, you may observe that your uninformed competitors use them interchangeably, but these are not words of similar import. Incorrectly using the term "trial" may attract regulatory harassment and fines.

Correct use of these terms will prevent legal problems without a loss of sales, since legal compliance means using the words in their logical context.

Again, you may not substitute a used product for a new one without disclosing this fact. Merchandise that has been used on a "trial" basis (for example, during a "15-day home trial") and then returned may not be offered for resale as anything but a used product. In an investigation, the FTC will review your inventory records and study the disposition of all your returned merchandise.

The FTC distinguishes between "trial" (which implies a sustained use) and "inspection" or "examination" (which indicate a mere looking at but not use). If your firm enters a joint promotion with another firm, it is coequally liable for the deceptive practice penalties incurred for disseminating used merchandise as new. Therefore, it is important to review contracts with vendors to make sure you have solid protection in your indemnification clause.

If you plan to refurbish and resell any returned merchandise, use the term "free examination." But realize that use of the word "examination" will not insulate you from a deceptive practice charge if it is apparent from a visual inspection that the products have been used or otherwise significantly handled. Don't try to replace visual inspection with words. Similarly, the legal result of using the word "trial" is never mitigated by a policy of visual inspection which eliminates obviously used products; *all* products are presumed tried and therefore used. In short, you must combine correct use of terminology with an adequate visual check of your returns.

> **TAX POINTER:** Have your counsel review the laws of the respective states in which your promotion is being run. In some states, a seller is not subject to sales and use tax on free promotional material because there is no sale or taxable use of such materials.

Other Promotional Wording

The standard for terms such as "cost," "wholesale," "mill," "leakproof," and "at a loss," is simple truth. However, one of the narrowest regulations on point for many of these terms is New York City's, and if you comply with it you'll be fairly safe—but check with your counsel about specific municipal and state regulations.

In New York City you may use terms such as "manufacturer's wholesale" or "factory price," only where your offering prices are compared to the prices currently and generally paid for such merchandise by retailers in the New York City trading area who also buy that category of merchandise directly from the manufacturer. Also, terms such as "below manufacturer's wholesale cost," "manufacturer's cost," and "our list price" are prohibited as inherently misleading terms.[80]

If you are running a "going-out-of-business sale," you must really be going out of business; the sale must be of limited duration and must not involve an early reopening under the same auspices. Again, check with your counsel as to whether a license is required—in some states and cities it is.[81]

The industry in which you are working may have its own trade regulation rule requirements. For example, in the textile industry the word "mill" indicates the ownership and operation of the manufacturing facility in which *all* textile materials sold under that name are produced.[82] Outside contracting will disqualify you from using the term "mill."[83] This guideline was a result of opinions of the FTC that such phrases as "Factory to You," "Direct to Consumer," "Factory Show Rooms" indicate that the advertiser owns and operates a factory and that the products are being sold at the same price as the factory would charge the wholesaler.

The use of the term "leakproof"[84] or "guaranteed leakproof" as descriptive of dry cell batteries is prohibited by the FTC. Nevertheless, the battery manufacturer is permitted to offer a guarantee to provide payment for damages or a refund to the consumer due to leakage.[85] Interestingly, the FTC leaves the door open for improvement. If any person develops a new or improved dry cell battery the Commission will reevaluate the rule.[86]

The list can go on and on, covering leather belts, tablecloths, sleeping bags, etc. Check with your counsel whether you have your "own" rule.

Use of Flag(s) in Advertisements

A federal statute prohibits the use of the American flag for advertising purposes,[87] and all states as well as the District of Columbia have statutes prohibiting the similar use of their own flag. Legislation designed to prevent the use of these flags for advertising purposes is not an infringement of the right of personal liberty or a violation of the guarantee of due process. An exception permitting newspapers, periodicals, books, pamphlets, and the like, to print a representation of the national flag, disconnected from any advertisement, does not make such statute repugnant to the equal protections of the law's clause.[88]

Use of Currency in Your Advertisements

Much attention was aroused by Time, Inc.'s challenge to a hundred-year-old law enacted during the Civil War to deter counterfeiting by prohibiting the printing or photographing of U.S. currency for any reason. In 1958 the law was amended to permit reproductions of currency for "philatelic, numismatic, educational, historical or newsworthy purposes" but not for advertising.

Sports Illustrated published a cover story with a photographic reproduction of $100 bills, in color and one-third their actual size. This stirred the wrath of the Treasury Department. Time, Inc. challenged the law in court.[89] Time won, but only to the extent that it was permitted to use currency reproductions. All other aspects of the law were upheld. For your purposes:

You *cannot* reproduce currency (paper money, checks, negotiable instruments and other obligations and securities of the U.S.) in any manner in its actual size. It should be larger than (at least one-and-a-half times) its original size or smaller (three-quarters the actual size or smaller). The Court still feels these obvious differences are needed to protect "unwary and inattentive" people from accepting a photograph of money as the "real thing."

Black-and-white reproductions must always be used—the color ban remains. The Court believed this secures a substantial government interest in protecting against counterfeiting.

The reproduction of coins is allowed.

You can use a drawing or photograph of phony (assuming it is false) currency.

If you violate the law, your plates may be destroyed before their use is finished, all your outside printers may be subpoenaed, and you may incur heavy fines.

Commercial free speech is an evolving body of law,[90] so be alert as to changes. However, as matters now stand, make sure your in-house and outside creative people comply with the law. If you're an advertising agency, you should keep the text of the law handy for reference if your client balks.

Major compliance issues arise when certain wording is used either orally or in print to capture the reader's interest or to break down buyer resistance. A premium is placed on clear and conspicuous accuracy. Ambiguity is no asset. A thorough knowledge of the subtleties of the words "sale," "free," "new," "at cost," "trial and examination," and other terms conveying similar meanings will greatly assist you in maximizing reader interest while minimizing the possibility of allegations of unfair and deceptive advertising.

Many other words have compliance variables. New York prohibits the use of the name "United Nations" in ads without the consent of the Secretary-General of the UN. Federal law has coronated "Woodsy Owl" and "Smokey the Bear" with specific protections. You must review your promotional copy with qualified counsel or risk myriad potential problems.

Demonstrating Your Product Visually

Demonstrating a product visually is in effect an "endorsement by sight" of the intended audience. Television is the ideal medium for this type of advertising. (Unless otherwise indicated, "television refers to both commercial and pay programming—cable, direct broadcast via satellite, or a related delivery source.) Viewing a television program requires no skills of the audience.

The product or service demonstration on television has the advantage of creating emotional involvement and of combining sight, sound, and motion, and it is particularly effective for selling "image" rather than utility. Because television air time is costly, the advertiser has little incentive to inform the target audience as to the detailed merits of the product. The advertiser is buying time, and desires to fill such time with promotional hooks, aware that the audience is captivated by variety and repelled by complexity.[91]

The advertiser must balance this desire to sell rapidly to a mass or semitargeted audience against the possibility that a premium on speech might result in a *material* omission that may incur the wrath of the FTC. Any advertiser disseminating a deceptive commercial over broadcast or cable television is subject to the FTC's jurisdiction. An important concept in the FTC's evaluation of ads is the element of materiality— does the error, omission, or deception affect the decision to buy? If it does, is it material?

Some points to consider when planning a visual demonstration include:

(1) Your demonstration must actually prove something relating to the quality of the product.

(2) Your demonstration must accurately reflect the honest experience a user would have. Any demonstrations performed must be able to be duplicated by the average member of your targeted audience.

(3) Consumers are entitled to see what they are told they are seeing.

(4) Your message should be presented in good taste. Further, there should be no visual misrepresentations of any premium, merchandise, or gifts that would distort or enlarge their value in the minds of your audience.

(5) Visual presentations should not utilize speed, color, sound, or other features to mislead viewers about product or performance characteristics.

(6) All demonstrations should be shown in safe environments and situations, i.e., those that don't encourage inappropriate use of your product.

(7) You must be able to substantiate any objective statements made about your product.

The sections following highlight each of these points. A bit of good news—the law here is fairly settled (note the dates in the references), so once you know it, you needn't expect rapid changes. To best appreciate these issues in their overall legal context, read the text on endorsements reviewed at length elsewhere in this chapter.

Does My Demonstration Actually Prove Something?

In print advertising, the FTC considers the advertisement as a whole. The FTC construes ambiguous statements against the advertiser and gears its review to the low-audience standard of the ignorant, credulous, and unthinking.[92] However, so long as the advertisement is true when read in the context of its entirety (qualified where necessary), the advertisement will pass muster.[93]

This is not true on television. When you seek to promote by sight, sound, and motion, your demonstration *must* be relevant to your product's major attribute. For example, a leading consumer products company marketed a product called "Baggies," designed to store food and prevent it from spoiling. The television demonstration focused on the visually more dramatic ability of Baggies to keep water off the contained food. The FTC obtained a consent order stating that the demonstration of Baggies' capacity to keep water out (though true) was irrelevant to its ability to prevent food spoilage. Here, an irrelevant demonstration, although true and accurate in its own right, might influence the purchase of an item not being sold for its primary purpose.[94]

Does My Demonstration Reflect the Honest Experience of the Typical User?

A toy company demonstrated its robot commando, representing that this toy would perform acts as directed by the user's vocal command.[95] In reality, each act was governed by a manual setting of a control on the toy; the toy would perform only the specific act set on the control. If the user wished to see a different act performed, using a "vocal command" was to no avail—the robot would not respond. Only when the user manually changed the setting would the robot perform a different act on command.

The FTC did not approve. It was a less assertive agency in those days and merely required the firm to cease and desist from "stating, implying or otherwise representing by words, pictures, depictions, demonstrations or any combination thereof, or otherwise, that any toy performs in any manner not in accordance with fact."[96]

It is important not to exaggerate or mislead in any demonstration. During the early 1970s, many gasoline additives were on the market in an attempt to capitalize on the post–1973 oil embargo and the ensuing gas price hikes, as well as to cultivate the environment-conscious market. In one advertisement, an oil company showed a car pulling two boxcars and a caboose—a load of more than 100 tons![97] The ad implied that the viewer's car could do this too if he or she used the company's 260 blended gasoline.

After the pitch appeared a repeat of the demonstration with the statement "You're seeing Sunoco premium delivery in this car."[98]

However, the consumer would find in typical driving that the gasoline did not have qualities unavailable in competitive brands. The blend did not consistently provide more engine power than a gasoline of a comparable octane rating.

There was no intent to deceive. The firm sought to capture customer attention by its demonstration. However, its demonstration misrepresented realistic consumer experience and was, at best, a gross exaggeration. The firm sought to enhance a product with a vivid visual image that would remain with the viewer. However, no such demonstration is permitted if it states or implies a material untruth.

Does the Demonstration Accurately Portray What the Viewer Is Seeing?

Prior to the advancements in lighting and photography that television put into place in the mid-1960's, mock-ups or props were widely used to compensate for technical deficiencies and to make products appear on television as they do in life.[99] This form of substantiation in demonstration advertising came to a head in a landmark Supreme Court decision in 1965.[100] Involved was a television demonstration in which Palmolive Rapid Shave shaving cream was applied to a substance that the viewer was told was sandpaper. The thrust of the commercial was to provide visual "proof" that Rapid Shave could soften the sandpaper. However, the shaving cream the viewer saw on TV did not actually come into contact with sandpaper but with a plexiglass prop to which sand had been applied.

The Court stated that the emphasis of a legal review should be on the impression the demonstration will have on the viewing public. Here the FTC had broad discretion due to its presumed expertise in this area.

> In commercials where the emphasis is on the seller's word, and not on the viewer's own perception, the respondents need not fear that an undisclosed use of props is prohibited by the present order. On the other hand, *when the commercial not only makes a claim, but also invites the viewer to rely on his own perception for demonstrative proof of the claim,* the respondents will be aware that the use of undisclosed props in strategic places might be a material deception.[101]

In the final analysis, it was decided that consumers are entitled to see what they are told they are seeing. The FTC need not prove actual deception or that the advertising actually influences consumer decisions. To measure deceptiveness, the FTC looks at the total impression and will reject "literal truth" as a defense if the overall impression is false or deceptive.

Although this was a tough, drawn-out case, in other cases the issues are less complicated. For example, an advertiser for a soup company placed marbles at the bottom of a bowl of soup to force the solid ingredients to the top.[102] The visual effect achieved by this demonstration was that of a bowl of piping hot soup jampacked with vegetables. The defense argued that if marbles were not used, the solid ingredients would sink to the bottom and this would lead viewers to believe that there were fewer ingredients than was actually the case. This argument did not hold water (or soup?). The technique was found to be deceptive since viewers were not seeing an accurate portrayal of what they would actually consume. Seeing is believing when it comes to a legal evaluation of your product demonstration.

In a more recent representative case a product demonstration depicted Bruce Jenner, a well-known Olympic athlete, squeezing an orange while claiming the juice was "pure pasteurized juice as it comes from the orange." He then poured the fresh-squeezed juice into a Tropicana container while the voice-over said, "It's the only leading brand not made with concentrate and water." The court held that the visual portion of the commercial was "not a true representation of how the product is prepared" because the juice was always pasteurized and sometimes frozen before it was put into the container. The appellate court ordered the district court to issue an order preventing Tropicana from running the "squeezing-pouring sequence"of the commercial.[103]

Are My Demonstrations in Good Taste?

The question of good taste involves trade practice and goodwill more than the law. You don't want to offend your audience by producing an ad with negative racial, sexual, or other overtones.

To get an idea of the boundaries of good taste in advertising, it is wise to follow the decisions of the National Advertising Division and the National Advertising Review Board (two self-regulating groups sponsored by the Council of Better Business Bureaus, which are discussed later in this chapter). You can track these organizations' findings by reading trade magazines and by getting on their mailing lists.

What Should You Do?

Tighten (or set up) internal and advertising agency procedures so that you can assure any regulatory or consumer group questioners that your TV commercials authentically depict what actually occurred. To accomplish this, require that an affidavit be provided for each television commercial produced for your company. The affidavit (which should be signed by two responsible people present during the filming) must outline the actual production steps, materials, and techniques that are relevant to the truth and accuracy of your commercial. No commercial should be aired unless an adequate affidavit has been provided in advance.

Finally, go through the checklist concerning visual demonstrations (at the end of this section) from time to time as a refresher on general points in this area.

New Technologies—New Laws?[104]

Computer data bases tied to interactive cable marketing, infomercials, home computers, videotext, etc., will personalize the ability to gear a demonstration to a much more targeted audience. Comparative pricing, demonstrations of utility, and in-depth warranty information will all enhance the knowledge of the consumer. The new technologies will present commercials your customers will want and possibly pay extra for!

This personalized marketing may make current laws on point obsolete. If a consumer can insert a personal shopping profile into a home computer and have a printout of purchase advice based on ad input, then what information is "material" to a purchase decision may be radically altered.

Increasingly, the legal environment you must comply with will be based on the advertising channel you use and the audience you reach through it. For example, the municipality granting your cable franchise agreement might contract for specific regulations governing product demonstrations. Your franchise agreement should be carefully reviewed with counsel as to regulations narrower than current federal and state laws.

It is obvious that nonselective product demonstration to a mass audience is in eclipse. Therefore, as you advertise through varied media (e.g., videotext), in the next few years it is imperative that you review your various contracts and ads with counsel. Don't merely carry over your commercial television marketing strategy and format that worked and were in legal compliance.

The following checklist contains questions you should consider in planning your visual demonstrations.

☐ If this is a simulation, will these words appear across the screen to inform our viewers?

☐ Will the demonstration disclose all relevant information so that the consumer can make an informed decision?

☐ Will the demonstration prove something that is material to the product's utility to the viewer?

☐ Did we carefully review the demonstration to eliminate any express or implied exaggerations or excessive puffery? If the demonstration asserts a scientific argument, have objective and well-controlled tests been performed and documented to verify *all* statements made or visually demonstrated?[105]

☐ Are we demonstrating a product requiring legal disclosures? For example, if the commercial involves the printing of "free" across the screen, do the qualifying terms appear in acceptable print size? Would they pass a Flesch readability test? If the presentation is spoken but requires disclosures, have your demonstration reviewed by one of the agencies that do audio recall tests as well as with your counsel.

☐ Do visual presentations utilize speed, color, sound, or other features to mislead viewers about product or performance characteristics? They shouldn't.

☐ Are all demonstrations shown in safe environments and situations—those that don't encourage inappropriate use of the product.

☐ Do demonstrations accurately reflect the honest experience a user would have? Any demonstrations performed must be able to be duplicated by the average member of your targeted audience.

☐ Is our demonstration in compliance with any FTC orders issued against our firm? If you subsequently violate such orders, *each* broadcast of your commercial may be considered a separate violation.

☐ Are we well versed on the endorsement issues when we're using a personality or spokesperson in the advertisement? The discussion on endorsements should be mastered so as to refine your questions for review with your counsel.

Don't forget that there are still consumer groups and individuals engaging in private verification of demonstrations. (They are usually looking for accuracy, not legal compliance.) Consumers Union, publisher of *Consumer Reports* magazine, is one large testing group, and individuals such as David Horowitz, whose show tests the claims of the advertisers, are also involved. One article quoted Horowitz as stating that one out of four ads flunk their own performance tests.[106] As briefly mentioned in the Colgate discussion, in all these areas more than dollar damages and nuisance penalties are involved. You should also check any self-regulatory codes in your own media—but with caution, to avoid antitrust complications.[107] You may encounter the problem of the emerging issue of *corrective advertising* and other remedial advertising.

COMPARATIVE ADVERTISING

Comparative advertising is a method of promotion whereby you compare the attributes of your product or service, expressly or impliedly, with those of a competitor. Many agree that the Avis "We Try Harder" campaign inaugurated the modern era of comparative advertising.[108] However, without the subsequent prodding by the Federal Trade Commission, the consumer would probably still be witnessing mostly "comparisons" with Brand X.

This section reviews how the FTC acted as a catalyst in this area in its positive desire to increase consumer information choices. It also examines how a variety of firms have used the courts to attack comparative ads; this can help you evaluate your legal exposure when you design your promotion.

Generic Standards for All Advertisers

The FTC has a broad mandate to root out "unfair methods of competition in or affecting commerce, and unfair or deceptive acts or practices in or affecting commerce."[109] It will act against materially deceptive speech (speech that may influence the consumer's purchasing decision) when the injury is to either the consumer or the advertiser's competitor and such action would be in the public interest.[110] This deception need not deal with substantive qualities of a product or service; *any* intrinsic fact that may influence the purchasing decision may be material.[111]

Throughout its history, the FTC has tried to follow the ideal that its regulation would serve two objectives—to provide useful and truthful data and to maintain effective competition. One way to accomplish this is to enforce minimal standards of marketplace compliance. Another way is to affirmatively encourage broader consumer information. One obvious strategy actively employed by the FTC since 1971 is to encourage truthful advertisements that make direct comparisons with competing products. The FTC believes this is socially beneficial because it puts more buying information into the public's hands.

Comparative Advertising—Why Did the FTC Want It?

Until the last decade, self-imposed media and professional regulations discouraged comparative advertising. At one time, CBS and ABC systematically rejected commercials that named competitors. Advertisers had little incentive to produce a comparative advertising campaign that would run only on one station. This policy changed in 1972, and now you can see "head-to-head" beer taste tests or firms comparing their prices to those of a named competitor.[112]

In 1972, the FTC directly intervened with a series of informal visits and correspondence by staff personnel, and the two recalcitrant networks agreed to allow specific comparative advertisements on the air.[113] NBC and ABC have subsequently issued guidelines that seek to ensure that comparative ads are both fair to competitors and of value to consumers. The American Association of Advertising Agencies has adopted a similar approach.[114] By 1978, most restrictions were eliminated, with the exception that comparative advertising must not be "disparaging." Further, all comparisons must be material and must relate to specified product characteristics or properties, and any differences highlighted or compared must be significant.

There were more than just legal hurdles. Market leaders didn't want to dignify their "lesser" competitors with comparisons. Parity competitors often felt they were granting free publicity. To this day you'll note that most comparative claims emulate Avis, in that they proclaim themselves the underdog versus the market leader or industry standard setter.

Advantages of Comparative Advertising

The FTC has taken an aggressive stance in promoting the use of nondeceptive comparative advertising because it has the potential to:

(1) Make the marketplace of commercial ideas self-correcting;

(2) Provide consumers with valuable information; and

(3) Facilitate free and fair competition.

First Amendment theory has traditionally encouraged "free and robust debate" so that all ideas can potentially generate opposing ideas and build from there. Comparative advertising, by providing a medium for commercial speakers to counter the false claims of competitors, could result in an analogous self-correcting marketplace of ideas. Further, it would reduce the general social cost of FTC policing and the specific cost to a firm of an FTC investigation. As one commentator succinctly put it: "Fears of legal problems will most likely impel advertisers to use greater caution in making sure their advertisements are based on clear, honest and substantiable facts, which is of course a major benefit the FTC hopes will come from greater use of comparison advertising."[115]

Such self-policing might have saved a number of firms much time, litigation, fines, and bad publicity. The self-correcting marketplace remains a theoretical goal at present, but it provides a firm philosophical basis for encouraging the development of comparative advertising in the future.

Valuable Source of Information

By contrasting the attributes of competing products in a single format, comparative advertising can provide a useful frame of reference for evaluating a seller's claims and can significantly reduce the cost to consumers of obtaining information.

The mere listing of product attributes is not enough. These attributes will be seen as significant by the consumer only when they are shown to meet the demands of the consumer's evaluative criteria for that specific decision. Comparative advertising can contribute to the total information environment in which consumers make purchase decisions.

The sequence of events that lead to a decision to purchase a product may be summarized as follows:

(1) Problem recognition: realization that a problem needs to be solved;

(2) Diagnosis: determining the cause of the problem;

(3) Examination of the alternatives: searching out possible solutions; and

(4) Product selection: termination of purchase decision when the consumer chooses one product from the alternatives examined.

Information from a wide variety of sources can be used by consumers at each step.[116] Consumers generally acquire information for decision-making through a combination of two basis types of search: (1) internal, through which the consumer retrieves previously acquired information from memory and (2) external, by which the consumer actively seeks information from a number of different sources.

In general, the FTC's position is as follows (emphasis added):

> . . .The Commission has supported the use of brand comparisons where the bases of comparison are clearly identified. Comparative advertising, when truthful and non-deceptive, is a source of important information to consumers and assists them in making rational purchase decisions. Comparative advertising encourages product improvement and innovation, and can lead to lower prices in the marketplace. For these reasons, the Commission will continue to scrutinize, carefully, restraints upon its use.
>
> (1) Disparagement—Some industry codes which prohibit practices such as 'disparagement,' 'disparagement of competitors,' 'improper disparagement,' 'unfairly attacking,' 'discrediting,' may operate as a restriction on comparative advertising. The Commission has previously held that disparaging advertising is permissible so long as it is truthful and not deceptive. . . .
>
> (2) Substantiation—On occasion, a higher standard of substantiation by advertisers using comparative advertising has been required by self-regulation entities. The Commission evaluates comparative advertising in the same manner as it evaluates all other advertising techniques. The ultimate question is whether or not the advertising has a tendency or capacity to be false or deceptive. This is a factual issue to be determined on a case-by-case basis. However, industry codes and interpretations that impose a higher standard of substantiation for comparative claims than for unilateral claims are inappropriate and should be revised.[117]

As the above language indicates, it is quite apparent that the FTC favors comparative advertisements and is loath to encourage narrower self-regulation by the industry. In this regard, two questions remain: Is the FTC's confidence justified? And what legal issues are specifically raised by comparative advertising? As to the utility of comparative advertising, other questions remain.

> (1) Some marketers fear sponsor misidentification (consumers may remember the competitor's brand, not their own).
>
> (2) Some market leaders fear a "ruboff" effect by publicizing the name of their competitor.
>
> (3) Comparative performance information programs could actually produce misinformation by placing an undue emphasis on a single product attribute (or a small number of attributes).

These factors (among others) will be tested and corrected in the marketplace. In the long run, consumer information presented in a clear comparison and stressing self-interest will produce results. An example of how markets respond dramatically to comparison information is provided by the recent surge in "light" cigarettes in response to comparisons between regular cigarettes and those with lower tar and nicotine content. However, while the market is working out all the kinks, you should be aware of the current law. Specifically, the pitfalls revolve around attribute and quality comparisons.

Quality Comparisons

Here there is latitude for "puffery"—our products are "better than our competitors'." However, puffery claims become subject to substantiation whenever they make representations of fact that are verifiable. For example, "our products are best" or our car "gets the most gas mileage" imply *overall* superiority and must be substantiated against all competitive products. Therefore, it goes without saying that the quality base against which a comparison is made must be identified clearly and conspicuously.

Whenever you make a quality comparison, you have the problem of standards. If you assert a claim against all your competitors, you must have objective evidence that you really tested *all* of them. If you did, fine. If you didn't, don't even imply that you did.

What about independent findings? Here you may quote them in a manner meaningful to your audience—and truthfully. This means you may not edit "in such a way as to create an entirely false and misleading impression."[118] Literal statements may not be truthful when they are taken out of context or when they contain deceptive omissions, or when measured against your targeted audience.

A specific example of this deceit by omission was the Lite Bread case.[119] Here the FTC found an implied comparison to white bread in the representation of Lite Diet bread that it could help control weight and that it contained only 45 calories per 17 gram slice. In fact, the only reason that a slice of Lite Diet contained fewer calories than ordinary bread was that the bread was sliced thinner. The omission obviously was a material one and therefore was deceptive.

The FTC has considered comparative advertising as misleading when this emphasizes immaterial differences between products. An immaterial claim is one that involves a distinction between the products that is so insignificant that it does not affect product performance. Here, an irrelevant comparison (though true and accurate in its own right) might influence the purchase of an item not for its primary purpose.

Further, expect particular scrutiny if the buyer (as determined by targeted audience) has a complex buying decision, your claim is serious (for example, if you're selling medical supplies), or your targeted audience will have difficulty ascertaining on its own the validity or correctness of your material claim.

Finally, if you are comparing "Brand X" to your product (and "Brand X" can be quite specific when there are relatively few competitors in your market), the appearance, size, or shape of "Brand X" in your copy or commercial must not be distorted. The impression conveyed must be similar to what your viewer would actually encounter upon visual purchase.

Disputing a Comparison: What the Courts Want You to Prove

The FTC may act on the complaint of an advertiser but is not obligated to do so. The primary vehicle utilized by those contesting the validity of a comparative ad is Section 43(a) of the Lanham Act. This was originally interpreted to apply to trademark infringements and "palming off" of products. It has been interpreted to apply to advertising in a number of cases over the past 15 years and is the most powerful weapon for an advertiser to contest a competitor's claim. If you're active in this field you should familiarize yourself with it. It reads as follows:

> *Any person* who shall affix, apply, or annex, or use in connection with any goods or services, or any container or containers for goods, a false designation or original, or any false description or representation, including words or other symbols tending falsely to describe or represent the same, and shall cause such goods or services to enter into commerce, and any person who shall with knowledge of the falsity of such designation of origin or description or representation cause or procure the same to be transported or used in commerce or deliver the same to any carrier to be transported or used, shall be liable to a civil action by any person doing business in the locality falsely indicated as that of origin or in the region in which said locality is situated, or by any person who believes that he is or is likely to be damaged by the use of any such false descriptions or representation.[120] (emphasis added)

"Any person" must be someone who has a commercial interest reasonably threatened by another's alleged false advertising.[121] Courts have restricted standing to commercial parties *excluding* consumers,[122] and you must show more than mere subjective belief about the promotion's injury to you.[123] A trade association has direct pecuniary interest (in advertising, tax issues, or any matter that threatens its members). In one case:

> [P]laintiff Association has a pecuniary interest in preventing the diversion of trade from its members to the defendants since in return for its services to its members it receives a percentage of the sales price of the pelts sold by them.[124]

Although the vast majority of comparative advertising cases do not involve business-to-business advertising but rather consumer product ads, the same law covers both types of advertising, unless the issue is the Lanham Act. *Consumers may not* assert this act in a false advertising action. Keep this in mind. As to causes of action the following (with their accompanying hurdles) are most frequently alleged in the 1980s.

False Advertising

The Lanham Act "marked the creation of a new statutory tort intended to secure a marketplace free from deceitful marketing practices." To obtain an injunction against an ad you believe false you need not require proof of the intent to deceive[125] but do need to prove the following:

(1) A claim was made about your product in a comparison by your competitor which made a false or deceitful representation about its product;

(2) The claim about your product was false (you need not prove the falsity was willful.)

(3) The deception was material.

(4) The goods or service compared are in interstate commerce.

(5) You are *likely* to be injured in the future by the wrongful diversion of a substantial part of your trade from you to your competitor.

This will be adequate for equitable relief, that is, an injunction to avoid loss of market share. If you wish to obtain damages you must be able to establish that your buying public was *actually* deceived.[126] The court will initially determine whether the representation is false on its face. [127] For example, false visual depictions (such as the color of a tablet) are covered as well as false statements. In reviewing a comparative promotion the court will view "the entire mosaic rather than each tile separately" looking for the "clever use of innuendo, indirect intimations and ambiguous suggestions."[128]

The court will also look at advertising that, although literally true on its face, is perceived by a significant proportion of the relevant market as making "subliminal" or "implicit" claims that are provably false. With regard to the second type of false advertising, the courts sometimes say that the advertising has a tendency to "mislead, confuse, or deceive."[129]

The correct standard of proof is whether it is *likely* the advertising has caused or will cause a loss of sales by showing a logical causal connection between the alleged false advertising and its own sales position. This can be accomplished by producing direct evidence such as testimony from individual members of your buying public or circumstantial evidence such as state-of-the-art audience reaction surveys and other market research setting forth a "qualitative showing that a not insubstantial number of consumers receive a false or misleading impression from it." You may want to show such consumers *believe* one product can be freely substituted for another if this is the false impression you believe your competitor sought to achieve with the comparative ad. You can also show that though the advertisement did not directly or explicitly compare your product, a substantial segment of the buying public perceived the comparison to be made between the two competitors.[130] Such consumers must obviously represent a significant portion of your audience unless you're a mass marketer marketing to everyone.

Your opponent will then counter with its own substantiation. It need not be flawless. Not every misrepresentation concerning consumer test methodology results in Lanham Act liability—only those so significicantly misleading that consumers would be deceived about a product's inherent quality or characteristics.[131]

Finally, to come under the provisions of the Lanham Act's protections you must be able to show that in the comparative ad your competitor made a false statement about its own goods or services. The act does not embrace misrepresentations about a competitor's products. If your competitor makes a false statement about your goods or services alone there is no cause of action under the Lanham Act (though there might be one for a disparagement suit).[132]

The courts are looking at the quality of the representative samples used in the tests (were they truly representative?); supervision, quality, and consistency of grading; time span utilized; bias, and the like. The courts take their role seriously though philosophically.

> . . . Although the task of evaluating scientific product tests may be challenging and distasteful because of the technical and theoretical nature of the procedures involved and the intricate statistical analysis needed to derive qualitative inferences and conclusions from the data, the court is under just as much of a duty to consider and weigh such evidence as it is to analyze economic or scientific evidence in a complicated patent or antitrust case.[133]

Trade Dress Infringement

This is another form of action by those alleging the unfair competitive nature of a comparative ad, and one that is growing in use. While there is no need to register your trademark to receive Section 43(a) Lanham Act protection,[134] this agreement is used by those whose mark is not on the primary register. Here you must allege and prove that:

> (1) The trade dress of the advertiser is so substantially similar to yours that there is a "likelihood that an appreciable number of ordinarily prudent purchasers are likely to be misled, or indeed simply confused, as to the source of the goods in question.[135]

> (2) The complained-of similarity in the appearance of the parties trade dress as to shape, size, or color is attributable to primarily nonfunctional features (there is no useful reason for the similarity except to "palm off" on your success).[136]

(3) Your trade dress has acquired a "secondary meaning" as a mark whose primary significance is identifying your product with a particular source (it's referential rather than functional).[137]

(4) Your trade dress acquired secondary meaning prior to the advertiser's use of the allegedly similar dress.[138]

When you demonstrate all of these elements— nonfunctionality, secondary meaning, and priority of use—you must then prove the substantial likelihood of confusion based on protectable product features. To satisfy the "likelihood of confusion" standard governing trade dress infringement, you must establish that:

(1) The confusion you allege pertains to the source of the product, not merely to its appearance or nature.[139]

(2) Consumer confusion as to source is not merely possible, but likely.

(3) This likelihood of confusion has reference to the "average" or "ordinarily prudent" consumer and not to the "wayfaring fool."[140]

(4) An "appreciable number" of such "ordinary" consumers are likely to be misled or confused.[141]

While no factor is considered dispositive, the courts have consistently reserved the right to decide whether a visual comparison of the products in question reveals such a lack of substantial similarity that confusion is unlikely.

The key to the court's determination as to the likelihood of confusion is whether the defendant manufacturer's or product brand name has been clearly displayed. The prevailing wisdom is that "the most common and effective means of apprising intended purchasers of the source of goods is a prominent disclosure on the container, package, wrapper, or label of the manufacturer's or trader's name . . . [and that when] that is done, there is no basis for a charge of unfair competition."[142] The more dissimilarities one can show the less chance there is that confusion is likely.[143] If the dissimilarities are not readily apparent, you are back to the need to provide specific scientific survey or market research evidence of consumer reaction.

Damages

Section 35 of the Lanham Act[144] provides for a variety of damages, and your chances of being awarded them depends on your ability to convince the court you've earned them.

Accounting for profits will be ordered if the defendant was unjustly enriched, if you sustained provable damages from your competitor's comparative promotion, or if the court feels it is a necessary deterrent to a willful infringer.[145] The latter will not be available if your competitor demonstrates good faith reliance on the opinion of an attorney who was consulted.[146]

Corrective advertising expenses may be awarded where actual confusion exists and there is evidence of wrongful conduct; theoretically, at least, you can remedy the confusion or lost business resulting from your competitor's comparative advertisement.[147]

Punitive damages may be awarded—up to three times the amount awarded for actual damages, based on the circumstances of the case (for example, larger damages may be appropriate for malicious, willful wrongdoing).[148]

Attorneys' fees may be awarded in an "exceptional case" (generally one that merits punitive damages).[149]

Conclusion

Make sure the attributes you stress in the comparison are of actual benefit to the purchaser and are truthful, and that you can objectively substantiate any comparison claims you make vis-a-vis a competitor. An advertising campaign that employs misleading statements or outright deception is as illegal today as ever. If you can make a quantitative case for your proportionately slipping sales, your competitor may suffer damages as well as an injunction.[150] Setting forth a full and accurate comparison is a problem on commercial TV. It is another opportunity for those of you in direct marketing, since the longer informercials and print are more effective media for presenting comparative advertising than the shorter time frames available on radio and commercial TV.

Finally, almost all other advertising law comes into play. If an ad is capable of being misread by the viewer, it may be misleading in the eyes of the FTC[151] and definitely will be in the eyes of your competitors.

Lingering False Beliefs—The Corrective Advertising Remedy

Those who followed the hamburger advertisement disputes in the early 1980s probably noticed that the debate focused on many issues relevant to managers.[152] The companies involved adopted the politician's tactic of turning their commercials into media events. McDonald's and Wendy's charges against Burger King attracted free media coverage and increased public attention to their respective commercials.

Burger King initiated the debate in September 1982, with an assertive comparative ad campaign. McDonald's sought an injunction, and Wendy's sought damages and corrective advertising as well as an injunction. McDonald's also countered with a wave of interview-format *customer testimonials.*[153] The debate involved three areas of interest: the limits of permissible comparative advertising, commercial free speech, and the much threatened, but rarely invoked, remedy of corrective advertising. Let's review just how this remedy has come about and your exposure to it (which will arise primarily if not exclusively from a regulatory body, since the remedy is rarely sought by a competitor).

FTC Remedies Against Deception

The FTC is charged with regulating trade practices, including advertising. The usual remedy in deceptive advertising cases has been the conventional cease and desist order, which defines in fairly broad terms those categories of claims that the FTC has found to be deceptive or unfair and proscribes similar conduct in the future. The FTC can move against all products sold by a party, even if false advertising has been found in the marketing of only one product or group of products, unless the party terminated the alleged practice before the consent order was issued or the party did not act in blatant disregard of the law. The consequence of failure to comply with such an order can be a penalty of up to $10,000 per day per violation.[154] The FTC's creativity in designing relief is broad though not unlimited. For example, it cannot order retroactive private relief such as, restitutionary relief or rescission of a contract in a cease and desist order.[155]

Traditional false advertising has been grouped into three areas: advertisements with misleading implications, advertisements that are deceptive by omission, and advertisements whose lingering effects require some form of correction. Advertisements in any of these categories have the tendency or capacity to mislead an appreciable or measurable segment of the consuming public (as noted, advertisements directed to a particularly vulnerable group such as children are subject to special scrutiny)[156] and the deception is material. The deceptive message need not deal with the substantive qualities of the product; any extrinsic fact that may influence the purchasing decision may be considered material.[157]

Deception by Misleading Implications

This area concerns advertisements that deceive through half-truths rather than outright lies, that is, through claims that are not actually false, but give a false impression. The adverstisement may contain affirmations that are themselves true but necessitate disclosure of further facts to avoid creating a misrepresentation in the minds of the consuming public.

The FTC's general approach has been to attempt to cure this type of deception through disclosures.[158] In a highly publicized case the FTC brought suit against an association making certain nutritional claims about eggs.[159] The association had argued to the effect that no scientific evidence existed that eating eggs increases the risk of cardiovascular disease. The FTC obtained an injunction against the ad as worded on the grounds that the company presented a one-sided opinion as fact (rather than as opinion) and that such presentation was misleading due to the divergence between the company's position and that of many, if not most, experts in the field.

Deception by Omission

An advertisement may be deceptive if it fails to disclose material facts necessary to correct a disparity between consumers' normal expectations about a product and its actual performance, for example, advertisements that do not disclose that clothing is made of flammable fabrics.[160] Similarly, deception by omission can stem from the customer's basic assumption about the condition of a product. For instance, the mere advertising of a product without qualification can raise the assumption in the minds of customers that the product is new.

This theory was codified in 1938 by the Wheeler-Lea amendments to the FTC Act, which defined false food and drug advertisements to include the failure to reveal material facts regarding the consequences of using a product in either the customary manner or under the conditions prescribed in the particular advertisement.[161]

Evolution of the Corrective Advertisement Remedy

The *Listerine* case discussed at the beginning of this section was not the beginning of the FTC's employment of the corrective advertising remedy; rather, the principles of this case had solid foundation in legal precedent ("the label may be newly coined but the concept is well established"),[162] although the Listerine case was the first corrective advertisement order to be approved by the courts.

Prior to "Listerine", the FTC had built precedent through affirmative disclosure cases, advertising announcing penalties imposed, and consent orders specifically requiring corrective advertising. One of the affirmative disclosure cases involved a baking powder company, which for 60 years had widely advertised that its product was superior because it contained cream of tartar rather than phosphate.[163] Eventually, prompted by rising costs, the firm changed its ingredients to include phosphate. It no longer claimed that its product contained cream of tartar and corrected the list of ingredients. However, its labels retained their original name, lettering, coloration, and design—they appeared exactly as they always had. A new advertising campaign stressed the new low cost of the product and dropped all reference to cream of tartar. But the advertisements were also silent on the subject of phosphate and did not disclose the change in product composition.

The FTC required and the court upheld an extended series of disclosures, including the mandatory use of the word "phosphate" as part of the name of the product. The court recognized that it "was proper to require the company to take affirmative steps to advise the public. To continue to sell the new powder on the strength of the reputation attained through 60 years of its manufacture and sale and wide advertising of its superior powder, under an impression induced by its advertisements that the product purchased was the same in kind and as superior as that which had been so long manufactured by it, was unfair alike to the public and to the competitors in the baking powder business."[164]

In a more recent but similar case, a long-established Massachusetts clock company (in business for 150 years) transferred its trade name, trademark, and goodwill to a successor corporation, which began to import clocks from Europe for resale in the United States.[165] The imported clocks were widely advertised as the "product of Waltham Watch Co., a famous 150-year-old company." To correct the false, lingering belief this created—that the clocks under the trade name were the same Massachusetts clock—the FTC ordered disclosures. The court upheld the FTC's order relying on "the well established general principle that the Commission may require affirmative disclosures for the purpose of preventing future deception."[166]

In both cases, the courts clearly recognized the latent effect of prior advertising on the purchasing habits of consumers. At the time of the *Listerine* case, the FTC established another form of corrective advertisement for lingering effects of prior advertising by requiring a manufacturer to pay for advertisements announcing the imposition of substantial civil penalties for making claims that the FTC alleged were not substantiated.[167]

The FTC first discussed its authority to impose corrective advertising in its 1970 consent order[168] regarding Campbell Soup Co.'s allegedly deceptive manner of advertising soup by placing marbles at the bottom of the bowl, forcing the vegetables upward to make the soup appear richer for a visual demonstration on camera. The FTC did not impose corrective advertising but did assert its right to do so in the future if the situation merited a stronger remedy than the traditional cease and desist or affirmative disclosure order.

The FTC's first corrective advertising consent order was obtained in 1971 from ITT Continental Baking Company.[169] The maker of the bread Profile was accused of deceptively advertising that its bread was a weight-control product when, in fact, the only reason Profile was less caloric than other breads was that a slice was only half the size of the other competing brands. The FTC's consent order required that at least 25% of the company's advertising for Profile read during the next year contain corrective advertising disclosures. Ten other consent orders followed from 1971, ranging from advertising to confirm that sugar is not a unique source of strength, energy, and stamina[170] to that explaining that cranberry juice does not contain more vitamins and minerals than tomato or orange juice.[171] In the juice case, the company used the words "high-energy food" to describe its product. The FTC charged that the words were misleading because, technically, high-energy food means food high in calories, a fact that is generally not recognized by consumers. The company was required to spend 25% of its advertising budget for one year to explain the meaning of "high-energy food" and to confess that this translates into calories.

In 1971, the FTC issued a complaint against Warner-Lambert Company, a pharmaceuticals manufacturer, alleging misrepresentation in the company's advertising of Listerine mouthwash.[172] As with all cases concerning comparative advertising, an important issue was how much do consumers really remember? In its defense, this marketing-driven firm protested that its sizable advertising budget creates fleeting impressions at best. The FTC countered with scientifically conducted consumer surveys showing that the ad campaign claims did stay in the public's mind. In affirming the power of the FTC to impose corrective advertising, the appeals court suggested that if advertisements do not have a long-lasting effect, companies everywhere may be "wasting their massive advertising budgets":

> We think this standard is entirely reasonable. It dictates two factual inquiries: (1) did Listerine's advertisements play a substantial role in creating or reinforcing in the public's mind a false belief about the product? and (2) would this belief linger on after the false advertising ceases? It strikes us that if the answer to both questions is not yes, companies everywhere may be wasting their massive advertising budgets. *Indeed, it is more than a little peculiar to hear petitioner assert that its commercials really have no effect on consumer belief* [173] (emphasis added).

This policy toward imposing corrective advertising orders has continued and evolved in recent years. Related remedies have varied from mandatory warning card disclosures to prospective book publishers[174] to the requirement of affirmative disclosures to past and prospective lot purchasers.[175] Finally you might wish to review whether Hertz had more cars than Avis, and who had to replace ads correcting their statements.[176] State agencies may also have the authority to impose affirmative disclosures such as "dieting is required" in advertisement of a weight-loss product and may invite complaints to be sent to its office.[177] This spinoff area is growing and may pose problems for multistate advertisers.

Burden on Commercial Free Speech

Certain critics have argued that corrective advertising is within the realm of prior restraint of advertising expression or, in effect, a form of censorship—the advertiser can avoid a corrective order only if it is willing to abandon its entire advertising campaign. However, this line of argument confuses the free expression of individual ideas with the commercial advertisers' presentment of facts. The Supreme Court has recognized that "the particular consumer's interest in the free flow of commercial information. . .may be as keen, if not keener by far, than his interest in the day's most urgent political debate".[178]

However, the opinion also recognized that the free flow of commercial speech was not incompatible with some forms of government regulation. Time, place, and manner restrictions as well as "truth-in-advertising" laws were deemed an acceptable "burden" on commercial free speech.[179] In another opinion the Court recognized in-person solicitation because its potential for abuse can be more strictly regulated than public advertising.[180]

Corrective advertising when used with proper restraint will prove to be an effective remedy to diminish if not eliminate the increased market share the advertiser has gained by its deception. Corrective ads involve an "unwanted message" (correction of past false claims), controlled by someone other than the advertiser (FTC negotiated or litigated), that must be disseminated at the advertiser's expense. They are imposed because of past deceptive claims that have resulted in present lingering consumer beliefs. If such a lingering effect is found, the remedy is imposed for a period necessary to reduce the incorrect or false beliefs to an "acceptable level."

Whether this remedy will be utilized often or selectively in the future by the FTC and private parties remains to be seen. In the interim, you're well advised to consider this potential penalty as you design your own advertisements.

ENDORSEMENTS AND TESTIMONIALS

At one time, commercial transactions involved face-to-face communication. Buyer and seller often knew each other personally, which heightened credibility. As we entered the world of impersonal sales, credible trademarks and brand names somewhat replaced this personal touch, although such marketing was still product-oriented. Endorsements by experts, celebrities, and the person on the street, however, can personalize a product as well as attract attention, and the endorser's credibility enhances your product's image. However, it's not all roses. In a promotional campaign you must carefully research the endorser's value to your target market, paying attention to age, sex, regionalism, and other factors influencing audience acceptance.

As a much publicized 1984 Video Storybook Tests/Campaign Monitor survey indicated,[181] commercials that employ humor, feature children, or portray real-life situations can be more successful. No number-crunching can compensate for the proper subjective analysis of what (if any) type of celebrity will assist your efforts. If you're seeking sound footing in this area you might consider retaining the services of an expert. [182]

Do endorsements work? Over 30% of advertising contains some form of endorsement. However, statistics aside, perhaps the best-run consumer-oriented company in the United States is Procter & Gamble. Two of their best-known products were given a decisive edge by endorsements, neither of which were the traditional celebrity endorsement.

Back in 1882 few people were aware of the benefits of an "absolutely" pure soap—that is, Ivory Soap. How could this asset best be conveyed? By getting an expert to say so. A chemical consultant performed tests on the soap. The analysis of B. Silliman, a professor of chemistry, was extensively advertised; along with his testimonial was born one of the most famous advertising slogans in history—Ivory Soap is "99 and $^{44}/_{100}$% pure."

Then Procter and Gamble added flouride to a toothpaste. Sales were initially disappointing because the benefit was not immediately observable. Since their potential customers couldn't see the benefit of flouride, they needed to hear of the benefit from an expert. Procter and Gamble submitted their product to the American Dental Association—a group which had never before endorsed a toothpaste. After six years of testing and efforts to seek its approval, on August 1, 1960, the *Journal of American Dentistry* reported the now familiar (though then landmark) "Crest has been shown to be an effective decay preventative that can be of significant value when used in a conscientiously applied program of oral hygiene and regular professional care."[183]

We've seen that endorsements work. However, not all firms do the leg work to make sure they work right.[184] Therefore, here are some regulations and quotes on point, because the FTC staff has consistently taken the position that, when an advertisement contains a reference to a source of authority, consumers are particularly likely to believe the claims asserted. This is especially true when such claims are directed to or involve the central attributes of your product.

The FTC has issued guides on point.[185] We'll review these guides as well as contractual pointers and some other issues. First, though, let's look briefly at endorsements in general.

Endorsements and Testimonials As Effective Promotional Devices

What does the use of a person's (especially a celebrity's) status contribute to an advertisement? It attracts attention. Any name—or, more particularly—any picture of a person attracts attention to an advertising message or, if used at the point of purchase, to a product or service. Attracting the potential customer's attention to a product is the first step in selling the product, and to the extent that the use of a likeness attracts attention to a product, that use benefits an advertiser.

Names and pictures do more than merely attract attention to an advertisement or product. They may suggest endorsement and otherwise influence decisions to purchase. They give the advertisement or product appeal that the advertiser's own statement about the product or organization may lack by itself.

The testimonial of a satisfied customer capitalizes on people's tendency to believe the words of one of their own, who had nothing to gain, rather than the words of the seller, who has a pecuniary interest in the product. Of course such testimonials must be true *and* must reflect the typical results that the average user of the product could expect to obtain.

When using endorsements or testimonials, remember the following points:

(1) Don't relate the comments out of context, or distort the opinion expressed.

(2) Don't attribute any particular experience, or competence, to a person's comments unless it is warranted.

(3) Don't use endorsements by anyone indicating approval of your product unless such a person is a bona fide user of your product.

(4) Don't use endorsements by persons no longer using your product or service (especially experts).

(5) Do get a signed release and contractual arrangement permitting the use of the endorser's name, comments, photographs, and illustrations (this requirement can't be emphasized enough). This should include a specimen or a precise description of the advertisement and its authorized use, such as print advertising, direct mail, and TV broadcast, as well as a detailed description of the product or service to be advertised. Your contract analysis (and draft) should also specify the following checklist points:

- *Services to be rendered:* Specify media (and limits on same), and all forms of promotional materials the endorser's name will be associated with (e.g., point of purchase materials, calendars, product packaging, videocassettes). Does the endorser have to attend specific functions for you such as dinners, trade shows, "grand openings," and press conferences? Define at the outset "personal appearances" as well as "media" and "promotional materials." Consider each broad grouping and each subsection as a form of subsidiary rights you're acquiring from your key person. Once you agree on the services, make sure you agree on a flexible but workable schedule so he or she is available for taping, photos, and other activities on the dates you need him or her.

- *Term:* Life of the product, specified initial term with a renewal option or other creative time period must be negotiated with a keen eye on overall strategic marketing plans and goals and how you hope this endorser will fit in. You also need immediate termination rights in case your endorser runs afoul of the law or otherwise violates some social norm in which business sense would dictate that you disassociate yourself as expeditiously as possible from his or her soiled image. This is basic contract law. You're contracting for an image enhancement, but this agreed-on performance is no longer possible if you are by association involved in some form of sordid publicity.

- *Grant of rights:* As mentioned in the discussion of photos and privacy rights, the laws are narrowly construed to protect individuals' names and likenesses from appropriation for commercial purposes. Specify how and when you can use your endorser's photo, name, likeness, and biography.

- *Products to be endorsed:* Do you want your company, product line, or specific product to receive the endorser's halo? Do you want an option on the key person's endorsement of new products?

- *Consideration:* In specifying each grant of right, services, and related efforts, you should tie in benchmark compensation, incentives, minimum fees, and travel and other expenses and also review any applicable union scale.

- *Exclusivity:* The norm (for credibility and often legal reasons) is that your star not endorse a competing product(s). If you don't negotiate the rights to prevent the celebrity from endorsing any other product (a term that is often not possible or may be prohibitively costly), make sure you clearly specify what the realm of competing products are. If you're in an industry that thrives on nominal adaptions you'd be wise to make this clause as flexible as possible.

- *Territory:* Related to exclusivity—are you getting worldwide rights, U.S. rights, or just rights in Hurricane, West Virginia? If you can't get (or don't desire) more, at the time of contract try to negotiate an option for other territories at an agreed-on compensation level.

- *Approval and consultation rights:* Your endorser may wish to have advance clearance approval of all artwork, media, cooperative advertising, and the like so as to protect his or her image. You should qualify this by wording such as "such approval shall not be unreasonably withheld." Further, make sure such approval's "negative option" is in your favor. For example, you agree to personally deliver or send certified mail (the return receipt "green card" is great protection here, as in any important mailing) with a specified number of days' advance approval. If you don't get a reply within the number of days specified, the endorser's silence is deemed to be approval. Finally, make sure you have agreed on flexibility as to legal and regulatory changes or mandated changes resulting from your agreed-to media's clearance and censorship departments.

- *Insurance/Indemnification:* Depending on need, value to you or whatever your marketing calls for, you may wish to take out life, accident, cost, or other form of insurance covering your endorser. You should get your personality to agree in advance to assist you in obtaining all reasonable insurance.

As a quid pro quo the endorser will want evidence of your Professional Errors and Omissions insurance policy and product liability policy both in a specified amount. Again, indemnification in these relationships is now essential. The endorser will wish the insurance policy to be expressly incorporated therein and probably will require a minimum of 30 days' notice from the *insurer* if the protection lapses. Your endorser will also insist on specific protection from claims made against you by third parties.

Review with counsel all other basic contractual pointers set forth in Section VIII as well as each specific agreement prior to signing it. As always, these checklists are for convenient information and are not meant as the final, all-inclusive word. The first four points above are required by the FTC.[186] The others are included to help protect you from marketplace realities as well as legal problems in your contractual relationships.

The FTC Speaks

Is there any difference between an endorsement and a testimonial? No. For your compliance purposes and its enforcement purposes, the FTC makes no distinction between the two.[187]

How does a slice-of-life advertisement differ from an endorsement? The former is an "obvious fictional dramatization of a real life situation." "A TV commercial depicts two women in a supermarket buying a laundry detergent. The women are not identified outside the context of the advertisement. One comments to the other how clean her brand makes her family's clothes, and the other then comments that she will try it because she has not been fully satisfied with her own brand. This obvious fictional dramatization of a real life situation would not be an endorsement."[188]

By contrast, an endorsement "means *any* advertising message. . .which message consumers are likely to believe reflects the opinions, beliefs, findings or experience of a party *other than the sponsoring advertiser*" (emphasis added). Such endorsement can be made without any verbal statement but merely by association or by the net impression conveyed through the context of the setting.[189]

Who is a spokesperson, and how does such person differ from an endorser? The endorser directly relates a *personal* opinion based on personal experience. A spokesperson does not do this. The spokesperson merely speaks in the place of or on behalf of the advertiser rather than on the basis of personal opinion. Such a person is usually not recognized by the public and makes no claims of special expertise. The FTC exempts spokespersons from the scrutiny that endorsers must pass under the guides. "In an advertisement for a pain remedy, an announcer who is not familiar to consumers except as a spokesperson for the advertising drug company praises the drug's ability to deliver fast and lasting pain relief. He purports to speak, not on the basis of his own opinions, but rather in the place of and on behalf of the drug company. Such an advertisement would not be an endorsement."[190]

How does an expert endorsement differ from that of an ordinary consumer? The expert must possess training or expertise greater than ordinary individuals. Such expertise must be relevant in terms of the particular product or service endorsed. For example, a leading case on point concerned certain toy products aimed at children (a vulnerable target audience enjoying great FTC protection).[191] In this specific area of endorsements, the FTC prohibits endorsements of the worth, value, or desirability of a particular toy to a child by famous celebrities unless they also have the experience, special competence, or expertise to form the judgment expressed in the endorsement.

For your compliance purposes, much depends on whether you are using an expert or an ordinary consumer, since significant guides distinguish the two, many of them developed since the 1980 guides. Following are specific compliance issues you must be aware of in evaluating whether to choose an expert or an ordinary consumer.

Consumer Endorsements

You probably have one type of consumer endorsement available in your mailroom each day. Unsolicited letters from your satisfied customers, quoted in context, help sell others on your product or service. Such letters capitalize on the human tendency to believe the statements of one's peers. One note of caution here: Obtain a written, detailed, irrevocable release and agreement (for valid consideration) for any use of another's name in endorsement promotions, including the use of your customer's address. This release and agreement should include a full description of the advertised product or service and nature of the intended use (see above discussion on general endorsement contractual situations).

Any endorsement by an individual consumer should typify what consumers in general will experience, that is, a "significant proportion." This point was discussed at length in *In re Porter & Dietsch, Inc.,* which concerned the promotion of a diet aid.[192] Several of the advertisements included testimonials reciting weight reduction or figure improvement attained by lay users of the preparation X-11. As indicated on the ad copy, the testimonials of ordinary consumers were presented, accompanied by statements such as "From Georgia to Nebraska to California." The net impression was the general nationwide success of the users of X-11. Such purported results (amount of weight lost) did not accurately reflect the typical or ordinary experience of consumers who used X-11 under circumstances similar to those depicted in the advertisements. The advertisements did not disclose or identify this difference.

Thus, a material fact (one likely to affect the purchase decision) was not disclosed in the advertisements. The ads were found to be false and misleading. The decision not only held the firm liable but maintained that any retailer that runs an ad prepared by a supplier is legally liable for the truthfulness of everything in it.

Another variation of the "typical and ordinary" theme was found in a case concerning the Ford Motor Company.[193] The company advertised mileage test results for five small cars; there was an implied "you" in the milage claims for driving performance, that is, "you" the purchaser will have a similar result if you drive the company's cars.

Here it was found that evidence of actual deception is not necessarily essential to a finding that an advertisement is unfair and deceptive. The capacity to deceive is important. Even if people submitting a testimonial honestly believe they obtained the results or that "you" will obtain similar results, consumers as a group are subject to too many variables that affect gas mileage, such as how fast they start and stop and actual driving conditions. Ford ceased advertising mileage claims that could be construed, with reference to the EPA mileage standards, as implying the success of a typical driver. Such problems have been alleviated by the federal EPA mileage standards.

Another case involved the National Dynamics Corporation,[194] whose published endorsements stated the history of select and highly successful performance incomes of users of a particular service. Although all statements were true, many were no longer current, and few releases had been obtained in writing. In the future, the firm's endorsements must be current, and each endorser must have given permission in a signed document.

The commission's experiences in these cases suggest that the more specific the endorsed experience is, the more likely that the representation will be considered a claim that the average consumer can expect similar results.

One of the changes to the 1980 guides concerns consumer endorsements. A disclaimer to product performance is now permitted, although not encouraged, when an advertiser is not sure it can expect equivalent performance by other consumers using the product.[195] A simple statement that "not all consumers will get this result" or a similar vague disclaimer will *not* be considered adequate. The overall net impression governs, and the FTC will expect to see such a disclaimer as to product performance prominently displayed and integrated with the endorsement. The burden of proof as to prominence and integration is on you, the advertiser, not on the FTC.

Formerly the advertiser was required to check at reasonable intervals to determine whether *all* endorsers continued to use the endorsed product. The 1980 guides were changed to *exempt consumer endorsement* from ongoing verification of whether the endorsers are still bona fide users.[196] This reflects the marketplace reality that most consumer endorsements are one-time encounters, and the expert or celebrity is more traceable as a public person or more likely to have signed a contract with the advertiser.

Another important change concerns compensation:

> When the endorser is neither represented in the advertisement as an expert nor is known to a significant portion of the viewing public, then the advertisers should clearly and conspicuously disclose either the payment or promise of compensation prior to and in exchange for the endorsement or the fact that the endorser knew or had reasons to know or to believe that if the endorsement favors the advertised product *some benefit, such as an appearance on TV, would be extended to the endorser.*[197] (Emphasis added.)

This change is significant. An expert or celebrity need only disclose an unusual connection to the endorsement, for example, one that "is not reasonably expected by the audience." Therefore, so long as such an expert or celebrity does not represent that an endorsement was given without compensation, no payment need be disclosed. However, this is *not* so for a consumer. The 1980 guides mark the first time that the FTC has required an *unpaid* consumer endorser to disclose any information in the endorsement. Intangible benefits, such as the opportunity to appear on television, are considered disclosable compensation.

The key here is prior knowledge, whether the consumer knows beforehand that an advertisement is being made. Personal notification or a sign in a window, for example, is prior compensation and must be disclosed. However, if consumers are filmed by a hidden camera or in some other way so that they "had no reason to know or believe that their response was being recorded for use in an advertisement," then no issue as to compensation need be disclosed.[198]

Two other pointers need to be mentioned. If actors are used to represent "ordinary consumers", the 1980 guides do not require that you state that they are actors, just that the persons depicted are not "actual consumers." Also, payment to these actors need not be disclosed. Finally, the new guides *permit* consumer endorsements of "any drug or device," if the *advertiser* has adequate scientific substantiation for the endorsement and such endorsement is not contrary to FDA determinations.[199]

Why the increasing regulatory attention? Quite simply, this form of promotion works well. For an excellent article on the utility of unprompted consumer responses providing more credibility than many script writers could hope to produce, consult an article by James P. Forkan.[200]

Expert Endorsements

Under the guides, two distinct types of expert endorsements are recognized: organizational and individual. A good example of the former is an endorsement by the American Dental Association. Such an endorsement is not given lightly. An organization's endorsement is perceived as less subjective because it embodies the varied opinions of many people. Specifically, the guides state that the organization's "collective experience exceeds that of any individual member and whose judgments are generally free of the sort of subjective factors which vary from individual to individual. Therefore, an organization's endorsement must be reached by a process sufficient to ensure that the endorsement fairly reflects the collective judgment of the organization."[201] Thus, it is improper to represent a minority opinion of an organization as the organization's official opinion.

The guides further require that when an organization is represented as being expert, it must use "an expert or experts recognized as such by the organization and suitable for judging the relative merits of such products."

> A mattress seller advertises that its product is endorsed by a chiropractic association. Since the association would be regarded as expert with respect to judging mattresses, its endorsement must be supported by an expert evaluation by an expert or experts recognized as such by the organization, or by compliance with standards previously adopted by the organization and aimed at measuring the performance of mattresses in general and not designed with the particular attributes of the advertised mattress in mind.[202]

> An association of professional athletes states in an advertisement that it has "selected" a particular brand of beverages as its "official breakfast drink." As in Example 4,[203] the association would be regarded as expert in the field of nutrition for the purposes of this section, because consumers would expect it to rely upon the selection of nutritious foods as part of its business needs. Consequently, the association's endorsement must be based upon an expert evaluation of the nutritional value of the endorsed beverage. Furthermore, unlike Example 4, the use of the words "selected" and "official" in this endorsement imply that it was given only after direct comparisons had been performed among competing brands. Hence, the advertisement would be deceptive unless the association has in fact performed such comparisons between the endorsed brand and its leading competitors in terms of nutritional criteria, and the results of such comparisons conform to the *net impression created by the advertisement*[204] (emphasis added).

The individual expert must actually possess the training and expertise he or she is purported to have, and such expertise must be relevant to the actual product endorsed (unless discussing taste or price). For example, the guides indicate that an "engineer" endorsing an automobile must be an expert in automobile engineering and not, say, chemical engineering.[205] Further, only unusual material connections between the advertiser and expert need be disclosed; routine compensation is presumed.

The advertiser must remain alert as to whether the celebrity or expert endorser continues to subscribe to the views presented. Once the endorser ceases to be a bona fide user of the product, the advertisement must cease. Depending on the nature of the promotion, you should formally contact your endorsers in writing as to their use of the product, every six months, but never delay longer than one year. (You might consider contractually obligating the endorser to contact you on cessation of use.) Supplying the endorser with your product will help ensure continued use.

Finally, endorsers must make objective inquiry into the truthfulness of their claims. This is particularly true in the case of an expert's endorsement, because the total impression created on the targeted audience is one of the expert's endorsing a product both from experience as an expert in the field *and* as a personal user.

The pitfalls of ignoring or haphazardly approaching such inquiry are illustrated in the *Coogo Moogo* decision.[206] *Coogo Moogo* was the first time in the history of the FTC that an endorser of a product agreed to be personally accountable for representations made in an advertisement. Pat Boone was prominently featured in a television and magazine advertising campaign to promote an acne remedy. The remedy failed to live up to the claims made for it. Boone agreed to personally pay a percentage of any restitution ordered against the manufacturer. He also agreed to make reasonable inquiry into the truthfulness of any products he would endorse in the future.

This decision supports the principle that an endorser must either verify the claims made for the advertised product before the first commercial goes on the air or appears in print, or risk FTC action. As to the means of verification, if endorsers are not experts, they must look to independent and reliable sources to objectively substantiate all material claims, tests, or studies supplied by the advertiser.

Conclusion

The guides we've just reviewed, while not carrying the force of substantive law such as a trade rule, nevertheless should be studied with caution. Read the guides with sections 5 and 12 of the FTC Act. Together they prohibit any unsubstantiated or deceptive representation made by an endorser in any form of advertisement or media.

Be aware of the related regulations, such as those promulgated by the Bureau of Alcohol, Tobacco and Firearms, which forbid an active athlete to endorse alcoholic beverages (that's why all the light-beer endorsements feature only retired athletes). There are also self-regulatory codes such as the advertising guidelines issued by the National Association of Broadcasters. Here, for example, endorsements by celebrities and "real-life authority figures" are not permitted in children's advertising. (Check with counsel as to the rules' current status, as some are in flux because of commercial free speech, antitrust, and other considerations).

The endorsement is an excellent vehicle for all media, especially commercial and targeted cable TV and mail. To best use this promotional device, carefully monitor FTC and other regulatory activity affecting these promotions. There were significant changes in the revised 1980 guidelines, and market place dynamics will undoubtedly dictate further interpretations. Not staying on top of these areas could be costly to you. You should review the following checklist along with the one on contractual pointers before beginning your endorsement promotion:

- Have you reviewed with your counsel whether this situation involves an endorser or a spokesperson? All promotions must be reviewed individually and specifically with counsel.

- How was the endorser selected and how was the contract prepared?

- Has your counsel signed off on the contract after a review of the agreement text and the marketing goals you hope to achieve by the endorsement?

- Was the endorser a user of the product or service prior to this promotion? Is he or she still a satisfied user?

- Has this person ever been employed by the promoting firm or in any other way possessed a pecuniary interest in the success of the firm or product?

- Is this person a professional performer? An "average" customer? Or merely a fictional personality? If the person is a fictional personality, a specific clause should be placed in the contract whereby a real and accountable person stands behind the fictional name.

- If performance claims are made, what competency or expertise (or lack of same) does the endorser have in evaluating this particular product?

- Is the total impression that this promotion creates on the targeted audience one of a person endorsing a product based on experience in the field (as an expert?) or on personal experience?

- Has an adequate written legal release been prepared, reviewed, and obtained for any and all names, photographs, and the like that are to be used?

- Has an affidavit been obtained and signed by the endorser, attesting to the truthfulness of the endorsement? Such affidavit should relate the full text of the endorser's comments to prevent any ambiguity.

- Have you consulted the self-regulatory guides of responsible groups such as the Children's Advertising Review Unit of the Council of Better Business Bureaus? For example, in a promotion targeted to children, have you refrained from using children's program personalities or characters to promote products in which they appear? Likewise for print promotions, a character or personality associated with the editorial content of a publication should not be used to promote your products.

Agency Liability for False Advertising—Boundaries of Risk

Since we're discussing advertising, we shouldn't forget the advertising agency (used here as a generic term for media-buying services, creative boutiques, etc., although their liability may differ depending on circumstances and function). These agencies have always been imbued with the mystique of high-pressure glamour in a creative and individualistic environment. However, nowadays the law can be as high a priority as the deadline.

No longer may the agency send out its account executive to work on ideas and services alone. The agency will probably share with the advertiser the responsibility for false, deceptive, or unfair advertisements concerning the product or service of the agency's client. Remember, the buying public is not under any duty to make reasonable inquiry into the truth of the advertising.[207] That is the responsibility of the marketer and the agency retained.

Now both the agency and its client must be able to substantiate each objective claim (performance, mileage, and other tangible attributes that are measurable and verifiable). If a claim needs qualification, then such qualification must be made in language understandable to the vast multitude of your audience, which includes the "ignorant, unthinking and credulous." [208]

This liability is a factor both sides must consider in drafting their contracts—particularly as the trend toward a la carte services develops. You and your counsel must get in writing exactly what you are doing together and what documentation and testing is available to substantiate the claims you are making.

Those who have been in advertising for a while will remember that at one time there was much greater latitude for puffery than today. Puffery is permissible but narrowly construed. Clearly subjective statements and hyperbole that are not provable are permissible. However, an opinion statement cannot be used as a subterfuge to transform an objective, verifiable claim into puffery. Superlatives, too, contain substantiation problems. If you claim to have the "most," "best," or "fastest" in comparison to the competition, you must exceed all competitors in the category to which your superlative statement refers.

An ad agency will need clear claim substantiation protection from the client also because its insurance liability policy may not provide protection in regard to an incorrect description of the article or commodity featured (it may not protect against trademark infringement or a mistake in the advertised price either).

A particular area of possible exposure nowadays involves claims arising from comparative advertising. The agency has a fairly complicated legal posture in presenting its client's message. How has this come about?

Agency Relationship

The position was in keeping with the traditional view of the agency relationship. Such relationship is a legal and fiduciary one created by an agreement or "implication" whereby one person (agent) is authorized to act for another (principal) in business transactions (usually in the area of some expertise) with third parties. Such agent must measure up to the standards of skill possessed by other agents engaged in the same business (as measured by customs of such business). Such customs must be universal so as to create a presumption that everyone knows the custom and contracts with reference to it.[209]

The agent must accept the authority voluntarily conferred by the principal and act upon it, and the intention of the parties must find expression either in their words or their conduct. When an agent, acting within the scope of his or her authority, contracts with a third party for a known principal, the principal and not the agent is liable. This issue frequently arises when an agency is retained to purchase media.[210]

Co-equal Liability

The idea of agency liability is about 25 years old. Once, the Federal Trade Commission dismissed complaints against agencies despite their clients' false and misleading advertising if it was determined that the agencies at all times acted upon their client's instruction and direction and were under the client's control.

It was held that the agency acted as an agent for media purchasing. At most, the agency only disseminated the advertising, and this was not enough to constitute deception. The client was held to have the final authority and responsibility for the advertising.[211]

The past 20 to 25 years have seen a continued legal tension and social transformation between increased individual "rights" (and accompanying freedom of expression) and greater institutional accountability. The advertising agency/client relationship did not escape this scrutiny. Promotional messages have expanded as have their channels (though the same may be said of commercial free speech protections).[212] At the same time, puffery has been less condoned, and any message conveying authority is increasingly held to a high standard of public accountability. The courts and regulatory agencies have begun to examine more closely the extent of what the agency actually knew independently or through the client (principal) concerning the promotion.

The first evolutionary standard was the "absence of reasonable suspicion" on the agency's part that the promotion it was assisting was not false or deceptive. There was no affirmative burden on an agency to substantiate the elements of a promotion its client held to be true. However, if the agency was actually a "prime mover" or "active participant" in the creation and implementation of a promotion, then the agency could have legal liability for its false aspects.[213]

One salient question controlling today's legal review was set forth in 1963: "Is one carrying out the will of another to be held responsible for the results of his actions?"[214] The court believed the proper criterion should be the extent to which the advertising agency actually participated in the deception. Here the agency was liable, as it worked with its client for years, developed the idea to emphasize a deceptive claim, wrote the storyboards, and assisted in other preparations for promoting the product.

Another controlling issue was whether there was a reasonable basis on which to rely. "The term reasonable basis may consist of an opinion, where appropriate, in writing signed by a person qualified by education or experience to render the opinion that a competent scientific test(s) or other objective data exist; *provided however,* that such opinion also discloses and describes the contents of such test(s) or other objective data."[215]

An agency will also be held liable when the deception found to exist stems not from the falsity of the information itself but from the use made of it by the agency. This can include a false impression made by words and sentences that are literally and technically true but are framed in such a way as to mislead or deceive.

In taking exception to the repeated use of unqualified medical claims by Merck & Co., the court said as follows (emphasis added):

> The skillful advertiser can mislead the consumer without misstating a single fact. *The shrewd use of exaggeration, innuendo, ambiguity and half-truth is more efficacious from the advertiser's standpoint than factual assertions.*

> Nothing in the information supplied by Merck indicated that Sucrets or Children's Sucrets would have any effect on the course of either a viral or bacterial infection of the throat. Nor was there anything to indicate that these products would promptly elimate severe pain, such as that symbolized by fire. To the contrary, *the agency knew* that the products were recommended only for the relief of minor sore throat irritations. *Despite this knowledge,* it developed advertising, which by the use of "exaggeration, innuendo, ambiguity and half-truth" conveyed the false impression that the products would cure or help cure existing throat infections and would be effective in relieving severe pain of sore throat. As found by the examiner, *the falsity of such advertisements should have been apparent to the creator.*

> Nor is it a defense to the agency that the advertising was approved by the client's legal and medical departments. The agency, more so than its principal, should have known whether the advertisements had the capacity to mislead or deceive the public. This is an area in which the agency has expertise. Its responsibility for creating deceptive advertising cannot be shifted to the principal who is liable in any event.[216]

Finally, in 1978 the general legal standard for all agencies was set forth in another opinion worth quoting at length:

> The standard of care to be exercised by an advertising agency in determining what express and implied representations are contained in an ad and in assessing the truth or falsity of those representations increase in direct relation to the advertising agencies' participation in the commercial project. The degree of its participation is measured by a number of factors including the agency's role in writing and editing the text of the ad, its work in creating and designing the graphic or audio-visual material, its research and analysis of public opinions and attitudes, and its selection of the appropriate audience for the advertising message. . . .

> Representatives of the agency were involved in the development of the advertising from the very earliest stages. They carefully reviewed all the

test results and were active participants in numerous meetings in which alternative advertising approaches were evaluated and ultimately accepted or rejected. The final determination to use the demonstration format of the advertisements was a joint decision of agency and principal, and after the final joint decision was made, the agency actively participated in the filming of the pictorial portions of the advertisements, the drafting of the verbal texts, the preparation of layouts and the promotion and distribution of the advertisements.[217]

This is where we are today. The advertising agency has an affirmative duty to ensure the truthfulness of claims made in the promotion it produces. For example, if the agency alleges the product contains any unusual or special ingredient or quality, it had better be unusual and not commonplace.[218]

If the agency makes representations, directly or by implication, by reference to a survey or test of "experts" or "consumers" or the results thereof, concerning the performance or any characteristic, benefit, recommendation, usage, or choice of or other preference for your product, it should be able to prove that the survey or test of experts or consumers:

(a) is designed, executed, and analyzed in a competent and reliable scientific manner;

(b) substantiates the claim(s) represented by providing a reasonable basis for such claims; and

(c) establishes, in regard to any claims of superiority based on surveys, that the product is superior to each compared product in respect to which the specific representation is made to a degree that will be discernible to or of benefit to consumers or potential consumers to whom the representation is directed.

In addition, all proper inquiries must be made to ascertain the accuracy of a study performed by the client.

The term *expert* is deemed to be an individual, group or institution, possessing as a result of experience, study, or training, knowledge of a particular subject that is superior to knowledge generally acquired by ordinary individuals. Experts should not be implied to have utilized their expertise unless all of the following can be demonstrated:

(a) Such experts in fact possess the expertise to evaluate the product with respect to the representations.

(b) Such experts actually exercised their expertise by evaluating or testing the product and, based on their stated preferences, findings, or opinions in performing the test or evaluation, exercise their expertise.

(c) Such representation, to the extent it expresses or implies product comparison, is supported by an actual comparative evaluation or test by such experts.

(d) Such representation, to the extent it express or implies that such product is superior to competing products, is supported by actual comparative evaluation or test by such experts which lead to the conclusion that the product is superior in fact to competing products with respect to the feature(s) compared.[219]

In fashioning a remedy, both the courts and the FTC have wide discretion and will impose one that has a reasonable relation to the unlawful practices found to exist in the specific circumstances of the case. An agency (as well as a client) with a solid track record and with written in-house procedures with which to evaluate promotions before they are disseminated will receive much more favorable treatment than firms characterized as habitual violators of objective truth-in-advertising standards.[220]

This underscores an agency's need to have a uniform procedure of verification, editing, and other in-house standards to check and recheck the veracity of both its own claims and those of its clients for each promotion. This checklist should be reviewed by counsel. Finally, advertising agencies have the same defenses available to them as their clients plus two additional ones:

(1) The agency can argue it was not an active partipant in the false advertisement or that it was only a secondary factor in its creation.

(2) The agency in good faith neither knew nor had reason to know of the falsity of the advertisement. Again, this defense has not fared well. The FTC *presumes* the agency was primarily responsible for the advertising approach selected.

Looking to the Future

The days of giving short shrift to legal compliance are long past. Attention to legal details makes good business sense. An agency is selling its reputation, and exposing itself and the client to adverse publicity due to questionable advertising means the possible loss of the client and additional clients (and may incur legal penalties).

In the 1980s the advertising agency is now a partner in legal liability when it lacks substantiation for any objective claims dealing with performance, efficacy, preference, mileage, taste, and other tangible attributes that are objectively measurable and verifiable. It is responsible for all other advertising legal compliance issues discussed in this chapter.

In proceedings against advertisers, it is now an acknowledged FTC staff procedure to include the advertising agency. Examples of liability can vary from being able to substantiate the nutritional value of the products intended as a central selling message[221] to being responsible for verifying that test results not only are accurate but do not convey a misleading impression.[222]

The FTC has stated that unless advertising agencies are under this duty to make independent checks of information relied upon in their advertising claims, the law would be placing a premium on ignorance. The practical effect of a court decision or FTC order against your agency, aside from its adverse effects on getting new clients, can include fines, being barred for a period of time from engaging in certain categories of product promotions, or even being barred from certain promotions themselves (e.g., sweepstakes, endorsements, or visual demonstrations).

It's good business for both the agency and its client to comply with the applicable legal rules affecting the particular promotion. It's also good business to investigate your legal exposure further. For example, unless it's contractually protected, the agency is liable to pay the media even if the advertiser fails to pay the agency. Written contractual protection with all parties is a must.

Written Contractual Protection Checklist

At a minimum, your written agreement (whether you represent the agency or principal) should include the following:

- Appointment of the agency. Is it the sole agency? If the issue of additional products or services might arise, you should address it here. The agency might limit its obligations to its "availability."
- Term of agreement. Set forth a commencement date, a termination date and a method to exercise an automatic or specific renewal procedure when so desired.
- Nature of the services to be performed by the agency.
  a. Routine:
- analyze your products in light of your contemplated and potential markets
- recommend the best cost/benefit media for your targeted audience
- provide for checking, billing, follow-up on contracts
  b. Negotiated as per need
- create messages (if advertiser, make sure they're subject to your approval)
- order the space, time, etc. from the agreed-on media
- program contracts, talent contracts, obtaining permissions and releases, and securing music and literary rights.
- Compensation. Whether payment for services will be in the form of commissions or fees, or a combination of the two. How do you intend to allocate costs? Receipts are a must, and requiring prior approval for any expense above a specified amount is recommended. You should specify how the billing should be itemized and procedures for dispute resolution.
- Commitments made to third parties
  a. An agency shouldn't handle competitive products—make sure your agency agrees;
  b. Any agreement the agency negotiates requires your prior approval;
  c. The advertiser may have to assume certain agreed-to liabilities of the agency to third parties;
  d. A clear division of property rights (characters, slogans, themes, etc.) on termination should be negotiated and set forth. (This can vary depending

on the choice of compensation, so consider this when agreeing on a fee or commission system).

- Indemnification

  a. Clearly define what each party is indemnifying;

  b. Set forth the manner of notice to the other party of a claim;

  c. The agency should receive indemnification for any good faith reliance on the advertiser's product claims, trademark infringement, as well as product liability in general (including a requirement of product liability insurance in which you're named as a co-insured);

  d. The advertiser should be protected against all copyright, plagiarism, and related claims concerning material prepared by the agency or a firm under its direction. Client should obtain a copy of the advertising agency liability insurance policy and review it as to its own needs. Indemnification protection should be drawn tightly in light of our society's gunshot approach to suing everyone in sight once these forms of action begin. Your indemnification protection should (where necessary) survive the termination of the agreement.

- Confidentiality. Each party should specifically set forth the general and precise properties the other has access to and that such unauthorized disclosure would cause irreparable harm. At a minimum, each party should provide a standard of care equal to its own in-place internal safeguards for property of equal value.

- Inspection of books. An advertiser will want some policing powers as to the agency's books and the right of inspection during ordinary business hours.

- No joint venture. Both parties will want language making it clear that the agency is an independent contractor.

- Governing law. Each party would prefer the governing law of its own jurisdiction. You should also consider an informal dispute resolution or arbitration.

- Integration clause. This states that what you see is what you get and no other letters, phone calls, etc., that are not expressly incorporated in the agreement can be used to modify the agreement.

The above checklist is advisory, with emphasis on minimum care protection. Obviously, each agreement you enter into will be modified in light of its unique objective, target audience, etc. The consultation of both parties, each with their own counsel, is imperative.

National Advertising Division (NAD) of the Council of Better Business Bureaus

It's a long title, but one worth remembering if you want an inexpensive and confidential alternative to certain of your legal problems. In 1971 the National Advertising Review Council (NARC) was established by the Council of Better Business Bureaus, Inc., in conjunction with the American Association of Advertising Agencies, the American Advertising Federation, and the Association of National

Advertisers. Its primary purpose is to promote and enforce standards of truth, accuracy, taste, morality, and social responsibility in advertising. Composed of members drawn from the leadership of these four organizations, NARC is regarded as the most comprehensive and effective regulatory mechanism in the advertising industry.

Under its direction, two regulatory divisions were established: the National Advertising Division (NAD), an investigative body, and the National Advertising Review Board (NARB), an appeals board for NAD decisions. The NAD monitors advertising industry practices. It reviews complaints received from consumers and consumer groups, brand competitors, Better Business Bureaus, NAD monitors, and others about objectionable advertisements. Its functions were glowingly endorsed in *AMF Incorporated v. Brunswick Corp.*[223] A review of that case is a good summary of this alternative channel. The case itself involved a contractual dispute over arbitration. One party ran a thinly veiled comparative ad,[224] and the other party sought to have the underlying substantiation examined in confidence by NAD.[225]

NAD publishes a monthly Case Report in which a wide range of topics are reviewed. In one[226] you'll see topics such as child-directed advertising, direct response, foods/beverages, and sport and hobby equipment. Some headings include "Advertising Substantiated," or "Advertising Modified or Discontinued." The advertiser, advertising agency, product and issue, response and resolution are all included. If the advertiser so desires, a concise statement of its views will be included.

It is a good idea to receive the NAD Case Report if you can. For further information write to the National Advertising Division Council of Better Business Bureaus, Inc., 845 Third Avenue, New York, N.Y. 10022, or call (212) 754-1358.

You might also ask for NAD's statement of organization and procedures and for the NAD Guide for Advertising and Advertising Agencies. Another useful guide put out by the Council of Better Business Bureaus (Children's Advertising Review Unit) is Self-Regulatory Guidelines for Children's Advertising. These are all helpful to your overall profit preservation center development and should be kept in its library. (See the discussion on profit preservation center in Chapter 24).

ENDNOTES

(1) U.S. Constitution Article I Section 8. *See also* 17 USC §§101 and 201.

(2) Write to: Copyright Office, Library of Congress, Washington DC 20559.

(3) 17 USC 102(a).

(4) 17 USC 411.

(5) 17 USC 412, 504, and 505.

(6) 17 USC 411(c).

(7) See Chickering, Robert, and Susan Hortmann, *How to Register a Copyright and Protect Your Creative Work*. Charles Scribner's Sons, 1980, pp. 8-9. Then read the other 200-plus pages.

(8) *Rosemont Enterprises, Inc. v. Random House, Inc.*, 336 F2d 303, 306 (2d Cir. 1966), *cert. den.* 385 US 1009; 87 S.Ct. 714; 17 L.Ed.2d 546 (1967).

(9) *Iowa State University Research Foundation, Inc. v. American Broadcasting Co.*, 621 F.2d 57 (2d Cir. 1980).

(10) 17 USC 107; this section affirms that fair use can apply to commercial advertising overruling questions raised by cases such as *Henry Holt & Co. v. Leggett & Myers Tobacco Co.*

(11) *[E]very commercial use of copyrighted material is presumptively an unfair exploitation of the monopoly privilege that belongs to the owner of the copyright. Sony Corp. v. Universal City Studios, Inc.*, 464 U.S., at 451, 104 S.Ct., at 793. (1984) *Marcus v. Rowley*, 695 F.2d 1171, 1175 (9th Cir. 1983); *see also Consumers Union, Inc. v. General Signal Corp.*, 724 F.2d 1044 (2nd Cir. 1983).

(12) *Universal City Studios, Inc. v. Sony Corp.*, 659 F.2d 963, 972 (9th Cir. 1981), *rev'd on other grounds*, 104 S.Ct. 774, 220 USPQ 665 (1984), *reh.den* (1984); see also *Rubin v. Boston Magazine Co.*, 645 F.2d 80, 84 (scientific material has limited fair use protection).

(13) 17 USC 107(4); *Harper & Row Publishers, Inc. v. Nation Enterprises*, 105 S.Ct. 2218 (1985); *Roy Export Co. v. CBS*, 503 F.Supp. 1137 (1980), *aff'd on other grounds* 672 F.2d 1095 (2d Cir. 1980); see also *Triangle Publications v. Knight-Ridder Newspapers*, 626 F.2d 1171 (5th Cir. 1980).

(14) *Salinger v. Random House, Inc.*, 811 F.2d 90 (2d Cir. 1987); *Time, Inc. v. Bernard Geis Associates*, 293 F.Supp. 130 (1968).

(15) *Metro-Goldwyn-Mayer, Inc. v. Showcase Atlanta Co-op Prod.*, 479 F.Supp. 351 (N.D. Ga. 1979).

(16) *Berlin v. E. C. Publications, Inc.*, 329 F.2d 541 (2d Cir.), *cert den.* 379 US 822 (1964); see also *Dr. Pepper Co. v. Sambo's Restaurant, Inc.*, 517 F.Supp. 1202 (N.D. Tex. 1981) and *D.C Comics, Inc. v. Crazy Eddie, Inc.*, 205 USPQ 1177 (S.D.N.Y. 1979).

(17) *Zacchini v. Scripps-Howard Broadcasting Co.*, 433 US 562, 577 and n.13, 97 S.Ct. 2849, 53 L.Ed.965 (1977).

(18) *Dallas Cowboys Cheerleaders, Inc. v. Scoreboard Posters, Inc.*, 600 F.2d 1184 (1979).

(19) *Walt Disney Productions v. Air Pirates*, 581 F.2d 751, 753 (9th Cir. 1978).

(20) *Laskowitz v. Marie Designer, Inc.*, 119 F.Supp. 541 (1954).

(21) *Brattleboro Publishing Co. v. Winmill Publishing Corp.*, 369 F.2d 565 (1966).

(22) *Blumcraft of Pittsburgh v. Newman Brothers, Inc.*, 373 F.2d 905 (1967).

(23) *B & S Auto Supply, Inc. v. Plesser*, 205 F.Supp. 36 (1962).

(24) *Rexnord, Inc. v. Modern Handling Systems, Inc.*, 379 F.Supp. 1190, 1195 (1976).

(25) *Markham v. A.E. Borden Co.*, 206 F.2d 199, 201 (1953).

(26) *Burndy Engineering Co. v. Penn-Union Electric Corp.*, 25 F.Supp. 507 (1938).

(27) *Day-Brite Lighting, Inc. v. Sta-Brite Flourescent Manufacturing Co.*, 308 F.2d 377, 379-380 (1962).

(28) *Southwestern Bell Telephone Co. v. Nationwide Independent Directory Service, Inc.*, 371 F.Supp. 900 (1975); *Micromanipulator Co. Inc. v. Bough*, 779 F.2d. 255 (5th Cir. 1985); *Hutchinson Tel. Co. v. Fronteer*, 770 F.2d 128 (8th Cir. 1985). For any compilation you must demonstrate "selection, coordination or arrangement" of the data. See also *Financial Information Inc. v. Moody's Investors Services, Inc.*, 808 F.2d 204 (2d Cir. 1986) and Eckes v. Card Prices Update, 736 F.2d 859 (2d Cir. 1984).

(29) *New Jersey Motor List Co. v. Barton Business Service,* 57 F.2d 353 (1931). See also *West Publishing Co. v. Mead Data Central, Inc.,* 799 F.2d 1219 (1986), *cert. den.,* 107 S.Ct. 962 (1987).

(30) *Burrow Giles Lithographic Co. v. Sarony,* 111 US 53, 60, 28 L.Ed. 349, 4 S.Ct. 279 (1884).

(31) *Jeweler's Circular Publishing Co. v. Keystone Publishing Co.,* 274 F 932, *cert den.* 259 US 581 (1922).

(32) *Habersham Plantation Corp. v. Country Concepts,* CCH Copyright Law Decisions, §25, 160 No. C80-146 (1980).

(33) For a good, representative article, see Nancy Madlin, "Photographer's Owner Rights Fading From Picture," *Adweek,* June 17, 1985, p. 36. See also *Peregrine v. Lauren Corp.,* 601 F.Supp. 828 (Col. 1985).

(34) 17 USC 205(d).

(35) *Durham Industries, Inc. v. Towy Corp.,* 630 F.2d 905, 913 (2d Cir. 1980); *Sid & Marty Krofft Television v. McDonald's Corp.,* 562 F.2d 1157 (1977); 17 USC 501(b).

(36) *Roth Greeting Cards v. United Card Co.,* 429 F.2d 1106 (9th Cir. 1970).

(37) *American Intern Pictures, Inc. v. Foreman, 576 F.2d 661 (1978).*

(38) 17 USC 101(b).

(39) *Roy Export Co. v. CBS, Inc.,* 503 F.Supp. 1137 (1980), *aff'd* 672 F.2d 1095 (2d Cir.), *cert den.,* 459 US 826, 103 S.Ct. 60, 74 L.Ed.2d 63 (1982).

(40) *Nucar Corp. v. Tennessee Forging Steel Service, Inc., 513 F.2d 151, 153 (8th Cir. 1975).*

(41) 17 USC 201(b).

(42) *Quinto v. Legal Times of Washington, Inc.,* 506 F.Supp. 554 (1981); see also *Aldon Accessories v. Spiegel Ltd.,* 738 F.2d 548 (2d Cir.) *cert. den.* 105 S.Ct. 387 (1984); *Easter Seal Society v. Playboy Enterprises,* 815 F.2d 323 (5th Cir. 1985).

(43) 17 USC 101.

(44) 17 USC 201(c).

(45) 17 USC 105.

(46) Labor Code Sec.3351.5 and Unemployment Code Sec.621.

(47) Sec. 397 of the General Business Law.

(48) You should check first to see if the law of your state permits a recovery on a theory of invasion of privacy.

(49) N. Y. Civil Rights Law Sec.50 and 51. Similar statutes in other states include (a) California Civil Code Sec.3344(a) (1986); includes privacy protection for a person's voice and signature.

(b) Kentucky Revised Statute Sec.391.170 (1984).

(c) Massachusetts Gen. Laws Annotated ch. 214 Sec.3A (1985).

(d) Nebraska Revised Statutes Sec.20-201 through 20-211 (1983).

(e) Oklahoma Statutes Annotated Title 21 Sec.839.1 through 839.2 (1985).

(f) Rhode Island General Laws Sec.9-1-28 (1985).

(g) Utah Code Annotated Sec.45-3-1 through 45-3-6 (1985).

(50) *Wojtowicz v. Delacorte Press,* 43 NY 2d 858, 374 NE 2d 129 (1978).

(51) *Onassis v. Christian Dior - New York, Inc.* 472 NYS 2d 254, 122 Misc. 2d 603 (1984). For a subsequent victory for free and open satire see *Moreno v. Time* (1985).

(52) *Allen v. National Video, Inc.,* 610 F.Supp. 612 (D. C. NY 1985).

(53) Id.p. 624.

(54) Id.p. 622.

(55) *Cohen Herbal Concepts,* 482 NYS 2d 457, 472 NE 2d 307, 63 NY 2d 379 (Ct. App. 1984), 473 NYS 2d 426, 100 AD 2d 175 (1984); but see *Fox v. Fixx et al* 183 *N.Y.L.U.* p. 6 col. 3 (S.Ct. N.Y. Co. Feb. 20, 1980).

(56) *Caesar v. Chemical Bank,* 483 NYS 2d 16 (1984). See also *Shields v. Gross,* 58 NY 2d 338, 461 NYS 2d 254 (1983); *Welch v. Mr. Christmas Tree, Inc.,* 57 NY 2D 143, 454 NYS 2d 971 (1982) (use after time period limitation in the written consent); *Dzurenko v. Jordache, Inc.,* 59 NY 2d 788, 464 NYS 2d 730 (1983) (use in media other than that specified in the written consent).

(57) See *Aniretti v. Rolex Watch, U.S.A, Inc.,* 56 NY 2d 284, NYS 2d 5 (1982) (any writing signed by the subject of the photograph intended as an expression of consent is sufficient to satisfy the statutory requirement) and *Freihofer v. Hearst Corp.,* 64 NY 2d 1161, 490 NYS 2d 735, 739 (1985); *Stephano v. News Group Publications, Inc.,* 64 NY 2d 174, 485 NYS 2d 220 (1984).

(58) *Sinatra v. The Goodyear Tire & Rubber Co.,* 435 F.2d 711 (1970).

(59) *Binns v. Vitagraph Co.,* 210 NY 51, 103 NE 1108 (1913) and *Murray v. New York Magazine Co.,* 27 NY 2d 406, 318 NYS 474, 267 NE 2d 256 (1971).

(60) *Pagan v. New York Herald Tribune,* 32 AD 2d 341, 301 NYS 2d 120, *aff'd* 26 NY 2d 941, 310 NYS 2d 327, 258 NE 2d 727.

(61) *Arrington v. New York Times Co.,* 55 NY 2d 440, 449 NYS 2d 941, 434 NE 2d 1319; *Stephano v. News Group Publications, Inc.,* 474 NE 2d 580 (N.Y. 1984). See also *Namath v. Sports Illustrated,* 48 A.D.2d 487, 371 N.Y.S. 2d10 (1975).

(62) For an excellent review of this area see Kent, Felix, "New Protections for Celebrity's Rights," *New York Law Journal,* 6/27/86, pp. 1-3.

(63) Kentucky Revised Statutes Chapter 391 (1) and (2).

(64) Oklahoma Statutes Sec. 1448 Title 12.

(65) *Lugosi v. Universal Pictures,* 25 Cal. 3d 813, 603 p.2d 425, 160 Cal. Rptr. 323 (1979) in contrast to *Estate of Presley v. Russen,* 513 F.Supp. 1339 (D.N.J. 1981).

(66) 15 USC, 45(a)(1) (1980).

(67) *In re Pfizer,* v. 81 Federal Trade Commission, p. 23 (1972).

(68) *FTC v. Colgate Palmolive Co.,* 380 US 344, 186 (1965).

(69) Chapter I, Title 16, Part 233 *Federal Trade Commission Guides Against Deceptive Pricing,* 1986.

(70) 16 CFR 233.1(c).

(71) See *FTC Advisory Opinions* 120, 246, and 325.

(72) See *Donovan v. Aclonian Co.,* 200 NE 815 (1936).

(73) For example, see New Jersey 5684, especially Sec. 13:45 A-0.2(7) and (8).

(74) 16 CFR 256.5, "Guides for the Law Book Industry." [Guide 5]

(75) Chapter I, Title 16, Part 251, Section 251.1(b)(1), *FTC Guide Concerning Use of the Word "Free" and Similar Representations.*

(76) *Spiegel, Inc. v. FTC,* (CA 7), 494 F.2d 59 (1975). This case presents an excellent discussion of the Free Rule.

(77) Oregon Attorney General Press Releases, 3/21/85.

(78) New York City Department of Consumer Affairs, Regulation 201.

(79) 16 CFR 251.1(2)(j).

(80) New York City Department of Consumer Affairs, Regulations 13.4, 13.5, and 13.6.

(81) See N.Y. General Business Law Sec. 581 and New York City Administrative Code Sec. B32-206, -209 and -214.

(82) 16 CFR 236.1.

(83) 16 CFR 236.2(a).

(84) 16 CFR 403.4(b).

(85) 16 CFR 403.5.

(86) 16 CFR 403.6.

(87) 36 USC 176(i).

(88) *Holter v. Nebraska,* 205 US 34, 51 L.Ed. 696, 27 SCt 419, (1907).

(89) *Regan v. Time, Inc.,* 468 US 641, 82 L.Ed. 2d 487, 104 S.Ct. 3262 (1984).

(90) Posch, Robert J. Jr., "Commercial Free Speech—The Argument for Our Side," *Direct Marketing,* February 1983, pp. 92-94.

(91) For an excellent book on the variety of negative implications TV presents for our society, see Postman, Neil, *The Disappearance of Childhood,* New York: Delacorte Press, 1982.

(92) *Charles of the Ritz Distribs. Corp. v. FTC,* 143 F.2d 676 (1944).

(93) *Aronberg v. FTC,* 32 F.2d 165, 167 (7th Cir. 1942).

(94) *Liggett & Myers Tobacco Co. v. FTC,* 55 FTC 354, 370 (1958).

(95) *In re Ideal Toy Co.,* 64 FTC 297 (1964).

(96) Id. at 316.

(97) *In re Sun Oil Co.,* 84 FTC 247 (1974).

(98) Id. at 249; 1974 was a bad year for additive claimants. See also *In re Standard Oil Co.of Cal.,* 84 FTC 1401 (1974) (concerning misrepresentations as to its F-310 gasoline additive) and *In re Crown Central Petroleum* Corp., 84 FTC 1493 (1974) (concerning misrepresentation of gasoline additive).

(99) Comment, *Illusion or Deception: The Use of "Props" and "Mock-ups" in Television Advertising,* 72 Yale LJ 145 (1962).

(100) *FTC v. Colgate Palmolive Co.,* 380 US 374 (1964).

(101) Id. at 393 (emphasis added).

(102) *FTC v. Campbell Soup Co.,* 77 FTC 664 (May 25, 1970).

(103) *Coca-Cola Co. v. Tropicana Products, Inc.,* 690 F.2d 312 2d Cir. 1982).

(104) Posch, Robert J. Jr., "The Technology Is Here—The Laws Aren't Yet," *Direct Marketing,* February 1982, pp. 86-101. See also Posch, Robert J, Jr., "Narrowcasting May Not Be the Future of Cable TV," *Direct Marketing,* October 1982, pp. 202-204, and Posch, Robert J. Jr., "Direct Broadcast Satellites: Marketing Tool of the Future," *Direct Marketing,* February, 1985, pp. 128-130.

(105) *ITT Continental Baking Co. v. FTC,* 532 F.2d 207 (1976).

(106) Marich, Bob, "Consumerist Earns Grudging Respect," *Advertising Age,* March 16, 1981, p. 12. Another article in this area that is well worth reading is Elrod, *The Federal Trade Commission: Deceptive Advertising and the Colgate-Palmolive Company,* 12 Washburn LJ 133 (1973).

(107) *United States v. National Association of Broadcasters,* 536 FSupp 149 (1982).

(108) Gaughan, "Advertisements Which Identify 'Brand X': A Trialogue on the Law and Policy," 35 *Fordham Law Review* 445, 57 TMR 309, 310 (1967).

(109) 15 USC 45(a)(1)(1976).

(110) *In re Pfizer,* 81 FTC 23 (1976).

(111) Pitofsky, *Network Policy of Preventing Advertising from Naming Competitors,* Memorandum to the FTC (March 6, 1977).

(112) *FTC v. Colgate Palmolive Co.* 380 US 344, 386 (1965).

(113) FTC News Release, March 30, 1972.

(114) Wilkie and Farris, "Comparison Advertising: Problems and Potential," *Journal of Marketing,* vol. 39 1975, p. 10.

(115) Rotfield and Hisrich, *Comparison Advertising: Preliminary Findings on Practitioner's Perspectives,* Working Paper, Marketing Department, Boston College (submitted for presentation to the American Academy of Advertising 1979 National Conference), 13. See also Posch, Robert J. Jr., "Commercial Free Speech—The Argument for OUR Side," *Direct Marketing,* February 1983 pp. 92-94.

(116) For our purposes, information is envisioned as any stimulus perceived by the consumer as potentially helpful in making a purchase or in using a product or service. Technically, a stimulus is not transformed into information until it is actively examined and assigned meaning by the consumer.

(117) 16 CFR 14, 15, 44 Federal Register 47378, August 13, 1979.

(118) *Lorillard Co. v. FTC,* 186 F.2d 52, 58 (4th Cir. 1950).

(119) *Bakers Franchise Corp. v. FTC,* 302 F2d 258 (3d Cir. 1962).

(120) 15 USC 1125(a).

(121) *PPX Enterprises, Inc. v. Audiofidelity, Inc.,* 746 F.2d 120, 125 (2d Cir. 1984); though you need not be a direct competitor. See *Dallas Cowboys Cheerleaders, Inc., v. Pussycat Cinema,* 467 F.Supp. 366 (1979), *aff'd* 604 F.2d 200 (2d Cir. 1979).

(122) *Colligan v. Activities Club of N.Y. Ltd.,* 442 F.2d 686, 692 (2d Cir.) *cert den,* 404 US 1004, 92 S. Ct. 559, 30 L. Ed. 2d 557 (1971); but see *Smith v. Montoro,* 648 F.2d 602 (9th Cir. 1981) and *Thorns v. Reliance Van Co., Inc.,* 7736 F.2d 929 (3d Cir. 1984).

(123) *Johnson & Johnson v. Carter-Wallace, Inc.,* 631 F.2d 186, 189 (2d Cir. 1980).

(124) In *Mutation Mink Breeders Association v. Neirenberg Corp.* 23 FRD 155, 1161-62 (SDNY 1959).

(125) *L'Aiglon Apparel v. Lana Lobell, Inc.,* 214 F.2d 649, 651 (3d Cir. 1954).

(126) *Alfred Dunhill Ltd. v. Interstate Cigar Co., Inc.,* 449 F.2d 232 (2d Cir. 1974).

(127) *Skil Corp. v. Rockwell International Corp.,* 375 F.Supp. 777, 783 (1974); see also *Avis Rent-a-Car Systems, Inc. v. The Hertz Corp.,* (S.D.N.Y. 1985); see also *Johnson & Johnson v. Carter-Wallace, Inc.,* 631 F.2d 186, 190 (1980).

(128) *Upjohn Co. v. American Home Products Corp.,* 598 F.Supp. 550, 556 (1984); see also *Coca Cola Co. v. Tropicana Products, Inc.,* 690 F.2d 312, 317 (1982); see also *American Home Products Corp. v. Johnson & Johnson.* 577 F.2d 160 (2d Cir 1978).

(129) *FTC v. Sterling Drug, Inc.,* 317 F.2d 669, 674 (2d Cir. 1963).

(130) *American Brands, Inc. v. R. J. Reynolds Co.,* 413 F.Supp. 1352, 1356-7 (SDNY 1976); see also *R. J. Reynolds Tobacco v. Loew's Theatres, Inc.,* 511 F.Supp. 867, 876 (1980); see also *McNeil, Inc. v. American Home Products Corp.,* 501 F.Supp. 517 (S.D.N.Y. 1980).

(131) *Vidal Sassoon, Inc. v. Bristol-Myers Co.* 661 F.2d 278 (1981); see also *Philip Morris, Inc. v. Loew's Theatres, Inc.,* 511 F.Supp. 855 (1980) and *Quaker State Oil Refining Corp. v. Burmah Castrol, Inc.,* 504 F.Supp. 178 (1980).

(132) *Bernard Food Industries, Inc. v. Dietene Co.,* 415 F.2d 7279 (7th Cir 1969), *cert den.* 397 US 912, 90 S.Ct. 911, 25 L. Ed 2d 92 (1970).

(133) *Procter & Gamble v. Chesebrough Pond's Inc.,* 558 F.Supp. 1082 (for an unprofessional view), *aff'd* (but with criticism of specious attacks on advertising), 747 F.2d 114, 120 (2d Cir. 1984).

(134) *Richard v. Auto Publisher, Inc.,* 735 F.2d 450 (1984); see also *Metric Multistandard Components v. Metric's,* 635 F.2d 710 (8th Cir. 1980).

(135) *Spring Mills, Inc. v. Ultracashmere House, Ltd.,* 689 F.2d 1127, 1129 (2d Cir. 1982).

(136) *Perfect Fit Industries, Inc. v. Acme Quilting Co., Inc.,* 618 F.2d 950, 955 (2d Cir. 1980) *cert den.,* 459 US 832, 103 S. Ct. 73, 74 L.Ed. 2d 71 (1982).

(137) *Warner Bros. Inc. v. Goy Toys, Inc.,* 724 F.2d 327, 332 (2d Cir. 1983).

(138) *Saratoga Vichy Springs Co. v. Lehman,* 625 F.2d 1037, 1043 (2d Cir. 1980).

(139) *Bi-Rite Enterprises v. Button Master,* 555 F.Supp. 1188, 1195 (1983).

(140) *Feathercombs, Inc. v. Solo Products Corp.,* 306 F.2d 251, 257 (2d Cir. 1962) *cert den.* 371 US 910 (83 S.Ct. 253, 9 L.Ed. 2d 170) (1962).

(141) *Mennen Co. v. Gillette Co.,* 565 F.Supp. 648, 653 (1983), *aff'd,* 742 F.2d 1437 (2d Cir. 1984).

(142) *Venn v. Goedert,* 319 F.2d 812, 816 (8th Cir. 1963).

(143) *PPG Industries, Inc. v. Clinical Data, Inc.,* 620 F.Supp. 604 (D.C. Mass. 1985).

(144) 15 USC 1117.

(145) *Burndy Corp. v. Teledyne Industries, Inc.,* 748 F.2d 767 (1984).

(146) *Cuisinart Inc. v. Robot-Coupe International Corp.,* 580 F.Supp. 634 (1984).

(147) Id. *See also Durbin Brass Works, Inc. v. Schuler,* 532 F.Supp. 41, 44 (E.D. Mo. 1982).

(148) 15 USC 1117.

(149) *Transgo, Inc.v. Ajac Transmission Parts Corp.,* 768 F.2d 1001 (9th Cir. 1985) *cert den.* 106 S.Ct. 802, 88 L.Ed.2d 778 (1986).

(150) *M & W Gear Co. v. AW Dynamoter, Inc.,* 424 NE2d 356 (1981). See also Posch, Robert J. Jr., "Comparative Advertising Yesterday and Today," *Direct Marketing,* May 1982, pp. 106-110.

(151) *Resort Car Rental Sys., Inc. v. FTC,* 518 F.2d 962 (1975).

(152) For example, "Wendy's Asks Damages", *Advertising Age,* October 4, 1982, p.3; and Marshall, C., and R. Kreisman, "Competitors to Fight Burger King Drive," *Advertising Age,* September 20, 1982, p.2.

(153) Kreisman, Richard, "Big Mac Ads Hit Back at BK," *Advertising Age,* November 1, 1982, p.1.

(154) 15 USC Secs. 45(1) and (m) (1) (B) (1978).

(155) *Heather v FTC,* 503 F.2d 321 (9th Cir. 1974).

(156) *U.S. v. J. B. Willliams,* 492 F.2d 414 (2d Cir. 1974) and *ITT Continental Baking Co. v. FTC,* 532 F.2d 207 (2d Cir. 1976).

(157) *FTC v. Colgate Palmolive Co.,* 380 US 374 (1965).

(158) *See J. B. Williams Co. v. FTC,* 381 F.2d 884 (6th Cir. 1967).

(159) *National Committee on Egg Nutrition v. FTC* (1977 CA7) 570 F.2d 157 *cert. den.* 439 US 821, 58 L.Ed. 2d 113, 99 S.Ct.86 (1970).

(160) *Fisher and Deritis,* 49 FTC 77 (1972).

(161) 15 USC Secs. 52, 55 (1978).

(162) Warner-Lambert Co v. FTC, 562 F.2d 749, 759 (1977).

(163) *Royal Baking Powder Co. v. FTC,* 281 F 744 (2d Cir. 1972).

(164) Id., p. 753.

(165) *Waltham Watch Co. v. FTC,* 318 F.2d 28 (7th Cir.) *cert. den.* 375 US 944 (1963).

(166) Id., 318 F.2d 32.

(167) *United States v. STP Corp.,* No. 78-559 (S.D.N.Y. 1978).

(168) *Campbell Soup* (1967-1970 Trans. Binder) *Trade Regulation Reporter* Paragraph 18,897 (1970).

(169) ITT Continental Baking Co., 70 FTC 248 (1971).

(170) *Amstar Corp.,* 83 FTC 659 (1973).

(171) *Ocean Spray Cranberries,* 80 FTC 975 (1972).

(172) See note 11 above.

(173) Id., p. 762.

(174) *Amrep Corp. v. FTC,* 768 F.2d 1171 (1985).

(175) *Encyclopaedia Britannica, Inc. v. FTC,* 605 F.2d 964 (7th Cir. 1979) *cert. den.* 445 US 934, 100 S.Ct. 1329, 63 L.Ed.770 (1980). See also *Grolier, Inc. v. FTC,* 699 F2d 983 (9th Cir.), *cert. den* 104 S.Ct. 235, 78 L.Ed. 2d 227 (1983). (Grolier also had to make up-front disclosures in lead gathering materials and to employment applicants).

(176) *Avis Rent-A-Car Systems Inc. v. The Hertz Corp.,* (S.D.N.Y. (1985).

(177) *Consumer Protection v. Consumer Publishing,* 501 A 2d 481 Md. (1985).

(178) *Virginia State Board of Pharmacy v. Virginia Citizens Consumer Council,* 425 US 748, 763 (1976).

(179) Id., p. 771.

(180) *Ohrolike v. Ohio State Bar Assoc.,* 436 US 447, 457, 98 S.Ct. 1912, 1919, 56 L.Ed. 2d 444 (1978).

(181) Vadehra, Dave "Pitches That Persuade Viewers," *Adweek,* 2/25/85, p. 48. See also Stratford, Sherman, "When You Wish Upon a Star," *Fortune,* 8/19/85, pp. 66—71.

(182) Milinkoff, Ellen, "Hiring A Celebrity," *A&SM,* Aug./Sept. 1985, pp. 9–14.

(183) For the best book you'll ever read on Procter & Gamble and maybe the best book you'll read on any corporation, see Shisgall, Oscar, *Eyes on Tomorrow: The Evolution of Procter & Gamble,* New York: Doubleday/Ferguson, 1981.

(184) For a good commentary on certain abuses see the editorial viewpoint "If the Shoe Fits," *Advertising Age,* July 5, 1982, p. 12. See also Posch, Robert J. Jr., "Check Revised FTC Guide before Planning Endorsements," *Direct Marketing,* July 1982, pp. 214–217.

(185) Guides Concerning the Use of Endorsements and Testimonials in Advertising, 16 CFR 255.

(186) 16 CFR 255.1.

(187) See 16 CFR 255.0: "(a) The Commission intends to treat endorsements and testimonials identically in the context of its enforcement of the Federal Trade Commission Act and for purposes of this part. The term "endorsement" is therefore generally used hereinafter to cover both terms and situations." This text uses both terms interchangeably.

(188) 16 CFR 255(b) and example 2.

(189) Id. and examples 1, 4, and 5.

(190) Id. and example 3

(191) *In re Mattel and Topper, Inc.,* [1970-1973 Transfer Binder] Trade Reg. Rep. (CCH) para. 19,735 (Consent Orders 1971).

(192) 3 Trade Reg. Rep. (CCH) para. 21,380 (FTC 1977).

(193) 87 FTC 756 (1976).

(194) 82 FTC 488 (1973), *mod. in part,* 442 F.2d 1333 (2d Cir. 1974), *cert.* den., 419 US 993 (1974), *order further mod.,* 85 FTC 1052 (1975).

(195) 16 CFR 255.2(a).

(196) 16 CFR 255.1(b).

(197) 16 CFR 255.5.

(198) 16 CFR 255.2(b) and example 3.

(199) 16 CFR 255.2(c).

(200) Forkan, James P., "Maysles Finds 'Great' Copy from Mouths of Real People," *Advertising Age,* November 8, 1982, p. 80. However, for a note of caution to this form of testimonial, review *Better Business of Metropolitan Houston, Inc. v. Medical Directors, Inc.,* 681 F.2d 397 (1982).

(201) 16 CFR 255.4.

(202) *Id.*

(203) 16 CFR 255.3, example 4.

(204) 16 CFR 255.3, example 5.

(205) 16 CFR 255.3, Example 1.

(206) 92 FTC 310 (1978). *See also* "Let the Stellar Seller Beware," *Time,* May 22, 1978, p. 66. The effect of this decision hung over the endorsement industry for a long time. For example, Marty Ingels of Ingels, Inc. (one of the agencies to contact for celebrity endorsers) was quoted in the February 8, 1982 *Advertising Age,* p. 50: "all this, despite the Pat Boone thing still hanging over our heads."

(207) *Resort Car Rental System, Inc. v. FTC,* 518 F.2d 962 (1965).

(208) *Sears, Roebuck and Co. v. FTC,* 676 F.2d 385 (1982).

(209) *Doyle Bernbach, Inc. v. Avis,* 526 F.Supp. 117 (1981).

(210) *Housatonic Valley Pub. Co. v. Citytrust,* 463 A.2d 262 (1983); *American Broadcasting Companies v. Climate Control Corporation,* 524 F.Supp. 1014 (1981); *American Broadcasting Paramount Theatres, Inc. v. American Mfrs. Mutual Insurance Co.,* 42 Misc. 2d 939 (1963); *Clark v. Watt,* 83 Misc. 404 (1913).

(211) *FTC v. Bristol Myers, Young and Rubicam, Inc. and Pedler & Ryan, Inc.,* 46 FTC 162, *aff'd,* (DA 4) 185 F.2d 58, 47 FTC 1749 (1949).

(212) *Beneficial Corp. v. FTC,* 542 F.2d 611 (1976).

(213) *Colgate v. FTC,* 310 F.2d 89 (1963) *rev'd* 380 US 1374 (1975); *Doherty, Clifford, Steers & Shenfield, Inc. v. FTC,* 392 F.2d 921 (1968).

(214) *Carter Products, Inc. v. FTC,* 523 F.2d 523, 534 (1963).

(215) *In re Block Drug Co., Inc. et al,* 92 FTC 852, 853 (1978).

(216) *FTC v. Merck & Co.,* 392 F.2d 921, 1929 (1968).

(217) *Standard Oil Company of California v. FTC* (CA 9) 577 F.2d 653, 659–660 (1978).

(218) *Bristol-Myers Co. v. FTC,* 738 F.2d 554 (1984).

(219) See generally *In re Ted Bates & Company, Inc.,* 97 FTC 220 (1981).

(220) Id., p. 663.

(221) *ITT Continental Baking Co.,* 83 FTC 865, 83 FTC 1105, 90 FTC 181 (1965).

(222) See note 213.

(223) 621 F.Supp. 456 (D.C.N.Y. 1985).

(224) Id., p. 458.

(225) Id., p. 462.

(226) May 19, 1986, pp. 1-4, NAD Case Report.

CHAPTER 16

PERSONAL PROMOTIONS

Your marketing strategy may include personal selling, in which your salespeople (or your current customers, as you will see in a moment) deal with potential customers on a one-to-one basis. Obviously included in this category are door-to-door sales and telephone sales (see Chapter 9). Other personal promotions are those in which you reward satisfied customers with a bonus or merchandise when they recruit new customers. Less obvious as a form of personal selling, but one that rightly belongs in this discussion, is the personal sales pitch your customers may get when they come into your store to buy an advertised item. Here you must be careful to keep the sales pitch from reverting to bait-and-switch tactics.

Each of these types of personal selling entails certain legal issues with which you should be familiar, since your marketing strategy probably does include at least one of these forms of promotion.

Door-to-Door Sales and the Three-Day Cooling-Off Period

For years you've seen the satirized confrontation between Dagwood Bumstead and his nemesis, the door-to-door salesman. The scene is familiar—the leg in the door, a chase from room to room, a fight in the bathtub and other physical confrontations, and various other exhibitions of the "hard sell." The FTC and other consumer groups have argued that a salesperson coming to your door represents an unplanned purchase and often is after a less dramatic but no less effective hard sell than that to which Dagwood was subjected.

To alleviate the perceived problem of deceptive door openers and high-pressure misrepresentations, the FTC[1] (and many states)[2] promulgated in 1974 a "cooling-off" rule for door-to-door sales. The salient parts of the rule are as follows:

(1) For purposes of the FTC regulation, a door-to-door sale is one that requires a purchase of $25 or more (some states may have a lower threshold)[3]

(2) The purchase must be made at a place other than the seller's place of business. A door-to-door sale does not include a sale made pursuant to prior negotiation in the course of a visit by the buyer to a retail business establishment with a fixed location and where the goods are available for inspection. The rule does not apply to a sale conducted and consummated entirely by mail (though states may vary).[4] However, it *does* apply to the growing practice of sales made at consumer product "parties" given in private homes, hotel rooms, or restaurants.

Consumers should note that they are *not* entitled to a refund under this law if the contract was signed at the seller's place of business. Many people erroneously believe that they can cancel any contract within three days, but that is not the case.

If your transaction falls into the category of a door-to-door sale, you must give your would-be buyer oral and written notification (see below for FTC wording) of the buyer's right to cancel anytime before midnight of the third business day following the date of the transaction. Any claim misrepresenting this right to cancel or cooling-off period is prohibited. The buyer must receive a copy of the contract or sales receipt before the three-day period is said to commence.

The written notification must be in the language used in negotiating the contract (for example, French or Spanish, if applicable), must be easily detachable, and must contain in *10-point* boldface type, a statement in substantially the following form:

"You, the buyer, may cancel this transaction at any time prior to midnight of the third business day after the date of this transaction. See the attached notice of cancellation form for an explanation of this right.[5]

You must then furnish a completed form in duplicate (one to return and one for the purchaser to keep for his or her records) captioned "Notice of Cancellation" and stating the following:

NOTICE OF CANCELLATION
[enter date of transaction]

———————

(Date)

YOU MAY CANCEL THIS TRANSACTION, WITHOUT ANY PENALTY OR OBLIGATION, WITHIN THREE BUSINESS DAYS FROM THE ABOVE DATE.

IF YOU CANCEL, ANY PROPERTY TRADED IN, ANY PAYMENTS MADE BY YOU UNDER THE CONTRACT OR SALE,

AND ANY NEGOTIABLE INSTRUMENT EXECUTED BY YOU WILL BE RETURNED WITHIN 10 BUSINESS DAYS FOLLOWING RECEIPT BY THE SELLER OF YOUR CANCELLATION NOTICE, AND ANY SECURITY INTEREST ARISING OUT OF THE TRANS-ACTION WILL BE CANCELED.

IF YOU CANCEL, YOU MUST MAKE AVAILABLE TO THE SELLER AT YOUR RESIDENCE, IN SUBSTANTIALLY AS GOOD CONDITION AS WHEN RECEIVED, ANY GOODS DELIVERED TO YOU UNDER THIS CONTRACT OR SALE; OR IF YOU WISH, COMPLY WITH THE INSTRUCTION OF THE SELLER REGARD-ING THE RETURN SHIPMENT OF THE GOODS AT THE SELL-ER'S EXPENSE AND RISK.

IF YOU DO MAKE THE GOODS AVAILABLE TO THE SELLER AND THE SELLER DOES NOT PICK THEM UP WITHIN 20 DAYS OF THE DATE OF YOUR NOTICE OF CANCELLATION, YOU MAY RETAIN OR DISPOSE OF THE GOODS WITHOUT ANY FURTHER OBLIGATION. IF YOU FAIL TO MAKE THE GOODS AVAILABLE TO THE SELLER, OR IF YOU AGREE TO RETURN THE GOODS TO THE SELLER AND FAIL TO DO SO, THEN YOU REMAIN LIABLE FOR PERFORMANCE OF ALL OBLIGATIONS UNDER THE CONTRACT.

TO CANCEL THIS TRANSACTION, MAIL OR DELIVER A SIGNED AND DATED COPY OF THIS CANCELLATION NOTICE OR ANY OTHER WRITTEN NOTICE, OR SEND A TELEGRAM, TO [Name of seller] AT [address of seller's place of business] NOT LATER THAN MIDNIGHT OF ___ [date]. I HEREBY CANCEL THIS TRANSACTION.

[Date] _____
[Buyer's signature][6]

Proof of mailing date and receipt are important, and thus a certified letter is your customer's best protection. You are not obligated to require certified mail on the form (though the FTC encourages its use).[7] Finally, your customer is not required to give a reason for cancelling—it can be blatantly arbitrary.

Generally if you've received nothing postmarked after three business days your worries are over. You've made a sale. On the other hand, if you do receive a cancellation from the consumer that meets the three-day requirement, you must, within 10 business days of receipt of the cancellation:

(1) Cancel and return any papers the consumer signed;

(2) Refund the consumer's money and indicate whether any product left with him or her will be picked up; and

(3) Return any trade-in.

What about work in progress? Some unscrupulous sellers of home improvements and solar devices have tried to get around the three-day rule by beginning work on the consumer's home before the three days have expired. Then, when the consumer asks to cancel the contract, he or she is told that it is "too late" because work has already begun. That is not allowed under the rule, however (or under any state law). The smart consumer will continue to assert his or her rights under these circumstances.

The seller is obligated to return a person's home to its original condition or work out some other solution that satisfies the customer if work has already started. For example, some solar water heater vendors install equipment that is attached to the roof. If the installation was done during the three-day cancellation period and the consumer wants to cancel before that time period is up, the seller must either remove the equipment or leave it on the roof.

With other goods, you must within 20 days either pick up the items or, if your customer agrees to send them back, reimburse him or her for mailing expenses. If 20 days pass without your picking up the goods, your customer can keep them as a gift. No dunning may be instituted.

The FTC exempted sales under $25 or those made totally by mail or phone.[8] The mail exemption is obvious, and the phone's should be too because the high pressure is greatly diminished by the safety valve of a simple hang-up (again, check each state you're doing business in). Further, there is no confrontational presence before the customer. However, many states have thought otherwise and have enacted laws that cool off the spontaneity of the telephone sale; telephone marketers should know which states impose various restrictions of this sort. Some require permits *prior* to solicitation of sales. For example, Florida will focus on the counties in which you're doing business.[9]

In addition to the under-$25 exemption, other exemptions include:
(a) purchases of real estate, insurance, or securities;
(b) transactions in which the consumer is accorded the right of recision by the provisions of the Consumer Credit Protection Act (15 USC 1635) or regulations issued pursuant thereto; or
(c) transactions in which the buyer has initiated the contact and the goods or services are needed to meet a bona fide immediate personal emergency of the buyer, and the buyer furnishes the seller with a separate dated and signed personal statement in the buyer's handwriting describing the situation requiring immediate remedy and expressly acknowledging and waiving the right to cancel the sale within three business days.[10]

As emphasized above, the FTC, while cognizant of the varied burdens of often inconsistent state laws, still endorses federalism. Specifically:

". . .except to the extent that such laws or ordinances, if they permit door-to-door selling, are directly inconsistent with the provisions of this section. Such laws or ordinances which do not accord the buyer, with respect to the particular transaction, a right to cancel a door-to-door sale which is substantially the same or greater than that provided in this section, or which permit the imposition of any fee or penalty on the buyer for the exercise of such right, or which do not provide for giving the buyer notice of his right to cancel the transaction in substantially the same form and manner provided for in this section, are among those which will be considered directly inconsistent.[11]

The above section is why states have the right under their police powers to have narrower or tougher laws than the FTC rule. A model state statute on point is the Ohio Home Sales Solicitation Act.[12] The state law is broader in many respects and is balanced as to the competing interests in areas the FTC doesn't address. For instance, it gives broader protections to the seller after cancellation by specifying that the buyer may not diminish the quality of the goods while they are in his or her custody.[13] At the same time it sets forth a legal *presumption* of a home solitation sales:

> "Where a sale is made pursuant to negotiations that occur at a place other than the seller's fixed location business establishment where goods or services are offered or exhibited for sale, but the agreement or offer to purchase is signed at a seller's fixed location business establishment, a presumption arises that the sale was a home solicitation sale."[14]

Two final areas of note in door-to-door sales are the *Britannica* and the *Grolier* cases.[15] Especially interesting is the up-front notice both firms originally were supposed to give the potential customer before beginning a sales presentation. Grolier also had further disclosure burdens in lead-generating ads and to employment applicants. The courts have been whittling down the FTC's penalties, and you should consult with counsel as to the final developments in these cases and their possible implications for your method of promotion.

At the same time you should be aware that the Court has gone on record as holding that in-person solicitation, because of its greater potential for abuse, can be more strictly regulated than public commercial advertising.[16] As usual, check your state laws. A number of states are tightening up their laws concerning licensing and sales by "transient sellers" of consumer merchandise by phone or in-person visits, but not those who sell exclusively by mail.[17]

Checklist for Door-to-Door Sales

The salient issues to remember for door-to-door sales include:

- Did we furnish each buyer at the time he or she signed the door-to-door sales contract a completed Notice of Cancellation in duplicate, in the form required by the Rule?[18]
- Did we, before furnishing copies of the Notice of Cancellation to the buyer, complete both copies by entering the name of the seller, the address of the

seller's place of business, the date of the transaction, and the date—not earlier than the third business day following the date of the transaction—by which the buyer may give notice of the cancellations?[19]

- Did we inform each buyer orally at the time he or she signed the contract of the right to cancel?[20]
- Did we misrepresent the buyer's right to cancel in any material way?[21]
- Did we properly honor all valid notices of cancellation by our buyers, at the time and in the form and manner required by the rule?[22]

Legitimate Multilevel Marketing, or Pyramid Sales Scheme?

Multilevel selling programs have swept the country during the last decade. They hold out the potential to be your own boss or at least an independent business person. These plans are used to market food products, financial plans, home furnishings, drug and beauty items, as well as hundreds of other consumer products.

There is often a great deal of confusion surrounding the actual implementation of these distributorships. Some of the plans are first established as legitimate businesses; however, as later generations of downlines of the program operate, they move further from the original design and can become illegal in one or all of the states in which they do business. Anyone interested in becoming involved in such a business operation should review the following before investing time, effort, and above all else, money.

The Pyramid Scheme

To distrubute their products, most conventional sellers (apart from direct marketers) use a system of intermediaries to reach the ultimate consumer. These are often referred to as jobbers or wholesalers and retailers, or a similar term. At each of these levels a profit is made on the product, reflecting each level's contribution toward getting the product to the consumer. Whether the contribution is warehousing, shipping, packaging, or selling, it enables the profit to be earned, and the product is marked up accordingly under the "value added" theory.

Multilevel marketing plans differ from the conventional distribution in that each level in the marketing network consists of independent contractors rather than employees. Each distributor buys the product from the distributor preceding him or her in the distribution network and then either retails it to consumers or wholesales it to those further down the distribution network, usually distributors whom he or she has recruited. Distributors profit from sales made by their own retail sales.

As you can see, the organization is designed to expand in a pyramid fashion (usually four-tiered). It is permissible to offer incentives to recruit what are in effect your employees. Incidental recruitment of more people is essential because of the high turnover. However, the incentives for recruitment must be primarily geared toward the sale of the product, not so that recruitment becomes an end in itself. (If this becomes the case, you probably will have a pyramid scheme.) The problem with these schemes is that for everyone to profit, there has to be a never-ending supply of potential and willing participants to push money up the pyramid. Obviously, each new level of participants has a lesser chance to recruit others and a greater chance of losing money.

While not yet illegal per se,[23] the FTC has defined an illegal pyramid scheme as one

> "characterized by the payment by participants of money to the company in return for which they receive (1) the right to sell a product and (2) the right to receive in return for recruiting other participants into the program rewards which are unrelated to the sale of the product to ultimate users . . . .As is apparent, the presence of this second element, recruitment with rewards unrelated to product sales, is nothing more than an elaborate chain letter device in which individuals who pay a valuable consideration with the expectation of recouping it to some degree via recruitment are bound to be disappointed."[24]

As is evident from the above, pyramid schemes are not true sales organizations, since the sale of a product is only an incidental part of the business;[25] the defendant in this case was primarily in the business of selling distributorships.[26] Recruiters were compensated based on this recruiting regardless of whether the actual products were sold.

Further indications of an illegal pyramid scheme are the required purchase of nonreturnable inventory and the requirement that upon joining the organization, the new members must buy in at various levels (in one case $4,500[27]) for the right to sell the product and recruit other distributors or for nonreturnable inventory ("inventory loading"). These are often referred to as entry or "headhunting" fees. In exchange, the new distributor receives the right to recruit others who will themselves pay a large sum of money. Recruiting new distributors is not a means of selling more of the product, but is itself a source (possibly the only source) of profit for the recruiter. It also, ironically, creates competition for the recruiter himself in the sale of the products. Eventually there is market saturation.

Pyramid schemes are analagous to chain letters, which are analogous to lotteries. All are illegal. All violate the lottery law, which makes illegal any promotion having all the following elements: prize, chance, and consideration. The lottery aspect was reviewed in detail in *People v. Koscot Interplanetary, Inc.* The "prize" is obvious. The participant hoped to receive a return higher than his initial investment by bringing prospects to a meeting where the company could sign them into the organization as distributors, thereby entitling the participants to commissions. Chance and consideration were discussed in the decision:

". . . Consideration is present in that a participant in the Koscot promotion pays a sum of money for the privilege of joining the marketing plan and is present in that the participant hopes to receive a return higher than his investment by bringing prospects to a Golden Opportunity meeting where the defendant may be able to sight one or more prospects into the operation, thereby allowing the participant to earn commissions on the earnings of those over whom he exercises no control. When one invites and brings a prospect to a Golden Opportunity meeting he is relying on the ability and efforts of the operators of that meeting, representing defendant, to persuade the prospects to join. This contingency satisfies the element of *chance.*"[28] (Emphasis added.)

Successful Multilevel Marketing Plans

One need go no further for a text case than the Amway decision.[29] After an extensive review of the Amway system in light of the law, the FTC held that Amway is not in business to sell distributorships and is not a pyramid scheme in any other respect. Amway avoided the usual abuses because:

(1) It does not have a "headhunting" fee.

(2) Amway makes product sales a precondition to receiving the performance bonus.

(3) Amway buys back excessive inventory—the converse of inventory loading.

(4) It requires that products be sold to consumers.

(5) Its training programs' main emphasis is on sales training and the Amway Way, not on recruiting new distributors.

(6) Amway maintains a variety of other internal management controls.

If your sellers work for no more than straight pay and are not entitled to recruit anyone, and the distributors are only recruiting replacements, the courts will probably look favorably upon your operations also.[30]

Referral Sales Agreements or Member-Get-A-Member Promotions

When using referral sales agreements, the key to running a successful promotion is to avoid running any form of direct or indirect chain referral or pyramid-type scheme. You should also become familiar with specific statutes regarding the traditional "member-get-a-member" promotions. The following is the type of wording included in many, if not most, state unfair trade practice statutes on point (consult your counsel for your state's exact wording):

It is considered an unlawful act when a person engages in a sale of goods or services, gives or offers to give a rebate or discount, or otherwise pays or offers to pay value to the buyer in consideration of the buyer giving to the seller the names of prospective purchasers, lessors, or borrowers, or otherwise ordering the seller in making a sale, lease, or loan to another person if the earning of the rebate, discount, or other value is *contingent* upon the occurrence of an event subsequent to the time the buyer enters into the transaction.

A member-get-a-member promotion is a bit different from a pyramid scheme in that in a referral agreement the party who supplies the names of potential buyers is normally purchasing a product for his or her own consumption, while under the pyramid program, the party who brings another into the program is normally purchasing products for resale. Also, the participant in a referral plan is merely a consumer who receives goods after they have gone through traditional distribution outlets, while in a pyramid distribution program, the participants constitute the entire distribution system for the manufacturer of the product.

As discussed earlier in this section, a satisfied customer is the *best* recommendation for your product. Many shrewd business people have established plans that encourage their firms' customers to recruit new customers to them. They know this personal trust relationship among friends and neighbors is an excellent market penetration device. In our society we encourage a fundamental law of behavior—that of reward spurring motivation. You wish to reward your customers who get other customers. You also wish to stay within the law. What is to be done?

First, the obvious: check your contract. If you are giving away rewards, review with your counsel whether such promotional giveaways are permissible in your state.

Second, review your promotional wording with counsel. As stressed throughout, keep in mind the maturity of your target audience. Then make sure that your wording cannot be construed as a false representation for the purpose of inducing consumers to participate in your plan.

You can give away a reward on receipt of a referral, or you might wish to qualify that the reward is *contingent* on the referral's action—buying your food plan or joining your record club, for example. If you do the latter, review the promotional copy with counsel, since all qualifying terms must be *clear and conspicuous—not* buried in the overall promotion piece. You and your counsel will work out a conspicuous layout (possibly similar to a "rule box" you'll use in your sweepstakes copy). The wording will contain terms such as "as soon as your friend pays." You will invite the recruiter to claim the gift or reward (not order it) when presenting the referral.

Remember that you are dealing with a *free* offer. As discussed in chapter 15, when you make so-called free or similar offers, all the terms, conditions, and obligations on which receipt and retention of the free item are contingent should be set forth clearly and conspicuously at the outset of your offer. Leave no reasonable probability that the terms of the offer might be misunderstood.[31] Further, remember that terms such as "gift," "given without charge," "bonus," or other words conveying the impression that the article is free are governed by the Free Rule.[32]

Third, for any promotion of this kind, make sure you review with your counsel whether you've obtained a valid certificate of authority to do business in the state[33] and that your agreements don't leave you open to adverse antitrust exposure.

Finally, always have a signature line on your order card for these promotions. The signature requirement discourages forgery by the recruiter and highlights the fact that the applicant is entering a potential business relationship and not merely helping a friend. If it's a juvenile promotion, you should have a parent or guardian sign. This will discourage lark entries by informed minors who know or may be told by your recruiter that their contractual obligations are generally voidable at *their* initiative.

Despite criticism to the contrary, these promotions work and, if you do them right, improve your bottom line while presenting no adverse legal exposure.[34]

Avoiding Legal Exposure

The following checklist questions should be reviewed against your copy, distribution agreements, training manuals, etc., before you initiate a promotion:

- Do we make claims as to earnings potential or legitimate recruitment potential with no adequate written substantiation to support our claims?
- What about our claims as to the potential market or geographic exclusivity for an individual distributor?
- Do we make statements that an official government agency has sponsored, approved, or certified any organization, our marketing plan, agents, employees, representatives, or products? A written copy of such approval must be on file.
- What is the real emphasis on bringing others into the program (in light of our targeted audience)? Even if the sale of a product is connected with the program, the primary focus of the plan should not be to bring others into the company. If the program is based on incentives, bonuses, or commissions to recruit others, no matter what other details are given, it could be a pyramid scheme and thus a violation of law.
- Have we analyzed the plan's structure as to its actual function? The number of levels a plan contains does not necessarily determine the plan's compliance with applicable laws or distinguish it from any other marketing plan.
- Do we make statements that our company's marketing plan is legal because it is similar to another, better-known company's marketing plan? This may not be true.
- Does our sales staff make verbal presentations that differ from the company's written materials? Verbal and written materials should be the same, and our sales manuals must stress this.

- Do we impose requirements of large or monthly purchases of our company's products? This could be a tool simply for the company to sell its products with no regard to its distributors or what they can reasonably sell in a given time.
- Do we accept returns of inventory, and is this clearly communicated?
- Can we prove our distributors are not saddled with unsold inventory?
- Will our records substantiate that we receive most of our profit from product sales and that the sale of distributorships is not the real source of our income?
- Are our training programs geared toward training (with a minimum of high pressure tactics) management and employees in product sales, not in recruiting new distributors?
- Has our ad copy been reviewed as to the basics: lottery factors, misrepresented facts, exaggeraged claims and statistics, undisclosed material facts, noncompliance with home solicitation laws (e.g., cooling-off periods), or false advertising?
- Has counsel signed off on our distribution agreements so that there is no restraint of trade present?
- Have we acquired all necessary certificates for doing business in the states we're entering?
- Are all our recruitment efforts fully in compliance with state and federal equal opportunity laws?

If you're in compliance with the above checklist, you're in good shape. Now you must make sure your people don't get involved in the messy area of bait and switch.

Bait-and-Switch Advertising

It's a familiar scenario: A customer walks into a store, drawn by an ad in the newspaper, and requests an item on sale. The seller informs him or her that the "bait" item isn't available, or that it lacks a guarantee, or that parts are hard to replace, or that it has some other shortcoming. The "switch" item, on the other hand, is available and has none of the failings of the bait item. Of course, it costs "a bit more," too. Maybe the salesperson gets a better commission on the particular item he or she is pushing.

The FTC guides against bait advertising should be studied by any manager attempting to trade up, even in good faith.[35] The FTC also audits these complaints. Any complaint to the FTC hurts your firm individually. A high volume of complaints hurts your industry. If you don't think the FTC audits and *adds up* all complaints, order a copy of the *Digest of Consumer Complaints and Inquiries*[36] and make it a part of your profit preservation center library (see chapter 24). You can expect similar problems with your state attorney general and the various related agencies. Try to get on their mailing list, too.

Since these guides are important to you and your goodwill, we'll review them here.[37] In general, this review applies to retail and telephone marketing as well as to any other personal contact promotional selling you devise.

What the FTC Says

The FTC defines bait advertising as an "alluring but insincere offer to sell a product or service which the advertiser in truth does not intend or want to sell. Its purpose is to switch consumers from buying the advertised merchandise, in order to sell something else, usually at a higher price or on a basis more advantageous to the advertiser. The primary aim of a bait advertisement is to obtain leads as to persons interested in buying merchandise of the type so advertised."[38]

In short, the offense entails advertising (which is defined as any form of public notice, however disseminated or used) in such an attractive way as to bring customers to your store or have them call, followed by sales staff disparagement of the advertised product to get customers to switch to a more expensive product (often with a more lucrative commission for the sales staff obtaining the order).

The initial order or interview that brings your customer to you must be truthful from the start, as stressed throughout this section. You *cannot* redeem a deceptive initial offer by presenting the facts to your customer on arrival.[39] In addition to the wording of the ad, the FTC requires that no statement or illustration may be used that creates a false impression to a reasonable person as to the make, value, newness of model, size, color, usability, or origin of the product offered, or that may otherwise misrepresent the product in such a manner that later, on disclosure of the true facts, the purchaser may be switched from the advertised product to another.[40] Many state deceptive-sales statutes specifically state that it is not necessary for a sale to actually take place before a supplier may be liable to a consumer for deceptive acts. A solicitation to sell goods or services intended primarily for personal, family, or household use may be sufficient to give rise to liability, even in the absence of an actual sale, if a deceptive act is committed in connection with the solicitation.

For example, a company circulated advertisements for a piano at a specific sale price. The ad featured a sketch of (presumably) the sale piano, which was actually a composite drawing of several more expensive pianos. The composite drawing was used even though a photograph of the piano on sale was available. The court found that this newspaper advertisement, announcing a special sale price on a particular piano model and containing a drawing that was a composite of several more expensive piano models, was a solicitation to supply, which could serve as a basis for a deceptive act for purposes of action under Indiana's Deceptive Consumer Sales Act.[41] The moral of this story is that your entire advertisement—not merely the price quote or salesperson's in-store conduct—can be part of the bait.

Assuming that your promotional vehicle is true in all respects, your sales staff cannot discourage a purchase when the customer arrives at your store or phones in the order. Among the acts or practices that will be considered in determining whether an advertisement is a bona fide offer or a "bait-and-switch" are the following:[42]

(1) Using statements or illustrations or other representation in any advertisement which would create in the mind of a reasonable consumer, a false impression as to the grade, quality, quantity, make, model, year, price, value, size, color, utility, origin, or any other material aspect of the offered goods or services in such a manner that, upon subsequent disclosure or discovery of the facts, the consumer may be induced to purchase goods or services other than those offered;

(2) Failing to show, demonstrate, or sell the advertised item in accordance with the terms of the offer;

(3) Disparaging the product, its warranty, availability of service, or other aspects of the product by actions or words (including exaggerated exclamations upon inquiry);

(4) Failing to make an affirmative offer to sell;

(5) Failing to have available a sufficient quantity of the advertised product to meet reasonably anticipated needs or to provide a raincheck[43]—unless your advertisement clearly and adequately discloses the *specific quantity* of advertised goods or services available, or that the supply is limited, or that your merchandise is available only at designated locations;

(6) Refusing to take orders for the advertised merchandise to be delivered within a reasonable period of time;

(7) Showing or demonstrating a product that is defective, unusable, or impractical for the purpose represented or implied in the advertisement;

(8) Using any commission or other sales plan that penalizes your sales force from selling the advertised product;

(9) Subjecting a customer who orders the advertised product to protracted delays in delivery, parts, service, etc. to discourage others from purchasing the product (i.e., general unethical business conduct)[44];

(10) Delivering offered goods or services that are materially different from the offered goods or services.

Switch After Sale

Obviously, you may not pursue any practice to "unsell" a product after its purchase with the intent to sell other merchandise in its place. This can occur when you've accepted a deposit and the customer returns to pay the balance or when you fail to make timely or adequate delivery or in any other way discourage the customer from obtaining the goods which you are actively trying to switch away from such customer. Again, at this time you are not permitted to disparage by acts or words the advertised product, guarantee, credit terms, availability of service, repairs, or any other related factor.

Finally, it almost goes without saying that the delivery of the advertised product that is defective, unusable, or impractical for the purpose represented or implied in the advertisement is not allowed.[45]

Trading Up Is Not a Bait-and-Switch Tactic

When people call or drop in (or you call them), you already have a buyer of predisposed interest at least in the product about which the potential customer is inquiring. Any additional soft sell will be treated as information. This is a good time to cross-sell. The customer wants a fishing rod—how about a tackle box? A *well-trained* marketer might also attempt to sell up or trade up. Be careful here: You must not get involved in the bait-and-switch areas or even offer the inference of such.

Trading up is not an illegal practice when done in conformity with the guides. What your salespeople actually do and say—not their intentions— determines whether you have a legal violation. If you're within the law, trading up is merely full-line selling, that is, giving customers the information and opportunity to learn about the various features available in the product line so that each customer can make an informed buying decision by matching his or her *individual* needs and budgetary requirements with the product and features you are offering in your total line. Your customer relations will be enhanced because your customer will appreciate making a buying decision based on personal attention to his or her own particular need.

For example, if a customer calls in to purchase an air conditioner, your informed salesperson may question his or her needs, such as the size of the room to be served. If the customer's original order is legitimately inadequate, you have the right if not the obligation to inform your customer of this fact and then attempt to sell a piece of equipment that would better fulfill your customer's needs. Such equipment might be a larger air conditioner, a ceiling fan, a dehumidifier, or whatever is applicable. Not only are you within the law, but you otherwise might have lost the customer's future patronage if he or she blamed your firm for selling an inadequate cooling device. Further, these judgment calls represent the service aspect of your business, the reason you have a sales staff and not an answering machine.

Another instance where trading up presents no bait-and-switch problems is when customers decide against your advertised offer or are truly undecided. You may then ask prospective buyers if they are interested in obtaining further information. If the answer is yes, you may trade up by making the person aware of the top-of-the-line products you are offering.

Dry Testing

This is a related bait-and-switch issue—at best the hook is baited. As discussed in Chapter 9, the social policy behind the mail-order merchandise rule was to discourage the practice of dry loans. We also stressed that the FTC considers it an unfair or deceptive act to solicit an order through the mails unless you have a reasonable basis to believe you can fulfill the order within a certain time. In light of all this, can you still "dry test" (test market response by soliciting orders for a product before it even tangibly exists)? Interestingly, the answer is yes— but in certain circumstances.

There is limited law on point, but you should be aware of FTC Advisory Opinion No. 753 7003:[46]

[T]he Commission does not object to the use of dry-testing a continuity book series marketed by mail order as long as the following conditions are observed:

(1) No representation, express or implied, is made in advertisements, brochures, or other promotional material, which has the *tendency or capacity* to mislead the public into believing that the books have been or will definitely be published, or that by expressing an interest in receiving the books a prospective purchaser will necessarily receive them.

(2) In all solicitations for subscriptions and other promotional material, *clear and conspicuous disclosure* is made of the terms and conditions of the publication, distribution, and other material aspects of the continuity book series program. Such disclosure must provide adequate notice of the *conditional nature* of publication of the book series, i.e., the fact that the book series is only planned and may not actually be published.

(3) If the decision is reached to not publish the book series, due notice is given to persons who have subscribed, within a reasonable time after the date of first mailing the solicitations for subscriptions. The *Commission considers four months or less to be a reasonable time,* unless extenuating circumstances exist. If the decision whether or not to publish the book series has not been made within that time period, persons who expressed a desire to subscribe should be notified of the fact that a decision has not yet been reached, and should be given an opportunity to cancel their order.

(4) There is no substitution of any books for those ordered.[47]

In terms of the clear and conspicuous disclosure discussed in point 2 above, stated elsewhere[48] and applicable here is the requirement that where the direct-mail advertising of specific products consists of a promotional package containing more than one advertising piece (e.g., brochure and cover letter with order form or reply card), the disclosure required by §§256.1-256.3, 256.5 through 256.8, and 256.17 must appear clearly and conspicuously where they are most likely to be noticed, on at least one piece of the promotional advertising package.

A related FTC guide also applies:

§256.7 Representations relative to works not yet published

Representations soliciting the sale of specific industry products should not expressly or impliedly hold out a publication as having been printed or published at the time of the offer when such is not the fact. Solicitations relative to works not yet published should clearly and conspicuously disclose that the publication is being planned or contemplated and that inquiries or orders are being solicited to determine demand for the publication, or words to that effect. [Guide 7][49]

As is generally advisable, you should have your counsel review any state law that places stricter requirements on or affords greater consumer protection from dry testing.

Checklist for Bait-and-Switch Compliance

The following should be incorporated into any serious in-house program to avoid even the inference of bait-and-switch tactics.

- Don't disparage *any* product you sell. Make your sales staff cognizant of your policy not to disparage or belittle any advertised product you are offering.

- Make sure that the issue of bait-and-switch tactics is *specifically* addressed by name in all your sales manuals. Include examples of acceptable and unacceptable practices. Make it clear that a violation will result in disciplinary action. Review such manuals (as well as all telephone-marketing sales scripts) with your counsel. If you are involved in telephone marketing and are employing outside service consultants, indicate your policy against bait-and-switch conduct in writing in your contract with each agency and protect yourself against such liability in the indemnification paragraph of your contract. Further, make sure such service acknowledges it will comply with all pertinent federal, state, and local laws and regulations.

- Coordinate your sales advertising campaign with your inventory department. If there are problems, make sure that you have a *communicated* policy of issuing rain checks to your customers whenever an advertised product becomes out of stock before the advertised termination date (or a reasonable time if no date is specified). If there is any margin for error, specify the quantity of goods available. Review with your counsel how specific your wording must be. For example, must you specify "sixteen televisions available," or would "limited quantity available today only" be satisfactory? You need your counsel's input on the varied state and municipal regulations you're dealing with at each store location.

- Make sure any photos or illustrations of your item on sale are as accurate as the price.

- Make sure your sales staff is committed to your corporate goals and knows that any comparison of the advertised product with another must be positively oriented. They must stress what each product will do in a positive manner—not what a product won't do.

- No personnel should contradict a promotional piece that has initiated the call or in-store visit unless there was an objective error (e.g., a typographical misprint). If such an error exists, put the prospective buyer in touch with a customer service professional, *not* another product.

- Obviously, no untrue or misrepresenting statements should be made by any personnel.

- Instruct salespersons that if there is any resistance at all to trading up, they must cease. Once a customer reviews your trade-up presentation and elects the original purchase, your salesperson must close the sale. The customer should not be requested or in any way encouraged to reconsider.

- Be sensitive to all bait-and-switch rules when designing any dry testing promotions.

These tips will help you to practice smart customer relations, not just legal compliance. Your customer knows this law from a barrage of consumer education leaflets and from simple, word-of-mouth education and expects compliance and fair treatment. If such expectations are not met, your customer will be someone else's customer in the future. And remember, many customers are no longer just walking away. They're contacting the newspaper, magazine, or other medium that carried your ad. Such media follow-up can turn one customer's bad experience into a cause celebre at your expense.

ENDNOTES

(1) "Cooling-off Period for Door-to-Door Sales," 16 CFR Sec.429. If you have problems here, a good group to contact (with an excellent newsletter) is the Direct Selling Association, 1730 M St., N.W., Suite 610, Washington, D.C., 20036.

(2) Some of these states include:

California. Cal. Civ. Code Sec.1689.5-.13 (Deering Supp. 1979): three-day cooling off; $25 minimum purchase; oral and written notice of right to cancel must be given in the same language used in the sales presentation; seller has 10 days to return down payment and 20 days to pick up canceled goods.

Florida. Fla. Stat. Ann. Sec.501.021-.035 (West Supp. 1981): three-day cooling off; $25 minimum purchase; seller may keep part of down payment as cancellation fee.

Georgia. Ga. Code Ann. Sec.96-902 to 96-906 (Supp. 1979): three-day cooling off; credit sales only; seller may assess a cancellation fee and pick up fee for canceled goods even if buyer made no down payment.

Mississippi. Miss. Code Ann. Sec.75-66-1 to -11 (Supp. 1980): three-day cooling off; credit sales only, cancellation fee, 40 days to pick up goods; excludes sales on buyer's initiative.

New York. N.Y. Pers. Prop. Law Sec.425-431 (McKinney Supp. 1980-1981): same provisions as the California Civil Code.

Remember that state legislative activity is a constant; monitor it and review your planning with your counsel.

However certain restrictions may violate First Amendment rights. See *Watska v. Illinois Public Action Council* (CA 7 Ill.) 796 F.2d 1547 (1987) (city ordinance which limited door-to-door solicitation to the hours between 9 A.M. and 5. P.M., Mon.-Sat.).

(3) See Arizona, Arkansas, Indiana, Louisiana, Michigan, North Dakota, Oregon, Wisconsin, Wyoming, and others. For a recently enacted law see Florida Statutes, Sec.501.021 et seq. A firm must file an application and obtain a permit from the sheriff in the county in which the firm intends to do business.

(4) For example, see Utah Code Ann. Sec.13-11-4(1)(k)(1), which is overkill, as mail by its nature is reflective, with no undue sales pressure.

(5) 16 CFR 429.1(a).

(6) 16 CFR 429.1(b).

(7) See FTC Bureau of Consumer Protection pamphlet "Door-to-Door Sale," as revised, third paragraph.

(8) The following states have telephone sales incorporated into their home solicitation laws. You should review these with counsel because they vary (e.g., some cover all calls, others cover orders over $25): Arizona, Arkansas, Indiana, Louisiana, Michigan, North Dakota, Ohio, Oregon, Utah, Virginia, Wisconsin, and Wyoming. Certain localities and municipalities also have regulations on point.

(9) Florida Statutes, Sec.501.021, 501.023, 501.046-7, 501.055 (1986).

(10) 16 CFR 429 note 1(a)(1)(b) and (c).

(11) 16 CFR 429 note 2(b).

(12) Ohio Revised Code 1345.21 et seq. (1986).

(13) Id., 1345.27.

(14) Id., 1345.25.

(15) *Encyclopaedia Britannica, Inc. v. FTC,* 605 F.2d 964 (7th Cir.1979).

(16) *Ohralik v. Ohio State Bar Association,* 436 US 447,457, 98 S.Ct. 1912,1919, 56 L.Ed.2d 444 (1978).

(17) 32 *Maine Revised Statutes Ann.* 4682 - B.

(18) 16 CFR 429.1(b).

(19) 16 CFR 429.1(c).

(20) 16 CFR 429.1(e).

(21) 16 CFR 429.1(f).

(22) 16 CFR 429.1(g).

(23) *United States v. Bestline Products Corp.,* 412 F.Supp. 754, 777 (N.D. Cal. 1976).

(24) *Koscot Interplanetary, Inc.,* 86 FTC 1106 (1975), *aff'd sub nom. Turner v. FTC,* 580 F.2d 701 (D.C. Cir. 1978).

(25) *Holiday Magic, Inc.,* 84 FTC 748, 1035 (1974).

(26) Id., see note 2, p. 1140.

(27) Id., see note 3.

(28) 37 Mich. App. 447, 459, 195 NW2d 43, 54 ALR3d 195, 208 (1972); see also *M. Lippincott Mortgage Investment Co. v. Childress,* 204 S.2d 919 (1968).

(29) *In re Amway Corp, Inc. et al.,* 93 FTC 618 (1979).

(30) *Holiday Magic, Inc. v. James,* 209 S.2d 47 (La. App. 1968).

(31) 16 CFR 251.1(c)—see discussion under "Copy Headliner Compliance."

(32) 16 CFR 251.1(i).

(33) *Thaxton v. Commonwealth,* 211 Va. 38, 175 SE2d 264 (1970), and *Kugler v. Koscot Interplanetary, Inc.,* 120 NJ Super. 216, 293 A2d 682 (1972).

(34) *Ammerman v. Bestline Products, Inc.,* 352 F.Supp. 1077 (1973). See also H. R. Ronich, "The Case Against Referral Sales," *Case and Comment,* December, 1973, p.20. For other views on this type of promotion, see Comment, *Let the "Seller" Beware -*

Another Approach to Referral Sales Scheme, 22 Miami L. Rev. 861 (1968) and *Pyramid Sales Participants: Victims or Perpetrators?,* 47 Temple L. Q. 697 (1974).

(35) Guides Against Bait Advertising, 16 CFR 238 (1981).

(36) The FTC publishes this every three months, and you may get it by writing to the Public Reference Branch, Room 130, Federal Trade Commission, Washington, D.C., 20580 or by calling them at (202)523-3598.

(37) Don't forget to review with your counsel applicable state and local laws. For example, the following codes are all in the New York City area: N.Y. Gen. Bus. Law Sec. 396; New York City Admin. Code Sec. 2203.d-2.0(a)(4); Nassau County Admin. Code Sec. 21-10.2(5); Westchester County Admin. Code Sec. 863.11(7)(c).

(38) 16 CFR 238.0.

(39) 16 CFR 238.2(b).

(40) 16 CFR 238.2(a).

(41) *McCormick Piano & Organ Co., Inc. v. Geiger,* 412 NE2d 842 (1980)

(42) 16 CFR 238.3.

(43) *Weaver v. J.C. Penney, Inc.,* 372 NE2d 663 (1977).

(44) *In People by Lefkowitz v. Levinson,* 23 Misc.2d 483, 199 N.Y.S.2d 625 (1960).

(45) 16 CFR 238.4.

(46) "Dry Testing" and "Bulk Loading" a Continuity Book Series by Mail Order, 85 FTC 1192-97 (1975).

(47) Guides for the Law Book Industry, 16 CFR 256.1.

(48) Id. at 1193-94.

(49) 16 CFR 256.7.

CHAPTER 17

NONPERSONAL
PROMOTIONS

Use of in-store promotions has remained fairly constant the last few years. What is said in Chapter 15 about coupons and price discounts, applies here. This chapter examines deceptive pricing schemes used to get people in the door and to perhaps buy incorrectly. It reviews general rules of legal advertising designed to keep people moving about the store. As a rule, such promotions are aimed at getting current customers to increase their purchases rather than at attracting new customers.

A favorite—and one of the safest—point-of-purchase displays is the matchbook. This can bear promotional wording or an 800 number, or it can simply act as a reminder of your business. Don't let anti-smoking sentiment throw you—the matchbook still has utility value to your customer, so it will be retained, if only for the pilot light or the barbeque grill. Each time your customer lights a match the matchbook will be read. This gives you 20 exposures before the book is used, and then there are the matchbook collectors. . . . From a legal point of view, keep in mind the copy-wording laws discussed in other sections.

How to Avoid Deceptive Pricing

People do love a bargain, but oh, how they hate to be conned! Examples of deceptive pricing abound in everyday life: the so-called going-out-of-business sale where everything is marked way up before the "25% off everything" signs go up, comparisons between a fictitious "former price" and the new "sale" price, "sales" that never end. These deceptive pricing schemes not only are aggravating to the consumer, they're also illegal.[1]

When it comes to pricing, this area permits no latitude for puffery, and you may have to stifle your creative urge just a bit. Objective accuracy is at a premium. Unlike the more subjective claims of quality, when you stress price you are in an objective area of substantiation. Let's review a few common questions on pricing.

What is deceptive pricing? This is any *unsubstantiated* price claim that would materially affect the purchaser's decision to buy your product.[2] Substantiation means you must maintain adequate records that disclose the factual basis for your representations.

What if I don't intend to deceive? Your intention to deceive is not a prerequisite to committing an unfair or deceptive trade practice. The test of a violation is the effect on your purchaser.[3] Further, although a false price may be obviously false to those in your trade, that is no defense if it deceives a particularly vulnerable group (such as children) or "that vast multitude which includes the ignorant, the unthinking and the credulous."[4]

What if my price is the actual value of the product? If you are selling a $35 grill for $35 and this is its genuine price—no problem. However, if you had previously marked up the grill to $60 and then "cut" the price to $35 to advertise a "sale," you are engaging in deceptive pricing.[5]

What former price comparisons may I use? In making comparisons to a former price, you must have made bona fide sales at the advertised former price in the *recent* past. If the product was offered for sale but no sales were made at that price or any other price in the recent past (the past thirty-day period, for instance), that fact must be disclosed in connection with any mention of the former price. This test is important: You must be able to demonstrate that the product was openly and actively offered for sale for a reasonably substantial period of time, in the regular course of business, honestly and in good faith—and, of course, not for the purpose of establishing a fictitious higher price on which is made a deceptive comparison.

The product must have been offered for sale in the same trade area (e.g., geographically comparable over the entire market area, which can be local, regional, or national), and not an "average" of all markets in general. The use of the words "usually" or "formerly" does not cure your situation if a fictitious price comparison is being made. The use of asterisks to contradict a statement in the advertisement may be misleading, but to use an asterisk to denote additional information or define a term may be permissible. Again, the totality of the advertisement must be examined.

If a savings cannot be substantiated over a significant geographic area, a disclaimer is advised. Sales records, checks, invoices, and even correspondence will be helpful here as objective evidence.[6]

Finally, don't forget qualitative aspects. If you have diluted the quality of your product you may not create the impression that the original product is being offered at a reduced price.[7] The standard of comparable product is a requirement for all price claims by you and your competitors.

What about just stating my "regular price?" This is all right if you use the word "regular" or other words of similar import and mean to refer to any price amount which is not in excess of the price at which any article, merchandise, or service has been sold or offered for sale in good faith by you for a reasonably substantial period of time in the recent, regular course of your business. Further, your business records must establish that this amount is the price at which your merchandise has been sold or is offered for sale in good faith by you for a reasonably substantial period of time in the recent, regular course of your business.

There are two points to keep in mind here. You must be able to demonstrate that you have a reasonable basis (scientific sampling) to substantiate that your sample is representative. Also, you must be careful that any sale prices do not exist for more than six months and that no more than 50% of the sales were at the sale price, because then the "sale price would become the regular price." If the same sale price is always maintained, the offer is merely deceptive advertising.

What about manufacturer's list prices? Use of manufacturer's list prices is acceptable *if* relevant to the area you do business in or the "trade area." The following are a few things to watch:

- If an article is seasonal, don't compare a "substantial markdown" due to seasonal preferences to the in-season price.
- Don't call yourself a "wholesaler" or imply that your large buying power enables you to eliminate the intermediary unless this is true or, in the latter case, such savings are *directly* passed on to the purchaser.

May I advertise the price of the item includes the sales tax? This area is in flux, but certain states permit it. For example, Washington[8] permits this but if the seller advertises the price as including the tax or that the seller is paying the tax, the advertised price shall not be considered the selling price.

May I charge more than list price? Yes, but you might have to say so. Many states and municipalities have disclosure laws on this. For example, a seller in New York City significantly marked up his calculators.[9] He was fined $2000 for violating the Administrative Code. The seller argued (correctly) that the higher rents in his area justified the higher price. He also alleged that his "customers are both willing and happy to pay its prices because of the store's convenient location and knowledgeable sales staff."[10]

Not good enough, said the court: "When a fact is material to a buying decision and consumers would not ordinarily discover that fact before buying, it is deceptive not to disclose such a fact. . . . To a consumer who wishes to make an informed choice, disclosure that the selling price far exceeds the manufacturer's suggested retail price is clearly material."[11] The court upheld the regulation on its merit insofar as it enhances comparative shopping and diminishes the vulnerability of the public.

In California it is an unfair or deceptive trade practice to advertise that a product is being offered at a specific price plus a specific percentage of that price unless (1) the total price is set forth in the advertisement, which may include, but is not limited to, shelf tags, displays, and media advertising, in a size larger than any other price in that advertisement, and (2) the specific price plus a specific percentage of that price represents a markup from the seller's costs or from the wholesale price of the product.[12] Check with your counsel about similar state and local laws.

What substantiation is required in comparative pricing? This topic always bears repeating. No comparisons should be made or implied between the price at which an article is offered for sale and some other reference price unless the nature of the reference price is explicitly identified and you have a reasonable basis to substantiate its accuracy in the sales area in which you are actually making the claim.[13] This substantiation must be undertaken *prior* to publishing the price comparison advertisement. It must be relevant to the area in which the audience will shop.

Can I charge shipping and handling, and does this affect my discount claim? Amazingly, no. You will often see that direct marketers' discount claims vis-a-vis their store competitors' do not factor in the fact that the store has *already paid* the shipping and handling charges to get the product in the store! Nevertheless the stores and agencies have never picked up on this. (Even if they did, perhaps the direct marketers could argue carfare to the store versus shipping and handling charges.) Have your counsel keep an eye on this discrepancy if this topic affects you.

What is "relevant" to my audience? What is your geographic drawing power? Is yours a national chain? If so, verification of prices is required using reasonable business methods in your trade, such as market surveys. If you are an independent, you should ascertain what prices are being charged at the principal retail outlets in the area.

What about free offers or two-for-one sales? These are fine (see discussion under "Copy Headliners" in Chapter 15) so long as care is taken not to mislead your customer and all the terms and conditions of the offer are made clear at the outset.[14]

What about media life? This can complicate the issue of what is a valid, current reference price for comparison purposes. For example, you base certain strategies on media exposure life. Newspapers may last a day, *TV Guide* a week, cable guide a month, and your annual catalog may be retained and browsed through over an entire year! Here, good faith and reasonable business practices in pricing are in order for the promotional vehicles with a longer life. Provided that the prices were substantiated as a reference at the time of publication, you will probably overcome this hurdle.

Can I apply limitations to the sale, such as certain hours or days, for example? Various nuances in state laws may affect issues such as this. For example, Ohio would require:[15]

- Advertisements for clothing must state if there is an additional charge for sizes above or below a certain size.

- If the advertised price is available only during certain hours of the day or certain days of the week, that fact must be stated along with the hours and days the price is available.

- If the advertisement involves or pictures more than one item of goods (for example, a table and chairs) and the advertised price applies only when the complete set is purchased, that fact must be stated.

- If a minimum amount (or maximum amount) must be purchased for the advertised price to apply, that fact must be stated.

Are there any special rules for "going-out-of business" sales? Arkansas has passed strict laws governing the "going-out-of-business" sale. Besides following the strict provisions of the statute, business planning sales, such as liquidation or "lost our lease" sales, must first obtain a license from the *county* in which the sale is to be conducted.[16] As usual, check all local and state laws applicable to your targeted markets.

May I guarantee a price or a percentage discount for one year or even indefinitely? Yes — this is simple truth in advertising if later events force an increase.

What if all my competitors are engaged in violations? Sorry — no defense. You still may be singled out. Even if all your competitors are *more* deceptive, this evidence is irrelevant to your defense.[17]

Summing Up Deceptive Pricing

The following checklist will help you avoid deceptive pricing claims in your promotions.

- The items you're comparing must be identical or substantially similar. For example, if you're comparing meats, they must be identical in cut and grade. You also can't offer imperfect or irregular clothing at a reduced price in comparison with regular goods.[18]

- All price comparisons (your own prior claims or comparisons with a competitor) must be based on "actual, bona fide prices at which the article was offered to the public in the trade area on a regular basis for a reasonably substantial period of time."[19]

- Geographic changes in pricing (if significant) must be accounted for or a disclaimer provided stating that such comparison prices do not mean that the consumer will always save by purchasing the item advertised.

- Terms such as "wholesale" or "factory" prices should not be used unless you are selling at prices a consumer would pay if they purchased directly from the supplier.[20]

- In order to establish the objective validity of your claims through market research, competitors to be surveyed must be selected in such a way as to provide a valid basis for any generalizations made from the results.

- All promotions must be conducted within the following guideline: "In every case act honestly and in good faith in advertising a list price and not with the intention of establishing a basis, or creating an instrumentality, for a deceptive comparison in any local or other trade area."[21]

- You should create internal checklists for promotion review that encompass and integrate all compliance areas. For example, the rules on "free," "new," "sale," etc. are relevant to an honest pricing policy.

- All pricing promotions should be reviewed with counsel in a systematic way — especially any new "creative" concepts.

Simulated Checks

Obviously you want to stimulate consumer interest in your products, but as discussed above, not by deceptive pricing schemes, which would be counterproductive at best. By the same token, when it comes to coupon promotions, don't make them appear as simulated checks, bonds, or other financial instruments, especially if you are mailing them to your target list in a traditional check-bearing envelope. The key is to offer a *bona fide check* as part of the promotion. Otherwise, you must avoid employing any promotion piece that could be interpreted as a "confusingly simulated item of value." Each of the following could be so interpreted:

- check-style paper (because of coloration, use of watermark, and so on),
- traditional check-style borders,
- wording that might give an air of authenticity to a final document,
- a traditional check-size and -style envelope, and
- other items normally found on checks, such as any reference to negotiability.

Obviously, the more of these items actually included, the more you have increased your exposure to marketplace confusion.

You can employ a check promotion using a negotiable document. The promotion may be qualified, provided that, in the final analysis, the check is *not. The check must have the value apart from its value as a reduction of the cost of membership or service.* A violation in this area can be quite costly. One firm paid a fine of over $1 million.[22] Eventually the ruling was overturned,[23] but the firm lost the money. You can expect rulings in this area to fluctuate with the agenda of those who sit on the FTC and other regulatory agencies.

This is not an issue against which your firm can indemnify itself contractually. Use of simulated checks is against public policy. If an outside creative firm creates your piece, you (and possibly they) are responsible for all public FTC decisions.

Remember what the FTC is looking for in *all* promotions:

(1) An act or practice is deceptive if it consists of a representation, omission, or practice that is both material *and* likely to mislead consumers acting reasonably under the circumstances.

(2) A representation that is likely to affect a consumer's choice or conduct regarding a product or service is material. Failure to disclose qualifying information constitutes an omission. All express representations are material. Implied representations and omissions are material when they pertain to the central characteristics of the products or services being marketed, such as their performance, quality, purpose, or (as with simulated checks) their cost or discount.

(3) The defense to unfairness is that (a) there is no substantial injury to consumers resulting from the promotion, and (b) it is *not* outweighed by any contervailing benefits to consumers or competition.

In-Store Advertising

Your point-of-purchase displays, premium discounts, and coupons must be in compliance with all relevant laws and guides discussed so far in this review of advertising. At a minimum you should review the deceptive pricing guides, free rule, and comparative advertising discussions.

You should also be aware of an FTC rule for "Retail Food Store Advertising and Marketing Practices."[24] Don't let the seemingly limited scope fool you. As with sweepstakes, there is a broad brush application. The FTC is on record that the legal principles are generally applicable to the advertising of other commodities. Consequently, in the future the commission will consider matters involving unavailability and mispricing of other advertised commodities in that spirit.[25]

The FTC will find it an unfair method of competition and an unfair or deceptive act or practice if you:

(1) Offer any products for sale at a stated price, by means of any advertisement disseminated in an area served by any of your stores covered by the advertisement if the products are not in stock and are not readily available to customers during the effective period of the advertisement. (If the items are in stock but are not readily available, clear and adequate notice must be provided that the items are in stock and may be obtained upon request.)

It will constitute a defense to a charge under the above if you maintain records sufficient to show that the advertised products were ordered in adequate time for delivery and delivered to the stores in quantities sufficient to meet reasonably anticipated demands.

(2) Fail to make the advertised items conspicuously and readily available for sale at or below the advertised prices. In each of the above cases, you are OK if you've clearly and conspicuously disclosed in all such

advertisements all exceptions and limitations or restrictions with respect to stores, products, or prices otherwise included within the advertisements.[26]

In analyzing the above, the FTC will consider:

(a) all circumstances surrounding non-delivery of advertised products which were actually ordered in quantities sufficient to meet reasonably anticipated demands but were not delivered due to circumstances beyond the advertiser's control, and (b) all circumstances surrounding failure to make advertised items conspicuously and readily available for sale at or below the advertised prices, but were not made available at those prices due to circumstances beyond the advertiser's control. In such cases, the availability of "rainchecks" will also be considered by the Commission as relevant. However, the existence of a "raincheck" policy, in and of itself, will not be considered as compliance with this section.

. . .General disclaimers in advertising relating to product availability will not be considered to be in compliance with the disclosure provisions of this section. Examples of such general disclaimers would be:

(a) "Not all items available at all stores."

(b) A statement that a particular item or group of items is "Available at most stores."

. . .Specific clear and conspicuous disclaimers in advertising relating to product availability only in those stores possessing particular facilities will be considered to be in compliance with the disclosure provisions of paragraph (b)(1)(i) of this section. An example of such a disclaimer would be:

"Available only at stores featuring delicatessen departments."[27]

Laws on Coupons, Trading Stamps, and Redeemable Devices

All these devices are designed to attract repeat business, especially as to retailers selling high volume, low-priced goods. Repeat business can be done with stamps where license agreements can encourage a "family of merchants"[28] in a given area, to obtain a unique advantage by differentiating their products. No laws ban coupons, though obviously they are regulated by the applicable laws/rules discussed earlier. No states have banned stamps despite court and FTC hostility.[29] However, the alleged consumerist interest in the late 1960s in the area of stamps has left a lot of diverse laws including tax issues. We'll take a look at eight representative regional samples (with commentary on coupons where relevant) to give you an idea of the regulations you should consider.

California[30] has as representative the following definition of "trading stamp":

"Trading stamp" means any stamp or similar device issued in connection with the retail sale of merchandise or service, as a cash discount or for any other marketing purpose, which entitles the rightful holder, on its due presentation for redemption, to receive merchandise, service or cash.[31]

. . . ."Trading stamp" also means any stamp or similar device issued as a gift or as a consideration in any transaction other than in connection with the retail sale of merchandise or service, by a trading stamp company which also issues such devices in connection with the retail sale of merchandise or service, as a cash discount or for any other marketing purpose, and which may be redeemed by the rightful holder on the same basis as, or interchangeably with, any trading stamp issued as described [above].[32]

For reference, it is similar in most respects to the New York statute.[33] For one, it defines a "trading stamp" as broadly as New York does but excludes from that classification redeemable devices issued by a manufacturer or packer of an article in advertising or selling it as well as any redeemable device issued and redeemed by a newspaper, magazine, or other publication.[34] It also excludes any coupon issued and distributed by merchants and redeemable by them with the purchase of merchandise from their stock.[35] The specific sections should be reviewed as to licensing and bond requirements.

Unlike New York, however, California also has a broadly worded statute relating to premium coupons.[36] This statute makes it unlawful for any person to issue a coupon unless there shall be specified in or upon such coupon the person with whom such coupon is redeemable. Specifically, "coupon"includes certificates, cards, package labels, wrappers, can covers, bottle caps, or other and similar devices that entitle the person holding, delivering, or surrendering them to have them exchanged for or redeemed in goods, wares, merchandise, or services of any kind free of charge or for less that the retail price of such goods, wares, merchandise, or services. "Person" includes persons, firm(s), and corporation(s). To "issue" means to use, distribute, give away, sell, or furnish.[37]

Pertaining to redemption information on coupons, this statute states[38] that it is unlawful for any person to issue coupons unless the coupon names, specifically or by class, the person(s) by whom or with whom the coupon is exchangeable or redeemable, and unless such person is:

(a) the person issuing the coupon, or

(b) a member or members of an association issuing such coupon, and the association is a bona fide organization in existence for a period of at least six months prior to issuing the coupon (the name and address of the association's principal place of business must also be specified in or on the coupon), or

(c) engaged in the business of issuing coupons for use or distribution by itself or by others.

Connecticut's[39] trading stamp statute appears designed to regulate the business of traditional trading stamp companies in the state and go on further. It deals with licensing and defining certain unfair or deceptive practices.

Florida's[40] trading stamp statute is analagous to New York's and Connecticut's statutes and is designed to regulate the business of traditional trading stamp companies in the state. It should be consulted as to definition, applications, bonds, declared face value, and possible tax exposure.

Maryland[41] does not have any coupon or trading stamp statute other than a licensing requirement for trading stamp companies doing business in the state. The definition of persons subject to the license requirement and annual fee is very broad. Moreover, unlike similar statutes of other states, under Maryland law, manufacturers who issue coupons in connection with the sale of their own products are subject to the *license* requirement. This statute is short but potentially wide-sweeping, and it is worth your review.

Massachusetts'[42] trading stamp company registration act sets forth cash value, bonding, and other requirements.

Mississippi,[43] similar to Alabama[44] and Maryland, does not have any trading stamp registration statute but does impose a license or privilege tax on trading stamps issued in the state. Unlike the Maryland statute, however, Mississippi's tax statute appears limited to traditional trading stamp companies.

Specifically, the persons subject to the tax must be engaged in the business of issuing trading stamps or other similar devices to tradesmen with the understanding that the stamps should be presented or given by them to their patrons as a discount, bonus, or premium or as an inducement to secure trade or patronage. The person who is engaged in the business of selling or delivering the stamps and is subject to the tax gives money or other things of value to the customer presenting the stamps for redemption.

Generally speaking, manufacturers who pack coupons in their merchandise to be redeemed by the consumer on purchasing more of the same, are not in the trading stamp business, and therefore are not subject to the privilege tax.

New Jersey's[45] traditional narrow trading stamp statute deals only with such areas as cash values on the stamp's face, filing of registration statement, the annual fee, and bonds.

Virginia[46] has a privilege tax. Under its statute, however, a manufacturer or packer who issues coupons in connection with goods may be exempt from the tax only if the coupon is attached to the goods she or he manufactures or packs.

Washington[47] makes it a misdemeanor for any person to issue trading stamps or other similar redeemable devices in any county of the state without first obtaining a license. This licensing requirement, however, does not apply to manufacturers' direct redemption of premium coupons, certificates, or similar devices issued by them in connection with the sale of their goods and contained in or attached to the original package. It requires also a cash redemption value printed on the face of the stamp or coupon. The exemptions for coupons and similar devices have recently been clarified as follows:

(1) Nothing in this chapter, or in any other statute or ordinance of this state, shall apply to:

(a) The issuance and direct redemption by a manufacturer of a premium coupon, certificate, or similar device; or prevent him from issuing and directly redeeming such premium coupon, certificate, or similar device, which, however, shall not be issued, circulated, or distributed by retail vendors except when contained in or attached to an original package;

(b) The publication by, or distribution through, newspaper or other publications of coupons, certificates, or similar devices; or

(c) A coupon, certificate, or similar device which is within, attached to, or a part of a package or container as packaged by the original manufacturer and which is to be redeemed by another manufacturer, if:

(i) The coupon, certificate, or similar device clearly states the names and addresses of both the issuing manufacturer and the redeeming manufacturer; and

(ii) The issuing manufacturer is responsible for redemption of the coupon, certificate, or similar device if the redeeming manufacturer fails to do so.

(2) The term "manufacturer," as used in this section, means any vendor of an article of merchandise which is put up by or for him in an original package and which is sold under his or its trade name, brand or mark.[48]

The laws as to trading stamps have long since settled in. Coupon regulation (particularly as states eagerly look to new revenue sources and as in-store coupon machines become more prevalent) has yet to see its heyday. As usual, the state and local laws of your area of business need to be systematically reviewed, especially when you're considering a new form of promotion and the relevant legal waters are as yet untested.

Outdoor Advertising

All that was covered regarding truth in advertising holds here. There is an expansion of the right to say what you wish to say within your broadened commercial free speech rights. You should review with your counsel any "nuisance" or zoning restriction that might impede your setting up your message outdoors.

Zoning. You wish to post a sign somewhere, for example, over your office door or on a billboard, i.e., "an erection annexed to the land for the purpose of posting advertising bills and posters".[49] You must review the applicable zoning ordinances. Since advertising is neither inherently dangerous nor a nuisance per se, it cannot be prohibited—only regulated.[50] A zoning ordinance will be upheld when it is a valid exercise of the state or municipal police power. When based on the nature or character of that power it must:

- be impartial,
- bear a substantial relation to the maintenance of the safety, health, security, morals, or general welfare of the affected area (including purely aesthetic criteria) and
- be published with criteria that prevents uncontrolled discretion or arbitrary enforcement by the enforcing officials.

If a zoning ordinance is valid, you're not going to circumvent it by arguing that it deprives you of the reasonable use of your property or violates your right of free expression.[51] Even a subsequent ordinace forcing you to remove an existing promotional sign may be valid if the above criteria are met.[52] You can try for a variance, but the hurdles can be quite formidable.[53]

Nuisance. Is it possible that your advertising might be construed as a "nuisance"? This term is used to cover a variety of acts that infringe on the enjoyment of someone's land in light of the neighborhood. To be deemed a nuisance, the act must be substantial and not the result of someone's hypersensitivity. Obviously, you don't want to aesthetically injure the neighborhood or interfere with the lawful interest of another, if for no other reason than because it's bad for business. In determining whether your advertisement is a "nuisance," evaluate the following:

- Will it block an entrance or exit to adjacent property?
- Will it block the light or air from an adjacent property, or the view of or from it?
- Will bright light or noise from the sign disturb the neighborhood?
- Could any part of the promotion be considered obscene in the locality you're putting up your sign, billboard, or other advertisement? (Keep in mind that in a major city a promotional vehicle may enter a variety of neighborhoods.)

Obscenity Standards

The standard for evaluating what is impermissible obscenity in advertising is one of the most important opinions handed down by former Supreme Court Justice Warren Burger. A state may choose not to control obscenity, but where it does choose to exercise such control, the three-fold standard for the law is as follows (emphasis added):

This much has been categorically settled by the Court, *that obscene material is unprotected by the First Amendment* . . . . We acknowledge, however, the inherent dangers of undertaking to regulate any form of expression. State statutes designed to regulate obscene materials must be carefully limited. As a result, we now confine the permissible scope of such regulation to works which depict or describe sexual conduct. *That conduct must be specifically defined by the applicable state law,* as written or authoritatively construed. A state offense must also be limited to works which, taken as a whole, appeal to the prurient interest in sex, which portray sexual conduct in a patently offensive way, and which, taken as a whole, do not have serious literary, artistic, political, or scientific value.

The basic guidelines for the trier of fact must be: (a) whether "the average person, applying contemporary community standards" would find that the work, taken as a whole, appeals to the prurient interest, (b) whether the work depicts or describes, in a patently obvious way, sexual conduct specifically defined by the applicable state law, and (c) whether the work, taken as a whole, lacks serious literary, artistic, political, or scientific value. We do not adopt as a constitutional standard the "utterly without redeeming social value" test. . . . If a state law that regulates obscene material is thus limited, as written or construed, [First Amendment values] are adequately protected by the ultimate power of appellate courts to conduct an independent review of constitutional claims where necessary.

We emphasize that it is not our function to propose regulatory schemes for the States. That must await their concrete legislative efforts.[54]

Approximately 38 states have wording along these lines.[55] Often a state (such as Connecticut)[56] specifies by law that in applying contemporary community standards, the state is deemed to be the community. Predominant appeal is to be judged with reference to ordinary, reasonable adults unless the material, its message, or its dissemination is designed for a specifically susceptible audience such as children. Many other states have specific protections for minors.[57] Finally, as often happens, California's law may move into broader territory, i.e., *"serious* literary, artistic, political, education or scientific value." The Statute now reads *"significant* literary . . ."[58] The sponsor of the bill to expand coverage hopes to broaden a prosecutor's ability to deal with "marginal works." A court challenge may settle the final wording.[59]

Obscenity is an issue that is constantly in flux and subject to current political winds at the state and federal level. You should review with your counsel your promotional wording for compliance with the current law as well as with the popular opinion of your targeted audience.

A Participation Promotion—Sweepstakes

For a time you couldn't go to many gas stations and supermarkets without being able to obtain tokens to save toward a prize. The sweepstakes promotion remains popular for its ability to sell a dream—of a vacation prize or other windfall "without paying for it." In general, cash is the preferred prize, followed by travel and then merchandise. However, no matter what prize you offer, you'll have people enter— especially when they know a purchase *cannot* be required. The market is so competitive that "contesters" have turned to specific literature on point, such as *And the Lucky Winner Is—The Complete Guide to Winning Sweepstakes and Contests.*[60]

Because of the popularity of sweepstakes, we shall review the rules here in detail and also distinguish a legal sweepstakes promotion from an illegal lottery or chain letter.

Chain Letter or Sweepstakes?

You have, no doubt, received chain letters in the mail at some time or another requesting that you send a dollar or more to one or more persons whose names appear in the letter and that you send copies of the letter with your name at the top of the list to a certain number of friends. Naturally, the financial remuneration you're promised is tremendous if "the chain is not broken." Fun and games? The government doesn't think so.

First, if you "played," you probably lost your money. Second, the use of the U.S. Postal Service to send chain letters involving money can result in civil or criminal penalties. Why? This scheme violates the lottery laws, which make illegal any promotion with *all* the following elements: prize, chance, and consideration. It has long been recognized that the law for the suppression of lotteries is in the interest of the morals and welfare of the people of a state and therefore is a legitimate exercise of the state's police power.[61]

If you understand the legal concept behind the chain letters, sweepstakes compliance will be fairly easy for you. A sweepstakes or other form of contest is illegal if it contains the "big three" named above—prize, chance, and consideration. In a legitimate sweepstakes no consideration (such as, payment of time or money) is required to enter. Make sure your participants will be spared undertaking "any effort" if they don't like the rules of the game. *Note:* "Any effort" beyond returning a first-class envelope should be reviewed by your counsel. Many "efforts" will result in being classified as "consideration" and will fall within the lottery laws.

Contests of Skill

Contests of skill are also distinguishable from sweepstakes. In a legitimate contest, winners are selected purely on the basis of skill, not *chance* (the classic country fair animal-raising or pie-baking contest are examples). If any element of chance is present, the contest is illegal, even if some skill is involved.

Sweepstakes are more popular because of the little effort involved. However, sometimes you'll want to run an event requiring writing skill, artistic expression, jingle or slogan writing, or something along this line. You may even require the submission of a proof-of-purchase or an entrance fee to cover the costs of evaluating the contest. Such activity to enter is consideration by your entrant. Do you now have a lottery (chance, consideration and prize)? No—*there is no chance or luck* because winners are selected purely on the basis of their individual skill, and without *all three* elements you can't have a lottery. To avoid even the appearance of chance you must make sure the selection of the winner is not beyond the control of the winner or judges (a tie-breaking flip of a coin would be considered a random drawing, for example).

To avoid the element of chance you must be able to demonstrate two criteria. First, you must base the winning selection on specified reasonable standards made known to your contestants (see discussion of general disclosure rules later in this chapter). Second, the contest must be judged by people whose qualifications have a reasonable relationship to the purpose of your contest's aims. *Each* entry must be evaluated regardless of how many people enter. This judgment based on merit by qualified people will eliminate any aspect of chance.

To fulfill FTC regulations, you should explain all aspects of the contest in the promotional material, including who is an eligible contestant, what the judging criteria for the contest are, what the prizes are and how many are awarded, who the judges are, when the contest will be conducted, and when the winners will be announced. Any other information that helps explain the contest and what is expected from contestants should also be included in the promotional material. This includes the precise scope of *your* rights to use the entrant's slogan, song, recipe, etc. if you wish. Either you'll need a release in the entry blank or the entry blank's rules should include as a condition of participation an agreement that the entrant will enter into a formal release if he or she wins.

To wrap it up, in a sweepstakes there can be no element of *consideration.*[62] In a contest of skill, there can be no element of *chance or luck.* As usual it is essential to check the particular laws of your state. For example, it is questionable whether any contest can be held in Florida or Vermont if any valid consideration by a participant is needed to enter.[63] Call the attorney general's office of these two states if you're contemplating this form of promotion.

Preparing for a Sweepstakes Promotion

You've researched your market and found that the breakdown of the profile of typical sweepstakes entrants is approximately 45% to 55%

female. In general, they are younger, have larger families, are slightly better educated, and are slightly more upscale in income than the population at large.

A marketer's first exposure to possible governmental and consumer complaints about a sweepstakes occurs upon the publication of the offer and the rules for participation. Therefore, care should be exercised to state clearly, fully, and accurately the terms and conditions for participation, and to avoid any misrepresentation. Ambiguity in the rules will be construed against the sponsor who drafted them and in favor of the participant. How to proceed?

A good idea is to enlist the aid of an independent, professional sweepstakes firm to advise and assist on all elements of your promotion—not merely as an independent judging body.[64] The firm will present you with a standard contract outlining its services. With its standard services the firm should, at a minimum:

- [ ] Provide advice on all phases of the offer during the planning of the promotion, including a screen of your copy.
- [ ] Provide advice on postal and certain legal and regulatory matters, including writing the rules for the promotion. Their advice is advisory only and no substitute for your own counsel.
- [ ] Handle all areas pertaining to the winners, such as generating the winners through a random drawing, notifying them, delivering the prizes, and preparing the formal list of winners to be available to the public.
- [ ] File surety bonds in states requiring them (at least two states—Florida and New York—do). These bond requirements are important.
- [ ] Consult your counsel and sweepstakes firm as to other local and state laws and rules affecting your planned area of operations. For Florida[65] you are also required to file the following at least 30 days before the game promotion begins:
  - A copy of the sweepstakes rules (which must indicate that no purhase is necessary).
  - The beginning and ending dates of the promotion.
  - A statement of trust account or other documentation from a national or state-chartered financial institution indicating the balance of a trust account which has been established in an amount equal to the total value of all prizes to be offered. (*In lieu* of establishing a trust account, a surety bond, with sufficient sureties, in the amount equivalent to the total value of all prizes, may be submitted. These need not be countersigned by a Florida resident agent.
  - A $100 nonrefundable registration fee. Checks must be made payable to the Division of Licensing Trust Fund. In New York,[66] you will want to ask for the filing forms to comply with Section 369-e of the New York State General Business Law.

As in any transaction, the boilerplate agreement you receive should be considered the beginning of negotiations, not the final word. For example, ask yourself whether the contract contains the following minimum points you need for your own protection:

☐ Are we being offered vague terms such as "practical knowledge"? Never accept these. Demand that your sweepstakes firm *warrant* all advice it offers. If the firm won't offer you such contractual protection, then your eyes are open and you should consider exactly what, if any, protection you are receiving.

☐ Do we retain the right of final approval as to all creative copy, promotional and rules wording, as well as layout and mailing dates?

☐ Does the sweepstakes firm have the right to assign the contract without our consent? Never accept this, because you could wind up paying for one firm while receiving the services of the later "assigned firm."

☐ Is our customer list valuable to us? Marketers are well aware of the advantages of the list potential sweepstakes entrants create—even the "no" respondents. More and more retail firms are developing sophisticated data bases. When in doubt have your counsel draft a tight confidentiality clause protecting your lists and any other trade secrets or "know-how" the independent firm may have access to. Specify what steps you expect them to take to keep it confidential, and make sure you make clear that its loss would cause you "irreparable harm."

☐ Have we carefully reviewed the indemnification clause as to all actions *both* private and governmental? Avoid language that states you'll only recover on "finally settled" claims. This hurts your cash flow as these matters drag on. Ask your counsel about your exposure to class actions. The recipients of your sweepstakes promotion could be a built-in class, and poor administration of the promotion could expose you to high financial and goodwill costs.

☐ Have we added specific language disclaiming any joint venture, or are we in fact specifically engaged in one? Particular attention must be paid to the tax implications of a joint venture with another firm if you are promoting by mail. Such cosponsoring of a sweepstakes might expose the firm to "doing business in the state" where the co-venturer is doing business. The tax issue is another reason to review with your counsel all promotions in this sensitive area.

☐ Have we made sure that the contract can't be assigned without our advanced notice and consent? You're hiring this firm for their track record, not to enhance their sales value to someone you had no choice in selecting.

None of these points is designed to reflect adversely in any way on the independent service you've chosen. They are designed to make you think of self-protection before you sign any form contract they devise. Their contracts are for their protection. You and your counsel have to protect you.

The Rules

We'll now examine in detail the aspects of what you might include in your rules. The following discussion is probably the broadest review of this topic you'll read anywhere.[67]

In addition to the input from your independent consulting firm and your counsel's review and sign-off, you'll have to develop your own philosophy about these promotions. For example, the law doesn't say it has to be easy to enter without a purchase. Provided that it is possible, and provided that a complete reading of the promotional copy and rules make that clear, you are covered legally. However, be aware that ambiguity in the rules will be construed against the sponsor who drafted them and in favor of the participant. Further, remember that customer goodwill is all-important.

To ensure that the future customers you are seeking feel that they have been dealt with fairly, it is essential to state clearly and conspicuously, in lay person's English, the rules of the sweepstakes and all conditions and terms that will govern the awarding of prizes. This information should be relayed at the time they are invited to take the first step necessary toward receiving a prize. What is "clear and conspicuous"? As a rule of thumb, terminology should be simple, nontechnical, and unambiguous. Typography in size, style, and location should be such that one can view the promotion piece at a glance, can see that the rules and conditions are there to be read if one chooses to do so, and can read those rules easily. It is to the sponsor's advantage to undertake a separate compliance review (for example, through an in-house checklist) so as to have all copy reviewed from an impartial viewpoint.

The following are the practical points to consider in drafting the rules. These elements are common to most sweepstakes and should be disclosed, in addition to any others that may be peculiar to a particular promotion.[68] Obviously, the rules of the sweepstakes must be set forth in an area of the copy easily accessible to the reader. The type size must be the same size as (or larger than) the type size used in the main body of the advertisement.

(1) **Yes or no box.** This often appears as a "check box" in the copy or on the envelope. The no and yes boxes must be equally conspicuous. Be clear here. If a purchase is required to win a prize, you are probably running afoul of the lottery laws. Even worse, it means you didn't OK your rules with counsel, who would have caught this. Also, being "cute" and offering two differently colored or sized envelopes for the return of yes and no entries is not a legal violation but might prompt a government agency or consumer group to monitor the outcome to see whether the percentage of winners was skewed in favor of the participants who checked yes.

(2) **Facsimile.** May a facsimile of the entry blank or promotional piece be used? If a facsimile in lieu of an official entry blank is made acceptable, a potential lottery violation is removed if a purchase is required to obtain the official entry blank. (Remember, prize, chance, and consideration must *all* be present for a promotion to be considered a lottery.) The rules should clearly indicate what the facsimile must state or reproduce. If a facsimile is not acceptable, the rules must specifically say so; for example, "Only official entry blanks will be accepted. No facsimiles permitted." If you do permit facsimiles make sure your systems are set up so that these entries have as much chance to winning as an official entry.

(3) "Lucky" or other number. If these are used, they must actually identify the individual and be directly related to the award of a prize.

(4) Simulated check. Avoid these as entry forms. If you must use them, remember that simulated checks may not be used unless they have value independent of the promotion, they impose no obligation on the recipient, and they may be cashed, redeemed, or exchanged by recipients for U.S. currency.

(5) Prizes. The following points should be considered:[69]

a. Listing of prizes. List all prizes by category in detail including their exact nature, the quantity to be awarded, and the odds of winning each prize of $25 or more. This disclosure must be revised each week the game extends beyond 30 days, to reflect the number of prizes still available and the odds of winning each such unredeemed prize.[70] If you're doing a mailing and the prizes will reflect response, you can consider this as one total contest.

b. Visual depictions. All visual depictions of prizes must be accurate (in correct proportion, for instance). Especially in sweepstakes promotions, you should be aware that, while photographs or printed illustrations of U.S. coins may be used for advertising purposes, printed illustrations of paper money, checks, and the like are *not* permitted. (This matter is in flux, and you should consult your counsel as to your current exposure.)

c. Specification of value. No award may be described as a prize unless it has a retail value greater then $1. No prize may be held forth, directly or by implication, to have substantial monetary value if it is of only nominal intrinsic worth. The value test must be substantiated by written records (for example, prize purchase receipts). Mere opinion is not permissible.

d. Purchase of prizes. All enumerated prizes must have been purchased prior to the commencement of the promotion, and you must be able to verify this with dated receipts. All prizes are then set aside until used for the specific awards.

e. Warranties. Are you prepared to make good on warranty offers? A few years ago a fast-food franchise sought to spur customer traffic with a contest. It offered among the prizes an auto that supposedly was a full-scale replica of the classic 1930 Bentley. The winner found that it was not in the condition promised and sued after numerous attempts to repair. He recovered damages because of the breach of contract.[71] The prizes you offer must be able to do what your promotion implies they do or what a reasonable person could infer they'd do.

f. Free-rule requirements.[72] Don't forget that the prizes you are offering are free and are regulated by the free rule. *All* free-rule requirements discussed earlier must be complied with. Any qualifications on the prize offered must be set forth immediately contingent at the outset of offer. Such qualifications must be set forth clearly and conspicuously to leave no reasonable probability that the offer might be misunderstood. For example, a free prize for two people to anywhere in the United States or to Tahiti, for instance is wide open, with you footing the bill. Phrases like "first class" "pampered," "travel in style," "all expenses paid," or "luxurious accomodations" will be interpreted literally, by the winner, and will work *against* you). You must disclose any qualifications immediately. Using an asterisk to indicate the qualifications elsewhere or setting them forth in the rules will only fail the contingency test and be disallowed as a violation of the FTC.

g. Personal and property injury. Protect yourself from potential claims of winners by stating that you are not liable for loss of property or personal injury incurred resulting from use of the prize. A clause negating liability for the recipient's personal negligence, liability, or property loss while on the trip is also advisable. You should consult with your counsel as to your total legal exposure in this often overlooked area.

h. Cash substitution. If you will not substitute cash, say so. Some winner might request this for various reasons, including tax liabilities. You're not legally required to state "no substitutions" upfront, but it is a wise move in terms of goodwill. Some firms are simply stating "Your Choice—Cash or Travel."

i. Expiration date. If the prize is a travel package, it is a good idea (in inflationary periods and a generally unstable geopolitical climate) to state the date by which the trip must be taken.

j. Prizes by gender (e.g., man's or woman's watches). These are fine provided that there is retail value parity in the prizes *and* that winners may elect either category at their option.

(6) Prize procedures. State the total number of prizes to be awarded and describe the procedures for the disposition of unclaimed prizes.

(7) Unclaimed prizes. You should state that all prizes will be awarded and describe the procedures for the disposition of unclaimed prizes.

(8) Odds of winning. Statements such as "the odds of winning depend on the number of entries received" or "we anticipate the odds to be . . ." may be sufficient for your promotion. (The specific details and procedure of your promotion may require different wording; review these with your counsel.)

(9) Age restrictions. Certain age restrictions are patently obvious and necessary (alcoholic beverages, tobacco, and so on). More subtle issues relate to the enjoyment of the prize (e.g., automobiles or vacations). In such a situation, you might wish to disqualify minors or restrict delivery to a parent or guardian. Again, all disqualification language must be clear and conspicuous.

(10) Restrictions on entries. Is entry restricted to one application per family or address, or may the consumer "enter as often as you wish but only one entry per envelope"? A good idea might be "one person per entry," which obviates the need to divide a prize between two or more winners on a single entry. 'A stipulation of one entry per address would create complications in view of the various living-together arrangements. The same issue is raised by 'one entry per family.' Can you really bar the entry of a 21-year-old son simply because his mother also entered? What about spouses living apart in legal separation? Any limitation other than one entry per person (18 or over) could present legal problems and create the potential for the loss of customer goodwill.

(11) Exclusions due to employment. Any member of the sponsoring firm and his or her family (plus your independent agency) is routinely disqualified.

(12) Voiding clause. As a voiding clause, "void where prohibited by law" is proper; I don't like "void where prohibited *or restricted* by law" because the word "restricted" is too vague. This is a fluid area and the state legislatures must be carefully monitored. Prior to December 1978, sweepstakes were effectively banned in Missouri by action of the state's attorney general. This was altered by a popular vote constitutional amendment ratified November 7, 1978, which redefined consideration (people *like and want* sweepstakes promotions.)[73] Utah at one time held that the expenditure of a first-class stamp was consideration enough to constitute a lottery. The rule was overturned by the state supreme court. Things are always in flux with the varied state laws and you should review them with your counsel before each promotion is mailed.

(13) Endorsements. If you are planning to use the winner's name or picture likeness for future publicity and promotion, notice must be set forth in the rules, especially if no further compensation is planned (if a contest is involved see the discussion earlier). The right to do this may vary from state to state.

(14) Other qualifications. State any geographic limitations (e.g., continental United States). Also, state your disqualification policy for entries which do not substantially conform to the rules of the promotional offer. A record of any disqualifications should be maintained for 30 days after the end of the promotion.

(15) Dates. State the *specific* commencement and termination postmark and/or receipt dates for eligibility and whether the termination date refers to mailing or of receipt of the entry.

(16) Total number of retail outlets. If applicable, specify all outlets (one figure) participating.

(17) Taxes. Contest awards and similar prize winnings are income subject to federal income tax.[74] Your winner will have to report the fair market value of the prizes won. This isn't your headache, but a statement to the effect that income tax liability is the responsibility of the winner is a good idea. However, you do have some tax exposure, and state sales or use taxes should be checked.

(18) Applicable law. State that all federal, state, and local laws and regulations apply. When running a sweepstakes promotion in any state, obviously you should comply with the rules of the particular states. For example, the New York General Business Law requires a game of chance bond be obtained and formal registration of the promotion be filed with the secretary of state. Florida requires a similar bond with certain qualifications.[75]

(19) Customer inquiries. Include in the rules the identity and address of a specific person to whom inquiries concerning the sweepstakes in general and how to obtain a list of winners in particular may be directed. Usually this is the independent judging organization you have retained to assist in the promotion. You can require the customer to send a self-addressed, stamped envelope to obtain the list of winners.

(20) Notification of winners. The method by which winners will be notified must be specified (for example, by a sign in a store or by mail). It is a good idea to obtain a signed affidavit of identity and acceptance, particularly for the large-dollar-value prizes.

(21) Proper Mixing. Be sure to mix, distribute, and disperse all game pieces totally and soley on a random basis throughout the game program and throughout the geographic area covered by the game, and to maintain proper records to demonstrate to the FTC that total randomness was used in such mixing, distribution, and dispersal. Also, don't promote, sell, or use any game that is capable of, or susceptible to, being solved or "broken" so that winning game pieces or prizes are predetermined or preidentified by such methods rather than by random distribution to the participating public.[76]

(22) Signature Line. You can require a signature line. There is no legal requirement for a signature on the entry blank, but it may be legally advantageous for you to obtain the signature of the sweepstakes subscriber. The signature is a specific manifestation of the customer's assent to the terms of the sweepstakes promotion. It helps to remove any ambiguity as to whether all terms and rules were definitely understood and agreed upon—including such issues as sales tax liability and any limitations concerning the recipient (for example, no minors).

(23) Delivery of Prizes. There is no legal requirement concerning payment and delivery of prizes so long as payment and delivery occurs promptly and as described in the contest materials.

(24) Affidavit of Eligibility. Regardless of any of the above you should state the prize winner will be asked to execute an affidavit of eligibility and release within 30 days of notification. The failure to comply will result in an alternate winner being selected.

Your promotion must be conducted strictly according to its published rules. If an unforeseen development mandates a change, timely notice must be given. This is legally required and important for customer satisfaction.

Finally, all statements made in connection with your promotional contest or game must be true and accurate to avoid civil and criminal liability for false advertising, misrepresentation, and fraud.

Recordkeeping

If you are the game promoter, you are required to maintain the following data in your records for three years after the published termination date for entries for submission on FTC request[77]. (Again, these requirements aren't carved in granite and are changed from time to time; ask your counsel for a current reading on your federal and state requirements).

- Approximate number of entries or game pieces distributed,
- Total number of prizes advertised in each category, which was made available in all participating retail outlets,
- Approximate number of participants,
- Name and address of each winner of a prize, together with a description and the approximate retail value of the prize given to each, and
- Method by which winners were determined.

Finally, consult your counsel as to the current rules on posting, length of time between games, and other procedural matters that have been subject to change in recent years. For instance, the requirement to forward a list of winners to the FTC has been eliminated.

After the Contest

It constitutes an unfair or deceptive trade practice for users, promoters or manufacturers of such games to:

(a) Promote or use any new game without a break in time between the new game and any game previously employed in the same retail establishment equivalent to the duration of the game previously employed or 30 days, whichever is less.[78]

(b) Terminate any game, regardless of the scheduled termination date, prior to the distribution of all game pieces to the participating public.[79]

(c) Add additional winning game pieces during the course of a game, or in any manner replenish the prize structure of a game in progress.[80]

Prizes for Property "Go Sees"

A growing form of promotion is the proliferation of offerings for one to see a vacation home, condominium development, and the like. The states are increasingly drawing the parameters of what you can offer and show. An excellent example of current regulation is Ohio's law:[81]

(A) It shall be a deceptive act or practice in connection with a consumer transaction for a supplier to in any way notify any consumer or prospective consumer that he has:

(1) Won a prize or will receive anything of value, or

(2) Been selected, or is eligible, to win a prize or receive anything of value, if the receipt of the prize or thing of value is conditioned upon the consumer's listening to or observing a sales promotional effort or entering into a consumer transaction, unless the supplier clearly and explicitly discloses, at the time of notification of the prize, that an attempt will be made to induce the consumer or prospective consumer to undertake a monetary obligation irrespective of whether that obligation constitutes a consumer transaction. The supplier must further disclose the market value of the prize or thing of value, that the prize or thing of value could not benefit the consumer or prospective consumer without the expenditure of the consumer of prospective consumer's time or transportation expense, or that a salesman will be visiting the consumer's or prospective consumer's residence, if such is the case.

(B) A statement to the effect that the consumer or prospective consumer must observe or listen to a "demonstration" or promotional effort in connection with a consumer transaction does not satisy the requirements of this rule, unless the consumer or prospective consumer is told that the purpose of the demonstration is to induce the consumer or prospective consumer to undertake a monetary obligation irrespective of whether that obligation constitutes a consumer transaction.

(C) The following example illustrates a violation of this rule as a result of lack of disclosure relative to a promotional presentation which is not a consumer transaction.

A free vacation is offered in connection with the purchase of a set of encyclopedias. All disclosures required by the rule are made except that during the vacation the consumer is required to observe a sales presentation for real estate. An offer to sell real estate is not a consumer transaction, but it is an attempt to induce the consumer to undertake a monetary obligation, and such attempt was initiated in connection with a consumer transaction (the sale of encyclopedias.)

(D) It shall be a deceptive act or practice in connection with a consumer transaction for a supplier to in any way notify any consumer or prospective consumer that he has:

(1) Won a prize or will receive anything of value, or

(2) Been selected, or is eligible, to win a prize or receive anything of value, if the receipt of the prize or thing of value is conditioned upon the payment of a service charge, handling charge, mailing charge, or other similar charge.

Conclusion

If these guidelines are mastered, you will have exhausted the problems inherent in today's state of the art. If you design your sweepstakes promotion in compliance with these guidelines (and a review with your counsel) you can be confident that your successful promotion won't be negated by fines, consent agreements, or an entrant's personal injury or property damage claims. Just as important, compliance will enhance your positive image to your extrants, retaining and building the goodwill of entrants (your future customers?) Who are knowledgeable about those rules from previous experience and expect you to be, too.

ENDNOTES

(1) Deceptive pricing relates to several topics covered in other chapters. You may wish to review the discussion of pricing allowances in the discussion of the Fair Packaging and Labeling Act (15 USC 1451) in Section I and see the discussions of bait advertising (16 CFR 238) in Chapter 16, free offers (16 CFR 251) and what a sale is in Chapter 10.

(2) A material term provides information that an ordinary, reasonable consumer would consider when deciding whether to purchase the particular product you are offering.

(3) We're referring to the FTC here, and particularly the agency's Guides against Deceptive Pricing, 16 CFR 233 (see distinction between guides and rules in the Glossary). However, most states have laws similar to or narrower than the guides. Consult with your counsel as to applicable laws for your promotion.

(4) *FTC v. Standard Education Society,* 302 US 113 (1937) and *P. Lorillard Co. v. FTC,* 186 F.2d 52, 58 (1950).

(5) 16 CFR 233.1(c).

(6) 16 CFR 233.1(b).

(7) *Royal Baking Co. v. FTC,* 281 F 744 (1922).

(8) Section 82.08.050 RCW, Sec. 1 and 2.

(9) *City of New York v. Toby's Elecs., Inc.,* 110 Misc. 2d 848, 443 NYS2d 561 (1981).

(10) Id. at 566.

(11) Id.

(12) Section 1770 (1) (t) of the Civil Code of California.

(13) 16 CFR 233.2(a).

(14) 16 CFR 233.4(a-c).

(15) Ohio Revised Code (1985) Chapter 109:4-3-02(2) (b), (e)—(g).

(16) For more information on this enforcement effort, contact the Consumer Protection Division in the Attorney General's Office at 201 East Markham, Little Rock, Arkansas 72201. The office can be reached at (501) 371-2341 or toll free for Arkansas residents at 1-800-482-8982. TDD service for use by the deaf and hearing-impaired consumer is available from both these numbers.

(17) *Spiegel, Inc. v. FTC,* 494 F.2d 59, 65 (1973).

(18) 16 CFR 233.5.

(19) 16 CFR 233.1(a).

(20) 16 CFR 233.5.

(21) 16 CFR 233.3(i).

(22) *United States v. Reader's Digest Ass'n, Inc.,* 464 F.Supp. 1037 (1979), 494 F.Supp. 770 (1980 DC Del), 662 F.2d 955 (1981), *cert. den.* 102 SCt 1253, 455 US 908 (1981).

(23) This area remains vague, so no similar promotions should be used without careful legal review.

(24) 16 CFR 424.

(25) 16 CFR 424.2(b).

(26) 16 CFR 424.1(b).

(27) 16 CFR 424.1 notes 1 and 2.

(28) *Sperry & Hutchinson Co.,* 73 FTC 1099, 1155 (1968).

(29) *Sperry & Hutchinson Co. v. FTC,* 405 US 244 (1971). *See also* "FTC Unfairness Doctrine," *Duke Law Journal* Vol. 1983 p. 903.

(30) *California Codes Ann,* Business and Professional Section, Sec. 17550 et seq. (1986).

(31) Id. Sec. 17550.

(32) Id. Sec. 17550.1.

(33) See the *Consolidated Laws of New York Ann.* General Business Law Sec. 570 et seq.

(34) Note 30, Sec. 17751.

(35) Id., Sec. 17552.

(36) Id., Secs. 17700–17702.

(37) Id., Sec. 17700.

(38) Id., Sec. 17701.

(39) *Connecticut General Statutes Ann.* Title 42 Sales and Collections (1986), Sec. 42-126(a).

(40) *Florida Statutes Annotated* (1986) Sec. 559.01-559.06.

(41) *Annotated Code of Maryland* (1983) Article 56 Sec. 172.

(42) *Massachusetts General Laws Annotated* (1986) Ch. 93 Sec. 14L-14R.

(43) *Mississippi Code Annotated* Title 27-17-387 (1985). See also *Craig v. Ballard and B. Co.,* 189 Misc. 60, 196 So. 238 (1940).

(44) *Alabama Code* Sec. 40-12-170 (1975). Coupons or stamps issued directly by a manufacturer or packer to the purchaser on its own goods are specifically excluded from the tax.

(45) *New Jersey Statutes Annotated* (1985) 45:23-1-13.

(46) *Code of Virginia* Sec. 58-354.1-7 (1985).

(47) *Revised Code of Washington Annotated* (1986) Chapter 19.83 et seq.

(48) Id., Sec. 19.83.040—Trading Stamp Licenses.

(49) *Cochrane v. McDermott Advertising Agency,* 60 So. 421, 422 (1912).

(50) *Central Outdoor Advertising Co. v. Evendale,* 354, 124 NE 189 (1954).

(51) *Metromedia, Inc. v. San Diego,* 453 US 490, 69 L.Ed. 2d 800, 101 S.Ct. 2882 (1980).

(52) *People ex rel Dept. of Transp. v. Hadley Fruit Orchards, Inc.,* 50 Cal. App. 3d 49, 130 Cal. Rptr. 287 (1976).

(53) *Silverman v. Keating,* 52 App. Div. 2d 1076, 384 NYS 2d 366 (1976).

(54) *Miller v. California,* 413 US 15, 93 S.Ct. 2607, 37 L.Ed. 2d 419 (1973).

(55) See note 56 plus the following representative samples:

Colorado Revised Statutes (1986) Article 7 of Title 18-7-101 et seq.

Consolidated Laws of New York Annotated (1986) Penal Law Sec. 235.

See also *People v. Heller,* 33 NY 2d 314 (1973) and *People v. Calbud,* 49 NY 2d 389 (1980).

Code of West Virginia (1986) Article 1 Chapter 7 County Commission and Chapter 8, Article 12 8-12-5(b).

Wyoming Statutes (1986) 6-5-303(a) (iii).

(56) *Connecticut General Statutes Annotated* 1986 Sec. 53a-193(a) (3).

(57) A few representative samples include:

Colorado Revised Statutes (1986) Article 7, Title 18-7-501 et seq.

Georgia Code (1986) Title 26-3502-3504.

Hawaii Revised Statutes (1986) Section 712-1210 et seq.

Annotated Code of Maryland (1983) Article 27 Section 419.

Massachusetts General Laws Annotated (1980) Chapter 49 A of the General Laws Sec. 28.

Nevada Revised Statutes (1986) Sec. 3201.257.

Consolidated Laws of New York Annotated (1986) Penal Law Sec. 235.23-25.

Code of Virginia (1985) Sec. 18.2-389.

(58) *Annotated California Code* Sec. 311, 312.1, and 313 of the Penal Code.

(59) Shirst, Douglas, "Law Likely to lead to Stronger Curbs on Pornographers," *Los Angeles Times,* 4/16/86, p.3.

(60) Tyndall, Carolyn and Roger Tyndall with Ted Tuleja, *And the Lucky Winner is —The Complete Guide to Winning Sweepstakes and Contests,* New York: St. Martin's, 1982.

(61) *Rast v. Van Dearan & Lewis Co.,* 240 US 342 (1915).

(62) *FCC v. American Broadcasting Co.,* 347 US 284 (1953) (goodwill provided sponsor by contest is not consideration flowing from entrant).

(63) Florida Dept. Leg. Aff. Admin. & Sales Rule 2-907 (12/20/73) and Attorney General of Vermont Rule DF 109.01 (6/15/78).

(64) Four reputable agencies to investigate for such assistance include:

- D. L. Blair Corporation, 185 Great Neck Road, Great Neck, NY 11021, (516) 487-9230.

- Marden Kane, Inc., 666 Fifth Avenue, New York, NY 10103, (212) 582-6600.

- Ventura Associates, Inc. 200 Madison Avenue, New York, NY 10016, (212) 689-0011.

- Weston Group, Inc., 44 Post Road West, Westport, CT, 06880, (203) 226-6933.

For further information, write to the Promotion Marketing Association of America, 420 Lexington Avenue, New York, NY 10170.

(65) Contact the Secretary of State or Sweepstakes Section Service Rep., Florida Department of State, Division of Licensing, The Capitol, Tallahassee, Florida, 32301, (904) 488-5381. Ask for a copy of Sec. 849.094 *Florida Statutes* and their handy sweepstakes packet, which contains the registration and surety bond forms.

(66) Call or write NY Department of State, Miscellaneous Records Unit, 162 Washington Ave., Albany, NY, 12231. Ask for the filing forms to comply with Sec. 369-e NYS General Business Law.

(67) Posch, Robert J. Jr., "Direct Marketing Compliance Guide for sweepstakes Promotions," *Do's and Don'ts in Advertising Copy,* recommended by DMA and reprinted by the Council of Better Business Bureaus, Inc. Even the best rules can be misunderstood, e.g., *Johnson v. NY Daily News,* 114 Misc. 2d, 450 N.Y.S. 2d 980 (1982).

(68) The body of law to be studied by managers desiring an in-depth knowledge of this area is as follows:

Mail Fraud Law	18 USC Sec. 1341
Fraud by Wire, Radio, TV	18 USC Sec. 1343
Federal Communications Act*	47 USC Sec. 509
Federal Alcohol Administration Act	27 USC Sec. 205c
Federal Food, Drug, and Cosmetic Act	21 USC Sec. 342
Fair Packaging and Labeling Act	15 USC Sec. 1451
FTC Guide on Use of Word "Free"‡	16 CFR Sec. 251
Robinson-Patman Act	15 USC Sec. 13
FTC Guides on Advertising Allowances	16 CFR Sec. 240
FTC Guide—Deceptive Pricing*	16 CFR Sec. 233
Hazardous Substances Act	15 USC Sec. 1261
Consumer Product Safety Act	15 USC Sec. 2051
Federal Bank Regulations	12 CFR Sec. 526
FTC Guidelines on Games of Chance in The Food Retailing and Gasoline Industries	16 CFR Sec. 419

(*) This act enforces a federal law that bars broadcast of lottery information or advertising except for state government-conducted lotteries.

‡ Generally applicable to all promotions. The others will vary by reason of the nature of the product being promoted or the article being awarded as a prize.

You should, of course, review the laws of the respective states you're doing business in. As demonstrated, the laws affecting this area are quite comprehensive. Do not think that the FTC rules will apply *only* to "Games of Chance in the Food Retailing and Gasoline Industries." Voluntarily comply, because the FTC has indicated that it expects other firms running similar promotions to take these guidelines under advisement. The commission still retains control over sweepstakes by virtue of its general jurisdiction over misleading and deceptive advertising, and it has exercised this jurisdiction in many instances. For example, between January 1970 and March 1977 the FTC was involved with nine cases relating to sweepstakes: *D'Arcy Advertising Co.,* 78 FTC 616 (1971); *McDonald's Corp.,* 78 FTC 606 (1971); *Reuben H, Donnelly Corp.,* 79 FTC 599 (1971); *Procter & Gamble Co.,* 79 FTC 589 (1971); *Reader's Digest Ass'n, Inc.,* 79 FTC 696 (1971); *Longines-Wittnauer, Inc.,* 79 FTC 964 (1971); *Revere Chem Corp.,* 80 FTC 85

(1972); *Lee Rogers d/b/a American Holiday Ass'n.*, 81 FTC 738 (1972); and *Coca-Cola Co.*, 88 FTC 656 (1976).

If you follow the FTC guidelines, you'll avoid complaints from entrants and be within almost all provisions of state law. Compliance follows the old axiom of "do thy patient no harm."

(69) 16 CFR 419.1(a).

(70) 16 CFR 419.1(b)(1).

(71) *Rutherford v. Whataburger, Inc.*, 601 SW 441 (1980); *Whataburger, Inc. v. Rutherford*, 642 SW2d 30 (1982).

(72) 16 CFR 251.

(73) Formerly Missouri did not recognize federal preemption of control over mailed offers (*Missouri v. Readers Digest Ass'n, Inc.*, 527 SW2d 355, 1975). Subsequently the people of the state endorsed sweepstakes promotions by popular referendum (1978). This was a demonstration that people *want* these promotions and don't regard them as junk mail.

(74) 96 L.Ed. 1242 (1952). Annotation "Contest Awards & Similar Prize Winnings As Subject to Federal Income Tax."

(75) The Games Registration Law, Sec. 849.094(4)(a) requires a 30-day advance registration of a sweepstakes promotion with the attorney general. Effective July 1, 1981, this was amended to permit the Department of Legal Affairs to waive the bond or trust account requirement for operators who have conducted game promotions in the state of Florida for not less than *five consecutive* years and who have stayed within the law during this period. Prior to 1967, Florida banned sweepstakes altogether.

Rhode Island requires registration if retail stores participate in the promotion. For a good overall marketing analysis of this promotional device, see Peterson, F. and J. Turkel, "Catching Customers with Sweepstakes," *Fortune*, February 8, 1982, p. 84.

(76) 16 CFR 419(4)(c)and(d).

(77) 16 CFR 419(4)(e).

(78) 16 CFR 419(4)(f).

(79) 16 CFR 419(4)(g).

(80) 16 CFR 419(4)(h).

(81) *Ohio Revised Code* Substantive Rules 109:4-3-06 (1986).

SECTION V

IMPLICATIONS OF THE
CREDIT DISCLOSURE
LAWS

This section is worth reading for your personal as well as professional benefit. These laws affect you every day in your daily life. You'll find it useful to update your knowledge of your rights from time to time. As to your professional benefit, in today's business environment, it is a dubious policy to assume that consumer credit laws are solely the province of your financial or credit departments. A serious marketing effort is impossible unless your customer has the abililty to purchase. The ability to borrow is a vital component in the consumer's purchase decision—consider Detroit's low-interest-rate promotions. Further, many payment options you offer are considered "credit." Therefore your credit policy is vital to your marketing effort. How your policy will benefit your consumer must be clearly conveyed both to boost sales and to avoid serious legal problems.

The FTC (whose Division of Credit Practices oversees enforcement by the commission) and other federal agencies have enforcement responsibilities in the area of credit regulations that affect you and your business. The regulations involved have an increasing impact on situations and practices far removed from those generally thought to involve either consumers or credit. This agency (and its state counterparts) has adopted the policy of "caveat vendor" (let the seller beware) in its truth-in-lending enforcement as well as in its truth-in-advertising role.

Credit is a marketing decision variable, but a right decision about your markets can be a wrong decision legally. Anyone involved directly or indirectly in the extension of credit should have an overview of the predominant laws on point. The essence of compliance with these laws is proper *notice,* full *disclosure,* and the facilitation of equal acess. For example, Truth-in-Lending stresses the informal selection and use of credit through clear and conspicuous up-front disclosures. The Fair Credit Billing Act and Fair Credit Reporting Act emphasize fairness in

521

access to and the content of negative credit information about an individual. All these laws are useless if the consumer is denied access to credit for arbitrary, nonbusiness-related criteria. Here's where the Equal Credit Opportunity Act figures in.

Today's Credit Evaluation Process: A Sensitivity to Rights

The laws and cases reviewed in this section all came about because society believes that credit applicants were often confronted with too many hurdles. Such hurdles arose upon application, acceptance, billing, and record retention. As in many other areas of law, clear, objectively worded (and substantiated) advertising is a partial remedy in itself.

Increasingly, too, the courts are viewing one's good name as a business asset recognized by law. This right has now been broadened for commercial credit. Can consumer credit be far behind? I doubt it and am sure the future will evidence a consumer version of the *Dun & Bradstreet, Inc. v. Greenmoss Builders*[1] decision.

How is this decision relevant to consumer, not commercial, credit? First, for the reason stated above—it is the future. One astute commentator has already commented: "Its threatening inplications will be tested in future cases, but it is already obvious that Dun & Bradstreet now ranks as one of the three most important libel decisions in history"[2] (the other two being *N. Y. Times v. Sullivan*[3] and *Gertz v. Welch*[4]). Further, it touches on a variety of other topics in this chapter:

- credit decision making
- credit record retention
- commercial free speech
- sensitivity to the individual's credit rights
- the inescapable intertwining of the issue of libel in the credit process. This is rarely commented on in credit law reviews. Yet, as individuals realize the harm done to them by negligent or malicious credit practices, they'll want to do a lot more than "set the record straight."

What Is Libel?

Libel is a false and defamatory statement (that tends to adversely affect reputation) recorded in writing or other permanent form. To recover you must plead and prove special damages unless the libel is defamatory on its face (sometimes call libel per se). There are five categories constituting libel per se. Injury to the reputation of a plaintiff is presumed by law.

One example of libel per se is when the defamatory statement adversely reflects on the plaintiff's abilities in his or her business, trade, or profession. Statements that one is dishonest or lacks the basic skill to perform his or her profession is probably libelous per se. Two defenses are truth and qualified privilege. The latter is inherent in a communication on any subject matter when the recipient has an interest in the information and when it is reasonable for the defendant to make the publication. Traditionally, a statement by a credit bureau to a customer is qualified privileged.[5] As to damages, traditionally the plaintiff could recover actual damages on a showing of mere negligence. To recover punitive or compensatory damages actual malice, falsity, or the *reckless* disregard for the truth against a media defendant must be shown. In *Greenmoss*, Dun & Bradstreet was such a media defendant.

From this brief run-through of traditional libel and damages relevant to *Greenmoss,* let's move on to what the Fair Credit Reporting Act says about this area.

Consumer Libel Under the Fair Credit Reporting Act (FCRA)

Generally, a consumer will not be successful if he/she brings a defamation, invasion of privacy, or negligence action or proceeding (with respect to the reporting of information) against a consumer reporting agency, user of information, or person who furnishes information to a consumer reporting agency, based on the information disclosed. To successfully recover there is an exception you can show if the information is furnished with malice or willful intent to injure the consumer.[6]

One individual did go this route against Dun & Bradstreet but lost.[7] However, the *dissent* may have the last word:

> Dun & Bradstreet was found liable because it published a libel which was the proximate cause of Oberman's injury. Foreseeing the republication of such a libel in a business context is anything but unreasonable; on the contrary, it would be unreasonable to assume that the bank's director, upon receiving a damaging credit report and not knowing it to be libelously false, would ignore it in the making of a decision in his other business. The contract provision against reproduction cannot absolve Dun & Bradstreet from responsibility for libel published via its credit reports; to guard against that, it must take care not to publish false reports in the first place.[8]

Let's look at the *Greenmoss* case in depth. We'll particularly review the Court's discussion of business operations as they are directly and indirectly related to several issues examined in this chapter.

What Does *Greenmoss* Tell Us?

Dun & Bradstreet (hereafter D & B) is a credit reporting agency, providing subscribers with financial and related information about business. All the information is confidential; under the terms of the subscription agreement the subscribers cannot reveal it to anyone else. On July 26, 1976, D & B sent a custom-made report to five subscribers indicating that Greenmoss Builders, a construction contractor, had filed a voluntary petition for bankruptcy. This report was false and grossly misrepresented respondent's assets and liabilities. It had not been verified. The error occurred because of the oversight of a 17-year-old student.

The same day, while discussing with its bank the possibility of future financing, the construction contractor's president was told that the bank had received the defamatory report. He immediately called D & B's regional office, explained the error, and asked for a correction. In addition, he requested the names of the firms that had received the false report in order to assure them that the company was solvent. D & B promised to look into the matter but *refused to divulge the names* of those who had received the report.[9]

D & B issued a correction a week later to the five subscribers. The correction did not satisfy Greenmoss, which *again* sought the names of the subscribers in order to contact them directly. When D & B refused to identify the subscribers, Greenmoss sued for defamation. The jury returned a verdict for Greenmoss, awarding $50,000 in compensatory or presumed damages and $300,000 in punitive damages.

The issue before the court was whether punitive damages could be assessed against D & B absent proof of actual malice in reporting the erroneous information. The Supreme Court held that "permitting recovery of actual and punitive damages in defamation cases absent a showing of actual malice" does not violate the First Amendment "when the defamatory statements do not involve matters of public concern,"[10] and that *Gertz* does not apply to this case because the defamatory publications did not relate to a matter of public concern. "We have long recognized that not all speech is of equal First Amendment importance. It is speech on 'matters of public concern' that is at the heart of the First Amendment's protection." The court correctly noted the numerous exceptions to free and robust free speech including (1) obscenity, (2) fighting words, and (3) certain forms of commercial speech.

As to public concern, the Court noted it must be determined by the "expression's content, form and context. . . .as revealed by the whole record." The factors found relevant in *Greenmoss* were that (1) the speech was solely in the individual interest of the speaker and its specific business audience; (2) the speech was wholly false and clearly damaging to the victim's business reputation; (3) the defaming credit report was made available only to five subscribers who were bound by agreement not to disseminate it further; (4) the speech was motivated solely by the desire for profit; and (5) arguably the speech was objectively verifiable, and the market provides a powerful incentive to a credit reporting agency to be accurate since false reporting is of no use to creditors.[11]

The dissent argued that financial data circulated by D & B is part of the fabric of national communication. It also sought to isolate this to a "Vermont holding" by stating that most states recognize a qualified privilege for these reports. A very real fact of life is that the dissent represents an older law written by the oldest judges. *Greenmoss* is the direction of the future.

A follow-up case went this way. An interoffice memorandum for use of only certain of an insurance company's employees in dealing with its insured's loss of personal property was held defamatory. There was no constitutional requirement of proof of actual malice. The evidence was sufficient to support a verdict for the insured for both compensatory and punitive damages for defamation. The defendant argued that the offending publication was "commercial speech" entitled to First Amendment protection and that it may be held liable to plaintiff only on clear and convincing proof of actual malice.[12] The Court cited *Greenmoss* and quite simply stated that that decision forecloses this form of argument.[13]

What This Case Stands For

Greenmoss gives private persons an opportunity to protect themselves against a secret information system that includes personal data to information concerning their credit rating. A private plaintiff need simply show some dissemination of the information coupled with a failure to use reasonable care in verifying the facts. This holding is in keeping with the general thrust of the commercial free speech evolution, (you can have a wrong verifiable fact in an advertisement—and now, credit report) as contrasted to personal speech, where no one can have a wrong idea. It is also in keeping with the credit laws, where each transaction is predicated on accurate information, with a premium placed on the consumer's ability to understand and access such information.

We'll stress these points wherever applicable as we run down your legal requirements. It is important to emphasize these points in all aspects and operations of your credit policy.

ENDNOTES

(1) __ US __ , 105 S.Ct. 2939, 86 L.Ed. 593 (1985).

(2) Denniston, Lyle, "The Perils of Private Concerns", *Washington Journalism Review*, 1985, p. 58.

(3) 376 US 254, 84 S.Ct. 710, 11 L.Ed. 686 (1964).

(4) 418 US 323, 94 S.Ct. 2997, 41 L.Ed. 789 (1974).

(5) *ABC Needlecraft v. Dun & Bradstreet, Inc.,* 245 F.2d 775 (1957).

(6) 15 USC 1681h(e). See also *Hansen v. Morgan,* 582 F.2d 1214 (1978).

(7) *Oberman v. Dun & Bradstreet, Inc.,* 586 F.2d 1173 (1978).

(8) Id., p. 1178. For a related decision on point, see *Mitchell v. First National Bank of Dover,* 525 F.Supp. 176 (M.D. Ala. 1981); FCRA sec. 610(e), 15 USC 1681h(e).

(9) See note 1, p. 2941-2.

(10) Id., p. 2945.

(11) Id., p. 2947.

(12) *Mutafis v. Erie Insurance Exchange,* WVa 775 F.2d 593, 594 (1985).

(13) Id., p. 594-5.

CHAPTER 18

TRUTH-IN-LENDING ACT AND REGULATION Z

In 1969, Congress passed the Consumer Credit Protection Act, one section of which is commonly referred to as the Truth-in-Lending Act.[1] Understanding the Truth-in-Lending Act (and the corresponding Regulation Z) is useful to you both personally and professionally since this law affects various aspects of your credit purchases. The Truth-in-Lending Act was designed to enable consumers (not businesses) to make meaningful comparisons between the rates charged by different lenders. It sought to specify and improve disclosure of credit terms by creditors who regularly extend consumer credit, and the FTC was given the jurisdiction to enforce the act.

In enacting the Truth-in-Lending Act, Congress felt that the best marketplace decisions are made by informed purchasers. Congress required that a consumer receive a full and detailed disclosure as to the full cost of consumer credit. The two most important figures are the finance charge and the annual percentage rate. These figures make the comparison of borrowing costs relatively simple. The finance charge is the total dollar amount the borrower pays to use credit. It includes interest costs and certain other costs such as service charges and appraisal fees. The annual percentage rate is the percentage cost of the credit on a yearly basis.

Other required disclosures include the cash price, down payment, payment schedule, deferred-payment price, and other financial information. The Truth-in-Lending Act does not govern charges themselves for consumer credit.[2] Each prospective purchaser of credit is to be treated on his or her merits without consideration of the economic bargaining power of such purchase. The purchaser should then be able to comparison shop among the various credit options available and avoid the uninformed use of credit. To accomplish this fundamental objective, the act imposes a fairly complex and technical set of rules, which contain many pitfalls for the unwary.

Must You Comply?

The Truth-in-Lending Act does *not* govern every extension of credit; it is *limited to* an extension of credit where a finance charge is imposed for such extension. The law likewise applies when there is no finance charge but payments will be made in *more* than four installments.[3] To best understand this area, it is necessary to labor through a few important definitions. To come within the provisions of the act, the transaction must contain *all four* of the following variables:

(1) The transaction must be a *credit transaction.* That is, it must involve a credit sale, which is the right to defer payment of debt or the right to incur debt and defer payment.[4]

(2) The consumer credit must be *offered by a creditor.* A creditor is one who regularly extends credit. Regularly is defined to mean that credit was extended more than 25 times (or more than five times for transactions secured by a dwelling) in the preceding or current calendar year.[5] The obligation must be initially payable to the creditor (even if it is simultaneously assigned to another creditor). *Note:* Congress has amended the act's definition of "creditor" to include only certain persons who *extend* credit; that is, the new definition "creditor" *excludes* those who merely *arrange* credit that someone else extends. (The latter were included in the act prior to October 1982.)

(3) Such arrangement or extension of credit must be payable by written agreement in *more than four installments or with a finance charge.*

(4) The transaction must be a *consumer credit* transaction, which is credit offered or extended to a consumer primarily for personal, family, or household purposes. (It must not be for business or commercial purposes.)[6]

The Federal Reserve Board's staff offers these guidelines,[7] among others, to determine "whether credit to finance an acquisition is primarily for business or commercial purposes" (as opposed to a consumer purpose):

- The relationship of the borrower's primary occupation to the acquisition. The more closely related, the more likely it is to be a business purpose.
- The degree to which the borrower will personally manage the acquisition. The more personal involvement there is, the more likely it is to be a business purpose.
- The ratio of income from the acquisition to the total income of the borrower. The higher the ratio, the more likely it is to be a business purpose.
- The size of the transaction. The larger the transaction, the more likely it is to be a business purpose.

The courts look to the primary purpose of the loan. You may take someone's word for it on an application without further inquiry. If someone both lives on a premises and uses it as a business, the courts will look at what the parties are focusing on, how the proceeds will be spent, and even whether the premium is deducted as a business expense.[8] The Truth-in-Lending Act does not apply to the loan in which the borrower claims that he wants the loan for business use and the lender does not know that the borrower needs the money to save his home by paying off a business creditor that is threatening to seize the debtor's home.[9]

The results might be different if the lender knew of the borrower's intent.[10] The Truth-in-Lending Act does not apply if a person is borrowing money to stake another in business, even if the loan is secured by a personal residence.[11] It is clear that "credit sale" is not applicable to periodic leases. Nor is it applicable to the issuance of credit cards to a corporation for the use of the corporation's officers.[12] Generally, loan brokers and real estate brokers are exempt from the Truth-in-Lending Act.

A creditor also includes a person who honors a credit card for certain purposes[13] or any card issuer that extends either open-end credit or credit that is not subject to a finance charge and not payable by written agreement in more than four installments.[14]

If *all* four of the above criteria are *not* met, the federal act does not cover you. If it does, you should also consult state law, since Regulation Z will defer to substantially similar and *consistent* state laws. A "consistent" state law is one that does not contradict current federal law.[15] Thus, the regulation leaves in effect state laws that require disclosures that the federal law no longer requires. For example, the federal law still requires disclosure of the amount financed, but it no longer requires an itemization of the components of the amount financed. If the state law, modeled on the old federal law, continues to require both, creditors must continue to make both disclosures to satisfy state law. Review applicable state law requirements with your counsel.

In addition to keeping an eye on state law, you must determine whether you (as a creditor) are offering "open-end" credit or "closed-end" credit. Open-end credit[16] is consumer credit extended to a customer under a plan in which the following:

> **(1)** The creditor reasonably expects the customer to make repeated transactions (for example, using a credit card) rather than a one-time credit purchase. This element of repeat transactions is based on good faith and the demonstration of your ongoing relationship with your borrower. (This would be easier for a financial institution to justify than a car dealer selling "one shots.")
>
> **(2)** The creditor may impose a finance charge from time to time on the unpaid balance. *Note* : your plan can meet the finance charge criterion even though most members actually pay no finance charge during their member life because they pay within 25 or 30 days of billing (or whatever the time necessary to avoid finance charges). The only way a plan fails to meet this criterion is if there is no possibility that a periodic finance charge may be imposed on the outstanding balance.
>
> **(3)** As the customer pays the outstanding balance, that amount of credit is, generally, once again made available to the customer. This criterion contemplates a credit limit (reusable line) under which amounts repaid

would generally be available for additional extensions of credit in the absence of individual credit problems.

Closed-end credit's coverage[17] is defined by exclusion. It includes all consumer credit that does not fit the definition of open-end credit; it consists of both sale credit and loans. In a typical closed-end credit transaction, credit is advanced for a specific time period, and the lender and the customer agree on the amount financed, the finance charge, and the schedule of payments. If a person borrows $1000 from the bank, and agrees to repay it in 12 months, this type of credit is called closed-end credit.

Now let's tie in these definitions with their practical impact on you, that is, what you must disclose. Credit decisions now affect not just legal compliance and your customer's ability to pay; they also affect a very real trade-off, copy space. If you comply with the Truth-in-Lending Act, you will sacrifice creative wording and copy space for required language and disclosures, which must be printed clearly and conspicuously. Some of the disclosure areas are discussed in the following pages. However, make sure you review all copy text with your counsel.

Open-End Credit Disclosures[18]

You must set forth your credit policy plan to your customers in a "clear and conspicuous" manner. The plan's wording must be presented legibly in a reasonably understandable form, though it need not be so clear that it cannot be improved on.[19] Such information must be furnished to your customer in a specific written disclosure statement prior to the consummation of the credit transaction. Your customer must be able to keep the full text of the disclosure form.

The prominence you must give to the terms "finance charge" and "annual percentage rate" (APR) depends on your particular communication vehicle. The terms need not be emphasized (though they may be) when used as a part of general informational material. Only the words "annual percentage rate" or "finance charge" should be accentuated or emphasized. For example, if the term "total finance charge" is used, *only* "finance charge" should be emphasized. These terms may be made more conspicuous in any way that highlights them in relation to the other required disclosures (for example, by the use of capital letters or larger or contrasting color type, by underlining or setting off by an asterisk, etc.).[20] However, when the annual percentage rate and finance charge are required to be disclosed with a number they must be more conspicuous than any other disclosure. You *must* consult counsel before publicly circulating your credit offer.

While certain terms are to be emphasized, you should not confuse this with any mandated type size. All type-size requirements were eliminated as of October 1982.

Location

The disclosures need not be segregated from other material or located in any particular place on the disclosure statement,[21] or that numerical amounts or percentages be in any particular type size. Such items as contractual provisions, explanations of contractual provisions, explanations of contract terms, state disclosures, and translations may be added to the required disclosures. The creditor may make both the initial disclosures and the periodic statement disclosures on more than one page and use both the front and the reverse sides so long as the pages constitute an integrated document. An integrated document would not include disclosure pages provided to the consumer at different times or disclosures interspersed on the same page with promotional material. An integrated document would include, for example:

- Multiple pages provided in the same envelope that cover related material and are folded together, numbered consecutively, or clearly labelled to show that they relate to one another;
- A brochure that contains disclosures and explanatory material about a range of services the creditor offers, such as credit, checking account, and electronic fund transfer features.[22]

Timing of First Disclosure

The initial disclosure statement must be delivered *before* the consummation of the first transaction under your plan and before your customer is obligated to the terms of the plan. There can be no violation of the act until the transaction is consummated.[23] Delivery of the disclosures is legally permissible at any time before this, even if a membership fee or advance charge has already been posted, provided that your customer may, after receiving the disclosures, reject your plan with no further prejudice or obligation.

It is not relevant whether the creditor has advanced any funds or delivered any goods under the agreement. More significant is the time when the consumer, on the basis of comparison shopping has made a choice and commits to the purchase of credit.[24] The creation of the contractual relationship, not the time of performance of either party is controlling.[25] The latest time a creditor may give a consumer a Truth-In-Lending disclosure statement is the moment before they consummate the transaction.

The violation of the act is not simply the inaccurate disclosure; it is the consummation of the new transaction without having made the required disclosure. Liability will flow from even minute deviations from the requirements of the statute and Regulation Z.[26] Since the precise content of an offer or the time a consumer actually becomes obligated on a credit transaction may vary, if you have any question as to the time of contracting, look to the law of the state.[27]

Further, a consumer may recover against you if you failed to provide the required disclosures, even if he or she later doesn't follow through on the contract through termination, substitution, etc.[28] This is not the case if an account is temporarily suspended for a valid reason. When it is reactivated no new disclosures are required.[29] In this area you must bend over backwards to be technically exact in following through on the requirements. The Commentary on the Regulations set forth a few more examples in this area for your consideration:

> **(1)** If the consumer pays a membership fee before receiving the Truth-in-Lending disclosures, or the consumer agrees to the imposition of a membership fee at the time of application and the Truth-in-Lending disclosures statement is not given at that time, disclosures are timely as long as the consumer, after receiving the disclosures, can reject the plan (a parallel to certain direct marketing book and record clubs). The creditor must refund the membership fee if it has been paid or clear the account if it has been debited to the customer's account.

> **(2)** If the consumer receives a cash advance check at the same time the Truth-in-Lending disclosures are provided, disclosures are still timely if the consumer can, after receiving the disclosures, return the cash advance check to the creditor without obligation (for example, without paying finance charges).[30]

Finally, what about "additional information"? Basically, the law is that no matter how unclear, confusing, or misleading the additional information is, it doesn't violate Truth-in-Lending as long as it befuddles the consumer only about matters not included in the required disclosures. But as soon as it confuses or misleads the consumer about a *required* disclosure, it causes a violation because it renders the disclosure unclear, and unclear disclosures do not satisfy the law.[31]

What Must the Initial Disclosure Statement Contain?

The initial disclosure must contain the following:[32]

(1) The circumstances under which a finance charge will be imposed and an explanation of how it will be determined, as follows:

- A statement of when the finance charge accrues. (You need not state a specific date. A general one, such as "30 days from billing statement date," is sufficient.)
- What "free period" (before imposition of finance charges) your plan is extending, if any.
- Each periodic rate, the range of balances to which it applies (if more than one), and the corresponding annual percentage rate.
- The corresponding annual percentage rate for each periodic rate.
- An explanation of the method used to determine the balance subject to the finance charge.
- If there is a variable rate plan, the circumstances under which the rate(s) may increase, limitations on the increase, and the effect(s) of an increase. (Variable rate plans are open-end credit plans under which rate changes are part of the plan and are tied to an index or formula.)

- A full explanation of how the finance charge will be determined by your plan, *including* the amount of any charge other than a finance charge that may be imposed.
- A statement outlining the creditor/member's respective rights and responsibilities under the Fair Credit Billing Act.
- Where the total charge consists of two or more types of charges, a description of each.

(2) The amount of any charge other than a finance charge that may be imposed as part of the plan, or an explanation of how the charge will be determined.[33]

The following are "other charges," that must be disclosed under an appropriate heading such as "other charges":

- late payment and over-the-credit-limit charges;
- fees for production of documents for billing error resolution;
- real estate charges;
- taxes and fees prescribed by law and filing or notary fees excluded from the finance charge;[34] and
- membership or participation fees.[35]

The following are not "other charges":

- collection fees after default;
- attorney's fees;
- credit insurance premiums excluded from the finance charge; and
- any other charge that a creditor may impose on cash and credit customers alike.

(3) Any other material facts of significance to a reasonable consumer in his or her "comparison shopping" for credit. A disclosure is material if "a reasonable consumer would find it significant in deciding whether to use credit."[36]

Finally, you might wish to be aware that a creditor is permitted to unilaterally reduce the annual percentage rate *without disclosure,* provided no other credit terms are altered. The annual percentage rate may be reduced, without disclosure, in one of two ways: by lowering the amount of the finance charge, or by extending the time period of the extension of credit.[37]

Security Interest

A security interest is an interest in property that secures performance of a consumer credit obligation and is recognized by state or federal law.[38] The term "security interest" is not found in all the states' laws.[39] Disclosure is not required about the type of security interest, or about the creditor's rights with respect to that collateral. In other words, the creditor need not expand on the term "security interest." Also, since no specified terminology is required, the creditor may designate its interests by using, for example, "pledge" or "mortgage" instead of security interest.

All the creditor need do to satisfy the current law is to disclose "the fact that the creditor has or will acquire a security interest in the property purchased as part of the transaction (a purchase money security interest), or in other property identified by item or type (a nonpurchase money security interest)." Security interest can be given in the goods or property being purchased, an automobile, or collectibles, for example. Such a security interest is valid for the items specified, and for any accessories or parts (in a car, for instance) that are added during the life of the agreement. The creditor is not obligated to disclose after-acquired property clauses in the security agreement.[40] Also not required to be disclosed are interests that arise solely by operation of law and incidental interests (proceeds, fixtures, insurance proceeds, etc.). They, like after-acquired property, are excluded because they exist only because of the primary security interest. If a creditor is unsure as to a classification, he or she is better off disclosing it as a security interest.

As is always the case, any waivers or modifications on possible consumer rights must be carefully drafted. A statement such as "all exemptions are hereby waived" without more detail will violate the act.[41]

Periodic Statements[42]

You must mail a periodic statement for each billing cycle for which there is an ending debit or credit balance of more than a dollar or on which a finance charge has been imposed (unless it is in the process of collection).[43] The language and terminology of all statements must be the same as that used in the initial disclosure.

The statement must be sent at least 14 days prior to the end of any "free period" you granted in the initial disclosure. Failure to meet the 14-day period will forfeit the right to collect a finance charge in that cycle. In general, the periodic statement need not be sent if you have begun dunning. Each periodic statement you send must include the following disclosures:

- Your customer's account balance at the beginning of the cycle. If it is a credit balance, it must be disclosed clearly as such. In a multifeatured plan, the previous balance may be disclosed as an aggregate balance or as separate balances for each feature.
- An easy-to-understand identification of each transaction on your customer's account.
- Each sale[44] and nonsale[45] credit to your customer's account during the billing cycle, including the amount and the date.[46]
- Each periodic rate that may be used to compute the finance charges, the range of balances to which each is applicable, and the corresponding annual percentage rate.
- The amount of each type of finance charge (if more than one) imposed during the billing cycle. These must be separately itemized.
- All other account debits.

- The closing date of the billing cycle and the outstanding balance on that date.
- The address to be used for notification of billing errors. (See the in-depth discussion of the Fair Credit Billing Act in this section.) A telephone number may also be given, but the number may *not* be in lieu of an address. Further, the number should be accompanied by a precautionary instruction that telephoning will not preserve your customer's rights. This latter instruction will also be stated in the initial disclosures.

Subsequent Disclosures

Other required disclosures include:

Annual Statement of Billing Rights.   Here you may elect to send out the same statement provided with the initial disclosure, or you may include a shorter statement on or with *each* periodic statement. The annual statement is sent to all your credit-qualified active customers for the particular billing cycle in which the annual statement is mailed.

Change in Terms.   The member must be notified (with certain exceptions) of any changes in credit features, terms, rates, etc.

Other Compliance Requirements

You will be required to credit your customer's payment as of the date of receipt. For instance, payment by check is received on the date of arrival, not when the funds are collected. However, you may impose a "no cash in the mail" policy and require that your customer include an account number on the check. If your customer's check is nonconforming, a reasonable inhouse processing delay may result during which finance charges accrue.

You must comply with the treatment of credit balances (more on this later in this section). The law here has been clarified. Whereas formerly the law spoke only of "payment balances," it now specifically includes balances resulting from *any* source, including returns. Also, the time to mail a refund specifically requested by a member has been extended from five to seven business days.

Finally, you should retain records evidencing your compliance for two years from the date the disclosures are required to be made or actions are required to be taken. A customer who catches you in violation of this act must sue you within a year of the alleged violation or be barred by the statute of limitations (see more on this in the section on Civil and Criminal Liability).

Closed-End Credit Disclosures

Unless they differ from open-end credit disclosures, we shall not distinguish or go into detail over any of the terms used (for example, definition of creditor or credit). Disclosures for closed-end credit must be made clearly and conspicuously in writing and in a form that your customers may keep. You can make specific terms, such as "amount financed," "finance charge," and "annual percentage rate," more conspicuous by printing them in bolder type or in colors different from other disclosures, by underlining them, or by putting them between asterisks. The disclosures must be grouped and *segregated* from all other materials (in contrast to open-end credit). You may include additional information only if it is "directly related" to the disclosure (again, in contrast to open-end credit).[47]

The notice of right to rescind "shall be on a separate document." This means that the notice of right to rescind must always be on a document seperate from the credit contract and the security agreement,[48] except that the notice may appear with other information, such as the itemization of the amount financed. Itemization of the amount financed must also be separate from the main body of disclosures.[49]

These segregation mandates may be accomplished by any of the following:

- Outlining them in a box;
- Using bold print dividing lines;
- Using a contrasting color background;
- Using a different style of type (e.g., elite or pica);
- Placing them on a separate sheet of paper.

As to location, the regulation imposes no specific location requirements on the segregated disclosures. For example:

(1) They may appear on a disclosure statement separate from all other material.

(2) They may be placed on the same document with the credit contract or other information, so long as they are segregated from that information.

(3) They may be shown on the front or back of a document.

(4) They need not begin at the top of a page.

(5) They may be continued from one page to another.

However, there are exceptions to the group and segregate requirements, and these should be reviewed with your counsel. One way a creditor can be sure that the notice contains what it is supposed to contain is to use the model forms devised by the Federal Reserve Board.[50]

Consummation—Again

As you saw earlier, this is a key determinative of exactly when disclosure should be provided[51] and when an aggrieved consumer's rights begin to run. For example, it is one of three factors which determines the time during which the consumer may rescind certain transactions involving an encumbrance on his home. The period during which the consumer may rescind runs for three business days from the last to occur of these three events:

- consummation of the transaction.
- delivery to the consumer of a Truth-in-Lending statement containing all material disclosures.
- delivery to the consumer of the notice of the right to rescind required by the law (a discussion of rescission follows in this chapter).[52]

Consummation is determined to be the time that a consumer becomes contractually obligated in a credit transaction. Moreover, it is not the federal Truth-in-Lending law that determines when a contract comes into being, it is the state law.[52] Let's see what closed-end credit disclosures are mandated prior to consummation.

Contents of the Disclosures

As applicable, the following disclosures should be made for each closed-end credit transaction:

(1) Identity of the creditor making the disclosure. You should include your firm's name and (optionally) address and telephone number. All the law specifically requires is that you state your correct name.[53]

(2) The total sale price (including the amount of any down payment, including trade-ins paid to reduce the price) and a descriptive explanation of all such charges.[54] The total sale price is the sum of the cash price plus the finance charge and any amounts other than the principle loan amount or cash price that are financed by the creditor and are not part of the finance charge.[55]

(3) The amount financed. The term "amount financed" must actually be used.[56] This must be accompanied by a brief description such as "the amount of credit provided to you or on your behalf." The exact computation is set forth in the statute.[57] It must also include any other amounts financed by the creditor and not part of the finance charge— e.g., real estate settlement charges and premiums for voluntary credit life and disability insurance. Then you must subtract any prepaid finance charges, such as points or service fees.[58]

(4) An itemization of the amount financed.[59] A creditor has two alternatives in complying:

a. He or she may inform the consumer, on the segregated disclosures, that a written itemization of the amount financed will be provided on request, furnishing the itemization only if the customer in fact requests it. If the consumer requests the itemization, he or she must immediately be provided with it (that is, at the same time as the other disclosures required by law are provided).

b. The creditor may provide an itemization as a matter of course, without notifying the consumer of the right to receive it or waiting for a request.

Whether given as a matter of course or only on request, the itemization must be provided at the same time as the other disclosures required, although separate from those disclosures. The information will include:

- proceeds distributed directly to the consumer;

- amounts credited to the consumer's account with the creditor;
- indentification of other persons to whom amounts are paid by the creditor on the consumer's behalf;
- prepaid finance charges.

(5) The finance charge. The term "finance charge" must be used with a brief description such as "the dollar amount this credit will cost you."[60] As with open-end credit, this term (like annual percentage rate), where required to be disclosed, must be more conspicuous than the other terms.[61] The finance charge disclosure requirements include:

a. In a transaction involving an amount financed of $1000 or less, the finance charge shall be considered accurate if it is not more than $5 above or below the exact finance charge.

b. In a transaction involving an amount financed of more than $1000, the finance charge shall be considered accurate if it is not more than $10 above or below the exact finance charge.

c. The creditor may modify the description for variable-rate transactions (e.g., "which is subject to change").

d. Only the total finance charge may be disclosed; the elements of the finance charge may not be itemized in the segregated disclosures.

e. The filing fee will probably wind up in the federal law.[62]

(6) Annual percentage rate. This term must be used with a brief description such as "the cost of your credit at a yearly rate." For variable rate transaction, this language may be modified.[63]

(7) The items required by Section 226.4(d) of the Truth-in-Lending Act in order to exclude certain insurance premiums from the finance charge.[64] The disclosure may, at the creditor's option, appear apart from the other disclosures. It may appear with any other information, including the amount financed, itemization, any information prescribed by state law, or other supplementary material. When this information is disclosed with the other segregated disclosures, however, no additional explanatory material may be included.

(8) Certain security interest charges (see open-end credit discussion). The disclosures required in order to exclude from the finance charge certain fees prescribed by law or certain premiums for insurance in lieu of perfecting a security interest.[65] No special format is required for these disclosures. They may appear, at the creditor's option, apart from the other required disclosures.

(9) Variable rate. The statute sets forth a number of disclosures if your annual percentage rate may increase after the consummation.[66]

(10) Payment schedule, including the number, amount, and timing of payments to repay the obligation. The repayment schedule should reflect all components of the finance charge, not merely interest.

(11) Total of payments. Use this specific term along with a brief explanation,[67] such as "the amount you will have paid when you have made all the scheduled payments." This must be disclosed unless it is a single-payment transaction. For variable-rate transactions the phrase may be modified.

(12) Demand feature, if any.

(13) Total sale price. Use this specific term and a descriptive explanation (including the amount of any down payment) such as "total price of your purchase on credit, including your down payment of $ __ ." The total sale price is the sum of the cash price, finance charge, and other items such as taxes, license fees, and insurance premiums that have not been included in the cash price or finance charge.

(14) Prepayment costs. You may be definite as to whether or not a penalty will be imposed or a rebate given.[68]

(15) Late-payment charge.[69]

(16) The security interest the creditor may or may not acquire in the property as part of the transaction.

(17) Contrast reference.

(18) Assumption policy.[70] Whether this is a non-negotiable note or one "subject to conditions."

(19) Required deposit. If the creditor requires the consumer to maintain a deposit as a condition of the specific transaction, it must make a statement that the annual percentage rate does not reflect the effect of the required deposit. A required deposit need not include:

- an escrow account for taxes, insurance, or repairs;
- a deposit that earns not less than 5% per year; or
- payments under a Morris Plan.[71]

As you may have gathered, this is a complicated area. Don't attempt to design the disclosure documents yourself without the assistance of counsel.[72]

Consider a Late Fee[73]

If you demand a late payment and want to avoid the Truth-in-Lending Act, make sure that your late fee is not a finance charge. A charge assessed for late payment is distinguishable from a finance charge in that it is imposed for an actual and *unanticipated* event. The pertinent citation reads as follows: "A late payment, delinquency, default, reinstatement or other such charge is not a finance charge if imposed for actual unanticipated late payment, delinquency, default or other such occurrence."[74]

To comply with the statutory exemption, your late fee plan must satisfy the following:

(1) The account must involve credit extended on a *single* occasion for a specified sum.

(2) The late charge may not be cumulative.

(3) Your bill must offer your customer no choice but full and immediate payment. I wouldn't stress a grace period if you offer one, since it might dilute the immediacy of your payment demand. You want no inference made that you are giving your customers any right to defer payment. You expect it now, and you demand it now.

(4) It can only be a one-time charge based on the amount of a monthly payment due and *not* on any general balance.

(5) Most important, your system must be one in which you can demonstrate that your late-payment charge assessment is not anticipated.

(6) Finally, you must be vigilant in pursuing collection.

If you satisfy the above your late-payment fee will be excluded from Truth-in-Lending, whether or not the creditor continues to extend credit or provide goods or services.

Implementation

State your payment policy up front, for example, "payment due on receipt." Then no late fee should be assessed until you consider an account in default and treat your customer accordingly (for example, by dunning). If you do not regard your customer's account in default in the event of a late payment but continue to service the customer, you will expose yourself to a finance charge disclosure problem. You will definitely have a finance charge if your policy is to continue servicing and assessing late fees from time to time until paid.

In short, you may use only one late fee per account until the account is paid in full. Service may then be resumed.

Civil Recovery Under the Truth-in-Lending Act

There is a range of civil and even criminal liability for the unwary or all-too-intentional violator. We'll review a few of the more significant areas here, but first let's see how much time a consumer has to pursue his or her action.

Tolling of the Statute of Limitations

The key operative statutes of limitation for the Truth-in-Lending Act are as follows:

(1) There is a three-day cooling-off period for certain rescindable transactions.

(2) There is an *absolute* three-year limitation on rescission actions. [75] It begins to run at the consummation of the transaction or on the sale of the property, whichever comes first.

(3) There is a one-year limitation on damages actions (generally from the date of consummation). [76]

Three rules have been formulated by the circuits to determine the commencement of action for purposes of the one-year statutory period: (a) the execution date of the contract; (b) the date of actual disclosure (the "continuing violation" theory); and (c) the date the contract is executed, subject to the doctrines of equitable tolling and fraudulent concealment. Under the third formulation, the period of limitation commences when a borrower discovers or should reasonably have discovered the violation.

At present, the "continuing violation" theory is being rejected and the one-year statutory limitation is viewed as too inflexible. Current decisions appear to be compromising between the two by upholding the one-year policy outright or permitting "equitable tolling," with the year to begin when the consumer could have discovered the fraud.[77] The controlling issue may be whether the omitted disclosures result from fraud or carelessness.

> In order to meet those standards, a plaintiff must show not only that he exercised due diligence to discover his cause of action prior to the running of the statute *but also* that the defendant was guilty of 'some affirmative act of fraudulent concealment [which] frustrated discovery notwithstanding such diligence. . . .'The fraudulent concealment doctrine therefore requires more than mere non-disclosure. Otherwise, the 1-year statute of limitations would be tolled in almost every Truth-in-Lending action in which a non-disclosure violation was found and the statutory limitations provision would be a nullity.[78]

Rights of Recovery — Merchandise Sold by Credit Card

Here is a lesser-utilized right by consumers, possibly because they don't know of it. Under the Truth-in-Lending Act, a consumer who purchases unsatisfactory goods using a credit card may withhold payment for such merchandise provided the purchaser has made a good faith effort to resolve the disagreement with the seller. This could have a major impact on catalog sellers.[79]

Damages

A creditor who fails to comply with any disclosure requirement or any requirement under the Truth-in-Lending Act Section 125 is liable to such person for (1) *actual* damages sustained by such person as a result of the failure and (2) *statutory* damages (twice the amount of any finance charge in connection with the transaction except that liability shall not be less than $100 or greater than $1,000).[80]

What conduct (or failure to act) exposes you to damages? The following checklist may be helpful.

☐ Did you fail to make the required disclosures clearly and conspicuously in writing? For closed-end credit, did you fail to group the required disclosures together, segregated from everything else, without the presence of unrelated (clutter) information?

☐ Did you itemize the amount financed, separate from other required disclosures?

☐ Did you fail to more conspicuously disclose the terms "finance charge" and "annual percentage rate" (together with corresponding amounts or percentage rates), when these are required to be disclosed by the act?

☐ Did you fail to make the proper disclosures prior to the actual consummation of the transaction?

☐ Did you fail to disclose any dollar or percentage charge that you may impose before maturity due to a late fee or payment?

☐ Did you fail to disclose (where applicable) that you as creditor will acquire a security interest in the property purchased as part of the transaction?

A creditor's violations of the current law's disclosure requirements will enable the consumer to recover actual damages. But violations of Truth-in- Lending never cause any *real* injury (in the traditional sense) to the consumer and, therefore, never give rise to actual damages. Consumers are finding statutory damages (that is, the damages measured by the familiar formula of twice the finance charge, with a minimum of $50 and a maximum of $1,000) harder to come by.[81]

Because of the lack of a "real" injury (physical or to reputation, for example), the creditor should always seek mitigation, especially to avoid punitive damages and bad publicity in the trade press. If available, consider setting forth the following defenses:

- The creditor is one who, in good faith, tries to comply with this complex law, although on this single occasion in question, he or she may have erred. (If available, bring in evidence of compliance efforts, such as compliance checklists, documentation of an operating system on point, employee manuals, etc.)

- The creditor's act or omission, even if it constitutes a breach of Truth-in-Lending, is a non-material matter, a mere technical violation.

- The consumer had all the information that the law requires the creditor to disclose, even if the creditor did not put it all in the disclosure statement prior to the consummation of the credit transaction. Consquently, the creditor's act or omission did not mislead the consumer. It's an attempt to play "gotcha".[82]

- The creditor's act or omission caused the consumer no real injury. The consumer induced the creditor to extend credit by false statements, or breached the credit agreement as soon as he or she entered it, or both.

- Basically, the consumer's position is "legal litter".[83]

Rescission

A significant and growing-in-favor equitable remedy is rescission. Rescission puts an end to a transaction and leaves the parties in a position as though it had never been made. For example, the Truth-in-Lending Act gives a right of rescission to a consumer debtor who gives a security interest in his principal residence in two circumstances: an unqualified right for three business days following the consummation of the transaction, *or* until three days after all *material* disclosures are delivered (including, of course, the disclosure of consumers's right of rescission).[84] The first is easy. It is the basic three-day cooling-off period. The issue as to the failure to deliver all material disclosures is more complicated (see earlier discussion of consummation and disclosure).

The law requires a Truth-in-Lending statement to disclose more than a dozen items. Some are more important than others, but the law requires a creditor's Truth-in-Lending statement to properly disclose them all. If a Truth-in-Lending statement incorrectly lists one of the relatively unimportant disclosures, the creditor's malfeasance will have no effect on the consumer's right to rescind: It will expire three business days after the parties consummate the transaction.

It is a much different matter when a Truth-in-Lending statement omits or incorrectly lists one of the more important, or "material," disclosures (information of the type that would affect a reasonable consumer's decision to use credit or to engage that creditor when "comparison shopping for credit").[85] This extends the time for rescission until three business days after the creditor gives the consumer a second, corrected disclosure statement.

The information need not be so important that a reasonable consumer would probably change creditors on the basis of it, but it must be relevant to the credit decision. An example of a material nondisclosure is the failure to identify the collateral (incidental interests are excluded— they exist only because of the primary security interest) the consumer is putting up to secure the loan.[86] Other material terms which must be conveyed to the borrower in a meaningful fashion include:

- the annual percentage rate
- the finance charge
- the amount financed
- the total of payments
- the payment schedule.[87]

On notification from the borrower that he or she elects to rescind, the creditor must act first in strict compliance with the statute.[88] He or she must, within 20 days (extended from 10 to enable the creditor to have a reasonable time to weigh his or her options) after the borrower exercises the right of rescission, return to the borrower any money or property given as earnest money, down payment, or otherwise (all payments of principal or interest made before rescission), and take any action necessary or appropriate to reflect the termination of any security interest created under the transaction (for example, remove from the public record the mortgage on the consumer's house).

Only when the creditor has returned all payments made by the consumer and removed all traces of the security interest does the borrower have to act. The borrower must then tender the property to the creditor, except that if return of the property in kind would be impracticable or inequitable; in those instances the borrower must tender its reasonable value. If the creditor doesn't take possession of the property within 20 days after tender by the consumer, the act provides that the ownership of the property vests in the consumer with no obligation on his/her part to pay for it.

The goal of this statute is to restore the parties to the status quo existing before the transaction. The creditor's failure to rescind at all or to act in a timely manner on the rescission can expose him or her to statutory damages equal to twice the finance charge, up to a maximum of $1,000 plus, generally, reasonable attorney's fees and costs.[89]

If a creditor feels uncomfortable about its ability to calculate properly any aspect of the rescission, it is free to petition the court within the 20-day statutory period to determine the rights and obligations of the parties. A creditor can avoid a breach of the act by commencing within 20 days a lawsuit against the consumer asking the court to determine just what the Truth-in-Lending Act requires of each. The court may end up finding that the consumer had every right to rescind. It may order the creditor to proceed with the rescission. But it should not find the creditor in breach of the Truth-in-Lending Act and should award no damages for such a breach.[90]

Note: The creditor need not complete within the 20-day period *all* the actions required under the statute. He or she is on safe ground by merely beginning the process within that period, as long as the required actions are followed through to completion.[91]

Finally, if you as a creditor elect to act within the 20 days in any manner other than going along with the rescission, you should put the disputed amount in a valid escrow account. The creditor should also place in escrow the documents needed to reflect the termination of the credit security interest, for example, the release of the deed of trust encumbering the consumer's home, and documents discontinuing the foreclosure proceeding that the creditor has begun.[92]

As with all of the Truth-in-Lending Act provisions, you must be in scrupulous compliance. A creditor's mistaken interpretation of the Truth-in-Lending Act, even if honest and reasonable, is generally no defense here as elsewhere.[93]

Damages and Attorney's Fees

The Truth-in-Lending Act restricts recovery to one penalty per transaction regardless of the number of violations the transaction contains.[94] The tolling provisions discussed earlier remain intact.[95] The Truth-in-Lending Act was designed to encourage consumers to act as private attorneys generally to enforce it[96] individually or as members of an aggrieved class.[97] Overall, the statutory recovery and actual damage limits are low. To preserve the self-policing policy, the Truth-in-Lending Act offers incentives to the plaintiff of the recovery of actual costs and reasonable attorney's fees.

The object of an award of attorney's fees in a Truth-in-Lending Act case is to compensate the attorney out of the assets of the violator so that the net damage recovery of the victim will not be diminished to pay his or her legal expenses.[98] Further, the "reward" must be available, since the statutory award allows little incentive to bring a contingency fee action. The courts, however, don't wish to see spurious claims or long-winded ones—a return to the days when lawyers were paid by the page. The courts don't want "legal litter."[99] A plaintiff can thus be forced to pay a creditor's legal fee.[100] A plaintiff may also waive his or her right to attorney's fees in a negotiated settlement.[101]

The significant standards a court will look to in awarding attorney's fees are as follows:

- the special skill, reputation, and experience of counsel;
- the quality of representation;
- the results obtained;
- the novelty and complexity of the issues;
- the preclusion of other employment by the attorney because of the time and effort required to handle this case;
- undesirability of the case within the legal community;
- time and labor expended; and
- customary fee for like work.[102]

In addition to the "core" Truth-in-Lending Act issues discussed above are others of interest, which will be reviewed here briefly.

Preservation of Consumer's Claims and Defenses[103]

This section of the federal regulations is related to the Truth-in-Lending Act but is broader because it defines the creditor as merely a person who, in the ordinary course of business, lends purchase money or finances the sale of goods or services to consumers on a deferred payment basis, *provided* such person is not acting, for the purposes of a particular transaction, in the capacity of a credit card issuer.[104]

As you can see, it is "any creditor" (almost) and there are no more than four installment or finance charge obligations. Other important definitions include:

Purchase money loan.   A cash advance received by a consumer in return for a "finance charge" within the meaning of the Truth-in-Lending Act and Regulation Z, and is applied, in whole or in part, to a purchase of goods or services from a seller who (1) refers consumers to the creditor or (2) is affiliated with the creditor by common control, contract, or business arrangement.

Financing a sale.   Extending credit to a consumer in connection with a "credit sale" within the meaning of the Truth-in-Lending Act and Regulation Z.

Contract.   Any oral or written agreement, formal or informal, between *a creditor and a seller,* that contemplates or provides for cooperative or concerted activity in connection with the sale of goods or services to consumers or the financing thereof.

Business arrangement.   Any understanding, procedure, course of dealing, or arrangement, formal or informal, between a creditor and a seller, in connection with the sale of goods or services to consumers or the financing thereof.[105]

Consumer credit contract. Any instrument that evidences or embodies a debt arising from a "purchase money loan" transaction or a "financed sale" as defined in paragraphs (d) and (e) of this section.

Seller. A person who, in the ordinary course of business, sells or leases goods or services to consumers.[106]

In connection with any sale or lease of goods or services to consumers, in or affecting commerce, as "commerce" is defined in the Federal Trade Commission Act, it is an unfair or deceptive act or practice within the meaning of Section 5 of that Act for a seller, directly or indirectly, to:

(a) Take or receive a consumer credit contract which fails to contain the following provision in at least ten point, bold face type:

NOTICE

ANY HOLDER OF THIS CONSUMER CREDIT CONTRACT IS SUBJECT TO ALL CLAIMS AND DEFENSES WHICH THE DEBTOR COULD ASSERT AGAINST THE SELLER OF GOODS OR SERVICES OBTAINED PURSUANT HERETO OR WITH THE PROCEEDS HEREOF, RECOVERY HEREUNDER BY THE DEBTOR SHALL NOT EXCEED AMOUNTS PAID BY THE DEBTOR HEREUNDER. or,

(b) Accept, as full or partial payment for such sale or lease, the proceeds of any purchase money loan (as purchase money loan is defined herein), unless any consumer credit contract made in connection with such purchase money loan contains the following provision in at least ten point, bold face, type:

NOTICE

ANY HOLDER OF THIS CONSUMER CREDIT CONTRACT IS SUBJECT TO ALL CLAIMS AND DEFENSES WHICH THE DEBTOR COULD ASSERT AGAINST THE SELLER OF GOODS OR SERVICES OBTAINED WITH THE PROCEEDS HEREOF. RECOVERY HEREUNDER BY THE DEBTOR SHALL NOT EXCEED AMOUNTS PAID BY THE DEBTOR HEREUNDER.[107]

This section prevents assignments to banks so that such banks may enjoin the holder in due course protections. This would enable the assignor to recover against a consumer borrower even if a seller/creditor had defaulted on its loan or the promised serviceability of its product. The FTC notice puts the assignee in the seller's shoes and, therefore, permits the consumer to assert against the assignee of the contract and note—the same defenses that the consumer would have had against the seller.

Credit Practices Rule

The Credit Practices Rule does not apply to a "pure" commercial loan, but may to a commercial consumer loan. It comes into play when a business subject to the FTC "extends credit to a consumer."[108] The rule defines "consumer"as a natural person who seeks or acquires goods, services, or money for personal, family, or household use.[109] That definition does not limit "consumer" to one who seeks goods, services, or money *primarily* for personal, family, or household use. Therefore, a loan to a natural person who will put even a part of the proceeds to personal, family, or household use seems an "extension of credit to a consumer," even though the borrower will put the greater portion to business use. A creditor must comply with the Credit Practices Rule whenever the debtor will put a part of the credit, however small, to a consumer use.

The rule also applies to all consumer credit transactions regardless of the amount.[110] The requirements: financial institutions must make sure that their consumer credit contracts contain no confession of judgment, no waiver of exemptions, no irrevocable wage assignment, and no nonpossessory interest in the consumer's household goods (except a purchase money security interest).[111] Further, the financial institution may not obligate a cosigner unless the creditors have explained to the cosigner in advance his or her potential liability. In the case of open-end credit, this means prior to the time that the agreement creating the cosigner's liability for future charges is executed.

This advance warning may take the form of a notice such as the following:

NOTICE TO COSIGNER

You are being asked to guarantee this debt. Think carefully before you do. If the borrower doesn't pay the debt, you will have to. Be sure you can afford to pay if you have to, and that you want to accept this responsibility.

You may have to pay up to the full amount of the debt if the borrower does not pay. You may also have to pay late fees or collection costs, which increase this amount.

The creditor can collect this debt from you without first trying to collect from the borrower. The creditor can use the same collection methods against you that can be used against the borrower, such as suing you, garnishing your wages, etc. If this debt is ever in default, that fact may become a part of *your* credit record.

This notice is not the contract that makes you liable for the debt.[112]

Finally, financial institutions are prohibited from pyramiding and other improper uses of late charges.[113]

State Law Not Preempted

The Truth-in-Lending Act does not alter, affect, or exempt a creditor from complying with any state law relating to the disclosure of information in connection with credit transactions except to the extent that they are inconsistent with the federal law.[114] In such case state law is nullified to the extent that it actually conflicts with federal law. Such a conflict arises when compliance with both federal and state regulations is a physical impossibility or when state law stands as an obstacle to the accomplishment and execution of the full purposes of the federal law and objectives of Congress.[115]

One recent example of this was when the FTC granted New York's request for an exemption from a provision of the FTC's Credit Practices Rule (see above). The state had asked the commission for an exemption from the rule's cosigner provision, which requires that creditors give potential cosigners notice about their obligation to pay if the borrower defaults. New York State law requires a notice similar to the one required by the FTC's rule.

According to the FTC, the State law affords consumers substantially equivalent protection against cosigner abuses and the state is effectively administering and enforcing the law. The FTC can grant an exemption from the rule or any of its provisions if these standards are met. However, the commission said, the federal rule will still be in effect for loans of *more* than $25,000 because the New York law covers only loans below that amount.

Another example of a consistent yet tighter law is the recently enacted Wisconsin act to require a creditor in an *open-end* credit plan to make certain disclosures in *all* applications and advertisements. It applies to all creditors whether or not they're located in Wisconsin. Part of it is set out below. Can you pick out the variances from federal law?

422.308 Open-end credit disclosures.

(1) With regard to every open-end credit plan between a creditor, wherever located, and a customer who is a resident of this state and who is applying for the open-end credit plan from this state, every application for the open-end credit plan, including every application contained in an advertisement, shall be appropriately divided and captioned by its various sections and shall set forth all of the following:

(a) The annual percentage rate or, if the rate may vary, a statement that it may do so and of the circumstances under which the rates may increase, any limitations on the increase and the effects of the increase.

(b) The date or occasion upon which the finance charge begins to accrue on a transaction.

(c) Whether any annual fee is charged and the amount of the fee.

(d) Whether any other charges or fees may be charged, what they may be charged for and the amounts of the charges or fees.

(2) With regard to every open-end credit plan between a creditor, wherever located, and a customer who is a resident of this state and who is given the opportunity to enter into an open-end credit plan while present in any establishment located in this state but who is not required to complete an application under sub. (1), the customer shall be given a notice prior to entering into the open-end credit plan. The notice shall be appropriately divided and captioned by its various sections and shall set forth all of the information in sub. (1)(a) to (d).

Cash Discounts

Another hybrid area worth discussing under the Truth-in-Lending Act is the Cash Discount Act, which amended the Truth-in-Lending Act. Its stated purpose was to "encourage" discounts for cash purchases. Accordingly, it removes the previous 5% limit on cash discounts. It also contains a definition of "regular price," which distinguishes permissible cash discounts and unlawful surcharges.

The Cash Discount Act[116] states in its entirety:

(a)(1) With respect to credit cards which may be used for extensions of credit in sales transactions in which the seller is a person other than the card issuer, the card issuer may not, by contract or otherwise, prohibit any such seller from offering a discount to a card holder to induce the card holder to pay by cash, check or similar means rather than use a credit card. (2) No seller in any sales transaction may impose a surcharge on a card holder who elects to use a credit card in lieu of payment by cash, check or similar means. (b) With respect to any sales transaction, any discount from the regular price offered by the seller for the purpose of inducing payment by cash, checks or other means not involving the use of an open-end credit plan or a credit card shall not constitute a finance charge as determined under section 1605 of this title if such discount is offered to all prospective buyers and its availability is disclosed clearly and conspicuously.

In addition, 15 USC Sec.1665j(c) states:

(c) Notwithstanding any other provisions of this subchapter, any discount offered under section 1666f(b) of this title shall not be considered a finance charge or other charge for credit under the usury laws of any state or under the laws of any state relating to disclosure of information in connection with credit transactions, or relating to the types, amounts or rates of charges, or to any element or elements of charges permissible under such laws in connection with the extension or use of credit.

On a reading of the Cash Discount Act and its legislative history, it is obvious that the provisions of Section 1666f were implemented by Congress to prevent credit card issuers from prohibiting retailers from offering discounts to consumers who elect to pay for goods or services with cash. Neither the Cash Discount Act nor any other provision of the Truth-in-Lending Act prohibits states from preventing credit card issuers from imposing processing charges on retailers.[117] Finally, you should be aware that the discounts must be available to all your customers — not just to those holding credit cards.

Besides lifting the ceiling on discounts, Congress has also lessened the posting disclosure requirements. A merchant can offer any amount of discount to cash customers. Customers may be informed of their discount in any manner so long as it's displayed "clearly and conspicuously."

You have the option of offering cash discounts only on certain types of products or services, or only at certain stores in a chain. For example, a gas station owner could decide to give discounts for cash purchases of gas but not for such purchases of items such as tires or batteries. Whatever your policy is, you must make it known to all customers.

At one time, the Truth-in-Lending Act prevented merchants, innkeepers, restauranteurs, and other sellers from imposing a surcharge on consumers who used a credit card, but that prohibition expired on February 27, 1984.[118] But a surcharge is a finance charge. A retailer who imposes a finance charge at the time of honoring a credit card which the retailer did not issue (e.g. a bank credit card) must disclose the amount of this finance charge prior to imposing the charge.[119]

This distinction between cash discounts and surcharges is important if you price the goods in a particular outlet as well as supervise the creative presentation of such price. This is another reason you should have your counsel work with you in designing all credit and discount promotion plans and copy.[120]

Conclusion

If your business practices are not within the realm of the areas covered in this chapter, the Truth-in-Lending Act does not directly affect you. If you are included or think you might be, consult your counsel. This is not an area where you can cross your fingers and "hope for the best"; most judges will demand literal compliance. Areas such as specific disclosures or even how such disclosures are placed on the copy become issues. For example, you may be required to use only one side of each piece of paper to avoid "hidden" disclosures on the back.[121]

Remember that with the Truth-in-Lending Act and all credit requirements discussed hereafter, more protective state statutes and regulations are usually permitted. In addition, the legislative and judicial dynamics at the federal and state levels are such that these laws and their interpretation constantly change through legislative amendment and court rulings.

ENDNOTES

(1) 15 USC Sec. 1601 et seq. as amended, 12 CFR 225 (1986) et seq.

(2) 12 CFR 226.1(b).

(3) Of course, state law may differ. For example, see California's "Unruh Act," i.e., California Civ. Code Sec. 1802.6 (payment is *four* or more, unlike TILA's more than four). See also *Crawford v. Farmer's Group, Inc.*, 207 Cal. Rptr. 155 (Cal App. 1 Dist. 1984).

(4) 12 CFR 226.2(a)14.

(5) 15 USC Sec. 1602(f), TILA Sec. 103, 12 CFR 226.2(a) (17) (i) and 226.2(a) (17) (i) (A) fn. 3. See also *Lowell & Austin, Inc. v. Truax*, 507 A2d 949 (1985) and *Eustace v. Cooper Agency Inc.*, 741 F.2d 294 (1984).

(6) 15 USC Sec. 1603, TILA Sec. 104, 12 CFR 226.2(a) (12) (i) and CFR 226.3(a). See also *Hawkeye Bank and Trust Company v. Michel*, 373 NW2d 127 (1985) and *Ator v. City Bank and Trust Company*, 749 F.2d 498 (8th Cir. 1984).

(7) Official FRB Staff Commentary No. 3(a)-2 construing 12 CFR 226.3(a).

(8) *Quinn v. A.I. Credit Corporation*, 615 F.Supp. 151 (E.D. Pa. 1985) , 15 USC Secs. 1602(h), 1603(l). See also *Anderson v. Foothills Indus. Bank*, 674 P.2d 22 (Wyo. 1984) and *Anderson v. Rocky Mountain Federal Savings and Loan Association*, 651 P.2d 269 (Wyo. 1982) and *Dougherty v. Houlihan, Neils & Boland, Ltd.*, 531 F.Supp. 717 (1982).

(9) *Conrad v. Smith*, 712 P.2d 866 (Wash. Ct. App. 1986). See also TILA Sec. 103(h), 15 USC Sec. 1602(h), and TILA Sec. 104(a), 15 USC 1603(l). See also *London v. Bank of the South*, 315 SE2d 924 (Ga. App. 1984).

(10) *Anderson v. Lester*, 382 S.2d 1019 (La. Ct. App. 1980), *cert. den., 450 US 1045, 101 S.Ct. 1767, 68 L.Ed.2d 244 (1981).*

(11) *Poe v. First National Bank*, 597 F.2d 895 (5th Cir. 1979); see also *Weingarten v. First Mortgage Co.*, 466 F.Supp. 349 (E.D. Pa. 1979).

(12) *American Express Co. v. Koerner*, 452 US 233 (1981).

(13) 15 USC Sec. 1602(f), 12 CFR 226.2(a)(17)(iii).

(14) 15 USC Sec. 1602(f), 12 CFR 226.2(a)(17)(iv). Effective 1/1/88 a new Section 520 is added to the NYS General Business Law that all mail application forms (including department store catalogs) contain specified information in chart form and in specified type size.

(15) 15 USC Sec. 1610.

(16) 15 USC Sec. 1602(i), TILA Sec. 103(i), 12 CFR 226.2(a) (20).

(17) 12 CFR 226.2(a) (10).

(18) TILA Sec. 121(a) and (b), 12 CFR 226.5(a). *Note :* Certain requirements common to both open- and closed-end credit disclosures are discussed here.

(19) *Dixon v. D.H. Holmes Co.*, 566 F.2d 571, 572-73 (5th Cir. 1978).

(20) TILA Sec. 122(a) and 12 CFR 226.5(a) (2). See also *Shroder v. Suburban Coastal Corp.*, 729 F.2d 1371, 1379 (1984).

(21) *Misher v. Household Finance Consumer Discount Co.*, 571 F.Supp. 726 (E.D. Pa. 1983).

(22) 12 CFR 226.5(a)(2).

(23) *Harman v. New Hampshire Savings Bank*, 638 F.2d 280 (1st Cir. 1981); *Waters v. Weyerhauser Mortgage Co.*, 582 F.2d 503, 505 (9th Cir. 1978) and *Chevalier v. Baird Savings Association*, 371 F.Supp. 1282, 1284 (E.D. Pa. 1974).

(24) *Bryson v. Bank of New York*, 584 F.Supp. 1306, 1317 (1984).

(25) 12 CFR 226.2(a)(13) and also 12 CFR 226.17 (b) for closed-end. See also *Nash v. First Financial Savings and Loan Association*, 703 F.2d 233, 238 (1983), *James v. City Home Service, Inc.*, 712 F.2d 193 (5th Cir. 1983) and *Super Chief Credit Union v. Gilchrist*, 653 P.2d 117 (Kan. 1982).

(26) *Charles v. Krauss Co., Ltd.*, 572 F.2d (5th Cir. 1978).

(27) *Bourgeois v. Haynes Construction Company*, 728 F.2d 719, 720 (5th Cir. 1984) and *Murphy v. Empire of America, FSA*, 746 F.2d 931, 934 (1984).

(28) *Marcano v. Northwestern Chrysler-Plymouth Sales, Inc.*, 550 F. Supp. 595 (N.D. Ill. 1982). Also note that if any existing extension of credit is *refinanced* this will be considered a new transaction subject to the disclosure requirements. See *Adiel v. Chase Federal Savings and Loan Association,* 586 F.Supp. 866 (1984).

(29) 12 CFR 226.5(b)(2).

(30) 12 CFR 226.5(b)(1).

(31) *Gambardella v. G. Fox Co.,* 716 F.2d 104,110-111 (1983).

(32) TILA Sec. 127(a)(1-4), 12 CFR 226.6(a). See also *Steele v. Ford Motor Credit Co.,* 783 F.2d 1016 (11th Cir. 1986).

(33) TILA Sec. 127(a)(5), 12 CFR 226.6(b).

(34) *Watts v. Key Dodge Sales, Inc.,* 707 F.2d 847, 849 (1983).

(35) *Lifschitz v. American Express Co.,* 560 F.Supp 458 (E.D. Pa. 1983).

(36) *Bustamente v. First Federal Savings and Loan Association,* 619 F.2d 360, 364 (1980). See also *Ivey v. United States Department of Housing and Urban Development,* 428 F.Supp 1337 (1977), *Davis v. FDIC,* 620 F.2d 489 (1980), and *Brown v. National Permanent Federal Savings and Loan Association,* 526 F.Supp. 815 (1981). See also *Dixey v. Idaho First National Bank,* 505 F.Supp. 846 (1981) ("technical errors" distinguished). Whether your customer can read or understand English is not relevant—the disclosure ritual is; see *Zamarippa v. Cy's Car Sales, Inc.,* 674 F.2d 877 (1982).

(37) *Krenisky v. Rollins Protective Services Co.,* 728 F.2d 64, 66 (1984).

(38) TILA Sec. 127(a)(6). 12 CFR 226.2(a)(25), 12 CFR 226.6(c).

(39) *First Guaranteed Bank v. Alford,* 470 S.2d 473, 475 (La. App. 1 Cir. 1985).

(40) 12 CFR 226.3(c), 226.18(m). See also *Varner v. Century Finance Co., Inc.,* 738 F.2d 1143 (11th Cir. 1984) and *Read v. Finance One of Virginia, Inc.,* 560 F.Supp. 2d 791, 794 (1983).

(41) *Stewart v. Abraham Lincoln Mercury, Inc.,* 698 F.2d 1289, 1294 (1983). See also *Williamson v. Lafferty,* 698 F.2d 767 (1983).

(42) TILA Sec. 127(b), 12 CFR 226.7.

(43) 12 CFR 226.5(b)(2).

(44) 12 CFR 226.7(a).

(45) 12 CFR 226.7(h).

(46) TILA Sec. 127(b)(2), 12 CFR 226.8(a).

(47) TILA Sec. 128, 12 CFR 226.17(a). This "segregation" includes the disclosures of the right to rescind and other required disclosures such as optional insurance. See *Palmucci v. General Motors Acceptance Corp.,* 618 F.Supp. 460 (D. Conn. 1985). This case is a step-by-step review of the compliance highlights of closed-end credit.

(48) 12 CFR 226.23(b). See also FRB Staff Commentary no. 23(b)-3.

(49) 12 CFR 226.17(a) (1).

(50) See Reg. Z appendix H, Model Forms.

(51) 12 CFR 226.17(b).

(52) 12 CFR 226.2(a) (13); Official FRB Staff Commentary no. 2(a) (13-1). See also *Murphy v. Empire of America, FSB,* 746 F.2d 931 (2d Cir. 1984).

(53) 15 USC 1638(a) (1); TILA Sec. 128(a)(1), 12 CFR 226.18(a). Once, failing to identify the creditor was a material nondisclosure. It no longer is. See 12 CFR 226.23 n. 48.

(54) TILA Sec. 128(a) (7-8), 12 CFR 226.18(j).

(55) 12 CFR 226.18(b) (2).

(56) 15 USC 1638(a) (2) (A); TILA Sec. 128(a) (2), 128(a) (8), 12 CFR 226.18 (b).

(57) Id.

(58) 12 CFR 226.2(a) (23).

(59) 15 USC Sec. 1638(a) (2) (B); TILA Sec. 128(a)(2) (B), 12 CFR 226.18(b).

(60) TILA Sec. 128(a)(3), 128(a)(8), 12 CFR 226.18(d).

(61) TILA Sec. 122(a), 12 CFR 226.17(a)(2).

(62) To comply with 12 CFR 226.18(o). See also *Lewis v. Award Dodge, Inc.,* 620 F.Supp. 135 (D. Conn. 1985).

(63) TILA Sec. 128(a) (4), 128(a) (8), 12 CFR 226.18(e). See also *Shroder v. Suburban Coastal Corp.,* 729 F.2d 1371 (11th Cir. 1984) — "annual percentage rate" must be printed more conspicuously than rest of text.

(64) 12 CFR 226.18(n).

(65) TILA Sec. 128(a) (9), 12 CFR 226.18(m), 12 CFR 226.2(a) (25).

(66) 12 CFR 226.18(f).

(67) 12 CFR 226.18(h). See also *Misher v. Household Finance Consumer Discount Co.,* 571 F.Supp. 726 (E.D. Pa. 1983).

(68) TILA Sec. 128(a) (11), 12 CFR 226.18(k).

(69) TILA Sec. 128(a) (10), 12 CFR 226.18(l).

(70) TILA Sec. 128(a) (13), 12 CFR 226.18(q).

(71) 12 CFR 226.18(r).

(72) For assistance in this area, you may wish to review *How to Advertise Consumer Credit,* which is an FTC Manual for Business. It contains a number of samples of disclosure wording you might find useful. To order it call or write to any FTC office listed in the Profit Preservation section or write to the Federal Trade Commission, Division of Credit Practices, Sixth and Pennsylvania Avenue, N.W., Washington, D.C. 20580.

(73) As opposed to a late charge. For a few cases on late charges see *Southern Discount Co. of Georgia v. Whitley,* 772 F.2d 815 (11th Cir 1985), *Watts v. Key Dodge Sales, Inc.,* 707 F.2d 847 (5th Cir. 1983), *Parry v. Ford Motor Credit Co.,* 575 F.Supp.204 (1983), and *Pittman v. Money Mart, Inc.,* 636 F.2d 993 (5th Cir. 1981).

(74) 12 CFR 226.4(c) (2).

(75) 15 USC Sec. 1635(f).

(76) 15 USC Sec. 1640(e), TILA Sec. 130(e).

(77) *King v. State of California,* 784 F.2d 910 (9th Cir. 1986); see also *Jones v. Transohio Savings Association,* 747 F.2d 1037 (6th Cir. 1984).

(78) Id. Contrast to *Hughes v. Cardinal Federal Savings and Loan Association,* 566 F.Supp.834, 838 (1983). See *Wachtel v. West,* 476 F.2d 1062 (6th Cir.), *cert. den.,* 414 US 874, 94 SCt 161, 38 L.Ed.2d 114 (1973).

(79) *Montgomery Ward Co. v. Horgan,* 448 A.2d 151 (Vt. 1982).

(80) 15 USC Sec. 1640(a) — under 1640a(2) (B) you also have class action exposure, TILA Sec. 130(a) (1-3).

(81) 15 USC Sec. 1640(a) (2) (A) (i) and 15 USC Sec. 1640 (a) (e), TILA Sec. 130(a). See also *Gambardella v. G. Fox Co.,* 716 F.2d 104 (2d Cir. 1983); *Huff v. Stewart-Gwinn Furniture Co.,* 713 F.2d 67 (4th Cir. 1983) and *Mars v. Spartanburg Chrysler Plymouth, Inc.,* 713 F.2d 65 (4th Cir. 1983).

(82) James C. Hill, Circuit Judge, commenting on TILA litigation becoming a game of "gotcha"; see *Shroder v. Suburban Coastal Corp.,* 729 F.2d 1371, 1386 (1984).

(83) More legal eloquence: see *Kramer v. Marine Midland Bank,* 559 F.Supp. 273, 293 (1983).

(84) 15 USC 1635(f); TILA Sec. 125(a); 12 CFR 226.23(a) (3). See also *Dawe v. Merchants Mortgage and Trust Corp.,* 683 P.2d 796, 799 (Colo. 1984); but note as with all TILA coverage herein there is no protection for commercial credit transactions so there is no rescission remedy, either. See Sherrill v. Verde Capital Corp., 719 F.2d 364 (11th Cir. 1983). Also it practically goes without saying that a borrower cannot rescind a loan secured by real property that is not the borrower's principle residence. See *Fleming v. Federal Bank of Georgia,* 306 SE2d 332 (Ga. App. 1983).

(85) *Davis v. Federal Deposit Insurance Co.,* 620 F.2d 489, 492 (citation omitted), *mod.,* 1981, 636 F.2d 1115 (1980).

(86) *Smith v. Capital Roofing Co. of Jackson, Inc.,* 622 F.Supp. 191 (SD Miss. 1985). See also *Cox v. First National Bank of Cincinnati,* 751 F.2d 815 (1985).

(87) TILA Sec. 103(u); 12 CFR 226.23(a) (3) n.48. See *King v. State of Col.,* 784 F.2d 910, 913 (9th Cir. 1986).

(88) 15 USC Sec. 1635(b). See also *Semar v. Platte Valley Federal Savings and Loan Association,* 791 F.2d 699 (9th Cir. 1986) and *Arnold v. W.D.L. Investments, Inc.,* 703 F.2d 848 (1983).

(89) 15 USC Sec. 1640(a). See also *Valentine v. Influential Savings and Loan Association,* 572 F.Supp. 36 (1983); *Brown v. National Permanent Federal Savings and Loan Association,* 683 F.2d 444 (1982); *Abbott v. Shaffer, 564 F.Supp. 1200 (1983); and Bookhart v. Mid-Penn Consumer Discount Co.,* 559 F.Supp. 208 (1983).

(90) 15 USC Sec. 1635(b), TILA Sec. 125(b). See *Acquino v. Public Finance Consumer Discount Co.,* 606 F.Supp.504, 509 (E.D. Pa. 1985).

(91) FRB Official Staff Interpretations para. 23(d) (2), 12 CFR Supp. 1 at 731 (1983).

(92) *Pearson v. Easy Living, Inc.,* 534 F.Supp. 884, 895 (S.D. Ohio 1981) but see also *Charles v. Krauss Co.,* 572 F.2d 544, 549 (5th Cir. 1978). See also *Reliable Finance Co. v. Jenkins,* 7 Ohio Misc. 2d 24, 454 NE2d 993 (Co. Ct. 1982)

(93) 15 USC Sec. 1640(c).

(94) *Moors v. Travelers Insurance Co.,* 784 F.2d 632 (5th Cir. 1986).

(95) *Davis v. Werne,* 673 F.2d 866, 869 (5th Cir. 1982); see also *Streit v. Fireside Chrysler-Plymouth, Inc.,* 697 F.2d 193 (1983).

(96) 15 USC Sec. 1640(a) (2) (B). See also *Ransom v. S & S Food Center, Inc.,* 700 F.2d 670 (11th Cir. 1983).

(97) TILA Sec. 130(a) (3). See *Mars v. Spartanburg Chrysler-Plymouth, Inc.,* 713 F.2d 67 (4th Cir. 1983). But see also *In re Wayne Strand Pontiac-GMC,* 653 SW 2d 45 (Tex. Ct. App. 1983).

(98) 15 US Sec. 1640(a) (3), TILA Sec. 130(a) (3). See also *Matter of Pine,* 705 F.2d 936 (1983). As to counterclaims see *Mortgage Mint Corp.,* 708 P.2d 1177 (1985). As for the right of an attorney to sue for his or her fee, see *James v. Home Construction Co. of Mobile, Inc.,* 689 F.2d 1357 (11th Cir. 1982).

(99) *Kramer v. Marine Midland Bank,* 559 F.Supp. 273, 293 (1983).

(100) *People's National Bank of Liberal v. Moly,* 718 P.2d 306 (Kan. 1986).

(101) *Gramm v. Bank of Louisana,* 691 F.2d 728, 730 (5th Cir. 1982). If not specifically omitted from a settlement, see *James v. Home Construction Co. of Mobile, Inc.,* 689 F.2d 1357 (11th Cir. 1982).

(102) *Hensley v. Ecberhart,* 103 S.Ct. 1933, 76 L.Ed.2d 40 (1983), *Redic v. Gary H. Watts Realty Co.,* 586 F.Supp. 699, 700-703 (1984); *Varner v. Century Finance Co., Inc.,* 738 F.2d 1143 (1984); and *Freeman v. B & B. Associates,* 595 F.Supp. 1338 (1984).

(103) 16 CFR 433.1-3.

(104) 16 CFR 433.1(c) — emphasis added.

(105) 16 CFR 433.1(d-g).

(106) 16 CFR 433.1(i-j).

(107) 16 CFR 433.2.

(108) 16 CFR 444.2(a), 444.3(a), 444.4(a).

(109) 16 CFR 444.1(d).

(110) TILA exempts unsecured transactions exceeding $25,000; 15 USC Sec. 1603(3), TILA Sec. 104(3), 12 CFR 226.3(a).

(111) 16 CFR 442.2(a)1-4.

(112) 16 CFR 443.(c).

(113) 16 CFR 444.4.

(114) 15 USC Sec. 1610.

(115) *Fidelity Federal Savings and Loan Association v. De La Cuesta,* 458 US 141, 102 S.Ct. 3014, 73 L.Ed. 2d 664 (1982).

(116) 15 USC Sec. 1666f.

(117) *Texaco, Inc. v. Hughes,* 572 F.Supp. 1, 7 (D.C. Md. 1982).

(118) 15 USC Sec. 1666f (2), TILA Sec. 167(a) (2).

(119) 12 CFR 226.9(d). *Note* : prior to its recent amendment, the Truth-in-Lending Act required retailers to treat discounts greater than 5% of the credit card price as a finance charge and disclose it as such to their credit card customers. Under current law, a lawful discount is not a finance charge no matter how large it is, e.g. *Minnesota Statutes* Chapter 325G.051.

(120) Check with your counsel as to whether a surcharge problem still exists according to federal law. Many, if not most, states prohibit it.

(121) *Chapman v. Miller,* 575 SW2d 581 (1978) and *Charles v. Krauss Co.,* 572 F.2d 544 (1978). For a pamphlet about what information the consumer may receive, contact the Director, Division of Consumer Affairs, Federal Reserve Systems, Washington, D.C., 20551, and ask for *How to File a Consumer Credit Complaint.*

CHAPTER 19

FAIR CREDIT BILLING ACT

Under early Roman law, creditors who could not obtain satisfaction from a debtor were allowed to cut up the debtor's body and divide the pieces. As an alternative, the Romans also allowed creditors to leave the debtor alive and sell him into slavery. Today, debtors are better off and have more protections. One of these protections is the Fair Credit Billing Act (FCBA).[1]

This act, an amendment to the Truth-in-Lending Act, is the law your customers are likely to be familiar with, because it is stated periodically in their credit card bills. Your customer is on top of this one, so you'd better be, too—both to protect yourself legally and to enhance customer relations.

The Fair Credit Billing Act was designed to protect customers against unfair practices of issuers of open-end credit and all those who issue credit cards.[2] The act requires credit grantors to inform debtors of their rights and responsibilities in a billing dispute. It also requires creditors to resolve billing disputes within a specific time period (whose onset is activated by the customer's written correspondence) by making appropriate account adjustments or explaining why the original bill is believed to have been correct.

For those with an electronic funds transfer (EFT) payment operation, or who otherwise fall within Regulation E's definition of "financial institution," the procedures for resolution of EFT billing errors are generally patterned after those found in the FCBA, and we'll discuss where they differ (see also the discussion of Electronic Fund Transfer Fraud in Chapter 22).

Electronic fund transfer exemptions and nuances that might affect your firm's operations should be discussed with your counsel; we'll assume compliance to cover all bases. For purposes of this discussion EFT means any transfer of funds

- other than one originated by check, draft, or similar paper instrument,
- that is initiated through an electronic terminal, telephone, computer, or magnetic tape,
- that orders or authorizes a financial institution to debit or credit an account.

The term includes most transfers that take place at automated teller machines (ATMs) or point-of-sale (POS) terminals (including deposits), payment by telephone or transfer plans, direct deposit of payroll, government benefits, or annuities and automatic payments of bills, such as insurance premiums or mortgages. If an extension of credit is incident to an electronic fund transfer, under an agreement between a consumer and financial institution to extend credit when the consumer's account is overdrawn or to maintain a specified minimum balance in the consumer's account, the creditor shall comply with the requirements of Regulation E (12 CFR 205.11) governing error resolution rather than those of the Fair Credit Billing Act.[3]

The term excludes cash or check payments at ATMs, wire transfers, certain telephone initiated transfers, most direct payments made by composite check and check truncation systems.[4] The Regulation E Commentary also excludes home banking terminals from the regulation's receipt requirement. Transfers initiated by means of home banking terminals, however, are subject to all of the regulation's other provisions.

Must You Comply?

You'll want to review the definitions contained in the Truth-in-Lending Act, particularly that of open-end credit.[5]

If your promotions do not fall within the definitions of open-end credit, you are not required to provide with your billing a statement informing the consumer of the right to dispute billing errors. However, if you honor credit cards in a consumer credit transaction, certain sections of the act should be reviewed with your counsel, specifically those that deal with open-end credit, credit card accounts,[6] and possible exceptions to the general rule.[7] Again, all state laws on point should also be reviewed.[8]

Once you are satisfied that you are within the area covered by law, you may become involved with a billing error situation. The term billing error can mean:

(1) Credit has been extended, but "not . . . to the consumer or to a person who has actual, implied, or apparent authority to use the consumer's credit card or open-end credit plan."[9] (This includes instances of lost or stolen credit cards.)

(2) Your consumer has refused to take delivery of goods because they were the wrong quantity, were delivered late, or otherwise did not comply with the contract.

(3) The creditor failed to properly credit a payment or credit the consumer's account.

(4) There was a mathematical error affecting the consumer's account.

(5) Incorrect or unauthorized electronic fund transfers took place.[10]

(6) Your consumer has requested additional clarification, including documentary evidence concerning an order.

(7) The creditor failed to mail or deliver a periodic statement to the consumer's last known address if that address was received by the creditor, in writing, at least 20 days before the end of the billing cycle for which the statement was required.

(8) Any other legitimate grievances affecting an open-end credit plan. Remember that you're selling customer service and satisfaction as well as marketing a product, so don't try to be technical here. Follow the mandated procedure for billing dispute resolution.

Keeping a Customer and Complying With the Law

If you and your counsel have determined that you must comply, you will be required to distribute a notice in the form prescribed informing all your customers of their rights under the act and the means to implement such rights.[11] You've probably received such notices in your own credit card bills every few months, so you are likely to be familiar with them.

You should acquaint yourself with the general and specific disclosure requirements of the Fair Credit Billing Act.[12] As a "covered" creditor, you are required to disclose to the consumer the following customer and creditor obligations under the act:

(1) The notice must be given by the consumer personally. The creditor is not "notified" by discovering the error itself. The customer is required to put the complaint in writing and send it to the address requested by the creditor.[13] The written correspondence must include information enabling the creditor to identify the consumer's name and account number as well as a description of the error, and any other pertinent information (such as type, date, amount or error) and be reviewed by the company within 60 days of transmittal of the alleged billing error. You have the right to require that it be received at the address designated for this purpose on the periodic statement. A telephone call will not preserve your customer's rights.[14]

EFT procedure: The notification may be oral or written. If the notice is oral, the institution may require a written confirmation to be received within 10 business days, if the consumer is advised of the requirement at the time of the call and given the appropriate mailing address to which a confirmation must be sent.[15]

(2) You, the creditor, must acknowledge the customer's written inquiry within 30 days of receipt. You must conduct a reasonable investigation concerning this dispute. Then, within two complete billing cycles after the end of the billing cycle in which the notification is received (and in no event more than 90 days), you must either correct the error or explain why you believe the bill was correct.[16] Correcting the error includes making all appropriate corrections necessary (and mailing such correction notice), including the crediting of any finance charges on amounts erroneously billed. The creditor must then transmit to the consumer a notification of such corrections with an explanation of any such change in the amount indicated by the consumer, if any such change is made, and, if the obligor so requests, copies of documentary evidence of the consumer's indebtedness.[17]

Explanations include sending a written explanation or clarification to the consumer, after having conducted an investigation, setting forth (to the extent applicable) the reasons the creditor believes the account of the consumer was correctly shown in the statement and, on request of the consumer, provide copies of documentary evidence of the consumer's indebtedness. In the case where the consumer alleges that the creditor's billing statement reflects goods not delivered to the consumer or a designee in accordance with the agreement made at the time of the transaction, the creditor may not construe such amount to be correctly shown unless he or she determines that the goods in question were actually delivered, mailed, or otherwise sent to the obligor and provides the obligor with a statement of such determination.

After complying with the provisions of this subsection with respect to an alleged billing error, a creditor has no further responsibility under this section if the obligor continues to make substantially the same allegation with respect to such error.[18] Further, the creditor need not send periodic billing statements to an open-end account once the creditor begins its collection efforts.[19]

EFT procedure : The institution has 10 business days to investigate, determine whether an error occurred, and transmit the results. It may extend this time up to 45 days, if it

- provisionally recredits within 10 business days of receipt of the error notice;
- recredits not only the disputed amount, but also interest, when applicable;
- promptly (within two business days) notifies the consumer of the amount and date of the credit and that he or she will have full use of the funds pending resolution.[20]

(3) During this interval, neither you nor a collection agency may take any collection action concerning any portion of the amount your customer believes to be in dispute (including related finance or other charges). Action includes imposing a finance charge or any other such charge or compelling payment of a minimum periodic payment when only such minimum is involved. Legal or other action includes threatening to damage a person's credit rating or report him or her as a delinquent to anyone. Action prohibited includes accelerating any part of the consumer's

indebtedness or restricting or closing a consumer's account solely because the consumer has exercised in good faith rights provided by this section.[21] This shall not prevent a creditor from applying against the credit limit of its customer's account the amount indicated to be in error.

The consumer is, however, obliged to pay all undisputed debts during this interval unless the dispute is the creditor's failure to send a periodic statement. The creditor can pursue any amount not paid that the consumer has not indicated to contain a billing error.[22] If the failure to send the periodic statement is the dispute, then it affects the entire balance owed, and your customer need pay none of the amount in question until he or she receives the statement. The customer then has the same amount of time to pay as he or she would have had if the statement had been received on time.

(4) One unfortunate reality of modern credit extension is when the consumer purchases defective merchandise[23] with a store (or in-house) account. If the seller refuses to remedy the problem or exchange the product for a new one, the consumer may generally withhold payment for the item. If the charge had been made with a national credit card rather than the in-house credit card, the consumer may take the same legal actions against the credit card issuer as he/she could under state law against the seller. However, the consumer must first give the seller a chance to remedy the problem. Also, when the card issuer is not the seller, to exercise these rights the item in question must have cost more than $50, and it must have been purchased in the purchaser's home state or within 100 miles of his or her home address. If this is not the case, the consumer must generally pay the card issuer regardless of any claims against the seller (see state law exemptions below).

The above rules are important especially in the case of direct marketers. "The geographical limitation serves to protect banks from consumers who may expose them to unlimited liability through dealings with merchants in faraway states where it is difficult to monitor a merchant's behavior."[24] For example, when a New York City-based customer calls a telephone number of a direct marketer in Hawaii and places an order, the transaction is considered to take place in Hawaii.

This is because when the consumer calls the seller, the consumer is making an offer to buy on the terms and conditions set out in the seller's catalogue. When the seller, on the other end of the line, accepts that offer, a contract arises in the place where the offer was accepted. Because of the obvious excess of the in-state or 100-mile limit, the consumer is not permitted to assert against the card issuer any claims and defenses he or she would have against the seller, *unless* state law differs.

In all Truth-in-Lending issues, the question of where the transaction occurs (as in mail or telephone order cases) is determined under state or other applicable law.[25] Furthermore, any state law permitting customers to assert claims and defenses against the card issuer would not be preempted, regardless of whether the place of transaction is at issue. In effect, the federal laws are viewed as bare minimum standards.

You should review with your counsel any limitations placed on your firm by your state laws. If you're the aggrieved consumer, your counsel may be able to provide you with a state law "loophole"– check in these situations:

If the creditor fails to comply with any of the above, it forfeits any right to collect from the consumer the amount indicated as a finance charge thereon. Such forfeiture is not to exceed fifty dollars ($50).[26]

EFT procedure : The institution must promptly (within one business day) correct the account. The customer must be informed of the correction orally or in writing within 10 business days (or 45 calendar days, if applicable—see item 2 above) of receipt of error notice. The amount of consumer liability for unauthorized use may be deducted from the amount to be recredited where appropriate.

(5) Once you have explained the bill in the correct manner, you may then proceed to collect in the normal manner. After compliance you have no further responsibility under this section if the consumer "continues to make substantially the same allegation with respect to such error."[27] If the creditor now wishes to resume its collection, it[28]

- must give prompt written notice of the time when payment is due and the amounts still owing, including related finance charges;

- shall allow any free ride period as disclosed under Sec. 226.6(a)(2) and 226.7(j), during which time the consumer may pay the amount due without incurring additional finance charges;

- may report the amount due as delinquent if unpaid after the expiration of the free ride period or 10 days (whichever is longer), unless the creditor receives further written notice that a portion of the billing error is still in dispute (but then the creditor may still report it if it follows the required steps);[29] and

- may not report that an amount or account is delinquent if the creditor receives (within the time allowed for payment by law)[30] further written notice from the consumer that any portion of the billing error is still in dispute, unless the creditor also:

(i) promptly reports that the amount or account is in dispute;

(ii) mails or delivers to the consumer (at the same time the report is made) a written notice of the name and address of each person to whom the creditor makes a report; and

(iii) promptly reports any subsequent resolution of the reported delinquency to all persons to whom the creditor has made a report.[31]

EFT procedure : If it is determined that no error occurred or that an error occurred but in a manner or amount different from that alleged by the customer, then the creditor institution:

- will mail a written explanation mentioning the consumer's right to request documentation within three business days of the determination.

- may immediately debit the recredited amount, but concurrently it must give oral or written notice of the date and the amount debited and must disclose the fact that the institution will honor preauthorized transfers and checks payable to third persons for five business days after transmitting the notice.

- must promptly mail or deliver the documents relied on, if the consumer requests them.[32]

Conclusion

The Fair Credit Billing Act is primarily self-enforcing. The FTC has favored an education campaign to inform consumers of their ability to use and enforce the act. To comply with the act, you must set up a system internally to resolve open-end credit transaction billing disputes. Your specific practices should be reviewed with your counsel in light of this act and applicable state law, and possibly in light of the provisions of the Electronic Funds Transfer Act. If you are not strictly within the definitions set forth, this act's provisions provide a workable model that your customers understand from purchasing activity elsewhere and one that the FTC endorses.

ENDNOTES

(1) 15 U.S.C. Sec. 1601, 12 C.F.R. Sec. 226.13. Since this is an amendment to the Truth-in-Lending Act, compliance is predicated on whether your practices come within the specifications of the definitions in that act governing open-end creditors (see discussion on point in previous chapter).

(2) 15 U.S.C. Sec. 1666, 12 C.F.R. Sec. 226.13, and *Jacobs v. Marine Midland Bank, N.A.*, 475 NYS 2d 1003 (Sup. Ct. 1984).

(3) 12 C.F.R. Sec. 226.13(i).

(4) Regulation E, 12 C.F.R. Sec. 205.3.

(5) 2 C.F.R. Sec. 226.2(20). "Open-end credit " means consumer credit.

(6) 12 C.F.R. Sec. 226.2(15).

(7) 12 C.F.R. Secs. 226.2(17) (i)–226.2(17) (v), 226.12.

(8) For example, N.Y. Gen. Bus. Law Secs. 701-707 (McKinney 1982).

(9) 12 C.F.R. Sec. 226.13(a)(6).

(10) Regulation E, 12 C.F.R. Sec. 205.11(a). As we discussed, if the extension of credit is incident to an electronic fund transfer, you must comply with these error resolution procedures rather than those of 12 C.F.R. Sec. 226.13(i). See Posch, Robert J. Jr. "Credit Card and Electronic Fund Transfer Fraud," *Direct Marketing,* November 1983, pp. 97-101.

(11) 12 C.F.R. Secs. 226.5, 226.6, 226.7, 226.8, and 226.9, should be reviewed.

(12) 12 C.F.R. Sec. 226.13.

(13) 12 C.F.R. Sec. 226.7(k).

(14) 12 C.F.R. Sec. 226.13(b)(i)–226.13(b)(3). *Himmelfarb v. American Express Co.* (1984) 301 Md 698, 484 A2d 1013.

(15) 12 C.F.R. Sec. 205.11(b)(2).

(16) 12 C.F.R. Sec. 206.13(c).

(17) 15 U.S.C. Sec. 1666 (a)(B)(i); 12 C.F.R. Sec. 226.13(f). See also *Saunders v. Ameritrust of Cincinnati,* 587 F.Supp. 896 (S.D. Ohio 1984) (a credit card holder has a cause of action against a card issuer who reports to a credit bureau that an account is delinquent after the account has been paid in full).

(18) 15 U.S.C. Sec. 1666 (a)(B)(ii); 12 C.F.R. Sec. 226.13(e).

(19) 12 C.F.R. Sec. 226.5. See also *Saunders v. Ameritrust of Cincinnati,* 587 F.Supp. 896 C.S.A. Ohio 1984.

(20) 12 C.F.R. Sec. 205.11(e)(2)(ii).

(21) 12 C.F.R. Secs. 226.13(d)(e), 226.13 fn.27, 15 U.S.C. 1666(d); see also *Gray v. American Express Co.,* 743 F.2d 10 (D.C. Cir. 1984) (contractual clause allowing card issuer to cancel account without cause or notice does not waive cardholder's rights under Fair Credit Billing Act).

(22) 12 C.F.R. Sec. 226.13(d) fn.30, and Sec. 226.13 fn.27.

(23) 15 U.S.C. Sec. 1666(i), 12 CFR Sec. 226.12(c).

(24) *Israelewitz v. Manufacturers Hanover Trust Company,* 465 NYS 2d 486, 488 (N.Y. City Ct. 1983).

(25) 12 C.F.R Sec. 226.12(c) *Weschitz v. American Express Co.,* 560 F.Supp. 458 (1983).

(26) 15 U.S.C. Sec. 1666(e)(i).

(27) 12 C.F.R. Sec. 226.13(b).

(28) 12 C.F.R. Sec. 226.13(g)(1-4).

(29) 12 C.F.R. Sec. 226.13(g)(4)(i).

(30) 12 C.F.R. Sec. 226.13(g)(3).

(31) 12 C.F.R. Sec. 226.13(g)(4)(i-iii).

(32) 12 C.F.R. Sec. 205.11(f)(2)(ii).

CHAPTER 20

EQUAL CREDIT OPPORTUNITY ACT (ECOA)

Congress intended the enactment of the Equal Credit Opportunity Act[1] (ECOA) primarily to benefit married women. At the time, some creditors would not extend credit to a married woman in her own right, even if she had ample income apart from her husband's income. These creditors refused, for example, to open charge accounts in a married woman's name. Some required her husband to open the account in his name; others required the couple to open a joint account in both their names. Finally, when a woman got over the initial hurdles, she often had to get her husband to cosign a note, loan, or whatever. Few of these burdens fell on married men, and single women often had an easier time of it than did their married counterparts.

The ECOA was appended to the Consumer Credit Protection Act in 1974. The act makes it unlawful for any creditor to discriminate or show any credit partiality against an applicant, with respect to any aspect of a credit transaction on the basis of race, color, religion, national origin, sex, marital status, or age (provided the applicant has the capacity to contract).[2] It also prohibits such adverse conduct against any applicant because all or part of his or her income is derived from public assistance (including social security) or because the applicant has in good faith exercised any right under the Consumer Credit Protection Act. The ECOA does not create a legal right to credit for anyone, just equal *access* to credit for everyone. The Equal Credit Opportunity Act governs *commercial* as well as consumer credit.

Note: At present, residence and geographic criteria have not been adopted federally, though some states have included such criteria in their TILA. There is activity at the congressional and FTC levels which might alter this. Be alert to this and review with your counsel.

The ECOA contains two separate sections for enforcement.[3] The first empowers 12 agencies to enforce the act's ban on discrimination. If you do business, one or more of the following is currently watching you.

- The Comptroller of the Currency;
- Board of Governors of the Federal Reserve System;
- Board of Directors of the Federal Deposit Insurance Corporation;
- Federal Home Loan Bank Board (acting directly or through the Federal Savings and Loan Insurance Corporation);
- Administrator of the National Credit Union Administration;
- Interstate Commerce Commission;
- Civil Aeronautics Board;
- Secretary of Agriculture;
- Farm Credit Administration;
- Securities and Exchange Commission;
- Small Business Administration;
- Federal Trade Commission.[4]

Each of the above has enforcement powers over the various creditors subject to its own regulatory authority. For example, the Federal Reserve Board, the Interstate Commerce Commission, and the Small Business Administration are empowered to enforce the ECOA against federal reserve banks, common carriers, and small business investment companies, respectively.

If you don't "fit in," the FTC enforces the act where you're concerned. The statute provides that the FTC shall enforce the ECOA "except to the extent that enforcement under the Act is specifically committed to some other government agency." This means the FTC is the "enforcer of last resort" for any creditor not clearly falling within the responsibility of any other agency.[5] So, plan on someone watching over your shoulder. What compliance issues are they concerned with? Here's a rundown.

The heart of the ECOA is a prohibition against credit discrimination in *any aspect* of a credit transaction. Examples include:

- Using discriminatory criteria in the credit evaluation decision.
- Discouraging applicants who are members of a protected group. Such protections bar discrimination based on race, color, religion, national origin, sex, marital status, and age (provided the applicant has the capacity to enter into a binding contract). Protection is also extended to applicants whose incomes derive entirely or in part from any public assistance program, and to applicants who have, in good faith, exercised any right under the Consumer Credit Protection Act.
- Imposing one or more onerous terms on a prohibited basis.
- Requiring cosigners on a prohibited basis (although cosigning may be permissible depending on your policy and the facts of the individual case).
- Failing to furnish adverse action notices to a rejected credit applicant.
- Failing to retain and report separate credit histories for married persons and other marital status issues.

Each of these prohibitions is covered in depth in this chapter. But first, a few key definitions and a discussion of your duty to comply.

What Is Credit? *Credit* means "the right granted by a creditor to an applicant to defer payment of a debt, incur debt and defer its payment, or purchase property or services and defer payment therefor."[6] You'll note this definition is a lot broader and more encompassing than those you've seen in the TILA topics. However, just as with the TILA, levying a fee for late payment does not bring you within the provisions of the ECOA either. A late payment, delinquency, default, reinstatement, or other such charge if imposed for actual unanticipated late payment, delinquency, default, or other such occurrence is not covered by the act.[7]

Who Is a Creditor? *"Creditor* means a person who, in the ordinary course of business, regularly participates in the decision of whether or not to extend credit. The term includes a creditor's assignee, transferee, or subrogee who so participates. For purposes of Sections 202.4 and 202.5(a), the term also includes a person who, in the ordinary course of business, regularly refers applicants or prospective applicants to creditors, or selects or offers to select creditors to whom request for credit may be made. A person is not a creditor regarding any violation of the act or this regulation committed by another creditor unless the person knew or had reasonable notice of the act, policy, or practice that constituted the violation before becoming involved in the credit transaction. The term does not include a person whose only participation in a credit transaction involves honoring a credit card."[8]

Who Is an Applicant? *"Applicant* means any person who requests or who has received an extension of credit from a creditor, and includes any person who is or may become contractually liable regarding an extension of credit. For purposes of Section 202.7(d), the term includes guarantors, sureties, endorsers, and similar parties." *Note:* This is a significant change. Under prior law, "applicant" included only the principal debtor or debtors; it did not include a guarantor, surety, endorser, or similar party. The practical effect is this: When a creditor violates Section 202.7 (d) by requiring a cosigner he or she should *not* have required, the cosigner as well as the principal debtor may recover damages from the creditor.

Must You Comply?

The ECOA sought to balance the often very real conflict between the rights of an applicant and the creditor's need to have discretion in making a credit decision. As a result of the balancing of interests and civil rights aspects of this law, the definitions and other key phrases may vary. Please read through carefully.

The ECOA requires *full* compliance from all creditors covered by the TILA. (Refer to Chapter 18 to determine if you must comply with

TILA.) Specialized treatment is afforded credit grantors who extend incidental credit to consumers or business credit for commercial purposes falling within any five categories.[9] This area has been amended from time to time, and you should update internal compliance with counsel. Creditors who fall within the limitations of this section should review carefully the extent to which Regulation B affects them. The five categories are:

- Public utility credit;[10]
- Securities credit transactions;[11]
- Credit transactions primarily for business or commercial purposes, including agricultural purposes;[12]
- Extensions of credit to governments or government agencies;[13]
- Incidental consumer credit transactions not involving credit card accounts or finance charges and not payable in more than four installments.[14]

The fifth category, comprising incidental consumer credit, is the one most likely to affect you if you are not covered by Truth-in-Lending. If it might, Section 202.3's definitions should be reviewed; specifically, "consumer credit," "credit," "creditor," and "extend credit."

The above sections read with Section 210(a) and 210(b) would define your inclusion as an incidental creditor under this act. It is important to note that the definition of "creditor" in this act may be broader than that of the TILA. It excludes a person who merely honors a credit card but nothing more. Check this out before you exempt yourself from compliance.

If your operations do exclude you from compliance, you're home free. If not, you are either an "incidental creditor" or a full creditor under the act. Either way, you should be aware of the prohibited areas to avoid and qualified areas to watch for (discussed later).

Incidental or Full Compliance?

Let's examine what the ECOA requires of an incidental or full creditor.

Incidental Creditor. If you fall into this category, you are effectively excluded from the more onerous sections of the ECOA we'll discuss. Essentially all that is left is the general rule prohibiting discrimination, which states that "a creditor shall not discriminate against an applicant on a prohibited basis regarding any aspect of a credit transaction" (i.e., race, color, religion, or any category mentioned).[15] However, one area not protected is that of the noncitizenship (alienage) of an applicant.[16] Here, the court made a point of noting that no showing was made that Vietnamese noncitizen aliens were less favorably treated than other groups of aliens. If such disparity existed, an argument for natural-origin discrimination *might* have existed. Otherwise, "neither the statute nor its legislative history shows an intent of Congress to proscribe the denial of credit on the ground of lack of citizenship. Moreover, the regulations promulgated pursuant to the Equal Credit Opportunity Act specifically provide that a creditor may take immigration status into account in evaluating a credit application."[17]

You should watch legislative developments in this area. There have been various efforts in Congress to amend this act's prohibited basis criteria to include residence and geographic location. If this takes place and you engage in address hits or zip code qualification criteria (see below), you may run into problems.

Further, as discussed, you may not make the existence of a telephone listing in your applicant's name or a specific telephone number a prerequisite for doing business.[18] Any question about a telephone listing or number is a red flag for a consumer agency. However, such a question may be labeled as "optional." (The number may be desired as intelligence for follow-up telephone marketing.) You may *ask* whether a telephone exists at the applicant's residence. (Creditors are leery of people with such shallow roots that they don't even have a telephone.) When you're done with the above, make sure you retain your records for a minimum of 25 months.

Finally, watch the laws of your state. Congress has steered clear of the states' traditional dominion in the area of property law and relations. The ECOA preempts only inconsistent state laws and only to the extent of the inconsistency. A state law is not inconsistent if it is more protective of the applicant.[19]

Full Compliance. If you're covered by the ECOA, but not as an incidental creditor, then you must undertake full compliance. Tight compliance is enforced both through the civil rights aspects discussed and through the authorization that the FTC has to enforce this act as if it were an FTC trade regulation rule.[20] Enforcement to date has resulted in stiff fines and penalties for alleged violations of the act.[21] The Justice Department also has been active in this area.[22] In addition to the fines (which are *not* deductible business expenses), the paperwork burden is considerable for all violators. In general, all fines are the result of alleged violations of the use of prohibited basis criteria (see further discussion below).

Now, let's see what you have to do (and avoid) to comply.

Prescreening Legal Exposure

Prohibited Areas. The determination of creditworthiness is singularly the most significant aspect of the credit extension process. A creditor may not make any oral or written statements in advertising or otherwise that would discourage on a prohibited basis a *reasonable* person from making or pursuing an application. You cannot permit any

of the following criteria to influence your process either in your
application forms or your interview with prospective applicants:

☐ You may not ask questions (orally or in your written forms) concerning
anything to do with an applicant's

- Race
- Color
- Religion
- National Origin
- Sex

☐ You may not ask questions referencing sex, such as titles of respect (Mr.,
Mrs., Miss, or Ms.). You are safest if you ask for just initials and a last
name. If you must for one reason or another place such titles on your
application form, you *must* state that such terms are optional. Otherwise
your application forms may include only sex-neutral terms. Courts have
indicated that where a violation is proven and the creditor has failed to
disclose the "optional" on the application, punitive damages and costs may
be recovered even when an applicant cannot prove actual damages. A
word to the wise: have each and every credit form you use reviewed by
your counsel.

☐ You must furnish separate credit histories for a husband and wife. Such
histories must stand separate and apart from each other. Therefore, avoid
credit criteria based on street address where the bad credit history of a
spouse could deny credit to another spouse with either no credit history or
a good credit rating.

☐ You may not discount an applicant's income on the basis of any of the
protected classes.

☐ You may not inquire into an applicant's birth control practices or family
plans, or use any similar criteria in your credit evaluation or credit-scoring
system.[23]

☐ You may not take the existence of a telephone listing in the applicant's
name as a valid criterion for evaluation in your credit-scoring system.[24]

Qualified Areas. These criteria can be used in credit evaluation, but
review all of them with counsel: (1) The presence of a telephone in the
applicant's home may be considered in the credit-scoring system and (2)
you may make limited inquiries into the applicant's age, marital status,
and receipt of public assistance benefits.

Age. Age can be a prohibited basis except when used to determine
whether the applicant is of the age of majority (that is, old enough to sign
binding, *not* voidable contracts). Usually this age is 18 or over, but the
law of each specific state should be reviewed. *Preference* to those 62
(defined as "elderly") or over is usually OK. Otherwise age is a
prohibited basis for various reasons. Many of those over 62 were the solid
citizens who paid as they went and never accepted credit. Now,
ironically, having no debts has hurt their credit history.[25] When they
apply for credit, many are on fixed incomes traceable to public sources,
unemployed, and prone to changing their residence after retirement

(having been "stable" homeowners, they become "transient" renters when they sell their homes).

Thus, you may not make an *arbitrary* credit decision based on age. You may use relevant statistical characteristics of a given age group provided that the age of an older applicant is not assigned a negative value.[26]

Public Assistance Income. This means any federal, state, or local government assistance program, including but *not limited to* Aid to Families with Dependent Children, food stamps, rent and mortgage supplement programs, Social Security, and unemployment compensation.[27] Unlike age, the applicant's receipt of public assistance income may not be used in any empirically derived credit system.

Marital Status. This is the big one. You must be particularly sensitive to what you do and don't ask about marital status, especially in a community property state. Even "innocent" things such as signature lines or courtesy titles can get you into trouble. You're not required to use any courtesy title even if it is supplied to you by your applicant.[28] You must grant individual credit to a creditworthy applicant who wants individual credit. It is a violation of the law to request that the spouse cosign the agreement *unless* the two spouses have applied for a joint credit.[29] Another limited exception is when state law requires the spouse's signature to create a valid lien to protect the creditor's security interest. The act expressly authorizes requests for the signature of the applicant's spouse on the security agreement when the spouse's signature is "reasonably believed by the creditor" to be necessary for a security interest free and clear of any claims the spouse may have on the collateral.[30]

"A request for the signature of both parties to a marriage for the purpose of creating a valid lien, passing clear title, waiving inchoate rights to property, or assigning earnings, shall not constitute discrimination under this subchapter. . . ."[31] This holds true even if the couple are currently separated and in the process of seeking a divorce.[32] However, keep in mind the creditor may not require the spouse's signature on the promissory note or installment sale contract, only on the security agreement.

A final exception is where the applicant does not qualify under the creditor's standards of credit worthiness for the amount in terms of the credit requested *but* could qualify if the other spouse signs on. [33] This situation fosters the congressional intent of making "credit equally available to all *creditworthy* customers without regard to sex or marital status." Here a creditor may only require a third party's signature on the credit instrument and may *not* require that the third party be the applicant's spouse. This election is for the applicant to decide individually.

Generally, it is not a violation to ask how many dependents an applicant has.[34] Further, to avoid problems with the marital status category, you must apply the same criteria to engaged couples (and possibly those simply living together) who apply for credit jointly (e.g., aggregate income) as you would married couples.[35]

Finally, don't put on the credit application any language implying that you will accept only one individual with the same last name from each address. This is "gender-neutral" as it is "first come, first served" and doesn't favor either spouse. However, this system will tend to discriminate against married individuals: when a married couple using the same last name applies for credit, one spouse would be denied credit that would be extended to both of two unmarried individuals living together.

Sensitivity as well as legal compliance with marital status, sex, and the other areas is good business and, as discussed later in this chapter, will save you from stiff penalties and damages. When in doubt, don't ask a creditworthy customer to get his or her spouse's signature on anything.

Even if you haven't directly utilized any overt discrimination against any of the protected classes, you run the risk of subtly discriminating, even inadvertently. One area of exposure you have to keep an eye on is zip codes. With nine-digit zip codes greatly segmenting your demographic pie, it is important that such codes are not used to "weed out" geographic areas on prohibited criteria.

Looking at Zip Codes

In most credit allocation systems, creditors take into account a number of elements; some are general standardized screening devices, but most are based on the creditor's own experience with others with whom an applicant shares certain key characteristics. Each criterion is weighed in accordance with the individual creditor's view of its importance to the credit-scoring decision.

One popular criterion today is a person's zip code (occasionally derogatorily referred to as a "surrogate for race"). An individual's zip code is considered to be a solid predicator of creditworthiness. With the advent of the nine-digit zip code, census tracts will provide even more useful credit applicant segmentation.

Although neutral on its face, use of zip codes in credit reporting *may* tend to lead to negative effects on a protected class. An obvious situation is the reality that races can be segmented or at least estimated by their addresses falling within certain zip codes due to the prevailing housing patterns in the United States. An interesting twist to this involved a case with Amoco Oil Company.[36] Amoco used a complex system to evaluate credit applications. It took into account 38 predictive and objective factors, including the applicant's level of income, occupation, and prior credit experience in the U.S. Postal Service zip code area where he or she resides.

Amoco received an application from a white female typesetter living in a predominantly nonwhite residential area of Atlanta. The applicant was denied credit in part because of Amoco's previous credit experience in her immediate geographical area, based on its use of zip code criteria. The woman argued that she was denied a credit card because of her residence. She alleged that the use of such zip code criteria was the equivalent of racial discrimination due to the segregated pattern of housing in the Atlanta area. Thus, her individual right to be evaluated on her own merit was denied.

The applicant argued that this policy disproportionately denied credit to blacks, members of a protected class. Amoco then proved a direct positive business purpose for the criterion (one of 38 used). The ECOA states that a statistically sound system must separate creditworthy from noncreditworthy applicants at a statistically significant rate (see below).[37]

Amoco effectively demonstrated that its zip code ratings did this, and did not tend to adversely affect black applicants disproportionately. Further, this geographic factor was more difficult to falsify than information about job or income, and since the ECOA prevented the company from asking about the race of the applicant, the company had no conscious idea or ability to create de facto discrimination by race in its rejections. Therefore, Amoco claimed, its credit scoring system for new applicants had no adverse intent or effect.

A lesson to learn from this is that, although your in-house system evidences no intent to discriminate, you must also carefully monitor *(at least annually)* the quantitative impact or effect on the various prohibited basis categories set forth in Regulation B. Here, you want the advice of your counsel and a statistician (preferably experienced in demographics) who can assist you in interpreting your numbers.

Finally, if you think all this sounds complex, you're right. The positive aspect of this complexity is that it will discourage private individuals from suing, since they are unlikely to possess the type of statistical analysis required to bring an effects test case.

Screening by Credit Scoring

Your applications pass the initial prescreening process. The regulations elaborate in detail upon what they want to see in your credit scoring system. They are directed largely at the perceived abuses once prevalent in judgmental methods of granting credit. Potential predictor characteristics are usually obtained from the application blank or an interview or both. The creditor sets cutoff values based on experience factors. One characteristic that is most often controlling is the zip code. Others often include occupation, whether applicants rent or own a home, length of time at such residence, etc.

The regs are quite clear on what they want you to demonstrate. You should read the following section carefully.

(1) *A credit scoring system* is a system that evaluates an applicant's creditworthiness mechanically, based on key attributes of the applicant and aspects of the transaction, and that determines, alone or in conjunction with an evaluation of additional information about the applicant, whether an applicant is deemed creditworthy. To qualify as an *empirically derived, demonstrably and statistically sound, credit scoring system,* the system must be:

(i) Based on data that are derived from an empirical comparison of sample groups or the population of creditworthy and noncreditworthy applicants who applied for credit within a reasonable preceding period of time;

(ii) Developed for the purpose of evaluating the creditworthiness of applicants with respect to the legitimate business interests of the creditor utilizing the system (including, but not limited to, minimizing bad debt losses and operating expenses in accordance with the creditor's business judgment);

(iii) Developed and validated using accepted statistical principles and methodology; and

(iv) Periodically revalidated by the use of appropriate statistical principles and methodology and adjusted as necessary to maintain predictive ability.

(2) A creditor may use an empirically derived, demonstrably and statistically sound, credit scoring system obtained from another person or may obtain credit experience from which to develop such a system. Any such system must satisfy the criteria set forth in paragraph (p) (1)(i) through (iv) of this section; if the creditor is unable during the development process to validate the system based on its own credit experience in accordance with paragraph (p) (1) of this section, the system must be validated when sufficient credit experience becomes available. A system that fails this validity test is no longer an empirically derived, demonstrably and statistically sound, credit scoring system for that creditor.[38]

As we'll discuss shortly, if your prescreening or rejection is challenged, you'll have to survive the "effects test." To best insulate yourself from a successful challenge, make sure you've reviewed your quantitative system for all subjective bias that could be built into the predicators. For example, your profile population criteria are based on a sample pool, which may weigh against certain protected classes. Past discrimination against minorities can be perpetuated by an overemphasis on rental v. ownership. Length of employment will discriminate against those who've only recently had access to certain jobs or to women who lost time in the work force because of pregnancy or raising children. In a quantitative vacuum, your samples may look good, but you should broaden and reevaluate your sample size to better survive a challenge.

Now, let's review the criteria on which you would be challenged. First, was your rejection in proper form? Second, did your rejection violate any rights of an individual in protected class?

Specific Reasons for Adverse Action

The statute defines adverse action in very broad terms:

. . ."adverse action" means a denial or revocation of credit, a change in the terms of an existing credit arrangement, or a refusal to grant credit in substantially the amount or on substantially the terms requested. . . ."[39]

The definition of adverse action was narrowed by the Federal Reserve Board in Regulation B:

(c) Adverse action. (1) For the purposes of notification of action taken, statement of reasons for denial, and record retention, the term means:

(i) A refusal to grant credit in substantially the amount or on substantially the terms requested by an applicant unless the creditor offers to grant credit other than in substantially the amount or on substantially the terms requested by the applicant and the applicant uses or expressly accepts the credit offered.[40]

The law requires that "each applicant against whom adverse action is taken shall be entitled to a statement of the reasons for such action from the creditor."[41] The act expects you to be quite specific concerning the reasons for the denial. If the terms are modified, state this, too.[42] Your notice must be timely and as follows:

(d) (1) Within thirty days (or such longer reasonable time as specified in regulations of the Board for any class of credit transaction) after receipt of a completed application for credit, a creditor shall notify the applicant of its action on the application.

(2) Each applicant against whom adverse action is taken shall be entitled to a statement of reasons for such action from the creditor. A creditor satisfies this obligation by —

(A) providing statements of reasons in writing as a matter of course to applicants against whom adverse action is taken; or

(B) giving written notification of adverse action which discloses (i) the applicant's right to a statement of reasons within thirty days after receipt by the creditor of a request made within sixty days after such notification, and (ii) the identity of a person or office from which such statement may be obtained. Such statement may be given orally if the written notification advises the applicant of his right to have the statement of reasons confirmed in writing on written request.

(3) A statement of reasons meets the requirements of this section only if it contains the specific reasons for the adverse action taken.[43]

There is a reason for all this detail. The legislative history of the 1976 amendments to the ECOA is particularly instructive in construing the congressional intent behind the passage of the act:

> The requirement that creditors give reasons for adverse action is, in the Committee's view, a strong and necessary adjunct to the antidiscrimination purpose of the legislation, for *only if creditors know they must explain their decisions will they effectively be discouraged from discriminatory practices. Yet this requirement fulfills a broader need*: rejected credit applicants will now be able to learn where and how their credit status is deficient and this information should have a pervasive and valuable educational benefit. Instead of being told only that they do not meet a particular creditor's standards, consumers particularly should benefit from knowing, for example, that the reason for the denial is their short residence in the area, or their recent change of employment, or their already overextended financial situation. In those cases where the creditor may have acted on misinformation or inadequate information, the statment of reasons gives the applicant a chance to rectify the mistake.[44]

Once a creditor is apprised of the error, he or she is obliged to correct it.

When you deny a young homeowner a new car loan, you need more than "credit references are insufficient." You had better specify the material relied on and the name and address of any credit bureau(s) utilized.[45] "Your past payment record" is OK if a firm is relying on its in-house records with a former customer. Just make sure your response is sufficiently lucid that your applicant need not "speculate" on the reasons for the denial.[46] If you fail to satisfy the notice requirements you are in violation of the ECOA regardless of whether you've actually engaged in any prohibited discriminatory conduct![47]

Further, make sure you're correct in everything you say. One firm established a credit-scoring system based on various factors. When denied credit (including the right to defer payment), an applicant would receive notice that credit was denied. He or she could then inquire into the specifics of the denial. Often, the reasons given in response to these queries were incorrect. Certain specific reasons for denial, such as the geographic area in which the applicant lived, determined by a zip code (a principal reason for taking adverse action against an applicant), were *never* disclosed. The FTC alleged that the firm violated the Equal Credit Opportunity Act. The civil penalty payment provided for by the resulting consent order was the largest to that date to involve either the ECOA or an FTC trade regulation rule.[48]

Finally, one last argument for truth is that almost any forum tolls the statute of limitations. Read into every federal statute of limitations . . .is the equitable doctrine that in case of [a creditor's] fraud or deliberate concealment of material facts relating to [the creditor's] wrongdoing, time does not begin to run until [the aggrieved person] discovers, or by reasonable diligence could have discovered, the basis of the lawsuit.[49]

The Effects Test

The following is one of the significant footnotes in the ECOA: "The legislative history of the Act indicates that the Congress intended an 'effects test' concept, as outlined in the employment field by the Supreme Court in the cases of *Griggs v. Duke Power Co*. . . .and *Albemarle Paper Co. v. Moody* . . . to be applicable to a creditor's determination of creditworthiness.[50] (This concept is similar to that approved by the Supreme Court for use in employment law cases.) The "effects test" deals with the information that may be requested in connection with an application for credit. If you fall into the category of creditor, you should be aware that the test for discrimination is the *use* of information. The coverage provided by the ECOA includes not only discriminatory motivation but also the discriminatory effects of facially neutral actions. Thus, there is no requirement that the creditor *intends* to discriminate, and applicants do not have to prove any motive to do so. The effects test, developed in employment discrimination law (although a slightly more lenient standard, as discussed below)[51] is incorporated into this act; the use of an otherwise neutral criterion may be illegal if it has a discriminatory impact and is not justified by business necessity.

The test requires that the plaintiff show that your credit policy criterion under attack hurts protected applicants (such as blacks and married couples) in disproportionately greater numbers than other applicants (such as whites and singles). The disproportionate numbers are "proof" of the "effect" of your intent to discriminate, and the burden is now on you to prove that the criteria were neutral as to the protected categories and that effect is accidental.

To bring an action, the aggrieved party must make out a prima facie case of discrimination, i.e., by showing that

- he or she belongs to a protected group;
- he or she applied for credit and was creditworthy;
- despite his or her qualifications, he or she was rejected; and
- after the applicant's rejection, others not in the protected group were accepted.

Yet, submission of proof on these four elements gives rise to only a rebuttable presumption of discriminatory intent. The defendant need only produce a basis other than discriminatory intent (i.e., all requirements have a manifest relationship to the creditworthiness of the applicant) to rebut that presumption. The burden then falls again on the plaintiff to show pretextual discrimination.[52]

The ECOA, unlike some other consumer protection laws such as the Truth-in-Lending Act, requires more than just that the creditor follow black letter rules. The ECOA proscribes not only overt discrimination but also practices that are fair in form but discriminatory in operation.

Consumer Remedies

How costly to the creditor is a finding of a violation of ECOA? Since the FTC is charged with the ECOA's overall enforcement, a violation of the ECOA is a violation of the FTC Act.[53] An applicant may also seek private enforcement (actual and punitive damages up to $10,000 per aggrieved individual) or a class action. Similar to the Fair Debt Collection Practices Act (reviewed in chapter 23), the aggrieved applicant may sue in any federal or state court of competent jurisdiction regardless of the amount in question.[54] Certain equitable relief is also available. It is even possible for the rejected applicant to recover for embarrassment, humiliation, and mental distress, plus damages to reputation and creditworthiness.[55] In any of these legal actions, the applicant is entitled to a trial by jury.[56] Last but not least, the resulting bad publicity may hurt your bottom line as well as current and possibly future marketing efforts. Following are the major forms of relief in detail.

Actual Damages may include out-of-pocket monetary losses, injury to credit reputation, and mental anguish, humiliation, or embarrassment.[57] All actual damages must be specifically proven.

Punitive Damages comprise the second type of relief available to the plaintiff under the ECOA. This is potentially the most ominous area. The act states that any creditor "who fails to comply with any requirement imposed under this subchapter shall be liable to the aggrieved applicant for punitive damages in an amount not greater than $10,000, in addition to any actual damages provided [elsewhere in this] section."[58] However, punitive damages may be awarded even without the showing of actual damages.

The act specifies certain factors to be considered when determining the appropriateness of punitive damages. The court is directed to consider all relevant factors, including "the amount of any actual damages awarded, the frequency and persistency of failures of compliance by the creditor, the resources of the creditor, the number of persons adversely affected, and the extent to which the creditor's failure of compliance was intentional.

Although the traditional word "punitive" is used, one of the factors to be considered is whether the creditor's noncompliance was intentional. This suggests that the courts are allowed to award punitive damages under Section 1691e(b) even when the creditor's conduct is not wanton, malicious, or oppressive, in order to increase the incentive for creditor compliance. This incentive is particularly appropriate when actual damages are difficult to prove. However, since punitive damages are awarded to punish the defendant and to serve as an example or warning to others not to engage in similar conduct, they are justified only when the defendant has committed a particularly blameworthy act.

Consequently, punitive damages may be awarded pursuant to the act if (1) the creditor wantonly, maliciously, or oppressively discriminates against an applicant, or (2) the creditor acts in "reckless disregard of the requirements of the law," even though there was no specific intention to discriminate on unlawful grounds. This determination is to be made by considering all the relevant factors, particularly those listed in the statute itself.[59]

Attorneys' Fees comprise the third type of relief available to the appellant under the ECOA. The applicable provision states that if there is a successul action under Section 1691e(a), (b), or (c), then the "costs of the action, together with a reasonable attorney's fee. . .shall be added to any damages awarded by the court. . ."[60] Thus, attorneys' fees are available only if there has been a "successful action," whether the success lies in obtaining actual or punitive damages, or injunctive or declaratory relief.

The size of the attorney's fee is to be determined by the court. The court will consider all the relevant factors on a case-by-case basis, including the amount of damages awarded, the number of past and future consumers affected by the creditor's discrimination, the complexity of the litigation, and the time expended. Plaintiffs who cause a creditor to halt an illegal practice should be compensated for their attorneys' fees.

Equitable Relief may include

- An *injunction* forbidding any breaches of the law in the future and telling the creditor what he or she must do to comply. This is available only where damages are too speculative or there is a need for an immediate remedy.
- *Consumer redress,* including things such as rescission of a contract, reformation of a contract, and the refund of money and return of property. The FTC, or the Attorney General, acting at the request of the FTC[61] (on his or her own initiative)[62] may bring against a creditor who has violated the ECOA a kind of class action on behalf of all the individuals aggrieved by the creditor's violations. But there is good news for those who are regulated by some administrative agency other than the FTC: No other governmental agency charged with enforcing ECOA may seek this remedy. The latter point was constitutionally challenged, but this challenge failed. [63]

The plaintiff complained that, of the 12 agencies given enforcement powers, only five have authority to seek civil penalties and only one, the FTC, has the authority to seek consumer redress. (The five agencies are the Federal Home Loan Bank Board, the Interstate Commerce Commission, the Secretary of Transportation (formerly was the Federal Aviation Administration), the Secretary of Agriculture, and the Federal Trade Commission.) Moreover, the size of the penalties varies from $100 to $20,000 per violation.

In holding against the plaintiff, the Court emphasized the vigor and diversity of targeted enforcement Congress intended:

> [Plaintiff's] argument that a statute cannot impose different penalties on different kinds of business enterprises engaged in the same activity has been consistently rejected by the courts and loses even more force in light of the varying characteristics that businesses engaged in the same basis activities might possess. . . .the ECOA enforcement scheme rests on the rational basis that compliance could best be achieved by subjecting each business to the enforcement mechanisms to which it was already subject through the regulatory control exercised by its primary regulatory agency. . . .It was hoped that the specialized expertise of these agencies could best be used in the enforcement of the ECOA.[64]

To prepare for any legal eventuality, the creditor must maintain certain records of each transaction: application forms, copy of notification of action taken and reasons for it, as well as any written statements disputing the decision filed by the applicant.[65]

Some Final Thoughts

The Equal Credit Opportunity Act is more understandable than others because it is based on "newspaper law," that is, the obvious, straightforward, nonesoteric legal debate you've witnessed unfolding and accelerating since the late 1950s.

Each person is uniquely different and must be considered for any granted credit solely on the basis of individual merit. Treat each as uniquely as a snowflake! You may not legally base your decisions concerning a particular credit applicant on your general experiences with persons sharing a characteristic of the applicant, whether it's race, sex, religion, address, or other prohibited criterion.

Although many managers will fall into the category of incidental creditors, be careful to understand the prohibited bases for discrimination as well as to refrain from requesting telephone numbers on ad copy unless the ad copy request specifically states "optional" and the answer, if given, does not impact the decision to extend credit.

The manager should remain vigilant at the state and federal levels to prevent the enactment of zip code and residence restrictions that would adversely affect lists in general and compiled lists in particular. (See discussions of how to systematically monitor such legislation in Chapter 24.) You might order the FTC's easy-to-read outline on point[66] or get on the Federal Reserve's mailing list.[67]

Even the best-intentioned firm may be at risk of violating the law if its application for credit is worded in a way that tends to discourage a particular group from applying. Again, counsel should read all "public" documents as well as all internal credit-granting criteria. The test of equal credit opportunity—at every stage of the process, from application through final notification to the applicant— revolves around the question: Have the avenues of acceptance been opened equally to all?

ENDNOTES

(1) 15 U.S.C. Sec. 1691 et seq., and its implementing regulations, 12 CFR Sec. 202 et seq. Also known as Regulation B, this was an amendment to the Truth-in-Lending Act.

(2) 15 U.S.C. Sec. 1691(a) (1-3).

(3) Section 704, 15 Sec. U.S.C. 1691(c) and Section 706, 15 USC Sec.1691(e).

(4) U.S.C. Sec. 1691, 12 C.F.R. Sec. 202.1(b).

(5) Section 704(c), 15 U.S.C. Sec. 1691c(c).

(6) 12 C.F.R. Sec. 202.2(j). As to whether leases of personal property are "credit," see Informal FTC Staff Opinion, 2/1/84, and *Brothers v. First Leasings,* 724 F.2d 789 (1984). As to whether and when debit cards are covered, see *Dunn v. American Express Co.,* 529 F.Supp. 633 (Colo. 1982).

(7) *Bright v. Ball Memorial Hospital Association,* 463 F.Supp. 152, 154 (S.D. Ind. 1979).

(8) 12 C.F.R. Sec. 202.2(1).

(9) 15 U.S.C. Sec. 1691(b), 12 C.F.R. Sec. 202.2(e). See also *Delta Diversified, Inc. v. Citizens & Southern National Bank,* 320 SE2d 767 (Ga. App. 1984); *Morse v. Mutual Federal Savings and Loan Association,* 536 F.Supp. 1271 (1982).

(10) 12 C.F.R. Sec. 202.3(a)(1).

(11) 12 C.F.R. Sec. 202.3(b).

(12) 12 C.F.R. Sec. 202.3(d).

(13) 12 C.F.R. Sec. 202.3(e).

(14) 12 C.F.R. Sec. 202.3(c) (1-2).

(15) 12 C.F.R. Sec. 202.4.

(16) *Nguyen v. Montgomery Ward & Co.,* 513 F.Supp. 1039 (1981).

(17) Id. p. 1040. See also *Espinoza v. Farah Manufacturing Co., Inc.,* 414 US 86, 94 S.Ct. 334, 38 L.Ed. 2d 287 (1973).

(18) 12 C.F.R. Sec. 202.6(b) (4).

(19) 15 U.S.C. Sec. 1691(d) (f); 12 C.F.R. Sec. 202.11(a).

(20) Two good articles on point are Capon, Noel, "Discrimination in Screening Credit Applicants," *Harvard Business Review,* May-June 1978, p. 76, and Capon, Noel, "Credit Ratings and Right," *Washington Post,* December 17, 1977.

(21) 15 U.S.C. Sec. 1671(d), 12 C.F.R. Sec. 704(c).

(22) See, e.g., *In re Aldens, Inc.,* 92 FTC 901 (1978) and 12 C.F.R. Sec. 202(b) (2).

(23) 12 C.F.R. Sec. 202.5(d) (4).

(24) 12 C.F.R. Sec. 202.6(b) (4).

(25) Certain evidence suggests that older applicants are more likely to repay than similarly situated younger ones. 12 C.F.R. Sec. 202.6(b) (2) (iv).

(26) 12 C.F.R. Sec. 202.6(b) (2) (ii).

(27) 12 C.F.R. Sec. 202.2(aa).

(28) *Harlough v. Continental Illinois National Bank & Trust Co.,* 615 F.2d 1169 (1980).

(29) *Cragin v. First Federal Savings and Loan Association,* 498 F. Supp. 379 (D.C. Nev. 1980).

(30) *Anderson v. United Finance Co.,* 666 F.2d 1274, 1276-77 and n.1 (9th Cir. 1982).

(31) 15 U.S.C. Sec. 1691(d) (a).

(32) *McKenzie v. U.S. Home Corp.,* 704 F.2d 778, 779 (1983).

(33) *Miller v. Elegant Junk,* 616 F.Supp. 551 (D.C. W. Va. 1985).

(34) But see *Cragin v. First Federal Savings and Loan Association,* 498 F.Supp. 379 (D.C. Nev. 1980).

(35) *Hess v. Fair Employment & Housing Commission,* 187 Cal. Rptr.712 (App. 1982). This area may be getting too far-fetched.: See "Credit Without Benefit of Clergy," *Consumer Credit and Truth-in-Lending Compliance Report,* vol. 10, no. 3, 1979, p. 1. The article discusses an unofficial FRT ECOA staff interpretation possibly suggesting that credit card issuers should give equal consideration to marriage and living-together arrangements. See also *Markham v. Colonial Mortgage Serv. Co. Assoc.,* 605 F.2d 566 (1979).

(36) *Claire Cherry v. Amoco Oil Co.,* 490 F.Supp.1026 (N.D. Ga. 1980). Eventually Amoco agreed to settle by discontinuing the use of a zip code or any other geographic unit smaller than the individual's state in detemining creditworthiness. The company also had to pay a stiff civil fine of $200,000 as part of the consent agreement. See also Capon, Noel, "Credit Scoring Systems: A Critical Analysis," *Journal of Marketing,* Spring 1982, p.41.

(37) 12 C.F.R. Sec. 202.2(p)(2).

(38) 12 C.F.R. Sec. 202.2(p)(1-2).

(39) 15 U.S.C. Sec. 1691(d)(6).

(40) 12 C.F.R. Sec. 202.2(c)(1-2). See also *Jockum v. Pico Credit Corp. of Westbury, Inc.,* 730 F.2d 1041 (1984).

(41) 15 U.S.C. Sec. 1691(d)(26) (emphasis added).

(42) *Dorsey v. Citizens & Southern Fin. Corp.,* 678 F.2d 137 (11th Cir., 1982), 12 C.F.R. Sec. 202.2(c)(1)(i).

(43) 15 U.S.C. Sec. 1691(d)(1-3).

(44) 1976 U.S. Code Cong. & Admin. News, p. 406 (emphasis added).

(45) *Fischl v. General Motors Acceptance Corp.,* 708 F.2d 143 (5th Cir. 1983), 12 C.F.R. Sec.202.9(b)(2) and ECOA Sec. 701(d)(3).

(46) *O'Dowd v. South Central Bell,* 729 F.2d 347 (5th Cir. 1984), 15 U.S.C. Sec. 1691(d)(3), 12 C.F.R. Secs.202.9(a)(2)(i), 202.9(b)(2); ECOA Sec. 701(d)(3).

(47) *Carroll v. Exxon Corp., U.S.A.,* 434 F.Supp. 557 (1977); *Sayers v. GMAC,* 522 F.Supp. 835 (1981).

(48) *United States v. Montgomery Ward & Co.,* No. 79-140 (D.D.C. 1979). Although not admitting guilt, Montgomery Ward agreed to do the following:

- Pay $175,000 in civil damages.
- Contact every applicant who had been denied credit since March 23, 1977, and had inquired as to the rejection. Such applicants would be informed that Montgomery Ward may have failed to comply with the Equal Credit Opportunity Act, provided with an FTC pamphlet informing them of their rights under the act, and invited to reapply for credit.
- Provide all applicants denied credit in the future with *specific* reasons for credit denial (e.g., age, number of dependents, rent).
- Make available to the FTC *all* credit-scoring records for the next 10 years.
- *Not* consider zip codes or any other geographic unit in evaluating future credit applications.

(49) *Fitzgerald v. Seamans,* 533 F.2d 220, 228 (D.C. Cir. 1977). See also *Birkett Williams Ford, Inc. v. East Woodworking Co.,* 456 NE2d 1304, 1307 (Ohio Ct. App. 1982), ECOA Sec. 706(f), 15 U.S.C. Sec 1691e(f).

(50) 12 C.F.R. Sec 202.9(o) n.7.

(51) The so-called effects test is derived from the decision of the U.S. Supreme Court in *Griggs v. Duke Power Co.,* 401 U.S. 424 (1971). Here, a high-school diploma was required for employment—the effect being to exclude a significantly greater percentage of black applicants. The Supreme Court stated that title VII (42 U.S.C Sec. 2000) not only proscribes intentionally discriminatory conduct but also looks to the consequences of conduct, whether or not the intent to discriminate is present. If the *effect* is discriminatory, it becomes the employer's burden to show that the job requirement was related to job performance. *Note:* of all the credit statutes enforced by the FTC, the ECOA is enforced the most vigorously precisely because of its civil rights background.

(52) *Lieberman v. Gant,* 630 F.2d 60, 65 (1980). See also *Williams v. First Federal Savings,* 554 F.Supp.447, 449 (1981).

(53) 15 U.S.C. Sec. 1691c(c).

(54) 15 U.S.C. Secs. 1691e(a), 1691e(c), and 1691e(f).

(55) *Schuman v. Standard Oil Co. of Cal.,* 453 F.Supp. 1150 (N.D. Ca. 1978) and *Sayers v. GMAC,* 522 F.Supp. 835 (1981).

(56) *Vander Missen v. Kellogg-Citizens National Bank of Green Bay,* 83 FRD 206 (1979).

(57) *Anderson v. United Finance Co.,* 666 F.2d 1274, 1277 (1982).

(58) 15 U.S.C. Sec. 1691(e)(b). See also *Schuman v. Standard Oil Co. of Cal.,* 453 F.Supp 1150 (N.D. Ca. 1978).

(59) Note 57, 1278.

(60) 15 U.S.C. Sec. 1691(e)(d).

(61) *U.S. v. Landmark Fin. Serv., Inc.,* 612 F.Supp. 623, 626 (Md. 1985); ECOA Sec. 704(c); 15 U.S.C. Sec. 1691(c).

(62) ECOA Sec. 706(h); 15 U.S.C. Sec. 1691e(h). See also *U.S. Beneficial Corp.,* 492 F.Supp. 682 (N.J. 1980), *aff'd* 673 F.2d 1302 (3d Cir. 1981).

(63) Note 61, p. 629.

(63) Id., p. 630.

(65) 12 C.F.R. Sec. 202.12.

(66) Equal Credit Opportunity Act, Federal Trade Commission, Equal Opportunity, Washington, D.C., 20580.

(67) Write to the Secretary, Board of Governors of the Federal Reserve System, Washington D.C. 20551. Refer to specific items by number.

CHAPTER 21
FAIR CREDIT REPORTING ACT

It's a fact of life that more and more information is being collected about individuals. For some, this constant computerization of credit and personal information raises the specter of an Orwellian nightmare where an individual's activities and even thoughts may be stored in someone's computer creating an objective or (even worse) subjective profile. This social tension will definitely increase. Once, you could follow Horace Greeley's advice and "go West" to make your fortune and, just as important, to escape your identity or past. The West was our equivalent of the foreign legion on a large scale. Now you can't escape your past, social security number, nor any of the other myriad indicia that bind us to our past.

Fingerprinting and the assignment of social security numbers set the stage to end all escape. What was lacking was the system to collect and instantly retrieve various files about a person. Now the computer offers this ability and has eliminated even the privacy potentially available through the haphazard collection of files.

As personal data is compressed, so is the individual's breadth of privacy and, potentially, freedom. If you have a charge account, home mortgage or life insurance policy, or have applied for a personal loan or a job, it is almost certain that somewhere there is a file that shows how promptly you pay your bills, whether you have been sued or arrested, or you have filed for bankruptcy. Such a file may include your neighbors' and friends' views of your character, general reputation, or manner of living. More insidiously, the information might be inaccurate or dated. Personal, targeted database marketing by its very nature requires the retention of as much relevant data about a customer as possible. This building, maintaining, and enriching the database of your customers now constitutes the leading debate in this channel.

Anyone who believes this debate will die should review the tremendous outpouring of public response concerning the proposed 10% withholding on interest earned in savings accounts, during the formative stages of the 1982 tax bill. All polls clearly demonstrated that the people flooding the Congress with letters, postcards and petitions perceived this to be a privacy issue. We can expect similar outpouring of privacy sentiment in related areas.

People care about the privacy (and accuracy) of their financial records. These people are your customers. Commercial data which is coded is clearly distinguishable from individual files maintained by public and quasi-public institutions.

In this chapter, we'll examine an information regulation law that has stood the test of time. The Fair Credit Reporting Act (FCRA)[1] became effective in 1971. It remains one of the few federal laws to regulate the collection and use of personal information in the private sector. It was passed by Congress to protect individuals against the dissemination, maintenance, circulation, or retention of inaccurate or obsolete credit information and to ensure that consumer reporting agencies adopt fair and equitable procedures for obtaining, maintaining, and disseminating information about consumers.[2] It also gives the individual the right to dispute the information in his or her file[3] and, where unsuccessful in having the disputed information removed, to have his or her own explanation included in the file as well.[4]

You should be interested in this law because of its potential effect on customer lists and, of course, because it is important to you *personally.* It is the vehicle by which you can effectively protect your credit reputation, which is extremely valuable to you in almost every aspect of your involvement in commercial America.

Compliance with this act turns on a precise reading of a number of definitions. Besides their literal wording, this section takes a look at how the courts are interpreting them.

Definitions You Should Know

As with most laws, the words and definitions you use must be precise.

Three key definitions are absolutely essential to your understanding of the FCRA: the definitions of "consumer report," and the definition as to what constitutes permissible purposes of reports.

At the heart of the FCRA is the term *consumer report,* which means:

"any written, oral, or other communication of any information by a consumer reporting agency bearing on a *consumer's* credit worthiness, credit standing, credit capacity, character, general reputation, personal characteristics, or mode of living which is used or expected to be used or collected *in whole or in part* for the purpose of serving as a *factor* in establishing the consumer's eligibility for

- credit or insurance to be used primarily for personal, family, or household purposes, or
- employment, or
- other purposes authorized under section 604 (15 USC 1681b)."

"The term does not include (a) any report containing information solely as to transactions or experiences between the consumer and the person making the report; (b) any authorization or approval of a specific extension of credit directly or indirectly by the issuer of a credit card or similar device; or (c) any report in which a person who has been requested by a third party to make a specific extension of credit directly or indirectly to a consumer conveys his decision with respect to such request, if the third party advises the consumer of the name and address of the person to whom the request was made and such person makes the disclosures to the consumer required under section 615 [16 USC 1681m]."[5]

A report on a natural person is a consumer report, and therefore governed by the FCRA, if either of the following is true:

(a) The one who ordered the report will use it to evaluate the subject's application for consumer credit, consumer insurance, a job, or one of the other consumer purposes,[6] or

(b) the agency disseminating the report originally collected the information for use in evaluating the subject's application for consumer credit, consumer insurance, a job, or one of the other consumer purposes.[7] What are a few examples of reports not governed by the FCRA?

- reports solely as to business or *commercial* transactions;[8]
- reports as to the "professional rating" of individuals;[9] or
- in response to a grand jury subpoena.[10]

Distinguishable from a consumer report is the term *investigative consumer report,* which means a consumer report or portion thereof in which information on a consumer's character, general reputation, personal characteristics, or mode of living is obtained through personal interviews with neighbors, friends, or associates of the consumer reported on or with others with whom she or he is acquainted or who may have knowledge concerning any such items of information.

However, such information shall not include specific factual information on a consumer's credit record obtained directly from a creditor of the consumer or from a consumer reporting agency when such information was obtained directly from a creditor of the consumer or from the consumer.[11]

If you're involved with the above you may be or may become a *consumer reporting agency,* which means any person that, for monetary fees or dues, or on a cooperative nonprofit basis, *regularly engages in whole or in part* in the practice of assembling or evaluating consumer credit information or other information on consumers for the purpose of *furnishing consumer reports to third parties,* and that uses any means or facility of interstate commerce for the purpose of preparing or furnishing consumer reports.[12]

Whether or not your firm operates for profit and whether this reporting constitutes a major part of your business has no bearing on determining whether you may be considered a consumer reporting agency. Most if not all law enforcement agencies would be excluded.[13] A consumer reporting agency may furnish a consumer report under the following circumstances *and no other:*

- In response to the order of a court having jurisdiction to issue such an order.
- In accordance with the written instructions of the consumer to whom it relates.
- To a person which it has reason to believe intends to use the information in any of the following ways or *otherwise has a legitimate business need for the information in connection with a business transaction involving the consumer.*[14]

(a) in connection with a credit transaction involving the consumer on whom the information is to be furnished and involving the extension of credit to, or review or collection of an account of that consumer's; or

(b) for employment purposes; or

(c) in connection with the underwriting of insurance involving the consumer; or

(d) in connection with a determination of the consumer's eligibility for a license or other benefit granted by a governmental instrumentality required by law to consider an applicant's financial responsibility or status.

Getting the Information You Want While Avoiding Problems With the FTC

Administrative enforcement to police credit-reporting agencies and all persons subject to the FCRA (but not lenders)[15] rests primarily with the FTC.[16]

For example, a firm may request, for its own use, information from another business concerning its dealings with a *particular* customer. As long as the original firm limits the use of the information received from the other business to its own application and does not disseminate it to third parties, it will not become a consumer reporting agency.[17] The act of seeking credit information from other businesses might appear to be "assembling or evaluating" consumer credit information; however, as long as the information is strictly for the firm's own use, such assembling or evaluating cannot be said to be for the purpose of furnishing consumer reports to third parties.[18]

Those that request and use reports have the easier role in the relationship. A consumer reporting agency must jump through a number of legal hoops; these are highlighted here.

Compliance Procedures

(1) Every consumer reporting agency must maintain reasonable procedures to ensure accuracy and to limit the furnishing of consumer reports to the purposes listed above. These procedures shall require that prospective users of the information identify themselves, certify the purposes for which the information is sought, and certify that the information will be used for no other purpose. Every consumer reporting agency shall make a *reasonable* effort to *verify* the identity of a new prospective user and the *uses* certified by such prospective user prior to furnishing such user a consumer report. No consumer reporting agency may furnish a consumer report to any person if it has reasonable grounds for believing that the consumer report will not be used for a permissible purpose.[19]

(2) Whenever a consumer reporting agency prepares a consumer report it shall follow reasonable procedures to ensure maximum possible accuracy of the information concerning the individual about whom the report relates.[20]

(3) Certain types of information may not be kept forever in the credit bureau's file. Most unfavorable credit information must be removed after seven years. Information concerning a bankruptcy must be removed from a person's file after 10 years.[21]

If you don't do the above (and more, which is reviewed below) you may have the consumer and possibly an administrative agency coming after you.

Now, some good news.

There is no right to inquire into the reasonableness of a credit reporting agency's procedures if it is demonstrated at the outset that the report in question is in fact true, even if the procedures in putting the report together left something to be desired.[22] In order to pursue a cause of action predicated on the FCRA, the credit report sought to be challenged must be inaccurate.[23]

There is *no automatic liability* merely because inaccurate information is contained in a credit report. Liability attaches only if the inaccuracy in a report is the result of a failure to follow reasonable procedures to assure the maximum possible accuracy of the information contained therein.[24]

You are not required to erase valuable information, merely to update it. For example, if a credit bureau includes the unpaid debt in the consumer's file, the consumer may require the credit bureau to also include the fact of discharge. However, he or she may not require the credit bureau to omit the debt and its discharge. The fact that the consumer did not pay is still information bearing on his or her creditworthiness. Consequently, the credit bureau may lawfully report it.[25]

You are not strictly liable for your inaccurate credit reports but must use reasonable care in their preparation; the standard of conduct by which a trier of fact must judge the adequacy of agency procedures is what a reasonably prudent person would do under the circumstances.[26]

Finally there is a flexible cost/benefit test presented in evaluating systems. The court, in determining whether a violation has occurred, would weigh the potential that the information will create a misleading impression against the availability of more accurate (or complete) information and the burden of providing such information. Clearly, the more misleading the information (i.e., the greater the harm it can cause the consumer) and the more easily available the clarifying information, the greater the burden on the consumer reporting agency to provide this clarification. Conversely, if the misleading information is of relatively insignificant value, a consumer reporting agency should not be required to take on a burdensome task in order to discover or provide additional or clarifying data, and it should not be penalized under this section if the procedures used are otherwise reasonable.[27]

In conclusion, a credit reporting agency has a fair degree of statutory and case law leeway so long as it has solid in-place procedures. But here are some cautions to bear in mind:

The FCRA requires vigilant updating procedures, because the preparation of a consumer report should be viewed as a continuing process with the obligation to insure accuracy with every additional item of information. If you fail to demonstrate this, especially as to matters you had actual knowledge of, you'll lose.[28]

You must have in place reinvestigation procedures that can follow up on consumer complaints. The standard of care can range from "not fundamentally incomplete"[29] to "maximum possible accuracy."[30] The more valuable the information the greater the standard of care required.[31] Merely making a few follow-up calls is not a system designed to ensure maximum possible accuracy.[32]

You must promptly delete misleading information. For example (see ECOA discussion in chapter 20), once a consumer reporting agency is on notice that a spouse's credit history does not reflect on the applicant's creditworthiness such information must be deleted.[33]

Special Compliance Procedures Involving Investigative Consumer Reports

The act designated a report that merely gathers information about a person's credit history as a consumer report. If the report in question deals with interviews with a third person concerning the character, general reputation, or manner of living of the person being investigated, it is referred to as an investigative consumer report.

A business that intends to seek an investigative consumer report concerning a person is required to inform the person before seeking the information. The person about whom the report will be made has a right to information about the nature and scope of the investigation. Following the investigation, the person has a right to learn the nature and substance of the information that was collected.

The relevant part of the FCRA reads as follows:

(a). Disclosure of fact of preparation. A person may not procure or cause to be prepared an investigative consumer report on any consumer unless—

> (1) It is clearly and accurately disclosed to the consumer that an investigative consumer report including information as to his character, general reputation, personal characteristics, and mode of living, whichever applicable, may be made, and such disclosure (A) is made in a writing mailed, or otherwise delivered, to the consumer, not later than three days after the date on which the report was first requested, and (B) includes a statement informing the consumer of his right to request the additional disclosures provided for; or

> (2) the report is to be used for employment purposes for which the consumer has not specifically applied.

(b). Disclosure on request of nature and scope of investigation. Any person who procures or causes to be prepared an investigative consumer report on any consumer shall, upon written request made by the consumer within a reasonable period of time after the receipt by him of the disclosure required by subsection (a) (1), [shall] make a complete and accurate disclosure of the nature and scope of the investigation requested. The disclosure shall be made in a writing mailed, or otherwise delivered, to the consumer not later than five days after the date on which the request for such disclosure was received from the consumer or such report was first requested, whichever is the later.[34]

A classic case, *Millstone v. O'Hanlon Reports, Inc.,*[35] provides guidance for what not to do:

> "In *Millstone,* an investigative consumer report was prepared in connection with the consumer's application for automobile insurance. The report contained several derogatory statements relating to the consumer's character, including rumored drug use, participation in demonstrations, eviction from prior residences, and complete lack of discipline of his children, all of which were false. The investigator's only source was a person with a strong bias against the consumer. On the basis of the report, the consumer's application for insurance was denied. The district court found the investigator's actions were "so heinous and reprehensible," "so slip-shod and slovenly," and "so wanton as to be clearly willful non-compliance with the Fair Credit Reporting Act."

You should also be aware that investigative reports you have prepared may not become stale. Whenever a consumer reporting agency prepares an investigative consumer report, no adverse information in the consumer report (other than information that is a matter of public record) may be included in a subsequent consumer report unless such adverse information has been verified in the process of making such subsequent consumer report, or the adverse information was received within the three-month period preceding the date the subsequent report is furnished.[36]

What happens if someone asks for a *copy* of a report done previously? A copy requested is not a new or "subsequent" report, it is merely a copy of a previously prepared report. The FCRA prohibits the inclusion of stale, unverified adverse personal information in new consumer reports. However, the law says nothing whatsoever about the reproduction of existing reports. In this case, the copies each indicated the date and circumstances of the report and could not be construed as providing new or fresh information.[37]

Obviously, an investigative report could be an embarrassment to the consumer. The mere threat by a creditor to order such an investigation could be a useful collection tactic in the case of a debtor in default. It might be enough to finally bring the debtor around to the creditor's office to pay up. Is this form of threat legal? (See chapter 23 on debt collection.)

Someone contemplating an investigative consumer report must warn the subject that such a report "may be made." On the other hand, the law does not require a person who gives this warning actually to go ahead; the person who gives such a warning does not have to have its own employees, or a reporting agency, or anyone else actually begin an investigation. This means that the failure to follow through on the warning is not a breach of the FCRA.[38]

Alert Lists

For example, a firm furnished merchants (by subscription) with "alert lists" of consumers who allegedly had passed bad checks.[39] The lists did not pertain to a particular customer a firm was preparing to do business with, but rather contained 30 to 500 names provided at random.

The firm did not have an adequate system either to check the allegations on its list or to delete the names of those incorrectly placed on the list. Further, the subscribers did not have a legitimate business need for the data, and the firm did not obtain certifications from its subscribers that such subscribers would use the lists only for permissible purposes.

The FTC held that such lists are not "consumer reports" because the information was not collected for consumer reporting purposes and because it could not be reasonably anticipated that they would be used in connection with a legitimate business transaction with persons in anticipation that a permissible purpose will subsequently arise.

The primary purpose of the alert lists was to warn potential victims of the habits, practices, and descriptions of alleged check forgers, swindlers, and other.

If such bulletins remain devoid of information collected or reasonably expected to be used for the purpose of establishing the subject's eligibility for consumer credit, insurance, employment, or other purpose, they cannot be afforded the protections of the FCRA.

Note: You might be able to overcome this problem of indiscriminate alert lists by designing a proper coding system.[40] The system you review with your counsel should consist of (at a minimum) a unique identifier, other than a name, through which the subscriber may identify the consumer and decode the information in connection with a business transaction. Thus, the decoded information will become available to the subscriber only when a legitimate business need for the information arises in connection with a business transaction involving the consumer.[41]

The FTC has stated that credit guides ("alert lists"), which are alphabetical listings of consumers assembled at random and sold to users, violate the FCRA. No recipient could conceivably have a transaction with every individual in the guides.[42]

If you are unsure whether your firm may be dealing in consumer reports, it would be a good idea to review a few other FTC decisions on this topic and, of course, to consult your own counsel. Be aware that this area is in flux and may be modified by the courts at any time.

Disclosures to Consumers

As a consumer reporting agency you must do whatever is reasonable under the circumstances to minimize the chances that an alleged debtor will be harmed by inaccurate reporting.[43] Your data subject has the right to the following services.

(1) When a consumer (alleged debtor) is adversely affected by information contained in the report, the user of the report must, without awaiting a request by the consumer, notify the consumer of the adverse action and provide him or her with the name and address of the consumer reporting agency making the report. The user may *not* wait for or require the rejected applicant or otherwise aggressed party to request the name and/address.[44]

(2) The consumer may then contact you and, when you're given proper identification, you must disclose the "nature and substance of all information in your files on the consumer" at the time the request is made, including the sources of such information (except as to investigative reports—see above).

The procedures of correcting disputed information extend to all the information in a consumer's file, not just to information included in a consumer report. The term "file," when used in connection with information on any consumer, means all the information on that consumer recorded and retained by a consumer reporting agency regardless of how the information is stored.[45]

(3) You must furnish the names of any person who have received a report on the consumer within the last six months,[46] and for employment two years.[47]

(4) You must make such disclosures to a consumer during normal business hours on reasonable notice and proper identification. Reasonable notice includes:

- in person, if he or she furnishes proper identification; or
- by telephone, if he or she has made a written request with proper identification for telephone disclosure, and if the toll charge, if any, for the telephone call is prepaid by or charged directly to the consumer.[48]

Note: A consumer's telephone conversation with a credit reporting agency, during which the consumer asked what was going on and was told by a receptionist that she didn't know but would have someone get in touch with consumer, does not constitute request for disclosure under the act.[49]

It is advisable, of course, to communicate in writing if you are involved personally (preferably by certified mail), but you can't *require* it of others.

(5) When giving consumers access to their files, you must provide trained personnel competent to explain their contents or use, or to decode any data.[50]

(6) The consumer shall be permitted to be accompanied by one other person of his choosing, who shall furnish reasonable identification. The consumer must furnish a written statement granting permission to the consumer reporting agency to discuss the consumer's file in such person's presence;[51] this avoids third-party communication and reduces your exposure for defamation.

(7) If the consumer disputes the completeness or accuracy of any item of information contained in his or her file, and such dispute is *directly* conveyed to the consumer reporting agency by the consumer, the consumer reporting agency shall within a reasonable period of time reinvestigate and record the current status of that information unless it has reasonable grounds to believe that the dispute is frivolous or irrelevant.

(a) If after such reinvestigation, the information is found to be inaccurate or can no longer be verified, the presence of contradictory information in the consumer's file does not in and of itself constitute reasonable grounds for believing the dispute is frivolous or irrelevant.

(b) If the reinvestigation does not resolve the dispute, the consumer may file a brief statement setting forth the nature of the dispute. The consumer reporting agency may limit such statements to not more than 100 words if it provides the consumer with assistance in writing a clear summary of the dispute. The FCRA does not put affirmative duty on reporting agency to advise consumer of consumer's right to include own statement about disputed transaction in consumer's credit file. While it is clearly better practice for a consumer reporting agency to inform consumer of his right to file such statement, the defendant in an illustrative case did not violate the statute by failing to so inform.[52] A consumer cannot complain that a credit bureau failed to include his full side of the story if the consumer has elected not to return a consumer statement form provided him in which he could have provided elaboration or correction of his file to be included in future credit reports.[53]

(c) Whenever a statement of a dispute is filed, unless there are reasonable grounds to believe that it is frivolous or irrelevant, the consumer reporting agency shall, in any subsequent consumer report containing the information in question, clearly note that it is disputed by the consumer and provide either the consumer's statement or a clear and accurate codification or summary thereof.

(d) Following any deletion of information found to be inaccurate or whose accuracy can no longer be verified or any notation as to disputed information, the consumer reporting agency shall, at the request of the consumer, furnish notification that the item has been deleted or the statement, codification or summary pursuant to subsection (b) or (c) to any person specifically designated by the consumer who has within two years prior thereto received a consumer report for employment purposes, or within six months prior thereto received a consumer report for any other purpose, which contained the deleted or disputed information. The consumer reporting agency shall clearly and conspicuously disclose to the consumer his rights to make such a request. Such disclosure shall be made at or prior to the time the information is deleted or the consumer's statement regarding the disputed information is received.[54]

The "maximum possible accuracy" provision[55] does not apply to dispute resolution and reinvestigation provisions in this section, and there is no claim for failure to maintain reasonable procedures to achieve maximum possible accuracy in relation to reinvestigation and dispute resolution procedures.[56]

A nominal, predisclosed charge may be levied on the consumer for the disclosure costs.[57]

(8) All adverse information must be deleted from the consumer's file after seven years except in certain situations. State laws may require deletions in a shorter period of time.[58] Further compliance includes proper encoding to ensure anonymity and to avoid involvement with the publication of overbroad "protective bulletins" or alert lists. Every name reported on must be an ascertainable individual person. "Address hits" if used (and many firms do) must produce specific information that concerns only the subject of an inquiry. Address hits that report on others at the same address are prohibited by the FTC. This is in keeping with the trend in the law to maintain credit histories on individuals and not family units.

Damages

The FCRA provides for recovery by a consumer on a showing of willful or negligent failure to follow reasonable procedures. On a showing of negligent noncompliance, a consumer may recover actual damages, costs, and attorney's fees.[59] The same recovery, and in addition punitive damages, may be awarded on a showing of willful noncompliance.[60]

A private enforcement action may be maintained by an injured consumer in the form of a civil suit for willful noncompliance with the

FCRA and for recovery of actual and punitive damages as well as attorney's fees. There is no ceiling on the amount of punitive damages a consumer may recover, and a suit may be brought in any appropriate court in the United States without regard to the amount in controversy.

A two-year statute of limitations from the date liability arises is provided for civil suits; however, where a defendant willfully misrepresented information required by the FCRA to be disclosed to a consumer, and the information is material to the establishment of the defendant's liability, the statute of limitations does not begin to run until the discovery of the misrepresentation.[61]

In order to recover under these sections, a plaintiff must prove:

(1) Defendant was negligent or willfully noncompliant (or both) in that it failed to follow reasonable procedures to assure maximum possible accuracy of information about the plaintiff;

(2) Defendant reported inaccurate information about the plaintiff;

(3) Plaintiff was injured; and

(4) Defendant's negligence and/or willful noncompliance was the proximate cause of such injury.

The failure to follow reasonable internal procedures as to accuracy, verification, reinvestigation, etc. will be held to be negligence.[62]

The FCRA permits recovery for humiliation and mental distress even when no pecuniary out-of-pocket loss is shown. Outrageous conduct or extreme conduct beyond the bounds of decency "will result in punitive damages." Malice or evil motive need not be established for a punitive damage award, but the violation must have been *willful.*[63]

Conversely, a plaintiff who brings a frivolous action may find himself having just damages, attorney's fees, and costs assessed against him.[64]

One way to play with fire is to obtain the information under false pretenses. Any person who knowingly and willfully obtains information on a consumer from a consumer reporting agency under false pretenses shall be fined not more than $5,000 or imprisoned not more than one year, or both.[65] The penalties are similar for any officer or employee of a consumer reporting agency who knowingly and willfully provides information concerning an individual from the agency's files to a person not authorized to receive that information; the person who does so will be fined not more than $5,000 or imprisoned not more than one year, or both.[66]

Civil actions are not precluded by the availability of penal sanctions.[67] The main thrust of the section is the reality that information obtained (or given) by false pretenses will frequently, if not always, be obtained for improper purposes.[68]

You have to be careful even in seemingly innocent transactions. If your agreement is that you can get only one form of employment report (such as a credit history) you may be in violation if you request another form. The courts have diverse opinions here.[69]

Relation to State Laws.   The FCRA does not annul, alter, affect, or exempt any person subject to the provisions of the act from complying with the laws of any state with respect to the collection, distribution, or use of any information on consumers, except to the extent that those laws are inconsistent with any provision of this act; and then only to the extent of the inconsistency.[70]

As always in our federalist system, take federal law as a guide but not as the final word. See your counsel as to the laws of your state(s).

Clear Contractual Protection

You will probably need the assistance of a credit bureau. Outside of your own in-house collection file, the bureau is your primary source of information about deadbeats or delinquent payers. However, a firm in your industry or product line (especially a competitor) might be preferable, because that firm is more likely to possess the bad file histories of consumers you wish to avoid. Set up a formal, written arrangement to exchange the information.

Whether you use the services of a credit bureau or exchange information with another firm, have your attorney draw up a basic contract to protect your interests. Your contract should state that all parties to the contract agree not to homogenize their lists. Otherwise, you will no longer be relating your respective individual experiences but the total experiences accumulated from your own lists and the lists of the other contract parties.

If you are dealing with credit bureaus, your contract should also have an air-tight indemnification clause. The credit bureau should protect you with the following warranties:

The credit bureau should warrant to you that it is not guilty of negligence (for example, in correcting its list, recording judgments, and removing stale names from its lists). These issues are important. In a recent decision the court noted that a credit-reporting agency is not automatically liable each time it reports inaccurate information, but it must do something reasonable to verify its information, especially after a consumer has refuted it.[71] An inaccurate list wastes your money on useless names.

The time for retaining adverse credit records may vary. The FTC's current position is seven years, but New York's is five.[72] Therefore, you don't want to keep New York State names for a day longer than five years (bankruptcies may be reported for 14 years.).

Your indemnification clause and related insurance coverage should specify protection against private actions, for example, libel protection.

Although administrative enforcement of the FCRA[73] rests primarily with the FTC, a private right of enforcement may be maintained by a consumer in the form of a civil suit for willful noncompliance with the FCRA. One such area of noncompliance you might be exposed to is libel.[74] Make sure you review their errors and omissions policy. Make sure the contract (and insurance policy) is worded so that you must be notified three days prior to any cancellation.

In general, a credit report sent by a commercial credit agency to an interested subscriber is privileged and immune to attack for libel. However, the report must have been furnished in good faith and not be the result of malice or a gross and reckless disregard of known facts.[75] However, although there is no strict liability for inaccuracies in a credit report, the credit agency must follow reasonable procedures to ensure the maximum possible accuracy of information concerning the individual about whom a credit report relates.[76] A consumer may also recover damages from a credit bureau for negligently releasing a report on a consumer to someone who has no right to it.[77] In one case, a court judged that a credit-reporting agency had properly refused to provide a credit report in response to a grand jury subpoena.[78]

The onus of any negative performance will probably be on your agency from the first instance, and you are well advised to clarify this in your contract with your agency.

The credit bureau must warrant to you that it is in compliance with all relevant federal, state, and local laws and regulations, and that it routinely monitors and updates its system to reflect changes. This warranty not only enhances the integrity of the names acquired but also follows the FTC's mandate that any firm acquiring credit information must use its best efforts to obtain only accurate information about delinquent debtors.

Finally, make sure there is language clearly spelling out your respective roles, and that the agency is not your agent or in a joint venture with you.

Impact on Commercial Free Speech

Commercial free speech rights have expanded by leaps and bounds over the last decade. Why, then, is this form of legitimate speech so much more regulated than newspapers or books? This section began with a review of *Greenmoss*. Now we will look further. This emerging doctrine has been useful for business advocates to date and will be even more useful in the future. All business leaders should be aware of it.

The First Amendment

The Supreme Court first encountered the issue of determining the first amendment status of commercial speech in 1942.[79] The court considered commercial speech to be outside the zone of First Amendment protection, though the court failed to address a constitutional distinction between commercial and private speech or, for that matter, even to define "commercial speech." This opinion was later characterized by Justice Douglas as "casual, almost offhand".[80]

Commercial speech protection began to emerge in *New York Times Company v. Sullivan,*[81] where the court distinguished between commercial speech and editorial advertising. The content of the advertising was found to convey more than a commercial purpose. Because the advertisement contained information of the "highest public interest and concern", it was constitutionally protected.[82]

Twelve years later came a decision that was squarely based on the principle that the free flow of information in the commercial sector is as much (or almost as much) a part of First Amendment values as the robust and open debate of political issues.[83] In fact, the court went so far as to state the "particular consumer's interest in the free flow of commercial information . . . may be as keen, if not keener by far, than his interest in the day's most urgent political debate".[84]

More people may remember a Lite Beer commercial than a news brief or even the name of their local assemblyman. More obvious, a lot more people actively shop during the December Christmas season than vote in the November elections, especially in "off years". There are no off-years for shopping.

However, the strongest endorsement from the court came in the following quote:

> Advertising, however tasteless and excessive it sometimes may seem, is nonetheless dissemination of information as to who is producing and selling what product, for what reason, and at what price. So long as we preserve a predominantly free enterprise economy, the allocation of our resources in large measure will be made through numerous private interest and that those decisions, in the aggregate, be intelligent and well-informed. To this end, the free flow of commercial information is indispensable . . . and if it is indispensable in the proper allocation of resources in a free enterprise system, it is also indispensable to the formation of intelligent opinions as to how that system ought to be regulated or altered."

This last point is important as to the content issue. If commercial information were outside the protection of the First Amendment, the consumer advocate as much as the commercial speaker would be left unprotected. Ralph Nader and Consumers Union are two "speakers" on commercial matters whose speech deserves (and receives) constitutional protection.

True, there are differences in the state's ability to regulate private and commercial speech. This is because the latter is more than mere content, but content leading to a sale. The states retain the right (under the Tenth Amendment police powers) to protect their citizens as to content that would mislead an individual into a contract or would jeopardize health and welfare to a serious extent. Most cases will turn on whether a regulation on commercial speech is based on the informative function or the contractual function of the message.

Context or Contract?

The test most useful was articulated by the Supreme Court in *U.S. v. O'Brien,* a case involving a private citizen's burning his draft card. Here was a case in which speech and nonspeech elements were combined in the same course of conduct. O'Brien lost. The test employed by the court was as follows:

> (a) government regulation is sufficiently justified if it . . . furthers an important or substantial government interest: if the government interest is unrelated to the suppression of free expression; and if the incidental restriction on alleged First Amendment freedoms is no greater than is essential to the furtherance of that interest.[85]

As part of "contractual regulation" government may regulate false or deceptive advertising. This is not a regulation of an advertiser's message content but of the fact the advertiser did not make do on the contract as promised subsequent to the content dissemination. Likewise, the state may compel affirmative disclosure where a deception might arise from incomplete disclosure. Such incomplete disclosure will not make itself apparent until the contractual state prompted by the message. Finally, corrective advertising might be ordered not as a regulation of content but as a remedy for inducing a contract by deceptive means. (See Section IV.)[86] There is, of course, such a thing as a wrong product claim. As the court noted:

> There is no First Amendment Rule . . . requiring a state to allow deceptive or misleading commercial speech whenever the publication of additional information can clarify or offset the effects of spurious communication.[87]

However, the existence of varied forms of truth-in-advertising regulations should be considered to result in commercial speech as a "secondary" speech. Commercial speech claims are more verifiable and true to a contractual relationship. They are more than mere "opinion". When it goes beyond mere opinion, private speech is not above its own standards. As stated, false statements of fact do not enjoy constitutional protection for their own sake. There is no constitutional value in false statements of fact,[88] as, for example, many "fighting words," or yelling "Fire!" in a crowded theatre.

When any regulation goes beyond the contractual aspects of the commercial speech it will be analyzed under general First Amendment principles. This is important to all marketers in defending overboard regulations on lists of all kinds involving credit lists (consumer reports). Almost all marketers in any media employ delinquent lists for rental or purchase. The communication of the consumer's address in and of itself is information bearing not only on credit worthiness but also on credit standing, credit capacity, general reputation, and mode of living. The type of neighborhood in which one lives and one's lifestyle both come from an address, which are important factors that influence a credit decision. None of these factors are yet illegal because they're considered positive criteria, though you should keep an eye on developments in the state legislatures.

Lists Are "Content"

The U.S. Supreme Court has held that the flow of commercial information is vital to free enterprise economy and as much a part of First Amendment values as the robust and open debate of political issues. Obviously targeted information is the most preferred commercial advertising in assisting a consumer to make a choice. By its very nature of customizing itself to a select audience, its message is more valuable to that audience's purchase decision.

Further, the content of the message is impossible to create without a thorough understanding of the targeted customer.

This is built in your database. Restrictions on the creation of your database constitute a prior restraint on the content of your message and a general restraint on the free flow of ideas in the commercial marketplace.

At present, the sale or rental of positive commercial information is permissible with certain qualifications. Further, if your firm keeps its own records about transactions between itself and a consumer, you need not comply with the FCRA so long as the information is being assembled or evaluated for the firm's own use and not for transmittal to third parties. However, once your firm sells, rents, or exchanges adverse credit criteria (such as a deadbeat list), it may subject itself to compliance with the FCRA.

As discussed, the FCRA is a legitimate, constitutionally balanced trade-off between commercial free speech and privacy. *Objectively,* accurate lists are commercial free speech. *Objectively,* wrong lists are not free speech but commercial hostility to privacy rights and an individual's good name.

It is important that you are alert to the issue of list erosion. The first state court to take up the constitutionality of the FCRA is in Maine.[89] The court invalidated provisions of the state statute that

- require users of investigative consumer reports to obtain the consumer's written authorization before obtaining a report;
- prohibit reporting of information about the consumer's race, religion, color, sexual preference or orientation, or political affiliation; and
- prohibit the reporting of specific categories of obsolete information.

Obviously this is not the last word. The Supreme Court ruled on advertising, not on the free speech of consumer reporting agencies. However, it should be noted that the Court had the opportunity to review the decision on certiorari, but did not.[90] As discussed below, the Supreme Court has spent the 1980s retreating on commercial free speech. Obviously, this matter is in flux, and you should anticipate future litigation to clarify certain areas. Stay abreast of the area with your counsel. Stay active with your trade association. Otherwise your marketing options will become more restricted.[91]

Is the Court Backing Off From Commercial Free Speech?

The *Equifax* case wasn't an isolated example of the Court's retreat from the possibility of full protection of commercial free speech raised in 1976 in the *Virginia Pharmacy*[92] decision.

The Court is fairly on record that commercial free speech is afforded a lesser degree of protection than other forms of speech under the First Amendment.[93] The Court has been set forth a four-part test for its analysis.

- Does the speech concern lawful activity *and* is not misleading?
- Does the government have a substantial interest in restricting the speech?
- Does the restriction directly advance the governmental interest?
- Is the regulation drawn as narrowly as possible?[94]

It is important that your speech conform with *all four elements* of the test. For example, the Supreme Court has upheld a ban on truthful commercial advertising[95] on the mere assertion (without specific objective evidence) that the government had an interest in protecting its citizens from gambling advertising. Here the plaintiffs sought to overturn the regulation by Puerto Rico of casino gambling. They claimed the right to advertise their business in media varying from print to matchbooks. The Supreme Court deferred to the judgment of the Puerto Rican legislature.

There are probably many "sin in business" products worth less to society than gambling. The court's rationale in this case and its overall trend during the last decade bodes ill for liquor, tobacco, and similar businesses. It might spur on regulation of sugar, "junk food,"or other "unhealthy" products. It could also give impetus to overreaching regulators such as those involved in "Kid-Vid" in the late 1970s.

This whole area bears close watching by you and your trade association. You should encourage your group to intervene as a friend of the court whenever your commercial free speech rights are directly or indirectly at risk. Watch for significant laws and decisions reported here in future supplements.

Conclusion

As discussed, compliance in the area of fair credit reporting will be altered by more definitive litigation and possibly narrower state statutes. In the interim, compliance with this law makes good business as well as legal sense. As discussed in Chapter 23 on debt collection, in-house creditors were exempted because these collectors generally want to do business with the alleged debtor again.

Accurate information is needed to avoid doing business with a deadbeat. But, what is more important, you need accurate information so that you do not lose a business opportunity with a good payer classified incorrectly by obsolete or erroneous information.

Finally, an unpleasant experience in this area will turn off a potential buyer who wants to do business with you. If the buyer is good, you want him or her as a customer. Demanding accurate information from your credit bureau is in the best interest of you and your customer. It is simply good business policy.

ENDNOTES

(1) 15 U.S.C. Sec. 1681 (1974). The FTC has an excellent report on point entitled "Compliance With the Fair Credit Reporting Act." You should order one from: Bureau of Consumer Protection, Federal Trade Commission, Washington, D.C., 20580.

(2) 15 U.S.C. Sec. 1681m. *Note:* there is a stricter law in California for certain notification (Civil Code Sec. 1785.10-.20) relating to such agency's automatically advising a consumer of the agency's obligation to make a written disclosure to the consumer. This disclosure should be made each time the agency gives information to a client. The law further increases consumers' access to their files, but at the same time appears to raise privacy concerns, since it permits a consumer to make contact by phone—a potentially improper way to access confidential information about another.

(3) 15 U.S.C. Sec. 1681i.

(4) 15 U.S.C. Sec. 1681i(c).

(5) 15 U.S.C. Sec. 1681a(d), emphasis added. See also *Houghton v. New Jersey Mfrs. Ins. Co.,* 615 F. Supp. 299 (D.C. Pa. 1985).

(6) FCRA Sec. 603 (d). See also *Boothe v. TRW Credit Data,* 557 F.Supp. 66 (S.D.N.Y. 1982); contra see *Matthews v. Northern Bank & Trust Co.,* 741 F.2d 217 (8th Cir. 1984).

(7) Id.

(8) *Matthews v. Northern Bank & Trust Co.,* 741 F.2d 217, 219 (1984); *Boothe v. TRW Credit Data,* 523 F. Supp. 631 (1981).

(9) *Bergen v. Martindale-Hubbell, Inc.,* 337 S.F.2d 770 (Ga. app. 1985). *Note:* the plaintiffs in both 8 and 9 above might be grateful. If the information or any part of it was collected for one of the consumer uses specified by FCRA Sec. 603 (d), it was a consumer report, regardless of the use to which it is put. "Expected to be used" must refer to what the credit reporting agency, not the requesting party, believed. See *Houghton v. N.J. Mfrs. Ins. Co.,* F.Supp. 299, 303 (E.D.A. 1985).

(10) *In re Grand Jury Subpoena to the Credit Bureau of Greater Harrisburg,* 594 F.Supp. 229 (M.D. Pa. 1984). See also *In re Gren,* 623 F.2d 825 (1980). FCRA Sec. 604(1), 15 U.S.C. Sec. 1681b(1).

(11) 15 U.S.C. Sec. 1681a(e).

(12) 15 U.S.C. Sec. 1681(f).

(13) *Ricci v. Key Bancshares of Maine, Inc.* 768 F.2d 456 (1985), *Oblestad v. Kelly,* 573 F.2d 1109 (9th Cir. 1978).

(14) 15 U.S.C. Sec. 1681(b).

(15) 15 U.S.C. Sec. 1681s(a).

(16) 15 U.S.C. Sec. 1681s(b).

(17) See FTC Informal Staff Opinion Letters, April 1971, and July 1971. 15 U.S.C. Sec. 1681(a)(d)(A).

(18) Hearings on S. 823 before the Subcomm. on Financial Institutions of the Senate Banking and Currency Comm., 91st Cong., 1st Sess. 62 (1969).

(19) 15 U.S.C. Sec. 1681e(a).

(20) 15 U.S.C. Sec. 1681(b). The report must also be limited to the *individual* . If you are investigating an individual for employment you may not investigate his/her spouse. See *Zomora v. Valley Fed. S&L Assn'n.*, 811 F.2d 1368 (10th Cir. 1987).

(21) 15 U.S.C. Sec. 1681c.

(22) *Tracy v. Credit Bureau of Georgia, Inc.* 330 S.E.2d 921 (1985); FCRA 607(b); 154 S.C. 1681e(b). See also *McPhee v. Chilton Corp.*, 468 F.Supp. 494 (D. Conn. 1978).

(23) *Lowry v. Credit Bureau of Georgia*, 494 F.Supp. 541 (N.D. Ga 1978). See also *Pendleton v. Trans. Union Systems Corp.*, 76 FRD 192 (E.D. Pa. 1977).

(24) *Swooger v. Credit Bureau of Greater St. Petersburg*, 608 F.Supp. 972 (M.D. Fla 1985); see also *Thompson v. San Antonio Retail Merchants Assn.*, 682 F.2d 509 (5th Cir. 1982).

(25) *Johnson v. Beneficial Fin. Corp.*, 466 N.Y.S. 2d 553, 554 (Sup. Ct. 1983); FCRA 605(a) (obsolete information), 607(b) (procedures required for maximum accuracy), 15 U.S.C. 1681c(a), 1681e(b).

(26) *Thompson v. San Antonio Retail Merchants Assn.* 682 F.2d 509 (5th Cir. 1982). See also *Hawser v. Equifax, Inc.*, 602 F.2d 811 (8th Cir. 1979).

(27) *Koropoulos v. Credit Bureau, Inc.*, 734 F.2d 37, 42 (1984).

(28) *Pinner v. Schmidt*, 617 F.Supp. 342 (D.C. La. 1985).

(29) *Stewart v. Credit Bureau, Inc.*, 734 F.2d 47, 55 (1984).

(30) *Alexander v. Moore & Associates, Inc.*, 553 F.Supp. 948, 951 (1982).

(31) Id. See also *Colletti v. Credit Bureau Services, Inc.*, 649 F.2d 1148 (1981).

(32) *Swooger v. Credit Bureau of Greater St. Petersburg*, 608 F.Supp. 972, 976 (D.C. Fla. 1985).

(33) *Morris v. Credit Bureau, Inc.*, 563 F.Supp. 962, 964 (S.D. Ohio 1983).

(34) 15 U.S.C. Sec. 1681d(a)-(b), FCRA Sec. 606(a)-(b).

(35) 383 F.Supp. 269 (E.D. Mo. 1974); aff. 528 F.2d 829 (8th Cir. 1976); see *Hauser v. Equifax, Inc.*, 602 F.2d 811, 815 (1979).

(36) 15 U.S.C. Sec. 16811, FCRA Sec. 614; see also *Miller v. Elegant Junk*, 616 F.Supp 551 (D.C.W.Va. 1985).

(37) *Equifax, Inc.*, 762 F.2d 952, 959 (11th Cir. 1985).

(38) *Kates v. Crocker National Bank*, 776 F.2d 1396 (1985).

(39) *In re Howard Enterprises, Inc.*, No. 9096 (June 12, 1979) [overturning a January 16, 1978, decision by FTC Administrative Judge Parker], 93 F.T.C. 901 (1979).

(40) Id.

(41) 16 C.F.R. Secs. 600.1(c), 600.1(d). Depending on circumstances, you should consult 16 C.F.R. Secs. 600.1-.8 (1982).

(42) *In re Hooper Holmes, Inc.*, No. C-3020, 45 Fed. Reg. 44260 (1980) (respondent furnishes information concerning individuals other than those inquired about—an allegation that if true is a clear violation of the Fair Credit Reporting Act) and *In re Equifax*, No. 8954 (1981).

(43) 15 U.S.C. Sec. 1681e.

(44) 15 U.S.C. Sec. 1681m. See also *Carroll v. Exxon Co., USA*, 434 F.Supp. 557, 560 (1977). As long as the decision to deny credit is attributable even in part, the creditor is required to disclose the use of the report. *Fischl v. General Motors Acceptance Corp.*, 708 F.2d 143 (1983). You are not responsible for a mechanical, electronic, or clerical error made in good faith [15 U.S.C. Sec. 1691(d)(3)]. See also *Bryant v. TRW*, 48 F.Supp. 1234 (1980).

(45) 15 U.S.C. Sec. 1681a(g).

(46) 15 U.S.C. Sec. 1681g(a)(3)(B), FCRA 609.

(47) 15 U.S.C. Sec. 1681g(a)(3)(A).

(48) 15 U.S.C. Sec. 1681h (a), (b).

(49) *Clay v. Equifax, Inc.,* (1985, 11th Cir. Ala.) 762 F.2d 952, 960.

(50) 15 U.S.C. 1681h (c).

(51) 15 U.S.C. 1681h (d).

(52) *Roseman v. Retail Credit Co.,* 428 F.Supp. 643 (1977, ED Pa). See also *Middlebrooks v. Retail Credit Co.,* 416 F.Supp. 1013 (N.D. Ga 1976).

(53) *Stewart v. Credit Bureau, Inc.* (1984, App D.C.) F.2d 47.

(54) 15 U.S.C. 1681 i (a)-(d), FCRA Sec. 611. See also *Freeman v. Southern National Bank,* 531 F.Supp. 94 (1982).

(55) See note 30 above.

(56) 15 U.S.C Sec. 1681 i.

(57) 15 U.S.C. Sec. 1681 j.

(58) For example, New York State mandates five years.

(59) 15 U.S.C. Sec. 1681 o.

(60) 15 U.S.C. Sec. 1681 n.

(61) 15 U.S.C. Sec. 1681 p.

(62) *Morris v. Credit Bureau of Cincinnati, Inc.,* 563 F.Supp. 962 (1983). However, see *Watson v. Credit Bureau, Inc. of Georgia,* 660 F. Supp. 48 (S.D.Miss. 1986).

(63) *Thornton v. Equifax, Inc.,* 619 F.2d 700 (8th Cir.), cert. den., 449 U.S. 835, 101 S.Ct. 108, 66 L.ED.2d 41 (1980).

(64) *Rush v. Macy's New York, Inc.,* 775 F.2d 1554 (1985.)

(65) 15 U.S. Sec. 1681 q., *Hansen v. Morgan,* 582 F.2d 1214 (9th Cir. Idaho 1978).

(66) 15 U.S.C. Sec. 1681 r.

(67) *Kennedy v. Border City Saving & Loan Ass'n.,* 747 F.2d 367 (1984).

(68) Id., pg. 369.

(69) See note 67 above; but see *Russell v. Shelter Fin. Serv.,* 604 F.Supp. 201 (W.D. Mo. 1984).

(70) 15 U.S.C. 1681 t.

(71) *In re Equifax,* 96 FTC 844 (1980).

(72) N.Y. Gen. Bus. Law Sec. 380 (j) (1) (f) (ii) from Assembly Bill 6051-A, effective January 1, 1980.

(73) 15 U.S.C. Sec. 1681.

(74) *Thornton v. Equifax,* 619 F.2d 700 (1980).

(75) *Oberman v. Dun & Bradstreet, Inc.,* 586 F.2d 1173 (1978) and *Peller v. Retail Credit Co.,* 359 F.Supp. 1235 (1974). See also 15 U.S.C. Secs. 1681n, 1681o. When there is no allegation of malice or willful intent, there can be no action for libel or invasion of privacy under the FCRA.

(76) *Millstone v. O'Hanlon Reports, Inc.,* 383 F.Supp. 269 (1974), 15 U.S.C. Secs. 1681(e)(b), 1681(m), and 1681(o). See also *Hauser v. Equifax, Inc.,* 602 F.2d 811 (1979). See also *Colletti v. Credit Bureau Serv.,* 644 F.2d 1148 (5th Cir. 1981).

(77) *Credit Bureau of Pulaski Co., Inc. v. LaVoie,* 627 S.W. 2d 49 (1982); but see *Freeman v. Southern National Bank,* 531 F.Supp. 94 (1982).

(78) *United States v. TRW,* 633 F.2d 825 (9th Cir. 1980).

(79) *Valentine v. Christensen,* 316 U.S. 52 (1942). See also *Beard v. Alexandria,* 341 U.S. 622 (1951).

(80) *Commarano v. U.S.,* 358 U.S. 498, 514 (1959).

(81) 376 U.S. 254 (1954).

(82) Id. at 266.

(83) *Virginia State Board of Pharmacy v. Virginia Citizens Consumer Council,* 425 U.S. 748 (1976).

(84) Id. at 763.

(85) 391 U.S. 367, 377 (1968) (emphasis added).

(86) Posch, Robert J., Jr., "Lingering False Beliefs: The Corrective Advertising Remedy." *Direct Marketing,* December 1981, pp. 88-91.

(87) *Friedman v. Rogers,* 440 U.S. 1,8 (1979).

(88) *Gertz v. Robert Welch, Inc.,* 418 U.S. 323, 340 (1974).

(89) *Equifax Serv. v. Cohen,* 420 A.2d 189 (1980), *cert. den.,* 450 U.S. 916 (1981).

(90) This is an appellate proceeding for the reexamination of a lower court's record to enable the higher court to review the questions of law.

(91) Posch, Robert J., Jr., "Speak Up: The Only Way To Counter Threat to List Usage" *Direct Marketing,* April 1984, p. 154-157, and "Commercial Free Speech: The Argument for Our Side" *Direct Marketing,* February 1983, pp. 89-95.

(92) See note 83 above.

(93) *Central Hudson Gas & Electric Corp. v. Public Service Commission,* 447 U.S. 540, 563 (1980).

(94) Id., p. 557. The Rehnquist dissent in this case is more important as to where the court is going. He argued that the regulation of advertising should be evaluated under a mere "rational basis" test rather than a First Amendment test. See also *Zouder v. Office of Disciplinary Council,* 1052 S.Ct. 2265, 2275 (1985); *Holger v. Youngs Drug Products Corp.,* 463 U.S. 66-68 (1983) and *In re R.M.J.,* 455 U.S. 191, 203 N.15 (1982). For a related decision see *Capital Cities Cable, Inc. v. Crisp,* 467 U.S. 691 (1984).

(95) *Posadas de Puerto Rico Associates v. Tourism Company of Puerto Rico,* 106 S.Ct. 2968 (1986).

CHAPTER 22

CREDIT CARD AND
ELECTRONIC FUND
TRANSFER FRAUD

The topical areas covered in this chapter are related to the interaction of payment for your product. These devices have greatly accelerated the ease of purchases, especially in today's world, where we are less likely to carry cash. It is important to both the seller and the customer that the integrity of these instruments remain intact. Recognizing this, Congress has set forth some lucid laws. We'll examine those related to credit cards first.

UNAUTHORIZED USE OF CREDIT CARDS

Background

In May 1968 Congress passed the Truth-in-Lending Act,[1] which requires that creditors disclose the true cost of consumer credit so that consumers can make informed credit decisions.[2] In 1970 Congress passed an amendment to the Truth-in-Lending Act to regulate the credit-card industry.[3] The amendment had three purposes—to prohibit the unsolicited distribution of credit cards,[4] to make the fraudulent use of credit cards a federal crime,[5] and to limit cardholder liability for the unauthorized use of a credit card to $50.[6] Before 1970, credit card agreements generally placed the burden of loss for unauthorized use on the cardholder. Then a variety of state courts and legislatures sought to give the consumer some protection. Congress acted to impose uniformity as well as equity.

The original Truth-in-Lending Act focused on consumer transactions and exempted extensions of credit for business purposes.[7] In 1974 the Congress added a section to the act stating that the business exemption does not apply to the credit-card legislation.[8] *All credit cards,* whether used for business or consumer purposes, are covered by the $50 limit (see below).

To avoid undue exposure, the law has banned the issuance of unsolicited cards. A credit card may be issued only to a person in response to an oral or written request or application for the card or as a renewal or substitute for an existing card.[9] All cases turn on whether the use was authorized. If so, the holder pays. If not, or if there is ambiguity, the issuer pays as a matter of social policy.

> The federal credit card statute reflects a policy decision that it is preferable for the issuer to bear fraud losses arising from credit card use. [I]ssuers are in a better position to control the occurrence of these losses. They not only select the merchants who may accept the card and the holders who may use it, but also design the security systems for card distribution, user identification, and loss notification. Hence, the statutory choice of issuer liability assures that the problem of credit card loss is the responsibility of the party most likely to take efficient steps in its resolution.[10]

The term *unauthorized use* means a use of a credit card by a person other than the cardholder who does not have actual, implied, or apparent authority for such use and from which the cardholder receives no benefit.[11]

As per the statute:

(a)(1) A cardholder shall be liable for the unauthorized use of a credit card only if—

(A) the card is an accepted credit card;

(B) the liability is not in excess of $50;

(C) the card issuer gives adequate notice to the cardholder of the potential liability;

(D) the card issuer has provided the cardholder with a description of a means by which the card issuer may be notified of loss or theft of the card, which description may be provided on the face or reverse side of the statement required by section 1637(b) of this title or on a separate notice accompanying such statement;

(E) the unauthorized use occurs before the card issuer has been notified that an unauthorized use of the credit card has occurred or may occur as the result of loss, theft, or otherwise; and

(F) the card issuer has provided a method whereby the user of such card can be identified as the person authorized to use it.

(2) For purposes of this section, a card issuer has been notified when such steps as may be reasonably required in the ordinary course of business to provide the card issuer with the pertinent information have been taken, whether or not any particular officer, employee, or agent of the card issuer does in fact receive such information.

(b) In any action by a card issuer to enforce liability for the use of a credit card, the burden of proof is upon the card issuer to show that the use was authorized or, if the use was unauthorized, then the burden of proof upon the card issuer to show that the conditions of liability for the unauthorized use of a credit card, as set forth in subsection (a) of this section, have been met.

(c) Nothing in this section imposes liability upon a cardholder for the unauthorized use of a credit card in excess of his liability for such use under other applicable law or under any agreement with the card issuer.

(d) Except as provided in this section, a cardholder incurs no liability from the unauthorized use of a credit card.

Thus, a cardholder is liable for a limited amount if certain conditions are met and if the use of the credit card was unauthorized. Pursuant to Sections 1643(b), (c), and (d), Title 15, U.S. Code, " . . . the burden of proof is upon the card issuer to show that the use was authorized or, if the use was unauthorized, then the burden of proof is upon the card issuer to show that the conditions of liability for the unauthorized use of a credit card have been met".[12]

Accordingly, the initial determination is whether the use of a credit card is unauthorized.[13] " . . . Whether actual, implied or apparent authority exists is to be determined under state or other applicable law. The test for determining unauthorized use is usually agency, and State agency law must be used to resolve this issue."[14]

Issues Raised

If actual authority is present, the credit card company can assert it. For example, if one spouse expressly authorizes another to use the card and the card is issued upon such authority, the authority ceases only when it is expressly withdrawn by contract.[15] This is usually easily proven by an application or credit authorization. Likewise, a spouse's actions may create apparent authority, making him or her liable whether or not the purchases were in fact authorized.[16]

In all areas of agency, the general principle is that actual and implied authority is revoked when the principal so notifies the agent. Revocation of actual or implied authority, however, does *not* revoke apparent authority, especially if the agent retains some indication of authority, such as a power of attorney or as, in regards to the current discussion, to credit cards. Apparent authority is revoked only when third parties have notice of the revocation of actual or implied authority.

As stressed throughout, in any action by a card issuer to enforce liability for the use of a credit card, the burden of proof is on the card issuer to show that the use of the card was authorized. The party who alleges the existence of agency based on apparent authority (the issuer) has the burden of proving agency by clear and convincing evidence.[17] (See the discussion of agency Chapter 15 on Traditional Advertising).

Apparent authority exists when a person has created such an appearance of things that it causes a third party reasonably and prudently to believe that a second party has the power to act on behalf of the first party. Again, if a spouse requests his or her spouse be issued a card bearing the spouse's own name and signature, the card is a representation to the merchant to whom the card was presented that the spouse was authorized to make charges on the card.

In one situation a cardholder gave his credit card to his associate for use in their joint business venture, but orally authorized the agent to only charge up to $500 on the card. When the associate ignored the cardholder's directions by charging in excess of this amount, the cardholder attempted to avoid payment by relying on the $50 maximum liability provision of the Truth-in-Lending statute on "unauthorized" use of the card.

In rejecting the cardholder's argument, the court concluded the statutory limit of liability for unauthorized use of a credit card may be warranted where the card is obtained from the cardholder "as a result of loss, theft or wrongdoing" but not "where a cardholder voluntarily and knowingly allows another to use his card and that person subsequently misuses the card."[18]

Generally, then, you are responsible for purchases charged to your credit card; misuse is no defense unless you can set forth evidence of loss, theft, or other wrongdoing. You should note that apparent authority on the part of the agent cannot be established solely by the conduct of the agent, but must be traced to some act of the principal who clothed the agent with apparent authority.

For example, your *minor* child takes your card without permission and blows a considerable amount of your money on frivolous purchases. In one case such as this,[19] the card issuer had to come up with evidence showing the parent authorized these purchases. The issuer could not. This isn't all that unjust, as the authority to use the card must be based on the parent's conduct which, reasonably interpreted, causes a third person to believe the agent (child) has authority to act for the principal (parent).

The vendors who dealt with the minor child could have questioned the child's right to use the card, name (child and parent were of different sexes), signature, etc. They failed to do so and, most likely, learned a lesson accordingly. The decision could have turned out differently. The daughter cross-claimed on the father's responsibility to provide necessaries for his minor child.[20] The law requires a father who is able to support his children to do so by supplying them with necessaries of life such as food, medicine, clothing, shelter, or personal services as are usually considered reasonably essential for the preservation and enjoyment of life. If the daughter had purchased necessaries, her father would have been providing credit that satisfied the father's legal obligation to his child. That would make the daughter's use of the card an authorized use for which the father would be responsible. Fortunately, for the father that was not the case here.

Finally, the issue may turn on when you notify the issuer.

▶ If the unscrupulous user of your *authorized* card has stepped beyond his or her authority, you may be liable for all losses accrued prior to your notification to the issuer.[21]

▶ In a reverse scenario, you may be free and clear until the card issuer sends you your billing statement with *unauthorized* charges clearly evident. Your failure to promptly follow up on these may make you liable for all subsequent charges.[22]

▶ Otherwise, a cardholder is not liable for "unauthorized" use of his or her card that occurs after he or she has notified the card issuer that an unauthorized use has or may occur. Furthermore, the cardholder's liability for unauthorized use occurring before such notification is limited to $50 and may be imposed only if the card issuer meets the conditions set forth in the statute.

Note: During any dispute whereby the cardholder is asserting a claim or defense against the card issuer, the card issuer may not report the amount in dispute as delinquent until it is settled or a final judgment is rendered. These rights apply only if:

• the cardholder has made a good faith attempt to resolve the dispute with the person honoring the credit card; and

• the amount of credit extended to obtain the property or services that result in the assertion of the claim or defense by the cardholder exceeds $50 and the disputed transaction occurred in the same state where the cardholder resides or within 100 miles from that address (unless the person honoring the credit card is the same person as the card issuer or is controlled by the card issuer).

Fraudulent Use of a Credit Card

The key here is showing the requisite intent, resolve, or determination to pursue a criminal scheme to illegally and wilfully use a credit card in a manner so as to steal $1000 or more (of aggregate goods and services) over a one-year period. The element of intent, not authority, is controlling.

The statute is quite clear and worth a line-by-line reading. The text of 15 USC Sec. 1644 is as follows:

Fraudulent use of credit cards; penalties

(a) Use, attempt or conspiracy to use card in transaction affecting interstate or foreign commerce. Whoever knowingly in a transaction affecting interstate or foreign commerce, uses or attempts or conspires to use any counterfeit, fictitious, altered, forged, lost, stolen, or fraudulently obtained credit card to obtain money, goods, services, or anything else of value which within any one-year period has a value aggregating $1,000 or more; or

(b) Transporting, attempting or conspiring to transport card in interstate commerce. Whoever, with unlawful or fraudulent intent, transports or attempts or conspires to transport in interstate or foreign commerce a counterfeit, fictitious, altered, forged, lost, stolen, or fraudulently obtained credit card knowing the same to be counterfeit, fictitious, altered, forged, lost, stolen, or fraudulently obtained; or

(c) Use of interstate commerce to sell or transport card. Whoever, with unlawful or fraudulent intent, uses any instrumentality of interstate or foreign commerce to sell or transport a counterfeit, fictitious, altered, forged, lost, stolen, or fraudulently obtained credit card knowing the same to be counterfeit, fictitious, altered, forged, lost, stolen, or fraudulently obtained; or

(d) Receipt, concealment, etc., of goods obtained by use of card. Whoever knowingly receives, conceals, uses, or transports money, goods, services, or anything else of value (except tickets for interstate or foreign transportation) which (1) within any one-year period has a value aggregating $1,000 or more, (2) has moved in or is part of, or which constitutes interstate or foreign commerce, and (3) has been obtained with a counterfeit, fictitious, altered, forged, lost, stolen, or fraudulently obtained credit card; or

(e) Receipt, concealment, etc., of tickets obtained by use of a card. Whoever knowingly receives, conceals, uses, sells, or transports in interstate or foreign commerce one or more tickets for interstate or foreign transportation, which (1) within any one-year period have a value aggregating $500 or more and (2) have been purchased or obtained with a counterfeit, fictitious, altered, forged, lost, stolen, or fraudulently obtained credit card; or

(f) Furnishing of money, etc., through use of a card. Whoever in a transaction affecting interstate or foreign commerce furnishes money, property, services, or anything else of value, which within any one-year period has a value aggregating $1,000 or more, through the use of any credit card knowing the same to be counterfeit, fictitious, altered, forged, lost, stolen, or fraudulently obtained — shall be fined not more than $10,000 or imprisoned not more than ten years, or both.

The courts are looking at substance over form when they interpret this statute. A defendant will not prosper arguing that he did not intend to exceed the jurisdictional thresholds ($1,000 aggregate, one year, etc.). A recent decision stated these issues are solely jurisdictional and need not be in the mind of one who knowingly joins a conspiracy to use counterfeit cards or otherwise defraud the public.[23]

The term "transaction" will be satisfied by charging the card or otherwise utilizing it for purchases. Interstate commerce is interpreted broadly, so that any use of a credit card will probably pass muster under section 1644(a), (b), and (c), even if you never leave the state and make purchases only from intrastate firms. Invariably the invoices issued after the credit card purchases will cross state lines in one manner or another, thereby meeting the interstate requirement. Finally, the fraudulent use of the credit card's account number will be held to constitute the fraudulent use of the card itself. This use of fraudulent numbers is a growing problem, particularly for direct marketers in mail, telephone, or other interactive media.

Electronic Fund Transfer Fraud

Whereas Truth-in-Lending governs unauthorized use of a credit card to obtain credit, the electronic fund transfer law governs the cardholder's liability in an unauthorized electronic fund transfer.

In November 1978, Congress enacted the Electronic Fund Transfer Act (EFTA). Congress found that the use of electronic systems to transfer funds provides the potential for substantial benefits to consumers, but that the unique characteristics of these systems make the application of existing consumer protection laws unclear, leaving the rights and liabilities of users of electronic fund transfer systems undefined. The act establishes the basic rights, liabilities, and responsibilities of consumers who use electronic money transfer services and of financial institutions that offer these services. This regulation is intended to carry out the purposes of the act, including, primarily, the protection of individual consumers engaging in electronic fund transfers.[24]

For the purposes of this regulation, the following definitions apply, unless the context indicates otherwise:

Access device means a card, code, or other means of access to a consumer's account, or any combination thereof, that may be used by the consumer for the purpose of initiating electronic fund transfers.[25] An access device becomes an "acceptable access device" when the consumer to whom the access device was issued:

- requests and receives, or signs, uses, or authorizes another to use the access device for the purpose of transferring money between accounts or obtaining money, property, labor, or services;
- requests validation of an access device issued on an unsolicited basis; or
- requests an access device issued in renewal of, or in substitution for, an accepted access device, whether such access device is issued by the initial financial institution or a successor.[26]

Account means a demand deposit (checking), savings, or other consumer asset account (other than an occasional or incidental credit balance in a credit plan) held either directly or indirectly by a financial institution and established primarily for personal, family, or household purposes.[27]

Credit means the right granted by a financial institution to a consumer to defer payment of debt, incur debt and defer its payment, or purchase property or services and defer payment therefor.[28]

Electronic fund transfer means *any* transfer of funds, other than a transaction originated by check, draft, or similar paper instrument, that is initiated through an electronic terminal, telephone, or computer or magnetic tape for the purpose of ordering, instructing, or authorizing a financial institution to debit or credit an account. The term includes, but is not limited to, point-of-sale transfers, automated teller machine transfers, direct deposits or withdrawals of funds, and transfers initiated by telephone. It includes all transfers resulting from debit card transactions, including those that do not involve an electronic terminal at the time of the transaction. The term does not include payments made by check, draft, or similar paper instrument at an electronic terminal.[29]

It has been made official: *All* electronic transfers of funds from a consumer's savings, checking, or asset management account in payment of a purchase made with a debit card are governed by the EFTA. Such a transfer is governed by EFTA regardless of whether the order for the transfer of funds comes from an electronic device at the point-of-sale or from one that comes into play at a later stage (for example, a transfer electronically requested by the seller's bank after the sale).

Electronic terminal means an electronic device, other than a telephone operated by a consumer, through which a consumer may initiate an electronic fund transfer. The term includes, but is not limited to, point-of-sale terminals, automated teller machines, and cash dispensing machines.[30]

Unauthorized electronic fund transfer means an electronic fund transfer from a consumer's account initiated by a person other than the consumer without actual authority to initiate the transfer and from which the consumer receives no benefit. The term does not include any electronic fund transfer that is (1) initiated by a person who was furnished by the consumer, with the access device to the consumer's account unless the consumer has notified the financial institution involved that transfers by that person are no longer authorized, or (2) initiated with fraudulent intent by the consumer or any other person acting in concert with the consumer, or (3) initiated by the financial institution or its employee.[31]

Electronic terminals can be key players in database marketing and home shopping networks by telephone and home computer through the potential of cable interaction. When are and aren't these vehicles governed by the act? The Official Staff interpretations are quite lucid.[32]

Q: *Electronic terminal* —telephone bill payment. If a consumer uses a pay-by-phone plan to initiate a payment, must the financial institution provide a terminal receipt?

A: No. A telephone is not an electronic terminal for purposes of the receipt requirement, although the transfer itself is subject to the regulation.

Q: *Home terminals.* Some financial institutions offer home banking services to their customers. The service will typically involve the use, for example, of a home computer terminal or a television set that is linked to the financial institution's computer by means of telephone or cable-television lines. Does the in-home equipment used by the consumer to initiate fund transfers qualify as an electronic terminal, and are the transfers subject to the terminal receipt requirement?

A: Any transfer, to or from the consumer's asset account, that is initiated by means of the home banking equipment is an electronic fund transfer and is subject to the regulation. However, although not expressly excluded from the definition of electronic terminal, the home banking equipment used by the consumer for initiating fund transfers is analogous to a telephone in function.

The definitions present three forms of unauthorized transfer exposure. The issue of internal employee theft is obvious. As to the other, the interpretations are again quite clear.[33]

Q: *Unauthorized transfers—access device obtained from the consumer.* A consumer is robbed or induced by fraud to furnish another person with an access device. Are transfers initiated at an ATM [automated teller machine] by the person who obtained the access device from the consumer "unauthorized electronic fund transfers?"

A: The transfers are unauthorized for purposes of Regulation E. Although the definition of "unauthorized electronic fund transfer" excludes any transfer initiated by a person "who was furnished with the access device to the consumer's account by the consumer," it assumes that the consumer has authorized the person to make transfers with the access device. This exclusion does not apply when the access device is "furnished" as the result of a robbery, or as the result of a fraud on the consumer in which the consumer does not authorize the use of the access device to make transfers. But if the consumer furnishes an access device to another person (a family member or coworker, for example) who then exceeds that authority, the consumer is liable for the transfers unless the financial institution has been notified that transfers by that person are no longer authorized.

Q: *Unauthorized transfers—forced initiation.* A consumer is forced by a robber (at gunpoint, for example) to withdraw cash at an ATM. Do the liability limits for unauthorized transfers apply?

A: Yes. The transfer is unauthorized for purposes of Regulation E. Under these circumstances, the actions of the robber are tantamount to use of a stolen access device.

As to unauthorized transfers, a transfer of funds effected by someone other than the cardholder is an authorized transfer for which the cardholder is liable if the cardholder furnished his debit card and

PIN (personal identification number) to the person who made the transfer. This refers to a situation in which the cardholder originally authorized someone, such as his or her child, to use the card. The parent gives the card and PIN to a child and authorizes the child to withdraw $100. The child, however, exceeds his or her authority and takes out $500. The bank will not have to reimburse the cardholder for any of the loss because the entire withdrawal by the child was authorized, because the cardholder furnished the child with the card and PIN and, at the same time, authorized a withdrawal.

The issue concerning unauthorized transfers is easier. A forced initiation occurs when:

(1) A thief begins the transfer by placing the consumer's debit card in an automated teller machine and punching the consumer's personal identification number (PIN); and

(2) The consumer has at no time given the one making the transfer actual authority to begin any transfer whatsoever; and

(3) The consumer derives no benefit from the transfer.[34]

What Is the Actual Liability of the Consumer?

The EFTA restricts the liability of consumers when someone acting without authority uses an automated teller or point-of-sale machine to transfer funds out of the consumer's account; it requires the financial institution to bear the loss.[35] The ground rules are as follows:

(1) If the cardholder notifies the financial institution within two business days of an unauthorized transfer, his or her maximum liability is $50.

(2) If the cardholder reports an unauthorized transfer within 60 days of the transmittal of the billing statement, his or her maximum liability is $500.

(3) If the cardholder fails to notify after 60 days then his or her liability may be unlimited.

The financial institution is deemed[36] to have received notice for purposes of limiting the consumer's liability if notice is given in a reasonable manner at some address or telephone number of the institution. As is often the case, state laws offering greater protection will require compliance even if they differ from the federal law.[37]

The Staff Commentary is helpful in setting forth examples of a consumer's exposure to the financial institution for unauthorized transfers.[38]

Situation 1—$500 Limit Applies

Date	Event
June 1	C's card is stolen
June 2	$100 unauthorized transfer.
June 3	C learns of theft.
June 4	$25 unauthorized transfer.
June 7-8	$600 in unauthorized transfers that could have been prevented had notice been given by June 5.
June 9	C notifies bank.

Computation of C's liability:

Paragraph (b)(1) will apply to determine C's liability for any unauthorized transfer that occurs before notice is given.

Amount of transfers before close of two business days: $125	$ 50*
Amount of transfers, after close of two days and before notice to institution, that would not have occurred but for C's failure to notify within two business days: $600	450**
C's total liability	$500

* Maximum liability for this period.
** Because maximum liability is $500.

Situation 2 — Both $500 Limit and Unlimited Liability Provisions Apply

Date	Event
June 1	C's card is stolen.
June 3	C learns of theft.
June 5	Close of two business days.
June 7	$200 unauthorized transfer that could have been prevented had notice been given by June 5.
June 10	Periodic statement is transmitted to C (for period from 5/10 to 6/9).
June 15	$200 unauthorized transfer that could have been prevented had notice been given by June 5.
July 10	Periodic statement of C's account is transmitted to C (for period from 6/10 to 7/9).
August 4	$300 unauthorized transfer that could have been prevented had notice been given by June 5.
August 9	Close of 60 days after transmittal of statement showing unauthorized transfer.

August 10	Periodic statement of C's account is transmitted to C (for period from 7/10 to 8/9).
August 15	$100 unauthorized transfer that could have been prevented had notice been given by August 9.
August 20	C notifies bank.

Computation of C's liability:

Paragraph (b)(1) will apply to determine C's liability for unauthorized transfers that appear on the periodic statement and unauthorized transfers that occur before the close of the 60-day period. (The transfers need not both appear on the periodic statement *and* occur before the close of the 60-day period.) The maximum liability under (b)(1) is $500.

Amount of transfers before close of two business days: $0	$ 0
Amount of transfers, after close of two business days and before close of 60-day period, that would not have occurred but for C's failure to notify within two business days: $700	500*

Paragraph (b)(2)(ii) will apply to determine C's liability for transfers occurring after the close of the 60-day period. There is no dollar ceiling on liability under paragraph (b)(2)(ii).

Amount of transfers, after close of 50 days and before notice, that would not have occurred but for C's failure to notify within 60 days: $100	$100
C's total liability	$600

* Maximum liability.

Situation 3 - $50/unlimited liability provisions apply

Facts same as in Situation 2, except that C does not learn of the card theft but questions that account balance and notifies bank on August 20 of possible unauthorized transfers.

Computation of C's liability:
  In this situation only paragraph (b)(2) applies.

Amount of transfers appearing on the periodic statement or occurring during the 60-day period: $700	$ 50*
Amount of transfers, after close of 60-day period and before notice, that would not have occurred but for C's failure to notify within 60 days: $100	100
C's total liability	$150

* Maximum liability for this period.

Conclusion

The much-touted myth of a cashless society isn't going to happen—at least not before the "paperless office" becomes the norm. Credit cards and, gradually, electronic fund transfers will grow as an essential convenience in purchasing. It is in the interest of all of marketers to back strict compliance with laws that give consumers confidence in the system. Confidence breeds use—and use, sales.

ENDNOTES

(1) 15 U.S.C. Sec.1601-1667e.

(2) 15 U.S.C. Sec.1601.

(3) 15 U.S.C. Sec.1602, 1642-1644.

(4) 15 U.S.C. Sec.1642.

(5) 15 U.S.C. Sec.1644.

(6) 15 U.S.C. Sec.1643.

(7) 15 U.S.C. Sec.1603(1).

(8) 15 U.S.C. Sec.1645.

(9) TILA Sec.132, 12 CFR 226.12(a). See also *Re Credit Card Service Corp.,* 98 FTC 887 (1984).

(10) *Walker Bank & Trust Co. v. Jones,* 672 P.2d 73, 77 (1983), *cert. den.;* 466 US 937, 104 S.Ct. 1911 (1984); TILA Sec.103(o), 12 CFR 226.12(b) n.22.

(11) 15 U.S.C. Sec.1602(o), TILA Sec.133, 12 C.F.R. 266.12(b). See also *Vaughn v. United States Bank of Oregon,* 718 P.2d 769 (Or. 1986).

(12) 15 U.S.C. Sec.1643; see also *Society National Bank v. Kienzle,* 463 NE2d 1261, 1264 (Ohio App. 1983).

(13) *Transamerica Ins. Co. v. Standard Oil Co.,* 325 NW2d 210, 213 (1982).

(14) Id., p. 214.

(15) Note 10 above. See also Note, "Walker Bank & Trust Co. v. Jones: New Meaning for the Phrase 'Don't Leave Home Without It,' *Utah Law Review,* 1984.

(16) *Oclander v. First National Bank of Louisville,* 700 SW2d 804, 806 (Ky.1985).

(17) *Farmers Union Oil Co. of Dickinson v. Wood,* 301 NW2d 129, 133 (N.D. 1980).

(18) *Cities Service Co. v. Poilet,* 452 So.2d 319, 321-22 (La. App. 4 Cir.), citing *Martin v. American Express, Inc.,* 361 S.2d 597 (Ala. Cir. App. 1978).

(19) *Fifth Third Bank/Visa v. Gilbert,* 478 NE2d 1324, 1326-27 (Mun. Ct. 1984).

(20) Id., p. 1326-27.

(21) See note 18 above. See also *Standard Oil Co. v. Steele,* 489 NE2d 842 (Ohio Mun. 1985).

(22) *Transamerica Ins. Co. v. Standard Oil Co.,* 325 NW2d 210, 214-15 (1982).

(23) *United States v. DeBiasi,* 712 F.2d 785 (CA,N.Y. 1983), *cert den.* , 78 L.Ed.2d 339, 104 S.Ct. 397 (1983).

(24) 12 C.F.R. 205.1(b).

(25) 12 C.F.R. 205.2(a)(1).

(26) 12 C.F.R. 205.2(a)(2).

(27) 12 C.F.R. 205.2(b).

(28) 12 C.F.R. 205.2(f).

(29) 12 C.F.R. 205.2(g). The law governs only electronic transfers of funds *from* a consumer's account and *into* a consumer's account.

(30) 12 C.F.R. 205.2(h).

(31) 12 C.F.R. 205.2(1).

(32) 12 C.F.R. Ch. II (1-1-86 Edition), 2-22 and 2-23.

(33) 12 C.F.R. Ch. II (1-1-86 Edition), 2-27 and 2-28. See also *Kashanchi v. Texas Commerce Medical Bank, N. A.,* 703 F.2d 936 (1983).

(34) But see *Ognibene v. Citibank, N.A.,* 446 NYS 2d 845 (Civ. Ct. 1981).

(35) 15 U.S.C. Sec.1693(g), 12 C.F.R. 205.6.

(36) 12 C.F.R. 205.6(c).

(37) 15 U.S.C. Sec.1693(f). See also *Goffrey v. Community Federal Savings and Loan Association,* 706 SW2d 530 (Mo. Ct. App. 1986) as to the EFTA's rules being a guide to states.

(38) 12 C.F.R. Ch. II (1-1-86 Edition), 6-5 as to the applicability of liability provisions.

SECTION VI

COLLECTING DEBTS

No legal experience is more common to marketers than the bad debt problem. It may influence your market and the medium you use, segments of the medium, and possibly even your product selection. The law has developed an increasing bias in favor of the debtor. If you want to be able to collect your debts, you need finesse to avoid not only corporate legal exposure but also personal legal exposure to allegations of "abusive, deceptive, and unfair debt collection practices."

The law is straightforward but exacting. If you don't comply literally, you're going to have problems. Let's look at a case that illustrates just how precise you must be in formulating your collection policy. A collection management firm was under a consent order of the FTC. The Government alleged that the firm subsequently violated the order as well as the Fair Debt Collection Practices Act (FDCPA).[1] The suit sought to determine the liability of the firm and of certain individual collectors and whether the owners of the corporation had personal liability.

Internal Operations of Defendant Firm

The activity of the collector's local agencies included correspondence with the debtor through form letters prepared by the home office and telephone calls made by an individual collector. If the collector assigned to the case failed to collect the debt, he or she could recommend to the office manager that legal action be taken to recover on the debt. If the office manager concurred, the account was referred to the home office for further consideration. If the home office agreed that legal action would be cost effective, the collection firm requested written authorization from the creditor to sue. On receipt of the authorization,

619

the matter was referred to an attorney.[2] The firm didn't always sue; it made a judgment call in any given case.[3] The firm utilized the following three letters (emphasis added). You may wish to compare these form letters with your own.

1. Letter 003

48-HOUR NOTICE

TAKE NOTICE . . . That your creditor alleges that you are justly indebted in the amount listed with us for collection. Further, we have been authorized to proceed with any necessary lawful action to effect such collection. Therefore, you have *48 hours* in which to pay the amount indicated above.

TIME IS OF THE ESSENCE!

IF YOU REMIT WITHIN *48 HOURS* NO ACTION WILL BE TAKEN

2. Letter 005

Your account has been referred to my desk for proceeding. In a percentage of cases referred to us, we find it necessary to resort to legal proceedings through attorneys and the civil courts.

If this account is referred to counsel, and he determines that suit should be filed against you, it may result in the recovery of a judgment which may, pursuant to law, include not only the amount of your indebtedness but, in addition, the amount of any statutory costs, legal interest, and where applicable, reasonable attorney's fees.

If the judgment is not thereon satisfied, it may be collected by attachment of and execution upon your real and personal property. Garnishment is also an available remedy to satisfy an unsatisfied judgment.

We, therefore, suggest two alternatives:

1. Bring or send this balance personally by return mail.

2. Come to this office personally to see and make arrangements for the satisfaction of this account.

We are not representing either directly or by implication that legal action has been or is being taken against you *at this time*.

We would appreciate hearing from you or your attorney within the next forty-eight (48) hours.

3. Letter 006 - identical to Letter 005 in all respects except the penultimate paragraph, which reads:

"We do not mean to represent directly or indirectly that legal action has been, is being *or will be taken* against you. We would, however, prefer that the money which is due be paid without necessity of further processing by us."

Case Holding

The Government alleged that all three letters threatened legal action and that the collection firm mailed these letters to debtors without any intention to bring a legal action against them. This violated the FDCPA, which prohibits "the threat to take any action that cannot legally be taken or that is not intended to be taken."[4]

The Government argued that three types of evidence established as an undisputed fact that the collector did not intend to bring legal action against the debtors who received one of the form letters. First, the individual collector, after sending the letter, did not initiate the internal procedure to procure authorization to sue by recommending to his office manager that suit be brought against the debtor. Second, the collector did not request authorization from the creditors to sue these debtors. (In some cases the record shows the clients forbade it.) Finally, the collector did not file suit against any of the debtors who received the letters.[5]

In certain cases it was clear the collector's employees acted without or against authorization. Fourteen were fired, but this was not a defense. The principal is bound by the acts of the employees he or she chooses. (See the discussion of agency in Chapter 15). All violations, even those that violated the collector's written and communicated collections policies, were within the apparent authority of the collectors because they were done in an effort to collect debts on behalf of the collector's local agencies.[6]

Generally, "a corporate executive will not be held vicariously liable, merely by virtue of his office, for the torts of the corporation . . . Personal liability must be founded upon specific acts by the individual director or officer."[7] However, here the firm was held to have violated an FTC order. Absent some changes in circumstances after the issuance of the order, a director or owner of a closely held corporation may be included in the order, which would expose him or her to personal liability for violations by the corporation's employees, if the individual is "in charge and control of the affairs of respondent corporation and if they were validly included as respondents to the order."[8]

The Court granted summary judgment as to the liability of certain top managers who were found to exercise sufficient participation and control. If you want to see just how public even lower-level employees can become in this form of lawsuit, you should consult the Appendix of this case. It lists the fired employees and their alleged violations of the Order or the FDCPA. The listing reads like a menu of all possible violations, including:

- calling at an inconvenient time—before 8:00 a.m. or after 9:00 p.m. (state law may vary);[9]

- calling the debtor directly after the debtor had retained an attorney in regard to the debt;[10]
- communication of the fact of the debt to a third party;[11]
- abusive calls;[12]
- threats of violence;[13]
- obscene calls;[14]
- repeated calls;[15]
- threat of arrest or imprisonment;[16]
- threat of garnishment of wages;[17]
- threat of attachment of property;[18]
- misrepresentation of the identity of the caller or the nature of the call;[19]
- acceptance of postdated checks;[20]
- solicitation of postdated checks;[21]
- deposit of postdated checks;[22] etc.

This case is a good introduction to this section because it demonstrates a number of important points:

☐ If you violate the FDCPA or an FTC order (or both) the government will pursue you in a big way.

☐ This law must be literally complied with. Its wording is precise and your compliance must be, too.

☐ Strict supervision of your employees (or your agency) is important, not just for legal compliance, but also for long-term goodwill.

☐ You must review your letters (and telephone scripts) before using them. For instance, the 48-hour contingency used in the letters might also be interpreted as a legal violation: It falsely implied an imminence of action. If a debtor's failure to meet such a "deadline" results in no more than the receipt of the next form letter in the series, such urgency is clearly a misrepresentation.[23]

☐ There are a variety of ways you can violate the FDCPA.

The material following reviews all of the above, and more, in depth.

ENDNOTES

(1) 15 U.S.C. Sec. 1692 (1986) et seq.

(2) *United States v. ACB Sales and Service, Inc.,* 590 F.Supp. 561, 566 (1984).

(3) Id., p. 566–567.

(4) 15 USC 1692e(5), FDCPA Sec. 807(5).

(5) See note 2, p. 571.

(6) Id, p. 572.

(7) Id., p. 573 *See also Murphy Tugboat Company, Ltd. v. Shipowners & Merchants Towboat Co., Ltd.,* 467 F.Supp. 841, 852 (N.D. Cal. 1979), *aff'd,* 658 F.2d 1256, 1257 (9th Cir. 1981), *cert.den.,* 455 US 1018, 102 S.Ct. 1713, 72 L.Ed.2d 135 (1982).

(8) Id., p. 573-4. See also *FTC v. Standard Education Society,* 302 US 112, 119, 58 S.Ct. 113, 116, 82 L.Ed. 141 (1937).

(9) FDCPA Sec.805(a)(1).

(10) FDCPA Sec.805(a)(2).

(11) FDCPA Sec.805(b).

(12) FDCPA Sec.806.

(13) FDCPA Sec.806(1).

(14) FDCPA Sec.806(2).

(15) FDCPA Sec.806(5).

(16) FDCPA Sec.807(3).

(17) FDCPA Sec.807(4).

(18) FDCPA Sec.807(4).

(19) FDCPA Sec.807(10).

(20) FDCPA Sec.808(2).

(21) FDCPA Sec.808(3).

(22) FDCPA Sec.808(4).

(23) *In re Capax,* 91 FTC 1048, *amended,* 92 FTC 871 (1978).

CHAPTER 23

COLLECTING CONSUMER DEBTS TODAY

The United States is now a credit-oriented consumer society. Credit is often the lifeblood necessary to sustain your customer's ability to purchase. Not all such customers prove honest, although more often than not they are. Sometimes adverse personal circumstances account for customers' inability to pay on time. Then, both they and the vendor of goods or services have a bad-debt problem.

A consumer having difficulty meeting debts can pick up any county Yellow Pages and find both private and public assistance. One national and regional nonprofit group, for example, Consumer Credit Counseling Services,[1] offers help (for a percentage fee) in working out a payment schedule between a debtor and creditors. This is a useful social function in times of economic uncertainty, when even the best-intentioned individual may suddenly face credit problems due to an unexpected loss of job or reduction in overtime. If the debt is large or the debtor acts in good faith in notifying you of his or her plight, recommending this service will assist the debtor to get back on his or her feet. It may also preserve a good customer who will make purchases again when paychecks begin arriving.

As for you, you want to recover the money. If the purchaser survived your in-house credit checking system, you'll want to review your loopholes. Then you'll probably begin sending biweekly four to six short dunning letters of maybe four to eight lines asking for and then gradually demanding payment. The interval between contacts with the debtor is often more important than the words you use. You don't want the debtor to believe you will forget his or her bill. In your last letter you may suggest the truthful consequences of nonpayment. If you have access to the debtor's phone number, and the amount of the debt makes it cost effective, you'll probably call a couple of times and then immediately follow up the call with a letter.

What are your legal requirements at this time? You must be fair and honest (at least within the parameters of the Federal Trade Commission Act).[2] Strictly speaking, you need not comply with the FDCPA because you're not a "debt collector" if you're collecting in-house (see below).[3] However, this area is in flux. A few bills introduced into the Congress seek to narrow this exclusion, and certain cities (such as New York City) already have narrowed it,[4] as have certain states (for example, Pennsylvania's law is tighter than most states' but not as all-inclusive as New York City's).[5]

All debt collectors must comply with the following FTC case law:[6]

☐ Layout. If your layout is a violation then you're in violation no matter how innocuous your dunning wording is. For example, the use of a speedgram or other form of simulated telegram "which form by its color and appearance, styling, printing and format simulates a telegraphic message and which, by virtue of said simulation, misleads the recipient as to its nature, import, purpose, and urgency" is prohibited.

☐ Legal action. Even the inference of legal or similar action is not permitted unless there is a "realistic possibility" that suit (or other threatened action) will be undertaken where it is threatened. (It's not a lottery, with many entrants but few selected to be sued.) Likewise, if a legal action is undertaken in certain states but never in others, you may not use legal threats in the states where you know you will never act.

- Other threats. The standard is truth; you can state only that you will do what you actually will do. If you threaten adverse impact on the debtor's credit rating, then you must be prepared to back up the validity of your claim.

- Imminence of action. You may not threaten action with a false sense of urgency. Unless you are prepared to carry out the threatened action if payment is not received by the stated deadline, you may not imply that immediate action is needed. Remember that wording such as "urgent," "imperative," "reply immediately," "reply within 48 hours" (a probable illegality not addressed by the court in the discussion at the beginning of this section), or "action will be taken if not paid within one week" may not be used unless such statements are true and the threatened action will occur if payment is not received by the stated deadline. If a debtor's failure to meet such a "deadline" or to act "immediately" results in no more than the receipt of the next form letter in the series, there is no urgency to reply.

- Internal organization. You may not use fictitious job titles or department designations (for example, a fictitious in-house legal department) in collection material, although you can use a "desk name" or alias for individual collectors (to protect them from retaliation), provided that all other descriptions are accurate.

- Test. The test is the *capacity* to deceive. The intent to deceive or actual deception is not necessary.

- Attorney letterheads. Attorney letterheads should be reviewed with counsel. In general, it is a misrepresentation for a debt collector to send out a collection letter under an attorney's letterhead, even if the attorney has approved the form you are using.

If you read just one decision, read the *Capax* decision (see note 6). With the exhaustive analysis presented in *Capax* and the enforcement powers granted by the Fair Debt Collection Practices Act, the FTC clearly sets forth in one decision most of your legal obligations in collection.

If the compliance problems seem complicated, then explore other options. One option is to buy "insurance" by using standard credit card payment options. Then American Express, banks, or other credit issuers absorb your bad debts after they approve the order. Offsetting this advantage, however, are certain disadvantages inherent in employing the credit card payment option, primarily the fees (5% to 7%). Although this figure is fixed (unlike the variable market bad-debt figure), it is a cost that must be built into the cost of your product and thus, taken off the bottom line.

A debt collector who must comply with the FDCPA (see below to find out whom this pertains to) must comply with such case history also. The new act *expands* already existing Federal Trade Commission jurisdiction over unfair or deceptive acts and practices of collection agencies; it is not written on a clean slate. The Federal Trade Commission's prior exercise of jurisdiction in this area is entitled to great weight.[7]

If a check comes in, make sure you deposit it quickly. If it bounces, make sure you put it on automatic redeposit immediately. If it still bounces or you never receive a satisfactory response, it is time to consider outside assistance.

Evaluating an Outside Professional Agency

If you are choosing a local firm to quarterback your outside collection, it is almost mandatory for you to visit its offices and observe the procedures, controls in place, type of personnel, sample dunning series, telephone scripts, etc. Ask whether the firm is representing companies similar to yours, and if so, find out which ones. If they don't currently have a similar client firm, ask for references they believe would be appropriate. Obviously, you should consult the local Council of Better Business Bureaus and consider a Dun-&-Bradstreet-type check. The FTC and the state attorney general's office can also be valuable sources of information. If the agency is out of state or otherwise inconvenient for a walk-through, you can obtain most of this information on request.

Then make sure the firm can give up-front assurances (later to be confirmed in your written contract—see below) that it will comply with *all* applicable state licensing requirements. Congress encourages each state to address the debt collection issue with stringent state legislation, and many states do. For example:

- In many states you cannot engage in the business of a collection agency or operate a collection business without a proper license.[8]

- In many states you cannot retain a firm that is not in compliance.[9]
- Some states attempt to mandate fees.[10]

Finally, if you're going to test, make sure you contract for it (see below). Don't just wait for the formal roll-out. If you're testing a few firms, make sure the timing, geography, and other comparisons[11] are a fair reflection of your business as it actually is. Testing one firm's 1987 results against another's 1988 results is a waste. Likewise, a southern regional firm's results may have no comparison value with a western firm.

Your collection agency (and, where applicable, you) must comply with laws such as these even if it has no offices, employees, or property in the state and seeks only to collect outstanding debts by mail and through telephone communications. If your agency believes this form of state-by-state regulation would duly hamper a national campaign, it had better be able to designate such burdensome laws as creating a specific burden through cumulative, disparate state regulation. So far, this case hasn't been made.[12]

Once you're happy with the method of operation and compliance with the applicable laws, you'll have to begin to review the agency's menu of services and proceed to negotiate what you want so you can set forth your respective needs, services, and obligations in your contract. One "service" you might wish to avoid is "flat rating," in which a collection firm merely sells you a set of dunning letters with its own letterhead (which would indicate that the sender is a collection agency), but you actually mail them out yourself. This gives the debtor the false impression that a third party—a professional debt collector, to boot—is attempting to collect the debt. In reality, you as creditor are trying to collect on your own.

If the firm you select offers a full range of services to the public, you may select only that it send the dunning letters on your letterhead and nothing more. Even though the collector will do nothing else for you, you really have involved a professional collector in your collection effort. This is not mere pretense.[13]

A debt collector that uses letters as the only collection tool does not violate the act merely because he or she charges a flat rate per letter, if he or she is meaningfully "participating in the collection of a debt." The consumer is not misled in such case, as he or she would be if the collector supplied the creditor with form letters and provided little or no additional service in the collection process. The performance of other tasks associated with collection (e.g., handling verification requests, negotiating payment arrangements, keeping individual records) is evidence that such a party is "participating in the collection."

It's not hard to avoid flat raters. Just select a reputable, full-service firm—then pick anything you want from its menu.

Minimal Contractual Protection from Your Agency

While the agencies are independent contractors, you have a right to insist they obey the law. The public will view the outside collection as an extension of your company's goodwill. Any adverse actions will reflect badly on you. By negotiating with the independent contractor to protect your good name, you will not upset a worthwhile independent contractor relationship but will be reinforcing a worthwhile one with the public. Therefore, you need to clarify your rights and what services you expect.

The following protections should be nailed down whether you're testing or ready for a full-scale roll-out. Obviously you'll negotiate the draft, and getting a solid draft up front means less attorney time, which equals less legal overhead for you.

☐ Article I—Relationship. Set forth the terms of your employment obligations and relationships of the parties:

- Provide a general statement of purpose.

- Specify that the agency is an independent contractor (unless you want otherwise) and is neither an employee nor an agent of your firm.

- Allow the agency as narrow authority as possible.

- Reserve the right to an advance clearance of dunning letters and telephone scripts. This should not upset the independent contractor status. The agency should warrant it will use only such communication vehicles you've approved. If the agency is uncomfortable doing this, find another.

☐ Article II—Term. Indicate the duration, how it will be renewed (automatically or by formal agreement), and how you can prematurely end it at your discretion or for cause (see also Article V below).

☐ Article III—Compliance. You must have the agency warrant it will comply with all laws, ordinances, regulations, etc. at the federal, state, and local levels. Specifically require literal compliance with the FDCPA and similar state laws. Beyond the words, make sure the agency has a system in place to monitor, update, and stay atop legislation and regulatory changes. Tell the agency to review chapter 24 as to profit preservation centers. Further, make sure you receive a warranty that the agency is licensed and bonded where applicable. Prudence indicates you should expressly incorporate these as exhibits to your contract. Finally, you should have them warrant compliance with published and customary professional ethical standards.

☐ Article IV—Services. Spell out and itemize the general and specific services you wish the agency to provide. You should spell out where the services will be provided, the record keeping you expect, and how you can obtain reasonable access to it. The record keeping should include any disputes that come in and a system you've specified as to how you wish to handle them (for example, the agency should cease all communication with the debtor until you advise it otherwise).

You can grant a wide variety of discretionary authority, too. For example, the FDCPA tells debt collectors that they may not collect "any amount (including any interest, fee, charge, or expense incidental to the principal obligation) unless such amount is expressly authorized by the agreement creating the debt or permitted by law." Therefore, if a credit sale contract specifies the exact amount recoverable as collection costs, the law permits the debt collector to recover that amount. The debt collector may recover the actual collection costs. It will have to have sufficient evidence proving the costs (e.g., parties agree in advance to a certain percentage).[14]

Review with your counsel the precise scope of what you want in this area as well as all others. Invariably the law will prove flexible for ordinary debt collection strategies and even a few creative ones.

☐ Article V—Compensation. Specify in your contract:
- Whether compensation is per letter (plus postage), per call, a percentage of the total, or other (unless a fee is otherwise mandated by state law);
- How billing will take place (e.g., monthly invoice);
- How rapidly you must pay;
- Whether there are any prompt payment discounts or late fees.

☐ Article VI—Insurance. Make sure you review a copy of the agency's errors and omissions insurance with your counsel or your in-house insurance manager as to its adequacy and coverage. Make sure it specifically covers libel, as you're dealing with each individual debtor's reputation. Then require that it contain a provision that no reduction in or termination of coverage take place without 30 days' written notice to you. Tie this in with Article II's Term so that such notice period is always longer than the time allowed for you to opt out at your discretion or for cause.

☐ Article VII—Indemnification. Specify that you want written notice of any action against you, and also indemnification (including reasonable costs and attorneys fees) as to all warranties plus any other exposure due to the agency's negligence or willful acts. At the end wrap it up with "the foregoing representations, warranties, and indemnities shall survive termination of this Agreement." The agency should also indemnify you from the actions of each secondary agency it employs.

☐ Article VIII—Assignment. Neither party should have the right to assign the Agreement without the written consent of the other.

☐ Article IX—Governing Law. Specify a convenient state to govern interpretation and performance. Obviously, it is easier to deal with a problem if you can ensure that the law you are most familiar with will be applied, rather than some other state's law.

☐ Article X—Benchmark Criteria (If a Test). Make sure you specify benchmark criteria as to what will lead to a further relationship and what results may mean adieu.

☐ Article XI—Confidentiality. If you are supplying a list of names, get a warranty specifying that such names are confidential and at all times your sole property. Your lawyer will write it in such a way that you'll obtain consequential damages, that is the loss of the list will be recognized as causing you "irreparable damage" and therefore compensable. At the end of your "Confidentiality" clause, make sure you state "The foregoing paragraph shall survive the termination of this Agreement."

Of course, as a prudent businessperson, you'll "seed" the names if you have the capacity, including a few "dummy" names or specific misspellings, which you can then trace and monitor.

Finally, depending on the relationship, your needs, etc., you should consider specifying what steps the agency must take to keep your data confidential (i.e., it will hold and use such information in the same manner and with the same safeguards as it uses for its own proprietary information).

☐ Article XII—Amendments. You will want all amendments in writing. This is fairly standard. You don't want the other party to be in a position to alter your rights without your approval. Therefore, no rights can be altered unless you agree (as confirmed by signature) in writing.

☐ Article XIII—Notices. You don't want notification of delays, lawsuits, and so forth, arriving at your firm addressed to no one in particular. You must specify a name and title to receive correspondence. The latter is more important, as names turn over much more readily than titles.

☐ Article XIV—Severability. In any state you might consult with your counsel whether a "severability" paragraph would enhance or diminish your protections. What severability does for you is to protect your overall agreement from being struck down by virtue of one or more nonenforceable paragraphs. Sample language:

If any provision of this Agreement shall be held invalid, illegal or unenforceable, the validity, legality, and enforceability of the remaining provisions shall not in any way be affected or impaired thereby and this Agreement shall be construed as if such invalid, illegal, or unenforceable provision had never been contained herein.

Severability can be a useful tool. However, never use this as a "throw-in" in a form contract you use, as you may find a court throwing out a paragraph that goes to the heart of why you want the contract. Then, you're struck with the remaining contract, which may not only go against your expectations, but may also be flat-out injurious to you. Severability should be used only as needed in your "non-form language" after a review with your counsel.

☐ Article XV—Arbitration. This can expedite disputes, because of its greater informality and may be desirable in *clearly defined* instances. It is particularly to your advantage if you lack the resources vis-a-vis the other party to endure a protracted litigation.

☐ Article XVI—Integration or Merger Clause. Here you'll see or use language such as "This contract constitutes the entire agreement between the parties with respect to the subject matter; all prior agreements, representations, statements, negotiations, and undertakings are superseded hereby." This means that all letters, brochures, demonstrations, sales pitches, and other prior representations you relied on are inoperative as to the contract obligations, unless you expressly incorporated these.

The above discussion is obviously not exhaustive. You'll want to review with your counsel some of the areas discussed above as well as other areas as they arise.

WHAT YOU NEED TO KNOW ABOUT THE FDCPA

The federal Fair Debt Collection Practices Act (FDCPA) was enacted on September 29, 1977 as an amendment to the Consumer Credit Protection Act to eliminate abusive, deceptive, and unfair debt collection practices by independent debt collectors. In a more positive light, Congress also went on record to state that the act was intended to insure that those debt collectors who refrain from using abusive debt collection practices are not competitively disadvantaged, and to promote consistent state action to protect consumers against debt collection abuses.[15] This was an acknowledgment that many responsible groups, such as the American Collectors Association and the Associated Credit Bureaus, *encouraged* legislation related to debt collection. What evolved was a controversial but workable law.

Unlike many federal credit laws, most of the provisions of the FDCPA are specific and clearly written and provide answers to what collection tactics are legal. Also, unlike other consumer laws, there was contemplated a reduced role for the FTC from the outset. Although the FTC is the agency charged with the administrative enforcement of the FDCPA, its power is clearly limited in this act. The act expressly prohibits the FTC from issuing additional rules or regulations concerning debt collection, because Congress thought the FDCPA "fully addresse[d] the problem of collection abuses."[16] It does permit the states the power to broaden their laws and expand enforcement. Finally, it grants the right of private enforcement to individuals, thus indirectly curtailing some of the need for an aggrieved debtor to fall back on the FTC.

It is imperative to conform literally to the act's wording. The FTC has initiated a number of formal actions against debt collectors in the years since the Fair Debt Collection Practices Act became effective, and the states are also active. Further, even if you are exempt from this act's coverage (see below), other consumer protection laws may apply similar restrictions to creditors. For example, the Federal Trade Commission Act[17] has prohibited particular collection tactics in a variety of cases, and it applies to most creditors. The FTC looks to the FDCPA when interpreting the FTC Act. All states now have their own consumer protection laws modeled after the FTC Act; most of these laws apply to creditors, and most look to the FTC Act for interpretation of their own statutes. Courts trying to apply those broad standards to specific conduct are likely to be influenced by specific provisions and interpretations of the FDCPA. Many states have enacted statutes regulating debt collection practices, and these statutes are often applicable to creditors. Many of the provisions of these statutes are similar to those of FDCPA, and interpretations of the FDCPA will influence courts' interpretations of state laws.

Finally, there is the issue of customer goodwill. Your customers are familiar with this law, and if you don't at least generally comply (regardless of legal exemptions that apply to you), you run the risk of losing their business or having them lodge complaints. You may prevail on your legal exemption, but is it worth it? It's a good idea to be very familiar with the following.

What Constitutes a Debt?

The act is controversial, since it applies only to *third-party* collectors and excludes the actual entity that extended the credit in the first place. Because the act focuses on the collection of debts by debt collectors, the statutory terms play a central role in delineating the scope and reach of the act. Specifically, the act applies to:

▶ Debts, defined as "any obligation or alleged obligation of a customer to pay money arising out of a transaction in which money, property, insurance or services which are the subject of the transaction are primarily for personal, family or household purposes, whether or not such obligation has been reduced to judgment."[18]

▶ Such debts must be consumer debts (the act does not apply to collecting debts from businesses), that is, the purchase of goods or services for primarily personal, family, or household services. For example, commercial debts were not covered, because it was thought that a commercial entity had more savvy to protect itself in the marketplace.

We are looking at obligations incurred primarily for personal, family, or household purposes. Then there are a variety of fine-tuning points rendered by the courts. For example, the act has no application to cash sales or commercial accounts.[19] It doesn't apply to unpaid taxes or fines, since the act contemplated that the debt must arise as a result of the rendition of a service or the purchase of property or some other item of value.[20] Neither does it apply to a credit card that a cardholder retains after the card issuer has demanded its return. The cardholder's account balance is the debt.

It does apply to student loans, since a student acts as a consumer of educational services, in securing a debt arising out of a transaction in which the service was obviously intended for personal use.[21] It also applies to overdue obligations such as medical bills that were originally payable in full within a certain time period (such as 30 days) and to dishonored checks that were tendered in payment for goods or services acquired or used primarily for personal, family, or household purposes.

Who Is Governed by This Law?

If you do not have a debt governed by the FDCPA, you need not comply. If you have such a debt, then you are liable under the act only if you fit its precise definition of a "debt collector."

Debt collector means any person who uses any instrumentality of interstate commerce or the mails in any business, the principal purpose of which is the collection of debts, or who regularly collects or attempts to collect, directly or indirectly, debts owed or due or asserted to be owed or due another. The term includes any creditor who, in collecting his own debts, uses a name other than his own, which would indicate that a third person is collecting or attempting to collect such debts. In addition, the term includes any person who uses any instrumentality of interstate commerce or the mails in any business the principal purpose of which is the enforcement of security interests.[22] Also included are the following:

- ☐ Employees of a debt collection business, including a corporation, partnership, or other entity whose business is the collection of debts owed another.

- ☐ A management firm that regularly collects overdue rent on behalf of real estate owners, because it "regularly collects . . . debts owed or due another."

- ☐ A party based in the United States who collects debts owed by consumers residing outside the United States, because he or she "uses . . . .the mails" in a collection business. The residence of the debtor is irrelevant.

- ☐ A firm that collects debts for a creditor solely by mechanical techniques, such as (1) placing phone calls with prerecorded messages and recording consumer responses, or (2) making computer-generated mailings.

Creditors are generally *excluded* from the definition of debt collector to the extent that they collect their own debts in their own name. However, the term *specifically applies* to "any creditor who, in the process of collecting his own debts, uses any name other than his own which would indicate that a third person is " involved in the collection. A creditor is a debt collector under this act if:

- ☐ He or she uses a name other than his or her own (including a fictitious name) to collect his or her debts.

- ☐ His or her salaried attorney-employees who collect debts use stationery that indicates that they are employed by someone other than the creditor or are independent or separate from the creditor.

- ☐ He or she regularly collects debts for another creditor. Note, however, he or she is a debt collector only for purposes of collecting these debts, and not when he or she collects his or her own debts in his or her own name.

- ☐ The creditor's collection division is not clearly designated as being affiliated with the creditor; however, the creditor is not a debt collector if the creditor's correspondence is clearly labeled as being from the "collection unit of the (creditor's name)," since the creditor is not using a "name other than his own" in that instance.

Exclusions

Banks, credit unions, loan companies, and retailers are excluded from the act as "debt collectors" because their primary business purpose is the extension of credit rather than the collection of debts. The statute does not apply to persons or businesses collecting debts on their own behalf because such person or business is presumed to do this in isolated instances. It is directed to persons engaged in business for the principal purpose of collecting debts.

Among the major *specific exemptions* to "debt collector" (and therefore excluded) are the following:

(a) " Any officer or employee of a creditor while, in the name of the creditor, collecting debts for such creditor."[23] This provision, though much criticized, clearly insures that in-house creditors and other officers and employees in a creditor's collection department are not covered by the act. The exemption includes a collection agency employee who works for a creditor to collect in the creditor's name at the creditor's office under the creditor's supervision, because he has become the *de facto* employee of the creditor. The exemption does not include a creditor's former employee who continues to collect accounts on the creditor's behalf, if acting under his or her own name rather than the creditor's.

The abnormal case in which a creditor *is* a "debt collector " and bound to comply with FDCPA is that in which the creditor uses a name other than his or her own, which would indicate that someone other than the creditor is dunning the debtor. This provision is designed to discourage creditors from pretending that a professional, independent collection agency is trying to collect.

(b) Any person while acting as a debt collector for another person, both of whom are related by common ownership or affiliated by corporate control, if the person acting as a debt collector does so only for persons to whom it is so related or affiliated and if the *principal business* of such person is not the collection of debts.[24] The "principal business" requirement is to be liberally construed.[25] The exemption applies where the collector and creditor have "common ownership or . . . corporate control." For example, a company is exempt when it attempts to collect debts of another company after the two entities have merged.

The exemption does not apply to an entity whose principal activity is debt collection, even if it is under common ownership with a differently named creditor and collects debts only for that party. Neither does the exemption apply to a party related to a creditor if the party collects debts for others in addition to the related creditor.

(c) Any officer or employee of the United States or any state to the extent that collecting or attempting to collect any debt is in the performance of his or her official duties.[26] Here, look for any form of a government official or other whose action constitutes official duties and you'll probably have an exemption.[27] "State" includes "subdivisions of same," such as counties.[28] Again, be aware that even in instances where the FDCPA does not apply to a government debt, some regulatory agencies look to the act as providing their policy for proper or ethical collection practices by the creditors they regulate. This exemption would not apply to governmental employees who "free lance" outside their official duties as debt collectors in their free time.

(d) Any person while serving or attempting to serve legal process on any other person in connection with the judicial enforcement of any debt,"[29] The exemption covers marshals, sheriffs, and any other process servers while conducting the normal duties relating to serving legal papers.

(e) Any nonprofit organization which, at the request of consumers, performs bona fide consumer credit counseling and assists consumers in the liquidation of their debts by receiving payments from such consumers and distributing such amounts to creditors.[30] The social policy for this is obvious. As to for-profit credit reporting agencies, the facts of their particular operations will control.[31]

There are a variety of other exemptions.[32] One exemption that was eliminated on July 9, 1986, was that for attorneys. The FDCPA now requires that any attorney who collects debts on behalf of a client be subject to the provisions of the act.[33]

Three questions might come to your mind about now.

▶ *Why were they all excluded?* Congress made a judgment that in-house and other collectors do not act abusively in attempting to collect debts because the creditor's primary business is to do more business with the debtor once the account is paid.

▶ *Who's left?* The third-party creditor who does debt collection for a living is left.[34] This includes certain domestic U.S. collectors of foreign accounts when, even though the debtor is in a foreign country, the collector would still use "instrumentalities of interstate commerce" such as the U.S. Postal Service and U.S.-based telephone systems. FDCPA applies to any efforts to locate and collect from a consumer debtor using such instrumentalities. The act regulates communications by the debt collector with the debtor, prohibits a number of debt-collecting practices, requires certain disclosures to be made to the debtor, and addresses legal actions available to the parties. We'll examine each of these areas in detail.

▶ *I'm not covered—why read on?* A few good reasons:

(a) Many provisions apply to in-house collectors as well (they're found in law and consent agreements).

(b) The FTC at times and certain members of Congress have indicated a desire to incorporate all collectors. Elsewhere, a few bills have been introduced into Congress to narrow this exclusion, and certain cities (e.g., New York City) already have.[35] In certain states (e.g., Pennsylvania) the law is tighter than in most states but is not as all-inclusive as New York City's.[36] Further, there is an increasing legislative trend to make firms more responsible for their outside collection efforts. You should also be aware that, although the act does not govern cash sales, it does govern efforts by a collection agency you hire to collect personal checks.[37]

(c) The outside collector your firm retains reflects on your firm's goodwill. You should screen all dunning letters and scripts employed before you pay a retainer and sign a contract. Although they are independent contractors, you certainly have a right to insist that they obey the law. The public will view the outside collector as an extension of your company's judgment. Any adverse actions will reflect badly on you. You will not upset a worthwhile relationship with an independent contractor by protecting the good name of your firm.

Although it's a good idea for anyone to read further, if you're a third-party collector, you *must* master the following concepts.

Communication Requirements

Your initial task as a debt collector is to discover your debtor's address and possibly a telephone number where he or she can be reached. This "location information" is the most valuable data a collector can possess.[38] Our society is mobile, and, to get the job done, the collector must keep up with the debtor. Therefore, for this and other reasons, both the profession and the law put a premium on knowing the individual circumstances of the debtor. To obtain such information you must be careful.

Location information includes a debtor's residence, home phone number, and place of employment. It does not cover work phone numbers, names of supervisors and their telephone numbers, salaries, or dates of paydays.[39] You are not permitted to contact third parties under the pretense of obtaining location (or other) information already in your possession.

Although a debt collector is permitted to contact third parties (e.g., employers) to obtain location information, the act provides certain guidelines that must be followed. This is to preserve the consumer's privacy and spare him or her the humiliation that could result if knowledge of the default were widespread. You should abide by the following pointers when attempting to acquire this information:

☐ *Identifying Yourself.* You as a debt collector must identify yourself (not necessarily by true name, provided that no deception is used) and state that you are looking for certain location information about an individual.[40] If you are contacting an employer, you must be very careful to do nothing that would interfere with the debtor's employment relationship. You must not state that you're a debt collector unless specifically asked. However, if so asked you must respond with the true and full name of your employer. Under current FTC policy, debt collectors probably can use aliases (in writing and calls) to protect themselves from disgruntled debtors who might approach them personally, as long as the alias is used consistently and does not interfere with another party's ability to identify the debt collector (e.g., the true identity can be ascertained from the employer).[41]

This provision overruled a number of state court decisions that allowed debt collectors to contact employers.[42] The argument in these rulings was that the debtor's right of privacy was superseded by the employer's interest in hiring qualified personnel and the collector's right to use reasonable, noncoercive means to secure payment. The act shows more sensitivity, not only as to privacy concerns but also in recognizing that a terminated employee can't pay debts.

Your exposure to such third-party contact can vary. A spouse or parent isn't a third party for purposes of the act, while your children, uncles, aunts, and grandparents may be.[43] Make sure you receive careful compliance to pursuing location information from third parties.

Other points to keep in mind concerning various third-party contacts are:

- Your debtor can consent to your specific third-party contact. While not required by law, make sure you get the consent in writing. Relying on the law's standard of "presumed from the circumstances" is too subjective in this era of high-volume and high-cost libel verdicts.

- You may contact an employee of a telephone or telegraph company in order to contact the debtor, without violating the prohibition on communication to third parties, if the *only* information exchanged is that necessary to enable you to transmit the message to, or make contact with, the debtor.

- You may use an "in care of" letter only if the consumer lives at, or accepts mail at, the other party's address and you know this in advance to be true.

- You may not send a copy of the judgment to an employer, except as part of a formal service of papers to achieve a garnishment or other remedy.

- You may disclose your files to a government official or an auditor, to respond to an inquiry or conduct an audit, because the disclosure would not be "in connection with the collection of any debt."

- You do not violate the act when you give a receipt to a consumer's friend or relative who makes a payment on a debt, as long as you do not convey information about the details of the debt to the payer.

☐ *Repetitive Contact.* You may not contact the third party more than once unless such contact is *absolutely* necessary to obtain more complete or correct information (or unless the third party can now supply complete information) or unless requested to do so by the debtor. A final exemption is where you're calling back after you had requested a third party to return your telephone call, if you do not refer to the debt or your status as (or affiliation with) a debt collector.

☐ *Stationery.* Collectors may not place an indication, mark, symbol, or any other language on the outside envelope of the letter or telegram that identifies the sender as a debt collector. A debt collector may *not ever use* his or her own name in the return address if the name indicates that the sender is in the business of collecting debts. An innocuous firm name or simple return address is all that is permitted. Obviously, you are prohibited from using postcards or transparent envelopes.[44] By the same token, a debt collection firm may not use its actual name in the letterhead or elsewhere in a written communication seeking location information, if the name states or indicates collection activity, such as a name containing the word "debt," "collector," or "collection." Remember to review with your counsel your exposure as to libel in this area and make sure your insurance policy protects you. If you're the principal, refer back to the earlier discussion in this chapter on debt collection agency contracts.

Then there is always the subtle problem of your public's marketplace experience. Say you have the name National Credit Approval Company. This is innocuous as to third parties—at first. As the years roll by the public will know what the National Credit Approval Company's business really is and will recognize a letter with National's return address as a dunning letter. What does debt collector do now to avoid violating the FDCPA? In determining whether a company's name indicates that the company collects debts, the FTC's staff has said that one must consider whether members of the community are aware of the company's business activities. You may well have to change your name.

Finally, don't try to be clever by sending computerized billing statements or "Personal and Confidential" letters that are easily recognizable (by a glance at the envelope or a "slight glance" through the letter) as a "Final Demand for Payment."[45]

☐ *Attorney on the Scene.* Collectors may not contact third parties for *any* reason (including all types of location information) once the collector knows that the debtor is represented by an attorney *with regard to the debt*[46] and can contact the attorney (that is, the collector knows or can readily obtain the attorney's name, address, or phone number) *unless* the attorney fails to respond to the debt collector's communication within a reasonable period of time.[47] Some would consider 14 days to be reasonable; whatever your policy, it should be consistent. Once contact with the attorney is made, you must direct all communications to the attorney *unless* the attorney consents to your communicating directly with the consumer. If this happens, get such consent in writing or confirm the conversation in a *certified* letter to the attorney and client debtor. [48]

Direct Communication With the Debtor

In evaluating your communications with the debtor, the courts will be looking at the tendency of the language to deceive *not* the most sophisticated or even the reasonable person, but the *least sophisticated person.*[49] The standard generally followed is to protect the debtor at the "low end of the spectrum of the reasonable person"[50] though some courts have adopted the reasonable person standard so long as the standard encompasses protection for "the unsophisticated or uneducated customer." [51] This latter position has been criticized as not protective enough, [52] so you are best advised to target your pitch to the least sophisticated element of your audience. Whether or not an alleged debt is valid will not bar a suit against you if you violate this standard.[53]

The above standards are important because many actions regarding your method of calls, wording of letters, etc. will turn on them. Now we'll move from the general standards to the specific rules you must obey in contacting the debtor.

The debt collector may not contact the debtor in regard to the collection of the debt at a place or time inconvenient to the debtor or at the debtor's place of employment if the employer does not allow such calls. A convenient time is assumed to be between 8:00 a.m. and 9:00 p.m. at the debtor's location (taking into account the different time zones).[54] Avoid placing calls on Sunday, though they are not per se illegal. If the debtor has indicated (or the collector discovers) that such hours are not convenient (if, for example, the debtor works at night and sleeps during the day), he or she has the right to be contacted at more convenient times. Finally, if you know or the debtor has informed you that he or she is represented by an attorney, you must deal directly with the attorney rather than the debtor.[55]

Two points concerning the attorney's arrival on the scene:

(1) A debt collector who knows a consumer is represented by an attorney with respect to a debt is not required to assume similar representation on other debts; however, if a consumer notifies the debt collector that the attorney has been retained to represent him or her for all current and future debts that may be placed with the debt collector, the debt collector must deal only with that attorney.

(2) The creditor's knowledge that the consumer has retained an attorney is not automatically imputed to the debt collector.

One final note on initial contact: if the debtor is a minor, you may contact the debtor's parents.[56]

After the initial oral communication, you must follow up *once* in writing (or in your first letter if you write directly) within five days and notify the debtor that if he or she disputes the validity of all *or any portion* (finance charges, for example, are a portion) of the debt, he or she *must* notify you within 30 days of receipt of this notice, or it will be assumed that the debt is valid. The act does not mandate any particular format, type size, sequence, location, etc. for the validation notice—only its specific content.[57] If you utilize the wording of the statute by simply quoting it, you may not be creative, but your letters will pass muster.[58]

If the debtor notifies you in writing (writing is not required under 15 U.S.C. Sec.1692q(a)(3) but is best for all concerned) within 30 days of the receipt of notice, you will obtain verification from the creditor or, if a judgment exists, a copy of same and mail the debtor a copy of the verification or judgment. This is to reduce the incidence of dunning the wrong person or attempting to collect previously paid debts. If the debtor cannot identify the current creditor and writes to you to that effect, you must provide the name and address of the original creditor if different from that listed.[59]

If the debtor does dispute your bill or asks for the identity of the original creditor in writing within 30 days of receiving the notice, the debt collector must stop all collection of the debt or any disputed portion of the debt. However, collection efforts may be resumed when the information requested by the debtor is *mailed* to the debtor.

It should be noted that even if a consumer does *not* dispute the debt within the 30-day period, that in itself is not an admission of guilt or any other waiver of rights on the consumer's part. In your communications you may never state or imply such failure to respond is an admission of liability.

Debtors may inform the debt collector *in writing* that they refuse to pay the debt or desire that further communication from the debt collector cease. In this event the debt collector's response is limited, and none of the statutory limitations permit even the suggestion of a demand for payment. The debt collector may *not* contact the debtor *except* to advise him or her that certain *specific* action will be taken by the debt collector or the creditor. This action *must* then actually happen. This section is strictly enforced; if even an innocent additional message is sent, the sender may be liable for breach of the law[60] as well as intentional infliction of emotional distress.[61]

This law puts the debtor in control of the collection process in another way: If a debtor owes more than one debt and makes a payment, the debt collector may not apply the payment toward the disputed debt and must, when directed, apply the payment according to the debtor's instructions.

If no response to your proper initial notification is received, you will begin the routine collection process. You need not disclose any specific debt collection caveats. A straightforward collection letter that demands payment of a debt by its nature informs the consumer that it is an attempt to collect a debt. And the consumer also knows very well that the debt collector would use any information that the consumer might supply to collect the debt.[62] You need now refrain only from using the statutory false representations discussed below.

Prohibited Practices

The act precludes the collector from engaging in any conduct "the natural consequences of which is to harass, oppress, or abuse any person in the collection of a debt."[63] The law presents a large yet nonexclusive list of examples of such conduct you must avoid, including:

☐ *Threats of or actual harassment or abuse.* This includes continual or repeated calls or personal contacts[64] as well as anonymous or "collect" calls. Abusive language includes religious slurs, profanity, obscenity, calling the consumer a liar or a deadbeat, and the use of racial or sexual epithets. Statements such as "You shouldn't have children if you can't afford them"[65] are improper. A letter that implies that a woman ignores her mail and her bills, and lacks the common sense to handle her financial matters properly is both abusive and illegal. And, of course, any threat of violence, physical harm, extortion, blackmail, or criminal prosecution is illegal.[66]

Finally, don't leave the recipient of your call dangling with a veiled though unspecified threat. "You owe it, you don't want to pay, so we're going to have to do something about it" is language that cannot be defended.[67]

☐ *Soliciting and depositing or threatening to deposit a postdated check before the designated date.*[68] The act prohibits debt collection agencies from *accepting* checks postdated by more than five days *unless* the agency notifies the debtor in writing at least three, and not more than ten, *business* days before it intends to deposit the check. Debt collectors must never deposit or threaten to deposit a postdated check before the date of the check.[69]

The social policy here is that debtors cannot always plan their economic futures with perfection, and they may run into trouble if they give checks that are postdated too far in the future. The act's solution to this kind of problem is to give consumers notice before their checks will be cashed, so that they can tell the collector not to go ahead.

☐ *Publication of deadbeat lists, except for consumer reporting agencies.* (See discussion of the Fair Credit Reporting Act, chapter 21.)[70] These provisions are designed to prohibit debt collectors from "shaming" a customer into payment by publicizing the debt. A debt collector may not exchange lists of consumers who allegedly refuse to pay their debts. Nor may a debt collector distribute a list of alleged debtors to its creditor subscribers, because the statute permits it to provide such information only to the consumer reporting agencies.

☐ *False or misleading threats.* This is an area reviewed in detail in the introductory case. The act prohibits false, deceptive, and misleading statements by debt collectors, including the threat to take action that the collector does not mean to take.[71] Even a tentative threat violates FDCPA if the collector has already decided not to sue.[72]

Obviously the threat of a lawsuit or damage to one's credit rating is more likely to grab the attention of your reader than the outcome, i.e., in today's world most debtors are savvy enough to know just how impotent the typical debt collector is. Terms like "lawsuit" in debt collection notices are similar to "free" in advertising. Both catch the eye and both are literally interpreted. A few points: Don't bluff. A letter such as "It is our policy to attempt to settle these matters out of court before making any decision whether to refer them to an attorney for collection . . . . Unless we receive your check or money order, we will proceed with collection procedures"[73] must be literally true *at the time it was mailed.* Likewise, stating that you will recommend legal action "unless satisfactory arrangements are made within five days" requires truth as to the action *and* that five days (or shortly thereafter) is actually a trigger date and not a false threat.[74]

Threats of unintended actions or misrepresenting the imminency of intended action violate the law. This is true for related terms, too, such as "criminal warrant pending"[75] or that you'll report a dishonored check to the police or other legal authority unless you actually intend to.

Finally, a debt collector's statement that legal action has been recommended is a representation that legal action may be taken, since such a recommendation implies that the creditor will act on it at least some significant percentage of the time. Lack of intent may be inferred when the amount of the debt is so small as to make the action totally unfeasible or when the debt collector is unable to take the action because the creditor has not authorized him or her to do so.

☐ *Any form of misrepresentation of the nature or urgency* of your communication or the speed of any action to be taken as a result of the nonpayment of the debt. For example:

- Dunning letters simulating the appearance of telegrams or court summonses or complaints violate the act.[76] "Some collectors seem to be foolishly fascinated with determining how close they can come to simulating a telegram or legal process without violating the law, or at least being caught. Common sense dictates that there is no violation if you use an *actual* telegram or similar service, notwithstanding a Western Union (or other provider) logo and the word "telegram" (or similar word) appear on the envelope.'

- Headlines such as "Urgent," "Immediate," "48 Hours," "Use Express Mail Only," etc. are illegal unless they have a consequence objectively and truthfully set forth. (They rarely do.)

- A debt collector may not falsely represent that a person named in a letter is his or her attorney or that attorney is doing anything more than collecting a debt (an attorney's letter is usually a problem but should always set forth at the outset his or her purpose is collection and *not* a lawsuit). A debt collector's employee who is an attorney may not use "attorney-at-law" stationery without referring to his or her employer, so as to falsely imply to the consumer that the debt collector has retained a private attorney to bring suit on the account.

Note: A "threat" that is a known fact (for example, that failure to pay one's debts would affect a future credit rating) does *not* violate the FDCPA.[77] Also, none of the above makes illegal subtle prodding such as having a high-ranking corporate official sign your letter, which may convey a sense of urgency without being illegal.

☐ *False claims of association memberships* that imply a national strength and perhaps a larger bad debt file.[78]

☐ *Misleading symbols on dunning notice.* A debt collector may not use a symbol in correspondence that makes him or her appear to be a government official. For example, a collection letter depicting a judge, or the scales of justice, violates this section. A creditor may not use any name that would falsely imply that a third party is involved in the collection. Only a bona fide consumer reporting agency may use names such as "Credit Bureau," "Credit Bureau Collection Agency," "General Credit Control," "Credit Bureau Rating, Inc.," or "National Debtors Rating." Whether you qualify as such is determined by your actual operations and not merely your choice of what name you elect to do business under.

A debt collector's disclaimer in the text of a letter that the debt collector is not affiliated with (or employed by) a consumer reporting agency, will not necessarily avoid a violation if the collector uses a name that indicates otherwise. The text of the letter, function of the firm, etc., all must be considered.[79] Naturally, none of these names, even if proper, can be used on the envelopes.

☐ *False allegations that the consumer has committed fraud.* A debt collector may not make a misleading statement of law, falsely implying that the consumer has committed a crime, or mischaracterize what constitutes an offense by misstating or omitting significant elements of the offense. For example, a debt collector may not tell the consumer that he or she has committed a crime by issuing a check that is a "scheme to defraud."

Again, what is misleading or deceptive generally relates to the total effect your message might have on a reasonable debtor. However, some courts will look less at the reasonable person standard and more at the reading comprehension and mental ability of the actual recipient of your message. The multitude of subsections cover a whole gamut of violations; if you have any doubt about whether you or your collection agency may be in violation here, review this section with your counsel.

A classic case of what *not* to do under this law is found in *Housh v. Peth:*[80]

> The record shows that the defendant deliberately planned a systematic campaign of harassment of the plaintiff, not only in numerous telephone calls to the plaintiff herself *every day* for a period of three weeks, some of which were *late at night,* but also calls to her superiors over the telephone, informing them of the debt, that she was called out of the classroom *three times within 15 minutes;* that she lost a roomer at her rooming house because of the repeated calls, and was threatened with loss of employment unless the telephone calls ceased. The calls to the employer, and the rooming house, were all part of the pattern to harass and humiliate the plaintiff and cause her mental pain and anguish and cause her emotional disturbance for the purpose of coercing her to pay the debt. [Emphasis added.]

Post Dunning

If you've collected your money—congratulations. If you haven't, what alternatives are left?

First, if you've properly gone through all the legal hoops discussed above, then feel free to deliver on your threats by reporting the debtor's name to a credit reporting agency. The only qualification is that if a debt is disputed by your debtor, either via written notice or other means, the debt must be reported as disputed.

Second, even if the debt is paid in full, you may still pursue a fee or charge (e.g., interest) in addition to the debt if either (a) the charge is expressly provided for in the contract creating the debt and the charge is not prohibited by state law, or (b) the contract is silent but the charge is otherwise expressly permitted by state law. If state law permits collection of reasonable fees, the reasonableness and consequential legality of these fees is determined by state law.

Third, if you've received some money, but not sufficient funds, you must, on multiple debts, honor your debtor's preference for payment if he or she informs you of such a preference.

Finally, you may sue the debtor, but only in the judicial district where the consumer resides or signed the contract sued upon. Exception: An action to enforce a security interest in real property that secures the obligation must be brought where the property is located.[81] Naturally you'll consult with counsel on these specifics.

Penalties/Civil Liability

The original House-passed version of the act contained a criminal law enforcement provision. This was dropped in favor of just civil enforcement by private individuals (both individually and as a class)[82] with the FTC as the major enforcement agency.[83]

The act was designed to be self-enforcing, so individuals are encouraged to seek redress for "unfair" and other conduct by a debt collector. Conduct will be deemed unfair if it causes injury to a debtor that is substantial, not reasonably avoidable, and not outweighed by countervailing benefits.

Individual debtors may bring suit (and in certain cases debtors can bring class actions) within one year of a violation in any appropriate U.S. district court without regard to the amount in controversy.[84] The consumer may collect actual damages (which may include emotional distress, embarrassment, or humiliation) caused by a collector's violation of the act, statutory damages up to $1000[85] (merely on proof of a violation—*no* actual damages are required), reasonable attorneys fees, and court costs.[86] In assessing damages, the court must take into account the nature of the violation, the frequency and persistence of noncompliance, and the extent to which the debt collector's noncompliance was *intentional* .[87] Debt collectors are in the clear if they can show that violations were not intentional *and* resulted from a bona fide error.[88] The act also shields from civil liability a collector who relies on an advisory FTC opinion.[89] If the court finds that any action was brought by a consumer in bad faith and for harassment purposes, the court may award the debt collector reasonable attorney fees and costs.[90] It is hoped that this will dissuade some nuisance suits by debtors. One final note: the individual debtor has the right to a jury trial.[91]

Don't forget the state laws. The act provides an exemption for state regulations and laws that are substantially similar to the act (which means that the laws of the state in which you are collecting may be narrower than the federal act).[92] Discuss with your counsel the laws of the states in which you do business.

TELEPHONE DUNNING

Because of the potentially more intrusive aspects of telephone dunning (compared with dunning by mail, for instance) and for other reasons, telephone dunning has caused much legal action in the last few years. There are certain public policy issues as to telephone intrusion. Allowing an interval of 3 to 10 days between calls may be the norm, but

I'd recommend an interval no shorter than one week (for the same debt). There is no prohibition of dunning if you place your dunning call the same day or the day after the arrival of your dunning letter. Likewise, you are permitted to follow up on any "promises to pay" with a letter confirming the conversation and amount and date of promised payment. A coordinated policy such as this, carried out with reasonable restraint, is not intrusion.

All dunning calls should be manually dialed unless you have carefully examined the law of the state your are calling. Certain states have restricted or banned automated dialing or - speaking calls. (See the discussion of telephone marketing as well as the discussion of unordered merchandise in Chapter 9.)

All the previously discussed points on debt collection (for example implied urgency) are relevant to the phone, if applicable (obviously the postcard issue is a moot point here, unless you follow up your calls with a mailing). If you are doing a national dunning campaign, no calls should be made before 8:00 a.m. or after 9:00 p.m. (8:00 p.m. in Pennsylvania and New York City check with counsel regarding time restrictions in your area). Avoid all Sunday calls. By calls, I mean actual discussions terminated by 9:00 p.m. Any calls "under the wire" risk violation. Individual state laws and regulations should be reviewed with your counsel, as the act permits narrower state enforcement.

Make sure you ask for the alleged debtor by full name and then say nothing until the debtor answers. Then politely ask if you are speaking to him or her. If the person is not in, you may leave a return number. Here you must not identify the nature of the call (this will better the chances of getting a return call). You need only state your name and the firm you represent. You might try to purge the debtor's place of employment telephone number from your file unless it is the only access you have to the debtor.

Once you are speaking with the debtor, you should identify yourself and the purpose of your call before starting your "pitch." Then, within five days of the first call, you should send the debtor a written notice of the right to verify the debt, dispute it, and possibly end communication altogether (see above).

No harassing or abusive calls are permitted. Immediately calling the debtor after the debtor has hung up the phone is an example of harassment. All calls should be made in a businesslike manner and with a subdued tone.

Finally, you are expected to use well-trained professionals in your debtor contact. Courts like to see a program of constant on-the-job training, coupled with telephone monitoring, supervision, and reference to a standardized manual as a procedure reasonably adopted to avoid violations of the act.[93] However, if you are thinking of taping or otherwise listening to employee calls for employment training purposes, first review the following discussion.

Monitoring Employee Calls

Congress passed a comprehensive electronic surveillance law in Title III of the Omnibus Crime Control and Safe Streets Act of 1968.[94] This act was intended to deal with the growing use of sophisticated electronic monitoring devices, which increasingly threatened an average citizen's reasonable expectation of privacy.

Unlike many pieces of legislative overkill, this act was worded to strike a fair balance between privacy rights and legitimate business practices. For your business needs, an understanding of certain definitions in 18 USC Sec.2510 is important. To violate the act, you must intercept an oral or wire communication. A telephone conversation is a wire communication. However, an interception does not occur unless an "electronic, mechanical, or other device" is employed. The definition of these devices specifically excluded a telephone used in the regular course of the subscriber's business. Specifically, the law grants an exception to

> any telephone or telegraph instrument, equipment or facility or any component thereof, ...furnished to the subscriber or user by a communications common carrier in the ordinary course of its business and being used by the subscriber for use in the ordinary course of its business.[95]

If you request that the telephone company install a monitoring device that will permit you to listen to telephone conversations between employees and customers in the ordinary course of business only, this will not be considered interception. This is predicated on the fact that duties in the ordinary course of business include only lawful and proper activities.

Lawful and Proper Activities

The courts that have reviewed the issue do not want to see evidence of surreptitious monitoring or monitoring for personal gain or gossip. At all times you should be able to demonstrate that the monitoring was undertaken for the sole interest of the company's business operations and for a limited purpose and time. At no time do you wish to appear to have monitored a strictly "private" call.

For example, a telephone system vendor installed monitoring equipment on telephones in those departments of a newspaper organization that had direct contact with the public. The business purpose of this monitoring was to assist the employee training program as well as to protect employees from abusive calls. The monitoring was not surreptitious; on the contrary, it was performed with the prior knowledge of management and all affected employees (who were informed in writing). The court held that there was no interception, since the equipment was used in the ordinary course of the employer's business.[96]

One sobering case involved monitoring performed over a simple extension phone. A supervisor was invited to listen to a call—the employee had been visibly upset by a previous call from this person, and the supervisor's curiosity had been aroused.[97] The caller issued a death threat to the employee, a threat he proved only too capable of following through on. The trial court convicted the murderer in part based on the supervisor's testimony.

This decision was reversed by the appellate court, but the Florida Supreme Court upheld the trial court's conclusion that there was no interception, despite the issue of the supervisor's "curiosity." The supervisor was acting in her official capacity, concerned with the employee's emotional state affecting her job. The employee gave prior consent. The business purpose performed during business hours satisfied the test for the ordinary course of business, establishing that there was no interception.

Is monitoring permitted without an employee's prior consent or notification? Yes, in limited circumstances. A manager had justifiable reason to suspect an employee was acting in concert with an agent of a competitor to the possible detriment of the manager's corporation. The manager warned the employee not to disclose confidential information to this outside party. The manager believed that something still was not right.

When the manager was subsequently informed that the parties were on the phone with each other, he decided to validate his suspicions. He listened to and recorded a part of a telephone conversation by means of an extension phone without the prior knowledge of the employee or the third party. The act of listening in was limited in purpose and time—just enough time to confirm his suspicions. The U.S. District Court held that there was no interception, because the manager was acting in what he legitimately believed was the company's best interests.[98] While in no way condoning the manager's actions, the court held that his use of the telephone satisfied the ordinary-course-of-business test.

Finally, note that the use of an extension telephone to intercept a phone call by someone who is not authorized to use the telephone (e.g., non-management employees, if phones are restricted to management) cannot be considered conduct "in the ordinary course of business" under any circumstances.[99]

Protecting Your Monitoring

If you can demonstrate that your procedures for monitoring employee telephones are lawful and proper and used in the ordinary course of business, you are in fairly good shape. However, your worries are not over, and the following precautions are in order.

☐ State and local legislative and regulatory activity should be routinely audited. The laws in place should be reviewed with counsel. The federal law we have discussed permits more stringent state standards, and some states do have more stringent laws on point.[100] For example, West Virginia prohibits the interception or monitoring of telephone conversations between an employee and a customer, *unless* the employer notifies employees that their telephone messages may be intercepted and provides telephones for the personal use of its employees that are not subject to monitoring.[101]

☐ Neither the surreptitious use of a telephone extension to record a private telephone conversation nor a general practice of surreptitious monitoring would qualify as a legal exception. You should never tape a call as "evidence" that a customer agreed to do something.

☐ Do not attempt to monitor personal calls to "prove" a violation of a legitimate business policy against such calls without extending prior warning to an individual concerning such violation.

☐ To meet the ordinary-course-of-business test:

a. State this purpose when you procure the equipment from the common carrier.

b. Give advance written notice to all managers and employees involved, stating the business purpose of the monitoring.

c. Obtain a written release from each employee involved, stating that they are aware of the fact that their supervisor will listen in unannounced and that they agree to this policy. For more information, see the discussion of contracts in Chapter 25.

☐ With the growth of international business in general and marketing in particular, one final comment is useful. The provisions of the Wire Interception and Interception of Oral Communications Act apply only within the territorial jurisdiction of the United States. The law of the nation where the monitoring takes place (situs) governs the validity of such monitoring, even if a United States citizen is involved or the intercepted telephone conversation travels in part over the U.S. communications system. Therefore, a firm physically located in the U.S. may monitor calls to Canadian customers subject to U.S. law. Likewise, a Canadian-based firm monitoring calls to U.S. customers is bound by Canadian law on this point.

Wrapping Up Telephone Monitoring

In monitoring any aspect of employee calls (such as in training), managers must be careful not to monitor in a manner that would "intercept" calls. There is no interception under federal law if the acquisition of the contents of the communication is accomplished through telephone equipment used in the ordinary course of business.

TREATMENT OF CREDIT BALANCES

Bad debts may not be the only problem related to credit purchases. Ironically perhaps, overpayment too may be a problem. Review your policy as to credit balances (these apply not just to credit card charges but to in-house charges as well, even if no finance charge, late fees, etc. are involved).

A credit balance is created when the creditor receives or holds funds in an account in excess of the total balance due from the customer on the account. The FTC requires that you provide charge or other credit account customers having credit balances with periodic statements setting forth credit balances no less than three times in a six-month period following the creation of the balance. Each statement must notify customers with credit balances of their right to an immediate cash refund of the balance. If your customer sends a written request for the money, you must refund it as soon as possible.

If you hear nothing from your customer, then, after the lapse of seven months, you must act. The law states that whenever a credit balance in *excess* of $1 is created as a credit account (for example, by overpayment or rebate), in connection with a consumer credit transaction through (1) transmittal of funds to a creditor in excess of the total balance due on an account, (2) rebates of unearned finance charges or insurance premiums, or (3) amounts otherwise owed to or held for the benefit of an obligor, the creditor must:

☐ credit the amount of the credit balance to the consumer's account;

☐ refund any part of the amount of the remaining credit balance within seven business days upon receipt of a written request from the consumer; and

☐ make a good-faith effort to refund to the consumer by cash, check, or money order any part of the amount of the credit balance remaining in the account for more than six months; however, no further action is required in any case in which the consumer's current location is not known by the creditor and cannot be traced through the consumer's last known address or telephone number.[102]

Credit balances under $1 may be written off, but you must be prepared to refund within 30 days any credit balance requested within five to six years of its creation.

What do you do after repeated good-faith efforts to refund the balance and the check is returned "addressee unknown" or "no forwarding address"? Here, the respective state escheat laws must be examined in light of your firm's specific business practices. You need not have all the checks pile up. However, to protect yourself you should keep a record of your effort. Both the check and the envelope showing attempted delivery should be microfilmed. Then retain it for the applicable period (five to six years). After that, if still unclaimed, it will probably be escheated to the respective state of the "owner." Your consolation is that you had the "float" value of the funds during this interval. The respective state and federal laws should be reviewed with counsel as to when and how such balances must be refunded.

Note: A creditor has to send a billing statement covering a particular period only if there is an outstanding balance at the end of the period or a finance charge. Otherwise, you can save the postage unless you want to initiate routine contact for goodwill or enclosure merchandising opportunities.

Your Dunning Checklist

As part of an overall systematic and professional management of your bad-debt problem, you'll want to create a checklist of legal compliance. You should do this whether or not you must comply with the act. Your checklist will include the following:

- ☐ Have we carefully reviewed with counsel what specific federal and state laws we must comply with and how? If we're "excluded," are we aware of what actions will result in our becoming "included"?
- ☐ Are we retaining an independent agency to collect for us? If so, have we confirmed in writing that the agency is licensed, bonded, insured and passes a Dun & Bradstreet, Better Business Bureau or other check? Have we thoroughly reviewed the agency services contract with our counsel?
- ☐ How are we handling person-to-person communications?
  - Are we careful *not* to tell third parties that the person we're looking for owes a debt?
  - Are we avoiding contacting third parties more than once in our location efforts unless absolutely necessary to get correct and complete information?
  - Are we truthful in response to inquiries from third parties?
  - Are we confining location information solely to a debtor's residence, home phone number, and place of employment?
  - Do we cease contacting the debtors directly when we know they are represented by an attorney with regard to the debt?
- ☐ Do we keep in mind that all our communication vehicles (letters, telephone scripts, etc.) must be targeted to the least sophisticated of our audience?
- ☐ How are we handling our written communications (e.g., dunning letters) both internally and those used by an outside agency?
  - Have we carefully examined all envelopes to make sure there is no reference of a collection effort visible on them, such as in the return address? Obviously, only opaque envelopes are considered, since all forms of postcards are prohibited.
  - Do any of our communication pieces misrepresent the nature and urgency of the communication, for example, are we sure not to use simulated telegrams, mailgrams, court process documents, or any wording such as "urgent," "immediate," or "10 days to reply" (unless such wording has legal significance)? Do we threaten *immediate* action? Even if such actions are eventually pursued, no likelihood of immediate

action can be indicated if no immediate action will take place (for example, the phrase "it must be settled immediately" is not acceptable if untrue).

- Does the wording of any communication misrepresent in any way, directly or by implication, the purpose, intent, and procedure of our collection efforts with the debtor or our affiliation?

- Do any communications threaten any consequence we do not *routinely* follow through on? For example:

(1) reporting the debtor to a consumer reporting agency,

(2) taking legal action, or

(3) arranging for attachment or garnishment.

- Does our use of an attorney's letterhead state directly or imply that legal action will result? If so, will we act accordingly? Have we confirmed in-house or with the outside agency that such attorney is a real living member of the bar and not some fictitious or deceased individual? Have we reviewed with counsel whether this form of letter in these circumstances is permissible at all?

- Are we sending the debtor a notice within five days of the first communication that includes all the following items?

(1) Name of the creditor owed

(2) Identification of the debt by amount and account number

(3) Nature of the default and how it can be cured

(4) Name, mailing address, and (where applicable) telephone number to contact for verification of the debt

(5) The right to obtain verification of the debt

(6) The procedure for verification

(7) The right (and consequences resulting from the exercise of such right) of the debtor to have the collector cease communication

- Are we making sure that there is no offensive, abusive, or threatening language in any contact?

- Are we careful to avoid inducing "shame" or similar tactics to encourage payment?

☐ How are we handling internal procedures?

- If the debtor disputes the debt or requests the name of the creditor, are we stopping our collection efforts until we have mailed the verification of the debt or the creditor's name? If the debtor disputes the debt, claiming unordered merchandise was sent, do we carefully confirm that this is not the case? (See discussion of laws on direct marketing of unordered merchandise in Chapter 9.) It is illegal to send collection letters demanding payment *or* return of merchandise that was never requested in the first place. If selling on approval or through negative option plans, you must carefully review the wording in your coupons or order forms with your counsel.

- Is every statement made in each follow-up letter or call true and in compliance?

- If we receive a check from the debtor, do we have a written screening policy for the following?

(1) What to do when a postdated check arrives.

(2) What do do when a check arrives that is insufficient payment but has "paid in full" written on the back. Merely crossing out such endorsement often is not enough; sometimes the best policy is to send back the check if it is for an unacceptable amount. Here you'll have to balance this with your own business judgment as well as your counsel's input.

(3) How to apply payment if the debtor owes multiple debts and makes a single payment with specific directions concerning how the payment should be applied.

(4) How to apply prompt internal controls as to the deposit of payment checks as well as the automatic redeposit of "bounced" checks.

☐ Regarding our telephone dunning procedures:

- Have counsel screened all our telephone scripts as to their legal compliance? Have we screened them for their readability to our callers and for comprehension by our debtors?

- Have all our employees been informed in writing of our policy (and the penalties) for obscene or profane language, use of threats, etc.?

- Do all our callers properly ask for and obtain the proper and specific person desired?

- Do our callers properly identify themselves and the nature of the call?

- Are all calls reasonably spaced and at a proper hour (time zones verified) to avoid harassment?

- Are our employee-testing procedures lawful?

- Have we established written systems, procedures, and checklists to demonstrate to an investigating body that any error was accidental and not a matter of policy of negligence?

- Within five days of the first call, are we sending the debtor a follow-up *written notice* of the right to verification of the debt, the right to dispute the debt, and the right to end communication?

- Finally, are all our internal employee monitoring procedures in accord with state and local law?

☐ Are our post-dunning procedures in compliance?

- In any reports to credit reporting agencies are we careful to include a report of a debtor's dispute of such debt?

- Are all our judicial follow-ups in strict accordance with the law?

Remember that, unless you are careful to document your employee training, these procedures may be of little assistance in a legal action. Remember, too, that the FTC takes a very literal view of the wording of laws on point. That "other firms are doing it" is no defense for non-compliance—they just haven't been caught yet!

ENDNOTES

(1) Consumer Credit Counseling Services, National Foundation for Consumer Credit, 1819 H Street N.W., Washington, D.C., 20006.

(2) 15 U.S.C. Sec. 41 et seq.

(3) FDCPA Sec. 803(6)(B).

(4) Regulation 10.1(4) of the New York City Consumer Protection Law provides for certain exclusions but not the exclusion of in-house collectors. It became effective on February 27, 1979 and applies to creditors located within the five boroughs.

(5) *Pennsylvania Code* Chapter 303, Debt Collection Practices, adopted July 27, 1979. This regulation requires your *outside agency* to include the name, mailing address, and telephone number of the debt collector and the creditor.

(6) *Trans World Accounts, Inc. v. FTC,* 90 FTC 350 (1977), 594 F.2d 212 (1979); *In re Capax,* 91 FTC 1084, *amended,* 92 FTC 871 (1978); *United Computered Collection, Inc.,* 87 FTC 541 (1976); *Encyclopedia Britannica, Inc.,* 87 FTC 421, 539-50 (1976); *New Process Co.,* 87 FTC 1359 (1976), *Pay 'N Save Corp.,* 86 FTC 688 (1975); and *Compact Electra Corp.,* 83 FTC 547 (1973).

(7) *State v. O'Neill Investigations, Inc.,* 609 P.2d 530.

(8) For Example:
Arizona Revised Statutes Sec. 32-1001, 32-1021-1022.
Arkansas Statutes 71-2006, 2007.
California Business and Professions Code Sec. 6894.2 et seq. (1986).
Annotated Code of Maryland Article 56-329 B and C (1986).
North Dakota Century Code 31-05-01 et seq. (1986).

(9) *California Civil Code* Sec. 1788.12 and *Business and Professions Code* Sec. 6871. *Connecticut General Statutes Annotated* Sec. 42-131 a (h).

(10) *Connecticut General Statutes Annotated* Sec. 42-131 (1986).

(11) *Silver v. Wolff,* 694 F.2d 8 (1982).

(12) *Scrimpsher v. Wegman's Food Markets, Inc.,* 17 B.R. 999 (1982), FDCPA sec. 812; 15 U.S.C. Sec. 1962j.

(13) 15 U.S.C. Sec. 1692.

(14) *Grant Road Lumber Co., Inc. v. Wystrach,* 682 P.2d 1146, 1148 (Ariz. App. 1984) FDCPA Sec. 808(1), 15 U.S.C. Sec. 1692(f). See also FDCPA Sec. 812(a).

(15) 15 U.S.C. Sec. 1692 (e).

(16) 15 U.S.C. Sec. 1692 (a), (c) and (d); see Sen. Rep. No. 95-382 at 6, reprinted in [1977] U.S. Code Cong. & Administrative News 1695 at 1700. *Staub v. Harris,* 275, 279 (3d Cir. 1980).

(17) 15 U.S.C. Sec. 45.

(18) 15 U.S.C. Sec. 1692 (a) (5), 803(5); see *In re Scrimpsher,* 17 B.R. 999 (N.D.N.Y. 1982).

(19) *Dun & Bradstreet, Inc. v. McEldowney,* 564 F.Supp. 357 (1983).

(20) *Staub v. Harris,* 626 F.2d 275 (3d Cir. 1980).

(21) *Carrigan v. Central Adjustment Bureau, Inc.,* 494 F.Supp. 824 (1980).

(22) 15 U.S.C. Sec. 1692 (a)(6), 808(6). For an example of a representative state law on point see 32 *Maine Revised Statutes Annotated* Chapter 111, Sec. 11001- 11054 (1986).

(23) 15 U.S.C. Sec. 1692(a)(6)(A), *Warren v. Bank of Marron,* 618 F.Supp. 317 (W.D.Va. 1985). This is true even if you run afoul of state law. See *Baldwin v. First National Bank of the Black Hills,* 362 NW2d 85 (S.D. 1985).

(24) 15 U.S.C. Sec. 1692(a)(6)(B).

(25) *Horne v. Farrell,* 560 F.Supp. 219 (1983); *Staub v. Harris,* 626 F.2d 275, 277 (3d Cir. 1980).

(26) 15 U.S.C. Sec. 1692(a)(6)(C).

(27) *Heredia v. Green,* 667 F.2d 392 (1981).

(28) *Gray v. Spires,* 473 F.Supp. 878 (1979), rev'd. on other grounds, 634 F.2d 772 (1979).

(29) 15 U.S.C. Sec. 1692(a)(6)(D).

(30) 15 U.S.C. Sec. 1692(a)(6)(E).

(31) *Alexander v. Moore Associates, Inc.,* 553 F.Supp. 948 (1982).

(32) For a good review of 15 U.S.C. Sec. 1692 (a)(6)(G); FDCPA Sec. 803 (6)(G), see *Perry v. Stewart Title Co.,* 756 F.2d 1197 (5th Cir. 1985).

(33) U.S.H.R. (sponsor Annuzio) 237, P.L. 99-361 (1986). See also *Annotated Code of Maryland* (1985) Article 56—Licenses, Section 324.

(34) *West v. Costen,* 558 F.Supp. 564 (W.D.Va. 1983).

(35) Regulation 10.1 (4) of the New York City Consumer Protection Law provides for certain exclusions but not the exclusion of in-house collectors (effective February 27, 1979). It applies to creditors located within the five boroughs.

(36) See note 5, above.

(37) *In re Scrimpsher,* 17 Barb. 999 (N.D.N.Y. 1982).

(38) 15 U.S.C. Sec. 1692(a)(7), 15 U.S.C. Sec. 1692(b), FDCPA Sec. 804.

(39) FDCPA Sec. 803(7).

(40) Section 806(6) requires that some identifiable name be given. The caller *must* correctly identify the collection agency as well as the fact that the call concerns the attempt to collect a debt. See *Wright v. Credit Bureau of Ga., Inc.,* 548 F.Supp. 591 (1982).

(41) *Kleczy v. First Federal Credit Control,* 486 NE2d 204, 206 (1984); but see *Bingham v. Collection Bureau, Inc.,* 505 F.Supp. 864 (N.D. 1981) (use of alias violates FDCPA but excused as a bona fide error).

(42) *Vogel v. W. T. Grant Co.,* 458 Pa. 124, 327 S.2d 133 (1974).

(43) *West v. Costen,* 558 F.Supp. 564, 575-581 (W.D. Va. 1983); FDCPA Sec. 803(6), 15 U.S.C. Sec. 1692 (a) (6), which took a broad view of who a "consumer" is. See also *Whitley v. Universal Collection Bureau,* 525 F.Supp. 1204 (1981) (contra opinion re parents and other "loved ones").

(44) FDCPA Sec. 808(7), 808(8); 15 U.S.C. Secs. 1692(f)(7), 1692(f)(8).

(45) *Kleczy v. First Federal Credit Control,* 486 NE2d 204 (1984); FDCPA Sec. 806, 808; 15 U.S.C. Sec. 1692(d), 15 U.S.C. Sec. 1692(f).

(46) A debtor's divorce or estate attorney, even if known to you, is not the debtor's attorney with regard to the debt unless such attorney informs you accordingly.

(47) The original bill in Congress stated "seven calendar days," but this was amended to "a reasonable time."

(48) Use certified mail in all legal matters; your receipt is proof that the party who signed for it received the letter. A secretary's signing for the letter will be acknowledgment for the attorney.

(49) *Exposition Press, Inc. v. FTC,* 296 F.2d 869, 873 (1961), *cert den.,* 370 US 917 (1962); *Charles of the Ritz Distributors Corp. v. FTC,* 143 F.2d 676 (2d Cir. 1944).

(50) *Bingham v. Collection Bureau, Inc.,* 505 F.Supp. 864 (N.D. 1981).

(51) *Wright v. Credit Bureau of Georgia, Inc.,* 555 F.Supp. 1005, 1007 (1983).

(52) *Jeter v. Credit Bureau, Inc.,* 760 F.2d 1168, 1174-1175 (1985).

(53) *Baker v. GC Services Corp.,* 677 F.2d 775 (1982).

(54) FDCPA Sec. 805(a)(1), 15 U.S.C. Sec. 1692(c).

(55) FDCPA Sec. 805(a)(2), 15 U.S.C. Sec. 1692(c).

(56) *Harvey v. United Adjusters,* 509 F.Supp. 1218 (1981). See elsewhere in this book, and consult your counsel for the applicable state laws concerning what is a legal, contracted-for debt as to a minor.

(57) FDCPA Sec. 809, 15 U.S.C. Sec. 1692(g). See also *Blockwell v. Professional Business Services of Georgia, Inc.,* 526 F.Supp. 535 (N.D. Ga. 1981) and *Harvey v. United Adjusters,* 509 F.Supp. 1218 (1981).

(58) *Check Center of Oregon, Inc. v. Barr,* 54 Bankruptcy Law Reporter 922 (D. Ore. 1984).

(59) 15 U.S.C. Sec. 1692(g) (a).

(60) *Bingham v. Collection Bureau, Inc.,* 505 F.Supp. 864 (N.D. 1981).

(61) *Carrigan v. Central Adjustment Bureau, Inc.,* 494 F.Supp. 824 (1980). The court also fined the firm for a violation of the state licensing law; such licensing laws held constitutional. See, for example, *Silver v. Woolf,* 694 F.2d 8 (1982).

(62) *Pressley v. Capital Credit & Collection Service,* 760 F.2d 922, 925 (1985); FDCPA Sec. 807(11), 15 U.S.C. Sec. 1692(e)(11).

(63) 15 U.S.C. Sec. 1692(d).

(64) 15 U.S.C. Sec. 1692(d)(1) - (d)(6), FDCPA Sec. 806(5). "Continuously" means making a series of telephone calls, one right after the other. "Repeatedly" means calling with excessive frequency, such as six phone calls in an hour. See also *Long v. Beneficial Finance Co. of New York,* 330 N.Y.S.2d 664 (1972).

(65) *Bingham v. Collection Bureau, Inc.,* 505 F.Supp. 864, 874 (N.D. 1981).

(66) *Harvey v. United Adjusters,* 509 F.Supp. 1218, 1221 (1981).

(67) *Rutyna v. Collection Accounts Terminal,* 478 F.Supp. 980, 981 (1979).

(68) 15 U.S.C. Sec. 1692(f)(2)(1) - 1692(f)(2)(4).

(69) 15 U.S.C. Sec. 1692(f)(2-4), FDCPA Sec. 808, (2-4).

(70) FDCPA Sec. 806(3); *Zaludek v. Atwood Oceanics International,* 553 F.Supp. 955 (1982).

(71) 15 U.S.C. Sec. 1692(e)(5), FDCPA Sec. 807(5).

(72) *Baker v. GC Services Corp.,* 677 F.2d 775 (CA Ore. 1982).

(73) Id.

(74) *Jeter v. Credit Bureau, Inc.,* 760 F.2d 1168, 1176 (1985).

(75) *West v. Costen,* 558 F.Supp. 564 (1983).

(76) 15 U.S.C. Sec. 1692(e) (10) and (13); see also *In re Scrimpsher,* 17 B.R. 999 (BC, NDNY 1982); and *Trans World Accounts Inc. v. FTC,* 594 F.2d 212 (1979).

(77) *Wright v. Credit Bureau of Georgia, Inc.,* 555 F.Supp. 1005.

(78) *Bingham v. Collection Bureau, Inc.,* 505 F.Supp. 864 (1981).

(79) See note 77 plus FDCPA Sec. 807.

(80) 165 Ohio St. 35, 133 NE2d 340 (1956).

(81) FDCPA Sec. 811.

(82) 15 U.S.C. Sec.1692(k)(a).

(83) You might want to get on the FTC's mailing list to stay abreast of current activities: FTC News Summary, Federal Trade Commission, Washington, D.C., 20580. You can call the general information number, (202) 523-3598, to order any cease and desist order from the FTC discussed in the FTC News Summary; you'll need to indicate the name of the firm and its assigned docket number.

(84) 15 U.S.C. Sec. 1692(k)(d).

(85) 15 U.S.C. Sec. 1692(k)(a)(1) - 1692(k)(a)(2); *Baker v. GC Services Corp.,* 677 F.2d 775 (1982).

(86) 15 U.S.C. Sec. 1692(k)(a).

(87) 15 U.S.C. Sec. 1692(k)(b)(1).

(88) 15 U.S.C. Sec. 1692(c). In addition to proving the existence of an unintentional clerical error, the debt collector must show that there existed systems and procedures reasonably adapted to avoid such error.

(89) FDCPA Sec. 813(E); see also 16 C.F.R. 1.1-1.4.

(90) 15 U.S.C. Sec. 1692(k)(a) (3), FDCPA Sec. 813(a) (3); *Penny v. Stewart Title Co.,* 756 F.2d 1197 (5th Cir. 1985).

(91) *Sibley v. Fulton DeKalb Collection Services,* 677 F.2d 830 (1982).

(92) 15 U.S.C. Sec. 1692(o), FDCPA Sec. 816-817.

(93) *Bingham v. Collection Bureau, Inc.,* 505 F.Supp. 864, 874 (1981).

(94) 18 U.S.C. Sec. 2510-2520.

(95) 18 U.S.C. Sec. 2510(5)(a)(i). *Note :* a "beep tone" is no longer required when recording *interstate* calls. However, it is necessary to get the other party's *consent.* You should review any narrower laws affecting local or *intrastate* calls with your counsel. Also review with your counsel any particular taping your firm considers. Privacy cases turn on the "reasonable expectation of privacy" of the person whose conversation is being recorded. Taping is rarely worth the exposure—monitor, don't tape. See *Moore v. Telfon Communications Corp.,* 589 F.2d 959 (1978).

(96) *James v. Newspaper Agency Corp.,* 591 F.2d 579 (10th Cir. 1979). See also *Stimmons v. Southwestern Bell Tel. Co.,* 452 F.Supp. 392 (1978).

(97) *State v. Nova,* 361 So.2d 411 (1978) (Florida).

(98) *Briggs v. American Air Filter Co.,* 630 F.2d 414 (1980).

(99) *State v. Harpel,* 493 F.2d 346 (10th Cir. 1974).

(100) For example, *Georgia Code Annotated,* Art. 26-3001-26-3010 or *Code of Virginia* Article 8 of Chapter 5 Title 18.2-167 (1986)—requires advance notice to employees.

(101) *Code of West Virginia* Article 3 Sec. 61-3-24(c) (1980).

(102) 15 U.S.C. Sec. 1666(d), 12 C.F.R. 226.11.

SECTION VII

PROFIT PRESERVATION
CENTER

CHAPTER 24

ESTABLISHING YOUR PROFIT PRESERVATION CENTER

What is a profit preservation center? A quick definition would be an integrated system whereby the activities of state and federal legislatures and regulatory bodies are monitored to avoid adverse exposure. Sound complicated? It's not, really. Depending on the size and scope of your operation, it doesn't have to be. A profit preservation center assists a modern firm's market research. It also performs its traditional function of anticipating and influencing the actions of public bodies. Any size firm can do it, and this chapter will show you how.

Where Do You Start?

Even if you're operating from a basement, you as an individual can call or write to your representatives at every level of government. First, you should find out who they are. You should be aware of those representing your business location as well as your residence. If you are not sure who represents your particular business location, contact your local Board of Elections, which should be able to provide you with the names of the representatives and districts for your location.

Once you have determined who your representatives are, it's time to build a relationship with them. After all, you are a constituent, and they will be representing your interest in Congress or the state legislature. Even if you can't get through to the representative personally, developing a rapport with a staff member can be helpful. The time to develop a relationship is now—*before* you need their help.

Your Representatives and Lobbying

Your legislative system should be integrated with your lobbying system. Politics, at its most effective, is persuasion. If you've educated yourself well on the merits of a bill, you're ready to persuade your antagonist to table, amend, or withdraw it.

If you support a bill, write your representative, the sponsor, and the head of the committee, in that order. If you don't think your opinion counts, try writing a personal letter (form letters, cards, and petitions are worthless). Your representative will respond to a personal letter from a constituent. Other representatives will respond to nonconstituents also.

Here's a case in point: I wrote to a number of senators concerning the Panama Canal treaties, including at least six out-of-state senators. I received in-depth responses from each in varying length. Senators Richard Schweiker, Paul Laxalt, Robert Dole, and Orrin Hatch agreed with me, and so their letters were barely a page. Then Senator Howard Baker disagreed and sent a three-page response apologizing for a three-week delay and candidly acknowledging that his Tennessee constituents come first. Remember, many of these people take their jobs as public servants seriously, as do their staffs. If you're cynical, remember that many Congressmen outside your district aspire to statewide office and that many representatives and senators consider running for president. Your state has a primary. Through the primaries your vote can carry more weight than you might think.

In your letter of support or opposition, inform your representative why the bill is bad for the district or state. Talk about lost jobs, investment, tourism, and so on. You'll be surprised by what *personal* letters from you, your friends, and trade associations can accomplish. Finally, don't forget the press—write to your local newspaper. Your local representatives don't want bad press, and an editorial may cause them to reconsider their votes. If that fails, you must employ the full triad and defeat the legislation. To do this, your system should be familiar with legislative specialists in your field. Your trade association should be able to assist you either directly as a lobbyist or, at minimum, as an information resource.

Your representatives can be a valuable information source on both the state and federal levels. Not only can they provide assistance and input into legislative matters, but they also can be a great help when you're confronted with problems dealing with state or federal bureaucracies.

Make Sure Your Trade Association Is Involved

If you haven't done so already, contact your trade association to find out what they're doing in these areas and what the credentials are of the people looking out for your interests. If you're not already a member, you may wish to join. Trade associations can be valuable assets in your lobbying efforts as they can carry greater weight and expertise than individual members. Such trade associations may represent all businesses of one type or all business interests within the state. Only you can determine which type of association best suits your needs.

The true purpose of an association is to provide for the industry's common defense. Social gatherings are, at best, of secondary priority. Leadership raises the money to do what is necessary. Without an adequate in-place political intelligence and lobbying effort, all other budgets can become academic. An organized legislative program acts like insurance to protect against the risks of the unknown, the unexpected. If your association doesn't do this or reacts to every adverse legislative or regulatory issue in a crisis atmosphere, then it has substandard management. Join another, more effective association. Your trade association adds a dimension to your lobbying effort. You can submit input through your trade association, whose larger membership and possibly greater expertise might afford greater accessibility to the necessary party. You may not get the rule you oppose discarded, but your input may contribute to a more finely worded and narrowly drawn rule. This is important, since you cannot be held to any standards not expressed in the final rule. Further, legalese is not favored, and courts will construe the language of the rule literally and "according to the natural meaning of the words." [1] So, it is in your best interest to contribute to the lobbying effort either individually or as a member of a trade association. The key is to be involved—whichever route you choose.

State Services

Now that you know whom to contact for your lobbying efforts, you need to know *how* to obtain your state legislative information. This is an important part of your profit preservation center because in certain areas the Congress will expressly permit "narrower" drafting of state legislation in the interest of the public (this is the trend, not the exception). In addition, there are areas in which the state alone may choose to act. This can be a problem for a nationwide business, since sales and use taxes, personnel policies, and advertising copy may vary from state to state.[2] It is in your best interest to stay abreast of the new state laws and, if possible, aid in the passage of laws that will not injure your current or proposed business—or better yet, that will help your business.

There are many ways to approach the state legislative hurdle without drowning in a sea of paper. Many states will provide you with legislative and regulatory calendars for a nominal charge (the references list state services that are free or cost less than $600 per year as of 1986).[3] Your trade association may be able to capsule a few specific topics as part of its dues. In many states, the attorney general's office has a *free* newsletter that will update you on their activity as to consumer fraud, antitrust, and other issues of interest to you.[4] Get on newsletter mailing lists of your state elected officials, as well as other key state representatives in both houses. They'll also send you bills free for the asking, so they are a useful resource for your operation to keep in mind. Finally, there are services that specialize in state reporting and lobbying. These services will probably cost in excess of $10,000 per client, which may be prohibitive for small businesses but excellent for a larger firm or a trade association.[5]

Don't overlook the obvious. Your local newspaper will cover state and local matters. All good business magazines cover broad general-interest legislative areas. For instance, each week you should make it a habit to skim *Business Week's* Table of Contents for "legal affairs." National magazines can be helpful in keeping track of foreign government activity. However, if a particular foreign nation or region is important to you, a magazine such as *The Economist* is a must. Trade magazines and newsletters are another good source of first-step information on legislative and regulatory activity affecting their constituents' business interests.

Federal Legislative and Regulatory Coverage

While in some instances states can narrow federal law, there are certain areas where the federal government preempts state authority. For this and many other reasons, it is important to keep a watchful eye on the activities of the federal government. While newspapers and the trade press are more inclined to pick up federal legislative activity, there are better sources—provided you or the person so appointed to handle this area has the time to wade through these volumes—namely the *Congressional Record*[6] and the *Federal Register*[7]. Each is a good reference and investment when staying abreast of federal activity that could directly impact your business.

The Congressional Record and How to Use It

The *Congressional Record* is the full text of everything said in Congress each day, including all legislation introduced, subsequent votes, and certain articles, stories, and the like introduced and read into the record by various senators and representatives. The latter are not to be overlooked. Inside the *Congressional Record* are the best newspaper and magazine articles, editorials, satire, etc., written on every issue before Congress. These are indexed periodically, which allows for easier reference to material on a particular subject, by a certain sponsor, etc.

You'll want to read this in greater depth than you do the *Federal Register.* Not only are there debates on bills that directly affect your business, but there also are daily debates on defense, taxes, water rights, highways, and other matters that will be of interest to you personally.

For a nominal price, you now have access to the public goings-on in Congress.

The Federal Register and How to Use It

Most of the federal regulatory activity affecting your business will be found in these papers. If your business is small or you simply can't afford more, these will probably be sufficient for your needs.

In 1935, Congress passed the Federal Register Act, setting up a basic centralized system to publicize government regulations. The *Federal Register* is published daily by the General Services Administration and is an indispensable bible for following the rule-making of any federal agency. It contains three types of documents: proposed rules, final rules, and notices (which are not rules but documents of general interest to the public). All agencies must give a 30-day notice in the *Federal Register* when a new rule is adopted. The agency is also required to include a summary of the comments received earlier in response to the proposed rule and state why it did or did not incorporate such comments. The language, although printed in small type, is straightforward and well indexed. It's important to follow the *Federal Register* so that you may proceed to areas of interest to you and your business.

You can use the *Federal Register* simply to follow the rulemaking procedures of federal agencies impacting your business. Or, if you have the resources, you might consider using it as an alarm. When an agency intends to promulgate a new rule, a general notice of the proposed rulemaking must be published in the *Federal Register*. The agency *must* allow those with an interest in the area to be regulated, an opportunity to submit written data, comments, amendments, or arguments, and it is within the agency's discretion to allow an oral presentation. This could be important if the proposed rule would have an adverse impact on your business. By the agency's notice process, you would at least be permitted to comment on your opposition to the proposed rule, which it will have to either rebut or accept. Either way, your comments would go on record should there be compliance problems with the rule down the road.

Free Federal Newsletters and How to Get Them

You may wish to take advantage of several free newsletters that are available. Newsletters are available from the Federal Trade Commission (a must if you advertise and also need to keep abreast of consent agreements), the Consumer Product Safety Commission, the Justice Department (especially for antitrust issues) and many others.[8] However, you should write to all federal agencies that affect your business—for example, the Federal Communications Commission (FCC) or the Department of Agriculture—to ask if they have a newsletter. These are all "free," paid for by tax dollars. Once you're on the list, you're routinely updated.

Next, write to all those in Congress who affect your business and get their newsletters and press releases. Since many senators and representatives distribute newsletters and press releases, you can receive these indefinitely for the price of a stamp. You should follow legislative positions of anyone who heads a committee that affects your business directly. You might also wish to use this method to track someone you're considering supporting for public office. Further check the footnotes to find out how to update the status of any legislation you're tracking.[9] Ask around. There are toll-free numbers for many of the above information resources and services. Finally, don't forget to document these compliance efforts, especially if you run a small business. This can be useful later if you need to show an agency you are making good-faith efforts within the limits of your resources to comply and monitor regulations.

Other Federal Resources

How do you contact your elected officials in Washington? There is no better book to answer this question than the *Almanac of American Politics.*[10] This reference contains the state and Washington, D.C. office addresses and phone numbers of all members of Congress as well as their voting records and ratings by various groups. You'll also find a detailed demographic study of every state and congressional district and how and why every key player got there. (If you're a politics "junkie" you won't be able to put this book down!)

This Almanac, the *Federal Register,* and the *Congressional Record* provide a strong basis from which to monitor the federal scene as it affects your business. Any congressional newsletters you receive are a bonus. They can provide valuable information on the interests of the Senator or Congressman as well as those of their constituents. As such, these are useful not only on the federal level but also on the state level as a measure of constituent interests.

Another book you should seriously consider adding to your profit preservation center library is the *Consumer Protection Directory.*[11] This is a comprehensive guide to federal and state agencies, as well as to consumer protection organizations in the United States and Canada. It provides the address, phone number, and often the name of a direct contact for every agency you might need in the consumer field. In any state in which you're doing business, you'll be able to contact, for example, the attorney general's office, all state consumer services offices, and all state licensing boards. You'll also have direct contact with all local government agencies and private organizations such as the Better Business Bureaus, credit unions, and consumer groups. This book is a necessary source for any firm doing business in more than one state and a useful one for intrastate business since it is better organized than a phone book.

Getting Information Through the Freedom of Information Act

Congress unanimously passed the Freedom of Information Act in 1966 to enable individual citizens to obtain information about the workings of their government.[12] You can use this act to find out *general* information about competitors. However, it is not the purpose of the act to allow individuals or companies access to *private competitive* information. Not only will you be unable to obtain it, but your efforts may result in litigation if your competitor discovers what you tried to do.

The Freedom of Information Act provides that each agency shall make available to "any person" all records requested if they are reasonably identified unless the information falls into one of the nine enumerated exemptions. For purposes of this act, "records" include more than written records; for example, films[13] and tape recordings[14] are records.

The exemption most clearly applicable to business information is Exemption 4, which excludes from mandatory disclosure "trade secrets" and commercial or financial information received that is privileged or confidential.[15] Another area of protection is Exemption 8, which protects the privacy of truth-in-lending compliance reports as well as reports concerning solvency.[16] You should be aware that the courts have generally construed such exemptions quite narrowly.[17]

Your first step is to write to the specific federal agency from which you want records. If you have any problem getting an address, just call (202)555-1212 to find the agency's phone number (often a toll-free one is available) and address. In your letter, be sure to include the following:

(1) Cite that you are writing pursuant to 5 U.S.C. Sec. 522 of the Freedom of Information Act.

(2) Identify the records you are requesting as clearly and narrowly as possible.

(3) State the limit of fees you are willing to pay.

(4) Ask for all records not exempt (in case some are).

The agency must determine within 10 working days whether it will comply.[18] The time limit may be extended another 10 days if the agency notifies you of certain specific circumstances. If the request is denied, a specific reason must be given for the denial, and you must be supplied with the name and title of the person responsible for the denial. You then have the right to appeal to a higher official in the agency. If your appeal is subsequently denied, you can file suit in a district court, where you may receive expedited preference under the law.

However, you'll usually get the information quite painlessly. A nominal fee to cover costs will be charged. The only possible drawback is that any requests made under this act become a matter of public record. If discretion is important, you might consider using private stationery or having your attorney inquire for you. Be aware that information provided under this act does not have to be investigated for accuracy by an agency before it is released.[19] Finally, if you yourself are submitting information to the government, and you need to maintain its confidentiality, it is imperative that you seek the assistance of an attorney who has expertise in preserving privileged or confidential material.[20]

Easing of Federal Burdens?

The flood of papers and overly broad agency investigations of the past may be receding. The following are a few areas you should be alert to.

Executive Order 12291 (1981). This executive order requires that regulatory action may not be undertaken unless the potential net benefits to society outweigh the potential costs to society. Furthermore, it directs the agencies to choose the least costly alternative among regulatory approaches and requires a regulatory impact analysis for every major rule that an agency intends to issue. This new emphasis on a cost-benefit approach amplifies the positive effects of conveying your firm's message when the agency first announces it is studying a rule.

Paperwork Reduction Act. This act requires that each form sent to you by an agency have the name, address, and telephone number of a person who can help with any questions you might have. Also, *all* federal forms must have an Office of Management and Budget clearance number on them (usually in the top right-hand corner). If they do not, you can legally ignore the form if your attorney so advises.[21] At a minimum you could consider contesting the form in a polite response letter.

Equal Access to Justice Act. This act became effective October 1, 1981, and provides that your business will be reimbursed for costs and fees if it prevails in litigation in certain suits involving the U.S. Government, unless the court holds the agency's position to be "substantially" justified *or* certain special circumstances make the award unjust. The burden is on the government to justify its actions—you don't have to prove them unjustified.

Previously, an agency with or without justification could conduct a fishing expedition into any business at the general taxpayer's expense. If the business "won," it had only the dubious satisfaction of winning a Pyrrhic victory, since the business was out all costs and attorneys' fees incurred in defending itself and since it lost goodwill through resulting bad publicity. This act lessens the government burden on qualifying parties in both civil and administrative cases.

Are you a "qualifying party"? Eligible parties include individuals whose net worth does not exceed $1 million and who are sole owners of unincorporated businesses, partnerships, corporations, and associations of public and private organizations whose net worth does not exceed $5 million. No business employing more than 500 employees may recover under this act regardless of net worth (part-time employees are included on a proportional basis, and temporary or seasonal workers are excluded). Further, this act seems to be under an almost continuous "sunset" threat. Review its status with your counsel before you hang your hat on it.

More About Federal In-House Compliance

The cost of federal regulatory compliance is now close to $130 billion per year (usually approximating the national debt, for obvious reasons).[22] This compliance does not include fines and other costs for violations (which are not tax-deductible).

Perhaps the most frustrating aspect of compliance is that it changes with each popular fad.

Remember the "population bomb scare"? You might have wondered what ever happened to the neo-Malthusian debate concerning overpopulation and no-growth. Fifteen years ago this was discussed in apocalyptical terms, and zero population growth became a popular, albeit anti-business goal. Business, however, soon regrouped and won this debate. No candidate in 1986, no matter how liberal, argued for a no-growth economy. One of the most fascinating arguments concerning population was given by economist Thomas Sowell of Stanford's Hoover Institution in *Harper's* November 1983 issue:

> To get some idea of how crowded the planet is in actuality, imagine that every man, woman and child on earth were placed in the state of Texas. There are 4,414 million people in the world and Texas has 262,134 square miles of land area. That works out to approximately 1,700 square feet per person. A family of four would thus have 6,800 square feet—about the size of a typical middle-class American home with front and back yards. In short, every human being on the face of the earth could be housed in the state of Texas in one-story, single family homes, each with a front and back yard.

While most industries regrouped rapidly to counter no-growth, the electric utilities generally failed to do so. Comfortable in their monopoly positions, they failed to evaluate their local constituencies as to their attitudes and then at least try to educate their customers in regard to the value of the nuclear reactors they were purchasing. The builders of such equipment adopted a similar policy toward their public constituencies.

The result was inevitable. As Japan, England, France and other nations pursue safe, clean, advanced power sources, the U.S. returns to fossil fuel while bemoaning its very real negative byproduct, acid rain. This accounts for some of the problems experienced now. Popular opinion can and does influence the government's regulatory climate. Therefore, it should not be ignored and should be monitored for opinions potentially adverse to your business or to the business climate in general.

Failing to anticipate a manipulated "public" outcry and regulations that followed, many firms had to have their product and marketing decisions imposed on them, and they paid accordingly—often drastically. The important thing to you is that government can make or break your marketing opportunities. Government's permitting of comparative advertising opened new opportunities while its ban on cigarette advertising on television destroyed some. How you'll word your copy, whether and what lists are available to rent, will in some cases be decided by government.

For this reason, it is important that you try to influence either public opinion or the regulatory agency that could regulate your industry through education efforts designed to give them the necessary knowledge to make informed decisions on the issues at hand. If influencing or educating isn't possible, be sure you keep attuned to public opinion, both that of your customers and that of the regulatory agencies that govern your business practices. Perhaps the best advice is to remain vigilant in your own education efforts to stay abreast of both the public's and government's views on your business and industry.

Adopt a system that will *anticipate, educate and defeat or revise legislation.* The anticipation function will provide immediate marketing information as to customer opinion absolutely essential to serious long-term planning for marketing and customer service. Any "planning" system you could employ that does not include this is simply operating in a vacuum.

You should interact with the legislative process. Once you have access to the proposed laws and rules coming to your desk, start writing—both for bills you support *and* for those you oppose. Write to the key people concerned. If feasible, ask for an appointment to see them. This will almost always be possible if you are a constituent. However, don't limit your contact to your representatives: Contact the sponsors and committee chairman where the legislation is pending, too. To track a particular piece of legislation that would affect you, a simple telephone call[23] will keep you alerted as to a bill's movement through the legislative process.

Last but not least, contribute to the campaigns of candidates who support the free-enterprise goals you live by. If the incumbent doesn't, then work for the opponent. Finally, if you have the resources, discuss with your attorney the possibility of your firm's forming a political action committee (PAC).[24]

Monitoring: As Valuable as Analysis of Trends

You *must* monitor the government activity that affects your business. Monitoring requires an understanding of what signals precede an event (or have done so in the past). This is important not only because you wish to stay within the law but also because knowledge of future trends enables you to adjust your corporate planning in advance with a minimum of dislocation and inconvenience.

The anticipation function, if properly used, will more than pay for itself, therefore justifying its costs. The education function lets management know what is happening and why. Another cost justification here is that if you can demonstrate a solid effort by management to keep abreast of the laws and regulations affecting your business, an agency or attorney general's office may consider this a mitigating factor if you accidentally run afoul of a government body. Besides the less appreciated (or less utilized) role of marketing research input from legislative analysis, there is the obvious need to preserve profits and marketing opportunities. The fines you incur for violation of laws (of which you may or may not be aware) are *not* deductible business expenses. The loss of goodwill can be a greater cost.

Market "research" in isolation is as invalid as a poll that doesn't measure public feeling and intensity. Firms that "researched" by number crunching discovered too late that big cars weren't wanted in the 1970s, that nuclear power plants have a weak constituency, and that "new Coke" wouldn't dominate the market. Such erstwhile products sit idle and drain firms as financing costs.

Market researchers that have adopted the market concept rather than the product concept in a firm strategically oriented for survival know that they interact with their legislative operation. This is because a skilled government affairs professional will provide analysis of how your market is thinking nationally, by state, or by municipality.

When a legislator introduces a bill, he or she knows there had better be a constituency for it because the legislator wants to be reelected. If you see several similar bills introduced or many cosponsors, consider this as valuable information on *your markets.* These individuals must know the pulse of their constituents to survive. *And their constituents are your customers.* You're depriving your firm of a wealth of market data if you don't factor legislative analysis into your marketing program. Plan for it.

Legislation is the best reflection of current mood, trend, and passion a marketer can get. If the political climate (read "popular will") is averse to a waste-treatment plant, then don't enter that area. If they're averse to your product (e.g., a potentially dangerous toy or flammable product), your marketing research had better account for this sentiment or you won't sell; in fact, you may suffer a backlash through picketing, demonstrations, or other states' picking up the legislative imperative. Finally, if you must sail against the wind of the current public mood, the advance input will be invaluable to you in planning a response to the customer service issues that will likely arise.

Planning ahead means planning for what the government is going to do. If you were selling cigarettes in the 1950s on TV you were testing alternative media in order to survive. The government was going to force you to. Any firm planning to market successfully in the long term had to view the long-term political analysis of their markets. How is this done?

Laws don't happen—*your customers make them happen.* If you see a candidate newly elected in a product market important to you, search out his or her past. Did the individual publish articles adverse to your position? Was the individual an active opponent of yours as a young attorney in an attorney general's office? Did this person run and get elected on an issue opposed to your current or contemplated marketing strategy?

If any of these factors exist, then you have information as to the direction that district is going in or will be guided toward by the new representative. You might anticipate your marketing strategy accordingly, or at least initially attempt to persuade the new representative of the error of a prior position. Your legislative analysis should provide you with the above type of information for each and every market segment important to you nationally and overseas.

In addition to monitoring state and federal activities, you should stay abreast of matters overseas. Surprisingly, people who are quick to agree that national economies are increasingly interdependent often belittle the legislative intelligence our neighbors overseas provide. You may leave your culture, but your culture doesn't leave you.[25] If your market research is using buzzwords such as demographics, ethnicity, pseudographics, etc., but is not interacting with your legislative department as to how comparable groups are thinking overseas, then you are receiving, at best, no input and possibly counterproductive input for your long-term market planning directed at these target groups.

Who Will Run Your System?

Your profit preservation center should have a broad, up-to-date data base covering the social, political, technological, and economic trends affecting your business. The manager you select for this function must be able to learn how to learn, since expertise in government affairs demands a lifelong education. Every election brings a new cast of elected and appointed officials at every level of local, state, and federal government.

Your manager could be a lawyer or paralegal, but certainly someone with business savvy. Otherwise he or she will bog you down in esoteric legalese rather than provide you with legal or legislative advice targeted to your products and markets. This person must know your business to isolate the key laws and rules that may or may not affect your business. The manager must also understand the government process—who is a key sponsor, what committees really count in a given state, and how receptive a sponsor's staff is to your input. Knowledge of computers also will help as more government bodies expand their electronic data transmission systems.

A premium must be given to personnel continuity because no bill ever dies. Winning one year is no guarantee that a bill won't be reintroduced. Ongoing legislative vigilance is essential. Your profit preservation center manager should be able to project for you which way the legislatures are heading.

Then there are the bills that start out innocuously. If they look remotely applicable, you must track them because amendments that are unfavorable to you can be tacked on. You must be prepared to react swiftly or accept the consequences to your bottom line. More ominous are the laws you worked for and now believe are safely on the books. Remember, all laws "on the books" can be amended. Any bill you permit to be enacted that can affect you *will* affect you. For example, in the early 1970s, most states enacted Home Solicitation Laws. Other direct marketers such as telephone sellers ignored them. There was little industry input, as many felt the law didn't affect them. Then suddenly in the late 1970s states rushed to incorporate telephone marketing in the "cooling off" and other provisions of the statutes. Almost 20 states now have these laws, which potentially reduce the advantage of the spontaneity of the telephone order process.

As you can see, it is important to choose the proper person for this task. If you're running a small business and must do this yourself and the previous description doesn't sound like you, don't despair. Much of the law involved is "newspaper law." A good selection of comprehensive newspapers and magazines, along with the materials mentioned earlier in the chapter, will assist you.

Conclusion

Today's manager who wants to be tomorrow's manager must know the current law and trends and how he or she can anticipate (and influence) the government before it jeopardizes marketing plans. Failure to anticipate and interact with government and other political environments can lead anyone in the 1980s and 1990s down the same path as the nuclear power industry followed in earlier decades. You can reduce your costs and lower your adverse visibility to the federal government by creating a profit preservation center. The previous comments are useful particularly to managers of smaller businesses. Managers also need knowledge about state rulings and legislation, which this section discusses.

If you are a committed professional, you cannot avoid being informed of and involved with legislative activity. You must plan for legislative change the same way you do for technological change, tax change, or competitive change.

If your business is large, you may be involved with as much as 5% to 10% of all state bills (and 150,000 to 200,000 are being introduced every two years in addition to those at the federal level). However, as a large industry you have the ability and the resources to develop an effective profit preservation center. If, on the other hand, your business is small, you may want to have input but may feel overwhelmed. Don't despair. You can stay abreast of and affect many issues without exorbitant cost. Our regulatory survival course can be self-taught, regardless of your background or previous experience.

While the principles expressed apply to firms of all sizes, this chapter is a primer for the businessperson in a small firm who doesn't believe interaction with government bodies can be so easy and so inexpensive. For less than $1000 (often tax deductible) you can accomplish a lot. Larger firms are already involved. Their interest may be yours generally but not specifically. It is important that you be heard. If you have any further questions or ideas, please write.[26]

ENDNOTES

(1) *Diamond Roofing Co. v. OSHRC* (1976) 528 F.2d 645.

(2) "Heads in the Ozone," *Wall Street Journal editorial,* March 6, 1984.

(3) Free state services include the following free publications, listed by state:

Florida - Daily Journal; Mr. Allen Morris, Clerk of the House, Florida House of Representatives, 427 The Capitol, Tallahassee, FL, 32301.

Kentucky - Weekly Legislative Calendar; Legislative Research Commission, State Capitol, Frankfort, KY 40601.

Maine - Weekly Legislative Calendar, Mr. Edwin H. Pert, Clerk of the House, House of Representatives, Augusta, ME 04333.

Minnesota - Weekly Wrap Up; House Information Office, Room 8 State Capitol, St. Paul, MN 55155.

Nebraska - Unicameral Update; Unicameral Information Office, State of Nebraska, State Capitol, Lincoln NB, 68509.

New Jersey - Legislative Calendar; Legislative Information Service, State House, CN-042, Trenton, NJ, 08625.

Washington - Legislative Meeting Schedule; Washington State Legislature, Legislative Building, Olympia, WA, 98504.

In addition to these free publications, there are other inexpensive state services available. The following states provide legislative subscription services for nominal fees; the addresses and telephone numbers needed to discover what available services fulfill your requirements are included.

Delaware - Ms. Hedgecock, Legislative Council, P.O. Box 1401, Dover, DE, 19901.

Illinois - Legislative Reference Bureau, Room 112, State House, Springfield, IL, 62706.

Indiana - Legislative Service Agency, 302 State House, Indianapolis, IN, 46204.

Maine - Mr. Edwin H. Pert, Clerk of the House, State House, Augusta, ME 04333.

Maryland - State Department of Legislative Reference, Attention: V. Tilghman, 90 State Circle, Room G-18, Annapolis, MD, 21401.

Missouri - Eric Luthi, Assistant Chief Clerk/House Administration, Missouri House of Representatives, State Capitol, Jefferson City, MO 65101; or call the Missouri House of Representatives Legislative Information System at (314)751-2357.

Montana - Legislative Bill Distribution, Capitol Station, Helena, MT 59601.

Nevada - Legislative Counsel Bureau, Legislative Building, Capitol Complex, Carson City, NV, 89710.

North Carolina - Publications Office, Institute of Government, Knapp Building 059A, The University of North Carolina at Chapel Hill, Chapel Hill, NC, 27514; or call (919)966-5381.

Oklahoma - Mr. LeRoy A. Ritter, Oklahoma Business News Co., P.O. Box 1177, 605 N.W. 13th, Suite C, Oklahoma City, OK 73101; or call (405)521-1405.

Oregon - Distribution Center, Room 49, State Captiol Building, Salem, OR 97310.

Utah - House of Representatives, State of Utah, 318 State Capitol, Salt Lake City, UT 84114.

Vermont - Vermont Legislative Council, State House, Montpelier, VT 05602.

Wisconsin - Legislative Document Room, State Capitol, Madison, WI 53702; or call (608)266-2400.

In addition to the specific state services mentioned, you might be interested in keeping abreast of national trends in the legislatures. Two magazines of interest in this area are *State Legislatures*, published by the National Conference of State Legislatures, 1125 Seventeenth Street, Suite 1500, Denver, CO, 80202, (303)623-6600 ($30 for a one-year subscription), and *State Government News*, published by the Council of State Governments, P.O. Box 11910, Lexington, KY, 40578 ($15 for a one-year subscription).

One final source for state legislative information is *The State Legislative Directory,* which is prepared by *Information for Public Affairs.* This contains the names, addresses, party affiliation, and committee membership of all legislators in the 50 states. The cost of a subscription is $165. To obtain more information or to order a copy, contact Laurie Brown, *Information for Public Affairs,* 1900 14th Street, Sacramento, CA, 95814, (916)444-0840.

(4) State attorney general and consumer protection newsletters that are available include the following, listed by the state:

Alaska - *Consumer Protection Newsletter;* Consumer Protection Section Department of Law, 1049 W. Fifth, Suite 101, Anchorage, AK 99501.

Arkansas - *Consumer Alert;* Consumer Protection Division, Justice Building, Little Rock, AR, 72201.

Colorado - *A.G. Legal Newsbriefs;* Colorado Department of Law, 1525 Sherman Street, 3d Floor, Denver, CO, 80203.

Iowa - *Department of Justice Press Releases;* Consumer Protection Division, Hoover Building, 2d Floor, 1300 East Walnut, Des Moines, IA, 50319.

Kentucky - *News Release;* Office of the Attorney General, Capitol Building, Frankfort, KY, 40601.

Maryland - *Attorney General's Digest;* Attorney General of Maryland, 1400 One South Calvert Building, Baltimore, MD, 21202.

Mississippi - *Report from the Office of Attorney General Ed Pittman;* Office of the Attorney General, State of Mississippi, P.O. Box 220, Jackson, MS, 39205-0220.

New Mexico - *In the Public Interest;* Office of the Attorney General, State of New Mexico, Post Office Drawer 1508, Santa Fe, NM, 87504.

Oregon - *Department of Justice Press Releases*; State of Oregon, Consumer Protection and Services Section, Justice Building, Salem, OR, 97310.

South Carolina - *Consumer Affairs Report;* South Carolina Department of Consumer Affairs, 2221 Devine Street, P.O. Box 5757, Columbia, SC, 29250.

Texas - *The Consumer Alert;* Office of the Attorney General, Supreme Court Building, P.O. Box 12548, Austin, TX, 78711-2548.

Wisconsin - *Consumer Protection Report;* Office of Consumer Protection, 114 East, State Capitol, Madison, WI, 53702.

For consumer news contact *Consumer News,* U.S. Office of Consumer Affairs, Washington, D.C., 20201. Should you be interested in a state not listed, address a letter to the attorney general of the state at the state capitol.

(5) These services include Information for Public Affairs, 1900 14th Street, Sacramento, CA, 95814, (916)444-0840; De Hart & Darr Associates, 1360 Beverly Rd., Suite 201, McLean, VA, 22101, (703)448-1000; and Legi-Slate, Suite 408, 444 North Capitol Street NW, Washington, D.C., 20001, (202)737-1888. Also, your trade association might have a targeted legislative service. An example would be the Business Council of New York State, 152 Washington Avenue, Albany, NY, 12210, (518)465-7511. This group can keep you abreast of all legislative activity in the state legislature as well as lobby your cause. Fees are based on the number of full-time employees in New York. Similar organizations are in place in many states and would be of value to your profit preservation program. The following are some examples:

Colorado - Colorado Association of Commerce and Industry, 1860 Lincoln St., Suite 550, Denver, CO, 80295, (303)831-7411.

Illinois - Illinois Manufacturers Association, 175 West Jackson Boulevard, Room 1321, Chicago, IL, 60604, (312)922-6575.

Michigan - Michigan Manufacturers Association, 124 East Kalamazoo Street, Lansing, MI, 48933, (517)372-5900.

Minnesota - Minnesota Association of Commerce and Industry, 300 Hanover Building, 480 Cedar Street, St Paul, MN, 55101, (612)292-4650.

New Jersey - New Jersey Business and Industry Association, P.O. Box 230, Trenton, NJ, 08602, (609)373-7707.

Pennsylvania - Pennsylvania Manufacturers Association, 925 Chestnut Street, Philadelphia, PA, 19103, (215)629-5080.

Virginia - Virginia Manufacturers Association, P.O. Box 412, Richmond, VA, 23202, (804)643-7480.

(6) The *Congressional Record* may be ordered by calling or writing the U.S. Government Printing Office at (202)783-3238 and charging the subscription to a VISA or Mastercard number (the present cost is $218, which is subject to change) or by ordering in writing with a prepayment to Superintendent of Documents, U.S. Government Printing Office, Washington, D.C. 20402-9371.

(7) The *Federal Register* can be ordered by calling the U.S. Government Printing Office. The present cost is $300, which is subject to change (for address see note 6). Another valuable tool is *The Business Action Network: Washington Watch,* a monthly newsletter published by the U.S. Chamber of Commerce. For more information and a price quote, call (202) 659-6000.

(8) To obtain press releases issued by the Department of Justice, write to the Attorney General, Antitrust Division, Department of Justice, Washington, D.C., 20530.

The FTC issues *News Notes,* which can be obtained by writing to the Office of Public Affairs, from Room 496, Federal Trade Commission, Sixth and Pennsylvania Avenue NW, Washington, D.C., 20580; (202)326-2222.

The National Advertising Division of the Council of Better Business Bureaus, Inc. issues a newsletter, *NAD Case Report,* which can be obtained by contacting the National Advertising Division, Council of Better Business Bureaus, Inc., 845 Third Avenue, New York, N.Y. 10022; (212)754-1358.

Copies of federal legislation may be obtained at no charge by contacting the sponsor's office or by writing to the following: Senate Document Room, Hart Senate Office Building, Room B-04, Washington, D.C., 20510. When writing to the Senate document room, provide a self-addressed label with your request. (If more than six documents are ordered per day fees are charged.)

For information on the status of federal legislation send the bill number or numbers along with a self-addressed, stamped envelope to Legis Office, House Office Building Annex 2, Second and D Streets SW, Room 696, Washington, D.C., 20515, and they will provide you with a printout of any activity on the bill or bills requested along with the current status. For mailed status reports, there is a charge of 10 cents per page. Also, for immediate updates on the status of a bill you can call (202)225-1772.

(9) The following listing should be of some assistance in obtaining the bill status. When calling, indicate that you wish to obtain the current status of some legislation; if this is not the direct line, they will be able to transfer you accordingly. Try to limit your status checks to between five and six bills per call so as to obtain the best cooperation from these offices. If you know the sponsor, you can also call that person's office.

State	Capital	Phone Number	Office Location
AL	Montgomery	(205)261-7826	Bill Status
AK	Juneau	(907)465-4648	Bill Status
AZ	Phoenix	(602)255-4221	House Bill Status
		(602)255-3559	Senate Bill Status
AR	Little Rock	(501)371-1937	Bill Status
CA	Sacramento	(916)445-3614	Bill Status
CO	Denver	(303)866-2317	Bill Status
CT	Hartford	(203)566-5736	Bill Status
DE	Dover	(302)736-5702	Bill Status
FL	Tallahassee	(904)488-4371	Bill Status
GA	Atlanta	(404)656-5015	Bill Status
HI	Honolulu	(808)548-4262	Bill Status
ID	Boise	(208)334-2411	General Legislature
IL	Springfield	(217)782-3944	Bill Status
IN	Indianapolis	(317)232-9856	Bill Status
IA	Des Moines	(515)281-5129	Bill Status
KS	Topeka	(913)296-2149	Bill Status
KY	Frankfort	(502)564-8100 X323	Bill Status
LA	Baton Rouge	(504)342-2456	Bill Status
ME	Augusta	(207)289-1110	Bill Status
MD	Annapolis	(301)841-3810	Bill Status
MA	Boston	(617)722-2356	House Bill Status
		(617)722-1276	Senate Bill Status
MI	Lansing	(517)373-0170	Bill Status
MN	St. Paul	(612)296-6646	House Bill Status
		(612)296-2337	Senate Bill Status
MS	Jackson	(601)354-7011	General Legislature
MO	Jefferson City	(314)751-2979	Bill Status
MT	Helena	(406)444-4853	Bill Status
NE	Lincoln	(402)471-2271	General Legislature
NV	Carson City	(702)885-5636	Bill Status
NH	Concord	(603)271-2239	Bill Status

State	Capital	Phone Number	Office Location
NJ	Trenton	(609)292-4840	Bill Status
NM	Santa Fe	(505)827-4011	General Legislature
NY	Albany	(518)455-2255	Bill Status
		(Toll-free NYS) 1-800-342-9860	
NC	Raleigh	(919)733-7779	Bill Status
ND	Bismarck	(701)224-2916	Bill Status
OH	Columbus	(614)466-8842	Bill Status
OK	Oklahoma City	(405)521-2733	Bill Status
OR	Salem	(503)378-8551	Bill Status
PA	Harrisburg	(717)787-5320	Bill Status
RI	Providence	(401)277-2473	Bill Status
SC	Columbia	(803)734-2060	Bill Status
SD	Pierre	(605)773-3251	Bill Status
TN	Nashville	(615)741-3511	Bill Status
TX	Austin	(512)463-1252	Bill Status
UT	Salt Lake City	(801)533-5481	Bill Status
VT	Montpelier	(802)828-2231	Bill Status
VA	Richmond	(804)786-5435	Bill Status
WA	Olympia	(206)786-7593	Bill Status
WV	Charleston	(304)340-3200	House Bill Status
		(304)357-7800	Senate Bill Status
WI	Madison	(608)266-0341	Bill Status
WY	Cheyenne	(307)777-7881	Bill Status
Federal Legislation		(202)225-1772	

(10) Barone, Michael and Grant Ujifusa, *The Almanac of American Politics 1988* (revised every two years). Can be ordered from National Journal, 1730 M St., NW, Washington, D.C., 20036; or call toll free 1-800-424-2921; in D.C. call (202)857-1400. The 1988 volume is $43. Should you need to contact any senator or representative and this book is unavailable, the Capitol switchboard, at (202)224-3121, will connect you with any senate or congressional office you specify.

(11) Write to Marquis Academic Media, Marquis Who's Who, Inc., 200 East Ohio Street, Chicago, Illinois, 60611.

(12) 5 USC Sec. 552.

(13) *Save the Dolphins v. Department of Commerce* (1975) 404 F.Supp. 407.

(14) *Hrynko v. Crawford (1975) 402 F.Supp. 1083.*

(15) 5 USC Sec. 552(b)(4). *See also Chrysler Corp. v. Brown* (1979) 441 US. 281.

(16) 5 USC Sec. 552(b)(8). *See also Consumers Union of the United States, Inc. v. Heimann,* (D.Ct. D.C. 1978) No. 77-2115.

(17) *Department of the Air Force v. Rose,* (1976) 425 US 352, 361. *See* McCarthy and Kornmeier, *Maintaining the Confidentiality of Confidential Business Information Submitted to the Federal Government,* 36 The Business Lawyer 57-78 (1980).

(18) 5 USC Sec. 552(6)(A).

(19) *Price & Stevens Chem. Corp. v. United States Consumer Product Safety Commission* (1978) 585 F.2d 1382.

(20) *Bristol Myers Co. v. FTC* (1978) 598 F.2d 18.

(21) For problems with federal department and agency forms, write or call the Office of Information and Regulatory Affairs, Office of Management and Budget, 726 Jackson Place NW, Room 3208, Washington, D.C., 20503, (202)395-6880. Also you might try the Business Advisory Council on Federal Reports, 1625 Eye St. NW, Suite 903, Washington, D.C., 20036, (202)331-1915. Finally, don't forget to call your local representative if you have an unresolved or burdensome problem with federal reports (obviously the same holds true for state reports, which will be discussed further).

(22) In addition to the *Almanac of American Politics,* you should obtain a copy of *Conquering Government Regulations - A Business Guide* (New York: McGraw-Hill, 1982) edited by McNeill Stokes assisted by 10 contributing authors who are experts in their fields. It contains a helpful jargon-free discussion of government regulations.

(23) See note 9 for phone numbers.

(24) For a lucid description of PACs, see Chapter 13 of Stokes's book, discussed in note 22.

(25) An interesting book that discusses the overseas influence on certain states and voting patterns is Phillips, Kevin, *The Emerging Republican Majority,* Doubleday/Anchor, 1970.

(26) If you have any questions about starting your profit preservation center, write the author at 242 Elsie Avenue, Merrick, New York, 11566, or call me at (516)868-9849 or (516)873-4628. Also see, Posch, Robert, "To Survive You Must Follow Current Legislative Trends," *Direct Marketing,* July 1983, pp. 138-140.

SECTION VIII

CONTRACTS

The days of sealing a business agreement with a handshake are over. Today's reality is that what's not in writing does not exist—at least from the perspective of your ability to enforce your contractual expectations. Like most topics covered in this book, these issues are important to you personally as well as professionally.

This section emphasizes the theory and suggests contractual language to cover a variety of typical scenarios, including computer-related agreements. It covers hardware, software, and their respective maintenance. And it recommends legal approaches to protecting your software in today's business environment.

Employees are the essence of a successful firm. A sign that U.S. firms recognize this is the flourishing headhunter business and the boom in related business books.[1] This section reviews covenants not to compete in the context of broader employee contractual issues.

As information is a resource, it must be guarded, or you will have no edge over your competition. This section reviews trade secrets as well as the theory and structure of confidentiality agreements. Finally, it reviews product and character licensing agreements. This spinning off of your various brands and capitalizing on characters you create is a flourishing source of subsidiary rights income.

Of all the contractual topics reviewed, none is more important to pure marketing than the boom in character licensing. Because of its importance, we'll take a look at a little-publicized case (at the time) which is gradually becoming a landmark in subsidiary rights expansion.

A Perpetual Monopoly in Your Character Rights

Frederick Warne[2] published the well-known series of children's books written and illustrated by Beatrix Potter, and sold under the

677

trademark "The Original Peter Rabbit Books." Warne was, in fact, Miss Potter's original publisher, printing the first volume of her series, *The Tale of Peter Rabbit,* in 1902.

For years, Warne and Miss Potter enjoyed the profits generated by their extraordinarily popular series. But because seven of the books, in issue here, are no longer—or never were—covered by copyright protection in the United States, several new editions of Miss Potter's works appeared on the market to compete with Warne's editions. Warne conceded that the seven works are in the public domain. Nevertheless, Warne claimed exclusive rights in the cover illustrations, and character marks derived from those illustrations, which were originally created by Miss Potter for Warne's editions of the seven books and do not appear within the text of the books themselves. In addition, it claimed exclusive trademark rights in an illustration appearing within *The Tale of Peter Rabbit,* referred to as the "sitting rabbit." Three of the covers have been registered under the Lanham Act as book trademarks.

Warne had creatively exploited public affection for Miss Potter's characters by using, and licensing the use of, the eight illustrations on a variety of commercial products. Thanks to its marketing efforts, Warne claimed the characters portrayed in the eight illustrations, "particularly the 'running rabbit', have attained a place in the public esteem comparable to Mickey Mouse, Peter Pan, and Raggedy Ann and Andy."[3]

The plaintiff was not asserting rights in the stories or under copyright. Instead, Frederick Warne asserted that the Beatrix Potter characters had acquired a secondary meaning as a result of its book sale and licensing efforts, and that the public recognized the existence of a single source of those products. It claimed, therefore, exclusive rights in the cover illustrations, the characters, and the character names. In short, the plaintiff was asserting the position that a trademark in characters will protect those characters beyond the term of the copyright applicable to the underlying work.[4]

Warne argued that the defendant had republished these seven works in one compilation, embellishing the cover and interior with redrawings of Warne's character illustrations. It also used, as part of its cover, a reproduction of the particular character design that had been the principal symbol of Warne's licensing activity (for toys, clothing, etc.).

The court agreed with Warne's argument in holding that the fact that a copyrightable character or design has fallen into the public domain should not preclude protection under the trademark laws so long as it is shown to have acquired independent trademark significance, identifying in some way the source or sponsorship of the goods. Because the nature of the property right conferred by copyright differs significantly from that of trademark, trademark protection should be able to coexist, and possibly to overlap, with copyright protection without posing preemption difficulties.[5] To hold otherwise would create the incongruous situation where trademarks in uncreative material could exist without limit, whereas such rights in creative material would be tied to copyright and would terminate accordingly.[6]

In quoting from a related case[7], the court succinctly distinguished the theory and practical impact of the respective rights:

> A trademark is a property right which is acquired by use. *Trade-Mark Cases,* 100 US 82, 25 LEd 550 (1879). It differs substantially from a copyright, in both its legal genesis and its scope of federal protection. The legal cornerstone for the protection of copyrights is Article I, section 8, clause 8 of the Constitution. In the case of a copyright, an individual creates a unique design and, because the Constitutional fathers saw fit to encourage creativity, he can secure a copyright for his creation for a [limited period of time]. After the expiration of the copyright, his creation becomes part of the public domain. In the case of a trademark, however, the process is reversed. An individual selects a word or design that might otherwise be in the public domain to represent his business or product. If that word or design comes to symbolize his product or business in the public mind, the individual acquires a property right in the mark. The acquisition of such a right through use represents the passage of a word or design out of the public domain into the protective ambits of trademark law. Under the provisions of the Lanham Act, the owner of a mark acquires a protectable [sic] property interest in his mark through registration and use.

> Dual protection under copyright and trademark laws is particularly appropriate for graphic representations of characters. A character deemed an artistic creation deserving copyright protection . . . may also serve to identify the creator, thus meriting protection under theories of trademark or unfair competition . . . . Indeed, because of their special value in distinguishing goods and services, names and pictorial representations of characters are often registered as trademarks under the Lanham Act.[8]

The court also applied its secondary meaning analysis to the defendant's contention that a book cover should be part of a copyrightable component of the copyrighted book. Once copyright protection ends, the entire book should be free to copy. The court stated:

> The proper factual inquiry in this case is not whether the cover illustrations were once copyrightable and have fallen into the public domain, but whether they have acquired secondary meaning, identifying Warne as the publisher or sponsor of goods bearing those illustrations, and if so, whether defendant's use of these illustrations in "packaging" or "dressing" its editions is likely to cause confusion.[9]

Finally the court argued that copying the covers is not crucial to the successful exploitation of the books since other publishers have reproduced the stories without copying the covers.

Conclusion

The appropriation of a character from a public domain work may constitute unfair competition or trademark infringement or both. The courts did not then (or since) address the issue of imposing limits on the scope of such trademark protection in order to harmonize trademark and copyright laws.

What should you do? If you are thinking of creating any form of marketing effort, you should follow the steps outlined in Section I's text on trademark searches. If you own a copyrighted property you should be alert to the fact that once the copyright on the underlying work expires, your property will be in the public domain subject to copying by anyone who chooses to do so. To avoid this fate, take these steps.

(1) Commercially (rather than literately) license your character as extensively as possible and document this.

(2) Graphically depict your character whenever possible.

(3) Feature the character prominently on all uses, even as to the copyrighted areas.

(4) Seek to formally trademark the name and (separately) the visual representation of your property.

(5) Put a TM after all uses.

In your commercial licensing efforts, assert your proprietary rights in the contract. Each contract will constitute an agreement by the licensee that you own rights in your character beyond "mere" copyright. Then specifically require the licensees to comply with steps 3 and 4 above in all its uses. Where possible, require them to meet step 2, too.

As you read through this part, you'll pick up a variety of ideas to use for all forms of your properties and confidential information.

ENDNOTES

(1) For example, O'Toole, James, *Vanguard Management,* (New York: Doubleday & Co., 1985).

(2) *Frederick Warne & Co., Inc. v. Book Sales, Inc.,* 481 F.Supp.1191, 1193 (S.D.N.Y.) 1979).

(3) Id., p. 1194.

(4) Id., p. 1197 n.3. See also *Silverman v. CBS,* 632 F.Supp.1344 (S.D.N.Y. 1986), *Universal City Studios v. Nintendo Co.,* 578 F.Supp 911 (1983) and *Toko Co., Ltd. v. Sears Roebuck Co.,* 645 F.2d 788 (1981).

(5) Id., p. 1196. See also Lanham Trade-Mark Act Sec. 1 et seq., 15 USC Sec. 1051 et seq.

(6) *Boston Professional Hockey Association, Inc. v. Dallas Cap & Emblem Manufacturing, Inc.,* 510 F.2d 1004, 1014 (5th Cir.), *cert. den.,* 423 US 868, 96 S.Ct.132, 46 L.Ed.2d 98 (1975).

(7) See note 2, p. 1197-98.

(8) Id., p. 1197. See also Lanham Trade-Mark Act Secs. 32(1), 43(a), 15 USC Secs. 1114(1), 1125(a).

(9) Id., p. 1198.

CHAPTER 25

IMPORTANT
CONTRACTUAL
RELATIONSHIPS

This chapter discusses the theory behind the basic contract and looks at the generic contract terms you'll encounter consistently in your personal as well as professional life. Here, traditional contract law is covered. The Uniform Commercial Code (see Chapter 8) sets out rules that considerably modify the rules applicable to other contracts. It might be a good idea to go back and distinguish this area once you've read through the chapters that follow.

The Thought and Theory Behind Contracts

Contracts are either unilateral or bilateral. If one party promises to do something in return for a specific act of the other party, we have the elements of a unilateral contract. No enforceable obligation is imposed on the promisor until the specified act is performed. When one party promises to do something in exchange for a promise, we have the elements of a bilateral contract. An enforceable obligation may arise based on the exchange of mutual promises.

The following are the core elements necessary for the formation of a contract:

(1) *Offer:*

- An expression of a promise, undertaking or commitment to enter into a contract;
- Definite, unqualified, and certain in its terms (e.g., in a requirements contract the quantity must be definite); and
- Communicated to the offeree.

(2) *Acceptance:*

- Acceptance made by one who has the power of acceptance;

681

- Conduct constituting an acceptance is present, that is, an act claimed to be the acceptance of an offer must be shown to have been made with the knowledge of the offer; and
- The terms of acceptance are unequivocal (in some states for an acceptance to be effective it must be an acceptance of the offer in its exact terms).

   (3) *Consideration:*

- Something must be bargained for, which can be the doing or promising to do what one is not legally obligated to do or the refraining from doing what one may legally do. The promise and the consideration must purport to be the motive for each other.
- There must be legal value; and
- There must be mutuality.

Note: In certain situations, "consideration" as defined above is not required to create contractual liability. In these cases, a "substitute" will suffice. For example, under the Uniform Commercial Code (UCC), promises in writing will suffice in lieu of consideration. This is just one way the UCC may vary the equation.

Before getting into the nitty-gritty of boilerplate text, you should be familiar with the following more global issues that determine the legality of a contract.

Defects in formation. Contracts entered into by *incompetent persons* are voidable at the option of the individual. A contract by a *minor* also is voidable, at the minor's election (but this can vary if necessities were provided).

Illegal contracts. These are usually void as a matter of public policy. For example, a loan shark will rarely gain redress in the courts. As to mistake, fraud, and duress, each situation depends on its own facts.

Mistake. Where there is a mutual mistake as to a basic element of fact in the contract, such contract may be voidable.

Fraud. A contract can be voidable if all of the following essential elements are present:

(1) There was a representation of a material fact.

(2) The representation was false.

(3) The representer knew it to be false, or in the alternative, must have asserted it as being of his own knowledge without having known whether it is true or false.

(4) The representer intends for the other party to rely on it, and this party acts in reliance.

(5) The party suffers damages and the damages are attributable to the misrepresentation, that is, the statement is the proximate cause of the injury.

If all of these five elements are present, then you probably can extract yourself from the offering agreement.

Duress. Did the party have free will—a real choice? Duress isn't necessarily a "gun to the head." It could also be economic pressure. Economic duress exists when a party to a contract threatens to withhold proper performance unless the other party submits to uncontracted-for demands. To be in a position to argue this, you must have fulfilled your contractual obligations up to the time of the attempted duress.

Statute of frauds. People have always known that a permanent commitment is worth a lot more than oral "assurances." Since the time of English Common Law, society has required certain agreements to be in writing, describing all the material terms and signed by the party to be charged. Examples of this legal requirement include a contract to transfer real property or a contract that, by its terms, is not to be completed before the end of a lifetime or not to be performed within one year of its effective date.

Note: Though an express contract is unenforceable because of its failure to comply with the statute of frauds, there may be a quasicontractual recovery for the reasonable value of services rendered.

Parol evidence. When the parties execute a written agreement which they intend to be a complete and accurate integration of their agreement, extrinsic evidence (oral or written) of prior or contemporaneous statements of the parties will not be admissible for the purpose of varying, contradicting, or supplementing the written agreement. However, if the parties have a final but not complete writing, it may not be contradicted or varied by extrinsic evidence. It may be *supplemented* by evidence of *consistent* additional terms. Most integration clauses expressly state that the writing is the entire agreement of the parties (see below).

The most important contract element is the quality of the firm you're contracting with. Promises from a shoddy, insolvent, or poorly managed firm will not be worth much, regardless of the quality of the contractual drafting. Quite simply put, a good contract with a bad firm has little or no value. Your attorney is not serving you well if he or she merely reviews the contract in isolation from this essential business reality. Before you read the language of a contract that is important to you, learn about the firm. Ask around the trade, get references, contact the references and ask meaningful questions, do a credit search, take a look at their insurance coverage, and if they're publicly traded, get all the appropriate SEC documents. If it all checks out, you'll more often than not be presented with some or all of the following terms. Make sure you get the agreement in writing. Don't rely on the fact that you have a good relationship with the other party now, because people, relationships, and companies change.

Besides exploring the other person's business you must know your own and its objectives in entering the transaction. If you're dealing with in-house counsel, you've made this cost-effective investment already. The more your attorney knows about the parties, the technical terms and jargon, and your goals, the better chance you have to get a contract that effectively protects your interests.

Finally, get your attorney involved early. If you present a completed deal for a mere legal sign-off, you'll lose in a variety of ways.

Primary Contract Clauses

Some of these clauses will also apply to other contractual relationships discussed in this section. Where necessary, you'll be able to distinguish the particular goals of your specific agreements.

A cardinal rule in drawing up a contract is that in an arms-length agreement it is best to volunteer to do the drafting. Often the other party will be glad to waive this tedious chore, figuring the agreement can be amended at will later. There is *always* an advantage in drafting in that your counsel has worked through the integrated whole. The only time this can hurt you is in situations where ambiguity is construed against the drafter. This is a rare situation in arms-length agreements (though it's a consumer's defense against you). VOLUNTEER TO HAVE YOUR ATTORNEY DRAFT THE AGREEMENT.

The agreement should lead off with a set of definitions so that there is no ambiguity as to any term. (This provides a more practical reference than defining the terms in the paragraphs in which they are used.) Have your counsel follow through and draft the contract so that it can be read and understood by both parties.

Further, each paragraph should be numbered and have a heading. A table of contents that lists the headings and their corresponding page references is also a handy device. And finally, be sure the contract identifies the parties and sets forth a statement of purpose in the opening paragraph. Your counsel should review this with you and the agreeing party to ensure that it is in line with your intentions.

Following are clauses your attorney may wish to include.

Term of the agreement. If you're purchasing anything, the term should expire only after the item has been delivered, accepted (either inspected or, if necessary, after tests have been run), and paid for and title has been transferred to you. The key wording is the acceptance. You can't generally begin the term of the agreement on the date of execution or delivery. You need to at least inspect the product delivered as to its conformity with the agreement (quantity, weight, color, and so forth) as well as to make sure it has arrived undamaged. If you're buying equipment or software, you'll want to establish benchmark tests and a payment schedule reflecting same. You want to see whether the product or service purchased fits in and meets the specific, written standards you require.

If you are renting or leasing something (equipment, software, consultant services, etc.), the term will run until expiration after proper acceptance (discussed above). However, in these agreements you should qualify the term by negotiating a right to cancel at, say, 30 to 60 days based on specified events.

Assignment. This is an important provision if you're leasing or if the seller retains an interest pending payment. These can contain subtle but very important downsides depending on what you're negotiating for. You rarely want to accept the assignment provision as drawn by another. At a minimum, you want to ensure that:

(1) Anything you license is not restricted to a single site if you need or could reasonably contemplate needing the product at other locations. A notice to the lessor is a reasonable requirement, but don't allow yourself to be subject to the lessor's arbitrary approval. The only condition that should reasonably be imposed is that on maintenance (if relevant to your agreement) if the product is moved beyond a certain radius.

(2) You need to have some veto power over the lessor's ability to assign the agreement without your advance approval. If the lease is silent on the right of assignment then you will have little recourse to prevent this. If the lessor assigns to a third party, usually you cannot assert any claims for improper performance against the third-party assignee. This may also impair your ability to assert any claims against the original lessor. More subtly, but just as ominously, you might find the agreement assigned to:

(a) A bank in your credit line—this could restrict your future borrowings with that bank—or

(b) A competitor's parent or subsidiary, with obvious implications as to confidentiality and other sensitive areas.

If you can't get a general veto over a licensor's assignment for reasonable cause, then you should attempt to negotiate and specify a few instances, such as those above, where assignment won't be permitted and then subject other instances to situations where your right to veto the assignment will not be "unreasonably withheld" by you. Then, at a minimum, get in a quiet enjoyment paragraph, to the effect that "The Customer shall be entitled during the term of this license, and all renewals to use the product without disturbance, subject only to its obligation to make the required payments. Licensor represents that this agreement provides for nondisturbance of the customer so long as it shall not be in default hereunder."

Finally, in a personal services agreement, the caliber of your consultant is what you're negotiating for. Each individual is unique. Make sure the service is not free to arbitrarily pull people out and replace them without your advanced consent and right to terminate the agreement.

Confidential property right to new ideas. In virtually every modern business, the user is in possession of information, the confidentiality of which is important to the user, both directly and because of potential liabilities to others. The former might include your mailing list, market surveys, or product development data. The latter might include a delinquent list or subjective analysis of personnel. It is imperative that you negotiate to include (it's rarely presented voluntarily) provisions protecting yourself against the misappropriation, misuse, disclosure, and loss of your critical data. You'll also want to include in your indemnification clause (see below) protection as to defamation and privacy matters that are increasingly costly (juries more readily empathize with injured parties). At a minimum you must specify:

(1) What data needs to be kept confidential;

(2) What steps the other party must take to keep it confidential (that is, it will hold and use such information in the same manner as it deals with its own proprietary information); and

(3) Its disclosure will result in irreparable harm to you and, as such, mere legal remedies are inadequate.

Indemnification. The scope should be specified. It should include all costs associated with the exercise of the remedy (e.g., attorneys fees and court costs). You'll also want protection against all claims whether or not successful. However, if you are drafting the initial agreement (again, a generally good position to be in), you wish to give protections as to *finally* settled claims only. This way you avoid paying out money on spurious suits that lead nowhere.

As part of any serious indemnification protection you must examine the quality of the firm you're considering doing business with. If there's any doubt, set forth minimal insurance requirements and expressly make the policy a part of the contract. The insurer must also be required to notify you immediately if the policy lapses. You should also retain the right to bridge the policy and to elect at your sole option to terminate the agreement as a material breach.

In general, indemnification provisions must survive the life of the contract (whether a purchase or license agreement).

Warranties. At the outset, make sure you retain and incorporate expressly into the agreement as warranties all brochures, letters, demonstrations, and like matter that the seller used to induce you to purchase the product. When you're negotiating, simply request this in good faith and if you meet resistance, ask why. This exercise helps you two ways. First, these will broaden the scope of protection you'll have as to unanticipated events that crop up in the system. Second, if your seller won't stand behind the written sales material or demonstrations (or backs off from some earlier promises), then you're going into the agreement with your eyes open.

Once the above are settled, attempt to negotiate a longer warranty. Often, you can extend these 30 or 90 days. Further, make sure your warranty begins on the date of acceptance, not the date of delivery, installation, or first testing. Finally, make sure you include a statement to the effect that "time is of the essence" for all warranty repairs.

Disclaimer of warranties. The seller always has a paragraph disclaiming warranties. You needn't be intimidated by these if the product you purchase or license fails.

(1) As discussed above, your seller won't insure you against all hazards, but written specifications of performance and any inducement brochures you can incorporate into the agreement contain warranties that the seller can't disclaim. These specific warranties rather than vague terms such as "merchantability" are what you want.

(2) If a dispute arises, have your counsel review the disclaimer language to see whether it's drafted properly. If it isn't, you may be able to break it in whole or in part.

(3) If you worked closely together in developing a customized product or service, then argue that you have an express warranty of fitness for a particular purpose.

(4) If there is any material malfunction, argue fraud, unconscionability, or material misrepresentation of fact.

If you're involved in a computer systems agreement, these tort areas are becoming of greater interest to you. Though the situations may vary from state to state, the trend of the courts in those areas is to give less latitude to a salesperson's "puffing" than in other commercial situations. In general, the decisions are holding that there is greater reliance on the expertise of the salesperson in areas of computer hardware and software purchase because of the sophistication of the product and the velocity at which the field is evolving.

You should be aware that if you seek remedies in tort, other contractual expectations such as choice of law may be affected.

Liquidation of damages. Many of the issues discussed in "Warranties" above are relevant here. The seller initially promises the world and then attempts to disclaim all promises of performance and any significant recovery. Request a liquidated damages provision for a seller's (or lessor's) breach as actual damages may be hard to determine. Make sure you state that such liquidated damages are an estimate of actual damages, not a penalty.

Statute of limitations. You may see language such as "No suit or action shall be brought against seller more than one year after the related cause of action has occurred." Under the UCC, the statute of limitations is four years and can be shortened to no less than one year. However, where state law controls, you have a new situation entirely, because certain states bar any restriction on their statute of limitations. Again, see your counsel. If you need to, breaking boilerplate language line by line is less difficult nowadays.

Force Majeure. Along the Atlantic seaboard this might be called the "Hurricane Gloria clause." It was once titled "Acts of God." What much of it means is that your business is not to be placed at risk because the drafter failed to anticipate a reasonable business eventuality.

The fact that a licensor or the maintenance firm did not intelligently plan for a strike, power failure, or other unforeseen eventuality may result in your system's being down or your missing a deadline. You lose both present income and future goodwill resulting in near/and long-term disaster.

You need not be conned into believing these are "reasonable" and "unavoidable." In general, a backup can be arranged for and specified in your agreement. New York is on record as stressing that such wording must not stand alone but must be read in context. Thus, the limitation of damages will apply to some extraordinary cause but *not* to problems in performance that might naturally have been anticipated. Absent more explicit terms, the release language, which is to be strictly construed, cannot be read to include delays caused by the defendant's breach of basic fundamental duty.[1]

Agree to release language only for real Acts of God or eventualities that can't be reasonably planned for by a business in its field (can you think of any?). Even here, make sure you've specified that you can terminate the agreement at no prejudice to yourself within __ days if the other party can't perform.

All amendments in writing. This is fairly standard. You don't want the other party to be in a position to alter your rights without your approval. Therefore, no rights can be altered unless you agree (as confirmed by signature) in writing. This complements your merger clause (see below).

Notices. You don't want notification of delays, lawsuits, and so forth, arriving at your firm addressed to no one in particular. You must specify a name and title to receive correspondence. (The latter is more important, as names turn over much more readily than titles). All material correspondence must be by certified mail. The little green receipt is an inexpensive investment in peace of mind. It provides you a guarantee of delivery and objective evidence of same.

Default. Here you want to specifically define how this occurs and, if the default is on your part, how to take steps (if you so elect) to cure the default (or appearance of same). It is particularly important that your attorney analyze any technical terms as to bankruptcy and insolvency triggering a default.

Termination. Here you'll specify how your purchase agreement can be terminated prior to a completed sale and how your license agreement can be terminated prior to, during, or on completion. The termination will include certain specific trigger events but must then also provide for an orderly wind-down, return of the other parties' assets, and so forth.

Governing law/venue. This paragraph defines the laws of the state under which your contract will be governed. You should specifically include the governing state law you want in your contract (such law should bear some reasonable relationship to the agreement, such as place where it is signed, performed, and so forth). You should be aware that if you commence a tort action, your original choice of law may go by the boards since contracting parties can't choose the law applicable to a tort claim arising from the relationship. A simple paragraph such as the following will save you from having the courts later impose a choice of state law you won't like:

"This Agreement will be governed according to the laws of the State of (blank) both as to interpretation and performance."

Don't confuse this with a mandated venue paragraph, which *obligates* you to travel to the other party's home state. Routinely object to these as circumstances warrant.

Integration or merger clause. Here you'll get language such as "This contract constitutes the entire agreement between the parties with respect to the subject matter; all prior agreement, representations, statements, negotiations, and undertakings are superseded hereby." This means that all letter, brochures, demonstrations, sales pitches, and other prior representations you relied on are inoperative as to the contract obligations, unless you followed the earlier recommendation of expressly incorporating these.

Signature line. Make sure all parties are correctly identified. Then just before you sign, do a quick count to make sure all required attachments are attached.

Secondary Contract Clauses

These issues are less important, or come up less often, but you should be aware of them:

Tax applicability. Coordinate language and effect with your tax department or CPA. Never accept a blanket clause that holds you responsible for all taxes levied. All taxes applicable must be defined and allocated by the parties in consultation with a tax professional.

Severability. In any state you might consult with your counsel whether a "severability" paragraph would enhance or diminish your protections. Severability protects your overall agreement from being struck down by virtue of one or more nonenforceable paragraphs, such as unconscionability (and its related doctrine) or other language found to be against public policy. Sample language is as follows:

"If any provision of this Agreement shall be held invalid, illegal, or unenforceable, the validity, legality, and enforceability of the remaining provisions shall not in any way be affected or impaired thereby and this Agreement shall be construed as if such invalid, illegal, or unenforceable provision had never been contained herein."

Severability can be a useful tool. However, never use this as a "throw-in" in a contract, as you may find a court throwing out a paragraph that goes to the heart of why you want the contract. Then, you're stuck with the remaining contract, which not only may go against your expectations, but also may be flat-out injurious to you. Severability should be used only as needed after a review with your counsel.

Maintenance. You'll want any free-maintenance period to begin only after your warranty expires (if applicable—see " Warranties" above). Otherwise, you would be paying for overlapping protection. You'll also want a "time is of the essence" provision to govern these.

Future maintenance obligations can be avoided by a bankruptcy trustee by declaring them executory (as in status of contract not trustee). Here, your greatest danger is that the entire maintenance agreement will be treated as a unitary executory contract; on rejection of such a contract, the trustee may demand the return of all previously completed maintenance work. This area gets complicated; see your counsel as to your specific needs.

Price protection. In a rental agreement, you'll want protection for at least some time. In addition, a notice requirement should exist in the event the lessor desires to increase rental rates after the expiration of the protected period. The notice period should give you the opportunity to cancel if the price increase is not acceptable. Finally, you should certainly negotiate to get the benefit of any price reductions that take effect during the term.

Most favored nations. Here you want the lessor to specify that if any better terms are offered to any other purchaser then such terms will in the future be passed on to you (automatically or as negotiated).

Arbitration. This can expedite disputes, because it is less formal than litigation and may be desirable in *clearly defined* instances. It would be advantageous if you lack the resources vis-a-vis the other party to endure a protracted litigation. However, consider that strict rules of evidence do not apply, e.g., there is no right of appeal. If you have a good case, arbitration should be avoided.

Compliance with all laws. This establishes a warranty from the other party that it will adhere to existing and future laws and regulations.

Waiver. It is desirable to point out that the waiver by one party of a breach by another does not establish a precedent under which other or subsequent breaches are excused.

Headings not controlling. An attorney adds this paragraph if he or she is being paid by the word. Sample language is as follows: "The headings in the Agreement are for convenience only, and shall not limit or otherwise affect the meaning hereof."

The above discussion is obviously not exhaustive. You'll want to review with your counsel some of the areas discussed above as well as other areas as they arise.

Check off the following points each time you approach a contract:

☐ Know what you need in advance.

☐ Search out, find, and negotiate only with reputable parties who have a reputation at stake in your satisfaction.

☐ Work through with the other party (in advance) all specifics you need.

☐ Reduce such specifics to writing and expressly incorporate them in the agreement.

☐ Negotiate any and all terms that represent a significant impediment to your present and reasonably anticipated future needs.

Such terms should include at a minimum:

- An opening section setting forth all definitions,
- A statement of what you intend to accomplish by your contract,
- All parties set forth by name and address,
- The term of your agreement, including the effective date of commencement, and how to terminate the term – automatically or by a certain event(s),
- Price/description of services/most favored firm,
- Warranties extended/disclaimed,
- Indemnification,
- Force majeure,
- Default provision,
- Assignment,
- Governing law,
- Integration or merger clause,
- Signature line.

The above are basic to all agreements. Your counsel should prepare an individual agreement according to the specific needs of the situation.

ENDNOTE

(1) *Forward Industries, Inc. v. Rolm of N.Y. Corp.*, AD 2d (2d Dept., 1986).

CHAPTER 26

COMPUTER HARDWARE AND SOFTWARE PROTECTION AGREEMENTS

All managers are selecting computer systems today for the home as well as the office. Computer literacy is a cliche, but one based on life's experience. Even if your data processing professionals do your legwork, you should have a working knowledge of the essentials so you can assist them as to your needs and free up some of their time to work on your specific needs. Then set up a negotiating team of your data processing professionals, legal staff and finance people.

This chapter reviews some unique elements of computer agreements and then shows how some of the basic contract provisions work in. It starts the review with hardware agreements, moves on to commercial software agreements, consumer software agreements, and options available to you to protect your software from infringement by others. Finally, it looks at a sobering case that addresses your potential liability for systems you design or supervise.

Note: The contractual wording is for general reference and not to be used as a "form" without consulting counsel as to your own needs.

Hardware Agreements

Initially, your finance people will determine the relative merits of a lease or sale. Here there will be trade-offs involving security, taxes, and potential technological obsolescence. Once this is decided, you work through the contract issues in the following sequence. Note: If you're presented with a preprinted boilerplate contract by the lessor, seller, or the vendor, just create an addendum with your counter-language and make acceptance conditional on the vendor's signing your addendum. Then, at the end of your addendum, add the following: "If there shall be any contradictions or inconsistencies between the printed portion of this

Agreement and the Addendum, the provisions of the Addendum shall control."

Parties. Specify each party by name, address, and so on. Define yourself as "Customer/Lessee/Buyer" (hereafter referred to as Customer) and state that Customer shall include any affiliates of the Customer in which Customer owns more than 50% of such affiliates or to an affiliate that owns more than 50% of Customer. This will facilitate the transfer of your leases, warranties, etc. in the event you sell your company or wish to transfer your equipment to other locations.

Effective date. Don't accept the delivery, installation, or date of execution as the effective date: None of these factors means that the hardware is operational to your satisfaction. You want the acceptance to be the date it is actually working. One good reason for this is you don't want your warranty to begin to run until the system is running to your agreed-to specifications. Use the following or similar language, depending on circumstances:

> The Effective Date of this Agreement for the purpose of determining when payment begins shall be the date the hardware has been accepted by the Customer on the successful conclusion of the thirty (30) day Acceptance Period.

Definitions. Define any term used that may be ambiguous or subject to trade jargon to avoid conflicting interpretations. "Understandings" alone aren't enough, as the parties may not be around when the need to interpret the agreement arises.

System identification and specification. Set forth precisely what you wish to receive, and attach a specific exhibit. Incorporate by reference and expressly make a part of the contract *all* material brochures, sales literature, technical specifications, letters, etc. that induced you to obtain this hardware. All these will be identified as Vendor "expressly warrants . . . " so that you create a warranty that the hardware is fit for the particular purposes the vendor specifies. At this time you'll be attempting to use contractual provisions precisely so as to promote performance and to minimize the risks associated with performance failure. Therefore, review with care your needs, the site preparation, appropriate acceptance testing, etc.

Site preparation. The vendor will specify the requirements for the hardware environment. Have the vendor (where cost effective) actually visit and inspect the site prior to delivery and get its OK at this time. Who pays can be negotiated. The most important thing you wish to negotiate here is that the specifications be worded so as to create an express warranty of fitness for your particular purposes once you've complied with the vendor's specifications and your site conforms to the established requirements.

Include a warranty as to the compatibility of components.

Price and payment terms. Establish a variety of benchmarks for your acceptance testing. Offer an up-front payment of perhaps 20% and then certain incremental payments at the completion of each benchmark. This way your initial outlay isn't excessive and the vendor has an incentive to get involved in modifications that may prove necessary. Your leverage to fall back on alternatives decreases with time and so your benchmark checkpoints and payment terms must reflect your increasingly precarious position. Anticipate a few disputes and add in protection against possible default accordingly. For example:

> Customer shall not be subject to any interest charge for failure to make a payment when the billing is the subject of a reasonable dispute by the Customer. In such event, Customer shall communicate in writing such dispute to Vendor within thirty (30) days after receipt of invoice, and Customer shall use due diligence to resolve the error.

You might also create a favorable schedule of payments if you're leasing, e.g.: "All payments due under this Agreement shall not be made until thirty (30) days after receipt of invoice by Customer."

In any leasing agreement, or where you might be purchasing a system with the right to obtain peripherals, you'll want to obtain most-favored-firm price protection. This language will state that if better terms are offered to any customer of the vendor for similar or the same equipment, you will automatically receive such better terms. This, by the way, should present no anticompetitive pricing exposure in antitrust terms.

You should try including the following or similar language depending on your circumstances:

> All of the prices, terms, warranties, and benefits granted by Vendor are comparable to or better than corresponding terms being offered by Vendor to any other Customer. If the Vendor has during the term of this Agreement or during the period this Agreement was being negotiated, entered into any agreement with any other Customer providing greater benefits or more favorable terms, this Agreement shall thereupon be deemed amended to provide the same to Customer as of the effective date of that agreement, or of this Agreement, whichever date is earlier.

Once you've agreed to the basic hardware and pricing, you're ready to move on to it's delivery.

Shipment. Avoid accepting the risk of loss or title to hardware, which you may not accept at all, and certainly will not accept until the effective date. If you are forced to take title or risk of loss on shipment, then negotiate to choose the carrier or at least have veto rights over the choice of carrier. And include a paragraph providing insurance protection to a lessor from delivery to return and to a seller from delivery until final acceptance. An example of the language is as follows:

Customer, at its own expense, shall insure the hardware against all risks and in such amount as Vendor shall reasonably require (but not less than the Stipulated Loss Value identified as of each Equipment Schedule) with carriers acceptable to Vendor, and shall maintain a loss payable endorsement in favor of Vendor and its successors and assigns affording to Vendor and its successors and assigns such additional protection as Vendor and its successors and assigns shall reasonably require, and shall maintain liability insurance satisfactory to Vendor. All such insurance shall name Vendor, its successors and assigns, and Customer as insureds and loss payees, and the policies shall provide that they may not be canceled or altered without at least 10 days' prior written notice to Vendor and its successors and assigns.

At a minimum you should have title and risk of loss revert back to the vendor if the hardware fails to live up to its warranted (promised) expectations. You should also receive a guarantee. You'll receive the benefit of any price decrease prior to delivery. Finally, deadlines should be established according to attached schedules. If you are in control of the equipment the vendor will wish to retain a security interest in the hardware until your full payment or its safe return. You'll agree to cooperate in assisting with the execution and filing of any reasonably necessary security documents. The lessor will utilize its UCC rights based on these documents if you default or go bankrupt, or in other specified contingencies (see below).

Address the issues of what to do when the hardware has arrived: installation, training, and vendor's indemnification for damage done on your premises. Add the following:

In the event the Vendor shall enter the premises where the hardware is located for the purpose of installing the hardware, the Vendor shall be liable for any loss, damages, injury, claim, demand or expense (including legal expenses) pursuant to the installation, resulting from the intentional or negligent act or omission of Vendor. Vendor warrants that it shall maintain, during the term of this Agreement, general public liability insurance and Worker's Compensation coverage and disability coverage for any of its employees assigned to perform any services for Customer. On request, Vendor shall furnish to Customer evidence that such insurance coverages are in effect.

Training. Before the hardware is installed you will want (when necessary) your operating people trained in its proper use. You'll agree to the cost, scope, and location of the training. If the location is remote you'll want to ensure a similar environment to your own. Finally, you'll want to know the qualifications of the instructors and whether they'll be available as on-site consultants. These people can facilitate the implementation as your operating people will (hopefully) have become comfortable with them during the training.

On a related issue, you'll wish to obtain copies of the manuals and the right to reproduce them. The vendor will, at a minimum, require a copyright notice to be placed on them and possibly some other confidentiality restraints (see discussion under "Commercial Software Agreements" below).

Installation. For the specifics as to the actual installation, you'll have to clearly set forth in your agreement:

☐ Who is in charge of the installation (and possibly the accompanying software package);

☐ Who is paying for the personnel and machine time;

☐ Your benchmark payment on satisfactory installation; and

☐ Your recovery of costs needlessly incurred if the hardware fails the acceptance tests.

Performance schedule. Provide for your benchmark tests, both as to hardware and software. You should also specify minimum up-time commitments. Specify grace periods so the vendor can cure any defect. Also state the "outside" date when the hardware must be both installed and ready for use.

If the performance period isn't specific, the law implies a "reasonable time." Reasonableness depends on factors such as the nature of the hardware and services to be furnished, transportation realities, etc. Thus if the delivery, installation, or performance are unreasonably late the customer may still be able to terminate the agreement for a breach even though no date was specified in the contract.

Finally, as in all your similar agreements, you might consider including a system of performance incentives. You'll be entitled to a schedule of agreed-on credits for any hardware/software maintenance that fails to meet the minimum performance criteria. You will also state that such credits are to be considered as liquidated damages and not construed to be or to involve a penalty of any kind.

Just as there are incentives offered for coming on-line rapidly, you may also consider penalties or liquidated damages for the failure of timely performance.

Warranty. Once your hardware has passed the applicable acceptance tests, interrelated warranty and maintenance provisions should kick in to govern the performance and reliability of the hardware on an ongoing basis. You already have established express warranties and warranties for a particular purpose in your specifications, attachments, benchmarks, etc. You will also want to include the following warranties in your contract.

☐ Vendor is free of any obligation that would prevent it from entering the agreement, has good and clear title to the products (sold or licensed), and will not make any commitments to others inconsistent or in conflict with your rights.

☐ The hardware is free of defects in material and workmanship when delivered.

☐ Impaired or defective hardware will be repaired or replaced.

☐ The warranty period shall not expire while any new error brought to the vendor's attention during the warranty period remains uncorrected. The failure of the vendor to make any and all such corrections shall constitute a material breach of the Agreement.

Be sure to get as long a warranty as possible for these reasons: (a) the free maintenance interval for itself; (b) if your maintenance is to be performed by another firm you'll lose the vendor's unique knowledge of your hardware as well as your status as a future customer to be satisfied; and perhaps most importantly, (c) the warranty period gives the customer who intends to perform his or her own maintenance a reasonable period in which to act.

The vendor will have a variety of disclaimers in boldface type. You must *precede* the disclaimer language with "Except as expressly set forth herein" so as to preserve all the express and subtle warranties you've gained through negotiations. If the vendor attempts to add in a disclaimer as to late delivery, add in language (here or in your Termination paragraph) that gives you the right to terminate after ___ days at your election.

The vendor will also disclaim the warranty where you have made "unauthorized changes." Where practical, try to limit this warranty loss to the equipment you actually alter.

If you are leasing from a lessor in a third-party financing arrangement, you'll also want the following warranty and related protections:

> "Lessor represents and warrants that it has purchased the Equipment leased hereunder from the Seller thereof. Lessor hereby assigns to Lessee all of Lessor's right, title, and interest in the Equipment listed herein and hereby appoints Lessee its attorney-in-fact, irrevocable during the term of the lease, and coupled with an interest to exercise and enforce all of the rights granted to Lessor."

If the vendor attempts any limitation of damages, make sure you make it *mutual,* for example: "Notwithstanding anything stated herein, neither party shall be liable for consequential, special, or exemplary damages, even if it has been advised of the possibilities of such damages."

Maintenance. Make sure any maintenance agreements you sign don't commence until the expiration of the applicable warranties. You'll want to use protective language such as this:

> In the event that Customer accepts the hardware, the ninety (90) day warranty shall commence the day following the expiration of the thirty (30) day Acceptance Period and the Maintenance Period will commence immediately on the termination of the warranty.

Then make sure the maintenance agreement is signed prior to or contemporaneously with the vendor if it is providing maintenance (either its own or through a third-party contractor). If this is a problem, use language such as: "In the event this Agreement and the _____ agreements are not all executed on or before _____ ,19 _____ , this Agreement and each of the above agreements will be voidable at Customer's sole election." Prior to the sale or lease of the hardware is when you have your greatest leverage as to ancillary agreements such as maintenance.

You'll want most-favored-firm language as to price increases (see above). In the interim, you'll want a specific hourly rate plus any material costs and reasonable travel and living expenses where necessary. (Use "reasonable" often in these agreements as to time, notice, costs, etc.; when in doubt, qualify what is meant by "reasonable".)

Then you'll want to specify:

(a) Response times and holidays (and availability on same, especially if you're using the equipment on conflicting days or the hardware is in continuous use). For example, consider language similar to the following:

> Within four hours after notification by Customer that the hardware is operating defectively or improperly, qualified Maintenance representatives of Vendor shall respond at the location of the hardware, and shall make all efforts to correct any errors or defects of the hardware, free from interruption until the hardware becomes operative. Vendor's normal working hours shall mean 8:30 a.m. to 5:00 p.m., Monday through Friday, excepting "Holidays," which shall be limited to Washington's Birthday, Memorial Day, Independence Day, Labor Day, Thanksgiving Day, Day after Thanksgiving, Christmas Holiday, New Year's Holiday.

(b) Schedule for routine, ongoing preventive maintenance. You might utilize language such as:

> Preventive maintenance shall be performed at least once monthly and may be performed concurrently with remedial services. Preventive maintenance shall consist of the scheduled procedures generally performed for other Customers of similar equipment and shall be carried out so as to assure optimal performance and availability of the equipment. Vendor shall cooperate with Customer in scheduling and rescheduling preventive maintenance so as not to unreasonably interfere with the required operation of the equipment. Preventive and remedial maintenance shall be performed by qualified employees of Vendor with a view toward maintaining the equipment in continuous working order, free from error and interruption of performance.

(c) If the lease or purchase justifies it, you may wish a full-time maintenance person to be assigned to your site for a fixed period. For all maintenance, you want to specify a qualified engineer totally familiar with the hardware.

(d) While you have leverage, you should tie in maintenance for the life of the agreement, the estimated useful life of the hardware, or some other minimum maintenance term or guaranteed renewal. Otherwise, on a given transaction date you may contractually lose your maintenance without any available substitute. You should try for the following:

"In the event that the Program product and or associated maintenance becomes unavailable on a commercial basis, then a current copy of the source code shall be sent to Customer by Vendor at a nominal cost to the Customer."

(e) Any enhancements to be provided on a most-favored-firm (sometimes referred to as most-favored-nation) basis.

(f) Finally, the vendor will want full and free access to the hardware during maintenance. You should qualify this a bit with language such as:

The "full and free access" to be afforded to Vendor for maintaining the Equipment shall be limited to such access as is reasonably necessary to perform maintenance on such equipment as required maintenance, and shall not be deemed to permit Vendor to disable or render unavailable the balance of the system except as is necessary for such maintenance and testing.

If all else fails, try for a parts availability covenant for the estimated useful life of the equipment or the term of your lease. For extended problems you'll want progress reports provided to you at specific, routine intervals. Finally, consider the problem of the firm's bankruptcy. Future maintenance obligations can be avoided by the bankruptcy trustee as executory. Here your greatest danger is that the entire maintenance agreement will be treated as a unitary executory contract; on rejection of such a contract, the trustee may demand the return of all previously completed maintenance work. This area becomes complicated. See your counsel as to your specific needs and make sure he or she has considered this matter to your satisfaction.

Indemnification. Your most important protection may be that related to intellectual-property infringement. You want protection along the following lines:

Vendor shall defend any suit or proceeding brought against the Customer so far as based on a claim that the hardware/software furnished under this Agreement constitutes an infringement of any patent, copyright, or trademark of the United States, or other proprietary right at common law, if notified promptly in writing and given authority, information, and assistance (at Vendor's expense) for the defense of same and will pay all damages and costs awarded therein against Customer. In case said hardware/software is enjoined, Vendor shall, using due diligence, at its own expense, with the approval of the Customer, which shall not be unreasonably withheld, either (a) procure for the Customer the right to continue using said hardware/software, or (b) replace same with noninfringing hardware/software, or (c) modify it so that it becomes noninfringing or (d) (i) provide the Customer a full refund of such hardware/software for the amounts paid Vendor by Customer, and (ii) pay all damages and costs awarded against the Customer as herein provided.

Vendor shall have no liability in respect to any infringement which results exclusively or is in significant part developed by Customer outside of Vendor's discretion or without Vendor's permission.

You'll also want quiet enjoyment tied in to your indemnification and warranty protection. For example:

The Customer shall be entitled to possess and use the hardware during the term of the Agreement without interruption by the Vendor or any person claiming under or through the Vendor, provided only that the Customer has duly performed its obligation under the Agreement. The Vendor warrants and represents that the leased/purchased hardware is not subject to any lien, claim, or encumbrance inconsistent herewith.

Again you'll want to include indemnification protection for the vendor's time on your property for training, installation, warranty, maintenance, or other reasons, e.g.:

In the event that the Vendor or the Vendor's assigns shall enter the Customer's premises where the hardware is located for the purpose of inspecting such hardware, the Vendor shall be liable for any loss, damages, injury, claim, demand, or expense (including legal expenses), pursuant to the inspection, resulting from the intentional or negligent act or omission of the Vendor or the Vendor's assigns.

Default. The vendor will protect itself against your bankruptcy, failure to pay as agreed, breach of other material terms, etc. You need a few hedges, for instance:

Vendor's right to terminate this Agreement for Customer's failure to comply with any terms or conditions shall not be exercised except after (a) thirty (30) days notice to Customer, which notice shall state in detail the nature of such alleged failure of compliance and (b) Customer's failure to correct such failure of compliance within the thirty-day period; provided, however, that if in the exercise of due diligence Customer's failure of compliance cannot be corrected within such thirty-day period, this Agreement may not be terminated by vendor and so long as Customer shall commence, and diligently continue to correct such failure of compliance.

As to any right of vendor to act against you for insolvency, make sure it is for *voluntary* bankruptcy or insolvency only. This prevents a nuisance suit or filing from triggering this paragraph.

Finally, you will never permit self-help entrance onto your premises. A vendor may only enter your premises "with appropriate legal process."

Assignment. Like the "generic" contract, your computer hardware agreement should avoid an assignment to a bank in your line of credit or to a competitor firm. You *do* wish to include the 50/50 language (see "Parties" above) to freely assign internally. Otherwise, any bars on assignment (written notice to other party, need to obtain permission) should be qualified by language as "such right to assignment shall not be unreasonably denied."

You should obtain the right to transfer the hardware to any temporary location without immediate notification to the vendor in the event of malfunction of normal computer operations at the licensed location. The purpose of this transference is to provide a backup contingency plan of operation in the event of such malfunctions.

Joint venture. You might not wish to create the appearance of this, especially if you're financing customized hardware. Consider language such as this:

> Nothing contained herein shall be construed to imply the existence of a joint venture, or principal and agent, and employer and employee relationship between the parties, and neither party shall have any rights, power, or authority to create any obligations express or implied on behalf of the other, except as expressly provided herein.

Taxes. Here you'll wish to exclude your paying for any taxes on vendor's net income. In the case of a lease, you wish to exclude any personal property taxes on the hardware. Then both parties will specify the current tax benefits available as to each party, depending on how the transaction is put together and what incentives (such as the investment tax credit) are available.

No waiver. Standard and reasonable language to include would be to the effect that "The waiver or failure of either party to exercise in any respect any right provided for herein shall not be deemed a waiver of any further right hereunder."

Termination. You will want to provide for an orderly termination (if necessary) by specifying all causes and cures (such as, defective warranty and time to correct same), effect on end users, and any possible escrows. All dates and time periods must be specific. Other paragraphs which will crop up include force majeure (Acts of God), severability, governing law, notice, arbitration (or some informal, agreed-on dispute resolution procedures), and integration (see discussion above under general contract law). You may wish to expand on the latter as follows:

> "This Agreement supersedes all proposals, oral and written, all negotiations, conversations, or discussions between the parties relating to the Agreement and all past course of dealing or industry custom. This Agreement, together with all subordinates and other documents incorporated by reference herein, constitutes the entire Agreement between the parties with respect to the subject matter contained herein and may only be modified by an amendment executed in writing by both parties hereto."

You'll end your addendum with the following: "If there shall be any contradictions or inconsistencies between the printed portion of the

Agreement and this Addendum, the provisions of the Addendum shall control.

Signatures. You'll sign below on both the boilerplate and addendum and possibly some or all of the attached schedules.

Now for a look at some unique issues that crop up when you acquire software.

COMMERCIAL SOFTWARE AGREEMENTS

Much of what was said concerning hardware agreements carries over to software agreements.[1] There are, however, important differences. Although the paragraphs that follow discuss these distinct areas, contract sections build on one another in sequence and do not stand alone.

Few important software packages are sold outright. Most transfers are by a nonexclusive, nontransferable license. This license grants the right to use the software in certain specified ways, but does not convey title or ownership. This is a major difference between software and many hardware contracts. Familiarity with a few basic concepts can alleviate much confusion in this area. The following discussion applies to most software licenses and acquisitions.

Before You Sign

Here are three questions to ask yourself at the start:

(1) Does the product meet my needs as proposed?

(2) What if bugs in the system are uncovered along the way?

(3) What if the licensor (again, you're usually licensing rather than purchasing) goes out of business after I've started to use his software?

It is usually less expensive to use packaged software. One reason is that preconstructed software can be tested and validated before your purchase. However, information is useless to you unless it is presented in a way that can easily be understood by your firm, enabling management to make decisions that are relevant to the firm's unique operations. Therefore, if you need customized software, you must be very clear as to *your* specifications (if this is a turnkey system,[2] define and select the software first). Good specifications form the basis for a good contract. Your machine won't work without instruction, and the usefulness of the system is directly related to the quality and effectiveness of the programs designed for it.

Your specifications should include:

☐ a functional description of the package that defines the tasks you need it to accomplish (inputs, outputs, processing requirements, etc.);

☐ a hardware environment description–if your hardware and software firm is the same, incorporate by reference; if not, then you must be precise as to restrictions, data transmission procedures, and related matters.

☐ a description of the software environment (languages, operating system, etc.);

☐ a definition of all documentation;

☐ any other internal, mechanical, or other factors necessary to make this software work in your environment; and

☐ a sign-off warranty by the licensor that he or she is familiar with your system requirements and that the system as set forth is adequate for your requirements.

All specifications must have measurable references. One way to assist both parties is to draw up a Request for Proposal (RFP) before negotiating. The best RFPs incorporate functional specifications and technical specifications. In the RFP, identify your needs as precisely as possible and then ask the software designer or seller if a product package can satisfy the specifically stated needs.

If you aren't too clear as to what you need, draw up an informal RFP and ask for the seller's views concerning appropriate software for your needs. Whether formal or informal, your RFP will then be negotiated, and the seller will conduct demonstrations so that both parties can get the specifications as clear as possible. Your payments should be tied to the completion of various benchmark tests.

Once the specifications are clear, commit them to writing. Eventually you'll attach these as part of a schedule. This accomplishes a number of things for you:

• You have reduced to writing exactly what you want and how it will develop.

• The development flow is underlined by payments tied to each step.

• The specifications you've agreed to create an express warranty, which will generally prevail[3] over an express disclaimer of all warranty liability found in the boilerplate. With this in mind, you might obtain language such as "Licensor recognizes that the software shall be a major factor utilized by the License in its operation. Failure to implement such would cause damage to Licensee."

All specifications are described in detail, attached as exhibits and expressly made a part of your agreement.

Software Agreements—Contractual Terms

Here are some of the specific software terms that you'll be presented and what you can do to modify them.

Grant and scope of license.[4] You'll be offered a perpetual or finite nonexclusive, nontransferable license. You'll want to receive:

• Any future enhancements and upgrades, i.e.:

The Licensee shall have the right, with the prior written consent of the Licensor, which approval shall not be unreasonably withheld or delayed, to make upgrades, attachments, and/or feature enhancements to the Equipment, at licensee's own expense. Licensee, at its own expense, shall remove such upgrades, attachments, and/or feature enhancements and return the Equipment to their normal condition. Title to all such upgrades, attachments, and/or feature enhancements will remain with Licensee. The foregoing shall not obligate Licensee to obtain any upgrade, attachment, and/or feature enhancements from Licensor. Desired upgrades, attachments, and/or feature enhancements may be obtained by Licensee from any third party.

- A most-favored-firm language as to such enhancements (see hardware agreements above).
- Use the "50/50 language" for ease of transfer internally or to facilitate the transfer of your systems intact if your firm is sold (it will also permit you to use the program on another computer if the identified computer is down for maintenance): "Licensee shall include any affiliates of the Licensee in which Licensee owns more than fifty percent (50%) of such affiliates or to an affiliate which owns more than fifty percent (50%) of Licensee." Then get in: "Licensee may use the Programs at any location whatsoever without restriction, subject only to the restrictions herein elsewhere contained with respect to Licensee disclosure, reproduction, or permitting others to use the Programs."

Definitions and Parties. See discussion of hardware terms above.

Effective or commencement date. As with hardware agreements, you don't want the contract term to commence until you're at least minimally satisfied. You need language similar to the following: "The Commencement Date of this Agreement for the purpose of determining when the monthly rental charges begin hereunder shall be the date the ___ listed herein is delivered, installed and accepted by Licensee."

Delivery. Be sure the delivery date is the date of physical delivery of not only the software, but also all manuals and anything else you need to complete your package. Here you'll wish to protect yourself from two types of delivery failure. First, and most obvious, is the absolute failure to deliver. Second is failure to deliver software that meets your specifications for reliability, function, or performance standards.

Acceptance provisions. You'll construct your own tests and specify the standards in the RFP and then, again, in your contract clause. Both parties are better protected if the Licensee notifies the Licensor in writing of the acceptance of the software or, where necessary, each item of the software package. The Licensee's acceptance is not valid unless in writing. If there is any objection, the Licensee should describe in detail any errors and defects discovered.

The provision for a written acceptance is preferable to any form of negative-option acceptance such as "If no written rejection is received by Licensor/Seller within thirty (30) days from the date of shipment to

Licensee/Buyer, the software will be deemed acceptable." You may want some downside "out" protection, such as this:

> If within ninety (90) days from the date Licensee expects delivery of the software, same has not been delivered, installed, and accepted by Licensee, Licensee may on ten (10) days' notice to the Licensor, terminate this lease and its obligations hereunder, and Licensor shall refund any advance rentals required under the Agreement to the Licensee.

Training. Hardware training focuses on the operations people. Software training, on the other hand, will often encompass higher management as well as other levels of management. You'll need to specify the time frame, price, and location for training level of user. You'll also have to address follow-up training. Finally, you'll have to specify how much latitude you'll have as to the circulation of manuals and related documents.

You might have the Licensor expressly warrant that its consulting and professional personnel provided shall have the appropriate technical and applications skills to enable them to perform their duties, satisfactory to your specified needs. You might also request in advance a background description or resume of the key people such as the project manager. You might require veto power over whom you receive as well as any replacements prior to the completion of their specified task(s).

Price of royalty provisions. Specify whether there is a flat rate, royalty on use, or other pricing provision (see also the discussion above on hardware agreements.)

Sales and property tax liability. See the discussion above on hardware agreements.

Trade secret acknowledgment. This area is covered extensively elsewhere in this section. Suffice it is to say here that the Licensor will establish that this material is of a confidential nature and its disclosure will cause the Licensor irreparable harm. The licensor will then state that such irreparable injury cannot be adequately compensable in damages. They'll get injunctive powers. Narrow these as much as possible, as an injunction can shut your system down. The best strategy is to negotiate a liquidated damages clause, setting a ceiling for unauthorized copying or related breaches of this warranty. You probably can hold these to 5 to 10 times the value of the license fee.

If you spend time developing improvements, modifications, training materials, etc., can you take these with you, or is this a breach of confidentiality or of another provision in the license? Specify your rights here if warranted. Finally, the Licensor will want a certain survival period for such confidence to extend beyond the termination of your license.

You want to know precisely which parts of the software package are subject to the alleged trade secret protection. For example, you might require that "the software and specimens of the software shall be clearly marked and identified as proprietary and confidential material of Licensor." You will honor their labels, but wouldn't obligate yourself to continuously put on new labels. You'll then want to restrict this by excluding:

(a) material you already know;

(b) material you learn from an independent or separate source entitled to disclose it;

(c) material in the public domain;

(d) material "leaked" by other licensees regardless of their intent (remember, you don't have an exclusive license, and your accountability should be reduced as a result) or by the Licensor without restriction on disclosure; and

(e) information developed by or for you, independent of the activities governed by this license agreement.

You won't want any undue or oppressive standard of care imposed on you for the protection of Licensor's trade secrets, title, and other proprietary rights. The following strikes a reasonable balance (and remember, this is *your* warranty): "Licensee agrees to exercise the same degree of care to safeguard Licensor's product as Licensee would exercise to safeguard the confidentiality of Licensee's confidential property."

You will want the following warranty from the Licensor as a trade-off to the burdens he or she is imposing on you. Consider the following:

> Licensor warrants that it is the sole owner of the software and has full power and authority to grant the rights herein granted without the consent of any person and will indemnify and hold the Licensee harmless from and against any loss, cost, liability and expense (including reasonable counsel fees) arising out of any breach or claimed breached of warranty.

Finally, if the Licensor will have access to your proprietary secrets, either in the creation or maintenance of your system, make sure your counsel includes in your Addendum confidentiality protection for your interests. Make sure you inform your counsel as to any customer lists, trade secrets, and other proprietary information involved. The language of your mutual nondisclosure agreement shall contain the following:

> Each party may disclose to the other information concerning its confidential know-how, trade secrets, and future product plans as may be necessary to further the performance of this Agreement. All such confidential know-how, trade secrets, and future product plans shall remain the sole property of the party disclosing same, and the receiving party shall have no interest in or rights with respect thereto except as set forth herein.

> Each party agrees to identify and mark (or itemize on a schedule to be incorporated) such information as proprietary and to maintain such information in confidence to the same extent that it protects its own proprietary information, and further agrees to take all reasonable

precautions to prevent any unauthorized disclosure of any such information. The obligations of this paragraph are to remain in effect until such time as the information becomes a matter of public knowledge, regardless of the termination of the Agreement for any reason whatsoever.

At the end you'll include the exceptions set forth in (a), (b), and (c) above or similar language so as to prevent any "confidentiality overkill."

Maintenance obligations and terms. See the discussion above on hardware agreements. To review a few highlights:

☐ Always negotiate your maintenance agreement before or as a condition to your software agreement. This maximizes your leverage.

☐ Make sure the maintenance term commences as your warranty period expires. Otherwise, you're paying for the overlap you don't need.

☐ Make sure you retain and incorporate expressly into your agreement as warranties all brochures, letters, demonstrations, and like matter that were used to induce you to purchase the product. This exercise helps you two ways: first, by broadening the scope of protection you'll have as to unanticipated events that may crop up in the system, and second, if your Licensor won't stand behind his or her written sales material, then you're going into any agreement with your eyes open.

☐ You'll want protection in case of the unforeseen loss of your maintenance, e.g. "In the event that the software and/or associated maintenance becomes unavailable on a commercial basis, then a current copy of the source code shall be sent to Licensee by Licensor at a nominal cost to the Licensee."

For software, consider the following special situations. First, will your maintenance people assume the responsibility for maintaining the initial software package (correction of errors or malfunctions) as well as any changes (including enhancements) necessitated as the system evolves? Also, will the Licensor see that you have free maintenance until at least the final acceptance of the system? You don't want to pay for their delays in setting up your system. More than hardware, the effectiveness of software maintenance is closely related to the timeliness of the quality repair. If possible, avoid terms such as "best efforts" and "expeditiously," and pin them down to precise times. For example (assuming Licensor is performing the maintenance):

During the term of this license, Licensor will correct all errors found by Licensee, any other user, or Licensor. Such corrections shall be made within twenty-four (24) hours after discovery and shall be at no cost to the Licensee.

If the Licensor says this is arbitrary, then build incentives such as penalties for __ hours downtime after 24 hours and penalties for __ hours downtime in a week, month, or year.

Warranties. See the discussion above on hardware agreements. At all times you want at least substantial conformance to the Agreement's specifications as published and its run time.

Disclaimer or limitations on warranties assumed. See the discussion above under hardware agreements. Also, always make sure you precede the boldprint disclaimer language paragraph(s) with "Except as expressly set forth herein." If your software fails, you needn't be intimidated by any disclaimers.

- Your Licensor won't insure you against all hazards, but written specifications of performance and any inducement brochures you can incorporate into the agreement contain warranties that the Licensor can't disclaim.
- If a dispute arises, have your counsel review whether the disclaimer language is drafted properly. If it isn't, you may be able to break it in whole or in part.
- If you worked closely together in developing the customized software, then argue that you have an express warranty of fitness for a particular purpose.[5]
- If there is any *material* malfunction, argue fraud, unconscionability (see discussion below), and material misrepresentation of fact.

These tort areas are increasingly of interest to you. Though the situations may vary from state to state, the trend has been for the courts to give less latitude to a salesperson's "puffing" in these areas than in other commercial situations. In general, the decisions are holding that there is greater reliance on the expertise of the salesperson in computer hardware/software purchases because of the sophistication of the product and the velocity at which the field is evolving.

If you seek remedies in tort, contractual expectations regarding matters such as choice of law may not apply. Tort remedies are useful in situations where you have been wronged or misled. In one recent case[6] a plaintiff argued that he wasn't "computer literate" and that the seller took advantage of this fact. This was found to be unconscionable.

Finally, you may see language such as "No suit or action shall be brought against seller more than one year after the related cause of action has occurred." Under the Uniform Commercial Code (UCC), the Statute of Limitations is four years and can be shortened to no less than one year. However, where state common law controls, you have a new situation entirely, because certain states bar any restriction of their statute of limitations. Again, see your counsel.

Indemnification. You'll want the indemnity as to the license's not infringing on a copyright, trade secret, etc. Review and adapt the language suggested in the hardware agreements discussion above. You'll also want specific indemnification for Licensor's errors in the data it supplied. And finally, you'll want a mutual indemnity catchall such as this:

Each party shall promptly notify the other by written, certified mail, all actions at law or otherwise arising out of all work in conjunction with this Agreement. Each party shall be liable for and shall indemnify and hold the other party harmless against any loss or damage arising from any and all finally settled and adjudicated claims by or on behalf of any person or persons for personal injury or property damage arising out of the fault or negligence of such party, its officers or employees. The foregoing representations, warranties and indemnities shall survive termination of this Agreement.

Bankruptcy/Insolvency. The Licensor will give you boilerplate protecting the Licensee's rights in these situations. Any third-party maintenance firm (in case of assignments—see below) will also have a lien on its work in these situations. This is an important area to review with your counsel. Again, the Licensor's reputation and solvency are issues you'll want to discuss. If there is any question of the Licensor's solvency, then you'll want your counsel to draft addendum language protection accordingly, such as the maintenance executory contract exposure discussed above.

In the event of the Licensor's bankruptcy you'll need to define the availability of and your access to the source code. You cannot simply hire a replacement if your Licensor goes bankrupt. Without the source code, it may be impossible for a programmer to modify another firm's program. You'll wish to specify here exactly what the source code is and that you are to receive the *current* source code. Your counsel will also draft language to facilitate its immediate transfer to you on a triggering event, rather than your having to line up at the door with the general creditors later.

Governing law. This paragraph defines the laws of the state under which the contract will be governed. You should be aware that if you commence a tort action, your original choice of law may go by the boards, since contracting parties can't choose the law applicable to a tort claim arising from the relationship.

Assignment clause. You rarely want to accept these as drawn. At a minimum, make sure that:

(1) The software license is not limited to a single site and that you have free transferability of the software among other entities you control. Requiring notice to the lessor is reasonable, but the lessor should not be able to restrict your transferring the software among your affiliates through any "special permission" language. (Though the seller might reasonably impose an additional maintenance charge on software located beyond an exact number of miles from seller's nearest office.)

(2) You negotiate for some veto power over the lessor's ability to assign the agreement without your advance approval. If the lease is silent on the right of assignment or reserves an unrestricted right of assignment, you will have little recourse to prevent this.

If the lessor assigns to a third party, you generally cannot assert any claims for improper performance against the third-party assignee. This may also impair your ability to assert any claims against the original seller.

More subtly but just as ominously, you might find the agreement assigned to:

- a bank in your credit line—this could restrict your future borrowings, or
- a competitor's parent or subsidiary—the implications are obvious.

If you can't get a general veto over a licensor's assignment for reasonable cause, then you should attempt to specify a few specific instances where assignment won't be permitted, such as: "Lessor acknowledges that the Lessor's Assignees or Transferees shall be restricted to a Bank or Financial Institution or noncompetitors of Lessee."

Finally, regardless of the final assignment clause wording, you must have good language as to quiet enjoyment. For example:

> The Lessee shall be entitled to possess and use the software during the Lease without interruption by the Lessor or any person claiming under or through the Lessor, provided only that the Lessee has duly performed its obligation under the lease. The Lessor warrants and represents that the leased software is not subject to any lien, claim, or encumbrance herewith.

Licensor's employees. There will be a paragraph that prohibits the licensee from offering direct or indirect employment to any person within one to two years of such person's employment by licensor (see discussion in Chapter 27 on employment contracts and covenants not to compete). In general, the employer can have a rough time sustaining this form of restriction on an employee without a showing of need plus that the duration and geographic restrictions are limited and reasonable.

Force majeure. This has been discussed under general contract terms. If you sign a standard force majeure claim, you may find yourself in the position where your system is down as a result of the licensor's or maintenance firm's failure to anticipate a foreseeable business eventuality. You could wind up missing deadlines and losing both present income and future goodwill. If you're a small user, you could go under, if you've committed your entire operation to this system.

In general, a backup could be arranged for and referred to in your agreement. In addition, or as a less desirable alternative, have your counsel draft a provision for recovery for catastrophic failure for the "Acts of God" that can be reasonably anticipated and planned for. This is a form of liquidated damages protection and will work wonders in discouraging extended downtime due to force majeure.

Merger or integration clause. Here you'll get language such as "This contract constitutes the entire agreement between the parties with respect to the subject matter; all prior agreements, representations, statements, negotiations, and undertakings are superseded hereby." This means that all letters, brochures, demonstrations, sales pitches, and other prior representations you relied on are inoperative as to the contract obligations, *unless* you followed the recommendation of expressly incorporating these.

If you already have signed a contract containing this form of language (and they always do), make a record of and retain all printed matter or anything else you relied on in negotiating with and then contracting with your seller.

These documents can still be valuable to you, because the merger clause has no effect on an allegation of fraud in the inducement. If you can demonstrate the existence of such fraud in the inducement, all limitations on liability enunciated in this clause are out, since fraud permeates the entire contract. One California decision that is a growing precedent case stated that fraud may be "inferred from the immediate failure to perform a promise."[7]

Finally, see the discussion of hardware agreements as to "Joint Venture," "Severability," "No Waiver," and other clauses.

Conclusion

The above discussion is obviously not exhaustive. You'll want to review with your counsel other possible proprietary rights protection, who gets to copyright software adaptations, sublicenses to permit consultants to get access, and many more areas. The purpose of this discussion has been to demonstrate that boilerplate is negotiable both before and after you receive it. Even after you've signed on, it is not a legal straightjacket. If you were materially wronged (as opposed to merely outnegotiated on a point), your legal counsel can probably find redress for you. However, the need for legal redress is greatly reduced if you:

(1) Know what you need in advance.

(2) Search out, find, and negotiate only with reputable sellers/licensors whose reputation is at stake in your satisfaction.

(3) Work through with the seller/licensor (in advance) all of your specifications.

(4) Reduce such specifications to writing and expressly incorporate them in the agreement.

(5) Negotiate any and all boilerplate terms that represent a significant impediment to your present and reasonably anticipated future needs.

The following boilerplate terms should be addressed in your hardware, software, and maintenance analysis prior to and during the drafting of your agreement *in addition* to the generic terms addressed in chapter 25.

☐ After you set forth the parties, definitions, and intent, and before you set forth the effective date, you'll want paragraphs setting forth in detail your method of delivery, installation, and acceptance. You'll also attach a variety of exhibits and performance schedules related to these areas.

☐ Your price and payment terms will, of course, differ depending on your utilization of a license or purchase agreement.

☐ Unlike most contracts you'll address the issue of personnel training.

☐ Your warranty period will tie in with the maintenance period. Both paragraphs will have to be drawn to your specific expectations and/or needs.

☐ Indemnification will include not only the routine mutual protections but specific intellectual property protections extended to the Licensee/Buyer.

☐ Default must be material due to the cost of these systems.

☐ Assignment should be more carefully qualified and at all times contain a paragraph setting forth in detail your right to quiet enjoyment. In all of these agreements, to allow flexibility you must have the right to transfer the agreements internally and to successor corporations if your business is sold.

☐ Taxes are always specified in these agreements, especially in third-party financing arrangements.

☐ Confidentiality is a must in every license agreement, especially one covering software.

☐ Bankruptcy is an important issue in these agreements, both as to the potential of certain aspects being considered executory and your need for immediate access to the source code.

SMALL FIRM AND CONSUMER SOFTWARE CONTRACTS—THE SHRINK-WRAPPED LICENSE ECLIPSES

Historically, commercial enterprises have been able to limit the extent of their warranty exposure in the consumer market so long as the product was not inherently dangerous. This situation is changing because of the complexity of software as a product.

It is no longer prophetic or revealing to discuss the information economy and its displacement of the familiar hard-goods manufacturing economy (which replaced the land economy). However, it is rarely questioned how long the competitive environment will remain healthy when the legal environment remains statically rooted in the manufacturing era.

One reads with amusement trade press's misconception that isolated updates of laws, such as those governing copyright and cable, are signs of a society comfortable with the new technological realities. The opposite is true. Laws change only when most people come to understand that they're locked out of the path to upward mobility.

The land economy was altered by Yorktowns and guillotines. The manufacturing economy was altered when the trusts were "busted". The information economy will be altered when all have at least proportionately equal access to the creation and retention of information. One way this will happen is when individuals and small firms begin to change the contra clause that often victimize them.

Almost all readers of this book are at a distinct disadvantage in the home-computer market—the generic term for the market that controls the gateway to the information economy as computers form the core of the high-tech economy. Let's look at the techniques for the individual and small firm to use to break the stronghold of contract boilerplate.

The antitrust analogy. A consensus came about during the manufacturing era that small firms could not compete in the capital and credit markets. Pressure from small businesses brought about a number of laws that curbed predatory pricing, blatant tie-ins, horizontal price fixing, and prohibited price discrimination between small and large firms where the effect was to substantially lessen, injure, or prevent competition. The antitrust laws worked fairly well when the U.S. was a self-contained manufacturing economy. They adapted slowly to the global economy, and only recently has rule of reason replaced per se analysis in evaluating most of these situations.

The dominant position of a few large firms in the computer industry goes beyond their power in the capital markets and extends to their monopoly of specialized knowledge. Only they have access to the knowledge of whether the system they sell will do what it is touted as being capable of doing. However, consumers have a few protections by law, and a computer system and its related software rarely affect their livelihood. A small firm doesn't have even this legal assistance. The consumer is confronted with no bargaining power and often must contend with a "shrink-wrapped" software license, in which he or she is "informed" (via a license visible through the product's cellophane wrapper) that on opening the package he or she becomes a licensee of the software.

It's Unconscionable

A small firm, unlike a consumer, has no Magnuson-Moss protection (see Section I) or related protections. Yet, the small firm often lacks the technical in-house expertise to evaluate its needs. It also lacks financial leverage in negotiation. Then, when the system the seller designed for the buyer is paid for and fails, the owner finds there is no protection in the boilerplate for the seller's failure to perform. The law tells the owner that business transactions are presumed to be between equals and at arm's length. In short, the realities a small business owner faces in trying to effectuate relief are quite simply unconscionable.

The laws governing computer systems require a new analysis because the traditional legal theories of fraud and breach of warranty ignore the inherent differences between computers and ordinary business purchases. Two primary factors control the market:

- The industry is dominated by a few large companies whose form contracts are the industry standard.
- These firms possess technological sophistication, or "computer literacy."

Unconscionability rarely exists in a commercial setting involving parties of equal bargaining power.[8] However, no small firm acquiring a computer system even approaches a semblance of equal bargaining power. When the small firm is acquiring a computer system for the first time or upgrading an existing one, the firm is in a weak position. When acquiring a system, the small firm may not know its precise needs and tends to rely on the seller's expertise. Yet, the boilerplate routinely disclaims any warranty for a particular purpose. If the firm has already purchased a system, it finds that switching sellers is difficult and so generally must negotiate with the existing one. The seller knows this. Remember, while this is your isolated case, the seller has a store of expertise developed in this specialized business.

To date, the small firm trying to obtain hardware and systems must approach the large sellers with great care. However, "great care" is enough when one party has access to knowledge that the other lacks and is computer literate while the other party's confined to English. Yet, the law generally views this situation in the same context as a firm's purchase of a company car or order of widgets. The "language barrier" alone should mandate these dealings be governed by the unconscionability standard. This standard would apply if a consumer were presented with a foreign-tongue boilerplate (see note 5). However, too often today the legislatures and the courts assume as a matter of law we're all computer experts.

Apart from the computer language barrier, most small business users are unable to assess their electronic data processing (EDP) needs and to choose the most suitable. They may be too small to have an EDP staff or their staff may lack the necessary sophistication. Therefore, a computer salesperson assesses the user's business requirements and works in good faith to develop a system. Assurances are given orally or in sales literature. If the purchased system fails, and perhaps takes the firm's business with it, the user may find that there are no effective warranties, a damage recovery is nonexistent, and all promises rendered were wiped out by the integration clause. The user could have read these and negotiated for broader terms. However, if there was no room to negotiate or the user lacked a meaningful competitive choice in entering the agreements, then unconscionability should be found on the basis that the user had no real choice, could not bargain, and in effect, did not agree to the onerous terms.

The doctrine of unconscionability in sophisticated commercial transactions is as necessary to small business users today as, say, the Robinson-Patman Act is to the same group—if not more so. The latter secured at least threshold protection as to price competition among small and large firms in the manufacturing economy. Unconscionability will (if argued properly) secure threshold protection as to knowledge access in the information economy.

Unconscionability

You can generally assume that the Uniform Commercial Code (UCC) will govern (outside of Louisiana) almost all of your varied computer transactions, as these inevitably are found to be dealings in goods. Hardware is obvious, as is the software licensed or sold with it as part of a package (turnkey system). Software is ordinarily distributed by license agreement. In certain cases (when not sold with hardware), a factual evaluation may be necessary, depending on whether it is a canned or custom product. A common example of canned software is the shrink-wrap license. Such a license, if enforceable at all, will be construed as a contract for sale of a good. Certain customized software purchased separately and independent maintenance agreements will generally be "services" and not goods, so there is no UCC exposure. Otherwise, look to and argue the UCC's philosophy and black letter law on unconscionability.[9]

Unconscionability has the potential to be an effective means for a small business user to challenge the validity of a clause or perhaps even the entire contract. In case of "extreme overreaching," you should demonstrate that the matter in question is unconscionable. The basic test is whether in the light of the general commercial climate then existing, and within the framework of a particular transaction, the clauses are so one-sided that they are unconscionable as of the *time of the making of the contract.*[10]

This time qualification is important because the UCC is not interested in propping up poor negotiators or someone who simply blew a deal for example, by simply making a low bid due to miscalculation. The courts won't rescue the business person from a negligent mistake that may not have been initially apparent but becomes obvious as the transaction proceeds.[11]

A court wants to see real pain suffered in a situation of *disparate sophistication* or bargaining power. A court will also review the representation of the seller and the reasonable expectations of the buyer. This setting can defeat the necessary mutuality of agreement and obligation. A good working definition for the theme of literacy is obtained from the court's decision in a case involving a *consumer* who couldn't speak English, much less read and understand the fine-print terms:

> . . . the doctrine of unconscionability is used by the courts to protect those who are unable to protect themselves and to prevent injustice . . . . Unequal bargaining powers and the absence of meaningful choice on the part of one of the parties, together with contract terms which unreasonably favor the other party may spell out unconscionability.[12]

The literacy analogy extends to computer literacy itself and technical sophistication in general. The reality is that software is usually very complex and the small business user may have little or no expertise in the field. The user is much more at the mercy of the seller than in other commercial transactions. As knowledge is power, unequal knowledge is unequal power. When you add lack of financial leverage and adhesion contract boilerplate to a small user's lack of technical knowledge, it becomes mandatory of the counsel retained by the user to scrutinize the agreement for unconscionable limitations.[13]

Finally, don't assume that this argument won't be held because you're a "merchant" dealing at arm's length. If the drafters of the UCC didn't want this remedy included in the Code, it wouldn't have been written in it—and in such flexible language.[14]

If you can get into court and uphold your argument, the UCC gives the court broad powers as to an unconscionable contract or clause. Specifically:

> "(1) If the court as a matter of law finds the contract or any clause of the contract to have been unconscionable at the time it was made the court may refuse to enforce the contract, or it may enforce the remainder of the contract without the unconscionable clause, or it may so limit the application of any unconscionable clause as to avoid any unconscionable result.

> (2) When it is claimed or appears to the court that the contract or any clause thereof may be unconscionable the parties shall be afforded a reasonable opportunity to present evidence as to its commercial setting, purpose and effect to aid the court in making the determination."[15]

The major argument against unconscionability is specious. For example, "A modern economy is characterized by its enormous specialization of functions. A business necessarily deals in many areas that are unfamiliar to him/her. His/her prime responsibility is acquiring or assembling the appropriate persons or expertise in each area. Literacy is the minimum requirement for all of these other tasks.[16]

I believe this standard summation argument fails for a number of reasons, including the following:

> (1) By analogy of the antitrust laws, our system of law has until now always provided a certain shelter to small businesses competing with the larger ones, especially as to prohibitions on entry.

> (2) Computer literacy/sophistication on a parity level is not affordable by the small firm, and yet if the small firm can't establish a working systems base it will never be able to afford such expertise even on a limited scale.

> (3) The argument begs the question of why the vendor doesn't have to provide a working system in the first place or, if it can't, then why it shouldn't pay on a reasonably negotiated consequential damage provision or even a refund in same cases!

This last issue gets lost in a philosophic debate. The issue for the user is that he/she is in court because he/she didn't get what was promised by a sales representative, advertising literature, and contractual specification. (As advised in other chapters, expressly incorporate these into your hardware/software agreement for their warranty value). In fact, computer performance is one area where users frequently seem to accept their fate whereas in any other they'd simply use the "radical" argument that they deserve to receive what the seller promised and was paid for.

The only rational argument for the adhesion boilerplate approach to limiting the user's remedy is that the seller/licensor can't be an insurer for all eventualities. However, while this may be applicable to a major corporation (which has the resources to protect itself in negotiation, anyway), the argument is inapplicable to a small firm, where the downside to the seller is finite and able to be anticipated. However, so long as the courts review each case as if there were no difference between a megabillion user and a Mom-and-Pop entrepreneur, the law will fail to provide a remedy essential to the health of small business growth in a knowledge economy.

The good news is that certain courts and legislatures are viewing a seller's sales puffery and adhesion contracts in light of modern commercial realities. Arguments of computer literacy, based on unconscionability and misrepresentation or fraud, are establishing precedents from which the computer seller may actually be made to perform its bargain as promised—or pay accordingly.

The Small Business User Begins to Win a Few

The scenario in which a user traditionally seeks a remedy is that in which he or she is confronted with a system that doesn't work or is deficient in some material respect. A careful reading of the boilerplate then reveals that the warranty and limitation of damages clauses afford no relief. What to do? One solution is to begin at Section 2-719 of the UCC.

Section 2-719 (1) of the UCC permits parties to a contract to fashion the remedies available in the event of a breach. But Section 2-719 recognizes two significant constraints on the power to limit remedies: Subsection 2 provides that "where circumstances cause an exclusive or limited remedy to fail of its essential purpose, remedy may be had as provided in Article II." Subsection 3 adds that *unconscionable* limitation or exclusion of party's right to recover consequential damages will not be enforced.

The comments[17] go further:

> It is of the very essence of a sale contract that at least minimum adequate remedies be available . . . .Thus, any clause purporting to modify or limit the remedial provision of this Article in an unconscionable manner is subject to deletion and in that event the remedies made available by this Article are applicable as if the stricken clause had never existed.

Below are two examples in which the courts focused on the parties' relative sophistication when deciding if an exculpatory clause is unconscionable. *Note:* The decisions came out of California—the state that tends to define the future direction in law.

In *Glovatorium*[18] the court focused on the reality that a seller has reason to know of the user's particular purpose for the system and that its reliance on the seller's skill was selected. Here, a buyer had been in business for 30 years, was familiar with commercial transactions generally, and had previously leased non-computer equipment of substantial value. The court held that the buyer's *computer illiteracy* overrode these other commercial experience factors. Candidly, the court said, "A purchaser who has no experience in computers does not have any inkling of how wrong these things can go."

In the absence of bona fide bargaining to exclude damages, a small business buyer should argue that the seller cannot rely on the general commercial sophistication of a user but must establish that the user is computer literate as well. Failing to establish this, a seller must be held accountable for what is in essence professional malpractice in recommending a deficient system.

In another (non-computer) case,[19] the court was faced with a business-to-business unconscionability issue. Here, a farming company was sold deficient equipment. Instead of passively accepting the boilerplate, the company sued. The court made a number of obvious (but rarely stated) comments:

(1) "With increasing frequency courts have begun to realize that experienced but legally unsophisticated businessmen may be surprised by what amounts to unconscionable boilerplate.[20]

(2) "The warranty allegedly breached by FMC went to the basic performance characteristics of the product. In attempting to disclaim this and all other warranties, FMC was in essence guarantying nothing about what the product would do. Since a product's performance forms the fundamental basis for a sales contract, it is patently unreasonable to assume that a buyer would purchase a standardized mass-produced product from an industry seller without any enforceable performance standards. From a social perspective, risk of loss is most appropriately borne by the party best able to prevent its occurrence . . . rarely would the buyer be in a better position than the manufacturer-seller to evaluate the performance characteristics of a machine.[21]

(3) "The burden should be on the party submitting (a standard contract) in printed form to show that the other party had knowledge of any unusual or unconscionable terms contained therein. The principle should be the same as that applicable to implied warranties, namely that a package of goods sold to a purchaser is fit for the purposes intended and contains no harmful materials other than that represented."[22]

(4) Some other points to argue include throwing back at the seller the salesperson's "I can't change the boilerplate". The court found that the nonnegotiability of the boilerplate terms constituted "ample evidence of unequal bargaining power here and a lack of any real negotiation over the

terms of the contract."[23] Cite this case to your next seller's salesperson who can't negotiate. Better still, if you're a small businessperson, don't cite the case, but get a letter stating this. Then if things go wrong, go to court and win.

(5) Finally, the court addressed the primary area that irks me, i.e., that certain sellers have for years said that they alone among all professionals and businesses are immune from giving you what they recommended, stated in brochures, etc., and you paid for. The court states:

"If there is a type of risk allocation that should be subjected to special scrutiny, it is probably the shifting to one party of a risk that only the other party can avoid.[24]

You should clip the court's summation below and take it with you to court:

In summary, our review of the totality of circumstances in this case, including the business environment within which the contract was executed, supports the trial court's determination that the disclaimer of warranties and the exclusion of consequential damages in FMC's form contract were unconscionable and, therefore, unenforceable. When non-negotiable terms on preprinted form agreements combine with disparate bargaining power, resulting in the allocation of commercial risks in a socially or economically unreasonable manner, the concept of unconscionability as codified in Uniform Commercial Code sections 2-301 and 2-719, subdivision (3), furnished legal justification for refusing enforcement of the offensive result.[25]

Whenever you fear you may have adverse legal exposure on these issues, make sure you explore with your counsel the utility of including a Severability Clause (see discussion in this section).

In a knowledge economy, grafting on the manufacturing economy's laws will retard progress and negatively affect competition as it will hurt small businesses. This trend will accelerate because, as computers become less expensive and the need for them is more apparent, progressively smaller firms (lacking in-house counsel and even the time and personnel for sophisticated negotiation) will enter into the market.

There is nothing all that radical in stating that a computer seller who understands the customer's business, induces reliance (as the sole possessor of the technological knowledge and computer literacy in the transaction), and then fails to deliver should be assessed damages just like any other seller or professional. If yours is a small business, you can take the seller to court and recover.

Conclusion

John Naisbett said in *Megatrends* that to be successful in the future you'll need to be fluent in three languages: English, Spanish, and Computer. Whether you buy this premise or not, there is no compelling argument that in the interim the student of "Computer" must be penalized by overbearing disclaimers.

PROTECTING YOUR SOFTWARE—COPYRIGHT, PATENTS, AND TRADE SECRETS

It is important that all professionals directly and indirectly involved in the computer field as well as all those in the much publicized "knowledge sector" understand when and how to use patents, copyrights, and trade secrets (manufacturing processes, product designs, customer lists) to protect the integrity of your computer goods and services as well as possible other intellectual property you might possess.

A knowledge of these areas can be critical to the competitive success of your business as well as to a user's understanding of the various contractual paragraphs a vendor employs in an attempt to protect its proprietary rights.

Copyright is reviewed elsewhere in this book, in relation to antitrust (Section III) and advertising (Section IV), but it is also of importance here because of the protection it can provide for computer software. As a general rule commercial agreements traditionally are the domain of state law. State law is not displaced merely because the contract relates to intellectual property. The states are free to regulate the use of intellectual property in any manner consistent with federal law.

Copyright Protection

Pursuant to the constitutional mandate "To promote the Progress of science and useful Arts,"[26] the federal copyright act provided that "any person entitled thereto, upon complying with the provision of this title, shall have the exclusive right to print, reprint, publish, copy, and vend the copyrighted work . . . ".

The act is designed to encourage and protect many forms of intellectual effort by giving the author the exclusive right to reproduce and sell his or her creative idea. The starting point of any analysis is the axiom that copyright protection extends only to particular "expression" and not to concepts or ideas that may be abstracted from concrete embodiment.[27] In no case may copyright protection for an original work of authorship extend to any idea, procedure, process, system, method of operation, concept, principle, or discovery, regardless of the form in which it is described, explained, illustrated, or embodied in such work.

Can a computer program[28] be copyrighted? Yes—copyright protection extends to works in *any* tangible form of expression from which they can be perceived, reproduced, or otherwise communicated, either directly or with the aid of a machine or other device. The computer program is copyrightable, whether in object code or source code, and is protected from unauthorized copying whether from its object or source code version.[29] Such protection extends beyond a program's line-by-line or element-by-element correspondence between two programs to general similarities that would reveal duplication. Therefore, copyright protection extends to a program's structure, sequence, and organization.[30]

What kind of a program can be copyrighted? The program must be original. However, the word "original" as used in this context does not mean that the work is novel or unique, but that it originates with the software developer (author). All that is required is that the software developer contribute something more than a "merely trivial" variation. Something that is recognizably his or her own must be contributed by the software developer for a computer program to qualify for copyright protection. The program must contain at least a certain minimum amount of authorship in the form of statements or instructions. In a computer program the expression used by the programmer is the copyrightable element of the program. The actual process or methods embodied in the program are not within the scope of the copyright law.

Such protection can even be extended to different expressions of the same idea written in different programming languages (or the translation from one programming language to another), which may each qualify for a separate copyright if the necessary originality and creativity elements are present. Screen outputs are considered audio-visual works under the Copyright Act[31] but are covered by a different copyright than are programs.

There are certain limitations by statute[32], namely:

It is not an infringement for the owner of a copy of a computer program to make or authorize the making of another copy or adaption of that computer program provided:

(1) that such a new copy or adaption is created as an essential step in the utilization of the computer program in conjunction with a machine and that it is used in no other manner, or

(2) that such new copy or adaptation is for archival purposes, and copies are destroyed in the event that continued possession of the computer program should cease to be rightful.

Certain non-copyrightable elements include algorithms, disks, encrypting, language alone, and software methodology. Once you've determined that your software qualifies for copyright protection, you next must consider whether it is worth registering. Registration at the Copyright Office is *not* a prerequisite to copyright protection. Copyright in your software exists immediately from its creation whether or not you take steps to actually register it.

There are certain statutory incentives to register the work (such as recovery of attorneys fees and statutory damages for infringement). However, the trade-off may not be worthwhile to you. Registration requires publication of the copyrightable material, thus exposing the idea or creation to public view, while protecting only its articulation and not the underlying idea.

The main problem is that the Copyright Act[33] says that the "best edition" of a work must be deposited for registration. The Copyright Office has interpreted this to mean, "The best representation of the authorship for which copyright is being claimed." Noting that copyright examiners are not programmers and that it is extremely difficult to examine programs in other than source code form (such as the object code, which is written in combinations of zeros and ones) to decide whether the program contains copyrightable authorship, the Examining Division has concluded that "the best representation" is a printout in source code format.

There are certain ways around this (for example, "partial" deposit with certain affidavits), which you should review with your counsel. This area is constantly in flux, but your confidentiality options are growing. However, to the extent you deposit all or part of your work, it is open to visual inspection (though not copying). You may expose for appropriation by others the logic, structure, method, and organization of your program. Another competitor can analyze it, identify its unique idea, and reproduce the idea in a new form of expression.

If you do obtain registration, you should include notice of copyright. The notice provision of the Copyright Act requires that whenever a copyrighted work is published, a copyright notice must be placed on "all publicly distributed copies from which the work can be visually perceived, either directly or with the aid of a machine or device."[34] Publication is defined as "the distribution of copies (or the offering to distribute copies) of a work to the public by sale or other transfer of ownership, or by rental, lease or lending."[35]

Prior to 1978, failure to include such notice was fatal to copyright protection. Today, by contrast, the failure to include the notice of copyright will *not* be fatal to securing copyright protection, provided:

- Notice was omitted from no more than a relatively small number of publicly-distributed copies;
- Registration has been made before or is made within five years of the publication without notice and a reasonable effort is made to add notice to all copies distributed in the U.S.; or
- The publication was done in violation of an agreement to publish only with notice.

The location of the notice will vary, depending on whether it can be visually perceived or not. If the notice cannot be visually perceived without the aid of a computer (for example, on disks), the notice should be affixed as follows:

- A notice embodied in the copies in machine-readable form in such a manner that on visually perceptible printouts it appears either with or near the title, or at the end of the work; or
- A notice displayed at the user's terminal at sign-on; or

- A notice continuously on terminal display; or
- A legible notice reproduced durably, so as to withstand normal use, on a gummed or other label securely affixed to the copies or to a box, reel, cartridge, cassette, or other container used as permanent receptacle for the copies.

For books and manuals, you should consider placing the notice on:

- The title page or the page immediately following it;
- Either side of the front or back cover, or the front or back leaf if there is no cover;
- The first or last page of the main body of the work.

Copyright protection may afford you valuable exclusive protections of your unique expressions. It is most useful for valuable software materials with a short life. It enables you to register the expression and capitalize on exclusive use without having to worry about the idea being expressed differently by a competitor; the short life of the software minimizes the potential damage of a competitor's adopting it.

Patent Protection

Patent protection is the area of least certainty and most rapid evolution under the law (see discussion in Chapter 4). Critics have charged that "patent law provides protection that is slow and expensive. Often by the time the patent is issued, the software is obsolete,"[36] and, therefore, less marketable. Further, during the period between the application for and the approval of the patent, the owner has no enforceable rights under the patent laws, rendering the software protection meaningless during the time it may be most valuable to the creator or seller. This is the traditional view.

Recent case law suggests that you should be able to get fairly good patent protection on most of your important pieces of software. This route should be considered only for software you're planning to use for some time without obsolescence (the application process can take two to three years) and is very valuable to you (the cost per patent begins at $7,500).

The source of federal authority to grant patents is the United States Constitution, which authorizes Congress "to promote the Progress of Science and useful Arts, by securing for limited Times to Authors and Inventors the exclusive Right to their respective Writings and Discoveries."[37] The current patent statute[38] enumerates in Section 101 the categories into which an invention must fall to qualify for patent protection. "Whoever invents or discovers any new and useful process, machine, manufacture, or composition of matter, or any new and useful improvement thereof, may obtain a patent therefor . . . ."

An invention not falling within one of these classes is deemed nonstatutory subject matter and ineligible for patent protection. Examples of such ineligibility include abstract principles and laws of nature such as mathematical laws. In addition to meeting the Section 101 requirements, an invention must also exhibit novelty and non-obviousness before a patent will be issued. Together, these three basic conditions determine whether you can patent your invention.

Your threshold question in evaluating an application for a patent is whether the subject matter presented in your claim is eligible for patent.[39] The patent laws are committed to the idea that "mere" abstract ideas, "scientific truths," laws of nature, physical phenomena, logical designs, or intellectual processes cannot be patented (here copyright may be useful, as discussed above).

The most common example of what *can't* be patented is a mathematical formula.[40] If the idea does not involve such a formula, you have a good chance to obtain a patent (assuming all of the above quoted statutory requirements are met). If your software involves a mathematical formula (algorithm), then you must show that your claim does not attempt to wholly preclude other people from using it, but is only one specific application of the mathematical formula.[41] Further, you must show that your computer program does more than merely present and solve the claimed invention. This eliminates most prepackaged software and much customized software where these programs are developed with the intent to distribute them to computer users as stand alone packages, rather than as part of a larger process or apparatus that is patentable. For example, you can show that while the mathematical formula you're using is well known, you've used it in a new and efficient way and that it is applied to the physical elements or process steps.[42] Computer programs are patentable when the programs are part of a larger process or apparatus that is patentable.

Another area to watch for is a program that merely recites a method of doing business. A bare set of instructions that doesn't set out the sequence of steps that accomplishes a specific purpose is non-statutory subject matter because it's a mere idea or an abstract intellectual concept of the programmer.

What protections does a patent afford that other alternatives don't? Depending on your particular needs, the most important factor for you is the following. An infringer can't appropriate your property "innocently." Of the three protections we'll discuss, this is the only one that protects you completely as to someone who develops your software completely independently.

If you have a patent monopoly, the person copying it later, no matter how innocently and independently, is as guilty of infringement as a deliberate infringer.

Here, "obsolescence" can work in your favor. Patent applications are secret until the patent is formally issued. Thus, for the two to three years the application is being processed, it is officially a secret. At this time, you'll enjoy trade-secret protection. You can couple trade-secret and patent protection so long as it is done in sequence and not in tandem.

When the patent finally becomes public, you have a two- to three-year jump on the market, and this time lag in a rapidly changing technological area will by itself discourage copying of the essentially "dated" software you invented. Patent protection (due to time and costs) is not a routine option. However, if you have a valuable software program that is worth a long-term investment or that offers a significant competitive advantage in marketing or sales then it is an option you should consider.

Trade Secret Protection

This will protect your idea so long as you take steps to preserve your "trade secret." Is your property a trade secret? A trade secret is a plan, process, formula, or other valuable information *that is not patented* but gives you, its possessor, *a competitive advantage* so long as it is kept secret. Trade secret protection (unlike the federal copyright and patent laws) is a creature of each state and thus can vary widely. Software that qualifies for protection in one state may not in another. You'll have to review with your counsel each state law important to you.

A trade secret is distinguished from a skill and intelligence acquired or increased and improved through experience or through instructions received in the course of employment, which you cannot protect and your employees are free to take away with them.

The line of demarcation between a trade secret and copyright protection is clear. Trade secret law protects content, irrespective of the form of expression.[43] Today, many if not most software products are marketed under license agreements that classify the software as a trade secret. Other forms of trade secrets can include internal processes and marketing research. The latter is often overlooked but may be your most important secret. Protection here covers not only the obvious but also categories such as the methodology by which consumer surveys were conducted to assure that the surveys were representative of the population as a whole.[44]

Can a person have a trade secret when all the elements of the program are common knowledge? Yes, it is the whole, as a combination in your precise form, not the sum of the parts that establishes whether you have a secret meriting protection.

The very nature of a trade secret is its secrecy, that is, difficulty to obtain other than by improper means. It must be a secret—with conscious, provable intent,[45] protected by confidential relationships among all the parties who deal with it. These relationships are usually recorded in a signed license or confidentiality agreement. Your protections will vary depending on whether a subsequent taker of the secret stands in a fiduciary or contractual relationship with the owner of the secret.

Besides these agreements, you must constantly monitor all parties having access to such information and bar access to others who have no need of access to this information. Similarly, no copying at will of the material can be tolerated—even by those who have authorized access.

Further, keep an eye on what you say in your promotional material. This is less of a problem in a consumer environment than a commercial marketing environment. Industrial buyers will put a premium on up-front knowledge of your product. Here, you will have to establish trade-off priorities between your marketing people, who will favor open disclosure to push sales, and your engineering people, who will favor secrecy.

It is essential that your people seriously appreciate that they are involved with a trade secret and must take time and effort to protect it. What steps should you take as part of your formalized trade secret protection program? Here are seven to consider:

(1) *Warning notice.* Every document, process or formula, list, etc. must have a confidential information warning notice prominently displayed on it.

(2) *Limited circulation.* You cannot have a trade secret manual that is distributed like a company's annual report. Documents containing sensitive information should not be reproduced or distributed except to those within the company who actually *must* have the information. You should not use such limited distribution of the document itself as a warning. You should keep track of how many copies you give to whom, making all recipients sign for their copies. Finally, make sure no employee is allowed to make a presentation or publish an article explaining your system.

(3) *Employee education.* Inform and warn your employees, when first employed, during employment, and particularly when the employee leaves, not to use or disclose confidential information learned at the company.

(4) *Signed contracts.* Have job applicants sign nondisclosure agreements containing a covenant not to compete (see discussion below) in consideration for employment prior to their hire. If you wait longer, the more likely it becomes that such employee may not be willing to sign. Have all other persons participating with or having access to your secrets (such as customers and consultants) sign confidentiality agreements.

(5) *Access control.* Have signs posted and set up a company procedure to limit visitor privileges as to the number, type, and access to the premises. Allow visitors through only those areas where their observations can cause you no loss of trade secrets. Be sure that all visitors are escorted by company personnel.

(6) *Restrictive licenses.* Make no sales of the secret. License it only by carefully worded restrictive licenses, acknowledging that the product

is a trade secret, that its use is restricted, and that the licensee must take certain steps to preserve the confidentiality of the trade secret.

(7) *No overkill.* Trying to stamp everything as confidential or a trade secret will lead a fact finder to conclude that you couldn't effectively discriminate between what is a valid trade secret and what is not. That, in turn, will make it hard for you to establish whether any of your information is proprietary.

In short, be consistent, be diligent, make no exceptions to your company polices about signing nondisclosure agreements and about respecting sensitive information. All of these efforts will document the value of the information to you and show you're willing to incur financial and administrative costs to keep it a secret. The primary rule to remember is: If you have a trade secret, treat it as a secret.

If your secret is misappropriated, you are entitled to a variety of remedies. An injunction is of particular importance to you if time is of the essence to stop the appropriator. You are generally entitled to injunctive relief (among other relief) for trade secret misappropriation[46] if you establish the following:

- a subject matter capable of protection as a trade secret;
- disclosure to defendants in circumstances giving rise to a contractual duty or other legal duty not to disclose or use the secret to your detriment; *and*
- the facts support the conclusion that the public policy favoring protection of your interest in maintaining the secret outweighs the interests of the defendants in using the knowledge.

For maximum protection, the trend today is to obtain "dual protection"[47] of software. Copyright and trade secret protection can be available simultaneously for works such as computer programs that embody trade secrets *if* the requirements for the maintenance of *each* are met.[48] With dual protection, both your software's means of expression and its underlying ideas might be legally protected.

Obviously, all these legal remedies are expensive. Your resources are best expended in an effective program of anticipatory steps that will act to avoid much legal exposure and, if you wind up in court, will diminish your opponent's case accordingly.

Your Personal Liability In Systems Design

It is standard tort law that a duty voluntarily assumed must be performed with care. A college[49] has designed a security system to protect its all-female resident student body. The college and its vice president of operations used gates, fences, locks, guards, etc. Yet, on the night of December 11, 1977, the system broke down in some way and a freshman co-ed was raped on their premises. (The freshmen were required by the college to live on the premises.) The court found that:

. . . implicit in Pine Manor's requirement that freshmen live in dormitories provided by the college is the representation that the college believed that it could provide adequately for the safety and well-being of its students.[50]

As to the issue of negligence the court found that the vice president for operations:

admitted that he designed and supervised the installation of the security system. He acknowledged that he was responsible for establishing the patrol pattern and the network of locks. The jury could have found the following deficiencies in the college's security system. An observation post near the main entrance is situated at such a distance from the fence that an intruder could climb over the fence without being detected by the guard on duty. The exterior gates leading into the courtyards were not difficult to scale or to open. The walls surrounding the courtyards were too low to be adequately protective. The college used a single key system whereby the same key would open the door to the dormitory and the door to the individual room. Only two security guards were performing their patrols around the campus. The locks on the doors to the dormitory and the individual rooms were easy to pick, and neither deadbolts nor chains were used. The jury also could have credited the opinion of the plaintiff's expert that the security provided by [the college] was inadequate to protect a student in the position of the plaintiff. Additionally, there was evidence that after the evening of the attack, the college hired two additional guards to patrol the villages from 11:30 p.m. to 7:30 a.m. and installed chains on the interior side of the doors to individual rooms. There was also ample evidence that the guards failed to perform their duties both prior to the attack and on the evening of the attack. There was evidence that the locks to the individual rooms could be opened with a credit card. There was also evidence that the door to [plaintiff's] dormitory lacked a knife guard which the defendant's expert witness indicated should have been present . . . .[51]

It reads like a detective story. Well, what did the college and the vice president do after the jury returned a $175,000 verdict? On appeal, the vice president found that though the college was largely protected by the doctrine of charitable immunity,

. . . the agent is not entitled to the protection of his principal's immunity even if the agent is acting on behalf of his principal[52] . . . .a corporate officer is not immune from liability for acts and omissions which occur while performing corporate business.[53]

In short, the vice president was not entitled to avoid liability on the grounds that he was an officer of a charitable (or other) corporation. Neither will you. Depending on your occupation and level of management, you will find potential *personal* exposure due to negligent supervision or pure negligence overall in such supervisory duties. The standard is broader than one that holds employees liable for many negligent acts of their agent:

Thus persons engaged in certain occupations may be held liable in contract for acts of their employees even if those employees are acting outside the scope of their duties.[54]

In today's world, the system you design or supervise may have consequences to you beyond mere administration. If you are in such a position you might consult your personal (not in-house) counsel as to your overall potential liability, if any.

ENDNOTES

(1) "Software" is the general term describing programs of instructions, languages, and routines or procedures that enable you to use your computer.

(2) A turnkey system is one that is predeveloped and virtually can be plugged right in and ready to function immediately.

(3) If you're licensing rather than buying, then state law, rather than the UCC, may apply; you should review this with your counsel. This is because a "pure" license transaction is not a sale of goods. If you're involved in a turnkey purchase (hardware/software together), then this is a "sale of goods" and thus covered by the UCC.

(4) We're using Licensee rather than Licensee/Buyer and Licensor rather than Licensor/Seller because almost all of these transactions deal with licenses.

(5) UCC Sec. 2-315.

(6) *Glovatorium, Inc v. NCR Corporation,* 684 F.2d 658, 661 (1982) (use this case for arguing against warranty disclaimers and limitations of damages). Alleging fraud or a similar tort may assist the settlement in another way. Reputable sellers do not like the publicity such allegations raise. See also *Suntogs of Miami, Inc. v. Burroughs Corp.,* 433 S.2d 581 (1981). See generally UCC Sec. 2-302.

(7) Id., p. 661.

(8) *U.S. Fibres, Inc. v. Proctor & Schwartz, Inc.,* 507 F.2d 1043, 1078 (1975).

(9) UCC Sec. 2-302 (1984) and Section III.

(10) *Industralese v. R.M.E. Enter.,* 58 AD 2d 48, 396 NYS 2d 427 (1977).

(11) *Tierney, Inc. v. T. Wellington Carpets, Inc.,* 392 NE 2d, 1066 (1979).

(12) *Brooklyn Union Gas Co. v. Jiminez,* 8 Misc. 2d 948, 951 (1975) (emphasis added).

(13) And such "addition" is necessary, as the mere disparity of bargaining power by itself is usually not enough for a finding of unconscionability. One has to make out a case of "oppression or unfair surprise" rather than disparity of bargaining power alone.

(14) For a good background on the drafting of UCC Sec. 2-302 see Leff, "Unconscionability and the Code—The Emperor's New Clause," 115 U. Pa. L. Rev., 485 (1967).

(15) UCC Sec. 2-302 (1984).

(16) Himelson, David, "Unconscionability," *Computer Law Journal,* Vol. IV, 712 (1983). This is a good article for an opposing view, but I believe it deficient insofar as the author's solution primarily rests on a small firm's becoming rich so it can afford the overhead specialists a large firm can (e.g., pp. 696, 712-714) or that the buyer—not the seller—should protect against the seller's risk (pp. 717-719). Neither position is sensitive to the needs of the small user in a 1980s knowledge economy.

(17) UCC Sec. 2-719 comment.

(18) *Glovatorium v. NCR Corp.,* Reporter Transcript, May 1, 1981 (N.D. Cal 1981), *aff'd on other grounds,* 684 F.2d 658 (9th Cir. 1982). This remedy will probably fail (as it should) for large, sophisticated buyers. See *AMF, Inc. v. Computer Automation, Inc.,* 57 F.Supp. 924 (1983).

(19) *A & M Product Co. v. FMC Corp.,* 18 Cal. Rptr. 114 (1982).

(20) Id., p.124.

(21) Id., p.125.

(22) Id., p.124.

(23) Id., p.125.

(24) Id., p.126.

(25) Id., p.126. If you're in New York and would like to break a disclaimer of an express warranty, take a look at *Consolidated Data Terminals v. Applied Digital Data Systems,* 708 F.2d 38 (1983).

(26) U.S. Constitution, Article I, Section 8.

(27) 17 USC Sec. 102(b).

(28) "A 'computer program' is a set of statements or instructions to be used directly or indirectly in a computer in order to bring about a certain results." [17 USC Sec. 101.]

(29) *Apple Computer, Inc. v. Franklin Computer Corp.,* 714 F.2d 1240 (1983).

(30) *Whelan Associates, Inc. v. Jaslow Dental Laboratories, Inc.,* 797 F.2d 1222 (3rd Cir. 1986). *Contra* see *In Plains Cotton Cooperative v. Goodposture Computer Service ,* 807 F.2d 1256 (5th Cir. 1987).

(31) *Williams Electronics, Inc. v. Arctic Interm, Inc.,* 685 F.2d 870, 874 (3d Cir. 1982); *Midway Manufacturing Co. v. Esrohon,* 564 F.Supp. 741, 749 (N.D. 1983).

(32) 17 USC Sec. 117. See also *Salinger v. Random House, Inc.,* 811 F.2d 90 (2d Cir. 1987); *Financial Information, Inc. v. Moody's Investors Service,* 751 F.2d 501 (2d Cir. 1984).

(33) 17 USC Sec. 408(b)(2).

(34) 17 USC Sec. 401(a).

(35) 17 USC Sec. 101.

(36) Brown, Peter and Richard Raysman, "Dual Protection for Software," *New York Law Journal,* July 11, 1984, p. 1.

(37) U.S. Constitution, Article I, Section 8, Clause 8.

(38) 35 USC Sec. 101 (1976).

(39) *Diamond v. Diehr,* 450 US 175, 182-84 (1981).

(40) Often referred to as an "algorithm," which the Supreme Court in *Gottshalk v. Benson,* 409 US 63, 65 (1972), defined as a "procedure for solving a given type of mathematical problem." See also *Parker v. Flock,* 437 US 584 (1978).

(41) *In re Freeman,* 573 F.2d, 1237 (C.C.P.A. 1978).

(42) See note 12.

(43) *Bryce & Assoc. v. William Gladstone,* 319 NW2d 907 (1982). See also *Aronson v. Quick Point Pencil Co.,* 440 U.S. 257 (1979).

(44) *Sum of Squares, Inc v. Market Research Corp. of America,* 401 F.Supp 53 (S.D.N.Y. 1975); but see also *McAlpine v. Aamco Automatic Transmissions, Inc.,* 46 F.Supp. 1232 (E.D. Mich 1978) and *Briggs v. Butler,* 45 NE2d 757 (Ohio 1942).

(45) *Jostens, Inc. v. National Computer Systems,* 318 NW2d 691 (1982); *J & K Computer Systems, Inc. v. Parrish,* 642 P.2d 732 (1982). See also *In the Matter of Innovative Construction Systems, Inc.,* 793 F.2d 880 (7th Cir. 1986).

(46) *GCA Corp. v. Chance,* 217 USPQ 718 (N.D. Cal. 1982).

(47) Clearly permitted under the 1980 Software Protection Act.

(48) Elements include an invasion of privacy, a trespass, a breach of a fiduciary relationship, or a breach of confidentiality.

(49) *Mullins v. Pine Manor College,* 449 NE2d 331 (1983); related cases include *Irwin v. Town of Ware,* 467 NE2d 1292 (Mass. Supp. Jud. Ct. 1984); *Magaw v. Mass. Bay Transp. Authority,* 485 NE2d 695, 697-98 (Mass. App. 1985); *Brighetti v. Consolidated Rail Corp.,* 479 NE2d 708 (Mass. App. 1985).

(50) Id., p. 337, n. 11.

(51) Id., p. 338.

(52) Id., p. 341.

(53) Id., p. 342.

(54) *O'Malley v. Putnam Safe Deposit Vaults,* 458 NE2d 752, 758 (Mass. App. 1983).

CHAPTER 27

EMPLOYMENT CONTRACTS AND CONTRACTUAL PROTECTION OF CONFIDENTIAL DATA

This chapter reviews the employment contract, the tort of wrongful discharge, and the erosion of the employment-at-will doctrine. It moves on to an in-depth look at covenants not to compete.

While you read this chapter recall that those individuals who know how you make your profits could be valuable to your competitors. You should consider whether you're taking adequate precautions to protect your competitive advantage from walking away with the next call from the headhunters.

Background to the Erosion of Employment-at-Will

Today, roughly one out of five employees is protected from arbitrary termination by collective bargaining agreements. Until recently, however, most other private-sector employees were governed by the at-will doctrine, limited by narrow statutory proscriptions against discrimination based on race, age, sex and some other characteristics unrelated to job performance.

Recent cases have begun to reexamine the termination-at-will doctrine in light of 20th century social and economic theories heavily influenced by European law and legislation and by Japanese custom. This influence had led many states to alter their law to reflect a change in social thinking. We have moved from a society where property defined one's position to one where your employment or profession defines your status. Employees are seen as having a property right in their job, something that cannot be taken from them except through a fair process. Such a fair process puts a premium on objective documentation as opposed to the traditional subjective evaluation.

Theories of Wrongful Discharge

Although the doctrines of wrongful discharge are rapidly evolving (and states vary widely in their acceptance of these doctrines), three theories have emerged:

(1) Retaliatory discharge that violates statutory or public policy;

(2) Breach of an implied contract requiring good cause for termination; and

(3) Bad faith or abusive discharge that violates an employer's duty of good faith and fair dealing.

The crux of an employee's case under the theory of retaliatory discharge is that the discharge was in retaliation for the employee's assertion of protected rights, or refusal to commit illegal or unethical acts (such as violating antitrust laws).

As to the implied contract, this is a growing issue. The courts in a number of states (California, Michigan, and Pennsylvania, for example) will examine *all* the surrounding circumstances to determine whether an implied contract existed. In addition to express representations made by the employer, the courts have examined the following (based on author's analysis, and in order of persuasion):

(a) Employer's personnel policies and practices (were employees told they'd be retained as long as they did good jobs or "you have a job here as long as you want it"?). Especially important are any promises implied in employee handbooks and employment application forms;

(b) Those practices of other employers in the trade;

(c) Length of the employee's service and quality of same;

(d) Whether an employee forgoes other employment at the urging of the employer;

(e) Promotions and merit increases that state or suggest approval of the employee's performance;

(f) Absence of warnings or criticism of the employee's performance; and

(g) Other types of implied assurances of continued employment.

If such an implied contract is found, then the employer will be found liable for breach of this contract unless a legitimate business reason justifies the discharge.

The issue in bad faith or abusive discharge revolves around the traditional tort theory of a breach of duty (express or implied) owed by the employer to the employee. The employee is harmed by the breach. By far the most common pattern arises when the motivation for discharge is to deprive the employee of accrued or about-to-accrue rights to deferred compensation. The classic case is when an employee is terminated shortly before pension rights vest.

The second pattern of the duty to act in good faith has been held to require documented good cause for termination where (1) the employee has a long history of service with the employer (California, for example, has held that the duty of good faith may be imposed solely because of the length of service) and (2) the employer's own personnel policies contemplate some sort of notice or procedural fairness prior to termination. The longer the service, the more suspect a sudden discharge will appear. When long service is combined with a documented history of satisfactory performance (regular receipt of merit increases, good to excellent annual performance evaluations, commendations from superiors), the inference of bad faith is greater.

The traditional employer defense that it had an unfettered discretion to terminate employees for any reason or no reason at all is fast being eclipsed. You should consider this as you evaluate whether to enter into written agreements clearly defining your individual relationship with your employee.

Employment Contracts—An Overview

Today, you might wish to extend employment contracts to rank and file employees. Such a contract would eliminate any ambiguity as to their at-will status *if* that is your goal. It would also clarify the precise limits of employees' rights to any ideas or inventions they bring to the job. Another candidate for an employment contract is your key employee, whose services are essential and whose ongoing employment with you is important. Such a contract is also necessary as a basis for an ancillary covenant not to compete.

In any agreement with an employee you'll want to cover the following items. Consult Chapter 25 on the "generic contract" for boilerplate provisions that would be applicable (that is definitions, identification of the parties, notices, the specific form of business the employer is engaged in, integration clause, etc.)

Definitions. Usually, this section expands the scope of a defined term beyond its ordinary meaning, answers questions in advance, or simply clarifies points. For example, "businessday" is not as precise as "business day," which means any day when the New York Stock Exchange is open. If you employ a term in accord with the meaning the dictionary gives, then *don't* define it.

Term of employment. Whether it is for a fixed period, purely at will, part-time, etc.

Duties of employment. This provision encompasses the where, when, and how of the job to be performed, specifically:

(a) place where duties are to be performed (if at home make sure you've reviewed the industrial homework hurdles);

If a worksite change is possible, or travel is involved, you'll need to address who covers the cost of relocation or of living expenses while the employee is away from the principal place of employment.

Further in this section you may wish to address, define, and permit the employee's actual or apparent authority to bind the employer.

In this era of telecommuters and other home-based workers, it is important that you are aware of certain restrictions that are often overlooked.

Workers are not taken from the scope of the Fair Labor Standards Act merely because their work is done in their own home without the immediate supervision and direction of the employer.

The Fair Labor Standards Act itself does not contain a definition of industrial homeworkers. It defines an "employer" as any person acting "in the interest of an employer in relation to an employee." It defines an "employee" as including "any individual employed by an employer." The term "employ" is defined as including "to suffer or permit to work." Finally, the definition of "home" is obvious, but it does not include living quarters allocated to a regular use for production purposes, where workers work regular schedules and are under constant supervision by the employer.

In 1949, Section 11(d) (29 U.S.C. Section 211) was added; it authorizes the Administrator to make "sure regulations and homework as are necessary or appropriate to prevent the circumvention or evasion of and to safeguard the minimum wage rate prescribed in" the act.

The Administrator's regulations define "industrial homeworker" and "homeworker" as meaning "any employee employed or suffered or permitted to perform industrial homework for an employer," and "industrial homework" as meaning "the production by any person in or about a home, apartment, or room in a residential establishment of goods for an employer who suffers or permits such production, regardless of the source (whether obtained from an employer or elsewhere) of the materials used by the homeworker in such production."

The regulations also provide that no work in the industry as defined in Section 530.1 (d) through (j) (not applicable to you) shall be done in or about a home, apartment, or room in a residential establishment unless a special homework certificate was issued and in effect has been obtained for each homeworker.

The FLSA specifically makes it unlawful for any person to violate any provisions of the act pertaining to records or industrial homework. The recordkeeping enforcement is strict (wages, hours, employment practices, etc.) but what is required is reasonable and familiar to you.

The area of industrial homework is currently in flux, check before you contract.

(b) hours of employment;

(c) whether outside duties or jobs or other potential conflict of interest is permitted (if your employees are required to devote full time to your corporate business you might consider a covenant not to compete *during* employment); and

(d) a precise description of just what duties the employee is temporarily or permanently expected to accomplish;

(e) catchall language such as "Employee agrees that he/she will at all times faithfully, industriously, and to the best of his/her ability, experience, and talent, perform all of the duties that may be required of and from him/her pursuant to the express and implicit terms hereof, to the reasonable satisfaction of the employer."

Compensation, benefits, and expenses. Include the following:

(a) terms of payment of wage, salary, or commissions;

(b) vacation pay or earned leave;

(c) sabbatical options with or without pay;

(d) overtime work and holiday or night differential;

(e) sick or disability pay;

(f) fringe benefit package;

(g) reimbursement of travel, meal and similar expenses;

(h) status of compensation if you breach the contract;

(i) severance pay and any continuation of the above;

(j) compensation, benefits, etc. to a surviving spouse or minor children.

Note: Since October 1, 1986, federal law[1] has required that most employers sponsoring group health plans offer employees and their families the opportunity for a temporary extension of health coverage (called "continuation coverage") at group rates in certain instances where coverage under the plan would otherwise end.

Remedies of breach and resolution of disputes. These may include

(a) liquidated damages,

(b) equitable remedies,

(c) a fidelity bond obtained by the employee in an amount as may be specified by the employer (and usually paid for by the employer), and

(d) arbitration.

Generally (b) will fail as to specific performance (thirteenth Amendment's prohibition against involuntary servitude) but you can obtain an injunction against someone working for a competitor depending on the circumstances, the uniqueness of the employee's services, and your properly drawn covenant not to compete. In most cases your remedy will be damages. To avoid the speculative court awards plus attendant costs both parties might consider a liquidated damages provision drawn so as to avoid the specter of appearing to be a penalty.

Extension and/or renewal.

Covenants not to compete or confidentiality agreements. (See discussion below).

Termination. Such may be terminated on __ days notice or in the event the employer discontinues operating its business at __ location.

You should also clearly define a few instances specifically important to your operations that would be a tortious interference with business relations.

The traditional rule for such tortious interference is set forth in the Restatement of Torts (III) 766, which provide "[O]ne who without a privilege to do so, induces or otherwise purposely causes a third person not to

(a) perform a contract with another, or

(b) enter into or continue a business relation with another is liable to the other for the harm caused thereby."

Section 768 enumerates the four requirements necessary to establish the defense of "privilege": (1) the business relation must concern a matter involved in the competition between the actor and the competitor; (2) the actor must not employ improper means; (3) the actor must not intend to create an illegal restraint of competition; and (4) the actor's purpose must be at least partially to advance his or her interest in competing with his competitor.

One can be held for punitive damages if they interfere with malice. It is well established that the term "malice" when used in the context of cause of action for interference with contractual relations does not require a showing of ill will, hostility, or an intent to injure. Rather, plaintiff must show that the defendant acted intentionally and without just cause.[2]

One common form of such tortious interference is a former key executive's violation of his or her constructive trust by pirating away other key executives if such transactions begin *during* the existence of the employment relationship or are founded on information or knowledge acquired during the relationship. As one court stated:

Significantly, the expectations of the parties to a voidable contract, which is for a prescribed duration, differ substantially from the expectations of parties to a terminable at will agreement. The latter are usually aware, when they enter into the contract, that their relationship is to continue only so long as is mutually agreeable and hence will refrain from relying on the agreement in planning future transactions. Parties to a voidable contract, on the other hand, believe that they have established a relationship which will span a period of time and may order their future conduct accordingly.[3]

You may have some other ideas as to what you need for your firm's protection. You might wonder why this whole area is governed by tort rather than contract tests? The primary reason is that in an arm's-length contractual situation, the other party can protect itself by providing for special or liquidated damages. This contemplation factor cannot enter the picture with a third party who interferes. Such party was not in the contemplation of the plaintiff, nor was his interference contemplated.

This is why there is exposure as to damages for loss of reputation and punitive damages—such damages are normally denied in traditional contractual claims.

Contractual Protection of Your Confidential Data or Key Interests by Means of a Covenant Not to Compete[4]

The following principles apply directly to confidential data protection but the overall discussion also relates to your retention of key employees for other reasons such as their unique business expertise.

What a trade secret is may not always be precisely defined. Whenever an employee, or more importantly an outside consultant, has access to systems and procedures you don't want leaked out, you should enter into a covenant not to compete. At one time these were looked on with disfavor, but a more enlightened view of antitrust law and equity will demonstrate that they are quite the opposite of a restraint of trade.

The paragraphs that follow review the history and philosophy behind covenants not to compete and the elements of a good one and they suggest some language you might consider. This is probably the core of your business and the prime contributor to your profit.

Restraint of Trade

Common law, early U.S. court decisions, and certain states[5] did not favor these contracts (other states specifically authorize them).[6] The argument was that they were a restraint of trade.

The courts felt that they restricted an individual employee's mobility and freedom to earn a living. It was also alleged that they sustained artificially high prices by prohibiting employees from setting up businesses in competition with their former employers or from competing against them in a rival's employ.

At the same time, it was argued that individual employees' salary growth was suppressed because employers knew that the employees' freedom to bargain was restricted by a lack of mobility. Finally, issues of involuntary servitude were often raised.

These arguments at first glance seem reasonable, but like much of antitrust law they do not reflect business as it actually is, especially in an information economy. What is the incentive for an employer to invest in employee training or permit access to information that will make an individual a key executive if he or she can then pick up and leave for another firm that pays a premium because of the value of the training?

Covenants not to compete encourage firms to invest in new technologies and costly research and to increase their employees' professional skills. And once employees have acquired this knowledge their worth to the firm is greater than it would otherwise be and their compensation will reflect this. These incentives to innovate and educate promote competition.

Courts have recognized the social value of this investment in human capital and now balance it against issues of restraint of trade. In doing so they've evolved a test which you should consider:

- The restraint must be no greater than required to protect the employer (a key element).
- There must be bargained-for consideration exchanged.
- The covenant must be ancillary (only) to the main agreement.
- It must not impose undue hardship on the employee's ability to earn a livelihood at his or her trade.[7] Here you should have the employee acknowledge that he or she is capable of obtaining other employment without the use of the confidential information.
- It must not be so broad in scope as to be injurious to the public's interest in unrestricted free trade.[8] The requirements are interrelated. A restriction on a wide geographic area, for example, may be reasonable if imposed for a short period of time. Also, the importance of an employee or his or her job will be factored into an analysis of reasonableness. Generally, you must show that the employee's services are unique, special, or extraordinary.

Let's look at some of these test elements and at what an employer must be able to show.

Legitimate protectable interest. You must have first and foremost an important interest that you have a legitimate need to protect. You cannot insulate yourself from ordinary competition from a departed employee. Any ordinary skill and experience obtained by the employee during employment does not, by itself, constitute a protectable interest. Three interests you can generally protect are:

- Customers,
- Confidential business matters or trade secrets,
- Information gained at your expense.[9]

You have goodwill built up in the acquisition and retention of your customers. You may contract to protect yourself against any pirating away of your customers, whether they be identified individuals or aggregate members of a mailing list.

Bargained-for consideration. Remember to set forth in the contract the consideration given. Such consideration must be adequate to support the restraints in the contract.

At the time of an initial hire, the employer's agreement to hire the individual satisfies this test. The mere fact that an employee was induced to sign a covenant by pressure to obtain a job is not considered "duress" that would make it voidable.[10] Any new consideration given to an existing employee (promotion, raise, etc.) also will satisfy this test, so long as the change in status of the employee can be attributed directly to the employment contract containing the restrictive covenant.

Mutual promises can establish consideration to support a covenant, but this theory is much criticized.[11] A better post-employment consideration would be to show the employer is providing continuous (and expensive) special training or that the parties have executed a mutual notice clause. Such notice of, say, 30 days is generally considered employment for term rather than at will and constitutes valid consideration.

If no new consideration is offered, you have a problem as to enforceability—until the employee actually performs under the terms of the covenant, that is he or she remains employed by the employer and receives the compensation normally attributable to such a relationship.

Ancillary to the main agreement. To be enforceable, a negative covenant restricting other employment must be ancillary to a valid affirmative covenant or contract.[12] The negative covenant will not be enforced if it appears to be the main purpose of the contract.[13]

Trade Secrets

A trade secret is a plan, process, formula, or other valuable information not readily available that is not patented but gives its possessor a competitive advantage or an opportunity to obtain an advantage so long as it is kept secret from competitors who do not know it or how to use it. Some factors to consider as to a trade secret include:

- The extent to which the information is known outside your business.
- The extent to which it is known by employees and others involved in your business.
- The extent of in-house measures taken by you to guard the secrecy of the information. At a minimum the employer must be thorough in restricting those employees who have access to the confidential information and must indicate to all employees the importance of the material. If some but not all affected employees sign covenants not to compete, these agreements will probably fail to be upheld in court.[14]
- The value of the information to you and to your competitors.
- The amount of effort or money expended by you in developing the information.

- The ease or difficulty with which the information could be properly acquired or duplicated by others.[15] A significant type of subject matter that cannot be maintained as a trade secret is information used in a business but nevertheless considered to belong to the firm's employees. Specifically, this refers to the skill, experience, and knowledge acquired by the employees over the course of their employment.

Once you've established a legitimate and reasonable business interest to protect, you should state this in the covenant. You should also relate how the employee had access to it.[16] Then you must make sure the covenant not to compete is narrowly drawn to legitimately protect you as to time and place.

Depending on the circumstances and your firm's methods of doing business, the failure to specify either an exact time frame or geographic area may result in your agreement's being struck down by the court reviewing it. Further, it is safe to assume that in any contract of this nature all ambiguity will be resolved against you—the drafter.

Reasonable time. What is "reasonable" will be decided in light of the particular facts of your situation. It also will vary from state to state, as the issue of unfair competition is one of state law.

An important trade-off will be the length of the employment relationship. If the employee had been employed by you for only a short period of time then he or she probably couldn't have learned your secrets. Unless you can prove otherwise, you have no valid interest to protect.[17] Two factors you must consider:

(1) How long is a reasonable transition period in which I could develop and train a replacement for this employee?

(2) Will the valuable secret knowledge the employee takes be obsolete after an estimable period of time? It may be helpful here to be able to argue that you are protecting not only your own business interests but also that of your customers or others with whom you may have entered into a confidential relationship. To quote one decision upholding a five-year limitation:

As is the case with territorial restrictions this court had not set any limitations on time restrictions which would, per se, be unreasonable and unenforceable. In this case, appellant had access to all of appellee's customer records and knew the dates that various maintenance contracts would be up for renewal or dates when warranties would terminate and new contracts would be unnecessary. Under these facts, the five-year limitation, which appellant agreed to in 1968, is not now unreasonable.[18]

The duration of time if reasonable in light of your objectively verifiable business activity will generally be upheld.

Reasonable area. This is a bit more tricky. At most you can restrict competition of a former employee in the area in which you are currently doing business at the time of the employee's departure (which could be worldwide). If you are doing business only in New England, you cannot bar access to California, even if you plan to do business there. If your business is conducted within a metropolitan area, that may be as far as your restriction can go. The employee may be barred only from areas actually worked in or from those which he or she had knowledge of your business.[19] A salesperson who worked in Maine only and never in the other five New England states, and who had no knowledge of the other areas, could be restricted only in Maine. Imposing a wider geographical limit than is necessary may scuttle your covenant with the employee. For example, barring one from a franchise radius of 25 miles without supplying more specifics could conceivably bar the employee from hundreds of such radiuses unless you define the precise site.[20]

If you, the employer, have a legitimate business interest to protect and draft the time and area restrictions carefully, you're almost home.

Reasonable to Employee and the Public

Employee. As a general rule, employers enjoy superior bargaining power. They have more experience with these covenants and are advised by attorneys. The employee may also be contending with an oversupply of labor. So he or she signs, then leaves.

The covenant will probably be enforced except where the employer has *knowingly* abused superior bargaining power. Examples of such abuse include:

- Where the employer has dealt unfairly with the employee in the circumstances surrounding the employee's departure (a good way to help control your exposure here is to have developed a viable exit interview policy as a defense in these situations).[21] You might also include a paragraph obligating the employee to inform you of his or her next employer.
- Where the covenant was imposed in a deliberately oppressive manner.[22]
- Where the employer's purpose in obtaining and enforcing the covenant is to create a monopoly.
- Where a specialist would be barred from his or her general area of expertise (e.g., a chemist at your firm moves into a new, distinguishable area of chemistry).[23]
- If a real possibility exists that enforcement would deprive the employee of a livelihood, resulting in the employee and employee's family becoming public charges.

The employee may attempt to show there was no opportunity to acquire the knowledge alleged. Some indicators may include the type or level of position held or the practical access to confidential knowledge actually possessed. In the absence of any of this or of an employee's otherwise proving the employer to have engaged in overreaching, the employer will probably be able to prevent the employee from competing.[24]

Public. Generally, if the court has scrutinized the covenant and found it reasonable as to the employer/employee relationship it will be upheld. However, certain statutory law has impeded such free drafting (which your counsel will alert you to). One example is the Employee Retirement Income Security Act, ERISA. Prior to the enactment of ERISA, pension plans frequently contained clauses that denied employees their otherwise nonforfeitable pension benefits if they competed with their former employer after termination.[25] Such covenants are not within the nonforfeitable provisions of ERISA[26] and are effectively banned by federal law.

The Courts Review Your Draft

Because the law of unfair competition is governed by the various states, you should specifically include the governing state law you want in your contract (such law should bear some reasonable relationship to the agreement, such as place where it is signed, performed, etc.). This will prevent your covenant from being voided or modified against your wishes. A simple paragraph such as the following will save you from having the courts later impose a choice of state law you won't like:

> This Agreement will be governed according to the laws of the State of __ both as to interpretation and performance.

However, generally contracting parties cannot choose the law applicable to a tort claim arising from their relationship. As a result, computer contracts—which typically contain numerous disclaimers, exclusions, and limitations—are particularly vulnerable. You must review this with your counsel.

If your covenant is contested, the court may take one of the following four approaches (again, these will vary by state, so you should plan accordingly in your choice of governing state law):

- Enforce the covenant as drafted.
- Use the "blue-pencil," whereby it will strike out objectionable language without changing the overall intent of the paragraph. This doctrine allows a court to modify an unreasonable covenant and enforce it to the extent where it is reasonable. It merely deletes the unreasonable restrictions and retains the rest.
- Reform (rewrite) an overly broad restraint without regard to the severability of the contract language. Unlike the approach above, the courts may add their own language to achieve the parties' intent within a lawful framework.
- Deny the enforcement of the entire covenant either by its own analysis or because of a governing statute in its jurisdiction. In certain states courts deny them as a matter of precedent, while other states have laws on the books declaring them void and unenforceable.

These possible actions show why it is important that you consult counsel before you attempt to draft one of these for an employee.

Enforcement is much less narrow when you're drafting a business-to-business commercial agreement. In any state, you might ask your counsel whether a "severability" paragraph would enhance your protections.

What severability does for you is to protect your overall agreement from being struck down by virtue of one or more nonenforceable paragraphs. Sample language is as follows:

> If any provision of this Agreement shall be held invalid, illegal or unenforceable, the validity, legality, and enforceability of the remaining provisions shall not in any way be affected or impaired thereby and this Agreement shall be construed as if such invalid, illegal, or unenforceable provision had never been contained herein.

Severability can be a useful tool in a covenant not to compete as well as in other agreements. However, never use this as a "throw in" in a form contract you use, as you may find a court throwing out a paragraph that goes to the heart of why you want the contract. In that case, you would be stuck with the remaining contract, which may not only go against your expectations, but also be flat-out injurious to you. Severability should be used only as needed in your "non-form language" after a review with your counsel.

Finally, you should review with your counsel the desirability of avoiding the courts altogether—if you are an employer. Arbitration may be a better route for you. An arbitrator is not bound to abide by principles of substantive law, and an arbitrator may enforce a noncompetition agreement that a court would not have enforced. Arbitration also offers many procedural advantages. For example, arbitrators are not bound by courtroom rules of evidence, arbitration proceedings can be held outside of the public eye, and there is no opportunity for appeal on the merits. Moreover, the arbitrator can be required to have certain qualifications and a general technical background or a background in the industry in which the agreement is being used, a clear advantage over the inexperience of a jury or a judge who are strangers to your business.

Sample Covenant Not to Compete

The following is a hypothetical covenant not to compete. Obviously you must carefully tailor your covenant to your specific needs and only after a review with your counsel.

You should include a "whereas" clause setting forth the employer's *specific* interest to be protected, how the employee might take it from you, and why it is vital to the employer that the employee not be permitted to do this.

> In consideration of hiring Employee by Employer, and of disclosures made to him concerning the company's business methods and trade secrets, the Employee agrees:

(a) During the term of his employment and for . . . years from and after the effective date of his termination for whatever cause that Employee will not compete with the Employer directly or indirectly, alone or with another, anywhere in the United States or its territories.

This would be the broadest language. As a general rule this should be more restrictive as to territory and only cover the exact area the employee actually worked in.

(b) The Employee agrees not to solicit directly or indirectly nor offer to provide nor agree to provide, nor actually provide (certain enumerated services).

(c) The Employee will not influence or attempt to influence any other employee of the company to terminate his employment to work for a competitor of the company.

(d) The Employee agrees the Employer's Customer List is confidential and unique to the Employer as it contains specialized and valuable data acquired over a substantial time period and which is not easily reproducible from other available sources and, therefore, the Employee will not make use of this list in any solicitational manner after his/her employment terminates. The Employee expressly agrees that this agreement shall survive the termination of the Employee's employment by the Employer, that the Employee fully understands its meaning and intent, and that it is reasonable as to time, area and all other respects.

Again, sample language is provided for general reference. Any specific covenant you need to protect your own business should be drafted by your counsel after an in-depth discussion of your personal requirements.

Tighten Covenant

Finally, consider some methods of tightening your covenant not to compete to further insulate it from attack.

- List the specific competitors you don't want the employee to go to work for during the reasonable time period. This specifically targets your restriction while lessening restrictions on the employee's economic mobility.

- Where such specification is not feasible, make sure (where applicable) that you restrict the competitors to the corporate entity actually affected. If a subsidiary is contracting, then the subsidiary should make sure the covenant clearly limits itself to the subsidiary's competitors only—to avoid being bound to the competitors of the other subsidiaries or the parent where such corporate units would not be directly affected by the employee's departure.

- You might consider stating that you'll pay an employee for the covenant's term if the covenant keeps such employee from finding suitable work.[27]

- Anticipate and set forth specific areas of damage you'll suffer, to help establish your case later on. In general, such damages will be measured by the employer's loss, not the employee's gain.

A covenant not to compete can be a valuable tool in protecting the security of your firm's competitive advantages in the marketplace. The courts are gradually coming to view these more favorably and to understand that society can no longer bear the cost of impeding an employer from having these assurances of protection, and that such assurances will tend to promote the free dissemination of ideas and knowledge between the employer and employee.

There are many variables involved (duration, geographical scope, quality of information sought to be protected, employee's access to such information, etc.). If you're the type of manager that protects his or her property through patents, trademarks, or copyrights, you should seek personal legal counsel as to how you can possibly protect what may be your most important property in an information society. Generally, you will want an agreement that:

(1) is not harsh, inequitable, or unconscionable for the affected employee,

(2) is valid as to new terms to continuing employees, and

(3) is carefully tailored to the circumstances.

It is a very complex area—as aptly summarized by Judge Hoover:

"An employee's covenant not to compete is not one of those questions on which the legal researcher cannot find enough to quench his thirst. To the contrary, there is so much authority it drowns him. It is a sea—vast and vacillating, overlapping and bewildering. One can fish out of it any kind of strange support for anything, if he lives so long."[28]

ENDNOTES

(1) Public Law 99-272, Title X.

(2) *Getschow v. Commonwealth Edison Co.,* 111 Ill. App. 3d 622, 67 1II. Dec. 343, 444 N.E.2d 579 (1982).

(3) *Guard Life Corp. v. Parker Hardware,* 50 N.Y.2d 183, 199 (from dissent but argued on other issues) 1980. See also *Smith Shrader Co., Inc. v. Smith,* 483 N.E.2d 283,289 (I11. App. Dist. 1985).

(4) See Valuihs, Anthony C., *Covenants Not to Compete: Forms, Tactics and the Law,* Wiley Law Publications (1986).

(5) For example, California generally proscribes covenants not to compete—see *California Business and Professions Code* 16600. But also see *Buskuhl v. Family Life Insurance Co.,* 271 Ca. App. 2d 514, 76 Cal. Rptr. 602 (1969).

(6) *Florida Statutes Annotated* 542.12.

(7) *J & H Goldberg Co., Inc. v. Stern,* 385 N.Y.2d 427, 53 A.D.2d 246 (1976).

(8) *Purchasing Associates, Inc. v. Weitz,* 13 N.Y.2d 267, 246 N.Y.S.2d 600, 196 N.E.2d 245 (1963).

(9) *Cherne Industries, Inc. v. Grounds Assoc.,* 278 N.W.2d 82, 90-91.

(10) *American Credit Bureau, Inc. v. Carter,* 11 Ariz. App. 145, 462 P.2d 838 (1968).

(11) *Leatherman v. Management Advisors, Inc.,* 448 N.E.2d 1048 (Ind. 1983). Pages 1050-1052 set forth a well written dissent for anyone considering this form of consideration standing alone. But see *Jones C. Green Co. v. Kelly,* 261 N.C. 166,168, 134 S.E.2d 166,167 (1964).

(12) *Collier Cobb & Associates, Inc. v. Leah,* 300 S.E.2d 583 (N.C. App. 1983).

(13) *Mastrom, Inc. v. Warren,* 18 N.C. App. 199, 196 S.E.2d 528 (1973).

(14) *Servomation Mathias, Inc. v. Englert,* 333 F.Supp. 9 (1971).

(15) *Forest Laboratories, Inc. v. Pillsbury Company,* 452 F.2d 621, 624 (1971).

(16) *Mixing Equipment Co., Inc. v. Philadelphia Gear, Inc.* 436 F2d 1308 3d Cir. 1971).

(17) *Rebsamen Insurance v. Milton,* 600 S.W.2d 441 (1980) (10 months not long enough to learn employer's system).

(18) *Johnson v. Lee,* 257 S.E.2d 273, 275 (1981).

(19) *Associates, Inc. v. Taylor,* 29 N.C. App. 679, 225 S.E.2d 602 (1976), *cert. den.* 290 N.C. 659, 228 S.E.2d 451 (1976).

(20) *Manpower of Guilford City v. Hedgecock,* 257 S.E.2d 109, 115 (1981).

(21) *Solari Industries, Inc. v. Malady,* 55 N.J. 571, 264 A.2d 53 (1970).

(22) Ibid. note 15 and 17 above.

(23) *Electronic Data Sys. Corp. v. Kinder,* 360 F.Supp. 1044 (N.D. Tex. 1973); *aff'd,* 497 F.2d 222 (5th Cir. 1974).

(24) *Lear Siegler, Inc. v. ARK-ELL Springs, Inc.,* 569 F.2d 286 (1978).

(25) *Winter v. Edison Brothers Stores Pension Plan,* 593 F.2d 307 (1979).

(26) 29 U.S.C. Sec. 1053(b). See also Coccoma, Ellen L., "ERISA and Anticompetitive Covenants," Albany Law Review, Vol. 45, pps. 410-435 (1981).

(27) *Modern Controls, Inc. v. Adreadakis,* 578 F.2d 1264 (1978).

(28) *B & Y Metal Painting, Inc. v. Ball,* 279 N.W.2d 813 (1981).

CHAPTER 28

PRODUCT AND
CHARACTER LICENSING
AGREEMENTS

An increasingly lucrative form of income, especially in these days of brand image and entertainment spinoffs, is subsidiary rights from licensing your tangible and intangible property. Merchandising properties include any word, name, symbol, or design that when used on or in association with a particular product or service, will create a demand for it from your targeted market. You might consider licensing to increase market penetration or because you lack the present capacity to begin large-scale manufacturing of your merchandising property.

Further, keep in mind that trademark rights cannot be bought and sold in the abstract, but may only be transferred by means of a controlled licensing program (uncontrolled licensing of a mark results in abandonment of the mark by the licensor) or along with the product the trademark identifies or with other assets or goodwill of the business that developed it.

Traditionally the most successful types of merchandise were low-priced, impulse products. However, this trend is changing, and higher mark-up items are becoming more successful. These properties can also be valuable to your competitors. All marketers who are considering developing properties for licensing or are about to embark on licensing existing properties should protect themselves as follows:

- ☐ Before making a sizable investment in the creation and exploitation of a potential merchandising property or character, review your proposals with an attorney skilled in licensing.

- ☐ Consider a merchandising program for each qualifying property and product.

- ☐ The properties should be analyzed with your counsel to identify what types of protection are available to you—patent, trademark, copyright, and the like—with appropriate steps taken as legally recommended.

☐ Your enforcement program should be agreed on and established prior to any infringement by a competitor.

☐ As a licensee, the agreement should be created or accepted only after a careful review with your counsel, reflecting the points above.

This chapter examines product and character licensing agreements, and ways to protect your merchandising properties in order of their general use. It also includes clauses to consider in drafting your license agreements and it raises issues unique to character retention and licensing. Finally, it suggests some ways you can protect your character rights.

Preparing the Agreement

You are the owner of a merchandising property who has both developed it and taken the steps to protect it. You now wish to exploit it by licensing.

There are several things to do before you work up the agreement. You must get a mental handle on the different natures of properties that may be licensed so as to be able to mold the license terms and related royalty and obligation of confidence terms into patterns that are compatible with each other, the law, the tax environment, and other realities of the marketplace (including distribution and servicing). You should also have considered whether such licensing may give away your know-how and eventually bolster your future competitor.

You must decide exactly what you are licensing. There may be many separate rights available to license, such as, the right to make, use, lease, or sell. Each right must be considered separately in your planning.

Check out the prospect. A license agreement is only as good for you as the firm standing behind it. Investigate your licensee's financial strength, sales capacity, familiarity with the subject matter to be licensed, and the geography of their market structure.

Be sure your counsel has a good understanding of contracts. Your agreement should cover the following terms at a minimum (you might want to refer to Chapter 25 on contracts in general):

Definitions. You should clearly set out in "plain English" the meaning of any trade jargon so as not to confuse the rights you're granting or the extent of the relationship. Remember, you wish to retain your rights in your product. That is one reason you're licensing rather than selling it.

Territory. Specify it—a state, region, U.S. and its territories, world rights—especially if you are granting exclusive rights to such territory. Any territorial controls or limits to be imposed on the licensee after the agreement expires should be reviewed for any anticompetitive factors and to establish whether there are rational, reasonable, and objectively verifiable justification for post-termination restrictions.

Preamble. The "Whereas" clause is a standard beginning. To avoid antitrust exposure and to preempt future disputes, you should recite specifically why the license is being granted and to whom.

License grant. Here, you should be clear as to what your grant of a license does *not* extend to or include. Then, one of the basic questions to be answered in a licensing agreement is whether the rights to be transferred are exclusive or nonexclusive.

The word "exclusive" raises the specter of antitrust (see below), since you're licensing an intellectual monopoly on property with unique economic power. Under an exclusive license, the licensee has been given the exclusive right to use, exclusive even as to the licensor—unless expressly provided for otherwise. Often, offering an exclusive license is the only way you'll generate any interest. The licensee may have to incur substantial costs to manufacture and develop a market for an untried product. The licensee will have enough worries about substitutes, and so will insist on some means to restrict the number of additional licensees.

A nonexclusive right is not without problems. For example, a trademark owner must maintain quality control. A situation could arise where one licensee demands you take legal action against another to enforce such controls.

Assignment. You want to have some or full veto power over the licensee's ability to sublicense the agreement without your advance approval. If the licensee is silent on the right of assignment or reserves an unrestricted right of assignment, then you may have little recourse to prevent this.

One situation you definitely want to control is closely related to quality control (see below). You don't want to have carefully screened a licensee to ensure it fits your firm's proper image only to have the licensee subsequently assign its rights to another firm you'd never consider entering into an original agreement with.

Strict quality control procedures. This is a must for certain licensees, especially trademarks. It is fundamental that a trademark license must obtain quality control provisions. Control is the key to uniformity and it enhances goodwill and maintains quality. However, not only must the provision be written into the agreement, it must be enforced.[1]

This relates back to the very basis on which trademarks are permitted to be licensed. Since trademarks represent source or origin, which to the public means goods of consistent quality, to prevent public deception the licensor must control the nature and quality of the goods. (See Chapter 5 on trademarks.)

To make sure there are no misrepresentations your license agreements must include a provision requiring the licensor's approval of all advertising and labeling. Such approval should not be unreasonably denied. A licensee will require that such approval be withheld within a specified time frame (for example, 10 days) or your silence will be deemed to constitute approval.

In addition, the licensor must vigorously follow up on this for the duration of the license, at adequate intervals, including visits to licensee's plants and warehouses. Direct mailers should also set up a few test accounts. Further, the licensor should be provided with current samples at specific intervals. The licensee must warrant that such samples reflect the current product as it is marketed, sold, packaged, etc.

The licensor will qualify all approvals (samples, advertising, etc.) by stating that such approval will not relieve the licensee of its responsibility to comply with all applicable law (see below) and shall not constitute a determination that such legal compliance thresholds have been met.

All of the above controls must be reviewed with counsel sensitive to your antitrust exposure in areas of pricing, territorial controls, tying, etc., and to the fact that you must assure your trademarked goods are of standard quality and character. Failure to enforce the latter could result in your mark's loss due to its becoming descriptive of its goods.

Indemnification. You should obtain indemnification from your licensee for a variety of forms of negligence as well as for product liability, and you should have such indemnification survive the term of the license. You should also require the licensee to name you, as licensor, co-insured in the licensee's insurance policy and to require the insurance company to notify you in the event the premiums are not paid or the policy is being revised, modified, or canceled. This will then allow you to pay the premiums or somehow otherwise insure yourself to avoid losing the benefits of insurance. You will reserve the right to examine such policy or require other evidence of insurance from the licensee. Failure to maintain such payments could also be grounds for termination of the license at your sole option.

Note: As licensor, you will probably be asked to warrant that your proprietary right does not infringe on or violate the right of any third party. You should require the licensee to promptly notify you if such action is commenced and that the licensee will cooperate (at your expense) in the defense. You should include language that if licensee on its own initiative settles any claims, demands, or action without your prior written consent, then you are released from this indemnity in this instance.

Confidential property. You'll want to specify that the licensee must use the same care in guarding your specified confidential property as the licensee would for its own proprietary information of like importance. The disclosure by licensee of any such property will cause you irreparable harm. Depending on the sensitivity of your needs, this is an important paragraph to review with your counsel.

Compliance with laws. A provision should be included that both parties will comply with all current laws and will monitor legislation so as to comply with future laws arising during the term of the license.

Registration. State that the licensee will not seek any copyright or trademark registration for the property without your prior written consent; will cooperate fully with reasonable requests by you in connection with any applications you may choose to file for such registrations; will execute any documents reasonably requested by you to confirm your rights; and will appoint you as its authorized attorney-in-fact to execute and deliver such documents in licensee's name should licensee fail or refuse to do so.

Royalties. To be negotiated as per your needs as to the type to be used, and whether you'll receive a guaranteed annual minimum in royalty as well as sales (to insure that the market is being adequately exploited). You might make such royalties contingent on a "best efforts" exploitation of all the significant markets or potential markets in the defined territory.

Finally, this paragraph should set forth all reporting requirement hurdles each party must meet, including what books and records of its transactions the licensee must keep updated and accurate.

Advertising. At a minimum you'll want language specifying that the licensee will in good faith use its best efforts to promote your product. You may also require the licensee to spend a certain stated minimum in advertising in a given market. You might also set forth a cooperative advertising plan (another area of antitrust exposure to review with your counsel).

Trademark and copyright notices. You should specifically set forth the licensee's requirement to cause each item to bear an appropriate trademark, copyright, or other notice. You might specifically state as to trademarks "Under license granted by (you)." For copyrights, you must make it clear that any copyrightable contributions licensees may make in any reproduction of your property will be deemed a work made for hire for you, or if it does not so qualify, all right, title, and interest in it shall be deemed automatically transferred to you, subject to the rights granted licensee under this agreement.

Reserved rights. Provide that all rights not expressly granted in the agreement are reserved by you, including without limitation . . . (set forth your rights in detail if you wish).

Termination. This should spell out that on the completion of a specified amount of time or on a specified event (e.g., licensee's insolvency, which would make it unlikely that the licensee can adequately market and protect your product) all rights granted will automatically revert to you as licensor. The licensee will immediately cease using your property. Some provision should also be made for disposing of the licensed products at termination.

Joint venture. You'll want specific language stating that your license in no way implies an agency relationship or joint venture between the parties.

Again, you should refer to the general discussion on contracts at the beginning of this section as to other terms you should include (and why) such as the Terms of Agreement, Governing Law, Force Majeure, Waiver, Notices, Severability, Merger or Integration Clause, etc.

The above discussion is not intended to cover all clauses that should be included in a license agreement, but it does cover many of the clauses that are more important to you. Each license situation involves unique considerations, and care must be exercised accordingly.

Protecting Character Rights

In today's lucrative merchandising license environment there is a scramble to license not only "hot," topical characters (such as movie spin-offs), but also formerly popular characters, literary characters, and even graphic characters designed on computer. This chapter suggests forms of protection for literary and graphic characters. At the conclusion it ties in suggestions for your contractual protection.

The situation is common to have a copyrighted character, and you know such protection in the underlying work has a finite life. You look to trademark protection while the copyright still subsists. This is the time to create a strong secondary meaning through separate merchandise licensing, giving the name a greater emphasis in promotional pieces (such as display posters), and, of course, making sure your various characters can be visualized and (where possible) are.[2] Then you can argue that any subsequent unauthorized use has caused a likelihood of confusion as to the *particular, single* source or sponsorship.[3] Essentially, you want to know whether a trademark in your characters can protect your rights in them beyond the term of copyright applicable to the underlying work.[4] Unlike copyright, trademark and unfair competition law is not inherently time limited.

Copyrightability of Characters

Where copyright exists, it may be the cornerstone of your protection. Once the copyright on the underlying work has expired, the character may be freely copied by anyone unless you have created some other protection. Two district holdings have emerged with respect to the copyrightability of literary or related characters. One circuit's test essentially prescribes two requirements which, if met, constitute copyright infringement:[5]

(1) The infringed character must be sufficiently delineated; and

(2) The infringing character must "closely imitate" the infringed character.

The other circuit's test is more stringent.[6] In this circuit a character is not copyrightable unless the character "constitutes the story being told." Mickey Mouse is a highly developed and publicly recognized character and entitled to copyright protection,[7] whereas the character Regan in the story of *The Exorcist* was not entitled to such protection, even though she was the main character. Perhaps the most dramatic example in this circuit was its holding that Dashiel Hammett's character Sam Spade was not protectable by copyright, and its suggestion that characters might be copyrightable if "they constituted the story being told" and were not merely chessmen in the game of telling the story.[8]

The creator or proprietor of character usually claims copyright protection in his or her characters. Reliance on copyright may be used to establish lone and exclusive use of the character resulting in secondary meaning. His or her opponent will usually take the position that the characters were never covered by copyright (e.g., they were mere ideas not entitled to protection) or that they were in the public domain. Because of the disparate viewpoints expressed as to the copyrightability of characters and the *ad hoc* nature of the decisions, the availability of trademark and unfair competition protection becomes all the more important.

Trademark and Unfair Competition Protection On Expiration of Copyright

Under trademark law and the broad umbrella of unfair competition law, particularly the Lanham Act,[9] it has become possible, in effect, to secure protection very much like copyright protection for your characters.

You don't keep it "all" intact. For example, on expiration of your copyright, the title of your work is "dedicated" to the public along with the work itself. Neither unfair competition nor trademark principles allow injunctions against reproducing the work under its original title. For example, you can probably publish your dictionary using the name Webster.[10]

To secure trademark protection, plan now. Seek suggestions from your counsel as to how you can keep your character rights existing separate from the story, script, and the like. One way to do this is to license such characters as separate property and clearly set forth this fact in such license agreements.

There have been cases which have protected literary characters under common-law unfair competition principles, Section 43(b) of the Lanham Act, or trademark infringement law. These are usually based on the underlying premise of trademark law that an unauthorized use will cause likelihood of confusion in two situations: (1) where the second user copies the first's character and gives it the same name so that it purports to be the first's character; and (2) where the character is differently portrayed and doesn't purport to be the plaintiff's character but has the same name.

The threshold question in these cases is whether the creator of the character has sufficiently used the character so that there is secondary meaning associated with it. If so, the creator is probably entitled to protection apart from copyright or contract law principles.[11] If not, any protection granted to the creator would be based on the contractual arrangement between the parties. In any situation you must be able to prove such use would cause confusion in *your* competitive market.

For example, in one case[12] plaintiff brought suit seeking a declaration that its production of toy dolls, sold under the trademark "Star Team," did not infringe any character rights possessed by the producer of the film "Star Wars" or by its toy manufacturer licensee. Defendants moved for a preliminary injunction based on copyright infringement and unfair competition under the Lanham Act and the common law.

The court characterized the unfair competition claim as a claim of "'misappropriation', or the unauthorized copying and use of that which belongs to a competitor, and 'misrepresentation', or the selling of another's goods as one's own." Although the court agreed that each of these theories stated a cause of action, it refused to find liability on either of them because of an absence of significant similarity between the parties' respective characters and the consequent absence of likelihood of confusion as to the source or sponsorship. Another illustrative case is *United Artists Corp. v. Ford Motor Co.*,[13] in which United Artists argued that its copyright in the animated Pink Panther character was infringed by the animated cat in the Lincoln-Mercury television advertisements. Not so, said the court, and Ford was permitted to continue its use of the Pink Panther animated character. The court found no copying, no unfair competition, no passing off, no misrepresentation or confusion of sponsorship, and no misappropriation of secondary meaning.

The above cases have generally dealt with the issue of concurrent trademark and copyright protection. Where characters were accorded trademark protection, the copyright on the work usually was still valid. For a case lacking such concurrency refer back to the discussion of *Frederick Warne and Co.*,[14] which opened this section. To recap, even though the copyrights had expired, the characters alone had clearly acquired secondary meaning as a result of book sales and licensing ventures. The public recognized the existence of a single source of those products.[15]

The crux of this extended protection is not that industrial property such as trademarks is favored over intellectual property or that it is possible to create perpetual copyright protection. Finally, disparate substantive results are not being created.

The courts are holding (when they grant "extended copyright" at all) simply that certain unfair trade practices are prohibited, and these prohibitions do not rise and fall within the life of a copyright. If it is wrong to use a mark in a deceptive manner during the term of the copyright, it is wrong to do so after the copyright has expired. The name or identity of the character is analogous to the name or mark of a product or business. Therefore, the proprietor must establish a sufficiently widespread use or publication of the name to get *secondary meaning* associated with the creator and publisher.[16] This requires proof that the owner of the story depicting the character has invested the name with a "commercial significance and goodwill that is attributable to [the name] itself."[17] This proof could include some demonstrated product merchandising or product licensing activity by the owner of the character, and it precludes any finding of a likelihood of confusion as to source or sponsorship. In the absence of secondary meaning or trademark use (i.e., use on goods or services), the names would be in the public domain and free for all to use.[18]

Finally, remember that trademark and unfair competition law prohibits consumer deception— *not* mere copying. Thus, where a competitor (especially a remote one) labels its product so as to clearly state it is the source of the product, there is little likelihood of confusion or any action based on appropriation or misrepresentation.[19]

Effect on Your Licensing Program

A character may be protected by copyright and unfair competition principles in addition to being used as a trademark on merchandise. Attempt to use a merchandising strategy as soon as practical. To maximize your protection, add the following to the licensing clauses discussed previously in this chapter:

(1) Use copyright notices (see Section IV) on the works in which the characters appear and on all promotion pieces as well as the actual merchandise items themselves. Require all your licensees to do likewise.

(2) Use trademark notices (see Section I) in conjunction with your characters when they are used as trademarks or service marks. To maximize your efforts here, try to have your character graphically depicted and have the thrust of your character's exploitation center on its promotional rather than literary or artistic merit. The visuals on your advertisement, display items, stationery, etc. not only strengthen your ability to protect your character per se, but also create another basis for trademark protection, namely the visual design features associated with the character. The physical picture could be registered as a trademark and protected under the trademark, Section 43(a), and unfair competition laws as well.

(3) In addition to requiring acknowledgment of your rights and the notice of same on all promotions and products (where applicable) in your license agreement you should also specify the following:

- *specific* quality control procedures and standards for each product;
- a registration policy for copyrights and trademarks;
- what rights you specifically reserve as well as your common-law rights; and
- indemnification protections you mutually offer each other customized around your ownership.

Antitrust Exposure in Licensing Agreements

Antitrust is generally discussed in Section II. However, a few points are emphasized here because of potential antitrust exposure in intellectual-property licensing.

The major issue is "tie-ins," which exist when the seller declines to sell a desired product unless the buyer is also willing to purchase an additional product or products that are not as desirable or that can be purchased from others at lower prices. A key to this is market power.

The crucial test is whether the tie-in involves one product or service in which the company enjoys substantial market power. In other words, does the tie-in represent an attempt by a firm to exert leverage so that its economic power in one market may be extended to another? Economic power here does not mean monopoly or even dominant power. The test is whether the firm "has sufficient economic power with respect to the tying product to appreciably restrain free competition in the market for the tied product."[20]

In addition to dollar power in a market, economic power can be inferred from the tying product's desirability, its uniqueness, or even its consumer appeal. Economic power is presumed if you possess a legal monopoly such as a patent, copyright, or trademark. Here, a competitor cannot have access to the property except through a license by the owner, and requiring additional purchases to license this product can invite antitrust exposure.

Copyrights are fairly straightforward. Each copyrighted work is unique, and no substitution in marketing is permitted. From our discussion above it is fairly obvious what goes into these licensing programs.

The mere refusal to license a lawfully acquired patent is no violation of the antitrust laws.[21] However, that may be challenged in some situations.

Dominant firm in the industry. Conduct that would be lawful for a smaller concern may be unlawful for a dominant one. Where a firm possessed monopoly power it may be sufficient for a plaintiff to show its acts "unnecessarily excluded competition" from the relevant market.[22] There traditionally has been a presumption of market power arising from a patent grant.[23] Concerted refusals to license patents may be as unlawful as a concerted refusal to deal.[24] Also under scrutiny will be whether the dominant firm has engaged in willful acts directed at maintaining its monopoly, such as:

(a) new product introduction utilized to stifle competition;

(b) utilizing rebate schemes to suppress competition;[25]

(c) becoming a "moving target" by frequently redesigning a product so competitors can't duplicate it;[26] and

(d) advanced publicity as to (a) or (c) above, calculated to preempt competition.

All of the above is effectively countered by the firm's demonstrating that its growth was a consequence of a superior product, business acumen, or historic accident[27] or that the innovation was not only a performance improvement but its success in the marketplace is proof positive that the public wanted or needed it.[28]

"Essential facility" doctrine. In today's world of increasingly sophisticated telecommunications and computer hook ups, new entrants can be barred forever unless they can interconnect with a dominant firm's services. A firm that controls such a facility must afford access to the facility on a reasonable basis if such is necessary and not merely convenient.[29] This access is the foundation on which telephone deregulation is built.

Once you've demonstrated you need access to an essential facility and such access was denied, you must argue and prove that (a) a monopolist controls the facility, (b) competitors cannot practically or reasonably duplicate the facility, (c) the monopolists actually denied its competitors use of the facility; *and* (d) that it would be feasible for the monopolist to provide access to the facility.[30]

Agreement on markets. In your licensing program (regardless of your size) you must be careful to make sure that any limitations you put on a licensee's ability to practice the patent for example, limiting the geographic area in which it may manufacture and sell) are limitations imposed by you alone and not as a result of an agreement between your firm and one or more or your licensees to carve up the markets.[31]

Differential royalties. Be careful—these are permitted where economically justified by market factors such as a favored firm's entering and developing a new market, sinking in a lot of development capital, and the like. A discriminatory royalty will be in violation of the law if it is found to suppress competition among competing licensees or to create a monopoly in a relevant market. However, the standard here is fairly loose. For example, a manufacturing patentee may set the price at which its licensee may sell[32] and may *require* that certain ancillary products be purchased by the licensee from the licensor.[33]

Grant-back or assignment-back clauses. These must be viewed with extreme caution. You don't wish to compete against your own licensees as to developments they make on your patent. However, you must be careful that these are not found to restrain trade. If you wish to minimize your risk, impose only a nonexclusive grant-back.

A trademark can also confer the presumption of economic power. However, it must be shown that the trademark is a distinctive representation of product quality or that it possesses requisite goodwill and public acceptance unique to it to restrain competition in the product market. A trademark representing only origin lacks this power.

This problem often arises in franchising. For example, ice-cream retailers brought suit against their franchisor, alleging maintenance of an illegal tying arrangement, illegal horizontal-market allocations, and wholesale price-fixing. The appellate court held that, since the *trademark served to identify the ice cream, and thus the trademark and ice cream were not separate products, the tying rules were inapplicable.* Rather than identifying a business format, the trademark represented the end product marketed by the system. The desirability of the trademark, therefore, was *utterly dependent on the perceived quality of the product it represented.* Therefore, in the court's view, tie-in doctrine had no application because the *prohibition of tying arrangements is designed to strike solely at the use of a dominant desired product to compel the purchase of a second, undesired commodity.* In addition, the desirability of the trademark and the quality of the product it represented were so inextricably interrelated in the mind of the consumer as to preclude any finding that the trademark was a separate item for tie-in analysis.[34]

You've no doubt eaten at a franchised "chain" restaurant at some time—possibly because of the goodwill of the franchisor's name. The franchisor may license its trademark (origin) and contract to sell any items unique to its particular operation. However, it may negotiate to sell but may not *require* you to purchase from it other items readily available in the open market from other competitors. For example, Howard Johnson's may not require its franchisees to purchase HoJo Cola, although through negotiations it may make this an attractive option for the franchisee. Again, consider whether the license pertains to one product or distinct products. If the items are sold as a unit in the marketplace, there is only one product. If they are sold as separate items, then the trademark and franchisee are tying products, and other required products are tied products and thus, probably illegal.

Another area of exposure is in *"dual distribution."* In "dual distribution" marketing systems, a manufacturer or supplier operates at more than one level of the distribution chain, thereby placing itself in actual or potential competition with distributors of its product or services. For example, a manufacturer that sells its product both to wholesale distributors for resale to retailers, and directly to retailers is engaged in dual distribution.[35] For example, a franchisor of a brand of ice cream that manufactures and sells the ice cream directly to retailers, while also licensing other manufacturers to produce and market the product to retailers, is a dual distributor.[36]

As discussed elsewhere, your nonprice restraints in your dual-distribution system will be judged under the rule of reason, while areas such as horizontal price-fixing remain, per se, illegal. A trademark cannot legally be used as a device to allow what would constitute a Sherman Act violation. More specifically, a trademark cannot be used for horizontal territorial allocation or solely to eliminate intrabrand competition and stabilize or maintain higher prices than would otherwise result.[37]

Antitrust penalties run the usual gamut in intellectual property areas, and then some. For example, the Lanham Act makes antitrust misuse of a trademark a special defense in infringement proceedings, even after the mark has become incontestable.[38]

Conclusion

There are a variety of economic benefits to be derived from a program of aggressive product and character licensing. To reap the rewards and avoid significant legal exposure, such agreements must be analyzed by your counsel *in advance*. This precaution will also help you avoid antitrust problems and develop a strategy to protect and extend your rights for as long as possible. Finally, care must be taken in the basic drafting of the agreement itself, on which all else may be judged.

ENDNOTES

(1) Quality control is incorporated in the Lanham Act's "related companies" doctrine. Sections 5 and 45 tacitly approve the use of a mark by someone other than the owner where the owner exercises control over what is sold under the mark (15 U.S.C. Sec 1055 and 1127). Without controls, the public cannot rely on the mark as a guarantee of quality and consistency or on its designation as a single source of origin. The trademark's owner risks losing his or her rights by abandonment by inadequately supervising the quality of the licensee's products. See also *Universal City Studios v. Nesitendo Co.,* 578 F.Supp.911 (1983), and *Haymaker Sports, Inc. v. Turian,* 581 F.2d 257 (Cust. & Pat. App. 1978).

(2) *Warner Brothers, Inc. v. American Broadcasting,* 530 F.Supp.1187 (S.D.N.Y. 1987). (After a lengthy comparison of the physical and personality attributes of these characters, the court concluded that they were so dissimilar as to preclude a finding of substantial similarity.) See also *Walt Disney Productions v. Air Pirates,* 581 F.2d 751 (9th Cir. 1978), *cert. den.,* 439 US 1132 (1979).

(3) Lanham Trademark Act Sec. 43(a), 15 U.S.C. Sec. 1125(a). Secondary meaning is the fundamental requisite of a Section 43(a) trademark. See also *Warner Brothers, Inc. v. Gay Toys, Inc.,* 513 F.Supp.1066 (S.D.N.Y. 1981) (2d Cir. 1981) and *Wyatt Earp Enterprises, Inc. v. Sackman, Inc.,* 147 F.Supp.621 (S.D.N.Y. 1958).

(4) *Frederick Warne & Co. v. Book Sales, Inc.,* 481 F.Supp.1191 (S.D.N.Y. 1979). See also Brown, "Eligibility for Copyright Protection: A Search for a Principled Standard," 70 *Minnesota Law Review* 579 (1985).

(5) *Nichols v. Universal Pictures Corp.,* 45 F.2d 119 (2d Cir. 1930), *cert. den.,* 282 US 902 (1931).

(6) *Warner Brothers Pictures, Inc. v. Columbia Broadcasting System, Inc.,* 102 F.Supp.141 (S.D. CA. 1951), *aff'd,* 216 F.2d 945 (9th Cir. 1954), *cert. den.,* 348 US 971 (1955).

(7) *Walt Disney Productions v. Air Pirates,* 581 F.2d 751 (9th Cir. 1978), *cert. den.,* 439 US 1132 (1979). Many states now incorporate independent contractors, e.g., *Florida Statutes,* 542.33(2)(a) (1987).

(8) *Warner Brothers Pictures, Inc. v. Columbia Broadcasting System, Inc.,* 216 F.2d 945, 950 (9th Cir. 1954).

(9) See note 3.

(10) *G & C Merriam Co. v. Ogilvie,* 159 F 638 (1st Cir. 1908), *cert. den.,* 209 US 551 (1908).

(11) *Toho Co. v. Sears, Roebuck & Co.,* 645 F.2d 788 (9th Cir. 1981), but see *American Broadcasting Co. v. World Mfg. Inc.,* 151 U.S.P.Q. 361 (N.Y. Sup. Ct. 1966).

(12) *Ideal Toy Corp. v. Kenner Products,* 443 F.Supp.291 (S.D.N.Y. 1977).

(13) 483 F.Supp.89 (S.D.N.Y. 1980).

(14) See note 4. See also *Silverman v. CBS, Inc.,* 632 F.Supp. 1344 (S.D.N.Y. 1986).

(15) Id., at 1194.

(16) See note 4.

(17) *Wyatt Earp Enterprises, Inc. v. Sackman, Inc.,* 157 F.Supp.621, 624 (1958).

(18) *Superior Models Inc. v. Tolkien Enterprises,* 211 U.S.P.Q. 587 (D. Del.), *mod. on other grounds,* 211 U.S.P.Q. 876 (D. Del. 1981).

(19) *Geisel v. Poynter Products, Inc.,* 295 F.Supp.331 (S.D.N.Y. 1968) (the Dr. Seuss dolls).

(20) *Northern Pacific Ry. Co. v. U.S.,* 337 US 293 (1949).

(21) *United States v. United Shoe Machinery Co.,* 247 US 32, 57 (1918); *SCM Corp. v. Xerox Corp.,* 645 F.2d 1195, 1212 (2d Cir. 1981), *cert. den.,* 455 US 1016 (1982); *E.I. du Pont de Nemours & Co.,* 96 FTC 653 (1980). For a case of general interest to patent licensing, see *Aronson v. Quick Point Pencil Co.,* 440 US 257 (1979).

(22) *Greyhound Computer Corp. v. IBM,* 559 F.2d 488, 498 (9th Cir. 1977), *cert. den.,* 434 US 1040 (1978).

(23) *Jefferson Parish Hospital District No. 2 v. Hyde,* 104 S.CT.1551 (1984).

(24) *SCM Corp. v. Xerox Corp., 645 F.2d 1195, 1212 (2d Cir. 1981), cert. den.,* 455 US 1016 (1982).

(25) *Smith Kline Corp. v. Eli Lilly & Co.,* 575 F.2d 1056 (3d Cir.), *cert. den.,* 439 US 838 (1978).

(26) *Bailey's Bakery, Ltd. v. Continental Baking Co.,* 235 F.Supp.705 (D. Hawaii 1964), *aff'd per curiam,* 401 F.2d 182 (9th Cir. 1968), *cert. den.,* 393 US 1086 (1969). (Court noted in dictum that frequent introduction of heavily advertised new bread lines over short period of time could constitute an unreasonable restraint of trade.)

(27) *U.S. v. Grinnel Corp.,* 384 US 563, 570-71 (1966).

(28) *Berkey Photo, Inc. v. Eastman Kodak Co.,* 603 F.2d 263, 287 (2d Cir. 1979), *cert den.,* 444 US 1093 (1980). See also *California Computer Products, Inc. v. IBM,* 613 F.2d 727 (9th Cir. 1979).

(29) *Southern Pacific Communications Co. v. AT&T,* 556 F.Supp.825, 972-73 (D.D.C. 1983).

(30) *MCI Communications Corp. v. AT&T,* 708 F.2d 1081, 1132-33 (7th Cir. 1983). *cert. den.,* 104 S.Ct. 234 (1983).

(31) *U.S. v. Krasnov,* 143 F.Supp.184 (E.D. Pa. 1956), *aff'd per curiam,* 355 US 5 (1957).

(32) *U.S. v. General Electric Co.,* 272 US 476 (1926).

(33) *Dawson Chemical Co. v. Rohm and Haas Co.,* 448 US 176 (1980).

(34) *Krehl v. Baskin-Robbins Ice Cream Co.,* 664 F.2d 1348 (9th Cir. 1982); see also *Power Test Petroleum Distributors, Inc. v. Calcu Gas, Inc. and Yonkers Overpass Equities Corp., (CA-2, Jan. 1985).*

(35) *Abadir & Co. v. First Mississippi Corp.,* 651 F.2d 422 (5th Cir 1981).

(36) *Krehl v. Baskin-Robbins Ice Cream Co.,* 664 F.2d 1348 (9th Cir. 1982). See also *American Motor Inns, Inc. v. Holiday Inns, Inc.,* 521 F.2d 1230 (3d Cir. 1975).

(37) *Sealy Mattress Co. of Michigan, Inc. v. Sealy, Inc.,* (Dec. 1984).

(38) 15 U.S.C. Sec. 1115(b)(7).

SECTION IX

EMERGING ISSUES

The computer, in general, and the database, in particular, are increasingly dominant influences in all forms of marketing.

This section discusses two emerging areas in computer law. One is demographics and market segmentation. The other is computer fraud and crimes.

CHAPTER 29

MARKET SEGMENTATION— FIND YOUR CUSTOMER, NOT A PROBLEM

The strategy of market segmentation recognizes that capturing bigger pieces of new markets may be preferable to gaining a share of all available markets. This strategy is based on the view that marketing to everyone is marketing to no one. Its goal is to locate groups of potential customers who are most likely to respond to particular marketing mixes. This area is developing rapidly for marketers because of both technological and legal changes.

The strategy of market segmentation has been made possible by expanded computer capacity, which has allowed marketers to sift through a vast amount of information to obtain precise profiles.

Marketers are well aware that households are shrinking in size yet growing in number. This marks families going through demographic as well as sociological transition. A walk in an urban area can further highlight the demographic diversity of residents. In some areas you can walk three blocks and find three totally different socioeconomic conditions.

Marketers counter this with expanded database criteria so as to stay atop group trends and make predictions about the individual living in such a group.

As input, we have not only increasingly sophisticated in-house database and private information sales, but the increased output and assistance of statistical data from all levels of government, particularly the federal government. The Census Bureau is a primary demographic source, as is the Department of Labor, for example. Then there is the expanded breakdown provided by zip codes.

Market segmentation has its critics. One commentator complains that her favorite magazine will disinvite most readers by avoidance with the help of a computer system that isolates rich readers by zip code.[1]

The most significant gray area of the law impacting market segmentation is that of residence/geographic area. At present marketers can treat people in geographic groups on an economic basis provided they treat each individual in such group similarly. Rejection based on the performance of the group in the area, rather than individual performance, is permitted within the bounds of the qualifications set forth in this chapter.

There are a variety of gradations of legal exposure in the demographic calculation. A fairly routine one with little legal exposure involves evaluating areas that are likely to have customers you want to serve and that will have the potential for supporting your business. A key question—Will this neighborhood support my business (available employee talent as well as customers)?—can be answered by tapping into the demographic data on your proposed site. This is all legal. Your only legal exposure would be if you treated employees or walk-in customers differently on prohibited basis criteria.

Section II discussed whether targeted, demographic/psychographic data[2] will be available in the late 1980s and into the 1990s, or whether the concerns over privacy make obtaining such data illegal, or at least counterproductive. Here we'll look at the variety of legal issues confronting a firm that seeks to use its own database rather than solicit outside data (though the principles are analogous for internal and external data use).

For example, you've probably had a newspaper come to you with its targeted distribution scheme. A glance at it may show how the marketer is able to exclude certain ethnic groups. Is this legal in our civil rights-conscious era? Later in the day your direct mail manager proposes you target only certain types of people based on their zip codes. Can you really mail solicitations for orders that obviously exclude certain groups?

The answer is yes, with some qualifications. The civil rights laws don't generally protect against discrimination based on geographic area of residence. The result is that marketing patterns as well as housing/mortgage patterns, credit extension, and many other facts of commercial life may be predicated on race and national origin.

The Effect of Zip Codes

In most credit allocation systems, creditors take into account a number of elements; some are general standardized screening devices, but most are based on the creditors' own experience with others with whom an applicant shares certain key characteristics. Each criterion is weighed in accordance with the individual creditor's view of its importance to the credit-scoring decision.

One popular criterion today is the person's zip code. An individual's zip code is considered to be a solid predictor of creditworthiness. With the advent of the 9-digit zip code (if it ever becomes popularly accepted), census tracts will provide even more useful credit applicant segmentation.

There is no requirement that a credit card company solicit applicants from certain zip codes, nor is there any prohibition against assigning a lower point-scoring criterion to them. Credit is the lifeblood of our market economy. Geographic discrimination generally overcomes the spirit of the civil rights-related laws, too. For example, the Equal Credit Opportunity Act (ECOA) requires notification when you deny someone credit.[3] Congress set forth its rationale as follows:

> Yet this requirement fulfills a broader need: rejected credit applicants will now be able to learn where and how their credit status is deficient and this information should have a pervasive and valuable educational benefit. Instead of being told only that they do not meet a particular creditor's standards, consumers particularly should benefit from knowing, for example, that the reason for the denial is their short residence in the area, or their recent change of employment, or their already over-extended financial situation. In those cases where the creditor may have acted on misinformation or inadequate information, the statement of reasons gives the applicant a chance to rectify the mistake.[4]

A careful reading of such denial statements can sometimes lead to court challenges by motivated applicants denied credit on arguably permissible criteria having an impermissible effect. The zip code criterion, for example, is one that has come under fire. The reality is that, due to the prevailing housing patterns in the United States, races can be segmented or at least estimated by their address falling within certain zip codes. An interesting twist to this involved a case filed against Amoco Oil Company.[5]

Amoco used a complex system to evaluate credit applicants. It took into account 38 predictive and objective factors, including the applicant's occupation, level of income, and prior credit experience in the U.S. Postal zip code area where the applicant resided. Amoco testified that its scoring system assigns a low rating to zip code areas in which it has had unfavorable delinquency experience.[6]

Amoco received an application for credit from a white female typesetter living in a predominantly non-white residential area of Atlanta. The applicant was denied a credit card in part because of Amoco's previous credit experience in her immediate geographical area, based on its use of zip code criteria.

The woman argued that she was denied a credit card because of her residence. She alleged that the use of such zip code criteria was the equivalent of racial discrimination due to the segregated pattern of housing in the Atlanta area. Thus, her individual right to be evaluated on the basis of her own merit was denied.[7]

The applicant argued that a disproportionate impact of this credit policy fell on a protected class. Amoco then proved a direct and positive business purpose for the criterion (one of 38 criteria used). The ECOA states that a statistically sound system must separate creditworthy from noncreditworthy applicants at a statistically significant rate. Amoco did this. Amoco demonstrated to the court's satisfaction that its zip code ratings did not tend to adversely affect black applicants disproportionately (though not to Sen. Levin's satisfaction, as he noted that exclusively white areas were excluded from the poor credit list while significantly or predominantly black areas were included[8]). Further, this geographic factor was more difficult to falsify than information about job or income, and since the ECOA prevents creditors from asking the race of the applicant, the company had no conscious idea or ability to create de facto race discrimination in its rejections. Therefore, Amoco proved that there was no adverse intent or effect accomplished by its credit-scoring system for new applicants.

The Court criticized the plaintiff's contention as follows:

> The Court agrees with Amoco's contention that Plaintiff's proof fails to show that the zip code ratings tend to adversely affect black applicants disproportionately. Rather, it shows only that the computerized grading system taken as a whole tends to reject a disproportionate number of persons living in predominantly black areas. In other words, it is deficient for two reasons: (1) It does not test the effect of zip code as a criterion involved but rather tests the effect of the overall 38-criteria grading scheme and (2) it does not deal with either an actual applicant pool or with one which could reasonably be assumed to possess the approximate characteristics of the applicant pool.[9]

Despite its win, eventually Amoco agreed to settle by discontinuing the use of a zip code or any other geographic unit smaller than the individual's state in determining creditworthiness. It also had to pay a civil fine of $200,000 as part of the consent agreement. Eventually Amoco was prohibited from considering an applicant's zip code or place of residence in terms of any geographical unit smaller than the applicant's state.[10]

The courts and the FTC have not favored residence/geographic discrimination, yet the legislatures have not acted at the state or federal level. This debate will continue on a case-by-case basis, whether the criteria comprise store-by-store variances, telephone area codes, or other geographic variations.

A lesson to learn is that, although your in-house system evidences no intent to discriminate, you must also carefully monitor (at least annually) the quantitative effect on the various prohibited basis categories set forth in Regulation B of the ECOA. Here you'd want the advice of your counsel and a statistician (preferably experienced in demographics), who could assist you in interpreting the numbers.

Finally, if you think all this sounds complex, you're right. One side of this complexity is that it will discourage private individuals from suing, since they are unlikely to possess the type of statistical analysis that is required to bring an effects test case.[11]

Designing Effective In-House Guidelines

Do you grant credit or incidental credit under the ECOA (see Chapter 20) in your *solicitation* or acceptance of customers? Generally you are free to solicit as you wish. What about acceptance criteria? The ECOA does not require that you guarantee credit—just that you cannot specifically deny it based on one of its prohibited basis criteria.

The following criteria are illegal:

- Race;
- Sex;
- Age over 62, unless such age is a positive credit score;
- Marital status. Questions regarding relationship to head of household, type of family, and number of own children, effectively indicate a marital status;
- Employment status as to married woman/husband present, married woman with children under six years old, etc.;
- Nativity, parentage, and country of origin (prohibited basis as to possibly race or religion and definitely as to national origin); and
- Receipt of public income.

The following criteria are presently legal:

- School enrollment;
- Years of school completed;
- Children (sufficiently vague so as not to reflect on a particular marital status; however, it may not be asked of just one sex in the application);
- Residence;
- Means of transportation and place of work;
- Employment status, when neutral as to gender;
- Occupation, when neutral as to gender, etc.;
- Industry—class of workers is also valid except as to "unpaid family workers";
- Income (type of income also valid as long as you do not adversely affect those receiving public assistance);
- Income below poverty level, as long as you do not adversely affect those receiving public aid, and such persons are classified in terms of neutral gender.
- Residence lacking some or all plumbing facilities, as long as there is no reference to race. The same as to kitchen facilities, rooms, person, persons per room, value, contract rent, units in structure, year structure built, heating equipment, basement, selected equipment, year of move into unit, automobile availability, gross rent, and gross rent as percentage of income.

In your applicant-screening methodology, you should be able to demonstrate legitimate reasons for your criteria, proven by your business experience, empirically derived and statistically sound. This is to avoid charges that criteria used were a mere pretext to discriminate against persons in prohibited categories. For example, in using residence/geographic area differences, be able to show neutral criteria such as:

- your proven in-house history with applicants from such source;
- history of media response in that area correlated to current applicants.

As has been discussed, you are free to solicit whomever you choose. The problem arises when an application for *credit* arrives in-house.

Make sure there is no reference to any pretextual motive in the systems' design memos and make sure you've stressed your opposition to the use of this screening for any but legitimate business experience reasons.

Finally, be able to prove that there is no less burdensome, cost effective way for you to evaluate these applicants. The FTC is on record that it will challenge (seek to ban) a system only where it can demonstrate that the creditor could have achieved much the same result without the use of an allegedly discriminatory characteristic. One suggestion was as follows:

> In determining whether a creditor has a sound justification for using a characteristic that may have a high predictive value, but no direct relationship to an applicant's ability or willingness to repay, the Committee may wish to consider the following factors: (1) whether the pool of applicants on which the system's empirical analysis is based is sufficient in terms of size and currency to reflect accurately the creditor's true loss experience; (2) whether the creditor can demonstrate with sound statistical methodology that the elimination of the objectionable characteristics would significantly increase the creditor's loss ratio; and (3) whether the creditor has designed its application process to solicit the categories of information that correlate most directly with its customers' willingness and ability to repay.[12]

ENDNOTES

(1) Fallon, Beth, "Pricing Us Out of House and Garden," *N. Y. Daily News,* July 12, 1982, p. 28. See also Allen, Henry, "You Are Where You Live," *Washington Post,* May 2, 1982, p. H1.

(2) Paris, James A., "How to Read a Demographic Report," *American Demographics,* April 1986, p. 22 et seq. This is a good article in a "must" magazine if you care about going beyond mere statistics to learn how your current and future customers are changing. For subscription information write to them at 127 W. State St., Ithaca, NY 14580.

(3) 15 U.S.C. Sec. 1691(d)(3).

(4) 1976 U.S. Code Cong. & Admin. News, p. 406. See also *Carroll v. Exxon Co. USA,* 434 F.Supp. 557 (1977).

(5) *Claire Cherry v. Amoco Oil Co.,* 490 F.Supp. 1026 (N.D. Ga. 1980).

(6) Id., p. 1028. See also Capon, Noel, "Credit Scoring Systems: A Critical Analysis," *Journal of Marketing,* Spring 1982, p. 41.

(7) Amoco's motion to dismiss the case for Cherry's lack of standing in a race bias suit (as a white) was earlier denied, *Cherry v. Amoco Oil Co.,* 481 F.Supp. 727, 732 (1979).

(8) U.S. Cong. Rec. S1480, Feb. 9, 1979.

(9) Note 5, p. 1030-31.

(10) *In re Amoco Oil Co.,* FTC File No. 792, 3088 (4/29/80).

(11) *O'Dowd v. South Central Bell,* 729, F.2d 347 (1984) (issue of allegedly unequal treatment by race segregated by telephone area exchange).

(12) This held true even under the Pertshuk FTC, e.g., Statement of David A. Clanton Before Subcommittee on Consumer Affairs Committee on Banking, Housing and Urban Affairs, U.S. Senate 6/5/79, p. 7.

CHAPTER 30

COMPUTER FRAUD

A significant problem in "computer law" has been the absence of laws involving the theft of computer time and programs. This is only now beginning to be rectified in the legislature. The following case is illustrative.[1]

A computer operator (McGraw) for the Indianapolis Department of Planning and Zoning was provided with a terminal at his desk and was assigned a portion of the computer's information storage capacity, called a "private library," for his use in performing his duties. No other employees were authorized to use his terminal or library.

From January 21, 1980 until March 26, 1981, McGraw used a computer in a private business operated by him involving the sale of a dietary product known as NaturSlim. Employees had no authority to use the computer for private business matters. At the time he was hired by the city, he received a handbook, as do all new employees, which discloses the general prohibition against the unauthorized use of city property. Nevertheless, McGraw used the computer in his NaturSlim business for client lists, inventory control, birthdates of clients, copies of letters of solicitation he was sending to customers and potential customers, and other allied material relating to the business. He also solicited co-workers. He had been previously reprimanded for selling his product in the office *and* on office time and was ultimately discharged for substandard job performance and for his failure to stop his personal business activities during office hours.

Following his discharge, McGraw applied for and received unemployment compensation benefits, over the protest of the City. He requested a former fellow employee to obtain a printout of his business data and then to erase it from what had been his library. Instead, the printout was turned over to McGraw's former supervisor and became the basis for criminal charges.

McGraw was charged and convicted by a jury in Superior Court. Yet the trial court overrode the jury's verdict and dismissed the charges. The Court of Appeals agreed with the reasoning of the jury. The law in Indiana was clear that "A person who knowingly and intentionally exerts unauthorized control over property of another person with intent to deprive the other person of any part of its value or use, commits theft, a Class D felony."[2]

> 'Property' means anything of value; and includes a gain or advantage or anything that might reasonably be regarded as such by the beneficiary; real property, personal property, money, labor and services; intangibles, commercial instruments, written instruments concerning labor, services, or property; written instruments otherwise of value to the owner, such as a public record, deed, will, credit card, or letter of credit; a signature to a written instrument; extension of credit; trade secrets; contract rights, choses-in-action, and other interests in or claims to wealth; electricity, gas, oil, and water; captured or domestic animals, birds, and fish; food and drink; and human remains.

The Court of Appeals clearly indicated that decisions should reflect the value of information devices in an information economy:

> Inasmuch as the evidence clearly supports the fact that McGraw knowingly and intentionally used the city-leased computer for his own monetary benefit, *the only real question is whether "use" of a computer is a property subject to theft*. The sufficiency question will not be discussed separately . . . .

> . . . Computer services, leased or owned, are a part of our market economy in huge dollar amounts. Like cable television, computer services are " . . . anything of value." Computer time is "services" for which money is paid. Such services may reasonably be regarded as valuable assets to the beneficiary. Thus, computer services are property within the meaning of the definition of property subject to theft.[3]

The Supreme Court reversed the Court of Appeals. The Court found "no distinction between Defendant's use of the City's computer and use, by a mechanic, of the employer's hammer, or a stenographer's use of the employer's typewriter, for other than the employer's purposes."

The Court did not distinguish the City's loss of the defendant's time, the co-worker's time, the diversion of resources, the cost of electricity, maintenance, paper, etc., most of which was covered by a flat fee. Most importantly, the Court seemingly did not recognize its message (given without regret, reservations, or deference to future legislative action) to thousands of employees in the computer field or the precedent it was establishing—in 1985!

The dissent well summed up the context of the majority's opinion:

In the first place, intent is clearly shown in that Defendant used the City computer system for his personal business, well knowing what he was doing and well knowing that it was unauthorized . . . . Time and use are at the very core of the value of a computer system. To say that only the information stored in the computer plus the tapes and discs and perhaps the machinery involved in the computer system, are the only elements that can be measured as the value or property feature of that system, is incorrect.

I think it is irrelevant that the computer processed the data from various terminals simultaneously and the limit of its capacity was never reached by any or all of the stations, included the defendant's. It is also irrelevant that the computer service was leased to the City at a fixed charge and that the tapes or discs upon which the imparted data was stored were erasable and reusable. The fact is the City owned the computer system of all the stations including the defendant's. The time and use of that equipment at that station belonged to the City. Thus, when the defendant used the computer system, putting on data from his private business and taking it out on printouts, he was taking that which was property of the City and converting it to his own use, thereby depriving the City of its use and value. The majority says: "Thus Defendant did not deprive the City of the 'use of computers and computer services' as the information alleged that he intended to do." I disagree. I feel that is exactly what he did and I think the Court of Appeals properly found so. I therefore would deny transfer and allow the Court of Appeals opinion to stand.[4]

The courts are not the final authority here, and the legislatures are acting—as the balance of this Chapter shows. Nevertheless, computer professionals can see the rough road of persuasion they must follow in protecting their systems from being appropriated by employees for an indefinite time.

If anything is more intrusive in society today than even television, it is the computer.[5] Intrusiveness invariably spurs a reaction in a variety of ways, including new laws.

The statutory law here is new and still in the process of being enacted. Court decisions will, of course, expand or alter some of the "black-letter" law. What is apparent is that society has finally recognized that it had left a huge gap in proprietary-rights protection. The law in this field, like the technology itself, is in a state of dynamic flux.

Harmful Access and Breach of Security

As the number and use of computers expanded, so did computer fraud, abuse, and damage. However, there was the legal problem that most value appropriated was intangible. Often the owner is not even aware that data has been stolen or otherwise appropriated or compromised. The courts had a difficult time determining what, if anything, was a "thing of value" in this context.

The courts could find that computer programs themselves were property subject to theft since they possess some ascertainable value.[6] However, most crimes did not involve the convenient theft of a physical item such as a program. More likely, the thing of value was the theft of computer time or the destruction or appropriation of confidential, proprietary data, which was difficult to try under existing laws.

Owners were baffled trying to convince the courts that these crimes were not new, just the same old crimes, committed in fresh and innovative ways. Relevant also was the lawyer's lack of a "comfort zone" when dealing with this unfamiliar technology.

The owners had to translate the fact pattern into conduct that the penal statutes classify as criminal. Courts found a computer programmer was not engaged in theft of services if he or she used the employer's internal office equipment without permission when such equipment was not used in making a profit.[7]

Other courts could find a "thing of value" in an intangible. In such courts, the definition of a thing of value could be broad enough to encompass amusement, sexual intercourse (or the promise of same), the promise to reinstate an employee, the testimony of a witness, an agreement not to run in a primary election, or the contents of unpublished writings.[8]

The information economy needed to remove the ambiguity concerning what was fast becoming its richest resource—information. The states began to act. Florida led the way with the first computer-crime law in 1978.[9] Most states followed, though not with any haste.[10] Finally, Congress enacted a modern statute in 1986.

General Protections

The various state statutes generally prohibit the following:

- "unauthorized access;"
- altering or destroying data;
- stealing computer time, services or software;
- fraud or extortion involving the use of a computer; and
- willful damage to hardware (negligence beyond wear and tear is addressed in routine boilerplate).

Other issues covered (but not unanimously) by the statutes include:

- value of loss or gain respectively;
- value of the equipment;
- location (computer and/or actors and/or crime if different from computer's physical location);
- proof of injury;

- whether parents/guardian can be held liable for unanticipated acts of minor;
- statute of limitations;
- whether civil remedies may be pursued;
- duty to report suspected theft; and
- the variances in sentences imposed.

One of the early examples of a computer-fraud statute is Delaware's.[11] The text as passed on July 21, 1982, is instructive.

Section 858. Computer Fraud and Computer Misuse

(a) Whoever knowingly and willfully, directly or indirectly, without proper authorization, accesses, causes to be accessed, or attempts to access any computer, computer system, computer network, or any part of same for the purpose of

(1) devising or executing any scheme to defraud the owner thereof or any company, government, client or person who may be so defrauded, or

(2) obtaining money, property, or services for themselves or another by means of false or fraudulent pretenses, representations or promises shall be guilty of computer fraud. Computer fraud is a Class C felony.

(b) Whoever intentionally and without proper authorization, directly or indirectly accesses, alters, damages, modifies, destroys, or attempts to damage or destroy any computer system network, software, program, or data or any computer for an improper purpose shall be guilty of computer misuse. Computer misuse is a Class E felony.

(c) For purposes of this section,

(1) 'computer' means an electronic device that performs logical, arithmetic, and memory functions by the manipulation of electronic or magnetic impulses;

(2) 'computer system' means a set of connected devices including a computer and all other devices such as data input, output, or storage devices; data communication circuits; and operating system computer programs, procedures, and associated documentation that make the system capable of performing general-purpose data processing tasks;

(3) 'computer network' means a set of two or more computer systems that automatically transmit data over communication circuits connecting them;

(4) 'property' includes, but is not limited to, financial instruments, data, computer programs, and documentation associated with data and computer systems and programs and any other tangible or intangible item of value;

(5) 'services' includes, but is not limited to, providing a computer system to perform tasks;

(6) 'access' means to approach, instruct, communicate with, store data in, retrieve data from, or otherwise make use of any resources of, a computer or computer system or network;

(7) 'software' means a set of computer programs, procedures, and associated documentation concerned with the processing of data on a computer or computer system;

(8) 'data' is information, knowledge, facts, concepts, or instructions or a representation thereof which is intended to be processed, is being processed, or has been processed in a computer or computer system. Data may be in any form including, but not limited to, computer printouts, microfilm, microfiche, magnetic storage media, or punched cards, or it may be stored internally in the memory of a computer. Data is classified as intellectual property.

. . . .

Section 2738. Venue for Computer Related Crimes

A person charged with computer fraud or misuse may be prosecuted *in the county where the act was committed,* in the county where the violator had possession of any proceeds or materials used in such violation, or in the county where the principal place of business of the owner or lessee of the computer or computer system is located.

The Delaware legislation as enacted was basic to this genre. It covered the main issues and provided flexibility. As experience in the courts expanded, other states added to their laws. For example, California defined "non-malicious" access: "Any person who intentionally accesses any computer system, computer network, computer program, or data, knowing that the access is prohibited by the owner or lessee, is guilty of a misdemeanor. This paragraph shall not apply to any person acting within the scope of his or her employment."[12]

New York finally enacted its long awaited computer crime law[13] in July 1986—almost four years to the date after Delaware's original statute. It is instructive to see how the laws have broadened with the courts' experience. "Computer data", "program", "service", and similar terms were added where applicable to the penal code concerning property, service, written instrument, and business records. The text of New York's law is as follows:

Section 156.00 Offenses involving computers; definition of terms

The following definitions are applicable to this chapter except where different meanings are expressly specified;

1. "Computer" means a device or group of devices which, by manipulation of electronic, magnetic, optical or electrochemical impulses, pursuant to a computer program, can automatically perform arithmetic, logical, storage or retrieval operations with or on computer data, and includes any connected or directly related device, equipment or facility which enables

such computer to store, retrieve or communicate to or from a person, another computer or another device the results of computer operations, computer programs or computer data.

2. "Computer program" is property and means an ordered set of data representing coded instructions or statements that, when executed by computer, cause the computer to process data or direct the computer to perform one or more computer operations or both and may be in any form, including magnetic storage media, punched cards, or stored internally in the memory of the computer.

3. "Computer data" is property and means a representation of information, knowledge, facts, concepts or instructions which are being processed, or have been processed in a computer and may be in any form, including magnetic storage media, punched cards, or stored internally in the memory of the computer.

4. "Computer service" means any and all services provided by or through the facilities of any computer communication system allowing the input, output, examination, or transfer, of computer data or computer programs from one computer to another.

5. "Computer material" is property and means any computer data or computer program which:

(a) contains records of the medical history or medical treatment of an identified or readily identifiable individual or individuals. This term shall not apply to the gaining access to or duplication solely of the medical history or medical treatment records of a person by that person or by another specifically authorized by the person whose records are gained access to or duplicated; or

(b) contains records maintained by the state or any political subdivision thereof or any governmental instrumentality within the state which contains any information concerning a person, as defined in subdivision seven of section 10.00 of this chapter, which because of name, number, symbol, mark or other identifier, can be used to identify the person and which is otherwise prohibited by law from being disclosed. This term shall not apply to the gaining access to or duplication solely of records of a person by that person or by another specifically authorized by the person whose records are gained access to or duplicated; or

(c) is not and is not intended to be available to anyone other than the person or persons rightfully in possession thereof or selected persons having access thereto with his or their consent and which accords or may accord such rightful possessors an advantage over competitors or other persons who do not have knowledge or the benefit thereof.

6. "Uses a computer or computer service without authorization" means the use of a computer or computer service without the permission of, or in excess of the permission of, the owner or lessor or someone licensed or

privileged by the owner or lessor after notice to that effect to the user of the computer or computer services has been given by:

(a) giving actual notice in writing or orally to the user; or

(b) prominently posting written notice adjacent to the computer being utilized by the user; or

(c) a notice that is displayed on, printed out on or announced by the computer being utilized by the user. Proof that the computer is programmed to automatically display, print or announce such notice or a notice prohibiting copying, reproduction or duplication shall be presumptive evidence that notice was displayed, printed out or announced.

7. "Felony" as used in this article means any felony defined in the laws of this state or any offense defined in the laws of any other jurisdiction for which a sentence to a term of imprisonment in excess of one year is authorized in this state.

Section 156.05 Unauthorized use of a computer

A person is guilty of unauthorized use of a computer when he knowingly uses or causes to be used a computer or computer service without authorization and the computer utilized is equipped or programmed with any device or coding system, a function of which is to prevent the unauthorized use of said computer or computer system.

Unauthorized use of a computer is a class A misdemeanor.

Section 156.10 Computer trespass

A person is guilty of computer trespass when he knowingly uses or causes to be used a computer or computer service without authorization and:

1. he does so with an intent to commit or attempt to commit or further the commission of any felony; or

2. he thereby knowingly gains access to computer material.

Computer trespass is a class E felony.

Section 156.20 Computer tampering in the second degree

A person is guilty of computer tampering in the second degree when he uses or causes to be used a computer or computer service and having no right to do so he intentionally alters in any manner or destroys computer data or a computer program of another person.

Computer tampering in the second degree is a class A misdemeanor.

Section 156.25 Computer tampering in the first degree

A person is guilty of computer tampering in the first degree when he commits the crime of computer tampering in the second degree and:

1. he does so with an intent to commit or attempt to commit or further the commission of any felony; or

2. he has been previously convicted of any crime under this article or subdivision ten of section 165.15 of this chapter; or

3. he intentionally alters in any manner or destroys computer material; or

4. he intentionally alters in any manner or destroys computer data or a computer program in an amount exceeding one thousand dollars.

Computer tampering in the first degree is a class E felony.

Section 156.30 Unlawful duplication of computer related material

A person is guilty of unlawful duplication of computer related material when having no right to do so, he copies, reproduces or duplicates in any manner:

1. any computer data or computer program and thereby intentionally and wrongfully deprives or appropriates from an owner thereof an economic value or benefit in excess of two thousand five hundred dollars; or

2. any computer data or computer program with an intent to commit or attempt to commit or further the commission of any felony.

Unlawful duplication of computer related material is a class E felony.

Section 156.35 Criminal possession of computer related material

A person is guilty of criminal possession of computer related material when having no right to do so, he knowingly possesses, in any form, any copy, reproduction or duplicate of any computer data or computer program which was copied, reproduced or duplicated in violation of section 156.30 of this article, with intent to benefit himself or a person other than an owner thereof.

Criminal possession of computer related material is a class E felony.

Section 156.50 Offenses involving computer; defenses

In any prosecution:

1. under section 156.50 or 156.10 of this article, it shall be a defense that the defendant had reasonable grounds to believe that he had authorization to use the computer;

2. under section 156.20 or 156.25 of this article it shall be a defense that the defendant had reasonable grounds to believe that he had the right to alter in any manner or destroy the computer data or the computer program;

3. under section 156.30 of this article it shall be a defense that the defendant had reasonable grounds to believe that he had the right to copy, reproduce or duplicate in any manner the computer data or the computer program.

. . . .

Section 4.   Section 165.15 of such law is amended by adding a new subdivision ten to read as follows:

10. With intent to avoid payment by himself or another person of the lawful charge for use of any computer or computer service which is provided for a charge or compensation he uses, causes to be used or attempts to use a computer or computer service and avoids or attempts to avoid payment therefor. In any prosecution under this subdivision proof that a person overcame or attempted to overcome any device or coding system a function of which is to prevent the unauthorized use of said computer or computer service shall be presumptive evidence of an intent to avoid payment for the computer or computer service.

. . . .

Section 7.   Section 20.60 of the criminal procedure law is amended by adding a new subdivision three to read as follows:

3. A person who causes by any means the use of a computer or computer service in one jurisdiction from another jurisdiction is deemed to have personally used the computer or computer service in each jurisdiction.

Section 8.   Subdivision one of section 240.20 of such law is amended by adding a new paragraph (j) to read as follows:

(j) In any prosecution under penal law section 156.05 or 156.10, the time, place and manner of notice is given pursuant to subdivision six of section 156.00 of such law.

Section 9.   Such law is amended by adding a new section 250.30 to read as follows:

Section 250.30 Notice of defenses in offenses involving computers

1. In any prosecution in which the defendant seeks to invoke any of the defenses specified in section 156.50 of the penal law, the defendant must within forty-five days after arraignment and not less than twenty days before the commencement of the trial serve upon the people and file with the court a written notice of his intention to present such defense.

For good cause shown, the court may extend the period for service of the notice.

2. The notice served must specify the subdivision or subdivisions upon which the defendant relies and must also state the reasonable grounds that led the defendant to believe that he had the authorization required by the statute or the right required by the statute to engage in such conduct.

3. If at the trial the defendant seeks to invoke any of the defenses specified in section 156.50 of the penal law without having served the notice as required, or seeks to invoke a subdivision of a ground not specified in the notice, the court may exclude any testimony or evidence in regard to the defense, or any subdivision or ground, not noticed. The court may in its discretion, for good cause shown, receive such testimony or evidence, but before doing so, it may, upon application of the people, grant an adjournment."

Problems Remain

The laws are flooding in—all within the last decade, and most within the last five years. However, there is no comparable computer literacy increase among prosecutors and judges. Because technology has outstripped the natural skills of the average state's attorney many experts in the field instruct their clients to be prepared to lend in-house legal and technical support to the public legal authorities.[14] In-house experts must be sensitized to the problems a public authority can have in detection or obtaining a warrant. In the interim, counsel should investigate computer-crime insurance, which is now offered by a few carriers. Because the laws are uncertain and their administration and enforcement is in a learning stage, the boilerplate is necessarily restrictive.

One in-house option for larger computer systems is to employ software locks to prevent at least certain unauthorized use. These locks establish an expiration date after which the program will no longer operate. Such lock must be carefully and unambiguously disclosed in your contract to prevent an accidental trigger-loss of a major system, which could cost the software owner/licensor a considerable amount in a damage suit.

Other protections involve basic contractual agreements prohibiting or carefully limiting duplication or disassembly, reverse-compiling, or otherwise tampering with software. Where possible, you can "seed" dummy names, errors, etc. that will be disclosed if use extends beyond a certain specified termination date.

The federal government enacted its long overdue "Electronic Communications Privacy Act,"[15] which extended the "Wire Communications Interception and Interception of Oral Communications Act."

Expanded Federal Law

Congress, in an attempt to secure the privacy of certain communications between people, had enacted the Federal Wiretap Law,[16] which prohibits the willful interception or willful use of "wire" or "oral" communications. "Wire communication" was defined as:

> . . . any communication made in whole or in part through the use of facilities for the transmission of communications by the aid of wire, cable, or other like connection between the point of origin and the point of reception furnished or operated by any person engaged as a common carrier in providing or operating such facilities for the transmission of interstate or foreign communications.[17]

"Oral communication" was defined as:

> . . . any oral communication uttered by a person exhibiting an expectation that such communication is not subject to interception under circumstances justifying such expectation.[18]

Congress prohibited the willful interception, willful disclosure, or willful use of any wire or oral communications.[19] The problem for computer systems owners is that they could not adequately be fitted into these protections. Whereas computer and electronic technologies advanced, the federal law stayed static.

Congress corrected this by its creation of an expanded and adaptable definition of electronic communication:

> . . . 'electronic communication' means any transfer of signs, signals, writing, images, sounds, data, or intelligence of any nature transmitted in whole or in part by a wire, radio, electromagnetic, photoelectronic or photo-optical system that affects interstate or foreign commerce, but does *not* include:
>
> (A) the radio portion of a cordless telephone communication that is transmitted between the cordless telephone handset and the base unit;
>
> (B) any wire or oral communication;
>
> (C) any communication made through a tone-only paging device; or
>
> (D) any communication from a tracking device (as defined in section 3117 of this title).[20]

No longer must the court attempt to pigeonhole new communication forms into the prior oral and wire communications categories. Further broadening is added by the definition of 'electronic communications system' which means:

> . . . any wire, radio, electromagnetic, photo-optical or photoelectric facilities for the transmission of electronic communications, and any computer facilities or related electronic equipment for the electronic storage of such communications;[21]

and 'electronic storage' which means:

. . . (A) any temporary, intermediate storage of a wire or electronic communication incidental to the electronic transmission thereof; and

(B) any storage of such communication by an electronic communication service for purposes of backup protection of such communications.[22]

To underscore that the *inadvertent* reception of a protected communication is not a crime, the required criminal state of mind has been modified from willful to intentional. Injunctions are now permitted, and prison terms of up to five years or fines or both are imposed.[23]

The new Title II concerns itself with "Stored Wire and Electronic Communications and Transactional Records Access." Unlawful access to stored communications is as follows:

. . . Except as provided in subsection (c) of this section, whoever-

(1) intentionally accesses without authorization a facility through which an electronic communication service is provided; or

(2) intentionally exceeds an authorization to access that facility; and thereby obtains, alters, or prevents authorized access to a wire or electronic communication while it is in electronic storage in such system shall be punished as provided in subsection (b) of this section.[24]

Punishments set forth in (b) include fines of up to $250,000 and imprisonment.[25]

Other issues addressed by the law include disclosure requirements for government access[26] and civil action.[27] The latter provides a right of civil enforcement to protect one's interest. Of specific interest as to government access is the requirement of backup preservation of data. Specifically:

(1) A governmental entity acting under section 2703(b) (2) may include in its subpoena or court order a requirement that the service provider to whom the request is directed create a backup copy of the contents of the electronic communications sought in order to preserve those communications. Without notifying the subscriber or customer of such subpoena or court order, such service provider shall create such backup copy as soon as practicable consistent with its regular business practices and shall confirm to the governmental entity that such backup copy has been made. Such backup copy shall be created within two business days after receipt by the service provider of the subpoena or court order.

(2) Notice to the subscriber or customer shall be made by the governmental entity within three days after receipt of such confirmation, unless such notice is delayed pursuant to section 2705(a).

(3) The service provider shall not destroy such backup copy until the later of-

(A) the delivery of the information; or

(B) the resolution of any proceedings (including appeals of any proceeding) concerning the government's subpoena or court order.[28]

To quote Congress:

A Summary of the Electronic Communications Privacy Act

The Electronic Communications Privacy Act amends Title III of the Omnibus Crime Control and Safe Streets Act of 1968—the federal wiretap law—to protect against the unauthorized interception of electronic communications. The bill amends the 1968 law to update and clarify federal privacy protections and standards in light of dramatic changes in new computer and telecommunications technologies. . . . . .

Currently, Title III covers only voice communications. The bill expands coverage to include video and data communications.

Currently, Title III covers only common carrier communications. The bill eliminates that restriction since private carriers and common carriers perform so many of the same functions today that the distinction no longer serves to justify a different privacy standard.

At the request of the Justice Department, the bill continues to distinguish between electronic communications (data and video) and wire or oral communications (voice) for purposes of some of the procedural restrictions currently contained in Title III. For example, court authorization for the interception of a wire or oral communication may only be issued to investigate certain crimes specified in Title III. An interception of an electronic communication pursuant to court order may be utilized during the investigation of any federal felony.

Wire communications in storage, like voice mail, remain wire communications. . . . .

Title II of the bill creates parallel privacy protection for the unauthorized access to the computers of an electronic communications system, if information is obtained or altered. It does little good to prohibit the unauthorized interception of information while it is being transmitted, if similar protection is not afforded to the information while it is being stored for later forwarding.

The bill establishes criminal penalties for any person who intentionally accesses without authorization a computer through which an electronic communication service is provided and obtains, alters or prevents authorized access to a stored electronic communication. The offense is punished as a felony if committed for purposes of commercial advantage, malicious destruction or damage, or private commercial gain; otherwise it is punished as a petty offense.

Providers of electronic communication services to the public and providers of remote computing services to the public are prohibited from intentionally divulging the contents of communications contained in their systems except under circumstances specified in the bill.

The contents of messages contained in electronic storage of electronic communications systems which have been in storage for 180 days or less may be obtained by a government entity from the provider of the system only pursuant to a warrant issued under the Federal Rules of Criminal Procedure or equivalent state warrant.

The content of messages stored more than 180 days and the contents of certain records stored by providers of remote computer processing services may be obtained from the provider of the service without notice to the subscriber if the government obtains a warrant under the Federal Rules of Criminal Procedure or with notice to the customer pursuant to an administrative subpoena, a grand jury subpoena, or a court order based on a showing that there is reason to believe that the contents of the communication are relevant to a legitimate law enforcement inquiry. Provisions for delay in notice are also included.

An electronic communications or remote computing service provider may disclose to a non-governmental entity customer information like mailing lists, but not the contents of the communication. Disclosure of such information to the government is required, but only when the government obtains a court order, warrant, subpoena, or customer consent.

At the FCC's request, a section was added to the bill to address problems highlighted by the recent Captain Midnight incident. The bill increases penalties for the intentional or malicious interference with satellite transmissions. . . .

The penalty structure under the Grassley and Simon amendments is:

A first offender will be subject to a suit by the federal government for injunctive relief. If injunctive relief is granted, the court may use whatever means in its authority, including civil and criminal contempt, to enforce that injunction. It must impose a $500 civil fine. In addition, the penalty for second and subsequent offenses is a $500 fine in a suit brought by the government.

Under the private civil damages provisions of the bill, the first offender may be sued for the greater of actual damages or statutory damages of $50 to $500. The second offender is subject to suit for the greater of actual damages or statutory damages of $100 to $1000. Third and subsequent offenders are subject to full civil damages under the bill.

The bill creates a statutory framework for the authorization and issuance of an order for a pen register or a trap and trace device based on a finding that such installation and use is relevant to an on-going criminal investigation.[29]

ENDNOTES

(1) *State v. McGraw,* 459 N.E.2d 61, 62 (Ind. App. 2 Dist. 1984); and *State v. McGraw,* 480 N.E.2d 552, 553 (Ind 1985).

(2) Id., 459 N.E.2d 63.

(3) Id., 459 N.E.2d 64-65.

(4) Id., 480 N.E.2d 555.

(5) Computers may be defined as systems of machines that process information in the form of letters, numbers, and other symbols, that are self-directing within predetermined limits. (16 *Am. Jur. Proof of Facts* 276.)

(6) See, e.g., *Harrioth v. State,* 402 SW 906, 18 ALR 3d 1113 (1966 Tex Crim.).

(7) *People v. Weg,* 113 Misc.2d 1017, 450 N.Y.S.2d 957 (N.Y. City Crim. Ct. 1982).

(8) *U.S. v. Gerard,* 601 F.2d 69, 71, *cert. den.,* 444 US 871 (1979). See also *U.S. v. Kelly,* 507 F.Supp. 495 (E.D.Pa. 1981) (convicted of mail fraud instead of computer services theft); *U.S. v. Jeter,* 775 F.2d 670 (1985) (grand jury information as a thing of value); *U.S. v. Schwartz,* 785 F2d 673 (9th 1986) and *Edwards v. Bardwell,* 632 F.Supp. 584 (M.D. La. 1986).

(9) Fla. Stat. Sec. 815.02 (1983).

(10) State computer crime laws—dates of enactment and cites:

Alaska - 1984 - *Alaska Statutes* Sec. 11.46.140 et seq. (1984).

Arizona - 1978 - *Ariz. Rev. Stat. Ann.* Sec. 13.2301 (Supp. 1984-85).

California - 1979 - *California Penal Code* Sec. 502 (West Supp. 1984).

Colorado - 1979 - *Colo. Rev. Stat. Ann.* Sec. 18.5.5-101 (Supp. 1984).

Connecticut - 1983 - *Conn. Gen. Stat.* Sec 53a-250 to 261 (1983).

Delaware - 1984 - *Del. Code Ann.* Tit. 11, Sec. 931, 939 (1984).

Florida - 1978 - *Fla. Stat.* Sec. 815.01 to .07 (West Supp. 1984).

Georgia - 1981 - *Ga. Code* Sec. 16-9-90, 95 (1984).

Idaho - 1984 - *Idaho Code* Sec. 18-2201 to 2202 (1984).

Illinois - 1979 - *Ill. Rev. Stat.* Ch. 38, Sec.16-9 (Smith-Hurd Supp. 1984-85).

Iowa - 1984 - *Iowa Code Ann.* Sec. 761A.1 to .16 (West 1984).

Kentucky - 1984 - *Ky. Rev. Stat.* Sec. 434.480-.860 (Supp. 1984).

Louisiana - 1984 - *La. Rev. Stat. Ann.* Sec. 14.73.1-.5 (West Supp. 1984).

Maine - 1983 - *Me. Rev. Stat. Ann.* Tit. 17-A, Sec. 357 (1983).

Maryland - 1984 - *Md. Crim. Law Code Ann.* Art. 27, Sec. 146 (1984).

Massachusetts - 1984 - *Mass. Gen. Laws Ann.* Ch. 266, Sec. 30 (West Supp. 1984-85).

Michigan - 1983 - *Mich. Comp. Laws Ann.* Sec. 752.791-.797 (West Supp. 1984-85).

Minnesota - 1982 - *Minn. Stat. Ann.* Sec. 609.87-.89 (West Supp. 1985).

Missouri - 1982 - *Mo. Rev. Stat.* Sec. 569.083-.089 (Vernon Supp. 1985).

Montana - 1981 - *Mont. Code Ann.* Sec. 45-2-101, 54 (k)(69)(a)(iii), 45-6-310-311 (1983).

New Jersey - 1984 - *N.J. Stat. Ann.* Sec. 38A-1 to -6 (West Supp. 1984-85).

New Mexico - 1979 - *N.M. Stat. Ann.* Sec. 30-16A-1 et seq. (1984).

New York - 1986 - *Penal Law* Art. 156.00-156.50 (1986).

Nevada - 1983 - *Nev. Rev. Stat.* Sec. 205.473 to .477 (1983).

North Carolina - 1980 - *N.C. Gen. Stat.* Sec. 14-453 (1983).

North Dakota - 1985 - *N.D. Cent. Code* 12.1.06 (1985).

Ohio - 1983 - *Ohio Rev. Code Ann.* Sec. 2901.01(J), 2913.01(L) (Page Supp. 1983).

Pennsylvania - 1983 - *Pa. Stat. Ann.* Tit. 18, Sec. 3933 (Purdon Supp. 1984-85).

Rhode Island - 1979 - *R.I. Gen. Laws* Sec. 11-52-1 to 5 (Supp. 1984).

South Carolina - 1984 - *S.C. Code Ann.* Sec. 16-16-10 to -40 (Law Co. 1985).

Tennessee - 1983 - *Tenn. Code Ann.* Sec. 39-3-1401 (Supp. 1984).

Texas - 1985 - *Texas Penal Code Ann.* Sec. 33.01-.02 (Vernon Supp. 1985).

Utah - 1979 - *Utah Code Ann.* Sec. 76-6-701-704 (Supp. 1983).

Virginia - 1984 - *Va. Code* Sec. 18.2-152.1 to .152.14 (1984).

Wisconsin - 1982 - *Wis. Stat. Ann.* Sec. 843.70 (West Supp. 1984-85).

Washington - 1984 - *Wash. Rev. Code* Sec. 9A.56.010 (Supp. 1984-85).

(11) Chapter 5, Title 11 *Delaware Code* Sec. 858 and 2738 (1984).

(12) *Cal. Penal Code* Sec. 502(d)(2) (West 1985).

(13) S.B. 5743-B amending penal law to add new Article 156 (1986).

(14) Cates, Homer W., CPP, "Computer Crime Law: A Review of State Statutes," *Data Processing and Communications Security,* Vol. 10 No. 2 p. 19-21 (1986).

(15) U.S. H.R. 4952 Amending Title 18 U.S.C. to add Sec. 2701 to 2710. For a related case under the original act see *Edwards v. Bardwell,* 632 F.Supp. 584 (M.D. La. 1986).

(16) 18 U.S.C. Sec. 2511.

(17) 18 U.S.C. Sec. 2510(1).

(18) 18 U.S.C. Sec. 2510(2).

(19) 18 U.S.C. Sec. 2511(1).

(20) 18 U.S.C. Sec. 2510(12).

(21) 18 U.S.C. Sec. 2510(14).

(22) 18 U.S.C. Sec. 2510(17).

(23) 18 U.S.C. Sec. 2511(4)(a) and 2520(b).

(24) 18 U.S.C. Sec. 2701(a).

(25) 18 U.S.C. Sec. 2701(b).

(26) 18 U.S.C. Sec. 2703.

(27) 18 U.S.C. Sec. 2707.

(28) 18 U.S.C. Sec. 2704(a).

(29) Congressional Record—S14450-14451, October 1, 1986.

GLOSSARY OF TERMS

These terms are defined to facilitate general reading of the text. They should not be considered a substitute for legal advice in any specific situation.

Acceleration — the shortening of the time for the performance of a contract or the payment of a note by the operation of some provision in the contract or note itself.

Acceptance — a manifestation of assent to the terms of an offer in the manner required or requested by the offer. The acceptance of an offer is the assent to an offer, which is requisite to the formation of a contract. It is either express or evidenced by circumstances from which such assent may be implied.

Act of God (Force Majeure) — an occurrence resulting exclusively from natural forces, which could not have been prevented or whose effects could not have been avoided by care or foresight.

Administrative Agencies — created by the state and federal legislative branches to carry out the laws they enact through rule implementation, oversight, and general administration.

Advertising — any paid form of nonpersonal presentation made by an identified sponsor through a mass communication medium on behalf of goods, services, or ideas.

Advertising Medium — the vehicle (e.g., newspaper or direct mail) used to carry the advertising message from the sender to the intended receiver.

Affidavit of Performance — a signed or notarized form sent by a television station to an advertiser or agency indicating what spots ran and when.

Agency — the relationship that results from the consent by one person (the principal) to another (the agent) that the latter will act on the principal's behalf in dealing with a third party.

Agent — one authorized to transact business for another (principal) within the scope of a defined authority.

Allowances — compensation (e.g., space or price discounts) by a wholesaler or manufacturer for services such as advertising or in-store point-of-purchase displays provided by a retailer or wholesaler. Such allowances must be generally available to all qualified customers on a proportionately equal basis.

Amicus Curiae Brief — a brief filed in a case by someone who is not a party to that case. Amicus curiae means "a friend of the court."

Antitrust Improvements Act of 1976 — empowered attorneys general at the state level to bring suit on behalf of injured consumers in their states.

Antitrust Law — the general body of law that regulates or prohibits combinations, conspiracies, agreements, monopolies, and certain distribution practices that restrain free trade.

Antitrust Procedures and Penalties Act of 1974 — an act increasing the fines for violation of Sherman Act provisions to $100,000 for individuals and to $10 million for corporations. It also made violation of the law a felony rather than a misdemeanor, with a maximum jail sentence of three years.

Arbitration — a proceeding used as a substitute for the more formal trial. An arbitrator hears a dispute and decides which person should prevail.

Attorney-in-Fact — a person who is authorized by his or her principal, either for some particular purpose, or to do a particular act, not of a legal character.

Attachment — a legal procedure through which the property of a debtor is taken.

Bad Faith — the term imports a person's actual intent to mislead or deceive another; an intent to take an unfair and unethical advantage of another.

Bailment — the transfer of the possession of personal property, in trust to another, without the transfer of title in which it is understood that the personal property is to be returned or duly accounted for to the owner after some period of time has elapsed or some particular purpose has been accomplished, or kept until the bailor reclaims it.

Bait and Switch — a bait offer is an alluring but insincere offer to sell a product or service that the seller does not intend to sell. Its primary purpose is to switch consumers from the advertised bait product or service to sell something else, usually at a higher price or on a basis more advantageous to the seller. Its secondary purpose is to increase store traffic (see Trading Up).

Bankruptcy — the condition of one lacking sufficient assets to pay due debts. The court will relieve the debts by dividing the remaining assets among creditors. There are two types:

> (a) *Involuntary Bankruptcy* - creditors file a petition to have a debtor declared bankrupt.

> (b) *Voluntary Bankruptcy* - a debtor's attempt to seek protection of bankruptcy laws on its own volition.

Bill of Lading — a written acknowledgment of the receipt of goods to be transported to a designated place and delivery to a named person or to his or her order.

Bill of Sale — a written agreement by which one person assigns or transfers interests or rights in personal property to another.

Bona Fide Prices — prices that under the Federal Trade Commission Act must represent the prices of actual purchases for a reasonable period of time in the same geographic area before they can be referred to in a sale that advertises price comparisons.

Boycott — an agreement or conspiracy to restrain or prevent the carrying on of a business by preventing or excluding potential competitors, suppliers, customers, or others from freely engaging in business or desired transactions with other businesses.

Brand — the name or symbol used to identify and differentiate a product or service from competing products or services.

Broker (Merchandise Agent) — a wholesaler who does not have title to the merchandise he or she sells. The broker is an agent who bargains or carries on negotiations on behalf of the principal as an intermediary between the latter and third persons in transacting business relative to the acquisition of contractual rights, or to the sale or purchase of property the custody of which is not entrusted to him or her for the purpose of discharging the agency.

Burden of Proof — the duty of a party to substantiate an allegation or issue to avoid dismissal of that issue early in the trial or in order to convince the trier of facts as to the truth of the claim and therefore win at trial.

Cable Television — television service with large antennae positioned to receive television broadcasts, amplify the signals and deliver them, via coaxial cable, to subscribers; originally designed to be a service to those unable to obtain adequate television reception. Increasingly cable systems are being used to deliver a wide selection of stations, features, and services (also referred to as CATV-Community Antenna Television).

Capacity/Legal — free from all natural or legal impediments that would bar competence to contract. (Minors, the insane, and others are considered competent to enter only into agreements for food, clothing, shelter, and medical care.)

Cartel — an association of producers that attempts to control a market by limiting output and dividing market shares among its members.

Case Law — the law extracted from decided cases.

Cash Discount — a reduction in price granted to buyers who pay cash.

Catalog Showroom — a system of retailing in which stock is sold from a nearby warehouse and the retail store is used to display sample merchandise only.

Cause of Action — a legal claim or complaint for which a party may seek redress in a court.

Caveat Emptor — literally, "Let the buyer beware." The buyer purchases at his or her peril, and there are no warranties, either express or implied, made by the seller.

Certiorari — a procedure whereby a higher court is given the opportunity to review a decision by a lower court. Most references herein are to the U.S. Supreme Court.

Channel of Distribution — the sequence of marketing agencies (such as wholesalers and retailers) through which a product passes on its way from the producer to the final user.

Chattel — an item of tangible personal property, that is, property other than land that has a physical existence. Examples include cars, books, and clothing.

C.I.F. — an abbreviation for cost, insurance, and freight; used in mercantile transactions, especially in import transactions.

Class Action — a lawsuit or legal action brought on behalf of a large number of people with similar claims.

Clayton Act of 1914 — an act amending the Sherman Antitrust Act, clearing up wording and forbidding specific actions that Congress saw as leading to monopoly.

C.O.D. (Cash on Delivery) — when goods are delivered to a carrier in this type of shipment, the carrier must not deliver without receiving payment of the amount due.

Collateral — a valuable item or items that can be seized by a lender should the borrower fail to repay a loan.

Collusion — a secret cooperation, usually in fraud or in illegal activities between two or more persons, to accomplish a common result, usually to injure a third party.

Commercial Law — rules governing business professionals.

Common Carrier — a firm obligated by the terms of a government license to transport goods under stated conditions for all of the public who wish to employ its services (see Contract Carrier).

Common Law — judge-made law based on precedents; contrasted with statutory law.

Comparative Pricing — pricing strategy that involves comparing the advertised low price with "normal" list prices in order to give the impression of overall discount prices.

Conditional Sale — the term is most frequently applied to a sale wherein the seller reserves the title to the goods, though the item is delivered to the buyer, until the purchase price is paid in full.

Consideration — bargained-for benefit or detriment which, given in exchange for a promise, makes the promise enforceable.

Consignment — a bailment for sale. Merchandise delivered or made available to an agent, with title or ownership to the goods remaining with the supplier. The cosignee does not undertake the obligation to sell or pay for the goods.

Conspiracy — a criminal partnership in which two or more people combine formally or informally to accomplish an unlawful act. In a price-fixing situation, there must be express or circumstantial proof that a combination was formed for the purpose of fixing prices and that it caused them to be fixed or contributed to that result.

Contest — a sales promotion device that offers prizes as a reward for some form of specific creativity or skill of the entrants.

Contract — enforceable agreement between two or more competent parties based on consideration to do or not do some particular legal thing.

Contract Carrier — a transportation company that provides its services to one or more shippers on an individual contract basis, usually does not operate on a regular schedule, and has rates more easily adapted to specific situations than those of common carriers (see Common Carrier).

Cooling-Off Period — the period (a certain number of business days) in which the buyer has the right to cancel after a sale. The buyer must receive written notification of this right and often must receive a copy of the contract or sales receipt.

Cooperative Advertising — advertising in which the supplier reimburses an agreed-on portion of buyer's advertising expenses for a certain product or service.

Copyright — a copyright gives its owner the exclusive right to reproduce ("copy"), sell, or adapt the work he or she has created for a limited time after the work has been fixed in a tangible medium.

Corporation — an artificial being, invisible, intangible and existing only in contemplation of law. It is exclusively the work of the law.

Coupon — a sales promotion certificate that entitles the holder to either a specified saving on a product or service or a cash refund.

Credit — deferred time to pay debt. May involve finance charges and/or installment payments.

Credit Bureau — an organization that collects credit information for dissemination to members or subscribers on request. Credit bureaus are sometimes cooperatives, owned by the users of the service.

Damages — monetary recovery of non-breaching party that is intended to put such party in as good a position as if the contract had been performed. Particular categories of "damages" are as follows:

> (a) *compensatory* — damages that will compensate a party for direct losses due to an injury suffered.

> (b) *consequential* — damages that are produced only with the concurrence of some other event attributable to the same origin or cause.

> (c) *liquidated* — a sum of money that the parties to a contract agree in advance will be paid to either as damages if the other is guilty of a breach of the contract.

> (d) *nominal* — damages that are recoverable where a legal right is to be vindicated against an invasion that has produced no actual present loss.

> (e) *punitive* — damages intended to punish a wrongdoer rather than simply to compensate the victim.

> (f) *special* — actual damages that would not necessarily flow from an injury but, because of special circumstances, do.

> (g) *treble* — damages given by statute in certain cases, consisting of the single damages found by the jury actually tripled in amount pursuant to that statute.

Debtor — a person who owes another anything, or who is under obligation, arising from express agreement, implication of law, or the principles of natural justice, to render and pay a sum of money to another.

Deceit — a tort involving intentional misrepresentation or cheating by means of some device.

Demographic Segmentation — selecting target markets on the basis of statistical information such as age, sex, income, or a geographical unit such as a zip code.

Direct Mail — mailing of advertising solicitations directly to consumers using the U.S. Postal Service or private direct-delivery service. The term may refer to a mail order firm selling only by mail and having no retail outlets as well as to a retail store that sells by mail.

Direct Marketing — a system in which a seller builds and maintains its own database of customers and uses a variety of media to communicate directly with those customers.

Direct-Response List — a list of persons who answered a direct-response offer of another firm. This list may be purchased from the firm directly or through a broker for a one-time promotion.

Disparagement — a statement about a competitor's goods that is deceptive or otherwise untrue and is asserted to influence the public not to buy such goods.

Distribution Center — a facility that resembles a private warehouse but also serves as a command post for moving products to customers.

Distribution Channel — route taken by a product as it passes from the original owner or maker to the ultimate consumer.

Divestiture — in antitrust law, an order by the court to a defendant to sell or otherwise dispose of property, securities, or other assets.

Draft — a written order drawn on one person by another, requesting him to pay money to a designated third person. A bill of exchange payable on demand.

Dual Distribution — use of two channels to market a product.

Due Process — a constitutional principle that requires that government actions not be arbitrary or capricious. Its concern is with establishing fundamental procedural fairness in our system of government.

Duress — a wrongful act or threat that overcomes a person's free will.

Endorsement — a product recommendation, usually paid for, given by a prominent celebrity or consumer targeted to the market segment(s) the advertiser is attempting to reach.

Escheat — the statutory reversion of property to the state after a specified period of time if the property holder or claimant cannot be located or if the property is abandoned.

Exclusive Distribution — a strategy used to maintain prestige, image, and premium prices by granting exclusive rights to a wholesaler or retailer to sell in one geographic region.

Executory — not yet executed; not yet fully performed, completed, fulfilled, or carried out; to be performed wholly or in part.

Express Warranty — actual statement made by the seller in reference to a material fact about the product.

Fair Packaging and Labeling Act — a truth-in-labeling law requiring manufacturers to state the contents of the package, who made it, and how much it contains.

Fair Trade Agreement — an agreement by which the manufacturer fixes the price at which the wholesaler or retailer can legally resell the product. Such an agreement, if otherwise lawful, binds not only the signers but the nonsigners of the contract.

Federal Communications Commission — the regulatory body with jurisdiction over the radio, TV, telephone, and telegraph industries.

Federal Trade Commission Act of 1914 — an act declaring that "unfair methods of competition in commerce are . . . illegal." In addition, it set up a five-member commission empowered to define, detect, and enforce compliance with this and the Clayton Act.

Fiduciary — one who holds goods in trust for another or one who holds a position of trust and confidence.

Flesch Formula — a means to check a communication's efficiency and understandability. Readability of advertising copy is assessed by determining the average number of syllables per 100 words, number of words per sentence, and other factors. The Flesch formula compares the results with predetermined norms for the target audience.

F.O.B. — an abbreviation for "free on board." A provision of the contract specifying at which point shipping costs are to be paid by the buyer.

Food and Drug Administration — the federal agency that has authority over the advertising, labeling, packaging, and branding of packaged foods and therapeutic devices.

Franchise — in marketing, a contract right or license granted by a franchisor for compensation, usually to multiple franchisees, to do business under a certain name legally controlled by the franchisor and usually involving specific territorial, field-of-use, and product-quality traits. A contractual relationship establishing a means of marketing goods or services giving certain elements of control to the supplier (franchisor) in return for the right of the franchisee to use the supplier's trade name or trademark, usually in a specific marketing area.

Fraud — a deliberate misrepresentation or nondisclosure of a material fact, made with the intent that the other party will rely on it, and in fact the party to whom the statement is made does rely on it to his or her detriment.

Free — a product or service that is an unconditional gift or, when a purchase is required, all the conditions to the receipt and retention of the product or service offered are clearly and conspicuously set forth in immediate conjunction with the first use of the word "free," leaving no reasonable probability that the terms of the offer will be misunderstood.

Frequency — the average number of times each household in the target population is exposed to a given ad message.

FTC Rules and Guidelines — refers to rules and guidelines adopted by the Federal Trade Commission. The terms "rules" and "guidelines" are not synonymous. Trade regulation rules define specifically which acts or practices are unfair or deceptive. Industry guides do not have the force of substantive law. However, the guides do advise the industry how the FTC will interpret the law. A violation of a guide may lead the FTC to issue a complaint.

Full-Service Agency — an advertising agency that has a full range of services for research and development.

Full Warranty — the Magnuson-Moss Act requires certain consumer products to be labeled as having either a full or limited warranty. Products with a full warranty must meet certain requirements specified in the act.

Functional Discounts — the means by which intermediaries are compensated for reselling to subsequent distributors in the distribution channel.

Fungible Goods — goods composed of units that are considered commercially alike, for example, a particular grade of wheat.

Game — in marketing use, a sales promotion device that requires no skill on the part of the participants, since pure chance determines the winner (see Contest).

Horizontal Agreements — agreements between competitors at the same level of market structure (for example, between two products or retail chains).

Horizontal Merger — the acquisition of one company by another company producing the same product and selling it in the same geographic market.

Horizontal Territorial Division of Markets — an agreement by which competitors on the same production or distribution level restrict their competitive activity to an agreed-on area.

Implied Contract — an agreement of the parties arrived at from their acts and conduct viewed in light of surrounding circumstances and not from spoken or written words.

Implied Warranty — an unwritten warranty that is created automatically when an item is sold: The item must perform the way it is supposed to.

Indemnity — a contractual relationship wherein one party agrees to reimburse the other party for losses or damages that may arise from that party's actions.

Independent Contractor — one who contracts to do a piece of work according to his or her own methods, and without being subject to the control of the employer except as to result.

Infomercial — a 5- to 15-minute hybrid cable program having an informational and entertainment component similar to a typical television program but designed as an extended advertisement for a particular product.

Injunction — an order by a court that prohibits or restrains a party from doing a particular act that threatens immediate harm.

Installment Buyer — one who orders goods or services and pays for them in two or more periodic payments after delivery of the products or services.

Intangible Assets — patents on a process or invention, copyrights to written or reproducible material, and trademarks; also, goodwill.

Interactive — a two-way information system whereby the information receiver can communicate directly with the information supplier.

Interbrand Competition — competition among the manufacturers of the same generic product. This area, under certain federal court decisions, can be important in evaluating vertical territorial marketing plans.

Internal Data — operational data on such items as sales, credit, and lists generated within the firm.

Interstate — operations crossing state lines or involving more than a single state. An important factor in many areas of law; whether you are selling interstate may determine whether you have antitrust exposure. For trademark registration, you must place your product in interstate commerce. Interstate telephone services come under the jurisdiction of the Federal Communications Commission.

Interstate Commerce Act of 1887 — the first U.S. law to regulate business practices.

Intrabrand Competition — competition between or among the distributors, wholesalers, or retailers of the product of a particular manufacturer of that product.

Intrastate — operations that remain within the boundaries of a specific state. Telephone services remaining intrastate are under the jurisdiction of the respective state's public service commission or board of public utilities.

Investigative Consumer Report — when a company gathers information about a person's credit history, the Fair Credit Reporting Act calls this an investigative consumer report.

Joint Venture — a company established for the cooperation of two or more companies in accomplishing a specific task.

Label—written, printed, or graphic matter attached to a product or inscribed on its package and used to give certain information about the producer, ingredients, weight, or how it should be used (see Warranty).

Law — set of rules that govern people and their institutions in their associations and dealings with one another.

Libel — malicious defamation of another's character expressed in writing.

Limited Warranty — the Magnuson-Moss Act requires certain consumer products to be labeled as having either a full or limited warranty. Limited warranties are those that do not comply with the act's requirement for a full warranty.

Liquidated Damages — a sum of money which the parties to a contract agree in advance will be paid to "the other" as damages if one of the parties is guilty of a breach of the contract.

List Price Comparison — may be advertised as comparable to the advertised sales price of another only to the extent that it is the actual selling price currently charged in the market area where the claim is made and the comparable products are of at least like grade and quality, demonstrable by objective evidence.

List Rental — an arrangement in which a list owner furnishes names and/or addresses on a list to a mailer, together with the privilege of using the list (unless specified) one time only. A list can be selected from a mass-compiled list on geographic, demographic, or psychographic bases, or it can be rented from a firm whose clientele closely resembles that desired (subject to the practice of many mailers and the Direct Marketing Association to permit consumers to remove their names from unwanted lists). The list owner is paid a royalty by the mailer, usually a specific fee per name. The list owner will establish a specific date on which the user has the obligation to mail to a specific list.

Lobbies — groups legally constituted to influence government decisions.

Location Clause — a clause that limits the area in which the distributor may establish a sales outlet but does not limit the distributor to servicing customers who live within that area.

Lottery — a sales promotion device offering to the public, illegal under most state and federal statutes (often ignored in the case of charitable or other nonprofit institutions), containing elements of chance, consideration, and prize.

Market Power — ability of producers to expand their share of a prevailing competitive market. Factors to consider include current market share of firm, degree of concentration in the industry, the extent of product differentiation, and actual or potential government regulation.

Material Statement — any statement in a promotion that is capable of affecting the decision to purchase.

Media — as used in promotion, all the different means by which advertising reaches its audience.

Member Get a Member — a phrase indicating a broad range of referral promotions by various firms whereby a current customer is offered free merchandise for soliciting other customers.

Merchantable — as applies to UCC, of good quality and salable, but not necessarily the best.

Misrepresentation — when a person by words or acts creates a false impression in the mind of another person.

Monopoly — Individual action, joint acquisition, or maintenance, by members of a conspiracy formed for purpose, of the power to control and dominate interstate trade and commerce in a commodity or service to such an extent that actual or potential competitors are excluded from the field; this action is accompanied by the intention and purpose to exercise such power.

Natural Monopolies — firms that, for the public good, are permitted to exclude competitors from a given field for social utility.

Negative Option — a buying plan in which a customer or club member agrees to accept and pay for merchandise announced in advance at regular intervals unless the individual formally notifies the company not to send the merchandise within the time period specified with the announcement.

Negligence — failure to observe the standard of care a reasonable person would in a specific situation.

Negotiable Instrument — a written evidence of a debt, i.e. a check, that can be used as a medium of exchange with practically the same freedom as money.

Oligopoly — market in which a few sellers control the supply of a product or service and, thus, its price or other terms of sale.

Out of Stock — merchandise that is not presently available but will be at some future date.

Parol Evidence Rule — this prevents the introduction of oral testimony in a court proceeding which adds to, alters, or varies the terms of a written agreement. Such terms may be explained or supplemented by (a) a course of dealing, (b) a usage of trade or business, (c) consistent additional terms or (d) a prior course of performance.

Patent — exclusive right (monopoly) to manufacture, sell, or otherwise use an invention for a limited period.

Per Se — literally, "by or through itself"; if an anticompetitive business activity is blatant in its intent and pernicious in its effect, a court need not inquire into the reasonableness of the case before determining that it is a violation of the antitrust laws.

Personal Property — all things that can be owned and which are not real property. The term includes tangible assets (such as manufactured goods) as well as intangible assets (such as stocks, bonds, patents, and trademarks).

Precedent — a previously decided case that serves as authority for a court's decision in a current dispute.

Place Utility — value added to a product by making it available to consumers at a convenient location, such as their homes.

Point-of-Purchase Advertising — a nonpersonal sales promotion implemented through window displays or counter set-ups in stores designed to provide the retailer with ready-made, professionally designed vehicles for selling more of the featured products.

Premium — a product offered free or at less than its usual price to encourage the consumer to buy another product or make a commitment to a membership.

Price Discrimination — generally, charging different prices to different customers.

Price Leader — a major producer in a given industry who tends to set the pace in establishing prices.

Prima Facie — at first sight; a fact that is presumed to be true unless disproved by contrary evidence.

Puffery — an expression of opinion (often exaggerated) by a seller, not made as a representation of fact.

Quantity Discount — a price allowance or deduction made from a gross sum given by manufacturers or wholesalers for purchases in large amounts.

Resale Price Maintenance Program — a situation in which a seller of goods, such as a manufacturer, regulates the price at which the goods may be resold by the retailer. Presently illegal under the antitrust laws in most cases.

Sale — a significant temporary reduction from the usual and customary price of the product or service offered.

Shipping and Handling — cost to seller of fulfilling and delivering orders. If an extra charge is required to make delivery of an advertised product, under FTC rules, that fact must be clearly and conspicuously stated in the offer.

Slice of Life — a type of commercial consisting of a short play that portrays a real-life situation in which the product is tried and becomes the solution to your buyer's need or problem.

Stare Decisis — a policy of courts to stand by previous judicial decisions.

Statute — a law enacted by a legislative body.

Statute of Frauds — a statute that requires that certain kinds of contracts be in writing to be enforceable.

Strict Liability — the standard of culpability to which a seller will be held for breach of an implied warranty that is imposed as a matter of public policy on a product he or she sells. Such liability is "strict liability" because it attaches even though the seller has exercised all possible care in the preparation and sale of his or her product.

Sweepstakes — a sales promotion device that offers prizes to participants but, unlike contests, requires no skill or analytical thinking. Consumers need only enter their name, an assigned number, or other identification symbol to qualify for random drawing. No purchase is necessary. The purpose is to encourage consumption of the product by creating consumer involvement.

Target Market — the most likely purchasers of your product.

Tie-In — express or implied contract arrangement whereby a party with significant economic power requires a purchaser, lessee, or licensor to purchase or acquire one or more additional products to be able to carry or deal in the desired product.

Title — legal ownership of property with the right to own and enjoy property and to transfer its ownership or possession to another. As to goods, title passes when the seller completes performance with respect to the physical delivery of the goods.

Tort — an injury or wrong committed, either with or without force, to the person or property of another.

Trademark — a brand (word, name, symbol, or device or any combination thereof) adopted and used by its owner to identify its goods and distinguish them from those sold by others. Usually given legal protection so that its owner has exclusive rights to its use.

Trading Up — attempting to interest your customers in better, and usually more expensive, goods than they expected to buy.

Unconscionable — a lack of meaningful choice in a contractual relationship coupled with a contract term that is so one-sided as to be oppressive.

Unique Selling Proposition — advertising claim concerning a product that is thought to be strong enough to cause customers to buy the product about which the claim is made rather than a rival product. To be unique, the proposition must be one that the competition either cannot or does not offer.

Vendor — seller of property.

Vertical Agreements — agreements between distributors at different levels of the market structure to cooperate closely with one another in selling, pricing, promotions, and advertising.

Vertical Territorial Restraint — specified territorial area imposed by a manufacturer or supplier as a condition of doing business with a customer such as a distributor or retailer.

Void — null; of no legal effect.

Waiver — the act of relinquishing or giving up some legal right.

Warehouse — a storage facility whose operators (if not the owner) do not take title to the goods they handle and whose receipts, if any, are often used as collateral for loans.

Warranty — a subsidiary promise or collateral agreement, the breach of which entitles the buyer to make certain claims for damages, replacement, or repair against the warrantor. The warranty may be full or limited (depending on the express agreement) or implied in law.

WATS — Wide Area Telephone Service, a long-distance service offered to business customers which enables them to use large amounts of long-distance service for high volume and short duration of conversation at a discount rate. Excellent service for any telephone-marketing program.

INDEX

INDEX